The Student Book 94

The indispensable applicant's guide to UK colleges and universities

Editors:

KLAUS BOEHM
JENNY LEES-SPALDING

First published 1979 by
PAPERMAC
a division of Pan Macmillan Publishers Limited
Cavaye Place London SW10 9PG
and Basingstoke
Associated companies throughout the world

Fifteenth edition 1993

ISBN 0-333-56700-5

A CIP catalogue record for this book is available from the British Library

Typeset by Florencetype Ltd, Kewstoke, Avon
Printed and bound in Great Britain by Cox and Wyman Limited, Reading

About the Editors

Klaus Boehm specialises in reference books and publishing sponsorship. He works with a number of publishing houses, developing titles including the *Dictionary of the History of Science*, *British Archives*, *The Royal and Ancient Golfer's Handbook*, *Macmillan and Silk Cut Nautical Almanac*, and two European titles *The European Community* ('the best single source on Europe') and *Business Europe*.

Jenny Lees-Spalding was academic registrar at London Guildhall University, then City Poly, where she was dealing with the students on first degree courses. She left to develop reference books with Klaus Boehm. Their current titles are *The Student Book*; a companion volume, *Independent Careers*, published for much the same readership but offering a unique guide to becoming your own boss (not a bureaucrat); and *The Equitable Schools Book*, the discriminating parents' guide to over 580 independent secondary schools ('the Wisden of the fee-paying circuit').

All three books share a non-prescriptive philosophy, that readers are intelligent people who make their own choices; reference books may be a good starting point for them but can never be a substitute for their own research and analysis of primary sources. And all three books have a European dimension – which led to the inclusion of Klaus Boehm Publications as one of two commended publishers in the 1991 European Information Association's Awards for European Sources.

Foreword

- **A Brave New World**
- **Student Hardship**
- **About the Book**

A Brave New World

It should be an exciting time to embark on higher education. Unless, of course, you are completely confused by what's happening and worried you can't afford it anyway.

You are among the first group able to choose your degree course from over 85 UK universities (as well as colleges of all sorts), without the ground shifting under your feet as it did last year. Gone are the old distinctions – universities are better than polys, polys better than colleges of HE. You might think this should make life much simpler, that there's little to choose between one place, or one course, and another. Not a bit of it. Whatever is claimed to the contrary, ignore it: the plain fact is that all universities and all degree courses are not all equal – some *are* better than others. And you'll be more suited to some than to others. It's up to you to choose from the huge range there is – old, new, large, small, conservative, innovative, static, vocationally based, research based . . . So what do *you* want? An established course in literae humaniores or a shiny new course in retail management?

The changing landscape of higher education hasn't, of course, just meant transforming polys into universities and allowing some colleges to award their own degrees. It goes hand in hand with a huge increase in student numbers – enough even to worry the government. The advantage of this is that it gives the opportunity of a degree course to many more people – although it's hard to see how employers and the public at large will value yet more graduates. It's partly a question of maintaining standards, partly of the sheer numbers of graduates hitting the labour market. Something like a third of each age group can be expected to get a first degree during your working life so, in principle, it's probably a good idea to jump on to the graduate bandwagon now, providing that makes good sense in your own personal circumstances.

One caveat. There is a possible downside for *you*. In many places growth in student numbers has not been matched by expansion of staff, teaching facilities and, more generally, student accommodation. For the most part, numbers in classes are increasing and small group teaching is on the decrease. It's up to you to make sure you're not short-changed. Whatever your abilities and ambitions – whether you're an academic flyer the admissions tutors scramble to recruit or a simple plodder – don't be fobbed off with something which is second-rate for you. It's *your* life, *your* degree course and *your* educational experience that count.

Student Hardship

We asked SUs to tell us about specific student problems. Their responses were terrific – for which many thanks – but we aren't going to name names for you. If you do want to know about student hardship at a particular university or college, you know what to do – check direct.

Don't let yourself be put off by what we present below or what you find out for yourself. Our advice is to get yourself a strategy for dealing with the problem. Then get your act together – preferably before you apply, certainly before you get there.

More equals less

From SUs' responses we distilled three general answers to three questions at the back of very many people's minds.

Question 1: Is student hardship widespread?

Answer: Yes, it's rife, it's almost universal, it's alive and kicking; indeed the monster grows and grows.

Question 2: Are students to blame? Has the government got a point, that it's down to individual fecklessness, laziness and welfare dependency?

Answer: No, no, no. Today's student hardship results from the drive to expand student numbers without a corresponding increase in public expenditure. There's little individual students can do about it. Literally, more equals less.

Question 3: How much less? Isn't higher education supposed to be free?

Answer: Ho! Ho! Ho! You must be joking! Yes, you'll probably get your fees paid, but you still have to live. 26% of students now receive no maintenance grant; 73% pay some or all of their notional maintenance costs; only 27% get the lot, and that isn't enough to keep body and soul together because you are expected to build up debts. Your grant (plus your parents' contribution, if any) should eventually be **no more** than your student loan (the government's loan, your debt). And that jolly little equation assumes that you only need to live for 30 weeks in the year, not 52; it also ignores the fact many of your costs may be determined by your university or college, so you can't control them.

Our SU reports paint a pretty grim picture. Student hardship is now a fact of student life. Many cope; a growing minority do not. Below we present a selection of specific points made by SUs from all over the country.

First, the bad news – A–Z student hardship

Academic demands 'The burden of work is such that many find it impossible to satisfy both their tutor and their bank manager. My tutor, for example, expected (demanded?) eight weeks' work (9–5) during the long vac' (Oxbridge).

Academic provision 'Staff/student ratios: more students, same number of staff.' 'Lecture theatres: gross overcrowding' (new univ). 'Semesterisation can cause financial hardship.'

Access funds 'Temporary reprieve, nothing long-term.' 'Small in relation to student numbers.' 'Does little to alleviate student poverty.' 'Large numbers of students apply.' 'Access fund cut by 10% while student numbers increased, therefore less hardship money per student' (Welsh coll).

Accommodation costs 'Main cause of hardship.' '51% of students' income goes on rent.' 'High rents account for more than entire grant.' 'College rents going up by 28% above inflation next six years' (Oxbridge coll). 'Rocketing cost of accommodation' (Midlands univ). 'Rapid rise in local rents compared with national rises' (Northern coll). 'Private rents £2,000 pa' (west country univ). 'Halls: none' (new univ). 'Expensive; must be self-financing.'

Accommodation – private 'Main problem is lack of affordable housing.' 'Living out can be ruinously expensive.' 'Private accommodation contracts 52 weeks in year, grant 30.' 'Off-site rents terrible problem.'

Additional study/electives 'Costs prohibitive.' '50% take self-funded BSc' (medical school).

Catch 22 'Students who are forced to drop out for financial reasons normally do so when their debts become intolerably high but dropping out doesn't cancel the debt. They thus leave without a degree which might have helped them get a job *and* heavily in debt.'

Causes of student hardship 'Basically being skint due to government education policy' (Scotland).

Debts 'Huge.' '£5–£10,000 average' (medical school). 'Average student debt on graduation, £1,122.40; expected to be £1,997.70 by 1993.' 'Loan of £2,000 plus substantial debts in final year not unusual.' 'Third years, £2,000 overdraft plus full student loans.' 'In a survey of 500 students, debts = £500,000.' 'Last year our student loans = £2.32 million!' (new northern univ).

Drop out for financial reasons 'The day a student is forced to drop out for financial reasons cannot be far off' (Oxbridge). 'Many forced to drop out a week BEFORE they start' (drama school). 'Many do' (northern univ). 'Small proportion do' (Welsh coll). 'Very few do' (western univ). 'Not many drop out on financial grounds' (HE coll). 'Drop-out rate in first week of term increasing significantly in recent years – probably due to financial hardship' (university). 'Estimated loss of students on financial grounds 50–60 pa' (art college). 'Often welfare and education bureau has to advise students to drop out of their courses due to current climate in education' (university). 'Expecting first drop-outs this year' (HE coll). 'Some students forced to leave because of financial problems' (drama school). 'Drop outs in plenty' (new univ). 'Students leaving because they cannot pay fees' (new univ in London).

Fatigue 'Students tired in class because of having to take a night job' (drama school). '47.5 hours teaching plus rehearsals leaves no time or energy to earn money too' (dance school).

Fear of future debts still to be incurred 'Many drop out because of fear of future debts piling up as well as hardship experienced from current lack of funds.'

Field trips/field work 'Compulsory on some courses and cost!' (London univ). 'Students particularly hard hit are those with field work *in vacs*' (new univ).

Financial problems 'Universal.' 'With fewer and fewer jobs and no benefits available, students are finding vacations particularly difficult. This problem often exacerbated by landlords charging full rent over summer vacation. Financial problems are a factor leading some students to drop out' (Midlands univ). 'Huge overdrafts. Low grants. No benefits. Lack of discretionary awards' (Welsh univ).

Grants: discretionary 'Discretionary grant students having huge problems both paying fees and living' (art college). 'Dancers often get no mandatory grant; discretionary if lucky' (dance school).

Grant levels 'LEA grants fall far short of cost of training a student for the ministry.' 'Living on £2,265 a joke' (Oxford). 'Grant far short of Oxford prices.' 'SE almost as expensive as London but no extra grant' (SE univ). 'Independent colleges get £660 mandatory grant fees only' (osteopathy college).

Grant nonsense 'Grant calculated on 30 weeks in year although the DFE appears not to have noticed there are 52. But private landlords know all about it and rent contracts often 52 weeks in year.' 'Students who are hard pushed to make a grant last 30 weeks cannot make it last 52 and so are endlessly paying off debts' (new univ in London).

Grant plus loan levels 'Total sum falls short of real costs by £15.00 per week in Liverpool' (univ). 'University acknowledges that students will have to pay £1,000 more than grant plus loan' (west country univ).

Hardship 'Rife.' 'A real issue.' 'Lots of it.' 'About 10% students.' 'Student poverty increasing' (Oxbridge). 'Fact of life here' (new univ). 'All students all over the country faced with hardship' (northern univ). (*NB Almost 100% report real hardship*). 'Life, financially, very tough in North' (northern univ). 'Absolutely intolerable situation over vacs' (new univ in London). 'More mature students face financial hardship.'

Hardship funds 'College fund confidential use only, eg parents made redundant' (Oxbridge coll). 'Can't cover everyone' (Oxbridge coll).

Hidden hardship 'Some students from wealthy backgrounds, therefore hardship not immediately identifiable here; but those who do suffer hardship suffer a lot' (southern coll).

Kids 'Students with kids face the greatest financial difficulties (northern univ). 'No crèche' (new univ). 'Child care appalling' (Oxbridge).

Late cheques 'More and more grants paid late.' 'Late cheques, especially from London LEAs.' 'Hardship can result because grants delayed: problem to find one month's rent PLUS deposit for accommodation' (new univ in London).

North v South 'Easier to survive than in the south' (northern univ). 'Accommodation costs very competitive in Hull compared with other universities.'

Overdrafts 'Overdrafts rising as access funds depleting' (new univ in London).

Overseas students 'No college accommodation, very hard on overseas students' (London). 'Delays in receiving o/s funds can cause incredible hardship.'

Parental generosity 'Essential during summer vac.' 'Recession making it impossible for some parents to help.' 'All students face hardship, especially those whose parents cannot support them financially' (Midland univ).

Part-time jobs 'With shortage of jobs, most part-time jobs lost' (Welsh univ).

Private colleges 'As a private college, mandatory awards considerably less than those of a university student.' 'As independent college, LEAs only obliged to pay £660 towards tuition fees for mandatory grant which leaves shortfall. Annual tuition fees now £5,200' (osteopathy college). 'Not able to claim student loans or access funds' (drama college). 'Privately funded, therefore fees high therefore difficult for students to pay fees.' 'Most have to find part-time work in order to survive' (drama college).

Recession 'Has hit Brighton badly as anywhere.' 'Killing off parents' ability to pay their contribution' (Oxbridge coll). 'Recession plus no vacation benefits means that many students have immense problems' (Welsh univ). 'Problem is that not everyone can get their course work placement (equals cash) in this recession' (univ in London).

Repayment of debts 'Main problem is no prospect of finding job after graduation' (southern univ). 'No difficulty in paying back £5,000–£10,000 after qualifying (medical school).

Social problems 'No money makes relating to others who have a few pence difficult' (northern univ).

Student town 'Town not geared to students (only small percentage of the population); not many NUS concessions, student housing etc' (northern coll).

Summer 'Dangerous. Many couldn't find any jobs at all' (northern coll). 'Hardship extreme as grant isn't even intended to cover it and jobs scarce. Lack of summer work' (Oxford coll). 'In summer, we ran student soup kitchen to provide at least one meal a day for students without vac work. About sixty students used it each day' (northern univ).

Travel 'Expansion of student numbers without increased accommodation means students being pushed out 10 miles or more' (Welsh univ). 'Living in London expensive; difficult to live near college therefore high travel costs' (univ in London). 'Housing major problem in Canterbury with students living some distance away and public transport expensive and no car a handicap.'

Trends 'Worse and worse.' 'More and more students having serious financial difficulties' (new univ in London). 'Dramatically increased hardship fund because of worsening student financial position.' 'Position deteriorating as recession kills off work opportunities (northern univ). 'Day when a student of this college is forced to drop out on financial grounds cannot be far off' (Oxbridge coll).

Welfare benefits 'Withdrawal of benefits from students is a major cause of real hardship' (Welsh univ).

Work experience/placements/teaching practice 'Work experience helps. Most have holiday jobs on farms as work experience' (veterinary coll). 'Placements ensure that students not as poor as others. Problem is that not everyone can get a placement in this recession' (univ in London). 'BEds find cost of teaching practice excessive.'

Working-class students 'No work, so students of working-class backgrounds drop out' (new univ in north). 'College has one of best state/independent school mixes in university, therefore more hardship than many colleges' (Oxbridge coll).

Working for money 'Students forced to work in vacs and often term time' (new univ). 'It's drying up' (northern coll).

Year 1 'No cheap accommodation for first years who accumulate large debts by end of three terms.'

Year 2 'Beware high rents when slung out of first-year halls' (northern univ). 'Some second years in expensive private accommodation get into financial trouble' (Oxbridge coll). 'Accommodation costs a problem for second years' (Oxbridge coll).

Year 3 'Grant and student loan assume you start a job the day after the end of the summer term.'

Years 4+ 'Vets find that in last three years of course money not easy.'

Then – the good news . . .

(much of it from Oxbridge)

Positive reports 'Three years in cheap college accommodation plus subsidised food (and hardship fund for extreme cases) means students are cushioned from spiralling costs in private sector' (Oxbridge coll). 'College loath to let students drop out on financial grounds so helps with hardship funds' (Oxbridge coll). 'I have not heard of anyone dropping out on financial grounds' (Oxbridge coll). 'Good hardship fund' (Oxbridge coll). 'Very sympathetic college authorities; relatively affluent college and can bail people out' (Oxbridge coll). 'College rich and cushions students, particularly the brightest, from hardship' (Oxbridge coll). 'University fund untouched last year' (Oxbridge coll). 'Banks – local branches very helpful: high debts (£5,000–£10,000) plus copper-bottomed employment prospects mean no drop outs on financial grounds' (London medical school). 'No drop outs for financial reasons despite real financial problems because students supported by church giving and friends' (theological college). 'Holiday town, good for summer jobs.' 'Most students get part-time jobs' (northern univ).

Financial workshops, tutors, counselling 'Financial workshops' (coll of London Univ). 'SU offers money management service' (Welsh univ). 'Over 50% welfare officers' workload is finance (southern univ). 'Finance tutor runs workshops' (Oxbridge coll). 'College helps find local jobs eg shops' (London art coll). 'Oxbridge – better off in college accommodation; therefore research your college!' (Oxbridge coll). 'Colleges help if desperate, therefore few drop out on financial grounds, but more mature students do' (Oxbridge univ).

And that's really all the Good News reported to us.

About The Student Book

The Student Book is a consumer book. To be precise, it is a book for potential consumers of first degree courses or equivalent in UK universities and colleges. The book makes no pretence to cover higher national diplomas or any further education. Nor is it a catalogue of degree course titles which you can find in excruciating detail elsewhere.

It's intended to do three things:

- to help you get a personal strategy;
- to help you make a shortlist of universities and colleges which you might like to go to;
- to help you shortlist what you might want to study.

After that, we think it's down to you to get stuck into the primary sources – the university and college prospectuses and alternative prospectuses – and work out your own final choices for yourself. We can't do it for you. Persevere – and good luck!

We are grateful for the help we have received from the named contributors and the administrators of over 250 universities and colleges – particularly Derek Pollard and also Julia Edwards, Martin Gaskell, Brian High, George Kiloh and Margaret Kilyon. The book would not be possible without the help of the student correspondents, especially those who have provided much valuable information on student hardship. Our special thanks go to Bryan Reading for the cartoons and to the many sixth formers who have written to us with suggestions for this edition.

Klaus Boehm & Jenny Lees-Spalding
c/o Pan Macmillan, 18–21 Cavaye Place
London SW10 9PG
30 November 1992

WHAT
YOU 1
NEED
TO 2
KNOW 3
IN 4
SIX 5
SECTIONS 6

GEOFFREY DIDN'T – 95% OF STUDENTS DID

An estimated 95% of higher education students are likely to be eligible for a student loan.

And it's easy to apply. Just bring along your birth certificate, award letter (if any) and bank / building society details to your student loans administrator.

To get full information call the Student Helpline on 0345 300 900 for a brochure with all the details, or read the "How to get the money" section of the Student Book.

HOW
TO GO
ABOUT
IT

BEFORE YOU APPLY

IS A DEGREE
WORTHWHILE?

SHOULD I DO A DEGREE
NOW OR LATER?

IF I WANT TO DO A
DEGREE NOW –
WHAT NEXT?

The Student Book

Basic reference books
worth getting

Library reference books
worth consulting

Prospectuses

Alternative prospectuses

Open days

Students with
disabilities:
extra checks

ENTRANCE
REQUIREMENTS

MAKING A SHORTLIST

GET A STRATEGY

Is a Degree Worthwhile?

You have to decide this for yourself. There are no useful general answers – the only worthwhile answer is one tailor-made for you.

If you are one of the very few who know what they want to do in life then you may be able to work it out from the qualifications needed to get there. A degree may be a legal requirement for entry into a profession such as medicine; *or* a selection criterion used by employers for shortlisting job applicants: no degree, no interview. A degree is more likely to be expected of those leaving school in the nineties than when your parents and teachers left school.

If you do not know what you want to be doing in three years' time then it's more complicated. There are lots of important factors to take into account including the cost; the opportunity to study in depth without the distraction of having to earn a living; the new range of talented people you will meet; the chance to develop your acting, musical, political or sporting prowess and of course the chance to keep your options open for another few years. And of course there's the hope that it'll be easier to find a job in three years' time.

So how do you begin to work it out for yourself? You could of course write to John Major and ask him whether he thinks he would have got further if he had a degree. Alternatively you could try looking at it as a personal investment decision – weighing the future benefits against the current sacrifices to decide whether your investment is likely to pay off. Admittedly this is a pretty dry approach but it might find some support in Downing Street.

If you want to look at the decision in purely financial terms you could use a framework commonly applied elsewhere. Try this:

A   Costs
B   Benefits
C   Net Balance

A.   Costs

1. Earnings.
   You lose income by studying, even with a grant, if you could otherwise have been earning. However, assess your chances of getting a job. If the alternative is unemployment you've nothing to lose.
2. Expenses.
   If you don't get a grant you'll have to pay fees (and you *may* have to, even with a grant). Everyone has to buy books, equipment etc. You may not need a suit but accommodation and travel is likely to be more expensive than if you were working or living at home.
3. Cost of Money.
   Overdrafts/loans have a finance cost or interest. Beware! Almost all students are now in debt by the end of their course; many in their first year.

4. Length of Course.
   The number of years your course lasts determines the total of these costs. Sandwich courses or courses involving languages usually mean more years of cost (but maybe higher future income to offset them).

B. Benefits

1. Better Chance of a Job.
   Graduates are less likely to be unemployed – in some areas there are real shortages of qualified graduates and it's likely to get worse.
2. Higher Income.
   Graduates tend to earn more than non-graduates. For some professions a degree is a prerequisite; for others it means higher entry on the promotion scale; for most it's a sign of ability.

C. Net Balance

If these benefits outweigh the costs, then acquiring a degree is worth it as a financial investment. Even if it isn't, take account of the non-pecuniary benefits (and costs) which cannot be valued directly in financial terms. A new college lifestyle, greater independence, satisfaction from study, longer holidays and the prospect of more interesting and satisfying work when you leave are all significant benefits. The downside includes prolonged financial dependence on parents, the shortage of cash while you're a student and the need to pay back your debts afterwards.

Allow for the benefits occurring later than the costs. Most of us would prefer to consume now rather than in the future. As a student you won't be able to maintain your desired level of consumption so the weight you give to present costs against future benefits depends on how much you value what you have to give up.

The cost benefit analysis framework is a valid economic approach for making your decision even if, for most, the motives are not solely financial. It should at least help you to identify the major reasons for and against studying further. If you don't know what you want to do now, you could do a lot worse than use the time at a university or college to find out.

Should I Do a Degree Now or Later?

Taking time off between school and going to college can mean deferring your entry for just a year or some longer period. Many universities favour one year off and will accept applications in 1993 for entry in 1995; for some subjects eg agriculture they may require it. If you have a year or more between, a degree course ceases to be the only alternative; the decision is made more by you rather than parents or teachers. You're likely to be more independent and better able to cope with the rigours of student life. Returning to old study habits may be difficult, but at least you're sure it's what you want.

A year off may help when you start looking for a job too; many leading industrialists are in favour of a year off between A-levels (or equivalents) and going to a degree course. But of course any time off must be well planned. Loafing about in sun-spots abroad won't count for much in career terms, however enjoyable. You can contact GAP Activity Projects Ltd (44 Queen's Road, Reading, Berkshire RG1 4BB; 0734 594914). They can set you up with 6 months' overseas voluntary work in schools, businesses, hospitals, farms . . . But apply early; they do not have unlimited places.

Abigail Dawson, who took a year off, writes:

'A whole year dossing. After the joys of A-levels that would probably sound a very enticing prospect, and it's quite feasible. There's nothing to stop you taking a year off and doing absolutely nothing with it. But what a waste. For the first and possibly last time in your life you have fifteen months at your disposal which, given money and parental support and sometimes without, you can spend exactly as you want.

'There are endless good reasons for taking the year. In my case it enabled me to leave the hassles of application until the relative calm of the post A-level period. It was a breather – I didn't feel I could go straight on from A-levels and start a degree course with much energy or enthusiasm. I'd heard how 'challenging and character-building' the year could be – at the time I took that with a deserved pinch of salt, but I have to report that it's probably true.

'I'm no expert – I can't tell you the ins and outs of how to go about planning what you will do. That's up to you, your inclination to use your local library or careers centre and, to an extent, your school or college. I was lucky enough to find a place teaching in a school in Malaysia before travelling round Singapore, Indonesia and Malaysia. The GAP scheme also provides openings, working abroad (with sheep in New Zealand, vines in France . . . or with a mission in Africa, at home in industry with INDEX) or doing voluntary work of some kind – a friend spent an unforgettable few months with down-and-outs in East London.

'Just about everything I encountered during the year was new: from a regular 9–5 job in a department store before Christmas and working behind a bar, to earn the cash to go away; to arriving in Malaysia expecting to give English conversation lessons and finding I was English teacher to 28 11-year-olds and general supply teacher to the rest of the school; travelling alone on decrepit buses full of livestock; accommodation at 30p per night; wonderful beaches; the odd volcano; religious ceremonies and festivals at which I was always made welcome; the humbling experience of fasting during the month of Ramadhan; beautiful temples, delicious (cheap!) food . . . and so on. I have met people who 'just' travelled during their years off. Looking back, most wish they'd taken some kind of job. But you can always play it by ear (two girls I met worked for bed and board for a week, teaching in a snow-bound Nepalese mountain village). I found the tourist trails of Malaysia and Indonesia so well trodden by back-packers that travel was easy, cheap and quite well organised (ignoring the odd breakdown and ubiquitous con-artists; a sense of humour and a good guide-book helped).

'So I started my degree course – refreshed and more self-confident and self-sufficient than a year before. There is an endless range of ways you can fill the year. If I have been preaching to the converted, I hope you have as good a time as I did. On the other hand you may be reading this in mid-October at 3pm, after your nth cup of coffee, sitting in your pyjamas and wondering what to do until it's time to go back to bed again. It's never too late. Get going and make the most of an invaluable opportunity.'

If I Want to do a Degree Now – What Next?

Find out as much as you can for yourself.

The Student Book

Once you've decided in general that you want to go on studying you need to be able to reduce the masses of information available to a shortlist of opportunities: where to study, what to study and how to go about it. *The Student Book* is the best place to start (obviously). It's divided into separate sections which give you this basic information:

- *How to go about it*
- *Where to Study (and maps)*
- *What to Study*

Look in the *Subject and Places Index* to see which prospectuses are worth looking at if you want to study a particular subject. Use it intelligently (browse, then read, then shortlist); then write direct for the prospectuses on your shortlist.

Basic reference books worth getting

Not a lot. Four are worth getting hold of for yourself if you are consider-ing their subject matter.

ADAR Registration Scheme for Applicants Handbook (BA/HND) (ADAR, Penn House, 9 Broad Street, Hereford HR4 9AP)

Student Grants and Loans (from Department for Education, Publications Despatch Centre, Honeypot Lane, Canons Park, Stanmore, Middlesex HA7 1AZ; also available from your local education authority or school; free leaflet)

Scottish Universities Entrance Guide (Scottish Universities Council on Entrance, 12 The Links, St Andrews, Fife KY16 9JB)
UCAS Handbook (Universities and Colleges Admissions Service, Fulton House, Jessop Avenue, Cheltenham, Glos GL50 3SH; free booklet within UK, £5 outside UK)

Library reference books worth consulting

These are books you might want to refer to in your school, careers or local library.
Commonwealth Universities Yearbook (London: Association of Commonwealth Universities)
University Entrance/The Official Guide (London: Association of Commonwealth Universities for the Committee of Vice-Chancellors and Principals)
Degree Course Offers (Trotman and Co Ltd, 12 Hill Rise, Richmond, Surrey TW10 6UA)
Designated Courses (Department for Education, Sanctuary Buildings, Great Smith Street, London SW1P 3BT; also available from your local education authority or school/college)
Guide to Courses and Careers in Art, Craft and Design (National Society for Education in Art and Design, The Gatehouse, Corsham Court, Corsham, Wiltshire SN13 0ES)
Design Courses in Britain (Design Council, 28 Haymarket, London SW1Y 4SU)

Prospectuses

Get hold of them; they're your best primary source on universities and colleges. Also, they are improving. Many are still glossy marketing documents, which are difficult to use for finding out real facts – an astonishing number lack even an index or list of subjects available. Some are works of art, especially for those of the more ambitious art schools, but more and more are well constructed documents which tell you what you want to know. Beware glossy photographs: a beautiful sylvan scene might not be the whole view; a turn of 180° may reveal the abattoir. Many prospectuses oversimplify and, while usually accurate in detail, sin by omission. (24% students surveyed this year said their courses failed to live up to promises in the prospectus). They may contain valuable information on courses, degrees, accommodation (or lack of it), fees, facilities, if you can find it among lists of staff and sales puff. Increasingly, they are full of disclaimers which say they may not be able to deliver what's described any way. ('This prospectus is provided for illustration purposes only . . .' Read your prospectuses several times – to make comparisons between them and for the detail (though they date quickly). Read between the lines. Try to identify the ethos. See what the prospectus says the strengths are (eg sport, religion); they may or may not match yours. Constituent colleges of universities (eg Cambridge, London, Oxford) have individual prospectuses, so get hold of these.

Departments/faculties often produce their own guides which list staff and research interests. You might be able to gauge the nature, direction and tone of a department from this. Some prospectuses/department guides are now giving the average entry A-levels, although these will change rapidly.

Alternative prospectuses

Some students unions (SUs) produce alternative prospectuses to give a 'truer' picture for potential applicants of what the place is actually like – at least one SU also has an alternative prospectus video. They can be bitchy, selectively informative and moderately amusing; on the whole they're good and useful. Well worth a look, particularly if you're applying for accommodation, want to know the political leaning of the SU, or the idiosyncrasies of the more obvious student cliques. If you want more information, many SUs are pleased to talk directly to sixth formers who take the trouble to phone them.

Open days

Most universities and colleges hold open days for prospective students. These give you the opportunity to see the campus and town as well as any facilities that are particularly relevant to your choice of course (computer centres, labs etc); a few charge for attendance. If your school doesn't have the details of these, contact the college direct to find out if and when they take place. They may only be available to those who have been offered a place. If open days are offered – **go**. Don't even think of spending three years of your life at a place you haven't visited.

Students with disabilities: extra checks

Like everyone else, you need to decide what you want to study and why, find out where it's taught and think about where in the country you would like to live. But you also need to know if the institutions offering the right course also have the facilities and support services that you need.

Check what facilities are like in universities or colleges before you make your final shortlist. Skill (National Bureau for Students with Disabilities; 336 Brixton Road, London SW9 7AA; 071 274 0565) recommends that you make direct contact with individual universities and colleges so you can discuss your needs, both for studying and daily living. You can then find out if you think that is the right place for you and also how they may be able to help you. Most universities and colleges have an adviser or co-ordinator for students with disabilities and learning difficulties who you can talk to. You will probably be able to arrange a 'fact-finding' visit if that would be helpful. Many establishments can now provide or help organise specialist support services eg readers, note-takers, transcription etc and many have specialist accommodation that they can make available to students throughout their course. Provision does vary, so always make individual enquiries. Make contact early, they may be able to improve their facilities in some way before you get there.

Entrance Requirements

You'll need to know about entrance requirements in general and the requirements of the courses that interest you in particular.

The present normal **minimum** for a first degree course (other than art & design) are: 5 subjects at GCSE to a minimum of grade C, of which 2 are passed at A-level; or 4 subjects at GCSE to a minimum of grade C, with 3 passed at A-level. (For the oldies, O-level passes grade C or above and CSE grade 1 passes are accepted in place of GCSE). Most universities will accept AS-levels in addition to the basic 2 A-levels; individual admissions tutors vary about accepting AS-levels instead of A-levels but most prefer old-fashioned A-levels. BTEC Certificates or Diplomas at a good standard are also accepted. 4 Scottish Highers are the minimum for Scottish universities but may not be acceptable without further study in the rest of the UK. A recognised qualification in English language, such as GCSE or the JMB test, is normally required. If you have qualifications which do not appear in the prospectus (eg Scottish Highers outside Scotland; International Baccalaureat) check directly with the college before you apply. In addition there may be special course or faculty requirements.

Remember that in practice most universities and colleges have higher requirements than these and they change yearly. Offers are expressed either specifically in terms of A-level grades you must actually get or a number of points your AS or A-level results add up to on a scale when:

for AS-level	for A-level
A = 5	A =10
B = 4	B = 8
C = 3	C = 6
D = 2	D = 4
E = 1	E = 2

Courses that are much in demand will be able to demand higher than average grades; some courses you're okay with the minimum requirements. The moral: badger and negotiate and remember A-level grades are not reliable pointers to future academic development. Don't waste applications; if in doubt consult the college. Have a look at *University Entrance* and Brian Heap's *Degree Course Offers* (Trotman & Co Ltd) in your school/college library. There are a few moves to judge you on a wider range of criteria than just your A-levels. If you have a Record of Achievement, make sure you say so on your application form.

Many colleges welcome applications from mature students and when you reach 21 (23 in some places) you may be accepted without all the formal entry requirements. If (but only if) you can prove your willingness and ability to learn, you could be accepted for a course you would have been unable to get on to at 18. Some universities and colleges have a policy of encouraging such applications; others are little interested.

There are increasing numbers of access courses, which help you return to study, or pick up eg science basics before starting a science degree. Some universities have their own so check direct – or consult *Access to Higher Education Courses Directory* (from ECCTIS, Fulton House, Jessop Avenue, Cheltenham, Gloucestershire GL50 3SH).

Making a Shortlist

There are lots of things you need to consider when you make a shortlist. It's very personal but here are some pointers:

University or College

Size and place: you need to find a congenial place to spend the next few years of your life. Do you want to be near home or are you hell bent on putting several hundred miles between you and your parents?

Facilities: find places that have not expanded so fast that their facilities and teaching staff have failed to keep up.

Teaching and research: there are moves to rank universities and colleges into those that teach, those that do research and those that do both; if you want to use your degree as a stepping stone to a research post, you would do well to find one that is good at research (in your chosen area). If you're really good, you will get into the really good places. If you're not, you are probably wasting a valuable choice if you apply there. It's all part of the game of accurately assessing yourself and your chances.

Employability: and which are the good ones? Well, employers are fairly conservative and still prefer graduates from Oxbridge or the universities well known in their field (eg Imperial for physics, LSE for economics). Ask about the employment record when you go for an open day.

Subject

Getting in: Some subjects are highly competitive; in others they are crying out for students. Bear this in mind although don't, of course, apply for something you can't do. It's well known that medicine and law are two of the most difficult subjects to get into but do you know that over 100,000 people apply for business studies? If you have the minimum A-levels – or a science access course – you can walk into physical science degrees all over the country. There are all kinds of incentives around to attract people to engineering courses, particularly if you missed out on the right A-levels.

Employability: There are lots of vocational degrees, which is fine if you *know* you want to stay in that area after graduation. Otherwise the subject you take probably doesn't matter very much (of the graduate recruits to many major accountancy firms, fewer than 20% have degrees in accountancy). What does matter is that you get a good degree; people with firsts really do earn more. And getting a good degree is partly dependent on selecting a subject that will grab you for the full duration of the degree course. So, if you **want** to read Akkadian, go for it – and worry about employers' demands later.

If you are going to be a mature student – beware. Employers (outside the civil service) don't treat you as equally recruitable after the age of 25. You'll need to talk to a careers adviser.

And don't forget Europe. Find out about language tuition and European exchanges – they can be combined with loads of subjects now.

Logistics

Don't forget the other factors such as the amount of university accommodation; can you afford the local rents; distance from home in terms of travel costs at the beginning and end of term; do the courses you are interested in attract a mandatory grant?

Get a Strategy

By now you'll be sick to death of prospectuses, teachers, careers services, relatives and 'friendly advice'. The golden rule is to listen to everything anybody can tell you and then ignore two-thirds of it. The choice of where to study and what to study is yours and yours alone. Avoid tunnel vision and don't be frightened of trying something you haven't done before. Don't be indoctrinated – no-one knows your strengths and weaknesses better than you. Remember, you're choosing how to spend the next 3 years or more of your life. So get a strategy.

This page could determine just how far you'll get as a student

Are you a student, young person aged 16 to 23 or a mature student in full time education?

If so you can get around 30% off most National Express fares to anywhere in mainland Britain.

With one of these it could be a very long way

All you need is a Discount Coach Card. It costs only £6 and is valid for a whole twelve months.

You can use it any time on any of our coaches to any of our hundreds of destinations time and time again. Most people save the cost of the card the first time they use it.

DISCOUNT COACH CARD »

To apply or get more details, see any National Express agent or most Student Travel offices, or write to National Express (TSB), 4 Vicarage Road, Edgbaston, Birmingham, B15 3ES

HOW

TO

APPLY

How to Apply in General

Where to apply

For the vast majority of degree courses you apply to a brand new clearing house called UCAS. The only exceptions are the handful of places to which you apply direct (see *Where To Study*) and most studio based art and design courses for which you apply through another clearing house, ADAR.

Clearing houses are like post offices; they process your applications and the responses but do not themselves take decisions on your application.

UCAS (Universities and Colleges Admissions Service) replaces UCCA and PCAS. Use it for courses starting in autumn 1994 onwards; for earlier courses use UCCA or PCAS (their systems are as described for UCAS here).

Check in *Where To Study* and in prospectuses to see where you should apply. For details on how the clearing houses work, see below in *How To Apply In Particular*.

Applicant's calendar for a 1994 start

1993

June–September:
Absolute must: get a strategy. Prepare your own shortlist. Write for prospectuses and spend your summer having a good read. Reduce your shortlist to eight applications through UCAS. There is no limit for those colleges not in clearing systems. Comb prospectuses.

From 1 September:
Application forms accepted by UCAS. You will need to pay an application fee (amount not yet known). Find out where to apply for grants – normally your LEA (local education authority). Write for forms and apply as soon as possible.

October:
Send applications direct to any colleges not in a clearing system.

15 October:
Last date for applications for Cambridge and Oxford to reach UCAS and the university from your educational referee.

15 December:
Last date for applications to reach UCAS. Remember your educational referee will need the form at least a week beforehand.

1994

February:
Application forms available for ADAR (for most studio based art and

design courses in England and Wales); write to ADAR with application fee of £16 plus £3 if you also need the *Handbook*.

31 March:
Last date for registration forms to reach ADAR and the last date for the other ADAR forms to reach first choice colleges, all to be sent by your educational referee.

February/March/April:
Interviews, if necessary, and offers of places.
For applications through ADAR, first choice interviews from 1 April (decision by 9 May).

31 May:
You won't be able to hold more than one conditional offer firmly through UCAS after this date with a further offer as an insurance.

May/June:
For ADAR applications, second choice interviews from 16 May (decision by 5 June).

16 June:
ADAR clearing; interviews held from 23 June.

30 June:
Normally the final deadline for submitting grant applications. Each LEA has its own date. Late applications are accepted but the grant may be paid late. So get yours in as early as you can.

August:
A-level results!

August/September:
UCAS clearing: if you do not have a place, you will be sent information about clearing. But anyway ring round the universities and colleges – they now fill vacancies, sometimes accepting lower grades than before. You can also get help from your school or your LEA. Information on unfilled places is widely available, including the national press and various databases (ECCTIS, Prestel, etc).

September/October:
Keep on ringing, there might still be places.

Allow for postal delays

Filling in forms

Just as the prospectus is the college's selling document, your own completed application form(s) is yours. Sell yourself. (But don't flannel – remember you may be interviewed by someone with your form in hand.) If you fail to do yourself justice, the chances are the selectors will reject you without giving you a second chance. Forget your reservations about the archaic school reward system (eg prefects) and write down any laurels you've earned. Remember selectors are looking for good grades; whether your reference indicates promise for the future; wide (but not necessarily 'straight') interests; and positions of responsibility. In short they want to know whether you are likely to benefit from their degree course. But getting a place is a worse lottery than marriage – so keep at it.

Print boldly and clearly in **black** ink/biro/Pentel. **Remember:** mess up an application form and you mess up your chances. Sign and date all application forms. Many applicants don't. This causes aggro and unsuccessful applications. If you think you need help, ask your teachers/tutors/careers officers.

The information you are usually asked for is this:

1. Personal details
Fairly straightforward unless you are an overseas student.

2. Address
Fairly straightforward unless your address for correspondence is different from your home address. If this is so, remember correspondence will continue until September next year. So make sure your correspondence address lasts this long or arrange for mail to be *efficiently* forwarded.

3. Choice of course
Browse through *The Student Book*. Then make a shortlist of about ten universities and colleges, consult prospectuses, reference books and **get it right for you**. Reduce to the relevant minimum and fill in using the correct codes. For UCAS, you can bracket HND and degree courses in the same subject at the same university/college; you may only include 5 medical or dental courses – check the *UCAS Handbook*.

4. Examinations for which results are known
Put down everything even failures/low grades. You must tell the whole story and it needn't seem all bad, eg coming back from a failure/disappointing result indicates persistence, motivation and determination. Remember: one poor performance earlier in your school/college career won't count against you.

5. Examinations to be taken
Again, put in everything even if not directly to do with your subjects.

6. Education and any employment, in date order
Straightforward – don't be too detailed.

7. Further information
This is the most difficult section but use the space positively. Make sure you draft it out in rough first. This is the only chance you've got to sell yourself, so give relevant and precise information. Include everything which gives you some 'depth' but don't put down (say) 'reading' as an interest; you're expected to read. Be specific. Then you can answer actual questions if you get an interview. The admissions tutors will read dozens of these, so make it interesting so you stand out from the crowd. Say if you have a career in mind (shows motivation) but don't lose sleep if you don't know.

Remember to alter the form if you are applying for deferred entry.

References

All applications must be supported by an educational reference. Increasing importance is being attached to it in selection procedures, so get the best you can. Your head teacher/tutor/lecturer will usually write the reference – and an academic reference carries more weight than one from a friendly clergyman. Don't go out of your way to flatter your teacher/tutor but show interest, motivation, persistence and that you're teachable. References are often held to be confidential, but some teachers/tutors show references to students and discuss them. Anyway badger whoever writes your reference to write a full and fair one. Make sure you give your referee enough time to write it, and that they send it in on time.

Interviews

If you are called for an interview, find out if it is part of the selection procedure rather than a visiting or open day. If it is part of the selection procedure then prepare for the interview by predicting questions like: why are you applying here, why have you particularly chosen this degree? Ask your teacher/tutor to give you a mock interview. When at the interview, show you have the personal qualities for a degree such as enjoying learning/reading/writing essays/lab work, wanting to argue and talk about new ideas, and being eager to find out new things for yourself. If you have more than one interviewer reply to the one who asks the questions and then bring the others in. Don't mumble, don't chew gum, don't pick your nose. Relax yourself as much as possible and wear what you feel most comfortable in. Wait to be told to sit down, and don't smoke. Try to repress all distracting mannerisms. Prepare questions for the interviewer at the end. Above all don't be cowed: you're interviewing them too.

How you are chosen

Being chosen implies some kind of rationality. Well, there isn't any. Each university sets itself a target number of new students and it will want to meet this target with the best applicants possible. They also want teachable students so they adopt one (or both) of two ways of going about this:

1) A-level offers, made to a large number of candidates; so the A-level exam results do the choosing.
2) More reliance on interviews and reports from heads/course tutors; so lower offers can be made with more assurance on final student numbers.

Remember that the college's predicament is to get acceptable candidates on to its courses while leaving not a single place unfilled. Their predicament could be your opportunity.

After the A-level results are known, some universities and colleges top up their targets with people they would have rejected earlier in the year. Don't lose heart if you haven't got a place at this stage; keep badgering, even after the beginning of the autumn term. Selectors usually try very hard to be fair. But they might as well use a pin.

Offers

You may be offered a place in one of two ways – **unconditionally** or **conditionally**. Unconditional offers are what they say – you're in! Conditional (or provisional) offers are dependent upon your getting, for example, specified A- or AS-level grades or points, and sometimes extra GCSEs. If they ask you for specified A-level grades, they will mean it (so you can't compensate for a poor grade in one subject by doing better than required in another). But there's no telling what they'll actually accept in August until the results are published and they can see what everyone has got.

The offers they made *last* year is catalogued annually by Brian Heap in *Degree Course Offers* (Careers Consultants Ltd). Use it with discretion: as in the Stock Exchange, today's actual price is not necessarily the price quoted in this morning's *Financial Times*! The permutations involved in the offer/acceptance bargaining are mind-boggling. It's all supply and demand; if you get an offer based on 2 As and a B, it **may** be a better course than one offering 3 Ds – it's certainly more popular.

After 15 May you will be restricted as to the number of offers you may hold through UCAS. If you have too many offers, you need to make your best guess as to what you will achieve in A-levels in the **future** in the light of your **current** offers. It is useful to have some sort of a multi-dimensional checklist in your head, or preferably on paper. If you are the sort of person who thinks better on paper than on your feet, why not try a do-it-yourself POP (Personal Offers Planner), using the proforma on p. 22 and tailoring it to your own personal needs?

When the crunch comes, choose the college and course you want. The rejected ones won't approve, but it's your life.

Mature students

Mature students are on the increase; some courses accept as many as 1 in 4; some are designed specially for them. If you are qualified for a degree course, you should have no problem. If you are not but you can persuade admissions tutors that you can benefit from the course and will be successful, you can still be accepted. For some you may have to take an exam; for others you will be interviewed. There is also an increasing number of access courses you can take to bring yourself up to the required standard. For advice and further information, approach LEA careers advisers; try any ECCTIS access joint.

If you have taken a course before – even if you did not complete it – you may be exempted from part of a degree. This is called 'advanced standing'. If you think you may qualify, make sure you say so on your form and expect to be asked for syllabuses, transcripts etc. If you want advice, you can contact CATS (Credit Accumulation and Transfer Scheme, Open University Validation Services, 344–354 Gray's Inn Road, London WC1X 8BP; 071 278 4411). It is probably better to write but telephone advice is available. In some cases you can get credit for work experience and in-service training courses – CATS can tell you about that too.

Disabled students

Once you are satisfied you have a shortlist of universities and colleges where your support needs can be met, fill in your UCAS application form. You can indicate the nature of your disability and your needs in question 8. Question 2 on the form includes a box about disability that **all** applicants fill in, disabled or not. This is to help monitor how many disabled people are applying and entering higher education. This, along with the information you give in question 8, should allow the admissions staff to gain a basic understanding of your disability and needs and prevent your being asked inappropriate questions at interview. If you attend an interview or open day and have any special requirements

POP
DIY – Personal Offers Planner

	What you think you'll get:			Points
A-level grade	Subject (1)	Subject (2)	Subject (3)	
A	10	10	10	
B	8	8	8	
C	6	6	6	
D	4	4	4	
E	2	2	2	
AS-level grade	Subject (4)	Subject (5)	Subject (6)	
A	5	5	5	
B	4	4	4	
C	3	3	3	
D	2	2	2	
E	1	1	1	Total: ____

Your own shortlist/offers	Grades needed for subjects						Points needed
	(1)	(2)	(3)	(4)	(5)	(6)	
COURSE (1)							
COURSE (2)							
COURSE (3)							
COURSE (4)							
COURSE (5)							
COURSE (6)							
COURSE (7)							
COURSE (8)							
COURSE (9)							

Instructions: Make up a POP when you are **beginning** to develop a strategy and keep it until August so that if you do not get the grades/points you need you can get cracking with clearing.

(communicators or parking facilities), make sure you let the college know in advance so it can be arranged.

Skill produces guidance notes on applying to higher education along with *A Guide to Higher Education for People with Disabilities*. (It also produces *Students with Disabilities in Higher Education: a guide for staff*. If you find a college without a copy perhaps you could let them know about it?) Skill: National Bureau for Students with Disabilities is at 336 Brixton Road, London SW9 7AA (tel 071 274 0565).

If you don't quite make it – action list

If you don't get the grades you have been asked for, first check they won't take you on the course anyway – if all their conditional offers have made the grade, they'll stick to the letter of that offer to you; if hardly any did, they'll be more flexible. Speak to course tutors – don't just assume you're not wanted. Then –

— Keep shopping around.
  UCAS will automatically send you details of clearing in August/September if your conditional offer is not confirmed. This gives you another chance to get a place, even if it is not at one of the colleges you originally chose.
— Keep up with last minute information available:
  – get in touch with your school/college
  – look in the national press – some list vacancies
  – look in local press for advertisements
  – listen to local radio services
  – use one of the electronic databases – ECCTIS, Prestel and Campus 2000 – which are constantly updated
  – ring the *Observer*/Middlesex University telephone vacancy service, which is constantly updated but better at giving general advice than a screen
  – ring universities and colleges direct – the more enterprising have specially staffed units.

Clearing is intended as a nice orderly filling of the last slots. In practice it can be mayhem (computer breakdowns, postal strikes or just life). Many colleges, desperate to meet targets precisely, take telephone applications (which are real) in preference to applications through clearing (which might not materialize). Some even by-pass the system and actively recruit by phone for hard-to-fill courses.

This leaves you in an impossible situation: do you run up a huge phone bill and maybe strike lucky; or do you wait your turn through clearing and not make it. It's up to you. Remember, you are not alone. 10%–20% places are still up for grabs at the start of clearing. Good luck!

What if you come completely unstuck?

Tough but not the end of the world. You can think about the following options –

— resit at school or a crammer (get a list from the Conference for Independent Further Education, c/o Buckhall Farm, Bull Lane, Bethersden, Nr Ashford, Kent; tel 0233 82797) or do something different at your local FE college.

— apply for a BTEC Higher Diploma if you have one A-level. If you choose somewhere with a diploma and a degree course in your subject you **might** be able to transfer later.

— forget all about it and do something else. There's always the chance you can come back to it later, when you're older and wiser. (Over 21 or, in some cases 23, the minimum entrance requirements can be waived on some courses, so long as you can persuade admissions tutors you will benefit.) Get a copy of *Independent Careers*, a companion book to *The Student Book* for all those who eventually want to become their own boss.

When you do have a place

As soon as you have a place, you will have dozens of things to do, apart from adjusting to it all becoming a reality at last. Don't panic. Start by confirming your place; make sure of your accommodation; tell your LEA, so your grant can be processed; arrange money for the start of term (even if you expect a full grant, it almost certainly won't have arrived when you do); get some passport photos done; read the joining instructions you'll be sent; find your exam certificates; buy supplies of stationery, suitable clothes etc. Try not to get rushed off your feet – you don't want to be in need of a holiday before you start and don't let the gigantic reading list you're sent put you into a cold sweat.

How to Apply in Particular

ADAR applications

Most studio based degree courses in art and design are run in art schools, colleges and some universities and you apply through ADAR. ADAR, the Art & Design Admissions Registry, is at Penn House, 9 Broad Street, Hereford HR4 9AP (0432 266653).

Write to ADAR in February with your fee of £16 for a package of forms: a registration form, Form B (for degree courses) and Form H (for HND courses); send a further £3 if you need the *UCAS Handbook* (Registration Scheme for applicants on BA and HND ADAR Handbook). Fill in the registration form and one or both of the other forms. Ask your referee to ensure the registration form reaches ADAR and forms B and H reach your first choice college no later than 31 March. Your first choice interviews start after 1 April and you should be told of their decisions by 9 May. Second choice interviews start after 16 May and you should be told **that** decision by 5 June. If you are still not successful, you go into clearing. You will be told of the remaining vacancies on 16 June and clearing interviews start after 23 June.

The minimum entrance requirements for art and design degree courses are not as inflexible as for other degree courses. After taking GCSEs, some students take A-levels, some BTEC diplomas, most a foundation course at an art college or university. Some are taken just on their portfolio. If you are one of the many who want to take a foundation course apply direct to the college – early.

Competition for art courses is stiff – make sure you know what you are going to do if you are turned down. You may find it useful to look at *Guide to Courses and Careers in Art, Craft and Design* (National Society for Education in Art & Design, The Gatehouse, Corsham Court, Corsham, Wiltshire SN13 0BZ) and *Design Courses in Britain* (Design Council, 28 Haymarket, London SW1), useful.

PCAS and UCCA

PCAS and UCCA are on their way out. It is only useful to know about them if you are still interested in a course starting in the academic year 1993/4. For courses starting September 1994 onwards, you need to know about UCAS, which takes over from both, adopting most of their procedures (and their address).

UCAS applications

The Universities and Colleges Admissions Service (UCAS), operates the central admissions scheme for full-time and sandwich first degree courses (as well as certain non-degree courses) at almost all UK universities and colleges of higher education. Its address is UCAS, PO Box 67, Cheltenham, Glos GL50 3SF.

Applicants fill in a single application form (see *Filling in forms*) and name a maximum of eight courses, usually at different places. UCAS forwards copies of the applicant's form to the named universities/colleges which send their decisions to you through UCAS. Applications for entry in autumn 1994 must be with UCAS by 15 December 1993 – or by 15 October 1993 if one of your choices is Oxford or Cambridge, when you must also apply direct to the university concerned (see Oxford and Cambridge prospectuses).

Normal application procedure is: obtain the application form and *UCAS Handbook* – you must have this because you can't fill in the form without it, as it has the all-important institution and course codes. You can get copies of the *Handbook* for the year you want to start your course from your school/college, or from UCAS if you have left school. This will cost you £5 if you are outside the UK. Consult prospectuses; choose eight courses (you can apply for a degree and HND course in the same subject at the same institution and count it as a single choice; no more than five if your choices are for medical or dental courses); fill in form (black ink only and be meticulous about reference codes); buy a postal order for the application fee (amount not known at the time of going to press) or check methods of paying with your school; give form and fee to a referee (usually your headteacher); ask referee to forward form, fee and confidential statement to UCAS. You will be sent an acknowledgment of your application (but not very quickly if your application goes in on 15 December). The acknowledgment letter will contain an application number and a list of the institutions to which the form has been forwarded. These details must be checked. You cannot change your mind or submit a second application until the following year. After 15 May, you will be restricted as to the number of conditional offers you may hold.

If you are unsuccessful in all eight choices, there is the summer scramble known as **clearing** when you might still find a place as the universities and colleges try to fill all remaining vacancies. You will be sent the information if you are eligible. Remember, universities know the number of places they have, but have no real idea of how many offers to make, so if you have no offer of a place do shop around during clearing. There is nothing to prevent you from getting in touch with any university or college direct and you might get a verbal offer which will later be confirmed through UCAS.

HOW

TO

GET

THE

MONEY

How Much Do I Need?

Income and expenditure budget

This sounds really boring. It is an accountant's device for discovering whether you can afford to do what you want to do. Try one out **before** you commit yourself to going to university and make sure your income and expenditure are not too far out of balance. Don't assume you don't need to do this because you expect an LEA grant and a student loan. **Your** view of your minimum expenditure is almost certainly not the same as the **government's** view of your necessary income.

Income each academic year		Expenditure each academic year	
Cash in bank	£	Tuition fees*	£ ....
Grant	£	Exam fees*	£ ....
Loan (don't underestimate)	£	Accommodation	£ ....
Parental contribution (actual)	£	Council Tax (if any)	£ ....
Earnings (vacation and term-time)	£	Food/drink	£ ....
		Daily travel	£ ....
		Travel (beginning and end term, any field courses, etc)	£ ....
		Vacation expenses	£ ....
		Books	£ ....
		Stationery	£ ....
		Clothes	£ ....
		Leisure (fags, flicks, contraceptives, societies etc)	£ ....
		Interest on overdraft/ credit cards	£ ....
TOTAL £		TOTAL £	
		BALANCE £	

*at present, normally paid direct if you are on an LEA grant, but check.

Don't forget to mutiply the resulting balance by the number of years of your course to see what the position will be at the end. You're bound to be in debt – all students are these days – but does it frighten you?

Fees

All universities and colleges charge fees but precisely what they are is often regarded as a trade secret ('Can I ask you why you want to know?') and their structure complex – one fees leaflet ran to 11 pages. The entries in *Where to Study* include the tuition fees for the academic year 1992/93.

In most cases, the basic **Home Fee** for home and EC students is set by the government, depending on the course. So classroom-based courses are £1,855; lab or studio courses £2,770; and clinical courses £4,985. Examination fees or registration fees are sometimes added to these and at Oxbridge, there is a college fee in addition to the university fee. Hard-pressed universities are rumoured to be considering 'top-up' fees – ie charging a higher fee for courses they can fill even if it's pricey.

If you are on a grant, your fees should be paid direct by your LEA (so far). There are some exceptions – your grant may be discretionary and so paltry that you/your parents are expected to pay the fees; there are some private colleges where the fees may not be covered in full; any top-up fees will not be covered. If you are not on a grant, some universities and colleges charge a special reduced fee (typically £750–£900 a year). Some don't, so it's well worth shopping around.

Students from the European Community pay the same Home Fee as UK students; and may not have to pay any fees at all if it appears they would have been eligible for a mandatory grant if they had been a UK student (now there's a bitter pill for UK students paying their own fees). EC students must apply to their LEA (normally the one local to the university) in order to have their fees paid.

Students from outside the EC pay fees which are set by the university and are intended to cover the full cost of the course – **Overseas Fees**. These range from around £5,500 for classroom-based courses, up to £7,500 for lab or studio courses to a staggering £12,500–£14,000 for clinical courses – and that's only for one year.

Make sure you know what has to be paid, by whom, when and where.

Council Tax

Council tax replaces poll tax from 1 April 1993. It is normally collected from the residents of each property and assumes that there are two of them; sole residents are, however, entitled to a 25% discount. Bills are based on the capital value of the property.

In a rare fit of empathy with students, the government that has prevented them from claiming housing benefit and is trying to ban them from squatting has **largely exempted students** from paying the tax at all. As we understand it, if you live in college, in a hall of residence, a student hostel or a flat/cottage/house where all the adult residents are students, you are **entirely exempt**.

If you live elsewhere, you may not be so lucky. The idea is that you get a 25% discount but the position is more complicated eg if two adults already live there, your presence won't add to the bill so the discount won't help; if there's only one person living there your arrival would mean they lose their sole occupant discount so the 25% discount should definitely help.

Whether landlords manage to pass on all or some of the tax to you will be a matter of personal bargaining. It's our bet that one way or the other they'll ensure that you pay more to reflect the new tax. How much more is in the lap of the gods, but at least you won't have to pay poll tax.

Where Do I Get It?

Grants of all sorts

Do not assume that a grant is your automatic right. In particular, watch out that you do not lose your grant if you change course. Most UK first degree students have their tuition fees paid and are awarded maintenance grants by their LEA, topped up with loans. EC students can get fees-only grants from their LEA. Overseas students have to depend on other sources such as the British Council (10 Spring Gardens, London SW1A 2BN) or World University Service (20 Compton Terrace, London N1 2UN). Some scholarships and loans are available from embassies and high commissions for their country's citizens; there are a few helpful charities, religious and others.

If your course is leading to a profession supplementary to medicine (eg physiotherapists, radiographers), grants are available from the DoH, Room 109, North Fylde Central Office, Norcross, Blackpool, Lancashire FY5 3YA (0253 856123), and in Scotland from the Scottish Education Department, Awards Branch, 2 South Charlotte Street, Edinburgh EH2 4AP.

NUS Information Service Sheets (on grants, loans, welfare benefits etc for students) are useful and available from NUS, 461 Holloway Road, London N7 6LJ, with a large sae. Look at *Money To Study* (published by Family Welfare) in your library.

LEA mandatory grants

Don't expect to survive on your grant alone. It won't go up however much the pound sterling goes down: the total you get from the grant (including parental income) is frozen at the 1990/91 level and student loans are intended to help you cope with the shortfall.

Regulations covering LEA awards are totally indigestible, but most straightforward questions are answered in the DFE booklet *Student Grants and Loans* sent to you by the LEA with your grant application form. Fundamentally you are eligible for a **mandatory** grant if you are ordinarily (but there are problems of definition) resident in the UK and have been so for at least three years; are doing a degree course or equivalent (DFE decide the qualifying courses; the jargon is 'designated courses'); and have not done a course of this kind before. If you don't meet these conditions then the LEA can still make a **discretionary** award but in the present financial climate you are lucky to get one. (The NUS has surveyed discretionary grant policies – see their LEA survey, from NUS, 461 Holloway Road, London N7 6LJ.) If you change courses or college with the approval of both course organisers and this is approved within 4 months of the end of your first year you should be able to transfer your grant too.

LEA discretionary grants

If you are not eligible for a 'mandatory' grant – either because you have held a grant before or because you are not on a 'designated course' (ie a degree course or similar, as judged by the DES), you are in the hands of your local authority – and the best of luck! Each local authority behaves differently, and they'll treat you differently if you're doing a 'non-designated' course such as a film course, foundation art, or Law Society course than if you are an HND student transferring to the second year of a degree course or repeating a year. Discretionary grants become more difficult each year as local authority finances are squeezed. Some authorities will give no discretionary grants or payments at all and they may not give you as much if you had a mandatory grant (it may not even cover your tuition fees). The policies of most LEAs are given in the NUS Local Education Awards Survey (from NUS, 461 Holloway Road, London N7 6LJ) and if they've changed, it'll be to give fewer.

The only general advice we can give to all students applying for a discretionary grant is:

- check direct with your LEA as soon as you think you may need a discretionary grant.
- expect to go through some arbitrary tests and assessment by the LEA (eg auditioning drama students) before you can even hope for financial assistance and then you may hear very late.
- get the LEA answer **in writing**.
- finally, don't forget that if you are turned down, LEAs always have an appeal procedure – however longwinded – which usually involves elected councillors who can legitimately be lobbied. Appeal and lobby!

LEA application procedure

If you live in England and Wales you write for grant application forms to the LEA in whose area you normally reside. (In Scotland write to the Scottish Education Department, Gyleview House, 3 Redheughs Rigg, Southgyle, Edinburgh EH12 9HH; in Northern Ireland to your Education and Library Board.) You should do this early. The completed forms often have to be returned to the LEA by the end of June (but closing dates vary) for a course starting in the autumn. Some authorities have a deadline irrespective of your having a place; others will not take your application unless you hold an offer. If you miss your LEA's deadline it can lead to delays, so find out their procedure and apply as **early** as you can. If yours is not a straightforward application, always confirm any conversations you have with your LEA in writing, or conduct dialogue by letters. LEAs do tend to say one thing and then several months later write something quite different. If your case is not straightforward, give **only** the information they ask for and get advice. LEAs have been known to turn down some applications on the basis of information which they needn't have been told in the first place.

If you have two possible LEAs, make enquiries and opt for the one which is the more reasonable. If you are moving, you should apply to the LEA where you will be resident on 30 June, prior to the autumn you start your course. LEAs often lose sight of their customers. Many have ansaphones to deter you from ringing from August to November and sometimes they don't reply to letters. So be persistent.

The number of students is increasing each year but the number of officials in the LEAs dealing with grants isn't, so treat them gently. Even if you get your forms in on time, you'll be lucky if your grant cheque is there at the start of term. One university started term in September with no first year students' grant cheques at all from over 60 LEAs. Your LEA could be one of those 60, so make sure you take some money to tide you over for a few weeks, or can get some from your bank; you'll need to eat as well as settle in!

Money to live on

UK students are expected to live on money from three sources.

- grant
- parental contribution
- loan

The grant and parental contribution are related so that, as one goes up, the other goes down (see our Rough and Ready Reckoner). Some 26% of students get no grant to live on, parents are expected to provide all; some 27% get a full grant, with no parental contribution payable so more than 70% get less than the full grant. The loan is extra but, since the total of grant and parental contribution is fixed at the 1990/91 rate, you will be more dependent on a loan each year.

The amount the government thinks you need to live on depends on whether you are in or out of London and whether you live at or away from home. You can see how much you could get for the 1992/93 year as a first year student from this table.

The Government expects you to live on:

	Grant plus parents	Loan	Total
In London	£2845	£830	£3675
Out of London	£2265	£715	£2980
Living at home (wherever that is)	£1795	£570	£2365

The loan will increase by the time you are a student but not the grant/parental contribution. You may get more if you study in certain places (eg year in Europe), you support dependants, you are over 26 and qualify for a mature student's grant or you qualify for a disabled student's allowance.

You may think it a joke but this figure is supposed to keep you all year round – term time and vacations (so you'll get less in your final year when you have no summer vacation). To survive, you'll need to be canny and resourceful, have generous parents, an understanding bank manager or try and find work in the vacations or part time in term time. Probably, you'll need them all. If your grant cheque comes in late (and loads do) or your parents don't pay up in full (loads of them too) you'll be in a heap of trouble. Universities and colleges almost all have hardship funds to bail out students but they're much in demand these days. Look at our Foreword for more grim details.

Parental contribution

Some 30% of students don't get money to live on from their LEA – their parents are expected to cough up the lot. Parents have to earn very little to avoid paying a contribution at all (see *Rough and Ready Reckoner*). Certain deductions can be made from parents' joint (or single) income, which then leaves something called the 'residual income'; and the greater the residual income, the greater the parental contribution is expected to be. All you can be sure of, of course, is that as the residual income goes up, your grant goes down. Your LEA (local education authority) will tell your parents how much they are to contribute but it's not a legally binding requirement. A recent survey reveals that 40% of students fail to receive their full parental contribution. This year's grant is based on your parents' income last year; the recession has made it impossible for many parents to pay up and more students are affected. Some parents even refuse to fill out the forms, so the grant is tiny. If your parents are expected to make a sizeable contribution and then don't pay, you'll be hard pressed to survive on your grant and loan, so work persuasively on your parents.

Your parents are not expected to contribute if you are over 25, you have been self supporting for three years or have been married for two years. Get in touch with your students' union (SU) if you are in difficulties. The NUS (National Union of Students) also provides helpful information.

Loans

Student loans come from the Student Loans Company, although you apply through your university or college. A loan is additional to your grant and parental contribution. You are eligible if you are a home student on a full-time designated course of at least one year. The good news is that more courses are designated for loan purposes than for grants – so you may qualify even though you've been refused a grant. If you're eligible, you can decide each year whether or not to apply for a loan – so

GRANTS ROUGH AND READY RECKONER (1992–93)
Grants for 30 week academic year for one student

Parents' income	Parental contribution	So your LEA will pay your fees and a grant of:-		
If your parents' residual income is:-	Your parents' contribution to you is supposed to be:-	For studying in London (£2,845 less parental contribution)	For studying outside London (£2,265 less parental contribution)	For studying while living at home (£1,795 less parental contribution)
up to £13,629	No contribution	£2,845	£2,265	£1,795
£13,630	£45	£2,800	£2,220	£1,750
£15,000	£169	£2,676	£2,096	£1,626
£20,000	£717	£2,128	£1,548	£1,078
£25,000	£1,354	£1,491	£911	£441
£30,000	£2,129	£716	£136	Nothing
£35,000	£2,923	Nothing	Nothing	Nothing
£53,000	£5,500	No grant, even if there are two students in your family		

Parental contributions

you can still apply in your second year, even though you didn't in your first.

The amount you can borrow is not related to any other income you may have; the government fixes the maximum loan you get in each year. This maximum goes up each year; the total of grant plus parental contribution does not. Beware – the government wants loans and grants to be almost equal. Your maximum depends on where you live while you are a student and on the year of the course (you get less in your final year because your academic career stops before your summer vacation). The most up-to-date figures available as we go to press are for 1992/93 when you could borrow any amount up to the following:

	Maximum loan	
	Full year in 1992/1993	Final year in 1992/1993
Students who live away from home:		
in London	£830	£605
or elsewhere	£715	£525
Students who live at home	£570	£415

The money is paid direct into your bank/building society account in one, two or three instalments (most students take the year's loan in one). You can apply for your loan any time during the academic year; if you get it all early in the year, you can stick the money into the building society until you need it. Don't drink it, the summer can be hard.

To apply, go to the office at your university or college which deals with loans (ask when you enrol). Before you go, check what to take with you – generally your birth certificate, the letter from your LEA offering a grant and evidence of your bank/building society account details. The office will check your eligibility and give you an application form to send to the Student Loans Company. You will then be sent a loan agreement to sign

ANDREA ANDREWS BA (ON LOAN)

and return and then you should get the money. Easy – so what about paying it back?

There is an interest charge. The amount you borrow is indexed to inflation. This means the amount you repay will have the same value in real terms as the sum you borrowed but you are not asked to pay more. So it's almost certainly lower than the interest you'll have to pay for any other interest-bearing loan. You start repaying in the April after you finish the course, normally over five years. In some cases deferral is possible but you must arrange it with the Student Loans Company or you could end up on a credit blacklist. To see how it really works, here are two examples provided by the Student Loans Company. They assume an inflation rate of 3.9% (for the purposes of illustration only; no-one would be so unwise as to **predict** the rate of inflation accurately, would they?).

FIRST EXAMPLE: In October 1992, a student in the first year of a 3-year course borrows £830. He completes his course. The repayments for that first year loan will be £17.36 a month for 60 months, starting in April 1996. The total amount payable by the student on that loan will be £1,041.60.

SECOND EXAMPLE: In June 1993, a student in the first year of a 5-year course borrows £570. She completes her course and borrows from SLC each year of her course. She will not commence repayment of the first year's loan of £570 until April 1998. Repayments for that loan will be 84 monthly payments of £9.30 including the payment for April 1998. The total amount payable by the student on that loan will be £781.20.

The Student Loan Company gives written quotations on request; there's also a helpline.

You can ring with your questions to the Student Loans Company Helpline – 0345 300 900.

Mature students

If you are over 26, you are eligible for a higher rate of grant – so long as your grant is mandatory; if it is discretionary, so is the amount. This age allowance is dependent upon your earnings in the three years before your course starts. It covers 52 weeks of the year. Even so, things will be tough. If you are supporting a family you may be able to claim extra amounts but mature students are more likely to end their course in debt than younger undergraduates.

Disabled students: extra money

If you are a student with disabilities, you may find you need to buy specialist equipment to enable you to study or you may incur other extra costs related to your disability. If you get a mandatory grant, you can also apply for extra money from three different disabled students' allowances. One is for general expenses (up to £1,110 per year in 1992/93); another for helpers eg interpreters, notetakers, readers, mobility helpers (up to £4,430 per year in 1992/93) and the third for specialist equipment eg computers, radio microphones, closed circuit televisions (up to £3,325 over the whole course in 1992/93). You apply for the disabled students' allowances directly to your LEA awards section. They may have an application form for you to fill in or they may ask you to write in giving details of what you wish to claim for. They may also ask for a letter from your college to vouch for your needs.

You may be able to claim reimbursement of any extra travelling costs due to your disability as part of your grant.

Some students with disabilities are still able to claim income support or housing benefit (not on college accommodation); find out if you may be able to qualify from your local benefits agency office, the college welfare office or from Skill. Both income support and housing benefit are means-tested so your grant and any other income will be taken into account.

You can get a range of information sheets about financial assistance for students with disabilities in higher education from Skill: National Bureau for Students with Disabilities, 336 Brixton Road, London SW9 7AA (071 274 0565).

Access funds and other hardship funds

There's a sweetie to help you swallow student loans, the freezing of grants, and the abolition of housing benefit – it's called an Access Fund. The government hands out money to universities and colleges, so they can distribute it to individual students who find the financial pressures too much. You may qualify for some money in one college and be ineligible in another; their criteria vary or, in some cases, appear to be non-existent. Some use criteria similar to those for housing benefit; others are using the money to reduce fees for self-financing students, help with childcare; they are encouraged to use at least some for short-term loans. The government is trying to make sure you can't get your hands on access money unless you have already applied for a loan.

Colleges often have their own hardship funds for students with short-term problems or those who come unstuck financially part way through their course. But you'll find there is rarely any long-term help for students at the start of their course, so don't bank on it.

Part-time work

Because you'll find yourself with too little money you'll probably have to look for work to supplement your income. But jobs for students are becoming scarce these days, as for everyone. You can work in the vacations (about 60% students do) and, if you're really pushed, during term-time as well (about 30% students do now). For summer vacation jobs, look at the guides produced by Vacation Work Publications (9 Park End Street, Oxford OX1 1HJ; 0865 241978) who produce a pretty impressive list (send sae). Also try your SU, Job Centre or commercial agencies. For opportunities during the rest of the year things are a little dicier. Your best bet is to try your students' union office. Some universities and colleges pay students to do work on campus through their own employment agencies. Be a little enterprising and look out for opportunities for part-time businesses such as car washing/window cleaning/

kissogram . . . Be prepared to experiment a bit by going outside the usual bar jobs or acting as hacks for academics. Two **awful warnings**: don't let your part-time work get in the way of your academic studies, **and** don't accept drug firms' money to act as human guinea pigs without checking carefully or you may risk your life. It is also probably a good idea to let your tutor know what you're up to, **but** informally.

Banks and building societies

You'll need one, and a sympathetic bank manager; most students need an overdraft to get through. Basic equipment: a cheque book and a bank card. Don't touch credit cards unless you're unusually organised about money and can pay them in full each month; the interest rates are ferocious. Handle cashpoint cards with extreme caution. **Shop around** – banks are wooing students with glossy brochures, filofax and member- ship of the Youth Hostelling Association – their student packages are unveiled each August. The building societies are into the market now too. Although all banks now offer free banking as long as you're in credit, or within your overdraft limit, it's well worth comparing what overdraft conditions you can get (several give overdrafts up to £400 interest free), and whether you'll get interest on any credit in your current account. The canny student applies for a student loan and leaves it earning interest while using the £400 interest free overdraft.

You could open an account at your parent(s)' bank; or find out which bank has a branch at your university and either open one there or at a branch of the same bank back home; it may help to have one with a specially appointed student adviser. Make sure you choose a bank with a branch on or near campus (the building societies are not seen on campus much yet). Open an account **before** you go or you may find yourself with a grant cheque in the bank but no cheque book to use the money. The table on pages 44 and 45 gives some idea of what banks offered to students in 1992. Check this year's glossies before taking action.

Charities, company educational trusts, sponsorship and scholarships

Charities
There are lots of impoverished students chasing the little money handed out by educational charities. So don't pin much hope on getting very much. Write to the Educational Grants Advisory Service, c/o Family Welfare Association, 501–505 Kingsland Road, Dalston, London E8 4AU (071 254 6251), which specialises in educational charities. It also produces *Money To Study* which you may find helpful.

Company educational trusts
Many large companies have these. Find out if the company where your parent(s) works makes grants to sons and daughters of its employees/staff (these are taxed as fringe benefits).

Banks And Building Societies

Summary Of Student Banking Services as at end 1992 – new whacky packages come out each August, so check

	Free Banking	Interest on Current Account	Cheap Overdraft	Student Advisers	Low Cost Graduate Loan	Cheque Card	Cashpoint Card	Low Cost Loan	Where to Write for Further Information
Abbey National	Yes	Yes	Yes	No	No	Yes	Yes	No	Abbey National plc, Abbey House, 201 Grafton Gate East, Central Milton Keynes MK9 1AN
Bank of Scotland	Yes (if in credit or agreed overdraft)	Yes	£200	No	Yes to £1,500	Yes	Yes	No	Marketing Department, Bank of Scotland, Uberior House, 61 Grassmarket, Edinburgh EH1 2JF
Barclays	Yes	Yes	Interest free to £300 for duration of student's course (on application)	Yes	Yes, up to £3,000	Yes (on application)	Yes	No	Student Account Service, Personal Sector Marketing Department, Barclays Bank PLC, PO Box 120, Longwood Close, Westwood Business Park, Coventry CV4 8JN
Clydesdale	Yes; if in credit or within agreed overdraft facility (but standard charge for eg direct debits)	Yes	Yes, interest free up to £400 for period of study (but not automatic)	Yes	Yes to £1,500	Yes (on receipt of grant and subject to status)	Yes		Clydesdale Bank plc, Marketing Department, 150 Buchanan Street, Glasgow G1 2HL
Co-operative (Nothing special for students)	Yes (if in credit)	Yes	No	No	No (but have career development loans)	Yes	Yes, cash cheques at Co-ops during shopping hours	No	The Co-operative Bank, Head Office, PO Box 101, 1 Balloon Street, Manchester M60 4EP
Girobank (Nothing	Yes (if in credit)	Yes	No	No	No	Yes (normally after 6 months)	Yes	No	Personal Banking Marketing, Girobank plc

	Free Banking	Interest on Current Account	Cheap Overdraft	Student Advisers	Low Cost Graduate Loan	Cheque Card	Cashpoint Card	Low Cost Loan	Where to Write for Further Information
Halifax	Yes	Yes	Yes; free to £300 for 12 months, preferential rate thereafter	No	No	Yes	Yes	No	Halifax Building Society Freepost Trinity Road Halifax West Yorkshire HX1 2BR
Lloyds	Yes	Yes	Yes; free to £400	No	Yes	Yes (on receipt of grant and subject to approval)	Yes	No	Lloyds Bank Plc Personal Banking PO Box 112 Canons House Canons Way Bristol BS99 7LB
Midland	Yes	Yes	Yes; free to £400, preferential rate thereafter, if agreed in advance	Yes	Yes	Yes (on receipt of grant)	Yes	No	Midland Bank plc Marketing Department Silver Street Head Sheffield S1 3GG
National Westminster	Yes	Yes	Interest free to £400 for duration of course	Yes	Yes	Yes (on receipt of grant)	Yes	No	National Westminster Bank PLC 41 Lothbury London EC2P 2BP
Royal Bank of Scotland	Yes (if in credit or if overdraft is prearranged)	Yes	£400 interest free if agreed in advance for first year students; base rate thereafter	No	Yes	Yes	Yes	No	The Royal Bank of Scotland plc FREEPOST Edinburgh EH2 0DG (no stamp required)
TSB	Yes	Yes	£400 interest free	No	No	Yes	Yes	No	TSB Bank plc Victoria House Victoria Square Birmingham B1 1BZ

Sponsorship

Sponsorships, and supplementary awards, are offered by employers (industry, government and professional organisations) – particularly for engineering students, where nearly 30% students are sponsored by large firms such as British Telecom. They are, of course, increasingly popular as a way of solving the dual problems of student hardship and difficulty of finding work on graduation; 12% of *all* graduates are recruited through sponsorship (63% of the construction sector). A common formula is a bursary (perhaps £1,000 pa) plus paid and structured vacation work. Beware – your grant will be reduced by the amount of the bursary – or even killed completely. Candidates are normally responsible for gaining their own admission to their degree course. *Sponsorships* is published by COIC; some schemes are also advertised in the press.

Scholarships

This is a complex area. Many universities and colleges offer scholarships of some sort either at entry or after a year; check prospectuses. There are also specialist scholarships (eg in arts and sport). If you go for a scholarship remember, it can affect the amount of your grant.

Social security benefits

Don't rely on them. The government is committed to removing almost all students' entitlements. Disabled students are the only ones recently to have got any extra cash.

Borrowing

A fact of student life these days. One business-like approach is to take the cheapest loan first.

Consider the costs carefully.

1. Overdraft. Should be interest free up to £400.
2. Student loan. Interest at inflation rate only.
3. Agreed overdraft. Variable interest rate, bank base rate plus.
4. Credit cards. Ferocious interest rates.

Overseas Students

If you are an overseas student, other than from the EC, you are expected to pay the full cost of your course without help from the British taxpayer. Legally you can be charged higher tuition fees (£5,500 pa for a classroom-based course, up to £7,500 if lab/studio based and £12,500–£14,000 for clinical courses) and are not entitled to an LEA award. Most colleges and universities have special overseas advisers and many of the staff make a special effort to be sympathetic towards your problems, so talk to them.

Like all DFE regulations, the rules defining overseas students are complicated. You may be charged the higher, overseas fee unless you qualify as a home student under one of the following definitions:

a) those who have been ordinarily resident in the UK for three years but **excluding** any time spent here primarily for the purpose of education;
b) EC nationals resident in the EC for the three years preceding the course;
c) UK citizens who have been abroad temporarily during the previous three years for the purpose of employment (or spouse's or parents' employment);
d) refugees, new immigrants and EC migrant workers.

Being classified as a home student for fees purposes does not necessarily make you eligible for an LEA grant. If you are not sure of your status, check with your LEA and with **each** university and college which offers you a place.

EC citizens resident in the EC pay the same fees as home students. But you pay no fees at all if you would have qualified for a mandatory grant had you been British. Apply to your LEA – it's normally where you will be studying.

If you want help in becoming/being an overseas student in the UK try contacting the British Council locally or, if there isn't one, the British High Commission or Embassy. If you are already in the UK, contact the British Council Information Centre, 10 Spring Gardens, London SW1A 2BN (071 389 4383), they have an educational enquiry service which you can phone or visit (though opening hours vary – so check); or try UKCOSA (United Kingdom Council for Overseas Student Affairs), 9 St Albans Place, London N1 0NX (071 226 3762); if you're a refugee, try WUS (World University Service), 20/21 Compton Terrace, London N1 2UN (071 226 6747).

HOW TO SURVIVE YOUR FIRST YEAR A–Z

Accommodation

Universities and colleges have responded to the government's enthusiasm for massive increases in student numbers but this has rarely been matched by increases in student accommodation. Some colleges believe that accommodation is their problem and will let new students sleep on library floors or increasingly bed and breakfast or holiday camps . . . Others pass the buck, believing that it is the students' problem and simply offer an advice and referral service. If you get a place at one of the few places with a policy of housing all new students, you can really gloat among your friends.

Your first assumption should be that the best accommodation will already have been nabbed. But get along there and sort out something before the start of term. You'll be at a long-term disadvantage if the course starts while you're still tramping the streets in search of a bed, however cosy your corner of the sports hall floor.

The only common factor shared by student accommodation is that it all costs a lot – and housing benefit is a thing of the past for all but a handful of students. Many SUs report students paying 50% grant on just a room – before they turn on a light, buy a book or eat. Average full board in halls of residence now is £52.21 per week – 74% student's income.

If you are lucky enough to have a choice, go for living in. The standard of accommodation is hugely variable but it's easier to make friends, you have more clout with the landlord and (in theory at least) should be closer to college and cheaper (although some are a rip off).

If college accommodation is beyond the pale or non-existent, you look outside. This gets harder every year although the recession has caused more landlords to appear. There are problems, particularly where there is a shortage of cheap private accommodation for rent (leafy suburbs) or where there are other sources of tenants (as in seaside resorts, where

TO HOLD
40 TINS OR
1 STUDENT

many holiday makers are still taking up valuable space at the start of term). Self catering accommodation is usually cheaper. The accommodation office should be able to give you a list of likely pads and, if you're lucky, a list of things to check when you're viewing. Get yourself a local map and off you go. If you find that at each place you're the last in a long queue of other hopefuls sent by the accommodation office, go to the local agencies. Remember to consider any travel costs when looking at the rent – no point in something dirt cheap if it costs a fortune getting to lectures. Another major consideration is how many weeks you have to pay for – rarely you can get away with paying only for term time; usually you pay a retainer during vacations while you're away; increasingly, you pay the full rent all year – so check carefully.

Your LEA will assume that you will live at home if you are studying close by, and so give you less grant. It is certainly cheaper but you may miss out on some of the social facilities and be less involved in college life, which is a mistake. You will need to get the support of your college to move away from home for 'educational reasons' – talk to the college office that deals with grants. You should definitely do this if you don't have proper facilities to study at home – a room of your own as a start.

Some mortgage companies have special packages for students if you can afford to buy a flat or house – maybe with two or three others. You need to know you can get on with your co-owners for the duration of the course and can cope with variable interest rates. You may need a parent to act as guarantor or your parents may find buying you a house the most cost-effective way of handing out their parental contribution.

If all else fails, you may still be able to join the student squatters, except in Scotland where it is already illegal, but the government is trying to close that bolt-hole soon. Get hold of the *Squatters' Handbook* from the Advisory Service for Squatters (ASS), 2 St Paul's Road, London N1 2QN; 071 359 8814 Monday, Wednesday and Friday afternoons. The ASS will help if you get in trouble in a squat, although you must act fast as you often only get two days before you are slung out.

You will, with luck, end up with at least a bed of your own, light, heat and somewhere to work. Cooking, washing and laundry facilities will invariably be shared. Find out if you need to take sheets, towels, saucepans, plates, cutlery, glasses . . . Plus whatever **you** need – garlic press, lemon squeezer, chip pan, cork-screw, water filter, favourite duvet. Don't take valuables unless you can't live without them, and your digs are really secure and you are well insured.

AIDS – Acquired Immunity Deficiency Syndrome

AIDS has, in recent years, become the concern of everyone. The great majority of cases have occurred in the high risk groups: male homosexuals, intravenous drug abusers and haemophiliacs. However, AIDS is now beginning to spread among heterosexuals and none of us can afford to be complacent.

As well as the clinical cases of AIDS, there are many thousands of people who are carrying HIV-1 (Human Immunosuppressive Virus) who may not develop the disease for up to ten years. During all this time they may infect others. There is at present no effective cure for AIDS and a vaccine protecting against it may take many years to develop. To complicate matters there is a variant virus, HIV-2, which is found mainly in Africa or in people who have been there and this is thought to be more transmissible by heterosexual intercourse.

For all these reasons we need to think more carefully about our sexual behaviour. Sticking to one sexual partner obviously helps. When there is any element of risk, with gay or bisexual men or intravenous drug abusers, it is safer to use a condom or sheath which acts as a physical barrier to the transmission of the AIDS virus.

AIDS victims suffer from many disadvantages on top of their inevitably fatal disease. They cannot get life insurance or mortgages and may be ostracised or persecuted by prejudiced people. Much of this prejudice is based on fear and ignorance. AIDS cannot be transmitted by normal social contact nor by sharing food, swimming pools or lavatory seats.

If you suspect that you may have been in contact with AIDS you should discuss this with your student health service or seek counselling at a sexually transmitted diseases (STD) clinic. Blood tests for HIV-1 antibodies can be arranged, anonymously if necessary. If you lose weight for no obvious reason, develop persistent swollen lymph glands or suffer from frequent unexplained infections, you will need to consult your student health service. Usually the cause will turn out not to be AIDS.

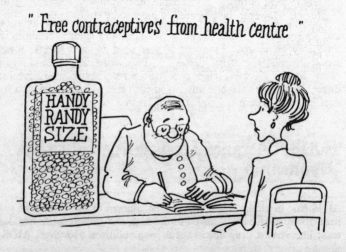

" Free contraceptives from health centre "

For advice ring AIDS Helpline at the Terence Higgins Trust Ltd, 071 242 1010 or send a large sae for leaflets from AIDS Helpline, The Terence Higgins Trust, 52 Grays Inn Road, London WC1X 8LT. A student information pack on HIV and AIDS is issued by the Health Education Authority, Hamilton House, Mabledon Place, London WC1H 9TX (071 383 3833).

Dr Peter Andersen,
Medical Administrator, Health Centre,
University College London

Arrival

Everyone experiences culture shock (especially overseas students) when they arrive at university or poly. Whatever the environment – red brick or ivory tower – it's new and it's unnerving. Don't worry, you'll get used to it. Make sure you register in the right place at the right time. At least then you should get your grant. Find out what you have to do and when and make yourself out a timetable. It's embarrassing to be late, or lost. Once that's over submerge yourself in the first week's entertainment – usually a 'freshers fair', endless discos, wine and cheese parties and bar promotion nights. Don't waste money by joining ludicrous societies. Induction meetings will bore you to death, but you'll see the faces in power and you might sit next to someone interesting.

Tom Dodd describes his experiences thus: 'On your first day, you will more than likely be overawed and a little intimidated – don't worry, all the other students will feel the same. (After going through the amazingly tedious registration procedure, anyone would feel at least stressed.) Try and talk to some of them – if you make the first move, people will gladly talk to you. However, be prepared to meet some strange people! You're bound to meet some cheery soul, who cracks obscure jokes and talks about Socrates.

'On the second day, you will get so sick of pamphlets, leaflets, booklets etc, that you'll more than likely dump the lot. Unfortunately, this means you will have no idea where your first introductory lecture is and it's embarrassing walking into a large lecture room full of people only to be told by the lecturer you are in the wrong place – I know!'

Books

In the first week of term if not before, you will be presented with an exhaustive reading list. Don't go to the bookshop and buy everything you're expected to – you'll never be able to afford it and they **should** all be in the library if they've kept their book purchasing budget abreast of the student intake. Second-hand text books are up for sale on most student union and department notice boards for a fraction of the price. If these are beyond your means try borrowing or splitting the cost with others on your course, or being inventive in your use of the library. Some books will have to be bought some time, but make sure they're essentials and not just your tutor's latest failed publication.

Changing Courses and Colleges

Once you've started, changing courses can be difficult, and practices vary. The dodges are known – getting on an undersubscribed course and then switching. But most places are sympathetic and the usual procedure is first to see tutors and then seek whatever permission is necessary. But watch out you do not lose your grant.

Transferring from one university to another can be more difficult and an agreed procedure doesn't exist. However, CATS' procedures are becoming more common – ask CATS (Open University Validation Services, 344–354 Gray's Inn Road, London WC1X 8BP). Different colleges, and different courses within them, will take different approaches to giving credit for earlier study. Check first before doing anything.

If you are on a grant, you should be able to transfer it to a new course – but only if **either** you get the timing right (the transfer must be approved by the universities concerned before a notional date which is 4 months after the end of your first year) **or** you would be due to complete your new course no later than you expected to complete your old course (eg moving from the end of the first year of one course to the beginning of the second year of your new course, if they are the same length and you don't take a year off between). But in either case, you can only transfer your grant if your course transfer is with the approval of **both** course organisers (or both institutions). So make sure you talk to everyone concerned before taking the plunge.

Disabled Students

Many disabled students have studied successfully for a degree and have enjoyed the time they spent doing so. Sometimes this has involved a great deal of organisation and some problems along the way, but most people say it has been well worth it. Sometimes disabled students do meet difficulties and barriers, possibly as a result of the physical environment, the attitude of staff or maybe financial difficulties but not all barriers are insuperable and many can be overcome.

Being well prepared is obviously an advantage, but you will not know exactly what your needs are until you have attended the course for a while. Make full use of any help and support available from the adviser for students with disabilities, welfare officer, student services officer or your personal tutor. There may be other resources such as the library or student union who can offer support too. Make sure you claim everything you need from the disabled students' allowances. There may also be support agencies outside the university or college which may be able to help you eg RNIB (Royal National Institute for the Blind), Access Centres (for computer assessments, advice) or the Dyslexia Institute. More information from **Skill**: National Bureau for Students with Disabilities, 336 Brixton Road, London SW9 7AA (071 274 0565).

Dropping Out

Only 6% students drop out prematurely at the moment – compared to nearly 50% in France and 60% in Italy. There are hundreds of reasons why students drop out – increasingly it's shortage of money; they may succumb to family pressure to do something else; fall ill or in love; or just not like the course or the subject or the place they've chosen. Maybe they decide they didn't want to do a degree course at all. Men are more likely to drop out of a first year course than women. If you hate your course and you're incurring frightening debts, the game's probably not worth the candle. But don't jump to conclusions too early – some students leave finding they've already incurred the debts and regret having nothing to show for them. If you're thinking of dropping out, make sure you talk to tutors and student advisers before you take irrevocable steps. And watch out that you don't jeopardise your future grant possibilities. Your debts, be warned, will leave with you.

Drugs

Many students will be tempted to experiment with drugs which alter their state of mind. Those that are legal, such as alcohol, nicotine and caffeine, will be sold in most Student Unions. Tobacco, particularly in the form of cigarettes, causes a great deal of long-term illness and increases the risk of circulatory side effects in those taking the contraceptive pill. Abuse of alcohol causes ill health and leads to loss of social inhibitions, sometimes with disastrous results, such as violence and unwanted pregnancies. Long-term alcohol abuse often leads to poor concentration and study difficulties. However, the temperate use of alcohol, particularly wine, can be the source of much civilized pleasure.

Experimenting with illegal drugs can be a very dangerous occupation – apart from the possibility of fines or imprisonment. Heroin, cocaine, amphetamines, barbiturates, LSD and marijuana are all illegal. New drugs of dependency keep cropping up, such as ecstasy which is an amphetamine derivative and crack which is a refined form of cocaine. Heroin is the most dangerous, particularly if it is taken intravenously. Dependency develops very rapidly and soon takes over the addict's life. Those who are hooked may have to find £80 a day to feed their habit. This can lead to dealing in heroin, prostitution and other crimes. The intravenous route also leads to the possibility of developing blood infections, Hepatitis B and AIDS.

One aspect of drug dependency is often forgotten. Addicts are at the mercy of their suppliers who may cut or contaminate what they sell. With LSD, for example, there is no way of knowing what dose is being taken. An overdose may cause very frightening 'bad trips' and lead to psychotic episodes.

Marijuana, although illegal, is in a rather different category. It is relatively harmless and does not often lead to antisocial behaviour. However, there is a risk of causing foetal abnormalities during pregnancy. In Holland it has been legalised without any great increase in its use.

If you feel under pressure to experiment with any illegal drug, the best advice is *'don't'*.

Students who get into trouble with the police for taking or supplying drugs can get advice from Release or Narcotics Anonymous.

Dr Peter Andersen,
Medical Administrator, Health Centre,
University College London

Gays

If you are gay, and it's estimated 5–10% of the population are, then the campus provides a better-than-average environment to come to terms with your own sexuality. Student trendiness promotes the cultivation of gay acquaintances: 'Some of my best friends . . .' Trendy tolerance is easy but public hostility is growing, especially in the light of AIDS statistics and it's worth remembering that landlords may not welcome overt gays. It is not necessarily easy for a gay to tell an uncomprehending Mum or Dad about it all, but you can get help from your college gay society: most universities have one. There you can meet other gays and, if you like, get into gay politics. But make sure you have read everything the government has dished up on the subject of AIDS and stick to safe sex.

The gay rights movement was triggered off by a riot in Stonewall's bar in New York about twenty-five years ago, but since then Oscar Wilde's 'love that dare not speak its name' has turned into the reactionary's 'love that does not shut up'. Although gays are sometimes overly paranoid, they are often victims of prejudice and fear. The 1967 Sexual Offences Act legalised sex between consenting males over the age of 21 in private. Lesbian sex has never been illegal, allegedly because of Queen Victoria's refusal to countenance that women would do such a thing. Groups like the Campaign for Homosexual Equality want an end to legal harassment and the age of consent lowered. More generally, gay groups are campaigning for society's acceptance, not just toleration, of homosexuals.

For gay students, London is reckoned to be the best bet for its variety of gay social life. Gritty macho areas like the North-east and strong church-going areas like North Wales and Northern Ireland are not advised.

Hardship Funds

Student hardship is now a universal problem – see our Foreword – and hardship funds are one of the most genuinely useful ways universities and colleges can tackle individual cases. Many have their own hardship funds, in addition to government access funds. These often allow small loans to tide you over if your grant is late (banks may also offer interest-free loans in these circumstances) or if your money from overseas is delayed by exchange control. Sometimes there are more substantial funds which allow reductions in tuition fees if you are not getting a grant or small cash handouts if you can prove hardship. In order to qualify for money from access funds, you normally need to have applied for a student loan. Other hardship funds may not be so restricted. Ask your tutor or your university or SU welfare staff if you're in difficulties. Some SUs have small hardship funds too.

Home-based Students

Living at home might have advantages and it's certainly likely to be cheaper but it doesn't help you to cut the apron strings and you might find that you are a second-class student by not being able to take advantage of all the academic and social facilities offered. It's also much more likely that you will turn your degree course into a continuation of school which is a great mistake. But a few colleges have large numbers of students living at home, where you would obviously fit in.

It is cheaper for LEAs if you are based at home rather than living in college accommodation. If you want to live away from home and your LEA has assessed you on a 'living at home' basis, talk to the office at your university or college which deals with grants. You may be able to get the LEA's assessment changed if the college supports your moving away from home on 'educational grounds'. You should definitely do this if you don't have proper facilities to study at home (a room of your own, for a start).

If your grant is discretionary, you are more in the hands of your LEA. If the course you want to do is offered locally, they may refuse to pay for you to study elsewhere (eg art foundation course).

Independence

Higher education will mean, for most, living away from home for the first time. Self-sufficiency both financial and emotional has to be learnt. Teach yourself to cook if you haven't already; budget your spending. Homesickness may be inevitable (it's said to affect some 60% students, though only some 12% suffer to the point they can't cope). For most it should gradually pass as you adapt to your surroundings. Making friends is important as you won't have parents, siblings or friends back home to rely on. Remember everyone's in the same boat. Don't rush into ephemeral friendships but equally don't avoid human contact for fear of getting hurt. Lasting friendships will form but not in the first five minutes. 'You'll find you spend half your second year shaking off the undesirable friends you made in the first.' (*Brideshead Revisited*.) If you find it hard to cope don't be frightened to use welfare services, or Niteline run by the SU at most universities, for advice and support. They'll be more use (and cheaper) than a bottle of Scotch.

Insurance

Best advice is not to take very expensive personal items with you – they might get nicked. It's worth getting anything you do take insured, whether you live in university accommodation or not. Try 'Possessions Insurance for Students' from Endsleigh Insurance Services, 20 The Promenade, Cheltenham GL50 1LR (0242 582563). SU or welfare services should be able to advise you on policies for musical instruments, bicycles etc. The most important thing is to get your insurance sorted out immediately so you are covered as quickly as possible. And the more broke you are, the more important it is to be insured if you are cleaned out.

There are occasional tales of unauthorised life insurance salesmen visiting halls and student flats. You are strongly advised not to sign anything and to inform the appropriate authorities. You'll also be sent unsolicited mail – ignore it. As a student any personal insurance policy you're offered is likely to be a waste of time and money.

Learning

Forget school and the way schoolteachers treated you. Teachers at degree level treat you as an adult. Having taken the trouble to get there, it is assumed that you enjoy your subject, are committed to it and want to find out more about it. If so, all well and good. But watch out – the pattern of work may be very different from what you've been used to. No spoonfeeding; you do it yourself. Before you go, you will probably be sent a booklist. You may not be advised which books to read, use your own judgement. You'll be given a timetable for lectures and tutorials, seminars and practicals. Some lectures and seminars aren't compulsory, but most tutorials and practicals are. It's quite easy not to attend lectures, but it's your loss if you don't. You will be expected to do a lot of written work and use a wide range of sources. Try to plan your time well, rushed work isn't usually good work. You might have to read your essay, for example, to your tutor or other students. Don't be put off by this. Criticism, painful as it can be, sharpens understanding. Don't be put off by more sophisticated students, they are not necessarily brighter. And the bright students can be haunted by the fear of failing and need time to adjust to new expectations. Use your own sense and go your own way. See D Rowntree, *Learn How to Study* (London: Macdonald); R A Carman and W R Adams, *Study Skills* (New York: Wiley & Sons). Sometimes there are courses for students who seem to lack study skills but if you need help get it while still at school or college. Have a look at Harry Maddox, *How to Study* (London: Pan Macmillan). Remember, you will have to handle much more information than you did for A-level.

Many universities and colleges have hugely increased their student numbers recently so you may find overflowing lectures, a shortage of books, overstretched specialist teaching space and inadequate contact with tutors. You'll just have to get good at working the system to make sure you don't lose out.

Libraries

Universities spend as much as £90 per student on books, or as little as £15. So not surprisingly, libraries vary in quality, quantity and size; some have specialist collections. Bear this in mind when you apply (see *Where to Study*). As libraries will loom large in your student life, suss out your college library very early on and make sure you know how to use it. If, like many, your university or college has increased the number of students and decreased its spending on books, you'll have to work out ways of reaching recommended books early. Also check opening times and days. Some are closed completely at weekends. It will probably use a different classification system from the one you were used to at school or college. Most libraries have information services and are only too pleased to explain how the library works and if there's a guide, get hold of it. Also ask other users about it – a useful topic of conversation at ghastly induction meetings.

London

London has over 60 universities and colleges and over 100,000 students – somewhere. It is clearly a magnet for students but there are difficulties.

Unless you're in student accommodation, being a student in London can be very isolated. London colleges tend to be splintered over various sites, and it's up to you to be in the right place at the right time both socially and academically. If you don't know your way around London or have never been there before, then you'll have to learn fast. Nobody is going to lead you round by the hand. Accommodation will be hugely expensive and may be difficult to find. Expect to travel some distance for work and play and that's expensive too. Opportunities for entertainment are great but so is the cost. SU facilities will be invaluable socially and financially, so use them. Guides and agencies for help do exist (through your SU), but your own resources will be your best asset.

Mature Students

Jeanette Dodd writes: 'It was a great surprise to find myself embarking upon a BA Honours degree course. Having waded through endless forms, interviews and exams, I felt I deserved a degree just for surviving the mature matriculation process; the passage of a mature student through the clearing system is both confusing and difficult, even with the aid of *The Student Book*.

'My friends had regarded me with suspicion when I announced my intention of giving up my job and entering higher education. 'On my first day at college, I met up with several other mature students who, I was relieved to see, looked as nervous as I did. Then we knuckled down to lectures, acquiring text books, and all that "studying stuff" we had heard about.

'So how did we all get on? Well, it became apparent that college was not the holiday camp it seemed at first after years of earning a living. We were actually expected to produce assignments, sometimes the first essays we had written for years. Families moaned they hardly saw us, and non-college friends complained we fell asleep in the pub after an exhausting week at college. We were usually found buried under piles of books in the library, that is when we were not raiding the younger brother's pencil case, or cramming a month's household chores into a thirty minute blitz! Meanwhile, on the campus the young students were very kind, opened doors for us and smiled encouragingly.

'College life is the most rewarding and stimulating experience. I enjoyed being part of a group, and the variety of people I came into contact with only served to increase my enthusiasm for learning. I even enjoyed all the reading and hard work – even after three years!'

Money Management

Expect to be broke; anybody with an IQ of $47^{3}/_{4}$ can see that the trivial sums the government expects you to live on are inadequate. Unless you're well heeled, you will almost certainly have to borrow more than your maximum student loan to stay afloat, so manage what money you have to keep debts at a minimum. The more forward-thinking colleges and universities believe that prevention is better than cure and run seminars on how to manage your money. Almost all try to apply a cure when things do go wrong – advice and, if you are lucky, money through (inadequate) hardship funds. Here are one or two considerations:

- Cheap accommodation that is expensive to get to is no help: budget for rent *plus* fares.
- Buying a second hand bike is usually cheaper than a year's bus fares.
- You will spend a fortune replacing your belongings if they are nicked and you're not insured.
- Most banks offer interest free overdrafts up to £400. This is (obviously) the cheapest way to borrow, when you get to that stage.
- A student loan costs you (later) an interest rate which is the same as inflation (currently around 4%). This is about as cheap as borrowed money comes once you start paying interest.
- If you agree an overdraft beyond £400 with your bank manager, it should be cheaper for you than for ordinary mortals. Credit cards are an outrageously expensive way to borrow.
- The astute student will apply early for a student loan and put it in the building society while living off the grant and interest free overdraft. There it will make a small amount of money – particularly for those who remember to arrange for it to be paid gross – until the grant and interest free overdraft are exhausted.
- If you find yourself overwhelmed go and see the student adviser at your college or university or in the SU. Don't consider leaving without

talking to those who may be able to help. Beware of dropping out because of money and ending up with the worst of all worlds – a few thousand pounds of debts and no degree to help you earn enough to pay it back.

Overcrowding

Recent government policy has been to increase the number of students and to reduce the amount it costs the government. You'll be astonished to learn that this has caused some problems and staff are having to be trained in how to cope with larger classes and mountains of marking.

Many of the more established universities with other sources of money (rich alumni, research money) have not been much affected. Some universities have increased their student numbers fairly steadily but some have grown very fast and are bursting at the seams (one or two colleges have doubled their student numbers in two years). So beware of over-crowded lectures, little personal tuition, insufficient study space, too few copies of standard texts, cramped student bars . . .

Overseas Students' Survival

The first few weeks at college can be disorientating for anybody. But students from overseas may have the additional problems of coping with a different language and culture (especially if you haven't already spent much time in the UK). And that's apart from the difficulties of coping with the immigration officials when you enter and re-enter the UK (absolute must: keep your visa up to date if you need one).

Many universities and colleges have special orientation programmes and societies for overseas students which offer counselling, help and support (as well as social events). You may not necessarily want to surround yourself with compatriots while you have the opportunity to meet the locals but it can be helpful to know that others share your specific worries/problems. The NUS produces good literature on every-thing from fees to what to do if the immigration authorities refuse to let you into the country; it also has a list of useful addresses (National Union of Students, 461 Holloway Road, London N7 6HT; 071 272 8900). You can also get useful advice and information and a contact at most colleges from UKCOSA (UK Council for Overseas Student Affairs, 9 St Albans Place, London N1 0NX; 071 226 3762). The British Council (10 Spring Gardens, London SW1A 2BN; 071 389 4383) runs an information service, which you can telephone or visit (though check their office opening hours). Two useful books – *Studying and Living in Britain* (published annually for the British Council, ISBN 0746306199) and

How To Study and Live in Britain (ISBN 0746303777) are both published by Northcote House Publishers Ltd.

Parents

Establish the ground rules before you go – parental contribution (when and how it's to be paid), frequency of correspondence, phone calls, visits home etc. You are now an adult with a separate life to lead. Preserve your independence but don't distance yourself too much, or it will make contact difficult and Christmas impossible. Pride and/or concern will mean they'll want to come and see how you're getting on. Warn them what to expect. Don't let them just turn up – it will be at the most inconvenient moment. Fix an exact time and date when your more disreputable friends are out of the way.

Poverty: Coping With It

The amount that students have to live on – whether it's from grants or loans – has failed to keep up with inflation over recent years so the romanticized image of student life on a shoe-string is now a harsh reality for many. Your allowance for the term (if you get it all at once) may seem like riches beyond measure; it isn't, so be careful you don't blow it all in one glorious fortnight only to spend the rest of term trying to avoid your bank manager.

One student writes: 'At the end of my first year, I had an overdraft of £500. This was rather in excess of what the banks generally like to allow.

The reason my bank was not attempting to lynch me was that I had got to know my student adviser by visiting him and he had got to know me personally. The moral is – get to know your student adviser. It keeps the bank happy if you have taken the trouble to discuss your finances with them.'

Depending on where and what you are studying, it is sometimes possible to supplement your income by finding part time work, maybe at the SU or in local pubs and restaurants. Your SU or nearest Job Centre may be able to help you with this. But there's less work around during a recession.

Students have tried living without their student loans. It's tough to do and some have regretted it by the time the next academic year comes round. If you don't want a loan, make sure you really can manage without it. If you do want a loan, apply early and let it earn you some interest before you spend it.

Wherever it comes from (grant, parent, loan, job) you will want your money to go as far as possible. The *Pauper Notes* in each profile in *Where to Study* will help by listing some of the cheapest local amenities. In general, college accommodation seems to be the best value although it is sometimes possible to find very cheap flat shares if you have the time and energy to hunt (and if you are lucky). Food, drink and entertainment are usually cheapest at the SU but keep an eye open for local alternatives (Chinese and Indian restaurants, student discounts at theatres, cinemas etc.). Some supermarkets produce student survival kits, including money-off vouchers and budget recipes.

This may all sound grim; try not to be put off. Although you won't have a lot of spare cash for clothes etc neither will anybody else; try not to skimp on books or food. Most students enjoy themselves in spite of their lack of money. After all, the best things in life are free . . . they say.

Pregnancy

Don't. It may seem like a good idea at the time but don't. For all but the most mature students there is plenty of time after you've graduated. Take one thing at a time and find out about contraception early. Many SUs report that it's students with kids who suffer the greatest student hardship.

Racism

Racial discrimination is still a sad fact of student life. Reports from the Commission for Racial Equality have shown that black students are discriminated against in some admissions procedures, that many colleges have no policies to deal with incidents of racism and that black graduates face discrimination in the labour market. That aside, black students are likely to find that they are confronted with less racial prejudice at a university or college than in many other walks of life.

Most universities now have well-organized Black, Jewish and Irish student groups, as well as societies representing overseas students and different national and religious minorities. Many of these groups are extremely active in the social and political life of the college and are a very good place to meet other students of a similar background. The existence of these groups, and national organizations such as the Anti-Racist Alliance and the Union of Jewish Students, has ensured that there is a constant challenge to racism wherever it appears on campus.

The desire to oppose racism wherever it occurs sometimes expresses itself in debates about whether people who are members of declared racist or fascist organisations should have the right to organize or speak at a university. Since the Government introduced a law safeguarding free speech on campus, students have found a variety of other means of showing their opposition to speakers who represent racist or fascist groups. The discussions about the issue still continue and often represent one of the most fascinating and educative debates on campus.

The black civil rights leader, Martin Luther King, once said, 'If you are not part of the solution you are part of the problem.' Student Unions go to great efforts to involve students in campaigns against racism, and anti-racism 'weeks of action' and international cultural evenings are now common features in a Student Union calendar. Indeed it is events like these which lead to an interaction of the experiences, histories and cultures of the different ethnic minority groups with those of the student body in general. This provides a dynamic and enriching aspect of student life and helps to ensure that universities remain relatively free from overt racism and a strong barrier against the spread of racial hatred and intolerance. Contact Student Union officers, or your tutor, if you have a problem on account of your race – on or off the campus.

Patrick Younge

Reading Difficulties

If you have difficulties with reading first have your eyes tested. Then get hold of M and E de Leeuw, *Read Better, Read Faster* (Penguin) or T Buzan, *Speed Reading* (David & Charles). And your local college of FE may run short helpful courses. If you are dyslexic there are special units at certain colleges and in extreme cases you may be able to dictate essays and exam papers. If all else fails, try READING UNIVERSITY.

Registration

Put up with registration and enrolment – it only happens once a year and the first year is worst. Expect queues (take books, crosswords or try busking). Make sure you take everything they ask for or it will be even more boring. If they ask for the original certificates they will mean it, so get duplicates in advance if you've lost them (most accept the slips you were sent by your exam board only for the most recent exams). Take your GCSE certificates along too, if they ask you to bring *all* your certificates. Take a pen and don't lose your papers. If you've got problems with eg your grant, tell registration staff. It's a hellish time for everyone – staff and students – so we advise patience and getting your act together before you reach the head of the queue. You'll find it useful to take four or five recent passport photographs for ID, membership cards etc.

Safety

This is becoming more of an issue, particularly (but not only) for women. Try and make sure you can get to and from your lectures/parties etc safely – ie that your lodgings are close to public transport and surrounding footpaths are well lit and you know which local routes are safe and which not. Many universities are very conscious of the problem and are running late night buses for women students only, issuing personal alarms and security leaflets and introducing 24-hour portering services. If these aren't available at your university or college – well, start badgering.

Self-catering Checklist

If you are in self-catering accommodation here are some points you may find useful:

– Find out what cooking facilities are available (oven, rings, grill, etc. gas or electricity?)
  How many others share them?
  Are there restrictions as to when they can be used?
  Make sure you know how to operate them properly.

– What about cooking utensils, pots, pans, cutlery, crockery etc?
  Make yourself a list of things you know you will need and check how many of them are provided. A basic list could start with:
    kettle
    frying pan
    sharp knife
    bread knife
    plates
    bowls
    jug
    ovenproof dish or bowl
    at least 1 saucepan
    chopping board/surface
    wooden spoon/spatula
    cutlery
    cups
    glasses
    dishtowels
    tin opener
  then add whatever else you expect to use: fish slice, lemon squeezer, garlic press, potato peeler, cheese grater, sieve, bottle opener and cork-screw.

– What food storage space is available? It can make a big difference if there is somewhere for you to store supplies (without fear of having them stolen) rather than having to dash to the shops every day. This is particularly noticeable during the summer if you don't have access to a fridge.

– Many students find it better to share cooking and food buying. This usually works quite well until somebody gets waylaid in the pub when it was their turn to cook. If you decide to take it in turns to cook (which will reduce considerably the time you spend cooking and shopping) it pays to be organized about it, especially where money is involved. Set up a kitty or an accounts book where everyone writes down how much they spend on communal food etc. It'll also save aggro later if you work out exactly what is communal and what isn't: milk, coffee, cleaning stuff etc. If possible keep some sort of emergency supplies so that you won't starve if your cook gets any last minute invitations on the way home.

– If you haven't done much cooking before, or even if you have and want some quick, inexpensive recipes then try some of these books:
> *The Students' Cookbook* by Jenny Baker (Faber)
> *Cooking for One* by Catherine Kirkpatrick (Hamlyn)
> *Cooking in a Bedsitter* by Katherine Whitehorn (Penguin)
> *Frugal Food* by Delia Smith (Coronet)
> *Not Just a Load of Old Lentils* by Rose Elliott (Fontana)

Many supermarkets have series of recipe books that cater for all sorts of tastes and pockets.

Sex

Many students spend much of their time thinking about sex, but relatively little time actually doing it. Nevertheless, liberal attitudes towards sex still prevail on campus; concerns about AIDS are reflected in the sales of condoms. The glib idea put about by certain sections of the press, that students have come full circle and now hold attitudes resembling those of Queen Victoria or Mary Whitehouse is simply not true. For students living in close proximity to each other, often for the first time free from parental control, the opportunity to experiment with sex is considerable.

Sexual Harassment

It probably happens everywhere to a greater or lesser extent. But the stories are most consistent and extreme in the old male preserves (medical schools; some recently co-ed Oxbridge colleges which still have a predominantly male staff and, therefore, ethos). Check the place out before you apply. If you do have trouble – from staff or fellow students – make sure you tell someone; there's usualy a staff code.

There's an officer responsible for women's issues in most SUs – that should be a good start. Or, like any other woman, telephone the local Rape Crisis Centre (in telephone book) or telephone the Rape Crisis Centre in London (tel: 071 837 1600). Men too get raped; there's a Male

Rape Centre in London (tel: 071 833 3737), Tuesday and Thursday evenings.

Sexually Transmitted Diseases (STDs)

STDs have always been a risk associated with sexual relationships. In 1913 about 10% of the British population had syphilis. By 1985 there were fewer than 3,000 cases of syphilis treated in STD clinics but the annual incidence of gonorrhoea was still over 50,000. Between the end of the last war until some ten years ago, the spread of STDs was contained by early diagnosis, effective treatment and contact tracing achieved by the STD clinics. In the past few years the AIDS epidemic has over-shadowed the other STDs but they are still a threat.

Syphilis was in several ways an earlier model of AIDS. It could be caught by sexual intercourse, it could lie dormant for years, it was often fatal and until the advent of antibiotics it was largely untreatable. There was a period in the 1960s and '70s when all STDs were thought to be treatable, which coincided with the introduction of the contraceptive pill and the breakdown of sexual taboos. However, the arrival of genital herpes on the scene changed all that.

The commonest STDs now are non-specific urethritis caused by chlamydial infection, gonorrhoea and monilial vulvo-vaginitis (thrush). The first two can unfortunately infect women without producing symptoms and are a risk to their future fertility. Human wart virus is also transmissible, from men to women and may be a causative factor in cervical cancer.

You can greatly reduce the chances of catching any STD including AIDS if you avoid promiscuity and use condoms or sheaths if your partner has been at risk of previous infection.

If you develop an unusual vaginal discharge, any genital sore or ulcer or unexplained lower abdominal pain, it is essential to consult your student health service or an STD clinic, also known as departments of genito-urinary medicine (GU Clinics). These departments offer free advice, investigations and treatment and you can refer yourself directly without going through your GP.

Dr Peter Andersen,
Medical Administrator, Health Centre,
University College London

Staff–Student Sex

It happens. Both male and female students can be at risk, heterosexually or homosexually. It can be very ego-boosting (but not much more) to be 'courted' by an older, and apparently wiser, person. At its worst it is simply sexual harassment.

An affair with a tutor can lead to awkwardness, and more importantly from your point of view it can increase pressure on you. And it can be very tacky if your tutor is your examiner. Permanent relationships have, very occasionally, been known but tread warily. Some colleges are introducing codes of conduct to regulate staff–student sexual conduct. If it happens to you and you don't welcome it, talk to your student counsellor (unless he/she is the offending party) or student union.

Student Concessions

Many shopkeepers will give you a discount on proof of student status, usually a NUS or ISIC card. You can also get some newspapers and journals cheap. Lists of local retailers offering discounts are available from your SU office, so use them. To get travel discounts you need an International Student Identity Card (ISIC) and to book your travel through a Student Travel Office. The ISIC is an internationally accepted proof of student status and is available to full-time students of any age for the price of £5.50 and a photo. It is valid from September to December of the following year and you will get free copies of the travel guide. Get details and an application card from your local SU or student travel office or NUS Services (Bleaklow House, Howard Town Mills, Mill Street, Glossop, Derbyshire SK13 8PT; 0457 868003).

Student Health

Most universities and colleges have their own student health services linked to the National Health Service. It is advisable for new students to register with them as NHS patients in the first week of term. Your medical records from your family doctor at home will then follow you in weeks or sometimes months. When you are at home during vacations you can still see your family doctor as a temporary resident.

All the information you give to doctors, nurses and counsellors remains confidential and will not be passed on to the college authorities without your specific consent. If you prefer to have your medical problems dealt with outside your place of study, you are free to register with any NHS general practitioner near where you are living.

The staff in student health services are experienced in dealing with your particular needs. They will be able to offer advice on contraception, unwanted pregnancies, study difficulties and eating problems such as anorexia nervosa. They will discuss with you how to avoid sexually transmitted diseases including AIDS and drug and alcohol problems. Information on healthy nutrition and keeping fit is available. Some centres also have attached dentists, opticians and physiotherapists.

Most health services will also have facilities for dealing with psychological problems. They employ counsellors, psychiatrists and psychotherapists who may normally be in short supply in the NHS as a whole. Again, it must be emphasised that these services are confidential.

Many colleges have special arrangements for the physically disabled or chronically ill students but it is important to inform them in advance of any difficulties you may have. Some groups of students, eg medics and dental students, need special immunisation cover for their clinical work.

Remember that the health centre staff are just as interested in preventing illness as in treating it, so feel free to consult them before health problems develop.

Dr Peter Andersen,
Medical Administrator, Health Centre,
University College London

Students' Unions

Almost all universities and colleges have their own SU (sometimes called guild or association) normally affiliated to the NUS. Every student is automatically a member of the SU, an arrangement the Tories want to end. Whatever the slant of the union (left, right or uncertain), it is run by students for students – more or less. It's usually responsible for entertainments (bands, discos, bars) and for funding clubs and societies. There is likely to be a union shop, which may be the cheapest place to buy stationery etc., 'Niteline' for personal problems, a bar and maybe other eating and drinking spots. They also often run and offer some form of welfare service which can be useful for advice and information on accommodation, work and money matters. (Most university and college authorities are unenthusiastic about taking over all these services.)

How much you get involved in union activities and politics is up to you, but life could be very dull without them. Don't necessarily be put off by a college's reputation for radical or conservative student politics but keep your eye on whether its SU engages in political censorship or racist or anti-middle-class activity. Things can change and your involvement could help to change them.

Studying

Do it! If you do not know how or want to improve on it, try reading *Study for Survival and Success* by Sander Meredeen (Paul Chapman Publishing Ltd). Many colleges run formal short courses at the beginning of the first term to help you develop study skills.

Travel

Local travel can be little or no problem at some universities and colleges but at others it can be horrendous. At some small, single campus colleges there is no need to travel at all while at others you may find that you are spending nearly as much time, energy and money on travel as the average local commuter. Check what's required before applying – you can get some idea from *Where to Study* and prospectuses.

Once you're living on your grant/loan/savings, you'll find you can walk much further than you ever thought possible; and, unless your nerve has completely failed you, a pushbike or pair of roller skates will be useful, if not essential. Hitching may be possible, depending on the area but it's not recommended for women alone after dark (some SUs run night-time minibuses for women). Buses are often cheaper than trains and both can be better than the Tube in London – but it will depend on your journey. Try to plan your local travel so that it does not eat into your grant/loan.

Travel further afield needs researching. You can start by looking for local opportunities on the college 'ride boards', advertising lifts to home, to London, to sporting events and cultural occasions. But to cut your travel costs usually means investing in one of the special cards offered by National Express Coaches and British Rail.

Cutting Your Coach Costs: National Express Coaches offers a Young Person's Card for £6.00 which gives you 30% off adult fares for one year in UK and reductions on some Eurolines fares. Regulations do change so check that you are getting what meets your own travel requirements. To get one you'll need a passport sized photograph and proof of age or if you're over 23, proof that you are a student eg a letter from your college. You can get your card locally from any National Express or Caledonian Express agents and you can find your nearest by telephoning National Express Coaches on 071 730 0202.

Cutting Your Rail Costs: British Rail offers a Young Person's Railcard for £16.00 which typically gives you a discount of 34% on all standard class fares, including savers, supersavers and cheap day returns (as at November 1992). You will need to check for full details at your local station as there may be certain ticket, route and time restrictions applicable. Keep an eye out for any discounts or special offers, particularly at the beginning of the academic year. Take two passport sized photographs with you and proof that you are either aged between 16–23 or a mature student. Young Persons' Railcards are sold at all BR railway stations with a ticket office and at British Rail appointed travel agencies.

Typing

Make sure you can.

Get a wordprocessor if you can; if you can't, you can probably use the ones at university.

Vacs

You'll never have holidays this long again until you retire, so make the most of them. It's probably essential to use them to inject some life into your bank balance as well, so look at some of the excellent books obtainable from **Vacation Work Publications** (9 Park End Street, Oxford OX1 1HJ; 0865 241078). The most general are *Directory of Summer Jobs in Britain* and *Directory of Summer Jobs Abroad*, £6.95 each. *Vacation Traineeships for Students* lists companies which will give you business experience to bolster your cv. Make sure you get the up-to-date editions, published in January.

If you are into travel, start with your Student Travel Office. They sell the products of the 10 or so main student travel operators and have heaps of good advice on student/youth travel. Or try the **Student Travel Centre, Tours and Travel** (STCTT, 18 Rupert Street, London W1V 7FN; 071 434 1306) or **Campus Travel** (headquarters at London Student Travel, 52 Grosvenor Gardens, London SW1W 0AG; 071 730 3402; and on 26 student campuses).

No student pays the full scheduled air fare. There are all the usual methods of getting cheaper flights – bucket shops, ads, charter flights, standby fares, and advance booking (APEX and ABC). In addition, there are lots of student specials. The most obvious are youth fares and student charters. Youth fares allow a range of reductions (up to 25%) off the standard economy fare to European countries and some others. Some have to be bought from the Student Travel Office, so ask there first. They are good value on long-haul and European flights, giving you full-fare service at student price. Student charter flights operate in each vacation to Europe, Israel and the USA. You can get on them with a valid International Student Identity Card (ISIC) – check your Student Travel Office.

Or you can take the train with a BIJ or Interrail ticket. BIJ (Billets International Jeunesse) issues a 2-month ticket which gives you up to 40% reductions on second-class train tickets (including the Channel crossing) to destinations in Europe and Morocco. You can stop-over and you don't need to come back the same way as you go; there's an Explorer's Ticket, linking 22 centres, for a round trip. If you're under 26, you can buy a ticket from any British Rail station or your Student Travel Office (or some other Eurotrain/British Rail/Sealink agents). If you want to hit the fleshpots of a number of European cities, you may prefer an Interrail card. This will currently set you back some £155 (less with a Student Rail Card), is valid for one calendar month and entitles you to unlimited travel on national rail networks in 22 countries on the Continent, as well as reductions on some hovercraft and ferry services. An Interrail and Boat card costs about £180 and adds free travel on some shipping routes; an Interrail Flexicard, at about £145, buys you the same for 10 days in any month. Go to your Student Travel Office or to British Rail or its agents.

There are some coach routes to Europe which are cheap.and cheaper still with a National Express Coach Card – get a brochure from Eurolines, 23 Crawley Road, Luton, Bedfordshire LU1 1HX.

Other thoughts: if you are interested in working in an American summer camp, contact **Camp America** (37a Queen's Gate, London SW7 5HR; 071 589 3223) or **BUNAC** (British Universities North America Club, 16 Bowling Green Lane, London EC1R 0BD; 071 251 3472) which also arranges other working holidays in North America.

Work on a kibbutz can be arranged through **Kibbutz Representatives** (1a Accommodation Road, London NW11 8ED; 081 458 9235) or **Project 67** (10 Hatton Garden, London EC1N 8JY; 071 831 7626).

And if you just want to bum around, you'll find cheap accommodation in youth hostels – contact the **Youth Hostel Association** Trevelyan

House, 8 St Stephen's Hill, St Albans, Hertfordshire, AL1 2DY
(0727 55215); in Scotland the **Scottish Youth Hostels Association**,
7 Glebe Crescent, Stirling SK8 2JA (0786 51181); in Northern Ireland,
YHANI (Youth Hostels Association of Northern Ireland), 56 Bradbury Place, Belfast BT7 1RU (0232 324733).

Victimisation

If you think you are being victimised for reasons of politics, race, religion
or sex you should contact your SU or try one of the following:

**Campaign for Homosexual
Equality (CHE)**
PO Box 342, London WC1X
0DU (071 833 3912)

Catholic Students Council
186 St Paul's Road, Balsall
Heath, Birmingham B12 8LZ
(021 440 3273)

Commission for Racial Equality
Elliot House, 10–12 Allington
Street, London SW1E 5EF
(071 828 7022)

**Democratic Left Youth and
Student Committee**
6 Cynthia Street, London N1 9JF
(071 278 4443)

**Equal Opportunities
Commission**
Overseas House, Quay Street,
Manchester M3 3NH
(061 833 9244)

Liberty (National Council for
Civil Liberties)
21 Tabard Street, London
SE1 4LA (071 403 3888)

**National Organisation of Labour
Students**
150 Walworth Road, London
SE17 1JT (071 701 1234)

National Union of Students
461 Holloway Road, London
N7 6HT
(071 272 8900)

Union of Jewish Students
Hillel House, 1/2 Endsleigh
Street, London WC1H 0DS
(071 380 0111)

**Youth Section Conservative
Central Office**
32 Smith Square, London
SW1P 3HH
(071 222 9000)

Welfare

Universities and colleges generally are supportive. They normally provide specialist help for a range of problems. The NUS publishes an
excellent Welfare Manual – intended for student advisers but you may be
able to consult a copy in your library or SU office or contact NUS
(461 Holloway Road, London N7 6LJ).

Scarcely any students are entitled to welfare benefits, with some exceptions eg disabled or single parents. More information from DSS leaflets from local DSS offices or Citizens Advice Bureaux.

DSS Information Service: dial 100 and ask for freefone DSS. Dental and eye checks are means tested once you are 19 – get the appropriate forms from your dentist and optician to claim free checks.

What If You Don't Survive Your First Year

Work out what went wrong

If you're not up to higher education, look for a job. If you fancy eventually becoming your own boss, buy *Independent Careers*.

If it was the wrong course, try changing course (fast, to keep your grant).

If it was the wrong college, or the wrong place, try changing (again fast, to keep your grant).

If the reasons are personal or financial, try giving it a break. You **may** be able to return later, transfer credit to another institution or continue part time somewhere else.

What You Call Them/What You Don't

(ie formal address for academics). Below are the terms for **formal** address in speech and writing – what you call academics **informally** is up to you.

Status	Speech	Writing
Vice-Chancellor	Vice-Chancellor	Dear Vice-Chancellor
Principal	Principal	Dear Principal
Director	Director	Dear Director
Master (applies to some women as well)	Master	Dear Master
Warden	Warden	Dear Warden
Professor (even if knighted)	Professor Bloggs	Dear Professor Bloggs
Readers		
Senior Lecturers	Dr/Mr/Ms/Mrs	Dear Dr/Mr/Ms/Mrs
Lecturers	Bloggs	Bloggs
Tutors		

Do not use Dear Sir, Dear Madam, or Dear Sir/Madam, when writing to tutors.

When You've Got Stuck In

When you've settled in, and before you forget *The Student Book* completely, how about writing to us? We'd particularly like to know of anything you wish you'd known about before you applied or when you got there.

Please write to Klaus Boehm and Jenny Lees-Spalding, The Student Book, c/o Pan Macmillan, 18–21 Cavaye Place, London SW10 9PG. If you're lucky, you might even get an acknowledgment – but no promises!

WHAT'S WHAT IN HIGHER EDUCATION

Abbreviations

Higher education is jargon-laden with a welter of confusing and confused abbreviations, acronyms and misleading terms (eg semester strictly speaking means a half academic year but in some places means a term, ie third of a year). Regrettably, the list continues to grow: 800 plus at the last count. Here are a few useful ones:

A-levels – GCE passes at advanced level; ADAR – Art and Design Admissions Registry; APEL – Assessment of Prior Experiential Learning; APL – Assessment of Prior Learning; AS-levels – Advanced Supplementary levels; BA – Bachelor of Arts; BBA – Bachelor of Business Administration; BSc – Bachelor of Science; BTEC – Business and Technology Education Council; CACC – Council for the Accreditation of Correspondence Colleges; CATS – Credit Accumulation and Transfer Scheme; CIFE – Conference for Independent Further Education; CNAA – Council for National Academic Awards; COMETT – Community Programme in Education and Training for Technology; DFE – Department for Education; EC – European Community; ECCTIS – Educational Counselling and Credit Transfer Information Service; ECTS – European Community Course Credit Transfer Systems; EGA – Educational Guidance for Adults; ERASMUS – European Community Action Scheme for the Mobility of University Students; FE – Further Education; FORCE – Formation Continuée en Europe; GCE – General Certificate of Education; GCSE – General Certificate of Secondary Education; GTTR – Graduate Teacher Training Register; HE – Higher Education; HEFC – Higher Education Funding Council; HEIST – Higher Education Information Service Unit; HNC – Higher National Certificate; HND – Higher National Diploma; IB – International Baccalaureate; ICP – Inter-University Co-operation Programme; IRT – Institution with Recognised Teachers (University of London); IT – Information Technology; JCR – Junior Common Room; LEA – Local Education Authority; LINGUA – Community Action Programmes to Promote Foreign Languages Competence in the European Community; MBA – Master's in Business Administration; NCDT – National Council for Drama Training; NUS – National Union of Students; NVQ – National Vocational Qualification; ONC – Ordinary National Certificate; OND – Ordinary National Diploma; PAMs – Professions Allied to Medicine; PCAS – Polytechnic Central Admissions System; PICKUP – Professional Industrial and Commercial Updating; Poly – Polytechnic; PSHE – Public Sector Higher Education; QTS – Qualified Teacher Status; SA – Students' Association; SCE – Scottish Certificate of Education; SCR – Senior Common Room; SED – Scottish Education Department; SRC – Students' Representative Council; STEP – Sixth Term Examination Papers (entrance exam for Cambridge University); SU – Students' Union; SWAS – Social Work Admissions System; UCAS – Universities and Colleges Admissions Service;

UCCA – University Central Council on Admissions; ULU – University of London Union.

Access

This means all things to all people. Widening access means opening up higher education, particularly to non-standard students or students from schools with no tradition of sending pupils on to university. There are access courses which are designed to prepare you for a degree course if you were not previously qualified – particularly science and engineering. Some are excellent, some are suspect. Check what extra qualifications you need for the degree course you want before you embark on an access course. Many access courses may be run at an FE college, in which case you can go for one near by. A useful directory to access courses is available from ECCTIS (Access to Higher Education Courses Directory).

There are also Access Funds – government money distributed to students by colleges, for those in financial hardship. In the *Where to Study* section, we use access to mean how you get there – bus, rail etc. How old fashioned.

ADAR

The Art and Design Admissions Registry, Penn House, 9 Broad Street, Hereford HR4 9AP (0432 266653). It processes applications for studio based art and design degree courses (and higher national diploma courses in design and associated studies) in universities, colleges and art schools in England and Wales.

Agriculture

Agriculture is taught both at first degree and higher national diploma. First degree courses are offered in much the same way as in any other science study area by universities and colleges. (You can look them up in the *Subject and Places Index*). In contrast, some agricultural colleges only teach for the higher national diploma and in general tend to be concerned more with vocational training and lay less emphasis on the scientific aspects of the subject. They are not included in *The Student Book*.

Six distinguished agricultural teaching institutions which are firmly rooted in both the scientific and the vocational traditions are: Harper Adams; Royal Agricultural College; Scottish Agricultural College; Seale Hayne (see Plymouth University); Welsh Agricultural College; Writtle. (Look them up in *Where to Study*.)

A-Level and AS-Level Grades

Grades A–E at A- and AS-level are accepted as passes; these are often turned into points. For AS-level, A = 5, B = 4, C = 3, D = 2, E = 1; for A-level, A = 10, B = 8, C = 6, D = 4, E = 2. If you have a conditional offer, you may well be asked to gain specific grades or a cumulative minimum number of points. A-level grades are not regarded as reliable pointers to future academic development but do help universities sort out students for places. *Your* job is to get your A-level grades. If you have to play the grades game, invaluable advice and information is given in Brian Heap, *Degree Course Offers* and also now in *University Entrance: The Official Guide*. Most admissions tutors will normally accept two AS-levels in place of a third A-level but not in place of the first two. But there may be additional course requirements, so check.

American Colleges

Many American colleges have a UK campus which admits British students. They are very variable and British students may find it difficult to get employers and professional bodies to accept a degree from some of them as equalling a British degree. Some of the American colleges represented in the UK are of course of international standing.

Art Colleges

Some, but not all, colleges of art offer degree courses. Where they do you'll find them in the *Subject and Places Index* together with university art courses. Many have become departments of universities; others remain independent but offer degrees of the Open University or another university. In some cases, several small art colleges have merged to form eg Kent Institute, Norfolk Institute. In London, a number have joined together in a loose federation called the London Institute; the individual colleges still maintain individual identities and you can look them up in *Where to Study*.

Work out what kind of institution you want to go to, but often grants for the foundation courses are not available for those outside your immediate area. Many offer foundation courses, which is one route to a degree. Our *Study Areas* distinguish between **fine arts**, which is art history, and **fine art** (which, together with graphic design, photography, textiles/fashion and three dimensional design, form the Art & Design *Study Area*).

Bogus Degrees

A number of bogus degrees are offered by post, mostly postgraduate degrees. Sometimes the degree is for sale, sometimes a thesis is required. There is seldom any course of instruction. No college in *The Student Book* offers or accepts them. Under the Education Reform Act 1988, it is a criminal offence to award or seek to offer to award a UK degree if you do not have express authority to award it, and the Secretary of State for Education provides lists of bodies authorised to award UK degrees. If in doubt contact the DFE. There is no such constraint on offering certificates or diplomas, so beware!

CATS

This is a national scheme operated by the Open University to help students transfer credit (see *Credit Transfer*). CATS stands for Credit Accumulation and Transfer Scheme. It should be able to help you if you:

- want to carry credit to a degree course, perhaps on the grounds that you have already taken part of a course or have work experience that duplicates part of the course;
- want to study for a degree at more than one college, perhaps because nowhere teaches the combination of studies you seek – eg Arabic and Hebrew;
- want to alternate periods of study with other activities – eg producing a family or earning your living.

You can make use of CATS in two different ways – either purely for obtaining advice before you apply for a degree course *or* by registering directly with CATS so that you become a CATS student and can then study at a number of places. A growing number of companies' in-house training schemes (eg IBM, W H Smith and even Wimpy) and professional bodies' qualifications (eg IPM, CIMA) can count for credit too.

Contact CATS at the Open University Validation Services, 344–354 Gray's Inn Road, London WC1X 8BP (071 278 4411).

CNAA

The CNAA is history. Up until this year, the CNAA (Council for National Academic Awards) awarded degrees to students who had satisfactorily completed CNAA-approved courses in polys and many colleges. Now the polys have become universities, some colleges can also award their own degrees and the others offer university degrees. So you can forget all about it.

There is a CNAA Aftercare Service for those who already have a CNAA qualification. So, if you're one of them and you lose your certificate or need independent evidence for an employer, contact the Open University Validation Services (344–354 Gray's Inn Road, London WC1X 8BP; 071 278 4411). They hold all the CNAA archives.

College

This is a portmanteau word. It can mean anything from the Garret Tutorial College, Hackney, to the Royal College of Surgeons. Some colleges teach first degrees, maybe as a constituent college of a university; most don't.

The colleges in *The Student Book* fall into several categories:

- colleges of higher education awarding their own degrees eg Bolton Institute and West Surrey College. These are not universities but have satisfied the various conditions laid down by the DFE to be able to award their own degrees. They run a variety of advanced (ie post A-level) and non-advanced courses; degree students may be in the minority;
- other colleges of higher education offering degrees awarded by a university eg West London Institute or Nene College. These are similar to those awarding their own degrees but they have some sort of a formal relationship with a university which awards its degrees. Some have considerable independence, some labelling themselves 'a college of —— University' whatever that *actually* means;
- specialist colleges, sometimes enormously distinguished and internationally known, which offer either degrees awarded by a university or their own qualifications – eg British School of Osteopathy, Jews' College, National Film School, Royal Academy of Music or the Royal Agricultural College;
- colleges that are part of a university but you are admitted to the college, typically Oxbridge.
- colleges of the federal universities such as London and Wales which are very independent; some would wish to be universities in their own right.

Community Service Volunteers

Are you uncertain about what to do when you leave school? Or have you decided, but would like to try something completely unconnected with work or college? Then community service volunteers could be the answer.

CSV is a national volunteer agency which involves young people in full-time community work in a wide range of projects throughout the UK, normally away from home. For example, volunteers are currently working with adults and children with learning difficulties or physical disabilities, with the homeless, the elderly, children whose families have broken up, young offenders, immigrants who want to learn English, battered wives and children on adventure playgrounds and play schemes.

You don't need experience or qualifications to become a CSV – just the enthusiasm to commit yourself to the community and to improving the quality of other people's lives. No offer of service is refused: provided you can give between 4 and 12 months' full-time and are over 16, CSV will find a project for you. As a volunteer, you'd receive full board and lodging plus £18.50 per week spending money and travelling expenses. If you think you might be interested in becoming a CSV, write for more information and an application form to CSV, 237 Pentonville Road, London N1 9NG (071 278 6601).

Continuing Education

Another educational term which means what its users want it to mean! Essentially it means that you can't expect your education to end when you've got your first degree (we thought that'd cheer you up) but you can expect periods of re-education and retraining during your working life. So you could be going back to college for up-dating in your subject. This contrasts with studying for a **higher** degree which is intended to take you **deeper** into your subject.

Correspondence Courses

These are essentially part-time courses by postal tuition. There have been abuses, and the responsible correspondence colleges have established the Council for the Accreditation of Correspondence Colleges (CACC). But accreditation is voluntary. CACC produces a list of colleges which it accredits. It's obtainable from CACC, 27 Marylebone Road, London NW1 5JS (071 935 5391). For advice on UK degrees available by correspondence, contact the DFE (Department for Education).

Credit Transfer

If you change course or return to higher education after a break you may be able to transfer the credit for the work you did in your earlier course to your new one so maybe take less time to complete your new course. The jargon for this is credit transfer. You can carry a credit from one university to another, or from one course to another within the same college. You will need the help (and maybe the approval) of the course tutor from your first course so make sure you keep him/her informed. Also, if you are on a grant, watch out you don't lose it when you change course (see separate entries).

Some transfers are easier than others – from a DipHE to a linked degree course in the same place will probably be automatic. But you wouldn't, of course, expect to carry any credit to a physics degree on the basis of previous study in the social sciences. You can now get credit (through CATS at the Open University Validation Services) for an increasing number of companies' in-house training courses though.

But the overlap in subject matter is not necessarily simple for admissions tutors to assess and there is often a noticeable reluctance even to try. Indeed, there can be a wide variation of approach to credit transfer between the different courses in a single university. Some modular courses can, and do, admit a large number of students with credit. So if you can't find (or don't want) a clone of your first course, start looking at them.

There are a number of developments aimed at breaking down some of the inflexibility of higher education. One is CATS (see separate entry). The other is the establishment of a number of local higher education consortia. In general these aim to ease transfer between the members and possibly lead to some common courses. Some consortia include local further education colleges, so it may be easier to move to local degree courses from these, possibly with some credit. If you want to find out whether your previous work will count for credit, ask when you apply. If that doesn't work, asks CATS.

If your college is part of the Erasmus Scheme, you can study somewhere else in the EC for credit – so long as you don't expect special treatment at the host institution because the assessment system and language are unfamiliar.

Degree-Equivalent Courses

To help you pick your way through the thickets of diplomas etc. the Department for Education provides a free publication *Student grants and loans* available from your local education authority or the DFE (Publication Despatch Centre, Honeypot Lane, Canons Park, Stanmore, Middlesex HA7 1AZ). Generally speaking, mandatory grants are available for first degree courses, Diploma of Higher Education (DipHE) courses, Higher National Diploma courses, and courses of initial teacher training. Some other degree-equivalent courses make you eligible for mandatory grants in the following subjects: accountancy, architecture, art and design, chemistry, drama, environmental health, landscape architecture/design, music, textiles and town and country planning. These are listed in a free leaflet, available from the DFE, *Designated Courses*. Scotland is different: contact the Scottish Education Department, Awards Branch, Gyleview House, 3 Redheughs Rigg, Southgyle, Edinburgh EH12 9HH (031 244 5823).

The degree-equivalent courses covered in *The Student Book* are not necessarily the same as those attracting mandatory grants. They are degree courses and those that, in the opinion of the editors, are real alternatives to a degree. No less valid than the DFE view!

Degrees

First degrees are the main concern of *The Student Book*, either honours or ordinary (sometimes called pass). Most degree courses are now honours, and ordinary degrees are awarded if a student fails to achieve honours standard. But there are some courses leading only to an ordinary degree, eg Open University and some part-time courses.

Usually first degrees lead to the award of bachelor status (BA, BSc, BEd or LLB) but there are many variants, eg many Scottish first degrees lead to an MA, and MEng and MPhys are first degrees going straight through to masters. And not all bachelor degrees are first degrees, eg BPhil. Higher degrees are usually masters or doctorates (MA, MSc, PhD), again with many variants. Don't get worried by the letters – course content matters much more. Honours degrees are usually classified into first, upper second (two one), lower second (two two) or third.

There are different types of degree depending on the course structure: **single** (where a single subject is studied for the length of the course, although a wide variety of topics may be covered and the first year may be broad); **joint** (where two subjects are taken; you don't do twice as much work – but check the proportions); **combined/multidisciplinary/ interdisciplinary** (where components from any number of subjects can be put together; check how the degrees are combined – are they just stitched together to appear trendy or do they cohere as a real educational whole?); **modular** (where students structure their own degrees from a range of units or modules). Nowadays you may be able to add study of a language to any of these.

There are also different kinds of approach: **theoretical** (a specialist study without immediate applications); **vocational** (the degree is directly linked to work applications); **sandwich** (part of the course is spent in a work placement). Think hard about what degree course structure and kind of approach will suit you best. Each university and college has its own language about its degrees so check thoroughly that it will provide what you expect. Check how the degree is assessed (eg examination, continuous assessment, project work). This can vary depending on the course. Make sure you find out the assessment procedure and that it suits you.

Commonly a degree course lasts three years. But there are now a few 'accelerated' courses lasting two years, typically 45 weeks a year. Many courses last four or more years – particularly if you spend a year abroad or in a work placement, you get an additional qualification (eg PGCE) as part of the course or if you are studying medicine or veterinary science. The course may also take more time if there is a foundation year or you start off on an access course.

Universities give their own degrees to their own students, those in affiliated colleges and maybe in some other colleges. Some colleges/ institutions of higher education also offer their own degrees, in others the degree is awarded by the Open University or another university. So check.

Degrees from foreign universities (eg American universities) are offered in the UK but *The Student Book* does not cover them. So long as the foreign university makes it clear that what is offered is not a UK degree but (say) a US degree, it is quite acceptable to the British authorities. But beware: the degree may not be acceptable to British employers or professional bodies. Check thoroughly before paying any fees.

DFE

The Department for Education, Sanctuary Buildings, Great Smith Street, Westminster, London SW1P 3BT (071 925 5000) is the central government department responsible for education in England and Wales. For Northern Ireland the equivalent is the Northern Ireland Department of Education, Rathgael House, Balloo Road, Bangor, County Down BT19 7PR (0247 270077), and for Scotland the Scottish Education Department, Gyleview House, 2 Redleuchs Rigg, Edinburgh EH12 9HH (031 556 8000). Most matters concerning grants are dealt with by your LEA.

Diploma in Higher Education (DipHE)

This is a two year diploma course which, in theory, is equivalent to the first two years of a degree course. They could be of interest to mature students not wishing to commit themselves to 3 years' study. Some colleges allow you to transfer from DipHE to degree courses; others haven't heard of them. **Don't** embark on a DipHE without ensuring that transfer to a degree is possible.

Drama

Because grants for drama students are discretionary (ie your LEA will decide for itself whether it will give you a grant and, if so, how much) it is particularly important that you give yourself a chance by going on an approved course. The National Council for Drama Training (5 Tavistock

Place, London WC1H 9SN, 071 387 3650) publishes a list of accredited courses (send sae). The NCDT list of accredited courses has included:

ALRA (Academy of Live and Recorded Arts); Arts Educational School; Birmingham School of Speech Training and Dramatic Art; Bristol Old Vic Theatre School; Central School of Speech and Drama; Drama Centre, London; Guildford School of Acting; Guildhall School of Music and Drama; London Academy of Music and Dramatic Art; Manchester Metropolitan University School of Theatre; Mountview Theatre School; Rose Bruford College of Speech and Drama (BA Theatre Arts); Royal Academy of Dramatic Art (RADA); Royal Scottish Academy of Music and Drama; Webber Douglas Academy of Dramatic Art; Welsh College of Music and Drama.

There are also lists of accredited courses in community theatre and stage management, and one year post-grad drama courses. Many of these colleges can be looked up in *Where To Study*.

ECCTIS 2000

ECCTIS stores information on 80,000 British and Irish courses, including entry requirements and courses content. It also catalogues credit transfers and credits for previous experience so you could find it useful if you are still at school, if you are a mature applicant, or if you are already doing a course and want to change to another.

You can only get your teeth into this mind-boggling mass of detail through an ECCTIS access point. These are rapidly being installed in schools and libraries and are already available in most careers offices (also British Council offices). To locate your nearest access point you can ask: ECCTIS, Fulton House, Jessup Avenue, Cheltenham, Gloucestershire, GL50 3SH (0242 518724).

European Community

Studying in Europe

By the time you finish your degree course, the single European market will be old hat. The people who are best equipped to work in it will be those who can speak European languages and, better still, understand the local environment, culture and networks in the different European countries. It is up to you to make your degree course help you survive in Europe.

In the past, it was only language specialists who had the opportunity to equip themselves with European languages and culture during their degree courses. All that is changing. There is a variety of Euro-opportunities in other degree courses, add-on languages are increasingly

available and exchanges to universities in other EC countries are growing. For example, many universities, polys and colleges now offer European studies or languages jointly with a range of other subjects; on a number of courses, you can add a European language as a supplementary subject and, at an increasing number of places, the aim is to make language teaching available to **all** students.

And then there are exchanges, which are as varied an assortment as you could imagine. They range from individual exchanges, to course based exchanges; some are effectively time out of your degree, some are an integral part of the course; on some you may get minimal or no credit for your work done abroad, on others the work can count towards your degree or you may be eligible for a qualification in your host country in addition to your degree. The European Commission is aiming for 10% first degree students to spend part of their course elsewhere in the Community. Erasmus now also covers the seven EFTA countries and there is scope for exchanges in eastern Europe too. At the moment, relatively few students from the UK go to the rest of Europe but large numbers are coming to the UK to improve their English – think of the implications of that for when you start your career in the single European market.

There is even lots of EC cash around to help student mobility, provided by Erasmus. In these cash-starved days, this means that some universities are better at counting the shekels that come to them from Europe than helping their own students to make use of the opportunities for going abroad. But many colleges and universities are imaginative and running well-organised exchanges. It's worth making sure they *are* well run. There's little point in going to Europe if, once you get there, your life is dogged by loneliness, you are living in a British ghetto, never meet local students and are locked out of overcrowded lectures – all of which happens. Some colleges and universities have been in Europe for a long time and are canny at making sure you get a worthwhile educational experience and an adequate roof over your head; others have cashed in on the bandwagon.

So, don't go through life blaming your lack of Euro-cred on the lousy language teaching at school. This could be your great opportunity to catch up and get ahead – go for it.

Erasmus: One British Student's Experience

Abby Innes. (BSc Econ, Government; LSE; Konstanz University, October–December 1990) writes:

If one year of life in a British university makes you yearn for distant shores and you're embarrassed about speaking only one language, or you never quite recovered from the wanderlust of your year out, then it is worth investigating *Erasmus*. Shirley Williams described the snappily named 'European Action Scheme for the Mobility of University Students' as a 'social revolution'. Williams may be exaggerating a wee bit but certainly in the colleges where it exists *Erasmus* offers a wonderful opportunity for broadening your horizons on the cheap.

The few months I spent at Konstanz university (southern Germany) turned out to be a glimpse of the 'campus' university life I thought I'd passed up by choosing somewhere like London to study. This didn't produce feelings of regret so much as amazement at quite how different (and easier!) life as a student can be. If you choose carefully you can do much to fill whatever 'gaps' you may have been noticing at home. For instance, if you usually study in the countryside why not give yourself a dose of some beautiful European city? Quite apart from learning another language, radically changing the college environment is a stimulating experience, not least in making one appreciate quite how privileged the British system is.

Success in creating mass universities does mean continental students get significantly less tutorial attention. In the German case, Konstanz at 9,000 students was pretty small when compared to Berlin which, at 44,000, has to provide video screens for those who forgot to book seats in the lecture theatre. On the whole this means *Erasmus* is good for painlessly improving your capacity for self-reliance. I say painless because there are other compensating luxuries. Lingering over seriously subsidised three-course meals in a canteen overlooking lake Konstanz, (drink-water clear blue and hugged by the looming figures of snow-capped mountains – which is odd if you're used to that pure London air) did truly wonderful things for the soul.

A break from your home university not only offers you a different style of study (assessment of long essays takes some of the strain from exams), but also a secure way of exploring another culture, new approaches to your subject and a chance to change your social life. Depending on how organized your home university is you can swap to a European university/polytechnic for anything between three months and a year. You can often participate without prior knowledge of the language, (especially where you can be assessed in English) though note: the better your language skills the greater your choice of course will be.

As social revolutions go the administrative problems could be worse, but still, beware, your *Erasmus* grant (full costs) often arrives late (even a year late!), and communication between universities can be dire. No one informed me as to when I should arrive at Konstanz and I went half expecting a professor in a rowing boat masquerading as a university! When you arrive the initial bureaucrat hassle of registration (particularly tortuous in Germany) can also be a bit daunting. However even the latter produced strange and wonderful bonding instincts. I know it's not what 'they' meant but breaking the Euro-ice sometimes meant standing in massive queues feeling touchingly 'European' and joking about the paperwork. But who knows, a bit of pressure on your own administration might even make them improve things.

When you think about it there are good reasons for being a 'fresher' again. There's a lot of satisfaction to be gained simply realising how far you've come in coping with strange situations. Nor, on a final note, do you necessarily 'miss out' by leaving your home university for a while. If anything *Erasmus* keeps the grass from growing under your feet and the experience can make you feel a good deal more confident about the friendships you come home to. It also lets you look abroad when it comes to leaving poly/university and finding work which, when you're British, could be useful!

Erasmus: A view from the Directorate

Fritz Dalichow writes:

Five hundred years ago, the Dutch humanist Desiderius Erasmus spent his school, university and working life as a university professor in different parts of Europe, moving freely both as a student and teacher. He learned and taught in places like Deventer/the Netherlands, Paris/France, Cambridge/England, Bologna, Turin and Venice/Italy, Leuven/Belgium and Basle/Switzerland. The Erasmus Programme (European Community Action Scheme for the Mobility of University Students) tries hard to bring back academic mobility in view of the Common Internal Market in 1993 and thereafter. This year there will be some 44,000 students spending a study period in an EC member state other than their own under Erasmus.

The Erasmus Programme was adopted on 15 June 1987 by the 12

member states of the European Community. As its name implies, the programme's main objective is to increase significantly the number of students who spend a period of study in one of the other European Community (EC) countries. However, the programme is broader than this in that it also provides funding for a wide range of other co-operative activities. Firstly, Erasmus provides grants to universities which, in this context, refers to all types of higher education institutions as defined nationally, for the purpose of designing, developing, operating, maintaining and evaluating programmes for the mobility of students and/or teaching staff. The totality of the programmes thus supported forms what is known as the European University Network. The emphasis is on programmes which enable students to spend a period of at least three months in another Community country for which they receive full academic credit from their home university. Tuition fees are mutually waived. In the case of the staff mobility programmes, preference is given to arrangements whereby the visiting staff members provide integrated teaching input of significant duration, ideally at least a month, into the programmes of the host institutions.

In addition, universities may receive support for the joint development of new curricula and for carrying out intensive programmes of short duration, involving students and teaching staff from several Community countries. All four types of programme are collectively known as inter-university co-operation programmes (ICPs). Grants for these various activities vary considerably depending on the nature and complexity of the programmes concerned. For establishing student mobility programmes, they average $9,300 per university, per programme, per year.

Secondly – and this is the element of Erasmus which gives the programme both its title and its main focus – Erasmus provides mobility grants to students in the form of top-up grants to help cover the additional costs incurred by students wishing to study in another Community country. These costs include such items as language preparation, cost-of-living differential and, of course, travel. The average grant, Community-wide, is around $2,000 for a full year's study, and students of all levels (up to doctorate) are eligible, though grants are not normally awarded to students in their first year of higher education. Priority is given to students moving to another EC country within the framework of ICPs supported under Erasmus.

Thirdly, the Erasmus Programme seeks to promote a number of measures designed to improve the possibilities for students to receive academic recognition or credit for study periods effected, and qualifications obtained, in other member states. In addition to the network of nationally based information centres on the assessment of foreign educational credentials which has been established for this purpose, a European Community course credit transfer system (ECTS) is now operational. Launched in 1989/90, the pilot phase of this project will span a six-year period. Within ECTS, automatic credit transfer arrangements are being progressively introduced in five subject areas (mechanical engineering, medicine, chemistry, business studies and history), between the total of some eighty institutions, which will form the core of the pilot project.

Finally, the programme encompasses a number of complementary measures designed to assist in creating a favourable climate for the future development of Erasmus. These include in particular a 'visits' scheme to enable university teachers and administrators to visit other Community countries for the purpose of preparing future exchange programmes, to carry out brief teaching assignments, or merely to familiarize themselves with aspects of the higher education systems in the countries visited. Support is also provided for specific projects of university associations and consortia operating at European level, for the preparation of publications related to university co-operation, and for various information activities.

The Commission of the European Communities is assisted in the operational implementation of the Erasmus programme by an agency called the Erasmus Bureau. The student grants' component of Erasmus is administered on a decentralized basis by nationally designated agencies, co-ordinated in Brussels and working according to jointly agreed guidelines.

Particularly important with regard to Erasmus is its comprehensive nature: it embraces twelve European countries and is open to all types of higher education institutions, all academic disciplines and levels of study, and provides support for a number of different types of co-operation activity.

Erasmus is by far the biggest programme for inter-university co-operation and exchange ever launched at European level, with a budget currently fixed at some 200 million ecu for the three year period 1990–92. Moreover, along with Comett, the EC programme for higher education-industry co-operation in the field of technology-related training, it has brought the higher education sector into the mainstream of policy-making for the EC as a whole. In helping to create a vastly increased pool of young people with first-hand experience of living and studying in another country, it has an important role to play in the run-up to 1993, the year in which internal barriers to trade and professional mobility within the Community should be dismantled, and takes its place alongside other measures designed to create what is becoming known as the 'People's Europe'.

An EC action programme, *Erasmus*, helps organize student mobility between member countries. Students can spend a fully recognized period of study in another member country. For information on schemes and grants approach your university or poly or UK Erasmus Students Grants Council (The University, Canterbury CT2 7PD; tel 0227 762712) or the Erasmus Bureau in Brussells (Rue Montoyer 70, B-1040 Bruxelles, Belgium; tel 0101.32.2.233.01.11).

[Fritz Dalichow is Assistant Director of the Erasmus Bureau in Brussels, responsible for academic recognition and credit transfer matters. This article is mainly based on an article written by Alan Smith (director of the Erasmus Bureau) for the review *Higher Education Policy* ('The Erasmus Programme of the European Community – Some Implications for International Exchange and Co-operation', in: Higher Education Policy, Vol 1 No.4 1988, pp 51–2). The views expressed in this article are those of the authors and do not necessarily represent those of the Commission of the European Communities or the European Cultural Foundation.]

European Languages

You don't need to be a language specialist to spend time in Europe. Even if you don't choose to specialize in modern languages for your first degree you'll probably be able to pick up some of the EC languages your school didn't get round to teaching you. Each university and college has its own approach and you'll have to check what's available directly but a good starting point is the profiles in *Where to Study* followed by a detailed search of individual prospectuses.

Language options for non-linguists and 'language for all' programmes are becoming much more common and one of the encouraging developments is that staff as well as students are taking up the new learning opportunities.

But what will be in place for your first degree course is another matter. In some institutions, an EC language component is now becoming an integral part of every one of their degree courses; in yet others it's an uphill struggle to get half an hour's use of a language laboratory before the long vacation. It's all changing so fast that you'll do best to ask direct what they'll be offering by the time you get there: the chances are that it will be more than they've got at the moment – so long as they can still find staff to teach languages.

External Degrees

These are issued by a university, eg Kent University, which validates the teaching at another college.

Film Education

Film education normally now includes TV film education. Two invaluable lists of film courses are sold by the Publications Department, British Film Institute, 29 Rathbone Street, London W1P 1AG. *Studying Film and Education* covers courses in which les than 50% of the work is practical; *Film and TV training* lists courses when over 50% of the work is practical. They cost £4.75 each (cheques to British Film Institute). See also Film Studies in *Subject and Places Index*.

Franchising

More commonly associated with fried chicken (Colonel Saunders) and health product retail outlets (Body Shop), franchising has recently become a feature of higher education. So, while the degree course you buy will be the genuine article, closely specified and monitored (like the Colonel's fried chicken) it can be taught (at least for the first year or two) in your own neighbourhood college of further education or even sixth form college.

This makes it possible to experience higher education locally for a year or two without committing yourself to the whole first degree curriculum in an inconvenient location. Access is the name of the game. You could for instance study at Salford University, which runs four-year first degree courses, the first two years are taught in local FE colleges, during which you aren't taught at Salford at all. The development of franchising could probably be of more interest to mature students than degree course applicants from school. Some courses make a mockery of the idea of higher education, so take a good look before you start.

LEA

This means your local education authority in England and Wales. It is to your LEA that you apply for a grant but also contact your LEA for advice (address in phone book). In Scotland apply for a grant to the Scottish Education Department, Awards Branch, Gyleview House, 3 Redheughs Rigg, Southgyle, Edinburgh EH12 9HH. In Northern Ireland apply to your area Education and Library Board.

London Institute

The largest school of art and design in Europe it is a combination of five famous London art colleges – Camberwell College of Arts, Central Saint Martins, Chelsea, London College of Fashion and London College of Printing.

Each college has its own identity, its own prospectus and you apply to the college not the Institute. But there is some Institute accommodation, an Institute Student Union (as well as individual college SUs) and it is beginning to gain an identity of its own. The degrees are awarded by the Open University.

Mature Students

For grants purposes, mature students are those over 26 on 1 September in the year they wish to start their degree and then they should get more money. You can have your grant assessed independently of your parents before that if you have worked for three years.

Entrance requirements for courses vary; so does the age at which you are classified as a 'mature student'. This can often be as low as 21, so check. Some universities are more flexible about entrance requirements for mature students than others – Oxbridge has colleges specially for mature students.

There is a useful Mature Students' Union but the president, and so the union's address, changes each year. Write to the NUS (executive member responsible for mature students) to find the current president.

Mergers

'Big is beautiful' is back. Size is the DFE's new criteria for an institution to become a university. So there have been mergers everywhere. The new generation of mergers make split city sites look like a tight-knit campus. Many merged institutions are spread over 50 miles.

UNIVERSITY OF
ALL THE LITTLE
BITS LEFT OVER

Military, Navy and Air Force Education

Look up Cranwell; Dartmouth; Manadon; Sandhurst; Shrivenham in *Where to Study*. See also Strategic Studies in *Subject and Places Index*. Military bursaries are paid to selected students in degree courses if you promise to go into the service when you graduate. If your heart is set on this, then go ahead. But don't forget that after three or four years as a student, service life may not have the same attraction. If you pull out you will probably have to pay the money back. Contact your local recruiting office for details of the various schemes.

Modular Degrees

Also called Course Unit Schemes. These are degrees where the stuff you get taught is parcelled up into little bits, called modules or units. To get a degree, you have to take a certain number of modules/units, some of which may be compulsory.

These degree schemes are becoming much more common. They have the advantage of allowing you more choice in the particular areas you cover (or don't cover) – for example you can include a language in your degree – and it is easier to transfer credit to another course if you need to.

Professor Laurie Taylor has described these schemes as like sweet counters – you can make up a pound of sweets by choosing equal amounts of liquorice all-sorts and toffees; stick to mint creams on their own; or you can go for fruit pastels with just a couple of chocolate truffles . . . What that means to you is that modularisation enhances your consumer choice.

Northern Ireland

Northern Ireland has two universities, Belfast and Ulster. Grants regulations are the same as for the rest of the UK although you apply to your Education and Library Board. Despite the political unrest student life is surprisingly normal. Students are affiliated to both the UK and the Eire NUS.

NUS

The National Union of Students, Nelson Mandela House, 461 Holloway Road, London N7 6HT (071 272 8900) is the central organization for UK students. You may or may not agree with its politics but student politics change rapidly – locally and nationally. NUS is a federation of students' unions. You join your local SU automatically and, as a collective body, it decides whether to join NUS – 98% UKCPUs do. If your SU is affiliated you will receive its benefits – its information services and student concessions are invaluable. Take grant and disciplinary problems to your local students' union.

The NUS is in the government's firing line. Watch this space.

Open University

Founded in 1969 to cater for part-time, mature students, the Open University (Walton Hall, Milton Keynes MK7 6AA; tel 0908 274066) now accepts applicants of 18 years and over on to degree courses. It also now runs the CATS scheme and validates degrees in a number of colleges.

Although OU degree courses usually take longer to complete than other full-time degree courses, the fact that they only require part-time study together with the flexibility of the inter-disciplinary course structures offered, makes the OU a good alternative for those who can't or don't want to commit themselves to a full-time degree course or who find it more satisfactory to study at home from the material provided by the OU. (See Open University in *Where to Study*.)

Oxbridge

There is no such thing as Oxbridge. There are two quite separate (and large) universities – Oxford and Cambridge, each comprising about 30 colleges which admit their own students. You go to a college at Oxford or Cambridge, not to Oxbridge, and it's worth taking the trouble to check out the colleges you are most likely to feel comfortable with.

If you think you might fit in – *don't let yourself be put off by their dodgy media reputations or by your schoolteachers*. Remember that Oxford and Cambridge are two of only a handful of British universities that are truly of international standing and that they are actively looking for bright students from the comprehensive schools.

These universities pre-date most of the others by several centuries. They have long and astonishingly prestigious histories and are still a primary training ground for cabinet ministers, headmasters, captains of industry, etc as well as more ordinary mortals. There are several ways in which they are still different: you need to apply earlier for example; both have an entrance exam as an alternative to the standard admission by A-level. They are both based on a collegiate system; some of your teaching will be college-based but much will be university based – as are the examinations.

Some schools have long traditions of sending people to Oxbridge. If yours doesn't, that's fine but you will have to do some research to discover what others will learn from their teachers. Find out which colleges are really good in your chosen subject and then decide whether you, too, are *really* good. If so, choose those colleges (as first choice, if you want them to look at you); any doubts, pick some completely different colleges. Don't be seduced by the buildings and the lawns. You may find the smaller, newer colleges less daunting than the big, grander ones. Find current students when you go up and visit – any students – and talk to them.

Women have been accepted in the universities since early this century – first in women's colleges and some 20 years ago the men's colleges began to accept women students. That may seem a long time ago to you but it's a relatively recent blip in the history of many colleges and most have at least one tame misogynist (is he in *your* subject?). It's hard to tell whether a college is truly co-ed or just a male bastion with some pix of female students in the prospectus – but you could start by looking at the number of male and female students they admit and, perhaps more revealing, the number of female members of staff. All but a handful of the women's colleges are also now mixed.

Last but not least, student hardship is less evident at Oxbridge than at many universities; the colleges have a great deal of accommodation and are sufficiently rich to ensure that virtually no students drop out because of financial problems.

PCAS

Polytechnics Central Admissions System, Fulton House, Jessop Avenue, Cheltenham, Gloucestershire GL50 3SH (0242 227788). PCAS is no use to you unless you are applying for a course starting in 1993/94. Everyone else turn to **UCAS**.

Performance Arts

This term has been coined through the need to find a description for an area of study that includes experience in those arts which involve an element of performance. The word **performance** rather than **performing** is generally used to make clear that courses so designated are not vocational courses of training for would-be professional actors, singers and dancers, but rather intended to provide opportunity for a practical and theoretical study of these arts in a non-vocational context. This does not mean that students who follow such courses are debarred from a professional career, if they have the necessary talent (and a high standard of performance is usually required); but that they are degree courses offering an education in the understanding of the arts rather than a training in their practice.

Performance arts courses are usually offered by polytechnics, rather than universities. This is a very complex area, study the various syllabuses with great care and write to the institutions to find out precisely the scope and objectives of the course and what options there may be.

John Allen

Polys

Polytechnics were mostly founded in the early seventies largely to teach vocationally oriented courses. They all turned into universities en masse in 1992. Another piece of educational history.

Professional Qualifications

Degrees in themselves do not normally license you to practise a profession. A professional qualification is also necessary. The list below gives enquiry points from which details of the qualifications necessary for practice are available. You will also be told how long professional qualifications take and what exemptions your degree will give you.

Accountants
(Certified): Chartered Association of Certified Accountants, 29 Lincoln's Inn Fields, London WC2A 3EE (071 242 6855); *(Chartered):* Institute of Chartered Accountants, Chartered Accountants Hall, Moorgate Place, London EC2P 2BJ (071 628 7060); *(Scotland):* Institute of Chartered Accountants of Scotland, 27 Queen Street, Edinburgh EH2 1LA (031 225 5673); *(Cost and Management):* Chartered Institute of Management Accountants, 63 Portland Place, London W1N 4AB (071 637 2311); *(Public Finance):* Chartered Institute of Public Finance and Accountancy, 2–3 Robert Street, London WC2N 6BH (071 895 8823)

Acoustics
Institute of Acoustics, PO Box 320, St Albans, Herts AL1 1PZ (0727 48195)

Actuaries
Institute of Actuaries, Staple Inn Hall, High Holborn, London WC1V 7QJ (071 242 0106)

Advocates
(Scotland): Faculty of Advocates, Advocates Library, Parliament House, 11 Parliament Square, Edinburgh EH1 1RF (031 226 5071)

Air Force
See Cranwell in *Where to Study*

Air Pilots, Engineers & Navigators
Guild of Air Pilots and Air Navigators, 291 Grays Inn Road, London WC1X 8QF (071 837 3323)

Architects
Royal Institute of British Architects, 66 Portland Place, London W1N 4AD (071 580 5533); Royal Incorporation of Architects in Scotland, 15 Rutland Square, Edinburgh EH1 2BE (031 229 7205)

Army
See Sandhurst and Shrivenham in *Where to Study*

Barristers
(England and Wales): Council of Legal Education, 4 Gray's Inn Place, London WC1R 5DU (071 405 4635)

(Northern Ireland): Council of Legal Education (Northern Ireland), Institute of Professional Legal Studies, Queen's University, Belfast BT7 1NN (0232 245133)

Chiropodists
Society of Chiropodists, 53 Welbeck Street, London W1M 7HE (071 486 3381)

Dentists
General Dental Council, 37 Wimpole Street, London W1M 8DQ (071 486 2171)

Dietitians
British Dietetic Association, Daimler House, Paradise Circus, Queensway, Birmingham, B1 2BJ

Doctors
General Medical Council, 44 Hallam Street, London W1N 6AE (071 580 7642)

Engineers
Engineering Council, 10 Maltravers Street, London WC2R 3ER (071 240 7891)

Mathematics
Institute of Mathematics and its Applications, 16 Nelson Street, Southend-on-Sea, Essex SS1 1EF (0702 354020)

Navy, Royal
See Dartmouth and Manadon in *Where to Study*

Navy, Merchant
Department of Transport (Marine Division), Sunley House, 90–93 High Holborn, London WC1V 6LP (071-405 6911)

Nurses
(England and Wales): UK Central Council for Nursing, Midwifery and Health Visiting for England and Wales, 23 Portland Place, London W1N 3AS (071 637 7181)

(Northern Ireland): National Board for Nursing, Midwifery and Health Visiting for Northern Ireland, RAC House, 79 Chichester Street, Belfast BT1 4JE (0232 238152)

(Scotland): National Board for Nursing, Midwifery and Health Visiting for Scotland, 22 Queen Street, Edinburgh EH2 1JX (031 226 7371)

Occupational Therapists
College of Occupational Therapists, 6–8 Marshalsea Road, London SE1 1HL (071 357 6480)

Opticians
General Optical Council, 41 Harley Street, London W1N 2DJ (071 580 3898)

Optometrists
British College of Optometrists, 10 Knaresborough Place, London SW5 0TG (071 835 1302)

Orthoptists
British Orthoptic Society, Tavistock House North, Tavistock Square, London WC1H 9HX (071 387 7992)

Pharmacists
Royal Pharmaceutical Society of Great Britain, 1 Lambeth High Street, London SE1 7JN (071 735 9141)

Physiotherapists
Chartered Society of Physiotherapy, 14 Bedford Row, London WC1R 4ED (071 242 1941)

Radiographers
College of Radiographers, 14 Upper Wimpole Street, London W1M 8BN (071 935 5726)

Social Workers
Central Council for Education and Training in Social Work, Derbyshire House, St Chad's Street, London WC1H 8AD (071 278 2455)

Solicitors
(England and Wales): Law Society, 113 Chancery Lane, London WC2A 1PL (071 242 1222)

(Northern Ireland): Council of Legal Education (Northern Ireland), Institute of Professional Legal Studies, Queen's University, Belfast BT7 1NN (0232 245133)

(Scotland): Law Society of Scotland, Law Society's Hall, 26 Drumsheugh Gardens, Edinburgh EH3 7YR (031 226 7411)

Speech Therapists
College of Speech and Language Therapists, Bath Place, Rivington Street, London EC2 (071 613 3855)

Surveyors
(Chartered): Royal Institution of Chartered Surveyors, 12 Great George Street, Parliament Square, London SW1P 3AE (071 222 7000);

(Quantity): Royal Institution of Chartered Surveyors (address as above)

Teachers
Teaching as a Career, Department for Education, Sanctionary Buildings, Great Smith Street, London SW1P 3BT (071 925 6617)

Town Planners
Royal Town Planning Institute, 26 Portland Place, London W1N 4BE (071 636 9107)

Transport
Chartered Institute of Transport, 80 Portland Place, London W1N 4DH (071 636 9952)

Veterinary Surgeons
Royal College of Veterinary Surgeons, 32 Belgrave Square, London SW1X 8QP (071 235 4971)

Sandwich Courses

These are ways of alternating courses of study with periods of professional/industrial training out at work (50,000 students do). Periods vary in length (eg one pattern is six months 'in' and six months 'out') and there are 'thick' and 'thin' sandwiches. Find out the pattern from the prospectus and ask for more details at the interview if you get one. Sandwich courses give good work experience and help your employability later; but some universities are finding it increasingly difficult to place their students, particularly those with work placements in Europe. One such course had to fold, so watch out.

Scotland

Scotland currently has twelve universities: Aberdeen, Dundee, Edinburgh, Glasgow, Heriot-Watt, Napier, Paisley, Robert Gordon, St Andrews, Stirling, Strathclyde and Glasgow Poly which has still to choose a new name. The Central Institutions, including art colleges; and the Royal Scottish Academy of Music and Drama. *The Scottish University Entrance Guide* gives details of university courses and requirements (available from Scottish Universities Council, Kinnessburn, Kennedy Gardens, St Andrews, Fife KY16 9DR; 0334 72406).

There has been a tradition of Scottish students going straight on to a degree course after taking Scottish Highers in the fifth form (and taking four years for an honours course). This does still survive but many universities and polys now require you to take A-levels or Certificate of Sixth Year Studies.

Semesters

This means half a year. Some that aren't classicists have three semesters in a year. Some universities divide the academic year into two semesters; more will in the future.

Skill: National Bureau for Students with Disabilities

Skill is a national charity that works to develop opportunities for people with disabilities and learning difficulties in all types of education and training over the age of 16. Amongst other activities, Skill runs an information service for individual students, their families or friends or people who work with them. A range of free information sheets are available as well as priced publications. You can write to Skill's Information Officer with enquiries or telephone (2pm–5pm, Monday–Friday). If necessary, it may be possible to visit Skill's office by appointment.

Skill: National Bureau for Students with Disabilities, is at 336 Brixton Road, London SW9 7AA (071 274 0565).

Students' Charter

No chance – they're still talking about it.

Teaching

If you want to teach there are two routes involving a first degree course: either get a degree in the subject you wish to teach, then take a PGCE – Postgraduate Certificate of Education. (You apply through the GTTR, PO Box 239, Cheltenham, Gloucestershire GL50 3SL.) Or you can take a bachelor of education; traditionally this has been a BEd but the trend now is towards a BA(Ed) or BSc(Ed) or BA/BSc(QTS); almost all the universities have made this change now because they believe the BA/BSc has higher standing.

Apply through UCAS for the places/courses you want in the same way as for any other first degree course – see *Where to Study*.

UCAS

The Universities and Colleges Admissions Service, PO Box 67, Cheltenham, Glos GL50 3SF takes over from PCAS and UCCA for courses starting in the autumn 1994 onwards. It operates the central admissions scheme for full-time and sandwich first degree courses (as well as some non-degree courses) at all universities and most colleges (but apply direct to the Open University and some colleges; through ADAR for studio-based art and design courses).

UCCA

The Universities Central Council on Admissions, PO Box 28, Cheltenham, Glos GL50 3SA is no use to you unless you are applying for a course starting in 1993/94. Otherwise look up UCAS.

Universities

Some universities have been around since the middle ages, some since last year so it's hardly surprising that they are a pretty mixed bunch. They do all have royal charters to award their own degrees. They are usually large, teach across a range of subjects to first degree level and have research students as well. Some of the newer universities also have some non-degree courses.

The number of universities has swelled since all the polytechnics and some colleges of higher education became universities in 1992, to the great benefit of those supplying academic gowns, maces etc. There are now often two universities in the same town. As the new universities struggle to distinguish themselves from their local university, they have increased the length of the average university name by 33% (the University of Northumbria at Newcastle, the University of Central England in Birmingham).

Wales

Wales has two universities: Glamorgan University and Wales University which is a federation of six institutions (Aberystwyth, Bangor, Cardiff, Lampeter, Swansea, Wales College of Medicine). There are also several institutes of higher education.

This section tells you about UK universities and colleges. Each has a map reference, so you can find it on the *maps* (next section). Each is profiled in two different ways; a Top and a Bottom.

TOP – from the relevant administration and/or prospectus.

BOTTOM – *What It's Like* and *Pauper Notes* usually derive from the students.

You should not necessarily expect a complete match between the TOP and the BOTTOM of each profile.

WHERE

TO

STUDY

WORCESTER COLLEGE
OF HIGHER EDUCATION

Bachelor of Arts, Bachelor of Education and Bachelor of Science Degrees
The Worcester Modular scheme offers the following first degrees:

B.A. (Honours) in	Combined Studies
	English Studies
	Geographical Studies
	Historical Studies
	Leisure Management*
	Social Science
B.Ed (Honours) in Primary	Art and Design
	Biological Science
	English Studies
	Studies in Geography and Society
	Studies in History and Society
	Mathematical Studies
	Music Studies
	Physical Education
B.Ed. (Honours) in Secondary	Biological Science
	Mathematics Studies
	Technology (Home Economics)
BSc(Honours) in	Combined Studies
	Biological Science
	Environmental Management*
	Environmental Science
	Geographical Studies
	Psychology Studies
	Sports Science*

*subject to validation

For further information and Prospectus please contact
Academic Registry, Worcester College of Higher Education,
Henwick Grove, Worcester WR2 6AJ   Telephone No. (0905) 748080 exts 205/225.

the MANCHESTER METROPOLITAN UNIVERSITY

Meeting your future needs

**with over 300 courses in 50 different subject areas...
... one of them will be right for you.**

The Manchester Metropolitan University's mission is to be an accessible institution of higher education meeting the needs of those with the ability to benefit, and of industry, commerce and the professions.

We are Britain's largest non-federal University and offer a wide variety of courses at undergraduate, postgraduate and professional level as well as an extensive portfolio of research and consultancy activities.

Many of our courses are available on both full-time and part-time modes and a Credit Accumulation & Transfer Scheme (CATS) is in place.

We have excellent library, computing and accommodation facilities and our Students' Union offers some of the best sporting and recreational activities to be found.

Our main location is in the centre of Manchester, a city renowned for its thriving cultural, social and sporting life.

Some of Britain's most beautiful countryside lies within easy reach of those who enjoy outdoor pursuits as do many other attractions and facilities of the region as a whole.

For more information call our 24 hour prospectus hotline: 061 247 1055, or write to us at The Manchester Metropolitan University, All Saints, Manchester M15 6BH.

formerly **MANCHESTER POLYTECHNIC**

LSU COLLEGE OF HIGHER EDUCATION
(University of Southampton)

NEW at LSU SOUTHAMPTON

Ten years ago LSU was one of the first colleges to recognise the importance of Europe when it introduced its innovative B.A. in Modern Languages and European Studies. In the 1990s we intend to respond to cultural and national needs.

In **1993** look out for the degrees which will be added to our existing programme, for example:

BSc Combined Honours – in this unique and exciting degree it will be possible to study less-traditional combinations of subjects.

For details of other new degrees and interesting combinations of subjects write to:

    The Registrar
    LSU College of Higher Education
    The Avenue
    Southampton SO9 5HB

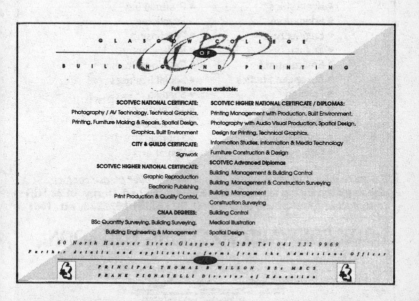

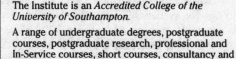

BATH COLLEGE
OF HIGHER EDUCATION

Courses at Bath College of Higher Education offer the opportunity to study and live in one of the most attractive and historic cities in the South West of England. A site in Georgian Bath, and a site in a country park on the edge of the city, offer a combination of urban and rural amenities to the College community. Bath College of Higher Education is a degree awarding body, by Order of the Privy Council.

The range of courses offered include:

BA (Honours)	Fine Art	(† three years, full time,*)
BA (Honours)	Graphic Design	(† three years, full time,*)
BA (Honours)	3D Design : Ceramics	(† three years, full time,*)
BA (Honours)	Music	(† three years, full time**)
BSc (Honours)	Human Ecology (Home Economics)	(† three years, full time‡)
BSc (Honours)	Food Management	(† three years, full time‡)

BA/BSc (Honours) Combined Studies (three years, full time,‡)
Major Subjects include: English Studies, Environmental Biology, Geography, History, Music, Sociology, Study of Religions;
Minor Subjects (one year only) include: Applicable Mathematics, Creative Studies in English, European Thought and Culture, Global Relationships, Japanese Studies.

BEd (Honours) (four years, full time)
The Primary course allows subject studies of an appropriate combination from:
Applicable Mathematics, Art, Creative Studies in English, Design & Technology, English Studies, Environmental Biology, European Thought and Culture, Geography, Global Relationships, Health Studies, History, Japanese Studies, Music, Sociology, Studies of Childhood, Study of Religions, Textile Design Studies.
The Secondary specialist course is for teachers of Home Economics in the context of Design and Technology.

BA (Honours) Creative Arts (proposed three years, full time)
Two major subjects chosen from: Art, Creative Studies in English, Music, Textile Design Studies.

BSc (Honours) Social Sciences (proposed three years, full time*)

DipHE (Diploma in Higher Education) (two years, full time‡)
Choice of subjects as for the BEd(Hons) Primary.

Post Graduate Courses
- PGCE (Primary)
- PGCE (Secondary): Design & Technology; Food & Textiles; Music; Religious Education; Science).
- PGDip/MA Visual Culture
- PGDip/MA Visual Culture (Fine Art)
- PGDip/MA Creative Writing
- PGDip/MA Irish Studies (proposed)
- PGCert/Dip/MSc Health Promotion

  * also available for part time study
** proposed part time route
  ‡ part time route only available through Credit Accumulation,
  † two year full-time Diploma in Higher Education also available

Enquiries and applications to:

**The Senior Registrar, Bath College of Higher Education,
Newton Park, Bath BA2 9BN.
Telephone enquiries on 0225 873701.
Fax enquiries on 0225 874123**
(except for Art & Design courses telephone 0225 425264 or fax 0225 445228)

ABERDEEN UNIVERSITY

University of Aberdeen, Regent Walk, Aberdeen AB9 1FX
(0224 272000) Map A, D2

Student enquiries: Schools liaison officer (0224 272090/272091)

Main study areas – as in What to Study section: *(First degree):* Accountancy, agriculture and forestry, anatomy, biochemistry, biology, botany, chemistry, civil engineering, computing, economics, electrical and electronic engineering, English, environmental sciences, environmental studies, European studies, fine arts, geography, geology, history, Latin-American studies, law, mathematical studies, mechanical and production engineering, medicine, microbiology, modern languages, pharmacology, philosophy, physiology, politics and government, psychology, religious studies and theology, sociology, zoology. *Also:* Aquaculture, land economy, marine resource management, safety engineering, women's studies.

European Community: 12% first degree students take EC language as part of course and 6% spend 6 months or more in another EC country. All first degree students have access to formal tuition in French, German, Spanish and Celtic at various levels including *ab initio*; 2 or 3 years study may be incorporated into degrees in arts and social services, law and science; in addition, university language centre is freely accessible to all students, with self tuition facilities in all EC languages. New courses in European studies; law with French/German law, involving a period of study at Grenoble or Regensburg to obtain a diploma. Formal exchange links with 54 EC and EFTA universities/colleges (of which only 6 are limited to language students): Austria (1); Belgium (4); Eire (3); France (11); Germany (11); Greece (3); Italy (6); Netherlands (4); Portugal (3); Spain (7); Switzerland (1). 25 approved Erasmus–Lingua programmes and links growing constantly.

Application: UCCA for 1993 start, UCAS thereafter. **Founded:** King's College 1495, Marischal College 1593 merging to one university in 1860. **Main awards:** MA, BSc, BD, BTh, LTh, LLB, BLE, MB ChB, BMedBiol, BEng, BScEng. **Awarding body:** Aberdeen University. **Special features:** Summer school for Baltimore and Maryland Law Schools. Visiting professors in engineering and international relations. Centres for the study of German and Austrian exiles in Great Britain; remote sensing and mapping science; philosophy, technology and society. **Academic features:** Access courses and summer school. Courses in tropical environmental science, Celtic civilisation, petroleum geology, Western Europe in the Renaissance, safety engineering, land use and marine resource management, countryside and environmental management. **Site:** 3 sites (King's College in Old Aberdeen, Marischal College in New Aberdeen, new medical buildings at Foresterhill). **Accommodation:** 2,400 places in halls, students houses and flats. **Library:** 5 library buildings, over 1,050,000 volumes, inter-library loan service, short loan collections for course books in heaviest demand; informal classes on use of library. **Specialist collections:** Jacobite material, transport and photographic collections, pre-1800 British and European works, first editions of early science and medical volumes. Almost 250,000 maps, many historical. **Other learning resources:** Interactive video; satellite TV for language teaching. **Welfare:** 3 doctors, dentist, health centre, university chaplaincy, academic and personal advisory systems at faculty and departmental levels; university counselling service. **Hardship funds:** Limited funds available. **Special category:** Every 3 years students elect Rector to represent them on university governing body. **Careers:** Information and advice service, regular vacancy bulletins. **Amenities:** Union building with snackbar, cafe, sewing room, launderette, 3 bars, music room with record library, supermarket; also large refectory with many facilities; SRC babysitting agency, vacation employment office, university symphony orchestra, choral society and chapel choir. **Sporting facilities:** Swimming pool, two extensive sports fields including running tracks, artificial ski slope, rowing on

River Dee, Cairngorms and Grampians (mountain hut) within easy reach for climbing and walking.

Duration of first degree course(s) or equivalent: 3 years ordinary/designated, 4 years honours; 5 years MB ChB; divinity 4 years. **Total first degree students 1992/93:** 6,887 **Overseas students:** 669 **Male/female ratio:** 1:1 **Teaching staff: full-time:** 461 **part-time:** 142 (plus research staff) **Total full-time students 1992/93:** 7,997 **Postgraduate students:** 1,540 **Tuition fees for 1992/93 (first degrees):** Home: £755 (if no grant), £1,855 (classroom), £2,770 (lab), £4,985 (clinical); Overseas: £5,633 (classroom), £7,470 (lab), £13,752 (clinical).

What it's like

Aberdeen, the silver or granite city, oil capital of Britain, is in NE Scotland with good access by rail and plane. Approaching its 500th anniversary. Based on medieval burgh with attractive landscaped campus. Main campus 10 minutes from halls and 5 minutes bus from city centre, where second site and union building are. About one-third housed in single study bedrooms and self-catering flats for 6 (same sex only). Hall place guaranteed for 1st year students. Private accommodation supply fluctuates; not too cheap. Student/admin relations good, SRC effective. Newly renovated SU building with 4 bars, function hall etc. 150 societies, sporting, political and many others. Some continuous assessment, more on the way. Failure and drop-out rate both below average. Changing courses is quite easy, as in Scotland you're admitted to a faculty, not a department. Most students are Scottish, but lots of English, Welsh, Irish and overseas. Less private school people than average. Some recognition given to Scottish Gaelic.

Pauper notes

Accommodation: Not much cheap accommodation but moderately priced is plenty enough. Lots of Hall places (squatting is illegal in Scotland). **Drink:** Real ale at various outlets and, of course, excellent range of whiskies almost everywhere. Regular cheap nights at the Union. **Eats:** Indian/Chinese/Italian very good, but not cheap. Radar's (pasta and American specialities) is always popular. Don't miss Jaws wholefood cafe. **Ents:** Several rock venues, including Union. Active folk scene, theatre, concert hall, arts centre, world cinema season (excellent value), alternative music festival. **Sports:** Facilities on campus (many free), for almost every sport imaginable. **Hardship funds:** Very little: university arranged access funds available. **Travel:** Scottish students can still claim travel awards, expensive to travel south by train. **Work:** A fair amount is available and the Students' Council runs a popular babysitting agency and lifts board.

More info?

Get students' Alternative Prospectus.
Enquiries to Stephen Reid (0224 272965).

Buzz-words

Fit like (how are you?); Nae baad (I'm fine, thank you); Quine (girl/lady); Loon (boy/man).

Alumni (Editors' pick)

Sandy Gall (ITV newscaster), Iain Cuthbertson (actor), Douglas Henderson, James Naughtie, Dr G Hadley (Convenor, Grampian Regional Council), David McLean MP, Alistair Darling, Denys Henderson (Chairman, ICI), Earl of Strathmore, Ian Crighton Smith, Catherine Gavin, Nikki Campbell (disc jockey), Kenneth McKeller, Gigi Callender, Glen O'Glaza, Dominic Addington, Evelyn Glenny (deaf percussionist).

ABERYSTWYTH

**University of Wales, PO Box 2, Aberystwyth, Dyfed
SY23 2AX (0970 622021) Map A, C7**

Student enquiries: Registrar

Main study areas – as in What to Study section: *(First degree):* Accountancy, agriculture & horticulture, American Studies, art & design, biochemistry, biology, botany, business studies, classics, computing, drama, economics, education, electrical and electronic engineering, English, environmental science, environmental studies, European studies, fine arts, geography, geology, history, information technology, law, library and information studies, mathematical studies, microbiology, modern languages, physics, politics and government, strategic studies, theology, zoology. *Also:* Celtic studies, environmental chemistry, space, Welsh studies.

European Community: Some 25% students have access to EC language tuition eg arts, economics and social studies students may take languages as a part one subject; computer science, biology and law may all be studied with an EC language. Formal exchange links with 8 EC universities/colleges in France (Le Havre, Lille, Marseilles) Italy (Siena) and Germany (Aachen, Heidelberg, Limburg, Mainz) all open to all undergraduates.

Application: UCCA for 1993 start, UCAS thereafter. **Structural features:** Part of Wales University. **Academic features:** Industrial year scheme, range of degree schemes relating to the study of the environment. New courses: in genetics and biochemistry, business and administration and Welsh, accounting and finance with Welsh, literature and history of Wales. Flexibility of degree schemes, students do not have to commit themselves until the end of their first or second year. **Special features:** Entrance scholarships worth £1,800 open to all UK candidates; biennial school on Dylan Thomas with internationally known experts on the poet. **Founded:** 1872, receiving charter in 1889, and joining with Bangor and Cardiff in 1893 to form Wales University. Merged with College of Librarianship 1988. **Main awards:** BA, BSc, BScEcon, LLB. **Awarding body:** Wales University. **Site:** Old College on sea front and Penglais campus of over 400 acres overlooking Cardigan Bay. Llanbadarn campus with accommodation within walking distance of Penglais. **Access:** Nearly all students live within walking distance of main teaching buildings. **Accommodation:** 2,322 places provided in halls and self-catering units, for 70% of student population. **Library:** 600,000 volumes, 3,000 periodicals; new library on Penglais site with over 500,000 volumes and 500 reader places; departmental collections. Access to National Library of Wales (copyright). **Specialist collections:** 600 books printed pre-1701; private press books; first editions collection (Matthew Arnold, Swinburne and Shelley), Catherine Lewis Gallery of prints and watercolours and 1747 edition of Shakespeare annotated by Samuel Johnson. **Other learning facilities:** Computer unit, microprocessor development laboratory, language laboratories with satellite receiving facilities. **Welfare:** College medical centre, college chapel (available for baptisms and marriages), Students' Union welfare service, children's centre, mature students' counsellor. **Hardship funds:** Keasbey Awards, Gwilym & Dilys Edmunds Awards, and Thomas Charles Edwards scholarships. **Careers:** Information and advice (also available to those who do not complete their courses). **Amenities:** SU buildings on Penglais campus include lounge bar, bank, shop selling reduced records, four student bars, restaurant, over 50 societies, studio theatre and college theatre (part of Aberystwyth Arts Centre), four student newspapers. **Sporting facilities:** Over 50 acres of playing fields on town outskirts; Cader Range and Snowdonia within easy reach. Outstanding new sports hall with wide range of indoor sports and heated indoor swimming pool; highest proportion in UK of sports teams per student population.

Duration of first degree course(s) or equivalent: 3 years; 4 years (modern languages) **Total first degree students 1991/92:** 3,330 **Overseas students:** 190 **Mature students:** 16% **Male/female ratio:** 1:1 **Teaching staff: full-time:** 326 **part-time:** 33 **Total full-time students 1991/92:** 4,126 **Postgraduate students:** 796 **Tuition fees for 1992/93 (first degrees):** Home: £1,855 (classroom), £2,770 (lab/studio), £755 (if no grant); Overseas: £5,320 (classroom), £7,055 (lab/studio).

What it's like

Founded in 1872 at a time of growing Welsh national consciousness, UW Aberystwyth is a small but close-knit university of 4,500 students. Most students are taught at the Penglais campus, built in the 1960s with a superb view of Aberystwyth town and Cardigan Bay, while some are taught at the small but beautifully sited campus at Llanbadarn (which also houses two other colleges).

Most students come from outside Wales. Approximately 10% of Aberystwyth students have Welsh as their first language, and there are plenty of courses available for those who want to learn Welsh. (The town itself is 50% Welsh speaking). 14% of the students are mature students, and 14% are from overseas.

Student accommodation is provided by the college for all first years (and covers 60% of total student population) and ranges from self-catering to pay-as-you-eat systems. Launderette facilities are available.

The college encourages students to take an industrial year out. Central library opens 9.00am–10.00pm.

Aberystwyth is about half way down the West Wales coast. Travel by rail or road is slow, but the scenery for miles around is beautiful. Most students stay in Aber over the weekends, and there are plenty of weekend ents and activities. The SU offers a wide entertainments package, 4 bars, 2 shops, travel bureau, insurance centre, 50 clubs and societies, a well-developed welfare service and opportunities for social, political and culture activities.

Sport is thriving with leagues in most sports. Students compete at local, Welsh and UK levels. Aber Rag is one of the world's biggest student charity appeals. It's great fun going on Rag trips collecting money anywhere in the UK!

The town has 1 cinema, an arts centre, 41 pubs, a weekly market. It is easy to meet other students. Family planning clinic offers advice on pregnancy and STDs. Hospital has an AIDS counsellor. Nightline is a student-run confidential advice service, and so is Lesbian and Gay Line.

Pauper notes

Accommodation: Variety of halls with different catering systems. A few married quarters available. **Drink:** Two new, very 'plush' Union bars serving good, cheap beer: Courage, Bass. Good town pubs – Bear, Rummers, Glengower etc. **Eats:** Good facilities, the 'Beacon' refectory, pizzeria and sandwich bar. **Sports:** Everything catered for at £10 pa. Large campus sports centre, track and pool. **Ents:** Regular live events and discos, variety of musical clubs and societies. Student discounts at Aberystwyth Arts Centre based on campus. **Hardship fund:** Interest-free loans and donations for extreme cases. **Travel:** Travel shop on campus offering advice on student travel. **Work:** Part-time work mainly in hotels, pubs and restaurants and SU.

CEFNDIR

Fe'i sefydlwyd yn 1872 ar gyfnod o ymwybyddiaeth genedlaethol Gymreig gynyddol, ac mae CPC Aberystwyth yn brifysgol fechan, glos o tua 4000 o fyfyrwyr. Dysgir y mwyafrif o'r myfyrwyr yng Nghampws Penglais, a adeiladwyd yn y 1960au ac sydd a golygfa wych o dref Aberystwyth a Bae Ceredigion, ac addysgir eraill ar y campws bychan, hardd yn Llanbadarn (Ile y mae hefyd 2 goleg arall).

Mae'r mwyafrif o fyfyrwyr yn dod o'r tu allan i Gymru. Cymraeg yw iaith gyntaf tua 10% o fyfyrwyr Aberystwyth, a threfnir digon o gyrsiau i rai sy'n awyddus i ddysgu Cymraeg. (Mae tua 50% o bobl y dref yn medru'r Gymraeg). Mae 14% o'r myfyrwyr yn fyfyrwyr hŷn, ac mae 14% yn fyfyrwyr tramor.

Darperir llety myfyrwyr gan y Coleg i fyfyrwyr y flwyddyn gyntaf i gyd (ac i tua

CAN'T FIND WHAT YOU'RE LOOKING FOR? USE THE INDEX!

60% o'r cyfanswm o'r boblogaeth fyfyrwyr) ac mae'n amrywio o lety hunan-arlwyol i systemau talu-wrth-fwyta. Darperir cyfleusterau golchi dillad.

Mae'r Coleg yn annog myfyrwyr i gymryd Blwyddyn Ddiwydianol Allan. Mae'r llyfrgell ganolog ar agor o 9.00am hyd 10.00pm.

Saif Aberystwyth tua hanner ffordd i lawr arfordir Gorllewin Cymru. Mae'n daith araf ar y rheilffordd neu'r ffordd, ond ceir golygfeydd hyfryd am filltiroedd o amgylch. Mae'r mwyafrif o'r myfyrwyr yn aros yn Aberystwyth dros y penwyth-nosau, ac mae digon o ddiscos ac adloniant byw ar gynnig yn Undeb y Myfyrwyr (UM) ar benwythnosau.

Mae UM yn cynnig pecyn adloniant eang, tri bar, dwy siop, Swyddfa Deithio, Canolfan Yswiriant, cant o glybiau a chymdeithasau, Gwasanaeth Lles da a chyfleoedd am weithgareddau cymdeithasol, gwleidyddol a diwylliannol.

Mae chwaraeon yn ffynnu a cheir cynghreiriau yn y mwyafrif o chwaraeon. Mae myfyrwyr yn cystadlu ar lefelau lleol, Cymreig ac o fewn y DU. Mae Rag Aber yn un o fudiadau elusennol myfyrwyr mwyaf y byd. Mae'n hwyl mynd ar deithiau Rag i gasglu arian unrhyw fan yn y DU!

Mae gan y dref 1 sinema, Canolfan Celfyddydau, 41 o dafarnau a marchnad wythnosol. Mae'n hawdd cyfarfod â myfyrwyr. Mae Clinig Cynllunio Teulu yn cynnig cyngor ynglyn â beichiogaeth a chlefydau rhywiol. Mae cynghorydd AIDS yn yr ysbyty. Mae Lein y Nos a'r Lein Lesbiaid a Hoywon yn wasanaethau cynghori cyfrinachol a redir gan fyfyrwyr.

Nodion Pauper

Llety (e.e. sgwatiau myfyrwyr, llety priod: Amrywiaeth o neuaddau gyda siste-mau arlwyo gwahanol. Ychydig o lety priod ar gael. **Diod (e.e. mannau rhesymol/da, bragdai da lleol):** Dau far Undeb Newydd gyda chwrw am bris rhesymol – Ushers, Banks etc.). **Bwydd (e.e. rhesymol/da yn y campws/y dref):** Microbeiotig/llysfwyd/ethnig. Cyfleusterau da i fyfyrwyr, yn Ffreutur y Beacon a Pizzeria arlderchog. **Adloniant (e.e. rhesymol, grwpiau newydd/ffilmiau/dramau ar/i ffwrdd o'r campws):** Neuadd gyngerdd fawr (1000 sedd) digwyddiadau byw rheolaidd, a discos, armywiaeth o glybiau a chlybiau cerddorol. **Chwaraeon (e.e. canolfannau chwaraeon rhesymol/da ar/i ffwrdd o'r campws, pyllau nofio, cyfleusterau trafnidiaeth):** Popeth ar gael am gost o £8 y flwyddyn. Canolfan Chwaraeon mawr ar y campws, trac a phwll. **Cronfeydd Caledi (i godi'r myfyrwyr tlawd ar eu traed):** Benthyciadau dilog a chyfraniadau i achosion eithaful o dlodi. **Teithio (e.e. ysgoloriaethau teithio, bodio, tocynnau myfyrwyr):** Swyddfa Deithio ar y campws, sy'n rhoddi cyngor ar deithio myfyrwyr. **Gwaith (i ychwa-negu at y grant yn ystod y tymor/gwyliau/ar/i ffwrdd o'r campws, agwedd i'r dol:** Gwaith rhan-amser yn bennaf mewn gwestair, tafarndai a thai bwyta.

Alumni (Editors' pick)

Lord Cledwyn, Arthur Emyr, Most Rev. George Noakes (Archbishop of Wales), Berwin Price, Angela Tooby.

ALRA

Academy of Live and Recorded Arts, Royal Victoria Building, Trinity Road, London SW18 3SX (081 870 6475) Map D, B3

Student enquiries: The Administrator

Main study areas – as in What to Study section: Dance, drama. *Also:* stage management, technical television.

European Community: Exchange visit to Paris theatre school funded by British Council.

Application: Direct. **Academic features:** Actor's course (3 years NCDT accre-dited or 1 year postgraduate); stage management course (1 year); performing arts dance course (3 years). ALRA has a modern approach and a concern for the individual student. The academy is personally supervised by its founder Sorrel Carson. Modern and classical theatre, television, dance, voice, singing and recorded arts. **Special features:** Guest speakers and directors from professional theatre and related fields. Guest lecturers from Cambridge University. Professional TV studio. **Largest fields of study:** Acting, performing arts, stage management. **Founded:** 1979. **Site:** In listed (Grade I) Victorian building on Wandsworth Common. **Access:** BR Clapham Junction or Wandsworth Common; bus to central London. **Accommodation:** Variety of private flats available for rent in locality; £40 exclusive of meals and public services. No academy-owned student accommodation. **Library and Learning Resources:** Two theatres, dance and rehearsal studios; stage management workshop; professional television studio; sound studio. **Careers:** Information and advice given; placement service when possible. **Welfare:** Active help with accommodation. Student welfare officers. Information pack given to new students regarding housing, public libraries, doctors and health centres, banks etc. Student social committee. **Hardship funds:** 3 scholarship places (up to value of £12,000 in fees) available each year. Bursaries for students encountering hardship awarded at Academy's discretion. **Amenities:** Active social life. Several plays produced each term. Showings of film and television productions. Student common room and bar. **Sports:** Good local sports facilities.

Duration of first degree course(s) or equivalent: 3 years **Others:** 1 year **Total first degree students 1991/92:** 115 **Overseas students:** Approx 5% **Male/female ratio:** 2:3 **Teaching staff:** full-time: 10; part-time: 30. **Total full-time students 1991/92:** 170 **Postgraduate students:** 15 **Tuition fees 1992/93:** £4,700–£6,573.

What it's like

Some drama schools take a selection of 'types', who are already 'good' young actors or good auditionees. ALRA looks at people as they are and finds the actor within them. It has no preconceptions of who will make an actor or who won't. The entry audition process does not use audition pieces but allows individuals to display their ability through improvisation, voice and movement workshops.

Royal Victoria Patriotic Building is beautiful, light and spacious. Good working environment. Comprehensive training has prepared me to enter the acting profession. Fully equipped TV studios give you the opportunity to realise yourself in the recorded medium and gives you the confidence to offer yourself and work in TV. Extensive movement and voice work – I enjoyed the special skills such as stage combat and mask work. Studying both classical and modern theatre very satisfying. Project work includes Greek theatre, Shakespeare and Restoration comedy as well as American, English and Irish drama. Working with guest directors and tutors who bring experience from their professional backgrounds means that students can make an immediate connection with what they learn in school and the reality of the profession.

ALRA is a young school – only 13 years old, constantly providing each new intake with a clear incentive and approach. It gives many students a chance where other schools have not. It's real. It's down to earth. It's genuine. And it wants to help.

Emily Murray
(now a graduate working at the
English Theatre in Vienna)

Pauper notes

Accommodation: Local help given. **Hardship funds:** Several scholarships and assisted places available; sympathetic approach to student finance. **Work:** Summer holiday work in academy; lots locally in bars, restaurants, etc. Most find part-time work in order to survive.

More info?

Enquiries to Gillian Davison (081 870 6475).

CAN'T FIND WHAT YOU'RE LOOKING FOR? USE THE INDEX!

Informal name
ALRA

Alumni (Editors' pick)
ALRA is a new institution. Graduates commencing their careers can be seen at the National Theatre, RSC, West End, BBC, ITV, American television and Hollywood.

ANGLIA POLY
See Anglia Poly University

ANGLIA POLY UNIVERSITY
Anglia Polytechnic University
(1) **Victoria Road South, Chelmsford, Essex CM1 1LL (0245 493131)**
(2) **East Road, Cambridge CB1 1PT (0223 63271)**
(3) **Sawyers Hall Lane, Brentwood, Essex CM15 9BT (0277 216971)**
(4) **Danbury Park Management Centre, Danbury, Chelmsford, Essex CM3 4AT (0245 415511)**
Map A, F7

Student enquiries: Student Administration (Admission)

Main study areas – as in What to Study section: *(First degree):* Accountancy, art & design, agriculture, biology, business studies, chemistry, communication studies, computing, economics, education, electrical & electronic engineering, English, environmental studies, environmental science, European studies, fine arts, geography, geology, history, information technology, law, mathematical studies, modern languages, music, nursing studies, philosophy, professions allied to medicine (PAMs), social policy and social welfare, sociology. *Also:* Building and construction, Japanese manufacturing engineering, personnel administration, quantity surveying, software engineering, telecommunications, women's studies.

European Community: 80% first degree students take EC language as part of course and 15% spend 6 months or more in another EC country. All first degree students have access to up to 3 language modules as part of their degree; a number of courses (eg European Business Administration) have more specific European and language study; specialist language programmes being developed in eg law, technology, rural resources development; European dimension being developed on all degree courses. Formal exchange links with some 5+ EC universities/colleges: in France (2), Germany (2) and Netherlands (1), mostly for business studies and technology students. Other links exist for eg language students to study at a wide range of institutions. Approved Erasmus programme 1992.

Application: PCAS for 1993 start, UCAS thereafter. **Academic features:** All courses available on modular, credit accumulation basis. Open course scheme allows individual negotiated pathways and accreditation of prior learning. **Founded:** 1992 as a university. Previously Anglia Poly founded 1989, ex Essex Institute and Cambridgeshire College of Arts and Technology. **Main awards:** LLB, BEd, BSc, BA. **Awarding body:** Anglia Poly University. **Site:** Chelmsford town centre, Cambridge city centre, Brentwood and Danbury Park. **Access:** Good train connections with London from all sites. **Accommodation:** 1,200 controlled bed spaces in hostels and college administered houses, 800 places in approved lodgings. **Library:** Library at all sites; 275,000 volumes, 650 periodicals, 700+ study places. **Other learning resources:** Computer centre; CAD/CAM centre; language centres. **Specialist collections:** Law, education and management, music, French Resistance Archive. **Welfare:** Counselling, medical and health education services. **Hardship funds:** None available but help given through student services and access funds. **Careers:** Information, advice and placement and Access funds. **Amenities:** SU bookshop on all main sites, SU buildings with bars, sports centre, soccer, table tennis, volleyball, judo, golf, hockey, netball, keep-fit, rugby, squash, fencing, horse-riding, karate, canoeing, trampolining, weight-training, yoga, drama, music, pottery and lots more! Mumford Theatre (at Cambridge), creche. Nursery (3–5 yr olds) on all sites.

Duration of first degree course(s) or equivalent: 3 and 4 years **Total first degree students 1991/92:** 3,382; **BEd students:** 432 **Number of overseas students:** 160; **Mature students:** 40% **Male/female ratio:** 1:1 **Teaching staff: full-time:** 515; **part-time:** 1,108 **Total full-time students 1991/92:** 3,928 **Postgraduate students:** 508 **Tuition fees for 1992/93 (first degrees):** Home: £1,855 (classroom), £2,775 (lab/studio), £1,855 (if no grant); Overseas: £4,950 (classroom), £5,300 (lab/studio).

What it's like (Cambridge)

Enjoys a sometimes uneasy, sometimes mutually beneficial relationship with Cambridge University, the more prestigious university. Many students use their rather more luxurious facilities, whilst many of theirs prefer Anglia's more relaxed and informal environment. Largely due to the efforts of the NUS area organisation a sense of homogeneity is gradually evolving amongst Cambridge students as a whole.

Excellent academic reputation, particularly for humanities/social studies; well developed and dynamic SU ensures that student services, entertainments and welfare issues are not neglected. Accommodation has improved with new halls of residence – *but* prohibitively expensive. The major problem is overcrowding – severe increase in students without similar increase in study spaces, library facilities, relaxation areas etc.

Wide variety of students from degree, through HND, A-level and day release. The opportunities are there for anyone with initiative to get on and pursue almost any field of endeavour they choose.

Pauper notes

Accommodation: Some cheap digs through housing associations. **Drink:** SU bar best value, local brews – Abbot Ale. **Eats:** The Tram Depot, SU Batman Cafe, the Corn Exchange. Veg: Arjuna, King's Pantry. **Ents:** Bands and gigs on campus, also at The Junction. New on-site Poly bar. **Sports:** *No* sports facilities on campus though active and successful sports teams nevertheless. Kelsey Kerridge sports hall and Parkside swimming pool (reduced rates to students at certain times). **Hardship funds:** SU will loan up to £700. **Travel:** STA Travel, Campus Travel, good hitching after long walk to starting points. **Work:** Pubs, shops, farms, factories.

Alumni (Editors' pick)

Sacha Count (own lingerie firm), John Swinfield (presenter of ITV programme, Enterprise), Pink Floyd, Adam Ant, Fluck and Law ('Spitting Image'), Tom Sharpe (lecturer).

What it's like (Essex)

Sites at Brentwood and Chelmsford; not very beautiful places. Chelmsford: small town, small campus but friendly. Most entertainment college based. Main courses – business studies, law, building studies, computer studies, nursing. Brentwood: quiet, mostly mature students, close to London. Teaching generally good. Small so atmosphere tends to be very friendly with everyone knowing each other. Students get involved in societies and college activities and most people enjoy their time here.

CAN'T FIND WHAT YOU'RE LOOKING FOR? USE THE INDEX!

Pauper notes

Accommodation: Halls of residence are small in Chelmsford. Accommodation generally quite expensive everywhere. **Drink:** Chelmsford Placcy (university bar) cheapest in town; local brew Ridleys and Crouch Vale. **Eats:** Small refectory at Chelmsford, good bar food; loads of pizza places and Indians. No vegetarian in Chelmsford. **Ents:** Small cinema and theatre in Chelmsford. **Sports:** Excellent leisure centre in Chelmsford – cheap tickets available from university sports department. Cambridge Utd – 2nd division. **Hardship funds:** Student services fund. **Travel:** Expensive bus fares and taxis. No student discounts. Brentwood – difficult to get to BR station from college. **Work:** Part-time work available term time and vacation in Chelmsford and Brentwood.

Alumni (Editors' pick)

Jerry Hayes (MP), Mike Smith, Tom Sharpe.

ARCHITECTURAL ASSOCIATION

Architectural Association School of Architecture, 34–36 Bedford Square, London WC1B 3ES (071 636 0974) Map E, C2

Student enquiries: Registrar's Office

Main study areas – as in What to Study section: *(First degree):* Architecture.

European Community: No students take languages as part of their course. No formal exchange links, but study trips may visit Europe.

Application: Direct. **Special features:** International character of school reflected by teaching staff offering a wide range of design options and teaching styles. Students recognised as individuals and expected to demonstrate a high level of self motivation to benefit from rich and varied programme which includes seminars and tutorials with professional consultants and members of allied disciplines. **Academic features:** 1-year foundation course is offered to develop creative skills in intensive programme of studio work. 5-year RIBA recognised course in architecture has emphasis on developing personal creativity with strong self-directed tutorials. **Founded:** 1847. **Main awards:** Exemption from RIBA Parts 1 and 2, AA Diploma. **Awarding body:** RIBA, AA. **Site:** Central London. **Access:** Tottenham Court Road underground station. **Accommodation:** None provided but advisory service. **Library:** 24,000 books, 75,000 slides, 50 study places. **Specialist collections:** Yerbury slide collection (3,000 slides on buildings of 1920s and 1930s). **Welfare:** Pastoral care and individual counselling available. **Careers:** Information and advice from Practical Training Adviser. **Amenities:** International exhibition gallery, specialist bookshop, brasserie, bar, darkroom, video studios, etching, workshop, computer facilities. **Employment:** Architecture.

Duration of first degree course(s) or equivalent: 5 years **Other:** 1 year **Total AA Diploma students 1991/92:** approx 260 **Overseas students:** 70% **Mature students:** 20% **Male/female ratio:** 2:1 **Teaching staff: part-time:** 120 **Total full-time students 1991/92:** 311 **Tuition fees, 1992/93:** (home and overseas) £7,900.

What it's like

Features a 5-year programme (plus a one-year foundation) for RIBA Parts I and II and AA Diploma. Choice of units (studios) ranging from conceptual to rigorously architectonic, all nevertheless experimental and none aim to advocate any house style. Pass from year to year based on quality of work presented in a final oral presentation of unit work as well as successful fulfilment of 3 other submissions: general studies, communications (life drawing, etching, video, photography, colour studio) and technical studies (including computer studio). Traditional university structure does not exist, as nothing is strictly compulsory during the year, but high standards are expected and students are given a great deal of independence which makes the system more difficult as it requires a great deal more resilience to maintain one's own standards without being spoon-fed – sometimes a mild shock to those arriving from A-level. An intense and sometimes competitive atmosphere prevails, diluted in the evenings as students and tutors collect themselves at the treasured school bar. The school year consists of very intense work alongside exhibitions, lectures, workshops and other events specially co-ordinated to complement study. Some are quite provocative and diverse. Student participation is sought and encouraged through the student forum.

In addition to small student exhibitions throughout the year, there is the final Year End Exhibition held in July which is the highlight of the London Architectural Calendar consuming all three Georgian buildings. The Exhibition is a place to see and be seen.

Students attend and occasionally vote at AA Council Meetings. No general student political affiliation or tendency. School attracts an international mix of students which creates a somewhat fragmented environment but at best brings a variety of influences and dialogues.

In addition to the basic school environment the AA features several superb evening lecture series, with speakers from all over the world in many different disciplines. There is a good but somewhat expensive bookstore, which includes in-house publications. The slide library is excellent. Decent workshop for working with metal and wood, and an ever-growing CAD studio.

There are problems. Darkroom is completely inadequate for serious work, etching studio closed three days a week, and library quite limited. No sense of campus, no extra-curricular organisation and no sport. No studio space provided by the school.

However, it's without doubt one of the best architecture schools in the world, if not the best. So if you really love the cutting edge of architecture, and you can't wait to express your commitment and fascination without being stifled by the inane requirements of what passes for education these days, then you must apply.

Pauper notes

Accommodation: As varied as London itself – students are seeming to prefer old factory buildings/loft spaces in Hackney and City. Very good accommodation service at beginning of term. SF and co-ordinators can advise house/flat shares. Watch school noticeboards. **Drink:** Love own bar, no time for anything else! **Eats:** Wagamama, Streatham Street – good cheap food, great architecture. Pollo Restaurant on Old Compton Street, Bar Italia on Frith Street. AA has its own lunchtime restaurant. **Ents:** Our Christmas party, workshop party, our Carnival – we're too busy! Students' standby at West End theatres and galleries (reduced rates). **Sports:** none at AA; ULU and YMCA facilities nearby. Local Camden facilities open to students. **Hardship funds:** Loans from AA. **Travel:** Travel scholarships from AA, other institutes (architectural). STA Travel. **Work:** Working within school part-time. Part-time in practices possible during term time.

More info?

Get students' Alternative Prospectus.
Enquiries to Sandra Morris, Registrar (071 636 0974).

Informal name

AA.

Buzz-words

You'll know soon enough – the list is endless.

Alumni (Editors' pick)

Richard Rogers (architect for Lloyds Building/Pompidou Centre), Mark Fisher (designer of Pink Floyd concerts), Ron Arad (furniture designer), Zaha Hadid (architect), Eileen Gray (architect, designer), Janet Street Porter (notorious).

CAN'T FIND WHAT YOU'RE LOOKING FOR? USE THE INDEX!

ASTON UNIVERSITY

Aston University, Aston Triangle, Birmingham B4 7ET
(021 359 3611) Map A, E7

Student enquiries: Admissions Officer

Main study areas – as in What to Study section: *(First degree):* Accountancy, administration, biology, business studies, chemical engineering, chemistry, civil engineering, computing, electrical & electronic engineering, European studies, mathematical studies, mechanical and production engineering, modern languages, pharmacy, physics, politics and government, psychology, town & country planning. *Also:* European/international business studies, ophthalmic optics, transport management.

European Community: 32% first degree students take EC language as part of course and 24% spend 6 months or more in another EC country. EC language tuition available to all students of business studies (including integrated international business and languages course), combined honours (languages may be combined with courses from across the university) and engineering (chemical, civil, computer, mechanical and manufacturing engineering may all be taken with European studies, including a 6 or 12 month placement in the EC). Formal exchange links with 24 EC universities/colleges: Belgium (1); Denmark (1); France (13); Germany (8); Spain (1). Approved Erasmus programme 1992.

Application: UCCA for 1993 start, UCAS thereafter. **Structural features:** Technological university. All departments in new or very recently modernised facilities. Excellent and extensive computing facilities. Aston Science Park adjacent to campus. **Academic features:** Strong European focus, eg international business and modern languages, European business management, wide range of engineering disciplines with European studies, computer science with European studies, transport management and modern languages. Most degree programmes have foreign language option. **Special features:** 65% of students are on 'sandwich' courses. Close links with industry and business. **Largest fields of study:** Engineering, management, modern languages and science, including pharmacy and ophthalmic optics. **Founded:** 1895. Central Technical School 1927. College of Technology 1951. College of Advanced Technology 1956. University Charter 1966. **Main awards:** BSc, BEng, MEng. **Awarding body:** Aston University. **Site:** Modern, increasingly green 40-acre campus. **Access:** Close to Birmingham city centre. **Accommodation:** Most live on campus; two-thirds of all students in university accommodation; all first years accommodated in university residence. **Library:** 215,000 monographs, 115,000 bound periodicals, 1,460 current periodicals; guides issued to students; computerised catalogues, circulation and information services, on-line access to databases throughout the world; audio-visual laboratory, 800 reader places. **Welfare:** Accommodation officer, doctor, dentist, FPA, psychiatrist, solicitor, chaplains, counsellor, careers & appointments officer. **Hardship funds:** A fund is available, and 3 annual travel scholarships. **Special category:** Married students' flats; accommodation for physically handicapped students; nursery facilities. **Amenities:** Guild of Students bookshop, arts centre, chapel, banks, travel agent, language laboratories, CAD laboratory, tutored video instruction system (TVI). **Sporting facilities:** Most indoor sports, including swimming pool, squash courts and two sports halls on campus. 90-acre centre for outdoor sports twenty minutes from campus. **Employment:** High graduate employment record in industry, commerce, the professions.

Duration of first degree course(s) or equivalent: BSc: 3 years full-time, 4 year (sandwich), BEng/MEng: 3–5 years full-time and sandwich **Total first degree students 1991/92:** 3,554 **Male/female ratio:** 3:2 **Number of overseas students:** 46 **Number of mature students:** 140 **Teaching staff:** full-time: 236; part-time: 18. **Total full-time students 1991/92:** 3,920 **Postgraduate students:** 1,300 (366 full-time) **Tuition fees for 1991/92 (first degrees):** Home: £750 (if no grant), £1,855 (classroom), £2,770 (lab/studio); Overseas: £5,910 (classroom), £7,819 (lab/studio).

What it's like

Easily accessible by coach, car or train. Small, compact campus; very friendly. Accommodation on campus in single-sex, self- and full-catering flats or 4 miles away in Handsworth Village (hall for first and final years and more self-catering flats). Both sites have launderettes. SU pioneered housing scheme for 200, 10 minutes walk from campus. Good city bus service, many all night routes.

Close to city centre facilities. SU active (about 70 societies, 40 sports clubs). Varied ents including one of the best student light shows in the country. Library open until 10 pm weekdays, 5 pm Saturday. Sunday opening in term 3. Campus health centre with full-time counsellor; understanding attitude towards contraception.

Courses increasingly modular usually with one year placements. Good graduate employment record. High entry grades but felt worth it by those that make it.

Pauper notes

Accommodation: Reasonable university accommodation. **Drink:** SU the best prices in town, regular promotions. Campus pubs also very popular with students. **Eats:** SU offers variety, reasonable prices, veggie food. In town – wide choice. **Ents:** SU provides films, discos, bands + cabaret. Campus Arts Centre caters for other tastes – good films (late night showings). **Sports:** 2 sports centres on campus plus swimming pool. University sports centre few miles out of town. **Hardship funds:** Only for the most deserving cases (mixture of grants and loans). **Travel:** University offers travel scholarships; travel bureau on campus offers student discounts etc. **Work:** Extremely hard to come by, SU, campus pubs offer bar jobs. Welfare now advertises jobs.

More info?

Get students' Alternative Prospectus.
Enquiries to Tom Conniffe, Schools Liaison Officer (021 359 6531 x 4062).

BANGOR

The University College of North Wales, Bangor, Gwynedd LL57 2DG (0248 351151) Map A, C6

Student enquiries: Academic Registrar

Main study areas – as in What to Study section: *(First degree):* Accountancy, agriculture, horticulture & forestry, biochemistry, biology, botany, chemistry, computing, economics, education, electrical & electronic engineering, English, history, linguistics, mathematical studies, modern languages, music, psychology, religious studies and theology, social policy and social welfare, sociology, zoology. *Also:* Banking, finance, nautical studies, oceanography, Russian, Welsh studies.

European Community: 6% first degree students take EC language as part of course and 4% spend 6 months or more in another EC country. All arts under-graduates may take an EC language at part 1; French and German available to

CAN'T FIND WHAT YOU'RE LOOKING FOR? USE THE INDEX!

science students; languages open to students in accounting, banking and economics in summer term continuing education programme. Degree in European financial management includes French/German/Russian and a year at European university. Formal exchange links with all EC countries except Luxembourg, and include placements in: Essen, Tubingen, Passau, Jena, Rennes (accounting, finance); Munster (accounting, banking); Mons, Siena (banking); Milan (banking); Namur (economics); Paris (banking, insurance, finance); Aarhus; Barcelona; Aveiro; Thessaloniki. EC initiatives: Staff/student exchanges (Tempus, Lingua, Erasmus).

Application: UCCA for 1993 start, UCAS thereafter. **Academic features:** Number of courses available through the medium of Welsh. **Structural features:** Part of Wales University. National Coaching Centre established (one of only two in UK universities), Centres of excellence in telecommunications and in structural biocomposites. School of Welsh Medium Studies. **Special features:** Sponsorship available with 4 major UK banks and a leading insurance company for degrees in banking, insurance and finance and with industrial companies for BEng/MEng. New degree course in history with nautical studies. **Largest fields of study:** Biological sciences, electronic engineering science, ocean science, accounting, banking, economics, psychology, agriculture and forestry. **Founded:** 1884. **Main awards:** BA, BD, BMus, BSc, BEng. **Awarding body:** University of Wales. **Site:** Town centre. **Access:** 2 hrs travelling distance from M56, which links with M6. A55 is coastal road and A5 the trunk road through N Wales. Regular fast trains to and from London, Birmingham, Manchester. **Accommodation:** 7 halls (including 1 self-catering) offering approx 1,300 places, 1,200 places in lodgings/flats. All first years normally accommodated in hall, £1,140–£1,383 pa. Rent: 48% in accommodation where rent controlled by college. **Library:** 6 library buildings including ocean sciences library. 400,000 volumes in total, 2,200 periodicals, 800 study places, short loan scheme for texts in heavy demand. **Other learning facilities:** Ocean-going research boats, college farms, botanical garden, field station, zoology museum, computer building, language labs. **Welfare:** 4 part-time doctors, psychiatrist, nursing sister, college chaplains, college counsellors, Students' Union welfare office. **Hardship funds:** Some bursaries available to help students in financial difficulties complete course; Access funds. Students' union interest free loan scheme for desperate cases. **Special categories:** Nursery run by Psychology Department, playgroup, SU 'Niteline'. **Careers:** Information, advice and placement. **Amenities:** Professional theatre, concert halls, museum, art gallery. **Sporting facilities:** Sports centre, 56 acres of playing fields, unparalleled opportunities for outdoor activities in Snowdonia. **Employment:** Teaching, manufacturing industry, management and administration plus specialist openings for graduates in banking and insurance, accountancy, electronic engineering, agriculture, fisheries and forestry.

Duration of first degree course(s) or equivalent: 3 years; 4 years (languages), 4½ years (BEng/MEng) **Total first degree students 1991/92:** 3,301 **Overseas students:** 455 **Mature students:** 1,112 **Male/female ratio:** 4:3 **Teaching staff: full-time:** 374 **part-time:** 6 **Total full-time students 1991/92:** 3,819 **Postgraduate students:** 646 **Tuition fees for 1992/93 (first degrees):** Home: £1,855 (classroom), £2,770 (lab/studio), £755 (if no grant); Overseas: £5,320 (classroom), £7,055 (lab/studio).

What it's like

Small coastal city, easily accessible by train, bus and car. 19th Century main building on hill overlooking town centre where other departmental buildings are situated. SU central to campus, all halls and departments within ten minutes (sometimes very hilly) walk. Regular bus service/easy hitch or cycle journey to Menai Bridge on Anglesey (for Marine School) three miles away.

College accommodation for 1/3 students – mainly in halls (mixed/single sex/self catered/catered) prioritised for mostly first years. College is building 800 hall places on one of the major hall sites. Private accommodation in very short supply (look early) and varies in quality. Launderettes on all hall sites and in SU, cooking facilities passable even in catered halls. Very wide variety of food shops (supermarkets, organic, Indian, Chinese) and restaurants (good prices).

Good mix of ages (28% mature students) and nationalities from Europe and further afield. All regions of Britain well represented. Very friendly atmosphere. Occasional trouble with locals, although extremely active Community Action organisation in SU to socialise and work with/for the local community.

Academically excellent in all areas – although cuts affect the number of courses offered and some study facilities. Arts, science and public libraries hold extensive (although sometimes dated) material and many periodicals. Departments such as Russian, electronic engineering, economics, marine studies and agriculture/forestry expanding, considered amongst the best in the UK.

Welfare services in SU run by sabbatical officer, permanent staff member, and volunteers giving confidential advice on academic, legal, financial, drugs, housing benefits (or lack of them!) and personal matters. Negotiations still in progress over the provision of a full-time counsellor to work in conjunction with moral tutors and college health centre.

SU houses travel office, shop, restaurant (all at discount rates) and secondhand bookshop. Other facilities include bank, insurance co., showers, laundry, snooker room, games room, television lounge and meeting rooms. SU creche near one hall. SU manages what was college refectory and serves cheap meals; five year refurbishment plan to turn it into a night time venue. Bars offer cheap drink and serve as venues for many and varied entertainments (recent appearances by The Waterboys, New Model Army, The Fall, Bliss, Spiritualised, Oceanic). SU clubs and societies cater for wide variety of cultural, social and political needs, from Real Ale, to Chess, Chinese to Afro-Caribbean, Labour to Plaid Cymru. The Athletic Union with Sports Hall and playing fields also provides a variety of activity from the more conventional hockey/football, to Ki Aikido. Excellent natural facilities for water sports and mountaineering make outdoor pursuits clubs very popular and very active. Other areas of interest include Seren (excellent student newspaper), Community Action, Rag and numerous opportunities to become involved with the running of the Union via General Meetings and campaigns as well as through Committees (such as Entertainments).

Not overtly political but facilities for students to become active in areas of interest or concern. Active bi-lingual policy.

Rachel Sethi

Pauper notes

Accommodation: Limited availability, especially at start of the year, mainly bedsits and shared houses, average £33 per week in Bangor (around £25 outside). College accommodation priority to 1st then 3rd years. **Drink:** SU bars cheapest. Extensive range of beers. **Eats:** SU Fat Freddies' and refectory omnivorous/veggie/vegan – both very cheap. Herbs Restaurant – wide range of salads and healthy foods. Various English/Italian/Greek/Indian/Chinese eats. **Ents:** SU major North Wales venue; many local Welsh bands and active folk club in Jocks bar where anyone gets up and performs; one nightclub, lots of pubs catering for every type of student. SU card gives discount at theatre, cinema and some restaurants. **Sports:** College centre (squash, weights, multigym, large multipurpose hall) with reductions for Athletic Union Members (join in the SU). Local pool with diving facilities. St Mary's gym for martial arts clubs etc. **Hardship Funds:** College access funds very limited. Loans Committee of SU can in exceptional circumstances of hardship give short term loans. **Travel:** Travel Office, with many discount schemes, in SU. Many overseas scholarships eg Canada/US/EC. Boats to and from Dublin very cheap. Intercity London–Bangor 3½ hrs, also National Express coaches. Local bus service reliable but limited. SU runs minibus lift service after Ents events. Hitching good (but as always not recommended to individuals). **Work:** Not much casual work available outside SU. Students employed as bar staff, stewards, catering casuals. Some pubs employ students.

CAN'T FIND WHAT YOU'RE LOOKING FOR? USE THE INDEX!

More info?
Enquiries to President SU (0248 353709).

Alumni (Editors' pick)
Dr Robert Edwards (pioneer of test-tube babies), Roger Whittaker (singer, songwriter), Dr David Rees (Director of National Inst for Medical Research), Ann Clwyd (MP), Robert Einion Holland (Chief General Manager, Pearl Assurance), Dr Dafydd Elis Thomas MP (President, Plaid Cymru), John Sessions (poet and impressionist).

BANGOR NORMAL COLLEGE

Bangor Normal College, Bangor, Gwynedd, N Wales LL57 2PX (0248 370171) Map A, C6

Student enquiries: Admissions Officer

Main study areas – as in What to Study section: *(First degree):* Art and design, communication studies, drama, education, English, environmental studies, history, humanities, mathematical studies, music, religious studies and theology. *Also* Administration, environmental planning, physical education, Welsh studies.

European Community: Administration students take EC language as part of course; no exchange links but short visits arranged within specific courses.

Application: PCAS for 1993 start, UCAS thereafter. **Structural features:** Associate institution of Wales University. **Largest fields of study:** Education (primary). **Founded:** 1858. **Main award:** BA, BEd. **Awarding body:** Wales University. **Site:** Two sites, one mile apart: residential site in Upper Bangor; other site (residential, teaching, recreational) on outskirts of Bangor, overlooking the Menai Straits. **Access:** Coach and train (Bangor station on London-Holyhead line). **Accommodation:** 450 places on site, additional places in flats and houses as need arises. **Approx cost:** £29 without meals; all accommodation self-catering. **Library:** 60,000 volumes, 200 periodicals, 175 study places. **Specialist collections:** Children's books, Welsh history and literature. **Other learning facilities:** TV and sound studios, editing suites, interactive video, CDROM, language centre with learning lab, resources centre with printing facilities, child-study centre, 2 open-access computer networks based on Acorn/Apple computers. Part of European Pluto network for teacher education. **Careers:** Personal tutors offer advice. **Employment:** Teaching (BEd); environmental centres, media, public and business administration (BA). **Welfare:** Nurse on site daily; college doctor's surgery weekly. Each student allocated a personal tutor; help also available from assistant principal. **Hardship funds:** Government access funds. **Amenities:** Variety of societies; SU bar; drama studies, hall. **Sports facilities:** Large sports hall, 2 gymnasia, multi-gym, playing fields, tennis courts on campus. Bangor city swimming pool and Snowdonia National Park within easy reach for walking, climbing etc.

Duration of first degree course(s) or equivalent: 3 years (BA), 4 years (BEd). **Total first degree students 1991/92:** 680 **Number of BEd students:** 456; **Number of mature students:** 134 **Male/female ratio:** 2:5 **Teaching staff: full-time:** 56; **part-time:** 6. **Total full-time students 1991/92:** 760 **Postgraduate students:** 80 **Tuition fees 1992/93 (first degrees):** Home: £1,855 (classroom), £2,770 (lab/studio).

GET HOLD OF THE PROSPECTUSES

BATH COLLEGE

Bath College of Higher Education
(1) **Newton Park, Bath BA2 9BN**
    (0225 873701; Fax: 0225 874123)
(2) **Sion Hill Place, Lansdown, Bath BA1 5SJ**
    (0225 425264; Fax 0225 445228)
Map A, D8

Student enquiries: Senior Registrar (Newton Park address)

Main study areas – as in What to Study section: *(First degree):* Art & design, education, food science and nutrition, music. *Also:* Human ecology (home economics).

European Community: 6% first degree students take EC language as part of course (German and/or Italian for music students; no other language tuition offered); none spend 6 months elsewhere in EC but home economics, science and humanities contacts in France, Germany and Netherlands resulting in short study exchanges. Formal exchange links with 2 EC universities/colleges: Hildesheim (art/music, combined studies); Munchen (graphic design). Erasmus and Tempus exchanges.

Application: PCAS for 1993 start, UCAS thereafter. ADAR for art and design. **Founded:** 1983 Ex Bath College of Higher Education and Bath Academy of Art. **Main awards:** BA, BEd, BSc. **Awarding body:** Bath College. **Site:** Newton Park and Sion Hill, about 3 and 1½ miles respectively from Bath city centre. **Access:** Rail, road (M4/A4), local buses. **Accommodation:** 595 places in college halls. Cost: £35.00 (single room); £30.50 (shared room). Rent: 40% in accommodation where rent controlled by college. **Library:** 1 library at each site; 146,000 volumes, 5,500 AV resources in total, 500 periodicals, 150 study places. **Other learning resources:** Computer systems; desk top publishing facilities, sound recording studio. **Welfare:** Doctor, student welfare officers, part-time counsellor. **Hardship funds:** Government access fund. **Careers:** Information and advice; placement. **Employment:** Teaching, home economics, music, art and design.

Duration of first degree course(s) or equivalent: 3 years; BEd 4 years **Total first degree students 1991/92:** 1,612 **Total BEd students:** 619 **Overseas students:** 104 **Mature students:** 520 **Male/female ratio:** 1:4 **Teaching staff: full-time:** 111; **Associate staff:** 22. **Total full-time students 1991/92:** 1,881 **Postgraduate students:** 111 **Tuition fees for 1992/93 (first degrees):** Home: £1,855 (classroom), £2,770 (lab/studio); Overseas: £5,319.

What it's like

It's divided between two sites: Sion Hill, 15 minutes walk from town; and Newton Park, four miles from Bath towards Bristol. There is a regular bus service from Bath to the college. Halls are for first years, all self catering. They are split into courts at Newton Park and houses at Sion Hill, where rooms are in a crescent, and each has its kitchen shared with other students. Each site has canteen open for lunch, coffee and snacks in the morning and afternoon. Bars on each site are subsidised. SU very active, holding events each week and liaising with university. At Newton Park there is a new sports hall and college teams hold matches, home or away, each week.

There is a strong student presence in Bath with students from university and college of further education all trying to share same pubs and clubs. There are a lot of very individual pubs; most popular with the college are: Salamander, Hatchets, Cellar Bar, Boater and the Hat and Feather. In accordance with an old by-law in Bath, many of the clubs are underground such as Tiergarten, Players, the Island Club and Moles, where you have to be a member. BCHE students have concessions Tuesday and Monday night respectively. There are several markets throughout week eg Great Western antique market, indoor market, and on

Saturdays a large flea market on Walcot Street. At the same time as living in Bath the college is on the bus route to Bristol, so you have the amenities of both a large town and city.

Rachel Hawkins

Pauper notes

Accommodation: Expensive and difficult to find. **Drink:** Good real ales, BX, Buttcombe, Eldridge Pope. Excellent pubs with atmosphere. The Bell, The Curfew, The Hat and Feathers, Hatchets. **Eats:** From veggie burgers to a-la-carte, eating places for all walks of life, eating habits and more importantly pockets. **Ents:** Venues for all tastes. Moles nightclub, gigs at the Uni and BCHE, much jazz, rock, pop and classics – Bristol 9 miles away. **Sports:** College teams play on a regular basis, also Bath leisure centre, with pool, squash and tennis. **Work:** Many bar and p-t jobs available throughout year.

Informal name

BCHE

Buzz-words

blads – white socks, lager swilling, permed hair, moustaches male persons frequently seen entering Cadillacs nightclub (avoid!).

Alumni (Editors' pick)

Anita Roddick (Body Shop), Mary Berry (cook), Sue Cuff (TV), Howard Hodgkin, Martin Potts (painters), Nicholas Pope, Veronica Ryan, Nigel Rolfe, Peter Randall-Page (sculptors).

BATH UNIVERSITY

The University of Bath, Claverton Down, Bath BA2 7AY
(0225 826826) Map A, D8

Student enquiries: Senior Assistant Registrar

Main study areas – as in What to Study section: *(First degree):* Aeronautical engineering, architecture, biochemistry, biology, business studies, chemical engineering, chemistry, computing, economics, education, electrical and electronic engineering, environmental science, European studies, mathematical studies, mechanical and production engineering, metallurgy and materials science, modern languages, pharmacology, pharmacy, physics, politics and government, professions allied to medicine (PAMs), social policy and social welfare, sociology. *Also:* Crop technology, quantity surveying.

European Community: 20% first degree students take EC language as part of course and 10% spend 6 months or more in another EC country. Most courses offer EC languages as an option. Formal Erasmus links with large number of EC universities/colleges: education (France, Germany, Greece, Netherlands); mechanical engineering (France, Germany, Greece, Portugal); languages (France, Germany, Italy, Spain); management (France, Germany, Netherlands); physics (Netherlands); electrical engineering (Eire, France, Germany, Greece, Italy); maths (Italy, France); social sciences (Eire, Greece, Netherlands, Portugal, Spain); architecture (Denmark); chemical engineering (Italy).

Application: UCCA for 1993 start, UCAS thereafter. **Largest fields of study:** Engineering, social sciences. **Founded:** 1894, as Merchant Venturers' Technical College, full university status 1966. **Main awards:** BA, BArch, BPharm, BSc, BEng, MEng. **Awarding body:** Bath University. **Site:** Campus 1 mile from Bath city centre. **Academic features:** Joint degree with Royal Agricultural College, in crop technology and resource management. **Access:** Buses. **Accommodation:**

1,600 residences, 300 lodgings (mixed and segregated). Approx cost: Average £34 pw. 50% students in accommodation where rent controlled by university. **Library:** 200,000 volumes, 3,000 periodicals, 500 study places, course books on short loan. **Welfare:** Counsellor, doctors, psychiatrist, chaplain, dentist. **Hardship funds:** Some funds available. **Special categories:** Some accommodation for married students, some facilities for disabled, nursery (15 places, £5 a day). **Amenities:** Bookshop, banks, general shop (SU), chapel, supermarket, travel agency, post office, newsagent and hairdresser. **Sporting facilities:** Include an excellent sports hall and swimming pool. All playing fields on campus. **Employment:** 80% of 1991 graduates employed. Strong tradition in engineering and pharmacy.

Duration of first degree course(s) or equivalent: 3 years full-time; 4 years (sandwich) **Total first degree students 1991/92:** 3,745 **Overseas students:** 222 **Mature students:** 338 **Male/female ratio:** 5:3 approx **Teaching staff: full-time:** 379 **part-time:** 10 **Total students 1991/92:** 5,082 **Postgraduate students:** 682 (+655 part-time) **Tuition fees for 1992/93 (first degrees):** Home: £1,855 (classroom), £2,770 (lab); Overseas: £5,390 (classroom), £7,125 (lab).

What it's like

650 feet above city of Bath. Exposed and windy, modern buildings are concentrated on central pedestrian area. Functional but not the most attractive setting. However, the city's beauty easily makes up for it.

Facilities on campus include medical centre, launderettes, banks (all with cash points). Residences all self-catering, low rise blocks, quiet, refectories with health food counters and fast food.

Academic concentration on science technology, especially sandwich courses hence strong links with industry. Employment prospects are excellent, Bath was highest in *Sunday Times* graduate employment league table in 1992. Varying proportion of continuous assessments, training course for new lecturers. Long library opening hours but shortage of reading space. Links with town good, majority of students live in town, so lots of opportunity to join in local life. Campus quiet at weekends. Small city but Bath has 3 cinemas, a theatre, 8 nightclubs, fairly good bookshops and excellent pubs. Good student town. SU facilities include shop, travel bureau and coffee bar but bar is not student run. Active, generally non-political SU with 70 clubs, 50 sporting clubs; high standard in teams and competitions.

Pauper notes

Accommodation: All first years live on campus; places for disabled students. About £34 per week. City accommodation often expensive, about £43 per week and hard to find, help given by university accommodation office. **Drink:** Plenty of pubs, lots of real ale pubs and student pubs. **Eats:** A range of food on campus, good selection of restaurants in town including vegetarian and wholefoods, Harvest and Huckleberry's, kebabs, curries and fish and chips, pizzas and burgers. **Ents:** SU night at club every Tuesday with live bands. Wednesday, disco in a club, Thursday, alternative disco. Few ents on campus due to lack of venue and no student-owned bar. Extensive freshers week, discount card for shops, cinemas, restaurants. **Sports:** Swimming pool and excellent facilities for squash and 8 tennis courts on campus free to students, many teams and clubs from snooker to hot-air ballooning, sports centre in town more expensive. Sports scholarships available. **Hardship funds:** University access fund for students, limited small loans from SU, good rights and advice from SU. **Travel:** Many hitch from town to campus as bus fares very expensive. Good rail and coach links but check Sundays. London 75 mins by train, Bristol 20 mins. SU travel shop on campus for discounts. **Work:** Some tourism work.

More info?

Get students' Alternative Prospectus from SU.
Enquiries to Buck Walsh (0225 826826).

CAN'T FIND WHAT YOU'RE LOOKING FOR? USE THE INDEX!

Alumni (Editors' pick)

John Kiddey (TV reporter), Martin Hedges (world champion canoeist), Chris Martin and David Trick (England Rugby Union internationals).

BEDFORD COLLEGE

Bedford College of Higher Education, Lansdowne Road, Bedford MK40 2BZ (0234 351966) Map A, F7

Student enquiries: Assistant Academic Registrar

Main study areas – as in What to Study section: *(First degree):* Business studies, dance, drama, education, English, environmental studies, European studies, geography, history, modern languages, sociology. *Also:* Sports studies.

European Community: Very small number of first degree students take EC language and spend time in another EC country. No formal exchange links.

Application: PCAS for 1993 start, UCAS thereafter. **Largest fields of study:** Education. **Founded:** 1976 by merger of 3 colleges. **Main awards:** BA, BEd, BSc. **Awarding body:** De Montfort University. **Site:** Split on 3 sites. **Accommodation:** 400 places in halls of residence. **Library:** 1 library on each site: 110,000 volumes in total; 880 periodicals; 190 study places. **Specialist collections:** Hockliffe collection of children's literature. **Welfare:** Doctor, FPA, psychiatrist, chaplain, counsellor, accommodation officer. **Careers:** Information and advice service. **Amenities:** Students' Union; close to town centre; theatre; day nursery. **Sporting facilities:** Playing-fields; gymnasia; dance/drama areas; swimming pool; sports halls.

Duration of first degree course(s) or equivalent: 3 years; 4 years BEd. **Total first degree students 1991/92:** 1,566 BEd students: 741 **Number of mature students:** 664 **Male/female ratio:** 2:5 **Teaching staff: full-time:** 95 **Total full-time students 1991/92:** 973 **Postgraduate students:** 156 **Tuition fees for 1992/93 (first degree):** Home: £1,855 (classroom), £2,770 (lab/studio); Overseas: £5,000 approx.

What it's like

Spiralling towers and crumbling edifices of Bedford symbolise its history and tradition. Timeless reputation for producing first-rate teachers and questioning graduates. Sporting reputation. Excellent standing nationally in producing primary teachers of outstanding calibre. BA course with new modular programme incorporates new teaching innovations alongside time honoured lecturing standards upheld by dedicated teaching staff.

Facilities for such a small college are plentiful and well maintained. Student accommodation recently refurbished to highest standard. Main student block set in beautiful surroundings of Victorian terrace housing with picturesque gardens.

Social life well supported by two bars with their convivial atmosphere; hectic entertainment calendar. Balls usually sell out and are always massively enjoyed. Variety is our middle name and recent events have included hypnotism, comedy, karaoke, pantomime and all manner of music. At Bedford College we don't mind working, but we do like to have a good time.

Pauper notes

Accommodation: Residence contract more expensive than many colleges. Accommodation register to assist students who wish to live out. **Drink:** 2 college bars recently refurbished. Bedford is the home of Red Stripe brewed by Charles Wells so has many thriving pubs. Greene King. Many excellent country pubs. **Eats:** Two new snack bars provide cheaper alternatives to the college facilities. Excellent pizza. Multi-racial town with varied eating establishments. **Sports:** Very good facilities (swimming pool needs upgrading). Local squash and golf at reduced rate.

Sports clubs run by students with expert staff coaching if wanted. High standard in teams. **Ents:** Varied with both local bands and big bands eg Amazulu, Geno Washington, Voice of the Beehive, Real Thing + Horizontal Favours. Also 3 colleges within 12 miles radius offering more events. **Societies:** Christian Union, film, women's group, drama etc. Also mountaineering society which travels somewhere (Scotland, Wales, Devon) at least every second weekend. **Hardship funds:** College fund now in operation. **Shops:** Student discount available in some. **Work:** Pubs, swimming pools, sports centres, taxis (if over 24). The Union now provides over seventy jobs on campus ranging from shop workers to stewards.

Pending merger

It is expected that in April 1993 Bedford College will be no more, and from its ashes will rise De Montfort University: Bedford. Although change will occur, the immediate changes will be few and far between.

Alumni (Editors' pick)

Mandy Pickles (England U-21 hockey team), Lisa Black (Olympic rhythmic gymnastics team).

BELFAST UNIVERSITY

Queen's University of Belfast, University Road, Belfast BT7 1NN, Northern Ireland (0232 245133) Map A, B4

Student enquiries: Admissions Officer

Main study areas – as in What to Study section: *(First degree):* Accountancy, aeronautical engineering, agriculture, American studies, anatomy, archaeology, architecture, biochemistry, biology, botany, business studies, chemical engineering, chemistry, civil engineering, classics, computing, dentistry, economics, education, electrical & electronic engineering, English, environmental studies, food science & nutrition, geography, geology, history, information technology, law, library & information studies, mathematical studies, mechanical & production engineering, medicine, microbiology, modern languages, music, pharmacy, philosophy, physics, physiology, professions allied to medicine (PAMs), psychology, religious studies & theology, sociology, zoology. *Also:* Byzantine studies, Celtic studies, Irish studies, history of science, Slavonic studies.

European Community: 4% first degree students take EC language as part of course and 5% spend 6 months or more in another EC country. Formal exchange links with 35 EC universities/colleges: social anthropology (Belgium, Denmark, France, Germany, Greece, Netherlands, Spain, Portugal); business studies and management science (Belgium, France, Spain); electrical engineering (Denmark, Eire, France, Germany, Italy, Netherlands); biochemistry (Belgium, Eire, France, Germany); mechanical engineering (Germany, Greece, Netherlands, Portugal). Non-specialist language unit provides language training additional to degree course (11 languages available) at various levels including Paris Chamber of Commerce and Institute of Linguists. New Institute of European Studies develops interdisciplinary courses relevant to Europe. A number of degree courses may be studied over 4 years of which one year spent at an institution abroad (eg Belgium, France, possibly Germany and Spain); subjects include law, information management, chemistry and physics. Approved Erasmus programme.

Application: UCCA for 1993 start, UCAS thereafter. **Special features:** Writer in residence, J Simmons. **Founded:** 1850. **Main awards:** BA, BAgr, BD, BDS, BEd, BEng, BMedSc, BMus, BSc, BSSc, LLB, MB, BCh, BAO, MEng. **Awarding body:** Queen's University of Belfast. **Site:** Main site with various buildings about 1 mile from city centre; medical site about 2 miles from main site. **Access:** Most live within 1 mile of main site. Public transport available, if necessary, to those coming from home. **Accommodation:** 1,700 places in halls and university houses, 150 reserved places in Biggart House for medical and dental students; 92 flats for married students and over 170 places in associated halls and hostels. **Library:** Main library (central site), science library, medical library and agriculture and food science library. Around 1 million books in main libraries, plus 80,000 in departmental libraries. **Other learning facilities:** Computer centre, marine biology station, astronomical observatory, audio resources centre, visual aids unit, conservation laboratory, phytotron, palaeoecology centre, Murlough Field Centre, electron microscope unit, microprocessor laboratory. Centre for Information Management, Information Technology Planning and Development Unit; Centre for Genetic Engineering (NICGENE), Technology Centre, Policy Research Institute; Queen's University Environmental Science and Technology Research Centre (QUESTOR). **Hardship funds:** Some funds for financial hardship. **Amenities:** SU building with supermarket, record shop, bars, discos, etc; cinema on campus, bookshop, appointments and careers advisory service, university health service, student counselling service, Officers' Training Corps, Air Squadron. **Sporting facilities:** Excellent playing fields and physical education centre.

Duration of first degree course(s) or equivalent: 3 or 4 years; 5 years for MB, BCh, BAO. **Total first degree students 1991/92:** 7,817 f-t; 1,010 p-t **Total BEd students:** 1,289 **Overseas students:** 600 (f-t), 50 (p-t) **Mature students:** 299 **Male/female ratio:** 6:5 **Teaching and research staff: full-time:** 970 **part-time:** 106 **Total full-time students 1991/92:** 9,259 **Postgraduate students:** 1,442 **Tuition fees for 1992/93 (first degrees): Home:** £1,885 (classroom), £2,770 (lab/studio), £4,985 (clinical); Overseas: £4,130 (classroom), £5,500 (lab/studio), £12,990 (clinical).

"Pubs not particularly welcoming ...."

OLD MALE CHAUVINIST

What it's like

Politically contentious city, student body holds itself apart from the troubles. Many students live at home. For many it's an extension of school and school friends. Most NI schools are single-sex and denominational although this is slowly changing. Academic standards high. Fair proportion of graduates go overseas for jobs, most remain at home. University area one of the most beautiful in Belfast, bordering posh Malone Road. Facilities good: 2 diners, coffee lounge, 2 bars renovated and a snack bar. Creche facilities. SU active. Some sectarianism. Accommodation improving, though many students live in poor privately rented accommodation. University area centre of night life. Public transport until 11.00 pm. Renaissance of pubs and eating places. Three major cinema complexes showing national releases. Excellent alternative films in Queen's Film Theatre. Annual festival, second only to Edinburgh in site and diversity. Major pop acts play in Belfast. Also regular discos and gigs in SU and town.

Main drug is alcohol. Police over-stretched but active in student area.

Pauper notes

Drink: Lots of good bars in university area. SU cheap. **Eats:** Pizza, kebabs, Wimpy, Kentucky fried chicken and burger joints abound. Most pubs do lunches. **Ents:** SU main venue for bands and discos. **Sports:** Excellent facilities on campus, leisure centres, ice rink and ten pin bowling. Sports shop in SU. **Hardship funds:** Bursar's loans. **Travel:** Cheap travel on railways. Hitching not practical for obvious reasons. **Work:** Bar work, cloakrooms, bouncers.

Alumni (Editors' pick)

Trevor Ringland, Nigel Carr and Philip Matthews (all rugby players), Brian Mawhinney (Minister of Education for N Ireland), Seamus Heaney (poet), Bernadette McAlliskey (nee Devlin), Kenneth Branagh (actor), Sir Francis Tombs (Chairman of Rolls Royce), Brian Moore (writer).

BIRKBECK COLLEGE

Birkbeck College, University of London, Malet Street, London WC1E 7HX (071 580 6622) Map E, C1

Student enquiries: Registrar

Main study areas – as in What to Study section: *(First degree):* Biology, botany, chemistry, classics, computing, economics, English, environmental science, fine arts, geography, geology, history, law, linguistics, mathematical studies, modern languages, physics, politics & government, psychology. Also Hispanic studies, management.

European Community: 11% first degree students take EC language as part of course; French, German and Spanish available to all humanities degree students (most take at least one); language centre provides facilities to all students on individual basis. No formal arrangements for periods abroad but French department has links in Toulouse, Spanish department in Saragossa and geology in Coimbra, Grenada, Lisbon, Lyon, Madrid and Torino. Approved Erasmus programme 1992/93.

Structural features: Part of London University. **Special features:** Birkbeck College (which is outside the UCCA/UCAS scheme) provides degree level teaching and research facilities for students 'engaged in earning their livelihood' – so is primarily part-time. There is provision to change from part-time to full-time study with the permission of the college. Applications from under-18 students not welcomed. **Application:** is direct but you will need to get hold of prospectus as qualifications for, and schemes of, admissions are complex. **Main awards:** BA, BSc, BSc(Econ), LLB. **Awarding Body:** London University. **Site:** In London University's central precinct in Bloomsbury. **Access:** Easily reached by underground (near Russell Square, Goodge Street, Warren Street and Euston stations) and close to a number of bus routes. **Library:** 250,000 books; 1,000 periodicals. Late opening hours particularly designed to provide good study conditions for part-time students. Students also use main London University library next door in Senate House. **Other learning resources:** Language Centre: self-tuition courses

CAN'T FIND WHAT YOU'RE LOOKING FOR? USE THE INDEX!

available in a number of languages, with a four-booth language laboratory; language teaching lab with computer-assisted language learning packages; expanding collection of recordings in major European languages, sound-recording studio and tape facilities; intensive taught course in English for academic purposes and study skills. **Computing facilities:** Access via terminals and micros to both college and university machines; advisory service; college central computing service produces range of technical bulletins and regular newsletter.

Duration of first degree course(s) or equivalent: 4 years: 3 years for some advanced students **Total first degree students 1991/92:** 2,188 **Mature students:** 90% **Male/female ratio:** 1:1 **Teaching staff: full-time:** 200 **part-time:** 20 approx **Total full-time students 1991/92:** 332 (mostly postgraduate) **Postgraduate students:** 1,759 **Tuition fees for 1992/93 (first degrees):** Part-time: £636–£1,080 (£498–£900 if not supported); Home: £1,855 (classroom), £2,770 (lab/studio), £696 (if no grant); Overseas: £5,856 (classroom), £7,200 (lab/studio).

What it's like

Unique college catering primarily for mature, working people who choose to gain a London University degree through part-time study; classes are held between 6 and 9 pm and students range from early 20s to late 70s. Students without formal qualifications are often accepted. Degrees take 4 years instead of 3 and students may transfer to full-time after two years. (Postgraduate and research degrees can also be gained through part-time and/or full-time study.)

Needs of both full-time and part-time students accommodated. Union office, library and snack bar are open in the evenings as well as daytime, also dining club, serving hot meals from 5 pm weekdays. Other facilities include a nursery, lively bar, SU magazine – *Owl* – encouraging student contribution, a freshers fair, and over 30 other SU funded clubs and societies, which include own sports ground, an active drama group. Birkbeck students highly motivated, so they still manage to put time into Union activities, clubs, and societies on top of work, study and family life; incredible, but true.

University of London Union (ULU) nearby, housing the major sports and social facilities; so are Senate House Library and Dillons bookshop. Located in the heart of academic London, Birkbeck is well served by public transport, and nearby shops, entertainments, and places of interest abound.

Pauper notes

Drink: SU bar. **Eats:** SU snack bars. ULU next door. **Ents:** Filmsoc – free film each week. Free live music/cabaret each week. **Sports:** Own sports association, own ground at Greenford, as used by QPR FC. **Hardship funds:** Some college assistance possible. **Travel:** ULU Travel is next door. **Work:** Ask SU for help – some casual work.

Alumni (Editors' pick)

Anthony Cornish, Baroness McFarlane of Llandaff (head of department of nursing, Manchester University), Elizabeth Esteve-Coll (Director of the V & A Museum), Frank Sidebottom (cabaret singer), Sidney Webb (founder of LSE and other things).

BIRMINGHAM CONSERVATOIRE

Birmingham Conservatoire, Paradise Place, Birmingham B3 3HG (021 331 5901/2) Map A, E7

Student enquiries: Director of Studies

Main study areas – as in What to Study section: *(First degree):* Music.

European Community: 20% of second-year BA students take French, German or Italian as an option; none spend 6 months or more in another EC country. No formal exchange links with EC universities/colleges yet but some informal exchanges.

Application: Direct (twice yearly, autumn and spring). **Structural features:** Part of Central England University, Birmingham. **Academic developments:** Initial full-time courses lead to BA Music or BMus on modular structure. Also postgraduate diploma in performance studies and BEd (Music). First study performance or composition with range of options on BMus including ethnic music, music administration, jazz, improvisation, conducting, music technology and recording teaching skills and school studies. Good record of professional placements. **Special features:** Distinguished teaching staff; workshops and master classes with internationally renowned musicians. Purpose built complex includes Adrian Boult Hall; also administrative headquarters of City of Birmingham Symphony Orchestra; many CBSO principals teach at conservatoire. **Founded:** 1886 as part of Birmingham and Midland Institute; 1992, faculty of Central England University. **Main awards:** BA, BEd, BMus. **Awarding body:** Central England University. **Access** 10 minutes' walk from railway station. **Site:** City centre. **Accommodation:** Places at Cambrian Hall; and halls of residence at faculty of education, Westbourne Road. **Library:** 41,000 volumes, 30 periodicals, 32 carrels. **Specialist collections:** Dodd Bows. **Welfare:** Medical facilities at Cambrian Hall nearby. **Hardship funds:** Harrod Bequest; Centenary Appeal Fund; also access funds. **Careers:** Information and advice, but no placement service.

Duration of first degree course(s) or equivalent: 3 years (BA (Hons)), BMus; **others:** 4 years (BMus (Hons)) **Total first degree students 1991/92:** 295; **Overseas students:** 9 **Mature students:** 4 **Male/female ratio:** 1:1; **Teaching staff: full-time:** 17 **part-time:** 91; **Total full-time students 1991/92:** 313; **Postgraduate students:** 20 **Tuition fees for 1992/93 (first degrees):** Home: £2,770; Overseas: £5,000.

What it's like

It's ideally situated in modern purpose-built city centre development, with easy access to transport and main arts centres including town hall, new symphony hall and repertory theatre. New concert hall and practice rooms should make it possibly best equipped UK music college. Most first years live in uni hostels (Cambrian Hall most accessible 4 mins walk). List of flats and digs available. Provides valuable opportunities for dedicated musicians with emphasis on professional discipline. Ample time for private practice. Staff/student relationships good. It combines a high practical and academic standard, with the centrality on the 1st study. Demand for places very high. Musical life centres around orchestras, choirs and bands, and growing chamber music dept. SU discos, and other ents. Birmingham night life ranges from cheap student bars to top international clubs. Very few students do not complete course.

Alison Knight

Pauper notes

Accommodation: Uni housing list very expensive. Better deals from private sector. **Drink:** The Shakespeare (M & B), Prince of Wales (Ansells), The Grapevine. New student bar opened in Notes wine bar next door. Cheap beer at SU. **Eats:** Lots of reasonable restaurants. College canteen reasonably priced – some vegetarian. **Ents:** Rock and classical concerts with regular big names. Loads of mad ents organised by SU. City centre excellent for a good night out. Everyone catered for. **Sports:** SU card and poly sports card get reductions at most sports centres and shops. **Hardship funds:** Difficult but not impossible to claim. Good advice given. Official fund for students without a grant. **Shops:** Very interesting shops in suburbs of Harborne and Moseley. **Travel:** Travel can work out expensive so best to live pretty close to site. Midlands travelcards cost about £25 a month for unlimited travel on bus and trains in region. **Work:** Some Xmas shows offer work plus chance to gain experience; pub work in term-time; many students get work stewarding at the new symphony hall.

Alumni (Editors' pick)

Ernest Elemont (violinist), Peter Aston, Paul Beard, Brian Ferneyhough, Jean Rigby, Nicholas Wood, orchestral musicians, singers in major opera companies, professors of music, music advisers, directors of music companies.

BIRMINGHAM POLY

See Central England University

BIRMINGHAM UNIVERSITY

The University of Birmingham, Edgbaston, Birmingham B15 2TT (021 414 3344) Map A, E7

Student enquiries: Academic Secretary (Prospectus)

Main study areas – as in What to Study section: *(First degree):* Accountancy, African studies, American studies, anatomy, archaeology, biochemistry, biology, biotechnology, botany, business studies, chemical engineering, chemistry, civil engineering, Classics, computing, dance, dentistry, drama, economics, education, electrical & electronic engineering, English, fine arts, geography, geology, history, law, mathematical studies, mechanical and production engineering, medicine, metallurgy and materials science, microbiology, modern languages, music, nursing, philosophy, physics, physiology, politics and government, professions allied to medicine (PAMs), psychology, public administration, religious studies and theology, social policy & social welfare, sociology, town and country planning. *Also:* Classical studies, medieval studies, physical education, sport and recreation studies, tourism.

European Community: Number of first degree students who take EC language as part of course unknown; 4% spend 6 months or more in another EC country. A number of degrees (in addition to language degrees) allow language study as subsidiary or option. Languages unit will provide language training for any student. Most degree programmes allow study abroad. Formal exchange links with 30 EC universities/colleges: Belgium (3); Denmark (2); France (7); Germany (5); Greece (3); Italy (5); Netherlands (3); Spain (2) and one EFTA university: Austria (1).

Application: UCCA for 1993 start, UCAS thereafter. **Academic features:** Degrees in fine arts and art history; East Mediterranean history; Greek and Roman studies; mechanical engineering and business studies; biomaterials, commerce with languages; public and social policy management. **Founded:** 1828, as Birmingham School of Medicine and Surgery, and 1875 Mason College; granted charter in 1900. **Main awards:** BA, BCom, BDS, BEng, MEng and Man, BEng & BCom, BEng and Com, MEng, BMedSc, BMus, BNurs, BPhys, BSc, BSocSc, LLB, MB/ChB. **Awarding body:** Birmingham University. **Site:** (Edgbaston) 2½ miles from city centre. **Access:** Just off A38; buses between university and city centre, trains between University Station (on campus) and New Street Station, in city centre. **Accommodation:** 2,000 places in halls, 2,100 in self-catering flats in three student villages; accommodation guaranteed for first year students. Independent hostels for Anglican, Jewish and Muslim students; university accommodation officer helps with flats and lodgings. 40% students in accommodation where rent controlled by university. **Library:** Main library with 1,600,000 volumes plus various subject libraries; guide issued to students. **Other learning facilities:** Computer centre, television and film unit, language laboratories, Barber Institute Art Gallery. **Welfare:** Student welfare officer. University health centre, counselling service, Guild of Students welfare service; medical and dental service both obtainable by telephone; all students asked to complete health questionnaire before coming up; sight testing by appointment at health centre. Day nursery for children of students and staff close to main campus. **Hardship funds:** A hardship fund, administered by the university, available for help in individual cases. **Careers:** Information and advice centre (including video-tape presentations of various careers). **Amenities:** Union building controlled by Guild of Students with hall, bars, etc; bookshop, banks and barbers on site; Barber Institute of Fine Arts. **Sporting facilities:** Multi-activity centre with swimming pool, gymnasia, etc; seventy acres of playing fields including all-weather pitches and running track; Raymond Priestley centre for rock climbing, sailing, and sub-aqua diving adjacent to Coniston Water in Lake District.

Duration of first degree course(s) or equivalent: 3 years; 4 years including language courses, MEng, MEng and Man, BCom, BNurs and BEng and Com; 5 years, and MB/CEB and BDS **Total first degree students 1991/92:** 9,017 **BEd students:** 979 **Overseas students:** 538 **Mature students:** 838 **Male/female ratio:** 6:5 **Teaching staff:** full-time: 1,087 part-time: 67 **Total full-time students 1991/92:** 11,202 **Postgraduate students:** 2,325 f-t, 1,464 p-t **Tuition fees for 1992/93 (first degrees):** Home: £1,855 (classroom), £2,770 (lab/studio), £4,985 (clinical); Overseas: £5,320 (classroom), £7,055 (lab/studio), £12,990 (clinical).

".....boasts curries so eerily cheap that one wonders what they put in them "

What it's like

The city of Birmingham is ideally located right at the centre of Britain. It's easily accessible from most parts of the country. University campus is situated 3 miles from the city centre in Edgbaston, one of the most attractive parts of the city. Excellent reputation academically. Impressive sporting facilities including two synthetic pitches on campus. Sports centre has a swimming pool, numerous squash courts, 2 sports halls and many other facilities.

The Guild of Students (SU) is housed in impressive building on campus. It provides all the usual bars, catering outlets and nightclubs, as well as substantial welfare facilities and academic representation. The Guild and students actively campaign on student issues, both within the university and nationally. Over 100 societies within the Guild which also funds extremely successful athletic union recognised as one of the best in the country.

Birmingham as a city is rapidly establishing itself as a cultural centre. There are a wide range of venues catering for all sorts of musical tastes, from the Symphony Hall to Ronnie Scott's Jazz Club. The city is doing a lot in an effort to lose its reputation for being a dull, grey city. Green areas are being developed all over and the canal which runs through the campus has just been renovated.

CAN'T FIND WHAT YOU'RE LOOKING FOR? USE THE INDEX!

The wide range of activities and opportunities at Birmingham University make it an ideal choice to maximise your time at university.

Joe Bourne
President of Guild of Students

Pauper notes

Accommodation: Wide range of both catered and self-catering accommodation on campus. Rented accommodation still fairly reasonably priced within walking distance of university and in Moseley, Harborne and Balsall Heath. **Drink:** Largely pubs in Selly Oak, as well as the bars within the Guild. Local beers are not up to much – the best real ale is at the Guild. **Eats:** In university accommodation – very basic. All tastes catered for in the Guild. The Bristol Road in Selly Oak is famous for its many curry houses. **Ents:** Jazz, rock, indie, raves, classical, etc all catered for at the Guild and within Birmingham. Stratford is within easy driving distance and the centre of Birmingham also houses many theatres. **Sports:** University facilities excellent, including the swimming pool. Edgbaston Cricket Ground within walking distance; Birmingham also has 3 first class football teams (NOT). **Hardship funds:** We do our best but things aren't getting any easier. **Travel:** Easy to all corners of the UK. Local buses and trains to city centre take 10 minutes. Cycling is quickest and most efficient way to get about campus. **Work:** Approaching 200 jobs within the Guild itself, eg working in bars, security, cleaning and catering. Also jobs in local bars and restaurants as well as some opportunity for temping during vacations.

More info?

Get students' Alternative Prospectus.
Enquiries to Student Reception (021 472 1841).

Informal name

Bugs (Birmingham University Guild of Students)

Alumni (Editors' pick)

Sir Alex Jarratt (Jarratt Report), Victoria Wood (comedienne/writer), Sir Austin Pierce (Chairman, British Aerospace), Desmond Morris (writer/broadcaster), Sir Peter Walters (Chairman, BP), Ross Whitley, The Hon J J Bossano (Chief Minister, Gibraltar), Dr D M Mutasa (Speaker of Parliament, Zimbabwe).

BOLTON INSTITUTE

Bolton Institute of Higher Education, Deane Road, Bolton BL3 5AB (0204 28851; Fax 0204 399074; Freephone 0800 262117)
Map A, D5

Student enquiries: The Marketing Officer

Main study areas – as in What to Study section: *(First degree):* Biology, business studies, civil engineering, computing, education, electrical & electronic engineering, English, environmental studies, history, mathematics, mechanical & production engineering, philosophy, psychology. *Also:* Building studies, gender studies, textiles, tourism and leisure studies.

European Community: 1% first degree students have the option of taking an EC language as part of course; less than 1% spend 6 months or more in another EC country. Some exchange links with France for business studies and civil engineering students.

Application: PCAS for 1993 start, UCAS thereafter. **Founded:** 1982, ex Bolton Institute of Technology and Bolton College of Education (Technical). **Main**

awards: BA, BEd, BEng, BSc. **Awarding body:** Bolton Institute; Manchester University (in-service teacher education degrees and research degrees). **Site:** Bolton town centre. **Access:** Easily reached by road and rail. 10 miles north of Manchester. **Accommodation:** Halls, hostels and private lodgings; accommodation manager. **Library:** 100,000 books and related materials together with microfilms, microfiches, audiocassettes and tape slide presentations. **Other learning resources:** Access to Prestel. Provision made for on-line access to major bibliographic machine readable databases. **Welfare:** Student services unit specialist staff; chaplain. **Careers:** Information, advice and placement. **Amenities:** SU with numerous clubs and societies. Octagon Theatre, Bolton Little Theatre, art gallery and museum, excellent shopping, indoor and outdoor markets, travel shop, Water Place. **Sporting facilities:** Sports hall, playing fields, squash court.

Duration of first degree course(s) or equivalent: 3 years full time; 4 years sandwich **Total first degree students 1991/92:** 2,800; **Total BEd students:** 24 **Overseas students:** 200 **Mature students:** 1,000 **Male/female ratio:** 3:2 **Teaching staff:** full-time: 300; part-time: 150. **Total full-time students 1991/92:** 3,000 **Postgraduate students:** 230 **Tuition fees for 1992/93 (first degrees):** Home: £1,855 (classroom), £2,770 (lab); Overseas: £4,700 (classroom), £5,250 (lab).

What it's like

It's a middle-sized seat of learning: not quite a university, yet bigger than most colleges of HE. BIHE has a lively SU with regular events throughout the week, ranging from discos and quizzes to live bands. The bar is open from 11.00am to 11.00pm selling food and cheap drinks.

SU runs shops and there are over 30 clubs and societies. SU is politically involved internally and externally, representing students at all levels of college management and taking part in national NUS campaigns.

Bolton's not a bad place to live: accommodation is cheap, but start looking a month or so before you come here. Bolton is full of pubs, so drinking is no problem. However the night life after 11.00pm is poor, but this can be overcome with Manchester only ten miles away.

So if you are thinking of coming to Bolton, it's not a bad choice: the facilities are here, it's just a case of making the most of them.

Buzz-words

BIHE – Bolton Institute of Higher Education.

Pauper notes

Accommodation: Private sector accommodation difficult; no married quarters. Approx 150 places in college accommodation. **Drink:** Loads of pubs. Greenhall Whitley, Witches, Pendles. **Eats:** Good SU pizza franchise and pies & peas. Refectory food is usually good, averagely priced. Reasonable veggy choice. **Ents:** Good on campus. Live bands (middle market), regular film nights, alternative discos, heavy etc. Apart from pubs local ents are negligible. **Sports:** On campus sports hall, squash courts. 1,000,001 local sports centres, gyms, swimming pools. **Work:** Bar work for hard-up students, also college shop.

BOURNEMOUTH POLY

See Bournemouth University

CAN'T FIND WHAT YOU'RE LOOKING FOR? USE THE INDEX!

BOURNEMOUTH UNIVERSITY

Bournemouth University, Talbot Campus, Fern Barrow, Poole, Dorset BH12 5BB (0202 524111) Fax: 0202 513293
Map A, E9

Student enquiries: Academic Secretary

Main study areas – as in What to Study section: *(First degree):* Accountancy, archaeology, business studies, communication studies, computing, electrical & electronic engineering, food science & nutrition; hotel & catering management, information technology, law, nursing studies. *Also:* Advertising, computer visualisation and animation, engineering business development, financial services, heritage conservation, public relations, tourism.

European Community: 14% first degree students learn an EC language as part of their course and 21% spend 6 months or more in another EC country. All students can study a language as an extra subject and work for certification of competence: languages form an integral part of courses in business studies and international marketing management. Currently, links with 36 EC universities/colleges: Belgium (1); France (14); Germany (4); Greece (4); Italy (5); Netherlands (3); Portugal (1); Spain (4) but number increasing. Undergraduates go on exchanges particularly in business management and tourism. Approved Erasmus programme.

Application: PCAS for 1993 start, UCAS thereafter. **Academic features:** Degrees in communication, retail management, electronic systems design, health and community studies, public relations, nursing. Sandwich courses in international marketing, engineering business development, product design, electronic systems design, information systems management. **Special features:** Visiting fellows: J Smith and I Swain (Institute of Health Services), W Vierich and Albert Roux (services industries), D Bebo, P Bird (management systems). **Founded:** As a university in 1992; previously Bournemouth Polytechnic. Founded as Dorset Institute in 1976, ex Bournemouth College of Technology and Weymouth College of Education. **Main awards:** BA, BSc, BEng, LLB. **Awarding body:** Bournemouth University. **Site:** 2 sites. **Access:** Buses. **Accommodation:** 250 places in student village, lodgings, self-catering flats and bedsits. **Library:** Libraries on each site; total of 130,000 volumes, 1,600 periodicals, 600 study places, restricted loan collection. **Welfare:** Doctors, nurses, counsellors, psychologist, chaplain, accommodation staff, family planning advisers. **Careers:** Information, advice and placement. **Amenities:** Good resort amenities, especially for sailing; arts centre and sports club (squash, swimming, gymnastics) at Poole; good sports halls, 2 squash courts and a weights room, together with cricket nets and wall-climbing facilities at Talbot campus. Large SU bar with refreshment and entertainment facilities.

Duration of first degree course(s) or equivalent: 3 years (full time); **Other:** 4 years sandwich **Total first degree students 1991/92:** 4,158 **Male/female ratio:** 1:1 **Teaching staff:** 270 **Part-time:** 50 **Total full-time students 1991/92:** 5,140 **Postgraduate students:** 550 **Tuition fees for 1992/93 (first degrees):** Home: £1,855 (classroom), £2,770 (lab/studio); Overseas: £5,319.

What it's like

It was Dorset Institute then changed its name and status to Bournemouth Poly and is now Bournemouth University. This has meant a huge increase in full- and part-time students and the rapid introduction of new and innovative courses (eg BA in public relations) and also better library. SU resources therefore strained; and left new university in poor position to cope due to limited facilities. Growth should stabilise as the goal has been reached. SU has been allocated a larger building. Houses of residence have a capacity of 250 only, so majority of freshers would continue to live in hotels for the first term, before moving out into fully furnished rented accommodation. Parking is getting worse.

University has 'hi-tech' 'hands-on' policy; personal computers on open access, though not enough to cope with peak times as most courses 'prefer' assignments done on the word processors. (Learn to type before coming if poss.)

It's a large concrete rabbit hutch and a smaller sci-fi building. Nearly all courses are practical (business studies and catering big) which makes this the government's model college, the fact that most students are white, middle class and either conservative or unconcerned probably helps too. High proportion of students own cars; parking a serious problem.

SU active although not radical, maintains a good relationship with college administration and provides a number of good services. SU provides a full-time sabbatical welfare officer, it is also a registered Citizens' Advice Bureau and so can give a high level of advice to students covering anything from housing to course work. The welfare service also produces its own student leaflets. Some counselling services are provided by university. Excellent welfare office.

Pauper notes

Accommodation: Houses of residence, B&B hotels for 1st term at college, then rented accom. **Drink:** University bar cheapest, although still not cheap. Some good clubs. Old Thumper good strong local beer. **Eats:** Refectory not cheap. SU special vegan/vegetarian meals. **Ents:** Lots of clubs. Bands play on Friday nights in SU bar. New groups on and off campus. **Sports:** Sports hall, multi-gym and squash courts on campus, off campus for playing fields and swimming pool (concessions). **Hardship funds:** Small fund operated under strict rules. Normally used for rent. **Travel:** Financial help: not known. Student travel is now on a par with outside outlets. **Work:** Part-time work in catering/bar establishments.

More info?

Enquiries to Michael Moss (0202 523755).

BRADFORD & ILKLEY

Bradford & Ilkley Community College, Great Horton Road, Bradford BD7 1AY (0274 753026) Map A, E5

Student enquiries: Admissions Officer

Main study areas – as in What to Study section: *(First degree):* Art and design, business studies, education, modern languages, social policy and social welfare. *Also:* Community studies, organisation studies.

European Community: Number of first degree students taking EC languages or spending time in EC, not known.

Application: UCCA for 1993 start, UCAS thereafter; ADAR for art courses. **Founded:** 1982 ex Bradford College and Ilkley College. **Main awards:** BA BEd. **Awarding body:** Bradford University. **Sites:** Bradford and Ilkley. **Academic features:** Open and distance learning facilities available. **Accommodation:** 400 single rooms; lodgings officer supplies list of flats. **Library:** 220,000 volumes; 1,250 journals. **Specialist collections:** Slide collection of over 60,000 journal reprints. **Welfare:** Student service centre (including tutor to West Indian youth, tutor for students with special needs, doctor and nursing staff). **Hardship funds:** Fully staffed student service gives advice and assistance. **Special categories:** Day nursery. **Careers:** Advisory service. **Amenities:** SU building with several bars; Bradford Alhambra Theatre, concerts, plays and recitals; library, theatre; National Photographic Museum. **Sporting facilities:** Shared with Bradford University; Richard Dunn Sports Centre in city of Bradford.

Duration of first degree course(s) or equivalent: 4 years; others: 3 years art and

CAN'T FIND WHAT YOU'RE LOOKING FOR? USE THE INDEX!

design, and organisation studies **Total first degree students 1991/92: 702; BEd students: 270 Overseas students: 3% Mature students: 300 Male/female ratio: 1:1 Teaching staff: Full-time: 550 Part-time: 1,000 Total full-time students 1991/92: 3,615 Postgraduate students: 110 Tuition fees for 1992/93 (first degrees):** Home: £1,855 (classroom), £2,770 (studio); Overseas: £5,000.

What it's like

Huge college (largest in UK? Europe?) – 33,000 students. Non-elitist community college. High proportion of overseas and mature students, with home students on minimum grant. SU active; on speaking terms with admin. Students represented on all college committees. Excellent counselling, careers accommodation services. Hall for 240, predominantly self-catering. Excellent social life.

Pauper notes

Accommodation: Housing lists from student services at the university. **Drinks:** SU building at Queens Hall and at Ilkley. Good local brews include Old Mill Bitter. Cellar Bar, Queene Hall: Old Mill, Ruddles, Courage, Theakstons, Batemans, Trough ales. **Eats:** Bradford home of foreign culinary delights at very cheap prices. 8 restaurants around union campus – inc vegetarian meals. Curry restaurants, Italia cafe, Last Pizza Show, Oasis (Arabian), Mayflower (Chinese) and Lunch Box. **Ents:** One of the best and cheapest SU live music venues in England at Queens Hall – close to Alhambra Theatre and St George's Hall – discounts available. **Sports:** Excellent sports facilities. A lot shared with university. **Hardship funds:** Access funds and student services hardship grant – college administered. **Travel:** Hitching OK, esp from Leeds (M1), cheap student bus/train passes for West Yorkshire; travel trust for course related trips. **Work:** Part-time bar work, some portering work in college, temping etc. Vacancy lists from SU.

Alumni (Editors' pick)

David Hockney – artist; New Model Army – group.

BRADFORD UNIVERSITY

University of Bradford, Bradford, West Yorkshire BD7 1DP
(0274 733466) Map A, E5

Student enquiries: Schools Liaison Office. Visitors welcome

Main study areas – as in What to Study section: *(First degree):* Archaeology, biochemistry, business studies, chemical engineering, chemistry, civil engineering, communication studies, computing, economics, electrical and electronic engineering, environmental science, environmental studies, European studies, food science and nutrition, geography, history, information technology, mathematical studies, mechanical and production engineering, microbiology, modern languages, nursing studies, pharmacology, pharmacy, philosophy, politics and government, professions allied to medicine (PAMs), psychology, social policy and social welfare, sociology, strategic studies. *Also:* Biomedical sciences, midwifery.

European Community: 13% first degree students take EC language as part of course and 13% spend 6 months or more in another EC country. EC language tuition is a full part of degrees in modern languages, European studies and management studies and French/German/Spanish; minor part of electrical engineering with European studies and European area studies; optional part of chemical and civil engineering degrees; all students can make private use of language facilities (not intended to make languages compulsory for all although provision is due to expand). Formal exchange links with 10 EC universities/ colleges: France (Montpellier, Nancy, Nice, Strasbourg, Toulouse); Germany (Hamburg, Munich, Rostock); Spain (Oviedo, Valladolid). Approved Erasmus programme 1992/93.

Application: UCCA for 1993 start, UCAS thereafter. **Special features:** Opportunity to add range of practical skills (team work, presentation, report writing etc) and to become computer literate. Fellowships in music and theatre ensure a very active student arts scene. **Founded:** 1966. **Main awards:** BA, BEng, BPharm, BSc. **Awarding body:** Bradford University. **Site:** Close to city centre. **Academic features:** A positive and encouraging attitude towards non-standard and mature applicants; wide range of qualifications and/or experience accepted for entry. 70% of students are on sandwich degree courses. Engineering courses with foundation year for applicants with non-standard qualifications; BSc in electronic imaging and media communications, BSc in pharmaceutical management. University also validates degrees for some courses at Bradford and Ilkley College, and degrees in physiotherapy and in radiography run by the Bradford Health Authority. **Accommodation:** 965 places for men, 660 for women in halls. Accommodation service for flats, bedsitters and furnished houses. Approx cost: £21–26 pw. 36% students in accommodation where rent controlled by university. **Library:** 2 sites; 500,000 volumes; 2,900 current periodicals; 750 study places. **Other learning resources:** Personal computer connections for all staff and students to a large campus network giving access to electronic mail, university library, campus computer hosts, information bulletin boards and other services. Network access points have been installed in offices, work areas and study bedrooms in student halls. Special prices and deferred payment terms available for personal computer purchases. **Welfare:** Student counselling service, overseas student advisers, student health service. 49-place day nursery. **Hardship funds:** Loans or small grants available from SU and from university in strictly defined circumstances. **Careers:** Information and advice service (with overseas section); annual recruitment fairs. **Amenities:** Communal building with 3 bar areas, dance floor, disco bar; SU travel office; bank and bookshop on campus; open air amphitheatre, studio theatre; campus radio; darkroom; SU shop and bar in Richmond Building. **Sporting facilities:** Indoor sports centre, plus solarium, sauna bath and 25 metre pool shared with Bradford College; sports grounds 3 miles away; additional squash courts and artificial turf areas at halls of residence.

Duration of first degree course(s) or equivalent: 4 years sandwich; **others:** 5 years (sandwich) **Total first degree students 1991/92:** 4,553 **Number of overseas students:** 332 **Male/female ratio:** 3:2 **Teaching staff:** full-time: 405 part-time: 175 **Total full-time students 1991/92:** 5,329 **Postgraduate students:** 776 **Tuition fees for 1992/93 (first degrees):** Home: £1,855 (classroom), £2,770 (lab), £755 (if no grant); Overseas: £5,300 (classroom), £6,900 (lab/studio).

What it's like

Small, friendly campus university, five minutes walk from city centre. 6,000 students, 600 of whom based at management centre, 2 miles from main campus, on main bus routes. Technological university awarded charter in 1966 (formerly Bradford College of Technology). Academic strengths – engineering, modern languages, business studies. Most courses include placement, either industrial or educational; many abroad.

Accommodation: 1,700 places in university halls of residence, mostly self-catering. Private accommodation averages £20–25 pw, mostly in large, Victorian terraced houses within 1 mile of campus.

SU offers 4 bars on campus, shop, travel agency, print shop, welfare service, wide range of clubs and societies and athletics clubs.

City – formerly Victorian textile capital, now extremely cosmopolitan and friendly. Cheap entertainment and food (cheapest and best curries in the country – try them or be forever socially inadequate!!). Products of 20 different real ale breweries can be sampled in the city.

CAN'T FIND WHAT YOU'RE LOOKING FOR? USE THE INDEX!

Students – friendly and down-to-earth, no failed Oxbridge complex here. Despite reputation as cheapest university city in the country, students rumoured to have largest per capita overdrafts (after London) – must be enjoying themselves.

Pauper notes

Accommodation: Halls places for the vast majority of first years. Housing in city cheap and local. Most non-Hall accommodation is in 4/8 bedroom houses. Cheap (£20–£25 pw) but you can get what you pay for. **Drink:** SU bars cheaper than local pubs. Watch for promos. Best beers are Tetleys, Websters, Theakstons and Youngers. **Eats:** The best curry houses in Britain. Great value Indian, Pakistani, Chinese, Greek, Arabian, Italian all close to campus. All the burger and pizza places in town. **Ents:** Gigs, films, discos, comedians every week on campus. Famous Alhambra Theatre and National Museum of Film Photography & Television nearby. 3 screen cinema near, ie it's brill. **Sports:** Cheap sports centre on campus ie swimming 40p. New astroturf pitches very near campus. Playing fields 3 miles away on direct bus route. **Hardship funds:** Funds run by Union and University. Excellent welfare department. **Travel:** Transport interchange and motorways. Campus travel provides great cheap student deals. **Work:** Temporary work available in bars/security.

More info?

Enquiries to Vikki Goddard, SU (0274 383300).

Buzz-words

FND = Friday night disco (1,200 raving students). Must learn all curry jargon!

Alumni (Editors' pick)

Dr Barry Seal MEP, Roland Boyes MP, Ian Bruce MP, David Hinchcliffe MP, Alice Mahon MP, Ann Taylor MP, Michael Meadowcroft (ex MP), Tony O'Riley (chairman of Heinz International).

BRETTON HALL

Bretton Hall, West Bretton, Wakefield, West Yorks WF4 4LG (0924 830261) Map A, E5

Student enquiries: Admissions Co-ordinator or Registrar

Main study areas – as in What to Study section: *(First degree):* Art and design, dance, drama, education, English, environmental studies, music. *Also:* Social studies.

European Community: No first degree students take EC language as part of course or spend time in another EC country.

Application: UCCA for 1993 start, UCAS thereafter. **Academic features:** Integrated arts course within BEd; BA dance centred on community dance, BA fashion, BA popular music. **Special features:** Over 20 visiting artists and writers in residence work and teach during the year. Lawrence Batley Centre for the National Arts Education Archive. **Founded:** 1949. **Main awards:** BA, BEd. **Awarding body:** Leeds University. **Site:** 18th century buildings in 260 acre rural setting. **Access:** 1 mile from M1 (Junction 38); public transport from Wakefield, Barnsley. **Accommodation:** 170 places on campus; excellent self-catering accommodation for 120 students off campus. College accommodation reserved for first-year students – 80% housed. 10% of students are home-based. **Library:** 70,000 volumes, 400 periodicals, 65 study places, reference or short term loan. Videos and microfiche reader facilities. **Other learning facilities:** Media resources centre. Apple Mac studio. **Welfare:** Doctor, chaplain, counsellors, sick bay (staffed). **Hardship funds:** A general fund available for extreme hardship cases. **Amenities:** Bookshop and art gallery on campus, playing fields; Yorkshire Sculpture Park; Bretton Lakes Nature Reserve. National Art Education Archive.

Duration of first degree course(s) or equivalent: 3 years (BA); 4 years (BEd); **Total first degree students 1991/92:** 346; **BEd students:** 114 **Overall overseas students:** 10 **Overall mature students:** 317 **Male/female ratio:** 1:3 **Teaching staff: full-time:** 88 **part-time:** 55 **Total full-time students 1991/92:** 1,097 **Postgraduate students:** 157 **Tuition fees for 1992/93 (first degrees):** Home: £1,855 (classroom), £2,770 (lab/studio); Overseas: £5,000. All first years pay £340 university fee.

"Lots of girl students go through initial heady Isadora Duncan-type period"

What it's like

Based around an 18th century mansion, set in 260 acres of beautiful landscaped parkland, which includes the Yorkshire Sculpture Park, country park, two lakes and a lot of squirrels!

Easy access from M1. 168 students on campus – catered, individual rooms, mixed hostels. Major housing area 10 miles away in Normanton – 3 students per self catering maisonette. Most students in private accommodation in 3 local villages and towns. A lot of mature students, some overseas. Small college, friendly relations with staff/students. Developing SU – students here tend not to be politically active.

Large amount of students with cars – useful because of isolated position. Number of societies gradually increasing – very easy to set up – a lot of SU and college backing. Good local markets in Barnsley, Wakefield and Huddersfield. Excellent multiscreen cinema 10 miles away. Campus is best meeting place as accommodation is so scattered.

Only arts courses available (BA, BEd, or PGCE). Course loads vary – BEd quite tough but very good. Lectures tend to be seminars, workshops and tutorials – quite small groups. Continuous assessment – few exams. Lots of practical experience.

Intake is from all over UK – mostly state schools. Typical student – 'arty'. Typical lecturer – 'arty'!

High BEd employment rate; BA rate difficult to say – arts jobs more difficult to get, a lot of BA students go on into post-graduate courses eg PGCE.

CAN'T FIND WHAT YOU'RE LOOKING FOR? USE THE INDEX!

Pauper notes

Accommodation: With increasing student numbers, accommodation very hard to find. *But* accommodation prices off-campus not too expensive. **Drink:** West Bretton one of only 3 dry villages in England! SU bar saves the world, with good selection of subsidised beers etc. John Smiths, Whitbreads, Youngers, Miller Lite, Taunton ciders, bar recently refurbished. **Eats:** Vegetarian food usually best bet in canteen. SU bar sells hot snacks. Good curry houses in Wakefield. Local real Italian pizzeria which will deliver to campus! **Ents:** Regular events, plus outside trips to Leeds, Sheffield etc. Increasing number of nightclubs in surrounding area have student nights; cheap entry and good music. **Sports:** All students entitled to free Passport to Leisure for Wakefield MDC's sport/leisure facilities. Local swimming pool small, cheap and very nice. Sport at Bretton depends on involvement of students. **Hardship funds:** PCFC Access Fund available plus short term loans from college. **Travel:** Student season tickets available for local buses and trains. **Work:** Even more difficult to get term/vac work. There is none available on campus at all. Possible to get bar/shop jobs part-time, transport permitting.

More info?

Enquiries to Natasha Cannell (0924 830282).

Alumni (Editors' pick)

Anne Collins (opera singer), Colin Welland (actor/playwright, author), David Rappaport (founder of Hull Truck), Nicholas Parsons (TV personality), John Godber (playwright), Ken Robinson (TIE/Arts in Education), Moira Stewart (newsreader).

BRIGHTON POLY

See Brighton University

BRIGHTON UNIVERSITY

University of Brighton, Lewes Road, Brighton, East Sussex BN2 4AT (0273 600900) Map A, F8

Student enquiries: The Academic Registrar

Main study areas – as in What to Study section: *(First degree):* Accountancy, architecture, art & design, biology, business studies, chemistry, civil engineering, computing, dance, drama, environmental science, economics, education, electrical & electronic engineering, English, fine arts, geography, history, hotel & catering management, information technology, library & information studies, linguistics, mathematical studies, mechanical and production engineering, music, pharmacy, physics, professions allied to medicine (PAMs), social policy and social welfare. *Also:* biomedical science, building and surveying, osteopathy, photography, sports science, tourism.

European Community: 20% first degree students take EC language as part of course and 5% spend 6 months or more in another EC country. EC language tuition available to all students. Formal exchange links with over 15 EC universities/colleges: France (6); Germany (2); Italy (1); Netherlands (1); Portugal (1); Spain (4); most open to non-language specialists. Approved Erasmus programme 1991.

Application: PCAS for 1993 start, UCAS thereafter; ADAR for art and design. **Academic features:** Courses in international tourism management; podiatry;

building surveying, editorial photography. **Largest fields of study:** Art, design and humanities; education (including physical education); engineering; business management; health; information technology. **Founded:** As a university 1992; previously Brighton Poly, formed ex-Brighton Colleges of Technology, Art and Education and East Sussex College of HE. **Main awards:** BA, BEd, BSc, BEng, MEng. **Awarding body:** Brighton University. **Site:** 3 major sites at Brighton; Eastbourne site. **Access:** Bus and train services provide regular inter-site travel. **Accommodation:** At least 30% of first year students housed by university, some catered, others self-catering. 25% students in accommodation where rent controlled by university. Accommodation officers help find lodgings in private sector. Approx cost: £35–£45 pw halls (with meals), £30–£35 pw (self-catering), £35–£50 pw (lodgings). **Library:** 7 libraries, over 500,000 volumes, 3,250 periodicals, 12,000 videotapes, 820 study places. **Other learning resources:** Media units for film and video, including darkroom and graphic design studio. 600 computer terminals/micros linked to each other and to VAX computers. Over 300 introductory documents to computing service. Advisory service also operates. **Welfare:** Welfare and accommodation officers, doctor, personal counsellor and chaplain on each site; recreation tutor. **Hardship funds:** Limited funds available for some final year students. **Careers:** Careers counsellor and careers information room for Brighton and Eastbourne campuses. **Amenities:** Bookshops at Moulsecoomb and Falmer sites; swimming pool (near Olympic standard) at Eastbourne campus; recreation facilities, including extensive playing fields in Brighton and Eastbourne, 6 gymnasia, dance studios, licensed bars.

Duration of first degree course(s) or equivalent: 3 years; **others:** 4 years (teacher training and sandwich) **Total first degree students 1991/92:** 5,639 **Total BEd students:** 847 **Number of overseas students:** 371 **Number of mature students:** 627 (in 1st year) **Male/female ratio:** 1:1 **Teaching staff: full-time:** 540 **part-time:** 550 **Total full-time students 1991/92:** 6,442 **Postgraduate students:** 698 **Tuition fees for 1992/93 (first degrees):** Home: £1,855 (classroom), £2,770 (lab/studio), £759 (if no grant); Overseas: £5,200 (classroom), £5,600 (lab/studio).

What it's like

Known as 'London by the sea', Brighton has an array of clubs, shops, restaurants, parks, cinemas, pubs and, of course, the beach – stony though it may be. It has two glorious piers – of which, unfortunately, only one is open to the public. A lively cosmopolitan town, Brighton also has the crunchy with the smooth, including high unemployment, homelessness, a degree of racism and terrace type violence. Yet it also has the bonus of a large gay and lesbian community and an overall breeze of liberty and freedom (could it be the sea air?). With two universities and a technical college, Brighton is very much a young town; its 20,000 students make up nearly 10% of its population. However, saying this, Brighton University has a high percentage of mature students, of which the majority blend almost unnoticeably into student life.

A poly until 1992, the university is based on four main sites:

1. Grand Parade – Placed in the centre of Brighton, diagonal to the infamous and exotically out of place Pavilion (also known as the Taj Mahal of the South). This is the home to most art based students and the SU nightclub/bar in town known as the Basement. An energetic part of the university, it also holds two galleries and a theatre for some of the best and cheapest shows in town.

2. Moulsecoomb – Placed 2 miles outside Brighton on 3 large sites, all within 2 minutes walk of each other, this holds the largest number of students (4,000 full-time), and courses include anything from business to pharmacy and law to architecture. Generally a busy hustle-bustle type of place, with the MTV blaring away, games being played and pizza being eaten in the main common room, this site also holds the main SU welfare unit as well as the sports office and the university-run nursery, for which the SU offers a limited number of single parents a subsidy.

3. Falmer – 4 miles out of town in the midst of the South Downs, directly

facing Sussex University, this site has a family atmosphere the size of all soap operas combined. It holds the SU half-term play scheme (far the cheapest in town); the Daisychain nursery (single parent students can obtain subsidised child care) 5 minutes walk away. Its playing fields are the venue for all university outdoor sports and its new SU bar/entertainments venue has a relaxed, friendly atmosphere, fast becoming the centre for students living in Falmer halls of residence as well as non-residential students. The main drawback of the site has always been and remains that of access for physically disabled students, with the layout making it nigh on impossible for anyone in a wheelchair to enter, get around or leave the site.

4. Eastbourne – 26 miles away – is based on various sites (which all look like private schools for girls), all within walking distance of each other. Despite this, students seem to enjoy the atmosphere of the place and, as a relatively small site, many students seem to get on together whilst getting down at the 'Deckchair Club' which, sited under the SU, is a hive of activity all year.

Untiring and fully comprehensive SU welfare office. SU is a small but developing entity with wonderful, hardworking staff and officers maximising services on ever tightening budget, including sports, clubs and societies, entertainments, food, campaigns (welfare and political), bars, nightclubs, and also representation both academically and in the outside world. It offers a Black South African student scholarship.

Pauper notes

Accommodation: Trying to find accommodation had turned into an art form over the last couple of years. The art of initially seeing a place before it's let, then sussing out the landlord/lady/agent, and finally deciphering the contract. The average rent for a student in Brighton is about £38 for a hell hole, £40–£45 for a reasonably nice place (slightly less in Eastbourne). University accommodation office holds many properties and should be seen early as they disappear faster than shell suits did. Student services also run a head lease scheme to keep a check on landlords and once again should be applied for sooner rather than later. University has halls of residence for just under 1,000 students dotted around Falmer, Eastbourne and Brighton seafront, both catering and self catering. Be warned – these rooms are small, but the community atmosphere can often make up for it.

Travel: Transport in Brighton is expensive. All sites can be reached by train or bus, although saver tickets and YP railcards are advised.

Work: As Brighton is almost as expensive as London, many students find themselves in dire need of a job – not easy in Brighton where with increasing numbers of students the jobs are in many cases simply not there. Despite this gloom, jobs do go begging at the end of summer so, as with the housing situation, *make moves early* before term starts.

Despite the doom and gloom Brighton is a truly amazing place, and needs visiting if nothing else. Try it – you'll love it!

Ian Carter
VP Welfare & Campaigns

BRISTOL OLD VIC

Bristol Old Vic Theatre School, 2 Downside Road, Clifton, Bristol BS8 2XF (0272 733535) Map A, D8

Student enquiries: The Principal

Main study areas – as in What to Study section: *(First degree):* Drama and theatre arts. *Also:* Movement studies, theatre design.

European Community: Number of students taking EC languages or spending time in another EC country, not known.

GET HOLD OF THE PROSPECTUSES

Application: Direct. **Academic features:** Strictly vocational training for theatre, and related media. **Structural features:** Close ties and working arrangements with the Bristol Old Vic Company, BBC Radio, HTV, both local universities. **Special features:** Visiting specialists in all fields of the profession. All permanent staff have wide professional experience. **Largest fields of study:** Acting and stage management, design and wardrobe. **Founded:** 1946. **Site:** Main Clifton site with other venues around the city. **Access:** Adjacent 'Dart' bus stop. **Accommodation:** Private accommodation in nearby areas. Apply to Accommodation Officer to help find digs 3 weeks before commencement. Approx cost: Allow £1,500+ per academic year. **Library:** No formal library, though the school stocks many play sets, individual texts and music. The central and reference libraries and the University theatre collection are open to certain student use. **Other specialist collections:** Sound and video editing, prop making etc. **Welfare:** Bristol University student health service is available. **Hardship funds:** No special hardship funds. Advice about grant-making trusts is available. **Careers:** Information and advice given. No guarantee of placement. Main areas of employment: theatre and related media. **Sporting facilities:** The usual city facilities.

Duration of first degree course(s) or equivalent: 3 years; **others:** 2 and 1 years **Male/female ratio:** 3:2 **Teaching staff: full-time:** 19; **part-time:** 12 **Total full-time students 1991/92:** 106 **Tuition fees, 1992/93:** £5,700.

What it's like

Training ground for all aspects of theatre/drama. Small institution with enormous amount of energy. Life can be emotionally and physically exhausting, yet rewarding and worthwhile. Claims to treat students as professionals, allowing them a glimpse of the biz: rigorous discipline; sometimes not enough room for error/human fallibility. Teaching is classically orientated; little radical input on the curriculum although this is gradually changing. Sometimes rewards outweighed by frustrations. Training realistic and totally practical.

Building is small but facilities are improving; the atmosphere is friendly, but intense.

Commitment to hard, penniless, unglamorous career in theatre has to be total, otherwise you will not endure the course.

Pauper notes

Accommodation: No college accommodation. **Drink:** Alma Tavern; Coronation Tap, University Union Bar. **Eats** Friary café (good, cheap, hearty meals). **Ents:** Watershed, Arnolfini, Old Vic. **Sports:** All Bristol SU facilities available. **Hardship funds:** The Madeleine Farrell Trust. **Work:** Front of house work at the Bristol Old Vic Theatre. Bar/restaurant work.

More info?

Enquiries to Erica Nellman (0272 733535).

Alumni (Editors' pick)

Daniel Day Lewis, Miranda Richardson, Jane Lapotaire, Christopher Cazenove, Jeremy Irons, Greta Scacchi, Gene Wilder, Simon Cadell.

BRISTOL POLY

See Bristol UWE

CAN'T FIND WHAT YOU'RE LOOKING FOR? USE THE INDEX!

BRISTOL UNIVERSITY

University of Bristol, Senate House, Tyndall Avenue, Bristol
BS8 1TH (0272 303030) Map A, D8

Student enquiries: The Registrar

Main study areas – as in What to Study section: *(First degree):* Accountancy, aeronautical engineering, anatomy, archaeology, biochemistry, biology, biotechnology, botany, chemistry, civil engineering, classics, computing, dentistry, drama, economics, education, electrical & electronic engineering, English, fine arts, geography, geology, history, Latin American studies, law, mathematical studies, mechanical and production engineering, medicine, microbiology, modern languages, music, pharmacology, philosophy, physics, physiology, psychology, politics and government, psychology, religious studies and theology, social policy and social welfare, sociology, veterinary science, zoology. *Also:* Astrophysics, chemistry, mechanical engineering with European studies, Mediterranean studies.

European Community: 11% first degree students take EC language as part of course and 12% spend 6 months or more in another EC country. EC language tuition available to engineering and science students on Euro-degrees in years 1 and 2; year 3 spent in EC. Language Centre caters for these students and eg Erasmus programme in law, history, economics, etc. Arrangements under Erasmus to send students to 70+ EC universities/colleges in 1992/93. Member of Santander Group (links 25 European universities) and Coimbra Group (links 30 universities) with aims of establishing special academic, cultural and socioeconomic ties. Founder member of Medical Schools' European Credit Transfer Scheme, allowing medical students to spend 1 term to 1 year at another EC university, which contributes to final degree. Range of innovative courses eg European legal studies; history, with year at Bordeaux; all branches of engineering and mathematics, physics or chemistry or psychology offered with European studies.

Application: UCCA for 1993 start, UCAS thereafter. **Academic features:** Degrees in music, philosophy, biology, botany, mathematics, zoology and computer science can be studied on a part-time basis by extended study and soon also in social science; biochemistry and chemistry with year in industry. Research centre on Mediterranean studies; Reckitt & Colman psycho-pharmacology research unit. New company called Language Consultants for Industry Ltd (in conjunction with Bath University and Bristol Polytechnic) so university's European expertise available to industry, providing linguistic teaching and support, such as translation for business. **Largest fields of study:** Science. **Founded:** 1876, charter granted 1909. **Main awards:** BA, BDS, BEng, MEng, BSc, BVSc, LLB, MB, ChB. **Awarding body:** Bristol University. **Site:** ¼ mile from Bristol city centre. **Access:** Walking, good bus services. **Accommodation:** 3,300 places in halls, flats and student houses. **Special categories:** Residential facilities for overseas married students and disabled students. **Library:** Main library (arts and social sciences and headquarters) and 14 branch libraries. 1,000,000 volumes, 6,100 periodicals, 2,250 study places. Late night opening in main library (term time). Short loan collections for heavily used course books. Library has own computer and an automated circulation system for issuing books in some libraries. On-line public access terminals in all libraries give access to information about books and periodicals. Strong emphasis on reader service and guided tours provided for new students. **Specialist collections:** Sir Allen Lane Penguin collection of autographed works, Wiglesworth ornithological collection, Exley mathematics library, medical library collections, manuscript and early printed rare books, original notebooks and sketch books of Isambard Kingdom Brunel, complete collection of election manifestos since 1892. **Other learning resources:** Computer centre; image analyser; Apollo Domain network for computer-aided design. **Welfare:** Health centre, chaplains, day nursery, counselling service, adviser to students with disabilities, adviser to overseas students. **Amenities:**

Three theatres, Van Dyck Gallery, university bookshop. Active SU with bars, restaurants, recreational facilities. **Sporting facilities:** Indoor sports facilities include full sized swimming pool, excellent indoor fitness training facilities, squash courts, martial arts areas and a multi-use modern synthetic hockey/soccer pitch and excellent grass pitches for rugby, soccer and cricket.

Duration of first degree course(s) or equivalent: 3 years; 4 years (MEng and degrees involving languages, study in Europe or industrial experience); 5 years (MB, ChB, BDS and BVSc) **Total first degree students 1991/92:** 7,949; **BEd students:** 30 **Overseas students:** 526 **Mature students:** 612 **Male/female ratio:** 4:3 **Teaching staff: full-time:** 740 **Total full-time students 1991/92:** 9,265 **Postgraduate students:** 1,316 **Tuition fees for 1992/93 (first degrees):** Home: £755 (if no grant), £1,855 (classroom), £2,770 (lab/studio), £4,985 (clinical); Overseas: £5,700 (classroom), £7,500 (lab/studio), £13,900 (pre-clinical).

What it's like

It's a very beautiful city with university located not far from both city centre and rural escape. It's quite lively with arts and cultural events – music, films, poetry at Watershed and Arnolfini exhibition centres. Clifton/Redland still student areas, increasing number moving to live further away as university grows.

Bristol University sprawls considerably, one of the first things to strike you. Departments embedded in the city – some in elegant Georgian squares, others in grey, square blocks called modern architecture. But never judge a book . . . most departments have excellent facilities and reputations, which keep student morale high and compensate those that are upset Oxbridge rejected them!

Most 1st years are accommodated in university accommodation some of which sprawls well away from the departments. Many of the first-years' halls are 2 miles away, but the Union runs an evening shuttle service. Some 1st years in lodgings. Some 2nd and 3rd years stay in hall but most find accommodation in the private sector – which can be expensive (can range from £25–£50/week). It usually costs more than a grant to live in Bristol.

Much of the student-sprawl is brought together by the SU – the largest SU building in Britain, so 9,500 students trek their way there to meet up. The SU is one of the wealthiest in NUS so lots of money is spent on hundreds of societies and entertainments. Good societies include ballooning, sky-diving, political (many MPs come to speak), dance and debating. The swimming-pool, bars, restaurant and burger-bar might appeal.

Some big name bands play at the Union but many more play in the city. Like London, Bristol has developed a number of centres rather than just one. Clifton is 'studentland', Broadmead is a shopping centre, St Pauls has a great annual festival. Look out for the Tropic club and Lakota. West country real-ale and scrumpy are pub specialities.

The general sprawl and vastness of Bristol mean that typical students are hard to define. The 'traditional' student, 18–19 year old grammar school and independents. Usually had a year out in India or similar exotic climes. New society called Geordie Soc has arrived to assert the mellifluous guttural tones of the Northener onto the university map.

Very good reputation on courses with most students showing keen and active interest in achieving good results. There are a few stereotypes (Sloanes and southerners; conservative and bookish; preoccupied with sex and rock 'n' roll) . . . Be wary of stereotypes . . . the university is ultimately cosmopolitan.

Courses vary – some lots of assessed course work, some heavily dependent on exams. All will be moving towards a modularised framework.

Graduates: engineers, doctors, dentists, etc, plus journalists and media people, not forgetting the management consultants.

Pauper notes

Accommodation: Some squats in Montpelier/St Paul's. House/flat shares for average £35–£40 pw in Clifton/Cotham/Redland/Hotwells. Normally have to pay

52 weeks in the year. **Drink:** Epicurean (Union) bar. Hall bars are cheapest. Smiles bitter popular local brew, sold widely but especially at The Highbury Vaults. Cider in Coronation Tap. Kings Street/Clifton popular but expensive. **Eats:** Union restaurant and burger bar. Good take-aways. **Ents:** SU bands, comedians etc. Lots of local/student bands in pubs (eg Bristol Bridge, Kings Arms). **Sports:** University sports centre at Woodland House (too small though); pool attached to Union; 46 sports clubs. Sports grounds 1 mile from halls, 4 miles from SU. **Hardship funds:** Emergency £50 loan from Union. Access funds average £20–£200. **Travel:** University scholarship schemes. Easy access for hitching to London. **Work:** Very little work available.

More info?

Get students' Alternative Prospectus.
Enquiries to Jessica Bowles (President SU) (0272 735035).

Alumni (Editors' pick)

Sue Lawley (BBC newsreader), Susan Engels (actress, RSC), Frances Horovitz (poet), Hugh Cornwell (lead singer with The Stranglers), Paul Boateng MP, David Hunt MP (Secretary of State for Wales), Alistair Stewart (newsreader).

BRISTOL UWE

University of the West of England, Bristol, Coldharbour Lane, Frenchay, Bristol BS16 1QY (0272 656261) Map A, D8

Student enquiries: Admissions Officer

Main study areas – as in What to Study section: *(First degree):* Accountancy, aeronautical engineering, art & design, biochemistry, biology, biotechnology, business studies, chemistry, civil engineering, communication studies, computing, economics, education, electrical & electronic engineering, English, environmental science, environmental studies, European studies, geography, history, information technology, law, mechanical & production engineering, microbiology, modern languages, nursing studies, physics, politics and government, professions allied to medicine (PAMs), psychology, sociology, town and country planning. *Also:* Biomedical sciences, estate management, housing and construction, surveying, time-based media.

European Community: 12% first degree students take EC language as part of course and 4% spend 6 months or more in another EC country. EC language modules available on a range of degrees in accounting, business, computing, social science, engineering and law; in addition, all students have access to self-tuition facilities. University is moving towards a language-for-all policy. Formal exchange links with many EC universities/colleges, eg Bologna, Catania, Haarlem, Lyons, Nice (all business school links); Barcelona, Bordeaux, Mainz, Rennes (languages); Marseille, Bologna, Rotterdam (art, media and design); Algarve and Faro (science); Thessalonika, Athens, Heraklion, Paris IUT and La Rochelle ITU (computing): Ollerup (education); Tours (town and country planning). Approved Erasmus programme 1992/93.

Application: PCAS for 1993 start, UCAS thereafter; ADAR for art and design. **Founded:** As a university, 1992; previously Bristol Poly, ex Bristol Technical College, College of Commerce and West of England College of Art and Redland and St Mathias colleges of education. **Main awards:** BA, BEd, BSc, BEng, BTP. **Awarding body:** Bristol UWE. **Site:** 4 main campuses. **Access:** Buses from Bristol city centre to all sites. **Accommodation:** 800 places in halls/hostels (90% reserved for first years). Approx cost: £34 pw (single, self-catering) to £60 (single, full-board), £31 pw (university residence). Rent: 40% in accommodation where housing controlled by university. **Library:** 4 libraries, total of 370,000 books,

2,700 periodicals, 1,100 study places, electronic information retrieval facilities available. **Welfare:** Student health service, welfare and counselling services, study advice for overseas students and others, two nurseries (student discount). **Hardship funds:** Some funds available. **Careers:** Information, recruitment fairs, careers and 'milk round' programme. **Amenities:** Bookshops on 4 sites, chaplaincy centre, student union shops, bank, centre for performing arts. SU: supermarket, bars, TV and games room, advisory services. **Sporting facilities:** Excellent volleyball facilities, gymnasium, playing fields (soccer, rugby, cricket, hockey), squash and tennis courts, provision by SU for large variety of minor sports e.g. canoeing, windsurfing, water-skiing.

Duration of first degree course(s) or equivalent: 3 years; 4 years (BEd & sandwich) **Total first degree students 1991/92:** 7,676 **Total BEd students:** 1,630 **Number of overseas students:** 130 (+ 80 EC students) **Male/female ratio:** 1:1 **Teaching staff: full-time:** 890 **Total full-time students 1991/92:** 9,280; (incl 2,821 sandwich) **Postgraduate students:** 1,921 **Tuition fees for 1992/93 (first degrees):** Home: £1,855 (classroom), £2,770 (lab/studio), £759 (if no grant); Overseas: £5,319.

What it's like

Six sites across the city. Main site, Coldharbour Lane, to the far north of the M4 and M32. Typical early seventies architecture offers little sympathy to the surroundings. 6 miles from city centre, transport can be a problem; slowly being rectified by new half hourly bus service and a late night and lunchtime minibus service run by the Students' Union. 550 residences on campus. Limited car parking for those off bus routes.

Other sites. *St Mathias* (humanities and health studies) in residential area, Fishponds. Beautiful old site, friendly atmosphere, good SU bar and shop, halls of residence. *Bower Ashton* (art, media and design). Set in peaceful landscape in middle of Ashton Court. SU bar and shop. Increasing media courses, good evening courses. *Glenside* (nursing) part of Avon College of Health just down the road from St Mathias. *Redland* (teaching department) located in 'posh' residential area. Halls of residence, SU bar and shop.

Outstanding academic reputation, especially in humanities, social sciences, law, many sciences and the arts.

Attractive and active student city. Wide range of pubs, nightclubs (including SU's nightclub 'The Tube' in city centre), theatres and cinemas. Rapidly becoming recognised as a centre for the arts, attracting international exhibitions and artistes throughout the year. SU is particularly active, politically and commercially. Bars, shops and services currently turn over nearly £2 million; greatly expanded shop. The education, welfare and information unit is rapidly expanding; SU nursery and playschemes. With over 80 different clubs and societies and UWESU magazine, Bacus, there is a fair deal of involvement in SU, which also means that campaigns are well supported.

Pauper notes

Accommodation: Increasingly limited. Gloucester Road and Bedminster areas cheaper housing. Montpelier and St Paul's licensed squats. Housing Association, Bristol rents high. **Drink:** SU does a lot of promotions on all drinks. Local pubs good; vary in price. Smiles – local bitter. Local cider, of course. commonly known as rough. Places depend on person – Sloane/Rugby Club; the Victoria in Clifton/hippy; Old England Montpelier/trendy. Expansion of non-alcoholic drink choices. **Eats:** SU shops good range of food. Pizza, sandwiches and specials. Canteen food fairly priced (including vegetarian). Gloucester Road and Whiteladies Road have many good cheap(ish) restaurants. York Cafe, Special K's, Cafe de Daphne. Refectory prices (university run) quite high. SU shop sells pasties etc. Bar sells pizzas and baked potatoes. **Ents:** SU nightclub in city centre. SU discos on 3 sites every week, gigs every week. Film club. SU has good reputation for promoting up and coming bands on Friday night at Coldharbour Lane – cheapest run ents by SU

– £3 for most bands. **Sports:** Plans for sports hall for 1993. Many different clubs play in BPSA and SWSSA. Transport provided. Good local clubs. SU subsidises many sports. Kingsdown Sports Centre in town is cheap. **Hardship funds:** Hardship loan fund; DES support fund. Max: £100 controlled by SU and Student Services. Must show severe conditions. Students with children £25 per dependant on top. Bank very good. **Travel:** Number of scholarships. Hitching from Coldharbour Lane OK. SU Travel Shop – only place in Bristol with genuine student discounts. Drive share scheme. **Work:** The usual bar work, temping, some in SU security.

Buzz-words
Colditz (Coldharbour Lane site).

Alumni (Editors' pick)
Jack Russell (England wicket keeper), Wreckless Eric (Stiff Records artiste).

BRITISH INSTITUTE IN PARIS

**British Institute in Paris, University of London,
11 rue de Constantine, 75340 Paris Cedex 07 (45 55 71 99)**

Student enquiries: *In Paris:* Secretary to French Department
In England: The London Secretary, British Institute in Paris, Senate House, Malet Street, London WC1E 7HU (071 636 8000, ext 3920)

Main study areas – as in What to Study section: Modern languages. *Also:* Aspects of French civilisation; literature, art, society and culture courses, translation studies, business studies.

European Community: 100% first degree students take EC language as part of course and 45% spend 6 months or more in another EC country.

Structural features: Part of London University. **Application:** Direct, to Paris or London office. **Academic features:** Courses leading to Certificate, Diploma and MA in French and English translation; Certificate of Proficiency in French in contemporary French studies; and in French for business. 1 year course in French language and literature and in political science, history or plastic arts for joint honours undergraduates taught partly at the Institute and partly at the Institut d'Etudes Politiques or the Universities of Paris I and IV. Distance education offered in translation and proficiency in contemporary French. The Certificate in French and English translation and of proficiency in French can be prepared fully by correspondence. Short refresher courses organised for teachers of French at secondary level. **Special features:** Institute has dual purpose: its French department for English-speaking students (age 18+) to study French language, literature and history; its English department for French students to study English language and literature. Many British universities give financial support, though London University is responsible for Institute as a whole. French language courses are at 5 levels: Preliminary, Elementary (first year degree or third year remedial), Advanced Level 1, 2 and 3 (degree level, majoring in French at third year level). French is language of instruction; minimum period one term. Also 3 intensive courses at Easter for finalists. Institute is recognised centre for London and Cambridge examinations. Publishes an academic journal, Franco-British Studies. **Founded:** 1894, as private organisation, becoming Senate Institute of London University in 1969. **Access:** Situated in Central Paris. On bus routes 63, 83, 93, 94, 69, 28, 49 and on metro routes 'B', Saint-Denis – Genevilliers – Montparnasse, and Balard-Créteil. **Accommodation:** Institute is non-residential, but accommodation secretary has address register. Some places for university students at Cites

Universitaires in the Paris area; good rooms and paying-guest accommodation for early birds. **Library:** British Institute French Library, Cultural Centre English/ Translation Library (lending and reference). **Other learning resources:** Tape and video-tape library, computer-assisted learning, film resources. **Welfare:** Best to take out insurance before you go. 'Mutuelle' (ie supplementary health scheme) available for full-time students. **Hardship funds:** Working scholarships available (full fees in exchange for light duties 2 hours a day). Access funds available to top up accommodation and food expenses. **Amenities:** Student club and cafeteria.

Duration of course(s): 1–2 years (Certificate/Diploma courses only) **Total first degree level students 1991/92:** 230 **Overseas students:** 47 **Mature students:** 15 **Male/female ratio:** 1:4 **Teaching staff: full-time:** 5 **part-time:** 14 **Total full-time students 1991/92:** 82 (full year), 181 (part year) **Postgraduate students:** 8 **Tuition fees for full-time courses 1992/93:** Home: £1,400, (£900 if no grant); Overseas: £1,300.

What it's like

Refreshingly different. The best of Britain-squeezed into a magnificent building overlooking the Esplanade des Invalides. For the English student abroad it offers a friendly and homely environment. Vast range of courses provide a very interesting and thorough insight into French culture and life, from Stendhal to the latest in arts, from commercial and contemporary French, to high-powered translation diplomas. Very important for the English student is the asset that classes are always conducted in French. All teaching staff are warm, friendly and make you feel at home; teachers are inspired and effective. BI library is small, however at a reduced rate, members can join the British Council Library which is in the same building and which is larger, lighter and has all English newspapers and periodicals. One slight disappointment; the Institute houses an English department for French students but English tend to keep with English and French with French. Institute accommodates every student's need and taste. One Cambridge student who strongly recommends the BI reports: 'Paris on a shoe-string is easy and rents lower than students pay in London. But rent direct from landlords if possible.' If you make the most of what it has to offer, your year will be rewarding, in terms of certificates and diplomas and also in terms of the many aspects of French life you are introduced to.

Pauper notes

Accommodation: Lots of garrets and rooms with French families available; only for very early birds. Some small reasonable flats to share. Best to be found on very useful American Church noticeboards, Quai d'Orsay. But beware that landlords can be rogues and are often unwilling to return deposits ('caution', as it is known there). **Drink:** Chartier restaurant, rue Montmartre, Café de la Paix, rue Montmartre, for drinks. French wine so prevalent that the Institute's Club serves English beer as a nostalgia jerker. **Eats:** French university restaurants excellent dietetically, and fairly cheap (15 francs a meal). Also cheap M&S dishes! For self-caterers, food and drink is SO cheap. Try 'Ed, l'épicier' supermarket. **Ents:** Plenty of student reductions for plays in the small playhouses. Cheap bowling (!) in the Mouffetard. There are choral groups and orchestras, who welcome foreigners. **Sports:** You have to be prepared to pay capital city prices for gym clubs, swimming clubs etc, of which every arrondissement has its own. There are football clubs, rugby clubs, skiing clubs, hiking clubs, etc. To find out about these go to the local arrondissement's Mairie, where there are all addresses and telephone numbers. Forest Hill Tennis Clubs are cheapest for students, though perhaps not cheap. Those interested in playing rugby, contact commercial clubs like France-Soir/Figaro Club. There are good walking areas within 15 minutes of centre, and swimming is plentiful. **Hardship funds:** For students who attend ALL lessons at BI and who prove lack of funds, there are generous meal/rent allowances. **Work:** American Church noticeboards have plenty of ads – notably babysitting. Ask for 35F/hr in interview, and then ask for pay rise to 40F/hr if you consider the family needs/appreciates you. Also, Institute bar, library etc, for deserving paupers.

Alumni (Editors' pick)

Poets: Carmela Moya, Adrian Mathews; Dramatist: Michael Sadler.

BRITISH SCHOOL OF OSTEOPATHY

The British School of Osteopathy, 1–4 Suffolk Street, London
SW1Y 4HG (071 930 9254) Map E, C3

Student enquiries: The Registrar

Main study areas: *(First degree):* Osteopathy.

European Community: No students take EC language as part of course or spend time in another EC country. No formal exchange links.

Application: Direct. **Academic features:** Course is student-centred with a focus on problem solving in a clinical context. **Structural features:** The School has links with eg medical schools and universities for specialist areas of the teaching course and research activities. **Special features:** The undergraduate programme includes contribution by eminent osteopaths and medical practitioners (UK and abroad). **Founded:** 1917. **Main award:** BSc. **Awarding body:** Open University. **Site:** Single site in central London (just off Trafalgar Square). **Access:** Underground and mainline stations within easy reach; also on various bus routes. **Accommodation:** Mainly private rented (especially shared) or hostel accommodation. Approx cost: £50; £55–£70 with meals. **Library:** 7,000 volumes, 110 periodicals, 70 study places. **Specialist collections:** Collections of rare books on osteopathy. **Other learning facilities:** Well-equipped human performance laboratory and anatomy resource room. **Careers:** Literature; promotional video and slides available; informal enquiries welcomed (any registered osteopath could provide information). **Employment:** Normally private practice as osteopaths. Some study for a higher degree and/or contribute to teaching. **Welfare:** Full-time counsellors. SU elects Welfare Officer each year and there is an active interest in student welfare through a committee of staff and students. **Special categories:** Local facilities for students with families (list available from Counsellor) but none yet on site. **Hardship funds:** Registered educational charities (lists from public reference libraries). On completion of first year, students may be eligible for support from the Osteopathic Educational Foundation (OEF). **Amenities:** Host of cultural facilities in central London. SU active in organising social functions with similar institutions. Squash court and weights room on-site. Student sports' clubs make arrangements externally for playing facilities with other institutions, eg local medical schools.

Duration of first degree course(s) or equivalent: 4 years **Total first degree students:** 305 **Number of mature students:** 50 **Overseas students:** 10 **Male/female ratio:** 1:1 **Teaching staff: full-time:** 2 **Teaching staff: part-time:** 110 **Postgraduate students:** None **Tuition fees, 1992/93:** Home and overseas: £5,200 – discount scheme available for early payment.

What it's like

With its out-patient clinics, it's the largest alternative medicine training centre in Europe, based in a large corner building of traditional architecture just off Trafalgar Square, central London. Inside it's a maze of staircases and corridors leading to lecture theatres, treatment rooms, administrative offices and library containing largest collection of osteopathic medical literature. Access easy; close to Piccadilly Circus and Charing Cross tube stations; many buses stop in Trafalgar Square; Charing Cross BR station nearby; many other mainline London stations are short walk away. Strong railings around the building for locking bicycles to, but cycling in London has its special dangers. School and SU help find accommodation. BSO is a private college; it has now achieved mandatory grant status but grant still considerably less than fees! So get additional financial backing before starting (eg low interest rate loans, similar to those offered to medics and law students).

SU is active in providing welfare advice, and is affiliated to NUS. Run by a non-sabbatical executive with no permanent employees, it concentrates on welfare, social activity, sport and maintaining relations with the BSO staff, with little time for political issues.

Loving: all lavatories in the building contain Mates condom machines; all forms of contraception are covered as part of the course, so no student can remain in ignorance for long. Course involves a great deal of physical contact between students while learning and practising osteopathic technique. Combined with the more formal lectures in anatomy, this means that all BSO students become remarkably relaxed about stripping off to their underwear in front of each other. But this does not mean that training at the BSO is akin to a four-year orgy. What it does mean is that sex, sexuality and intimacy become demystified and pointless social mores become recognised for what they are – an essential part of training for a lifetime of treating semi-naked patients and a valuable part of students' personal development.

Counselling: part-time counsellor provides confidential support over any personal problems, not just on sexual relationships. Four years of a heavy course, often with financial problems too, can wear down even the most resilient of characters.

Central London's cheapest booze in BSO's bar, a club with membership restricted to staff and students (guests can be signed in). Events throughout the year, main ones Christmas and graduation balls. Central London's cheapest grub in basement canteen. Squash court and a weights room (and showers!) in building; any other sports or activities can be organised if enough people interested. Most popular sports are horse-riding and hang-gliding. Being based right in the middle of London, the BSO is in the centre of the country's largest entertainment complex! Everything is on offer somewhere. The National Gallery and St Martin's in the Fields, with its lunchtime concerts, are 30 seconds walk; the Coliseum about a minute away; Theatre Royal Haymarket just around the corner; countless cinemas nearby. Pubs, wine-bars, restaurants and nightclubs too numerous to be counted, but geared up for tourists/people with incomes, and pretty pricey.

Workload phenomenal. The course is much the same as at medical school except with one year less to do it in! However, there are some important differences: training takes an 'holistic' approach, ie health and illness are looked at in terms of the patient rather than the disease. Instead of treating the disease with drugs or surgery, the osteopath treats the patient in order to activate his/her own healing ability; there is slightly less emphasis on biochemistry and pharmacology than there is at medical school, since osteopathy is a drug-free system of medicine. Anatomy is of vital importance and students should know the entire body at a level of detail that doctors only approach when doing postgraduate surgical training. Large part of course is osteopathic technique; new techniques are always practised on fellow students before being used in school's clinic on actual patients. Clinical training takes place throughout course, including during so-called 'holidays'. It starts with observation in first year and gradually increases, under supervision, until fourth year students are taking patients all the way through from taking case history to providing the final treatment session. Most training in BSO premises but some physiology practicals at South Bank Poly and dissection classes at Guy's Hospital Medical School.

Most clinical staff part-time; as qualified osteopaths they have their own practices to run. Work assessed by combination of written exams, viva voces, essays and 'Objective Structured Practical Examinations' (or 'OSPEs'). Large-scale projects in second and third years; 'final' exams throughout fourth year. With such a heavy workload there is inevitably some attrition, mostly in the first year.

Four hundred students from a very wide age range can be divided into three groups: about a third to a half are 18- to 22-year-olds who have come straight from sixth form or who have changed from another degree course elsewhere; another third to a half are between 25–35, for many of them this is their second degree, after a non-medical first degree/occupation; and the remainder are in their late 30s, even into their 40s, having decided to do what they have always wanted to do before it gets too late! It is worth noting that because this is an independent college there is a very great discrepancy between what you get from a grant for fees (£660) and what is charged. You'll be left with a shortfall of over £5,000 to fund yourself!

Upon graduation, most start as an assistant in an existing practice, using any spare time for building up their own practice. Osteopathy still has no statutory legal status, so all practices are necessarily private. European standardisation in 1992 will before long probably enable osteopaths to offer their skills through NHS. All in all, BSO provides vocational training for a career of self-employment (ie freedom!) that provides a comfortable living from relieving suffering. What could be better!

Martin Preston

Pauper notes

Accommodation: College doesn't provide accommodation but it offers help in finding it, as does SU. **Drink:** SU has cheapest drinks in central London. Fullers, from west London brewery, is the main beer but bar is fully-stocked with a wide range of drinks. **Eats:** Large canteen in basement. Very good value. **Ents:** Lots of SU social events, plus whole of London! **Sports:** Squash court, gym, weight-training room, all on campus. Off campus access to any sport you can think of if enough people interested. **Hardship funds:** Two welfare officers in Union. Osteopathic Education Foundation can help some students from 2nd year. **Travel:** Close to Charing Cross & Piccadilly Circus tube stations. Lots of bus routes. Railings to lock cycles to (for suicidal!). **Work:** It's a heavyweight course and students do clinical work during the so-called 'holidays'. Good time-management and masses of energy should enable people to earn some money if needed.

More info?

Enquiries to any SU member (071 930 6093).

Informal name

BSO.

BRUNEL UNIVERSITY

Brunel University, Uxbridge, Middlesex UB8 3PH (0895 274000)
Map A, F8

Student enquiries: Academic Secretary

Main study areas – as in What to Study section: *(First degree):* Anthropology, biochemistry, biology or business studies, chemistry, communication studies, computing, economics, education, electrical and electronic engineering, environmental science, European studies, information technology, law, mathematical studies, mechanical and production engineering, metallurgy and materials science, microbiology, modern languages, physics, politics and government, psychology, public administration, sociology. *Also:* design & technology, or natural sciences, with education; industrial design, medical biochemistry.

European Community: 10% first degree students take EC language as part of course and 5% spend 6 months or more in another EC country. All students may take French or German as assessed part of their degree; many opt for extra-curricular courses leading to certificate in proficiency. Formal exchange links with Lille and Stuttgart. Approved Erasmus programme 1991; individual departmental links in Eindhoven, Hanover, Milan and Paris, Cork and Denmark.

GET HOLD OF THE PROSPECTUSES

Application: UCCA for 1993 start, UCAS thereafter. **Academic features 1992/93:** Most degree courses follow thin-sandwich pattern though many may *also* be taken in 3-year, full-time or 4-year thick-sandwich. Modular structure allows students to take subjects other than their own eg languages, management, computer science, as an assessed part of their course. Student exchanges with most EC countries under Erasmus and with USA. Engineering course with options in French or German; optional 1 year extensions to BEng courses for MEng or Diploma in engineering management. One-year foundation courses in engineering or science for applicants with non-science A-levels. New 3-year, broad-based courses in natural sciences and in engineering science and technology. **Structural features:** Management input from Brunel Centre for Business and Management Studies into some courses. **Research centres in:** research into innovation and the culture of technology; materials processing; bioengineering; youth work studies; design research; criminal justice research; consumer law. **Largest fields of study:** Engineering, mathematics, social sciences, law and management. **Founded:** 1966. **Main awards:** BSc, BA, BEng, LLB. **Awarding body:** Brunel University. **Site:** Main campus near Uxbridge, West London; second campus near Egham, Surrey. **Access:** Uxbridge underground, West Drayton and Egham main line stations, M4, M25 and M40. **Accommodation:** 925 study bedrooms, 645 places in self-catering flats, 430 study bedrooms on Runnymede campus. First years through *main* UCCA/UCAS scheme offered accommodation. Approx cost: £33 pw. Rent: 55% in accommodation where rent controlled by university. **Libraries:** 350,000 volumes, 1,800 periodicals, 2,500 items of AV and microfilm material. **Other learning facilities:** Computer centre, audiovisual centre, EFL/Language Centre, experimental techniques centre, Metrology Centre. **Welfare:** Medical centre, chaplaincy, counsellors, nursery, welfare unit. **Hardship funds:** SU operate welfare loans up to £100. **Careers:** Information and advice services (many Brunel graduates are offered posts by companies that provide their periods of industrial training). **Amenities:** Bookshop, supermarket, travel shop, newspapers, radio station, nursery, coffee and snack bars, university art gallery, art and music classes, student music bursaries. **Sporting facilities:** Sports centres, squash courts, climbing wall, playing fields, all-weather playing surface. Programmes of coaching, classes, etc. Centre of excellence for weightlifting, basketball. Rowing, sailing, canoeing. Dry ski slope in Uxbridge. Students' sports bursaries.

Duration of first degree course(s) or equivalent: 3 or 4 years **Total first degree students 1991/92:** 3,235; **Overseas students:** 163 **Mature students:** 387 **Male/female ratio:** 2:1 **Teaching staff:** full-time: 260 part-time: 24 **Total full-time students 1991/92:** 3,889 **Postgraduate students:** 1,641; 952 p/t **Tuition fees for 1992/93 (first degrees):** Home: £1,855 (classroom), £2,770 (lab), £755 (if no grant); Overseas: £5,320 (classroom), £7,055 (lab).

What it's like

It's a fast expanding institution in the outer reaches of West London, ideally situated on the Metropolitan and Piccadilly tube lines but far away from any tourists.

Brunel is the only university in the country which operates the thin-sandwich degree system in large-size proportions. Students spend four years at Brunel, three of which are divided into 6 months study and 6 months related work experience. The advantage is that Brunel students do very well in the employment stakes. Brunel is currently undergoing semesterisation and introducing some 3 year courses.

Brunel is on two sites: Uxbridge, built during the swinging 60's, i.e. dire concrete monoliths, and also at beautiful Runnymede near Egham – where the St Trinians films were made.

The SU is one of the best related to its size. It has four bars, two band/disco venues, a nursery, a welfare unit, catering outlets and a printshop which produces the student newspaper. The backbone of the Union is its 100 sporting and cultural societies. There's anonymity at the larger universities if that's what you want, but at Brunel there is a closer community atmosphere – even more so at the Runnymede campus.

Pauper notes

Accommodation: Cheapest areas on campus. Other areas – Hayes, Southall. **Drink:** SU bar presently stocks mainly Allied and Bass and a small amount of Courage and S&N. Good selection. **Eats:** Fast food – Gallery; bar food – (both on campus). **Ents:** Nightclub venue – The Academy. On campus include regular bands, 'Now Dance!', 'Saturday Nites Alright!'; alternative cabaret plus clubs and societies events. **Sports:** Sports centre on campus. Swimming pool – nearest Uxbridge. **Hardship funds:** Short term welfare loans from SU. **Travel:** Service on campus. **Work:** As all students are on sandwich courses, they should be in full-time employment during summer term and holidays.

More info?

Enquiries to Jim Pressley (0895 239125 x 141).

BUCKINGHAM UNIVERSITY

The University of Buckingham, Hunter Street, Buckingham MK18 1EG (0280 814080) Map A, E7

Student enquiries: Admissions Office

Main study areas – as in What to Study section: *(First degree):* Accountancy, biochemistry, biology, business studies, computing, dance, economics, English, European studies, fine arts, history, hotel & catering management, law, mathematical studies, modern languages, politics and government, psychology. *Also:* Heritage studies.

European Community: 11% first degree students take EC language as main part of course, 50% as supporting course. All students have to take, and be examined in, a 6-month foreign language course, unless they are already proficient in 2 languages. 4% spend 6 months or more in another EC country. Formal exchange links with 7 EC universities/colleges in France (Lille and Strasbourg), Germany (Augsburg, Holstein Tubingen and Wedel) and Spain (Salamanca). Some students can transfer onto MBA programme at Strasbourg or Tubingen after graduating, completing within year.

Application: UCCA for 1993 start, UCAS thereafter. **Academic features:** Degree courses in business economics, European business management with French or German, dance and related arts. **Special features:** Britain's only independent university receives no direct government financial support. 2-year degree courses, and a range of cross-disciplinary supporting courses. Academic year is 4 terms long and runs January–December. Law course entry also available in July. Applications welcomed from mature students. University has funds for scholarships and bursaries. **Structural features:** Validates degree course in dance at London College of Dance and 3 degrees for the Royal Agricultural College (agriculture and land management; equine business management; and international agribusiness management). **Largest fields of study:** Law, accounting and financial management, business studies. **Founded:** 1974. **Main awards:** BA, BSc, BSc(Econ), LLB. **Awarding body:** Buckingham University. **Site:** 2 sites near Buckingham town centre. **Access:** Buses from Aylesbury and Milton Keynes (both have main line railway stations). **Accommodation:** Accommodation guaranteed to all first year students, thereafter help given by accommodation officer. Approx cost: £50–60 pw. 60% students in accommodation where rent controlled by university. **Library:** 2 libraries; 65,000 volumes in total, 495 periodicals, computerised catalogue, 207 study places, short loan collection. **Other learning resources:** include audio-lingual language labs; satellite TV viewing room for live broadcasts in 6 European languages; video facilities; library of audio and video recorded materials in over 12 languages. Computer labs with IBM-compatible microcomputers, peripherals connected to Orion minicomputer. **Welfare:** University medical officer, student advisory system, student counsellor. **Hardship funds:** Student hardship fund in operation: scholarship, bursary system and loan system; bursaries adviser. **Careers:** Information and advice service, full-time careers adviser. **Amenities:** Student social centre; concert hall; on-campus accommodation; Oxford 23 miles away; Milton Keynes 12 miles away. **Sporting facilities:** Access to sports and recreational facilities.

Duration of first degree course(s) or equivalent: 2 years (8 terms) **Others:** 9 terms; 3 years **Total first degree students 1992:** 808 **Number of overseas students:** 467 **Number of mature students:** 437 **Male/female ratio:** approx 3:2 **Teaching staff: full-time:** 83 **part-time:** 24 **Total full-time students 1992:** 851 **Postgraduate students:** 54 **Tuition fees, first degrees, 1992:** Home and Overseas: £8,052.

What it's like

It's between the stately city of Oxford and the butt-of-all-jokes Milton Keynes, lies the former market town of Buckingham, still getting used to being a university town. UB (as it is known) has much to offer – a small, compact campus, a dazzlingly cosmopolitan student body, and a succinct two-year degree course (Jan–Dec academic year) which dispenses with the lazy, hazy days of summer and delivers you into your chosen career in the time it takes you to say 'graduate' (almost). Not too many distractions from study but with ingenuity (and wheels) it doesn't take too long to reach culture in Oxford or the cinema in the great MK. Although predominantly lawyers, the student body abandons all labels (and many other things) during the yearly Rag Week – all in aid of charity and local breweries. Mega-Graduation Ball (February) and Summer Ball provide excellent outlets for pent-up emotions of two years' hard labour.

Pauper notes

Accommodation: Private accommodation but not easy to find. **Drink:** University bar. **Eats:** Local ethnics. **Sports:** On campus – all-weather tennis courts, multi-gym, snooker room, fencing, martial arts. Off campus – swimming pools, squash and badminton courts.

Informal name

UB.

BUCKINGHAMSHIRE COLLEGE

The Buckinghamshire College
(1) Queen Alexandra Road, High Wycombe, Bucks HP11 2JZ (0494 522141)
(2) Newland Park, Chalfont St Giles, Bucks HP8 4AD (0494 874441)
(3) Missenden Abbey Management Centre, Great Missenden, Bucks HP16 0BD (Map A, E8)

Student enquiries: Admissions Registrar (address 1)

Main study areas – as in What to Study section: *(First degree):* Art & design, business studies, computing, European studies, environmental studies, information technology, nursing, social policy and social welfare, sociology. *Also:* Building processes, furniture production, forest products technology, leisure studies.

CAN'T FIND WHAT YOU'RE LOOKING FOR? USE THE INDEX!

European Community: 60% first degree students take EC language as part of course and 50% spend 6 months or more in another EC country. Formal exchange links with some 12 EC universities/colleges: Denmark (2); France (3); Germany (2); Italy (1); Netherlands (1); Spain (3); many open to non-language specialists.

Application: PCAS for 1993 start, UCAS thereafter. **Structural features:** a college of Brunel University. **Academic features:** Degree in European business studies includes a year in France/Germany/Italy/Spain; International business administration includes year in the USA; business administration/studies; international office management; business environmental management; forest products technology and 3-dimensional design, and furniture design and production industry. **Largest fields of study:** Art and design, business studies, furniture and timber. **Founded:** 1975, ex High Wycombe College of Technology and Art and Newland Park College of Education. **Main awards:** BA, BSc. **Awarding body:** Brunel University. **Site:** 3 sites: near High Wycombe town centre; Newland Park, 12 miles from High Wycombe, near Chalfont St Giles; Missenden Abbey, near Great Missenden. **Access:** All sites served by excellent roads and railways; about 40 mins from London. **Accommodation:** 560 places in halls. Approx cost: £36 pw residence only, meals at cost. Rent: 50% in accommodation where rent controlled by college. **Library:** 3 libraries, over 100,000 volumes, multi-media services, 700 periodicals, 350 study places. **Welfare:** Doctor, dentist, FPA, psychiatrist, solicitor, chaplain. **Careers:** Information, workshops, vocational counselling and placement service. **Amenities:** SU bar, theatre. **Sporting facilities:** Sports centre, gymnasium, and playing fields at Newland Park.

Duration of first degree course(s) or equivalent: 3 years full-time, 4 years (sandwich) **Total first degree students 1991/92** 2,227 **Overseas students:** 17 **Male/female ratio:** 3:2 **Total full-time students 1991/92:** 3,400 **Postgraduate students:** 592 **Tuition fees for 1992/93 (first degrees):** Home: £1,855 (classroom), £2,770 (lab/studio); Overseas: £5,500.

What it's like

It's on 2 sites connected by union: Newland Park and High Wycombe.

Newland Park fairly isolated near Chalfont St Giles village. Life mostly campus-based in pleasant rural setting. Buildings mainly 1960s, grouped around Georgian mansion. Many on campus, some in comfortable modern accommodation, some in prefabs. Students mostly at degree/diploma level – courses include: business, management and social studies. Newland Park has college bar, student centre, sports and drama: it's the most attractive campus but far from any other major signs of life.

High Wycombe site is mostly 1950s buildings with recent extensions in town centre. Fairly attractive town with some social life – pubs, sports centre, college bar, film club, and furniture industry providing jobs for students finishing art/design and furniture courses. HND/degree students aged 19–23 (plus mature students) come from around the country – rooms in halls for 96 first years. Halls of residence are comfortable, generally not over-exciting. College and town fairly pleasant and bearable; strong SU; growing and expanding clubs and societies; many student services eg help for overseas students, accommodation advice.

Pauper notes

Accommodation: Off-campus expensive, some reasonable, others dire. College accommodation reasonable – no married quarters. **Drink:** College bar cheap – main brewery names, pubs are not cheap. **Eats:** College refectory. High Wycombe site greater choice, as in town. Newland Park more difficult to go off campus unless you have transport. Off campus food – good variety. **Ents:** Student Bar is where most ents go on – bands, quizzes, discos etc. Off campus not an exciting place – pubs have bands on. **Sports:** High Wycombe site – good sports centre (quite expensive) next to halls. Normal sports offered at college. Newland Park has reasonable facilities. **Hardship funds:** SU has emergency loan fund. **Travel:**

Shuttle bus between sites. **Work:** Temporary work through agencies; some part-time work available during term-time.

Alumni (Editors' pick)

Howard Jones, Martin Grierson.

BUCKLAND

**Buckland University College, Ewert Place, Oxford OX2 7YT
(0865 53570) Telex: 449793 TELSER G; Fax: 0865 52961**
Map A, E7

Student enquiries: Academic Registrar
Main study areas – as in What to Study section: *(First degree):* Law.

European Community: No first degree students take EC language or spend time in another EC country.

Application: Direct. **Largest field of study:** Law. **Founded:** 1963. **Main awards:** LLB. **Awarding body:** London University. **Site:** Oxford, a mile north of city centre. **Access:** Fast London-Oxford coach and rail links; local buses. **Accommodation:** college assists with finding accommodation locally and has links with halls of residence in Oxford. Rent: no accommodation where rent is controlled by university. **Library:** 30 study places; open 9-6; special short-term loan scheme. **Welfare:** College welfare officer. **Careers:** Information, advice and placement service provided by London University. **Amenities:** Common rooms; leisure centres and sports facilities nearby, cultural and social amenities of Oxford. **Employment:** Law, commerce, teaching.

Duration of first degree course(s) or equivalent: 3 years **Total first degree students 1991/92:** 82 **Number of overseas students:** 33 **Number of mature students:** 18 **Male/female ratio:** 1:1 **Teaching staff: full-time:** 2 **part-time:** 16 **Total full-time students 1991/92:** 100 **Number of postgraduate students:** 15 **Tuition fees, first degrees, 1992/93:** £3,100 (Home students on LEA grant, fee reduced by £95); Overseas: £3,100.

What it's like

Small, independent specialist law school providing courses for London University degrees and the Bar Final examination. Classes are small: lectures of 30 students, seminars in groups of circa 8 or 9. Visiting lecturers from other universities or colleges, but small scale means staff take a personal interest in students' progress. Lot of stress on full attendance and submission of written work. Reference and lending law library in college and access to other libraries in Oxford.

Located in a pleasant, modern building round a small, quiet quadrangle in the Summertown district of Oxford, its facilities for socialising are modest, but there are pubs, restaurants and shops just a few yards away. Programme of social events and sports fixtures with other colleges. Good mix of overseas students and mature students as well as 'home' students straight from school.

Pauper notes

Accommodation: College links with inexpensive hostels, especially for overseas students. **Work:** Some still find vacation work in Oxford.

Informal name

BUC.

CAMBERWELL COLLEGE OF ARTS

**Camberwell College of Arts, Peckham Road, London SE5 8UF
(071 703 0987)** Map D, C2

Student enquiries: College Administrator
Main study areas – as in What to Study section: *(First degree):* Art & design, fine arts. *Also:* Conservation (paper artefacts/library materials).

CAN'T FIND WHAT YOU'RE LOOKING FOR? USE THE INDEX!

European Community: Number of students taking EC language and spending time in another EC country, not known.

Application: ADAR; PCAS for the history of drawing & printmaking for 1993 start, UCAS thereafter. **Structural features:** Constituent college of the London Institute. **Largest fields of study:** Fine art painting/sculpture, graphic design, 3-dimensional design, history of drawing and printmaking, conservation. **Founded:** 1898. **Main awards:** BA. **Awarding body:** Open University. **Site:** Main building and 2 annexes. **Access:** Waterloo, Peckham Rye, Elephant & Castle stations, then bus; bus from Oval, Vauxhall, or Victoria station. **Accommodation:** Limited places in the London Institute's halls of residence. Approx cost: £45–£65 pw. Rent: proportion of students housed in accommodation where rent is controlled by college, not known. **Library:** 40,000 volumes, 85 periodicals, 40 study places. **Other learning resources:** Word processing, video viewing, photographic and computer facilities, media resources unit. **Welfare:** Easy access to all facilities, consult professional student counsellor. **Careers:** Information and advice service. **Amenities:** college shop. **Employment:** Graphics, ceramics, silversmithing, metalwork and paper conservation; students are successful in finding employment in craft or design studies related to their training.

Duration of first degree course(s) or equivalent: 3 years **Total first degree students 1991/92:** 565 **Overseas students:** 28 **Mature students:** 45 **Male/female ratio:** 2:3 **Teaching staff: full-time:** 36 **part-time:** 120 **Total full-time students 1991/92:** 908 **Postgraduate students:** 68 **Tuition fees for 1992/93 (first degrees):** Home: £2,770; Overseas: £5,950.

What it's like

Built on 3 sites. The main one on Peckham Road is an ugly sixties monstrosity tacked on, rather uncomfortably, to a beautiful, Victorian purpose-built art school. The other two sites are a prefab sculpture annexe and an old grammar school. The diversity of the architecture is outdone only by the diversity of the students. Courses range from art history to paper conservation.

SU provides opportunities for meeting in a crowded, smoky atmosphere to

" Main building looks like abandoned transistor radio "

BIG TURN OFF

GET HOLD OF THE PROSPECTUSES

exchange drunken conversations over loud music in friendly and inexpensive bar. Regular termly bashes with bands, cabarets etc. SU flourishing after a few bad years; the number of clubs is growing by the minute.

Accommodation in London is expensive and difficult to find but it is probably easier to find somewhere to live near Camberwell than other London art schools. Being in the capital means almost every type of entertainment is available (at a price).

All the courses require hard work, application and self-motivation. Support facilities, such as the library and media resources departments are stretched. There's not much space; studios are very cramped. Most of the staff are highly respected practitioners in their field.

Pauper notes

Accommodation: Some flats available through college; local council; squats in SE London: rented accommodation expensive but available. **Drink:** Popular SU bar cheap. Popular pubs: Grove, Phoenix and Firkin. **Eats:** College canteen. **Ents:** SU provides entertainment and Camberwell is very close to the centre of London. **Sports:** New sports centre 5 mins away in Peckham. 2 mins swimming pool. SU cricket and football teams. **Hardship funds:** See student welfare officer. **Travel:** Some college trips abroad: possibility of exchange trips to America. **Work:** Jobs in SU bar. Part-time work not difficult to find in London if you don't mind what you do.

CAMBORNE SCHOOL OF MINES

Camborne School of Mines, Trevensen, Pool, Redruth, Cornwall TR15 3SE (0209 714866) Map A, B9

Student enquiries: The Academic Registry

Main study areas: *(First degree):* Mining engineering, minerals engineering and industrial geology.

European Community: 30% first degree students take EC language as part of course. French for Engineers is integral part of industrial geology degree; includes French tuition in second and third years and 5-week residential course in Alès, France. German, Portuguese and Spanish to be offered in future. Formal exchange links with EC universities/colleges being developed; current feasibility study for mining engineering at school of mines in France.

Application: UCCA for 1993 start, UCAS thereafter. **Structural features:** Part of Exeter University from 1992. **Special features:** Experimental mine. Occasional lectures from visiting industrial consultants. **Largest fields of study:** Mining engineering; minerals engineering, industrial geology. **Founded:** 1859. **Main awards:** BEng. **Awarding body:** Exeter University. **Site:** Outskirts of Camborne, Cornwall. **Accommodation:** 50 single study bedrooms (priority to 1st year students); wide variety of furnished accommodation including 4 flats for married students (unsuitable for children). Approx cost: £26–£42 pw. 24% students in accommodation where rent controlled by college. **Library:** 8,000 volumes, 168 periodicals, 40 study places, course books kept in closed access. **Specialist collections:** Rare early mining publications. **Welfare:** Personal tutor system. **Hardship funds:** Student hardship fund. **Careers:** Exeter University careers service with on-site office at Camborne. **Amenities:** Carn Brea leisure centre and purpose built student club with squash court, bar, TV and billiards room. **Employment:** Mining and mineral, UK and worldwide. Tunnelling, quarrying, exploration (mineral).

Duration of first degree course(s) or equivalent: 3 years **Total first degree students 1991/92:** 133 **Overseas students:** 20 **Mature students:** 35 **Male/female ratio:** 14:1 **Teaching staff: full-time:** 26 **part-time:** 8 **Total full-time students 1991/92:** 350 **Postgraduate students:** 45 **Tuition fees for 1992/93 (first degrees):** Home: £2,770; Overseas: £6,890.

CAN'T FIND WHAT YOU'RE LOOKING FOR? USE THE INDEX!

What it's like

There cannot be too many places of higher education where the President of the SU is on first name terms with all students and academic staff. I, at the Camborne School of Mines, am. Briefly put, the CSM is more of a community of students than a gathering or crowd of students. Please do not misunderstand me. There are enough students at CSM to offer a wide range of activities and societies. Being mining, minerals, mineral surveying or geological engineers, most students are generally involved with outdoor activities. Therefore sports have a large influence with what CSM students do in their spare time. CSM provides teams for all major sports along with other minority sports such as surfing (CSM is only 4 miles from best surf beach in Europe), rock-climbing (the School has its own climbing wall), scuba-diving, gliding etc.

The School is situated in UK's main tourism area. It is thus able to offer students the chance to study in an area of outstanding natural beauty that also has a thriving night-life. The School is less than 3 miles away from both the grandeur of the Cornish coastline and entertainment at the best nightclub in south-west.

Students run own social club which contains a bar, squash courts and other less physical pursuits, as well as acting as headquarters for many a night out.

Impending merger with Exeter University: CSM seeks to retain traditional warm family atmosphere but hopes to gain from a larger SU providing a wider and more varied range of activities to suit the needs of any student coming to CSM.

Danny Callow

Pauper notes

Accommodation: Cheap modern hostel and married quarters provided by the college. Numerous low-priced holiday houses during autumn, winter and spring. Building in progress; rapidly expanding to accommodate increased intake. **Drink:** Cheap comprehensive bar in students' club with choice of ales to rival any larger institution. Numerous friendly pubs within easy staggering distance. Drink well below national average price – St Austell brewery. **Eats:** Cheap on-campus food at catering department of Cornwall Technical College, including vegetarian. Vegetarians well catered for in Cornwall. **Ents:** Recently modernised, well equipped students' social club. Regular very successful SU functions. Several good local discos. **Sports:** College rugby, soccer, hockey, squash, cricket, badminton, weight training. All major sports catered for, as well as more unusual such as scuba diving, all watersports, surfing, caving, climbing. Large sports centre near campus – free use to students once weekly. Strong Outward Bound. **Hardship funds:** Co-operative local bank managers. College hardship fund for those in dire straits. **Travel:** Regular international exchange schemes with other mining institutions worldwide. Nearby main-line station and direct intercity coach service. **Work:** Industrial vacation work in relevant subjects, often overseas during second year summer vacation. Local mining operations. Excellent vacation opportunities – mostly Australia/Africa, often leading to full-time employment.

More info?

Enquiries to Danny Callow, SU President (0209 714866).

Informal name

CSM.

Buzz-words

Emmet (person from east of Tamar river).

CAMBRIDGE UNIVERSITY

University of Cambridge, Cambridge, England CB2 1TN
(Registry 0223 332200) Map A, F7

Student enquiries: The Tutor for Admissions, ... College, Cambridge

Main study areas – as in What to Study section: *(First degree):* Aeronautical engineering, anatomy, anthropology, archaeology, architecture, Asian studies, biochemistry, biology, botany, chemical engineering, chemistry, civil engineering, classics, computing, economics, education, electrical & electronic engineering, English, environmental science, fine arts, geography, geology, history, industrial relations, Latin American studies, law, linguistics, mathematical studies, mechanical and production engineering, medicine, metallurgy and materials science, microbiology, modern languages, music, Near East & Islamic studies, pharmacology, philosophy, physics, physiology, politics and government, psychology, religious studies and theology, sociology, veterinary studies, zoology. *Also:* Astrophysics, history of medicine, history and philosophy of science, land economy, pathology, Serbo-Croat, Slavonic studies, Turkish.

European Community: 7% first degree students take EC language as part of their course and spend 6 months or more in another EC country. No formal exchange links with EC universities/colleges at university level. Approved Erasmus programme 1992.

All students have access to the private study facilities and language learning materials of the Language Centre – which are popular; students may also take courses in most EC languages (in addition to their degree work, subject to approval from the faculty and the college) leading to a diploma (for students with A-level) or certificate (beginners or those with GCSE; not available in French). In addition to specialist language degrees, languages are involved in the English and historical triposes and there are language courses for scientists and engineers.

The University and Colleges: Each college is a self-governing community which elects its own fellows, admits its own undergraduates and provides academic, sporting and social facilities. Colleges are not confined to particular subjects although some acquire a reputation in a particular subject. Most admit undergraduates to read all the subjects at Cambridge. For most undergraduates the college is the focal point of their life at Cambridge.

THE COLLEGES

There are 28 undergraduate colleges:

Men and Women:

Christ's	Peterhouse
Churchill	Queens'
Clare	Robinson
Corpus Christi	St Catharine's
Downing	St Edmund's (mature only)
Emmanuel	St John's
Fitzwilliam	Selwyn
Girton	Sidney Sussex
Gonville & Caius	Trinity
Homerton (separate profile which	Trinity Hall
you can find under 'H')	Wolfson (mature only)
Jesus	
King's	*Women only:*
Magdalene	Lucy Cavendish (mature only)
Pembroke	New Hall
	Newnham

CAN'T FIND WHAT YOU'RE LOOKING FOR? USE THE INDEX!

HOW TO APPLY TO CAMBRIDGE UNIVERSITY

Entry is on the basis of results of A-level papers already taken or to be taken, sometimes in conjunction with S-papers or Sixth Term Examination Papers (STEP). It is possible to apply either to a college of first preference or by submitting an Open Application not naming any colleges of preference. For details refer to the *Cambridge Admissions Prospectus* which you should consult as early as possible. In either case a preliminary application form should be submitted as early as possible, and by 15 October at the latest. The form may be obtained either from your school or from the Admissions Tutor of any Cambridge college, or from the Cambridge Intercollegiate Applications Office. You have also to submit a completed UCCA form (for 1993 start, UCAS form thereafter) in which you should name Cambridge as one of your university choices: **THIS MUST REACH UCCA/UCAS BY 15 OCTOBER.** You may not apply to Oxford as well as Cambridge in the same year unless you are a candidate for an organ award.

All schools on the UCCA/UCAS mailing list are invited annually to order copies of the *Cambridge Admissions Prospectus*. To obtain a copy for yourself, write to Cambridge Intercollegiate Applications Office, Tennis Court Road, Cambridge CB2 1QJ (0223 333308). Students' Alternative Prospectus available from Cambridge University Students' Union, 11/12 Trumpington Street, Cambridge CB2 1QA, price including p&p £3.50 to UK (£4.50 to Europe; £6.00 overseas). Cheques made payable to Cambridge University Students' Union.

Duration of first degree course or equivalent: 3 or 4 years. **Total first degree students:** 10,447 **Total number of BEd students:** 266 **Overseas students:** 595 plus 272 EC **Mature students:** 328 **Male/female ratio:** 3:2 **Teaching staff:** 2,800 **Postgraduates:** 3,473 **Total full-time students:** 13,920 **Tuition fees 1992/93:** Home: £1,855 (classroom), £2,770 (lab), £4,985 (clinical); Overseas: £5,247 (classroom), £6,882 (lab), £12,732 (clinical). College fees of £2,500–£3,000 are paid *in addition* to tuition fees.

What it's like

It is its collegiate structure that makes Cambridge 'different'. Colleges largely self-contained (eg sports clubs and facilities and a larger amount of teaching). Don't spend too much time worrying about which college to apply to. The main points to consider are whether a college is mixed or single sex; its size; its location; its wealth; whether it is old or new. Teaching in science subjects is mainly through lectures (6 mornings a week), supervisions and practicals. In arts, lectures are often ignored (very few are well integrated into the course) but students on average write 2 essays per week for supervisions. Seminars are virtually non-existent, supervisions in small groups. Work-load is usually very heavy. Courses are assessed by exams. Changing courses is not too difficult. Drop-out and failure rates are low. Social life can often become too intense. There is a distinct pressure on students to cram a wide variety of activities into a very short space of time. University and college societies cater for every possible interest from drama to tiddlywinks. Cambridge lacks a central focus for social activities – there is no central SU building and no central venue for gigs, discos or for meeting. College life therefore like extended family, basically very friendly but can be claustrophobic.

Nicole Smith writes, 'Some general points about Cambridge: Central town entirely geared towards students (and tourists) – allegedly more pubs per head of population than any other town in England. Also market town – good fruit 'n' veg plus second-hand clothes stalls. The Corn Exchange attracts motley variety of bands. 'The Junction' attracts more indie bands and 'alternative' theatre/dance groups.'

GET HOLD OF THE PROSPECTUSES

Pauper notes

Accommodation: Most students live in college or in hostels. Students wanting to live out tend to congregate in the Chesterton Rd or 'trendy' Mill Road areas. **Drink:** College bars tend to be popular and cheaper. Cambridge is reputed to have more pubs per square mile than other towns. Popular pubs include the Maypole, the Salisbury Arms, King Street pubs, The Mill and a couple of lesbian/gay pubs. **Eats:** College food varies from OK to stodgy to good. Most do vegetarian. Nettles good veggie food. Good late night kebabs Gardenia and Omars and pizzas (ditto most shops in Mill Rd). Town is crammed full of Pizza Huts etc. Most deliver as do curry houses. **Ents:** College Bobs, occasional college ents. Local bands at pubs. No university venue for larger bands or nationally known big names but Corn Exchange in town sees most tours, and the Junction. Arts cinemas very good (not always cheap). **Sports:** Most colleges have own sports facilities – eg there are 20 boathouses in Cambridge and as many rugby pitches. **Hardship funds:** Access funds are being used to help students in hardship. Colleges are able to give assistance in exceptional cases. **Travel:** Most colleges have funds – ask tutor. **Work:** Term-time work not permitted by university regulations unless tutorial permission given. Some vacation work in and around Cambridge for determined/resourceful, eg fruit-packing, teaching in language schools and tutorial colleges, punting tourists in summer, college kitchens (boosts your street credibility to mingle with workers). Post Office at Christmas. Tory Reform Group personal assistant scheme can offer stimulation (at Westminster) rather than money.

More info?

Get students' Alternative Prospectus.
Enquiries to CUSU (0223 356454).

Alumni (Editors' pick)

Milton, Darwin, Marlowe, Steve Coleridge, Brooke, Forster, Keynes, Pepys, Plath, Hughes, Erasmus, Wilberforce, Wordsworth, Palmerston, Cromwell, Bacon, Marvell, Dryden, Newton, Macaulay, Byron, Thackeray, Tennyson, Cleese, Frost, Burgess, McLean, Philby, Blunt, Drabble, Pitt the Younger, Trevelyan, Trollope, A A Milne, HM King Edward VII, Lord Owen, Rajiv Gandhi, Lord Mountbatten of Burma, Bertrand Russell, E M Forster, Ian McKellan, Sir Arthur Bliss, Griff Rhys Jones, Graham Greene, Stephen Fry, Emma Thompson, Germaine Greer.

CHRIST'S

Christ's College, Cambridge CB2 3BU
(0223 334953; Fax 0223 334967)

Founded: 1439; women undergraduates first admitted 1978. **Accommodation:** All students can be accommodated in college or college-owned property. Most undergraduates charged £760 pa (range £514–£960), inclusive of heat, light, cleaning etc. **Eating arrangements:** Choice of formal or informal meals. Fixed charge of £66 per term for meals, plus breakfast (£1.10), lunch (£1.48), dinner (£2.05). **Gate/guest hours:** None. **Admission:** Pre A-level, by matriculation or conditional offers; some places offered on A-level results, school reports and interview. **Scholarships:** Unlimited number of scholarships (£100) mainly awarded on results of university examinations (approx 95 awarded for 1992/93). **Travel grants:** Approx 100 available each year (from £50 to £1,000). **Library:** Modern (1976) college working library; old library with antiquarian collection; separate law library. **Other college facilities:** Theatre, concert hall, auditorium, playing fields, boathouse, squash courts, and modern public rooms. Medieval Dining Hall. Chapel.

European Community: 30 students learn an EC language or spend time in another EC country.

CAN'T FIND WHAT YOU'RE LOOKING FOR? USE THE INDEX!

College fees for 1992/93 (undergraduate) £2,542.

Undergraduates: *Men:* 235 *Women:* 134

Postgraduates: *Men:* 55 *Women:* 33

What it's like

A medium-sized college, enjoying an excellent location in the centre of town, with shops, market, pubs and cinema all close at hand. The college combines old and new: the 16th-century First Court and the Fellows' Garden are very picturesque, whilst New Court, built in the 70s and known as 'The Typewriter', is less universal in its appeal.

There are 390 undergraduates with a broad mix of subjects and social backgrounds. About 35% are women – room for improvement but reflects the university average. Above all, Christ's is a friendly and tolerant student community.

Practically all first and third years live in college; most second years live in college-owned hostels. Size and quality of rooms vary considerably; best facilities usually come with more modern rooms, although these often lack space and character. Cooking facilities are limited. 40 new student rooms with excellent facilities should be ready for '93 and improve the aesthetics at the back of college.

Food in college is subsidised by a fixed charge levied on all students. The Upper Hall (canteen) is cheap-ish and convenient but food tends to be stodgy and repetitive. Or you can dine in Formal Hall which is enjoyable and filling. There are two bars: the Buttery has a good, cosy atmosphere and provides a social mecca for college but restricted hours (6–8.30 pm), whilst the Wine Bar is lively if you can stand the appalling interior design.

Just about every sport or interest is catered for at university level, and Christ's has many of its own clubs and societies. Standards aren't always exceptional but the motivation is there. Rugby and soccer are played at a level to compete with the very best 'sporty' colleges, while rowing is less successful but popular. Drama is strong with a very active college group and the film society shows a good selection of alternatiave and mainstream films. Christ's has its own squash courts, library and theatre.

Pauper notes

Accommodation: College provides accommodation for everyone at reasonable prices, far cheaper than can be found in the town though likely to rise steeply over the next few years. **Drink:** Cheap in college bars (£1.10 per pint) but otherwise usual south of England prices. Many good pubs, especially off the beaten track. **Eats:** Cheap food in college. Variety of cafes and restaurants, prices correspondingly more. 'Nettles' and 'King's Pantry' for vegetarians. Pub lunches good. **Ents:** SU Friday night mini-ents and twice termly ents. College amateur dramatics strong. College film society costs £1.00. A few pubs have live music evenings. ADC Theatre for student productions. 'Cinderella's' student night is popular, being cheap, tacky and opposite college. 'The Corn Exchange' is more expensive but has a few biggish names a term, as does 'The Junction' a bit further out. **Sports:** Free squash courts in college. Excellently equipped college sports ground 10 minutes cycle up a small hill and boathouse accessible to students throughout the year. **Hardship funds:** Hardship funds though small are readily available if you go and see your tutor. New funds are being made available to those on grants, in addition to hardship funds. Having an overdraft is probably an unfortunate necessity. **Travel:** Travel grants, varying from £50 to several hundred pounds easy to obtain. **Work:** During term time frowned upon.

Cambridge speak

Buttery (college bar); bedders (women who make beds every day).

Alumni (Editors' pick)

General Smuts, John Milton, Charles Darwin, Mountbatten, C P Snow, David Mellor.

GET HOLD OF THE PROSPECTUSES

CHURCHILL
Churchill College, Cambridge CB3 0DS (0223 336202)

Founded: 1960; women undergraduates first admitted 1972. **Academic features:** Word-processing and computing courses. Churchill Archives Centre: 20th-century British history. **Accommodation available:** Modern bedsitting rooms or sets. Undergraduates in college all 3 years; most charged £260 per 10 week term (range £160–£360). **Eating arrangements:** Self-service breakfast, lunch and dinner; formal dinner. Vegetarian available. **Gate/guest hours:** None. **Admission:** Conditional offers: usually AAA (no S-level or Step) for sciences; usually AAB (no S papers) for arts. Virtually all candidates interviewed. Undergraduates not admitted for education, land economy, theology. **Travel grants:** Small long vacation travel fund. **Hardship funds:** Some available. **Library:** 2 undergraduate libraries open 24 hours a day. Books in greatest demand lent during limited period only. **Other college facilities:** Buttery, bar, theatre; extensive playing fields and tennis and squash courts within college grounds; multi-gym; boathouse (rowing); 8 BBC computers, 7 PC workstations and 14 AppleMacs for student use; music recital and practice rooms. Late night taxi service to provide safe travel back to college at college expense.

European Community: 4% students learn an EC language as part of their course and spend 6 months or more in EC country. Formal exchange links for engineering, computing and natural science students with Ecole Centrale, Paris.

College fees for 1992/93 (undergraduate) £2,529.

Undergraduates: *Men:* 296 *Women:* 96

Postgraduates: *Men:* 151 *Women:* 65

Teaching staff: *Men:* 86 fellows, 20 research fellows, 48 lecturers, 1 lector *Women:* 10 fellows, 2 research fellows, 5 lecturers

What it's like
Founded in 1962 as the national memorial to Churchill, it quickly adopted a liberal approach; among the first to admit women. Very few restrictions, a relaxed friendly and unpretentious atmosphere. Strong science bias but arts still alive and kicking. High proportion of state school students; less cliquey and much more friendly than many other Cambridge colleges.

An example of fine modern architecture, with open quads and a new modern conference centre. Inside, the rooms are light, airy, with all mod-cons; no visiting restrictions enforced. Dining hall serves a wide range of food (including salads and sandwiches), sometimes a little stodgy. Also a kitchen with phone (!) for every dozen students.

Large playing fields, tennis and squash courts and a multi-gym. Opportunities are numerous and include a thriving boat club, 4 football (1 women's), 2 hockey (one of each), 3 cricket (1 women's), 3 rugby (1 women's) and 1 American football team.

Large, well-equipped, air-conditioned lecture theatre-cum-cinema, which shows 3–5 films each week. Also a frequently packed bar and weekly discos.

Excellent library open 24 hours a day and caters well for most subjects; librarian very willing to fill any gaps. Excellent computer facilities – 3 computer rooms. College has its own professional counsellors.

Although over a mile from the town centre, not as isolated as many would have you believe. The guaranteed accommodation and the fact that everything is on site makes up for the distance from town. Almost everyone enjoys their 3 years here.

Pauper notes
Accommodation: Churchill houses all undergraduates; Wolfson Flats, and college-owned houses, for married students. **Drink:** College bar big and popular. The Cow and Calf college local. **Eats:** College food much complained about but

not that bad. Chips ad infinitum (well almost). Lots of cheap curry houses and kebab emporia in town. **Ents:** Excellent bar lively (and very friendly) most nights with an excellent free weekly disco (the 'Pav'). 3–5 films a week. The annual Spring Ball (in February!?) is renowned as the best value in Cambridge. Numerous cocktail parties in college. Lots of ents at all the other colleges, so you'll never be short of something to do! **Sports:** Good multigym in college, so you don't have to cycle to the other side of town to Kelsey Kerridge gym. New artificial nets. Good well kept college pitches. Tennis, squash courts, boat club, rugby, football, hockey, American football. Churchill quite 'sporty' (with the emphasis on taking part and on the post-match drinks). Chess, aerobics, canoeing, mountaineering, badminton, sailing – you name it! **Hardship funds:** Yes, but you need to be in very dire straits. **Travel:** Generous travel grants, both for study and for recreation. (Only once in three years, on submission of a report.) Easy to hitch – close to M11. Rail station 4 miles, bus station 2 miles. **Work:** During term-time actively discouraged. Vac work available in college particularly over summer. But work load too great to give you much time to earn vac money whatever your subject.

Buzz-words

Winston (college magazine), Pav (weekly disco).

Alumni

No alumni as yet, but fellows are exceptionally distinguished. We have had 12 Nobel prize winners through our gates.

CLARE

Clare College, Cambridge CB2 1TL (0223 333246)

Founded: 1326; women undergraduates first admitted 1972. **Accommodation:** Mixture of sets, bedsitters and hostels available in all 3 years. Most undergraduates charged £690 pa (range £600–£789). 2 room set and all meals in college, £1,280 pa. **Eating arrangements:** Self-service buttery, formal dinner in hall Mondays–Thursdays. Ticket system. **Gate/guest hours:** Porter lets college members in all night; guests not booked in overnight expected to leave by 2 am. **Admission:** Most candidates apply during fourth term in sixth form. A-levels plus Step is the most common method of entry but many offers are based on A-levels or A plus S-levels. **Scholarships:** Organ scholarship (£250 pa) every other year; an average of 7 choral and 2 instrumental exhibitions (£100 pa). **Travel grants:** Funds available at college's discretion; 3 major Parkin Grants, and 8 Thirkill Grants for those who have played a prominent part in college life; Mellon Fellowship for third year undergraduates who spend 2 years at Yale. **Library:** Forbes Mellon Library new building. 20,000 volumes, collection of past examination papers, law reading room. **Other college facilities:** Music and record libraries, music room, music practice rooms, computing and word-processing facilities and link to university mainframe, picture guild, pianos, harpsichord, meeting rooms, darkroom, studio and pottery room (with wheel and kiln); squash courts near college, outstanding playing fields (about 1½ miles away), rowing, punts available in summertime. **Hardship funds:** Available in cases of unavoidable hardship.

European Community: 10% first degree students take EC language as part of course and 10% spend 6 months or more in another EC country. Formal exchange links with 2 EC universities/colleges (Heidelberg, Paris); both open generally but Paris usually taken by a linguist, Heidelberg by a lawyer.

College fees for 1992/93 (undergraduate) £2,555.

Undergraduates: *Men:* 230 *Women:* 174

Postgraduates *Men:* 96 *Women:* 65

Teaching staff *Men:* 67 fellows, 8 research fellows *Women:* 6 fellows, 3 research fellows.

What it's like

It's a central, beautiful college on 'the Backs' – has an old bridge over the willow- and garden-bordered Cam. Closeish to shops/lectures: foot or bike always adequate. 99% of undergraduates live in – all have the option. Accommodation varies from tiny bedsits (few) to spacious sets (also few) to houses for groups of c. six: most rooms are middling/good, generally very good value. Minimal cooking facilities; coin-op washing and drying machines. No problems with mixed accommodation.

Keen on attracting overseas students. Very good relations between the college authorities and students, though sometimes borders on the paternal. Porters/catering/maintenance staff are excellent, friendly people.

Hours of libraries/labs/gyms/shops generally convenient. SU active in providing facilities, running social events, improving quality of life (eg low rents); politically reflects college's centre-left apathy, with a radical rump! Active Green group.

No visiting restrictions. Cambridge students not allowed cars – biking is better/easier anyway. Counselling/advice services overstretched, but comprehensive, confidential, helpful. 'Little Blue Book' of info on contraception/sex etc sent free to all first years. Clare SU provides free condoms. Active societies: rowing, mountaineering/hillwalking, music, football; plus inevitable (and nasty) drinking societies. Central Cambridge dominated by students in term, but relations not always easy between town and gown: university students seen as an 'overprivileged few' – justifiably! Good cinemas, market, usual chain stores, odd shops, many pubs.

It's fairly easy to meet students from other colleges, but most people's time is largely spent within college: Clare offers a lot; can sometimes be infuriatingly 'nice' in a claustrophobic sort of way.

University courses mainly academic rather than practical, often frustratingly so. Easy to switch subject. Work loads vary considerably, can (esp in sciences) be pretty heavy. No sandwich courses. Language courses have year abroad. Lecturers vary a lot: some very good, some not. Work is assessed (in terms of degree results – the only measurement in which the colleges seem really interested) only at the end of each year, in what can be very unpleasant competitive exams. Supervisors, one for each area of your course, see you fortnightly, arranged by Director of Studies in College. There's student pressure for course reform.

Most Clare students from south; approx 45% from public schools (Clare has a higher proportion from state schools than most colleges). Approaching 55/45 male/female ratio (again good for Cambridge). Failure rate low, not fixed. Courses (esp. Arts) are often dull and traditional at first, but after first year they can get more interesting. Resources and facilities (libraries/faculties etc) are, however, superb. Incidents of sexist/racist/homophobic discrimination relatively rare. Active Women's Group. Typical student has very high A-level grades, various non-academic interests/talents, will work in mainstream careers – financial services, industry, after graduating (but many do much more 'right-on' things).

Pauper notes

Accommodation: Varies in quality, but very cheap, large choice (eg house, single room, shared set). Enough accommodation owned by college for 3 years 'living in'. **Drink:** Greene King, Tolly Cobbold, and a few pub-cum-breweries. **Eats:** College canteen keeps students alive, sometimes pleasantly: vegan choices available (if you warn the Catering Manager in advance). Good markets, restaurants and pub lunches nearby. **Ents:** Clare has the best reputation of Cambridge colleges for rock, jazz, folk and blues nights – all cheap, brilliant performances in underground Cellars. Loads of music of every sort! Also film, video, arts societies. **Sports:** Good college/university facilities. **Hardship funds:** College is often sympathetic/helpful. University administers central Access Funds. But times are very hard (no state benefits available to students) – so debt is inevitable. **Travel:**

No transport apart from bikes necessary in Cambridge. **Work:** You won't have time during term-time anyway.

Alumni (Editors' pick)

David Attenborough (naturalist and broadcaster), Paul Mellon (philanthropist), Harvey & one of his Wallbangers, Richard Stilgoe (entertainer), James Watson (Nobel Laureate – DNA), Chris Kelly (broadcaster), Hugh Latimer (martyr), Cecil Sharp (folk songs), Siegfried Sassoon (poet), Peter Lilley MP, Matthew Paris (journalist), Norman Ramsey (Nobel Laureate).

CORPUS CHRISTI

Corpus Christi College, Cambridge CB2 1RH (0223 338056)

Founded: 1352; women undergraduates first admitted 1983. **Accommodation:** Sets and single rooms for all college members during 3 years' Cambridge residence. Most undergraduates charged £825 pa (range £435–£1,170). Room, rent and meals approximately £2,055 pa. **Eating arrangements:** All meals provided in hall and/or bar. **Gate/guest hours:** Entry after 11.00/11.30pm by key. **Admission:** Primarily based on public examination results, school report and interview. **Scholarships:** Awarded to those already in residence on the basis of academic performance. **Travel grants:** Considerable sums annually. **Library:** Butler Library (working undergraduate library); Parker Library (medieval manuscripts and early books). **Other college facilities:** Extensive sports grounds; 7-acre garden with open air swimming pool; river boathouse.

European Community: 25% first degree students take EC language as part of course and 5% spend 6 months or more in another EC country. Formal exchange links with various EC universities/colleges.

College fees for 1992/93 (undergraduate) £2,637.

Undergraduates: *Men:* 159 *Women:* 88

Postgraduates: *Men:* 93 *Women:* 48

Teaching staff: *Men:* 34 fellows, 7 research fellows, 19 lecturers, 18 life fellows, 14 honorary fellows *Women:* 6 fellows, 1 research fellow, 2 lecturers, 1 life fellow.

What it's like

Small and central, the main buildings comprise Old Court, Cambridge's oldest and arguably prettiest court, and gothic style New Court. 2nd years live in college hostels up to a third of a mile away, including the new comfortable Bene't Street development. Old Court rooms range from pokey to palatial, but can involve long wintry walks to the bathroom. 13-amp electricity, sinks and basic kitchens have all been recently installed.

Simple self-catering facilities are gradually being fitted throughout college. Food in Hall is generally good, but pricey; hefty fixed charge whether you eat or not. Regular Guest Nights are lavish, reasonable, very popular, but not as good value as they once were. The Buttery and Bar (refurbished) are extensively used. Lunchtime snacks (baked potatoes, burgers, rolls etc) are further victims of recent price rises, but still provide a cheaper alternative to lunch in Hall. The Bar is open late and serves several beers, lagers and wines from the college's extensive cellars.

Excellent sports facilities are 15 minutes away – squash courts, tennis courts, and in summer an open-air swimming pool. Sporting standards vary but in general emphasis is on taking part rather than winning.

Strong college drama, history, literary and wine societies. Video always available in the TV room. Impressive computing facility has just been installed.

Academic standards are fairly high – Corpus is in the top of Cambridge academic league table. College can provide supervisors for most subjects, though some may be farmed off to surrounding colleges. Top for law. Undergraduate relations with fellows are good. Money, or your lack of it, will always be dealt with sympathetically. Guest restrictions are minimal – just sign in. The college library is small, but about to be drastically expanded. Most departmental libraries are close by. The JCR has shaken off its former apathy and is now active in student politics.

No undergraduate group is dominant – good mix from all backgrounds. Corpus was one of the last colleges to become mixed, and the proportion of female undergraduates is still below the university average, but college is aiming to rectify this position.

College is surrounded by a welter of good pubs, and the Corn Exchange (an emerging venue for national name bands) is less than 100 yards away.

Richard Stephens

Pauper notes

Accommodation: New college hostel for 2nd year accommodation. Some rooms available 2nd/3rd years for c£15 per week. **Drink:** Several good 'student' pubs within 100 yards of college. Wide variety of brews can be found. 'The Bath' specialises in cider. **Eats:** College food relatively expensive for a Cambridge college. Vegetarians have a lot to moan about. Cambridge itself has a huge variety of eating places at all price ranges. **Ents:** College video club and college drama and music are both very active. **Sports:** Good college facilities, univ/town facilities limited. **Travel:** College awards two sets of travel scholarships (several awards each of anything from £100 to £900). **Work:** Some work usually available in college during long vac.

Alumni (Editors' pick)

Christopher Isherwood, Sir Frederick Lawton (Lord Justice of Appeal), Lord Sieff of Brimpton (Marks & Spencer), Sir Eric Faulkner (Lloyds Bank), Mark Elder, Joe Farman (discoverer of hole in ozone layer), Christopher Booker (journalist/writer), E P Thompson (historian/nuclear disarmer).

DOWNING

Downing College, Cambridge CB2 1DQ (0223 334800)

Founded: 1800; women undergraduates first admitted 1978. **Accommodation:** All undergraduates may live in college for three years or in adjacent college hostels where rent controlled by college. Most charges £780 pa (range £627–£894). **Eating arrangements:** Undergraduates may take all meals in hall. Limited facilities provided for self-catering. **Gate/guest hours:** Gates always open. Guests not booked in overnight must leave by 1.45 am. **Admission:** All offers based on school reference, interviews and A-levels or equivalent. **Structural features:** New library, undergraduate common room and theatre/concert hall. **Scholarships:** Scholarships and exhibitions on performance in university exams. Organ scholarship, choral and instrumental awards every year. Substantial awards available for Downing graduates intending to train for the legal and medical professions. **Travel grants:** Endowed trust funds. **Hardship funds:** Some funds available.

CAN'T FIND WHAT YOU'RE LOOKING FOR? USE THE INDEX!

Library: Well-stocked college library. **Other college facilities:** Coffee and reading room, bar; 2 tennis courts and 2 squash courts in college precincts; sports ground 10 min cycle ride away; boathouse. **Largest fields of study:** Natural sciences, law, engineering, medicine but applications welcome in all subjects.

European Community: 7% first degree students take EC language as part of course and 7% spend 6 months or more in another EC country. No formal exchange links with EC universities/colleges.

College fees for 1992/93 (undergraduate) £2,727.

Undergraduates: *Men:* 240 *Women:* 130

Postgraduates: *Men:* 70 *Women:* 20

Teaching staff: *Men:* 33 fellows, 1 research fellow, 3 lecturers *Women:* 7 fellows, 3 research fellows.

What it's like

In the south centre of Cambridge, next door to science sites and only a short walk from all faculties. Academically particularly strong in law, medicine, natural sciences and geography; thrives in all areas.

Outstanding open spaces and austere classical design. Much recent building in keeping with style. Howard Building provides a luxurious Junior Combination Room and a theatre/lecture hall; new JCR bar and party room; computer room equipped with latest IBM PC network hardware. Two-thirds live in college accommodation; all in their first year.

Active JCR concerned primarily with student problems rather than wider political issues. Good relationship between JCR and college authorities, eg co-operation over improvements in security for women. JCR bar, wholly run and staffed by students, is second cheapest in university.

Sporting reputation is well-deserved – champion rugby and football college, winners of the tennis and skiing university cup competitions, 2nd in May Bumps rowing competition, captain of the university cricket team, and of both university tennis teams, karate internationals . . . the list goes on. Emphasis on participation rather than success, with most students joining in for fun rather than serious competition.

Music Society has weekly concerts of an excellent standard; Drama Society puts on a number of excellent productions each year. Journalism thrives in the form of a termly college magazine and a fortnightly newsletter. A stimulating and active atmosphere for students.

Pauper notes

Accommodation: Many rooms recently refurbished; 30 new rooms built for 30 students; ⅓ live out and that is expensive. **Drink:** College bar cheap and good; Greene King IPA & Abbot, hand-pulled. The Alma Brewery nearby for scrumpy. **Eats:** (In college) middling to good, wide choice, excellent salads, generous portions, vegetarian every day; (outside) many jacket potato, pizza and other restaurants. **Ents:** Parties, sweaty bops; bands in corn exchange; pub crawls; plays in new theatre. Many productions and revues throughout Cambridge. **Sports:** College sports ground some distance but paddock in college for practices and tennis and squash courts on campus. Uni sports centre, gym & weights free; swimming pool nearby (£1.10). **Hardship funds:** Funds available; application to impartial Vice Master who considers individual cases. **Travel:** Travel scholarships available; some standard links with USA. **Work:** Bar work in college.

Alumni (Editors' pick)

Sir Graham Smith (Astronomer Royal), John Cleese, F R Leavis, Lord Goodman, Prof Lord John Butterfield, Brian Redhead, Michael Winner, Mark Cox, Michael Atherton, Dr Alan Howard, Sir Peter Hall, Trevor Nunn.

GET HOLD OF THE PROSPECTUSES

EMMANUEL

Emmanuel College, Cambridge CB2 3AP (0223 334200)

Founded: 1584; women undergraduates first admitted 1979. **Accommodation:** All first and third year undergraduates accommodated in college (old or modern rooms); second year undergraduates in college or college hostels. Rent: all undergraduates housed in accommodation where rent is controlled by college. Rent for 1992/93: ranges £291–£348; for room and 3 meals daily, approx £2,406 pa. **Eating arrangements:** No compulsory eating arrangements. **Gate/guest hours:** No gate hours but guests must leave by 2 am (unless registered as overnight guests). **Admission:** Conditional and unconditional offers only. **Travel grants:** 30 awarded annually to resident undergraduates. **Library:** Large college library; Sancroft Library (old books) and Watson Collection (illustrated books). **Hardship funds:** Funds available to both undergraduate and graduate students. **Other college facilities:** Grand piano, harpsichord and organ; 2 squash courts, table tennis room, tennis courts and open air swimming pool in college precincts; nearby playing fields and boat house.

European Community: 12% first degree students take EC language as part of course and 3% spend 6 months or more in another EC country.

College fees for 1992/93 (undergraduate) £2,586.

Undergraduates: *Men:* 256 *Women:* 139
Postgraduates: *Men:* 94 *Women:* 64

Teaching staff: *Men:* 39 fellows, 5 research fellows, 2 lecturers *Women:* 4 fellows, 2 research fellows.

What it's like

Known principally for its ducks, but also for being friendly and unpretentious, Emma has a strong college identity – caused in part by the best student-run bar in Cambridge. Students here are drawn from a large range of backgrounds – 40% are women and applications from state schools are actively encouraged. Though one of the richer Cambridge colleges, this will not affect your rent bill. However, it is reflected in full undergraduate housing for three years, generous travel awards, a commitment to tutorial teaching and an increasing provision for hardship funds.

The college SU is politically and socially very active and there are a lot of well-financed clubs.

It is not hard to enjoy Emma – its grounds and students, and the food should be best in Cambridge by the time you arrive – the college is fully modernising the kitchens this year.

Pauper notes

Accommodation: All 1st and 3rd and most 2nd years in college accommodation. Living out very expensive and rare. **Drink:** Student run college bar cheapest in Cambridge (111p–120p a pint). No local brew of note. **Eats:** Compulsory fixed termly charge a bone of contention. Quality varies. Many places nearby in town. **Ents:** Ents every Sunday night free, 2 good venues in town. Drama Society. **Sports:** Good free sportsground 15 min away by bike. Closest college to sports hall and swimming pool. **Hardship funds:** Extensive facilities available via tutorial system – useful to have a good tutor. **Travel:** Fairly generous travel grants. Travelling in Cambridge easy. No cars allowed. **Work:** Not encouraged during term. Some services/office vacancies in vacations.

Informal name

Emma

CAN'T FIND WHAT YOU'RE LOOKING FOR? USE THE INDEX!

Alumni (Editors' pick)

Michael Frayn, Eldon Griffiths MP, Professor Sir Fred Hoyle, Tom King MP, Cecil Parkinson MP, Sir George Porter, Griff Rhys Jones, Graeme Garden.

FITZWILLIAM

Fitzwilliam College, Cambridge CB3 0DG (0223 332000)

Founded: 1869; women undergraduates first admitted 1978. **Accommodation:** 317 rooms in college, college houses and hostel, some college-rented flats; all first and third year, and some second year undergraduates accommodated. 61% in accommodation where rent controlled by college. Most undergraduates charged £750 pa (range £654–£1,044). **Eating arrangements:** Continental breakfast and lunch in hall, choice of self-service and formal dinner. Small house charge but most meals paid for as required. Some overnight accommodation is available for guests if certain conditions satisfied. **Admission:** By A-level results: conditional and unconditional offers on basis of interview and school report only. **Scholarships:** Scholarships and exhibitions awarded on university examinations. **Travel grants:** Contributions to travel costs made from Sir John Stratton Travel Fund and other college sources. **Hardship funds:** Small amounts (£100–£200) through the Tutors Fund and University's Bell, Abbott, and Barnes Funds. **Library:** College library (open all evening and in Easter term until 2 am). **Other college facilities:** Bar, laundry, guest rooms, music room, squash courts, playing fields near college, photographic darkroom, weights room.

European Community: 9% first degree students take EC language as part of course and 9% spend 6 months or more in another EC country. No formal exchange links; modern linguists study at EC university of their choice. EC students welcomed at college.

College fees for 1992/93 (undergraduate) £2,715.

Undergraduates: *Men:* 268 *Women:* 130

Postgraduates: *Men:* 109 *Women:* 25

Teaching staff: *Men:* 50 fellows, 5 research fellows, 4 lecturers, 47 teaching officers, including externals *Women:* 5 fellows, 3 lecturers, 8 teaching officers.

What it's like

It's not only Fitzwilliam's red-brick exterior that distinguishes it from the 'traditional' Cambridge college – the student intake helps too, since students from state schools make up 70% of the undergraduate population. The atmosphere is down-to-earth and friendly and there is a strong sense of community, perhaps due to the college's location slightly out of town. It is, however, still only a five-minute cycle ride into the centre, and the rest of the colleges are close enough to be able to enjoy what the university as a whole has to offer.

Academically, Fitz is rising rapidly in the university ratings and has done particularly well recently in modern languages, law, and natural sciences. The student population is diverse and the number of women and black students has increased significantly in the past two years.

Accommodation is guaranteed for first and third years, consisting of corridors with eight rooms, a kitchen (two ring burners but no oven) and adequate bathroom facilities. Third-year rooms in New Court are palatial and trendily done out in black pine, hence a higher rent. Most second years and graduates live in privately rented accommodation, and this can prove expensive. New building work about to start will soon mean that most people will be able to live-in in second year if desired. This new block promises even better quality modern rooms.

On the social front, Fitz has the reputation for having probably the best Ents in town. These take place twice termly, and are only a small part of the social life on offer, should you wish it. Clubs and societies range from martial arts to aerobics, with music and drama growing quickly. Sport is extremely well catered for, with opportunities for all; three squash courts in college, and a college-owned ground near by. The traditional sports are all very popular and cater for all standards; along with some minor sports such as volleyball and basketball.

An active JMA (SU) involves itself with a wide range of issues, and an excellent welfare system provides each student with a tutor (there to help and listen in any situation, fully confidentially) as well as access to a women's tutor and a chaplain. Though fairly apathetic politically, attitudes in general are healthy and egalitarian.

Also worth noting: there are few restrictions on visitors or overnight guests. Contraceptive machines can be found in central block toilets and advice is also readily available. All students have access to computing facilities – Apple Macs and BBC model Bs. A spectacular new chapel has been recently opened and is available for use by the students. Bar has two full-time bar staff, one of the best in the university.

Colin Read

Pauper notes

Accommodation: No married quarters, rooms with and without basins. Good new block rooms. More being built. **Drink:** Bar cheaper than pubs (not as cheap as student run bars in Cambridge). **Eats:** Cafeteria good. Varying standard but always a salad bar. Veggie options. **Ents:** 2 excellent Ents per term. Films etc. One play in Michaelmas term. **Sports:** All sports free. Sports ground 5 minutes walk from college, unusually close for Cambridge. Basketball, badminton, athletics, tennis, squash (3 courts), rugby, football, hockey, netball, darts, softball. **Hardship funds:** On individual basis. **Travel:** Number of college and university awards. **Work:** No term-time employment (University regulations), some holiday jobs in kitchen and maintenance staff.

More info?

Enquiries to JMA President 0223 332081.

Informal name

Fitz

Alumni (Editors' pick)

Lord St John of Fawsley, Norman Lamont, Dr A Szent-Gyorgi (Nobel prize-winner), Derek Pringle, Phil Edmonds (cricketers), Christopher Martin Jenkins (cricket commentator), President Sharma of India, Nick Clarke (Radio 4 news-caster), Dr David English (President of Methodist Conference).

GIRTON

Girton College, Cambridge CB3 0JG (0223 338999)

Founded: 1869; men undergraduates first admitted 1979. **Accommodation:** 442 rooms (mostly single bedsits but some sets) available for undergraduates in college. 70 rooms in college houses. Rent: 98% in accommodation where rent controlled by college. All undergraduates charged £247.50 per term + £64.00 heating and £61.00 kitchen overheads; and gas and electricity as used. **Eating arrangements:** Optional books of meal tickets valid for academic year. No compulsory meals. Lunch arrangements with Clare, Downing and Pembroke colleges. Formal dinner in hall once a week. **Guest/gate hours:** College members must be back in college by 6 am (if without overnight exeats); guests after 10.30 pm only if accompanied by college member. **Academic features:** Mathematics Tripos course to take account of candidates with single subject mathematics.

CAN'T FIND WHAT YOU'RE LOOKING FOR? USE THE INDEX!

Engineering course now 4 years. **Structural features:** Besides the main college, Girton has Wolfson Court in Clarkson Road, in the centre of Cambridge for both graduates and undergraduates. **Admission:** Conditional offers on A-level with some matriculation offers. Post A-level and candidates for deferred entry welcomed. **Scholarships:** Scholarships and exhibitions awarded on results of Tripos examinations; organ scholarships, choral and instrumental awards. **Travel grants:** Some available. **Library:** College library (80,000 volumes). **Hardship funds:** The Buss Fund for undergraduates; The Pillman Fund for research and graduates; overseas bursaries for overseas students. **Other college facilities:** Playing fields, croquet lawns, swimming pool, cricket, soccer and rugger pitches, boathouse, tennis courts, squash court. **Largest fields of study:** Biological and physical sciences; engineering; also high intake in English, history, geography, economics, law, mathematics, medical sciences, modern languages and veterinary medicine.

European Community: 8% first degree students take EC language and spend a year in another EC country as part of their course (modern and medieval languages students). Formal exchange link with Utrecht University (for modern language students).

College fees for 1992/93 (undergraduate) £2,634.

Undergraduates: *Men:* 283 *Women:* 211

Postgraduates: *Men:* 62 *Women:* 45

Teaching staff: *Men:* 16 fellows, 12 research fellows, 16 lecturers, 3 professional fellows, 1 supernumerary fellow, 6 bye-fellows, 1 life fellow, 4 honorary fellows *Women:* 18 fellows, 4 research fellows, 22 lecturers, 3 professional fellows, 1 supernumerary fellow, 2 bye-fellows, 14 life fellows, 12 honorary fellows.

What it's like

Set in pleasant, extensive grounds about 2.5 miles from city centre; most find bikes essential. Friendly and relaxed atmosphere. Vast majority of undergraduates live in; most second and third years have good accommodation. Wolfson Court houses 100, is more modern. New law library, reading room and computer room complex opens this year at Wolfson Court. Several college houses available, all next to college. Fixed rent for all rooms (inc college houses), regardless of size. Good male:female ratio. Strong overseas contingent. No breakfasts; no Saturday or Sunday evening meal. Food quite cheap and quite good. Several choices and salads available. Vegetarian meals provided; vegan on request. Self-catering facilities on each corridor; coin operated washing machines provided. Extensive, good library, with convenient opening hours. Friendly relations between senior and junior college members. College societies range from subject-related to music, drama and film club. Sports available on site – most facilities good: hockey, lacrosse, tennis, netball, Rugby, soccer, squash, cricket, croquet. Also heated indoor swimming pool (water polo), multigym and successful rowing club. Lively bar in atmospheric college cellars with pool table, darts board, etc. Busy most times, cheap. Serves Abbott and Ruddles; unique barman. Party rooms available; TV room. JCR hires out discotheque and organises annual ball, garden party and band nights and discos.

Academic standards average, but improving. Fairly easy to change subjects. Workloads realistic and despite traditional atmosphere of degrees, interesting and unpressurised. Part One (first year) engineering and some sciences have a heavy workload (be prepared). Friendly and relaxed atmosphere. Very mixed intake – varied educational and home backgrounds; down-to-earth and unpretentious.

No restrictions on entry into college but after 12 pm entrance is by front gate only. Gate locked at 2 am but porter always on duty to open it. New security system about to be installed on an 'intelligent key basis' which will facilitate entry to college at night (system like that at Worcester College, Oxford). Can also be used as a charge up card – students can assign money to their key (maximum £30) which can be used in the canteen and bar. System should be installed by January 1993.

WANT TO HELP WITH THE NEXT EDITION – SEE PAGE 76

All rooms, facilities, library, bar etc contained within one building (which can be cold in winter as it's all brick and wood although major conversion of the boilers from oil to gas is well under way to improve heating efficiency). Frequent buses but not always running to time-table: approx cost 70p. CUSU taxi deal to town at flat rate of £3.00 (with CUSU card). JCR bikes available for students. Small JCR-run shop sells very cheap stationery, food and other essentials. Free taxi from town 12 am Friday and Saturday.

Pauper notes

Accommodation: Accommodation for most undergraduates – some 2nd years live out. No married quarters but houses available (rooms same rent as room in college) very near to college. **Drink:** Abbott, Ruddles, Newquay – good selection of bottled and tap beers. College bars (have to know people in other colleges to drink in their college bars). **Eats:** Best eating places in town, some on Castle Hill, thatched pub on Madingley 2 miles away serves cheap food. College meals about £1.50 each, vegetarian available. **Ents:** Local bands in college bars – some more famous play in Corn Exchange – fairly expensive – film, bop, band or other ents (eg bingo, generation game) each week in Girton. **Sports:** Very good facilities – swimming pool on cool side. New astro-turf cricket nets. Univ sports advertised at societies fair, realistic prices. **Hardship funds:** Access funds. Pay bill in instalments if negotiated (rare). **Travel:** Bicycles essential. Bus frequent but not always regular. Taxi to town £3.00. Travel grants available for summer vacation. **Work:** Some work in college kitchens – otherwise during term not officially allowed – temping possible in holidays.

Buzz-words

Mathmo (mathematician); Nat Sci (natural scientist); Comp Sci (computer scientist); JCR (student union).

Alumni (Editors' pick)

Arianna Stassinopoulos (writer and broadcaster), Angela Tilby (writer and TV producer), HM Queen Margarethe of Denmark, Prof Rosalyn Higgins (professor of international law, University College, London), Mrs Doris Wheatley (chairman and managing director, Cambridge Communications Ltd), Prof Dorothy Wedderburn, Joan Robinson (economics), Baroness Warnock (Warnock Committee, Question Time); Professor Gillian Beer, Mrs Juliet d'A Campbell – current mistress – (Ambassador to Luxembourg).

GONVILLE & CAIUS

Gonville & Caius College, Cambridge CB2 1TA (0223 332447)

Founded: 1348. **Accommodation available:** All unmarried students allocated room in college in first and third year; second years housed in college lodgings. **Eating arrangements:** Self-service breakfast and lunch; undergraduates encouraged to dine in hall as often as possible and there is minimum dining requirement. **Gate/guest hours:** No restrictions. **Admission:** On basis of A-level results already obtained; increasingly high proportion of places also offered to pre A-level candidates conditional on certain grades in A-level examinations. Candidates are usually asked to offer 1 or 2 subjects at S-level or Step if they wish to study maths or medicine. **Scholarships:** Unlimited scholarships and exhibitions on university examinations. **Travel grants:** Numerous minor travel grants plus Paton-Taylor travelling scholarship for projects of an academic nature; awards from Leonard Gluckstein Memorial Fund for travel associated with historical or archaeological studies; grants from Handson Bequest for medical projects (eg recent expedition to South America). **Library:** College library contains collection of modern books; also largest surviving medieval collection in university and various collections bequeathed by Fellows. **Other college facilities:** College boathouse and boatman;

CAN'T FIND WHAT YOU'RE LOOKING FOR? USE THE INDEX!

cricket pitch; sports ground. **Academic features:** Caius has more medical students than other colleges, and a teaching Fellow in every pre-clinical medical subject. It is one of the very few colleges with a French and German Lector in addition to modern languages teaching Fellows.

European Community: Number of students learning an EC language or spending time in another EC country, not known.

College fees for 1992/93 (undergraduate) £2,589.

Undergraduates: *Men:* 300 *Women:* 150

Postgraduates: *Men:* 80 *Women:* 70

What it's like

The main college buildings (the 'Old Courts') are in the centre of town – beautifully situated; next to the Squire Law Library. The buildings are attractive and ornate – pretty flower beds! Most first years live in Harvey Court (1960s halls – but admired by architects) – 10 minutes' walk away – on the Backs, and next to the arts faculties and university library. 2nd years 'live-out' in college houses, allocated by ballot; ballot order is reversed to choose 3rd year rooms in the Old Courts. Gate hours not 'unrestricted' – porters' lodges close 2 am. After that climb in over Gate of Honour.

Washing machines/irons etc are readily available (if rather antiquated) and 3-5 people share a 'gyp-room' (kitchen) which contains a fridge and cooking rings. Officially only 'minor cooking' is allowed, as it is compulsory to eat in hall 45 times a term. All staircases are now mixed. Approx 5–10% students are from overseas, more in the MCR. Special efforts are made to ensure their integration into college life. Little ostentatious wealth among students – few leave without an overdraft! Relations between the administration and students are friendly (each student has a personal tutor). The college SU is active and well-regarded: affiliated to CUSU and NUS it concentrates more on welfare issues than party politics – although members of the college are involved in all political spheres – from CUCA through the Greens to Uni-left. Much like other Cambridge colleges, the character of the college changes with each new intake of students – but generally thought of as a tolerant and relaxed atmosphere. Courts tend to be very sociable – there are three bars – 2 student run. Everyone knows everyone else because of the compulsory dinner system which brings the college together once a day. Some find it insular – but many current Caians are involved on a university level in various activities from the President of the ADC Theatre to the CU 'Hands On' Massage Society.

Strong subjects are history (15 firsts in 1992) and medicine; economics, engineering and law are also well-represented. It is very easy to change subject for Part II (eg law to English, economics to SPS). Workloads vary hugely from individual to individual and between courses: arts subjects require self-reliance (1–2 supervisions a week, few lectures); natural sciences and medicine are much more structured. The standard of teaching is excellent, though important to note that courses are fairly theoretical and can be stuffy and restricting. The college library is open 24 hours a day, and there is a separate law library.

Rowing and hockey are sports at which Caius excels – but most other sports are played at a more laid-back level. If your interest is not represented among the 40+ clubs and societies in college, it is easy to start up a new one (eg women's Rugby and mixed netball last year). Debating, music and drama are all thriving! The majority of students are from London/Home Counties: college is keen to attract more state school entrants but currently large majority public/private and grammar schools. Drop-out rate approx 1 a year (from 150). Lively women's group – women prominent in college, although only 45% of student body. The college Students' Union now has its first ever female President.

Pauper notes

Accommodation: Balloted accommodation, 95% excellent. £170–£340 per term. Married quarters. All students housed in college-owned property. Modern 1st year halls; 2nd year houses; 3rd year 'Old Courts'. New development at Harvey Court will provide extra 90 rooms late nineties. **Drink:** 3 college bars – good, vary a lot in character, not cheap £1.40 pint. Student run 'Late Night Bar' has dance floor and seedy atmosphere. **Eats:** College caters for all diets although dinners not great; good vegetarian restaurants and health food shops in town. **Ents:** Frequent (cheap) college bops and other events. Thriving drama society; regular (classical) concerts, plays. 'Arts' cinema in town is excellent; also Cannon cinema for mainstream films. No auditorium or practice rooms for non-classical music (ie band). However, plans going ahead for a new accommodation and amenities block to be completed by 1996. **Sports:** Excellent sports ground with clubhouse (the best in Cambridge) – contains signable drinks (ie not cash!) and a yard! – and squash/tennis courts. Good standard. Town sports centre has good indoor facilities (swimming, badminton etc). Also open-air pool in town. **Hardship funds:** College actually recognising the financial stress put on students due to frozen grant and loans, and responding with more grants and bursaries and leniency on paying bills. **Travel:** William Wade Travel Grants of up to £200 each for approximately 15–20 people. Approx £6 return to London (coach). **Work:** Possible to work in college bars (for a pittance) but otherwise work is officially prohibited during term.

Informal name

Caius (pronounced 'Keys')

Alumni (Editors' pick)

Titus Oates, David Frost, Captain Wilson, Venn (of Venn diagrams), Harold Abrahams, Sir Nevill Mott (Nobel Laureate, physics), Kenneth Clarke MP, Mark Bailey (England Rugby player).

JESUS

Jesus College, Cambridge CB5 8BL (0223 357626)

Founded: 1496; women undergraduates first admitted 1979. **Accommodation:** All first years and most third years accommodated in college. Second years in bedsitters and sets of rooms in adjacent external staircases or lodging houses. Rent: 98% in accommodation where rent controlled by college. Most undergraduates charged £738 pa in 1991/92: range £374–£1,071. **Eating arrangements:** Self-service with alternative formal Hall dinner. Each undergraduate pays kitchen fixed charge plus cost of meals taken. **Gate/guest hours:** Free access until 2 am. Overnight guests have to be signed in. **Admission:** By conditional offer, using Step or S papers in certain cases. Post A-level candidates admitted on basis of A-levels, school reports and interview. **Hardship funds:** Named funds plus college loans. **Travel grants:** Usually available for application in Lent term. **Library:** College library. **Other college facilities:** Bar, junior common room, party room, TV room, stereo-reproduction room, multi-gym, billiards room, launderette, sports fields within the college.

European Community: 20–25% students learning an EC language as part of their course and 10% spend 6 months or more in another EC country.

College fees for 1992/93 (undergraduate) £2,616.

Undergraduates: *Men:* 281 *Women:* 165

Postgraduates: *Men:* 128 *Women:* 55

Teaching staff: *Men:* 42 fellows, 2 research fellows, 31 lecturers, 1 lector *Women:* 6 fellows, 6 research fellows, 5 lecturers

CAN'T FIND WHAT YOU'RE LOOKING FOR? USE THE INDEX!

What it's like

Medium sized college just off the tourist track (an advantage in summer). Only 3 minutes' walk to city centre with full range of shopping facilities. College is one of the few in Cambridge that has all its sports grounds and facilities on site giving an atmosphere of openness as well as producing a strong sporting tradition, particularly in rugby, hockey and rowing. (The boathouse and river is again about 3 minutes away.)

Students are well-integrated from all social backgrounds, very active in university activities. Flourishing college music society and drama has received a recent revival.

Accommodation good though not the cheapest around; very few students have a landlady in any of their 3 years here. 1st year spent in; 2nd year out – literally opposite the College; 3rd year either in or out, with a number of 3 room sets available for 3rd years. Rooms tend to be warm and well-furnished, about 85% have washbasins. Food is quite good with Formal Hall (3 course waitress served meal to which gowns must be worn) rated as one of the best in Cambridge and only £2.50. Student bar is both lively and popular, with many outside visitors frequenting it regularly. Current price for a pint of bitter £1.15. Also a full-sized snooker table, reading room, TV room and computer room.

Jesus positively encourages applications from state sector and across the board in terms of subjects; no strict quotas in operation. English and history are particular strengths, but overall well-placed in the academic stakes with perhaps one of the more friendly Fellowships, always approachable and willing to listen to students and their problems.

Pauper notes

Drink: Cheap bitter, good brands. **Sports:** Sport free on college site. **Supplementary maintenance:** Mostly loans from college fund of £50,000. **Travel:** Travel scholarships available.

More info?

Enquiries to President JCR (0223 68611 ext 247).

Alumni (Editors' pick)

Alastair Cooke, W John Biffen MP, Bronowski, Raymond Williams, Sam Brittan, Sir Peter Gadsden, Sir David Trench, S T Coleridge, Archbishop Cranmer, Sterne, Malthus, Prince Edward.

KING'S

King's College, Cambridge CB2 1ST (0223 350411)

Founded: 1441; women undergraduates first admitted 1972. **Accommodation:** All undergraduates offered accommodation for 3 years – mostly study bedrooms, some sets of living room and bedroom. Charges range from £663–£786 pa plus heating. **Eating arrangements:** Self-service cafeteria. Standing charge covers kitchen overheads, individual meals are paid for. **Gate/guest hours:** None. **Admission:** Great majority by conditional pre A-level offers; some places offered to post A-level applicants with high exam grades. Undergraduates not admitted for law or veterinary science. King's encourages applicants from all backgrounds and all kinds of school and, by interviewing every candidate, attempts to assess potential rather than examination performance. **Scholarships:** Choral scholarships and organ studentships awarded at entrance; academic scholarships also awarded on university examinations. **Travel grants:** Many undergraduates awarded travel grants (about £120), usually for second year summer vacation.

GET HOLD OF THE PROSPECTUSES

Library: College library (110,000 volumes); extensive music section. Record library. **Other college facilities:** 2 bars, launderette, darkroom, arts centre, computer room, film projection room, picture loan collection, croquet garden, punts, sports grounds. No compulsory gowns or formal meals.

European Community: 9% first degree students take EC language as part of course and 9% spend 6 months or more in another EC country. No formal exchange links with EC universities/colleges.

College fees for 1992/93 (undergraduate) £2,453.

Undergraduates: *Men:* 230 *Women:* 153

Postgraduates: *Men:* 154 *Women:* 54

Teaching staff: *Men:* 47 fellows, 14 research fellows, 2 lecturers
Women: 6 fellows, 6 research fellows, 3 lecturers.

What it's like

King's effectively has the best of both worlds – from outside it presents the best known and most impressive exterior in Cambridge; within it's informal and relaxed.

In every field: social, academic, artistic, sports, King's can hold its own (at least) with the rest of the university. It is King's breakdown of Cambridge cliché that makes it stand out – here students, staff and fellows do actually achieve some sense of community.

King's offers high ratios for women, state school, mature and graduate intake, resulting in a mature and well-balanced student body. Minority subjects are a King's speciality. Accommodation, music, food and virtually everything else are the equal of anywhere in Cambridge.

The student activism of the 60s and 70s that gained us the tag of 'Red King's' has left its legacy – the college offers a unique degree of student representation and involvement both within Cambridge and the UK as a whole. The college is home to most shades of opinion and is best seen as a tolerant place to be.

King's actively welcomes and encourages applicants from all backgrounds. Student hardship is taken seriously at King's. It has a very sympathetic finance tutor who'll be running workshops during freshers week (though not just for freshers) with help and advice. The college is relatively affluent and can bale people out. It also welcomes the disabled – King's offers a set of rooms specially converted for wheelchair access.

So come on over and try finding out for yourself at our open days. It's a nice place.

Pauper notes

Accommodation: All undergraduates can live in. Town accommodation expensive. College accommodation ranges from not bad to expensive (which is very good – bedroom plus sitting room for many final years). **Drink:** College bar the only financial relief for the real drinker. **Eats:** Good choice in canteen, vegetarians well catered for and not too expensive. Town tends to be either McDonalds or expensive, with lots of restaurants, loads of curries, and one good kebab shop. **Ents:** Ents is good for films and student plays both on and off campus, with music generally agreed to be naf. **Sports:** Loads of very cheap sports facilities because colleges are rich and like sporty people. **Hardship funds:** Lots and lots of lovely lolly. **Travel:** Town is compact so little need for transport. Travel abroad can be easily funded by colleges. **Work:** Lots of badly paid tourist industry work in summer, also colleges themselves are quite good.

Alumni (Editors' pick)

Sir Robert Walpole, Rupert Brooke, J M Keynes, E M Forster, The King's Singers, Michael Mates MP, Salman Rushdie, Alan Turing.

CAN'T FIND WHAT YOU'RE LOOKING FOR? USE THE INDEX!

LUCY CAVENDISH

**Lucy Cavendish College, Lady Margaret Road, Cambridge CB3 0BU
(0223 332190)**

Founded: 1965; women only. **Accommodation:** Two-thirds offered accommodation. Standard annual rent, £1,005 if paid in termly instalments (£1,239.50 if
paid in monthly instalments). **Eating arrangements:** Lunches every day; evening
meal twice a week. Cooking facilities for residents. **Admission:** Normally
2 A-levels or equivalent recognised qualifications, and evidence of recent academic
achievement. Access courses can be a useful additional element. College written
test and interviews. College is for women only and admits mature (21 and over)
and affiliated undergraduates and also graduates. **Scholarships:** Some scholarships and smaller awards (details available from college). **Hardship funds:** Very
limited. **Travel grants:** Limited number of smaller grants. **Library:** College
library (12,000 books, currently expanding). **Other facilities:** Computer facilities.
Fine gardens. **Largest fields of study:** Law, English.

European Community: 28% first degree students take EC language as part of
course and 6% spend 6 months or more in another EC country. No formal
exchange links with EC universities/colleges.

College fees for 1992/93 (undergraduate) £2,631.

Undergraduates: *Women:* 60

Postgraduates: *Women:* 31

Teaching staff: *Women:* 22 fellows, 3 research fellows, 4 lecturers.

What it's like

It's a unique college within Cambridge University in that it caters exclusively for
mature female undergraduates and postgraduates. The age for entry is now 21
(down from 25) though in practice most students are 25–55. Undergraduate
numbers expected to expand to 100 over the next few years. Staff are used to
coping with the particular problems of mature students and are very supportive.

Lucy Cavendish has an excellent atmosphere, and being small it is possible to
know everyone. It consists of 4 old houses, one of which contains the library, one
the dining hall and there is a purpose-built new building. The majority of students
live in, accommodation being either study bedrooms in the older houses, or shared
flats in new Oldham Hall. It is a short walk or bicycle ride to centre of Cambridge.
Lectures and teaching take place around university, some at faculty buildings and
within other colleges. In all respects Lucy Cavendish is a full Cambridge college
and all the facilities of Cambridge are available for students. A degree course at
Cambridge carries a very intense workload but most mature students take their
work seriously and despite family and other commitments, do well in their
degrees.

Food is excellent – there is always a vegetarian option and plenty of salads.
Lunch available every day, with one formal dinner a week. The Students'
Association of the college is social, rather than political, and organises parties,
links with other mature students in the university and weekly aerobic and yoga
classes. As it is a small college there are few facilities for team sports but many
students row, play hockey, lacrosse etc in other college teams.

For many students the second chance Lucy Cavendish offers revolutionises
their lives and many go on to careers in law, teaching, medicine and management
in industry.

Pauper notes

Accommodation: Very nice study bedrooms about £33/week including heating,
but no married or family accommodation. **Eats:** College food some of best in
the university; vegetarian option. **Ents:** Cambridge and other colleges full of

entertainment. **Sports:** Lucy Cavendish joins other colleges for most sport. **Hardship funds:** College bursaries help.

Informal name
Lucy

MAGDALENE

Magdalene College, Cambridge CB3 0AG
(Switchboard 0223 332100, admissions 332135, fax 63637)

Re-founded: 1542; women undergraduates first admitted 1988. **Accommodation available:** Approx 404 rooms; accommodation in college or college hostels nearby available to all undergraduates who want it. Rent: 100% in accommodation where rent controlled by college. Most undergraduates charged £846 pa (range £753–£930). Average room rent plus heat/light/kitchen fixed charge approx £1,400 pa. **Eating arrangements:** Meals at cost (dinner £2.15), both formal and self-service facilities. **Gate/guest hours:** Gates shut 2 till 6 am. **Admission:** Conditional offers of a fairly high standard involving one Step or S paper grade in about 15% of cases. Rarely are two such grades required. All candidates interviewed. Further mathematics A-level not required for mathematics or engineering. **Hardship funds:** Various special funds of moderate value exist. **Scholarships:** Choral and music awards every year and an organ scholarship every second year. Generous scholarships and bursaries available in all subjects. Scholarships awarded to those gaining first in Tripos. At least one full-cost research scholarship each year, plus some bursaries for overseas students. **Travel grants:** Available (including research) in all subjects. **Library:** Over 25,000 volumes; also Wigglesworth Law Library, Pepys library (including the diaries) and Old Library. **Other college facilities:** Bar, film society; 2 grand pianos, harpsichord and organs; launderettes; photographic darkroom; boathouse; squash court, fives court, gym, table tennis room; 25 acres of playing fields nearby (shared), 3 computer terminals. **Largest fields of study:** Natural sciences, engineering, law. **Hardship funds:** Available; plus various dedicated trust funds. **Specialist subjects:** Architecture, land economy, law, natural sciences.

European Community: 4% first degree students take EC language as part of course and 4% spend 6 months or more in another EC country. No formal exchange links with EC universities/colleges.

College fees for 1992/93 (undergraduate) £2,730.

Undergraduates: *Men:* 208 *Women:* 108

Postgraduates: *Men:* 81 *Women:* 39

Teaching staff: *Men:* 31 fellows, 8 research fellows, 55 lecturers (including fellows) *Women:* 2 fellows, 4 lecturers (including fellows), 2 bye-fellows.

What it's like

It's a mixed college with about 420 students. With the longest river frontage of any college, it is an extremely attractive place to read for a degree.

Magdalene has successfully shaken off its image as a haven for public school chauvinists. The majority of students come from the state sector.

Sporting provision continues to be of the highest order; rugby is the sport where Magdalene truly excels with numerous Blues coming from the college. Rowing is growing and standard has increased dramatically. For the less active drama, music and journalism are fully catered for.

Law and engineering are particularly strong – the dons being very interested in their students. As the college does not have a don for all subjects, care must be taken to ensure adequate teaching will be forthcoming.

CAN'T FIND WHAT YOU'RE LOOKING FOR? USE THE INDEX!

The bar is popular – particularly as no money need change hands. Formal has a deservedly good reputation, the only candlelit hall in Cambridge is cheap and on every night.

Every student housed due to large investment in property and renovation work, not least the splendid Quayside. Magdalene's college bill is high but the standard of rooms is above average.

The most memorable aspect of college: it is friendly and relaxed.

Pauper notes

Accommodation: Room quality varies greatly from the very plush to store-box; all are comfortable. Because of its all male heritage, there is a dearth of cooking facilities. Washing machine provision has improved and there is a laundry service. Married quarters to those merely contemplating marriage. **Drink:** Excellent bar. Pickerel is **the** Magdalene pub. **Eats:** Hall: good value. Beware however of the fixed kitchen charge paid on the bill by everyone however often, or not, they eat in college. **Ents:** Limited in college. Excellent student bands regularly round town. **Sports:** Facilities – excellent and free at college/university level for major field sports; free playing fields, squash, swimming and most others. **Hardship funds:** College is poor but helps out readily. **Travel:** Excellent scholarships – especially the Power Scholarship to Michigan. Funds for individual travel are increasing with more endowment becoming available. **Work:** No term time work allowed officially. During vac college employs staff to help.

Alumni (Editors' pick)

Lord Ezra, Lord Justice Cumming-Bruce, Professor J Boardman, Sir Michael Redgrave, Lord Ramsay, Nick Estcourt, Gavin Hastings, Anthony Jay, Bamber Gascoigne, Samuel Pepys, I A Richards, Charles Kingsley, Lord Pilkington, Jonathan Ridgeon, William Burt, Viscount Melia, Lord Derby, Prince Szudek (of Poland).

NEW HALL

New Hall, Huntingdon Road, Cambridge CB3 0DF (0223 351721)

Founded: 1954, women only. **Accommodation:** All first and third years in college (some shared, split-level rooms). Rent: 88% in accommodation where rent controlled by college. Most undergraduates charged £684 pa, (range £504–£1,165). Single room, including background heating and cleaning approx £315 per term plus £78 kitchen overheads charge. **Eating arrangements:** Cafeteria system (pay as you eat), formal meals and self-catering, including vegetarian (special arrangements for particular requirements). **Gate/guest hours:** None. **Special features:** One of the newer colleges of the university and intends to continue to admit only women. **Admission:** Most candidates admitted on conditional offer largely based on A-level, IB, CSYS only, although maths candidates will be asked to take Step or S-level. Some candidates, post A-level, admitted on school record and interview. Mature candidates assessed on individual basis. **Academic features:** Library, computer facilities with links to University computer. **Scholarships:** Given to students in residence. **Hardship funds:** Funds available for personal maintenance, travel, equipment etc, for home and overseas students, but not full funding. **Travel grants:** Awarded annually. **Other college facilities:** Lecture room with projector, party room, bar, art studio, sewing room, darkroom, video room, squash court, tennis courts and croquet lawn; sports ground shared with Fitzwilliam and Churchill. **Largest fields of study:** English, modern & medieval languages, natural sciences.

European Community: 10% first degree students take EC language and spend 6 months or more in another EC country as part of course. No formal exchange links with EC universities/colleges. Participates in Erasmus scheme. Students may study for certificate or diploma in European language. Language options available in English and History Tripos.

College fees for 1992/93 (undergraduate) £2,727.

Undergraduates: 314 (Women only)

Postgraduates: 82

Teaching staff: *Men:* 11 fellows, 2 research fellows, 10 lecturers, 1 appointed supervisor, 6 external directors of studies *Women:* 24 fellows, 5 research fellows, 18 lecturers, 4 appointed supervisors, 5 external directors of studies.

What it's like

Set in beautiful gardens, New Hall is known for its Dome (strikingly modern art collection) and the fact it is an all-women's college. The atmosphere is friendly and relaxed and student/Fellow relationships are better than average. The college has many thriving societies including a boat club, music society, photographic society and many sports teams. There is a chance to get involved with the running of college by joining one of the liaison committees or the college union. As well as looking after the welfare of the students NH Union organises regular entertainment including the summer event in May Week. All college facilities, including the library, computer room and laundry are accessible 24 hours a day. The cafeteria food is fine but if you prefer to cook for yourself there are kitchens throughout the college. As well as cheap drinks, the bar has a pool table and juke box but most students seem to socialise in other colleges. (It is said they have the 'best of both worlds'.) New Hall students are well represented in the university societies and sports team. The college offers all tripos subjects and will arrange supervisors from outside college who are specialists in particular subjects.

Pauper notes

Accommodation: College or college hostel accommodation for all 1st and 3rd years. **Drink:** New Hall bar cheap. **Eats:** Cafeteria system (meal costs just over £1). Good vegetarian selection. Formal hall with waitress service on a Tuesday evening. No breakfast provided. Large selection of restaurants in town. **Ents:** Bands/discos evening twice a term – cost £1–£1.50; easy to go to discos, films at other colleges. 2 cinemas in town. **Sports:** Squash court, 2 tennis courts, table tennis table, large boat club. Most sports represented by college teams. **Hardship funds:** Hardship fund. **Travel:** Travel grants and vacation study grants available. **Work:** Not allowed during term.

Alumni (Editors' pick)

Tilda Swinton (film star), Joanna MacGregor (concert pianist), Sonia Ruseler (presenter of 12.30 pm News).

NEWNHAM

Newnham College, Cambridge CB3 9DF (0223 335700)

Founded: 1871, women only. **Special features:** Large grounds with plenty of accommodation and sports facilities on site. Artist in residence. **Academic features:** Good balance of academic subjects. **Accommodation:** Most undergraduates are given their own study-bedroom in college for all three years (no shared rooms). Rent: 95% in accommodation where rent controlled by college. All undergraduates charged £1,105 pa, including heating and subsidised buttery.

CAN'T FIND WHAT YOU'RE LOOKING FOR? USE THE INDEX!

Eating arrangements: Modern dining room for cafeteria service, and hall for formal dinners. All meals paid for in cash. Guests welcomed. Undergraduates may also cater for themselves. **Gate/guest hours:** Students and their guests are free to come and go at all times. **Admission:** Mainly on A-level grades and interviews, with some use of S-papers or Step. **Scholarships:** Scholarships and exhibitions awarded on results of University exams. **Travel and book grants:** Funds available. **Hardship funds:** Several College and University funds available. **Library:** 85,000 volumes, large antiquarian collection. **Other college facilities:** Bar, undergraduate kitchens; launderette; sewing machines; a music room with harpsichord; practice rooms with pianos; table tennis room, nearby squash court, playing fields in college grounds; punt hire scheme in summer. Microcomputer and word processor with link to university's main frame computer. Multi-gym.

European Community: 15% first degree students take EC language as part of course and 10% spend 6 months or more in another EC country. Formal exchange links with large number of EC universities/colleges including Rome (all students may go in the summer); classics link with the British School in Rome and Athens.

College fees for 1992/93 (undergraduate) £2,724.

Undergraduates: 390 (Women only)

Postgraduates: 90

Teaching staff: *Men:* 3 college lecturers, 4 special supervisors *Women:* 37 fellows, 6 research fellows, 4 special supervisors.

What it's like

One of the two remaining single sex colleges, it's a newish college by Cambridge standards. Victorian red brick buildings covered in climbing ivy enclose large gardens which are used by undergraduates for sunbathing and garden parties in summer. However our long corridor makes it possible to avoid the cold in winter.

It's just off the tourist trail so is left relatively undisturbed, but it is close to the Sidgwick Site of the university and about five minutes by bike from other faculties and town centre. The gardens are some of the most beautiful in Cambridge.

Newnhamites are a very diverse bunch including the most extrovert to the most reserved. Most undergraduates choose to live in for all three years, reflecting the high standard of accommodation and the relaxed rules. Rooms are large, fully furnished and well heated. First-year rooms are allocated, in subsequent years they are chosen by a ballot system. One modern building has rooms with sinks. No rooms are shared. There are no bedders which gives added privacy. Cooking facilities are above average in Cambridge and the buttery is reasonably priced, with vegetarian options.

In sport, Newnham has an active boat club with one of the fastest ladies' crews on the river. (It shares boathouse with Jesus.) College teams also do well in tennis, cricket, football, netball, hockey, cross-country running and netball. All standards are welcome and for the very keen there are university teams in most sports. The college has its own multigym, as well as sports fields within college grounds.

The Raleigh Music Society has a large membership and gives weekly recitals in college hall. Drama is catered for by the Anonymous Players, newly formed but very active.

Newnham is politically apathetic, but is well represented in university societies. Many Newnhamites are involved in student journalism.

Newnham's student-run bar is very lively, with special events and weekly promotions. It is very popular for socialising after the weekly formal hall, to which undergraduates often bring guests. The regular bops are always well attended. JCR organises regular ents, often with Robinson. The first two Newnham May Balls (in 1988 and 1990) were student organised and hugely successful and there is due to be another one in 1992.

Academically, Newnham is very supportive and students have less pressure on them than in other colleges; standards are high in both arts and sciences with one of the best equipped libraries in Cambridge. If anyone gets into financial difficulty it's generous with its funds. Students are not known to drop out due to money problems.

Newnham students socialise widely outside the college and tend to go home when they want to get away from the pressure of a predominantly male university.

The JCR encourages recycling schemes for paper and glass.

Pauper notes

Accommodation: Live in all 3 years, but possible to live out. 3 graduate houses. **Drink:** Cheap college bars. Many town pubs – The Bath, The Anchor (jazz live), Cambridge Arms, The Granta (on the River Cam). **Eats:** Veggie: King's Pantry; Clowns; Tatties; The Little Rose Restaurant; Eraina. **Ents:** Cheap college 'bops' and bands in most colleges each term – Christ's and Robinson College film societies. Night Clubs – Route 66, Cinderella Rockerfellas. **Sports:** At Newnham – free multigym; hockey pitch/football, tennis courts, shared squash courts, University badminton courts. Kelsey Kerridge sports hall and swimming pool. **Hardship funds:** Lots – college and university. Access grants, discretionary college loans, books, vacation grants. **Travel:** Travel grants available. Bike hire scheme, student rates with NUS card. **Work:** College bar, catering during term. Work (eg in pubs) available in town. Vacation: catering dept, housekeeping, library.

More info?

Get students' Alternative Prospectus.
Enquiries to Claire L Nortcliffe 0223 335761.

Alumni (Editors' pick)

Baroness Seear, Baroness David, Julia Neuberger, Frances Gumley, Sarah Rowland Jones, Dorothy Hodgkin, Margaret Drabble, A.S. Byatt, Germaine Greer, Sylvia Plath, Joan Bakewell, Susie Menkes, Miriam Margolis, Katharine Whitehorn, Shirley Williams, Emma Thompson, Ann Mallalieu, Mary Archer.

PEMBROKE

Pembroke College, Cambridge CB2 1RF (0223 338100)

Founded: 1347. Women undergraduates first admitted 1984. **Accommodation:** Mainly single study bedrooms centrally heated with wash basins; some 2-roomed sets. All first years live in college; others in college or nearby college hostels. Some married accommodation in flats and houses. Rent: 95% in accommodation where rent controlled by college. Most undergraduates charged £900 pa (range £870– £1,080). **Eating arrangements:** Self-service breakfast, lunch and evening meal. Formal dinner. Fixed charge (1992/93) of £222 pa; in addition meals are paid for as taken (eg dinner £2.70). **Gate/guest hours:** Gates closed 2 till 6 am, but with access for keyholders. Overnight guests permitted by prior arrangement; other guests leave by 2 am. **Admission:** Write to Tutor for Admissions to apply or for advice. Applications for admission on A-level or equivalent results or by conditional offer. **Scholarships:** College and Foundation scholarships, exhibitions and prizes awarded for merit in university examinations. **Hardship funds:** Some assistance may be given from Trust Funds. **Travel grants:** Grants towards cost of vacation travel for suitable projects, and to graduate students for research visits. **Library:** Reading and borrowing facilities in all degree subjects. Word processing and computing rooms, linked to CU data network.**Other college facilities:** Sports (cricket, hockey, rowing, rugby, soccer, squash, netball, tennis, table tennis), music (rehearsal rooms, pianos, organ, Instrumental Awards scheme), drama room, photographic darkroom. **Social:** Junior parlour, bar, party cellar, extensive gardens.

European Community: 15% first degree students take EC language as part of course and 6% spend 6 months or more in another EC country. No formal exchange links with EC universities/colleges.

College fees for 1992/93 (undergraduate) £2,709.

Undergraduates: *Men:* 224 *Women:* 128

Postgraduates: *Men:* 100 *Women:* 40

Teaching staff: *Men:* 37 fellows, 5 research fellows *Women:* 3 fellows, 1 research fellow.

What it's like

Founded 1347: medieval courtyard, architecture pleasant and homely, beautiful gardens. Very central and well located for most subjects. College accommodation for all 1st years; in total 45% live in, others live in nearby college owned hostels. Standard variable but on the whole good. No provision for married students. Food available on a cafeteria basis; breakfast good, lunch and supper dull though an alternative waitress-service dinner (Formal Hall) each night is good. Cooking facilities are limited. JP (Junior Parlour – College SU) active socially rather than politically and relations with the fellows are good. Undergraduates are outgoing, friendly and going places. Bicycles necessary (car ownership is very limited for Cambridge undergrads). Fine college library, bar, soundproof music rooms, video room, party rooms, college catered private functions and a large sports ground. Officially no overnight guests of opposite sex but very rarely enforced (condom machine provided). Sport is very strong, especially rowing, cricket and rugby. Opportunities are also plentiful in the arts, notably drama and music. Strong subjects: natural science, English, economics, engineering, oriental studies. Changing subject fairly easy. 10% overseas.

Pauper notes

Accommodation: Virtually everyone in relatively cheap college rooms or college hostels. **Drink:** Excellent cheap bar with very friendly barman. Cross Keys very popular with all sports clubs. **Eats:** Market is very good for fruit. Cheap student restaurants nearby. Reciprocal arrangements with other colleges, particularly Girton where food excellent and cheaper. **Ents:** Regular college films and free video room for hire. Much cheap and often good student theatre and close to Arts Theatre. Weekly university wide student night at local nightclub and regular college discos. **Sports:** Wide range of facilities although not always in top condition – own boathouse with rowing machine; football/rugby/cricket grounds, squash and tennis courts. University gym free. **Hardship funds:** Access funds well organised but no specific college funds unless you get a first. **Travel:** Number of travel awards – easy to get one. **Work:** Pembroke library supervision £1/hour to sit and study.

Alumni (Editors' pick)

R Porter, Peter May, Ted Hughes, Tom Sharpe, Christopher Hogwood, Clive James, Peter Cook, Eric Idle, Bill Oddie, Tim Brooke-Taylor, Ray Dolby, R A Butler, David Monroe, William Pitt, Thomas Gray, Edmund Spenser, Sir Robert Sainsbury, Lord Prior.

GET HOLD OF THE PROSPECTUSES

PETERHOUSE

Peterhouse, Cambridge CB2 1RD (0223 338200)

Admissions Tutor (0223) 338273

Admissions Secretary (0223) 338201

Founded: 1284; women undergraduates first admitted 1985. **Accommodation:** All first and third years offered rooms in college. All second years live in college accommodation, adjacent to Peterhouse. Most undergraduates charged £280 per term (range £175–£327). **Eating arrangements:** All meals provided in hall (breakfast 95p or £1.40, lunch £1.40, dinner £2.10). **Gate/guest hours:** Gates close at 2 am, when guests, other than overnight guests, required to leave; gate keys issued for out-of-hours use. **Admission:** Flexible admissions policy. Realistic level of offers, with low ratio of offers to places. All candidates interviewed: mode of admission tailored to individual cases. No undergraduates admitted for geography, land economy or veterinary medicine. **Scholarships:** Examination, prizes, scholarships and exhibitions (£50 to £150) for performance in tripos; annual organ scholarship (£250); music awards (£50 plus tuition); further named college examination prizes in history, law, mathematics, engineering, medicine and music. **Hardship funds:** Fund administered by Tutors. **Travel grants:** Approx 30 travel grants awarded pa (average value £200). **Library:** Approx 35,000 volumes. **Other college facilities:** Bar, croquet lawns, squash court, multi-gym, computer room, punts, washing machines, playing fields, boathouse. New library, theatre and concert hall. **Largest fields of study:** History, natural sciences, engineering.

European Community: 3% first degree students take EC language as part of course and 2% spend 6 months or more in another EC country. No formal exchange links with EC universities/colleges.

College fees for 1991/92 (undergraduate) £2,547.

Undergraduates: *Men:* 169 *Women:* 64

Postgraduates: *Men:* 64 *Women:* 19

Teaching staff: *Men:* 27 fellows, 7 research fellows, 2 bye-fellows *Women:* 1 fellow, 2 research fellows.

What it's like

Peterhouse has a lively and friendly student community. We are the oldest and smallest Cambridge college, and as such provide an excellent launch-pad to university life. Peterhouse students do not conform to the most common Oxbridge stereotypes. The college authorities do not believe in positive discrimination assuring the diversity of the student body. If they think you are bright enough they'll offer you a place, regardless of your ethnic, social or religious background.

We have no pretensions (or desire) to be at the intellectual cutting edge of Cambridge, and languish in glorious anonymity in the middle of the academic table. However, Peterhouse students perform consistently well in certain subject areas, most notoriously, history and law.

Accommodation is of a high standard, and the college provides undergraduates with rooms for all three years. Perhaps surprisingly, Peterhouse rents are not too expensive (an average room costing about £280 per term). Indeed, this year's JCR negotiated the lowest rent rise in the university. All meals take place in the college's thirteenth-century hall. Food varies from being curious to identifiable, but standards are improving, particularly for vegetarians.

The JCR suffers from perennial financial difficulties which the college take delight in ignoring, but basic services are provided. These include an excellent bar, a common room with television and daily newspapers, a pool room and a launderette. Microwave ovens are a recent and welcome improvement. A new computer room offers state-of-the-art word processing equipment for student use.

CAN'T FIND WHAT YOU'RE LOOKING FOR? USE THE INDEX!

Peterhouse has its own boat club and is steadily improving its stature in college rowing. We also share a sports ground with Clare College which boasts two football pitches, a Rugby pitch and an all-weather tennis court. There is a well-equipped multi-gym within the college buildings.

Above all else, Peterhouse is a tolerant college. Apathy (be it political or social) can sometimes be a problem, but the college is very much on the up. Comfortable and unpretentious, Peterhouse is a great place to spend your university career.

Edward O'Connor, JCR President

Pauper notes

Accommodation: Some shared same-sex sets and married quarters for graduates only. **Drink:** College bar is loud and cheap. Ace local pubs The Cross Keys and The Mill. **Eats:** Cambridge is expensive but there are some cheap spots – Curry Centre and The Little Rose. **Ents:** Film Society Bops, Bar and Pool Room. **Sports:** Kelsey Kerridge Sports Hall is a cheap supplement to college facilities. **Hardship funds:** Some available. **Travel:** Excellent travel grants, usually around £100–£200. **Work:** Vacation grants for work in college over the holidays.

Informal name

(i) Pothouse; (ii) Piphouse; (iii) Pettyhouse.

QUEENS'

Queens' College, Cambridge CB3 9ET
(0223 335540; Fax 0223 335522)

Founded: 1446; women undergraduates first admitted 1980. **Accommodation:** All undergraduates can live in college for all 3 years (sets and bedsits, medieval and modern, all with central heating and modern bathrooms). 90% in accommodation where rent controlled by college. Most undergraduates charged £260 per term (range £230–£320). **Eating arrangements:** Self-service for all meals; formal dinner also available. **Gate/guest hours:** Very relaxed. **Admission:** Entry in all subjects is via conditional offers based on A-levels. For mathematics, medicine and natural sciences only S-levels or Step are used, according to candidate's choice. All candidates interviewed. Several open days each year for prospective candidates. Undergraduates not admitted to study following in first year: chemical engineering, education, electrical & information sciences, history of art, manufacturing engineering, management studies. **Scholarships:** Not awarded on entrance but on subsequent university examinations. Bursaries available for eligible overseas students. **Travel grants:** Awards made from college expedition fund and other funds as well as grants to individuals. **Library:** Undergraduate library with copies of all course books; full borrowing facilities both in term and over vacation. Law library. Micro-computers and terminals with access to University main frame. **Hardship funds:** Several funds to help those who suffer financial difficulty. **Other college facilities:** Bar, 220-seat theatre, squash courts, table tennis, croquet, punts, organ, piano, harpsichord, record library, dark room, launderette, rooms for TV; new boathouse and playing fields nearby.

European Community: Number of students learning an EC language or spending time in another EC country, not known.

College fees for 1992/93 (undergraduate) £2,667.

Undergraduates: *Men:* 261 *Women:* 181

Postgraduates: *Men:* 168 *Women:* 76

Teaching staff: *Men:* 42 fellows, 5 research fellows, 37 lecturers
Women: 5 fellows, 5 lecturers, 1 lector

What it's like

It's a centrally located college containing about 450 undergraduates from a good mixture of backgrounds. For Oxbridge it has a high proportion of state school entrants and female students. Academically the college performs consistently well (usually featuring in the top 4), but the students are bright rather than self-consciously intellectual. The college is socially very active and a newly built multi-purpose hall has created one of the best theatre, cinema and disco locations in Cambridge.

The buildings cover a wide variety of ages and styles, from the medieval Old Court through to the very much twentieth-century Cripps development. The college straddles the river Cam and is famous for the misnamed Mathematical Bridge, which was not in fact designed by Newton.

Accommodation tends to be either beautiful or have good facilities, though not usually both. Rooms are on the whole large but self catering is discouraged and difficult (though by no means impossible).

The best way to judge the atmosphere of the college is to attend an open day. If possible come and have a look around and see for yourself why this is now the most popular college in Cambridge.

James Robertson

Pauper notes

Accommodation: Accommodation for all students, some in a disused nurses' home. No mixed sharing, but rents still fairly reasonable; college crêche. **Drink:** Local brews: Greene King, Tolly Cobbold. Bar relatively cheap – pubs in town varied. **Eats:** Town: wide variety from Pizza Hut to high class dining clubs. College: standard high – increasingly varied options, caters for vegetarians – attempts some more ethnic options. **Ents:** College discos – 2 every weekend, varied music; bands in the bar. Town: 2 large clubs and the gig venues – Corn Exchange and The Junction. **Sports:** Cheap/good sports centre 10 min walk. On college site: squash, badminton, gym – sports ground 1.5 miles. All major sports (even Tiddlywinks! European championships held in old hall!); strengths – rugby, football, rowing, squash and basketball and open air swimming pool nearby. **Hardship funds:** College very accommodating – quiet word to tutor goes a long way. **Travel:** STA Travel in town very cheap; college gives limited grants. **Work:** Some bar work/guided punting in summer – work during May Balls.

More info?

Enquiries to Sophie Webster, JCR President (0223 335511).

Informal name

Queen's

Buzz-words

Plodge (Porters' Lodge); JCR/Junior Combination Room (Students' Union).

Alumni (Editors' pick)

Archbishop of Sydney, Stephen Fry, Erasmus, Graham Swift.

ROBINSON
Robinson College, Cambridge CB3 9AN (0223 311431)

Founded: 1977; women undergraduates first admitted 1979. **Accommodation:** Study bedrooms, majority with own bathroom for approximately 340 undergraduates. Rent: 85% in accommodation where rent controlled by college. Most undergraduates charged £876 pa (range £498–£1,143). **Eating arrangements:** Both cafeteria and formal Hall; residents required to pay fixed kitchen charge. **Gate/guest hours:** Unaccompanied guests not allowed after midnight.

CAN'T FIND WHAT YOU'RE LOOKING FOR? USE THE INDEX!

Admission: Applicants considered by all available entry routes. **Scholarships:** Scholarships awarded on tripos results. **Hardship funds:** A Hardship Fund is available. **Other college facilities:** Cafeteria, bar, music rooms, auditorium; joint sports ground with Queens'; boathouse shared.

European Community: 10% first degree students take EC language as part of course and 3% spend 6 months+ in another EC country. No formal exchange links with EC universities/colleges; small numbers of visiting EC students.

College fees for 1992/93 (undergraduate) £2,682.

Undergraduates: *Men:* 266 *Women:* 126

Postgraduates: *Men:* 62 *Women:* 24

Teaching staff: *Men:* 31 fellows, 6 research fellows, 2 lecturers *Women:* 10 fellows, 1 research fellow, 3 lecturers.

What it's like

Robinson has none of the imagined hallmarks of a Cambridge college – Chariots of Fire, picturesque courtyards, crusty porters, students in tweeds and cravats. Built 17 years ago, funded by a man who made his money in radio rentals and racehorses, it makes up in originality what it lacks in tradition and antiquity. Average student is not the eccentric, loaded Oxbridge undergraduate many imagine; admissions procedure discriminates positively towards applicants from state schools, which makes for a good mix and friendly atmosphere. A policy combating sexual, racial, religious harassment recently introduced.

Predominantly red brick, very unusual architecture; also built to be a conference centre, so superb accommodation: all rooms are centrally heated (not the norm in Cambridge), comfortably furnished. About 50% first year have a private bathroom. Dual-purpose nature also provides excellent facilities: best auditorium in Cambridge, well-equipped party room, record library and hi-fi room and dark room plus the usual music rooms, games room, laundry, common rooms etc. Bar is run by paid staff rather than students; very much the focus of college life – people go there to be sociable, not just to drink! Food fairly expensive but good.

Very active students' association aims to represent and campaign for students; provides a forum for students' views, a variety of social events and funds college sports clubs and societies. Rowing, rugby and hockey teams recently hot competition in their fields; anyone with an interest, however humble, can enjoy the excellent facilities provided. Chapel choir and music society, and the dramatic society all active. Other societies, include debating, films, art, photographic; you are sure to find something to your taste. Above all, Robinson is a college where anyone can fit in and feel they belong.

Pauper notes

Accommodation: Expensive but most people live in. Two flats for married students. **Drink:** Bar good, but not cheap by other student bars' standards. **Eats:** Good, if pricey cafeteria. Exceptional Hall twice a week. Vegetarian OK; reduced kitchen charges for orthodox Jews and Moslems. Bar snacks. **Ents:** Regular on campus films, bands, discos and 'events'. **Sports:** Boathouse, playing fields, squash and tennis courts, volleyball, table tennis room all nearby. **Hardship funds:** Many available, widely publicised; college authorities seriously addressing the problem and have made substantial funds available. **Work:** College employs 20 students each vacation at good wage, with rent free accommodation.

ST CATHARINE'S

St Catharine's College, Cambridge CB2 1RL (0223 338300)

Founded: 1473; women undergraduates first admitted 1979. **Accommodation:** Most undergraduates spend 3 years in college accommodation; current charge

£850 pa (range £600–£945). **Eating arrangements:** All meals available in college dining hall. No compulsory meals. **Gate/guest hours:** Keys issued on payment of deposit; guest rooms for limited periods. **Admission:** College makes conditional offers on A-level results, and occasionally also on S-level or Step examinations. **Travel grants:** Various grants available. **Hardship funds:** Various funds available. **Library:** 3 college libraries. **Other college facilities:** Large new 3 manual organ, music practice room with grand piano; sports field with pavilion, squash, badminton, and tennis courts; boathouse; computer facilities; new graduate common room.

European Community: 8% first degree students take EC language as part of course and 8% spend 6 months or more in another EC country. Formal exchange links with Heidelberg (open to all undergraduates).

College fees for 1992/93 (undergraduate) £2,622.

Undergraduates: *Men:* 259 *Women:* 165

Postgraduates: *Men:* 95 *Women:* 34

Teaching staff: *Men:* 41 fellows, 8 research fellows, 1 lecturer *Women:* 5 fellows, 1 research fellow.

What it's like

Visually not one of the most impressive Cambridge colleges, its relatively small size makes St Catharine's one of the most friendly. Most students are able to live in college accommodation for all three years of their degree course, accommodation which ranges from decidedly poky to well above average; for the unfortunate few who have to live out however accommodation can be difficult to find in Cambridge, and is often fairly pricey.

Students come from a very wide range of backgrounds and most tend to accept one another regardless of social background. Politically the college's reputation seems to be shifting from that of a notoriously apathetic college to one with a very strong and active left wing, many students being actively involved in the university Labour students' group. As with any college, however, the students hold a very wide range of views and there is the inevitable handful of bigots.

The JCR committee, elected by and from the undergraduate body represents students in all aspects of college life, including organising a wide range of entertainments, financing the numerous college sports clubs and societies, and negotiating with the fellows of the college via the College Consultative Committee, a body comprising the JCR committee and several selected fellows.

Within the university itself it is possible to become involved in virtually any activity you could wish for, including a wide range of sports, drama, film-making, the list is almost endless. There is also a very strong network of support groups to make a student's life at Cambridge bearable in times of stress, including an eating-disorder group, several women's groups, gay and lesbian societies and an overseas students' society.

Students discover their own niches no matter what their background or beliefs; the intimate atmosphere of St Catharine's provides a valuable sense of security whilst incorporating the obvious benefits of a large university.

Ruth Entwistle

Pauper notes

Accommodation: Cheap Cambridge accommodation very hard to find but it can be done if you look early and hard enough. **Drink:** A number of good pubs in Cambridge (The Mill being the closest to Cats) but tend to be quite expensive – college bars cheaper. **Eats:** All colleges cater for vegetarians; very wide range of restaurants in town, varying price ranges and qualities. **Ents:** Very good for films and plays, not so good for nightclubs, although college ents committees arrange regular bops. New venue 'The Junction' very good. **Sports:** Very strong in university. Town facilities good but fairly expensive. **Hardship funds:** Students have to be very definitely in need. **Travel:** Travel scholarships easily available. **Work:** During term frowned upon, not available in college. Vacation jobs can be found both in town and college.

Alumni (Editors' pick)

Howard Brenton (controversial playwright), Emma Thompson and Ian McKellan (actors).

ST EDMUND'S

St Edmund's College, Cambridge CB3 0BN (0223 350398)

Founded: 1896; women undergraduates first admitted 1975. **Accommodation:** 80 single students in college rooms plus 5 apartments for married students with children. Most undergraduates charged £990 pa (range £750–£1,200). **Admission:** Primarily a graduate college. Admits some mature and affiliated undergraduates (21 and over) for any subject except medicine, veterinary medicine. **Other college facilities:** Micro-computing facilities (terminal to university mainframe); bar; football pitch, tennis courts, croquet lawn, boat club.

College fees for 1992/93 (undergraduate) £2,445.

Teaching staff: *Men:* 23 fellows, 4 research fellows, 12 lecturers, 3 research assistants *Women:* 4 fellows, 1 research fellow, 1 research assistant.

ST JOHN'S

St John's College, Cambridge CB2 1TP (0223 338600)

Founded: 1511; women undergraduates first admitted 1981. **Accommodation:** Normally accommodation in college is available to undergraduates in all three years. Most undergraduates charged £1,362 pa (range £1,245–£1,425). **Eating arrangements:** Self-service buttery dining room; formal dinner also available 6 evenings a week. **Gate/guest hours:** College members may come and go as they wish; certain regulations regarding overnight guests. **Admission:** Candidates are welcome to apply for conditional offers (which may include S or Step grades) or on the basis of A-levels already taken. **Scholarships:** Scholarships awarded to members of the college on the basis of examinations. Scholars receive generous book grants and other privileges. **Travel grants:** Available. **Library:** College library (early 17th century) with over 100,000 volumes, ranging from medieval manuscripts to modern university textbooks; reading rooms; full set of Law Reports; skeletons for medical students. A new library building is under construction. **Other college facilities:** Bar, college orchestra and musical society, theatre in School of Pythagoras; Fisher Building including music practice rooms, art studio, drawing office and large auditorium; 26-acre playing fields near college; modern squash courts, table tennis and billiards rooms, pool for college punts. Book grants available for textbooks; computer room with data links to University network.

European Community: Number of students learning an EC language or spending time in another EC country, not known.

College fees for 1992/93 (undergraduate) £2,502.

Undergraduates: *Men:* 372 *Women:* 160

Postgraduates: *Men:* 163 *Women:* 72

Teaching staff: *Men:* 61 fellows, 11 research fellows, 7 college lecturers *Women:* 5 fellows, 4 research fellows, 2 college lecturers, 1 lector.

What it's like

Architecturally beautiful and can accommodate undergraduates for all 3 years often in large, comfortable sets of rooms. Excellent on-site facilities: theatre/cinema, sportsfields and squash courts, fleet of punts, bar and music rooms. College academically strong. Generous book grants and travel scholarships (college is rich). Strong rowing tradition. Active JCR committee puts on events throughout year. Being in town centre, access to everything in Cambridge easy: most get involved in activities outside college. Major acting, debating and political societies currently run by St John's. College choir world-famous.

Pauper notes

Accommodation: More expensive than many colleges but excellent. You may find cheaper but not better elsewhere, and there's college accommodation for all 3 years. **Drink:** Quite cheap in college bar. **Eats:** Cheap in college buttery; vegetarians catered for. **Ents:** Good cheap ents in college most weekends. **Hardship funds:** Available from the college in real case of hardship. **Work:** Not really available or encouraged during term-time.

Alumni (Editors' pick)

Jonathan Miller (author, producer, broadcaster), J Michael Brearley (former England cricket captain), Piers Paul Read (novelist), William Wordsworth, Trevor Bailey, Douglas Adams, Rob Andrew, Derek Jacobi.

SELWYN

Selwyn College, Cambridge CB3 9DQ (0223 335846)

Founded: 1882; women undergraduates first admitted 1976. **Accommodation:** All unmarried undergraduates live in college rooms for all 3 years. Most charged £850 pa (range £490–£1,070). **Eating arrangements:** Breakfast, lunch and dinner taken in hall; informal self-service and formal dinner. **Gate/guest hours:** College gates closed between 2 and 6 am; late keys obtainable. Undergraduates permitted to put up a guest in their own rooms. **Admission:** By conditional pre A-level offer after interview; some places offered on A-levels, school reports and interviews. All applicants resident in the UK are invited for interview. **Scholarships:** Organ scholarships awarded 2 years out of 3; annual choral exhibitions; annual instrumental exhibitions; book prizes, scholarships and exhibitions awarded to firsts and other outstanding performances in university examinations. **Hardship funds:** Chadwick Fund, Keasbey awards. **Travel grants:** Available. **Other college facilities:** Bar, undergraduate shop, 3 rooms for private functions, drama facilities; music practice rooms; photographic dark room; shared sports ground with King's College. Newly extended library with law reading room; computer room. Choral evensong 3 times weekly, new organ being installed. **Largest fields of study:** Engineering, history, modern languages, natural sciences.

European Community: 25% students study an EC language as part of their course; 10% spend a period in another EC country. College has foreign national lecturers in French and German.

College fees: for 1992/93 (undergraduate) £2,721.

Undergraduates: *Men:* 198 *Women:* 133

Postgraduates: *Men:* 73 *Women:* 27

Teaching staff: *Men:* 55 fellows, 2 research fellows, 35 lecturers
Women: 5 fellows, 3 research fellows, 2 lecturers.

CAN'T FIND WHAT YOU'RE LOOKING FOR? USE THE INDEX!

What it's like

It's next to the Sidgewick (arts) site and the University Library, well off the tourist routes. Buildings are a mixture: neo-gothic to 1960s. Bravery, brashness and broccoli is the stuff of which men and women of Selwyn are made.

Most introspective, and least overtly intellectual of Cambridge colleges; life lived at high speed. With term lasting a mere eight weeks, the lecturers' determination to cram as much information into students' skulls is only matched by the same students' desire to put such cerebral pursuits firmly in their place and spend their time on the more important things of life. Most reach a suitable balance, thus satisfying both the expectations of their tutors and the demands of, for example, the determined and successful Boat Club.

What else? Musical menageries, variously attended societies, pointless parties, pseudo-intellectuals, committed Christians, strange slang, friendly Fellows, the cheapest (and best) Ball in town, a magazine named after the national bird of New Zealand. All this, and a library with a goldfish bowl extension that is almost impossible to get into. Truly a place with plenty of character, and a lot of fun.

Pauper notes

Accommodation: College houses all undergraduates in good quality rooms £160–£320 for term. £80 kitchen fixed charge. **Drink:** Selwyn bar good atmosphere – cheaper than pubs but not subsidised. Good local breweries inc Greene King, Abbot, Tolly Cobbold. **Eats:** College canteen has good range of dishes, including vegetarian, vegan (on request) and kosher (on request and expensive). Most meals cost £1–£1.50. **Ents:** College – cheap and regular eg 4 per term: discos, bands, cocktail parties etc. Univ – sparse but improving. Ents tend to be college based and run. **Sports:** College – lively, good participation. Good place to learn to row. Excellent facilities – ¾ mile from college. Univ sports centre 1.5 miles. Town sports centre 1.5 miles. **Hardship funds:** Selwyn College has two hardship funds. Students apply via their tutor. **Travel:** College **very** generous with scholarships for vac travel. **Work:** Univ/college authorities don't object. Work in pubs/restaurants easy to find.

More info?

Enquiries to First Year Representative (0223 335846).

Alumni (Editors' pick)

Malcolm Muggeridge, E R Nixon, Lord Rayner, D Trelford, D Lumsden, Simon Hughes MP, Rt Hon John Selwyn Gummer, Huw Davies.

SIDNEY SUSSEX
Sidney Sussex College, Cambridge CB2 3HU (0223 338800)

Founded: 1596; women undergraduates first admitted 1976. **Accommodation:** All undergraduates may spend all three years in college accommodation without sharing rooms. Most charged £720 pa (range £600–£960). **Eating arrangements:** All meals may be taken in hall; also self-catering facilities. **Gate/guest hours:** Until 2 am; keys available for late admission. **Admission:** Places are given on the basis of performance in public examinations. Detailed advice is available from the Admissions Tutors. **Scholarships:** Unlimited number of scholarships, exhibitions and prizes awarded on performance in university examinations; Evan Lewis-Thomas Law Studentships for law graduates to prepare for practice as barristers and solicitors. **Travel grants:** Available. **Hardship funds:** Funds available to assist undergraduate and graduate students. **Library:** Modern, open 24 hours. **Other college facilities:** Music practice room with piano, grand piano and harpsichord, new organ; sports field and pavilion shared with Christ's College; modern boat-house shared with Corpus Christi and Girton, and squash and tennis courts; two common rooms, two bars.

WANT TO HELP WITH THE NEXT EDITION – SEE PAGE 76

European Community: 10% study an EC language and spend a period in another EC country as part of their course. Informal exchange links with European Universities being established. 1–2 European students come to the college for one year.

College fees for 1992/93 (undergraduate) £2,724.

Undergraduates: *Men:* 200 *Women:* 105

Postgraduates: *Men:* 64 *Women:* 28

Teaching staff: *Men:* 32 fellows, 7 research fellows *Women:* 4 fellows, 2 research fellows, 1 lecturer.

What it's like

Small (300 undergraduates), co-residential college with pleasant architecture/ gardens and central location. Accommodation is among the cheapest in the university but is good quality and guaranteed to all undergraduates, either in college or in nearby house/hostel. All staircases have washing and catering facilities, though these vary enormously from staircase to staircase. Hall serves three self-service meals a day (except Sundays) and optional formal supper; culinary standard is also variable, but receptive to student suggestions; reasonable choice provided (including vegetarian and choice of salads). Laundry room. Wide and popular range of extra-curricular activities in which anyone, no matter what standard, can participate. Student-run bar doubles as a venue for fortnightly bops; sports facilities include playing-fields and tennis courts (a mile away), a boathouse and squash court; a very successful drama society, plus chapel choir and orchestra. Academically, a gifted Fellowship, reasonable library (open 24 hours/day) and good Tripos results, especially in geography, engineering, classics and economics. Reasonable relations with Fellows – students enjoy full representation on Governing Body and other college committees. Socially, very easy-going with few of the cliques found in other colleges. Probably the friendliest college. A very fair admissions policy means no-one should be discouraged from applying. College keen to obtain as many applicants as possible. SU President available to talk informally about college life and Cambridge in general. Open days from Christmas for sixth-formers. Thriving SU promotes student welfare and provides some focus for limited political debate and activity. Less political apathy than at other colleges.

Pauper notes

Accommodation: Guaranteed for all undergraduates, married accommodation available. Graduates: some rooms available. **Drink:** College bar very cheap, recently refurbished. Lots of pubs near by because college is centrally located. Greene King beers recommended. Good pub: Cambridge Arms. **Eats:** Not very good value – very touristy. Not many take-aways. **Ents:** University theatre (ADC) nearby, weekly productions. Arts Cinema across the road – excellent variety. Bops organised by different colleges and advertised throughout. No good nightclubs. **Sports:** No University sports centre. Cambridge town sports centre relatively expensive. No great skill required to play sport at college level. Wide variety of sports available – emphasis on fun. **Hardship funds:** Fund has been increased to £7,500 a year, administered by tutors. **Travel:** For vacation travel small amount (about £100) available quite easily for second years. £300 for 'deserving cases'. **Work:** Work discouraged during term. However, nights available in college bar.

More info?

Enquiries to Chris Jones, President SSCSU (0223 338860).

Alumni (Editors' pick)

John Patten, David Thomson, C T R Wilson, C F Powell, David Owen, Oliver Cromwell, Asa Briggs (historian).

CAN'T FIND WHAT YOU'RE LOOKING FOR? USE THE INDEX!

TRINITY

Trinity College, Cambridge CB2 1TQ (0223 338400)

Founded: 1546; women undergraduates first admitted 1977. **Accommodation:** All undergraduates are offered rooms in college or college hostels for 3 years. Most charged £600 pa (range £450–£800); £775 with heat and light. **Eating arrangements:** Breakfast, lunch and dinner available in hall on cafeteria system, plus formal dinner. Fixed annual price of £204 plus cash payment for individual meals. Small kitchens on all staircases. **Gate/guest hours:** Great Gate locked at 2 am but college members may enter or leave at any time. **Admission:** Pre A-level candidates considered for conditional offers which may include S-level papers or Step. Post A-level candidates considered on their record. Most candidates will be interviewed. **Scholarships:** Scholarships on university examinations; organ scholarship (£250 pa) offered in alternate years, 6 choral exhibitions (£100 pa) offered annually; numerous college prizes. **Travel grants:** Grants for projects and research; small grants for vacation travel. **Library:** Magnificent Wren Library with over 50,000 volumes plus a reading room; separate law reading room. **Other college facilities:** 3 large common rooms, bar, games and party rooms, buttery, 2 launderettes, record lending library, music room with pianos and harpsichord, small theatre; 3 sports grounds, squash, tennis and badminton courts; boathouse with excellent modern facilities. **Largest fields of study:** Natural sciences, medical sciences, mathematics, economics, English, engineering, law, modern languages, history.

European Community: 10% first degree students take EC language as part of course and 7% spend 6 months or more in another EC country. No formal exchange links with EC universities/colleges.

College fees for 1992/93 (undergraduate) £2,487.

Undergraduates: *Men:* 504 *Women:* 144

Postgraduates: *Men:* 192 *Women:* 71

Teaching staff: *Men:* 56 fellows, 16 research fellows, 15 professional fellows *Women:* 4 fellows, 5 research fellows, 1 professional fellow.

What it's like

Big's the first word that comes into peoples heads if asked to describe Trinity. It's also the only specific comment that you can make about this college. As the largest in Cambridge (just under a thousand at last count) it is the most diverse. Although the stereotype image is that Trinity's full of wealthy public school types this has little basis in fact. It's only partly full of them. There are a wealth of others too. There is none of the claustrophobia of a small college where everyone knows everything about everyone else. There is a tendency towards cliquey groups forming but there are so many of them that there are enough for everyone to settle in and do their own thing, from all night work sessions to just all night sessions.

Academically, it's often thought of as a mathematicians' and scientists' college but the English department is strong, if quirky, and arts students are just as plentiful and beautiful as anyone else. Traditionally music too is strong.

Financially, Trinity can't be faulted. There's a wide range of potential funds, grants, prizes and so on, to be tapped. The rooms are almost all excellent, with some rooms having en suite facilities and shared kitchens (called gyp rooms). The rooms are priced o.k. and an average college bill will come to £320. (This sounds like a bed and breakfast review).

The SU has had a reputation of apathy that is now being shaken off. Things are changing and the SU was even seen running campaigns last year and winning victories for its students. Representation with the college is limited but effective liaison committees exist to address matters of joint concern. The SU also does an excellent line in fine bops and cocktails.

In short Trinity won't stamp a distinctive flavour of life on you but rather it will offer a variety of spices for you to choose and mix into your life as widely as the metaphors are mixed in this sentence.

Alistair Land

Pauper notes

Accommodation: First and third years live in the college, in three years' time all students should be living in college, in the meantime use is made of dispersed lodging houses. Rents have an accessible range from £160 to £300. **Drink:** Cheap college bar that is often packed, interior improving as is stock range; handsome range of take away booze when bar shuts (11.30). **Eats:** Reasonable food in hall, cheap, filling but bland, vegetarian options are improving steadily. No provision is made for vegans or for kosher or halal food. **Ents:** T.C.S.U. Ents acquiring justifiably infamous status, drawing from all over the university. Massive range of clubs and societies all operating on site. **Sports:** Three sports fields with a pavilion, boathouse, squash courts, tennis courts, multigym and badminton court. College sports teams cater for all levels of skill and enthusiasm and are very active in inter college leagues. **Hardship funds:** Good hardship funds; tutors sympathetic to substantiated claims. **Travel:** Diverse range of wealthy funds to apply to for all sorts of vacation activities. **Work:** Many seek work in vacations but success here is declining. Work in term time is not feasible.

TRINITY HALL

Trinity Hall, Cambridge CB2 1TJ
(0223 332500; Fax: 0223 332537)

Admissions Office 0223 332535

Founded: 1350; women undergraduates first admitted 1977. **Accommodation:** All undergraduates accommodated in college or college hostels. Most charged £900 pa (range £720–£1,125). **Eating arrangements:** All meals available in hall; paid for by computer card. Super Hall (special dinner) on Thursdays. **Gate/guest hours:** Gate closed at 2 am; undergraduates intending to return later borrow a night key. Guests may not enter college after 1 am and must leave before 2 am. **Scholarships:** Scholarships and exhibitions awarded on the results of university examinations taken while in residence; numerous college prizes. **Hardship funds:** Funds are available. **Travel grants:** Elmore travel exhibition annually on result of modern and medieval languages tripos; grants from Benn and Gregson funds for vacation travel of educational or adventurous nature. **Library:** Separate law reading room; also historic library (chained books). **Other college facilities:** Bar, music room with piano and harpsichord; washing machines and driers; boathouse; squash and tennis courts; playing fields; micro-computers and main-frame terminals. **Largest fields of study:** Natural sciences, law, engineering, modern languages.

European Community: 10% students study an EC language and spend a period of time in another EC country as part of their course. No formal exchange links with EC universities/colleges.

College fees for 1992/93 (undergraduate) £2,658.

Undergraduates: *Men:* 197 *Women:* 125

Postgraduates: *Men:* 112 *Women:* 49

Teaching staff: *Men:* 32 fellows, 3 research fellows *Women:* 4 fellows, 2 research fellows.

CAN'T FIND WHAT YOU'RE LOOKING FOR? USE THE INDEX!

What it's like

Small college in pleasant setting on the Backs. Very central, yet relatively quiet. Friendly atmosphere; relations between staff and students relaxed (notably helpful porters). Amenities include a modern JCR complex of common room, theatre, music room – all adjoin the popular bar. New computer room. Accommodation varies considerably, but rents are reasonable: 1st years and some 3rd years live in college, everyone else on two other college sites. Limited self-catering and washing facilities are installed on each site. College food is tolerable: cafeteria every day, as well as the occasional formal and supper halls (usually good value), vegetarian alternatives usually available but not vegan.

Most sports catered for; playing fields, tennis and squash courts 10 mins from college. Women's rugby and football team a success. Several active societies: outstanding in music and drama. Apolitical JCR coordinates many of the college activities, as well as representing students in the governing body.

Fair proportion of public school descent; college seeks a wider range of applicants. Male:female ratio 2:1, relaxed attitude to co-residence. Academically high, main subject, law, though most mainstream subjects catered for. Size and good internal facilities make the college rather insular, perhaps even a little claustrophobic.

Pauper notes

Accommodation: Can get cheap rooms, £200 a term. OK, so long as you aren't married, disabled or have kids. **Drink:** No cheap places in Cambridge. Bar is reasonable but goes for quality not cheapness, Bop's exceptional value. **Eats:** Canteen cheap but subsidised by kitchen charge £200 p.a. **Ents:** Good for film buffs, but the town is dead for music. College ents very cheap, active discos, films and plays. **Sports:** A mecca for sports (apparently). Main sports (hockey, rugby etc) are free at college level. **Hardship funds:** Available. **Travel:** No need for public transport during term – everywhere is walkable. Travel bursaries available. **Work:** Not much in Cambridge, but being an undergraduate does help with getting summer work.

More info?

Enquiries to JCR President 0223 65561.

Alumni (Editors' pick)

Robert Runcie, Sir Geoffrey Howe, Norman Fowler, Samuel Silkin, A Nunn May, Rev. David Sheppard, Nicholas Hytner, A H Mars-Jones, Lord Simon of Glaisdale, J B Priestley, Tony Slattery.

WOLFSON

Wolfson College, Cambridge CB3 9BB (0223 335900)

Founded: 1965. **Accommodation:** 42% in accommodation where rent controlled by college. Rent not known. **Eating arrangements:** Meals in hall. Chocolate machine, cafeteria in club room. **Admission:** Primarily graduate college but mature undergraduates admitted. **Scholarships:** No scholarships. Some bursaries and awards. **Hardship funds:** College hardship fund. **Travel grants:** College travel fund. **Library:** 10,414 books, 44 periodicals, 20 study places. **Other college facilities:** Tennis court, multigym. **Largest fields of study:** Law.

European Community: No students study an EC language, but 1.6% spend time in another EC country as part of their course. No formal exchange links.

College fees for 1991/92 (undergraduate) £2,439. 1992/93 level not known.

Undergraduates: *Men:* 35 *Women:* 30

Postgraduates: *Men:* 174 *Women:* 138

What it's like

It's cosmopolitan, relaxed, unpretentious and friendly. Students are over 21, doing every imaginable degree (mostly postgraduate), from every corner of the world, lawyers and land economists, particularly strong. Food OK. Twice weekly formal halls popular. Limited college accommodation. Excellent May Ball (in April).

Pauper notes

Accommodation: Some flats and single accommodation for all first years and some others. **Drink:** College bar good, local pub 'Hat & Feathers' serves food also. **Ents:** Rest of Cambridge and internal college events. **Sports:** Best gym in Cambridge college. **Hardship funds:** Some; more available via university. **Travel:** Some assistance. **Work:** Some bar work.

Informal name

Very formal, ie Wolfson

Alumni (Editors' pick)

C Bowman (singer/entertainer, well-known in Ireland), Steve Richards (Channel 4 'Garden Club' presenter).

CANTERBURY CHRIST CHURCH COLLEGE

Canterbury Christ Church College, Canterbury, Kent CT1 1QU
(0227 767700) Map A, G8

Student enquiries: Admissions Office

Main study areas – as in What to Study section: *(First degree):* American studies, art & design, business studies, education, English, geography, history, information technology, mathematical studies, music, nursing studies, professions allied to medicine (PAMs), religious studies and theology. *Also:* Radio, film and TV studies, sports science, tourism.

European Community: 7% first degree students learn an EC language as part of their course – built into some courses eg business studies, tourism studies as well as language studies; language tuition available to all students.

Application: PCAS for 1993 start, UCAS thereafter. **Academic features:** New degree courses in American studies and language studies. **Special features:** College's own radio station now broadcasting. Mature students with one A-level or from an Access course accepted. **Largest fields of study:** Education, English. **Founded:** 1962; merged with Canterbury School of Radiography in 1988. **Main awards:** BA, BA(Ed), BSc. **Structural features:** Link now established with local hospitals to develop degree and other courses in nursing. **Awarding body:** Kent University. **Site:** 10 min gentle walk from Canterbury city centre. **Accommodation:** 200 places in mixed and segregated halls, accommodation officer will advise on lodgings. Special feature: head-leased houses – ie college rents houses from landlords and sub-lets to students. **Library:** 160,000 volumes, 400 periodicals, 200 study places, short term loan collection. **Welfare:** Doctor, nurse, sick bay, chaplain, nursery facilities nearby. **Careers:** Information and advice. **Amenities:** Spacious student building. **Sporting facilities:** 16-acre playing fields, tennis courts, squash courts and gymnasium. **Employment:** Teaching, commerce, civil service, research, management, media, occupational therapy, radiography, nursing etc.

Duration of first degree course(s) or equivalent: 3 years BA/BSc; 4 years BA(Ed) **Total first degree students 1991/92:** 3,000; **Total BA(Ed) students:** 1,000 **Male/female ratio:** 1:4 **Teaching staff:** full-time: 150 part-time: 40 **Total full-time students 1991/92:** 4,000 **Postgraduate students:** 500. **Tuition fees for 1992/93**

(first degrees): Home: £1,855 (classroom), £2,770 (lab/studio), £715 (if no grant); Overseas: £4,805. All first year students pay £340 registration fee in addition to these fees.

What it's like

Although expanding its campus, student numbers and course diversification Canterbury Christ Church College (C4) manages to maintain a friendly and personal atmosphere. Located in the city centre overlooking the cathedral, it's a very cosmopolitan college. An active international programmes office integrates students from all over the world into a range of C4 courses and co-ordinates visits and exchanges under the Erasmus scheme etc.

Originally a teacher training college, it has diversified into BA/BSc courses including media, industry, tourism and, most significantly recently, into nursing and PAMs.

Only 20% of the first year students are housed on campus, the remainder being accommodated in bed and breakfasts by the college. Canterbury has a large student population so accommodation is expensive and relatively hard to find (approx. £40 per week + bills). This historic city wasn't designed with traffic numbers in mind. C4 has no on-site student parking and the city also has a parking problem.

The SU building is the centre of most student activity and social life. Purpose built 6 years ago it contains a large bar area, a recently refurbished smaller bar, disco/band/event area, games room, 2 TV lounges complete with satellite facilities. The SU has many flourishing clubs and societies, all run by students for students, including a campus radio station. Events are renowned as some of the best in Canterbury, attracting visits from both the university and art college, with annual fixtures such as the Christmas ball, carnival, and summer ball.

Students come from all over the country and there seems to be no 'typical' student. C4 is ideal for those who enjoy a life away from the hustle and bustle of large inner cities.

Nic Peters

Pauper notes

Accommodation: No married quarters, very few squatting opportunities. **Drink:** Large and varied selection of pubs in the city, one of most crowded in England! **Eats:** A variety of food available in the college, many restaurants offering student discount in close proximity. **Ents:** Union has events at least 4 nights per week including discos, films, bands (both college and from outside), 'alternative' entertainment and a summer ball. **Sports:** Many thriving sports clubs, including highly successful swim team. **Travel:** Hitching opportunities to both London and the continent. **Work:** Mainly found in pubs, restaurants & supermarkets. Seasonal fruit picking and teaching English in language schools very popular in the summer.

More info?

Enquiries to Nic Peters (0227 782416).

Informal name

Christ Church; C4.

CARDIFF

University of Wales College of Cardiff, PO Box 68, Cardiff CF1 3XA (0222 874000) Map A, D8

Student enquiries: The Admissions Office

Main study areas – as in What to Study section: *(First degree):* Accountancy, anatomy, archaeology, architecture, biochemistry, biology, biotechnology, botany, business studies, chemistry, civil engineering, communication studies, computing, economics, education, electrical & electronic engineering, English, environmental studies, European studies, food science & nutrition, geology, history, hotel & catering management, industrial relations, law, maritime studies, mathematical studies, mechanical and production engineering, microbiology, modern languages, music, Near East & Islamic studies, pharmacology, pharmacy, philosophy, physics, physiology, politics and government, psychology, religious studies and theology, social policy and social welfare, sociology, town and country planning, zoology. *Also:* Astrophysics, banking, Catalan, conservation, journalism and broadcasting, ophthalmic optics, Welsh studies.

European Community: 7% first degree students take an EC language as part of their course, 2% spend 6 months or more in another EC country. Students on some courses required to study a language which may be formally assessed. Language Centre offers language tuition to all other students. Formal exchange links with 8 EC universities/colleges in Denmark, France, Germany and Italy of which 4 are open to non-language specialists; in addition, college is involved in 25 Erasmus schemes, of which 13 involve non-language specialists. Approved Erasmus programmes 1992/93. European office actively promotes teaching and research programmes in Europe.

Application: UCCA for 1993 start, UCAS thereafter. **Structural features:** Part of Wales University. **Academic features:** 4 year integrated sandwich courses, 5 year two-tier courses in architecture and town planning. **Largest fields of study:** Business studies, engineering, law. **Founded:** 1988 through merger of University College, Cardiff (founded 1883) and UWIST (founded 1866). **Main awards:** BA, BD, BEd, BMus, BSc, BEng, BScEcon, LLB, BPharm. **Awarding body:** Wales University. **Site:** Close to Cardiff city centre. **Accommodation:** Over 1,320 places in halls of residence; approximately 2,600 places in self-catering flats; all accommodation mixed, except for one females-only hall of residence. Sufficient college accommodation to meet expected demand from all first year undergraduates. Approx cost: £53 pw halls, from £27 to £41 pw self-catering flats. Some new en-suite rooms in self-catering residences, approx cost £35 pw. Limited accommodation for married students and postgraduates. **Library:** 9 libraries; over 550,000 volumes for loan, 5,000 periodicals, 2,000 study places. **Specialist collections:** Salisbury Library of Celtic and Welsh material. Deposit library for UN and EC official publications. Technical Reference Bureau; Company Information Unit; Thomson Foundation Bureau (journalism); Robbins-Langdon Collection (music). **Welfare:** Students' advisory, counselling and health services; international section to assist overseas students. **Other learning resources:** Computing service on campus, used for teaching and research by staff and students of all disciplines. **Hardship funds:** Funds are available for interest-free loans, remission of fees and maintenance grants. **Special categories:** Residential facilities for married and disabled students; nursery and playgroup. **Careers:** Information, advice and placement. **Amenities:** Anglican, Catholic, Baptist, Methodist and United Reformed chaplaincies; large SU with bars, nightclub, dining facilities, TV and reading rooms, snooker and pool room, general store, printshop, travel shop, launderette, banks etc; university bookshop on campus; Wales University Air Squadron; Officer Training Corps. **Sporting facilities:** Gymnasium; indoor and outdoor sports complex (about 1 mile away); extensive playing fields (about 4 miles away); boat houses on river Taff; 8 squash courts; very wide range of sport including rugby, hockey, sport-para, cricket.

Duration of first degree course(s) or equivalent: 3 years; others: 4 years, 5 years **Total first degree students 1991/92:** 7,731; **total BEd students** 58 **Overseas students:** 456 (u/g) and 541 (p/g) Mature students: c.500 **Male/female ratio:** approx 10:9 **Teaching staff: full-time:** 896 **part-time:** 33 **Total full-time students 1991/92:** 9,711 **Postgraduate students:** 1,785 **Tuition fees for 1992/93 (first degrees):** Home: £755 (if no grant), £1,855 (classroom), £2,770 (lab/studio); Overseas: £5,320 (classroom), £7,055 (lab/studio).

CAN'T FIND WHAT YOU'RE LOOKING FOR? USE THE INDEX!

What it's like

Main college looks pretty impressive, Union looks like a pile of shoe boxes. Easy to reach, at end of M4; M5 accesses north–south. Most of campus easy to get to and close (5 mins) to city centre. College accommodation available for most first years. There are now over a dozen halls of residence, including 1 women only and 1 Welsh speaking hall. Most students move out after 1st year. High proportion of overseas (approx 12%) and mature students.

Amicable relations with college, whose generosity with block grant has helped make Cardiff Union one of the country's best. Very active SU with over 200 social/sporting societies, nightclub complex, new bars and shopping area. Astroturf hockey pitch and indoor sports hall – all worth £1.25 million.

Aberdare Hall (women only), University Hall Tower Wing (women only) restrictive on male guests. FPA clinic 5 minutes from SU. Confidential union and college counselling available.

Union welfare and advice centre; private interview room available. Not much mixing with town. All the advantages of a capital city – covered shopping areas, cinemas, theatres, museums, galleries, castles, docklands, arts centres and night-life. Gay scene small (3 pubs/clubs exclusively gay) but well patronised.

3 subjects taken in 1st year, easy to swap if you pass exams and A-levels high enough. Language courses with 3rd year abroad. Lecturers slowly coming round to the idea of training. Degree assessment a mix of exams and continuous. Fail mark in first year about 40%, usually retakes allowed in September. Engineering building recently renovated and extended (excellent mobility disability access here: rest of college not very accessible). Home economics offered as a degree course. English department very innovative with some excellent (and famous!) lecturers (eg Chris Norris, Terence Hawkes, Catherine Belsey). European community studies a small close-knit degree course (3rd year away).

Students mostly from Wales and England, mixed backgrounds, approximately 10% Welsh speaking. Most famous student – Neil Kinnock (pass degree in economics). Some scholarships (£100 usually) and prizes available. Careers service available.

Pauper notes

Accommodation: Expensive (from £25 pw cheapest s/c to £48 pw dearest catered). Cheap, acceptable accommodation getting harder to find as student numbers increase. Halls contracts last whole year. **Drink:** Union one of cheapest in town. Mainly Bass and Courage with regular promotions. Brains is local brewery and worth getting to know as they own most local pubs. **Eats:** 2 Welsh, 2 Greek restaurants (although Greek society doesn't rate them very highly), 1 Portuguese (great!) and lots of Italian restaurants. SU one of cheapest, but lots of cafes and veggie/wholefood places. Lots of chippies, Chinese and Indian take-aways. **Ents:** Union nightclub and bars; entry £1.60 Tues to Fri, Mon free. Cheap films in town with NUS card (£2.00). Nightclub, new pa system in concert venue. Usually discounts available for theatres, concerts etc for students. **Sports:** Squash courts in SU, gym and weights room – all well used. National swimming pool, ice rink; very active athletic union. **Hardship funds:** College can give interest free loans or grants of up to £500. **Travel:** Travel shop in syndicate with Warwick and Sheffield and offers very good deals; member of ABTA. Some scholarships available depending on course for overseas travel. **Work:** Plenty of bar and casual work, in SU, college and in town. Other work hard to find.

Informal name

UWCC

Alumni (Editors' pick)

Rt Rev Derrick Childs (Bishop of Monmouth), Professor Alun Hoddinott (composer and professor of music at Cardiff), Neil Kinnock MP, Tim Sebastian, Ian Edwards, Sian Phillips, Philip Madoc, Bernice Rubens, Sir Graham Day, Sir Ronald Mason, Sir David Phillips, Vincent Kane.

GET HOLD OF THE PROSPECTUSES

CARDIFF INSTITUTE

Cardiff Institute of HE, Western Avenue, Llandaff, Cardiff CF5 2YB
(0222 551111) Map A, D8

Student enquiries: Information Office

Main study areas – as in What to Study section: *(First degree):* Art & design, biology, business studies, communication studies, computing, education, electrical and electronics engineering, fine arts, food science & nutrition, hotel & catering management, information technology, mechanical and production engineering, professions allied to medicine (PAMs), psychology, social policy and social welfare, speech sciences. *Also:* Biomedical sciences, electrical engineering, environmental risk management, manufacturing engineering, movement studies, professional studies (learning difficulties), sports studies, tourism, Welsh.

European Community: 10% first degree students take an EC language as part of course and spend 6 months or more in another EC country. Language tuition available to students in business information and management and those involved in exchanges. Formal exchange links with a number of EC universities/colleges in France, Germany, Netherlands, Portugal and Spain – open to students in art and design, industry, hotel and catering management. Approved Erasmus programme 1992. New French and Spanish language options for BEd.

Application: PCAS for 1993 start, UCAS thereafter; ADAR for art and design. **Main awards:** BA, BEd, BSc, BEng. **Awarding body:** Wales University. **Site:** 7 centres in or near Cardiff city centre. **Accommodation:** 450 places in two halls of residence. Approx cost: £60 pw. 17% students housed in accommodation where rent is controlled by the Institute. **Library:** 4 libraries, total of 210,000 volumes, 1,000 periodicals, 430 study places; reference and short term collections; access, through library computer, to British Library and Library of Congress (London). **Special collections:** Permanent collection of prints and books on the work of the designer Erte. Extensive collection of slides. **Welfare:** Doctors, nurses, chaplains, professional welfare and accommodation officer. **Hardship funds:** Student loan fund and Access fund. **Careers:** Careers advisory officer. **Sporting facilities:** Sports halls, gymnasia, swimming pool, athletic track (international standard), rugby and football pitches, etc, access to all sporting facilities of Cardiff University and to National Sports Centre. **Employment:** Art and design, education, design and manufacturing industry, paramedical sciences, hospitals, hotels, sports, environmental health, museums/galleries/arts administration, tourism.

Duration of first degree course(s) or equivalent: 3 years; **others:** 4 years (BEd, BEng, BSc nutrition and dietetics, speech therapy, environmental health, tourism). **Total first degree students 1991/92:** 2,249 **Total BEd students:** 509 **Number of overseas (non EC) students:** 10 **Number of mature students:** 525 **Male/female ratio:** 1:2 **Teaching staff:** 374 **Total full-time students 1991/92:** 4,861 **Postgraduate students:** 217 **Tuition fees for 1992/93 (first degrees):** Home: £1,855 (classroom), £2,770 (lab/studio); Overseas: £5,000.

What it's like

Formerly South Glamorgan Institute of Higher Education, it's still on 4 sites. Accommodation, generally very good, reasonable cost, reasonable quality. Good access to all 4 college centres. 2 halls of residence – warm, reasonably priced – good community atmosphere with lots of trust, team spirit and fun!

Travel – cheap and accessible (taxi and bus), regular use of SU minibuses but nowhere is too far on a bicycle.

Entertainment – very strong. Serious drinking and eating more than most student institutions. Great atmosphere; very friendly and easy going. Constant bombardment from SU with dances, games, shows, bands, discos. Students from all sites are given access to all 'gigs' due to use of SU minibuses. Lots of drinks promotions with prizes and freebies.

CAN'T FIND WHAT YOU'RE LOOKING FOR? USE THE INDEX!

Local areas (pubs, clubs etc) – good pubs with very good beer (price and quality). Claude Hotel – best student pub – landlord loves us; constantly provides for bands, sponsorship for SU clubs, freebies, fancy dress and parties (all because of liaison with SU). Clubs – quite expensive but good to visit in groups. Student nights very good.

Places of interest – beaches, hills, nature paths, rugby, football, skating, swimming, all strong in Cardiff and within its vicinity. Castles, museums, cinemas – you name it we've got it! Very much a student orientated city, with citizens of all nationalities. Very good relationship between students and locals.

Facilities at SU – sports excellent: swimming pool, physiotherapy service, squash courts, gymnasiums, sports hall, multigym, hockey pitches, football, cricket and first class rugby pitches. Best college rugby union and league sides in Britain. Clubs and societies provide equal sporting opportunities for men and women and there are plenty.

Students come from all over Britain, from all backgrounds. There is a highly impressive pass rate – FE courses as well as HE which range right across the board from PE to fine art. Regular exchange programme all over the world.

Pauper notes

Accommodation: Good accommodation, but must be searched for. **Drink:** Claude Hotel, Poets' Corner, Philharmonic, Brains Beers good, and SA very strong. For mega blitz try Hurlimans Lager at Roath Park. 42nd Street, Brain's concession to yuppie market. **Eats:** Campus food varies – Colchester Avenue and tuck shop good. Eating out: Broadway Steak Bar, Patrice (cheap), Bently's (cheap and late). Good for vegetarians and ethnic eats. **Ents:** Cardiff offers all facilities of large city. Chapter and Sherman theatres good for students. Nightclubs, cinemas etc. **Sports:** Plentiful and free on campus, also plentiful in city, eg National Sports Centre. Various leisure centres, swimming pools, golf club etc. **Travel:** Accessible and easy for hitching, trains and good bus service. **Work:** Pubs and restaurants, youth club coaching etc. Reasonably accessible during vacation time.

Informal name

CIHE

Alumni (Editors' pick)

Dewi Bebb, Lynn Davies, Peter Radford, David Pittaway, Gareth Edwards, Rhodri Lewis, Stuart Baxter, Sian Williams, Kevin Hopkins, Hugh Morris, Mike Pereybrune, John Devereux, David James, Grey Thomas, Sally Hodge, Nigel Cousins, Martyn Geraint, Robert Norster, Richie Collins, John Bevan, Jamie Hughes, Anne Diamond, Jill Dando, Michael Buerk, David Bryant, Paul John, Colin Laity, James Charles, Maxine Lock, Sean McGaughie (Pontypool rugby star), Tony Copsey (Llanelli rugby star), Mathew Lloyd, David Manley.

CENTRAL ENGLAND UNIVERSITY, BIRMINGHAM

University of Central England in Birmingham, Perry Barr, Birmingham B42 2SU (021 331 5000) Map A, E7

Student enquiries: Recruitment Unit, Registry

Main study areas – as in What to Study section: *(First degree):* Accountancy, architecture, art & design, building studies, business studies, communication studies, computing, economics, education, electrical & electronic engineering, English, fine arts, hotel & catering management, information technology, law, library & information studies, mechanical & production engineering, music, nursing studies, politics and government, professions allied to medicine (PAMs), sociology, speech sciences, town and country planning. *Also* criminal justice and policing, export engineering, landscape architecture, quantity surveying.

European Community: Less than 1% first degree students take EC language as part of course; number spending 6 months or more in another EC country not known. German language available on all engineering courses; French/German/Spanish options on degrees in business studies, economics, government, law, banking, accountancy, hotel & catering. Formal exchange links with EC universities/colleges in Denmark, France, Netherlands, Spain; also for engineering students in Germany.

Application: PCAS for 1993 start, UCAS thereafter; ADAR for art & design. **Academic features:** Current study on the needs of women engineers. New course in criminal justice and policing, export engineering. **Structural features:** Birmingham Business School. William Kenrick Library. **Largest fields of study:** Business studies, engineering, art & design, built environment. **Founded:** As a university in 1992. Previously Birmingham Polytechnic, founded 1971, from a number of colleges of art, commerce, education, music and PE. **Main awards:** BA, BEd, BSc, BEng. **Awarding body:** Central England University. **Site:** Split on several sites. **Access:** Buses and railway from Birmingham city centre. **Accommodation:** approx 650 study/bedsits. Halls of residence reserved for first year students. Approx 10% students in accommodation where rent controlled by polytechnic. **Library:** Six specialist libraries containing 400,000 volumes, 2,000 periodicals, 140,000 non-book materials, 800 study places, course books on reference. **Specialist collections:** Rare books collection; collection of children's books; large collection of sheet music; Marion Richardson archive. **Other learning resources:** Computer Services Department (IBM 9370 system, 3 Prime 50 series mini computers plus workstations with access to institutional, national and international networks); Learning Methods Unit (research on improving teaching methods and offering study skills services). **Welfare:** SU welfare services. Student Services Centre at Perry Barr. **Hardship funds:** Limited fund at SU and Student Services; also access funds. **Careers:** Information, advice and placement. **Amenities:** Bookshop, general shop, bank, travel shop, insurance broker, legal advice, medical services, creche.

Duration of first degree course(s) or equivalent: 3 years **Other:** 4 years **Total first degree students 1991/92:** 7,200; **BEd students:** 447 **Overseas students:** 374; **Mature students:** 2,058; **Male/female ratio:** 10:9 **Teaching staff: full-time:** 640 **part-time:** 85 **Total full-time students 1991/92:** 8,734 **Postgraduate students:** 1,593; **Tuition fees for 1992/93 (first degrees):** Home: £1,855 (classroom), £2,770 (lab/studio); Overseas: £5,000.

What it's like

An amalgam of modern/old buildings split over seven sites, the largest being Perry Barr, then Gosta Green (arts), Westbourne Road (teacher training), Conservatoire (music school), Bourneville, Margaret Street (arts), and the jewellery school. Halls places very limited but improving (new halls on the way). Most students share houses. Communication helped by SU magazine. SU runs 2 shops, also bank, bookshop and Endsleigh. 2 very successful SU entertainments venues, recently refurbished. All sports and societies run by SU – now has full-time sports officer and 40 teams in a range of sports. Entertainments cater for diversity of students. Large student population – many part-time/mature. Access to sites good, problems with car parking. Many good courses – business and music school especially. Birmingham is a student city (40,000 students in total) – many cheap 'student nights' in clubs, also some discounts on theatres, cinemas. Many cheap shops and a square mile of markets in the centre, selling everything you can imagine.

WANT TO HELP WITH THE NEXT EDITION – SEE PAGE 76

Pauper notes

Accommodation: Halls places extremely limited, university housing scheme: very restrictive contracts; accommodation available around main site. **Drink:** SU bar cheaper than all neighbouring bars; many real ale pubs, Black Country Beers. **Eats:** B'ham renowned for its curry houses, Balti houses. **Ents:** Many local events, bands, especially own student events and those at Birmingham and Aston Univs. Student discounts at nightclubs, theatres, cinemas. **Sports:** SU hires good pitches/halls from city. **Hardship funds:** University provides emergency cover (minimum) from government access funds. **Travel:** Cheap, good buses and trains in city, B'ham is easy to get to and from! **Work:** Usual – pubs and clubs, and anywhere.

Alumni (Editors' pick)

Alfred Bestall (the creator of Rupert Bear), Judy Simpson, Kathy Cook (Olympic athletes), Betty Jackson (fashion designer), Larry (cartoonist).

CENTRAL LANCASHIRE UNIVERSITY

University of Central Lancashire, Preston PR1 2TQ (0772 201201)
Map A, D5

Student enquiries: Student Recruitment

Main study areas – as in What to Study section: *(First degree):* Accountancy, agriculture and horticulture, American studies, art and design, biochemistry, biology, biotechnology, business studies, chemistry, computing, economics, education, electrical and electronic engineering, English, environmental science, environmental studies, European studies, fine arts, geography, history, hotel and catering management, information technology, law, linguistics, mathematical studies, mechanical and production engineering, microbiology, modern languages, nursing studies, pharmacology, physics, physiology, politics and government, psychology, social policy and social welfare, sociology. *Also:* Astrophysics, building technology, European business studies, health studies, journalism, midwifery, visual studies, women's studies.

European Community: 10% first degree students take EC language and 5% spend 6 months or more in another EC country as part of course. Language training is available for all students at a variety of levels, examined or not. Formal exchange links with some 44 EC universities/colleges: Belgium (3); Denmark (1); Eire (2); France (16); Germany (7); Greece (3); Netherlands (4); Portugal (2); Spain (6). Approved Erasmus programme. Opportunity to work abroad on Commett grant.

Application: PCAS for 1993 start, UCAS thereafter; ADAR for art and design. **Academic features:** New courses include fashion promotion, product design, employee relations, financial services, community studies, horticultural technology and management, applied physics for Europe with business skills, electronic design, medical electronics, design and manufacture; combined honours programme of 60+ subjects. Work studio approach to teaching of BEng (mechanical engineering), CATS (Credit Accumulation and Transfer Scheme) being introduced. ACOL (Analytical Chemistry by Open Learning). Languages for all initiative. **Special features:** John Thompson (IBA), first visiting professor in journalism and broadcasting; Ian McDiarmid (British Aerospace), visiting research fellow. Links with universities in China, USA and Europe where students may take part of their course. **Founded:** 1992 as a university, previously Lancashire Poly and Preston Poly, founded 1973. **Main awards:** BA, BSc, BEng. **Awarding body:** Central Lancashire University. **Site:** Central site of c. 38 acres. **Access:** Road and rail. **Accommodation:** 1,000 places in halls, 700 (approx) in university owned or controlled hostels/houses. Approx cost: Halls/hostels £35 pw, university houses £20 pw (both self-catering). Rent: 20% in accommodation where rent controlled by university. **Library:** 300,000 volumes in total, 1,700 periodicals, 700 study places; restricted loan collection; slide library, video & audio cassettes. **Specialist collections:** Preston Incorporated Law Society Library; collections of illustrated books and local history. **Welfare:** 2 counsellors and 3 accommodation officers, health centre, FPA, legal advice centre, multi-faith centre, creche, adviser for overseas students and adviser for students with special needs, racial equality unit. **Hardship funds:** Individual cases of financial hardship considered for assistance. **Careers:** Information Officer; advice and placement service; 2 careers advisers. **Amenities:** Arts centre, sailing centre, sports centre with human performance laboratory, good outdoor sports facilities, observatories, bookshop, pre-school centre, health centre, students' union with shops and travel agency, banking facilities, conference facilities, catering service.

Duration of first degree course(s) or equivalent: 3 years; **others:** 4 years (sandwich) **Total first degree students 1991/92:** 7,175 (full-time and sandwich), 4,351 (part-time) **Overseas students:** 97 **Mature students:** 2,202 (full-time), 3,480 (p-t) **Male/female ratio:** 1:1 **Teaching staff: full-time:** 500 **part-time:** 175 **Total full-time students 1991/92:** 8,000 **Postgraduate students:** 300 (full-time); 450 (part-time) **Tuition fees for 1992/93 (first degrees):** Home: £1,855 (classroom), £2,770 (lab/studio); Overseas £5,319.

What it's like

Preston is undergoing large re-development that makes it quite a busy town. Still maintains its friendly atmosphere without letting its abundance of rain dampen the spirit. University also expanding, taking on new students and new courses each year (though not increasing accommodation and library resources to go hand in hand with that!).

Purpose built Union building houses 3 bars, food outlets, admin offices, plus 950 capacity 'Venue'. (This is proving inadequate for the increasing number of students.) New 'Polygon' bar.

Pauper notes

Accommodation: New 400-bed halls (1991). Another new block 1992 – 450 places – Pontins at Southport is used as 'temporary' accommodation. University expensive – private sector not much better; squats impossible. **Drink:** SU bars reasonable, good selection. Lots of local pubs: Robinsons, Theakstons, Thwaites and Matty Brown. The Variety is best pub – it's a free house. **Eats:** SU offers a good range of burgers – few vegetarian restaurants, many Indian, few Chinese. Roobarb for vegetarian near university library. Lots of reasonably priced places to eat. **Ents:** SU good, Guild Hall, Charter Theatre, new 8 screen Warner. **Sports:** University has no playing fields of its own. **Hardship funds:** Access funds; none from SU. **Travel:** Good for hitching (M6/M61); main line rail; bus. **Work:** Difficult at the moment but work available in pubs, stores, restaurants, etc.

Informal name

Most local people still call it Preston Poly.

Buzz-word

Love (get used to being called 'love').

Alumni (Editors' pick)

Joe Lydon (rugby league international).

CENTRAL LONDON POLY

See Westminster University

CAN'T FIND WHAT YOU'RE LOOKING FOR? USE THE INDEX!

CENTRAL SAINT MARTINS

Central Saint Martins College of Art and Design
(1) **Southampton Row, London WC1B 4AP (071 753 9090)**
(2) **107/109 Charing Cross Road, London WC2H 0DU**
(3) **3/27 Long Acre, London WC2E 9LA**
(4) **Back Hill, Clerkenwell, London EC1R JEN (071 713 0865)**
Map E, C2

Student enquiries: Registrar of each School (Art; Fashion & Textiles; Graphic & Industrial Design)

Main study areas – as in What to Study section: *(First degree):* Art & design, fine arts.

European Community: 15% of first degree students learn an EC language as part of their course and 33% spend 6 months or more in another EC country. Programme of language support for first degree students. Formal exchange links with France through Artaccord and with 14 EC universities/colleges through Erasmus: Belgium (2); Eire (2); France (4); Germany (4); Netherlands (1); Spain (1).

Application: ADAR. **Founded:** 1989, from merger of Central School of Art & Design with St Martin's School of Art. **Structural features:** Part of The London Institute. Organised as three schools: fashion and textiles (Charing Cross Road); graphic and industrial design (Long Acre); art (Charing Cross Road). **Largest fields of study:** Design, fashion and textiles. **Main awards:** BA. **Awarding body:** Open University. **Site:** Central London. **Accommodation:** 35 places in hostels, 50 in mixed halls. Number of students in accommodation where rent is controlled by the school, not known. **Library:** Libraries on main sites; 80,000 volumes, 250 periodicals, 126 study places, slide libraries, 100,000 transparencies. **Welfare:** London Institute student services. **Hardship funds:** Access fund. **Careers:** Students use the London Institute careers service. **Amenities:** Shop selling course materials; common room, canteen and coffee bar; dances, films etc organised by SU; TV and cine equipment; reprographic centre.

Duration of first degree course(s) or equivalent: 3 years, 4 years sandwich, 5 years part-time **Total first degree students 1991/92:** 1,316 **Male/female ratio:** Not known **Teaching staff:** full-time 70 part-time; many visiting lecturers **Total full-time students 1991/92:** 1,551 **Postgraduate students:** 267 **Tuition fees for 1992/93 (first degrees):** Home: £2,770; Overseas: £5,950.

What it's like

It's the result of the merger of Central School of Art & Design, and St Martins School of Art. Based on 4 main sites in the heart of London, producing an art and design college which is both ancient and modern, true of the buildings and the staff alike. There are over 2,000 students, with more than two-thirds on degree or higher level courses. Courses are positively forward looking (as far as the financial constraints will allow) maintaining close links with industry and the arts through visiting professionals and being in the centre of London. Students are a mix of ages, backgrounds and interests, reflected in a diversity of personal styles.

No bars at the college; the bar at Westminster University, Red Lion Square (alongside Southampton Row site) shared by CSM students and staff. It's a friendly bar with cheap and plentiful drinks. Good sounds, a party every Friday which is very popular with a regular crowd. SU holds parties approximately once a fortnight at one of the main sites. Also nights are arranged at various nightclubs eg 'The Kevin Club' – a travelling venue.

Pauper notes

Accommodation: Limited access to halls of residence. London Institute has accommodation officer. **Drink:** Westminster University bar, shared with CSM.

" absinthe in glasses has been superseded by Nescafé in polystyrene cups"

Eats: Rosie's Restaurant, Southampton Row site. Surrounded by sandwich shops and greasy-spoons. **Ents:** Cheap and cheerful college ents. Film club shows cheap and unusual films every other Tuesday. **Hardship funds:** Access funds. **Travel:** Expensive London Transport. **Work:** Work available in bar and coffee bars and at college ents.

Informal name
CSM.

Alumni (Editors' pick)
Zandra Rhodes, Ralph Koltai (set designer for National Theatre), John Napier (set designer for RSC), Rachel Wilson (printmaker), Adam Elliott (actor), Lionel Bart (composer/playwright), Robyn Denny (fashion designer), Linda Kitson (Falklands war artist), Bruce Oldfield (fashion designer).

CENTRAL SCHOOL OF SPEECH AND DRAMA

The Central School of Speech and Drama, The Embassy Theatre, 64 Eton Avenue, London NW3 3HY (071 722 8183) Map D, B1

Student enquiries: Registrar

Main study areas – as in What to Study section: *(First degree):* Communication studies, drama, education, speech sciences. *Also:* Theatre design.

European Community: No students study an EC language or spend time in another EC country as part of their course (language tuition not currently available).

Application: UCCA for 1993 start, UCAS thereafter; except theatre design (ADAR) and acting (direct). **Academic features:** Many well-known guest

CAN'T FIND WHAT YOU'RE LOOKING FOR? USE THE INDEX!

directors and tutors from the theatre, teaching and speech therapy professions. **Special features:** Many new courses; major building programme to accommodate increased student numbers. Unique provision of academic study and practical training in fields of performance, presentation and communication studies. BA in drama and a language run jointly with Queen Mary & Westfield. **Founded:** 1906. **Main awards:** BA, BSc. **Awarding body:** London University, Open University. **Site:** Swiss Cottage. **Access:** Swiss Cottage station, buses. **Accommodation:** School is non-residential. Student services unit helps to find lodgings within half hour of School. Approx cost: £50 pw. **Library:** 30,000 volumes, 30 study places. Computerised subject searching (CD-Rom and on-line); book ordering service and stationery shop. **Specialist collections:** Drama, speech pathology. **Other learning resources:** Well-stocked Audio Visual Unit. **Welfare:** Student services unit, including counselling facility; ecumenical chaplaincy. **Hardship funds:** Limited loans from a special fund; also Access funds. **Amenities:** Fully equipped proscenium theatre (seating 274); 2 modern studios, range of design studios, workshop facilities.

Duration of first degree course(s) or equivalent: BA 3 years; 4 years BSc clinical communication sciences, BA with PGCE. **Total first degree students 1991/92:** 318 but increasing. **BEd students:** 92 **Overseas students:** 2 **Mature students:** 52 **Male/female ratio:** 1:3 **Teaching staff: full-time:** 23 **part-time:** 7 **Total full-time students 1991/92:** 526 (expected to be 1025 in 1994) **Postgraduate students:** 2 **Tuition fees, first degrees, 1992/93:** Home: £2,770; Overseas: £5,330.

What it's like

Main site at Swiss Cottage is centred around the Embassy Theatre. Stage management workshops, three drama studios, large library, speech therapy and teacher training facilities all adjoin. Small and friendly college of some 500 students split into acting, stage management, teacher training (BEd), speech therapy (BSc), ACSD, ADVS, foundation arts and design courses. All makes for a better social life than most drama schools or colleges. New student common room and bar. No halls but SU helps in finding accommodation. SU runs discos, dances, cabarets, bands; also good football and volleyball teams. Easy access to other sports facilities and also to West End. Workload heavy. Continual assessment. Failure/drop-out rate low. Changing courses virtually unknown.

Jonathan Peters

Pauper notes

Accommodation: No halls but a large number of housing agencies willing to accommodate students; very helpful, popular, and offer low rents within easy distance. **Drink:** Swiss Cottage (pub), SU bar for cheap booze. **Eats:** 'Booba's' on the Finchley Road for take-away snacks and Hollywood for fruit & veg. Usual fast food places and health food shops, bakeries, etc, various take-aways. College canteen offers wholesome meals, reasonable prices. **Ents:** All performances in Embassy Theatre and studios are free to CSSD students. SU holds regular functions. Off campus, local cinema, Freud museum, Hampstead theatre, etc. **Sports:** Sports centre across the road: swimming, aerobics, weights, badminton; discount on prices for Camden students. New volleyball team on campus. **Hardship funds:** Governors' hardship fund on a loan basis; Access funds – government. **Travel:** Reimbursements in some cases for fares, otherwise loan system. **Work:** Cleaning jobs, bar and waiter work, ushering, shop work – on and off campus.

Informal name

CSSD.

Alumni (Editors' pick)

Laurence Olivier, Peggy Ashcroft, Vanessa Redgrave, Judi Dench, French & Saunders, Robin Nedwell, Barry Foster, Wendy Craig, Deborah Warner, Carrie Fisher, Amanda Donahoe, Michael Elphick, Jeremy Brett, Cameron Macintosh.

GET HOLD OF THE PROSPECTUSES

CHARING CROSS AND WESTMINSTER

**Charing Cross and Westminster Medical School,
University of London, The Reynolds Building, St Dunstan's Road,
London W6 8RP (081 846 1234)** Map D, A2

Student enquiries: Admissions Officer (081 846 7202)

Main study areas – as in What to Study section: *(First degree):* Medicine.

European Community: No students take EC language or spend time in another EC country.

Application: UCCA for 1993 start, UCAS thereafter. **Structural features:** Part of London University. **Special features:** Recent introduction of a fibre-optic remote teaching system which enables clinical students on 4 hospital sites to receive lectures by cable from one centre at one time and also to communicate between sites. **Founded:** 1818 and 1834. **Main awards:** MB; BS; BSc. **Awarding body:** London University. **Site:** Fulham, Westminster and Chelsea. **Access:** Hammersmith and Baron's Court underground stations; Westminster underground station. **Accommodation:** 259 places in halls (accommodation nearly always provided for first year students). **Library:** 42,000 volumes, 300 periodicals; 250 study places. **Specialist collections:** History of medicine. **Welfare:** Doctor, dentist, FPA, psychiatrist, chaplain. **Hardship fund:** Dean's discretionary fund. **Careers:** Advice and limited placement service. **Amenities:** All resources of London University. **Sporting facilities:** International size swimming-pool on site, squash courts and extensive playing fields. **Employment:** Medical practitioners.

Duration of first degree course(s) or equivalent: 5 years (MB, BS); 1 year (Intercalated BSc) **Total first degree students 1991/92:** 846 **Overseas students:** 28 **Mature students:** approx 78 **Male/female ratio:** 9:8 **Teaching staff: full-time:** approx 120 **part-time:** approx 200 **Total full-time students 1991/92:** 872 **Postgraduate students:** 26 f-t; 75 p-t **Tuition fees for 1992/93 (first degrees):** Home: £2,770 (pre-clinical), £4,985 (clinical); Overseas: £7,500 (pre-clinical), £13,500 (clinical).

What it's like

A very active and friendly medical school situated at two contrasting sites: Charing Cross Hospital, in Hammersmith, is a 15 storey modern building in the shape of a cross; Westminster Hospital is a gothic brown brick building in the heart of Westminster. However, Westminster Hospital will be replaced in spring 1993 by the new Chelsea & Westminster Hospital being built on the Fulham Road. Both Charing Cross and Westminster are linked with associated teaching hospitals via a unique fibre-optic TV network allowing one to be taught by a lecturer ten miles away using 2-way audiovisual communication.

Modern SU building at the Charing Cross site. SU runs bar and bookshop and is responsible for maintaining the usual packed social calendar as well as representing students on various Medical School committees. The Union is also active in initiating and co-ordinating campaigns on any issues affecting student welfare. Extremely good facilities including library, TV and snooker rooms, cafeteria, gym and weights room, changing rooms. Sports complex situated on site with swimming pool, squash courts and concert hall. Active clubs and societies include drama, light operatic, rugby, soccer, hockey, water polo, squash, tennis, basketball, rowing, mountaineering, film, Christian Union and Catholic Society. 'Camp Cando' is a residential summer camp for mentally handicapped people organised and run by students.

Halls of residence at Notting Hill Gate and Westminster. All students promised first year in Hall. Afterwards most find private rented accommodation around Hammersmith. Medical School is noted for its progressive selection policy. No offers are made without interview; year out is favoured; and a large number of graduates are considered (20 selected each year). Good opportunities for an intercalated BSc degree, which is encouraged (86 students this year).

Pauper notes

Accommodation: Hard-to-let council accommodation. **Drink:** SU bar is easily cheapest (£1.20/pint) otherwise pubs are quite expensive. **Eats:** Veg! The Windmill (Fulham Broadway), Tea House (Ravenscourt Park), The Galleon (Notting Hill Gate), Hospital canteen and medical school refectory. **Ents:** Riverside Studios (Film and theatre) and The Lyric (Hammersmith) have student standby tickets, Brentford Waterman's Art Centre. **Sports:** On site swimming pool and sports club. **Hardship funds:** Access funds. **Travel:** Scholarships for electives; good hitching for M4/M3. **Work:** Good jobs in Hammersmith, temp jobs at the local Exhibition Centre.

Informal name

CXWMS; The Cross and Wesso.

Buzz-words

Trap – 'to pull'; Stiff – someone who contributes nothing to the life of the medical school; Fissure – to crack under stress eg at exams; Reynolds veg – group of students who sit in the common room and vegetate; Mary's Bears – St Mary's mascot, stolen by the Cross years ago (or so we're told!); Totty – something to trap; Moose – something you don't want to trap, but invariably do after ten pints; Ectopic – a person not from the Cross.

Alumni (Editors' pick)

Professor Harold Ellis (world famous general surgeon).

CHARLOTTE MASON

Lancaster University, Faculty of Teacher Education & Training, Charlotte Mason College, Ambleside, Cumbria LA22 9BB (05394 33066) Map A, D5

Student enquiries: Academic Services Officer

Main study areas – as in What to Study section: *(First degree):* Education, environmental studies.

European Community: No first degree education students take EC language as part of course; 1% spend 6 months or more in another EC country. All environmental studies students spend part of their course in Spain. Formal exchange links with colleges in Chartres and Heidelberg.

Application: UCCA for 1993 start, UCAS thereafter. **Structural features:** Faculty of Lancaster University. Some BA(QTS) students and all environmental studies students study at Lancaster for part of their course. **Special features:** Occasional artists/crafts person in residence. **Largest field of study:** Primary teacher training. **Founded:** 1892. **Main awards:** BA (QTS). **Awarding body:** Lancaster University. **Site:** Lake District Campus of Lancaster University. Two sites, a mile apart (Scale How and Kelsick). **Access:** Close to M6 (Kendal turnoff) and BR station at

Windermere. **Accommodation:** 148 places on-site, 220 off-site (approx cost £58 incl meals); 265 in private accommodation (approx cost £30.35 excl meals). 47% students in accommodation where the rent is under college control. **Library:** 80,000 books, 280 periodicals, 50 study places. **Specialist collections:** Children's books and learning materials. **Other learning facilities:** Primary teaching subject study resources centres. **Careers:** Information and advice service. **Employment:** Teaching, working in the environment. **Welfare:** Counselling service and accommodation officer. **Hardship funds:** Access fund. **Amenities:** Student union building, wide range of clubs and societies. **Sporting facilities:** Sports hall, tennis courts on campus and climbing wall; Lake District for sporting activities.

Duration of first degree course(s) or equivalent: 4 years BA (QTS), 3 years (BA). **Total first degree students 1991/92:** 605. **BA(QTS) students:** 585. **Number of overseas students:** 13 **Male/female ratio:** 1:7 **Teaching staff: full-time:** 36 **part-time:** 16 **Total full-time students 1991/92:** 713 **Postgraduate students:** 295 **Tuition fees for 1992/93 (first degrees):** Home: £1,855 (classroom), £2,770 (lab/studio); Overseas: £4,750.

What it's like

Now officially Lancaster University Lake District Campus, but still known as Charlotte Mason College, most students spend 4 years here working towards a BA (QTS). The college itself was originally a large country house in the heart of the Lake District. Kelsick, the second site, is about a mile away past Stock Ghyll Waterfall.

With only 666 students the college is a close knit and friendly community. Courses are of a good standard, with the second year of four being spent at Lancaster University, with the exception of outdoor education students who stay in Ambleside to gain valuable experience in the Lakeland fells. Teaching is tough but rewarding, not a soft option.

Most first years live in halls of residence and pay for their accommodation and two meals a day, all meals must be paid for whether the student eats them or not. It's expensive at £66 per week, sharing a room, but all rooms are of a good standard and clean, with good views. The hostels are converted houses around Ambleside holding up to 33 students, so making friends is easy. Rented accommodation around Ambleside is reasonable, at around £30–£40 per week plus bills. The nearest supermarket is in Windermere, four miles away, but the SU takes a minibus to Asda in Kendal for those interested in cheaper food bills. Some local outdoor shops offer a 10% discount for students.

There are 8 pubs of varying character in Ambleside, ranging from quiet country pubs to loud town pubs – choose one to suit your mood! The SU bar, 'The Overdraught', is renowned to sell the cheapest beer in Cumbria, so most students drink here. It is open every night, with an event once a week such as Karaoke, live bands and drink promotions. Students can try their hand at pulling a pint in the bar as a volunteer working on a rota system. The bar and disco is all 'No Smoking' due to fire regulations, so very good for the health conscious student.

The town caters for tourists so there is a wide variety of eating establishments such as Italian, Chinese, Vegetarian, Pub Grub, chip shops and lots of cheap cafes.

Not much entertainment really, but with so many students in a small town, there is always fun to be found! We have one small cinema which offers recent films at £3. The SU offers trips to the 'Sugarhouse', the university nightclub, theatre trips and other events. The Barn and Overdraught are the main source of entertainment.

The Athletics Union was set up last year and is going well, with fixtures at home and away. The college has a sports hall and climbing wall in the grounds and tennis courts, rugby, hockey and football pitches nearby. The swimming pool is 4 miles away in Windermere. The AU also arranges trips to the university to take advantage of their vast sports facilities. The possibilities for outdoor recreation are endless with kit available from college, friends and the AU.

Public transport in the Lakes is very expensive, the 8 mile round trip to

Windermere costs £2.52! Hitching is quite easy due to lots of kind tourists and locals.

Being in a tourist area there are plenty of hotels, guest houses, restaurants and shops so jobs have been easy to find, although recent feedback suggests they may be beginning to dry up. It's more difficult during the winter months but usually if you want work you will find it.

CHELSEA

Chelsea College of Art and Design, Manresa Road, London SW3 6LS (071 351 3844) Map E, B4

Student enquiries: Manresa Road for fine art. Lime Grove (081 749 3236) for design.

Main study areas – as in What to Study section: *(First degree):* Art & design.

European Community: No students take EC languages or spend time in another EC country as part of their course.

Application: ADAR. **Largest fields of study:** Painting, sculpture, printmaking, alternative media, design (design options: textiles, interiors, murals). **Founded:** 1891, later incorporating art departments of Regent Street Polytechnic and Hammersmith College of Arts and Crafts. **Structural features:** Part of the London Institute. **Main awards:** BA. **Awarding body:** Open University. **Site:** 4 sites in Chelsea/Fulham/Shepherd's Bush. **Access:** Tube (South Kensington/Sloane Square); buses along King's Road for Chelsea/Fulham. Tube (Shepherd's Bush/Goldhawk Road) for Shepherd's Bush. **Accommodation:** Limited number of hostel places. Rent: 10% in accommodation where rent controlled by college. **Library:** 3 libraries at Manresa Road, South Park and Lime Grove Buildings; 70,000 volumes, 200 periodicals, 30 study places. **Specialist collections:** Fine art at Manresa Road. **Welfare:** Student services officer. **Careers:** Information and advice. **Amenities:** Shops for students' materials on all sites. **Employment:** Strong tradition of freelance work in fine art, industrial employment in design.

Duration of first degree course(s) or equivalent: 3 years **Other:** part-time or mixed mode 4-5 years **Total first degree students 1991/92:** 450 **Overseas students:** 31 **Mature students:** 53 **Male/female ratio:** 2:3 **Teaching staff: full-time:** 41 **part-time:** 120 **Total full-time students 1991/92:** 780 **Postgraduate students:** 43 **Tuition fees, first degrees, 1992/93:** Home: £2,770; Overseas: £5,950.

What it's like

It's a small college, spread over 4 sites: Manresa Road (behind Chelsea Fire Station), Hugon Road (just off the Wandsworth Bridge Road), Bagley's Lane (near Chelsea Harbour) and Lime Grove (shared with Hammersmith & West London College) behind the BBC in Shepherd's Bush. This means it lacks strong single identity despite efforts of staff and SU. Make sure you look round the site you're actually applying to. Chelsea site, housing the fine art courses, has the best facilities (most 'events' take place here) and the academic reputation to match. Beware, students are expected to motivate themselves and tutors with famous names can prove elusive. If you do the Foundation Course at Bagley's Lane you'll probably have a great time, and get a place on a higher course but you may have to create your own social life. Look carefully at where the BA Graphic Design course is, before you sign up for three years in Hugon Road, SW6. It's a converted school, with the atmosphere to match; shared uneasily with over a hundred BTEC students and a long walk from the tube.

Being in central London, Chelsea has a problem with accommodation. There are 400 places in 2 halls of residence; however, competition for these places with

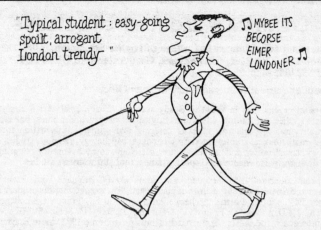

"Typical student: easy-going spoilt, arrogant London trendy"

♫ MYBEE ITS BECORSE EIMER LONDONER ♫

the other 20,000 students of the London Institute is stiff. Important to start looking early, it may take a few months to find adequate accommodation, years to find sought after housing co-op or council housing. Typical student is middle class (though that seems to be changing), easy going, pretentious but friendly and clad in shabby chic.

Welfare and amenities are not priority of college. There is one student services officer for 780 full-time and 300 part-time students, a small careers unit and overcrowded canteens. Student shops are open from a couple of hours a week to half-day every day and along with every other service are run in order to make a profit. However, SU has concrete plans to make bars on 2 sites. Chelsea concentrates its meagre resources on the libraries. There are financial difficulties in studying at Chelsea but millionaires are certainly encouraged to apply! Chelsea's results are excellent due to the few quality staff and the excellent quality of students Chelsea has been able to attract.

Pauper notes

Accommodation: Widely available – at a price. Expect to pay £40–£50 per week. Sharing cuts costs. Hall accommodation for out-of-town first years only. **Drink:** Pubs expensive, 2 SU bars, reasonable prices, open intermittently. **Eats:** Canteens quite good, reasonably priced – can lack ambience! **Ents:** Parties, bands, hoping for varied clubs and societies this year. **Sports:** Very limited. Student prices normally available in the borough you live in. SU currently working on several discount packages. **Hardship funds:** Minimal to non-existent – understanding bank manager and careful budgeting essential. Student loans and access fund. **Travel:** London Transport and British Rail, ie 3 Zone, 1 week card £14.90. Cycling dangerous, wet and cold in winter. Hobson's choice! **Work:** Don't bank on finding part-time work to supplement your grant.

More info?

Get students' Alternative Prospectus.
Enquiries to Students Union (071 371 9532).

Alumni (Editors' pick)

Notorious: Alexei Sayle – Throbbing Gristle, Graham Gough. Famous students: Tom Dixon (bass with Funkapolitan), Simon Edmonson (painter), Sarah Jane Hoare (stylist with Harpers & Queen). Famous students (from the past): Henry Moore, Vincent Price, Patrick Caulfield, Howard Hodgkin, John Berger.

CAN'T FIND WHAT YOU'RE LOOKING FOR? USE THE INDEX!

CHELTENHAM & GLOUCESTER COLLEGE

Cheltenham and Gloucester College of Higher Education, PO Box 220, The Park, Cheltenham, Gloucestershire GL50 2QF (0242 532700) Map A, D7

Student enquiries: Admissions or Publicity Office

Main study areas – as in What to Study section: *(First degree):* Art & design, business studies, computing, education, English, environmental studies, fine arts, geography, geology, history, hotel & catering management, information technology, mathematical studies, modern languages, psychology, religious studies & theology, social policy and social welfare, sociology, town & country planning. *Also:* Fashion, performance arts, sports studies, tourism, women's studies.

European Community: 5% first degree students take EC language (some French, German and Spanish taught) as part of course and ½% spend 6 months or more in another EC country. Formal exchange links with 10 EC universities/colleges: Belgium (1); Denmark (1); France (1); Germany (1); Italy (1); Spain (5). All open to non-language specialists. Approved Erasmus programme 1992; more Erasmus exchanges being developed.

Application: PCAS for 1993 start, UCAS thereafter; ADAR for art & design. **Special features:** American professor plus exchange students each academic year. Voluntary C of E Foundation. **Academic features:** Modular structure for undergraduate courses. Links with industry and commerce. **Founded:** 1990, from merger of College of St Paul and St Mary with GlosCAT. **Main awards:** BA, BEd, BSc. **Awarding body:** Cheltenham & Gloucester College, Bristol University. **Site:** Cheltenham and Gloucester. **Access:** Train, coach, M5 motorway, Birmingham and Bristol airports. **Accommodation:** Over 657 places in halls of residence (priority given to first year students). Cost: £51 pw (full board) £39 pw (self-catering). Over 50% first year students, 10% others, in accommodation where rent controlled by college. **Library:** 300,000 volumes, 1,900 periodical titles. **Specialist collections:** Early children's books; College archives from 1847; history of sport collection, slide collection of fine art and fashion, British Standards and defence standards, Database-Fame (details of UK companies). **Other learning facilities:** Resource centres with film and TV, dance and drama studios; microcomputer facilities. **Welfare:** Director of student services and college counsellor; medical officer and nursing staff, academic counsellors, chaplain, personal tutors. **Hardship funds:** Chapel Council, bursaries for projects/visits, access funds. **Careers:** College careers officers. **Sporting facilities:** 40 acres playing fields, swimming pool (near Olympic standard), sports hall. **Employment:** Less than 12% of recent graduates failed to gain employment.

Duration of first degree course(s) or equivalent: standard: 3 years; 4 years (BEd and BA/BSc with work placement) **Total first degree students 1992/93:** 3,500 **BEd students:** 960 **Overseas students:** 50 **Mature students:** 1,100 **Male/female ratio:** 1:2 **Teaching staff: full-time:** 248 **part-time:** 37 **Total full-time students 1991/92:** 2,100 **Postgraduate students:** 191 **Tuition fees 1992/93 (first degrees):** Home: £759 (if no grant), £1,885 (classroom), £2,770 (lab/studio); Overseas: £5,100.

What it's like

It's the product of the merging of GlosCAT and St Paul and St Mary in 1990, and now caters for 3,500 full-time students and 2,500 part-time students. Five separate sites are spread over the two towns; a fast growing and dynamic institution, it hopes to gain university status. At present the college is undergoing a great period of change, with new buildings for academic and accommodation space. Excellent academic record for teacher training, business courses and art based programmes.

GET HOLD OF THE PROSPECTUSES

There are also opportunities to study abroad for a term on many courses. The modular scheme adopted in 1990/91 provides greater choice and power for the student. On-site accommodation for approximately 500 students, both catering and self-catering available. Good areas for shopping and leisure activity close to the main sites with pleasant Cotswold countryside surrounding both towns.

Progressive SU runs 4 bars, 3 shops, a welfare advice centre, 28 Sports clubs, 19 societies and regular entertainment.

Pauper notes

Accommodation: Halls of Residence: 1st years priority. Shortfall made up from individual flats to terrace type housing. Rents average out at £35 per week. **Drink:** Multitude of pubs and wine bars. Expensive prices in comparison to SU bars. **Eats:** Impressive variety (price and nationality), Cantonese, Greek, French. **Ents:** SU events of good value, ie hypnotists, comedians, discos, bands, and 6 formals. Town entertainments include nightclubs, fringe theatre, Everyman theatre, literature and music festivals, town hall events, art galleries and museums. **Sports:** Excellent facilities. SU clubs regularly successful in national competitions, ie British Colleges Champions 1992 – badminton, cricket, women's hockey, swimming, water-polo, and tennis. Recreation centre, National Hunt Racecourses in Cheltenham and ski centre in Gloucester. **Hardship Funds:** Access funds administered by college. **Travel:** Bicycle almost essential in Cheltenham. Buses relatively efficient, making car ownership unnecessary. **Work:** Some bar, restaurant and clerical jobs.

Alumni (Editors' pick)

Omar Arteh, Samuel Baldeh, David Bryant, P H Newby, Sarah Potter, Graham Brookhouse, Don Hale, Chris Broad.

CHESTER COLLEGE

Chester College, Cheyney Road, Chester CH1 4BJ (0244 375444)
Map A, D6

Student enquiries: The Registry

Main study areas – as in What to Study section: *(First degree):* Biology, computing, drama, education, English, fine arts, geography, history, mathematical studies, psychology, religious studies and theology. *Also:* Health and community studies, physical education and sports science.

European Community: 12% first degree students take an EC language as part of their course and 1% spend 6 months or more in another EC country. French and German for communication available to all BA/BSc students in first year. French, German and Spanish for beginners available for 1 term. No formal exchange links but possibility of new European links for work experience.

Application: UCCA for 1993 start, UCAS thereafter. **Academic features:** BA (health and community studies). All BA/BSc students have work-experience placements; employment-related 'enterprise' modules in first-year course. **Special features:** Staff and BEd student exchange with State University of New York Plattsburg. **Largest fields of study:** Education, English, PE, psychology. **Founded:** 1839 by Church of England. **Main awards:** BA, BSc, BEd. **Awarding body:** Liverpool University. **Site:** 30 acre campus within walking distance of

Chester centre. **Access:** 15 mins from M56, 45 mins from M6, buses from town centre to site. **Accommodation:** 300 places in halls of residence on campus; 150 places in college houses on campus. Approx cost: £42 per week. Rent: 40% in accommodation where rent controlled by college. **Library:** 120,000 volumes, 550 periodicals, 200 study places. **Other learning resources:** Human performance laboratory; satellite remote-sensing suite; CCTV studio and media centre; new gym; multi media art building and drama building. **Welfare:** Chaplaincy; student counsellor, student services centre on campus; personal tutorial system. **Careers:** Full-time careers service; work experience for all undergraduates. **Amenities:** 25 metre pool, squash courts, sauna/solarium and all-weather pitches. **Employment:** Wide range in the professions, business, commerce, media, personnel etc.

Duration of first degree course(s) or equivalent: BA/BSc 3 years; BEd 4 years; 6 years part-time **Total first degree students 1991/92:** 1,666; **total BEd students:** 619 **Male/female ratio:** 1:3 **Teaching staff: full-time:** 102 **part-time:** 15 **Total full-time students 1991/92:** 1,703 **Postgraduate students:** 37 (full-time); 1,230 (part-time) **Tuition fees for 1992/93 (first degrees):** Home: £1,855 (classroom), £2,770 (lab); Overseas: £5,320 (classroom), £7,055 (lab). All students also pay £370 validation fee.

What it's like

Founded in 1839, situated on a 30 acre site ten minutes' walk from the town centre. All facilities are on the one campus and include library and media centre, health centre just off campus (with confidential counselling, pregnancy and contraception advice), bookshop, union shop, launderette and social club bar. Sports facilities include 2 squash courts, 2 gymnasia, swimming pool, sauna and solarium, 6 tennis courts, all weather pitch and various grass pitches. Also Northgate Arena, five minutes' walk away. Sports teams are all above average as PE is a major subject. 460 first years are accommodated in the nine halls of residence, many in single study bedrooms, the dining-halls cater for all dietary needs. Student village on campus accommodates 84 final year students in self-catering houses. The college owns several houses for self-catering students a few minutes walk away. Most 2nd and 3rd and 4th years live in the nearby Garden Lane area, which has varying standards and prices of accommodation. Because the majority of students live so close to college there is a great community atmosphere. Mix of students has a cosmopolitan feel with regular intakes of Hong Kong students and an exchange programme with the State University of New York, Plattsburgh. Clubs and societies are administered by a generally non-political SU, whose elected representatives sit on all major college committees. Entertainment-wise there are twice weekly bops and films on campus as well as visiting bands, novelty acts and theme nights with quiz nights in the bar. English, PE and primary education are the most popular courses all leading to a combined studies degree from Liverpool University.

Pauper notes

Accommodation: If it's cheap it usually looks it. **Drink:** College bar. 'Old Peculiar' at Telfords Warehouse, 'Moonraker' at Clavertons, otherwise loads of pubs, mainly Greenhalls, although better beer can easily be found. **Eats:** Bombay Palace, Sixties, Muswells. Wide variety of burgers, pizzas etc and lots of good restaurants. **Ents:** Nominal charge for college ents, discount at theatres, cinemas, etc. **Sports:** Campus swimming pool, gyms and squash courts. Northgate Arena. **Travel:** National Express coach cards, ISIC and Railcards available from SU. **Hardship funds:** Access funding. **Work:** Bunacamp, Camp America, Camp Beaumont. Bar and restaurant work in city centre.

Alumni (Editors' pick)

John Carlton (rugby international), Carol Lewis (assistant governor, HM Borstal), Walter Winterbottom (director of Sports Council), Richard Palmer (Secretary

GET HOLD OF THE PROSPECTUSES

British Olympic Committee), Eric Bolton (ex-HMI), The Venerable Francis William Harvey (Archdeacon of London), Lynn Davies (British long jump record-holder), George Courtney (top British football referee), Jim Bowen (super, smashing, great).

CITY POLY

See London Guildhall University

CITY UNIVERSITY

City University, Northampton Square, London EC1V 0HB
(071 477 8022) Map E, D1

Student enquiries: Academic Registrar

Main study areas – as in What to Study section: *(First degree):* Accountancy, aeronautical engineering, business studies, civil engineering, computing, economics, electrical & electronic engineering, law, mathematical studies, mechanical and production engineering, music, nursing studies, philosophy, professions allied to medicine (PAMs), psychology, sociology, speech sciences. *Also:* Actuarial science, insurance and investment, journalism, media studies.

European Community: Number of students taking EC languages or spending time in another EC country, not known. Language tuition available on all courses. Approved Erasmus programme 1992.

Application: UCCA for 1993 start, UCAS thereafter. **Largest fields of study:** Business studies, engineering, computing, IT, clinical and health-related subjects. **Founded:** 1894 as Northampton Institute, university status in 1966. **Main awards:** BA, BSc, BEng, LLB, MEng. **Awarding body:** City University. **Academic features:** Courses available as full-time or on sandwich basis. All offer introduction to information technology and development of communication skills. Degree courses in business law; journalism; sociology and media studies; physiotherapy with human sciences. **Site:** Islington, close to City of London. **Access:** Angel or Barbican underground stations. **Accommodation:** 810 places in hall (priority given to first and final year students). University accommodation service administers 199 places in self-catering flats and maintains register of private accommodation. Approx cost: around £55 pw self-catering; £70–£160 pw b&b or b&b with evening meal. Hall fee £647 per 10-week term. 40% students in accommodation where rent controlled by university. **Library:** 303,000 volumes, 1,800 periodicals currently taken. **Specialist collections:** Anderson Music Library, Erna Auerbach Collection, London Society Library, Walter Fincham Optics Collection. **Other learning resources:** Non-book media with listening and viewing facilities; Business School Library. **Welfare:** University health centre, counselling service and chaplaincy. **Careers:** Information, advice and placement service. **Amenities:** Bookshop on site, SU recreational facilities. **Sporting facilities:** Saddlers sports centre (good indoor sports and sauna); swimming pool; squash courts; major playing fields in South London.

Duration of first degree course(s) or equivalent: 3–4 years; **others:** 4–5 years
Total first degree students 1991/92: 2,648 **Overseas students:** 754 **Mature students:** 905 **Male/female ratio:** 2:1 **Teaching and research staff:** 536 **Total full-time students 1991/92:** 5,136 **Postgraduate students:** 2,378 **Tuition fees for 1992/93 (first degrees):** Home: £755 (if no grant), £1,855 (classroom), £2,770 (lab); Overseas: £5,320 (classroom), £7,055 (lab).

CAN'T FIND WHAT YOU'RE LOOKING FOR? USE THE INDEX!

What it's like

In the triangle formed by Angel, Old St and Barbican tubes – each 5/10 minutes walk away. Not a campus, but most activity takes place in main building; halls and academic sites also within the triangle. Main building 1960s brick and concrete; accessible by numerous buses. First and final year students, who want to, live in halls; others rent flats/houses in N or E London. Overnight guests allowed in halls for two nights in any one week – but no one ever checks. Counselling and advice on mating/contraception available from SU, university health centre or Barts Hospital clinic (very close and very busy). SU active; tasteful left wing bias. Runs a community action project and a creche for working/student mothers in the half term holidays. Discos/bands on Fridays, films on Thursdays and other ents during the week. Islington's pubs are a walk away and the West End is accessible. Top subjects are banking and finance, business, engineering, computing, optics and social sciences. Many students are sponsored (though fewer in a recession). Most students are here because of a desire to see London Town or sponsorship.

Pauper notes

Accommodation: All 1st and 3rd years in hall. Block of flats close to the university. Rents high. **Drink:** 2 Union bars – approx 20% off a pint. Bars in both halls of residence. **Eats:** Best to shop at the markets (Chapel & Whitecross Streets). Good veg curry house – lunch – as much as you can eat for £3.95+. Campus food missable. **Ents:** Ents card at least one-third off all City ents. Club atmosphere + appropriate music; venue refurbished. **Sports:** University sports centre very nearby + cheap for students. Swimming pool in main building. Sports ground (not close but coach transport arranged by SU). **Hardship funds:** Union will haggle with finance office/banks on students' behalf – good relationship with both. **Travel:** Travelling bursaries awarded by ex-student club (The N'ions). London fares high – get a bike or be prepared for the costs. **Work:** Work for Union in bars or ents, or for university in halls of residence kitchens.

Alumni (Editors' pick)

Charles Farnecombe (conductor), John Alvey, Michael Fish.

COLCHESTER INSTITUTE

Colchester Institute, Sheepen Road, Colchester, Essex CO3 3LL (0206 761660) Map A, F7

Student enquiries: Enquiries Office

Main study areas – as in What to Study section: *(First degree):* Art and design, environmental science, hotel and catering management, music.

European Community: 10% first degree students take EC language as part of course. Language tuition available to all students on full-time courses. Some work placements available in EC.

Application: PCAS for 1993 start, UCAS thereafter; ADAR for artwork and design. **Special features:** Ensemble in residence, master classes. **Structural features:** Links with Britten-Pears School at Snape and joint courses with Anglia Poly University and Essex University. **Founded:** 1976 ex North East Essex Technical College and School of Art, Colchester, and St Osyth's College, Clacton. **Main awards:** BA, BSc. **Awarding body:** Anglia Poly University. **Site:** Colchester and Clacton sites. **Access:** Both sites near town centres and railway stations. **Accommodation:** 180 places in halls of residence at Clacton. Approx cost: £46 pw including 5 evening meals. Well established network of student lodgings in Colchester and Clacton. **Library:** Libraries at Colchester and at Clacton; c.127,000 items including audio-visual materials; 500+ periodicals, 270 study places. **Welfare:** Qualified nurses, medical room, student counsellor. **Hardship funds:** Local authority support for handicapped students. Local charities also available. **Special categories:** Residential facilities for disabled students. **Careers:** Information and advice. **Amenities:** SU shop and handbook. **Sporting facilities:** Gymnasia, judo, fencing, etc; tennis, playing fields, weight training room, dance studio. **Employment:** Music performance/teaching/music industry; management; hospitality industry; environmental health.

Duration of first degree course(s) or equivalent: 3 years; others 4 years **Total first degree students 1991/92:** 450 **Overseas students:** 10 **Mature students:** 30 **Male/female ratio:** 1:2 **Teaching staff: full-time:** 300 **part-time:** 200 **Total full-time students 1991/92:** 3,000 **Tuition fees, first degrees, 1992/93:** Home: £1,855 (classroom), £2,770 (lab/studio); Overseas: £5,319.

What it's like

It's on 2 sites – Colchester (Sheepen Road) and Clacton. The Sheepen Road site was built primarily in the late 50s and early 60s although there is an excellent new library. The nationally respected School of Music and the North East Essex Art College are based here (the latter also at Braintree FE college). There are excellent welfare facilities and a relaxed, informal atmosphere; a new daytime student social area provides video games, pool tables etc. Refectory and snack facilities are very good. Sheepen Road caters for day students only, covering FE and HE – from GCSE resits to BA courses. Unfortunately this causes some elitism and segregation within the student body, something which is not helped by the fact that there is no bar and few evening socials. Clacton site is on the sea front, and is smaller but has residential facilities. It has a bar, but this is provided for residents only.

SU is well-developed but has some difficulties due to the large number of students and the seventeen mile distance between sites. Full sports facilities on both sites. There are some disabled facilities. Mature students are very welcome.

Pauper notes

Accommodation: Clacton has some residential accommodation (depending on student's course); Sheepen Road has only a token amount. However, Sheepen Road has an accommodation officer for houseshares and digs. **Drink:** Student pubs (Hole in the Wall, Fagin's Den, Oliver Twist, The Cups) are plentiful in Colchester. Clacton has its own bar (see above). **Eats:** Lots of good, cheap restaurants about (Clowns, Muswell's, Tilly's, Carol's) + the usual high street fast-food fodder. Both sites have training restaurants which are very cheap and very good. **Ents:** Colchester is (despite what Blur say) a good place for going out. Essex University in Wivenhoe (2 miles from town centre), Colchester Arts Centre, Hippodrome nightclub, Mercury Theatre, 4-screen Odeon, Minories Art Gallery, 7 museums. Good local bands: watch out for The Druids, Moonage Productions, Mysterie Boys, Penny Arcade. The SU at Sheepen Road runs major socials (bands etc) approx once per month; Clacton run smaller events much more frequently. **Sports:** Both sites have well-equipped gyms. Colchester has a brand new leisure centre, with gym, swimming pool, ten-pin bowling etc. Clacton has a sports centre with swimming pool 3 minutes from site. **Hardship funds:** The college has an access fund for hardship cases with around £30,000 per year, but don't rely on it as there are hundreds of applicants; SU extremely reluctant to loan money but it is capable of doing so in extreme cases. **Travel:** Inter-site transport available and free. Exchange visit to Germany every year. **Work:** As, and if, you find it.

Alumni (Editors' pick)

Graham Coxon (Blur's guitarist), Martin Litton (jazz pianist), Farnaby Brass Quartet, Ebony Wind Quartet.

CAN'T FIND WHAT YOU'RE LOOKING FOR? USE THE INDEX!

COURTAULD INSTITUTE

Courtauld Institute of Art, University of London, Somerset House, Strand, London WC2R ORN (071 872 0220) Map E, C2

Student enquiries: Registrar and Secretary

Main study areas – as in What to Study section: *(First degree):* Fine arts.

European Community: All first degree students take EC language as part of course but none spend time in another EC country.

Application: UCCA for 1993 start, UCAS thereafter. **Structural features:** Part of London University. **Largest fields of study:** History of European Art. **Founded:** 1931. **Main awards:** BA. **Awarding body:** London University. **Academic features:** Postgraduate courses in the history of art, conservation, art museum studies and the history of dress. **Site:** Central London. **Accommodation:** Apply to London University accommodation office (Malet Street, London WC1E 7HU). **Library:** Over 115,000 volumes, 220+ current periodicals, approx 200 study places; a slide library with over 250,000 b/w and coloured slides. **Specialist collections:** Witt Library (photographs and reproductions of paintings, drawings and graphics), Conway Library (photographs of sculpture and architecture). **Centres of excellence:** Courtauld Galleries (French impressionist and post impressionist paintings, Flemish and Italian Old Master paintings and drawings, Turner watercolours). **Welfare:** London University facilities. **Careers:** Information and advice service. **Amenities:** SU is affiliated to ULU and students can make use of their gymnasium, swimming pool, squash, etc. **Employment:** Museums and art galleries.

Duration of first degree course(s) or equivalent: 3 years **Total first degree students 1991/92:** 97 **Overseas students:** 6 **Mature students:** 15 **Male/female ratio:** 1:2 **Teaching staff:** full-time: 21 part-time: 1 **Total full-time students 1991/92:** 256 **Postgraduate students:** 167 f-t; 89 p-t **Tuition fees 1992/93 (first degrees):** Home: £1,855; Overseas: £5,690.

What it's like

It's in Somerset House, one of the most splendid houses in London, located close to the Strand and by the Thames. Spacious, good facilities, and the Courtauld's world famous art collection. Very good library facilities – beautiful library, great to work in. Good teaching rooms; own fully modernised lecture theatre. Students have large comfortable common room space and a smart refectory selling cheap food.

Small, friendly atmosphere. Large cross-section of students; the 'finishing school' reputation is long gone. High standard academically; all tutors expect complete dedication.

Social life revolves around frequent parties and Christmas and summer balls. Added to this is the more informal quaffing club whereby, when the college closes, anyone left in the building is encouraged to go to the pub. Much use is made of King's College Union, next door. Many theatre outings arranged. College magazine, life drawing club.

The Courtauld has no accommodation and refers its students to the intercollegiate halls. As members of London University, students can make use of all ULU sporting facilities at Malet Street.

It's within walking distance of London's galleries and libraries and, of course, the West End and all the entertainments London has to offer.

Pauper notes

Accommodation: Intercollegiate halls. **Drink:** King's College bar next door. **Eats:** Cheap refectory. **Ents:** Parties in college. **Sport:** ULU facilities. **Hardship funds:** Emergency hardship loans. **Work:** Several jobs in libraries and galleries for those that need them.

GET HOLD OF THE PROSPECTUSES

Alumni (Editors' pick)

Giles Waterfield, Neil McGregor, Alan Bowness, Anthony Blunt, Anita Brookner, Vincent Price, James Sainsbury.

COVENTRY POLY

See Coventry University

COVENTRY UNIVERSITY

Coventry University, Priory Street, Coventry CV1 5FB
(0203 631313) Map A, E7

Student enquiries: Registry Services Manager

Main study areas – as in What to Study section: *(First degree):* Accountancy, aeronautical engineering, art & design, biochemistry, biology, business studies, chemistry, civil engineering, communication studies, computing, economics, electrical & electronic engineering, environmental science, European studies, fine arts, geography, history, information technology, law, mathematical studies, mechanical and production engineering, modern languages, nursing studies, physics, politics and government, professions allied to medicine (PAMs), social policy and social welfare, town and country planning. *Also:* Equine studies, materials science, performing arts, recreation studies, women's studies.

European Community: 25% first degree students take EC language as part of course and 10% spend 6 months or more in another EC country. EC language tuition available to all students in first and second years as part of main programme. Several courses have European routes, with year abroad eg European business studies, European business law, building/civil engineering with European studies, European applied biology. Formal exchange links with over 25 EC universities/colleges, including some open to non-language specialists: Belgium (Brussels); Denmark (Odense); France (Strasbourg); Germany (Aachen); Spain (Valencia). Approved Erasmus programme 1992.

Application: PCAS for 1993 start, UCAS thereafter; ADAR for art and design. **Special features:** Admissions policy for mature and handicapped students. **Academic features:** Increasing modular provision; credit transfer; links with European institutions. **Founded:** As a university in 1992. Previously Coventry Poly, formed 1970 ex Lanchester College of Technology, Coventry College of Art and Design, and Rugby College of Engineering Technology. **Main awards:** BA, BSc, BEng, MEng, LLB, BTP. **Awarding body:** Coventry University. **Site:** Coventry city centre; large modern campus. **Access:** 5 miles M6/M1 intersection; 30 mins Birmingham by train, 75 mins London Euston; adjacent to National Express coach station. **Accommodation:** 737 places in halls of residence; 922 in bedsitters/houses; 300 places in lodgings. Approx cost: £27.50 pw room, £39.75 full board and lodgings. Rent: 20% in accommodation where rent controlled by university. **Library:** Main library and art and design library; 192,250 volumes in total; 3,020 periodicals, 1,100 study places; short loan collection of 8,000 course books and articles. **Welfare:** Doctor, FPA, psychiatrist, multi-faith chaplaincy; international office; educational guidance, student counselling service. **Special categories:** Residential facilities for disabled students. **Careers:** Information and advice service. **Amenities:** SU building with 3-bar complex, shopping area and travel bureau; nursery. **Sporting facilities:** 37 acre playing field, sports centre; Coventry swimming pool (Olympic standard) and city sports centre adjoin campus.

CAN'T FIND WHAT YOU'RE LOOKING FOR? USE THE INDEX!

Duration of first degree course(s) or equivalent: 3 years; **others:** 4 years (sandwich) **Total first degree students 1991/92:** 6,000 **Overseas students:** 650 **Male/female ratio:** 2:1 **Teaching staff: full-time:** 600 **part-time:** 50 **Total full-time students 1991/92:** 900 **Postgraduate students:** 550 **Tuition fees, first degrees, 1992/93:** Home: £1,855 (classroom), £2,770 (lab/studio); Overseas: £5,500.

What it's like

Convenient for city centre, adjacent to cathedral. Easy to get to – M1, M6, very near to bus station and about 15 mins walk to train station. Poly accommodation – very expensive – 1st year students in most cases – priority to overseas and particular courses, eg occupational therapy. Priory Hall – expensive, pay as you eat – poor cooking facilities. Laundry facilities recently renewed – still inadequate. Catering – little vegan and some vegetarian. Most students live in private rented accommodation. Still fairly cheap on national scale.

Greater number of part-time students and also mature students. Inadequate nursery facilities although nursery is excellent. SU runs half-term play schemes for 5–11 year olds. Library – opens longer near exam time – inadequate books due to increasing student numbers. SU – good socially and good ents. 3 bars with catering facilities; excellent refurbished gig venue. Over 120 societies. Good campaigning. Excellent welfare bureau. Women's priority transport provided every night. Coventry City – not particularly safe at night. Not really a student town but plenty of pubs where students are welcome. Good transport links with Birmingham for concerts, theatre etc. Very close to Warwick University. Warwick Arts Centre good. Many courses have national representation. Several specialist courses, eg horse studies. Many courses now modular. Reasonable teaching facilities. Lecturers have good relationships with students. Good relationship with administration. Generally, good standard of education and good social life.

Pauper notes

Accommodation: Introducing new head tenancy scheme for 1st year students. Priory Hall – fully catered and expensive; Caradoc Hall – 4 miles out but OK, dodgy neighbourhood; 50 poly houses in various states of repair, mostly good; River House – some like it, some don't, self-catering as is Caradoc and Poly houses. **Drinks:** SU cheapest beer – 3 bars. Warwick Uni only 3 miles away on No.12 bus. Pubs mostly M&B, with some Courage and Ansells. **Eats:** Granny's Restaurant popular, Sir Colin Campbell, Hope & Anchor, good, cheap for lunch. Vegetarian – The Wedge. **Ents:** SU – largest venue, Belgrade Theatre. The Filling Station – free delivery in city centre. **Sports:** SU runs comprehensive keep-fit programme. **Hardship funds:** Trouble at beginning of academic year, usually runs out by Easter. **Travel:** Hitching is easy from Coventry but obviously not recommended, especially for women students. **Work:** University runs employment bureau.

Alumni (Editors' pick)

John Kettley (TV weatherman), Steve Ogrizovic (Coventry City FC goalkeeper), Alan Smith (Arsenal footballer), Peter Hadfield (founder of Two Tone), Jerry Dammers (The Specials).

CRANFIELD

Cranfield Institute of Technology, Cranfield, Bedford MK43 0AL (0234 750111) Map A, F7

Student enquiries: Assistant Academic Registrar

Main study areas – as in What to Study section: *(Not at first degree):* Aeronautical engineering, biotechnology, business studies, marine technology, mechanical and production engineering, metallurgy and materials science. *Also:* avionics, energy engineering and the environment, manufacturing systems and designs.

European Community: Many double degree programmes with institutions in France, Belgium, Germany, Greece and Spain. Major European management school.

Structural features: A largely postgraduate institute; first degrees are taught at *Shrivenham* and *Silsoe* – look them up separately. **Application:** Direct. **Largest field of study:** Applied science engineering, technology, manufacturing and management. **Founded:** 1943, obtained Charter in 1969. **Main awards:** MBA, MSc, PhD. **Awarding body:** Cranfield Institute. **Site:** Single campus. **Access:** M1; BR station at Milton Keynes. **Accommodation:** On-site accommodation for 750. **Approx cost:** £50 with some meals. Private landlords in and around Bedford. **Library:** 800 periodicals. **Other learning resources:** Wind tunnel, airfield. **Careers:** Information, advice and placement service. **Welfare:** Welfare office and medical centre. **Special facilities:** Married accommodation, play groups, creches, local schools. **Hardship funds:** Help arranged as needed. **Amenities:** Many and varied student societies and student union. **Sporting facilities:** Gym, multi-gym and playing fields.

Staff: Academic/research: 650. **Postgraduate students:** 1,500 **Overseas students:** 20%. **Tuition fees for 1992/93:** Home: £9,500 (MBA); £2,200 (MSc, MPhil & PhD); Overseas: £14,500 (MBA), £9,500–£13,650 (MSc, MPhil & PhD).

CRANWELL

The Royal Air Force College, Cranwell, Sleaford, Lincolnshire NG34 8HB (0400 61201) Map A, F6

Student enquiries: Local RAF Careers Information Office (see Yellow Pages). No prospectus for Cranwell is issued.

Main study areas – as in What to Study section: Aeronautical engineering, computing, electrical and electronics engineering, strategic studies.

European Community: No students take an EC language as part of their course or spend time in another EC country.

Site: Rural setting 7 miles from Sleaford and 15 miles from Grantham. **Access:** Situated on B1429, just off the A17. Nearest British Rail station is Sleaford with connecting bus service to college. **Accommodation:** Cadets live in single-room permanent accommodation throughout their period of training. Officers attending specialist and postgraduate courses live in one of the 3 student officers' messes. **Library:** 2 extensive libraries covering all aspects of military aviation and associated technical subjects, together with a wide collection of historic documents connected with the early days of the RAF. **Welfare:** Medical, dental and chaplaincy services. **Amenities:** Wide range of sports facilities include gymnasium and competition standard indoor swimming pool. Also riding, flying and gliding, and extensive range of hobbies.

What it's like

RAF officers have been trained at Cranwell since 1920. The college is set in fine grounds of which the central feature is the imposing College Hall building. All officer cadets and student officers wear uniform. Initial officer training is both mentally and physically demanding, and the course is designed to make cadets into leaders and fit them for role as junior RAF officers. Courses run by other departments at the college or Flying Training School last from a few weeks to a year and are also challenging.

Alumni (Editors' pick)

Sir Frank Whittle, HRH The Prince of Wales.

CREWE & ALSAGER

Crewe & Alsager College of Higher Education, Crewe CW1 1DU (0270 500661 (College Office); 0270 589995 (Admissions)) Map A, D6

Student enquiries: Admissions Office

Main study areas – as in What to Study section: *(First degree):* American studies, art & design, biology, chemistry, dance, drama, education, English, environmental science, environmental studies, geography, history, mathematical studies, modern languages, music, philosophy, physics, physiology, psychology, religious studies and theology, sociology. *Also:* Crafts, physical education, sports science.

European Community: 5% first degree students take EC language as part of course and 5% spend 6 months or more in another EC country. No formal exchange links. French language tuition available to first degree students on BEd and BA humanities.

Application: PCAS for 1993 start, UCAS thereafter; ADAR for BA crafts. **Structural features:** Faculty of Manchester Metropolitan University. **Academic features:** Writing option offered as part of BA creative arts. Modular degree allows combination of subjects. BA Cert Ed for intending primary teachers. **Special features:** Nationally known artists and craftsmen teach part-time on courses; usually an artist or craftsman in residence. Resident theatre company (Theatre Exchange) and dance company. **Founded:** 1974, ex Colleges of Education of Crewe and Alsager. **Main awards:** BA, BEd, BSc, BA with Cert Ed. **Awarding body:** Manchester Metropolitan University. **Site:** 2 sites 6 miles apart. **Access:** M6 and railway stations near both campuses; regular inter-site transport. **Accommodation:** 900 places in both mixed and segregated halls of residence (can normally accommodate all first year students). Rent: 40% in accommodation where rent controlled by college. **Library:** Library on each campus; 200,000 volumes, 1,000 current journal subscriptions, plus collection of microfilms and audio-visual materials, 260 study places. **Welfare:** Centre on each campus, visiting doctors and psychiatrist; professional welfare officers. **Hardship funds:** From LEA on recommendation from college. **Careers:** Information and advice service from professional careers officer. **Amenities:** Bookshops, shops and launderettes; SU with bars, TV rooms, etc; arts centre at Alsager site: studio theatre, dance and drama studios. **Sporting facilities:** Extensive playing fields, swimming pool, squash court and weight-lifting/training rooms, including a twelve station multi-gym, national coaching centre and sports injuries clinic.

Duration of first degree course(s) or equivalent: 3 years; **others:** 4 years (BEd; BA Cert Ed) **Total first degree students 1991/92:** 2,000 **Total BEd students:** 600 **Overseas students:** 30 **Mature students:** 600 **Male/female ratio:** 1:1 **Teaching staff: full-time:** 170 **part-time:** c65 **Total full-time students 1991/92:** 2,700 **Postgraduate students:** c250 **Tuition fees for 1992/93 (first degrees):** Home: £1,855; Overseas: £5,288.

What it's like

Now a faculty of Manchester Metropolitan University, its original two sites are approx 6 miles apart. Crewe campus on outskirts of small, industrial town, pleasantly landscaped with good road and rail links. Alsager campus, in rural, rolling Staffordshire is less accessible but good services to Crewe and Hanley. Intersite bus service provided by college which include limited night services.

Halls on both sites, 5 at Crewe and 9 at Alsager; all are mixed. First years entitled to places; 2nd and final years live out. All halls are fully furnished with cooking facilities; no self-catering option and no creche facilities. Very good management/student relations. SU very active on both sites.

Officially no overnight visitors allowed – unregistered cars are liable to be clamped. Good medical services in Crewe and Leighton hospital, and student services provide a student counsellor for confidential counselling.

Active and successful sports clubs, particularly football, rugby, hockey, netball, lacrosse, volley ball etc. Also active social clubs, eg Christian Union, Women's Group, Lesbian and Gay Group and living colour group. Certain areas of Crewe town, eg Walthall Street inhabited almost entirely by students. Accommodation in Alsager is sparse. Other areas of Crewe not so friendly. Students living out generally meet up at college discos.

Crewe campus mainly HND business studies, environmental studies. Alsager mainly sports science, arts & humanity degrees (BEds on both). Work load depends on course. Assessments based on course work and examinations. The college has a National Coaching Centre, run by the National Coaching Foundation.

Pauper notes

Accommodation: Plenty of accommodation in Crewe, if sometimes rather expensive (£25–£50/week). **Drink:** The Vine, Earl of Crewe, Barrel, Brunswick, Belle Vue and the Victoria in Crewe (just a few of many). In Alsager: The Arms, The Lodge, The Mill and the Plough. **Eats:** Plenty of chippies, Chinese and Indian takeaways and kebab houses. Lakeside Chippie in Alsager does particularly good pizzas. **Ents:** Local Oakley Centre for bands etc. Alsager has drama facilities. Ents on campus have vastly improved. **Sports:** Good facilities at Alsager for a wide range of sports, but little on Crewe campus. Leisure centres, pools, etc both towns. **Hardship fund:** Access funds only. **Travel:** Exchanges with Bridgewater State University, Boston. Excellent for rail travel and Sandbach service station is a useful hitching point. **Work:** Very little locally, only bar work.

Informal name

C+ACHE

Buzz-word

CASU (Students' Union)

Alumni (Editors' pick)

Peter Purves, Mary Whitehouse, Steve Bainbridge, Dewi Morris, Matt Duncan, Phil Lewis, Ian Bucket, Sue Metcalf, Martin Grimley, Max Robertson, Tom Bailey (Thompson twins).

DARTINGTON

Dartington College of Arts, Totnes, Devon TQ9 6EJ (0803 862224)
Map A, C9

Student enquiries: Senior Administration Assistant (Registry & Examinations)

Main study areas – as in What to Study section: *(First degree):* Drama and theatre arts, music. *Also* Arts management, community arts, performance arts, visual performance.

European Community: Formal exchange links with universities/colleges in

Denmark (Aarhus), Germany (Berlin) and Netherlands (Utrecht). Lead workshops at international performing arts festival in German (1992); Research into integration of theatre, music and visual arts within European higher education. Approved Erasmus programme 1992/93.

Application: PCAS for 1993 start, UCAS thereafter. **Academic developments:** College now associated with Plymouth University, offering modular programmes in performance arts and single/combined honours in music, theatre, visual performance. **Special features:** College enjoys a close relationship with the Dartington Hall Trust; a unique establishment concerned with industry, education, arts and community development in rural area. Known for interest in Indian and other cultures. **Founded:** 1961. **Main awards:** BA. **Awarding body:** Plymouth University. **Site:** In beautiful grounds on River Dart. **Access:** Road and rail access to Plymouth and Exeter (within half hour), 10 mins from Totnes. **Accommodation:** 68 single study rooms on campus, accommodation officer helps with flats and lodgings in district. **Library:** 40,000 books and scores, 3,000 sound recordings, slides, films. **Other learning resources:** specialist performance technology centre, studios, workshops and practice rooms. **Welfare:** Nurse/health centre. **Careers:** Emphasis on preparing students for arts work in community. **Amenities:** Social centre with common room, bar, laundry, theatre, cinema; extensive grounds and garden.

Duration of first degree course(s) or equivalent: 3 years **Total first degree students 1991/92:** 353 **Overseas students:** 2 **Mature students:** 180 **Male/female ratio:** 2:1 **Teaching staff: full-time:** 33 **part-time:** 63 **Total full-time students 1991/92:** 367 **Tuition fees for 1992/93 (first degrees):** Home: £2,770; Overseas: £4,550.

What it's like

Beautiful, isolated campus, 20-minute walk from Totnes. Picturesque gardens, old buildings and trees. Small campus, intimate and comforting but claustrophobic at times – 370 full-time students. Provision for disabled students improving on a difficult campus – on the side of a hill. Child-care provision not good, means single parent families could find difficulty coping with courses and running a home. A small college, not a lot of money put into SU but still provides a variety of events from cabaret, folk nights and music in the bar to regular bands and discos. Student President and Executive look after SU affairs.

Easy reach of Torbay, Plymouth, Exeter and Dartmoor, though local bus service not too frequent. Totnes has great second hand market every Friday and main line railway station.

Staff/student relationships are good within college's friendly atmosphere. In Totnes, town and college mix well. Good pubs, eateries and every type of therapy you can think of – and then some.

Attracts European and Asian students; positively encourages applications from mature students. Excellent relations between SU and Admin. Library hours good; provision of texts/recorded material very good. Overnight visitors restricted to weekends. College nurse present each morning and two GP surgeries per week. Information readily available and comprehensive. As well as academic counsellors there is a counsellor on site for confidential and personal problems and visiting counsellor once a week.

Accommodation off campus improving, but rents can be more than you feel you want to pay. Rooms in family houses, flats, houses in Totnes and surrounding districts are the norm. Rural, so own transport a definite advantage. Not a lot of family housing available, and none on campus; so mature family students beware! Good college accommodation officer. 1991/92 is first year of revalidated course and work-load is high. High class visiting lecturers ensure that courses relate to current thinking in all subject areas. Few find the combination of work-load and campus conditions unbearable and leave. Failure rate low.

Students from a wide variety of social and educational backgrounds. Good visual and sound studios. More male than female lecturers but this deficiency is under constant appraisal. Female principal. Easy going college with no racism or calculated sexism. It's a beautiful place if you're up to here with pavements and exhaust fumes.

Pauper notes

Accommodation: 3 residential blocks for 68 students plus block for another 18 15-minute walk from main site. Latter is self catering. Blocks have fridge, toaster and kettle. No other personal cooking appliances are allowed. All single rooms with wash basins; kitchenette and 2 showers per 12 students. Other temporary accommodation is provided to cater for overflow. First years have priority for on site accommodation. **Drink:** Student club sells variety of beers and lagers but is not cheap. Public house also on campus but more expensive. Depends what you call a good pub, but ones in Totnes are well used both by students and locals. **Eats:** Cafeteria on campus not subsidised. Usual moans about prices and standard of food. Wide variety of vegan/vegetarian eating in Totnes. Also Chinese, fish and chips. Good value in local pubs. **Ents:** Visiting theatre companies, dance, concerts of all kinds, art exhibitions run by Dartington Arts Society; almost 100% on campus. Students are all members and further concessions are available. SU organises bands, discos, cabaret, gong shows, etc. Lots of home-grown entertainment, classical and bop most of the night away. No cinema in town but arts society has cinema on campus. **Sports:** Squash courts, outdoor pool and tennis in summer term. Indoor swimming pool in Totnes. Plenty of countryside to jog in or river walks. **Hardship funds:** Not a lot, so doesn't go far. **Work:** Some on campus (bar and library). This is Devon: work scarce.

Informal name

DCA

DARTMOUTH

Britannia Royal Naval College, Dartmouth, Devon Map A, C9

Student enquiries: Commander Graham Kemp RN, The Officer Enquiry Section, Old Admiralty Buildings, Spring Gardens, London SW1A 2BE.

Main study areas: Computing, electrical and electronic engineering, Navy studies, strategic studies.

European Community: Number of students taking EC languages or spending time in another EC country, not known.

Entry conditions: Candidates must be at least 17 years old and under 22, 23 or 26 (dependent on the type of entry). Minimum entrance requirements: 5 GCSE or equivalent (grade C or better), including English language and maths; 2 A-levels required for full career commissions; A-level passes in physics and maths for engineering specialisation for both full and medium career commissions; many graduate entrants. Before entry candidates must pass Admiralty Interview Board and medical examination. **Entry dates:** Main entries in September, January and May. **Special features:** All naval officers start their careers at Dartmouth, as do many officers of foreign navies. The time spent at Dartmouth depends upon course taken. After period of general naval training, students go on to specialist training either at sea, at Dartmouth, at Royal Naval Engineering College, Manadon (see Manadon), or at universities. **Founded:** Training on River Dart since 1863. College buildings completed in 1905. **Site:** Beautiful hillside setting overlooking the Dart estuary. **Access:** Nearest British Rail stations at Paignton and Totnes. **Accommodation:** Single or shared cabins for all students. **Welfare:** Excellent, including full medical and dental facilities. **Amenities:** Full range of sporting and recreational facilities, including gymnasium, swimming pool, sports grounds with hard hockey pitch; over 100 boats and yachts and a beagle pack.

CAN'T FIND WHAT YOU'RE LOOKING FOR? USE THE INDEX!

Duration of first degree course(s) or equivalent: up to 4 terms. **Male/female ratio:** 10:1. **Total full-time students 1992/93:** approx 400.

What it's like

Dartmouth is the Royal Naval Officers' new entry training establishment. As such day-to-day life at BRNC is very different from that of a normal university as the students are here to learn how to be leaders in the Royal Navy as well as to acquire the academic knowledge that will equip them for their future careers.

The student population is male and female and includes a number of international students. Daily routine is full, varied and demanding, geared to producing a healthy body and an agile mind. Teaching staff is comprised of full-time civilian lecturers and serving naval personnel and the academic courses cover a wide range of subjects from international affairs to celestial navigation.

Most students are accommodated in either single or double rooms and full board is provided. Visitors are welcome but no provision made for their overnight accommodation (abundance of small hotels and guest houses in the holiday town of Dartmouth). College is poorly served by public transport and although the town is an easy walk away, those wishing to venture further afield will find their own transport a necessity.

Wide range of cultural, recreational and sporting activities which include music, drama, sailing, rugby, riding, cricket and squash to name but a few.

Alumni (Editors' pick)

HRH Duke of Edinburgh, HRH the Prince of Wales, HRH the Duke of York.

DE MONTFORT UNIVERSITY

De Montfort University, The Gateway, Leicester LE1 9BH
(0533 551551) Map A, E6 and
**De Montfort University: Milton Keynes, Hammerwood Gate,
Kents Hill, Milton Keynes MK7 6HP** (0908 695511)

Student enquiries: Academic Registrar

Main study areas – as in What to Study section: *(First degree):* Accountancy, agriculture and horticulture, architecture, art & design, Asian studies, biology, biotechnology, business studies, chemistry, computing, dance, drama, economics, electrical & electronic engineering, English, environmental studies, fine arts, history, information technology, law, mathematical studies, mechanical and production engineering, modern languages, music, pharmacy, physics, politics and government, public administration, social policy and social welfare, speech sciences. *Also:* Building, equine studies, estate management, footwear, furniture design, performance arts, surveying, textiles.

European Community: 20% first degree students learn an EC language as part of their course, ½% spend time in another EC country. Languages available on courses in economics, business studies, public administration, business information systems, electronic engineering, industrial and business systems. Formal exchange links with over 40 EC universities/colleges: Denmark (1, design and manufacture); Eire (3, for fine arts, public policy and management studies); France (6, for eg economics, health and community studies, performing arts); Germany (12, for eg architecture, chemistry, human resource management, design and manufacture, engineering, textile design); Greece (1, design and manufacture); Italy (3, performing arts, design and manufacture, electrical & electronic engineering); Netherlands (6, for eg architecture, fine art, engineering, human resource management); Portugal (2, electrical & electronic engineering); Spain (6, eg for health and community studies, architecture, managerial studies). Approved Erasmus programme 1992.

Application: PCAS for 1993 start, UCAS thereafter; ADAR for art and design. **Special features:** Policy of encouraging mature students and disabled students where feasible. **Largest fields of study:** Business, technology, construction. **Founded:** 1992, as a university; previously Leicester Poly, founded 1969. **Main awards:** BA, BSc, BEng. **Awarding body:** De Montfort University. **Site:** Split on 2 sites; at or within easy reach of Leicester city centre; plus another site in Milton Keynes. **Academic features:** Semester structure operates for combined studies and engineering technology. Year 1 of combined studies available at franchise centres around the country (check with university for nearest). **Access:** Central position, easy access by rail and road. **Accommodation:** 1,270 places in halls of residence; 500+ approved lodgings; university housing 400+ places; monthly private housing list published; flats also available through the Student Housing Association. **Library:** on both Leicester sites, City campus and Scraptoft site; 276,000 volumes in total, 2,076 periodicals, 995 study places; collection of audio-visual material; micro-lab. **Other learning resources:** Excellent computing facilities. **Careers:** Information, advice and placement service. **Welfare:** Counselling; student health service; chaplaincy; legal information service. **Amenities:** Bookshop; exhibition hall; SU; expanding computer facilities. **Sporting facilities:** Good sporting facilities. **Employment:** Strong links with textile and fashion, and engineering industries (excellent employment record).

Duration of first degree course(s) or equivalent: 3 years; **others:** 4 years sandwich, 5 years extended **Total first degree students 1991/92:** 9,360 incl. all franchise centres **Overseas students:** 281 **Mature students:** 2,656 **Male/female ratio:** 5:4 **Teaching staff: full-time:** 700 **part-time:** 550 **Total full-time students 1991/92:** 11,221 **Postgraduate students:** 285 **Tuition fees for 1992/93 (first degrees):** Home: £759 (if no grant), £1,855 (classroom), £2,770 (lab/studio); Overseas: £4,900 (classroom), £5,300 (lab/studio).

What it's like

Living: Not a very attractive campus – one remaining patch of grass has recently been covered up with a new engineering block (*enormous* building and very environmentally friendly – solar panels, etc to tie in with the City Challenge idea). Canal runs next to the Union – some nice walks and cycle paths in the immediate area. Also castle gardens – attractive and a couple of mins from the Union. Campus can be a bit depressing at first glance, but is actually much nicer than you first think once you've seen it in sunshine etc!

Accommodation generally good. Lots of terraced houses (boasts longest row of terraces in Britain – Tudor Road). Average rent £25–£35/wk. I think Leicester's an excellent place to live. Narborough Road is a complete student community: shops, chippies, pubs, launderettes etc, and all open at unsociable hours. Alternatively, big student community up near the *other uni* – London Road area. Highfields can be very dodgy, but parts of it are great – very multicultural. Victoria Park/Queens Road area is lovely – bit far from DSU unless you've got a bike though, and houses can be pricey. Route into centre is down New Walk – attractive tree-lined path.

Library: recently obscured from view by the engineering block. Open 9am to 9pm Monday to Friday, 9 to 5 Saturday, and I'm told that it now opens Sunday too, although I've not tried this yet! Union shop opens till 6.00pm. Travel shop shuts 5.30pm. Neither open weekends.

SU: Apathetic in the extreme politically. UGMs attract a handful of SWSS extremists who use the meetings as platforms for their personal causes while the rest of the student body eats its lunch and wonders what all the noise is about. Politically active people should go somewhere else, unless they fancy taking on a challenge!

Socially: DSU is excellent – John Peel's favourite student venue! Attracts some big names – Arena has recently had a state-of-the-art PA installed; sounds brilliant. Only problem is that smaller bands fail to fill the Arena, so can look a bit like a cow barn unless it's more than half full. When it *is* full though it's a great venue – big stage, upper viewing area around dancefloor, and an enormous bar adjacent to stage. Smaller gigs can be catered for in the Red Chair Area. Big bands: tickets average £6 to £8. Disco nights: Wed, Fri, Sat (Wed and Sat mainstream; Fri alternative). Sat is always a sell-out (a recent change: 12 months ago Wed and Fri were sell-outs but are now pretty unpopular).

Inta-site: union magazine (edited by me). Editor's job is sabbatical, so changes every 1 to 2 years depending on whether you want to re-stand. Since I've been doing the job, it's gone from glossy paper into newsprint – more student-orientated. Feeling was it'd got a bit stuffy and Sunday-supplement-ish. Student input is improving but, to be honest, mag doesn't count for much in the average student's scheme of things.

Student cars: Few have them, probably because it's such a hassle to park *anywhere* in Leicester, especially on campus! And then there's the dreaded ring road . . . Football days: don't even think about it . . . you won't find a space within a 5-mile radius of Filbert Street.

Health etc: There's a student counselling service separate from the SU. Health centre is opposite SU and is friendly and helpful, but with the inevitable waiting list. New chaplaincy is being built at the moment in the Fletcher Building quad to replace the Portacabin.

Shops: Great student city, although shops leave a little something to be desired. Silver Arcade – 4 floors of 'arty' and interesting shops. Good for secondhand clothes and jewellery etc. **The Market:** Amazing. Has to be seen to be believed. Enormous fruit and vegetable market – includes florists, secondhand and new clothes (more of these on a particular day). You can eat so cheaply here; come 5 o'clock, they're giving the stuff away! You can buy enough vegetables to last at least a week for a fiver or less. Also sells 'exotic' fruit and veg: papayas, plantains, mangoes etc due to large black and Asian community. Also a massive indoor market – several floors high – and a great fish, meat and cheese market. Again, silly prices.

Pubs, Clubs etc: Student favourites are: The Princess Charlotte: live gigs every night, attracts big names and makes the national music press. Free soup Sunday lunchtime. Pump and Tap: live music most nights, free food Sundays, nice atmosphere. Hosts some great all-dayers. Closest pub to the 'Narby'. The Magazine: recently re-done, an *excellent* place and my fave. Great decor, nice beer, live music upstairs and a big beer yard. Free condoms on bar. Very much a pub based around certain political and social ideals, but these are not rammed down your throat. Love it. Oooh, good food too. The Globe, city centre: bit nondescript, but nice. Eight clubs (some studenty, one gay, some ravey, some less so).

Food: You're better off going to the market and cooking your own! Good places though are Mrs Bridge's tea rooms, the Devil's Kitchen for a good cheap and greasy meal, Blossom's (veggie), Bread and Roses, Que Pasa and Rum Runner (Mexican and good fun). Some good Indian restaurants and kebab shops.

Theatres: Phoenix Arts, always popular. Nice cafe, and a full timetable of events, films, etc. Good late showings, start 11pm. Haymarket, good but a bit pricey. Haymarket Studio has some interesting stuff – of more interest to students than the bigger productions.

Local community: good relations. Very little student bashing – you really have to *look* for trouble. Many of the student hangouts aren't in the town centre, which is where most trouble occurs, usually between non-students. Some complaints about noise from SU-area residents. SU takes active part in local residents' group to deal with these and maintain good relations. Only real threat to students comes from the more dodgy parts of Highfields where you need to be careful.

Generally, a great place to live. All the benefits of a cosmopolitan city, but with the feel of a big town. A good place to be in for your first time away from home – not in the least intimidating or threatening (easy to get lost in though). Lots of green bits – parks etc. and everything is within easy reach. Leicester people are generally very friendly. Not a million miles from some nice countryside if you're that way inclined.

Sue Lee, Vice President Communications

GET HOLD OF THE PROSPECTUSES

Pauper notes

Accommodation: Good – hundreds of terraced houses. New halls recently built at Milton Keynes campus and more are planned at city campus. **Drink:** SU is good and cheap. Good selection of local pubs who cater specifically for student style groups. **Eats:** SU food is good and cheap, as are the takeouts in Narborough Road. Couple of local pubs do vegetarian and vegan food – look out for the magazine. **Ents:** Princess Charlotte 5 mins from SU and is famous on the low key/indie/thrash/rock circuit. **Sports:** Uni sports centre does good selection of keep fit classes such as step-aerobics etc. **Hardship funds:** Done via the welfare officer in the SU. **Travel:** Good local bus service. Midland Fox operate cheap season tickets for students – good relations with SU travel shop. **Work:** Loads of pubs. Work in the SU – waiting list can be anything from 1 to 6 months. Pay = standard, ie £3/hr or less.

More info?

Enquiries to SU (0533 555576).

Buzz-words

DSU (De Montfort Students Union), Mi'duck (term of address by Leicester residents), 'Narby' (abbreviation of Narborough Road – the student area of the city), also 'yoh' (to rhyme with 'o'range), eg hiyoh! see yoh! ooh, yoh! (exclamation of surprise . . .).

Alumni (Editors' pick)

Charles Dance (actor).

DERBYSHIRE COLLEGE

See Derby University

DERBY UNIVERSITY

University of Derby, Kedleston Road, Derby DE3 1GB (0332 47181)
Map A, E6

Student enquiries: The Registry

Main study areas – as in What to Study section: *(First degree):* Accountancy, American studies, art & design, biology, business studies, chemistry, computing, drama, economics, education, electrical & electronic engineering, English, environmental studies, European studies, fine arts, geography, geology, history, information technology, law, mathematical studies, mechanical & production engineering, modern languages, music, nursing studies, physics, professions allied to medicine (PAMs), religious studies & theology, social policy and social welfare. *Also:* Film studies, tourism, photography.

European Community: 6% first degree students take EC language as part of course and 3% spend 6 months or more in another EC country. Formal exchange links with some 5 EC universities/colleges, including: Belgium (Nemours); France (Caen, Paris and Tours) and Netherlands (Breda). Planned expansion of modern languages learning and extension of range of languages available.

Application: PCAS for 1993 start, UCAS thereafter; ADAR for photographic studies and textile design. **Largest fields of study:** Design (textiles, fashion, graphic), education, earth & life studies. **Academic features:** New modular degree with 50 options; degrees in nursing, occupational therapy, accountancy and environmental monitoring. Biological imaging degree. **Structural features:**

Institute of Health and Community Studies, in collaboration with health authority. **Special features:** Artist-in-residence. **Founded:** 1992. Previously Derbyshire College, founded 1983, ex Derby Lonsdale and Matlock Colleges of Higher Education. **Main awards:** BA, BEd, BSc. **Awarding body:** Derby University. **Site:** Split on 3 sites. **Access:** Buses from Derby city centre. **Accommodation:** 2,000 places in halls, places in registered lodgings (priority given to first year students). Approx cost: £38 pw self-catering halls, £30 pw lodgings. Rent: 30% in accommodation where rent controlled by college. **Library:** Main libraries at Kedleston Road and Mickleover sites; 315,000 volumes, 1,900 periodicals, 500 study places. **Other Learning Resources:** Computer centre and media services centre. **Welfare:** Head of student services, assistant deans, wardens and college nurse, chaplaincy, student counsellors. **Hardship funds:** Directors administer a hardship fund. **Careers:** Information and advisory service. **Amenities:** SU shop and bar, bookshops and stationery kiosks at main campuses, vending machines. **Sporting facilities:** Gymnasia, heated indoor swimming pool at Mickleover site.

Duration of first degree course(s) or equivalent: 3 years; **others:** 4 years (sandwich) **Total first degree students 1990/91:** 5,000; **BEd students:** 800 **Overseas students:** 120 **Mature students:** 600 **Male/female ratio:** 6:5 **Teaching staff: full-time:** 300 **part-time:** 200 **Total full-time students:** 4,000 **Postgraduate students:** 2,000 **Tuition fees 1992/93 first degrees:** Home: £1,855 (classroom), £2,770 (lab/studio); Overseas: £4,850.

What it's like

It's concentrated on 7 sites in Derby. Main site, Kedleston Road on a hill, with magnificent views of the countryside from upper floors. All sites on main bus routes from town centre, with one, Green Lane, actually in town centre.

College accommodation varies from purpose built blocks eg Fitzherbert Hall and Lonsdale Hall to converted Victorian residences along Uttoxeter New Road. Most people live in private rented accommodation.

The student body is individual in its variety: a large proportion of women (balance has been addressed), many overseas students from countries as far apart as Ghana and Malaysia; also American and EC students.

Library on 3 sites. Gymnasium and a multi-gym for weight training on the Kedleston Road site. SU has developed rapidly in recent years and continues to be very progressive. There is a recreation room at Kedleston Road with a bar in separate building, and an SU block at Mickleover (recent facelift) where many events held. SU particularly effective representing student point of view on university committees; co-ordinates effective campaigns on multitude of issues; also runs variety of clubs and societies – the most active being mountaineering and caving, students against bloodsports, football and rugby. SU discounts for students in the city include Derby Playhouse, the Showcase cinema, sports and record shops. Wide range of pubs to choose from in town centre and plenty of country pubs. Most are supplied by Bass, Ind Coope, Marstons and Wards.

Nationally renowned art and design faculty and photography courses; geography option in earth and life studies degrees offers a field trip to Morocco.

Students friendly, not that politically active; everyone seems to get on very well. Community spirit maintained during expansion. People find it easy to settle in and have a very enjoyable time.

Pauper notes

Accommodation: Prices going up due to expansion of college and new Toyota car plant. **Drink:** SU bar cheapest drinks in town – Wards and Courage bitter. Other good places are Ye Olde Dolphin Inn (oldest pub in Derby), The Spa Inn in Abbey Street – serves Burton ale, and the students' favourite – the Great Northern on Junction Street. **Eats:** College restaurant now with edible food. Best takeaway Tuminose on St Peter's Street (pizzas and bolognese burgers a speciality), Ronos on Abbey Street. Many good Indian restaurants – many give student discount. Abbey Street kebab shops best. **Ents:** Theme discos. Annual favourites – Freshers Ball, Halloween Party and Bonfire Night. Bands recently already included Asia Fields, Lilac Time and Ska Boom. Also many bands at the assembly rooms; new venues, Wherehouse and Indie give student discounts. College radio. **Sports:** On campus – 2 gyms and multigym. College swimming pool – free to students. In town City Recreation Centre; Rollerworld, Roos Sports Centre and Moorways Sports Stadium. **Hardship funds:** SU offers loans – up to £30, also directors fund. **Travel:** Intersite buses. Centre of country so easy for all transport networks. Railcards and ISIC from SU Office. **Work:** Very little or poorly paid.

Informal name

DCHE

Buzz-words

UNR (Uttoxeter New Road); G/L (Green Lane); K/R or Keddy (Kedleston Road).

Alumni (Editors' pick)

Russell Harty, Barry Evans (Leicester/England – rugby), John Blakemore (photographer/lecturer), Berni Yates (fashion designer).

DUNCAN OF JORDANSTONE

Duncan of Jordanstone College of Art, Perth Road, Dundee DD1 4HT (0382 23261) Map A, D2

Student enquiries: Assistant Registrar

Main study areas – as in What to Study section: *(First degree):* Architecture, art & design, food science & nutrition, hotel & catering management, town and country planning. *Also:* Home economics.

European Community: 8% first degree students take EC language as part of course and 1% spend 6 months or more in another EC country. Language teaching available for all degree students as extra. Formal exchange links with several European institutions. Approved Erasmus programme 1992/93.

Application: UCCA for architecture, town planning, hotel and catering manage-

CAN'T FIND WHAT YOU'RE LOOKING FOR? USE THE INDEX!

ment and food and welfare studies for 1993 start, UCAS thereafter; direct other degrees. **Academic features:** Degree courses in art and design from common foundation course. Professional video and microcomputer centre available to students as a secondary study. **Special features:** Writer in residence. Staff/student exchanges with Nova Scotia College of Art & Design (Canada); School of the Art Institute of Chicago (USA). **Largest fields of study:** Architecture, art and design. **Main awards:** BArch, BDes, BA, BSc(Arch), BSc. **Awarding body:** Dundee University. **Site:** Dundee city centre. **Accommodation:** 156 hostel places (80% for first year students). Approx cost: £26 pw. Rent: 15% in accommodation where rent controlled by college. **Library:** 36,000 volumes, 180 periodicals, 130 study places. **Other learning resources:** Computer facilities. **Welfare:** No on-campus facilities. Assistant Registrar provides advice and assistance whenever possible. Access to Dundee University student welfare service. **Hardship funds:** College and SU offer loan scheme. Access funds available. **Careers:** Information service. **Amenities:** Shop, student common room, refectory and coffee bar. University SU and sports facilities.

Duration of first degree course(s) or equivalent: 4 years; **others:** 5 + 1 years for architecture **Total first degree students 1991/92:** 1,110 **Number of overseas students:** 39 **Male/female ratio:** 1:1 **Teaching staff: full-time:** 85 **part-time:** 70 **Total full-time students 1991/92:** 1,280 **Postgraduate students:** 75 **Tuition fees for 1992/93 (first degrees):** Home: £696 (if no grant), £1,855 (classroom), £2,770 (studio); Overseas: £5,500.

What it's like

Surrounded by university buildings, 5 mins walk from the city centre, with access to major shopping precincts (three in all). The original building was erected in 1955 to house mainly art-orientated courses but as the college's reputation gradually grew it became necessary to expand the premises; new building opened in 1974 housing a further 400 students on eg architecture and home economics. Social life is as good as you make it. 2 college functions a week, Wednesday night fund raiser discos for students and Friday night disco, with live music when affordable. Accommodation difficult to find but college has blocks of flats shared with local technical college (200 places) mostly for first and second year students. Rent includes lighting, heating and hot water but an off-putting contract has to be signed. Welfare officer will discuss financial or personal problems as will student president if preferred. Continual assessment on most courses with an end of term show of work. Changing courses or taking a year out is possible but not encouraged. Student association representation on all major governing bodies including appeals.

Pauper notes

Accommodation: Fairly hard to find – increased college residential accommodation. **Drink:** College surrounded by student pubs, SA coffee bar, external bar – competitive prices. **Eats:** Variety of Indian, Chinese, vegetarian within immediate vicinity. **Ents:** College discos twice weekly, theatre, cinema. **Sports:** University sports complex, leisure centre. **Hardship funds:** Dependent on availability of funds. **Travel:** University housed campus travel. **Work:** Bar work.

Alumni (Editors' pick)

Albert Watson (royal photographer), David Leslie (rugby international).

DUNDEE INSTITUTE

Dundee Institute of Technology, Bell Street, Dundee DD1 1HG
(0382 308000) Map A, D2

Student enquiries: Registry

Main study areas – as in What to Study section: *(First degree):* Accountancy, biology, biotechnology, business studies, chemistry, civil engineering, computing, economics, electrical & electronic engineering, environmental science, mathematical studies, mechanical and production engineering, nursing studies, physics. *Also:* Quantity surveying, environmental technology, retail & distribution management.

European Community: Approx 25% first degree students take EC language as part of course. Those studying European business administration spend 1 year in another EC country; shorter period in EC an option in applied economics. EC language tuition available as an option in a range of other degrees.

Application: PCAS for 1993 start, UCAS thereafter. **Academic features:** Biotechnology: chemistry with business studies: legal studies; building engineering and management; European business administration. **Special features:** All courses have strong vocational bias; good staff links with commerce and industry. Class sizes are small. **Largest fields of study:** Engineering, science, business and other professional disciplines. **Main awards:** BA, BSc, BEng. **Awarding body:** Dundee Institute. **Site:** Main building plus 2 other sites in Dundee city centre, 2 others being prepared. **Accommodation:** 390 places in institute flats; 170 places in hall of residence (particularly suitable for first year students); over 150 places in lodgings plus accommodation in private flats. Rent: 26% in accommodation where rent controlled by institute. **Library:** 100,000 volumes, 15,500 journals and periodicals, 400 study places, tied book system, audio-visual material. **Specialist collections:** Annual reports of 3,000–4,000 companies. **Other learning facilities:** Media centre; computer centre with powerful VAX system, available for use by all students. **Welfare:** Counselling and advice, medical and health, accommodation, chaplaincy. All students have personal tutor. **Hardship funds:** City of Dundee Educational Trust; Angus Educational Trust; access fund. **Careers:** Information, advice and placement service. **Amenities:** Bookshop; SU building with bars, games rooms, etc. **Sporting facilities:** Indoor facilities at SU.

Duration of first degree course(s) or equivalent: 4 years; **others:** 5 years (sandwich degrees), 1 yr less for unclassified.**Total first degree students 1991/92:** 1,780 **Overseas students:** 97 **Mature students:** 181 **Male/female ratio:** 3:1 **Teaching staff: full-time:** 199 **part-time:** 0 **Total full-time students 1991/92:** 2,520 **Postgraduate students:** 206 **Tuition fees for 1992/93 (first degrees):** Home: £666; Overseas: £3,570. All first year students pay £50 registration fee.

What it's like

Situated in Dundee city centre; one of Scotland's Central Institutions offering degree and HND courses. Accommodation is all around Dundee; college accommodation is in city centre, or 2–4 miles outside. Private accommodation is fairly easy to get but can be expensive. All college accommodation has laundry facilities, mostly self catering but halls of residence places are available. Overnight guests not allowed in college accommodation without prior permission and no mixed accommodation available.

SU (recently refurbished) has variety of facilities including two bars, games room (snooker, fully equipped leisure centre, table tennis) well-stocked shop and an excellent food service. Variety of clubs and societies, all very active.

Student welfare excellent and all counselling confidential.

Students regarded by Dundonians passively. Relations between other Dundee colleges and university good.

Approximately 15% of students receive minimum grant and an overseas student population of about 6%. The student population is varied and comes from many different backgrounds and social groups.

Pauper notes

Accommodation: Private accommodation only for mixed couples. **Drink:** SU cheapest. Several good real ale pubs. Beer usually of high standard and a wide variety. **Eats:** SU cheap and varied. Many pubs do good meals. **Ents:** Steps

Theatre, cinemas and rep all have discounts. Good live bands both major and minor. **Sports:** City council has good facilities and a Scottish Premier league team. **Hardship funds:** SA operates loan fund. **Travel:** Student fare system in operation. On main routes for easy hitching. **Work:** Pubs, PO at Christmas, potato and fruit picking during summer.

DUNDEE UNIVERSITY

University of Dundee, Dundee DD1 4HN (0382 23181) Map A, D2

Student enquiries: University Admissions Officer

Main study areas – as in What to Study section: *(First degree):* Accountancy, American studies, anatomy, architecture, art & design, biochemistry, biology, botany, chemistry, civil engineering, computing, dentistry, economics, electrical and electronic engineering, English, environmental science, European studies, fine arts, food science & nutrition, geography, history, hotel and catering management, law, mathematical studies, mechanical and production engineering, medicine, microbiology, pharmacology, philosophy, physics, physiology, politics and government, psychology, social policy and social welfare, town and country planning, zoology. *Also:* molecular science.

European Community: 2% first degree students take EC language as part of course and 1% spend 6 months or more in another EC country. Formal exchange links with a number of EC universities/colleges in Denmark (architecture), France (economics, European studies, law, modern languages and other arts subjects); Germany (English); Italy (pharmacology); Netherlands (architecture, law, town planning); Spain (law, pharmacology, economics and management); various countries for remote sensing. All students have access to language unit which offers practical skills in a wide range of languages, as non-examined option. French may be integral part of degrees in law and hotel and catering management; French, German or Spanish may be involved in all arts and social science degrees including European studies. Approved Erasmus programme 1992.

Application: UCCA for 1993 start, UCAS thereafter. **Academic features:** Students able to switch between arts and social sciences and science and engineering subjects respectively before entering the second year. New courses in accountancy and chemistry or computer science or mathematics, environmental biology and ecology, microbiology with biotechnology or genetics, molecular cell biology, molecular genetics, environmental management. **Founded:** 1882. **Main awards:** BA, BAcc, BArch, BDes, BDS, BEng, BMSc, BSc, LLB, MA, MB, ChB. **Awarding body:** Dundee University. **Site:** Near city centre. **Access:** By foot, rail and road. **Accommodation:** 860 places in mixed halls; over 950 places in university houses (over 50% students are accommodated, approximately 20% are home-based); 40% in accommodation where rent controlled by university. **Library:** Main library with approx 500,000 volumes; medical, law and departmental libraries; archives department; inter-library loan scheme. **Other learning facilities:** Computing service; microcomputer centre, Tay estuary research centre; central media service unit; language unit. **Welfare:** Student counselling service. Health service offers routine medical examinations by local GP. **Hardship funds:** Loans may be available to students who encounter financial hardship. **Careers:** Information and advice service. **Amenities:** SU building with swimming pool, shop, bars, restaurant, bookshop, coin laundry; chaplaincy centre; civic repertory theatre adjoining campus. **Sporting facilities:** Indoor sports complex; university sports grounds and water sports centre; more than 20 golf courses including St Andrews and Carnoustie within half an hour's drive; skiing, climbing and hill walking in surrounding countryside.

Duration of first degree course(s) or equivalent: 4 years; **others:** 5 years (architecture, dentistry and medicine) **Total first degree students 1991/92:** 4,973

Overseas students: 9% **Mature students:** 17% **Male/female ratio:** 3:2 **Teaching staff: full-time:** 360 **part-time:** 45 **honorary:** 380 (mainly in medicine and dentistry and courses taught at Duncan of Jordanstone College of Art) **Total full-time students 1991/92:** 5,599 **Postgraduate students:** 626 **Tuition fees for 1992/93 (first degrees):** Home: £760 (if no grant), £1,855 (classroom), £2,770 (lab), £4,985 (clinical); Overseas: £5,320 (classroom), £7,055 (lab), £12,990 (clinical).

What it's like

Campus a mixture of modern and 18th-century buildings. City centre 2 mins away, but no through traffic allowed. All facilities on campus with the exception of medical faculty which is on a separate campus 3 miles away. Ninewells Hospital is the largest teaching hospital in Europe. Plentiful accommodation, but not always the best. Excellent relationship between university and students – community atmosphere, close liaison with city. High proportion of mature students. Students from all over the country. Low drop out rate. Large, new library and excellent sports centre on campus. SU is centre of students' social life; politically fairly quiet.

Most courses are very flexible; transfers are easy at beginning of each year. Many field trips, several abroad. Work load really what you make it. Work assessment varies from course to course – all include exams but large move towards continual assessment.

Complete student support network. Full-time student counsellor, careers service, health service, plus SU run welfare team. Free dental treatment provided in campus dental hospital.

Over 70 active societies – many sports orientated. City geared towards students who form about 5% of population. Many pubs, two theatres, couple of cinemas (one devoted to showing 'alternative' films). Easy to meet other students.

Pauper notes

Accommodation: Univ accommodation. Cheapest private flats found by word of mouth. **Drink:** Union definitely cheapest – famous for 'Green Monsters'. Excellent Heavy throughout city. Most pubs do special promos from time to time – watch noticeboards. **Eats:** Union pizza parlour. **Ents:** Union; Dundee rep theatre. **Sports:** Sports centre on campus. Swimming pool in Association; new leisure centre 10 mins from campus. Ice rink in city. **Hardship funds:** Summer hardship fund, access fund, Lang Trust. **Travel:** No travel scholarships. Cheap fares available through Campus Travel in Union. **Work:** Association – bars, security, ents, DJs, painting, decorating, advertising etc. Other work difficult.

More info?

Get students' Alternative Prospectus.
Enquiries to A. Lamont (0382 21841).

Alumni (Editors' pick)

David Leslie (Scottish rugby captain; member of 1984 'Grand Slam' team), George Robertson MP, Selina Scott.

DURHAM UNIVERSITY

University of Durham, Old Shire Hall, Durham DH1 3HP
(091 374 2000) Map A, E4

Student enquiries: Academic Registrar

Main study areas – as in What to Study section: *(First degree):* Anthropology, archaeology, Asian studies, biochemistry, biology, botany, chemistry, civil engineering, classics, computing, economics, education, electrical and electronic engineering, English, geography, geology, history, law, linguistics, mathematical studies, mechanical and production engineering, microbiology, modern languages, music, Near East and Islamic studies, philosophy, physics, politics and government, psychology, religious studies and theology, social policy and social welfare, sociology. *Also:* Chinese, Japanese.

European Community: 10% first degree students take EC language as part of course and 4% spend 6 months or more in another EC country. Formal exchange links with increasing number of EC universities/colleges including: geography – 8 universities – main exchange with Tubingen (Germany), Barcelona (Spain); history – Roskilde (Denmark); theology – Aarhus and Tubingen (Germany); engineering – Nat Univ of Greece; education – Duisburg (Germany). New language centre where all students can learn EC languages in their free time. Approved Erasmus programme 1992.

Application: UCCA for 1993 start, UCAS thereafter. **Special features:** University consists of 12 colleges and 2 societies, largely self-governing, although teaching organised centrally. **Founded:** 1832. **Main awards:** BA, BSc. **Awarding body:** Durham University. **Site:** Durham city centre and south of river. **Accommodation:** Accommodation provided for 80% of undergraduate student body. **Library:** Main library has over 780,000 volumes, plus departmental and college libraries. **Welfare:** Student health centre; sick-bay facilities in each college, particular concern with deaf students with special adviser. **Careers:** Advisory service. **Amenities:** Wide range of facilities in both colleges and centrally (bar, bookshop, minibus) at Dunelm House, modern SU building; small theatre; museum of oriental art. **Sporting facilities:** Sports hall; 60 acres of playing fields.

Duration of first degree course(s) or equivalent: 3 years; **others:** 4 years **Total first degree students 1991/92:** 5,248; **BA (Ed) students:** 362 **Overseas students:** 234 **Mature students:** 487 **Male/female ratio:** 7:6 **Teaching staff: full-time:** 719 **Total full-time students 1991/92:** 6,061 **Postgraduate students:** 813 **Tuition fees for 1992/93 (first degrees):** Home: £1,855 (classroom), £2,770 (lab); Overseas: £5,320 (classroom), £7,055 (lab).

What it's like

An attractive medieval city with cobbled streets, dominated by an impressive cathedral. Often referred to as the oasis of the north. University made up of 12 colleges. Vary from the Castle (almost as old as the cathedral), old houses along the North Bailey to attractive modern buildings designed in the '60s. All colleges but one now co-ed; St Mary's will remain all female. Academic departments housed in old buildings in town or on the modern purpose built science site.

Colleges are important aspect of Durham student life; majority of undergraduates live in for whole three years; social life tends to be centred in colleges with active theatre and arts groups, regular social events such as discos and bands. SU provides central ents in the form of bigger name bands. Rag Week organised centrally as are clubs and societies which range from the cultural (Arts groups) to the political (all major parties, Amnesty International, Greenpeace etc) and social. SU welfare department for personal, academic, financial, legal etc advice and professional counselling.

For those wishing to escape from Durham's peaceful atmosphere, Newcastle is only 20 minutes by train and has three excellent theatres (RSC, National opera and ballet, visit regularly). Professional orchestras visit and big name pop bands. A range of cinemas (including alternative cinema) and many night clubs.

Sport a major part of Durham life. University teams very high standard but colleges provide for all standards. Sports range from hockey to hang-gliding and from rowing to rugby. Town has ice rink.

Students in Durham tend to be conventional with more Sloanes than usual. However, university widening the mix of students – hoping to take more overseas, mature and state school applicants.

Pauper notes

Drink: All colleges have bars; Castle (in the undercroft) best surroundings; van Mildert, best selection of real ales. Good pubs with real ale and student/town mix – Vic and Colpitts; other student pubs Dun Cow, New Inn, Swan + Three Sygnets.
Eats: Riverside (SU), Old Post Office Restaurant (Indian), Hong Sing (Chinese inc take-away), Castle Tandoori (Indian take-away), plus six Italian restaurants.
Ents: SU provides cheapest ents – mainly local bands, comedy etc; Film Society screens films(!). **Sports:** Graham Sports Centre (university); council swimming baths. **Travel:** SU travel bureau; some colleges give small travel scholarships.
Work: Little opportunity of local employment to supplement grant.

Alumni (Editors' pick)

Judith Hann (presenter, Tomorrow's World), Harold Evans (ex-editor of *The Times*), Will Carling (England rugby captain), Nasser Hussain (England test cricketer), Hunter Davies (writer, *Punch*).

EAST ANGLIA UNIVERSITY

University of East Anglia, Norwich, Norfolk NR4 7TJ (0603 56161)
Map A, G6

Student enquiries: Registrar and Secretary

Main study areas – as in What to Study section: *(First degree):* Accountancy, American studies, anthropology, biochemistry, biology, botany, business studies, chemistry, computing, drama, economics, education, electrical and electronic engineering, English, environmental science, environmental studies, European studies, fine arts, geography, geology, history, law, linguistics, mathematical studies, microbiology, modern languages, music, philosophy, physics, physiology, politics and government, professions allied to medicine (PAMs), social policy and social welfare, sociology, zoology. *Also:* Comparative literature, film studies, oceanography, law with European legal systems, Russian studies, Scandinavian studies.

European Community: 14% first degree students take EC language as part of course and 3% spend 6 months or more in another EC country. Approved Erasmus programme 1992. Also participates in many EC research projects, from information technology to greenhouse warming.

Application: UCCA for 1993 start, UCAS thereafter. **Special features:** Excellent links with contemporary writers; past fellows in creative writing include Adam Mars-Jones, Maggie Gee, David Lodge, Anthony Thwaite, the poet Matthew Sweeney, Gore Vidal and Stuart Frost (ice sculptor). With associated institutes (John Innes, Food Research, British Sugar Technical Centre and MAFF Food Science Laboratory) forms largest concentration of research scientists working on plant and food science in Europe. Also Climatic Research Unit. **Academic features:** Most degree courses combine study of several related disciplines, and include continuous assessment. **Founded:** 1963. **Main awards:** BA, LLB, BSc, BEng. **Awarding body:** East Anglia University. **Site:** 2 miles from centre of Norwich. **Access:** Frequent bus service. **Accommodation:** 1,450 study bedrooms on campus (further 1,100 under construction), 600+ on outskirts of Norwich, 100 in centre of Norwich, lodgings (addresses from accommodation centre). All first year students guaranteed accommodation. Approx cost (1991/92): £921 per 30 week licence. 60% students in accommodation where rent controlled by university. **Library:** Over 625,000 volumes, including books, volumes of periodicals, music scores and material in microform. 1,000 reading places, 100 study carrels; restricted loan collection of books in heavy demand, computerised catalogue system. **Other learning facilities:** Computing centre, James Platt language learning centre. **Welfare:** Medical centre on campus with sick bay and dental service.

CAN'T FIND WHAT YOU'RE LOOKING FOR? USE THE INDEX!

Hardship funds: Small fund available. **Special categories:** Nursery and play-group on campus, plus some accommodation for married students. **Careers:** Information and advice service. **Amenities:** Union House with common rooms, printing rooms, television studios, student radio station; bookshop, newsagent, supermarket, post office, banks, launderette, pub, cafeterias on site, coffee shop, Sainsbury Centre restaurant, carvery and buffet; music centre; Sainsbury Centre for Visual Arts (19th and 20th century European paintings and sculpture plus outstanding ethnographic collection); university art collection (20th century). **Sporting facilities:** Indoor and outdoor sports facilities.

Duration of first degree course(s) or equivalent: 3 years; **others:** 4 years (for courses involving study abroad) **Total first degree students 1991/92:** 5,809 **Total BEd students:** 88 **Overseas students:** 574 **Male/female ratio:** 1:1 **Teaching staff: full-time:** 407 **Total full-time students 1991/92:** 5,125 **Postgraduate students:** 1,482 **Tuition fees for 1992/93 (first degrees):** Home: £1,855 (classroom), £2,770 (lab/studio); Overseas: £5,320–£7,055 (classroom), £6,188–£7,055 (lab/studio).

What it's like

UEA started up in the mid-sixties and still growing today. New courses in occupational therapy and physiotherapy bringing more new students and building to the campus to improve upon already impressive facilities. Approximately 2 miles from centre of historic Norwich; easy access to the countryside and city. Although relatively small Norwich offers its students a massive range of entertainments so much so that many graduates stay in the city to live after their degrees.

On campus the Union of Students provides for all the students' non-academic needs, running several shops, bars, sports clubs, clubs and societies as well as a major concert venue which is renowned for attracting major names each term. With so much on offer three years at UEA need not be spent solely in study. The University has excellent record of academic achievement and has produced experts in fields as diverse as landscape archaeology and development studies. UEA allows a high degree of inter-disciplinary study often enabling students to tailor their degrees to suit their personal interests. Also by accepting students from a wide variety of academic backgrounds, instead of accepting the standard three 'A' Levels, UEA is as stimulating socially as it is academically.

All-in-all UEA allows for personal as well as academic advancement and is an excellent place to study for a degree. Come here – nowhere else will do!

Pauper notes

Accommodation: Accommodation for c1,400 students on campus and over 600 off, mostly in single rooms, some shared and married quarters available. Prices are falling in private rented sector. **Drink:** Cheapest pint at the union pubs, but good pubs include The Belle Vue, Reindeer (for real ales), Ironmongers, Garden House. **Eats:** Eat Naturally and Tree House for veggie; many Indian, Chinese, Mexican, Italian restaurants. **Ents:** Union provides best large venue in Norfolk, the Water-Front also runs an excellent range of gigs with famous bands. Good town for jazz, Cinema City for art films and others. **Sports:** Athletics track next to campus; good sports centre and 20 sports clubs. Bad city for swimming pools. **Hardship funds:** Available from Dean of Students, also distributes access funds. **Travel:** No motorways in Norfolk, poor rail links, hence takes time to get out of. Hitching good to London/M1. Union runs excellent travel shop. **Work:** Bar work is it during this recession.

More info?

Get students' Alternative Prospectus.
Enquiries to Nicola Sainsbury (0603 503711).

Informal name

University of Easy Access/UEA

GET HOLD OF THE PROSPECTUSES

Alumni (Editors' pick)

Jonathan Powell (BBC), Selina Scott (TV presenter), Jenny Abramsky (Radio 4), Ian McEwan, Kazuo Ishiguro (author), Noelle Walsh (Editor, *Good Housekeeping*), Vanessa Evans (Editor, *Country Homes & Interiors*), Tim Bentinck & David Vann (actors), Andy Ripley (rugby player), J Richard Sandbrook (International Institute for the Environment & Development), Dennis Callopy (MD, E6 Music Group), Martin Tyler, Peter Rose, Clive Sinclair.

EAST LONDON POLY

See East London University

EAST LONDON UNIVERSITY

University of East London
(1) **Stratford Campus, Romford Road, London E15 4LZ**
(2) **Barking Campus, University of East London, Longbridge Road, Dagenham, Essex RM8 2AS** Map D, D1
  (081 590 7722)

Student enquiries: Campus Registrar.

Main study areas – as in What to Study section: *(First degree):* Accountancy, architecture and landscape, art & design, biochemistry, biology, biotechnology, business studies, civil engineering, computing, economics, education, electrical & electronic engineering, environmental science, law, mathematical studies, microbiology, modern languages, nursing studies, pharmacology, physiology, professions allied to medicine (PAMs), psychology, social policy and social welfare, sociology. *Also:* Cultural studies, engineering and management, humanities, industrial design, manufacturing systems, production engineering, surveying – general practice.

European Community: Some first degree students take a second EC language as part of course and spend 6 months or more in another EC country. All students have access to language tuition (French, German, Italian, Portuguese, Spanish) at various levels. Language tuition encouraged for combined studies and engineering students; compulsory for sociology/new technology with European studies and business studies with French/German. Formal exchange links with a number of EC universities/colleges: 1 in France (manufacturing systems); 3 in Germany (business studies and manufacturing systems). Approved Erasmus programme 1992.

Application: PCAS for 1993 start, UCAS thereafter; ADAR for art and design. **Academic features:** BA/BSc by independent study (full-time or part-time); BSc biophysical science (sandwich course). Courses in biomarketing management; product design; geographical and land information management. **Founded:** 1992, as a university, previously East London Poly, founded 1970. **Main awards:** BA, BSc, BEng, LLB. **Awarding body:** East London University. **Site:** Split on 6 sites; divided into 2 campuses (Barking and Stratford). **Access:** Close to BR station, underground and bus routes. **Accommodation:** 500 places on campus, 800 places in housing association student flats, 60 YMCA places. Approx cost: £30–£50 pw. 12% students in accommodation where rent controlled by university. **Library:** Several libraries with subject bias; over 300,000 books in total, 1,000 study places. **Specialist collections:** Charles Myers Library of industrial psychology. **Welfare:** Professional welfare officers, with access to external agencies, eg charities and aid centres; also doctor, FPA, chaplain. **Hardship funds:** South Africa scholarship. **Special categories:** Playgroup at West Ham and Barking campuses and at Holbrook Centre. **Careers:** Information, advice and placement service. **Amenities:** SU officers and premises on each campus, choir of over 60, music centre at Barking campus. **Sporting facilities:** Wide range of sporting activities, swimming pool, fitness centre, playing fields.

Duration of first degree course(s) or equivalent: 3 years; **others:** 4 years; 5 years part time **Total first degree students 1991/92:** 6,800 **Overseas students:** 720 **Mature students:** 4,500 (ft & sw) **Male/female ratio:** 1:1 **Teaching staff: full-time:** 450 **part-time:** 30 **Total number of students:** approx 9,500 **Postgraduate students:** 1,400 **Tuition fees for 1992/93 (first degrees):** Home: £1,855 (classroom), £2,770 (lab/studio); Overseas: £5,200.

What it's like

East London University stretches across five sites in East London, with one other site just touching Essex in Barking. But before you get any cute ideas about East End Cockneys and Albert Square cliches, here's a closer look at life and study in this capital institution. From the tumbling down ex-school house of 'Holbrook' (architecture is based here!) to the plush conference halls of Duncan House (business), or the stern schoolness of Barking (law) the university has courses and atmosphere to suit every student. Courses range from the conventional teaching and accountancy to the unconventional independent study and cultural studies. London students have the good fortune (or financial frustration) of living in a capital where entertainment can be pursued in any sphere. Ents are sound with the plus that a 'closed' building brings ie safer/less harassed, plus some of the cheapest beer prices around. SU runs a huge range of clubs and societies from the Ravers to land surveying.

Lucy Bishop

Pauper notes

Accommodation: No shortage of private housing in East London; prices are not always realistic. **Drinks:** Two SU run bars – Barking and Maryland, beer cheap and atmosphere unharassed. The 'Eddie' popular student pub in Stratford. **Eats:** Uni food varies from the scarcely edible of Holbrook to the amazing cuisine of Duncan House. Has to be tasted to be believed. **Ents:** Good for supporting new (and often local) bands, cabaret excellent, good local theatres. **Sports:** Excellent range of facilities available at Barking. West Ham's sport is non-existent. **Hardship funds:** Ha ha ha ha ha! This has never been more relevant since the withdrawal of students from the benefit system. A hardship fund does exist for the desperate; you'll have plenty of company. **Travel:** Only railcards, Isic-cards and National Express. **Work:** Bar work and telephone research popular.

Informal name:

PEL.

Alumni (Editors' pick)

Garry Bushell (TV editor of 'The Sun'), Mark Frith (freelance journalist with 'Smash Hits').

EDGE HILL

Edge Hill College of Higher Education, St Helen's Road, Ormskirk, Lancashire L39 4QP (0695 575171) Map A, D5

Student enquiries: Admissions Officer

Main study areas – as in What to Study section: *(First degree):* Biology, communication studies, drama and theatre arts, education, English, European studies, geography, history, information technology, mathematical studies, social policy and social welfare. *Also:* Humanities, organisation and management, physical education, religious studies, urban policy and race relations, women's studies.

European Community: Number of students taking EC languages or spending time in another EC country as part of their course, not known. Language tuition available for language specialists and modern European culture students.

Application: UCCA for 1993 start, UCAS thereafter. **Academic features:** Common first year for BA and BSc + BA/BSc (QTS) courses. **Special features:** Links with the open college scheme operated by colleges in Lancashire and the north west. **Founded:** 1885. **Main awards:** BA, BA(QTS), BSc, BSc (QTS). **Awarding body:** Lancaster University. **Site:** Open rural site edge of Ormskirk. **Access:** Motorway, rail link with Liverpool. **Accommodation:** 450 places in halls, 750 flats/bedsitters/lodgings. All first year students offered accommodation. Approx cost: Halls £1,496 pa (b&b plus evening meal); lodgings £15–£25 pw (b&b). **Library:** 130,000 volumes, 650 periodicals, 166 study places, reference and short loan collections. **Other learning facilities:** Educational resources centre; closed circuit TV and studio, computer centre. College a national centre for UK Reading Association. **Welfare:** Full-time counsellor, college health centre, creche facilities. **Careers:** Information, advice and placement. **Amenities:** SU building with bar, snack bar and games room; bookshop on campus; good sporting facilities including a double gym and heated swimming pool.

Duration of first degree course(s) or equivalent: BA/BSc 3 years; others: BA/BSc (QTS) 4 years **Total first degree students 1991/92:** 1,513; **BA/BSc (QTS) students:** 715 **Overseas students:** 5 **Mature students:** 392 **Male/female ratio:** 2:5 **Teaching staff: full-time:** 158 **part-time:** 75 **Total full-time students 1991/92:** 2,300 **Postgraduate students:** 140 **Tuition fees for 1992/93 (first degrees):** Home: £1,855; Overseas £5,100.

What it's like

Campus with attractive buildings, ranging from 1930's to modern smoked glass and steel. 45 acres of playing fields and beautiful gardens. A very relaxing and attractive place to study, just outside Ormskirk (a small ancient market town). Within easy reach of Southport (7 miles) and Liverpool (15 miles). Both provide excellent nightlife; clubs, cinemas, theatres, restaurants, etc. Also good shopping facilities. Ormskirk has a cheap market on Thursdays and Saturdays and a small indoor market.

Campus life very easy-going. Students generally settle in very quickly. Low drop-out rate. College rooms comfortable, warm and nicely furnished. Meals provided in refectory and cooking facilities available in Halls.

Twice weekly entertainments organised. Films on Thursdays. SU societies are all active, especially in the Athletic Union. Folk, alternative music, anti-Apartheid, Arts, drama societies very active. SU finances societies and provides an excellent welfare service. Very active community work scheme and a child care facility on campus.

Students seem happy with courses. Nearly 50% on QTS courses. English, geography, social sciences also have large intakes. Courses assessed on 40% coursework, 60% exam. Good staff/student relations – each student allocated a studies adviser. Degrees validated by Lancaster University.

Pauper notes

Accommodation: Most non-resident students live in Southport. 85% first years in halls. Approx 500 in 10 halls (8 mixed, 2 single sex). Derby Hall for non-res close. **Drink:** College club on campus (Tetleys bitter, Skol and Castlemaine XXXX lager is main attraction). Favourite haunt – Buck'n'th'Vine, serves Addlestones. Ormskirk has 13 pubs ranging from wine bars to scruffy and cosy. **Eats:** Good value lunchtime snack – campus coffee bar, veggies catered for. Café bar, several good Chinese and Indian take out. Good variety of pub lunches in Ormskirk.

WANT TO HELP WITH THE NEXT EDITION – SEE PAGE 76

Couple of good pizza/pasta places plus dial-a-pizza service in Ormskirk. **Ents:** Disco every Wednesday. Bands etc on Fridays – frequent off-campus trips to local nightclubs, student discounts at two multi-play cinemas. **Sports:** Athletic union. Very good facilities; gym, swimming pool, tennis courts, weights room, hockey, rugby, football pitches, local swimming with squash and sauna. **Hardship funds:** Provided by SU; Access fund. **Travel:** Quite good hitching between Ormskirk and Southport as bus fares expensive (service every half hour). Trains to Liverpool every 15 minutes. **Work:** Some students manage to get work in Ormskirk or Southport. Limited term-time work.

Alumni (Editors' pick)

Francis Harmer (LEA careers officer), Ann McCormack (commercial planner, Metal Box Co), Duncan Pybus (area manager, Hornsea Pottery), Jonathan Pryce (actor).

EDINBURGH COLLEGE OF ART

Edinburgh College of Art, Lauriston Place, Edinburgh EH3 9DF (031 229 9311) Map A, D3

Student enquiries: Admissions Office

Main study areas – as in What to Study section: *(First degree):* Architecture, art & design, environmental studies, fine arts, town and country planning. *Also:* Architectural glass, film and TV, illustration, landscape architecture, tapestry, theatre costume design.

European Community: No students learn an EC language or spend time in another EC country as part of their course. College has educational links with European institutions in Czechoslovakia, Denmark, France, Greece, Hungary, Ireland and Spain. Erasmus and Tempus programmes.

Application: UCCA for 1993 start, UCAS thereafter; direct for art and design. **Structural features:** a constituent college of Heriot-Watt University. **Largest fields of study:** Art and design, architecture, landscape architecture and town planning. **Founded:** 1909. **Main awards:** BA, BArch, BSc, MA (Fine Arts). **Awarding body:** Heriot-Watt University, Edinburgh University. **Site:** Edinburgh city centre. **Accommodation:** 64 places in self-catering flats. Further information on halls of residence and lodgings available from Accommodation and Welfare Officer. 10% students in accommodation where rent controlled by college. **Library:** 83,500 volumes, 110,000 slides; 483 periodicals, 140 study places. **Other learning resources:** Computer facilities. **Welfare:** Counselling and welfare services available. **Amenities:** College shop, student common room, student snack bar, music room and photographic dark room. Clubs and societies provide a wide range of social activities. **Hardship funds:** Some discretionary funds.

Duration of first degree course(s) or equivalent: 4 years; **Others:** 5 years **Total first degree students 1991/92:** 1,200 **Number of overseas students:** 100 **Number of mature students:** 150 **Male/female ratio:** 3:7 **Teaching staff: full-time:** 80; **part-time:** 88 **Total full-time students 1991/92:** 1,300 **Postgraduate students:** 46 **Tuition fees for 1992/93 (first degrees):** £755 (if no grant), Home: £2,770; Overseas: £6,288.

What it's like

Established in 1909, built in the shadow of Edinburgh Castle it's near just about everything in Edinburgh including: art galleries; a huge library; and lots of shops and pubs. Inside it tends to be a bit confusing with loads of different stairways and corridors but you'll find your way eventually.

Associated with Heriot-Watt University, it still retains its own governing body and is independently funded. It also retains its own identity rather than being swallowed up by the larger institution.

The college consists of two faculties – environmental, and art and design. Apparently both of the faculties are very highly thought of.

SU is very active within the college and enables students from all the different departments to get together. We are always busy and active and have a high media profile. We are active on most world issues, particularly on human rights and environmental issues. Internally we have quite a few clubs and societies including: a women's group, a lesbian and gay society; a Christian union; and various departmental ones too. We also have facilities such as a darkroom, an occasional bar, a music room, Albertina's (the student run cafe) and a very friendly office.

Edinburgh College of Art is affiliated to the NUS, with which we work closely.

Pauper notes

Accommodation: Cowgate flats, central and cheap; usually allocated to students leaving home for the first time and to overseas students. Excellent college accommodation service. **Drink:** Variety of different pubs; Edinburgh is renowned for its lenient licensing laws and has so many bars that a pub crawl could turn into a lost weekend. Although the college only has a temporary bar there's the 'Tap O'Lauriston' across the road and the excellent 'International Bar' just round the corner. **Eats:** Albertina's, the student union cafe, has to be the cheapest place to eat in Edinburgh. Lots of health food restaurants and cafes such as Seeds Cafe in West Nicholson Street. **Ents:** Many different clubs in Edinburgh cater for all different tastes although most are dance orientated. Most good Scottish bands play here. Two superb cinemas near the college. **Sports:** Heriot-Watt University sports facilities at Riccarton (seven miles out of Edinburgh) tend not to be used by the students here. Numerous Victorian swimming pools of which Infirmary Street is the best. **Hardship funds:** A loan of £75 available immediately from college welfare.

Alumni (Editors' pick)

John Bellamy, John Houston, Gwen Hardy and Elizabeth Blackadder (painters); Sean Connery, Suzie Wighton (primary health care worker Palestinian camps), Ron Brown and Roy Williamson ('The Corries').

EDINBURGH UNIVERSITY

The University of Edinburgh, Old College, South Bridge, Edinburgh EH8 9YL (031-650 1000) Map A, D3

Student enquiries: Schools Liaison Office (031-650 4360)

Main study areas – as in What to Study section: *(First degree):* Accountancy, agriculture, horticulture and forestry, anthropology, archaeology, architecture, Asian studies, biochemistry, biology, biotechnology, botany, business studies, chemical engineering, chemistry, civil engineering, classics, computing, economics, electrical and electronic engineering, English, environmental science, European studies, fine arts, geography, geology, history, law, linguistics, mathematical studies, mechanical and production engineering, medicine, microbiology, modern languages, music, Near East and Islamic studies, nursing studies, pharmacology, philosophy, physics, physiology, politics and government, psychology, religious studies and theology, social policy and social welfare, sociology, veterinary studies, zoology. *Also:* Celtic studies, European community studies, fire safety engineering, gender studies, Scandinavian studies, Scottish ethnology, Scottish studies, wild life and fisheries management.

European Community: 10% first degree students take an EC language as part of their course and 1% spend 6 months or more in another EC country. All EC languages (except modern Greek) available on graduating or non-graduating basis (modern Greek available only as an option to Classical Greek students). Many degree courses allow students to add a language in first or second year. French, German, Spanish and Italian available for non-language specialists and special French and German courses for law students. Formal exchange links with over 50 EC universities/colleges, most of which are open to non-language specialists. Participant in ECTS History Pilot Project. Member of Coimbra Group and UNICA (capital cities network).

Application: UCCA for 1993 start, UCAS thereafter. **Academic features:** New courses in ancient civilisations, music technology, agricultural and mechanical engineering, environmental geoscience. **Founded:** 1583. **Main awards:** BA, BCom, BD, BDS, BEng, BMus, BSc, BVMS, LLB, MA, MBChB. **Awarding body:** Edinburgh University. **Site:** Edinburgh city centre (arts, law, music, social sciences, veterinary medicine and medicine); science 2 miles south. **Access:** Waverley BR station and central bus station (St Andrew Square) nearby. **Accommodation 1991/92:** 4,860 students in university controlled accommodation – halls of residence, student houses and flats; 4,250 in private sector accommodation (flats). Remainder at home or in lodgings. 50% students in accommodation where rent controlled by university. **Library:** Main library is largest university library building in UK, also various faculty libraries. Over 2 million volumes and pamphlets, long and short loan services. **Specialist collections:** Online computing network & associated facilities; Reid music library, Erskine medical library, European Institute library, law library, New College (Divinity) library, science libraries, veterinary library; Russell collection of early keyboard instruments; also historic collection of wind instruments; Talbot Rice Gallery with permanent Torrie Collection of painting and sculpture and visiting exhibitions. **Careers:** Advice and placement. **Amenities:** SA bars and shops, over 140 clubs, sports centre, playing fields and Firbush Point field centre on Loch Tayside for climbing and water sports. **Hardship funds:** Government access funds; limited assistance also available from university bequests.

Duration of first degree course(s) or equivalent: 4 years (hons), 3 years (general); **others:** 5 years (medicine and veterinary medicine) **Total first degree students 1991/92:** 10,372 **Overseas students:** 2,244 **Mature students:** 1,113 **Male/female ratio 1990/91:** 6:5 **Teaching staff: full-time:** 1,390 **part-time:** 178 **Total full-time students 1991/92:** 12,608 **Postgraduate students:** 3,496 **Tuition fees for 1992/93 (first degrees): Home:** £1,855 (classroom), £2,770 (lab/studio), £4,985 (clinical), £755 (if no grant); **Overseas:** £5,520 (classroom), £7,255 (lab/studio), £13,190 (clinical).

What it's like

Edinburgh is a very special place: no other city centre resembles it, with its main street exposed on one side, to reveal the famous castle overlooking Princes Street Gardens.

The university itself is almost entirely located in the centre, apart from the main Science Campus (Kings Buildings), which is well connected, by bus, to the centre. The university with some 14,500 students, boasts 3 student unions: EUSA (The Edinburgh University Students' Association), by far the largest of the 3, provides most of the welfare services, including 4 student union houses, and does this so effectively that most students believe that the services are actually provided by the university, and not the students. EUSA also incorporates the Students' Representative Council, which performs the majority of the representational work for the students. A nightbus service connects the centre with the Science Campus and the main University-controlled accommodation (Pollock Halls) until early in the morning.

Course-wise, the best advice for a student entering Edinburgh is to take advantage of the extremely wide range of academic courses, as it is generally easy to change course if one finds that things do not work out for you quite as the prospectus implied they might.

Welfare/AIDS/contraceptive/pregnancy-related advice/counselling is supplied by 3 main outlets: the University's SACS (Student Advisory Counselling Service), the much-used student-run telephone 'Nightline' and walk-in information centre, and the EUSA 'Advice Place' advice shop. As one might expect from the Festival City, Edinburgh is hardly underprovided for. It is exceptionally well endowed with theatres, museums, cinemas and galleries and the wide range of pubs, with Scotland's civilised licensing hours, proves a winner with most students. Common meeting-places for students are in the union houses: with the popular Rock Night at Chambers Street, and Teviot Row which sports the biggest disco light rig in Scotland.

Pauper Notes

Accommodation: All first year students are prioritised for halls of residence. The student accommodation service owns and approves a large number of fully furnished flats and houses, married students are catered for in certain buildings. **Drink:** Union bars – frequent promotions and a Happy Hour at every club night. **Eats:** Unions again during the day. At night the best eats are found at Pachuko Cantina (Mexican), Al Tabaq (Indian), Parrots (Vegetarian and anything else). **Ents:** All Unions have clubs at night, Potterrow especially, is venue to a lot of Indie bands. Filmsoc, the biggest film society in Europe shows 130 films a year for £14 membership. **Sports:** Sports Union boasts huge range of facilities and clubs. Free sports facilities at KBU, and the Commonwealth Pool resides next to Pollock Halls of Residence. **Hardship funds:** University provides small loans to help ease short-term financial strain and Crisis Funds for students in desperate long-term financial need. **Travel:** University has many exchange schemes; SA operates Edinburgh Travel Centre which offers many discounts. **Work:** A limited number of on-campus jobs, and a shrinking number off-campus.

Buzz-words

EUSA 'yoo-sah' (Edinburgh University Students' Association); KBU (Kings Buildings Union); Pollock (Main halls of residence).

Alumni (Editors' pick)

Elizabeth Blackadder (artist), David Daiches (author), Arnold Kemp (editor – Glasgow Herald), Neil MacGregor (director – National Gallery), James Africanus Horton (first African graduate from a British University), Sally Magnusson (TV journalist), Kirsty Wark (TV journalist), Gordon Wilson (former leader of SNP), Ian Charleson (actor – *Chariots of Fire*), Peter Roget (of Thesaurus), Sir David Steele, Sir Walter Scott, Sir James Barrie, R L Stevenson, Sir Arthur Conan Doyle, Malcolm Rifkind, David Livingstone, Gordon Brown, Sheena McDonald.

ESSEX UNIVERSITY

University of Essex, Wivenhoe Park, Colchester CO4 3SQ
(0206 873333) Map A, F7

Student enquiries: Admissions Officer

Main study areas – as in What to Study section: *(First degree):* Accountancy, American studies, biochemistry, biology, chemistry, computing, economics, electrical & electronic engineering, English, environmental science, European studies, fine arts, history, Latin American studies, law, linguistics, mathematical studies, modern languages, music, philosophy, physics, politics and government, psychology, public administration, social policy and social welfare, sociology. *Also:* Operational research, telecommunication engineering.

European Community: 9% first degree students take EC language as part of course and 2% spend 6 months or more in another EC country. Formal exchange links with some 40 EC universities/colleges: Belgium (3, including for law and history); Denmark (3, including for law and government); France (7, including history, law, literature, physics); Germany (7, including history, law); Greece (4, including literature, law, physics); Italy (7, including law, history, literature, physics); Netherlands (2, including history, law); Portugal (2, including physics); Spain (4, including history, law). Approved Erasmus programme 1992/93.

Application: UCCA for 1993 start, UCAS thereafter. **Academic features:** New degrees in history (European exchange); mathematics and French/German/Spanish/Russian; physics (European study option), psychology. **Founded:** 1962, Royal Charter received 1965. **Main awards:** BA, BSc, LLB, BEng, MEng. **Awarding body:** Essex University. **Site:** 2 miles east of Colchester. **Access:** Bus service from Colchester station and from town centre. **Accommodation:** 1,927 places in university-owned accommodation, 463 places in houses and flats leased by university. Guarantee of accommodation for single first year students. Approx cost: £30–£37 pw for 39 weeks (October–July). Rent: 60% in accommodation where rent controlled by university. **Library:** 500,000 volumes, 3,000 periodicals, 650 study places; 3-hour loan system for course books. **Specialist collections:** Latin American and Slavonic collections. **Welfare:** Doctor, FPA, chaplain, student counsellor, welfare rights advice. **Special categories:** Some residential facilities for married and disabled students; 50 nursery/playgroup places. **Careers:** Information, advice and placement service. **Amenities:** Bookshop, general shop, banks and post office; 217 seat theatre, exhibitions gallery; SU building with shop, bar, travel centre, print room, newsletter etc; film society; University Radio Essex; art studio. **Sporting facilities:** Sports hall; floodlit, all-weather playing area; gymnasium; wide range of sports including water sports association with club house and dinghies.

Duration of first degree course(s) or equivalent: 3 years; **others:** 4 years (eg languages, environmental and industrial chemistry, information and business systems technology) **Total first degree students 1991/92:** 3,282 **Overseas students:** 498 **Mature students:** 851 **Male/female ratio:** 1:1 **Teaching staff: full-time:** 296 **Total full-time students 1991/92:** 4,075 **Postgraduate students:** 793 **Tuition fees for 1992/93 (first degrees):** Home: £755 (if no grant), £1,855 (classroom), £2,770 (lab/studio); Overseas: £5,320 (classroom), £7,055 (lab/studio).

"If you come from public school, you're advised to keep quiet about it"

GET HOLD OF THE PROSPECTUSES

What it's like

Campus university, about 2 miles from Colchester, built in large park. Compact, with friendly atmosphere. Main features of concrete skyline are 6 residential towers. Accommodation on campus – supplemented by 600 rooms in purpose built flats on estate down the road. Towers divided into 14/16 flats with 13/16 people sharing kitchen; some flats mixed. Double flats and married flats at top of some towers. Also flats (for 4 people) in new houses on campus. Single 1st years guaranteed campus accommodation. Like other universities, visiting restrictions officially in force but nobody takes any notice. Off-campus accommodation varied; university owns property in Colchester; also operates contract housing scheme; otherwise private market. Distances 1 to 9 miles from university. Bus sporadic, especially to main BR station (no service after 9 pm on Sundays).

Live groups and discos, own radio station, newspaper plus sporting, cultural, practical and political societies, as well as student help and advice. Colchester garrison town 55 miles from London; relations with town okay, less good with squaddies. Wivenhoe, couple miles away, trendy ex-fishing village, now thriving port. Some reasonable pubs if prepared to look for them. During winter it is cold and very windy with North Sea winds prevailing.

Relations between students and university administration fairly good. Result of degree depends on continuous assessment and more traditional annual sit-down exams. Easy to change course. Almost all first-year courses unspecialised leaving open as many options as possible for final degree. Students mixed; some yuppies; many yearning for old, radical days of Essex students.

Pauper notes

Accommodation: No student squats; cheap accommodation difficult. **Drink:** SU bar biggest and cheapest in East Anglia; many good pubs in Wivenhoe ('Sociology on Sea') and surrounding area. Many good local real ales – Greene King, Adnams. **Eats:** SU food good and cheap. Veggie food catered for. **Shops:** Second hand bookshop and SU shop (alternative food) on campus. SU travel agent, proliferation of Oxfam, Help the Aged shops etc in area. **Ents:** Very good uni film soc. Good uni theatre. Fairly good ents, but not many student campus bands. **Sports:** No swimming pool. Astroturf and cheap facilities. Fifth best university at sport. **Hardship fund:** Both university and SU funds available. **Travel:** Most travel scholarships abolished. Good SU travel shop. **Work:** Still some summer work on campus and jobs off campus in term.

Alumni (Editors' pick)

Brian Hanrahan, Virginia Bottomley MP, President Oscar Arias of Costa Rica (Nobel Peace Prize 1987), Peter Joslin (Chief Constable of Warwickshire), Gwyn Jones (Welsh Development Agency), Rodolfo Neri Vela (Mexico's only astronaut).

EUROPEAN BUSINESS SCHOOL

European Business School, Regent's College, Inner Circle, Regent's Park, London NW1 4NS (071 487 7400) Map E, B1

Student enquiries: The Admissions Officer

Main study areas – as in What to Study section: *(First degree):* Accountancy, business studies, economics, information technology, modern languages, public administration.

European Community: All students take EC languages as part of the European

CAN'T FIND WHAT YOU'RE LOOKING FOR? USE THE INDEX!

business administration course and spend two 6-month periods in two different countries in the EC as well as gaining 48 weeks of work experience in at least three countries and five companies. International network with affiliated centres in France, Italy, Germany and Spain. New courses include a 3-language with business course, and business administration with one language. 'Eurostart' allows 16–19 year olds to come to London on a short course in business studies and languages as a taster course or prior to university.

Application: Direct. **Academic features:** Integrated language and business course: two foreign languages; study abroad; courses in leadership, public speaking, computer skills and management techniques. **Structural features:** Part of an international network with centres in France, Germany, Spain and Italy. Associated centres in Czechoslovakia, Hungary and Ukraine. **Special features:** 48 weeks in-company training in at least 3 countries and 5 companies. **Largest field of study:** Business administration, modern languages, finance, marketing and management. **Founded:** 1967. **Main awards:** BA. **Awarding body:** Open University. **Site:** Single 11 acre campus in the heart of Regent's Park, London. Other educational institutions on campus include the School of Psychotherapy & Counselling and Regent's College School of Arts & Sciences. **Access:** 5 minutes walk from Baker Street underground and buses. **Accommodation:** Residence hall on site. Help with bed-sits, flats etc in central London. Approx cost: £140 per week with good meal plan. **Library:** 40,000 volumes, 900 periodicals, 120 study places. **Specialist collections:** Royal Institute of Public Administration, Overseas Development Institute, College of Homeopathy and Institute of Linguists libraries. **Other learning facilities:** IBM and Apple computer laboratories; CALL and language laboratories. **Careers:** Information, advice and placement service. **Main areas of employment:** Managerial positions throughout Europe and the rest of the world: 30% in financial services & banking, 20% in marketing & advertising, 15% in manufacturing, 12% self-employed, 8% in information technology, 5% in pharmaceutical, 5% family business, 5% in travel industry. **Welfare:** Full facilities available on campus-wide basis through student services; personal tutors for counselling. **Hardship funds:** Scholarships and bursaries on application. **Amenities:** Music, art gallery, weights room and other activities on campus. **Sporting facilities:** Access to football and tennis in Regent's Park; indoor facilities in central London, through student services.

Duration of first degree course(s) or equivalent: 4 years **Total first degree students 1992/93:** 450 **Overseas students:** 70% **Male/female ratio:** 3:2 **Teaching staff: full-time:** 50 **part-time:** 30 **Total full-time students 1991/92:** 450 **Tuition fees 1993/94 (first degrees):** £6,000 (Home and Overseas).

What it's like

Situated in Regent's Park, one of the most beautiful parks in London. Excellent campus with first class facilities including large common room, bar, tennis courts, refectory, library; acres of park in centre of London. Emphasis on international business and professionalism. Four-year degree course in European business administration involves studying in three of the five EBS centres: London, Paris, Frankfurt, Madrid and Parma – and 48 weeks in-company training. All students develop fluency in two foreign languages, so even with the mix of European nationalities, you'll find communications no problem at EBS. Pace of work and life is demanding. Course very practical, not all theory, the main subjects are economics, law, finance, marketing, information technology (IT), international business. Special attention paid to personal skills for management, managerial skills and two languages. Graduate employment depends on 4th year specialisation. Some graduates continue businesses they founded at EBS, others go straight to management in international companies. To date c.3,000 EBS graduates managing companies all over world. EBS graduates command high starting salaries. You can meet students, see college and get advice from the Admissions Officer.

GET HOLD OF THE PROSPECTUSES

Pauper notes

Accommodation: Very expensive, single, double and triple rooms. **Drink:** College bar – nice cork-panelled – reasonable prices. Drummonds. **Eats:** Regent's College refectory – very good food – great variety – nice surroundings – reasonable prices. Also restaurant and a coffee/lunch bar now on campus. **Ents:** Student centre organizes trips, theatre, etc. **Sports:** On campus tennis courts (2 grass, 1 hard), fitness centre, basketball court. Football pitches in Regent's Park. Off campus: Seymour Leisure Centre. **Ents:** Student centre organises trips, theatres etc. **Work:** 48 weeks in 3 countries and 5 companies during the 4 year course. **Student European (Links):** SMILE (Student Marketing Initiative Linking Europe) is a student organisation that exists at EBS Frankfurt and London and is involved in arranging marketing and Europe-related activities. The long-term goal is to establish a European network in at least all the EBS centres. All outside EBS-students are welcome – co-operation with other universities etc is welcome in order to fulfil the European idea behind the organisation.

Informal name

EBS

Alumni (Editors' pick)

Felix Meyer-Morn (DEBA 1986), John Jesser (DEBA 1986), Nicholas J Davies (DEBA 1985), Georgina Swift (DEBA 1988).

EXETER UNIVERSITY

University of Exeter, Northcote House, The Queen's Drive, Exeter EX4 4QJ (0392 263263) Map A, D9

Student enquiries: Academic Secretary

Main study areas – as in What to Study section: *(First degree):* Accountancy, American studies, archaeology, biology, botany, business studies, chemical engineering, chemistry, civil engineering, classics, computing, drama, economics, education, electrical and electronic engineering, English, fine arts, geography, history, information technology, law, linguistics, mathematical studies, mechanical & production engineering, modern languages, music, Near East and Islamic studies, physics, politics and government, professions allied to medicine (PAMs), psychology, religious studies and theology, sociology.

European Community: Number of students taking EC language or spending time in another EC country not known. Some students may spend a year in the EC and be awarded a degree 'with European Study', eg students in accountancy and economics, geography, food and natural resources, law, physics, politics, psychology, statistics. Students in engineering encouraged to spend a year elsewhere in the EC. Foreign language centre offers courses to all such students. Large number of formal links with EC universities/colleges. Approved Erasmus programme 1992.

Application: UCCA for 1993 start, UCAS thereafter. **Academic features:** New degree courses in French & Arabic; 4-year courses in physics; physics with medical physics, physics with opto-electronics and theoretical physics, leading to MPhys; business economics. **Founded:** 1955. **Main awards:** BA, BEd, BSc, BEng, LLB, LLB (Eur), BA(Ed), BSc(Ed), BMus, MPhys. **Awarding body:** Exeter University. **Site:** Modern campus. 1 mile from city centre. **Access:** Bus from city centre. **Accommodation:** Around 50% of students accommodated.

CAN'T FIND WHAT YOU'RE LOOKING FOR? USE THE INDEX!

Library: Over 700,000 volumes and journals, separate faculty libraries, especially law and education. **Specialist collections:** Rare editions, examples of early printing. University houses Cathedral Library (distinguished collections of Anglo Saxon and medieval works); and the Devon and Exeter Institution Library (West Country material). **Welfare:** Health centre; counselling service and family centre for 28 children run jointly by Guild of Students and University; chaplaincy. **Amenities:** Shops, bank, etc on campus; Guild buildings with licensed bars, launderettes, etc; Northcott Theatre which has its own professional company but also provides for amateur productions. **Sporting facilities:** Sports hall on main site, offering wide range of facilities; indoor heated swimming pool and gymnasia at the school of education; open air pool during summer.

Duration of first degree course(s) or equivalent: 3 years; others: 4 years **Total first degree students 1991/92:** 5,425; **BA/BSc(Ed) students:** 1,441 **Overseas students (outside Europe):** 435 **Mature students:** Approx 500 **Male/female ratio:** 1:1 **Teaching staff: full-time:** 547 **part-time:** 42 **Total full-time students 1991/92:** 6,908 **Postgraduate students (including part-time):** 1,882 **Tuition fees for 1992/93 (first degrees): Home:** £1,855 (classroom), £2,770 (lab/studio); **Overseas:** £5,320 (classroom), £7,055 (lab/studio).

What it's like

Two sites: Main site (Streatham) set in beautiful grounds close to city centre with two SU buildings incorporating bars, coffee bars, refectories, shops, outdoor swimming pool, plus sports complex and theatre. School of education sited at St Luke's, about a mile away and also close to town. Luke's houses PE school and has excellent sports facilities, plus coffee bar, bar and shops. Most first years in hall; some purpose-built but comfortable, some converted 19th Century houses which are more attractive. Campus self-catering flats on campus vary from luxurious with en-suite facilities, to cheap, cheerful and convenient but cramped. Guild of Students is politically neutral as student membership tends to be from a varied social and geographical base; provides excellent ents programme and welfare services. Superb sporting reputation and over 100 clubs and societies. Exams: mainly unseens but also dissertation work. Personal tutor system could be improved. Teaching services centre provides study methods counselling. High academic standard; drop-out and failure rates relatively low, but difficult to change course. 'Town-gown' relationship seems to be improving, particularly amongst the younger people. Climate good; beautiful countryside and beaches close at hand.

Pauper notes

Accommodation: Due to rising student numbers, accommodation becoming scarcer – several 'student areas' off campus, and many live in the country. No squats. Halls expensive but good. **Drink:** Ram and Ewe still best bet, Ram having regular guest bitters. Otherwise old favourites the Red Cow and the Black Horse. **Eats:** Best restaurants include Harpoon Lovies for fish and steak; Crockers for posher meals and On the Waterfront for 'dustbin lid' pizzas. Vegetarian restaurants 'Herbies' and 'Brambles' incredibly cheap. **Ents:** Best ents programme in S.W. good up-coming bands. Cheap arts events and good student theatre. **Sports:** Two pools; cheap equipment hire rates; and campus gym, weights, dance studio etc. **Hardship fund:** Access fund (apply a.s.a.p.); £50 loans available from Guild. **Travel:** Some travel scholarships. M4/M5/A30, good rail links, Guild travel shop on campus. Good hitching. (Success in Rag Hitches in past.) **Work:** Guild bars, pubs and restaurants in town; also tele-sales company with large freelance staff. Otherwise fairly scarce.

Alumni (Editors' pick)

Richard Hill, Mike Slemen (England Rugby players), Paul Jackson (BBC comedy producer), Tony Speller and Boner Wells (Tory MPs).

WANT TO HELP WITH THE NEXT EDITION – SEE PAGE 76

FALMOUTH

Falmouth School of Art and Design, Woodlane, Falmouth, Cornwall TR11 4RA (0326 211077) Map A, B9

Student enquiries: Academic Registrar

Main study areas – as in What to Study section: *(First degree):* Art & design, fine arts. *Also:* Communication.

European Community: No first degree students take an EC language as part of course; 2% spend 3 months or more in another EC country. Formal exchange links with 4 EC universities/colleges in France (Ecole des Beaux Arts in Strasbourg, Caen, Poitiers and Tours). Industrial placement in Europe through Comett.

Application: ADAR and PCAS (for 1993 start, UCAS thereafter). **Academic features:** Courses include information and graphic design, copywriting, illustration, fine art, broadcast journalism, photographic communication and ceramics. Trend towards student centred learning. **Founded:** As private venture, taken over by local authority in 1938. Became Falmouth School of Art and Design in 1987. **Main awards:** BA. **Awarding body:** Plymouth University. **Site:** Near Falmouth town centre; 5 minutes from sea. **Accommodation:** 1 student hostel; list of approved lodgings sent to students. Approx cost: £30–35 pw. **Library:** 20,000 volumes, 160 periodicals. **Careers:** Advice service. **Amenities:** SU arranges social and sports activities; excellent sailing.

Duration of first degree course(s) or equivalent: 3 years; **others:** 4 years (sandwich course in graphic information design) **Total first degree students 1991/92:** 310 **Overseas students:** 35 **Mature students:** 80 **Male/female ratio:** 1:1 **Teaching staff:** full-time: 50 part-time: 30 **Total full-time students 1991/92:** 1,250 **Postgraduate students:** 58 **Tuition fees for 1992/93 (first degrees):** Home: £2,770; Overseas: £5,995.

What it's like

Fourth biggest art and design college in the UK recently affiliated with Plymouth University. Set in the picturesque South Western peninsula of Cornwall. Some first year accommodation (31) with priority to disabled students in one college hostel. Excellent facilities, including workshops and audio visual computer centre. Diversity of styles.

Space available for students to exhibit in our college gallery. Design courses have excellent industrial contacts, regular term-time placements (found by students and staff) and good career prospects. A rapidly expanding college with construction of new buildings including library, and increased studio space. SU very active, organises film clubs, and recently has established a sports society due to popular demand, local discount scheme, boat parties, bands, dance music in local clubs and trips to a variety of local events.

Pauper notes

Accommodation: Hostel £26.00 shared, £35.00 single (£54.00 deposit). Private sector accommodation, towns lowest price £25.00–£30.00. **Drink:** Jacobs Ladder, The Crab and Ale, Seven Stars, Kings Head, good speciality brews. **Eats:** Good on campus, especially catered for vegetarians. Completion due on a fast food canteen in refectory/student centre. Local restaurants for diverse tastes, check out the Bon Ton Roulet for student discount (£1.50 special meals). **Ents:** SU Film Club, (£1.00 every week), a variety of films; lively parties plus trips to concerts. Touring bands on campus. Falmouth Art Centre. **Sport:** Establishing a society which will offer students free membership and the access to a variety of sports. Current discounts at St Michaels hotel (weights/sauna) and Carn Brea Leisure

Centre (interdepartmental sports). **Hardship:** FACT hardship fund – SU – repayable. **Travel:** Isic cards available. **Work:** Scarce, however some bar work, tourist industry, bars, hotels etc.

Alison Love
Student Union President

More info?
Enquiries to Student Union (0326 319443).

Alumni (Editors' pick)
Fergus Walsh (BBC Radio 4 home affairs correspondent), Juliet Morris (BBC TV presenter).

FARNBOROUGH COLLEGE

Farnborough College of Technology, Boundary Road, Farnborough, Hampshire GU14 6SB (0252 515511) Map A, E8

Student enquiries: Information Office/Admissions Office (0252 391391)

Main study areas – as in What to Study section: *(First degree):* Aeronautical engineering, business studies, environmental studies. *Also:* Aerospace, leisure management.

European Community: No first degree students take EC language as part of course; few spend 6 months or more in another EC country. No formal exchange links with EC universities/colleges at present.

Application: PCAS for 1993 start, UCAS thereafter. **Academic features:** Wide range of courses (A-levels, vocational and professional courses, first degrees, masters degrees). New degree courses in environmental protection, computing, business administration, leisure management. **Special features:** Maintains close links with industry, commerce and local community. **Founded:** 1961. Began as training wing of former Royal Aircraft Establishment. **Main awards:** BA, BSc. **Awarding body:** Surrey University. **Site:** Two sites, Farnborough and Aldershot (all degree courses at Farnborough). **Access:** Easy reach of London; Farnborough campus on A325, close to junction 4 on M3; short walk to railway station. Good local bus service. **Accommodation:** Private accommodation locally, including flats, houses and in private homes. Approx cost: £40 pw for a room; £60 pw for room with meals. Advice and help from college accommodation officer. **Rent:** No students in accommodation where rent controlled by the college. **Library:** 50,000 books, 250 periodicals, 320 study places. Dialog and Profile offered on line. **Other learning facilities:** Computer facilities, language and science laboratories, engineering workshops, 3 wind tunnels, training kitchens, specialist beauty salons, audio-visual section. **Careers:** Information, advice and placement service. **Employment:** Public service, professions, industry, VSO. **Welfare:** Counselling service, occupational health unit, accommodation officer, learning support unit. **Special facilities:** Kindergarten (ages 2–5) on weekdays throughout the year. **Hardship funds:** Access fund; student union hardship fund. **Amenities:** SU arranges live bands, discos, theatre, films, charity and fund-raising events. Also sponsors clubs and societies eg rock climbing, conservation. **Sporting facilities:** Good health and fitness suite. Farnborough Recreation Centre within a few minutes has indoor sports.

Duration of first degree course or equivalent: 3 or 4 years. **Total first degree students 1991/92:** 10 now; numbers will be much greater by 1994. **BEd students:** 0. **Overseas students:** 0. **Mature students:** 3. **Male/female ratio:** 1:1 **Teaching staff: full-time:** 8 **part-time:** 0 **Total full-time students 1991/92:** 2,600 **Postgraduate students:** 170 **Tuition fees for 1992/93 (first degrees):** Home: £1,855 (classroom), £2,770 (lab/studio); Overseas: £5,319.

Alumni (Editors' pick)

Verity Larby-Walker (1992 Olympics), Beverley Kinch (long jump and 100 metres), Steve Benton (national cyclist).

FRENCH INSTITUTE

Institut Français, 14 Cromwell Place, South Kensington, London SW7 2JR (071 581 2701) Map E, A4

Student enquiries: Mrs Towers

Main study areas – as in What to Study section: Business studies, modern languages.

European Community: 100% students take French as part of course; none spend time in another EC country. Diploma is awarded by University of Lille III and allows access to second year of degree course in modern languages or French at the University. Part time Diploma in French and European studies offered, also awarded by University of Lille III. Cultural centre stages regular seminars and lectures, addressing wide range of European issues.

Application: Direct. **Academic features:** Completely bilingual courses, open to both English and French native speakers. University diploma, 1 and 2 year bilingual secretarial and business courses. **Structural features:** Institut Français is official French government centre of language and culture in London (one of 150 in 50 countries throughout the world). **Largest field of study:** French, European studies, bilingual secretarial skills. **Founded:** 1930s. **Main awards:** Diplome de Secretariat Bilingue; Certificate. **Awarding body:** University of Lille III, French Institute. **Site:** Single site in South Kensington, central London. **Access:** Underground, buses and BR (Victoria). **Accommodation:** None provided; Institute provides list of hostels. **Library:** 78,000 books (French), 400 periodicals, 50 study places. Institute houses Britain's largest French reference and lending library. **Other learning facilities:** Language lab, satellite link with French television, French language videos. **Careers:** Recruitment consultants attend to give guidance and help. **Employment:** Secretarial/PA. **Welfare:** All students have a pastoral care tutor. **Hardship funds:** None. Students may apply for discretionary grants from LEA. **Amenities:** Institute has own theatre and art gallery; cultural activities organised by the Institute include films, theatres, concerts, lectures and seminars; fully licensed cafe. SU offers full social calendar, is associated with London University and maintains links with Imperial College. **Sporting facilities:** Imperial College sports and leisure facilities.

Duration of first degree course or equivalent: 1 or 2 years. **Total students 1991/92:** 70 **BEd students:** 0 **Overseas students:** 14 **Mature students:** 25 **Male/female ratio:** Almost all female. **Teaching staff: full-time:** 5 **part-time:** 9 **Postgraduate students:** 5 **Tuition fees for 1992/93:** £2,400 (£2,650, 1 year intensive).

Alumni (Editors' pick)

Judith Kozlowska (winner) and Sue Lang (co-finalist) 1992 Times European Executive Secretary Competition; Sophie Hirman, former Business Woman of the Year.

GLAMORGAN UNIVERSITY

The University of Glamorgan, Pontypridd, Mid Glamorgan CF37 1DL (0443 480480) Map A, D7

Student enquiries: Admissions Officer

CAN'T FIND WHAT YOU'RE LOOKING FOR? USE THE INDEX!

Main study areas – as in What to Study section: *(First degree):* Accountancy, biology, biotechnology, business studies, chemical engineering, chemistry, civil engineering, communication studies, computing, drama, electrical & electronic engineering, English, environmental science, fine arts, geography, geology, history, information technology, law, mathematical studies, mechanical and production engineering, philosophy, psychology, public administration, religious studies and theology, sociology. *Also:* Building, energy studies, estate management, pollution, Welsh studies, women's studies.

European Community: 12% first degree students take EC language as part of course; 45% have the option, as part of their course. French, German, Italian, Spanish and Welsh available to all students. 12% spend 6 months or more in another EC country (60% have the option as part of course). Active collaboration with large number of institutions in most EC countries. Formal Erasmus links with 31 EC universities/colleges: Belgium (1); Denmark (3); Eire (2); France (5); Germany (8); Greece (1); Italy (4); Netherlands (3); Portugal (1); Spain (3). Approved Erasmus programme. European business studies introduced into a number of courses. New modular structure will allow more students to add a language.

Application: PCAS for 1993 start, UCAS thereafter. **Academic features:** Many courses are modular, so students can design own study programme. **Founded:** 1992 as a university; previously Wales Poly. **Main awards:** BA, BSc, BEng, MEng, LLB. **Awarding body:** Glamorgan University. **Site:** Single campus situated in Treforest, Pontypridd. **Access:** Good road and rail links. **Accommodation:** 484 single study, 4 twin-bedded bedrooms (catered); 76 single, 19 twin-bedded self-catering. Approx cost: £52.25 pw single study, £33 self-catering. Rent: 13% in accommodation where rent controlled by university. **Library:** Over 150,000 volumes, 1,000 serial publications, 730 study places. **Specialist collections:** Welsh writing in English, statistics. **Other learning facilities:** Computer centre, media services. **Welfare:** Health centre; 2 student advisers; 2 counsellors; 1 full-time, 2 part-time chaplains; playcentre. **Hardship funds:** None, but sympathetic consideration given to individual cases of genuine hardship. **Careers:** Information, advice and placement (2 careers advisers). **Amenities:** SU with discos, films, etc, sports fields, tennis courts; recreation centre with squash/ badminton courts, multi-gym, trimnasium, sauna, solarium, campus general shop, bookshop.

Duration of first degree course(s) or equivalent: 3 and 4 years **Total first degree students 1991/92:** 4,452 **Overseas students:** 339 **Mature students:** 1,942 **Male/female ratio:** 2:1 **Teaching staff:** full-time: 404 part-time: 90 **Total full-time and sandwich students 1991/92:** 5,897 **Postgraduate students:** 843 **Tuition fees for 1992/93** (first degrees): Home: £1,855 (classroom), £2,770 (lab/studio); Overseas: £5,300.

What it's like

Newly renamed the University of Glamorgan, the old Polytechnic of Wales is situated in the valleys on the outskirts of Pontypridd, a market town 12 miles between Merthyr Tydfil and Cardiff. Just off the campus, Treforest has its own valley line train station. Campus pleasant, green and built very much on the side of the hill, which may pose access problems for people with disabilities. It's probably the only campus with resident sheep, but at least the grass is always short.

On campus halls of residence accommodate approx. 500 out of the 7,000 full-time students, hopefully this will be 700 by September. A smaller number of places available in off-campus self-catering halls. Majority of students live in local private rented accommodation. Some live in Cardiff, only 20 mins. train journey away. Growing number of overseas students, currently around 10%. Students come from all over Britain, with a fairly high percentage being Welsh. The library stays open until 11.45pm weekdays. Links with the local community are improving all the time.

The union is the main focal point. It has many facilities: the shop (stationery, confectionery, essentials) incorporates travel shop and insurance office. The union houses 'Suds' (launderette), 'The Green' (fast food eatery), 'The George Knox' (tavern bar) and 'Shafts' (live music venue and club). There's a varied entertainments programme, with something on every night of the week; also a host of sporting and non-sporting clubs and societies.

Pauper Notes

Accommodation: Fairly good campus halls; self-catering off-campus halls; majority in private rented accommodation in Cardiff. **Drink:** Union 'George Knox' bar the cheapest. Plenty of good local pubs. Local(ish) brews include Brains, Buckleys, Felinfoel, Hancock's, Crown, plus a new local brew previously unnamed Welsh Bitter. **Eats:** Union 'The Green' fast food eatery caters for vegetarians. Two on-campus refectories. Surrounding area not brilliant – plenty in Cardiff. **Ents:** Union nightclub/disco 'Shafts'; varied acts programme with regular bands, discos, cabaret and films, close to Cardiff. Municipal hall in Pontypridd now shows films cheaply twice a week, the union also hires municipal hall for larger capacity events. **Sports:** Excellent on-campus new sports centre plus very active union sports facilities. 3 local swimming pools. **Hardship fund:** Union hardship loans system when you hit rock bottom (limited). Visit the welfare officer. College access funds organised on need basis. **Travel:** Good train service to Pontypridd and Cardiff. Buses locally. Union travel shop covers local and overseas travel.

More info?

Get students' Alternative Prospectus.
Enquiries to President/Deputy President Education and Welfare (0443 408227).

GLASGOW COLLEGE OF BUILDING

Glasgow College of Building & Printing, 60 North Hanover Street, Glasgow G1 2BP (041 332 9969) Map A, C3

Student enquiries: Academic Registrar

Main study areas – as in What to Study section: *(First degree):* Civil engineering. Also: Quantity surveying.

European Community: No students take EC languages or spend time in another EC country as part of their course.

Application: Direct. **Largest fields of study:** Quantity surveying and building, (non-degree courses in printing, photography, interior design). **Main awards:** BSc. **Awarding body:** Glasgow Poly. **Accommodation:** No college accommodation. **Library:** 30,000 volumes, 200 periodicals, 100 study places. **Careers:** Information and advice service. **Amenities:** Design centre, Scottish Exhibition Centre, public libraries, museums, workshops. **Employment:** Quantity surveying, construction management, interior and graphic design, building, photography, printing, surveying.

Duration of first degree course(s) or equivalent: 4 years; **others:** 3 years **Total first degree students 1991/92:** 170 **Overseas students:** 40 **Mature students:** 26 **Male/female ratio:** 6:1 **Teaching staff: full-time:** 150 **Total full-time students 1991/92:** 1,400 **Postgraduate students:** 20 **Tuition fees for 1991/92 (first degrees):** Home: £1,855 (classroom), £2,770 (lab); Overseas: £5,319.

What it's like

14 storey glass-fronted tower block overlooking George Square. Well placed for transport and faculties. Close to Glasgow College and Strathclyde University: reciprocal agreements. Parking at college impossible. Accommodation register compiled by SRC at start of academic year; no halls of residence. 3% overseas students. Approx 1,200 full-time and 3,200 part-time students.

CAN'T FIND WHAT YOU'RE LOOKING FOR? USE THE INDEX!

Active students' association with shop, photocopier, common room, welfare office, pool tables. Wide range of students due to variety of courses. Employment rate is high. Most students straight from schools in West, North and Central Scotland, many stay at home with parents and aspire to job, family, car etc. Average drop out rate. Ratio of male to female in full-time courses is 2:1. On part-time courses it is 7:1. SRC active in all areas affecting students.

Pauper notes

Accommodation: Shared in local authority flats or private sector if lucky. **Drink:** Cheapest at other SUs, plenty of trendy pubs nearby but the less trendy the pub, the cheaper the prices. **Eats:** Canteen average, some vegetarian. Fast food readily available nearby. **Ents:** Plenty of discos/clubs around city centre. Local theatre and cinema. **Sports:** Underused college PE dept, with facilities. **Travel:** Travel services at Strathclyde Univ Union. **Work:** High unemployment and skint student population makes work hard to find and you'll get paid next to nothing.

More info?

Enquiries to Students Association (041-331 1355).

Informal name

GCBP.

Buzz-words

If you come from outside the West of Scotland too many to make a list viable.

GLASGOW POLY

STOP PRESS: *Glasgow Poly is now a university; new title just approved as Glasgow Caledonian University.*

Glasgow Caledonian University, Cowcaddens Road, Glasgow G4 0BA (041 331 3000) Map A, C3

Student enquiries: Academic Registrar/Education Officer

Main study areas – as in What to Study section: *(First degree):* Accountancy, biochemistry, biology, business studies, chemistry, civil engineering, communications studies, computing, economics, electrical & electronic engineering, geography, food science and nutrition, hotel and catering management, information technology, law, mathematical studies, mechanical and production engineering, microbiology, modern languages, nursing studies, physics, politics and government, professions allied to medicine (PAMs), psychology, public administration, social policy and social welfare, sociology. *Also:* Actuarial studies, building, quantity surveying, risk management.

European Community: 25% first degree students take EC language as part of course and 10% spend 6 months or more in another EC country. Formal exchange links established in most EC countries.

Application: PCAS for 1993 start, UCAS thereafter. **Academic features:** BEng sandwich courses with electronic and manufacturing options. Degrees in chemistry with information technology and instrumentation; risk management; applied physics and instrumentation. Integrated management development programme leading to MBA. **Founded:** As a university 1992. Previously Glasgow Poly founded 1971. **Main awards:** BA, BSc, BEng. **Awarding body:** Glasgow Poly. **Site:** City centre West End. **Access:** Bus, underground, rail. **Accommodation:** 137-bed residence + further access to student flats. Accommodation officer will advise. **Library:** 150,000 volumes, 1,200 periodicals, 750 study places; study copies held. **Other learning resources:** Computer intensive environment, learning resources unit. **Welfare:** Doctor, chaplains, welfare advisers. **Hardship funds:** SA provides short term loans; additional fund for direct emergencies. **Careers:** Information, advice and placement service (most courses are vocational). **Sporting facilities:** Sports hall, gym.

Duration of first degree course(s) or equivalent: 3 or 4 years **Total first degree students 1991/92:** 5,035 **Overseas students:** 180 **Mature students:** 1,473 **Male/female ratio:** 1:1 **Teaching staff: full-time:** 350 **Total full-time students 1991/92:** 6,035 **Postgraduate students:** 1,005 **Tuition fees 1992/93 (first degrees):** Home: £770 (if no grant), £1,855 (classroom), £2,770 (lab); Overseas: £5,000.

What it's like

Built in 1971 it borders on the city centre with easy access to buses, trains and underground. Close to shopping precinct with cinemas, theatres, pubs and discos. Association provides a lively union with cheap entertainments, booze and food. Also produces a magazine, has a welfare office and two sabbaticals who represent students on college committees, etc. Runs many clubs, societies and sports clubs, from political to sub-aqua. However, there is a lack of sports facilities (a sports hall with a games hall and a weights room). Union shop sells confectionery, cigarettes and stationery at reasonable prices.

Very little accommodation but, being in the city, there are many good flats and bedsits within easy travelling distance. Library situated in a modern building provides study areas etc, on campus. Buildings are all situated on a compact campus and have just about everything a student needs within it.

Pauper notes

Accommodation: West end of city and south side popular. Red Road flats and Cobbington Place with Glasgow District Council, David Naismith Building with YMCA. **Drink:** Union for good cheap spirits and beers – Becks, Bellhaven, McEwans Export, Budweiser. **Eats:** Union snack bar for tasty cheap food. Always has at least 1 vegetarian dish. **Ents:** Discos every weekend, 4 'all-nighters' a year and bands. **Sports:** Easy transport to sports facilities off campus. Sports Club go on day/weekend trips. Games hall and weights room on campus (free to students). **Hardship funds:** Short term loans and has fund for direct emergencies. **Travel:** Transcard system for buses, trains and underground – all stopping near college. **Work:** Difficult to get vacation work as Glasgow has high unemployment.

Alumni (Editors' pick)

Alan Christie (ex-chairman NUS UK, general secretary of British Youth Council), James Doran (Nationwide journalist), Pat Nevin (Chelsea FC and Scotland), Colin Calder (Radio Producer with BBC), Denise Holt (AA Roadwatch), Claire English (TV presenter), Peter Lawwell (Celtic FC).

GLASGOW SCHOOL OF ART

Glasgow School of Art, 167 Renfrew Street, Glasgow G3 6RQ (041 332 9797) Map A, C3

Student enquiries: Academic Registrar

Main study areas – as in What to Study section: *(First degree):* Architecture, art & design.

European Community: No students take EC languages or spend time in another EC country. Approved Erasmus programme 1992.

Application: Direct. **Largest fields of study:** Architecture, art and design. **Founded:** 1840. **Main awards:** BA, B.Arch. **Awarding body:** Glasgow University. **Site:** Glasgow city centre. **Accommodation:** 80 hostel places. Approx

CAN'T FIND WHAT YOU'RE LOOKING FOR? USE THE INDEX!

cost: £18.50–£23.50 pw. Rent: no students housed in accommodation where rent controlled by college. **Library:** 50,000 volumes, 257 periodicals, 150 study places, 60,000 slides, 200 videocassettes. **Welfare:** Full-time welfare officer. **Careers:** Information and advice service. **Amenities:** Active student union, activities committee organises a comprehensive programme of exhibitions, annual fashion show and social functions including dances, gigs and clubs. **Employment:** All areas of fine art practice, design and architecture.

Duration of first degree course(s) or equivalent: 4 years **Total first degree students 1991/92:** 1,000 **Male/female ratio:** 1:2 **Overseas students:** 17 **Mature students:** 184 **Teaching staff: full-time:** 85 **part-time:** 35 **Total full-time students:** 1,200 **Number of postgraduate students:** 100 **Tuition fees 1992/93 (first degrees):** Home: £2,770; Overseas: £5,500.

What it's like

Centrally located for major shops, cinemas, theatres and nightclubs, although the school itself has regular film shows, courtesy of the Mackintosh Film Society, twice weekly discos with regular clubs, 'Unity Reggae' on Friday nights, 'Divine' on Saturday nights; highly successful annual fashion show and activities week (lectures, workshops, recitals, gigs, talent show). Clubs and societies, partly funded by the SU range from Karate Club to the French Cultural Society.

   Own student pub, where most of our activities take place, the 'Vic Cafe Bar' open 6 days a week and offers a full range of food and drink.

   As well as fine art and design, the college includes the Mackintosh Architecture School, and industrial and interior design courses. All materials for all courses are paid for by students.

   Welfare services and counselling are available and are, of course, confidential. Limited self-catering hostel accommodation.

Pauper notes

Accommodation: Expensive; cheap rented accommodation usually substandard and limited to bare essentials. Art school hostel. **Drink:** Vic Cafe Bar, Art School bar. Bars eg 'Porters' and 'Nico's'. **Eats:** Sauchiehall Street (various Chinese, Indian, Turkish, Thai, traditional cafe's, most offer veg food). **Ents:** Art School Union, GFT (student rate) cinema, RSAMD (regular theatre). **Sports:** Kelvin Hall Sports Centre, swimming pool (Woodside Baths). **Hardship funds:** Available on first come, first served basis. **Travel:** Many student discount schemes. **Work:** Difficult to find.

Alumni (Editors' pick)

Steven Cambel, Peter Howson, Adrian Wyzsenski, Ken Curry (painters), Robbie Coltrane, John Byrne, Pam Hogg.

GLASGOW UNIVERSITY

University of Glasgow, Glasgow G12 8QQ (041 339 8855)
Telex: 778421 GlasuL-G Map A, C3

Student enquiries: Registrar

Main study areas – as in What to Study section: *(First degree):* Accountancy, aeronautical engineering, agriculture, anatomy, archaeology, architecture, biochemistry, biology, botany, business studies, chemistry, civil engineering, classics, computing, dentistry, drama, economics, education, electrical & electronic engineering, English, fine arts, geography, geology, history, Latin American studies, law, marine technology, mathematical studies, mechanical and production engineering, medicine, microbiology, modern languages, music, Near East and Islamic studies, nursing studies, pharmacology, philosophy, physics, physiology, politics and government, psychology, religious studies and theology, sociology, veterinary studies, social policy and social welfare, zoology. *Also:* Aquatic bioscience, astronomy, Celtic studies, electronics with music, film and TV studies, Gaelic, Scottish language, Scottish literature, Slavonic studies, sports studies, topographical science.

European Community: 20% first degree students take EC language as part of course and 5% spend 6 months or more in another EC country. A wide range of exchanges exist with EC universities/colleges including: Belgium (Liège, performing arts; Ghent, dentistry); Eire (Dublin, performing arts); France (Grenoble and Toulouse, engineering; Strasbourg, dentistry, business and management); Germany (Mainz, dentistry and law; Kassel, language); Italy (Florence, education; Modena, law; Milan, economics); Netherlands (Antwerp, maths; Rotterdam, sociology, Nijmegen, biology and dentistry; Utrecht, performing arts and literature); Spain (Zaragoza, veterinary medicine; Barcelona, geography; Pamplona, philosophy). Most first degree students have access to EC language tuition. Approved Erasmus programme 1992.

Application: UCCA for 1993 start, UCAS thereafter. **Founded:** 1451. **Main awards:** BA, BAcc, BArch, BD, BDS, BEd, BMus, BN, BSc, BEng, MEng, LLB, MA, MB, ChB, BVMS. **Awarding body:** Glasgow University. **Site:** Compact central campus. **Access:** Within easy reach of bus and rail stations. **Accommodation:** 4,000+ places in halls and student houses. Approx cost: £50 pw (most meals), £30 pw (self-catering). 30% in accommodation where rent controlled by university. **Library:** Main and departmental libraries with around 1.5 million volumes; separate reading room with all first year texts. **Specialist collections:** Extensive and valuable collection of books and manuscripts. *Also:* Hunterian Museum (anatomical and surgical drawings, instruments etc); Hunterian Art Gallery (old masters, Whistlers, Chardins, Charles Rennie Mackintosh House), ethnographic and Roman collections. **Other learning facilities:** Computer centre, language laboratories. **Welfare:** Student health centre (works in co-operation with students' own local doctor). Student counselling service, academic advisers for all students. **Careers:** Advice (including summer vacation jobs) and placement service. **Amenities:** SRC shops, travel bureau, bank, insurance bureau, printing and photocopying facilities; 2 student unions with lounges, bars, TV rooms, etc. **Sporting facilities:** Stevenson Physical Education Building offering wide range of indoor sports, 25 m swimming pool and fitness training programmes. Athletic grounds with bar and pavilion about 2 miles from campus. Access to Kelvin Hall Sports Arena (most modern UK university sports facilities).

Duration of first degree course(s) or equivalent: 4 years (hons); **others:** 3 years and 5 years **Total first degree students (full-time) 1991/92:** 11,398 **Overseas students:** 1,067 **Mature students:** 22% **Male/female ratio:** 11:10 **Teaching staff: full-time:** 1,256 **Total full-time students 1991/92:** 12,826 **Postgraduate students:** 1,428 (ft), 1,148 (pt) **Tuition fees for 1992/93 (first degrees):** Home: £1,855 (classroom), £2770 (lab/studio), £4,985 (clinical); Overseas: £5,320 (classroom), £7,055–£7,205 (lab/studio), £12,990 (clinical).

What it's like

It comes as a surprise to many freshers that Glasgow University has two independent student unions. The first major decision that a fresher has to make is not what courses to study, but which union to join. Glasgow University Union (GUU), is the bigger, and many say the better of the two. Within this grade II listed building at the foot of University Avenue, the best and cheapest watering hole on campus can be found in the form of the internationally renowned Beer Bar or 'Beerie'. On further inspection of the union 5 other bars can be found as well as libraries, dining room, smoke room, buffet (excellent filled rolls), snooker hall (10 full size tables), pool hall, disco, bedrooms and last but by no means least the debates chamber where big bands have been known to play and as its name suggests, debates are also held. The Union enjoys the position of being one of the top debating unions in the world.

The Queen Margaret Union (QM), is situated on the other side of the hill from

CAN'T FIND WHAT YOU'RE LOOKING FOR? USE THE INDEX!

the GUU. Here members of either union can enjoy several facilities, but being on a smaller scale than the GUU choice is limited. Athletic club's excellent Stevenson Building contains Olympic swimming pool and many indoor sports, as well as assisting university's teams and sporting clubs. All students automatically join one of unions and athletic club on matriculation. Glasgow makes no concessions to trendy innovations but gives security of ancient Scottish university education, with wide-ranging chances in corporate life. Cultural and educational opportunities set in Gothic grandeur of 'varsity buildings refute slum-bound image of Glasgow; city (especially West End) where university situated, very attractive.

Pauper notes

Accommodation: 15 bedrooms at cheap rates in union for members 'too drunk to go home'. **Drink:** GUU beer bar and lounge bar cheapest on campus with excellent promotions. **Eats:** GUU catering – fresh filled rolls, vegetarian dishes, halal meat and normal meat-catering also in Beer Bar. **Ents:** Theatre Royal, Glasgow Film Theatre and Citizens Theatre all offer student discounts. **Sports:** Kelvin Hall and Stevenson Building. **Shops:** Union barber (John) for short back and sides. **Travel:** Scholarships on offer include McGill, Georgetown and Freiburg universities. **Work:** Large number of student bar-tenders needed in summer.

Alumni (Editors' pick)

Ian McGregor, Teddy Taylor (MP, Conservative), John Smith (leader of the Opposition), William Boyd (novelist and short story writer), Pat Kane ('Hue and Cry'), Donald Dewer.

GOLDSMITHS' COLLEGE

Goldsmiths' College, University of London, New Cross, London SE14 6NW (081 692 7171) Map D, C3

Student enquiries: Registry

Main study areas – as in What to Study section: *(First degree):* Art & design, anthropology, communication studies, computing, drama, economics, education, English, fine arts, history, Latin-American studies, mathematical studies, modern languages, music, politics & government, psychology, social policy and social work, sociology. *Also:* Art, craft studies, studio practice, textiles.

European Community: 15% first degree students take EC language as part of course and 15% spend 6 months or more in another EC country. EC languages available to language specialists and as options for students on other degrees. Formal exchange links with some 8 EC universities/colleges: France (Avignon, Paris, Toulouse); Germany (Berlin, Koumln, Marburg, Tubingen) and Spain. Approved Erasmus programme 1992/93.

Application: UCCA for 1993 start, UCAS thereafter; design studies and textiles through UCCA/UCAS or ADAR. **Structural features:** Part of London University. **Academic features:** Access to extensive evening study programme for all students. Many degree courses available part-time; many in combined subjects. Increasing student choice in degree courses. **Largest fields of study:** Art, English, communication studies, drama, mathematics, psychology, social sciences, music, education and European languages. **Founded:** 1891, incorporated in London University 1904. Royal Charter in 1990. **Main awards:** BA, BA(Ed), BMus, BSc. **Awarding body:** London University. **Site:** South-east London. **Access:** New Cross Gate or New Cross station (British Rail and underground) and buses. **Accommodation:** 1,032 places in halls (preference given to first years not within easy travelling distance, 85% of whom are housed). Approx cost: £41 pw (self-catering), £56 (five day catering). **Library:** Purpose-built central library; 333,000 volumes, 1,500 periodicals, audio visual collections with facilities, Prestel, computer-based literature search, 400 study places. **Other learning resources:** Languages resource centre with language laboratories, computer-enhanced learning facilities, studios, satellite reception, audio and video cassettes. **Welfare:** Doctors, counsellors, psychiatrist, physiotherapist, solicitor (via SU), chaplains. **Special categories:** Nursery (30 places). **Careers:** Careers adviser; London University appointments board. **Amenities:** College bookshop, refectory and bar; audio visual facilities, theatre; SU building with launderette, coffee bar etc. **Sporting facilities:** Sports campus and playing fields near Sidcup (30 minutes) and on site, swimming pool nearby. **Employment:** Teaching, media, public service, administration, banking, commerce and industry.

Duration of first degree course(s) or equivalent: 3 years; **others:** 4 years (European languages, BA(Ed), design studies, mathematics with work experience, extension degrees in psychology, fine art, textiles, art and art history) **Total first degree students 1991/92:** 2,736 **Total first year BA/BSc/BA(Ed) students:** 1,023 **Overseas students:** 86 **Mature students:** approx 15% **Male/female ratio:** 2:3 **Teaching staff:** full-time: 310 **Total full-time students 1991/92:** 3,736 **Postgraduate students:** 925 **Tuition fees for 1992/93 (first degrees):** Home: £775 (if no grant), £1,855 (classroom), £2,770 (lab/studio); Overseas: £5,500 (classroom), £6,630 (lab/studio).

What it's like

Very attractive Victorian red brick building, surrounded by very modern library, halls of residence and administration block etc in the heart of a gradually yuppifying, though shabby inner city area – enough to make Prince Charles wince! 3 faculties: arts, education and social and mathematical sciences. Good reputation for drama, music, visual art, communications and sociology – makes for a very diverse and interesting, though terminally trendy, student population. Most first years guaranteed hall place, though there is an accommodation crisis. Halls range from very attractive, converted houses in rather desirable areas, to utilitarian monolithic concrete blocks overlooking main London–Deal road on one side and scrapmetal yard on other. Teaching is done on one site, at New Cross, though history students sometimes venture into other London colleges for lectures; on-campus teaching space is often cramped. Many overseas students further enrich cultural diversity within college.

SU has earned reputation as one of the most politically vocal in the university; also at great pains to provide 3 bars, coffee shop, launderette, welfare services, clubs and societies (most popular athletics union, drama, soul club, lesbian and gay), sports and entertainments. *Time Out* once described it as 'the best student venue for bands in London'.

Local points of interest: Greenwich, for its park, historic ships and buildings, pubs and market; Blackheath, for its wide open space, where Cornish rebels fought in 1493 with 'such valour and stoutness', and its striking architecture; Lewisham, for its shops; Brockley, for virtually nothing; and New Cross, for Goldsmiths' and economically feasible Chinese and Indian takeaways.

Conveniently situated close to central London, trains from New Cross to Waterloo/Charing Cross (journey time – 12 mins) are frequent and it is well served by buses even late at night. On the whole, a good place to study for those city lovers who hate isolated, tight campus universities.

A student view: 'Basically Goldsmiths' is a completely cool place if you fancy being patronised by 3rd years during Freshers' Week, getting flanned by people in rabbit suits and sleeping in a toll booth rest room on the jail break during Rag Week. It's a laugh, come and join us, it's better than every other college under the sun. And no, I'm not biased!!'

Pauper notes

Accommodation: Hard to find. Squats – conditions improving; SU going to run squatting workshops and advice groups for students who squat. In SE London married quarters are rare. **Drink:** Pubs are usually friendly if you respect the locals. Union bar the cheapest by far. **Eats:** Many restaurants in surrounding areas: Italian, Chinese, Indian, Caribbean, Thai – you name it, SE London has it. **Ents:** *Time Out* said: 'Goldsmiths' still pursuing its excellent policy of being the place where you see big bands first.' Cheap and excellent also for budding cabaret stars. Of course, the delights of the capital city are also just a train ride and an overdraft away. **Sports:** Active athletics union. **Hardship funds:** Limited access fund, at discretion of college, with guidelines agreed by SU for distribution to worthy students. **Travel:** Near A2 – lots of traffic – cheap train and coaches. **Work:** Temping and part-time in local businesses can be hard to find.

More info?

Enquiries to Sara Ragab (081 692 1406).

Alumni (Editors' pick)

Vic Charles (world karate champion), Linton Kwesi Johnson (poet and musician), Mary Quant (fashion designer), Merlyn Rees MP, Colin Welland, Jack Brymer, Graham Sutherland, Malcolm McLaren (former Union VP), John Cale (Velvet Underground), Tom Keating (artist), Derek Hatton (politician), Julian Clary.

GREENWICH UNIVERSITY

University of Greenwich, Wellington Street, London SE18 6PF (081 316 8590) Map D, D2

Student enquiries: Course Enquiries Officer (081-316 8590)

Main study areas – as in What to Study section: *(First degree):* Accountancy, architecture, biochemistry, biology, business studies, chemistry, civil engineering, computing, economics, education, electrical & electronic engineering, environmental science, environmental studies, European studies, geography, geology, information technology, law, mathematical studies, mechanical and production engineering, metallurgy and materials science, nursing studies, physics, politics and government, religious studies and theology, sociology, town and county planning. *Also:* Building surveying, estate management, horticulture, landscape architecture, quantity surveying.

European Community: 2% first degree students take EC language as part of course and spend 6 months or more in another EC country. Formal exchange links with 6 EC universities/colleges: Eire (Limerick); France (Paris); Germany (Berlin & Stuttgart); Greece (Athens); Spain (Madrid). EC study available with chemistry, biological sciences, business studies, architecture and landscape architecture. BA International marketing (sandwich course) includes French/German/Spanish. Language labs open to all students. Approved Erasmus programme 1992/93.

Application: PCAS for 1993 start, UCAS thereafter. **Special features:** Mature students may be admitted without normal entry requirements if university satisfied they suit the course. Considerable transferability between courses allowed. **Largest fields of study:** Business, social sciences, humanities, education, computing and surveying. **Founded:** 1992 as a university; previously Thames Poly, founded 1970, ex Woolwich Polytechnic, Hammersmith College of Building and Art, Dartford College of Education, Avery Hill College and Garnett College. **Main awards:** BA, BSc, BEd, BEng. **Awarding body:** Greenwich University. **Site:** 7 sites (Woolwich, Dartford, Eltham, Wapping, Roehampton, Deptford and Shadwell). **Accommodation:** Over 1,200 places in own halls or affiliated halls; wide range of private sector rented accommodation close to university. All new students guaranteed accommodation. **Library:** 7 libraries; 400,000 volumes, 2,000 periodicals, 850 study places; short loan for course texts; photocopying; on-line information services. **Other learning facilities:** Computer centre, microcomputer facilities on all sites. **Welfare:** 2 counsellors, nursing officer and nurses, medical officers and consultant psychiatrist, Anglican and RC chaplains. **Careers:** Information, advice and placement. **Amenities:** Students' union, stationery and bookshop; dance and drama hall; creche on Woolwich campus. **Sporting facilities:** Gymnasia, heated indoor swimming pool, playing fields including all-weather surfaces, tennis, netball and squash courts.

Duration of first degree course(s) or equivalent: 3 years (full-time), 4 years (sandwich) **Total first degree students 1991/92:** 6,972 **BEd students:** 850 **Overseas students:** 323 **Male/female ratio:** 4:3 **Teaching staff:** 520 **Total full-time students 1991/92:** 8,546 **Postgraduate students:** 1,750 **Tuition fees for 1992/93** (first degrees): Home: £759 (if no grant), £1,855 (classroom), £2,770 (lab/studio); Overseas: £5,000.

What it's like

Spread over 6 sites, Uni stretches from Wapping (just east of the City of London) in fast-growing yuppy docklands area, to Dartford in Kent. Each site specialises in different types of courses – Wapping: accountancy, Shadwell: geology & earth sciences, Deptford: environmental, Woolwich: arts & sciences, Avery Hill: teacher training, and Dartford: architecture & surveying.

Uni accommodation reasonable, all rooms are single; uni guarantees accommodation for all first years.

Uni and highly active SU strictly enforce policies of equality of opportunity, which give rise to a pleasant, friendly, cosmopolitan community. Thames is a lively, fun and safe place to study, live and meet interesting people from a large cross-section of the community.

Pauper notes

Accommodation: Uni accommodation office does all it can, but it's still a little expensive. Student squats in Wickham Lane/Southwood Lodge; no married quarters. **Drink:** SU bars are the only place to be. SU opening new bar at Eltham – cheap, fun and friendly. **Eats:** Refectories on all sites; 10% discount with SU card at Cuisine of India; some reasonably priced restaurants around. **Ents:** Bands and cabaret at SU regularly. SU film society shows a film every Monday night. New ents manager promises bigger and better things than before. **Sports:** Excellent sporting facilities incl squash courts, tennis courts, swimming pool, football, hockey, lacrosse and rugby pitches. **Work:** Some SU bar work – loads of p-t off campus work available.

Alumni (Editors' pick)

Hale & Pace (TV comedians), Brian Jacks (Olympic judo medallist), Ann Packer (Olympic athletics medallist), Rachel Heyhoe-Flint (cricketer), Prof Ian McAllister (Prof of politics, Univ of New South Wales), Graham Ingham (BBC2 economics correspondent – Newsnight).

GUILDHALL SCHOOL

Guildhall School of Music & Drama, Silk Street, Barbican, London EC2Y 8DT (071 628 2571; Fax 071 256 9438) Map E, D2

Student enquiries: Registrar

Main study areas – as in What to Study section: *(First degree):* Drama, music. Also: Technical theatre – stage management.

European Community: No students take EC language. No exchange links.

Application: Direct. **Special features:** All teachers active in their professions outside the School. The Takacs Quartet, quartet-in-residence. **Founded:** 1880, degree status granted 1945. **Main award:** BMus. **Awarding body:** Guildhall

CAN'T FIND WHAT YOU'RE LOOKING FOR? USE THE INDEX!

School of Music & Drama. **Site:** Barbican, central London. **Access:** Moorgate underground station. **Accommodation:** Welfare Officer helps with accommodation. Approx cost: £55–£60 pw. Private lodgings, hostel and self-catering accommodation and flats. Proportion of students housed in accommodation where rent is controlled by school, not known. **Library:** over 60,000 volumes, 50 periodicals, 44 study places; listening facilities. Audio visual room with 17 study carrels, special resources room with computer facilities and multimedia/electronic music workstations; separate drama library and study area. **Specialist collections:** Alkan Society Collection, Appleby Collection (guitar music), Harris Collection (opera vocal scores), Merrett Collection (double bass), Rosenweig Jewish Collection, Worshipful Company of Musicians Westrup Collection. **Other learning resources:** Professional 16-track recording studio. **Welfare:** Welfare officer, doctor, counsellor, chaplain. **Hardship fund:** Limited funds available. **Careers:** Advice from Principal and senior members of staff. **Amenities:** Music hall, theatre (orchestra pit of 80), lecture recital room, John Hosier Practice Annexe (46 practice studios), theatre-training gymnasium, Barbican Centre. **Employment:** Music specialists in schools.

Duration of first degree course(s) or equivalent: 4 years (BMus) 3 years (AGSM acting) 2 years (CSM GSM stage management) **Total first degree students 1991/92:** 459 **Male/female ratio:** 1:1 **Teaching staff: full-time:** 12 **part-time:** 275 **Total full-time students 1991/92:** 698 **Postgraduate students:** 239 **Tuition fees for 1992/93 (first degrees):** Home: £3,010–£3,550; Overseas: £5,800.

What it's like

Modern building of deep red brick and grey stone/concrete in the bowels of the Barbican Centre. (With the LSO and RSC so free/reduced tickets and rehearsal passes.) Practice bunker near Barbican tube station, with 46 rooms of varying shapes and sizes.

No halls of residence – some live at Barbican YMCA – around £60 per week for a double room, including all meals and no travelling expenses (eligible for single room after 6 months; visitors must be out by 10 pm). Other accommodation includes Henry Wood House in Camberwell (shared with other music colleges) – cheaper than the YMCA, but further out and self-catering; visitors may stay overnight for a small fee. Otherwise look through papers, agencies, adverts or word of mouth. School Welfare Officer has an accommodation list.

Relations between admin and students generally good. Teaching staff, on the whole, are excellent personally and professionally – most are working with top orchestras, opera and theatre companies, so know the problems which students face.

Courses cover all aspects of the performing arts – music, drama, stage management and scene painting. Not much collaboration between courses, except for timetabled musicals/operas etc. Relatively easy to change courses/teachers; motives, personality clashes and ability all play a part. Exams are mainly sit-down, but trend towards continuous assessment. Dropout rate is virtually nil; general attitude is happy, and social activity is on the increase. 12% of students come from outside the EC; 3–4% from Europe. School Library is open until 7.15pm Mon–Thurs. Access to University of London Library at Senate House and the magnificent Barbican Library.

No sports facilities but thriving football teams, darts etc. Access to nearby City University Sports Centre and swimming pool.

School snack bar open 8.30 am–4.30 pm. Lauderdale Tower (a 5 minutes' walk through the Barbican) houses refectory, open 12 noon–2.00 pm and SU Bar Club (excellent, with a full range of drinks including real ales). Atmosphere very good and good range of food served in the evenings. Discos, jazz nights and other events held in main college Music Hall. Bar open Mon–Fri 12 noon–3 pm and 5.00 pm–11.00 pm.

SU helpful and efficient, strictly non-political. Publishes a regular newsletter and information sheet for freshers. Societies include Student Theatre Society,

Contemporary Music Society, Early Music Society, Christian Union, Overseas Students Association etc.

Ian Gardner and Andrew Bullough

Pauper notes

Accommodation: Barbican YMCA – no real halls of residence for Guildhall students. Henry Wood House takes a number of Guildhall students. **Drink:** Subsidised SU bar at Lauderdale Tower. **Eats:** Canteen at Lauderdale Tower 5 minutes' walk from school. Food in SU bar in evenings. **Ents:** Cheap tickets for concerts, operas, shows, plays, etc through SU. **Sports:** Swimming pool and sports facilities at City University. **Hardship funds:** Many scholarships available. **Work:** Some private teaching; busking; outside engagements (mostly City Livery Company dinners); depping in West End shows; gigs. Stewarding work: occasionally in college; regular at Barbican Centre, Colliseum, Southbank.

Alumni (Editors' pick)

Sir Geraint Evans, Fred Astaire, James Galway, Claire Bloom, Dudley Moore, Jacqueline du Pré, Peter Skellern, Max Jaffa, Mollie Sugden, Julia MacKenzie, Benjamin Luxon.

HARPER ADAMS

Harper Adams Agricultural College, Newport, Shropshire TF10 8NB (0952 820280) Map A, D6

Student enquiries: Admissions Secretary

Main study areas – as in What to Study section: *(First degree):* Agriculture, horticulture and forestry, business studies. *Also:* Agri-food marketing, agricultural engineering, animal science, land management, rural environmental protection, rural technology.

European Community: 8% first degree students take an EC language as part of their course and 1% spend 6 months or more in another EC country. Language options available to all students on agri-food marketing and business studies degrees. Formal exchange links with colleges in Belgium, France, Germany and Netherlands. Approved Erasmus programme.

Application: PCAS for 1993 start, UCAS thereafter (or direct if early). **Academic features:** A modular system for most courses, allowing a range of options. All degree courses are sandwich courses; teaching links with appropriate universities. **Founded:** 1901. **Main awards:** BSc. **Awarding body:** Open University. **Site:** Single campus for all teaching, living accommodation and recreation. College farm surrounds the campus. **Access:** M54 from the south; M6 and A519 from North. **Accommodation:** On-site accommodation for most first years and 50% of all students; 50% in private accommodation nearby. *Approx cost:* £58 pw (meals included at weekends). **Library:** 32,000 volumes, 700 periodicals. **Specialist collections:** Links with university libraries on joint courses. **Other learning facilities:** Covered soil working area, specialised laboratories, glasshouse complex, mixed commercial farm. **Welfare:** Regular surgeries held at college. **Special facilities:** Some college houses available for mature students with families; en-suite facilities in some college rooms. **Careers:** Information, advice and placement service. **Amenities:** 2 common rooms, SU bars, stage and auditorium, hall for dances etc. **Sporting facilities:** Squash and tennis courts, swimming pool, sports hall, sports fields – all on campus. **Employment:** Careers in marketing, farming, engineering and land management.

Duration of first degree course(s) or equivalent: 4 years sandwich **Total first degree students 1992/93:** 400 **Overseas students:** 25 **Mature students:** 20 **Male/**

CAN'T FIND WHAT YOU'RE LOOKING FOR? USE THE INDEX!

female ratio: 2:1 **full-time students 1992/93:** 1,200 **Postgraduate students:** 15
Tuition fees 1992/93 (first degrees): Home: £2,770; Overseas: £5,319.

What it's like

It's the biggest and soon to be the *only* independent agricultural college in
England. Life's hard and fast and you're here to work hard and play hard. Always
something to do with usual agric antics. Worst rivals, Cirencester. Best rivals,
Seale Hayne. 'Hey, we're still here and going strong. Forget the rest and hit the
best . . .' Harper spirit means you give as good as you get and *never, ever* lose your
sense of humour. See you in '94.

Pauper notes

Accommodation: Victorian, New Cambrian and up to date hostels. New hostel
with en suite bathrooms. **Drink:** New bar (48 pumps). Sutherland Arms (also
good for food). **Eats:** Cafeteria on campus. Town: 2 curry houses; 2 chip shops; 3
Chinese. **Ents:** Social fund £20 per semester. All bands free. **Sports:** Rugby,
football, hockey, netball, shooting, basketball, outdoor swimming pool, aerobics,
Gaelic football, snooker, squash. **Hardship funds:** No information. **Travel:** No
information. **Work:** Available locally.

Informal name

HAAC; Harper.

Buzz-words

NFI (no invite); SEP (someone else's problem); DBI (Daddy bought it); FBOT
(Fat Boys on tour); STNUS (Sod the NUS).

Alumni (Editors' pick)

Barbara Woodhouse.

HATFIELD POLY

See Hertfordshire University

HERIOT-WATT UNIVERSITY

Heriot-Watt University, Riccarton, Edinburgh EH14 4AS
(031 449 5111) Map A, D3

Student enquiries: Admissions Officer/Education Liaison Officer

Main study areas – as in What to Study section: *(First degree):* Accountancy,
architecture, art and design, biochemistry, biology, business studies, chemical
engineering, chemistry, civil engineering, computing, economics, education, electrical & electronic engineering, environmental science, information technology,
mathematical studies, mechanical and production engineering, microbiology,
modern languages, physics, social policy and social welfare, town and country
planning. *Also:* Actuarial studies, brewing, building, energy studies, estate management, interpretation & translation, offshore engineering, quantity surveying,
sports studies, textile technology.

European Community: 5% first degree students (plus language specialists) take
EC language as part of course and 3% (plus language specialists) spend 6 months
or more in another EC country. Language tuition (French, German, Spanish)
available to students of any subject; in particular, it is offered to students wishing
to combine maths, chemistry, accountancy, economics or international business,

with a language in a joint degree and students going on Erasmus exchanges, as well as to language specialists. Large number of formal exchange links in France, Spain and Germany. Some double degrees, where students can gain degree from Heriot-Watt and equivalent qualification from partner institution in EC. Some industrial placements abroad with study at partner institutions, eg degree in chemistry with European language. Approved Erasmus programme 1992/93.

Application: UCCA for 1993 start, UCAS thereafter. **Structural features:** Faculties of environmental studies (architecture, landscape, planning and housing) and art and design are joint with Edinburgh College of Art; faculty of textiles (industrial design, colour science, textiles & clothing studies) joint with Scottish College of Textiles; Institute of Education (teacher-training, social work, leisure studies, physical education) joint with Moray House College. All can be looked up separately. **Founded:** 1821, granted charter in 1966. **Main awards:** BA, BArch, BEd, BEng, BSc, MEng. **Awarding body:** Heriot-Watt University. **Academic features:** Combined studies degrees offer scope for choice and flexibility. Specialist degrees in brewing & distilling (Heriot-Watt is base of industry-backed International Centre for Brewing and Distilling), energy resources engineering, housing studies, manufacturing computing, quality management; industrial and business studies. **Site:** Modern campus at Riccarton, 8 miles from central Edinburgh. **Access:** Bus from central Edinburgh. **Accommodation:** c.1,000 places at Riccarton, in single and double study bedrooms, with full board or in self-catering student flats, plus further university accommodation off-campus. Accommodation and welfare officer assists with lodgings. Rent: 35% students in accommodation where rent is controlled by university. **Library:** 150,000 volumes, 2,500 periodicals; on-line information system. **Other learning facilities:** Television centre, computer centre, computer-based learning. **Welfare:** GP and dental services. Personal counselling by accommodation and welfare officer, tutor/mentor, university chaplains. **Careers:** Information and advice service. University has an excellent record of graduate placement in employment. **Amenities:** New purpose-built SU at Riccarton; numerous clubs and societies. **Sporting facilities:** Excellent sports centre on Riccarton campus.

Duration of first degree course(s) or equivalent: 4 years; 3 years for some ordinary degrees; 5 years for some MEng **Total first degree students, including associated colleges 1991/92:** 6,650 **Overseas students 1991/92:** 750 **Mature students 1991/92:** 950 **Male/female ratio 1990/91:** 3:2 **Teaching staff: full-time:** c700 **part-time:** c75 **Total students 1991/92:** 8,150 (full & part-time) **Postgraduate students:** 1,500 (full & part-time) **Tuition fees for 1992/93 (first degrees):** Home: £1,855 (classroom), £2,770 (lab/studio); Overseas: £5,420 (classroom), £7,155 (lab/studio).

What it's like

Split-site campus. Travel between sites by bus; train service to campus.

Campus probably one of the most striking but not well designed. Accommodation reasonable: full board, self-catering flats and self-catering single rooms. Central laundry facilities and spin driers in each hall. All blocks mixed (corridors single-sex); no visiting restrictions. All the problems of campus universities; student ghetto etc, but advantage of being close to one of the most exciting cities in Europe. Limited residences, mainly for College of Art students. University leases flats from private landlords, most of which are very reasonable. Overseas students predominantly from Malaysia and Norway, also from south (similar proportion). Many overseas students mature, fewer home students are. Main sports facilities on campus open 9–9 seven days a week; well used by students, staff and local community. Other facilities on campus; shop (open 7 days a week); library (7 days) are well used. In most matters relations with university administration are reasonably good.

Courses predominantly science and engineering; highly thought of business courses, economics, accountancy and finance and business organisation; highly respected interpreting course (one of very few in UK). Campus is science dominated and town, social sciences. Many unusual/unique courses including actuarial

CAN'T FIND WHAT YOU'RE LOOKING FOR? USE THE INDEX!

mathematics, marine biology and interpreting. All have high international standing, renowned as a technological institution. Heavy workload and specialised vocational courses. Scope for transfer (easiest in first or second year) to general degree provides a good safety net for those who have made the wrong choice or wish to keep their horizons broad. Main assessment by exam, some continuous. Much teaching goes alongside research so quite a few progress to further study.

New union building on campus. Free buses provided on major function nights. Entertainments range from bands, folk singers, drinks promotions to regular discos. Many active societies hold events such as speakers (debates), cheese and wine, pub crawls; cover wide range of interests. Edinburgh is a student city with three universities and several colleges. Excellent opportunity to meet and mix with other institutions. Many pubs, cinemas and theatres and reciprocal agreements allow students to use other unions.

Heriot-Watt provides the pleasant combination of city night life and a peaceful campus environment.

Pauper notes

Accommodation: Careful reading of adverts in papers may yield bargains. No knowledge of squats. **Drink:** Union provides cheapest pint in town, other reasonable places selling local brews, for example The Athletic Arms. **Eats:** Food in residences is fair. Union provides wide range of cheap meals and snacks. **Ents:** Many local pubs offer free bands midweek and weekends. Several 'alternative' theatres and cinemas. **Sports:** Several good sports centres in city including ice rinks, swimming pools and all-round complexes. **Hardship funds:** Students' Association can loan £75. **Work:** Vacation jobs harder to come by but many departments help with course-related jobs.

HERTFORDSHIRE UNIVERSITY

University of Hertfordshire, College Lane, Hatfield, Herts AL10 9AB (0707 284000) Map A, F7

Student enquiries: UK Development Manager (0707 284458), or appropriate Admissions Office

Main study areas – as in What to Study section: *(First degree):* Accountancy, aeronautical engineering, biology, biochemistry, biotechnology, business studies, chemistry, civil engineering, computing, economics, education, electrical & electronic engineering, English, environmental science, environmental studies, geology, history, law, linguistics, mathematical studies, mechanical and production engineering, microbiology, nursing, pharmacology, philosophy, physics, physiology, professions allied to medicine (PAMs), psychology, social policy and social welfare. *Also:* Contemporary studies, horticulture, medical electronics, software engineering.

European Community: 40% first degree students take EC language as part of course; very few spend time in another EC country. Formal exchange links with 40 EC universities/colleges in Belgium (1); Denmark (2); France (12); Germany (7); Greece (2); Italy (5); Netherlands (6); Portugal (1); Spain (4). Approved Erasmus programme. Member of ECTS for mechanical engineering. University policy that all students should have possibility of a European dimension to their studies. EC language tuition offered on wide range of courses in engineering, chemistry, environmental studies, business and humanities. Students can also work abroad through Comett.

Application: PCAS for 1993 start, UCAS thereafter. **Academic features:** High proportion of sandwich courses; most courses based on a common modular structure. Students over 25 make up about 40% of all students. **Founded:** 1992 as a university; previously Hatfield Poly, founded 1952. **Main awards:** BA, BEd, BEng, MEng, BSc. **Awarding body:** Hertfordshire University. **Site:** Three campuses all some 20 miles north of London. **Access:** Hatfield campus next to A1(M); Wall Hall campus near M1; Hertford campus near A10. All three campuses fairly near railway stations with regular fast services to London. Local buses between campuses and nearby towns like St Albans, Watford and Welwyn Garden City. **Accommodation:** 1,600 places in halls of residence (1,200 reserved for first-year students). Approx cost: £24–£29 pw (self-catering). New student village on Hatfield campus houses nearly 500 students, allocations are mostly to seniors. **Library:** 250,000 volumes – on all three campuses. Full CD-ROM and database facilities. **Other learning facilities:** Observatory, computer centre, audio/visual aids service. **Welfare:** Personal Services Unit providing specialist help, in addition to personal tutorial system. General medical and nursing facilities, professional counsellors, chaplaincy and day nursery, financial and legal advisory services. **Hardship funds:** Reduction or deferment of fees in cases of unforeseen hardship (after first year). University and SU have small loan funds to help students overcome temporary hardship. **Special categories:** Residential facilities for disabled and families. **Careers:** Advisory and placement service; recruitment fair. **Amenities:** Modern purpose built sports hall and SU building; music and drama centres; wide range of sports.

Duration of first degree course(s) or equivalent: 3 years (full-time; accelerated computer science sandwich); **others:** 4 years (sandwich), 2 years (accelerated LLB); **Total first degree students 1991/92:** 6,775 **Total BEd students:** 481 **Overseas students:** 304 **Mature students:** 3,217 **Male/female ratio:** 3:2 **Teaching staff:** 460 **Total full-time students 1991/92:** 9,264 **Postgraduate students:** 1,153 **Tuition fees for 1992/93 (first degrees):** Home: £1,855 (classroom), £2,770 (lab/studio); Overseas: £5,130 (classroom), £5,290 (lab/studio).

What it's like

Very accessible to London from all sites. Excellent SU facilities: Hatfield – snack bar, shop, travel office, the Font bar and Mandela bar. Excellent ents facilities in form of Hutton Hall. Balls Park – Boathouse Bar; Wall Hall – Bar/refectory, central hall ents venue. SU funds all the clubs and societies on campus which number over 70. Greenfield university, 3 campuses are spread about 12 miles apart with bad public transport. Poor transport service it is not as good as it could be and you must pay £30/year for it. Wall Hall and Balls Park are set in attractive park areas with ornate mansion buildings but Wall Hall is very isolated.

Hatfield campus has good library and computer facilities.

SU tries to make up for general facilities and offers an excellent entertainment programme.

Pauper notes

Accommodation: Not bad but distanced from university through inadequate transport system; few squats. **Drink:** The Font, Boathouse, Wall Hall bar – SU bars. Otherwise expensive area; White Horse, Hertford for excellent trad. beers. **Eats:** Hatfield naf, but St Albans good. Sloppy Joes in Hertford US theme bar. **Ents:** Brand new UCI 9-screen cinema, student cheap prices. Excellent SU ents. **Sports:** On campus – good sports centre though no artificial pitches. Off campus – Gosling Stadium, Welwyn Garden City. Numerous sports teams in area, giving student discount. **Hardship fund:** Very limited; access funds. **Travel:** Inadequate. Uni bus service that you now pay for; skeletal public service. Excellent trains to London, 20 minutes. **Work:** New shopping centre and employment agencies but limited.

Buzz-words

Hilltop (loutish git likely to smash in head); Skint (universally known, we are told!).

CAN'T FIND WHAT YOU'RE LOOKING FOR? USE THE INDEX!

Alumni (Editors' pick)

Martin Dew (badminton), Delroy Alexander (student DJ of the year), Helen Ledderer (Founder, Phileas Fog snacks).

HEYTHROP COLLEGE

Heythrop College, University of London, Kensington Square, London W8 5HQ (071 580 6941) Map E, A3

Student enquiries: Secretary and Registrar

Main study areas – as in What to Study section: *(First degree):* Philosophy, religious studies and theology.

European Community: No students take an EC language or spend time in another EC country as part of their course.

Application: UCCA for 1993 start, UCAS thereafter. **Structural features:** Part of London University. **Founded:** In 17th century Liège as a Jesuit college. Later providing a residential seminary for Jesuits and other students in Oxfordshire until transfer to London premises in 1970. Became college of London University in 1970. **Main awards:** BA, BD. **Awarding body:** London University. **Site:** Attractive Central London site. Collegiate scheduled buildings in Kensington Square. **Access:** Kensington High Street underground station. **Accommodation:** Non-residential students are advised to apply to a London University hall of residence or to one of the university chaplaincies in London. No students housed in accommodation where rent controlled by college. **Library:** 250,000 items (many 17th century), 150 study places. **Welfare:** Students use the facility of the University Health Service. **Amenities:** College choir; proximity to theatres, cinemas, museums, galleries; refectory including staff–student lunch facilities. **Sporting facilities:** Tennis courts; football and cricket teams. **Employment:** Christian ministry, teaching, social work, media, police force etc.

Duration of first degree course(s) or equivalent: 3 years **Total first degree students 1991/92:** 110 **Overseas students:** 13 **Mature students:** 55 **Male/female ratio:** 3:2 **Teaching staff: full-time:** 20 **part-time:** 9 **Total full-time students 1991/92:** 218 **Postgraduate students:** 108 **Tuition fees for first degrees 1992/93:** £1,545 (home & overseas).

What it's like

Around 250 students; in the last few years has taken on more younger students and a more vibrant atmosphere. Many students are members of religious orders and many studying towards some sort of church ministry. This, together with the close-knit atmosphere means it's not the average arty-student type place. Very friendly; most social life revolves around SU.

Library probably the best in the country for theology; stocked well for philosophy. 2 JCR's incorporating chocolate and drinks machines, microwave, TV and stereo. There's a shared refectory but no bar.

Heythrop is remarkable for its one-to-one tutorial system, giving priority to the individual. Lecturers are specialist and skilled. The college provides an unusual mix of age groups, nationalities and outlooks on life. Close friendships are readily formed.

Pauper notes

Accommodation: Catholic chaplaincies and inter-collegiate halls of residence. ULU accommodation office very helpful. **Drink:** ULU, Catholic chaplaincy, many pubs. **Eats:** ULU. **Ents:** Cinemas cheaper in the daytime during the week.

WANT TO HELP WITH THE NEXT EDITION – SEE PAGE 76

Bloomsbury Theatre very cheap for students. ULU gig night. **Sports:** ULU and sports centres out of Central London. **Hardship funds:** Discretionary college fund. **Travel:** Excellent but expensive; travel cards save a good amount of money. **Work:** Times are hard, but no harder than elsewhere.

HOLBORN COLLEGE

Holborn College, 200 Greyhound Road, London W14 9RY
(071 385 3377) Map D, B2

Student enquiries: Registrar

Main study areas – as in What to Study section: *(First degree):* Accountancy, business studies, economics, law. *Also:* Courses for professional law exams.

European Community: No students take EC language or spend time in another EC country.

Application: Direct. **Academic features:** Full-time, part-time, distance learning and intensive revision courses available for most study programmes. LLB in collaboration with Wolverhampton University offered, in addition to external degree from London University. **Founded:** 1970, as an independent college to provide courses for London University LLB external degree and for English Bar examinations. **Main awards:** LLB, BSc (Econ). **Awarding body:** London University; Wolverhampton University. **Sites:** West Kensington, adjacent to Queens Club. **Access:** Baron's Court, West Kensington, West Brompton underground; buses. **Accommodation:** Student Information and Welfare Officer gives advice. No college accommodation. **Library:** Own reference library and reading room. **Other learning resources:** Group publishes own textbooks and course materials, Lawtel. **Careers:** Information and advice on legal, accountancy, economics and business careers. **Amenities:** Bookshop (textbooks, stationery), dining room, library, sports facilities, students' common rooms. Extra-curricular academic and social activities.

Duration of first degree course(s) or equivalent: 3 years **Total first degree students 1991/92:** 870 **Overseas students:** 500 **Mature students:** 55 **Male/female ratio:** 1:1 **Teaching staff: full-time:** c43 **part-time:** c50 **Total full-time students 1990/91:** 970 **Postgraduate students:** 100 **Tuition fees for 1992/93 (first degrees):** £4,250 (home and overseas).

What it's like

It's not Holborn. It's in Fulham, London – and it's an associate college of the Wolverhampton University. Housed in former premises of Chelsea School of Art converted with excellent facilities; main block houses 20 teaching rooms, a dining room, students' common rooms, bookshop and academic offices. Outside blocks contain a library, reading rooms and administrative offices. There is a multi-purpose recreation area on site. Syllabus is covered by a mix of lectures, seminars, written assignments with mock examinations. Lecturers and tutors from all branches of the legal profession and academic fraternity give a healthy mix of practitioners and academics. Staff very friendly, there is a welfare and information officer, so together with academic and registrary staff there is always somebody available to discuss problems. The college produces a unique range of law textbooks, case books, revision workbooks and suggested solutions to previous examination papers, these are supplied to students within their course fees. Extracurricular activities include mooting, mock trials, guest lectures and court visits.

Pauper notes

Accommodation: Nearby student hostels; shared flats relatively easy to find in area. Student information and welfare officer helps. **Drink:** Good local pubs. **Eats:** College restaurant provides excellent food from around the world at reasonable

"Canteen serves both English and Oriental food "

TANDOORI CHICKEN

THE TRADE DESCRIPTIONS ACT

prices. Bargains at North End Road market. **Ents:** Trips to theatre, concerts, weekends away, discos etc. Students' society organises special events and annual glitter ball. **Sports:** Use of International Students House, Fulham swimming pools and local sports facilities. **Hardship funds:** Genuine cases – always some help available. **Travel:** Discounts with student ID, NUS discount card and ISIC card for cheap travel. **Work:** Assistance and advice given. A few on-campus summer vacation jobs available.

More info?

Enquiries to Paul Little 071 385 3377.

HOMERTON

Homerton College, Hills Road, Cambridge CB2 2PH (0223 411141)
Map A, F7

Student enquiries: Admissions Secretary

Main study areas – as in What to Study section: *(First degree):* Education.

European Community: No students take EC language or spend time in another EC country.

Application: UCCA for 1993 start, UCAS thereafter. **Structural features:** Part of Cambridge University. **Academic features:** BEd degree of Cambridge which incorporates 'qualified teacher status' including lower primary (4–8) or upper primary (7–12) age ranges. The BEd degree of the University is an internal degree with students studying tripos courses of the University in years 3 and 4. **Special features:** Links with Kokebe College (Ethiopia), Vanderbilt Univ (USA) and the Faculty of Education of the University of Guyana. **Founded:** Origins go back to 1695; in Cambridge since 1894. **Main awards:** BEd. **Awarding body:** Cambridge University. **Site:** A single site of 30 acres, with garden, playing fields and orchards, about one mile south of the city centre, and within easy reach of the railway station. **Access:** By rail, on the Liverpool Street–King's Lynn or Kings

GET HOLD OF THE PROSPECTUSES

Cross–Cambridge line. By road, via the M11 or A604/A1. **Accommodation:** 182 single study bedrooms; 71 single and double study bedrooms in college-owned houses nearby. Approx cost: £1,510 pa including 1 meal per day. Rent: 35% in accommodation where rent controlled by college. **Library:** 100,000 volumes, 300 current periodicals. About 100 study places. **Specialist collections:** Education and Teaching Practice. **Other learning facilities:** Computing/Resources Centre. Physics, chemistry and biology laboratories. Drama studio. 3 art studios. 3 primary bases. Specialist room for geography, English, maths and history. **Welfare:** College sick bay on site, with nursing sister. Own doctor holds regular surgeries. Full range of University medical and counselling services. **Careers:** Information, advice and placement service. **Amenities:** All the societies of the University of Cambridge. **Sporting facilities:** Squash courts, playing fields for soccer and hockey, indoor facilities for badminton and gym. **Employment:** Mainly teaching in the maintained sector.

Duration of first degree course(s) or equivalent: 4 years; **Total first degree students 1991/92:** 600 **BEd students:** 740 **Overseas students:** 20 **Mature students:** 40 **Male/female ratio:** 1:10 **Teaching staff: Full-time:** 51 **Part-time:** 20 **Total full-time students 1991/92:** 900 **Postgraduate students:** 260 **Tuition fees for 1992/93 (first degrees):** Home: £1,855 (classroom), £2,770 (lab/studio); Overseas: £5,247. In addition, all first year students pay a validation fee £340.

What it's like

Homerton is an independent voluntary college which is also an approved college of the University of Cambridge.

It's situated in spacious and attractive grounds one and a half miles from city centre, within easy reach of other university buildings. Facilities include science labs, art studios, drama and music workshops, language laboratory, new technical resources centre and dance studio which blend in well with lovely old red-brick buildings. Good library with well-stocked teaching practice section; *very* lively college bar and union room complete with new stationery shop. Residential accommodation in college or nearby college houses, guaranteed for all first year BEd students; rooms cosy, with brand new furniture, fitted carpets and new decor. Other students live in – 4th years priority – about 250 rooms. Finding somewhere to live in Cambridge a problem and expensive. Food generally good. Buttery open daily, serving snacks, filled rolls, sticky buns; cafeteria lunchtime. In good old Cambridge tradition 'Formal Hall' takes place about once a week and the Principal invites every 1st year to sit at 'High Table' for one evening – together with their supervisor and other guests. It's popular to invite friends from other colleges or for eg rugby club or Homerton Men's Sports and Drinking Society (Blaggards) or Homerton Ladies Wining and Dining Society (Thunderbirds) or the Canaries (all infamous in their own right) to reserve a block booking for a meal.

Mixed residency: Homerton is actually very relaxed about this – probably due to the very small number of male students on BEd course. No-one seems to think twice about having mixed washing facilities on all corridors!

Unusually high intake of mature students; PGCE students greater number of mature students. Very few overseas students apart from annual intake of about 15–20 JYA's (Junior Year Abroad Students) – spending year doing some main subject work, generally living it up in Cambridge – mainly from America – certainly add atmosphere to college life. Students from all parts of Britain, majority from 'south', background 50% private/50% state comprehensive. Less than 10% males on BEd course means atmosphere can be a bit like girls' boarding school in the first year. Homertonians are noted for their apolitical natures – but also for their involvement in many campaigns affecting both students and the public in general. Relations between admin and students are good.

Libraries open 9.00am–8.00pm Mon–Fri, Sat am and Sun pm. SU high profile, affiliated to CUSU (16 executive members, full-time sabbatical president). All main college entertainment provided by SU – freshers' bop, wine tasting,

Christmas events, jazz and cocktail evenings, local bands and a May Ball (first organised last year).

Resident students must sign out to be out later than midnight (or 2am Fri/Sat) – for fire regulations. College never shut at night, students free to come and go. Guests are supposed to be 'registered' simply by writing the number of extra persons in a student's room on a slip and leaving at porter's lodge.

Contraception and pregnancy advice – either through SU welfare team, resident sister, CUFU or advice centres in town. Counselling entirely confidential – Cambridge services include 'Linkline' and University Counselling Service.

Sport: right through from college teams and practises to representation on university teams where many Homerton students gain 'blues' eg rugby, cricket, netball. Sports range from water polo to highly popular women's football and rowing teams, to mountain club (where are the hills in Cambridge . . . ?!). Great variety of activities including music, religious organisations, social groups, political parties at college/university level, not forgetting 'wacky' clubs such as Cupboard Society to serious philosophical groups. Wealth of opportunities is overwhelming.

Homerton has long-established reputation for education and training of teachers of highest calibre; it attracts well-motivated students who become full members of the university.

Students have personal tutor to look after their welfare and eventually write job references/reports; quality of lectures very good; work loads about right. Student representation on college committees excellent. Work continually assessed with a number of assignments counting towards grades of 2nd year intermediate examination. Main subject lectures in university departments. Students would welcome a more practical approach with lots of ideas for classroom activities – though things are improving eg with new computer/word processing/display course in 1st year. 75–80% of 4th years go on to teach immediately. Very very low failure rate – students tend to leave if they are dissatisfied. Teaching practice soons sorts out weeds!

Homerton has a fast-rising reputation for very high standards – academically, sportswise and socially, within the vast framework of Cambridge University.

Pauper notes

Accommodation: Some shared double rooms; college houses. **Drink:** Homerton Bar – very cheap, lively atmosphere, juke box, darts, pool, games, live bands; Ruddles, Fosters, draught cider, lots of spirits. **Eats:** College 'trough' – good variety, meal ticket system in main hall. Formal halls; buttery for snacks, lots of local restaurants and take-aways. **Ents:** Film society, regular discos, May Ball, live bands, party rooms, dance studio, regular plays, CCTV. All university ents available local venues. **Sports:** All form of sports in college. Good liaison with university pool close by. Sports centres, 'Blues' varsity award. **Hardship funds:** College hardship fund – application system. **Travel:** 'Pilkington Travel Awards' for educational travel/teaching holidays. **Work:** Bar work within college and cleaning jobs. Ed bookstore, library, stationery shop, post sorting (summer), catering department. Formal hall silver service work, local pub work, vacation work.

More info?

Enquiries to Karl Brown (0223 411217).

Alumni (Editors' pick)

Julie Covington, Cherie Lunghi.

HUDDERSFIELD POLY

See Huddersfield University

HUDDERSFIELD UNIVERSITY

The University of Huddersfield, Queensgate, Huddersfield HD1 3DH (0484 422288) Map A, E5

Student enquiries: Assistant Registrar (Admissions)

Main study areas – as in What to Study section: *(First degree):* Accountancy, architecture, biochemistry, biotechnology, business studies, chemical engineering, chemistry, communications studies, computing, drama, education, electrical & electronic engineering, environmental science, English, food science & nutrition, geography, history, hotel & catering management, information technology, law, mechanical & production engineering, modern languages, music, politics & government, professions allied to medicine (PAMs), psychology, sociology. *Also:* Product design, textile management and design.

European Community: 10% first degree students take EC language as part of course and 2% spend 6 months or more in another EC country. Formal exchange links with 3 EC universities/colleges in Denmark (South Danish Business School for business studies students); and France (Besançon and Rennes). Plans to make an EC language available in a wider range of courses; language tuition available to all as an additional option, through open learning facility.

Application: PCAS for 1993 start, UCAS thereafter; ADAR for product design and textile design. **Academic features:** BSc environmental analysis. **Special features:** Hosts annual Huddersfield Festival of Contemporary Music. **Largest fields of study:** Engineering, business studies, catering studies, music. **Founded:** 1992 as a university, previously Huddersfield Poly, founded 1841. **Main awards:** BA, BSc, BEng, LLB, BMus, BEd. **Awarding body:** Huddersfield University. **Site:** Huddersfield town centre. **Access:** Within walking distance of main bus and railway stations. **Accommodation:** 1,000 places in halls of residence, average cost £33.50 per week; first year students given priority. Rent: 18% in accommodation where rent controlled by polytechnic. **Library:** 275,000 volumes, 2,200 periodicals, 750 study places; multiple copies of recommended books, including copies for reference use only; separate music library. **Other learning resources:** Wide range of computing facilities **Welfare:** Counsellors, chaplain, overseas students' adviser, health centre. **Special categories:** Residential facilities for disabled students. **Careers:** Information, advice and placement service. **Amenities:** SU with bar, films, disco, etc. **Sporting facilities:** Polytechnic sports hall and playing fields. Municipal sports centre with Olympic standard facilities.

Duration of first degree course(s) or equivalent: 3 years; **others:** 4 years (sandwich); 2 years BEd **Total first degree students 1991/92:** 4,730 (full-time), 620 (part-time); **Total BEd students:** 105 (full-time), 170 (part-time) **Overseas students:** 260 **Male/female ratio 1991/92:** 11:9 **Teaching staff: full-time:** 390 **part-time:** 80 **Total full-time students 1991/92:** 5,800 **Postgraduate students:** 450 **Tuition fees for 1992/93 (first degrees):** Home: £1,855 (classroom), £2,770 (lab/studio); Overseas: £5,000 (classroom), £5,250 (lab/studio).

What it's like

It's in the centre of Huddersfield (Hudds) close to the main shopping area and 10–15 minutes' walk from the bus and train stations. Four major supermarkets (one next to campus), a range of independent shops, and excellent markets – indoor/outdoor and secondhand. Student discounts at many shops, eg clothes, stationery, hairdressers.

Halls of residence are generally good quality but limited (only half the first years get a place). Some halls are on or close to campus, others a bus journey. All except Holly Bank are self-catering. Private accommodation is improving in supply but not in quality. Most students live about 20 minutes' walk away but some much further. Prices are increasing.

Sports facilities limited, with sports hall on campus and playing fields an expedition away. Municipal facilities better and widely used via Kirklees Passport discount scheme. The SU supports sports clubs and societies (over 50) although funds are limited.

SU provides entertainment, including live bands and the legendary 'Bop til ya Cop' nights. The SU is now based in Milton Hall with new offices, coffee bar, etc, and 'pub'. The disco venue, 'The Black Hole', is a dump and due to be knocked down; a new venue has been promised.

University refectory provides snacks and 'school dinners' of limited quality. On campus there is a bookshop and shop. The library is overstretched but does open over weekends. Computing facilities are okay in most departments.

SU apolitical – mostly social. Milton Hall has a coffee bar, shop, travel office, insurance office and two bars. 'The Black Hole' ents venue has two bars.

Students come from all over the country and overseas, and most courses have a good mix of students from different backgrounds. Relationship with the community is improving although some areas/pubs should be avoided. Large student population in town. Hudds itself is quite small but close to Leeds and Manchester, and overall has good facilities for students.

Stephen Hubbard

Pauper notes

Accommodation: Mostly private sector – average cost £30 per week (prices creeping up). Married accommodation limited. **Drink:** Beer prices not particularly cheap. Range of student pubs across the road from the main campus. Mainly Bass and Tetley houses. Some real ale (Rat & Ratchet). **Eats:** SU coffee bar in Milton Hall, Blue Rooms (vegetarian), numerous curry houses and take-away pizzas. **Ents:** Union live bands most Weds, some Sats. Most clubs have student nights, which vary in popularity. One cinema (mainstream) plus fringe theatre. **Sports:** SU clubs for most things. Good municipal sports centres, pools, etc. **Hardship funds:** SU welfare loan fund, very stringent and limited. **Travel:** M1 and M62 excellent hitching. Good public transport. SU travel office cheap deals. **Work:** Some pub and union bars; otherwise limited. Summer – forget it really.

More info?

Enquiries to Adam Waterman/Steve Hubbard (0484 538516).

Informal name

Hudds Univ.

HULL UNIVERSITY

University of Hull, Hull HU6 7RX (0482 46311) Map A, F5

Student enquiries: Academic Registrar

Main study areas – as in What to Study section: *(First degree):* Accountancy, American studies, anthropology, Asian studies, biology, business studies, chemistry, computing, drama, economics, education, electronic engineering, English, environmental science, European studies, geography, history, law, mathematical studies, mechanical & production engineering, modern languages, music, nursing studies, philosophy, physics, politics and government, psychology, public administration, religious studies and theology, social policy and social welfare, sociology. *Also:* Criminology.

European Community: 12% first degree students take EC language as part of course and 11% spend 6 months or more in another EC country. Formal exchange links with over 30 EC universities/colleges: Belgium (4); Denmark (1); France (9);

Germany (6); Italy (5); Netherlands (4); Spain (3) – all open in theory to students other than language specialists. EC language tuition available to all students, as part of their course or option; all major EC languages available including Dutch, Danish, Portuguese. Approved Erasmus programme.

Application: UCCA for 1993 start, UCAS thereafter. **Academic features:** BSc engineering sciences for students without science A-levels. Many part-time degrees, some taught at Doughty Centre, Grimsby. **Special features:** Distinguished art collection, specialising in British art 1890–1940; and Thompson collection of 17th-century Chinese ceramics. **Largest fields of study:** Engineering, English, law, modern languages. **Founded:** 1927, charter granted 1954. **Main awards:** BA, BEng, BMus, BSc, LLB. **Awarding body:** Hull University. **Site:** North of Hull. **Access:** Easy access from Hull town centre. **Accommodation:** 1,583 places in halls, 1,193 places in student houses. All first years accommodated. Rent: 65% in accommodation where rent controlled by university. **Library:** 750,000 volumes, 5,800 periodicals, 1,750 study places, reserve collection of course books. **Other learning resources:** Audio-visual centre, language teaching centre, computer centre. **Specialist collections:** Philip Larkin collection, history of Labour and left-wing movements, 20th century social and political archives, 20th century poetry, emigration to North America, South-East Asian studies, fine printing 1890–1940, German expressionism, medieval France. **Welfare:** Doctor, FPA (referral system), psychiatrist, solicitor, chaplain. Nursery with 42 places (cost according to income), facilities for disabled students. **Careers:** Information, advice and placement service. **Amenities:** Bookshop on campus; SU bar, launderette, television rooms; Middleton Hall (auditorium of over 500). **Sporting facilities:** Indoor purpose-built sports centre and all playing fields on campus. **Employment:** Law, chartered accountancy, computing, electronic engineering, education.

Duration of first degree course(s) or equivalent: 3 years; **others:** 4 years **Total first degree students 1991/92:** 5,747 **Overseas students:** 10% **Mature students:** 9% **Male/female ratio:** 1:1 **Teaching staff: full-time:** 352 **part-time:** 104 **Total full-time students 1991/92:** 6,673 **Postgraduate students:** 926 **Tuition fees for 1992/93 (first degrees): Home:** £1,855 (classroom), £2,770 (lab/studio); **Overseas:** £5,300 (classroom), £6,950 (lab/studio).

What it's like

It has always had a reputation for being a friendly place, something you can only experience for yourself, so take up any opportunities you may get to visit on an Open Day and have a look for yourself. It's expanding fast. All academic departments are on one campus about two miles out of the city centre. University accommodation is situated around this, and student houses (around £25/week) back onto the central site – new campus accommodation with en suite bathrooms ready for October 1992 (£37/week). 3 miles away, the halls of residence stand in a local village, Cottingham (the biggest village in the country, more like a small town). University accommodation is about £55, that includes meals. The modern Lawns Halls are particularly popular, boasting their own balconies with each room. Being so flat, Hull is a 'cycling city' and therefore you don't tend to notice the distance.

Many 2nd and 3rd years leave university-owned accommodation and move into private accommodation. Places in shared houses are around £27/week. Such private accommodation can best be described as cheap and cheerful, certainly not luxurious.

Most social events centre around the halls in Cottingham, or more particularly, the SU. The SU is one of the best equipped in the country, and the vast majority of students use it as their evening meeting place. The Union Ents committee put on many bands throughout the term, some pop/chart material, and run lots of films. SU also acts as a centre for some 160 societies, and also 55 sporting clubs as part of an active athletic union. SU manages the sports centre; new health and fitness centre which includes spa pool, saunas and sun beds. Union building has just undergone a £400,000 refurbishment/extension.

Unemployment has hit Hull hard; the city *is* recovering, capitalising on new industries and on links with Europe. However, many local clubs and pubs do seem to be doing well. Local venues provide a stream of lesser known acts which lead to a cheap, good night out. A wide choice of good clubs all offer student nights, and with the expansion in student numbers the city is becoming far more 'student-orientated', and the student is far better catered for now than five years ago. Theatre is extremely good in Hull, particularly Spring Street Theatre, home to Hull Truck Company (of Bouncers and Up and Under fame) which puts on late night cabarets, comedy, music and drama. The Film Theatre at the City Library shows films not on general release, which is always a good night out. Two multiplex cinemas, an ice arena, Megabowl and Princes Quay (the biggest shopping centre built on water!) recent additions.

Pauper notes

Accommodation: Basic – very few squats and no married quarters. **Drink:** SU bar – very cheap. Schnapps bar in town, the Minerva (at the marina) brews own beer. **Eats:** SU (food hall with international dishes including veggie food) and cheap Italian restaurants in town. Hull Food vegetarian restaurant. **Ents:** Fantastic band scene. Hull home of Kingmaker and the Beautiful South. SU films, discos and concerts. Fortnightly 'comedy store'. **Sports:** Excellently equipped sports centre on campus. Numerous centres in local areas. **Hardship funds:** VC's Hardship as well as Union loans. Could be a lot better. **Travel:** Expedition Fund. Travel Centre in SU. **Work:** Getting better. Not bad if you like pubs and hamburgers.

More info?

Enquiries to Siân Heffey (0482 466266).

Alumni (Editors' pick)

Sir Ron Dearing, Tony Galvin, Sarah Greene, Roy Hattersley MP, Chris Mullin, Roger McGough, Philip Larkin (was librarian), Ben Watt/Tracy Thorne (Everything but the Girl), John McCarthy, Jill Morrell.

HUMBERSIDE POLY

See Humberside University

HUMBERSIDE UNIVERSITY

University of Humberside, Cottingham Road, Hull HU6 7RT (0482 440550) Map A, F5

Student enquiries: Marketing and Student Services

Main study areas – as in What to Study section: *(First degree):* Accountancy, architecture, art & design, business studies, communication studies, electrical & electronic engineering, English, environmental studies, fine arts, food science & nutrition, geography, history, information technology, mechanical & production engineering, modern languages, psychology, social policy and social welfare. *Also:* Equine studies, fishery science, rural studies, tourism.

European Community: 25% first degree students take EC language as part of course and 15% spend 6 months or more in another EC country. Formal exchange links with 45 EC universities/colleges: business studies exchanges in France, Germany and Spain; European audio-visual production in Grenoble, Aix,

Marseille, Toulouse (France) or Barcelona; European contemporary studies in France (Savoie) or Germany (Chemnitz). Students on BA European business studies spend half time in Germany/France/Netherlands/Spain. European Food Studies involves a 6 or 12 month work placement in Germany, Spain, Portugal or Greece. Language tuition available only to those on courses with European element. Students admitted to European courses should usually have a language to A-level standard. Approved Erasmus programme.

Application: PCAS for 1993 start, UCAS thereafter; ADAR for art and design courses. **Academic features** Students on several business and humanities courses can spend a year in America. Encourages applications from those without formal entrance requirements; guarantees place on degree course to those passing Humberside-validated access course. **Largest fields of study:** Business, food science/technology, arts, social sciences. **Founded:** 1992, as a university; previously Humberside Poly, founded 1976. **Main awards:** BA, BSc, BEng. **Awarding body:** Humberside University. **Site:** In and around Hull city centre and Grimsby. **Accommodation:** 636 places in halls of residence. Approx cost: £54 pw. 11% students in accommodation where rent controlled by university. **Library:** 200,000 volumes, 1,560 periodicals, 750 study places and Learning Resource Centres. **Other learning facilities:** Computer centre, sound and TV studios. **Welfare:** Medical, chaplain, independent financial adviser, student counselling service, student advice centre, international office. **Careers:** Information, advice and placement service. **Amenities:** Sound and TV studios, students' union centre with shop, snack bar and bar, computer centre, health and fitness club.

Duration of first degree course(s) or equivalent: 3 years; **others:** 4 years (sandwich) **Total first degree students 1991/92:** 6,879 **Overseas students:** 870 **Mature students** 3,000 **Male/female ratio:** 1:1 **Teaching staff: full-time:** 323 **part-time:** 43 **Total full-time students 1991/92:** 10,341 **Postgraduate students:** 608 **Tuition fees for 1992/93 (first degrees):** Home: £759 (if no grant), £1,855 (classroom), £2,770 (lab/studio); Overseas: £4,720 (classroom), £5,120 (lab/studio).

What it's like

On seven sites – six in Hull, one in Grimsby. These range from the picturesque to the practical. The university boasts an impressive range of courses (which are highly respected). These focus on everything from fine art to business studies and engineering, as well as the social and professional studies.

Halls good but overpriced. Atmosphere in halls lively and liberal.

Increasing number of overseas students, particularly European. Access for non-traditional students actively encouraged.

SU has an excellent advice service. Active societies include hockey, rugby, football, drama and ski club. While having a large student body (two universities), Hull has little student culture but several student venues; Grimsby has fewer, with no SU bar or shops. This (along with distance) makes for an occasionally strained relationship. SU, affiliated to NUS and not politically biased, works mainly for improved student welfare and strives for equal provision on all seven sites. It provides cheap ents, drinks etc. and involves itself in campaigning work from welfare and sports facilities to grants and sexual politics.

Pauper notes

Accommodation: From £30 per week in Hull, expensive and limited in Grimsby. **Drink:** Cheap at SU. Hull Old Town and Cleethorpes pubs best, Minerva's Pilots Pride best real ale. Mostly Mansfield Brewery. Check out the Mainbrace and the Haworth for good student pubs. **Eats:** Lots of chippies, but also Italian, Indian, Chinese, Mandarin, Lebanese, kebabs – all excellent and cheap. Good, cheap snack bars and shops at SU (all diets catered for). **Ents:** Wide range of Hull nightclubs – the most popular is The Tower, Lexington Avenue, Studio Circus and Spiders. Grimsby clubs include Gullivers and Grinders. There is Hull Spring Street and Hull New Theatre, 2 multi-screen cinemas (Odeon & UCI). The

Central Library has an unusual film programme. Hull also boasts the Adelphi Club – the best live independent venue in the North East. SU ents have included Jools Holland, The Shamen, Kingmaker, Frank Sidebottom, and Half Man Half Biscuit. **Sports:** UHSU health and fitness club, sporting clubs (football to parachuting). **Hardship funds:** SU resources very limited but can help occasionally. **Travel:** Easy access by motorway (M62), Humber Bridge, rail network and cheap ferries to Europe – also Humberside Airport nearby.

Alumni (Editors' pick)

Ann Brown and Christine Ford (England Women's Basketball team), Mary Parkinson (TV presenter/interviewer), Eliot Morley MP, Death by Milkfloat (independent pop band).

IMPERIAL COLLEGE

(1) **Imperial College of Science, Technology and Medicine, University of London, London SW7 2AZ**
   (071 589 5111; Telex: 929484 IMPCOL G; Fax: 071 584 7596)
   Map E, A3
(2) **The Medical School, Norfolk Place, Paddington, London W2 1PG (071 723 1252; Fax: 071 724 7349)**
   (You can look up St Mary's Hospital Medical School separately)

Student enquiries: Assistant Registrar (Admissions)

Main study areas – as in What to Study section: *(First degree):* Aeronautical engineering, biochemistry, biology, biotechnology, botany, chemical engineering, chemistry, civil engineering, computing, electrical & electronic engineering, geology, information technology, mathematical studies, mechanical and production engineering, medicine, metallurgy and materials science, microbiology, physics, zoology. *Also:* Energy engineering, mineral processing technology, mining, petroleum engineering.

European Community: Approx 5% first degree students take EC language as a formal part of course; 7% spend 3–12 months or more in another EC country but increasing amount. Wide range of exchange schemes for undergraduates with prestigious technological institutions in Belgium, Denmark, Eire, France, Germany, Italy, Netherlands, Spain; over 20 approved Erasmus programmes in 1992–93. Strong commitment to 'Year Abroad' courses (available in aeronautical engineering, biochemistry, biology, biotechnology, chemical engineering, chemistry, civil engineering, computing, electrical and electronic engineering, materials, mathematics and physics and materials). Students taking 'Year Abroad' courses are required to take language tuition. All other students have access to formal or casual access to language laboratory facilities.

Application: UCCA for 1993 start, UCAS thereafter. **Structural features:** Part of London University. **Academic features:** 4 year engineering courses, MEng; 3 year courses, BEng. New courses with a year in industry in biochemistry, biotechnology, biochemistry and management; courses in biotechnology and mathematics with a year in Europe; other new courses in computing (European programme of study), environmental and earth resources engineering, physics with theoretical physics, physics and studies in musical performance. Humanities programme offering weekly lectures in associated studies and foreign language courses. **Special features:** Imperial College established by Royal Charter 'to give the highest specialised instruction and to provide the fullest equipment for the most advanced training and research in various branches of science especially in its application to industry'. Applications from women are strongly encouraged. Visiting lecturer and musician-in-residence leads a variety of musical activities. Some 78 visiting professors. **Founded:** 1907, from Royal College of Science, Royal School of Mines, City and Guilds College. Amalgamated with St Mary's Hospital Medical School, 1988. **Undergraduate awards:** MEng, BEng, BSc, MSci, MB BS. **Awarding body:** University of London. **Site:** 25 acre site in South Kensington. Medical School in Paddington. **Access:** South Kensington underground station; Paddington or Edgware Road underground stations for medical school; buses. **Accommodation:** Over 2,000 places on or near campus. All first year undergraduates are guaranteed accommodation. **Libraries:** Lyon Playfair Library for all course books: 250,000 volumes, 500 places; individual department libraries. For older material, college relies on Science Museum Library which shares the building and some facilities with college library: 600,000 volumes, 20,000 periodicals. Haldane Library (humanities and general reading): 35,000 volumes; music library, containing lending collection of records, tapes, CDs and scores. Medical School Library: 30,000 volumes and bound journals. **Other learning facilities:** College mine in Cornwall; computer centre on South Kensington campus; 240 acre college field station at Silwood Park (near Ascot). **Welfare:** Advisory committee; vacation training scheme; careers advisory service; student accommodation office; health centre, student counsellor, welfare adviser, 'Nightline', nursery. **Hardship funds:** Government access funds; also a number of funds available to MB BS course students. **Amenities:** SU building with refectory, bar, bookshop, etc; wide range of societies. Recreation centre also on Paddington campus. **Sporting facilities:** Sports centre on campus with indoor swimming pool; boathouse at Putney; 60-acre sports ground near Heathrow Airport; athletic ground at Teddington. **Employment:** Traditionally industry; but increasing number of graduates enter banking, insurance etc, as well as general commercial areas. Medicine.

Duration of first degree course(s) or equivalent: 3 or 4 years (science and engineering); 5 years (medicine) **Total first degree students 1991/92:** 4,414 **First degree overseas students:** 701 **First degree mature students:** 148 **Male/female ratio:** 3:1 **Teaching staff: total:** over 650 **Total full-time students 1991/92:** 6,525 **Postgraduate students:** 2,111 **Tuition fees for 1992/93 (first degrees)** (excluding Medical School fees): Home: £755 (if no grant), £1,855 (classroom), £2,770 (lab/studio); Overseas: £6,100 (classroom), £7,750 (lab/studio).

"Preponderance of 'grey' scientists...."

WANT TO HELP WITH THE NEXT EDITION – SEE PAGE 76

What it's like

It's in South Kensington near Hyde Park and the museums. All the benefits of central London and usual drawbacks of expense and accommodation. Halls off Exhibition Road; houses 20 mins walk away – most self-catering. Places also available at London University halls, a tube trip away. All first years offered places in IC residences, all undergraduates can spend at least one year in college accommodation. International reputation and very high academic standards. Courses fairly intensive, but lower than average failure rate. Men still outnumber women (26% of students are women). 35% of students are postgraduates. SU not affiliated to NUS, mainly apolitical, tends to concentrate on college matters: supports a wide range of clubs from sporting motorcycle to Amnesty International, as well as social clubs for most cultural and ethnic groups (24% of students from overseas). Excellent student media led by weekly newspaper, *Felix*, radio station and television network. ULU facilities and events at Malet Street are open to IC students. 4 constituent colleges (City & Guilds College, Royal College of Science, Royal School of Mines, St Mary's Hospital Medical School) organise rag stunts, such as tiddly-winking down Oxford Street, and other social events. The Medical School (St Mary's, Paddington), is the most popular medical school on UCCA applications with friendly atmosphere and strong traditions for revues and rugby. IC adage: 'Work hard, play hard' – balance often difficult but student life very much what you make of it.

Pauper notes

Accommodation: Never cheap, single room in college halls typically approx. £52 pw. Small chance of married quarters. **Drink:** College bar + 2 Union bars – very cheap. Guest ales. Queens Arms – good atmosphere. **Eats:** Campus all cheap – Da Vinci's Café/Bar, burger bar, pizza bar, refectory. Local area expensive except Indian and pasta bar in South Kensington. Best: veggie and Indians in Euston/Notting Hill etc. **Ents:** Weekly free discos and bands (c £2.50). Cheap events on campus. Still many free gigs/exhibitions in London. Pub gigs good value. **Sports:** Campus sports centre very cheap for swimming, squash, weights. Group transport to excellent college grounds at Heathrow. **Hardship funds:** Access fund arranged by College. **Travel:** Bicycle + A–Z London essential! Car parking only possible with disability/medical. For longer distances get coach card, rail savers. STA branch on campus, expedition fund available. **Work:** Good temping prospects vacation either London general or on campus cleaning residences, UROP program, clerical (including tutoring) in London.

Informal name

IC.

Alumni (Editors' pick)

H G Wells, Sir Lewis Casson, Sir Granville Bantock, Joan Ruddock MP, Sir John Egan, Trevor Phillips, Francis Wilson, Brian May.

INSTITUTE OF ARCHAEOLOGY

**Institute of Archaeology, University College London,
31–34 Gordon Square, London WC1H 0PY (071 387 7050)**
Map E, C1

Student enquiries: Registrar, University College London, Gower Street, London WC1E 6BT

Main study areas – as in What to Study section: *(First degree):* Archaeology. *Also:* Archaeological conservation, environmental archaeology.

European Community: No students take an EC language as compulsory part of their degree course. Variable number of students spend time on fieldwork in another EC country (no formal links). Erasmus schemes with Denmark and Portugal.

Application: UCCA for 1993 start, UCAS thereafter. **Structural features:** Part of University College, London University. **Founded:** 1937. Joined University College London in 1986. **Main awards:** BA, BSc. **Awarding body:** London University. **Site:** Central London. **Access:** Warren Street and Euston Square underground stations. **Academic features:** 60+ optional course units available. 3-year courses in W. Asia archaeology include language options and some ancient history. 3-year specialist BSc in archaeological conservation; environmental archaeology options available to BSc and BA students; computer facilities open to all undergraduates. All staff are practising archaeologists or archaeological scientists. **Accommodation:** Students can apply to University intercollegiate halls of residence, University College London Student Residence Office and University accommodation officer. **Library:** Specialist archaeology library: 27,000 volumes (6,000 in store), 22,000 pamphlets, 850 periodicals, 60 study places; recommended books temporarily restricted for use of students. **Welfare:** College Health Centre, health service nearby. **Careers:** Advice on careers in archaeology. **Amenities:** The Institute's Society of Archaeology Students affiliated to University College London union and to ULU, so students can make use of their facilities and the sports ground at Motspur Park.

Duration of first degree course(s) or equivalent: 3 years **Total first degree students 1991/92:** 230 **Overseas students:** 30 **Mature students:** 70 **Male/female ratio:** 1:1 **Teaching staff: full-time:** 30 **part-time:** 50 **Total full-time students 1991/92:** 325 **Postgraduate students:** 120 **Tuition fees for 1992/93 (first degrees):** Home: £795 (if no grant), £2,770; Overseas: £6,250 (standard), £7,995 (archaeological conservation).

What it's like

Building very late 50s and box like, but in an excellent position in the heart of the University of London at one end of the very pleasant Gordon Square. Within 2 minutes of UCLU and ULU bars and facilities. The Institute has its own well lived in and popular common room in the basement where drinks and snacks are provided.

There is a lively society in the form of the SAS (Society of Archaeological Students) which organises regular wild parties in the basement attended by staff and ex-students as well as everybody else.

The library is excellent but hectic, although other libraries in the university will often have the books that you need.

The very wide range of courses cover more or less the whole world at all time periods plus you may choose to take related courses in other departments.

Lots of field trips including the unique primitive technology course run by the SAS which involves the new undergraduate intake being primitive in a field in Kent for four days at the beginning of term.

With students of all nationalities, ages and backgrounds the atmosphere is cosmopolitan and welcoming.

Matthew Reynolds

Pauper notes

Accommodation: UCL and intercollegiate halls, cheapest accom in SE London, some halls just under £30 per week. **Drink:** Union bars cheapest, and there are lots of them. **Eats:** Union bars again and the college refectories for a wide selection of hot and cold foods; also departmental facilities. **Ents:** Cheap films at the Bloomsbury Theatre, plus the usual range of social events provided by the unions. Institute parties of course eclipse all other events. **Sports:** Facilities to satisfy most sports at ULU. **Travel:** Fieldwork grants for those in receipt of LEA grants. Various grants for travel/fieldwork.

CAN'T FIND WHAT YOU'RE LOOKING FOR? USE THE INDEX!

More info?

Get students' Alternative Prospectus.

Alumni (Editors' pick)

James Coppice Norman, Nick Branch, Andrew Hobley.

INSTITUTE OF EDUCATION

Institute of Education, University of London, 20 Bedford Way, London WC1H 0AL (071 580 1122) Map E, C1

This is postgraduate only.

Student enquiries: Deputy Registrar

Main study areas – as in What to Study section: *(Not at first degree):* Education.

European Community: Some students take an EC language or spend time in another EC country.

Special features: Postgraduate only, including research. **Application:** Direct; except PGCE to GTTR. **Structural features:** Part of London University. **Academic features:** Postgraduate teacher training course involving close partnership with schools. Modular masters and diploma courses in most educational specialisms, enabling students to accumulate credits over a period of time. Various short courses. **Founded:** 1902, became Institute of Education in 1932. **Main awards:** PGCE, MA, MSc, MPhil, PhD, specialist diploma courses. **Site:** Bedford Way. **Access:** Russell Square underground. **Accommodation:** Institute has an accommodation officer and students use London University accommodation office. 230 places in halls; a number of self-contained flats available. Approx cost: £63.70 per person pw. **Library:** 220,000 volumes, 1,900 periodicals, 240 study places. **Specialist collections:** ILEA Resources Collection. **Welfare:** London University health service, university chaplain, student adviser, nursery facilities (£59.50 pw for Institute students). **Hardship funds:** Loans available for students in temporary financial difficulties. **Special categories:** Facilities for married students. **Careers:** Information and advice. 90% of those on initial training course employed within 6 months. **Amenities:** Central London and London University. Dillon's 5 mins walk. **Employment:** Education.

Male/female ratio: slightly more female students **Teaching staff: full-time:** 175 **part-time:** 40 **Total full-time students 1991/92:** 1,360 (1,592 part-time) **Tuition fees, 1992/93:** Home: £2,770 (PGCE); £2,200 (Diploma); £2,200 (higher degree); Overseas: £5,320.

What it's like

Unlike most London University colleges, it's purely postgraduate. A world centre for study of education. Work falls into three broad categories: initial professional training; advanced courses for experienced qualified teachers; and research degrees – MPhil, PhD. The Institute has a high reputation for research and, occasionally, this filters down to practical training. It is a fairly strange place to spend a year.

The SU Society is a fairly liberated union, offering wide variety of services in the minute space allowed – a bar, snack bar, lunch counter and shop. Good relationship with the Institute, and many joint ventures are undertaken, such as the South African Scholarship Scheme. A lot of activity centres around educational issues, such as anti-racist and anti-sexist education. SU has cheap bar, free discos on a Friday, and general non-threatening environment.

Situated just off Russell Square, in a huge concrete and tinted glass monstrosity, it's near Euston & King's Cross BR stations. Nearby is Dillon's, also seriously trendy Lumiere Cinema, and the seriously untrendy ULU. The SU Society is popular with students from other colleges.

Pauper notes

Accommodation: Flats, self-catering accommodation and single/double rooms with food and heating included. **Drink:** Varies, but usually at least 2 real ales and 3 lagers. **Eats:** Cheapish meals in snack bar/lunch counter. A good variety of vegetarian and salads. **Ents:** Regular discos and sometimes bands are invited – cheap or free entrances. **Sports:** Join ULU facilities. **Hardship funds:** Hardship fund administered by college. Nursery subsidy. **Travel:** Cheap fares available from STA (round corner). **Work:** Bar work, stewarding, kitchen work for special events.

JEWS' COLLEGE

Jews' College, Albert Road, Hendon, London NW4 (081 203 6427)
Map A, F8

Student enquiries: Academic Registrar

Main study areas: *(First degree):* Biblical studies, Jewish history, Jewish law, philosophy, Talmud.

European Community: No students take EC language or spend time in another EC country as part of their course (although most students spend at least 1 year in Israel prior to their degree course).

Application: Direct. **Academic features:** Students not committed to any profession when they arrive. College linked to London University for all degrees. **Special features:** Lecturers regularly visit from Bar-lan University, Israel. **Founded:** 1855, to train rabbis, leaders and teachers for the Anglo-Jewish community and overseas. **Main awards:** BA. **Awarding body:** London University. **Access:** Buses from central London. **Accommodation:** Students accommodated with local families or flats in area; no college accommodation. **Library:** Outstanding reference and information centre for all things Jewish; 75,000 volumes, 142 periodicals; priceless 15th and 16th century manuscripts. **Welfare:** Student counsellor; honorary medical officer available for consultation. **Security:** Entrance door locked at all times. **Special categories:** Special arrangements for mature students. **Hardship funds:** Grants and scholarships available in appropriate cases. **Careers:** Direct links to United Synagogue for those wishing to pursue the ministry. **Amenities:** SU provides range of services.

Duration of first degree course(s) or equivalent: 3 years **Total first degree students 1991/92:** 20 **Mature students:** 2 **Overseas students:** 3 **Male/female ratio:** 3:2 **Teaching staff: full-time:** 12 **part-time:** 12 **Total full-time students 1991/92:** 32 **Postgraduate students:** 81 **Tuition fees for 1992/93 (first degrees):** £1,850 (fees for overseas students by negotiation).

What it's like

Small, cosy college, with warm, friendly atmosphere. Good student/staff relationships. Modern purpose-built campus boasts the most extensive Judaica library in Europe, numerous conference rooms and the London based Institute of Jewish Education. Host to educational sixth form centre and various Jewish Youth organisations, making available our services and facilities for week-end and evening seminars. SU offers programme of social and cultural events in conjunction with the Union of Jewish Students. College has enjoyed close contact with NUS and is represented at its Annual Conference. Degrees can lead to teaching, administrative, or ministerial posts within the community. Some graduates use their degree as a basis for entrance into the professions.

Location means most forms of entertainment are nearby. Prospective students are in for a busy and enjoyable time.

CAN'T FIND WHAT YOU'RE LOOKING FOR? USE THE INDEX!

Pauper notes

Accommodation: College helps find kosher accommodation locally. **Eats:** Discounts at some kosher restaurants. **Work:** Bursaries available for needy students. Some vacation work etc available.

Informal name:

JC.

Alumni (Editors' pick)

Lord Jakobovits, Rabbi Dr Jonathan Sacks, Prof S Greenbaum (London University), Dr Stefan Reif (Director, Taylor Schechter Geniza Research Unit, Cambridge), Prof Alan Corre, Dov Zackheim.

KEELE UNIVERSITY

Keele University, Staffordshire ST5 5BG (0782 621111) Map A, D6

Student enquiries: Head of Admissions

Main study areas – as in What to Study section: *(First degree):* American studies, anthropology, biochemistry, biology, business studies, chemistry, computing, economics, education, English, environmental studies, European studies, geography, geology, history, law, mathematical studies, modern languages, music, philosophy, physics, politics and government, professions allied to medicine (PAMs), psychology, sociology. *Also:* Astronomy, biomedical sciences, criminology, electronics, engineering physics, human resource management, international relations.

European Community: 16% first degree students take EC language as part of course and 12% spend 6 months or more in another EC (or EFTA) country. Formal exchange links with 25 EC universities/colleges: Belgium (2); Denmark (1); Eire (1); France (7); Germany (5); Italy (1); Netherlands (2); Portugal (1); Spain (5); of these, 16 are open to non-language specialists. 11 approved Erasmus programmes 1992/93. French and German may be studied on their own in combination with another subject; or as a double language combination with/without another subject. French, German and Spanish are offered as subsidiary courses, open to all undergraduates; Certificate in Language Competence may be reached by taking a subsidiary language over several years.

Application: UCCA for 1993 start, UCAS thereafter. **Special academic features:** 4-year course (foundation year + 3 years) with few course requirements. 330+ dual honours combinations available and concurrent Cert Ed possible; over 300 3-year dual honours courses. New courses in ancient history, physics with astronomy, engineering physics. **Special features:** Visiting Professors: J Bordas (physics from SERC Daresbury); K A Chittenden (electronics); G N Greaves (chemistry from SERC Daresbury); J F Hallstrom (music from Colby College, Maine); P E Secker (electronics from Royal Doulton); A M Stoneham (chemistry from AEA, Harwell). **Largest fields of study:** Computer science, English, law, management science, psychology. **Founded:** 1949, ex University College of North Staffordshire. **Main awards:** BA, BSc. **Awarding body:** Keele University. **Site:** Campus 2 miles from Newcastle-under-Lyme. **Access:** M6, buses to campus from Stoke station. **Accommodation:** 2,950 rooms. Approx cost: £28 pw. All first years and most others accommodated (83% in accommodation where rent controlled by university). **Library:** 500,000 volumes, 1,500 periodicals, 685 study places, separate foundation year library. **Specialist collections:** Turner mathematics collection, Wedgwood archives.**Welfare:** Doctor, dentist, FPA, psychiatrist, solicitor (SU), chaplains, financial adviser, counselling service. **Special categories:** Nursery (50 places); playgroup (25 places). **Careers:** Information and appointments service. **Amenities:** Bookshop on campus, SU premises with bookshop, launderettes, supermarket, newsagent and banks. Italian pizzeria with bar, unisex hairdressing salon, sunbeds. **Sporting facilities:** Multi-purpose sports centre with adjoining playing fields, tennis courts and athletics track; 7 squash courts, climbing wall and fitness centre gymnasium; sports shop.

Duration of first degree course(s) or equivalent: 4 years (with foundation year); 3 years (without foundation year) **Total first degree students 1991/92:** 3,405 **Overseas students:** 390 **Mature students:** 338 **Male/female ratio:** 1:1 **Teaching staff: full-time:** 295 **part-time:** 27 **Total full-time students 1991/92:** 4,907 **Postgraduate students:** 1,502 **Tuition fees for 1992/93 (first degrees):** Home: £1,855 (classroom), £2,770 (lab/studio); Overseas: £5,320 (classroom), £6,188 (one principal science), £7,055 (two or more principal sciences or single honours science).

What it's like

'Keele? OK, the one stuck on the top of a hill in the middle of nowhere!!', a narrow-minded view held by the ill-informed. Keele is, admittedly, on top of a hill so a supply of woolly jumpers wouldn't go amiss, but it's also the largest campus in England and by far the most picturesque.

The majority of full-time students are resident on campus so there's a good community atmosphere. Priority for on-campus accommodation is given to freshers and finalists. However, if you register for foundation year (and thus take a 4-year course) you will be required to live off campus for one year.

Courses at Keele are joint honours, and you also have to pass a subsidiary course. Assessment: Varies between departments. Modularisation introduced in 1993. Library: opens 7 days a week, although at weekends counter service is only available on Saturday morning. Includes a short loan library for books in high demand.

Regarding the social life, there's a variety of entertainments, from gigs and balls through comedy, plays and jazz nights to discos.

All in all, Keele is a brilliant university, and all who leave miss the lifestyle and the friends they make here.

Pauper notes

Accommodation: Majority of full-time undergraduates live on-campus. University supplies off-campus housing lists. Off-campus housing is some of the cheapest in the country. **Drink:** 5 bars in SU and 4 halls bars. University bar more expensive. Two pubs nearby, one close to each entrance to campus. **Eats:** 3 refectories. Pizza place in sports centre which will deliver. Snack bar and health food bar (including vegetarian and vegan food) in SU and catering in university bar. Off-campus: some local places will deliver pizza, curries, etc. Various pubs and bars of differing price ranges. **Ents:** SU ents include 3 main discos per week, gigs, comedy, karaoke and termly balls. Localwise: New Vic Theatre, gigs at Victoria Hall in Hanley, Stoke Beer Festival. Nightclubs: Fatty Arbuckles, Hippodrome, Maxims (but no student night), Peppers, Room 101, Valentinos in Newcastle, The Place in Hanley. Gay clubs in Hanley. **Sports:** Excellent facilities on campus except swimming – that's in Newcastle near the bus station. **Hardship funds:** Available but preference given to students in exceptional financial need due to lack of funds. SU can offer limited loans, funds permitting. **Travel:** New travel bureau in SU. Two bus routes (PMT and Midland Red) on campus. Last PMT bus to Keele leaves Hanley at 11.40pm Monday to Saturday. Limited car park spaces. **Work:** University and Union catering and bars offer employment. Limited security and ents work in SU.

More info?

Get students' Alternative Prospectus.
Enquiries to Anthony Hatter (SU 0782 711411).

Buzzwords

Potters (locals), Duck (what Potters call everyone), Hanley-Duck (Hanley).

CAN'T FIND WHAT YOU'RE LOOKING FOR? USE THE INDEX!

Alumni (Editors' pick)

John Golding, David Pownall, Bamber Gascoigne, Jack Straw, Gerry Northam, Sue Robbie, Alan Michael, Ian Taylor, Bernard Lloyd.

KENT INSTITUTE

Kent Institute of Art and Design, Oakwood Park, Oakwood Road, Maidstone, Kent ME16 8AG (0622 757286) Map A, F8

Student enquiries: Marketing Officer

Main study areas – as in What to Study section: *(First degree):* Architecture, art & design. *Also:* communication media.

European Community: Some students take EC language or spend time in another EC country as part of degree course. EC language tuition to be a compulsory component of all degree courses. Exchanges with Düsseldorf (architecture) and links with colleges in France, Germany, Italy, Netherlands and Spain. Approved Erasmus programme 1992/93.

Application: ADAR; PCAS for architecture for 1993 start, UCAS thereafter. **Academic features:** New degrees in European fashion design technology; three dimensional design (interior architecture); fine art includes pathway in public art; all degrees being converted to unitised structure to allow greater student choice. **Founded:** 1987 by merger of Canterbury College of Art, Maidstone College of Art and Medway College of Design. **Main awards:** BA. **Awarding body:** Kent University. **Site:** Three separate campuses, each shared with other educational establishments and close to a town or city centre (Canterbury, Maidstone, Rochester). **Accommodation:** Full-time officers arrange student accommodation. Rent: Proportion of students in accommodation where rent controlled by institute not known. **Library:** Three separate libraries, each approximately 20,000 volumes.

Duration of first degree course(s) or equivalent: 3 years **Other:** 5 years (part-time) **Total first degree students 1991/92:** 607 **Overseas students:** 48 **Mature students:** approx 80 **Male/female ratio:** 1:1 **Teaching staff: full-time:** 30 **part-time:** 200 **Total full-time students 1991/92:** 1,823 **Postgraduate students:** 84 **Tuition fees for 1992/93 (first degrees):** Home: £2,770; Overseas: £6,750.

What it's like – Maidstone

On the edge of town. Looks terrible; don't be put off, there are very good courses in illustration, graphics, film, video and foundation. Quite small population of students so no first year/second year cliqueness. Everyone mixes with everyone. Course facilities excellent. SU active. Own canteen/common room and bar; runs own gigs and parties. Quite near London but there's lots going on in college. Cheap market on Tuesdays.

Pauper notes

Accommodation: Student rented accommodation. Lodging with families. Student, college-owned houses. **Drink:** College bar – cheap. In town 'The Minstrel' – scrumpy cider very strong! Banks Wine Bar trendy beers. The Hog's Head; student night at 'Viennas' (Mon). **Eats:** Canteen very good. In town fast food, vegetarian restaurant and pizza places. **Ents:** College organizes parties, comedians, bands, pool challenges. In town cinema, theatre, bars with karaoke, parties, bands. There's always a new band to see each week. Cheap nights in nightclubs with SU card. **Sports:** Mote Park new leisure centre – excellent. Westbourne sports centre on campus. Active college football team. **Hardship fund:** College Access fund. Welfare and accommodation officers very helpful. **Work:** Part-time work in bars, pubs, supermarket, fast-food places.

More info?
Enquiries to SU President (0622 679685).

What it's like – Canterbury
1960s type building, with view of cathedral. Canterbury has large student population. College shares campus with tech. Little accommodation, but there are a few good student houses through college. Whitstable is cheap place to live. Foundation (GAD) students mostly home based.

Many students from north and Ireland, and quite a few foreign students (large Japanese community at university; many European students also live in Canterbury).

Good facilities in computers and technical based departments. Good welfare officer.

Mike Steel

Pauper notes
Accommodation: Through college or private; Canterbury rent is £30–£45; Whitstable £20–£35. Quite a few student houses near college (through college welfare officer). **Drink:** College bar cheap; the bar and canteen at college is now run by a local pub 'The Jolly Sailor'. 'City Arms', 'Millers Arms', 'Simple Simons', 'Jolly Sailor', 'Dolphin' most popular pubs in Canterbury. The 'Neptune', 'Tankerton Arms' in Whitstable. **Eats:** Good veg food in college canteen; many good restaurants in Canterbury (some cheap, some not). Cafe des Amies is popular (many of staff are art students). Good health food shop 'Canterbury Wholefoods'. **Ents:** Gigs, rave, etc every Thursday; films, cabaret on Tuesdays; uni has lots of gigs; tech now and then. **Sports:** Tech sports hall; university gym can be used (for a small fee). Art College has its own football club. **Hardship funds:** There is a fund available through college welfare officer. **Travel:** Some scholarships and exchanges to Europe and America. Hitching good and fairly safe between Canterbury and Whitstable and Herne Bay. Bus frequent but expensive. **Work:** Some work in SU canteen bar, and helping at gigs; restaurant work available; good town for busking, selling drawings on street, etc (big middle class 'arty' population here). **SU:** SU is now more organised politically: fighting sexism and racism and campaigning against student poverty. Developing strong links with other Kent student unions and nationally.

Informal name
Canterbury Art College; KIAD.

Alumni (Editors' pick)
Ian Dury.

KENT UNIVERSITY

University of Kent at Canterbury, Canterbury, Kent CT2 7NZ
(0227 764000) Map A, G8

Student enquiries: Office for Undergraduate Recruitment Services, University Registry

Main study areas – as in What to Study section: *(First degree):* Accountancy, African studies, American studies, anthropology, biochemistry, biology, biotechnology, business studies, chemistry, classics, communication studies, computing, drama, economics, electrical and electronic engineering, English, environmental science, European studies, geography, history, industrial relations, law, linguistics, mathematical studies, materials science, microbiology, modern languages, philosophy, physics, politics and government, psychology, public administration, religious studies and theology, social policy and social welfare, sociology. *Also:* Actuarial studies, business mathematics, Caribbean studies, film, microbial technology, management science, Renaissance studies, visual and performed arts.

European Community: 22% first degree students learning EC language (some 700 students); 4% (168 students) spend time in another EC country as part of their course. Formal exchange links with many EC universities/colleges: France (15+); Germany (10+); Italy (4+); Netherlands (4+); Spain (5+) – open to students in a range of disciplines eg computer science (Aachen), drama (Dublin), economics (Madrid), law (Amsterdam), maths (Liège), social psychology (Tilburg). Approved Erasmus programme. 1992/93. 4-year courses in English and French/German/Spanish/Italian law; 4-year BA course in French with 2 years at the University Stendhal (Grenoble III) to include award of Maïtrise de Lettres Modernes. National Erasmus office for UK housed at university. County council and university share services of Brussels representative. French, German and Italian available as 4-year degrees involving 1 year in country concerned. Most degrees in natural sciences, IT, social science may be taken with a language as 4-year degree. Languages not available as supplementary, non-examined courses but students in humanities and social science may be able to add language course as part of their degree work.

Application: UCCA for 1993 start, UCAS thereafter. **Academic features:** 4-year course, with 1 year abroad, offered for BA European management science, BSc in biochemistry, chemistry, electronics, microbiology and physics, as an alternative to normal 3-year courses. Unique course in African and Caribbean studies; 4-year course, with 1 year abroad for BA American Studies; electronic engineering with medical electronics BSc. New degrees in communication and image studies and physics with space science and systems astrophysics or optoelectronics. **Special features:** Number of distinguished scholars from various parts of world in residence for all or part of the year as visiting professors/scholars. **Structural features:** Institute of Social and Applied Psychology; Canterbury Business School; Space Sciences Research Unit; Channel Tunnel Research Unit. **Largest fields of study:** English and American literature, biochemistry, computer science, law, electronic engineering. **Founded:** 1965. **Main awards:** BA, BEng, BSc, LLB. **Awarding body:** Kent University. **Site:** 300 acre campus, on outskirts of Canterbury. **Access:** Good road and rail links with London and Europe. **Accommodation:** All first years guaranteed accommodation in 1 of 4 colleges, self-catering accommodation or university owned accommodation. Approx cost: £400 per term (single room in college), £33 pw (self-catering). **Library:** 650,000 volumes, 115,000 pamphlets and official publications, 148,000 microfilms and related materials, 126,000 slides, 4,000 periodical titles. **Specialist collections:** Links with the Library of Canterbury Cathedral; university library houses Lloyd George Collection (signed copies), Pettingell Collection (19th century plays), Maddison Collection (history of science), John Crow Collection (English literature); and Centre for Cartoons and Caricature (75,000 originals). **Welfare:** Personal tutorial system; medical service; SU provides legal and financial advice; student counselling service, travel bureau. **Careers:** Information and advisory service. **Amenities:** Dillon's bookshop on site; Gulbenkian Theatre; Cinema 3 (The Regional Film Theatre). **Sporting facilities:** Sports centre provides facilities for over 30 different activities (including coaching to international standard).

Duration of first degree course(s) or equivalent: 3 years; **others:** 4 years **Total first degree students 1991/92:** 4,264 **Overseas students:** 825 **Male/female ratio:** 5:4 **Teaching staff: full-time:** 370 **part-time:** 14 **Total full-time students 1991/92:** 5,312 **Postgraduate students:** 1,048 **Tuition fees for 1992/93 (first degrees):**

Home: £760 (if no grant), £1,855 (classroom), £2,770 (lab/studio); Overseas: £5,320 (classroom), £7,055 (lab/studio). £153 college fee added to all fees.

What it's like

It's a campus university, with central campus based on four colleges, plus extensive self-catering accommodation forming a 'sub-campus' with own bar/ social area. Access good, with two bus stops on campus, a regular service up to around last orders and a free late night minibus run jointly by university and union. Central campus small and compact, with even the full campus quite easy to negotiate and within walking distance.

Accommodation varied: colleges offer single rooms on corridors with breakfast included; a new college extension offers ensuite rooms at a cost. Most new accommodation is self-catering houses consisting of shared kitchen and single rooms. Accommodation not keeping track with student numbers, the proportion living in therefore decreasing. Washing facilities provided through coin-operated laundries in each college and one for self-catering housing. Cooking not allowed in the colleges, a hotplate is provided on each corridor purely for soup/hot drinks, but no fridge. Self-catering kitchens basic and barely adequate for the number of people. Mixed residencies rare. Corridors in college and houses generally single sex. Accommodation for couples/families very limited and priority often given to overseas students.

Students: Proportion of mature students increasing; overseas students roughly 25% of population, and not predominantly EC. Reasonable mix of students, many from southern England; mix of private and state-school backgrounds. Drop-out rate increasing, mainly due to financial hardship. Discrimination a problem, like anywhere, but generally we are quite a 'right-on' Union and campus life is quite tolerant.

Every student allocated personal tutor, but system not very effective; quality of pastoral care largely depends on the individual student forming a relationship with a member of staff. Collegiate system supposed to bring students and staff together but ineffective: overall structures fail but desired results achieved informally. The library is open long hours during the week (term-time) and acceptable hours at weekends. It is only closed for any length of time between Saturday afternoon and Sunday afternoon. The college shops are notorious for eclectic opening hours, especially at weekends, when the Union shop is currently also closed. The sports centre opens evenings.

Union is active, providing often the cheapest social events of any in the country, but is extremely limited by lack of a central union building/venue. It is political, naturally, but not dominated by any party political grouping.

College residents allowed guests for four nights at a time who must be signed in. Regulations for houses not clear, but virtually impossible to enforce. In practise it should not be a problem. Cars are useful when living out and many have them. College residents not allowed cars, because parking so congested.

Union's welfare department provides all the advice anyone could need, and there is a university counselling service if needed. Condom dispensers are in college toilets.

Having fun? Overseas cultural societies usually amongst the most active. Canterbury is student town in terms of population, but there is a definite division, with student and non-student pubs. There are some areas where mixing does occur. Plenty of pubs but most are expensive, theatre with a very mainstream programme, a two-screen cinema in town, but little in the way of markets. Car Boot Sales do occur. Campus has a small theatre and a drama studio. There are films aplenty, with union films and the campus art cinema ensuring that you can see at least four films a week if you wish. College bars social areas, but Kent suffers terribly from the lack of central union building. Students do visit from elsewhere, but geographical position tends to reduce Kent's popularity. Bands tend to be on the way up rather than well known because of venue limitations, but the quality is high and we are on the N.M.E./M.M. circuit.

Working? Modular(ish) system gives a lot of freedom of choice, and there is a wide range of courses, some unusual, some traditional. Four year language degrees involve a year in the relevant countries. Course changes are quite easy, particularly during the first year, and work loads vary greatly with the heaviest for natural science and the lowest for humanities. It's impossible to generalise about quality of teaching, but the union is trying to get student assessment increased. Courses seem generally well thought of and assessment is by coursework and exams. The balance varies but both are usually involved.

Pauper notes

Accommodation: Nothing cheap in Canterbury. **Drink:** Bass Masterbrew, Canterbury Ale. **Pubs:** Rose and Crown/Simple Simons/Falstaff and Tap/Three Compasses. **Eats:** Marlowe's, The Front Page, Sweeney Todds, all the usual nationals. **Ents:** Penny Theatre good off-campus. **Sports:** Sports Centre on campus. Only swimming pool in the area about to close for a year. **Hardship funds:** Union has welfare fund – limited budget. Access funds. **Travel:** Buses cheap, trains convenient but Network South East appalling. **Work:** Pub/ restaurant work available. Little else, pay is not great.

More info?

Get students' Alternative Prospectus.
Enquiries (preferably written) to Daniel Adamson, President SU (0227 765224).

Informal name

UKC.

Buzz-words

LBG – Lesbian and Bisexual and Gay Group. KRED – Keynes, Rutherford, Eliot, Darwin (the four colleges). All references to rooms abbreviate the college names. PW – Park Wood ('Brookside' housing estate).

Alumni (Editors' pick)

Kazuo Ishiguro, Ted Harrison, Colin Lazzerini (founder of Loose Tubes).

KING ALFRED'S COLLEGE

King Alfred's College, Sparkford Road, Winchester SO22 4NR (0962 841515) Map A, E8

Student enquiries: Admissions Officer

Main study areas – as in What to Study section: *(First degree):* American studies, archaeology, drama, education, English, history, nursing. *Also:* Design and technology.

European Community: A few students learn an EC language (French available in the first year of combined studies degree) or spend time in another EC country as part of their course. Exchange with university in Spain open to BEd (primary) students.

Application: UCCA for 1993 start, UCAS thereafter. **Academic features:** Computer studies built into BEd for all students. BA design and technology. **Founded:** 1840, as diocesan training college for teachers. **Main awards:** BA, BSc, BEd. **Awarding body:** Southampton University. **Site:** Overlooking city of Winchester. **Accommodation:** 560 places in halls of residence (accommodation provided for most first year students). Approx cost: £48 board and lodging. **Rent:** 50% in accommodation where rent controlled by college. **Library:** 100,000 volumes, 565 periodicals, 300 study places. **Welfare:** Health and counselling committee. **Special categories:** Some residential facilities for married students. **Careers:** Information, advice and placement service. **Amenities:** Theatre; television centre, learning resources centre, computer studies centre, library, art/design workshop, arts centre, human movement studio, sports hall, SU building with bar, laundry, bank, etc. **Sporting facilities:** Gymnasium, sports hall, squash courts, playing fields. **Employment:** Teaching, industry, commerce, civil service, media etc.

Duration of first degree course(s) or equivalent: 3 years; **others:** 4 years for BEd, BA design and technology; 2 years BEd design and technology. **Total first degree students 1991/92:** 1,990 **Total BEd students:** 950 **Overseas students:** 19 **Mature students:** 447 **Male/female ratio:** 1:3 **Teaching staff: full-time:** 108 **part-time:** 28 **Total full-time students 1992:** 2,350 **Postgraduate students:** 55 **Tuition fees for 1992/93 (first degrees):** Home: £1,855 (classroom), £2,770 (lab/studio); Overseas: £3,500 (classroom), £5,500 (lab/studio).

What it's like

It's attractively situated on a hillside 10 minutes walk from Winchester city centre. Modern blocks contrast with traditional stone buildings. Accommodation varies. 500 places in halls of residence and converted houses within half a mile of college. These places are mainly given to first years and a small proportion of third and fourth years. Everyone not given places informed in the July before they arrive and given accommodation lists by accommodation officer. Advice can also be obtained from the SU which also runs the union shop. Well developed and confidential counselling service. Social life centres around the SU. Discos, dances, bands, parties, quizzes, promotions, film showings and occasional excursions. Winchester has a fine selection of pubs, a theatre, disco, good but expensive shops and a market. Southampton is 12 miles away, 20 minutes by train. Good rail links with London, approx 1 hour away.

Free sports complex on site, playing fields a mile from campus. Strong reputation for drama – regular student productions and visiting companies.

Exchange scheme available in 1st term of the second year to Canada, USA and Poland. Shoei College for Japanese students.

Relatively easy to change courses during the first year. Quality of staff high. Workload reasonable to heavy, emphasised by use of continuous assessment as well as exams. Good academic reputation. SU active both socially and politically: gay and lesbian society, aids and welfare committees, anti racism group; also provides welfare and marketing services, free legal advice, social and sporting amenities, fortnightly TV programme 'Pulse', magazine 'Hard Times' and annual handbook. Students come from all over Britain with a wide variety of backgrounds. College has a very close-knit atmosphere, drop out rate low.

Pauper notes

Accommodation: Hard to find in town. Very expensive, college married quarters available but limited. College accommodation includes meals on card system. Creche available for 3–5 year olds. **Drink:** Union cheapest place, County Arms and The Exchange very student friendly. Winchester pub prices, average to high. **Eats:** Canteen food on card system and includes vegetarian. Good selection in town. County Arms gives student discount on food. **Ents:** Active ents committee. Film Soc, SU theatre productions, abundant theatre groups on and off campus. Good range of active clubs and societies. **Sports:** Free sports complex on campus. Various sports clubs. Recreation centre and swimming pool in town – student discounts. **Hardship fund:** Available. Heavily in demand. Short term loans in the direst of emergencies. **Travel:** Hitching relatively easy but definitely not advised. Travel scheme run by SU, with minibus runs on Ents nights. **Work:** Usually plenty – but recession has hit this area very hard.

More info?

Get students' Alternative Prospectus.
Enquiries to Peter Watt (Union Secretary) 0962 853144.

CAN'T FIND WHAT YOU'RE LOOKING FOR? USE THE INDEX!

Informal name

KAC.

Buzz-words

JST (John Stripe Theatre); TAB (Tom Atkinson Building); PA (public address system); PE (physical education); TP (teaching practice); ONIFMTP (Oh no, I've failed my TP); CF (Christian Fellowship); MS (market services).

KING'S COLLEGE HOSPITAL

**King's College School of Medicine & Dentistry,
University of London, Bessemer Road, London SE5 9PJ
(071 274 6222)** Map D, C3

Student enquiries: Medical School Office (ext 4017) or Dental School Office (ext 2528)

Main study areas – as in What to Study section: *(First degree):* Dentistry, medicine.

European Community: No students learn an EC language as part of their course but they may choose to spend time in another EC country as part of their elective period.

Application: UCCA for 1993 start, UCAS thereafter. **Structural features:** Part of King's College, London University. **Special features:** Densely populated urban area with some 1,000 beds, and over 100,000 dental patient attendances, so both medical and dental students have clinical contact with many patients. **Founded:** 1831. **Main awards:** BDS, MBBS. **Awarding body:** London University. **Site:** College in the Strand and in Camberwell Green/Denmark Hill area. **Access:** British Rail from Victoria, Holborn or London Bridge stations to Denmark Hill station; underground to Brixton, Elephant & Castle, or Oval, and then bus; various buses from central London. **Academic features:** Basic medical and dental sciences taught in multi-faculty environment of King's College London. Medical students also admitted from Oxford and Cambridge Universities for clinical studies only. **Accommodation:** Halls of residence of King's College London and the University of London. **Library:** 30,000 books and bound journals, 65 study places at Denmark Hill. **Other learning resources:** Use made of videos and computer-assisted learning packages. **Welfare:** Doctor, dentist, FPA, psychiatrist, counsellor, chaplain, independent financial adviser, hospital chapel. **Careers:** Information, advice and resident appointments service. **Amenities:** All facilities of London University, King's College London as well as the School of Medicine and Dentistry. **Employment:** Medicine and dentistry.

Duration of first degree course(s) or equivalent: 5 years **Total first degree students 1992/93:** 820 **Overseas students:** 40 **Male/female ratio:** 1:1 **Teaching staff: full-time:** 111 **part-time:** 30 (clinical only); **Postgraduate students:** 140 **Tuition fees for 1992/93 (first degrees):** Home: £760 (if no grant), £2,770 (pre-clinical), £4,985 (clinical); Overseas: £7,404 (pre-clinical), £13,275 (clinical).

What it's like

Spending two (or three) years in King's College on the Strand before coming down to the Hospital in Camberwell does make life rather interesting, since King's College London is one of the largest multi-faculty colleges of London University. Two or three years spent with non medics or dentists tends to broaden one's outlook and gives an experience of 'student life'. As well as being just down the road from Covent Garden, National Theatre and the whole West End, it means that while one still has some overdraft facilities, London life is there to be enjoyed.

Once finished in the Strand, students come down to Camberwell, to meet patients and be assimilated into hospital life. Rather than lectures, as at the Strand, learning is emphasised at the bedside, with importance being attached to speaking to and examining patients, so that a 'whole' view of the patient is obtained. A lot of learning is absorbed by a sort of osmosis as students are expected to spend some time following House Officers. This is exciting as patients are seen first-hand as they appear in casualty with anything from haemorrhages or heart attacks to knife wounds. Not all the course is in King's – two months are spent in outside district hospitals which is popular as teaching is generally enthusiastic and atmosphere more relaxed.

Once at the hospital students are also members of SU, called the Guild. Apart from one of the most pleasant bars in London, it also boasts one of the best mobile discos in south London, and provides cheap entertainment every week plus many bands during year. Also provided in 'The Penthouse' are TV/games rooms. The Guild has many clubs and societies, as well as brand new sports ground in Dulwich Village, which makes us rather unique in that students walk to 'the Griffin' rather than overcoming an obstacle course provided by London Transport and BR!

Outside the hospital, Camberwell and Brixton, while not being the West End, do provide many alternative night spots which are fairly cheap such as 'the Fridge' in Brixton and the Ritzy – an independent cinema. It's obviously an up and coming area judging by the wine bars springing up everywhere. Student reductions available at sports centres locally.

A few general points. Once outside King's the label 'student' is not automatically applied which provides independence with the friendly back-up of large student body. Accommodation provided in first year at least, free advice and information provided thereafter. Life is more expensive than outside London but Camberwell is cheaper than many other areas; there is a 'community' feeling in Camberwell not the 'lost in London' effect which is found in other areas. And because the hospital is in a varied community, medical teaching is varied, interesting and of a high standard.

Pauper notes

Accommodation: Squats through King's College London – £15-20/week. Short life because houses are condemned and to be demolished but this rarely occurs. **Drink:** Penthouse and Strand bars – £1/pint Kronenburg/Courage best. **Eats:** Cheap refectory at hospital, local kebab houses. Cheap pasta locally and excellent Thai food. Wine bars. **Ents:** Penthouse on campus plus Brixton Ritzy – alternative and box-office hit films cheap and interesting. Student reductions in London for plays. **Sports:** Brixton Sports Club – all sports. Cheap membership gives reductions. Griffin Sports Club – tennis, netball, hockey, rugby, multigym, bowls and squash courts. **Hardship Funds:** Some for poverty-stricken students. Apart from KCL Hardship Fund, there are some companies providing help. **Travel:** 15 seater minibus. Few travel scholarships for elective students; many local second-hand bike dealers. **Work:** Working on the bar, waitering/waitressing – very easy to find work, fairly well paid.

Alumni (Editors' pick)

Dr Reita Faria (ex-Miss World, now practising doctor), J L Dawson (Surgeon to Royal Household), Sir R M Feroze (President, Royal College of Obstetricians and Gynaecologists), Graeme Garden ('The Goodies').

KING'S COLLEGE LONDON

King's College London, Strand, London WC2R 2LS (071 836 5454)
Map E, C2

Student enquiries: Central Registry

CAN'T FIND WHAT YOU'RE LOOKING FOR? USE THE INDEX!

You can look up King's College School of Medicine and Dentistry separately.

Main study areas – as in What to Study section: *(First degree):* Anatomy, archaeology, biochemistry, biology, biotechnology, botany, business studies, chemistry, classics, computing, dentistry, education, English, environmental science, European studies, food science and nutrition, geography, history, humanities, Latin American studies, law, mathematical studies, mechanical and production engineering, medicine, microbiology, modern languages, music, nursing studies, pharmacology, pharmacy, philosophy, physics, physiology, professions allied to medicine (PAMs), religious studies and theology, strategic studies, zoology. *Also:* Electronic engineering.

European Community: 10% first degree students take EC language as part of course and 6% spend 6 months or more in another EC country. Formal exchange links with a large number of EC universities/colleges; most open to all undergraduates. Single or combined courses in French, German, Greek, Portuguese and Spanish; these languages, plus Italian, offered to students in modular programmes whatever their discipline; some courses, eg business management, have compulsory language element. Approved Erasmus programme.

Application: UCCA for 1993 start, UCAS thereafter. **Structural features:** Part of London University. **Founded:** 1829. **Main awards:** BA, BMus, BSc, BEng, MEng, BSc(Eng), LLB, MBBS, BDS, BPharm, BSc with RGN, BSc with PGCE. **Awarding body:** London University. **Special features:** Number of visiting professors contribute to the life of the college by giving lectures, participating in seminars, symposia etc. **Site:** 4 sites, one each in Strand, Kensington, Chelsea and Waterloo. **Access:** Good underground and bus services to all campuses. **Accommodation:** Over 1,900 places in college halls and a further 300 in intercollegiate halls; approx 95% first years who apply are offered a hall place. Approx cost (1992/93): £1,300 self-catering, £2,238 (fully catered) for a 30 week session. Rent: approx 27% students live in accommodation where rent is controlled by college. **Library:** Book stock of over 800,000, periodicals, microfilms, tapes, videos, computer tapes, slides and filmstrips; reserved collections in most popular subjects. **Specialist collections:** Eng (classics); Burrows (modern Greek and Byzantine studies); Box (Old Testament); Liddell Hart (military studies); Ford (science); Adam Archive (Portuguese). **Welfare:** Doctors, psychotherapists, chaplains, student advisers. **Hardship funds:** Every effort made to help students who encounter financial hardship; government access fund. **Careers:** Information, advice and placement service. **Amenities and sporting facilities:** All facilities of ULU (including swimming pool); King's College union of students buildings; sports ground, boat club and sailing club; a particularly central position for London's cultural amenities.

Duration of first degree course(s) or equivalent: 3 years; **others:** 4 years **Total first degree students 1991/92:** 5,567 **Number of BSc + P.G.C.E. students:** 37 **Overseas students:** 543 **Mature students:** 30 **Male/female ratio:** 1:1 **Total teaching staff: full-time:** 543 **part-time:** 75 **Total full-time students 1991/92:** 6,850 **Postgraduate students:** 2,148 **Tuition fees for 1992/93 (first degrees):** Home: £760 (if no grant), £1,855 (classroom), £2,770 (lab/studio), £4,985 (clinical); Overseas: £5,856 (classroom), £7,404 (lab/studio), £13,275 (clinical).

What it's like

A multi-sited institution right in the heart of London, King's is a vibrant go-ahead college of London University. Impressive academic standards are reached in a wide range of subjects with diverse course structures. A varied and high quality ents programme centres mainly on the Strand campus and Tutu's – the student nightclub – with 'Unity' the popular Saturday 'night'. Strand and Cornwall House campuses are within walking distance of the major tourist attractions and theatreland. Chelsea campus provides the unique and bizarre atmosphere of the King's Road, while Kensington is well situated between Notting Hill Gate and High

Street Kensington. Each site has its own distinctive flavour. Chelsea and Kensington are quieter but many enjoy the self contained 'small college' feel in the daytime. All in all KCL is an exciting and stimulating place to enjoy student life.

Ben Elger

Pauper notes

Accommodation: Halls – varied, some expensive. New 'student village' at Hampstead. Excellent head-leasing scheme run by college accommodation office. **Drink:** SU run Strand bar, 'The Waterfront' and 'Tutu's' and also Kensington bar. College runs Chelsea bar. All much cheaper than London pubs. **Eats:** SU has original and varied menu at Tutu's Cafe. College outlets on the Strand, Kensington, Chelsea and Hampstead. **Sports:** College sports ground at Berrylands, gym at Chelsea and weights room at Kensington. Also good indoor sports facilities at the ULU. **Hardship funds:** As well as Access Funds, there are educational trust/loans available – see college registry for details. **Travel:** Extensive exchange programme, scholarships, ULU travel shop at the Strand. **Work:** SU offers casual work in bars, catering, shop and at ents.

More info?

Enquiries to Ben Elger 071 836 7132.

Informal name

KCL/King's.

Alumni (Editors' pick)

Archbishop Desmond Tutu, Sir Shridath Ramphal, Chapman Pincher, Lord Edmund-Davies, Susan Hill, Angela Rumbold, Arthur C Clarke, Pat Reid, John McGregor, Ivison Macadars (founder NUS).

KINGSTON POLY

See Kingston University

KINGSTON UNIVERSITY

Kingston University, Penrhyn Road, Kingston upon Thames KT1 2EE (081-547 2000) Map D, A4

Student enquiries: Admissions Office

Main study areas – as in What to Study section: *(First degree):* Accountancy, aeronautical engineering, architecture, art & design, biochemistry, biology, business studies, chemistry, civil engineering, computing, economics, education, electrical and electronic engineering, English, environmental science, fine arts, geography, geology, history, information technology, law, mathematical studies, mechanical and production engineering, microbiology, modern languages, music, physics, politics and government, professions allied to medicine (PAMs), social policy and social welfare, sociology. *Also:* Estate management, human sciences, osteopathy, quantity surveying.

European Community: 25% first degree students take EC language (open to all as a non-examined subject) and 25% spend 6 months or more in another EC country. Formal Erasmus links with a number of EC universities/colleges: in economics (Spain); politics (France, Germany, Spain); business (France, Germany,

Netherlands, Spain); information systems (Eire, France, Greece, Spain); design (Eire, France, Netherlands, Spain); public administration (Belgium, Denmark, Eire, France, Germany, Greece, Italy, Netherlands, Spain); chemistry (Germany). Approved Erasmus programme.

Application: PCAS for 1993 start, UCAS thereafter; ADAR for art and design. **Academic features:** Courses in information systems design, business information technology, aerospace engineering, geographic information systems, manufacturing engineering, cell and molecular biology, biomedical science, business studies (European programme), music technology. **Special features:** Medici string quartet. Links with Gateway School of Music/modern music rehearsal centre and recording studio. Two Picker Fellows in art and sculpture. Three visiting professors in physical science, aerospace engineering and business. **Largest fields of study:** Applied science, business studies, engineering and modern arts. **Founded:** 1992, as a university; previously Kingston Poly, founded 1970, ex Kingston Colleges of Technology and Art and Gipsy Hill College of Education. **Main awards:** BA, BEd, BSc, BEng, MEng. **Awarding body:** Kingston University. **Site:** Kingston area. **Access:** British Rail (Kingston or Surbiton stations), buses. **Accommodation:** 1,250 hostel places cost c£50 pw; 600 headed tenancy cost £40–50. Accommodation usually found for first years, who have priority for hostel places. Rent: proportion of students in accommodation where rent controlled by university not known. **Library:** On 4 sites, total of 350,000 items consisting of books, periodicals, tapes, records; 930 study places; short loan service for course books; slide library at Knights Park Centre, music library at Gipsy Hill Centre. **Other learning resources:** One of largest academic computing facilities in Europe. **Welfare:** Full-time welfare unit, part-time doctors; counselling service, student services department. **Hardship funds:** Dealt with by student services department. **Careers:** Information, advice and placement service. **Amenities:** SU building with bar, common room, etc. SU bars on all four sites. **Sporting facilities:** Gymnasiums, playing fields, wide range of sporting activities. University teams have excellent records at national level.

Duration of first degree course(s) or equivalent: 3 years; **others:** 4 years (sandwich) **Total first degree students 1991/92:** 6,897; **total BEd students:** 120 **Overseas students (including EC):** 522 **Mature students:** approx 650 **Teaching staff: full-time:** 507 **part-time:** 200 **Total full-time students 1991/92:** 9,564 **Postgraduate students:** approx 1,833 **Tuition fees for 1992/93 (first degrees): Home:** £903 (if no grant), £1,885 (classroom), £2,770 (lab/studio); **Overseas:** £5,755.

What it's like

Contrary to the appearance of the official prospectus, Kingston is not all romantic sunsets over the Thames and peaceful strolls down tree-lined boulevards. Want to know the truth? Well, here it is in all its naked glory.

Kingston town centre is a road planner's disaster area with traffic wardens to match. Too many cars, too many buses, and far too many students but shopping facilities are excellent and so is public transport into central London (Waterloo 20 mins – no tube). Many good restaurants to suit all tastes and budgets; several popular student pubs although London prices make Guild bars the usual alternative; two very average night clubs with occasional student nights and the three-screen cinema 'Options'.

The university is most renowned for its fashion and engineering depts. Many sandwich and modular courses, work experience opportunities and field trips. The Erasmus scheme means good relations with European academic institutions and strong language dept. Also linked to some American colleges. Changing course obviously depends on requirements and subscriptions but generally university is very helpful. Highest drop-out rate is on HND courses because of extremely high workload. Overall academic standard is very good but food is dreadful (go to Guild snack bars instead: better quality and inexpensive).

Kingston University Guild of Students is very active, although not very radical.

Provides major Kingston venues and ents: weekly bands, discos, comedians, cabarets and films. There are 5 bars, 3 shops, over 70 social, cultural, sporting and political clubs; a confidential welfare service; campus banking and insurance; travel agency and many part time jobs. Most active societies are rugby, law, sub-aqua, surfing (trips to S of F), canoeing and mountaineering.

The main drawback for Kingston University is accommodation. A very lucky few may manage to get into halls of residence for their first year, but most students live out. However the situation has improved considerably this year with the university managing to find accommodation for the entire first year. Although rented accommodation is usually of quite a good standard it is scarce and very expensive (approx £50 pw) and since the abolition of housing benefit things are getting harder. It's not all bad though: bus services are good and many students live in slightly cheaper surrounding areas of New Malden, Surbiton, Tolworth and Norbiton.

There is no such thing as a 'typical' student at Kingston other than the fact that most are from south and south-east and private or grammar schools. There is every type here ranging from the hyper trendy art students at Knights Park to conscientious engineers at Canbury Park and finally to the Golf GTI brigade in the law dept at Kingston Hill. Anything goes here.

Money is the bane of every student's life and Kingston is not a cheap place to live; however if you do find somewhere to sleep and don't own a car, it's a great place to spend your degree years. Most students who come here end up staying in the area, so it can't be all bad!

Pauper notes

Accommodation: Expensive. **Drink:** Guild bars average 30–35p per pint cheaper. Popular student pubs include The Kingston Mill, The Ram and The Railway. **Eats:** Good Guild snacks available (pizzas, rolls, samosas etc). Good restaurants, Indian, Italian, Chinese, everywhere. **Ents:** Options cinema half price twilight shows around 6.00pm (3 films). Guild provides major Kingston venues – weekly bands, discos, films. **Sports:** Squash, tennis, golf clubs – cheaper if used through the Guild. University fitness rooms, squash courts, gyms, playing fields, tennis courts. **Hardship funds:** Small Guild loans. **Travel:** Guild travel office (STA). Hitching bad. **Work:** Many part time jobs in the Guild plus many others in Kingston pubs, shops, restaurants.

Alumni (Editors' pick)

Penny Jones (VP).

LA SAINTE UNION

See LSU Southampton

LABAN CENTRE

Laban Centre for Movement and Dance, Laurie Grove, New Cross, London SE14 6NH (Tel 081 692 4070; Fax 081 694 8749) Map D, C3

Student enquiries: Course Enquiries

Main study areas – as in What to Study section: *(First degree):* Dance. *Also:* Dance theatre.

European Community: No students learn an EC language or spend time in another EC country.

Application: Direct. **Academic features:** MA in dance studies, dance movement therapy. Also PhD offered in dance; other courses include professional diploma, community dance, diploma in dance teaching, diploma in dance in local, national and European government. **Special features:** Visiting artists as teachers and performers. Annual international summer school, junior year abroad scheme for US students. Access to buildings for the disabled. **Main awards:** BA. **Awarding body:** City University. **Site:** South East London. **Access:** New Cross or New Cross Gate stations (British Rail from Charing Cross); various buses. **Accommodation:** Private locally; no college (or college rent controlled) accommodation. **Library:** Dance collection, related subjects, notation scores, periodicals, record collection, Peter Williams dance archive, 40–45 study places, access to Goldsmiths' College libraries. **Welfare:** Doctor, psychiatrist, chaplain, solicitor through SU. **Hardship funds:** Small interest-free loans available for short term. **Careers:** Information and advice. **Amenities:** Purpose-built studios, sound studio, music rooms, well-equipped modern studio theatre and wardrobe department. Fully equipped pilates studio for body training. In-house publications: *Dance Theatre Journal* and *International Working Papers*. **Employment:** Performing arts and teaching. Community art. Dance animateurs. Choreography. Notation. Research.

Duration of first degree course(s) or equivalent: 3 years **Total first degree students 1991/92:** 140 **Overseas students:** 15 **Mature students:** 0 **Male/female ratio:** 1:10 **Teaching staff: full-time:** 16 **part-time:** 25 **Total full-time students 1990/91:** 215 **Postgraduate students:** 27 **Tuition fees for 1992/93 (first degrees):** £6,500.

What it's like

Housed in a converted church with purpose built dance studios and pilates studio, attached to the Goldsmiths' College campus. BR and tube available for easy access to central London. SU has no sabbatical officer, but is run by a committee of present students. Laban students have the chance to use many of the Goldsmiths' facilities. Timetable heavy – 9 am until 6 pm Monday–Friday and weekends when necessary, plus written work especially for BA students. Drop out rate high. Student hardship causing more to drop out. Many overseas students. Wide range of courses available and overall teaching standard is high, but relations between students and administration staff can be distant.

Pauper notes

Accommodation: See accommodation board in college, or ask to speak to accommodation officer. Average prices £35–£50 per week. **Drink:** Goldsmiths' SU bar next door, many local pubs. Rosemary Branch, Fox 'n' Firkin, Studio Bar, Gipsy Moth, Rose Inn. **Eats:** Goldsmiths' provide vegetarian food. Wholefood Cafe, Mary's Cafe, Coffee Shak, Bullfrogs, Ye Olde Pie Shoppe. Many Indian/Chinese/Italian restaurants (reasonably priced) nearby. **Ents:** Goldsmiths SU very active with discos and bands quite regularly. Barrie Bird theatre has dance companies regularly. The Venue (for bands). **Sports:** Ladywell Leisure Centre, with vantage card, half price admission for 1 year. Deptford swimming baths. **Hardship funds:** College provides loans fund, not very large amounts and has to be payed back within fairly short time. **Travel:** Lisa Ullman fund provides opportunity for dance students to travel abroad. Goldsmiths' SU provide safe women's transport after social events. Bus routes, 53, 36, 177, 171, 21. **Train/tube:** New Cross, New Cross Gate. **Work:** Local work in pubs, restaurants. Jobs in college, eg office work, stuffing envelopes to help with fees if needed.

More info?

Get students' Alternative Prospectus.
Enquiries to Students Union (081 691 7840).

Alumni (Editors' pick)

The Cholmondeleys, David Massingham, Matthew Bourne, Geographical Duvet, Adventures in Motion Pictures, Action Syndicate (all ex-Laban BA students), Lea Anderson, Jacob Marley (choreographers), Mark Murphy (V-tol dance company).

GET HOLD OF THE PROSPECTUSES

LAMPETER

St David's University College, Lampeter University of Wales, Dyfed, SA48 7ED (0570 422351) Map A, C7

Student enquiries: Admissions Officer

Main study areas – as in What to Study section: *(First degree):* Archaeology, classics, English, geography, history, modern languages, Near East and Islamic studies, philosophy, religious studies and theology. *Also:* Environmental archaeology, human geography, informatics, Swedish, Victorian studies, Welsh (Cymraeg), Welsh studies.

European Community: 10% first degree students take EC language as part of course and 5% spend 6 months or more in another EC country. Formal exchange links with Germany (Bayreuth) and Netherlands (Nijmegen). Approved Erasmus programme. French and German available as part-time courses.

Application: UCCA for 1993 start, UCAS thereafter. **Structural features:** Part of Wales University. **Academic features:** Joint honours courses in archaeology, church history, informatics, Victorian studies, Swedish and Islamic studies; first year has 3 subjects of equal weight including main degree subject(s) and possibly language. Information studies available to all first year students and as part of joint degree in informatics. **Largest fields of study:** English, history, geography, theology and religious studies, modern languages. **Founded:** 1822, becoming part of Wales University in 1971. **Main awards:** BA, BD. **Awarding body:** Wales University. **Site:** Lampeter town centre. **Accommodation:** 400 places in halls of residence; 250 places in self-catering hostels; rooms in halls of residence automatically allocated to all first year, non mature, students. Approx cost: Full board £1,700, Pay as you Eat £1,000, Self Catering £1,200. Meals paid for as taken in the refectory. Rent: 60% in accommodation where rent controlled by university. **Library:** Main library and old library; 200,000 volumes in total, 950 periodicals, 190 study places. **Specialist collections:** Tracts collection; early Welsh periodicals; Bibles, prayerbooks, hymnals, catechisms and ballads; mss collection including 15th century Books of Hours. **Welfare:** All facilities available in Lampeter; chaplain. **Hardship funds:** Principal's hardship fund and government access fund. **Special categories:** Residential facilities for disabled students; children's playgroup. **Careers:** Information, advice and placement service. **Amenities:** Bookshop on campus; purpose-built SU. New purpose-built medical centre. **Sporting facilities:** Sports hall; playing fields less than 5 mins from campus; free use of town swimming pool; college sailing club at Aberaeron.

Duration of first degree course(s) or equivalent: 3 years; **others:** 4 years (philosophy, Welsh, modern languages) **Total first degree students 1991/92:** 1,030 **Male/female ratio:** 1:1 **Teaching staff: full-time:** 80 **part-time:** 25 **Total full-time students 1990/91:** 1,100 **Postgraduate students:** 115 **Tuition fees for 1992/93 (first degrees):** Home: £1,855 (classroom), £2,770 (lab/studio); Overseas: £4,250.

What it's like

It is situated within the beautiful setting of rural West Wales on a very pleasant single site campus with all the amenities necessary to have a good social and academic time. Accommodation good, but on the small side; competition growing for on-campus accommodation as numbers grow without increasing correspondingly. Students being pushed out even further – some 10 miles or more. Rents relatively cheap on and off campus but some off-campus housing pretty grim.

Student population mixed. High percentage of mature students (not that you'd notice most of the time). About 10–15% are Welsh with half of them being Welsh speaking. There is an exchange scheme with Canadian and Swedish universities. About another 50% of students are from the Home Counties.

There are no visiting restrictions and few other restrictions although there are quiet halls for those who enjoy tranquillity.

Due to isolated position of Lampeter many students have cars. The remoteness of the place means that much of the entertainment is home-grown although some surprisingly large name bands have played here. Entertainment is centred on the Union building and arts hall. The Union itself is quite active but not at all party-political.

There are many clubs and societies from rugby club to shopping society. On campus squash and tennis courts, gym and all-weather hockey pitch. Off campus 3–5 minutes' walk major college sports pitches.

Pauper notes

Accommodation: College building new halls, though aimed at conferences market rather than students. Increasing amount of isolated cottages, very cheap, middle of woods, coming onto student market. Also caravans becoming available. **Drinks:** Bar is cheapest hostelry around and has good atmosphere. Beer prices dismal. **Eats:** SU Pooh's Corner best catering facility in Wales: cheap, wholemeal, vegetarian, vegan and meat eaters provided for. **Ents:** Regular bands, cabaret and comedy club. Films twice a week. Lots of discos. **Sports:** Sports hall on campus – students free use of squash courts, town swimming pool. **Hardship funds:** College own fund; Union fund, but only for dire cases. **Travel:** Isolated so difficult. No BR station in Lampeter; Aberystwyth and Carmarthen nearest BR stations. Hitching is good. **Work:** SU work in bar, shop and catering; also as security. Work occasionally in town, eg chip shops etc.

Alumni (Editors' pick)

T E Lawrence (of Arabian fame), Sulak Sivaraska (Thai human rights campaigner), Sue Slipman (former NUS chief).

LANCASHIRE COLLEGE

The Lancashire College of Agriculture and Horticulture, Myerscough Hall, Bilsborrow, Preston PR3 0RY (0995 640611) Map A, D5

Student enquiries: Admissions Officer

Main study areas (*First degree*): Horticultural technology and management.

European Community: No students take EC language as part of their course but industrial placements are available throughout EC. Formal links with Portugal. European studies built into some courses.

Application: PCAS for 1993 start, UCAS thereafter; or direct. **Academic features:** Modular courses allowing a range of options. BSc in Horticultural Management offered in conjunction with Central Lancashire University. **Special features:** Strong links with allied industries. **Founded:** 1894. **Main award:** BSc. **Awarding body:** Central Lancashire University. **Site:** Three campuses – main site (Myerscough) 6 miles north of Preston. **Access:** Easily accessible from M6 motorway/A6 Preston-Lancaster road. BR station at Preston. **Accommodation:** 70% on-site accommodation. Private accommodation available in surrounding areas. **Library:** 30,000 volumes, 190 periodicals taken. **Other learning facilities:** 3 lowland farms/1 hill farm, embryo transfer unit, 2ha nursery, 0.3ha glass, 5ha landscaped grounds, 20ha sportsgrounds, 30ha woodland, conservation areas, comprehensive range of irrigation systems and constructions on own 9-hole Golf Course, specialised workshops, indoor/outdoor schools and equestrian unit, laboratories, computer centre, audio-visual suite and library. **Welfare:** Residential wardens; full-time student counsellor. **Amenities:** TV/common rooms, college bar, stage and auditorium, active sports and social club. **Sporting facilities:** Sports hall, tennis courts, football, rugby, cricket, hockey, bowling, golf and horse riding. **Employment:** Advisory, consultancy, research or management positions in land-based industries.

Duration of first degree courses (or equivalent): 4 years. **Mature students:** 20% **Male/female ratio 1991/92:** 3:1 **Total full-time students:** 550. **Tuition fees 1992/93 (first degree):** Home £2,770.

What it's like

One of the oldest agricultural colleges in the country, it will celebrate its centenary in 1994. Based on three sites – Hutton, (just south of Preston), Winmarleigh and Myerscough (both north of Preston). It provides training and education for a wide range of land-based and rural leisure careers. High standard facilities and teaching resources. Courses have strong practical element and generally include a total of one year's industrial placement in Britain or abroad.

Good student social life including discos, films, bands, live entertainment, plus lively night-life in nearby university town of Preston. Excellent shops, restaurants, cinemas. Good road/rail access; Lake District, Fylde coast, and all major NW cities nearby.

LANCASHIRE POLY

See Central Lancashire University

LANCASTER UNIVERSITY

Lancaster University, University House, Lancaster LA1 4YW (0524 65201) Map A, D5

Student enquiries: Undergraduate Admissions Office

Main study areas – as in What to Study section: *(First degree):* Accountancy, American studies, art & design, Asian studies, biochemistry, biology, business studies, chemistry, communication studies, computing, drama, economics, education, electrical & electronic engineering, English, environmental science, geography, history, industrial relations, information technology, law, linguistics, mathematical studies, mechanical and production engineering, modern languages, music, philosophy, physics, politics and government, psychology, religious studies and theology, social policy and social welfare, sociology. *Also:* Japanese, medieval studies, operational research and operations management, women's studies.

European Community: 15% first degree students take EC language as part of course and 8% spend 6 months or more in another EC country. A wide range of opportunities; particularly strong links with Copenhagen University and

CAN'T FIND WHAT YOU'RE LOOKING FOR? USE THE INDEX!

Copenhagen Business School. There are programmes in (among others) management, medieval studies, geography, linguistics and law. Approved Erasmus programme 1992/93. Member of the European Credit Transfer System in business administration.

Application: UCCA for 1993 start, UCAS thereafter. **Academic features:** Flexible course structure makes it easy to change course and allows specialisation. Flexible BSc combined science; BA in culture and communication; BSc in environmental science; new BA in Women's Studies. Admission policy welcomes mature students (details from Director of Admissions). **Structural features:** Merged with Charlotte Mason College, producing new faculty of teacher education and training (you can look up Charlotte Mason separately). **Special features:** Medici String Quartet (artists-in-residence); John Clegg (pianist-in-residence). Exchange programme in many subjects with US universities, as well as Erasmus and Comett programmes in Europe. **Largest fields of study:** English, history, management, biological and environmental sciences. **Founded:** 1964. **Main awards:** BA, BBA, BMus, BSc, LLB, BEng, MEng. **Awarding body:** Lancaster University. **Site:** Bailrigg, south of Lancaster. **Access:** On main London–Glasgow line; A6 and M6 main roads. **Accommodation:** 2,800 rooms on campus (accommodation available for all first years). Rent: 57% in accommodation where rent controlled by university. **Library:** About 800,000 items, over 3,000 periodicals, 800 reader places; short loan system for course books. **Specialist collections:** Redlich collection (music); Quaker collection; library of Burnley Grammar School. **Other learning resources:** Language resource centre, TV studio. **Welfare:** Collegiate advisers, doctors, psychiatrist, chaplains, professional student counsellors. **Hardship funds:** Student aid fund assists students with unforeseen financial difficulties. **Special categories:** Residential facilities for disabled and some married students; nursery (40 places, subsidised for students). **Careers:** Information, placement and advice service. **Amenities:** Bookshop; second-hand bookshop run by students; various shops and banks on campus; Peter Scott art gallery; Jack Hylton music rooms; Nuffield theatre studio. **Sporting facilities:** Wide range of sporting and recreational facilities (including swimming pool, sauna, solarium, and rock-climbing wall); outdoor centre in the Yorkshire Dales.

Duration of first degree course(s) or equivalent: 3 years; **others:** 4 years (MEng, languages and sandwich courses); 5 years (sandwich MEng) **Total first degree students 1991/92:** 4,474 **Overseas students:** 1,000 **Mature students:** 21% **Male/female ratio:** 1:1 **Total teaching staff:** 424 **Total full-time students 1991/92:** 5,746 **Postgraduate students:** 2,346 (inc part-time) **Tuition fees for 1992/93 (first degrees):** Home: £1,855 (classroom), £2,770 (lab/studio); Overseas: £5,320 (classroom), £7,055 (lab/studio).

What it's like

Attractive modern on-campus university in pleasant grounds 2 miles south of Lancaster. Very accessible – M6 and maritime London-Scotland rail link. Excellent location for outdoor activity – sea, Lake District and good access to other major cities.

Reasonable accommodation for 1st and some 3rd year students, on campus in colleges. Each of the 8 colleges has own bar, student run JCR and tradition. Keen rivalry between colleges producing a very good atmosphere. Active and powerful SU campaigning and providing information including: education and welfare department, Athletic union (over 30 clubs), non sporting and cultural societies. Social events (Sugar House nightclub, on campus concerts, balls etc). No visiting restrictions.

Courses extremely flexible – three subjects in first year. Staff generally very helpful and friendly. Almost all courses have some continued assessment (alternative prospectuses available from SU). Chance to study abroad in 2nd year.

Friendly university; excellent atmosphere, international flavour.

GET HOLD OF THE PROSPECTUSES

Pauper notes

Accommodation: University headlease scheme; flats on campus. Married flats available. Graduate college on campus. **Drink:** 9 bars on campus and lots of local pubs provide good choice at reasonable prices. **Eats:** Cheap chippy and pizza place on campus. Usual fast food, takeaways etc plus good international selection of restaurants in town. **Ents:** Excellent off-campus student nightclub, good bands on and off campus; film club showing latest releases; theatre group excellent. **Sports:** Excellent sports centre on campus; swimming pool; good athletic union. **Hardship funds:** Limited funds available from university and from individual colleges. **Travel:** Good hitching. Buses expensive but regular, can get weekly/monthly passes. Some travel scholarships in colleges. **Work:** Some in Sugar House in term and in bars. Much tourist and conference trade, also catering department, in vacation.

Buzz-words

JCR (Junior Common Room), SCR (Senior Common Room.

Alumni (Editors' pick)

Eric Bolton (Senior Chief Inspector of Schools); Robert Fisk (award winning Middle East correspondent of *The Times*); Simon Smith (RU England International); Linda Lewis (reporter, BBC Television News); Gary Waller, MP; Michael Handley, MEP; Green (Scritti Politi, rock band).

LEEDS METROPOLITAN UNIVERSITY

Leeds Metropolitan University, Calverley Street, Leeds LS1 3HE (0532 832600)
Map A, E5

Student enquiries: Course Enquiries

Main study areas – as in What to Study section: *(First degree):* Accountancy, architecture, art & design, business studies, chemistry, computing, economics, education, electrical and electronic engineering, fine arts, food science & nutrition, history, hotel and catering management, law, library & information studies, modern languages, nursing studies, professions allied to medicine (PAMs), social policy and social welfare, sociology, speech sciences. *Also:* Construction management, informatics, human biology, music and media technology, sports studies, tourism management.

European Community: 15% first degree students take EC language as part of course and 12% spend 6 months or more in another EC country. Formal exchange links with over 40 EC universities/colleges: Belgium (4); Eire (3); France (13); Germany (6); Greece (6); Italy (1); Netherlands (3); Portugal (1) and Spain (6). Subject areas include: nursing, education, leisure studies, environmental health, European languages and business, European finance, information technology, graphic design, social work. Approved Erasmus programme 1991.

Application: PCAS for 1993 start, UCAS thereafter; ADAR for art and design (SWAS for DipHE social work). **Academic features:** BA consumer services management, European marketing and public relations; BSc courses in health sciences and health studies, physiotherapy, information systems for business; DipHE courses in playwork, social work and youth and community work. Several 4 year sandwich degrees. **Largest fields of study:** Education, European languages and business, business studies, hospitality management, engineering, informatics, law. **Founded:** 1992, as a university; previously Leeds Poly, founded 1970, from 4 existing colleges and 2 colleges of education. **Main awards:** BA, BEd, BSc, BEng, LLB. **Awarding body:** Leeds Metropolitan University. **Site:** 2 campuses, in or near Leeds town centre. **Access:** Good road, rail and air links. **Accommodation:** 800 places in halls (priority given to first years); other places in hostels, approved lodgings, and by Unipol agency for private rented accommodation. First year students apply to accommodation officer. **Rent:** Proportion of students in accommodation where rent controlled by university, not known. **Library:** Central library, plus smaller campus and subject libraries; 500,000 volumes in total, 2,500 periodicals; extensive AV and IT-based resources; over 1,000 study places. **Welfare:** 2 student health centres staffed by nurses; FPA; physiotherapy service; counsellors; budget adviser; students union welfare officer. **Hardship funds:** Student financial support scheme for existing students. **Special categories:** Childminding facilities available; 'night line' service; international students advisory group; chaplaincy. **Careers:** Information, advice and placement service. **Amenities:** Bank and shop on central campus; SU building with bars and other recreational facilities; health and fitness suite. **Sporting facilities:** Specialist PE facilities, including swimming pool, dance studio, floodlit all weather athletics track and field, regional gymnastics centre, tennis courts, health and fitness suite. **Employment:** Most courses vocationally slanted, excellent graduate employment record.

Duration of first degree course(s) or equivalent: 3 years full-time; 4 years sandwich **Total first degree students 1991/92:** 6,675 (full-time and sandwich); **BEd students:** 834 **Overseas students:** 395; **Mature students:** 2,725; **Male/female ratio:** 1:1 **Teaching staff: full-time:** 645 **part-time:** 250 **Total full time and sandwich students 1991/92:** 8,600 **Postgraduate students:** 1,250 **Tuition fees for 1992/93 (first degrees):** Home: £759 (if no grant), £1,855 (classroom), £2,770 (lab/studio); Overseas: £5,152 (classroom), £5,983 (lab/studio).

What it's like

Leeds is not only the gateway to the north, but a greatly expanding city. The city consists of two universities, many shopping precincts, side streets, Victorian arcade, a huge market, and has a championship winning football team!

Many shops, cinemas and theatres offer discounts to students.

Leeds Metropolitan Uni is growing rapidly with three main sites and a number of smaller ones. Many students live in Headingley and Hyde Park. Most uni halls of residence are at Beckett Park Site, Headingley (the house of Carnegie Sports College). There is always plenty to do with many facilities geared towards students.

SU provides two recently refurbished bars, cafes, shops, sports and cultural clubs, discos, concerts, alternative comedy, bank, discounts, a fully confidential student advice service and almost everything you need to survive your student life. No, not money!

If you want to make a success of your student life, Leeds is the city and the Metro Uni is the happening place!

Pauper notes

Accommodation: Headingley is getting expensive, other areas are cheaper but beware. **Drink:** SU cheaper than pubs, 2 bars refurbished in last two years. Fox and Newt on Burley Road brews its own lethal brews. **Eats:** Cheap hot and cold food on campus, with everything else available nearby. **Ents:** Regular free bands at Beckett Park Site. Cheap major bands and comedy on campus. Free quizzes and karaoke. Discounts offered by most cinemas. **Sports:** Probably the best sports facilities in Yorkshire on campus. Swimming pools, weights room, regular aerobics, gyms, majority of sports catered for. **Hardship funds:** Not much. **Travel:** Usual discounts. **Work:** On site – security/bar staff; off campus – pubs, restaurants, fast food outlets.

GET HOLD OF THE PROSPECTUSES

Alumni (Editors' pick)
Marc Almond (Soft Cell), Sir Henry Moore, Ron Pickering, Mick Hill, Bill Slater, Les Bettinson.

LEEDS POLY
See Leeds Metropolitan University

LEEDS UNIVERSITY
University of Leeds, Leeds LS2 9JT (0532 431751) Map A, E5

Student enquiries: Undergraduate Office (Admissions)

Main study areas – as in What to Study section: *(First degree):* Accountancy, American studies, anatomy, architecture, art and design, Asian studies, biochemistry, biology, biotechnology, botany, business studies, chemical engineering, chemistry, civil engineering, classics, communication studies, computing, dentistry, drama, economics, electrical & electronic engineering, English, environmental science, environmental studies, European studies, fine arts, food science & nutrition, geography, geology, history, industrial relations, Latin American studies, law, linguistics, mathematical studies, mechanical & production engineering, medicine, metallurgy and materials science, microbiology, modern languages, music, Near East and Islamic studies, pharmacology, philosophy, physics, physiology, politics and government, psychology, public administration, religious studies and theology, social policy and social welfare, sociology, zoology. *Also:* Broadcasting studies, ceramics, colour chemistry, energy studies, fire engineering, minerals processing technology, mining, operational research, textile technology.

European Community: 10% first degree students study an EC language, most of whom spend 3–6 months in another EC country. Language tuition available for intending Erasmus students and others interested (eg maths, engineering, geography students) as well as language specialists. Formal exchange links with more than 100 EC universities/colleges, both Erasmus and other, covering all countries of the European community. Active exchange links also with Ukraine, Bulgaria and Czechoslovakia. Erasmus exchanges approved in 1992/93 cover: business and economic studies, biochemistry, chemical engineering, chemistry, classics, electronic and electrical engineering, English, food science, geography, history, Italian, law, materials, mathematics, mechanical engineering, medicine, philosophy, Portuguese, public health, medicine and Spanish. Also involved in ECTS Tempus, Comett and FORCE.

Application: UCCA for 1993 start, UCAS thereafter. **Academic features:** Part-time degrees, modularisation of undergraduate degree schemes. **Founded:** 1904. **Main awards:** BA, BChD, BEng, MEng, BSc, MBChB, LLB. **Awarding body:** Leeds University. **Site:** Main central site close to city centre. **Access:** Nearby bus and railway stations; bus, or within walking distance of halls of residence. **Accommodation:** 1,800 places in halls, 3,000 places in university flats; almost all first year students accommodated. Approx cost: £1,500 for 30.5 weeks (full board). Rent: 48% in accommodation where rent controlled by university.

CAN'T FIND WHAT YOU'RE LOOKING FOR? USE THE INDEX!

Library: Over 2,500,000 volumes including microfilm, 2,500 study places. **Other learning facilities:** Audio-visual centre; central language laboratory (taped courses in over 40 languages available to all); computing service. **Welfare:** Health centre, advisers for handicapped and overseas students, day nursery, chaplaincies. **Hardship funds:** Students in financial hardship may make use of the Union's grant enquiry service or apply for a student loan or to Geoffrey Spink Hardship Fund. **Careers:** Advice and placement service. **Amenities:** Union with bars, coffee lounges, discos, newspaper; 600-seat theatre. **Sporting facilities:** Two sports halls on campus; sports ground within 3 miles; outdoor huts in Lake District and Pennines; Olympic standard swimming pool and golf in Leeds.

Duration of first degree course(s) or equivalent: 3 or 4 years; **others:** 5 years **Total first degree students 1991/92:** 11,443 **Overseas students:** 1,600 **Mature students:** approx. 800 **Male/female ratio:** 5:4 **Teaching staff:** 1,648 **Total full-time students 1991/92:** 13,553 **Postgraduate students:** 2,110 (full-time) **Tuition fees for 1992/93 (first degrees):** Home: £755 (if no grant), £1,855 (classroom), £2,770 (lab/studio), £4,985 (clinical); Overseas: £5,320 (classroom), £7,055 (lab/studio), £6,188 (classroom and lab combined), £12,990 (clinical).

What it's like

It's one of Britain's largest universities with over 15,000 attending courses. Vast range of courses cater for most tastes. Campus is about 10 minutes' walk from city centre, avoiding isolation of some campus universities, yet retaining a separate identity. University accommodation is in halls and flats which stretch from the campus to the north of the city, about 4 miles away. Most first years live in and then move out into private accommodation which is mainly concentrated in the Hyde Park area, 10 mins walk from the university.

SU is one of the country's biggest. Supports 180 societies and 52 sports clubs including sub aqua, hunt saboteurs, ballroom dancing and lacrosse. SU boasts 4 bars (and is Britain's biggest bitter retail outlet!), its own stationery shop, ABTA registered travel shop, print room and exam paper sales, bookshop, card and ticket shop, fully equipped games room and a concert venue which has put on acts such as EMF, Manic Street Preachers, Charter USM, and Billy Bragg. Range of welfare services impressive; 5 full-time permanent members of staff advise on all aspects. Range of facilities is probably unmatched by any other SU.

Leeds is a large city of ¾ million people, with a well-equipped city centre. For those of sporting bent there's football at Elland Road, rugby league and cricket at Headingley and an international swimming pool. Reasonable choice of theatres and cinemas, both large and small, with a new complex, the West Yorkshire Playhouse, recently built. Leeds is a lively and diverse city which can be recommended to anyone.

Andrew Berman

Pauper notes

Accommodation: All first years guaranteed a place in university accommodation. Private sector average rent is £32.50. **Drink:** 4 bars in SU, with cheap beer. Plenty of nearby friendly student orientated pubs, several good 'real ale' pubs. **Eats:** Many Indian and Italian restaurants. Some very cheap. Six restaurants/take-outs opposite university. **Ents:** Regular gigs in the SU. Many clubs every night in town. Local bands include Utah Saints, Pale Saints, Wedding Present, CUD. **Sports:** 53 sports clubs. Well-equipped sports centre on campus. International swimming pool just down the road. **Hardship funds:** Welfare loans available to everyone. Larger grants and loans available for worst cases. **Travel:** Some scholarships. Travel shop in the SU building. Leeds is on the M1 excellent rail and coach links. Easy hitching out of Leeds on M1. **Work:** Part-time work in union bars, security team and minibus driving. Bar work available in town pubs and clubs.

GET HOLD OF THE PROSPECTUSES

More info?

Get students' Alternative Prospectus.
Enquiries to Jon Jacobs, SU Education Secretary, (0532 431751).

Alumni (Editors' pick)

Sir Geoffrey Allen FRS, Sir George Porter, Mark Knopfler (Dire Straits), Nicholas Witchel (BBC newsreader), Jack Straw MP, Andy Kershaw, Andrew Eldritch (of Sisters of Mercy), Marc Almond.

LEICESTER POLY

See De Montfort University

LEICESTER UNIVERSITY

University of Leicester, University Road, Leicester LE1 7RH (0533 522522; Fax: 0533 522200) Map A, E6

Student enquiries: Admissions Officer (0533 522295)

Main study areas – as in What to Study section: *(First degree):* American studies, archaeology, biochemistry, biology, biotechnology, botany, chemistry, computing, communications studies, economics, electrical & electronic engineering, English, European studies, fine arts, geography, geology, history, law, mathematical studies, mechanical engineering, medicine, microbiology, modern languages, physics, physiology, politics and government, psychology, sociology, zoology. *Also:* astronomy, space and technology.

European Community: 14% first degree students take EC language as part of course and 7½% spend 6 months or more in another EC country. EC languages built into a number of degree courses (eg BSc chemistry/Europe, combined arts, European studies); also available to all students of university language centre including Institute of Linguists exams. French, German and Italian offered; occasional classes in eg Danish, Dutch, Spanish and cassettes available for eg Portuguese, Greek, Welsh. Formal exchange links with over 35 EC universities/colleges: Belgium (sociology, biology, chemistry, history); Denmark (archaeology, history of art, genetics, maths); Eire (geography, genetics, Italian, English); France (genetics, biology, law, English, arts, history, geography, French, archaeology, chemistry); Germany (medicine, English, arts, history, German); Greece (sociology, English); Italy (law, English, Italian, politics, genetics, arts); Netherlands (biology, history, genetics); Portugal (genetics, history, chemistry); Spain (history, geography, genetics, chemistry, English). Approved Erasmus programmes 1992/93.

Application: UCCA for 1993 start, UCAS thereafter; or direct if foundation/occasional/study abroad/part-time. **Largest fields of study:** Law, medicine, engineering, biological sciences. **Founded:** 1919, receiving charter in 1957. **Main awards:** BA, BSc, BEng, LLB, MBChB. **Awarding body:** Leicester University. **Site:** 1 mile from Leicester city centre. **Access:** Railway station (15 mins walk); M1 and M69 motorways 5 miles from campus. **Academic features:** 3 types of first degree; single, joint and combined honours. Combined honours provides flexible choice of 3 subjects (arts) or 2 to 5 subjects (science). **Special features:** Research centres focusing on football hooliganism, youth employment, public order, federalism. Genetic fingerprinting discovered here by Prof Alec

Jeffreys. **Accommodation:** 2,290 places in hall; 1,280 flats/bedsits (accommodation provided for 60%). Cost: (£1,418–£1,850 max) approx pa halls, £1,005 approx pa self-catering. **Library:** Main library has 923,000 volumes, 1,085 study places, multiple copies of prescribed textbooks on short loan. Also 3 subsidiary libraries. **Specialist collections:** Robjohn's Collection of Bibles; Works of Bunyan; English local history. **Other learning resources:** Audio-visual services, computer centre, language laboratory, university bookshop, Leicester University Press. **Welfare:** Doctors, welfare officers, personal tutors, FPA, psychiatrist, counsellors, chaplains, student legal advice centre, 'night line' telephone contact service. **Hardship funds:** Vice-Chancellor and SU both have modest funds for loans/grants for students in financial difficulties. **Special categories:** Nursery (independent) with favourable terms for student parents. **Careers:** Information and advice service. **Amenities:** Bookshop, travel centre, disco, general shops and banks on site; Leicester University Theatre (strong links with Haymarket and Phoenix professional theatres in Leicester); Archduke Trio (resident chamber music group). **Sporting facilities:** Excellent sports facilities including one of the finest athletics tracks in Midlands and two sports halls. **Employment:** 31% further study and training; 16% public sector; 24% industry and commerce.

Duration of first degree course(s) or equivalent: 3 years; **others:** 4 years (Chemistry/Europe, Combined Arts (Europe), European studies, modern languages, mathematics (European Community), mathematics + astronomy (EC), mathematics + computing (EC)); 5 years (medicine) **Total first degree students 1991/92:** 5,421 **Overseas students:** 711 **Mature students:** 942 **Male/female ratio:** 1:1 **Teaching staff: full-time:** 520 **part-time:** 43 **Total full-time students 1991/92:** 6,893 **Postgraduate students:** 2,397 **Tuition fees for 1992/93 (first degrees):** Home: £756 (if no grant), £1,885 (classroom), £2,770 (lab/studio), £4,985 (clinical); Overseas: £5,320 (classroom), £7,055 (lab), £12,990 (clinical).

What it's like

The university is close to the city centre. Self-catering houses closest to campus and halls of residence about 3 miles away in pleasant foliage-adorned residential area. Most first years stay in university accommodation, second and third years have choice to move out into private accommodation, helped by SU's private accommodation service. All halls/self-catering are mixed, some single sex houses, students can indicate preference on admission.

Large proportion of overseas students; SU sabbatical overseas officer to look after their interests. Growing number of mature students; half-term play schemes offered as well as nursery subsidy provision.

The campus is busy most of the time – library and SU open at weekends; restaurants for evening meals open during weekdays. SU has over 60 clubs and societies and runs a very active sports association. Students have many opportunities to become 'politically' involved; fortnightly general meetings, union council, various committees. Political orientation tends to be of moderate outlook. SU has extremely successful and progressive entertainments programme including weekly discos, rock discos, pub quizzes, comedians, films and top name bands. Runs very good 'Intro Week' for first years. SU boasts own nightclub, travel agent and union shop.

Plenty of opportunity to meet 'other halves' – no restrictions in halls and houses for visiting them once you've met them. Students with cars are few and far between because of parking restrictions on campus and halls of residence. Advice on contraception and pregnancy is offered both by student health centre and SU, all advice free and confidential.

Leicester is definitely a student town, loads of pubs and restaurants on the cheaper side! Number of shops, cinemas, theatres in a student discount scheme – need NUS card (available at registration). Can also use this card to get into other universities. SU on NME/MM circuit.

Biggest departments are medicine and law and there tends to be a concentration on scientific subjects, despite thriving arts and humanities courses. Trendy subjects include astronomy, astrophysics and mass communications; university building a much publicised 'Space Centre'. All courses have opportunities for field trips etc and university has many guest lecturers. Good choice of subsidiary subject in first year. Subject changes are fairly easy depending a lot however on A-level grades. Work assessed by combination of examination and course work. Opportunities to resit exams are good. Very low degree failure rate. Workload can be heavy in first year for combined subjects, but varied coursework complements this.

Students come from all over the country and world! Mixture of state/private school; few public school. Drop-out rate is low. Discrimination by staff/students whether sexual, racial or religious can be dealt with by formal procedures. Help and confidential counselling always available at SU. Typical student takes work fairly seriously – aims for a 2:2 degree. Spends free time playing sport or drinking in the bar, and organising round-the-world back packing trip for summer vacation.

Many graduates go on to teacher training in the school of education or other postgraduate work. Popular course with students who 'don't know what to do' when they've graduated is information technology.

Pauper notes

Accommodation: Catering hall accommodation for c1500 students. Self-catering flats for approx 1200. Others live in private accommodation. SU runs flat-finding service. **Drink:** SU bars cheapest in city. Local breweries Hoskins, HOB (notable real ales), Everards (large Midlands brewery). **Eats:** SU refectory seats over 1,000 diners. University catering service provides a large central restaurant plus numerous coffee bars around campus. Leicester notable for Indian food. Rise of Mexican, Cajun food restaurants in town – good atmosphere. **Ents:** New SU nightclub. SU runs popular discos on Fridays and Saturdays and films on Mondays. Leicester University Theatre is funded by SU and provides regular performances, as does the Revue and Theatre Society. Haymarket Theatre in Leicester nationally famous for touring productions. Halls and s/c houses organise their own entertainments frequently. **Sports:** University has 2 large sports grounds about 3 miles from campus, 1 adjacent to halls of residence. SU runs over 40 sports clubs. **Hardship funds:** SU hardship fund and Vice-Chancellor's fund. Grants above £200 are rare. **Travel:** Regular bus service from halls to campus (3 miles). Leicester being central is well connected for trains. London St Pancras is 1¼ hrs. Brand new travel agent. **Work:** Union employs evening bar staff. Part-time work plentiful in Leicester. Union has in-house job agency. Plenty of agencies in town centre which are 'student friendly', but the recession has hit **very** hard.

Alumni (Editors' pick)

Professor John Ashworth, Professor Laurie Taylor, Professor Alan Walters (Economist), Professor Malcolm Bradbury, Heather Cowper, David Puttnam, J H Plumb, C P Snow, Ron Pickering, Mike Nicholson, Sue Cook, John McVicker.

LIVERPOOL INSTITUTE

Liverpool Institute of Higher Education
(1) **St Katharine's College, Stand Park Road, Liverpool LI6 9JD**
    (051 737 3000)
(2) **Christ's & Notre Dame College, Woolton Road, Liverpool 16**
    (051 737 3000) Map A, D6

Student enquiries: Admissions Office, PO Box 6, (Address 1)

CAN'T FIND WHAT YOU'RE LOOKING FOR? USE THE INDEX!

Main study areas – as in What to Study section: *(First degree):* American studies, art and design, drama, education, English, environmental studies, European studies, geography, history, information technology, mathematical studies, modern languages, music, psychology, religious studies and theology, sociology. *Also:* Human biology, physical education.

European Community: 5% first degree students take EC language as part of course and 3% spend 6 months or more in another EC country. Formal exchange links in EC under development; currently in Belgium (1) and France (2). French is part of European studies and combined subjects degrees; also optional extra for all students, as are German, Spanish and Italian.

Application: UCCA for 1993 start, UCAS thereafter. **Academic features:** Degree courses in combined subjects, American studies, theology and religious studies, design, European studies. **Special features:** First ecumenical institute of HE. **Largest fields of study:** English, psychology, education. **Founded:** 1980. **Main awards:** BA, BEd, BSc, BDesign. **Awarding body:** Liverpool University. **Site:** Rural outskirts of Liverpool. **Access:** Bus to Liverpool city centre; M62 within one mile. **Accommodation:** Over 900 places in hall on both campuses (all first year students can be accommodated). Rent: Approx 40% in accommodation where rent controlled by institute. **Library:** 2 libraries; 210,000 volumes, separate reference/reading room for first degree students; resource centre. **Other learning facilities:** Computer laboratory for interactive learning. Primary Resource Centre and Religious Education Centre. Students have use of Liverpool University library. **Welfare:** Doctor, 3 chaplains, counsellor, two chapels (C of E and RC). **Careers:** Information, advice, work experience and placements. **Amenities:** SU common rooms, bookshop on campus, banking, playgroup. **Sporting facilities:** Gymnasia, squash and tennis courts, outdoor pursuits centre. **Employment:** Teaching (BEd). Wide range of employment (BA, BSc, BDes).

Duration of first degree course(s) or equivalent: 3 years; others: 4 years (BEd; BA American studies and European studies) **Total first degree students 1991/92:** 2,740; **BEd students:** 850 **Overseas students:** 50 **Mature students:** 600 **Male/female ratio:** 1:3 **Teaching staff: full-time:** 186 **part-time:** 5 **Total full-time students 1991/92:** 2,950 **Postgraduate students:** 610 **Tuition fees for 1992/93 (first degrees):** Home: £1,855 (classroom), £2,770 (lab/studio); Overseas: £4,166. All first years pay a registration fee of £340.

What it's like

It can be found in Childwall (posh suburb!) within a 20 minute bus ride from city centre. Easy access to M62 and Speke Airport. Newly refurbished and extended Derwent House (SU building) – caters for 500(+) with 2 bars. Reg's Bettabuys (the student shop) opened in September '92 by Bad Manners boasts a large range of stock from newspapers to Panadol – from bread to A4 file pads. All at very low prices. Half-term creche available. Car parking restricted. Good atmosphere at Institute – a 'happy' place to live and study. Opportunity to travel – European countries on Erasmus schemes plus assistantships; USA with American Studies. Student numbers indicate popularity – first year intake has almost doubled in the past three years – which can cause difficulty with accommodation. However this year practically all first years who required accommodation actually got it. Accommodation advice and help available from SU plus Institute accommodation office. Living in Liverpool is not too expensive – all items much cheaper than in south or midlands. In college – bars very cheap – eg in 1991/92 – pint of bitter 89p – pint of lager £1.07 – Newcastle Brown £1.12. Shop prices – heavily reduced.

Pauper notes

Accommodation: Halls of residence. **Drink:** Derwent, SU building – one of the largest and cheapest in Liverpool, 2 bars – 1 open lunchtime. **Eats:** 2 hot/cold servery/snack facilities plus sandwich and salad bar in Derwent. All at reasonable cost. Reg's Bettabuys student shop stocks extensive range of eats at rock bottom prices. **Ents:** Derwent House – extensive ents. Disco/bands 3/4 nights a week – one of the best light systems plus PA in Liverpool. Following have appeared: Carter, Thomas Lanc, Bad Manners, Comedy Club. City centre nightlife vibrant. Numerous pubs and clubs. Varied night life available in Liverpool city centre. **Sports:** Sports hall, gym, 2 squash courts, tennis courts, all-weather pitch as well as sports field. Numerous athletic clubs and nonsporting societies through SU. **Hardship funds:** Usual student hardship arrangements – access funds etc. **Travel:** Possible to European countries through Erasmus and Assistantships possible to USA through American studies. **Work:** Jobs few and far between.

More info?

Get students' Alternative Prospectus.
Enquiries to Patrick S. Kelly (V/P Welfare) 051 737 3634.

Informal Name

LIHE (pronounced 'Lie Hee').

Alumni (Editors' pick)

David Alton MP, Willy Russell (playwright).

LIVERPOOL JOHN MOORES UNIVERSITY

Liverpool John Moores University, Rodney House, 70 Mount Pleasant, Liverpool L3 5UX (051 231 2121) Map A, D6

Student enquiries: Academic Services – Admissions Centre

Main study areas – as in What to Study section: *(First degree):* Accountancy, architecture, art & design, biochemistry, biology, business studies, chemistry, civil engineering, computing, drama, economics, education, electrical & electronic engineering, English, environmental science, fine arts, geography, geology, history, law, library & information studies, marine technology, maritime studies, mathematical studies, mechanical and production engineering, microbiology, modern languages, nursing studies, pharmacy, physics, politics and government, psychology, social policy and social welfare, sociology. *Also:* Astrophysics, building, criminal justice, estate management, Japanese, sports science, surveying, women's studies.

European Community: 6% first degree students learn an EC language as part of their course and spend 6 months or more in another EC country. Approved Erasmus programme 1992. International business studies degree courses with French, German, Spanish (also Japanese). All students on integrated credit scheme have option of studying a language. French, German and Spanish offered to other students.

Application: PCAS for 1993 start, UCAS thereafter; ADAR for art and design. **Special features:** Has links to 20+ access courses in the Merseyside region (through the Merseyside Open College Federation); has long experience of supporting and positively welcomes mature students with non-standard qualifications or on access courses. **Academic features:** Integrated credit scheme offers range of subjects, single and joint honours, major/minor degree choice. **Largest fields of study:** Law, business studies, engineering. **Founded:** 1992 as a university; previously Liverpool Poly, founded 1970. **Main awards:** BA, BEd, BSc, BEng, LLB, MEng. **Awarding body:** Liverpool John Moores University. **Site:**

CAN'T FIND WHAT YOU'RE LOOKING FOR? USE THE INDEX!

Various sites in Liverpool city centre and southern suburbs. **Accommodation:** 1,200 places in halls, and flats/bedsitters. Approx cost: £45 pw halls, £24–£35 pw flats/bedsits. **Library:** On all sites; 550,000 volumes in total, 3,000 periodicals, 1,209 study places. **Other learning resources:** Audio-visual centres. **Welfare:** Doctor, chaplain, counsellor, accommodation officer. **Special categories:** Nursery. **Careers:** Information, advice and placement service. **Amenities:** SU wine bar, book and stationery shop, bank, bars on 3 other sites, 70 clubs and societies.

Duration of first degree course(s) or equivalent: 3 years (full-time); 4 years (sandwich) **other:** extended degree courses 4 years (full-time), 5 years (sandwich) **Total first degree students 1991/92:** 15,954 **BEd students:** 800 **Overseas students:** 389 **Male/female ratio:** 6:5 **Teaching staff:** approx 600 **Total full-time students 1991:** 11,201 **Postgraduate students:** 869 **Tuition fees for 1992/93 (first degrees):** Home: £1,855 (classroom), £2,770 (lab/studio); Overseas: £5,319.

What it's like

Spread over 11 sites, most in city centre. Accommodation varies from poor to excellent – self-catered flats and traditional halls; over 1,000 places provided. Active SU with social/political balance. More than 70 sporting, social and political clubs and societies, magazine, regular, quality entertainments, 8 shops and 6 bars (cheap and plush), and the Haigh. SU stretched to the limits; ents very popular and queues are a regular feature.

Wide range of subjects. Good staff/student relations. Course manoeuvres arranged. Work load depends on course. Industry years and field trips on some courses. Excellent staff. Continual assessment plus exams. Facilities average – libraries, recreation, student services and careers service. No visiting restrictions. Comprehensive welfare advice from university and SU – strictly confidential. SU Handbook. Good relationship with community. Wide range of theatres – from enormous Empire to tiny Unity. Art galleries and museums and a good shopping centre from the Albert Dock to the St John's Centre and Church Street. 2 large cinemas, including one 8-screen, and SU film nights. SU bars and good pubs in abundance. Excellent town clubs.

40% students from Liverpool, high North West intake. Ugly racism minimal, sexism more blatant but still minimal. SU always on lookout for either. Typical student – science/beer/rugby or humanities/trendy/politics – wide range!

Easy to get attached to Liverpool which is a vibrant and exciting city despite what the media says.

Pauper notes

Accommodation: Poly accommodation in city centre called Cathedral campus, excellent standard only five minutes from SU building. **Drink:** Places: Casablanca, Haigh Building. Brews: Higsons, Stones, Whitbread. **Eats:** On campus: The Venue and wine bar in the Haigh Building, various site canteens. **Ents:** On campus: Haigh Building, wine bar. **Sports:** Everton Sports Centre, Kirkby Sports Centre, Toxteth Sports Centre. **Travel:** Campus travel shop. **Work:** In city – bars to clothes shops!

Alumni (Editors' pick)

Debbie Greenwood, Martin Offiah, Julian Cope, Con McConville.

LIVERPOOL POLY

See Liverpool John Moores University

GET HOLD OF THE PROSPECTUSES

LIVERPOOL UNIVERSITY

University of Liverpool, PO Box 147, Liverpool L69 3BX
(051 794 2000) Map A, D6

Student enquiries: Schools Relations Office

Main study areas – as in What to Study section: *(First degree):* Accountancy, African studies, American studies, archaeology, architecture, biochemistry, biology, biotechnology, botany, business studies, chemistry, civil engineering, classics, communication studies, computing, dentistry, economics, education, electrical & electronic engineering, English, environmental science, geography, geology, history, Latin American studies, law, marine technology, mathematical studies, mechanical and production engineering, medicine, metallurgy and materials science, microbiology, modern languages, music, Near East and Islamic studies, nursing studies, pharmacology, philosophy, physics, physiology, politics and government, professions allied to medicine (PAMs), psychology, public administration, religious studies & theology, social policy and social welfare, sociology, veterinary studies, zoology. *Also:* women's studies.

European Community: Number of students learning an EC language or spending time in another EC country, not known. Approved Erasmus programme.

Application: UCCA for 1993 start, UCAS thereafter. **Founded:** 1881. **Main awards:** BA, BArch, BCom, BDS, BEd, BEng, BMus, BSc, BVSc, LLB, MBChB. **Awarding body:** Liverpool University. **Site:** 85 acres in city centre. **Accommodation:** 2,300 places in halls of residence on two sites near campus. Approx cost: £1,536 pa. First years normally live in if accepted through main UCCA system (except students living at home); 600 places in self-catering accommodation. Approx cost: £1,119 for 39 weeks. **Library:** 2 main libraries; 1,100,000 books; 1,100 study places. **Other learning resources:** Computing service. **Welfare:** 2 student counsellors, student health service, chaplains.

Duration of first degree course(s) or equivalent: 3 years and 4 years; **others:** 5 years (medicine), 5+ years (dentistry) **Total first degree students 1991/92:** 8,800 **Overseas students:** 4% **Mature students:** 15% **Male/female ratio:** 4:3 **Total full-time students 1990/91:** 7,370 **Postgraduate students:** 1,600 **Tuition fees for 1992/93 (first degrees):** Home: £1,855 (classroom), £2,770 (lab/studio), £4,985 (clinical); Overseas: £5,000 (classroom), £6,630 (lab/studio), £12,210 (clinical).

What it's like

With the main campus less than half a mile from the city centre, student life in Liverpool is amongst the best you'll find anywhere. The city has exciting politics, an extremely varied culture and people are warm and friendly.

The Guild of Students is the same as a Union (the name is different for historical reasons) and has second largest SU building in Europe. It houses a cafe, dining room, 1,500 capacity hall for major acts (like James, EMF, or Carter USM), a snooker room, table tennis and four bars. The Guild has a welfare department which is run partly by students, partly by staff including a brand new welfare advice centre. The majority of first years get place in halls of residence, which offer quite good accommodation – but food isn't haute cuisine! Living out is the option for most second years onwards and there is still adequate housing to choose from which is fairly cheap.

Socially, there is so much to do, loads of nightclubs, at least eight of which are tuned to student tastes (honestly!). 3 theatres – the Everyman, Playhouse and Unity, an opera house and the Royal Court – a 2,200 capacity live music venue. Add to that the Philharmonic Orchestra, the Tate and other galleries, Bluecoat Film Theatre and 3 other cinemas and you've got a city that offers plenty for everyone.

CAN'T FIND WHAT YOU'RE LOOKING FOR? USE THE INDEX!

Pauper notes

Accommodation: University accommodation for married students limited. Much less accommodation than before – harder to find places. **Drink:** Guild's good for cheap drink, many Yorkshire beers. **Eats:** Vegetarian restaurants and food shops in town. Good food on campus – but rarely open at awkward hours. **Ents:** Many new and 'up and coming' groups play, two films in Guild every week. **Sports:** Excellent university sports centre and swimming pool – free to students. **Hardship funds:** Student Support Fund unfortunately cannot offer hardship funds. **Travel:** Lime St. Station can get you anywhere, most places direct. Student travel shop in Guild offers many reductions. **Work:** Average opportunities for restaurant/bar work during term off campus. Little full-time holiday work.

More info?

Get students' Alternative Prospectus.
Enquiries to Steve Roden, Schools Liaison Officer (051 794 4141).

Informal name

Liverpool Uni.

Buzz-words

Guild (the Students Union); most people refer to its buildings as 'the union'.

Alumni (Editors' pick)

Hugh Jones (marathon runner), Judge O'Donoghue, Dr N Cossons (Director of Science Museum), Joan Rodgers (opera singer), Patricia Routledge (actress), Jon Snow (ITN reporter), Robert Kilroy-Silk (TV presenter), Steve Coppell (footballer), Dame Rose Heilbron (Lady High Court Judge), Phil Redmond (TV writer – Brookside), Lord Evans of Claughton, Graham Leach (BBC reporter), Ann Leuchars (TV newscaster), Maeve Sherlock (ex NUS President).

LONDON BIBLE COLLEGE

London Bible College, Green Lane, Northwood, Middlesex HA6 2UW (0923 826061) Map A, F8

Student enquiries: Academic Dean

Main study areas – as in What to Study section: *(First degree):* Philosophy, religious studies and theology.

European Community: No students learn an EC language or spend time in another EC country.

Application: Direct. **Academic features:** MA in aspects of biblical interpretation. Part-time MA. **Special features:** Number of subjects available unusual in theology degrees, eg sociology of religion, missiology, linguistics and pastoral theology. **Largest fields of study:** Theology. **Founded:** 1943. **Main awards:** BA. **Awarding body:** Brunel University. **Site:** 9 acres. **Access:** Metropolitan line to Northwood; by road off A404 Rickmansworth Road. **Accommodation:**

Places in halls of residence (priority to first year, overseas and mature students). Rent: 50% in accommodation where rent controlled by college. **Library:** 23,000 volumes, 100 periodicals, 100 study places. **Welfare:** Doctor, chaplain. **Hardship funds:** Some bursary funds available. **Careers:** Information, advice and informal placement service. **Amenities:** Bookshop on college premises; games room, tennis courts. **Employment:** Christian ministry, overseas missionary work, and RE teaching.

Duration of first degree course(s) or equivalent: 3 years **Total first degree students 1991/92:** 150 **Overseas students:** 55 **Mature students:** 120 **Male/ female ratio:** 3:2 **Teaching staff: full-time:** 16 **part-time:** 4 **Total full-time students 1991/92:** 226 **Postgraduate students:** 20 **Tuition fees for 1992/93 (first degrees):** £2,430.

What it's like

An international, interdenominational college community of 286 students from all 5 continents and 30 countries (including Eastern European) all over the world. 25% students from overseas. The residential suburb of Northwood, 30 mins from central London on the Metropolitan Line, and conveniently close to the M25.

One third of the students live on campus in pleasant, spacious grounds; onsite facilities include a launderette, football pitch, tennis courts, a well-stocked bookshop (some publishers' discounts), a student-run stationery shop, and a modern student centre with TV lounges, kitchen, music rooms, table-tennis room, weightlifting equipment, a pool table and changing rooms. (No accommodation for married students on campus.) Average age of students is 28.9, almost all have some work-experience before coming here. Good academic standard, excellent library facilities.

High motivation and commitment characteristic of students, who in addition to academic work perform some practical Christian activity each week, either in a local church or in a college team – drama, open-air evangelism, schools work, producing videos, preaching, children's work etc. Some practical assignments – sometimes overseas eg Southern Africa, Asia, Europe (E & W) – during the vacations, especially in summer.

Student–faculty relations are excellent; student reps sit on faculty and Governors' Board meetings.

Practical training department gives guidance for future work; students enter a wide range of full-time Christian (or secular) employment, several each year go on to post-graduate studies.

Overall the college has a very warm and friendly atmosphere, mutual respect and encouragement, groups of approx 15 act as support groups and provide forum for social events. Confidential counselling available.

Pauper notes

Accommodation: Not cheap in the area. Often local church members will rent rooms to LBC students at below the market rate. (College has a list of digs.) **Eats:** College meals very good; offers vegetarian food. Few cheap eating places in the area; non-resident students can sometimes get an evening meal in college free if a resident student is absent. **Ents:** Evening concerts by students several times a year. **Sports:** Soccer, rugger, cricket, volleyball teams; local squash courts and swimming pools have cheap afternoon slots which students can use. **Hardship funds:** College provides bursary funds to help with tuition fees (mostly for overseas students); students run a gift-fund to help day-to-day expenses if needed. **Travel:** Normal student discount schemes apply.

More info?

Enquiries to Anna Lapage (0923 825904).

CAN'T FIND WHAT YOU'RE LOOKING FOR? USE THE INDEX!

Informal name:
LBC.

Alumni (Editors' pick)
Os Guinness, Derek Tidball, Clive Calver, Terry Virgo.

LONDON BUSINESS SCHOOL

London Business School, Sussex Place, Regent's Park, London NW1 4SA (071 262 5050) Map E B1

Student enquiries: Information Officer, MBA Programme

Main study area: *(Not at first degree):* Business and management studies. Languages, including German, French, Japanese, Spanish as electives.

European Community: 40% students learn an EC language; 80 students spend 1 term in another EC country. Large number of exchange links in EC. Approved Erasmus programme.

Special feature: Postgraduate only.

Application: Direct. **Academic features:** Case teaching, group assignments, visiting speakers, student consultancy projects, assessed class participation, videos. Formal exams at the end of every term. 40% of MBA programme go on exchange for a term with eg Amos Tuck, Berkeley, NYU, Chicago, Wharton, Cornell, North Western, MIT, British Columbia, Sao Paulo, Barcelona, Cologne, HEC (Paris), ISA (Paris), Milan and Japan. Significant number of visiting professors from abroad as teaching exchange – lots of guest speakers. **Special features:** Research centres include economic forecasting, small business, finance and business strategy. **Founded:** 1965. **Main awards:** MBA, MSc, PhD. **Awarding body:** University of London. **Site:** Located at Regent's Park in an elegant Nash terrace overlooking the lake. 1 site. **Access:** Tube: Baker Street; road via Regent's Park. **Accommodation:** Many students have their own homes – which they often share with other MBAs. **Library:** Corporate library includes comprehensive stock of annual reports and extel cards – online data base facilities available. **Other facilities:** Computer room; close-circuit TV centre. **Careers:** Information, advice and placement service. **Employment:** Merchant banking, finance, strategy consulting, manufacturing. **Welfare:** None on site – Lisson Grove Health Centre nearby. Students have personal faculty advisers if needed. **Hardship funds:** Some scholarships and prizes are awarded by the school but no hardship fund. **Amenities:** Close to West End. **Sports:** On campus – gym and aerobics room; off campus – squash at Lord's cricket ground, soccer in the park.

Duration of courses: 21 months full-time; 30 months part-time; **others:** PhD 3 years plus **Male/female ratio:** 4:1 **Teaching staff: full-time:** 106 **research:** 50 **Total full-time students 1992/93:** 400 MBA **Tuition fees, 1992/93:** £9,100.

What it's like

A Nash terrace overlooking Regent's Park lake. An elegant facade hiding very well-equipped lecture theatres and computer rooms. Supposedly the best business library in Europe. On campus bedrooms small but functional. A well catered, subsidised restaurant and cafeteria, two bars and wine bar.

Fun but incredibly demanding. Not for the faint hearted. Students typically put in 80–90 hour weeks during the first year; weekends and evenings off are rare! A top business school; both students and faculty totally motivated and committed, with a strong career ethos among students, although not as deadly competitive as their Harvard counterparts. (These ones put high emphasis on team-work and group experience.)

A very international school; 60% students come from 35 different countries; international focus in curriculum as well as in various international projects and overseas field visits. An international exchange programme with students spending a term in other top business schools in continental Europe, Asia, North and South America: and probably highest percentage of women (30%) among world's best business schools.

Average graduating salary – £35,000 plus, although they will swear that is **not** why they are here! An exclusive, multi-layer admissions procedure with tough entry requirements, including minimum of two years' professional experience. Early application is essential as places on the programme are quickly filled. Low drop-out rate and few overall failures. Part-timers on MBA programme are usually sponsored and take three years to complete course.

Minimum of 4 years work experience needed. Average age of entrants is 28. Almost everyone is there to work hard – not for fun.

A great emphasis is put on high quality of teaching and research. Most have had experience in business schools abroad and close links with industry/commerce through their consulting activities. Students are very vocal if they are not getting value for time or money and formal assessments by students of lecturers each term.

Football, aerobics and squash are popular and there's a lot of swimming, jogging and boating around Regent's Park. LBS has own gymnasium.

Careers clubs (such as finance and consultancy) are well attended and enable students to mix freely with guest speakers. Students' association non-political, purely administrative and social. 3 or 4 large events per term, well attended, especially the summer ball!

Pauper notes

Clearing banks offer low interest loans to UK students which most take up. All students earn money for their project works and in summer vacations.

Alumni (Editors' pick)

John Egan (Chairman, Jaguar Cars), Iain Vallance (BT Chairman), Matthew Carrington MP, Sir Ronald Deering (Post Office Chairman), Brian Taylor (CEO Glaxo), Richard Greenbury (MD Marks & Spencer).

LONDON COLLEGE OF DANCE

London College of Dance, 10 Linden Road, Bedford MK40 2DA (0234 213331) Map A F7

Student enquiries: The Principal

Main study areas – as in What to Study section: *(First degree):* Dance.

European Community: 40% students learn an EC language (French and Italian).

Application: Direct. **Academic features:** BA Dance, with classical ballet and American modern dance as core discipline. Both degree and diploma courses focus on dance as a performing art open to talented male and female students seeking an intensive training in a variety of dance styles. Strong emphasis is placed on developing the individual dance potential of each student. In-depth preparation in the theory and practice of teaching is integrated with the practical dance studies in the diploma course. **Special features:** Most members of the vocational staff have had careers in ballet, contemporary companies and the musical theatre. **Largest fields of study:** Dance studies and teacher training. **Founded:** 1944 as London College of Dance and Drama; became London College of Dance in 1986. **Main awards:** BA, Diploma. **Awarding body:** University of Buckingham (BA), London College of Dance (Diploma). **Site:** In a pleasant part of Bedford. **Access:** British Rail (direct Bedford/St Pancras line); easy access to M1 and A1. **Accommodation:** Private accommodation in town. **Library:** Own library on site. **Specialist collections:** London College dance collection. **Careers:** Prospective employers apply direct to the college. Students are placed in these posts. **Employment:** Teachers of dancing; administration and theatrical performers. **Welfare:** Welfare and counselling facilities available to college students. **Amenities:** All SU facilities plus private college events. **Sports:** Sports facilities available via Bedford College.

Duration of first degree course(s) or equivalent: 3 years **Total number of degree and diploma students 1991/92:** 90 **Overseas students:** 10 **Mature students:** 5 **Male/female ratio:** 1:8 **Teaching staff: full-time:** 9 **part-time:** 12 **Total full-time students 1991/92:** 91 **Postgraduate students:** 2 **Tuition fees for 1992/93 (first degrees):** £5,100.

What it's like

It's quite small, at present only 95 students, but that's how it's intended and leads to a friendly and intimate atmosphere. LCD is not a stage school as such. It is primarily a teaching college although students are taught to such a high standard that a dancing career is often possible.

Good student/teacher ratio. Music staff particularly helpful and very talented and often compose pieces for students to use in teaching practice etc. Small number of mature students seem to fit in quite well.

Very well equipped. Spacious mirrored studios with sprung floors, air-conditioning, piano and music system. The Bowen-West Community Theatre is a stone's throw away, for student performances and many other shows.

Attractive setting in leafy square only ten minutes walk from the hustle and bustle of the town centre. SU small, organises parties and represents students at meetings with staff but no facilities/bars (we use Bedford College bar and disco).

Courses are particularly good. The work load is quite hard and there's continuous assessment. It's widely recognised that the college produces good teachers. Most students look upon dance as a form of bringing enjoyment to anyone, whatever age or ability, and strive to keep it a recognised, worthwhile art form. LCD involves a lot of hard work but it's also a lot of fun.

Hilary Needham

Pauper notes

Accommodation: No halls of residence; plenty of outside accommodation at decent prices but inspect it personally. **Drink:** Bedford College bar (reduced prices), good local pubs (including country ones if you have a car), one popular nightclub and one popular but expensive disco pub. **Eats:** College meals; subsidised tuck shop. Plenty of local choice, especially pizzas and Indian. Pubs also (close to college) have good, cheap meals. **Ents:** Bedford College disco; own Xmas/Halloween parties. **Sports:** Use of Bedford College sports facilities, public swimming pool, squash courts, leisure complex. **Hardship funds:** SU helps people in great difficulty. **Travel:** Usually by bike – but good bus services. SU cards for reduced coach travel. **Work:** Part-time jobs, including teaching dance.

Informal name:
LCD.

GET HOLD OF THE PROSPECTUSES

LONDON COLLEGE OF FASHION

The London College of Fashion, 20 John Princes Street, London W1M 0BJ (071 629 9401) Map E, B2

Student enquiries: School Administrator

Main study areas *(First degree):* Fashion, textiles.

European Community: 100% first degree students take EC language as part of course and 5% spend 6 months or more in another EC country. No formal exchange links with EC universities/colleges.

Application: PCAS for 1993 start, UCAS thereafter, ADAR or direct. **Structural features:** College of the London Institute. **Academic features:** 4-year sandwich course, related to fashion industry with emphasis on product development. **Special features:** Largest UK college covering whole of fashion industry. **Largest field of study:** Fashion design, clothing technology, fashion promotion and journalism, theatre studies. **Founded:** 1910; became part of London Institute 1986. **Main awards:** BA. **Awarding body:** Open University. **Site:** 4 sites in Central London. **Access:** Oxford Circus underground station and bus terminus. **Accommodation:** 2 halls of residence. Approx cost: £65.50 pw (b&b and evening meal); £45 pw (b&b only). Help from student accommodation officer in finding private accommodation. Approx cost: £45–£50 pw. **Rent:** 10% in accommodation where rent controlled by London Institute. **Library:** 40,000 books, 250 periodicals, 157 study places. Specialist fashion collection of unique interest. **Other learning facilities:** Textile lab, computer centres, all specialist fashion facilities. **Careers:** Information and advice service; specialist college placements officer. **Employment:** Fashion and clothing industry, UK and overseas. **Welfare:** Student services, advice and counselling. **Special facilities:** Creche available through London Institute (not on site). **Hardship funds:** Access funds, charities and specialist bursaries. **Amenities:** All cultural facilities of central London. **Sporting facilities:** None on site.

Duration of first degree course (or equivalent): 4 years. **Total first degree students 1991/92:** 212 **BEd students:** None. **Overseas students:** 5 **Mature students:** 4 **Male/female ratio:** 1:4 **Teaching staff: full-time:** 10 **part-time:** 5 **Total full-time students 1991/92:** 212 **Postgraduate students:** 0 **Tuition fees for 1992/93 (first degree):** Home: £2,770; Overseas: £5,950.

LONDON COLLEGE OF MUSIC

London College of Music at Thames Valley University, St Mary's Road, Ealing, London W5 5RF (081 231 2364; Fax: 081 566 1353) Map D, A2

Student enquiries: Warden

Main study areas – as in What to Study section: *(First degree):* Music.

European Community: 20% students learn an EC language; French, German and Italian available to all singing students and to other undergraduates if places available. No students spend time in another EC country.

Application: Direct. **Academic features:** 3-year undergraduate academic/performing course; post-graduate course for singers, accompanists and in writing music for films & TV; Music-in-Schools Programme. Music theatre class. **Special features:** Emphasis on wide range of relationships within whole music industry, and with community needs. Audio Visual Unit. **Largest fields of study:** Music. **Founded:** 1887, became part of Thames Valley University in 1991. **Main awards:** GLCM; Bmus, FLCM; Certificate of Advanced Study. **Awarding body:** Thames Valley University. **Site:** West London. **Access:** South Ealing and/or Ealing Broadway (BR and Tube) station. **Accommodation:** Hostels etc, apply to Warden. **Library:** c30,000 volumes, study places. **Welfare:** Doctor. **Careers:** Information and advice service. **Employment:** Teaching music, and all areas of music industry.

Duration of first degree course(s) or equivalent: 3 years **Others:** 1 year **Total first degree students 1991/92:** 106 **Overseas students:** 18 **Male/female ratio:** 1:2 **Teaching staff: part-time:** 60 **Total full-time students 1991/92:** 141 **Postgraduate students:** 30 **Tuition fees for 1992/93 (first degrees):** Home: £2,770; Overseas: £5,319.

Alumni (Editors' pick)

David Caddick (musical director, Royal Shakespeare Co), Martin Ellerby (composer), Raphael Terroni (pianist), Edward Blakeman (flautist, Head of Woodwind, LCM, Radio 3 presenter), John Treleaven (international tenor).

LONDON COLLEGE OF PRINTING

London College of Printing and Distributive Trades
(1) **Elephant & Castle, London SE1 6SB (071 735 8484)** Map E, D4
(2) **30 Leicester Square, London WC2H 7LE (071 735 8484)**
(3) **Herbal House, Back Hill, Clerkenwell, London EC1R 5EN**
    (071 735 8484)

Student enquiries: College Administrator

Main study areas – as in What to Study section: *(First degree):* Art and design, business studies. *Also:* Film and video, journalism, printing, publishing, radio journalism, retail management.

European Community: Number of students learning an EC language or spending time in another EC country, not known.

Application: PCAS for 1993 start, UCAS thereafter, ADAR or direct. **Structural Feature:** Part of the London Institute. **Founded:** 1990, ex London College of Printing and London College for the Distributive Trades. **Main awards:** BA. **Awarding body:** Open University. **Site:** Elephant & Castle; annexes at Clerkenwell and Leicester Square. **Access:** Elephant & Castle underground station (Bakerloo and Northern lines). **Academic features:** BA media production and design is 4 year sandwich course with periods of 3 months spent in industry. Part-time BA in book production. Degrees in film and video, and photography, journalism and media studies. Postgraduate diplomas in radio journalism and scriptwriting. **Accommodation:** 115 places in hall (reserved for students residing outside Greater London). **Library:** Main library at Elephant & Castle, 100,000 volumes in total, 580 periodicals, 70 study places; textbook reference collection. **Specialist collections:** History of the book. **Welfare:** Literature concerning welfare and accommodation is available; majority of advice facilities. **Careers:** Information and advice service. **Amenities:** Resident bookseller; students through membership of college library have access to all major art centres in London. **Employment:** Design and printing; photography, film and television industries; teaching; journalism; publishing; retailing.

Duration of first degree course(s) or equivalent: 3 years **Total first degree**

students 1992/93: 660 **Male/female ratio:** 3:2 **Teaching staff: full-time:** 270; **Total full-time students 1991/92:** 2,384 **Postgraduate students:** 102 **Tuition fees 1992/93 (first degrees):** Home: £2,770; Overseas: £5,250–£5,950.

What it's like
We don't know.

It's a new college by combining the London College of Printing with the College of Distributive Trades. The London College of Printing was a leading graphic arts college that evolved into teaching all-round media and communications; the College of Distributive Trades provided business studies/management courses for the distributive trade and broadened its interests to embrace food, travel, tourism, fashion and furnishing.

So on the face of it an odd marriage. The new college spreads over three sites. Two do first degree work: Elephant and Castle and Clerkenwell (Back Hill); the other, Leicester Square, does not. Printing management, graphic and also media design degree students are at the Elephant site; retail management first degree students at Clerkenwell. How the new college works for undergraduates will doubtless emerge in due course. Meanwhile we would be glad to hear from current students.

London student accommodation is scarce, difficult to find and expensive. The college does not accept any responsibility for finding student accommodation but tries to help students find somewhere to live. We would be glad to hear from students about accommodation, food, drink, etc.

Alumni (Editors' pick)
Trevor McDonald (newsreader), Neville Brody (designer 'City Limits', 'The Face'), Dave King (Arts Council Designer).

LONDON CONTEMPORARY DANCE SCHOOL

London Contemporary Dance School, 16 Flaxman Terrace, London WC1H 9AT (071 387 0152; Fax 071 383 4851) Map E, C1

Student enquiries: School Office

Main study areas – as in What to Study section: *(First degree):* Dance.

European Community: No students learn an EC language or spend time in another EC country.

Application: Direct, followed by practical auditions (some auditions held regionally and overseas). Candidates for degree courses must pass the dance audition, although academic qualifications are not necessarily required. **Academic features:** Parts of the degree course are taught in liaison with other institutions including Central Saint Martins School of Art and Design and Guildhall School of Music and Drama. **Special features:** Part of Contemporary Dance Trust which also embraces a performing company, London Contemporary Dance Theatre (also The Place Theatre, The Video Place and The Data Place). Leading centre for training professional dancers in contemporary dance and choreography in Europe. **Founded:** 1966. **Main awards:** BA. **Awarding body:** Kent University. **Site:** Off Euston Road. **Access:** King's Cross and Euston tube and BR stations, buses. **Accommodation:** Student services officer gives advice on accommodation. **Library:** Extensive collection of dance, arts, psychology and related studies in addition to a general collection. **Welfare:** School osteopath visits weekly, school doctor in NW1. Resident full-time student services officer.

CAN'T FIND WHAT YOU'RE LOOKING FOR? USE THE INDEX!

Hardship funds: For 2nd and 3rd year students only – competitive scholarship/ endowment fund. **Careers:** Personal contact service for jobs. **Amenities:** 9 dance studios, music studio, The Place Theatre for student workshop performances; restaurant, student common rooms. **Employment:** Combination of performance and teaching, further studies.

Duration of first degree course(s) or equivalent: 3 years; **others:** 1 year **Total first degree students 1991/92:** 80 **Overseas students:** 55 **Mature students:** 25 **Male/female ratio:** 1:7 **Teaching staff: full-time:** 15 **part-time:** 6 **Total full-time students 1991/92:** 155 **Postgraduate students:** 4 **Tuition fees for 1992/93 (first degrees):** £6,750.

What it's like

Large building in central London known as The Place. It's home of The Place theatre and London Contemporary Dance Theatre, a professional dance company. Euston and King's Cross stations only a few minutes' walk away. Hostels very close. Helpful student adviser/counsellor. 25% recruitment from overseas. School library open throughout college hours. SU very active, particularly in providing link between students and admin. Each year given different tutor and every group covers different topics throughout year. Degree course consists of practical work with theoretical contexts of dance, and is for professional dance students only. Generally, employment for successful candidates good, but training very rigorous and suited to dedicated dancers wishing for professional careers, prepared to work extremely hard. Drop-out rate 30%–40%.

Pauper notes

Eats: Restaurant, cafeteria for school and theatre on premises (caters for vegetarians) – cheap, healthy food. Also many local cafes. **Drink:** Local pub Mabels just across road. **Work:** Some available in theatre, theatre bar and in admin for students. Occasional teaching and demonstrating work.

Alumni (Editors' pick)

Richard Alston, Siobhain Davies, Robert North, Anthony Van Laast, Linda Gibbs, Ian Spink; entire performing members of London Contemporary Dance Theatre.

LONDON GUILDHALL UNIVERSITY

London Guildhall University, 117 Houndsditch, London EC3A 7BU (tel: 071 320 1000; fax: 071 320 1337) Map E, D2

Student enquiries: Admissions Officer, India House, 139 Minories, London EC3N 1NL

Main study areas – as in What to Study section: *(First degree):* Accountancy, art & design, business studies, communication studies, computing, economics, environmental studies, geography, information technology, law, mathematical studies, modern languages, politics and government, psychology, sociology. *Also:* furniture design, interior design, music technology, silversmithing and jewellery.

European Community: 10% first degree students take EC language as part of course and ½% spend 6 months or more in another EC country. French, German and Spanish may be studied *ab initio*. All three languages may be incorporated in degrees across all faculties. Formal exchange links with 13 EC universities/colleges: in Denmark (2); Eire (1); France (4); Germany (3); Italy

(1); Spain (2) – all open to non-language specialists who are suitably qualified linguistically. Dual qualification open to geography students – BA/BSc and Licence de Geographie from University of Caen. Approved Erasmus programme 1992. Also involved in Comett and Tempus.

Application: PCAS for 1993 start, UCAS thereafter; ADAR for art design. **Special features:** Credit Accumulation System (CAS) enables students to specialise from the beginning of their course, or delay final decisions until the end of year 1; includes flexible modular programme. Positive attitude to mature and local students with disabilities through equal opportunities, access and community liaison programmes. **Academic features:** New BSc restoration and conservation. **Founded:** 1992 as university. Previously City of London Poly, formed 1970 from City of London College, Sir John Cass College and, in 1990, London College of Furniture. **Main awards:** BA, BSc. **Awarding body:** London Guildhall University. **Site:** 8 teaching sites in City and Whitechapel. **Access:** British Rail, London Docklands Railway, underground and bus services. **Accommodation:** 380 self-contained flats; 99 in hall of residence. Approx cost 1992/93: £36–£44 pw (accommodation only), £62 pw (in hall). **Library:** 6 libraries; 260,000 volumes in total, 2,000 periodicals, 700 study places, slide collections (art), map collection. **Specialist collections:** Fawcett Library (women's studies). **Other learning facilities:** Computer centre, TV studio, language laboratories, GIS. **Welfare:** Student counsellors; chaplain; full-time nurse; AIDS adviser; access to solicitor and doctor. **Hardship funds:** Modest annual fund to help students facing financial hardship during their course, as well as government access funds. **Careers:** Information, advice and placement. **Amenities:** Refectories or snack bars on all teaching sites; SU building with bars, TV and games rooms, discos etc. **Sporting facilities:** Gymnasium, activities room, 2 fitness rooms with multigym facilities, 2 outdoor sports grounds.

Duration of first degree course(s) or equivalent: 3 years; **others:** 4 years (sandwich and language) **Total first degree students 1991/92:** 4,517 **Overseas students:** 440 **Mature students:** 1,492 **Male/female ratio:** 1:1 **Teaching staff: full-time:** 346 **part-time:** 52 **Total full-time students 1991/92:** 5,476 **Postgraduate students:** 510 **Tuition fees for 1992/93 (first degrees):** Home: £760 (if no grant), £1,855 (classroom), £2,770 (lab/studio); Overseas: £5,250.

What it's like

Spread over 8 sites in the City and East End; facilities such as libraries split and shared. Sites quite cramped, many facilities inadequate. Accommodation a problem, as it is everywhere in London. No students live less than 2 miles away, most commute much further. Housing expensive, many live with their parents. Distances affect academic and social life but Queen Mary and Westfield (Mile End) and Goldsmiths (New Cross) nearby and their students regularly visit the university.

Academically, standards are high; most staff are amenable and good teachers. Reasonable teaching and workload. Most subjects excellent. The modular degree scheme, probably the most flexible in the country, very popular. Proximity to the City ensures business and law related courses have the best teachers and are highly respected. Work placement and study abroad arranged. Student population contains high proportion of mature students; also American and EC students. No typical student. SU executive turning away from political infighting towards student needs. SU welfare officer full-time. Particular priorities are welfare, integration with local community, educational issues, student representation and active involvement in the academic affairs of the university at all levels. Campaigns eg for Gay rights; against racism in the East End, sexism. SU supports political societies across the political spectrum; a musicians' society with its own rehearsal facilities, and sports including caving, surfing and subaqua societies. 3 Union bars, 3 shops, a bookshop and 2 (healthy!) fast food bars. Active ents programme. Visiting bands have recently included: Carter the

Unstoppable Sex Machine, Store Roses, Revenge, Slow Bongo Floyd, Magic Mushroom Band. Also regular sports club discos – Friday Frenzys – and ents four times a week.

Pauper notes

Accommodation: University provides about 500 places. Otherwise accommodation can be difficult to find and expensive. Try areas like Leytonstone, Plaistow and the Isle of Dogs first; be prepared to have to live further afield. Start looking early. **Drinks:** 3 excellent SU bars (Fairholt House, Moorgate and Commercial Road); both the City and East End abound in pubs famous and infamous. Most, though, are expensive. SU bar in Fairholt House cheapest in city. **Eats:** Most university sites have refectories providing cheap, canteen-type food. SU runs coffee bar (Moorgate) and Buttery/Snack Bar (Fairholt). Also plenty of snackbars in the City, and lots of good 'ethnic' food (try Bloom's kosher takeaways and curries at Dee Daas and Nazrul, both in Brick Lane). **Ents:** SU provides full programme of Ents – something most days. Not just bands, but film shows, cabaret and outings. Fairholt SU building – cabaret etc. Also a lot of cheap, varied and different cultural activities in the East End, and the West End is only half an hour away. **Sports:** Full-time sports organiser and many clubs – but not great facilities. 2 university sports grounds – Chigwell, Essex, and Grove Park, Kent – both quite a long way. However, Wapping Sports Centre, and Sedgwick Centre are close by. **Hardship funds:** University hardship fund; access fund; small amounts from other university-linked sources. **Travel:** Central location makes travel quite easy. All sites close to tube and buses. Also near Liverpool St, Fenchurch St and Moorgate BR termini, Docklands light railway. **Work:** Plenty of work in 10 student trading shops and bars. Quite a lot of summer and weekend work in Central London. East End is unemployment blackspot.

Informal name

City Poly, *pro tem.*

Alumni (Editors pick)

Kate Hoey MP (Vauxhall); Jim Moir *alias* Vic Reeves (entertainer).

LONDON HOSPITAL

London Hospital Medical College, Turner Street, London E1 2AD (071 377 7000) Map D, C2

Student enquiries: Sub-dean for Admissions

Main study areas – as in What to Study section: *(First degree):* Dentistry, medicine.

European Community: Number of students learning an EC language or spending time in another EC country, not known. Exchanges with Denmark (Copenhagen Dental School), Eire (Cork), France (Rennes). Approved Erasmus programme; expanding involvement in Erasmus and becoming involved in Tempus scheme.

Application: UCCA for 1993 start, UCAS thereafter. **Structural features:** Part of London University. **Academic features:** Full medical course for MBBS degree; 23 pa students join clinical course after pre-clinical studies at eg Oxbridge. **Special features:** Pre-clinical teaching centred on Queen Mary and Westfield College. **Largest fields of study:** Medicine, dentistry. **Founded:** 1785; joined London University in 1900. **Main awards:** MBBS, BDS, BSc. **Awarding body:**

London University. **Site:** Off Whitechapel Road. **Access:** Whitechapel under-ground station. **Accommodation:** 235 places in halls, 93 flat/bedsitter places (preference given to those living outside London and with domestic or personal difficulties). Approx cost: £210–£245 pm halls, £70–£100 pm flats. **Rent:** 26% in accommodation where rent controlled by university. **Library:** Main library + several departmental libraries; 32,000 volumes, 350 periodicals, 100 study places. **Welfare:** Doctor, dentist, FPA, psychiatrist, chaplain. **Hardship funds:** Funds available in cases of special financial hardship. **Amenities:** SU building providing common rooms, shop with supply of textbooks. **Sporting facilities:** Athletics ground at Hale End; rowing club with boats at Chiswick, own cottage and boats at Burnham-on-Crouch. **Employment:** College provides approx 120 pre-registration house appointments.

Duration of first degree course(s) or equivalent: 5 years (MBBS); **others:** Intercalated BSc 1 year **Total first degree clinical students 1991/92:** 588 **Overseas students:** 28 **Mature students:** 196 **Male/female ratio:** 3:2 **Teaching staff: full-time:** 196 **part-time:** 131 **Total full-time students 1991/92:** 733 plus 218 part-time **Postgraduate students:** 363 **Tuition fees for 1992/93 (first degrees):** £755 (if no grant), £2,770 (pre-clinical), £4,985 (clinical); Overseas: £7,500 (pre-clinical), £13,600 (clinical).

What it's like

Noted for its friendly, informal atmosphere. London Hospital serves the East End community (including Dockland Yuppies) which provides an enormous variety of patients and disease for the clinical student. The oldest English medical school. Clubs Union, a union of 39 vibrant clubs, from bridge to drama (6–7 productions per year); sailing (own cottage at Burnham); various sporting clubs based at beautiful grounds at Hale End. Student life centres around SU building and lively bar in the hospital and college campus. Medical, dental and paramedical students and staff mix at discos, live concerts, balls and cabaret.

Famous Rag Week raises more than £60,000 in one week by entertaining and shocking the London public. Whitechapel tube (across the road) allows rapid access to the West End. East also has much to offer, street markets eg Brick Lane, cheap Indian restaurants, Greenwich and docklands. As far as pubs are concerned the East End 'lock-in' is not a thing of the past.

New and imaginative modular curriculum; preclinical students taught with Barts students at Queen Mary & Westfield, Mile End. About ⅓ of students are offered an intercalated BSc in their 3rd or 4th year.

A number of overseas and mature students. Selection Committee looks for students with interests and achievements outside medicine.

Come and join us!!

Pauper notes

Accommodation: 1st year accommodated in college hostel, Pooley Hall (QMW + LHMC) or intercollegiate halls. Clinical students eligible for cheap college housing. Many students in cheap council housing or college. Rent approx £15.00 pw. **Drink:** Club Union cheap and friendly. Traditional East End pubs with friendly atmosphere, eg The Lord Rodneys Head, Prospect of Whitby, Falcon & Firkin, Blind Beggar (of Kray Brothers fame). **Eats:** Good canteen food for around £1, Carlo's Cafe opposite the hospital for the true fry up. Many cheap Indian and Chinese restaurants as well as Pizza One, Pancake Two in Bethnal Green. **Ents:** Union events, usually once a week, bands, cabaret, discos etc plus 4 balls per year, rag week and fresher's fortnight. Cheap high quality off campus theatre, cinema. **Sports:** Hospital swimming pool, excellent sports clubs and grounds. City squash club and tennis courts. **Hardship funds:** Access fund available to all students. College helps. **Travel:** Some elective scholarships. STA Travel down the road. **Work:** Bar work, portering/agency nursing, drug and research trials, library attendants.

CAN'T FIND WHAT YOU'RE LOOKING FOR? USE THE INDEX!

More info?
Get students' Alternative Prospectus.
Enquiries to Simon Bott (071 377 7641).

Informal name:
LHMC; The London.

Buzz-words:
Mile End Run (beer race along Mile End Road).

Alumni (Editors' pick)
Frederick Treaves (physician to John Merrick 'The Elephant Man'), Dr
Barnardo.

LONDON INTERNATIONAL FILM SCHOOL

**London International Film School, 24 Shelton Street, London
WC2H 9HP (071 836 9642) Map E, C2**

Student enquiries: The Administrator

Main study areas: Film studies.

European Community: An international student body with increasing numbers
from Europe. Opportunities exist to make films in EC (and other) countries in
the final term.

Application: Direct. (Courses begin each term). **Academic features:** Writing
drama for film scripts. Directing workshops. Practical sessions with actors.
Extra-mural course in music for films. Time equally divided between practical
film-making and formal tuition. **Special features:** Acceptance depends upon
educational achievement and examples of relevant work, eg photography, previous films, video, film scripts, story boards; experience in film, TV or related
areas taken into account. **Main fields:** include script writing, direction, camera
work, art direction, sound recording and editing. **Founded:** 1956 as London
School of Film Technique. **Main awards:** Diploma, Certificate. **Awarding body:**
LIFS. **Site:** Covent Garden area. **Access:** Covent Garden tube station. **Accommodation:** None. **Library:** Technical books, periodicals, 17 study places.
Welfare: National health services nearby. **Careers:** Graduates are automatically
acceptable as members of BECTU, with access to vacancy registers covering
film and TV. **Amenities:** Two viewing theatres, two fully equipped studios,
video rehearsal studio, comprehensively equipped camera, sound and editing
departments. Equipment includes 35 mm Panavision, 16 mm and 35 mm
Arriflex cameras, Nagra sound recorders, Steenbeck and Magnasync editing
tables, video camera and editing equipment. LIFS Film Society run by students. SU plays large part in school. **Employment:** Film industry.

Duration of courses: 2 years **Total students (all full-time) 1991/92:** 120
Overseas students: 95 **Mature students:** 9 **Male/female ratio:** 4:1 **Teaching
staff: full-time:** 27 **part-time:** 24 **Tuition fees for 1992/93 (first degrees):**
£10,599.

What it's like

Housed in a former banana warehouse on the corner of Shelton and Langley
Streets, Covent Garden, right in the heart of the theatrical and film world.
Easily accessible by tube (Covent Garden, Leicester Square, Tottenham Court
Road) and various bus routes into West End. No students live in. Some are on

grants, mainly from governments of their countries of origin. Many UK students on discretionary LEA grants. School runs as co-op/charity by students, SU, administration and board of governors. One governor is student. SU lately gaining more influence. Film society very active. Various events have included sneak previews of 'Cafe Fears' and 'The Playboys' whose respective film makers were present and open to questions, and John Ward, the renowned Steadycam operator demonstrated steadycam and his work on *Robin Hood Prince of Thieves*. Main student meeting place school coffee shop. Covent Garden area abounds in pubs, cafes, coffee shops. LIFS has high reputation for technical expertise. Course primarily technical – how to make film, use cameras, sound equipment, edit, dub sound, build sets, lighting, directing etc. Quality of lectures variable. LIFS diploma has high local and international standing; diploma recognised by ACTT and membership automatically available to graduates who find work. About 140 students including 40 different nationalities. Women and ethnic minorities now particularly encouraged to apply. Students passionate about film: some want glittering prizes, others want monk-like quiet. LIFS graduate should be able to handle any aspect of film-making, in 16 mm or 35 mm, as well as the principles of video. Most work in film/TV industry. Many students would like to see more money put into equipment and facilities. Recent student work appearing in numerous festivals.

Pauper notes

This is an expensive school in an expensive area.
Drink: The Two Brewers, Seven Dials, Café Boheme, Bar Sol Ona, Freuds; various places around Covent Garden. **Eats:** Cheapest but not worst: LIFS coffee shop; various places around Covent Garden and Soho. **Ents:** Film society evening screenings; numerous cinemas and theatres around London.

Informal name

LIFS.

Alumni (Editors' pick)

Arnold Wesker, Mark Forstater, George Cosmatos, John Irvin, Franc Roddam, Les Blair, Mike Leigh, Michael Mann, Mark Kasdan, Don Boyd, Bill Douglas, Horace Ove, Simon Lourish, Tak Fujomoto.

LONDON UNIVERSITY

University of London, Senate House, Malet Street, London WC1E 7HU (071 636 8000) Maps D and E

Main study areas – as in What to Study section: *(First degree):* All study areas are taught in London University – see the entries for the constituent colleges.

European Community: 5% first degree students learn an EC language as part of their course, 1–2% spend 6 months or more in another EC country. Most schools of the university have well equipped language courses for those wishing to develop their language skills. Course unit structure allows languages to be taken as part of a degree course, particularly in the early years. A number of degree courses involve a year abroad, eg chemical engineering with a year in France, offered by Imperial College and University College. Several schools offer European Studies degrees. University is involved in over 100 Erasmus programmes, including almost all major European universities. Member of UNICA (universities in capital cities in Europe) which is considering the special problems of studying in a capital city.

CAN'T FIND WHAT YOU'RE LOOKING FOR? USE THE INDEX!

Academic features: Colleges, Schools, Institutes and London's unique external system offer over 900 undergraduate and 400 Master's degree courses, and many Diploma and Certificate courses via the Birkbeck College/Centre for Extra-Mural Studies. London offers the biggest choice of courses in the UK. Science degrees on modular system. **Special features:** Don't bother about the university's bureaucratic structure but concentrate on its separate teaching institutions, all of which select their first degree students themselves.

You can look up the following profiles:
Birkbeck College
British Institute in Paris
Charing Cross and Westminster (Medical School)
Courtauld Institute
Goldsmiths' College
Heythrop College
Imperial College
Institute of Archaeology (part of University College)
Institute of Education
Jews' College
King's College Hospital (School of Medicine and Dentistry; part of King's College)
King's College London
London Hospital (Medical College)
LSE (London School of Economics)
Queen Mary & Westfield (College)
Royal Free (Hospital School of Medicine)
Royal Holloway and Bedford (New College)
Royal Veterinary College
St Bartholomew's (Hospital Medical School)
St George's (Hospital Medical School)
St Mary's Hospital Medical School (part of Imperial College)
School of Pharmacy
Slade (School of Fine Art; part of University College)
SOAS (School of Oriental and African Studies)
SSEES (School of Slavonic & East European Studies)
UMDS (United Medical and Dental Schools)
University College London
Wye College

Application: Mostly through UCCA/UCAS. See individual profiles. **Awarding body:** London University. **External students:** The University will register and examine eligible students world-wide who are not registered at schools/colleges of London University. First degrees in divinity, arts subjects, laws, music (examinations in UK only), economics. Diplomas include education, public administration. Higher degrees restricted to London graduates. Enquiries to Secretary for External Students, at Senate House. **Site:** Bloomsbury, including 35 acres between British Museum and Euston Road, on which University College, Birkbeck, SOAS and Institute of Education are located. Almost all London University schools/colleges are within a radius of 3 miles of this site except for Royal Holloway and Bedford New College in Surrey and Wye College in Kent. **Central Library:** 1,300,000 books and 5,500 current periodicals; particularly strong in the humanities. Many distinguished specialist collections. Schools/colleges have own libraries. **Students' union:** University union (ULU) is in Malet Street. Most colleges have their own unions. Athletic ground in Motspur Park, Surrey; university boathouse at Hartington Road, Chiswick; sailing clubhouse at Welsh Harp Reservoir, Brent. **Welfare:** Central Institutions Health Service for the Institute of Education, Birkbeck College, SSEES, School of Pharmacy and SOAS. Other colleges make their own arrangements. **Hardship funds:** Vice-Chancellor's discretionary fund: unforeseen hardship **after** commencing a course of study. **Accommodation:** Enquiries to Accommo-

"... *private accommodation scarce and very expensive*"

dation Officer, Room 5, Senate House, Malet Street, London WC1E 7HU (071 636 2818). 37% in accommodation where rent controlled by university (varies from college to college). **Other learning resources:** The University has an excellent computer centre, one of two national facilities providing resources to university users all over the UK. It also has its own specialist collections and galleries as well being within easy reach of all London's museums and galleries.

Duration of first degree course(s) or equivalent: 3 years; **others:** medicine/dentistry 5 years **Total first degree students 1991/92:** 38,665 (full-time); 3,395 (part-time); **total BEd students:** 115 **Overseas students:** 8,765 **Mature students:** 3,980 (full-time), 2,228 (part-time) **Male/female ratio:** 1:1 **Teaching staff: full-time:** approx 9,913 **part-time:** 1,219 **Total full-time students 1991/92:** 64,744 **External students:** 16,807 **Extra-mural students:** 21,599 **Postgraduate students:** 12,727 full-time; 9,957 part-time **Tuition fees:** each college sets own fee.

Alumni (Editors' pick)

Rt Rev George Carey, Archibishop of Canterbury (King's), Edwina Curry (LSE), Bob Geldof (honorary graduate), Robert Mugabe, President of Zimbabwe (external system), David Owen (UMDS), Jonathon Ross (SSEES).

LOUGHBOROUGH COLLEGE OF ART AND DESIGN

Loughborough College of Art and Design, Radmoor, Loughborough, Leics LE11 3BT (0509 261515; Fax 0509 265515) Map A, E6

Student enquiries: Admissions Officer

Main study areas – as in What to Study section: *(First degree):* Art & design.

European Community: Some students learn an EC language and spend time in

CAN'T FIND WHAT YOU'RE LOOKING FOR? USE THE INDEX!

another EC country. Exchange links with Spain (University of Granada; fine art undergraduate numbers increasing); informal exchanges of art and design undergraduates with various schools of fine and applied arts in EC art colleges. Proposed links with France and Germany. Approved Erasmus programme 1992/93. Credit rating of courses underway to facilitate exchanges.

Application: ADAR. **Academic developments:** Flexible course arrangements. **Largest fields of study:** Textiles. **Founded:** 1958. **Main awards:** BA. **Awarding body:** Nottingham Trent University. **Accommodation:** 277 places in halls. Rent: 50% in accommodation where rent controlled by college. **Library:** 50,000 volumes, 400 periodicals, 150 study places; extensive slide collection and video library. **Other learning resources:** Artists' books collection, IT facilities. **Welfare:** Chaplain, counselling service. **Careers:** Information and advice service. **Amenities:** Bookshop in SU building. **Sporting facilities:** Swimming pool, running track, sports hall, sports pitches, squash courts, etc available to all students as members of the Loughborough SU.

Duration of first degree course(s) or equivalent: 3 years **Total first degree students 1991/92:** 541 **Overseas students:** 8 **Mature students:** 45 **Male/female ratio:** 2:3 **Teaching staff: full-time:** 49 **part-time:** 60 **Total full-time students 1991/92:** 888 **Tuition fees for 1992/93 (first degrees):** Home: £2,770; Overseas: £6,300.

What it's like

Shares campus with FE college, across the road from university. 10 minutes' walk from town centre. Usual facilities of a medium sized market town. Markets every Thursday and Saturday. Small shopping precinct off the market place. Equidistant from Nottingham, Derby and Leicester. SU one of the largest, over 12,500 student members from university, FE college, college of art and design and RNIB vocational college. Building three minutes' walk from college with bars, travel bureau, fast food outlet, 7 shops and a nursery.

Many students are local. Courses are strongly vocational for practising artists, industrial designers and teachers.

12 halls of residence for approximately 180 students. Large houses on main roads into town. Some are mixed; none are self-catering. Most have kitchens for supplementary cooking. Refectory adjacent to main site, less than a minute's walk from all the buildings. Students not in hall either live in lodgings or at home.

Own student-run internal affairs committee to promote and represent the general interests of students and to keep them informed on academic matters.

Pauper notes

Accommodation: No married quarters in residential accommodation but available for tenants in town houses. Certain student streets in area – small ghettos, good atmosphere – always near a pub!! **Drink:** 5 bars in SU building – drinks up to 20p cheaper. Regular drinks promotions, guest beers and a wide selection of soft drinks. A number of student pubs in town. Marstons Pedigree (real ale) still popular local beer. **Eats:** College refectory. SU fast food outlet, baked potatoes, burgers, pizzas. Wine/bottle lounge bar in SU provides traditional and continental cuisine. A number of curry houses, Chinese and fish and chip shops in town. One vegetarian restaurant and a number of whole-food shops. Town has a profusion of supermarkets. **Ents:** Excellent – lot of top groups tour here; regular films, SU discos. Drama on university campus as well as in town and adjacent cities. Three nightclubs within area which offer student rates, also a six screen cinema. **Sports:** Best college/university facilities in country. Need look no further. University facilities open to SU Club members. **Hardship funds:** £50 interest free loans from SU; nursery funding assistance, sliding scale of charges based on parental income. **Travel:** Travel bureau recently opened in SU –

provides cheap holidays for all students – can buy rail, coach and air tickets over the counter. Close to M1 for hitching. **Work:** Some part-time work available in the bars and shops plus occasional casual work and some work in the town's bars.

LOUGHBOROUGH UNIVERSITY

Loughborough University of Technology, Loughborough, Leics LE11 3TU (0509 263171) Map A, E6

Student enquiries: Senior Assistant Registrar (Admissions)

Main study areas – as in What to Study section: *(First degree):* Accountancy, aeronautical engineering, building services engineering, building engineering, business studies, chemical engineering, chemistry, civil engineering, communication studies, computing, dance, design, industrial design, drama, economics, education, electrical & electronic engineering, English, environmental science, European studies, geography, information technology, library & information studies, mathematical studies, mechanical and production engineering, metallurgy and materials science, modern languages, physics, physiology, politics and government, psychology, quantity surveying, social policy and social welfare, sociology. *Also:* Building technology, design, food science, operational research, physical education, recreation management, sports studies, systems engineering, surveying, transport studies, urban studies.

European Community: 5% first degree students take EC language (French/German) as part of course and 1% spend 6 months or more in another EC country. Formal exchange links with 29 EC universities/colleges (number increasing): Belgium (6; economics, design, PE, social sciences, business studies); Denmark (3; civil and mechanical engineering); Eire (1; civil engineering); France (3; European studies); Germany (5; economics, European studies, business studies, mechanical engineering); Greece (1; mechanical engineering); Italy (4; chemical and mechanical engineering, polymer technology); Netherlands (4; design, social sciences, business studies, recreation management); Spain (2; civil engineering, recreation management). Approved Erasmus programmes. Increased language teaching planned (70% students currently have access to French/German as part of their degree) and more opportunities to combine languages with other subjects.

Application: UCCA for 1993 start, UCAS thereafter. **Academic features:** New courses in recreation management; retail management; communications and media studies; physics and mathematics, mechanical and optical engineering, chemical engineering with food and bioprocessing and polymer technology and engineering, systems engineering, manufacturing and computing. **Special features:** Industrial professors (3-year appointments, several hours' teaching per week): chemical engineering, H A Duxbury; economics, J H B Tew; geography, J Sheail; management studies, D Allen; physics, J M Walls; transport technology, G L Wilde. **Largest fields of study:** English, Mechanical Engineering, civil engineering. **Main awards:** BA, BSc, BEng, MEng. **Awarding body:** Loughborough University. **Site:** 216 acres about a mile from town centre. **Access:** 1 mile from M1; 1½ miles from railway station; 8 miles from East Midlands airport; bus service between town and campus. **Accommodation:** 4,000 places. Rent: 80% in accommodation where rent controlled by university. **Library:** Pilkington Library has 600,000 volumes, 700 study places. **Other learning facilities:** Computer Centre. **Structural features:** Wide range of specialised centres and institutes including those in polymer technology and materials engineering; water engineering and development; computer-human interface research; parallel algorithm research, landscape ecology; coaching and recreation management; consumer ergonomics; surface science and technology. **Welfare:** Medical services, counsellors, chaplains, wardens. **Careers:** Active careers service. **Amenities:** Purpose-built SU building with 4 bars, wine/cocktail lounge bar, shop, travel office, banks, bookshop, performance area; day nursery/playgroup; student arts centre with darkroom, studio equipment, record and cassette library; associated music centre; drama studio with workshop; campus radio station. **Sporting facilities:** Excellent sports facilities including 3 sports halls, 2 gymnasia, 2 swimming pools, 7 squash courts, 2 floodlit all-weather areas, all-weather athletics stadium and tennis courts, dance studio, numerous major games-playing pitches.

Duration of first degree course(s) or equivalent: 3 or 4 years **others:** 4 or 5 years **Total first degree students 1991/92:** 5,895 **Overseas students:** 800 **Mature students:** 9% **Male/female ratio:** 2:1 **Teaching staff: full-time:** 510 **part-time:** 46 **Total full-time students 1991/92:** 6,892 **Postgraduate students:** 1,926 **Tuition fees for 1992/93 (first degrees): Home:** £755 (if no grant), £1,855 (classroom), £2,770 (lab/studio); Overseas: £5,280 (classroom), £6,920 (lab/studio).

What it's like

SU derives membership from 4 constituent student bodies (including university, art college, FE college and RNIB vocational college; 12,000 members in all, 15% overseas, 10% mature, mixture of private, state and comprehensive schools. Many part-time students. 25% university students own cars. Good SU facilities for students with disabilities. New nursery. Accommodation good, mixed; launderettes in SU and on campus. Bike or local bus company's campus service.

SU active. Confidential advice and welfare unit and hardship fund. Union on NME/MM circuits. Students meet easily, SU is centre of activity; good touring bands. Good town/student relations; student community action group. Lots of pubs, theatres (in town and 2 on campus), markets. Most active societies are the athletics union (50+ clubs) and Rag (largest in the country).

Engineering, technology and PE most popular subject areas, still plenty of arts students. Changing course in first year possible; workloads vary, science courses require a lot of time in practicals. Many courses have years abroad or in industry. Assessment through course work, exams and practical. No fixed failure rate. Students are hardworking.

Pauper notes

Accommodation: Halls, many 2nd/3rd year students choose to live-out. Large number of student 'ghettos' – streets that primarily house students. Very few student squats. Little or no accommodation for married students in hall. Finding somewhere in the private sector sometimes difficult. **Drink:** SU cheapest – 5 bars in SU building. Regular promotions and wide selection of wine and soft drinks. Numerous pubs in town. **Eats:** Hall food OK– good vegetarian options. SU food outlets including breakfast bar fastfood restaurant type and pizza, baked potatoes etc. A number of curry houses, Chinese and fish & chip shops in town. One vegetarian restaurant and a number of whole-food shops. Town has a profusion of supermarkets. **Ents:** Excellent – a lot of top groups tour here; regular films in SU, discos. Also Rag and Hall events. Drama on university campus as well as in town and adjacent cities. 3 night clubs in area which offer student rates, also a 6-screen cinema. **Sports:** Best university sporting facilities in country – open to Loughborough Students Athletics Club members. University Athletic Union Champions for a number of years. **Hardship funds:** £50 interest free loans available on delivery of post-dated cheque. Nursery funding assistance available sliding scale of charges based on parental income. **Travel:** ABTA Travel Bureau in SU – provides cheap holidays for students – can buy coach, rail, air tickets over the counter. **Work:** Casual work available at SU, also variety of part-time jobs in shops in town.

GET HOLD OF THE PROSPECTUSES

Alumni (Editors' pick)

Alastair Biggart (Channel Tunnel), Peter Bonfield (ICL), Rob Dickens (British Phonographic Industry), Sebastian Coe, David Moorcroft, Christina Boxer, Danny Nightingale and Steve Scutt, Sue Shoblon, Forbes Robinson, Jack Buckner, Tim Hutchings, Ernie Obeng, Bob Wilson, Tania Rodrigues.

LSE

London School of Economics & Political Science,
University of London, Houghton Street, London WC2A 1AE
(071 405 7686) Map E, C2

Student enquiries: Assistant Registrar (Admissions)

Main study areas – as in What to Study section: *(First degree):* Accountancy, anthropology, computing, economics, geography, history, industrial relations, law, mathematical studies, philosophy, politics and government, psychology, public administration, social policy and social welfare, sociology. *Also:* Actuarial sciences, management.

European Community: 3% first degree students take EC language as part of course and 1% spend 6 months or more in another EC country. Formal exchange links with 15 EC universities/colleges under Erasmus scheme; all open to non-language specialists (some for postgraduates only). Language studies centre provides tuition in English, French, Spanish as part of some degrees or additional courses.

Application: UCCA for 1993 start, UCAS thereafter. **Structural features:** Part of London University. **Academic features:** Unique concentration on economic and social sciences, taught in 15 departments. **Special features:** Numerous visitors attend every academic year. One-year courses for overseas students. **Founded:** 1895, joined London University in 1900. **Main awards:** BA, BSc, BSc(Econ), LLB. **Awarding body:** London University. **Site:** Central London (just off Aldwych). **Access:** Aldwych, Holborn and Temple underground stations; buses. **Accommodation:** Halls and flats to accommodate approx 25% of student body (apply to accommodation office). Approx cost: £47–£60 pw. Rent: approximately 25% students housed in accommodation where rent is under school's control. London University will advise on lodgings. **Library:** British Library of Political and Economic Science is a national collection in field of social science as well as School's working library; 881,000 volumes, 4,600 current periodicals. Teaching library: 31,500 volumes, with additional copies of more important course books; short loan collections of periodicals. Shaw Library: collection of general literature. **Centre of excellence:** Internationally renowned in social sciences. **Welfare:** Doctor, dentist, FPA, psychiatrist, nursing sister, chaplains, women's adviser, disabled students' adviser. **Hardship funds:** LSE 1990's Fund and other funds to help students facing hardship. **Special categories:** Nursery with 24 places. **Careers:** Information and advice service. **Amenities:** SU with restaurant, bar, shop, legal advice centre, newspaper and magazine; facilities of London University union in Malet Street. **Sporting facilities:** Sports grounds at New Malden; circuit-room, squash court and gymnasium on site.

Duration of first degree course(s) or equivalent: 3 or 4 years; **others:** 1 year **Total first degree students 1991/92:** 2,638 **Overseas students:** 2,558 **Mature students:** Large number **Male/female ratio:** 3:2 **Teaching staff: full-time:** 310 **part-time:** c200 **Total full-time students 1991/92:** 4,204 **Postgraduate students:**

CAN'T FIND WHAT YOU'RE LOOKING FOR? USE THE INDEX!

2,336 (incl 716 part-time) **Tuition fees for 1992/93 (first degrees):** Home: £1,855; Overseas: £6,560.

What it's like

Truly unique and cosmopolitan institution. High percentage of overseas and postgraduate students. Buildings lack the grandeur of Oxbridge (basically they are ugly, but lovely warren-like); academic tradition strong. It's an 'international centre of excellence'. Most departments very strong: economics + international relations + government in top three in world, law department one of most radical in UK, social policy, accounting, government and social admin all strong. Virtually all assessment is exam based, no opportunity for September resits (apart from law). Difficult to fail first year but could change soon. SU: bar, cafe and shop and excellent welfare service with specialist advice on money problems and cheapish available housing in London. Politically as stimulating as ever. SU policy decided at weekly UGMs, often of 400 students. Only university in England to hold quorate union meetings regularly. Wide range of political opinions, ferocious debates and fusillades of paper aeroplanes. Students in large departments can find relationships with academics distant. The library is the largest collection of social, economic and political material in Europe: tremendous asset but books are in constant demand, can be hard to get required course texts. Sporting facilities relatively good. Social life based on London facilities, SU bar, societies and also SU politics.

Pauper notes

Accommodation: Poor but trying. Squats all over London. ULU provides accommodation lists + houses; also SU accommodation lists. Only 20% in halls. Accommodation in London always available but often pricey. **Drink:** Cheap places – ULU bar, LSE Three Tuns, Hall Bars. **Eats:** SU cafe – good vegetarian 'Bethnal's' in Bethnal Green, pizza and pasta, reductions for students. 'Pollo's' – Italian, Soho, all fast-food chains. **Ents:** Cinema, Prince Charles, Leicester Sq – £1 all films, UCI Whitelys £3 before 4.00pm – theatres, student standbys particularly RSC + NT. **Bands:** Marquee + ULU, Underworld in Camden, Powerhous in Islington. Hall discos, film soc etc. **Sports:** ULU – swimming pool, LSE: gym + squash courts, tennis courts nearby. Sports ground in New Malden. Senegal Fields – community sports centre, Rotherhithe. The Oasis – Shaftesbury Ave. Gym on campus, playing fields at New Malden, Surrey. **Hardship funds:** SU Hardship fund. School access funds. School student support funds. 'Women's right to choose fund'. **Travel:** Some travel scholarships controlled by School scholarships office. Rail cards, ISIC cards available – STA branch on campus. **Work:** Some casual work in Union – whole of London casual market.

More info?

Get students' Alternative Prospectus.

Alumni (Editors' pick)

Neil Andrews, Fazile Zahir, John Moore, Lord Young, John Tower, John F. Kennedy, Ralph Dahrendorf, Roland Dumas, David Attenborough, Frank Dobson, Clare Francis, Bernard Levin, Robert Kilroy-Silk, Mick Jagger, Pierre Trudeau, Edwina Currie, Maurice Saatchi, Michael Meacher, Ron Moody, Ralph Brown (playwright/actor), B.K. Nehru.

LSU SOUTHAMPTON

LSU College of Higher Education, The Avenue, Southampton SO9 5HB (0703 228761) Map A, E8

Student enquiries: Registrar

Main study areas – as in What to Study section: *(First degree):* Biology, education, English, European studies, geography, history, mathematical studies, modern languages, politics and government, professions allied to medicine (PAMs), religious studies and theology, sociology.

European Community: 15% first degree students take EC language as part of course and 15% spend 6 months or more in another EC country. Formal exchange links with 5 EC universities/colleges in France and Germany.

Application: UCCA for 1993 start, UCAS thereafter. **Academic features:** New BSc podiatry gives eligibility for State-Registered status (joint venture with Wessex Regional Health Authority). **Special features:** Visiting literary figures and lecturers. **Founded:** 1904, by LSU sisters. **Main awards:** BA, BEd, BTh. **Awarding body:** Southampton University. **Site:** Southampton town centre. **Access:** 5 minutes from centre of Southampton. **Accommodation:** 360 places in college houses and hostels. (One third of students home based.) **Library:** 90,000 volumes, 366 periodicals, 142 study places, temporary reference collection. **Welfare:** Doctor, chaplain, nursery school. **Special categories:** RC and ecumenical services. **Careers:** Full advisory service. **Amenities:** SU coffee bar and bar, bookshop on campus, SU, CCTV. **Sporting facilities:** Heated indoor swimming pool, 2 gyms, tennis. **Employment:** Teaching; graduate careers in usual range for BA, BTh students.

Duration of first degree course(s) or equivalent: 3 years; 4 years languages **Total first degree students 1991/92:** 934 **Total BEd students:** 581 **Mature students:** 167 **Male/female ratio:** 3:7 **Teaching staff: full-time:** 67 **part-time:** 2 **Total full-time students 1991/92:** 1,203 **Postgraduate students:** 97 **Tuition fees 1992/93 (first degrees):** Home: £1,855 (classroom), £2,770 (lab), plus £321 for first year only.

What it's like

Compact campus close to train and coach station. Hostel accommodation limited, mostly single rooms – refectory caters for all resident students. Priority given to first and final years. City centre campus means restricted car parking but public transport good. Mainly BEd, but growing number of other courses. Language students take year abroad. Approx 33% mature students on courses. College degrees validated by Southampton University. Personal tutor system works well and builds excellent staff/student relationships. Catholic college, but open to students of all faiths or none. Strong sense of community without being claustrophobic. Professional counselling service available on campus. Good academic reputation but difficult to change course. Careers advice available and well co-ordinated. Media resources centre offers cost price stationery. Audio-visual resources and technician available. Library staff helpful. Students have access to university library. Liaison between university and institute improving especially over sports facilities and events. SU very supportive, union has welfare women's officers. Both offer advice on contraception, but careful due to Catholic nature of college. College clubs and societies growing each year – easy to get involved or establish new clubs. Events run by union but limited by space restriction; good use made of outside venues throughout Southampton. Staff/student social club charges competitive prices, guests must be signed in by a student. Southampton has large student population. Good pubs close to college and student nightclubs. Three theatres all offer student discounts.

Pauper notes

Accommodation: Mostly single rooms in hostels – first and final years only. First years guaranteed hostel accommodation. **Drink:** 2 student only night clubs, number of pubs close to college welcome students. **Eats:** SU coffee bar, good vegetarian food. Refectory OK, bar food or lunchtime. Good selection of restaurants in city. **Ents:** Local pubs put on live bands. Multiplex cinema, annual film festival, 3 theatres. **Sports:** College swimming pool, sports centre

CAN'T FIND WHAT YOU'RE LOOKING FOR? USE THE INDEX!

close by, county cricket ground. **Hardship funds:** College runs access fund. SU offer support and advice. **Travel:** Central campus – good bus and train services. **Work:** Most students do part-time work, but difficult to find. Opportunities in student bar.

More info?

Enquiries to SU President, (0703 226379).

Informal name

LSU.

LUTON COLLEGE

Luton College of Higher Education, Park Square, Luton LU1 3JU and
Putteridge Bury, Hitchin Road, Luton, Beds (0582 34111) Map A, F7

Student enquiries: The Information Officer, Marketing Dept, 75 Castle Street, Luton LU1 3AJ (0582) 401401)

Main study areas – as in What to Study section: *(First degree):* Accountancy, biochemistry, biology, business studies, communication studies, computing, electrical and electronic engineering, English, environmental science, geography, geology, history, information technology, linguistics, law, mechanical and production engineering, modern languages, nursing studies, professions allied to medicine (PAMs), psychology, public administration, social policy and social welfare, sociology. *Also:* Building studies, instrumentation, mapping, Urdu.

European Community: 15% first degree students take EC language as part of course (including building and engineering students) and 7% spend 6 weeks in another EC country. Formal exchange links with EC universities/colleges in Belgium, France and Spain – open to non-language specialists. Approved Erasmus and Tempus programmes. Development of language and exchanges in every faculty.

Application: PCAS for 1993 start, UCAS thereafter. **Main awards:** BSc, BA, LLB. **Awarding body:** Luton College. **Site:** Town centre. Putteridge Bury site 4 miles from main campus. **Access:** 5 mins from M1, bus and railway stations and international airport. **Accommodation:** 200 places in self-catering halls; college managed houses also available via Accommodation Office. Approx cost £32–£45 pw. Rent: 20% in accommodation where rent controlled by college. **Library:** 140,000 volumes, 800 periodicals, 500 study places; microfilm and video facilities. New £3 million library. **Other learning resources:** Computer services: approximately 600 PCs for student use; communication services: TV, video and radio stations. **Welfare:** Senior tutor, personal tutor for each student, doctor, FPA, independent adviser, on-site nurse seconded from local practice. **Careers:** Information and advice service. **Amenities:** College bookshop, closed circuit TV, regional sports centre; Olympic standard swimming pool, library, theatre in Luton, first division soccer. **Employment:** Wide range of careers in science, business and public services.

Duration of first degree course(s) or equivalent: 3 years **Others:** 4 years (sandwich) **Total first degree students 1991/92:** 1,341 **Overseas students:** 282 **Mature students:** 7,185 **Male/female ratio:** 9:5 **Teaching staff: full-time:** 825 **part-time:** 700 **Total full-time students 1991/92:** 4,147 **Postgraduate students:**

533 **Tuition fees for 1992/93 (first degrees):** Home: £1,855 (classroom), £2,770 (lab/studio); Overseas: £5,319.

What it's like

It's got three campuses. Main campus situated at Park Square, right in centre of Luton, next to parish church and Arndale Shopping Centre, which boasts all usual shops and good indoor market. Putteridge Bury campus, four miles away, a magnificent neo-Elizabethan mansion set in very attractive grounds, serves as a management centre. Third campus, next to Dunstable town centre, caters for vocational courses. Student population has increased by 53% over past 3 years and is forecast to increase further over next couple of years.

Main campus is about two minutes (by taxi) from coach and railway stations and about 10 minutes (by taxi) from Luton International Airport. For those wanting excitement and who have money to spend, London is only half an hour away by train.

One hall of residence opposite main campus provides ninety single study bedrooms with shared kitchens. Downs Road provides further sixteen self-catering places. A head tenancy scheme run by college accommodation office provides shared housing for majority of student population, plus large percentage in private sector. Average rent works out between £30 and £35 pw with bills on top usually.

Socially, SU centre of all activities; being cheapest place to drink in town it is always packed out. Union building just revamped, resulting in two bars which sell all usual plus a number of real ales. Within the bar you can play pool, bar billiards, darts, watch television and videos on a large screen and deafen yourself listening to the CD jukebox. Regular discos weekly and a number of live bands every term plus all the usual things that happen within a thriving SU!

In town, Cannon cinema receives all latest releases very quickly; an arts cinema in town library shows unusual but usually brilliant films. Also arts centre near town centre has regular programme of live music, comics, exhibitions etc. A number of nightclubs in town; more popular have student night every week.

All usual fast food joints and pizza places scattered through town; excellent Chinese and Indian restaurants; odd Italian and French restaurants, usually hidden up some obscure little side street.

Contrary to popular belief, Luton is a fun place to go to college. The typical Luton student can be described as conscientious and hard-working but when necessary can go through a metamorphic change and become the ultimate party animal.

Pauper notes

Accommodation: Mostly average – same price, varying standard. Private accommodation generally poor and over priced; new head tenancy scheme helps but still needs a lot of work. **Drink:** SU bar cheap, good atmosphere and friendly. Pubs generally don't cater for students but the Cock good local. **Eats:** Two refectories on campus: Church Street fast food; Vicarage Street, good food but vegetarian provision not good. Plenty of chip shops, kebab, Chinese and Indian. Good veggie curry houses Leagrave Road. **Ents:** 1 cinema and town library has good cheap plays and films. SU is main source of ents but more student support needed. **Sports:** Local sports facilities backed by college contacts. Within radius of 3 miles: 3 sports centres and baths and college playing fields. **Hardship funds:** Access fund (government); college welfare section. **Travel:** Mostly walking; poor college transport; local transport good but expensive. Get a coach and rail card. Hitching fairly easy on M1. **Work:** Mostly pub/bar work, stewarding in SU etc.

Alumni (Editors' pick)

Paul Young (pop singer), Sir David Plaistow (Chairman of Vickers).

CAN'T FIND WHAT YOU'RE LOOKING FOR? USE THE INDEX!

MANADON

The Royal Naval Engineering College, Manadon, Plymouth PL5 3AQ
(0752 553740 Ext 81213) Map A, C9

Student enquiries: Academic Registrar

Main study areas: *(First degree):* Engineering including aeronautical engineering, electrical and electronic engineering, marine technology, mechanical engineering, strategic studies.

European Community: No students learn an EC language or spend time in another EC country.

Special features: 3 year full-time residential engineering degree course (covering mechanical, electrical and control engineering), followed by up to a year's post-degree application training. New 2-year BA in maritime defence, management and technology. **Entry conditions:** Mainly RN engineering officers but also open to officers of the other armed services, and civilians sponsored by LEAs. **Founded:** 1880. **Main awards:** BEng, BA. **Awarding body:** Plymouth University. **Site:** Campus at Manadon, Plymouth. **Access:** Via Crownhill, 4 miles north of Plymouth city centre (regular bus services). **Accommodation:** 400 places in single rooms. Rent: 40% in accommodation where rent controlled by college. **Library:** 70,000 volumes, 500 periodicals, 90 study places. Microfilm and microfiche reader/printers, video cassette players for publications in non-book format. **Welfare:** Medical and dental facilities on site. Strong tradition of pastoral care. **Amenities:** Bank; sundries shop; theatre/cinema. **Sporting facilities:** Open air swimming pool; squash courts; full range of sporting facilities with gymnasium, excellent grounds and hard hockey pitch; recreational facilities covering a wide range of subsidised activities, including off-shore sailing.

Duration of first degree course(s) or equivalent: 3 years **other:** 2 years (BA) **Total first degree students 1991/92:** 210 **Overseas students:** 20 **Male/female ratio:** 25:1 **Teaching staff: full-time:** 70 **Total full-time students 1991/92:** 400 **Postgraduate students:** 20 **Tuition fees, first degrees, 1991/92:** £2,650.

What it's like

Set in 100 acres of wooded grounds between the Dartmoor National Park and the City of Plymouth. The high academic standard and low failure rate are as a result of a well structured course, regular assessments and excellent student/tutor ratio. The BEng course has been running for five years and its flexibility enables the course to take account of the changes in engineering. The structure of the degree is such that the first and second years are lecture/tutorial intensive with the third year based around individual projects, undertaken in the well equipped labs. A powerful mainframe computer and the VAX systems provide software to complement many of the subjects run in the college. An 11-week workshop course runs in conjunction with the degree to provide engineering application training as required by the Engineering Council for registration. BA degree course in management and defence studies is also available.

All first year students live in the officers' mess, with the equivalent facilities of a good students' union, where accommodation, food and facilities are provided well within the students' means. There are frequent, well attended social events at the college, including the more traditional naval occasions. Many social clubs also run including sporting, theatrical, political and musical.

Staff and students mix socially both in the mess and in the many sports the college caters for. Tennis/squash courts, playing fields, all weather astroturf pitch, 9-hole golf course, swimming pool and multigym are all available within the college. Sailing, rowing, flying and riding are all available through the college at little or no extra cost.

Plymouth, because of its location and size offers many facilities normally only available in much larger cities; these include cinemas, excellent theatre, concert

GET HOLD OF THE PROSPECTUSES

hall and leisure complex, dry ski slope, busy night life and Dartmoor nearby. The Barbican is particularly popular with its character pubs and restaurants set in the historic port of Plymouth. Bus services are good as are the road and rail links into the city.

The majority of the students are Royal Naval officers with varied social and academic backgrounds, but civilian students are welcomed and enjoy all the facilities on an equal basis. This contributes to a well-balanced, friendly professional atmosphere.

Pauper notes

Accommodation: There is ample rented accommodation on campus and in Plymouth at reasonable rates. **Drink:** Manadon bars are busy and inexpensive. Plymouth and Dartmoor also have a wide range of historic ale houses and pubs. **Eats:** All meals are catered for on campus at good rates and there is a large selection of restaurants/pubs in Plymouth to suit all tastes. **Ents:** There are frequent social gatherings on campus. Plymouth Theatre Royal and Drum Theatre are easily accessible. New concert and leisure complex opened with ice rink, leisure pools and restaurants. **Sports:** All sports and outdoor activities are catered for at any level and all at minimal cost. **Travel:** Ferry service Plymouth–France, Channel Islands, Spain. **Work:** Holiday resort – summer work in pubs, shops etc.

Informal name:

RNEC.

MANCHESTER BUSINESS SCHOOL

Manchester Business School, Booth Street West, Manchester M15 6PB (061 275 6311) Map A, D6

This is a postgraduate institution.

Student enquiries: Admissions Officer, MBA Office

Main study areas – as in What to Study section: *(Not at first degree):* Business Studies.

European Community: 80% students take EC language as part of course (French, German, Italian and Spanish available in MBA). Formal exchange links with 6 EC universities/colleges in France, Italy, Netherlands and Spain.

Application: Direct. **Special features:** Postgraduate only. Manchester Business School is Faculty of Business Administration of Manchester University. MBA course combines management theory and practice leading in the second year to consultancy-type projects within organisations. Doctoral programme involves one year of taught courses followed by a research project leading to the thesis. **Founded:** 1965. **Academic features:** 2-year MBA, 1-year Diploma in Business Administration and 3-year doctoral programme in business administration – all postgraduate and all available on part-time basis. Part-time Master in Business Management post-experience course. **Main awards:** MBA, PhD, Diploma in Business Administration, Master in Business Management. **Awarding body:** Manchester University. **Site:** University area of Manchester Education Precinct, 1 mile from city centre. **Access:** Regular bus service from most parts of the city. **Accommodation:** No accommodation within the school for graduates; advice from the university accommodation office. **Library:** 30,000 volumes, 800 journals, over 100 databases, newsclippings and annual report files. **Other learning facilities:** Advanced computing facilities; commercial information services. **Welfare:**

WANT TO HELP WITH THE NEXT EDITION – SEE PAGE 76

Emergency doctor, psychiatrist, chaplain, solicitor. **Careers:** career development centre. **Amenities:** University sports centre nearby (swimming pool, sauna, squash, etc). **Employment:** International commerce, finance, consultancy, marketing, line management (for case histories of graduates see prospectus).

Male/female ratio: 5:1 **Teaching staff: full-time:** 55 **Total full-time students 1991/92:** 300 **Total part-time students 1991/92:** 140 **Doctoral students:** 70 **Tuition fees for 1992/93:** Home: £7,500; Overseas: £9,000.

".... its all about pursuit of Mammon"

M B A
IN MEMORIAM
1976-82
REDUNDANT
BANKRUPT

What it's like

Emphasis on putting theory into practice; use of projects as a major teaching tool, with less emphasis on more traditional exam and case study approach. Formal training in all the basic aspects of management, but the 'MBS project' dominates course. Subject matter varies but working with groups of fellow students is always required. This can be rewarding or frustrating – sometimes both, and teaches you how to rely on other people in pressurised situations. Strong individualists who find it difficult to work in teams have a tough time. Students are **all** postgraduate; from a wide range of backgrounds with degrees ranging from medieval English literature to banking. Most have had significant work experience varying from being a diplomat in Peking to being a small businessman. Two years with this body of students is a great source of learning. Courses require mental stamina and considerable personal commitment; the rewards in terms of personal achievement and learning within a group environment cannot be denied. Good chance of getting on the international exchange programme, to spend one term at a prestigious business school in the USA, Europe or Japan. MBS international club is affiliated to a network of European business school student clubs.

Pauper notes

Drink: MBS club non-profitmaking (Newcastle Bitter). **Eats:** Cooked lunch cheap. On the Eighth Day for vegetarian. **Ents:** University Theatre, postgrad film society, Royal Exchange Theatre and Space Capsule in Old Cotton Exchange, Halle Orchestra, Palace Theatre (Grand Opera and Ballet), Royal Northern College of Music, just across the road. Peak District close at hand, and sailing at nearby Tatton Mere. **Sports:** MacDougall Centre (plus swimming pool) within walking distance. **Work:** Almost all take on summer jobs with UK and overseas companies, as a basis for a dissertation.

GET HOLD OF THE PROSPECTUSES

More info?

Get students' Alternative Prospectus.

Alumni (Editors' pick)

Joe Matthews (managing director, Adamson-Butterley), Terence Riorden (managing director, Benrose Ltd), Andrew Slinn (general manager for Europe – Readicut International), Chris Kirkland (business development executive, Burmah Oil), Tim O'Brian (project manager, Norcros), James Ross (chief executive, Cable and Wireless), John Ward (president of Midland Montagu, America).

MANCHESTER METROPOLITAN UNIVERSITY

The Manchester Metropolitan University, All Saints, Manchester M15 6BH (061 247 2000; fax 061 236 7383) Map A, D6

Student enquiries: Academic Registrar

Main study areas – as in What to Study section: *(First degree):* Accountancy, architecture, art & design, biochemistry, biology, business studies, chemistry, computing, drama, economics, education, electrical & electronic engineering, English, environmental studies, European studies, fine arts, geography, history, hotel & catering management, information technology, law, library & information studies, mathematical studies, mechanical & production engineering, metallurgy and materials science, microbiology, modern languages, nursing studies, philosophy, physics, physiology, politics and government, psychology, public administration, social policy and social welfare, sociology, speech sciences. *Also:* Film studies, international studies, landscape design.

European Community: 18% first degree students take EC language as part of course and 11% spend 6 months or more in another EC country. Formal exchange links with 21 EC universities/colleges in France (8, 2 open to non-language specialists); Germany (9, 2 open to non-language specialists); Spain (4, 3 open to non-language specialists). 30 approved Erasmus programmes 1992/93. Courses with EC links include international hotel management; business in Europe (with Université de Savoie, France; Fachhochschule Bochum, Germany; University 'G D'Annunzio' Csede Pescara, Italy; Universidad de Murcia, Spain); international economic studies (with university of Caen). 2,000 students expected to be taking a language as part of their course by 1994. Language tuition available to specialist language students (of which German or Spanish may be studied from scratch); combined with another subject, eg international hotel management, LLB with French/German/Spanish (some of which lead to a French/German/Spanish qualification as well as the degree); on most courses, languages at different levels can be included as accredited elective unit.

Application: PCAS for 1993 start, UCAS thereafter; ADAR for art and design. **Special features:** Some transfers possible between HND/HD and parallel degree courses for good students. **Founded:** 1992, as a university; previously Manchester Poly, founded 1970. **Main awards:** BA, BEd, BSc, BEng, LLB. **Awarding body:** Manchester Metropolitan University. **Site:** In or near city centre, except for Didsbury site (6 miles away), Hollings (3 miles) and Elizabeth Gaskell (2 miles). **Access:** Regular bus service to Didsbury, Hollings and Elizabeth Gaskell sites. **Accommodation:** 1,430 places in halls (90% for first year students). Accommodation office helps with flats, bedsits, lodgings and council flats. Approx cost: catered hall £58 pw, self-catered hall £38 pw, full board/lodging £45 pw, private self-contained flat £30–35 pw (excl heating/lighting). **Library:** 6 libraries, total of 750,000 volumes, 3,500 periodicals, 1,600 study places. **Specialist collections:** Including book design, children's literature 1870–1930, local collections. **Other**

learning facilities: Supermini computer system. **Welfare:** Counsellors, chaplains, educational adviser, learning skills adviser, nurse. Doctors (day emergencies only), FPA and nursery shared with Manchester University. All students required to register with local GP. Legal advice available from solicitors via SU. **Special categories:** Some accommodation for physically handicapped students in halls. **Careers:** Information and advice. **Amenities:** Horniman Theatre, art galleries and studios. SU building including bar, restaurant, shop, launderette and games room. **Sporting facilities:** Excellent sports facilities, including gymnasia, sports halls, tennis and squash courts, weight training and swimming pool. **Employment:** Public service, industry, commerce and professions.

Duration of first degree course(s) or equivalent: 3 years; **others:** 4 years (sandwich); up to 7 years (part-time) **Total first degree students 1991/92:** 11,800; **BEd students:** 932 **Overseas students:** 274 **Mature students:** 2,238 **Male/female ratio:** 5:6 **Teaching staff: full-time:** 948 **part-time:** 600 **Total full-time students 1991/92:** 13,613 **Postgraduate students:** 2,721 **Tuition fees for 1992/93 (first degrees):** Home: £1,855 (classroom), £2,770 (lab/studio); Overseas: £4,950 (£5,400 if paid in instalments).

What it's like

Split site, spread over 6 miles. Main site in middle of Manchester, 200 yards from Manchester University, UMIST and the Royal Northern College of Music. It's got approximately 18,000 students: mixed backgrounds, races, religions, nearly 51% mature students. SU facilities on 5 sites, main purpose built building on main site. SU runs 6 bars, 3 catering outlets, 6 shops, 2 launderettes, 1 bank and travel service, many machine services and socials and events of all sorts. Manchester is an active and popular city with highest student population anywhere in Europe, so caters for most tastes. City has lot to offer but is ideally situated for trips to countryside. Many specialised and interesting courses. Union active.

Pauper notes

Accommodation: Even more difficult this year – rents higher, no longer eligible for housing benefit – students are beginning to move into accommodation they would have rejected previously because of their lack of funds. **Drink:** Trendy: Dry 201, Archies, Flea & Firkin, Red Lion – Withington, Queen of Hearts – Fallowfield, the Didsbury Dozen (well known pub crawl), The Barleycorn – West Didsbury, The Beech and Dog and Trumpet – Chorlton. **Eats:** Rusholme for Asian food – vegetarian: Pie in the Sky (Withington), Greens, 8th Day, Billies (Chorlton). Good and cheap: Howling Smith Cafe, Basta Pasta, Corner House and Lime Tree Cafe. **Ents:** Weekly films, disco, gigs, bands, fashion show, comedy nights – all in main poly SU building. **Sports:** Moss Side Centre, Chorlton – swimming/badminton; Withington – karate, sauna, weightlifting, turkish bath, swimming and Victoria Baths; the poly's own All Saints Centre. **Hardship Funds:** Some available; contact welfare office or student services. **Travel:** Buses expensive – buy 'clipper cards' or use a bike whenever possible. **Work:** Bar work, fast food chains, supermarkets, waiting, waitressing, washing-up, security (in uni).

Alumni (Editors' pick)

L S Lowry (painter), Ossie Clark (fashion designer), Julie Walters (actress), Bryan Robson (footballer) Mick Hucknall (lead singer of 'Simply Red').

MANCHESTER POLY

See Manchester Metropolitan University

MANCHESTER UNIVERSITY

University of Manchester, Manchester M13 9PL (061 275 2000)
Map A, D6

Student enquiries: The Registrar

Main study areas – as in What to Study section: *(First degree):* Accountancy, aeronautical engineering, American studies, anatomy, anthropology, archaeology, architecture, biochemistry, biology, business studies, chemistry, civil engineering, classics, computing, dentistry, drama, economics, education, electrical & electronic engineering, English, environmental science, European studies, fine arts, geography, geology, history, information technology, Latin American studies, law, linguistics, mathematical studies, mechanical and production engineering, medicine, metallurgy and materials science, microbiology, modern languages, music, Near East and Islamic studies, nursing studies, pharmacology, pharmacy, philosophy, physics, physiology, politics and government, professions allied to medicine (PAMs), psychology, public administration, religious studies and theology, social policy and social welfare, sociology, speech sciences, strategic studies, town and country planning, zoology. *Also:* Hispanic studies, neuroscience, Russian studies.

European Community: Number of students learning an EC language or spending time in another EC country, not known. Approved Erasmus programme.

Application: UCCA for 1993 start, UCAS thereafter. **Special features:** Jodrell Bank Radio Telescope; University Theatre, Science Park, Manchester Museum, Whitworth Art Gallery. Lindsay String Quartet in residence. International Development Centre; Joint Centre for European Studies. **Largest fields of study:** Science and technology. **Founded:** 1851, charter granted in 1903. **Main awards:** BA, BA(Accg & Law), BA(Econ), BSc, BScBEng, BScMEng, BSocSci, BDS, BEd, BNurs, LLB, MBChB, MusB. **Awarding body:** Manchester University. **Site:** Centre of Manchester Education Precinct. **Access:** Bus. **Accommodation:** 8,880 places in halls, flats and self catering accommodation (all single first year students accommodated). Approx cost: £855–£1,820. **Library:** John Rylands University library, over 3 million volumes, 8,000 periodicals, 650 study places, course books on reference. Also over 1 million mss and 800,000 microform titles. **Specialist collections:** Charters, early printed and rare books, manuscripts, military documents, archives (eg of Manchester Guardian). **Centres of excellence:** University Library, Nuffield radio astronomy laboratories at Jodrell Bank, department of computer science, department of audiology and education of the deaf. **Welfare:** Central academic advisory service, student health service, SU welfare office, inter-denominational chapel, SU creche. **Careers:** Information, advice and placement service. **Amenities:** SU bars, second-hand bookshop etc, McDougall Centre and Armitage Centre (indoor sports), wide range of outdoor sport, all cultural and recreational facilities of Manchester.

Duration of first degree course(s) or equivalent: 3 years; **others:** 4 years (some arts and science courses and nursing); 4/5 years (dentistry); 5/6 years (medicine) **Total first degree students 1991/92:** 11,123 **Total overseas students:** 2,218 **Male/female ratio:** 5:4 **Total full-time students 1991/92:** 13,455 **Postgraduate students:** 4,262 (full-time) 2,150 (part-time) **Tuition fees for 1992/93 (first degrees):** Home: £755 (if no grant), £1,855 (classroom), £2,770 (lab/studio), £4,985 (pre-clinical); Overseas: £5,320 (classroom), £7,055–£7,205 (lab/studio), £12,990 (pre-clinical).

What it's like

Screw up your eyes and Manchester in May could look like Venice in January – university's central square shows more than passing resemblance to St Mark's Square for romantically inclined (difference being that one is surrounded by water, the other suffused in drizzle). Owens (as university is, for some impenetrable reason, called) takes many of its characteristics from its mother city; it's gruff, grandly built, hard-working and friendly. 13,000-strong student body allows for huge range of tastes; somewhere in mass of Manch. Univ. there is someone who shares your interests and desires, whatever they may be. Halls of residence, especially Whitworth Park, known as The Toblerones, good bet for first years trying to establish social niche, but not cheap. Don't be fooled by southern jessy agitprop: students here are as sophisticated, polished and clever as any in home counties. Manchester University kicked off social science revolution in 60s – Anna Ford is one of its most agreeable alumnae. Before that, Owens had established firm reputation in classics, arts and sciences. Course-switching easy, though lectures often remote, and being increasingly pressed by increased numbers.

Pauper notes

Accommodation: City council provides cheap flats in run-down areas eg Hulme.

Alumni (Editors' pick)

Mark Carlisle MP, Sir Rhodes Boyson MP, Sir Maurice Oldfield (MI6), Robert Bolt (playwright), Anthony Burgess (novelist), Christabel Pankhurst (suffragette), Peter Maxwell Davies (composer), Sir Frank Worrall (sport), Lord Lever (politician), Lord Winstanley (politician), Alan Gowling (sport), John Tomlinson (music), Anna Ford (broadcaster), C A Lejeune (film critic), Rik Mayall (actor), Francis Thompson (poet), Ian McNaught Davis.

MIDDLESEX POLY

See Middlesex University

MIDDLESEX UNIVERSITY

Middlesex University, White Hart Lane, London N17 8HR (081 362 5000) Map A, F8

Student enquiries: Admissions Enquiries

Main study areas – as in What to Study section: *(First degree):* Accountancy, American studies, art & design, business studies, civil engineering, communication studies, computing, dance, drama, economics, education, electrical & electronic engineering, English, environmental science, fine arts, geography, geology, history, hotel & catering management, information technology, law, mathematical studies, mechanical and production engineering, modern languages, music, nursing, philosophy, politics & government, psychology, religious studies and theology, social policy and social welfare, sociology. *Also:* Artificial intelligence, cultural studies, European business administration, film studies, performance studies.

European Community: 10% first degree students take EC language as part of course and 10% spend 6 months or more in another EC country. Formal exchange links with large number of EC universities/colleges including: Denmark (1); France (13); Germany (7); Greece (2); Netherlands (3); Spain (3). Approved Erasmus programme. Language skills available on every course. All disciplines can be partly studied at an institution outside UK. Many work placements can be in EC. On some courses, students can graduate with both UK degree and qualification elsewhere simultaneously.

Application: PCAS for 1993 start, UCAS thereafter; ADAR for art and design.
Academic features: New courses in manufacturing, construction, electronic

engineering and management; environmental technology; foundation engineering; modularised courses offer wide range of joint honours degrees, including pathways in English literary studies, money, banking and finance, artificial intelligence, society and technology, studies in contemporary writing and historical studies. **Special features:** Special entry procedures for mature students including those without formal qualifications. **Largest fields of study:** Art and design, business studies and management, education, performing arts, engineering, humanities, social science. **Founded:** 1992, as a university, previously Middlesex Poly founded 1973, ex Enfield and Hendon colleges of technology, Hornsey College of Art, Trent Park College of Education, New College of Speech & Drama, and College of All Saints. **Main awards:** BA, BEd, BSc, BEng. **Awarding body:** Middlesex University. **Site:** 8 campuses in North London/Middlesex area. **Access:** All campuses served by tube, bus or British Rail. Inter-campus transport. **Accommodation:** 600 mixed places in halls; campus accommodation officers help with private rented accommodation. Approx cost: From £42 pw (hall); from £40 pw plus bills (private/self catering). **Library:** 6 main libraries, total of 400,000 volumes, 2,200 periodicals, 1,150 study places, 6,000 video tapes, course books for reference. Audio-visual library at Trent Park with 7,000 records and tapes, 6,000 books on music. Art and design library at Cat Hill has 240,000 slides and illustrations. **Specialist collections:** Silver Studio Collection – complete archive of a London design studio 1880–1960. **Centres of excellence:** Microelectronics, high level tennis, design, computer graphics, flood hazard research, health research, criminology research, language centre at Enfield. **Welfare:** 4 student counsellors, 1 student advisory assistant, 6 health centres, co-ordinator for students with disabilities, nursery (15 places), playgroup (18 places). Ecumenical chaplaincy. **Careers:** 3 careers advisers providing guidance and advice to four campuses, and 2 careers information libraries based at Enfield and Hendon. **Amenities:** Bookshops at Bounds Green, Enfield, Hendon, Tottenham and Trent Park. **Sporting facilities:** Indoor and outdoor tennis courts, squash courts, saunas, indoor and outdoor swimming pools, playing fields, gymnasia including multigym.

Duration of first degree course(s) or equivalent: 3 years, 4 years (sandwich, BEd, MEng and part-time courses), modular courses part-time 5–8 years **Total first degree students 1991/92:** 8,572; **BEd students:** 492 **Overseas students:** 502 **Mature students:** 46% intake **Male/female ratio:** 1:1 **Teaching staff: full-time:** 467 **part-time:** 33 **Total full-time students 1991/92:** 9,258 **Postgraduate students:** 1,334 **Tuition fees for 1992/93 (first degrees):** Home: £1,855 (classroom), £2,770 (lab/studio); Overseas: £3,500 (classroom), £4,900 (lab/studio).

What it's like

The 8 sites, up to ten miles apart, range from the most beautiful campus in London (Trent Park) to converted grammar schools and the prototype for the Pompidou Centre in Paris (Bounds Green). Communication and travel between sites are erratic: societies and student social life suffer as a result although the SU (its politics swinging annually between moderate and revolutionary) does its best to provide decent entertainments on its meagre budget. 600 halls rooms spread around the sites, supposedly reserved for first years although others get places; otherwise accommodation is at prohibitive London prices. Sports facilities are good; tennis team is nationally renowned. Art and design faculty (Cat Hill), said to be one of the best in the country.

Pauper notes

Accommodation: Halls of residence far cheaper than rented accommodation but limited places. **Drink:** Cheap bars on each site, SU bar at Trent Park. **Eats:** SU shops sell food at reasonable prices including veggie/vegan products. **Ents:** Two SU discos per week at Trent Park. College ents usually much cheaper than London prices. **Sports:** Wide range of poly sports facilities available to all students. **Hardship funds:** SU can give loans of c£50 and can give general financial advice. **Travel:** Limited minibus service between sites. Bicycle (and strong padlock) recommended. **Work:** Some temporary work with SU or in poly facilities during term.

Alumni (Editors' pick)

Adam Ant (pop star), Ally Capellino (Alison Lloyd and Jonathan Platt), Wendy Dagworthy (fashion); Ray Davies (pop star – Kinks), Lynsey de Paul (pop star), Richard Torry; Gerald Hoffnung, Anish Kapoor (international artist), Richard Wilson (sculptor).

MORAY HOUSE

Moray House Institute of Education, Heriot Watt University, Holyrood Road, Edinburgh EH8 8AG (031 556 8455) Map A, D3

Student enquiries: Registrar

Main study areas – as in What to Study section: *(First degree):* Education, social policy and social welfare. *Also* Community education, leisure studies, movement studies, physical education, sports studies.

European Community: Some language training available for students going on exchanges. Some formal exchange links with universities/colleges in France, Germany, Italy and Spain. Approved Erasmus programme.

Application: Direct. **Structural features:** Part of Heriot Watt University. Moray House incorporates Scottish Centre for Physical Education, Movement and Leisure Studies, Centre for Leisure Research, National Coaching Centre, Scottish Centre for Sensory Impairment, Scottish Centre for Education Overseas. **Largest field of study:** Teacher training, physical education, recreation and leisure, social work, community education. **Founded:** 1835, incorporating Dunfermline College of PE in 1987; became Institute of Education, part of Heriot Watt University in 1991. **Main awards:** BA, BEd. **Awarding body:** Heriot Watt University. **Site:** Holyrood Campus in Edinburgh; Cramond Campus (physical education, movement and leisure) 6 miles west of city centre. **Access:** Holyrood Campus within walking distance of Waverley station; Cramond Campus on a bus route. **Accommodation:** 180 places at Cramond, 300 in halls 2 miles from Holyrood. Approx cost: £46 for accommodation and 1 main meal. 25% students are in accommodation with rent controlled by the college. Accommodation Officer will arrange private accommodation. **Library:** 135,000 books, 800 periodicals, 240 study places. Short loan collection of books in heaviest demand; microfilm and microfiche facilities, teaching practice collection, community studies collection, physical education library. **Other learning facilities:** Outdoor centre in Inverness-shire; resource centres for AV and computing; closed circuit television. **Careers:** Information and advice service. **Employment:** Teaching, social work, community education, recreation management. **Welfare:** Medical officers, physiotherapist, welfare officer, accommodation officer, counsellor, chaplains for various religions. **Hardship funds:** Access funds. **Amenities:** Student unions on both campuses; variety of sports and other clubs. **Sporting facilities:** Swimming pool, gyms, games hall on both campuses. Squash courts at Holyrood, playing fields at Cramond.

Duration of first degree course (or equivalent): Standard 4 years, others 3 years **Total first degree students 1991/92:** 1,424; **BEd students:** 1,061 **Overseas students:** 30 **Mature students:** 235 **Male/female ratio:** 1:4 **Teaching staff: full-time:** 95; **part-time:** 20 **Total full-time students 1991/92:** 2,056 **Postgraduate students:** 632 **Tuition fees for 1992/93 (first degrees):** Home: £696 (if no grant),

£1,855 (classroom), £2,770 (lab/studio); Overseas: £5,420 (classroom), £7,155 (lab/studio).

What it's like

It's on two contrasting campuses some eight miles apart: Holyrood, period buildings, just off Edinburgh's Royal Mile and half way between Edinburgh Castle and the Parliament; and Cramond, on the north-west outskirts of the town, a purpose built college for PE, leisure management and movement.

Halls of residence accommodate c.300 students from a mixture of courses, countries and ages. Holyrood halls two miles from campus; Cramond hall on campus. Costs of breakfast and dinner are incorporated in the hall fees. Laundry on site, common room; plus ents committee. No visiting restrictions but after 10 pm overnight visitors should book a guest room.

Rented accommodation for those preferring to live out not always easy to find with help of accommodation officer's list of what's available. Travel easy, good bus service into town.

Edinburgh huge city, c.40,000 students. Vast number of pubs, theatres, cinemas. Within the campuses many student societies. SU open most nights with variety of clubs, bands, discos, parties, etc, also during day for rolls, coffee and cheap pint.

Students' Association busy political hive of activity internally and working externally with NUS. Staff/student relations good; happy atmosphere. Two counsellors in college handle all student problems; contraceptive/pregnancy advice from medical staff or SA advice centre; sabbaticals also offer support and advice.

Work assessed differently within different courses: some by continuous assessment; some by examination. Academic links now established with university; all degrees now university status.

Students come from all over Scotland and England, also from Sri Lanka, Malaysia and USA. Anti-racist and antisexist policies within college/SA. Employment prospects good: teachers, social workers, community workers.

Pauper notes

Drink: SU on both campuses; various other institution's SUs. **Eats:** Moray House SU selection of sandwiches, etc. Blue Blanket, World's End and Holyrood Tavern pubs give student discount on lunches. **Ents:** Moray House SU – both campuses – bands, clubs, parties. Party Ceilid Disco, FBI & Shaft – very popular Union events. **Sports:** Cramond campus is sport and physical education centre; Holyrood campus, pool, gym, squash etc. **Hardship funds:** Access fund; loans. **Travel:** For those on Scottish Education Dept grants, excellent buses from Edinburgh to anywhere; likewise trains. **Work:** Both campuses: student wardens – free digs. Moray House SU – bar work, also during vacation; pub work. Executive officers of SA get honorarium.

Informal name

Moray House.

Alumni (Editors' pick)

Elaine C Smith, Danny Munro (Runrig and other members).

NAPIER POLY

See Napier University

CAN'T FIND WHAT YOU'RE LOOKING FOR? USE THE INDEX!

NAPIER UNIVERSITY

**Napier University, Edinburgh, Craiglockhart Campus,
219 Colinton Road, Edinburgh EH14 1DJ (031 444 2266)** Map A, D3

Student enquiries: Information Office, Freepost, Edinburgh EH14 0PA
(031 444 2266 ext 4330).

Main study areas – as in What to Study section: *(First degree):* Accountancy, biology, business studies, chemistry, civil engineering, communication studies, computing, electrical and electronic engineering, hotel & catering management, information technology, law, mathematical studies, physics. *Also:* Building, film studies, industrial design (technology), photography, publishing, quantity surveying, transport studies.

European Community: Number of students learning an EC language or spending time in another EC country as part of their course, not known. All students offered language tuition, if it is not included in their course. Approved Erasmus programme.

Application: Direct for 1993; may change for 1994, so check. **Largest fields of study:** Accounting, business studies, science, engineering, commerce. **Founded:** 1992, as a university. Previously Napier Poly, founded 1964. **Main awards:** BA, BEng, BSc. **Awarding body:** Napier University. **Site:** 3 major sites with four annexes. **Academic features:** Degree courses include interior design; applied physics with microelectronics; quantity surveying (multi-mode attendance); publishing; hospitality management; engineering systems; BEng electronic and communication engineering; BEd technology (with Moray House). Most courses are sandwich, **all** are vocationally oriented. **Special features:** Access courses in engineering, electronics, sciences, physics for those without formal entry qualifications. **Accommodation:** All students are helped to find accommodation if they wish. Full time accommodation officer. **Library:** 3 libraries; 2,130,000 volumes in total, 1,600 periodicals, 800 study places. **Welfare:** Medical officers, nurse, student advisers, chaplains. **Hardship funds:** Limited assistance can be given. **Careers:** Information, advice and placement service. Three full-time careers advisers on campus plus careers information assistant. **Amenities:** SU facilities at all main sites, sports dome, swimming pool; cultural facilities at Edinburgh.

Duration of first degree course(s) or equivalent: 3 or 4 years; **Others:** 4 or 5 years **Total first degree students 1991/92:** 2,450 **Male/female ratio:** 2:1 **Teaching staff:** 490 **Total full-time students 1991/92:** 5,500 **Postgraduate students:** 334 **Tuition fees for 1992/93 (first degrees):** Home: £1,855 (classroom), £2,770 (lab/studio); Overseas: £5,000.

What it's like

Well since last year we have had a change of name; now it's Napier University. We have around 9,000 students spread over 6 sites throughout Edinburgh; a fact that, in itself, creates obvious communication problems.

Napier Students' Association (NSA) has bars and shops at each of its 3 main sites but has no venue large enough to stage bands. Uni halls of residence provide places for a total of 173 students, and state of repair is pretty poor. NSA is currently campaigning for a central site union, better halls and an expansion of student services.

Academically emphasis is placed on science, technology and commercial disciplines. The most significant increase is in the number of short, high turnover, money spinning post-paid courses being offered mainly by the faculty of professional studies.

As with most other institutions, the Uni is expanding its student intake although funding and facilities are not increasing proportionately. The Uni at the moment appears to be filled past capacity and a large question mark hangs over its

GET HOLD OF THE PROSPECTUSES

ability to maintain, far less improve, the teaching standards and resources on offer – although to its credit, the Uni has prioritised development in this area.

Pauper notes

Accommodation: Edinburgh expensive; advisable to view potential flats. Getting hard to find considering student numbers in the city are rising. Uni flats and halls of residences reasonably priced. **Drink:** NSA bars at each main site, prices amongst cheapest in Edinburgh. McEwan's 80 shilling excellent, Scrumpy Jack Cider not to be missed (especially in Snakebite form). Each bar has its own atmosphere and range of alcoholic and non-alcoholic cocktails. Edinburgh is a city that is not short of pubs; other places to try include: any pub in The Grassmarket or Rose Street, Bennets Bar, the Malt Shovel, Berties and of course the famous Diggers (The Athletic Arms) which serves the best beer in town! **Eats:** Merky Bar (NSA bar at Merchiston) for quality cheap food; traditional chippies, Kalpna (voted best vegetarian restaurant in Britain). There are restaurants to suit every taste from Mexican to American and from Spanish to Armenian. **Ents:** Tons of cinemas including a 12 screen UCI and a 6 screen Odeon. Also the Filmhouse and Cameo independent cinemas. Many theatres from the Lyceum to the Bedlam theatre. Edinburgh nightclubs getting better, from mainstream Century 2000 to the more student orientated Shag and Shady Ladies. NSA ents – discos, ceilidhs, all-nighters etc. – high quality, quantity and variety. **Sports:** University sports dome at Sighthill, many active sports clubs. District council run free low cost sports centres and swimming pools. **Hardship funds:** Access fund; NSA also runs hardship loan fund managed by our welfare adviser. **Travel:** NSA sells ISIC, rail and NUS cards and has details of student bargains. As a whole Edinburgh has a good bus network and fairly reasonable fares. **Work:** Not guaranteed or well paid, but good jobs to be had. Try pubs, hotels, bookshops, shops or even McDonald's!

More info?

Get students' Alternative Prospectus, currently being compiled.
Enquiries to Andrew Mitchell 031 229 8791.

Buzz-words

Merky Bar (Merchiston Union), Shitehill (Sighthill campus), The Prince (our beloved Principal)

Alumni (Editors' pick)

Ian Buchanan (Edinburgh Councillor), Steve Jacks (Radio Forth DJ), Jane Franchie (BBC Scotland), Greg Kane (Hue & Cry), Gavin Hastings (Scottish rugby).

NATIONAL EXTENSION COLLEGE

National Extension College, 18 Brooklands Avenue, Cambridge CB2 2HN (0223 316644; fax 0223 313586) Map A, F7

Student enquiries: Head of Degree & Professional Services

Main study areas – as in What to Study section: *(First degree – correspondence):* Classics, English, geography, history, law, modern languages, philosophy, religious studies and theology.

European Community: 25% first degree students take EC language as part of their course; none spend time in another EC country.

Application: First – Secretary for External Studies, London University, Senate House, Malet Street, London WC1 7HU (071-636 8000). Then – NEC. **Special features:** Home-based teaching by correspondence. Most NEC students are mature and teaching is by NEC tutors; work schedules are individually worked

WANT TO HELP WITH THE NEXT EDITION – SEE PAGE 76

out. Assignments are sent regularly to tutors. Some courses designed to prepare students for degree work. **Largest fields of study:** Divinity, law. **Founded:** 1963, ex University Correspondence College. **Main awards:** BA, BD, LLB. **Awarding body:** London University (external). **Welfare:** Subject tutors are also personal tutors.

Duration of first degree course(s) or equivalent: 5 years **Total first degree students 1991/92:** 600 **Overseas students:** 150 **Mature students:** Most **Male/female ratio:** 1:1 **Teaching staff: Part-time:** c75 **Tuition fees for 1992/93** (first degrees): £130 plus approx £300 pa for assignments (£25 per assignment, UK students; £27 per assignment, overseas students).

What it's like

Reg Hutchings got his O and A levels in French through the NEC. He was then accepted as an external student (BA French) of London University. He writes:

'Whereas for A level, the limited choice of literary works had been made for me, the responsibility of choosing from the entire range of literature from medieval times to the present day was now entirely my own. My tutors were most helpful in discussing the implications of my choices of individual works and with the French language paper, but always strictly in the role of adviser.

Initially it was a journey into the unknown but gradually a pattern of work emerged. Tutors set a range of questions, marked papers and commented on them. Criticism, which must be no less rigorous than the examiner's, is the life-blood of the student/tutor relationship and that relationship is the crucial element in study by correspondence.

Oral work presents a special problem as it relies on tapes, radio, TV and films. Trips to France become more important, contact with other students is improved by the annual weekend course run by Bristol University. A good library is vital. I am most grateful for the use of Exeter University's library and the Devon library service's range of books, many of which are held in reserve.

My journey continues. It demands considerable self-discipline but is most rewarding. It takes a lot of one's time and calls for family support, but it enriches life without dominating it.'

Pam Osborne, an American registered as a London University external LLB student writes from a different standpoint:

'I originally trained and qualified as a registered nurse yet was always interested in studying for a law degree. Because of eye operations, I had to have a form of study which I could do at home and do at my own pace.

I studied GCSE law and A level law and obtained wonderful grades due to the fullest support of NEC's tutors. They helped me learn the 'subjects' but also taught me how to 'sit the exams'.

NEC is wonderful because it is user-friendly! They are geared for people who have just come out of school but also for those of us who have had quite a gap. Tutors really care about their students and about their getting good exam results. If any problems ever arise, which they seldom do, there is always a friendly voice on the phone at NEC anxious to help.'

NATIONAL FILM SCHOOL

National Film and Television School, Beaconsfield Studios, Station Road, Beaconsfield, Bucks HP9 1LG (04946 71234; Fax 0494 674042) Map A, E8

Student enquiries: Admissions Secretary.

Main study area: *(Not at first degree):* Film studies.

European Community: School has strong links with other film-schools worldwide

(Director is Vice-President of CILECT – Centre International des Ecoles de Cinema et Television). School is a founding member of GEECT – European Association of Film and Television Schools; frequent exchanges of students and staff from other European Schools. Other links include Council of Europe; MEDIA '95.

Special features: postgraduate only. **Application:** Direct (on basis of previous experience and/or supporting material). **Entrance:** Approx 35 students admitted annually (some places reserved for overseas students). Average age, 27 years; previous experience in film or a related field expected. **Academic features:** 3 year course which has postgraduate status leading to an Associateship (ANFTS) with specialisation in training of producers, directors, directors of photography, editors, animators, art directors, sound recordists, documentary and film composers. 1-year course in script writing is also available. Students encouraged to interchange roles in any practical activity at same time as developing their specialisation. Resident tutors include: Danny Boon, Toni de Bromhead, Rob Buckler, Henning Camre, Roger Crittenden, Chuck Despins, Herb DiGioia, Jan Fleischer, Gareth Heywood, Richard Jenkins, Simon Mallin, Wojciech Marczewski, Jim O'Brien, Paddy Seale, Francis Shaw, Moira Tait, Barry Vince, Paul Wheeler. Visiting tutors include: Andrzej Mellin, Gaby Prekop, Maureen Thomas, Ernest Walter, Colin Young. **Founded:** 1970. **Main awards:** Associate of NFTS. **Awarding body:** National Film and Television School. **Site:** Beaconsfield. **Access:** British Rail. **Accommodation:** Not provided. **Library:** 2,500+ volumes, 35 periodicals. (Entire collection film-oriented.) **Careers:** Advice service. **Amenities:** Student membership of British Academy of Film and Television Art; Corporate membership of British Film Institute, and CILECT (Centre International des Ecoles de Cinema et Television). **Hardship funds:** Own scholarship fund. **Employment:** Film-making for cinema and television (usually on a freelance basis).

Duration of post-graduate course(s) or equivalent: 3 years **Male/female ratio:** 2:3 **Teaching staff: full-time:** 18 **part-time:** as required **Postgraduate students:** 100 **Tuition fees for 1992/93:** Home: £2,200; Overseas: £5,325.

What it's like

Fully equipped school, having taken over the British Lion studio in Beaconsfield. Provides practical hands-on film training for a small number of students in all the major disciplines of film making: producing, writing, directing, camera, animation, editing, design, music, sound and documentary. Allows students to gain a considerable amount of useful experience, and to build up a showreel of work to promote oneself in the professional industry.

Being relatively young, the school has yet to sort out a structure which properly supports all students. It is left largely to the individual to structure his or her course, with little in the way of an organised curriculum. Although this provides great freedom, it also leads to considerable problems, and many students find it hard to work effectively in this environment. The first year is becoming increasingly structured as efforts are made each year to improve the curriculum. Definitely not a 9–5 place; most students come in a few days a week to make use of it as a facilities centre.

Beaconsfield is isolated. Most students live in London and commute out. There's little social life there – bar Christmas and summer parties. Reviving contacts with ULU. There is the possibility (long term) of the school moving into London.

A film course is only as good as the people who run it, whatever the structure. The NFTS has a certain amount of complacency in its staffing, and the few excellent tutors need their numbers boosting. Some are full time; some part time because they are working, which is good for contacts in the industry. At the end of the day, whatever the problems of the school, the level of practical film making experience is enormous.

CAN'T FIND WHAT YOU'RE LOOKING FOR? USE THE INDEX!

Alumni (Editors' pick)

Directors: Mike Radford, Malcolm Mowbray, Brian Gilbert, Ben Bolt, Conny Templeman; Documentary: Nick Broomfield, Jeff Perks, Jana Bokova; Camera: Roger Deakins, Dianne Tammes, Oliver Stapleton; Animators: Phil Austin, Derek Hayes, David Anderson; Music: Trevor Jones; Writers: Shawn Slovo; Also Michael Caton Jones, Harry Hook, Terence Davies, Molly Dineen, Beeban Kidron, Jennifer Howarth, Nick Park, Mark Baker, John Keane, Steve Morrison.

NATIONAL HOSPITALS COLLEGE

National Hospitals College of Speech Sciences, 2 Wakefield Street, London WC1N 1PG (071 837 0113) Map E, C1

Student enquiries: BSc Admissions Tutor

Main study areas – as in What to Study section: *(First degree):* Speech sciences.

European Community: 10% first degree students take EC language as part of course (not compatible with the clinical speech therapy qualification); none spend time in another EC country. Language tuition available at University College. Phonetics for foreign students may be taken in first year. Individual tutorials provided since intelligibility of expression as important as language proficiency for clinical purposes. Informal links in EC.

Application: UCCA for 1993 start, UCAS thereafter. **Special features:** Students are simultaneously undergraduates at University College London and at National Hospitals College. Students whose clinical profile is satisfactory are recommended to College of Speech Therapists for licence to practise. **Founded:** 1974, ex West End Hospital Speech Therapy Training School and Oldrey-Fleming School of Speech Therapy. **Main awards:** BSc. **Awarding body:** London University. **Site:** Bloomsbury (near St Pancras) – located at the former Royal Free Hospital School of Medicine building. **Access:** King's Cross, Euston, Russell Square underground stations; buses 18, 30, 73, 172. **Library:** Specialised library. **Specialist facilities:** Collection of language and speech assessments in test library; voice laboratory; adjacent clinic (with local DHA). **Amenities:** Students' common room and refectory on site; University College with students' union facilities and ULU (swimming pool etc) within walking distance. **Hardship funds:** Limited charitable funds to assist students. **Employment:** Speech therapy, home and abroad (students must register with the College of Speech Therapists); some 10% take up other employment in eg teaching, audiology, management consultancy.

Duration of first degree course(s) or equivalent: 4 years **Other:** 3 years (non-clinical course) **Total first degree students 1991/92:** 168 **Overseas students:** 10 **Mature students:** 36 **Male/female ratio:** 1:40 **Teaching staff: full-time:** 22 plus full-time U.C. staff who teach 40-50% of course **Total full-time students 1991/92:** 180 **Postgraduate students:** 19 **Tuition fees for 1992/93 (first degrees):** Home: £2,770, £795 (if no grant); Overseas: £7,995.

What it's like

Situated near King's Cross, ten minutes walk from University College in Gower Street. First year spent mainly at University College; subsequent years more time is spent at NHCSS, which has a common room, subsidised canteen and library. All UCL facilities – sport, libraries and union are available for our use. Friendly students – mature, overseas or straight from school. Good teaching and support from staff. Course is modular and from the second year onwards some time is spent on clinic placements. It is hard work, but worth it!

Pauper notes

Accommodation: Should be able to get UCL accommodation in first and final years, which is cheap and cheerful. In between you're on your own, which is hard in London, but everyone manages either through the accommodation office or other agencies. **Eats:** London University has many cheap places to eat and drink, but if these don't appeal, there are millions of other places all over London. **Ents:** Societies to suit all. Bloomsbury Theatre on site for films and theatre, but you always have the West End! **Health:** Health Centre and dentist on site. Counselling services are available. **Sport:** Good facilities at UCL and ULU. **Travel:** Expensive, but travel cards allowing unlimited travel on tubes and buses. Buses provided by UCL and general transport. **Hardship funds:** UCL hardship fund may help. **Work:** London is expensive, many students have to work part-time.

NENE COLLEGE

Nene College, Moulton Park, Boughton Green Road, Northampton NN2 7AL (0604 715000) Map A, E7

Student enquiries: Academic Registrar.

Main study areas – as in What to Study section: *(First degree):* Accountancy, art and design, American studies, biology, business studies, civil engineering, computing, drama, economics, education, English, environmental science, geography, history, law, mathematical studies, modern languages, music, nursing, professions allied to medicine (PAMs), psychology, sociology. *Also:* Building and construction, communications engineering, equine studies, European business, leather technology, quantity surveying.

European Community: 5% first degree students take EC language as part of course (French/German/Italian/Spanish for European business studies; French/German for combined studies); 5% spend 6 months or more in another EC country. Formal exchange links with 4 EC universities/colleges: in France (Poitiers); Germany (Trier), Italy (Florence) and Spain (Salamanca) – all for European business students; French/German/Spanish/Italian diplomas awarded as well as degree. Approved Erasmus programme.

Application: PCAS for 1993 start, UCAS thereafter. **Academic features:** Combined studies degree, including European business studies. Degree in podiatry. **Special features:** International centre for leather technology in English-speaking world. **Founded:** 1975, ex colleges of education, art and technology. **Main awards:** BA, BEd, BSc, LLB. **Awarding body:** Leicester University. **Site:** Outskirts of Northampton. **Access:** Public transport; 5 miles from M1. **Accommodation:** 470 places in halls. Approx cost: £42 pw (self-catering). Rent: 18% in accommodation where rent controlled by college. **Library:** 2 libraries; 200,000 volumes, 800 periodicals, 280 study places. **Other learning resources:** Resource centres at both campuses; computer centre; AVA; language labs. **Welfare:** Doctor, dentist, FPA, solicitor, chaplains, counsellor, dean of students. **Hardship funds:** Extreme hardship fund (loans on limited basis) plus access funds. **Careers:** Full-time careers officer. **Amenities:** SU building and rooms, also bookshop on both sites, banking facilities. VAX 11/780 computer with extensive terminal network. Additional laboratories and teaching block completed 1985. **Sporting facilities:** 2 sports halls, all-weather pitch, playing fields, tennis courts. **Employment:** Teaching or related personal services; social and health services, chiropody, leather technology, industry and commerce.

Duration of first degree course(s) or equivalent: 3 and 4 years **Total first degree students 1991/92:** 4,040 **Total BEd students:** 520 **Overseas students:** 80 **Mature students:** 450 **Male/female ratio:** 1:1 **Teaching staff: full-time:** 297 **part-time:** 8 **Total full-time students 1991/92:** 5,059 **Postgraduate students:** 80 **Tuition fees for 1992/93 (first degrees):** Home: £759 (if no grant), £1,855 (classroom), £2,770 (lab/studio); Overseas: £5,319. Additional £340 registration fee for all students in their first year only.

CAN'T FIND WHAT YOU'RE LOOKING FOR? USE THE INDEX!

What it's like

It's on two campuses, with a student population that includes a large mature student intake. Crèche facilities available. Halls have recently been refurbished. Extended library services, including disabled computer link on campus. Adequate sporting facilities with plans for development.

Both campuses have their own new SU site offices, bars and canteens. Currently over 50 clubs and societies cater for all, from parachutist to film buffs (showing new release films every Sunday). The SU operates a hectic social scene for all tastes, with top names throughout the year. SU also offers full welfare and support services to help you through your time at college. We have good ties with NUS and are very involved in campaigning on student issues.

As Nene expands so too does the Union. So get involved and have a whale of a time in Northampton.

Kenan Osborne

Pauper notes

Accommodation: £42 single room, £20 shared Old Halls, £32 shared New Halls.
Drink: Both main SU bars and Gig Centre (ex Sports Hall) offer cheap beers and spirits. Favourite student pubs – Kingsley Park Tavern, the Racehorse, King Billy, Shipmans. Many Mann's houses. Abington Hotel amazing home brew.
Eats: Campus college canteen OK. SU canteens (one at each site) superb value. Town has good vegetarian, burger/pizza places, with discounts. Cagney's Diner, Heros, Buddies. **Ents:** Ents go on all week with 3 or 4 late bars a week and 4 balls a year. Societies run promos and contact with local theatre and major transport link to London and Birmingham for concerts, plays etc. **Sports:** SU parachutes, sailing, canoeing, fencing etc. **Hardship fund:** SU hardship fund. **Travel:** Northampton accessible via M1 and A45. Hitching easy – be careful! Good bus service/easy rail links with London and Birmingham. No student travel service. **Work:** Fairly easy (low local unemployment).

More info?

Get students' Alternative Prospectus.
Enquiries to Kenan Osborne, President SU (0604 711697).

Alumni (Editors' pick)

David J. (Bauhaus), Daniel Ash (Love & Rockets), Derek Redmond, John (Neds Atomic Dustbin).

NEWCASTLE POLY

See Northumbria University, Newcastle

NEWCASTLE UNIVERSITY

University of Newcastle upon Tyne, 6 Kensington Terrace, Newcastle upon Tyne NE1 7RU (091 222 6000) Map A, E4

Student enquiries: Admissions Officer

Main study areas – as in What to Study section: *(First degree):* Accountancy, agriculture, anatomy, archaeology, architecture, art & design, Asian studies, biochemistry, biology, botany, chemical engineering, chemistry, civil engineering, classics, computing, dentistry, economics, electrical & electronic engineering, English, environmental science, fine arts, food science & nutrition, geography, history, Latin American studies, law, linguistics, marine technology, mathematical studies, mechanical & production engineering, medicine, metallurgy and materials science, microbiology, modern languages, music, Near East & Islamic studies, physics, physiology, politics and government, psychology, religious studies and theology, social policy and social welfare, sociology, speech sciences, town & country planning, zoology. *Also:* Agricultural engineering, astronomy, film studies, management, marine biology, materials design, midwifery.

European Community: 8% first degree students take EC language as part of course and 5% spend 6 months or more in another EC country. Formal Erasmus links with a large number of EC universities/colleges including languages, computer science, politics, chemistry, urban planning, neurolinguistics, theology, soil sciences, literature, civil engineering, medicine, chemical engineering, microbiology, chemistry, public administration, marine technology, geography, biology, architecture, education, mechanical engineering, business studies, materials science. Approved Erasmus programme 1991/92.

Application: UCCA for 1993 start, UCAS thereafter. **Academic features:** Courses in: accounting and law; agricultural and environmental science; natural resources; molecular biology; 4-year engineering degrees for those without maths/science A-levels. **Largest fields of study:** Science, engineering, arts, medicine and dentistry, agriculture, economics and social sciences. **Founded:** Early 19th century, present title 1963 (formerly the Newcastle Division of Durham University). **Main awards:** BA, BSc, BEng, MEng, LLB, MBBS, BDS. **Awarding body:** Newcastle University. **Site:** City centre. **Accommodation:** Approx 1,800 places in halls, about 800 in self-catering flats and 300 in student houses. Approx cost: £546–£1,197 pa. Rent: 44% in accommodation where rent controlled by university. **Library:** 800,000 volumes, 5,000 periodicals, 700 study places. **Specialist collections:** Archaeology (Gertrude Bell); History of Medicine (Pybus); English Literature (Robert White); Japanese Science and Technology (Robert Phillifent). **Other learning facilities:** Espin Observatory (largest telescope in north of England), Computing Laboratory, Museum of Antiquities, Greek Museum, Hatton Gallery, 2 farms, marine biological station, Moorbank Gardens. **Welfare:** Sick bay, counselling service, Union Society welfare adviser, chaplaincy. **Careers:** Careers advisory service, wide range of facilities including personal interviews, careers education programmes, talks, seminars, library and information service and employer contact. **Employment:** 1991 graduates – 62% direct into employment, 4% into professional training or further academic study, 5% unplaced, 3.5% unknown. **Amenities:** Newcastle is regional capital of NE (excellent theatres, cinemas, bars, concert halls). SU one of largest in UK with wide range of facilities including 13 food and drink outlets, tennis courts, shops, sporting and cultural facilities, an 18 hole golf course, extensive outside sporting facilities and new sports hall.

Duration of first degree course(s) or equivalent: 3 & 4 years; **others:** 5 years town & country planning **Total first degree students 1991/92:** 7,437 **Overseas students:** 1,038 **Male/female ratio:** 3:2 **Teaching staff: full-time:** 820 **part-time:** 67 **Total full-time students 1991/92:** 9,861 **Postgraduate students:** 2,424 **Tuition fees for 1992/93 (first degrees):** Home: £1,885 (classroom), £2,770 (lab/studio), £4,985 (clinical); Overseas: £5,320 (classroom), £7,055 (lab/studio), £12,990 (clinical).

What it's like

Attractive city, close to the beautiful countryside of Northumbria and the coast, easily accessible by rail, coach and Metro – Newcastle's very own underground system. Excellent social life – many good pubs and restaurants offer happy hours and/or student discounts. Especially good for live music, cinema and the theatre – many local and two 10-screen cinemas in the area, plus the Tyneside cinema which shows a wide selection of foreign and artistic films. Good nightclubs eg Rockshots, Ritzy's, Tuxedo Royale.

SU impressive listed building – six bars, provides a wide range of reasonably priced hot and cold food, wide variety of ents – live bands, Friday night disco, quizzes, bingo and drinks promotions. Runs a huge range of social, political and sporting clubs and societies. Students conservative (with a small c) but union still runs campaigns on most issues affecting students and tries to involve as many students as possible. Excellent welfare service. Good mix of students, just under 10% are from overseas.

Accommodation, private sector has been cheap and plentiful, however rents are starting to go up and there is more pressure on places. University accommodation – too little in the past but more has recently been built.

Courses – many excellent ones but style and quality of teaching varies from dept to dept, eg economics has a high failure rate but is recognised as an excellent department nationally. Big for medicine, agriculture, engineering.

Pauper notes

Accommodation: Private sector: very cheap and plentiful. Halls of Residence: as everywhere else. **Drink:** University Union **now** cheapest drinking venue in the city. 6 SU bars: wide range of atmospheres with frequent promotions. **Eats:** SU main provider of campus; cheap and wide range; pizzas, salads, hot food, stotties, vegetarian and whole-food. Lots of vegetarian/vegan places to eat out. **Ents:** Friday night discos, live bands in SU. Studio Theatre on campus. Tyneside cinema: cheap off circuit. Good local venues, eg 'Broken Doll' and Riverside for bands and City Hall, the two universities for bigger outfits. **Sports:** Off campus swimming, on campus excellent cheap/free sports facilities. **Hardship funds:** Access Fund. **Work:** Average opportunities.

More info?

Get students' Alternative Prospectus (in video form).
Enquiries to Heather Saville, Union President (091 232 8402 ext. 281).

Alumni (Editors' pick)

Rowan Atkinson (comedian), Bryan Ferry (musician), Miriam Stoppard (TV doctor), Richard Hamilton (painter), Kate Adie.

NORFOLK INSTITUTE

Norfolk Institute of Art and Design

(1) **Great Yarmouth Campus, Trafalgar Road, Great Yarmouth NR30 2LB (0493 843557);**
(2) **Norwich Campus, St George Street, Norwich NR3 1BB (0603 610561) Map A, G6**

Student enquiries: Chief Administrative Officer

Main study areas – as in What to Study section: *(First degree):* Art & design *Also:* Cultural studies.

European Community: No students learn an EC language or spend time in another EC country as part of their course although language tuition available as supplementary subject to all students. Formal exchange links with 5 EC universities/colleges: Germany (Aachen, Karlsruhe, Kiel); Netherlands; Portugal. Approved Erasmus programme. Further links proposed with France and Italy.

Application: ADAR. **Founded:** 1989 ex Norwich School of Art and Great Yarmouth College of Art and Design. **Main awards:** BA. **Awarding body:** Anglia Poly University. **Site:** Norwich city centre and Great Yarmouth. **Accommodation:** Very limited hostel accommodation; a register of landladies is maintained by the college. Rent: 1% in accommodation where rent controlled by institute. **Library:** 24,000 volumes, 120 periodicals, 45 study places; slide library: 135,000 slides. **Welfare:** Student counselling service available. **Amenities:** Norfolk Museums Services; East Anglia University library; Norwich Gallery; Sainsbury Art Centre at UEA.

Duration of first degree course(s) or equivalent: 3 years **Total first degree students 1991/92:** 361 **Overseas students:** 6 **Male/female ratio:** 1:1 **Teaching staff: full-time:** 41 **part-time:** 100 **Total full-time students 1991/92:** 686 **Tuition fees for 1992/93 (first degrees):** Home: £2,770; Overseas £5,319.

What it's like

A friendly place. Norwich Art School in town centre overlooking River Wensum. Facilities improving: new library, many new studio spaces. Several students live in boats on the river but most opt for private rented housing – limited college accommodation. Good staff/student relationships unique to smaller colleges. Merged with Great Yarmouth College of Art and Design 1989 to form Norfolk Institute.

Gigs and alternative music Jaquard Club, big name bands at nearby UEA. Various other venues throughout city. Theatre and cinemas offer student discounts. Art school football team only team in college. Successful women's group; environmental group works with local conservation group.

Erasmus European exchange scheme offers the opportunity to learn a European language and study abroad for a term. Easy access to London (2 hrs train). Majority of students come from Home Counties. Student welfare has contracted out financial counselling to Norwich Centre; free and fully confidential to full-time students. Union invites students experiencing difficulty with their courses (eg unsatisfactory term assessments) to discuss their problems with them.

Pauper notes (Norwich)

Drink: Real ale: White Lion, Ten Bells, Golden Star, Ferryboat. Trendy – Murderers, La Rouen, Central Park, Ritzy Nightclub, Jolly Butcher Nightclub. The Red Lion unofficial SU bar, actively supports students with cheap nights, promo's, cheap nosh. **Eats:** Many places offering all types of food. Too many to list. Also ethnic, Mexican, Lebanese, Greek, Italian, veggie, Chinese, Indian, fish (through the price range). **Ents:** Film society provides constant pulp viewing, fringe cinema over the road, plus Cannons, Odeons etc. **Sports:** Loads of community centres plus UEA facility. **Hardship funds:** Hardship loans suspended, but SU arrangements with the big 4 banks. **Work:** Part-time bar work readily available.

Informal name:

NIAD.

NORTH CHESHIRE COLLEGE

North Cheshire College, Padgate Campus, Fearnhead, Warrington WA2 0DB (0925 814343) Map A, D6

Student enquiries: Admissions Officer

Main study areas – as in What to Study section: *(First degree):* Business studies, drama and theatre studies, communication studies, information technology. *Also:* film studies, leisure and recreation.

European Community: 5% first degree students take EC language as part of course and 5% spend 6 months or more in another EC country on work-based assignments. No formal exchange links with EC universities/colleges.

Application: PCAS for 1993 start, UCAS thereafter. **Academic features:** Three modular joint honours degrees and a combined honours degree for mature stu-

CAN'T FIND WHAT YOU'RE LOOKING FOR? USE THE INDEX!

dents, with wide range of modules and a work-based assignment. Courses in media with business management; recreation with business management; performing arts with business management. **Largest fields of study:** Media studies, leisure & recreation, performing arts, business management, information technology. **Main awards:** BA. **Awarding body:** Manchester University. **Site:** Extensive landscaped site, close to new shopping and leisure facilities. **Access:** Within easy reach of M6, M56 and M62 motorways. **Accommodation:** All years can be accommodated in single and shared study bedrooms. **Library:** Number of libraries; over 95,000 books, range of periodicals, reading rights at Manchester Univ library. **Other learning resources:** Computer facilities; TV and sound studios, darkroom etc; desktop publishing; fully equipped theatre for use by students and touring companies. **Welfare:** Student Services Centre offers careers guidance, counselling and welfare services. **Amenities:** Good sporting facilities; own SU complex; within easy reach of Manchester and Liverpool; town a short bus ride away.

Duration of first degree course(s) or equivalent: 3 years **Total first degree students 1991/92:** 390 **Mature students:** 120 **Male/female ratio:** 1:1 **Teaching staff: full-time:** 50 **part-time:** 5 **Total full-time students 1991/92:** 390 **Tuition fees for 1992/93 (first degrees):** Home: £1,855; Overseas: £5,319.

What it's like

A smallish college on the edge of Warrington. Higher education currently focuses on business management with media, leisure studies or performing arts, all of which are becoming bigger and better, and facilities are (we're told) catching up. On-site students have gone up in number recently to about 500 (a vast amount for us with which to infiltrate the locals).

Warrington's best entertainment generally takes place on campus during weekdays, so most students stick around until the weekend, when they tend to 'hit the city'. Everybody knows everybody, and we have a great sense of community (alongside a notorious grapevine). Main gathering point on campus is new SU bar: probably the best of recent brilliant initiatives thought up by hardworking, forever active, always caring SU executive committee. Athletics union is equally active and well organised.

Friends and visitors are always welcome and can be entertained in town centre (20 minutes bus ride) or in Manchester (15 mins by train), which is probably as good as London for pubs, clubs, eats and other cultural activities.

NCC graduates have been known to go into all walks of life from working in burger bars to executive stress. A few have even come back as lecturers most of whom are 'okay' but the Old Boys are naturally the most understanding.

The drop-out rate is considerably low, and if you can cope with your lectures, your finances and your neighbours, your three years here will be an experience you will carry with you fondly for the rest of your life.

Pip Hunt

Pauper notes

Accommodation: Halls of residence quite cheap – often shared, very little accommodation in Warrington. All second years must now live off campus. **Drinks:** Tetley Walker, Scottish & Newcastle and special beers in (very cheap) SU bar. **Eats:** New pizza place (Munchies in SU Bar) very cheap. Nice Greek/Indian and veggie. **Ents:** Close to Manchester. Cinema reductions with SU card. Local theatre. **Sports:** Sports hall and multigym on campus – free. **Hardship Funds:** Limited but available from college. **Travel:** Close to M6, convenient for hitching. **Work:** Bar work in SU and locally; cinema likes students in evenings – work always available.

More info?

Enquiries to Alan Tomlinson (0925 821336).

WANT TO HELP WITH THE NEXT EDITION – SEE PAGE 76

Informal name:
NCC.

Alumni (Editors' pick)
Alan Bleasdale.

NORTH EAST WALES INSTITUTE

The North East Wales Institute (NEWI), Plas Coch, Mold Road, Wrexham, Clwyd LL11 2AW (0978 290666) Map A, D6

Student enquiries: Admissions Office

Main study areas – as in What to Study section: *(First degree):* Aeronautical engineering, biochemistry, biology, business studies, chemistry, civil engineering, computing, education, electrical & electronic engineering, English, environmental science, environmental studies, history, information technology, metallurgy and materials science, mechanical and production engineering, nursing studies, physics, social policy and social welfare. *Also:* Estate management, quantity surveying, Welsh studies.

European Community: Opportunities to learn an EC language (including Welsh) or spend time in another EC country.

Application: PCAS for 1993 start, UCAS thereafter. **Academic features:** New courses in aeronautical engineering, computing and European studies, business management, youth, community and education. **Special features:** Mature students may be exempted from normal entry requirements. Specialist BEd business studies; possibility of some study in the United States. 1 A-level entry for BSc/BEng (2 + 2) courses – these include study time also at Bangor, UMIST, Salford, Liverpool or Manchester universities. **Founded:** 1975; formed from two technical colleges and a teacher training college. **Main awards:** BA, BEd, BEng, BNursing, BSc. **Awarding body:** Universities of Liverpool, Manchester, UMIST, Salford, Wales. **Site:** 4 sites – main site plus admissions office at NEWI Plas Coch. **Access:** Public transport to each site; train service nearby Deeside site and Wrexham sites. Good rail and bus links to Chester. **Accommodation:** 245 places in halls, 135 hostel places (20% of students home-based). **Library:** Library on each site with subject bias – approx 10,000 volumes, 500 periodicals, 350 study places. £3.6 million library + resources centre being built. **Other learning facilities:** Resources laboratories, computer links, TV studios. **Welfare:** Welfare officer, qualified nurses, doctor on call, chaplain, counsellors, on-campus nurseries. **Careers:** Information and advice service. **Amenities:** SU common rooms, bar and shops. Concert venue on Plas Coch campus and Theatre Clwyd at Mold. Leisure centres: Plas Madoc (8 miles), Deeside. Deeside Ice Rink. **Sporting facilities:** Excellent boating and mountaineering. Good sporting facilities on campus, including weight training, gym and dry ski slope at Deeside. **Employment:** Good employment prospects due to high proportion of vocational courses.

Duration of first degree course(s) or equivalent: 4 years; **others:** 3 years (computing with European Studies, combined studies) **Total first degree students 1991/92:** 841; **Total BEd students:** 436 **Overseas students:** 55 **Mature students:** 449 **Male/female ratio:** 1:1 **Total full-time students 1991/92:** 3,518 **Postgraduate students:** 124 **Tuition fees for 1992/93 (first degrees):** Home: £1,855 (classroom), £2,770 (lab/studio); Overseas: £5,319 (classroom).

What it's like

It's a multi-site institute based at 7 different locations. At the time of writing NEWI is being incorporated and at the same time being disaggregated with the most 'out on a limb' site at Deeside becoming a separate college. Thus NEWI will be based solely in and around Wrexham.

CAN'T FIND WHAT YOU'RE LOOKING FOR? USE THE INDEX!

There is a huge variety of sites ranging from a converted army barracks to a purpose built campus, from an 18th century building to an old hospital. Each site has its own special character! The distance between the sites varies from half a mile to two miles – walkable but bus services do exist.

Student population surprisingly large, about 11,000. A lot come from the local area but the HE students come from the length and breadth of the UK. Significant numbers of overseas students include Omanis, Nigerians, Japanese, American and French. The student population is also characterised by a huge diversity of age groups. 18s to 22 year olds dominate but all other age groups are well represented.

The Institute provides accommodation for about 500 students. Most of FE students and mature students live locally, the rest are housed by the private rented sector which is, largely, cheap and adequate. All institute accommodation is self catering, on and off campus single sex hostels. Hostels comfortable, not too expensive and very warm. Kitchens well equipped but very crowded, good for social gatherings. Most of the institute is 9am to 5pm, however the library stays open until 8pm, the gym until 12pm and of course the bar which abides by the licensing laws!

SU comparatively small but very active, runs all the entertainment and sport as well as the bar and some retail facilities. It supports all the clubs and societies. It is headed towards massive development with the possibility of operating a multi million pound complex. Crèche facilities are available but very limited; you must apply for a place very early. Counselling and welfare advice is sufficient. On site counsellors nurses act in the strictest confidence. Wrexham itself has a good range of clinics and health centres.

NEWI courses are continually expanding and progressing towards being more science based. Tuition is generally good which makes up for the poor libraries; lectures are similar to sixth form classes, student input into lectures is high and lectures often go on for up to 3 hours. Student/staff relationships good; racism, sexism, agism and intimidation practically unheard of. Course rep networks are in existence so any complaints will reach those 'up top'. Workload sporadic; not difficult, just time consuming. It is a good idea to pace yourself throughout the year. Assessment increasingly towards course work although exams still dominate. Degrees are validated by the Wales University which unfortunately doesn't carry any extra clout. The drop out scenario is low and invariably related to financial difficulties rather than course issues.

Wrexham is a bit of a cultural desert. However there are plenty of good pubs. It's not a student town but most of the community welcomes students. Chester offers a wealth of entertainment which is only a bus ride away. SU provides most of the entertainment which is popular but not extravagant.

NEWI is a friendly institute and has a number of internal close-knit communities. Making friends is very easy. Some of the more technical courses often end with employment; non-vocational courses lead to further education or training. Many ex-students however find the pull of the bar too much and return once in a while to meet old friends and reminisce.

Alistair Chambers

Pauper notes

Accommodation: Private rented sector locally: cheap and sufficient but under increasing pressure. **Drinks:** SU bar, plenty of pubs, coffee shops, local brews Marston's Pedigree. **Eats:** Okay for junk food, eg burger joints and pizzas, chip shops, also Chinese and Indian restaurants. Excellent sandwich shops. **Ents:** Good, popular but not extravagant, discos three times a week in SU bar, live bands, theme nights, comedians, shows etc. Good fun. **Sports:** SU organises a lot of clubs; good facilities offered in Wrexham. Olympic baths and diving boards; college teams have the reputation for having fun but not being any good! **Hardship funds:** Access fund offered by college – restricted applicability: students must be over 19. SU has hardship fund: £50 loans. **Travel:** Not good: once you're here you're stuck. National Express and BR stations. Hundreds of taxis (very competitive). SU has free minibus service. **Work:** Unemployment in area high;

however with industrial estate, superstore chains and fast food outlets always have a few jobs going.

More info?
Enquiries to Alistair Chambers (0978 357319).

Informal name
NEWI.

NORTH LONDON POLY

See North London University

NORTH LONDON UNIVERSITY

University of North London, 166–220 Holloway Road, London N7 8DB (071 607 2789) Map D, B1

Student enquiries: Course Enquiries Office 071 753 5066/7 (24 hour answering service 071 607 5755)

Main study areas – as in What to Study section: *(First degree):* Accountancy, architecture, Asian studies, biochemistry, biology, business studies, chemistry, classics, communication studies, computing, economics, education, electrical and electronic engineering, English, environmental studies, European studies, food science & nutrition, geography, history, hotel & catering management, information technology, Latin American studies, law, library & information studies, mathematical studies, microbiology, modern languages, philosophy, professions allied to medicine (PAMs), psychology, physics, sociology. *Also:* Consumer studies, film studies, Irish studies, leisure and tourism management, sports studies, theatre studies, women's studies.

European Community: 16% first degree students take EC language as part of course and 16% spend 6 months or more in another EC country. Formal exchange links with 10 EC universities/colleges: Belgium (3); France (1); Germany (1); Greece (1); Italy (4). Approved Erasmus programme 1992/93. Increasing opportunities for language study.

Application: PCAS for 1993 start, UCAS thereafter. **Academic developments:** Newly structured modular courses in business; new subject combinations within the BSc science modular scheme. **Special features:** Development of flexible entry criteria and of foundation year programmes; commitment to mature students; strong local community involvement. **Largest fields of study:** Science and technology. **Founded:** 1992 as a university; previously North London Poly founded 1971, ex Northern and North Western Polytechnics. **Main awards:** BA, BEd, BEng, BSc, LLB. **Awarding body:** North London University. **Site:** Split on 3 sites. **Access:** Good rail, underground and bus connections. **Accommodation:** Over 400 places in halls plus a range of university managed council flats. Rent: 10% in accommodation where rent controlled by university. **Library:** 4 libraries; 300,000 volumes in total, 2,100 periodicals. **Specialist collections:** Information

CAN'T FIND WHAT YOU'RE LOOKING FOR? USE THE INDEX!

studies, polymers, H G Wells. **Welfare:** Chaplain, student services office including advisers, counsellors and accommodation officer. **Hardship fund:** Fund for
Hong Kong students. **Special categories:** Residential facilities for students with
disabilities; limited childcare facilities. **Careers:** Information, advice and placement service. **Amenities:** University theatre, The Rocket, a multi-purpose venue
with an emphasis on music and dance; SU with own paper, offices and shops on all
sites; bookshop, bank and British Rail agency at Holloway Road. **Sporting
facilities:** Sobell Sports Centre near by; dance studio and gymnasia on 2 sites;
playing fields close to main sites.

Duration of first degree course(s) or equivalent: 3 years; **others:** 4 years
(sandwich) **Total first degree students 1991/92:** 5,256 **Total BEd students:** 475
approx **Male/female ratio:** 1:1 **Teaching staff: full-time:** 400+ approx; **part-
time:** Over 200 **Total full-time students 1991/92:** 6,000 **Postgraduate students:**
685 app. **Tuition fees for 1992/93 (first degrees):** Home: £800 (if no grant),
£1,885 (classroom), £2,770 (lab/studio); Overseas: £5,200 (£4,940 if paid before 16
October).

What it's like

Coming to study in London can be daunting – there is no relief when you
first encounter this 'new university'. The former PNL hasn't changed much
except for a new logo and everything is painted blue. A new site, Spring House, to
add to the other six, has eased some of the chronic overcrowding. Facilities
thought to be poor, libraries tend to be understocked, computers overused and
rooms overflowing.

A good mix of overseas, mature and 'conventional' students, everyone is
welcomed equally. There are some very good and interesting courses though – all
moving towards a modular/semester approach making it less hassle to change
courses, and there are a very wide range of options as to what you want to study.

Good student support services provided both by the university and the traditionally active SU (which has successfully fought on many issues). Good inter-
site mix of entertainments so you can have a good social life if you want. Buy a
travelcard and get to each site as regularly as possible and make the most of your
time here.

Simon Evans

Pauper notes

Accommodation: Hardly any space in halls of residence – not very good housing
on Trowbridge Estate in Hackney. About 90% students live in private rented
sector. Uni accommodation reserved for 1st and 3rd years: apply early. **Drink:** SU
has bars at Ladbroke House and Kentish Town sites. Also try the Flounder &
Firkin on Holloway Road. **Eats:** Try Mick's café or at least eat the sandwiches in
the SU bar. **Ents:** Good on campus. Ents at least twice a week in the SU bars. Off
campus – well, it's London, so take your pick. **Sports:** Uni sports clubs. **Hardship
funds:** Limited funds; slow to administer. **Travel:** Hitch; buy a travelcard or
Young Person's Railcard. **Work:** Summer work is increasingly hard to find – bar
work in term time is the traditional stopgap. Library takes on some students in
term time as does the SU but there are always too many students and not enough
jobs.

More info?

Get the *Handbook of UNL Students Union* direct from SU, Ladbroke House,
62–66 Highbury Grove, London N5 2AD (071 359 6174).
Enquiries to Simon Evans, President SU.

Alumni (Editors' pick)

Jeremy Corbyn MP, Garth Crooks (Tottenham Hotspur), Malcolm Fraser, Claire
Rayner, Neil Tennant (Pet Shop Boys).

GET HOLD OF THE PROSPECTUSES

NORTHERN SCHOOL OF CONTEMPORARY DANCE

Northern School of Contemporary Dance, 98 Chapeltown Road, Leeds LS7 4BH (0532 625359) Map A, E5

Student enquiries: The Administrator

Main study areas – as in What to Study section: *(First degree):* Dance.

European Community: No students learn an EC language or spend time in another EC country.

Application: Direct. **Academic features:** Classical and contemporary dance; choreography and allied arts; performance and related studies; theory and practice of dance in education design. **Structural features:** Collaboration on costume design with Leeds Metropolitan University. **Special features:** Strong links with local artists and musicians. **Largest fields of study:** Contemporary dance. **Main award:** BA. **Awarding body:** Leeds University. **Founded:** 1985. **Site:** Leeds city centre, close to city library/art gallery and universities. **Access:** Very accessible. **Accommodation:** Private accommodation available. Approx cost: £20.00 pw (excluding meals). **Welfare:** Own physiotherapist in attendance; counselling on tutorial system. **Careers:** Information, advice and placement service available. **Hardship funds:** Small student assistance fund. **Amenities:** Cultural and social facilities of Leeds. **Sporting facilities:** City facilities. **Employment:** Professional dance companies in UK and abroad.

Duration of first degree course(s) or equivalent: 3 years (full-time); **Total full-time students 1992/93:** 120 **Male/female ratio:** 2:3 **Teaching staff: full-time:** 10 **part-time:** 6 **Tuition fees for 1992/93 (first degrees):** Home: £2,770; Overseas: £5,319.

What it's like

It's quite different to most colleges and universities despite producing similar qualifications and the inhabitants (students) are far from 'normal'. Based in a beautiful green domed synagogue converted to a working theatre, we shed tears, blood, sweat and laughter from 8.30am to 6.00pm (excluding evening rehearsals). The college takes pride in accommodating a hotch-potch of people – all ages, sexes, creeds and colours – creating a rare environment where you can be yourself and learn about others.

Despite this diversity of people, backgrounds and ideals everyone has a common denominator – commitment. You have to be committed to survive the time-table, eg 4 classes a day; ballet, contemporary dance, jazz, body, music, lighting and design, creative arts, teaching practice, anatomy, choreography, performance, dance history, etc. It couldn't be more intense, which makes for the universal feeling of being completely knackered. Everyone is in the same boat so there is a very close-knit feeling in the college. Everyone knows everyone, so no-one is isolated but gossip is rife. There are close staff–pupil relationships too but you can't hide much when standing in a 10m by 6m studio in a leotard and tights all day every day.

Although this all creates an insular atmosphere, the college is part of Leeds University, which provides a short but essential break from 'dancers' and gives access to university libraries, SUs, etc. Our size means our SU is not politically or socially active but we are welcome to join in university student activities.

Technical progress is continually assessed and written assignments are set half-termly with exams at the end of the year. The graduation performance is the 'biggy'; people come from all over to watch, admire and criticise, the most ruthless examination of all – the public eye.

It's a vocational course and the academic demands are not great. However it's terrifically demanding, mentally and physically, and although you don't need

CAN'T FIND WHAT YOU'RE LOOKING FOR? USE THE INDEX!

previous dance training, in your audition they look for someone with spirit, the will to dance, and perhaps a masochistic streak. Dance students are usually very short of money because grants are only discretionary, and you don't get much if you are lucky enough to have one, and there is no time or energy left to work in the evenings.

But don't let me frighten you off, we have lots of fun. Leeds has a massive student population so there are loads of good pubs, clubs, theatre and cinema. But time to appreciate/abuse them is limited for dancers working 47.5 hours per week excluding rehearsals! That aside a pint in your local is highly recommended of an evening – to help you relax and *try* to be 'normal'.

Charlotte Darbyshire – President SU

Pauper notes

Accommodation: Student digs. **Drink:** Good mixture of pubs, cheap/good atmosphere. **Eats:** Cheap, informal – Indian, vegetarian. **Ents:** Cheap student nightclubs/plays/theatre/bars. **Sports:** No time for extra sports – occasional swim/sauna and gym workout. **Hardship funds:** Scarce. **Travel:** Student fares/hitching.

More info?

Enquiries to Charlotte Darbyshire (0532 374101).

NORTHUMBRIA UNIVERSITY, NEWCASTLE

University of Northumbria at Newcastle, Ellison Building, Ellison Place, Newcastle upon Tyne NE1 8ST (091 232 6002) Map A, E4

Student enquiries: Assistant Registrar (Registry)

Main study areas – as in What to Study section: *(First degree):* Accountancy, art & design, business studies, chemistry, computing, drama, economics, education, electrical & electronic engineering, English, environmental studies, European studies, fine arts, geography, history, information technology, law, library & information studies, mathematical studies, mechanical and production engineering, modern languages, music, nursing studies, physics, politics and government, professions allied to medicine (PAMs), psychology, sociology. *Also:* Building studies, consumer studies, estate management, media studies, quantity surveying, secretarial studies, sports studies.

European Community: 10% first degree students take EC language as part of course (and increasing); 4½% spend 6 months or more in another EC country. Formal exchange links with a number of EC universities/colleges in Belgium, Denmark, France, Germany, Italy, Netherlands, Portugal, Spain. Approved Erasmus programme 1992/93. 10+ degree courses contain language element either compulsory (eg business information technology, international business studies) or as an option (eg computing, information and library management). All students can use university's 'Telelang', language lab, where use of recorded audio or video material allows a language to be started at any time of the year at any level.

Application: PCAS for 1993 start, UCAS thereafter; ADAR for art and design. **Academic features:** Degree courses in media production, travel & tourism, history of modern art, design and film; business information technology, fashion promotion, communication engineering. **Special features:** National coaching centre. **Founded:** 1992 as a university; previously Newcastle Poly, founded 1969. **Main awards:** BA, BEd, BSc, BEng, LLB and MEng. **Awarding body:** Northumbria University. **Site:** 3 sites (Newcastle city centre; Coach Lane campus 3 miles away; new campus at Carlisle, 50 miles from Newcastle). **Accommodation:** 1,900 places available (1,100 places in hall; others in lodgings and tenancies). Priority given to first years. Halls mixed or female only. Approx cost: £50 pw (full board), £30 pw (self-catering). **Library:** Library at each site; total of 500,000 volumes, 3,750 periodicals, 1,100 study places, short loan only for recommended volumes. **Specialist collections:** EC Documentation Centre. **Specialist Centres:** Microelectronics education centre, small business unit, special needs research unit, European law centre, optoelectronics research group, Newcastle Fashion Centre. **Welfare:** Health services, welfare officer, student counsellor, accommodation service, chaplains. **Special categories:** Some places in hall for disabled students, 24 places in local authority flats for married students, playgroup. **Careers:** Information, advice and placement service. **Amenities:** One of the largest SU buildings in UK (300-seat theatre, ballroom, second-hand book shop). **Sporting facilities:** Indoor sports on city campus, outdoor sports 2 miles away, Newcastle swimming baths.

Duration of first degree course(s) or equivalent: 3 years (full-time); 4 years (sandwich), 3–6 years (part-time), **Total first degree students 1991/92:** 7,950; **BEd students:** 550 **Overseas students:** 360 **Mature students:** approx 25% **Male/female ratio:** 1:1 **Teaching staff: full- and part-time** approx 700 **Total full-time students 1991/92:** 9,222 **Postgraduate students:** 824 **Tuition fees for 1992/93 (first degrees):** Home: £1,855 (classroom), £2,770 (lab/studio); Overseas: £4,500 (classroom), £4,800 (lab/studio).

What it's like

Nestles between A1 flyover and civic centre: main site conglomerate of burnt brick and paving slabs. Campus handy for city centre, metro, buses. Also several suburban sites. Halls split between sites and 'residential' area: some self-catering places, personalisation possible with ingenuity.

Social life good with one of the biggest SUs in UK providing bands and discos every week, and facilities for many clubs and societies. SU a good mixture of political/social.

Many students are not straight from school, gives a more mature attitude. Many students from local community and region, and large population of part-time students; makes for less 'ivory-tower' atmosphere. SU has fully equipped theatre, bars, dark room, sports centre, playgroup (run by SU) and XL newspaper. Town has plenty of cinemas, nightclubs, pubs, community groups and special-interest activities. Metro has put campus within 20 mins of Whitley Bay and coast.

Useful welfare services include SU welfare officer, personal tutors, counsellor, accommodation officer and chaplains. SU has women's officer, and contact persons available for sexual and racial harassment procedures.

Term varies from 10 to 13 weeks and assessment is a mixture of continuous assessment and sit-down exams depending on course. New courses being set up include varied teaching modes. Authorities sympathetic to requests to change course if students genuinely unhappy. Appeals procedure for failure exists but is inadequate.

Several courses considered 'centres of excellence'. Library good – is best in region. SU tries to build and develop strong links with local community, to widen access to building and resources to groups in the city. Strong commitment to taking students 'out' into the community.

Pauper notes

Accommodation: Keelmans flats and Garth heads. **Drink:** Three bars on main site, one at Coach Lane serving cheap beer. Good places Barley Mow and 'trendy' Egypt Cottage. Newcastle Brown. **Eats:** A variety of excellent food on SU; veggie, vegan, kosher. Good places to eat in town Starlings, Breadcrumbs. **Ents:** Excellent range of ents including 'Ripe' – a mix of jazzy groups. Good films at Tyneside Art House cinema. Big name bands in town. **Sports:** Good sports centres all over region including Gateshead Stadium. **Hardship funds:** Minimal hardship funds available. **Travel:** Not known. **Work:** Very little work available.

More info?

Enquiries to Tom Robin, Union President (091 232 8761 ext. 441).

CAN'T FIND WHAT YOU'RE LOOKING FOR? USE THE INDEX!

Alumni (Editors' pick)
Steve Cram, Paul Shriek (fashion designer), Rodney Bickerstaff, Karen Boyd (designer), Jeff Banks.

NOTTINGHAM POLY
See Nottingham Trent University

NOTTINGHAM TRENT UNIVERSITY

Nottingham Trent University
(1) **City Centre Site, Burton Street, Nottingham NG1 4BU**
    (0602 418418)
(2) **Clifton Campus, Clifton Lane, Nottingham NG11 8NS**
(3) **Clifton Hall, Clifton Village, Nottingham NG11 8NJ**
Map A, E6

Student enquiries: Academic Registrar

Main study areas – as in What to Study section: *(First degree):* Accountancy, art & design, biology, biochemistry, business studies, chemistry, civil engineering, communication studies, computing, drama, economics, education, electrical & electronic engineering, English, European studies, fine arts, hotel & catering management, information technology, law, mathematical studies, mechanical and production engineering, modern languages, music, physics, politics and government, psychology, public administration, social policy and social welfare. *Also:* Broadcast journalism, estate management, operational research, performance arts, sports studies, surveying, textiles, theatre design.

European Community: Language certificate scheme offers French/German/Italian/Spanish at various levels to all students. Open access to language facilities for wider range of languages. 17% first degree students take an EC language as part of their course; 4% spend 6 months or more in another EC country. Formal exchange links with 11 EC colleges/universities, all open to non-specialists: Denmark (1), France (4), Germany (5), Spain (1). Many student exchanges eg electronic engineering in Karlsruhe, theatre design in Nice, education in Crete, construction management in Waterford.

Application: PCAS for 1993 start, UCAS thereafter; ADAR for art and design. **Academic features:** MEng in computer aided engineering and manufacturing systems engineering with management. Part-time MBA. BA business and quality management. **Special features:** Credit accumulation and negotiated study programmes. **Founded:** 1992, as a university; previously Nottingham Poly. **Main awards:** BEd, BA, BSc, BEng, LLB, MEng. **Awarding body:** Nottingham Trent University. **Site:** Nottingham city centre and Clifton. **Access:** City centre site near rail and coach stations; bus services from Clifton sites. Near M1 and East Midlands Airport. **Accommodation:** 1,000 places in halls and self-catering accommodation. **Library:** Main library on each site plus number of small reference libraries; 400,000 volumes in total, 2,500 periodicals, 1,250 study places. **Other learning resources:** Extensive computing facilities for all students; modern, open-access language laboratories; science and engineering laboratories. **Welfare:** Doctors, nurses, counsellors, chaplains, welfare officer. **Hardship funds:** Fund available to alleviate cases of temporary financial hardship. **Careers:** Information, advice and placement. **Amenities:** Students' union with films, concerts, subsidised social evenings, shop bar, hairdresser, bookshop and bank on each site; travel bureau, sports facilities, playgroup at all sites; closed circuit television studio, playing fields and athletic track at Clifton; cultural resources of Nottingham (museums, theatres, cinemas).

Duration of first degree course(s) or equivalent: 3 or 4 years **Total first degree students 1991/92:** 9,881 **BEd students:** 783 (full and part-time) **Overseas students:** 299 **Mature students:** 8,637 (full- and part-time) **Male/female ratio:** 3:2 **Teaching staff: full-time:** 770 **part-time:** not known **Total full-time students 1991/92:** 10,969 **Postgraduate students:** 762 **Tuition fees for 1992/93 (first degrees):** Home: £1,855 (classroom), £2,770 (lab/studio); Overseas: £5,000.

What it's like

It has the highest rate of students in the country who stay on after completion of their degree. Students arrive in Nottingham and don't want to leave . . . must be good.

The University is split between 2 sites. City site is in the city centre whilst Clifton (D H Lawrence) lies 4 miles away. Both sites house SU buildings, the centres for all student activities.

NPSU's large commercial wing generates profits which are all pumped back into Union services. This enables the SU to offer help, advice and support to all students. Its welfare department encompasses a free women's mini bus, a playgroup and ½ term playscheme. Niteline info. and listening phone service and also student community action, an organisation to get student volunteers to work within Nottingham on welfare projects.

Over 80 clubs and societies. Literally something for everyone – whether you fancy yourself as a budding hang glider or mystic then this is the place for you. SU's Gigs'N'Things Entertainments Department has blossomed and aims to provide something for everyone. Free and varied ents. on offer on a Monday night at the city site, backed up by a huge ents. programme throughout the year.

Nottingham itself is just the right size, enough shops to shop till you drop (grant sufficing) and small enough to get around on foot. Untold clubs, pubs, cinemas and theatres leave little time left for study . . . best years of your life.

Matt Oransfield

Pauper notes

Accommodation: Limited places in halls of residence but an 'adequate' private sector. **Drink:** Too many pubs to mention, I've been in Nottingham 3 years and still keep finding new ones. **Ents:** SU's Gigs'N'Things lead the way in live entertainments. There are more clubs in Nottingham per person than anywhere in the country. All offer student nights and specialist nights, be you a raver or a rocker you will be welcome in Nottingham. **Eats:** Untold eateries & bistros grace Nottingham, therefore lots of competition, therefore cheap! **Sports:** National Water Sports Centre, Trent Bridge, Notts. County & Brian Clough. **Travel:** NPSU's very own travel shop caters for all student travel needs. **Work:** Pubs & obligatory stint at Pork Farms (smelly, messy, dehumanizing but good for the overdraft). **Hardship Funds:** University has 22k to distribute according to need. SU has very small emergency fund.

NOTTINGHAM UNIVERSITY

University of Nottingham, Nottingham NG7 2RD (0602 484848)
Map A, E6

Student enquiries: Registrar

Main study areas – as in What to Study section: *(First degree):* Accountancy, agriculture, horticulture & forestry, American studies, archaeology, architecture, biochemistry, biology, botany, business studies, chemical engineering, chemistry,

CAN'T FIND WHAT YOU'RE LOOKING FOR? USE THE INDEX!

civil engineering, classics, computing, economics, electrical & electronic engineering, English, environmental science, fine arts, food science & nutrition, geography, history, law, mathematical studies, mechanical and production engineering, medicine, metallurgy and materials science, microbiology, modern languages, music, nursing studies, pharmacology, pharmacy, philosophy, physics, politics and government, professions allied to medicine (PAMs), psychology, religious studies and theology, social policy and social welfare, sociology, town and country planning, zoology. *Also:* Agricultural economics, horticulture, mining, Slavonic studies.

European Community: Subsidiary languages tuition available on many courses in arts, law and social science; increasing in engineering. All students may use the language centre. Increasing number of degrees combining languages with other subjects eg electrical and electronic engineering with French/German/Spanish; management studies with French/German; modern European studies; agricultural and food sciences with European studies; French/German with history/politics. 21 departments have established Erasmus links; other schemes in the pipeline.

Application: UCCA for 1993 start, UCAS thereafter. **Academic features:** Courses in modern European studies, Soviet and East European studies, law with American/European law, social and cultural studies, chemistry and molecular physics, materials chemistry, neuroscience, minerals engineering, environmental engineering and resources management. **Founded:** 1881. **Main awards:** BA, LLB, BSc, BEng, MEng, BPharm, BM, BS, BN. **Awarding body:** Nottingham University. **Site:** 330-acre campus to west of city centre. **Access:** Buses from city centre and railway station; campus 4 miles from M1. **Accommodation:** 12 halls of residence on campus; all first year students can be accommodated. **Library:** Over 1,000,000 volumes and pamphlets, over 5,000 periodicals; short loan collection for books most in demand. **Other learning facilities:** Cripps computing centre; university museum and arts centre. **Welfare:** Health service and chaplaincy, counselling service. **Careers:** Advisory service. **Amenities:** SU with shop, minibuses, travel agency, hairdressers; 200 clubs and societies; campus bookshop; performing arts studio, theatre. **Sporting facilities:** Indoor sports centre, excellent playing fields, 2,000 metre international rowing course near by.

Duration of first degree course(s) or equivalent: 3 years; others: 4 years; 5 years (medicine); 6 years (architecture) **Total first degree students 1991/92:** 7,814 **Overseas students:** 1,000 **Mature students:** 700 **Male/female ratio:** 6:4 (first degree) **Teaching staff: full-time:** 750 **Total full-time students 1991/92:** 9,520 **Postgraduate students:** 1,706 **Tuition fees for 1992/93 (first degrees):** Home: £1,855 (classroom), £2,769 (lab/studio), £4,985 (clinical); Overseas: £5,320 (classroom), £7,055 (lab/studio), £12,990 (clinical).

What it's like

Nottingham University is one of the most pleasant working environments. Being campus based it's very much self contained, with most amenities available within easy walking distance but can lead to a feeling of encroaching suburbia!

Campus social life is improving. The twelve halls of residence have a long-established events programme, culminating in summer hall party extravaganzas. Almost all first years are placed in halls, but shortages of accommodation do occur. The SU have recently acquired and refurbished a large union bar and this, added to their other amenities of travel bureau, shop, printing unit, student advice centre, make the Union an integral part of university life. Participation in activities is high, especially in sport, Union clubs and societies, hall life, community work and charity fund raising.

The city centre is a ten-minute bus journey away and has a wide range of pubs, clubs, cinemas, theatres, art galleries and shopping centres. Student discounts are available at many restaurants, theatres etc. Student housing is becoming less easy to obtain; prices are reasonable but rising fast. 51% of student income goes on rent alone – student areas are buzzing with atmosphere.

GET HOLD OF THE PROSPECTUSES

The university has a strong community atmosphere and three years here are well spent.

Pauper notes

Accommodation: Generally good but always a rush to find houses in January/ February. Landlord problems always exist but major problems are rare. **Drink:** Cheap hall bars and Union bar. Local pubs popular with students: Happy Return, Three Wheatsheaves (Lenton), Greyhound (Beeston), Yates's Wine Lodge, Trip to Jerusalem. Local brew: Home Ales. **Eats:** Lots of Indian and Chinese restaurants as well as pizza joints – all do student discount. **Ents:** Midland is 'trendy arts' theatre. Cheap student nights at Rock City, Zhivago's, Irish Social Centre. Reduced cinema prices at the Odeon, Savoy, also Unifilms – run by Students Union. **Sports:** Local swimming pools; on-campus well-equipped sports centre, University sports fields adjacent to campus and inter-Hall sports grounds about 1 mile away. **Hardship funds:** 2 Union-employed welfare assistants, and a full time sabbatical Union officer. **Travel:** Cheap bus travel offered for regular users. **Work:** Temping available but low-paid. Bar jobs, local pork pie companies. Some theatre and sports concessions for UB40s.

Alumni (Editors' pick)

D H Lawrence, Brian Moore (England Rugby international).

OAK HILL COLLEGE

Oak Hill College, Chase Side, Southgate, London N14 4PS
(081 449 0467) Map A, E8

Student enquiries: Admissions Officer

Main study areas – as in What to Study section: *(First degree):* Religious studies & theology. *Also:* Pastoral studies.

European Community: No students learn an EC language or spend time in another EC country. Some language tuition possible at Middlesex University but not as part of course.

Application: Direct. **Founded:** 1932. **Main awards:** BA. **Awarding body:** Middlesex University. **Site:** Cockfosters/Southgate area. **Access:** Underground to Southgate (Piccadilly line); then walk or bus (about 1 hr from Westminster). **Academic features:** Module in homiletics. Successful DipHE candidates can transfer to degree course. Number of mature students admitted without the formal qualifications. **Special features:** Some modules may be taken with the Middlesex University American exchange programme. **Accommodation:** 47 places in hall; 60 houses for married students; 8 flats/bedsitters. Approx cost: Maintenance fee £2,199 pa, £60 pw (average) for married accommodation. **Library:** 18,000 volumes, 182 periodicals, 30 study places; course books placed on temporary reference; tape library, video library. Access to major London libraries. **Welfare:** Doctor, chaplain. **Special categories:** Houses for married couples plus families. **Careers:** Advice service. Vocational placement scheme. **Sporting facilities:** All weather tennis courts; football/rugby field on site; municipal squash courts and swimming pool near by; also cricket pitch. **Employment:** Christian ministry and various community services.

Duration of first degree course(s) or equivalent: 3 years **Total first degree students 1991/92:** 80 **Overseas students:** 10% **Mature students:** 100% **Male/ female ratio:** 4:3 **Teaching staff: full-time:** 12 **part-time:** 2 **Total full-time students 1991/92:** 115 **Postgraduate students:** 4 **Tuition fees, first degrees, 1992/93:** Home and Overseas: £3,591.

What it's like

It is first and foremost an Anglican training college and those students training for the ministry are supported by their diocese. It is housed in a compact, much extended former stately home in 60 acres of parkland and woods. All singles accommodated in rooms in main building; most married couples in college-owned houses and flats on campus or near by. Individual studies available. Good food. Good washing and cooking facilities.

While majority of 130 students training for Church of England ministry, some are from other denominations, some studying to test vocation. About 30 on part-time course. All studying theological and pastoral studies.

Expanding library; good bookshop.

Relations with all staff on first-name basis. Student representation on all committees. Prayer and worship an integral part of day when college meets together. All students in tutorial groups for pastoral care.

Long-standing links with colleges in US (with which student exchanges can be arranged) and Africa (students fundraise for training college in Uganda).

Two semesters per year. Courses usually run one semester. Some can be taken at Middlesex University. College courses include: biblical studies, counselling, sociology, world religions, communication, Greek, Church history, doctrine, liturgy, preaching, philosophy, ethics. Assessment is continuous and/or by exam. Varied teaching styles: seminars, lectures, workshops, role play, videos, tutorials.

Good placement scheme with churches within 15 miles. College missions, block placements, and courses in hospital chaplaincy and urban studies in vacations.

Families well catered for. Green spaces and equipment for children to play, crèche for children up to 2½ years, babysitting rota. Programme in evening for wives. Spouses welcome at all lectures.

Pauper notes

Accommodation: Study bedrooms for singles. Year-round accommodation for singles available in some cases. Houses for marrieds on and off campus. **Drink:** Good local pubs, especially in countryside few miles to north. **Eats:** College offers good meals, often seconds. Includes vegetarian meals and fresh fruit or pudding for desert. **Ents:** TV and video room. Social committee organise events throughout year, inc. College Ball, panto, reviews. Two miles to nearest cinema in Barnet. One mile to nearest station for 45-minute journey to central London. Classical music programme organised. **Sports:** On site: tennis, football, rugby, cricket, snooker, croquet, table tennis. Near by: squash (courts booked by college), swimming (Southgate Leisure Centre one mile away), running club, fishing. All sports subsidised by college. **Hardship funds:** College Bursary Fund. In cases of real need the college community will almost invariably try to meet the need itself. **Travel:** Expenses reimbursed for Sunday and block placements. **Work:** Paid manual vacation-work available.

Informal name:

'Oak Hill'; (former students known as 'Old Oaks').

Alumni (Editors' pick)

Include Rt. Rev. George Carey (former tutor).

OPEN UNIVERSITY

Open University, Walton Hall, Milton Keynes MK7 6AA (0908 274066)

Student enquiries: Central Enquiry Service (0908 653231 – answering service out of office hours)

Main study areas – as in What to Study section: *(First degree):* Biochemistry, biology, chemistry, computing, economics, education, English, environmental science, environmental studies, European studies, fine arts, geography, geology, history, humanities, information technology, mathematical studies, materials science, music, philosophy, physics, politics and government, psychology, public administration, social policy and social welfare, sociology. *Also:* Classical studies, design, electronics, engineering mechanics, micro-electronics, social studies, systems. Very many specialised subjects in course unit system.

European Community: No students learn an EC language or spend time in another EC country. University is establishing study centres in various parts of the EC and hopes to increase considerably its recruitment of students living in other EC countries.

Application: Direct. No educational qualifications required but students should be 18 or over and resident in the European Community. Early applications take precedence over later ones, so apply early. **Academic features:** Approx 130 courses, many multi- or inter-disciplinary, in arts, social sciences, mathematics, science, educational studies and technology. Degrees built up on course credits (6 for degree, 8 for honours) or individual courses may be taken on one-off basis for vocational, updating or as refreshers. Community education study packs available in eg parent education, energy saving, consumer decisions. Wide range of courses provided for professionals in commerce, industry, education, and the caring services, (including a certificate, diploma and Masters degree in management). Postgraduate study also possible (taught and research based). **Special features:** Students study at home from specially written course texts, set books, radio and television broadcasts, other audio-visual materials and home kits. Also face-to-face tuition at regional study centres, where appropriate; for some courses, home computing and annual residential summer schools. **Founded:** 1969. **Main awards:** BA. **Awarding body:** Open University. **Centres of excellence:** Centre for advice to others wishing to set up similar institutions. **Library:** For staff and full-time students only. **Careers:** Information booklet 'Career choices and degree planning' and a series of leaflets. **Hardship funds:** Funds for students experiencing financial hardship. Some LEAs may help also and give funds for residential school. **Amenities:** Set book stockists from whom students can obtain essential texts; network of more than 250 study centres. The Open University Students' Association, whose membership includes all currently registered students, provides support services in both education and welfare.

Duration of first degree course(s) or equivalent: 4–5 years average, 5–6 years average for honours **Total first degree students 1991:** 75,076 **Mature students:** Almost all **Male/female ratio:** 1:1 **Teaching staff: full-time:** approx 800 **part-time:** approx 6,700 **Total full-time students (all post-grad) 1991:** approx 150 **Postgraduate students:** approx 6,500 **Tuition fees 1993 (first degrees): UK students 1993:** £260 for each full credit; £130 for each half credit (plus £180 if a residential school is involved). Higher fees are charged for students resident outside the UK.

What it's like

A large-scale distance teaching organisation; studying with it is a unique experience. The student is recommended to spend 10–15 hours a week studying, but this varies greatly. The well-organised and self-disciplined do just that, others cram everything into a frantic weekend of study closeted away from family and friends. The OU provides students with units of written information and details of set books; these are supported with radio and television broadcasts. Unfortunately, the broadcasts are becoming increasingly inaccessible due to very unsocial transmission times. They are, however, available on video. All courses have tutorials. These vary greatly in frequency. The foundation course, for example, has considerably more than third and fourth level courses. Some courses also have summer schools (all the foundation courses do) held at universities throughout the country. The prospect of spending a week away from home with hundreds of strangers can be daunting, but everyone's in the same situation and most enjoy the intensive study and social life. Many OU students have problems with isolation. It's very easy to feel that you are the only OU student in your area (this is very unlikely to be true). One source of support is the Students'

Association (OUSA) which exists to serve the needs of OU students through its welfare and services provisions; to promote the student voice by its representation and education function on OU boards and committees; and to fight for lower fees and mandatory grants for part-time students through campaigning. Most study centres have an OUSA branch where students can not only meet like-minded people but derive inspiration and stimulation for further study. Studying with the OU is not cheap. Fees continue to rise but help is available for the unemployed and low-waged by application to OU. There is also a fund administered by the Students' Association to help with the other study related costs: details from OUSA, c/o The Open University, Walton Hall, Milton Keynes MK7 6AA. Being an OU student means being in charge of your own learning experiences. You can study what you want when you want; cross discipline areas and even take a year off. Study can be fitted into odd moments through the day or in the evening, weekend or holiday periods. The OU is no easy option. It's difficult to cope with all the demands on your time and keep up with the deadlines. However, its very popularity indicates how worthwhile its students feel it to be – not only in the acquisition of a qualification, but in proving to yourself that you can do it.

OXFORD BROOKES UNIVERSITY

Oxford Brookes University, Headington, Oxford OX3 0BP
(0865 741111) Map A, E7

Student enquiries: Registry

Main study areas – as in What to Study section: *(First degree):* Accountancy, anthropology, architecture, biology, business studies, chemistry, civil engineering, computing, economics, education, electrical & electronic engineering, English, environmental science, environmental studies, fine arts, food science & nutrition, geography, geology, history, hotel & catering management, law, mathematical studies, mechanical & production engineering, modern languages, music, nursing studies, physics, politics and government, professions allied to medicine (PAMs), psychology, sociology, town and country planning. *Also:* Building, cartography, estate management, publishing, tourism.

European Community: 11% first degree students take EC language as part of course and 7% spend 6 months or more in another EC country. Formal exchange links with 108 EC universities/colleges in all EC countries except Luxembourg. Approved Erasmus programme.

Application: PCAS for 1993 start, UCAS thereafter. **Academic features:** Modular course allows study on a full-time, part-time or mixed-mode basis including nursing and midwifery, visual studies or cartography. New courses in exercise and health science, geotechnics, and marketing. Access courses at seven local centres give entry to university courses. **Founded:** 1992 as a university; previously Oxford Poly, founded 1865, as school of art, becoming polytechnic in 1970. **Main awards:** BA, BEd, BSc, BEng, LLB. **Awarding body:** Oxford Brookes University. **Site:** Headington (1 mile from city centre) and Wheatley (6 miles from city centre). **Access:** Transport between sites. **Accommodation:** 1,600 hall places; 350 places in university housing association; other students in lodgings or shared houses. Average rent for private accommodation in Oxford £42 self catering, £56 full board. **Rent:** 27% in accommodation where rent controlled by university; 50% first years accommodated in hall. **Library:** 2 libraries, 280,000 volumes, 2,000 periodicals, 760 study places. **Other learning resources:** Computer centre: SUN 6/70 Unix host, over 300 PC workstations, 10,300 registered users. PC and Unix networks available 24 hours a day, 7 days a week. Educational methods unit: TV, graphics and photography. Consultancy and training in teaching methods, course design and evaluation. **Welfare:** Student services centre with 30 professional staff (counsellors, careers, accommodation, housing and chaplaincy staff, nurses, FPA, visiting GPs and specialist advisers for international students, mature students and students with disabilities). **Amenities:** SU with bars and shop, banks, outdoor sports, fitness training room and multi-gym, choirs and orchestra, nursery. **Hardship funds:** A fund is available.

Duration of first degree course(s) or equivalent: 3 years; **others:** 4 years **Total first degree students 1991/92:** 8,020 **BEd students:** 210 (70 in-service BEd) **Overseas students:** 800 **Mature students:** Approx 3,300 **Male/female ratio:** 1:1 **Teaching staff: full-time:** 390 **part-time:** 70 **Total full-time students 1991/92:** 6,139 **Postgraduate students:** 1,585 **Tuition fees for 1992/93 (first degrees):** Home: £1,855 (classroom), £2,770 (lab/studio); Overseas: £5,250.

What it's like

Two sites, Headington and Wheatley; buildings on both sites functional. Access to Headington site average from city centre, excellent from London (190 bus stops outside). Intersite transport free and frequent: half-hourly, and hourly after 6pm. Halls of residence (full board and self-catering) and shared houses fiercely competed for and prices high (around £40+ pw, excluding bills). After much recent building, most first year students can find a place in halls.

Based on modular course system – most advanced in the country. Successful and popular. Non-modular courses available. Library and labs well-equipped and stay open late. Sports facilities average but dwindling – no central sports hall. Student services and SU both have good counselling service. SU organises good quality ents; bars on both sites and in 2 halls. Top subjects: architecture, education, estate management, town planning, catering, business studies although most others of very high quality. Oxford is student city and geared to students' needs but expensive! Drop-out rate is low and most enjoy life. Social mix – mostly middle class – 60% students from independent schools, but becoming more varied.

Pauper notes

Accommodation: Expensive in private rented sector, average for halls/hostels. **Drink:** SU has cheapest, otherwise average–high. **Eats:** Campus food average, and improving after massive refurbishment. Good choice in town. **Ents:** Good SU ents. **Sports:** Considering poor facilities, great range and quite cheap. Good teams. **Hardship funds:** Available. **Travel:** Easy hitch to London, regular buses, trains. **Work:** Uni takes part-time and full-time staff during vacations, locally jobs available but not mind-bending, usually barperson, salesperson, waiting etc.

More info?

Get students' Alternative Prospectus. Enquiries to President SU (0865 794773).

Alumni (Editors' pick)

Adrian Reynard (Reynard Racing), Tim Rodber (England Rugby).

OXFORD POLY
See Oxford Brookes University

OXFORD UNIVERSITY

University of Oxford, Oxford, England OX1 2JD
(Registry 0865 270000) Map A, E7

Student enquiries: (1) (University) Oxford Colleges Admissions Office, University Offices, Wellington Square, Oxford OX1 2JD
(2) (Colleges) The Tutor for Admissions, ... College, Oxford.

Main study areas – as in What to Study section: *(First degree):* Archaeology, anthropology, Asian studies, biochemistry, biology, botany, chemistry, chemical engineering, civil engineering, classics, computing, economics, electrical & electronic engineering, English, fine arts, geography, geology, history, law, mathematical studies, mechanical & production engineering, medicine, metallurgy & materials science, modern languages, music, Near East and Islamic studies, philosophy, politics and government, physics, physiology, psychology, religious studies and theology, zoology. *Also:* Human sciences, management.

European Community: 9% first degree students take EC language as part of course and spend 6 months or more in another EC country. University has links with large number of EC universities. Most exchanges at undergraduate level are for language specialists although number of opportunities in other subjects is increasing. All undergraduates have access to self instruction courses and language laboratories in the language teaching centre; and to classes (1–2 hours/week) in main EC languages (priority given to students needing classes as part of their course). As well as the specialist modern languages degree, there are joint schools of modern languages with classics, English, modern history or philosophy.

The University and the Colleges

Oxford is not a campus university – university and college buildings are scattered throughout the town centre. It is a federation of 35 colleges, 28 of which admit first degree undergraduates, together with 6 private halls and 1 society for continuing education. Each college selects its own students, houses them (for at least 2 out of 3 years), provides meals, common rooms, libraries, sports and social facilities and is responsible, through the tutorial system, for academic work. You apply to colleges for a BA degree. Your college will be the hub of your life.

The Colleges

You can look up these colleges and private halls:

Women only:
St Hilda's
Somerville

Men and women:
Balliol
Brasenose
Christ Church
Corpus Christi
Exeter
Hertford
Jesus
Keble
Lady Margaret Hall
Lincoln
Magdalen
Manchester (permanent private hall for mature students)
Mansfield (permanent private hall)
Merton
New College
Oriel
Pembroke
Queen's
Regent's Park (permanent private hall)
St Anne's
St Catherine's
St Edmund Hall
St Hugh's
St John's
St Peter's
Trinity
University College
Wadham
Worcester

There are three other permanent private halls – Campion Hall (men only, principally members of the Society of Jesus); Greyfriars (principally members of the Franciscan Order); St Benet's Hall (men only, principally for Benedictines).

GET HOLD OF THE PROSPECTUSES

How to apply to Oxford University

Critical dates: Oxford Colleges Admissions Office must receive your completed application card and UCCA (for 1993 start, UCAS thereafter) must receive your application form, both by 15 October.

You may choose up to three colleges if you wish, or put in an open application to the university. (The Admissions Office will advise you; or see the *Undergraduate Prospectus*.) All candidates will be considered by the colleges named in order of preference. Candidates not accepted by any of the colleges so named will then be available to all other colleges for consideration. You must complete your application in the calendar year before the year in which you wish to enter the University. The procedures are different from most other universities and you should study the *Undergraduate Prospectus* carefully. There is a choice of application routes – Mode N (conditional offers or post A level) or the Entrance Examination, Mode E. There are 2 forms to be submitted:

Form 1: *The Oxford Application Card* – You must return this to the Oxford Colleges Admissions Office (University Offices, Wellington Square, Oxford OX1 2JD) by 15 October. There is an application fee of £10.00. Instructions for completing the cards are given in the *Undergraduate Prospectus* which is distributed, with the card, by the Admissions Office to schools or, for candidates who have left school, by application to the Secretary of the Oxford Colleges Admissions Office.

Form 2: *The UCCA/UCAS Form* – You must return this to UCCA/UCAS before 15 October.

Applications to both Oxford and Cambridge:
It is no longer possible to apply to both Oxford and Cambridge in the same admissions year, unless you are a candidate for an organ award.

Duration of first degree course(s) or equivalent: 3 and 4 years **Total first degree students 1991/92:** 10,326 **Overseas students:** 655 **Male/female ratio:** 3:2 **Teaching staff: full-time:** 1,500 **part-time:** 200 **Total full-time students 1991/92:** 14,228 **Postgraduate students:** 3,902 **University tuition fees for 1992/93 (first degrees):** Home: £1,855 (classroom), £2,770 (lab/studio), £4,985 (clinical); a reduction of some £1,000 if no grant. Overseas: £5,320 (classroom), £7,055 (lab/studio), £12,990 (pre-clinical). In addition, college fees are charged – some £2,000–£3,400.

What it's like

Consists of over 30 semi-autonomous colleges scattered around the centre of city; many beautiful old buildings, some modern. Easily accessible by rail from London, the south-west and anywhere via Birmingham. There's also a cheap and frequent bus link to London. In Oxford cars are impractical and most students cycle, though there is a reasonable bus service. Accommodation (quality and quantity) varies from college to college; but everyone gets at least their first year in, some all three. Private rented sector is expensive. Two all-female colleges; the rest are mixed. A high percentage of overseas students, particularly graduates, but few mature students. Library opening hours vary from college to college; some 24 hour. Excellent university libraries too.

Without a large central site the student union tends to be a campaigning and representative force rather than a social one; though it has a cheap stationery shop and is the largest student union publisher in the country. Currently Labour-led. Visiting restrictions vary from college to college but most fairly lenient. Contraception and pregnancy advice available in city; many colleges have condom machines; university has own confidential counselling service and there are numerous telephone help lines too. Enormous range of societies; ranging from things you've always wanted to be involved in to those you've never heard of. Relationship with the town is fairly good. Lots of pubs, student plays, excellent cinemas showing new releases, stuff that you missed first time around and trendy, arty films.

All subjects highly rated though courses generally traditional. You can change

CAN'T FIND WHAT YOU'RE LOOKING FOR? USE THE INDEX!

subject reasonably easily if it's because you want to rather than because you're terrible at your present one. Work load . . . some people claim they don't have one, others spend all their time in the library. In the end most people get seconds. Degrees awarded solely on performance in exams at the end of your final year (a stressful time!). Lectures vary from interesting to abysmal but few people attend anyway (especially arts subjects). It's your tutorials that matter and you can change tutor if you really don't get on.

The south and private schools are over-represented but this is changing (at present 43% state schools). The university has recently produced a code which aims to protect students from any harrassment on the grounds of gender, race, religion or sexual orientation.

There's no such thing as a typical Oxford student; everyone finds their niche be it in the library, the bar, the theatre etc, and whether they become a high-earning merchant banker, an unpaid voluntary worker or something in between.

Vicki Howe

Pauper notes

Accommodation: Houses outside city centre cheaper; area called Jericho (western edge of city) traditionally popular; Cowley Road is student-inhabited. **Drink:** College bars (especially St Catz & Somerville) cheapest – Morrells best beer; many pubs but surprisingly few outstanding ones: though all visit central Turf and King's Arms. **Eats:** Pak Fook (Chinese, on Cowley Road), number of good Indian restaurants on Cowley Road, particularly Aziz. Burger vans in High Street. Best college food in St. Hilda's and Lincoln. Vegetarian served almost everywhere. **Ents:** College discos cheapest, Oxford discos towny (as opposed to gowny) but can be fun, eg Downtown Manhattan on George Street. Playhouse, good cinema (Phoenix in Walton Street carries on independent tradition of old Scala, which formed British Cinema – John Schlesinger, Lindsay Anderson). Also Penultimate Picture Palace (PPP) on Cowley Road. Oxford Brookes University often has good bands to which all NUS members can go; also Jericho Tavern and The Venue. **Sport:** Most colleges have good sports facilities – but no swimming pool in university as yet. **Hardship funds:** Most colleges have them. Money supplied as a grant or loan. Those eligible and amounts paid out vary widely from college to college. Also Access Fund: aimed at those living out. Amount varies from £25 to £600. Means tested. **Shops:** Covered market (fruit and veg, Camembert and well-hung game), Gloucester Green market (Weds), 3 Oxfam shops, contraceptive vending machines now in many colleges. **Travel:** All colleges have some funds (however piddling), most students too languid to claim them. Cheap coach travel to London (£5 period return) by Citylink. **Work:** Students rarely take on paid work in term time. Quite a lot of part time shop and pub work, some teaching in summer and 'Undergraduate tours' (London-based) if you have car.

More info?

Alternative Students' Prospectus available from OUSU, New Barnett House, 28 Little Clarendon Street, Oxford OX1 2HU (0865 270777).
Sixth-former enquiries to Vicki Howe.

Alumni (Editors' pick)

Oscar Wilde, Margaret Thatcher, Roy Jenkins, Harold Wilson, Michael Heseltine, Denis Healey, Benazir Bhutto, Roger Bannister, Rowan Atkinson, Dudley Moore, Willy Rushton, Melvyn Bragg, Sir Robin Day, Tony Benn, Kris Kristofferson, Bill Clinton, Barbara Castle.

Buzz-words

Loads, eg subfusc (cap and gown); the High (High Street); collections (college set exams)

GET HOLD OF THE PROSPECTUSES

BALLIOL

Balliol College, Oxford OX1 3BJ (0865 277777)

Founded: 1263; women undergraduates first admitted 1979. **Accommodation:** All undergraduates offered rooms in college (usually bedsits) for their 1st year and either their 2nd or 3rd year and possibly both. Rent: 75% in accommodation where rent controlled by college. More accommodation being built. Rent and establishment charges vary, £585 to £960; average £799 for 25 weeks; average expenditure on laundry and electricity £116 for 25 weeks. **Eating arrangements:** Undergraduates not required to take meals in college but the average expenditure by undergraduates in hall likely to be £503. All meals taken in hall on cafeteria basis, JCR pantry for snacks and breakfast. **Gate/guest hours:** Gate locked at midnight. All students have keys. 2 guest rooms. **Admission:** Mainly by Mode N or Mode E except pre-A level candidates in modern languages who must apply by Mode E. No undergraduates admitted for biological sciences, earth sciences, geography, human sciences or theology. **Scholarships:** None at entrance. Awards made at end of first year. **Travel:** Grants for academic purposes awarded annually on tutors' recommendations. **Library:** Library aims to provide at least basic coverage in all main subjects. **Hardship funds:** Hardship fund available. **Other college facilities:** Nearby sports field and pavilion (with 2 squash courts).

European Community: 8% students study an EC language and spend a period in another EC country as part of the formal requirements of their courses. All undergraduates have access to language tuition at the university language laboratory. Formal exchange links in Paris and Munich.

College fees for 1992/93 (undergraduate) £2,966.

Undergraduates: *Men:* 276 *Women:* 106

Postgraduates: *Men:* 92 *Women:* 47

Teaching staff: *Men:* 57 fellows, 10 research fellows, 19 lecturers
Women: 6 fellows, 2 research fellows, 8 lecturers.

What it's like

Good academically (especially in social sciences and classics) and active and energetic in other aspects. Co-residential, guaranteed 2-years-living in, some for 3 years. Separate graduate centre and middle common room. Lots of overseas students. Hall dining facilities and JCR pantry service (best and latest breakfast in town). Lively JCR both socially and politically. Excellent drama, sport and music facilities. Central sports field. Sunday night concerts free and famous in Oxford. Music room and Lindsay drama room are very actively used. Good library facilities (all-night law library). Active women's group – regular speakers and meetings. Progressive college with high academic standards and friendly and active atmosphere to suit all needs and interests.

Pauper notes

Accommodation: In college quite cheap, most live out one year. More building planned. **Drink:** Cheap bar, good atmosphere, new bar (spring '92). **Eats:** Hall provides cheap food, JCR alternative – cheap and good; some vegetarian choices. **Ents:** Big summer event, discos, famous cocktail parties, plays, Christmas panto. **Sports:** Close sports field with football, squash, tennis, Rugby. Also darts, pool and video games. Nearest pool about 2 m away. **Hardship funds:** College loans/ grants help those living out. Book grants. Grants, loans and short-term cash loans always available to needy cases. **Travel:** Grants, travel scholarships, 8 yearly awards to USA for summer. **Work:** Not in term; considerable competition for holiday work. Some vacation grants.

Alumni (Editors' pick)

Harold Macmillan, Ted Heath, Bryan Gould, Graham Greene, H H Asquith, the Huxleys, Gerard Manley Hopkins, Peter Snow, Anthony Powell, John Schlesinger, Denis Healey.

BRASENOSE

Brasenose College, Oxford OX1 4AJ (0865 277823)

Founded: 1509; women undergraduates first admitted 1974. **Accommodation:** All undergraduates can live in for two years, and some (if they wish) for a third year. Rent: 75% in accommodation where rent controlled by college. Most undergraduates charged £671 pa (range £372–£1,110). **Eating arrangements:** Breakfast, lunch and dinner in hall; tea available in New Buttery. **Gate/guest hours:** Unrestricted. **Admission:** Standard Oxford arrangements. No undergraduates admitted to earth sciences; human sciences; metallurgy, economics and management; or history with English. **Scholarships:** Made at the end of the first year. **Hardship funds:** The college has discretionary funds for assistance in case of hardship. **Library:** About 30,000 volumes – on open shelves and a further collection of about 12,000 older books; 90 periodical subscriptions; separate history and law reading rooms. **Other college facilities:** Shop, bar, sports ground, pavilion, squash and tennis courts about 10 mins walk from college; boathouse. **Largest fields of study:** PPE, law, modern history.

European Community: 10% students take EC language as part of course and spend 6 months or more in another EC country. Formal exchange links in Strasbourg.

College fees for 1992/93 (undergraduate) £2,985.

Undergraduates: *Men:* 230 *Women:* 106

Postgraduates: *Men:* 90 *Women:* 28

Teaching staff: *Men:* 23 fellows, 11 research fellows, 22 lecturers
Women: No fellows, 1 research fellow, 6 lecturers.

What it's like

Positioned along one side of Radcliffe Square, in the wake of the towering dome of the Camera, Brasenose is ideally situated. All main libraries, the Bodleian, the Codrington and the Radcliffe Camera are extremely convenient; very close to shops, pubs and nightclubs. Though not one of the most imposing or palatial of the Oxford colleges, the 16th-century Old Quad and adjoining, ironically named, miniature Deer Park are very picturesque. Small enough for a sense of community; large enough not to be claustrophobic. Some modern rooms – warm and ugly – but mainly old 'character' rooms which are being steadily renovated to very high standard (ensuite bathrooms for finalists). Undergraduates guaranteed accommodation for two out of three years. This may include a year in Frewin, the college annexe.

Academically variable, lodged in the middle of the Norrington Table, after a brief spate of success. Widely known as the place for law and PPE. Tutors and library facilities are excellent in these areas. College library is more comprehensive than it looks in most other subjects, and has extensive reserve stacks. Historians have own specialist library, one of the largest in the university.

JCR generally moderate, incorporates students from a variety of backgrounds, schools and regions. In the past, however, the 2:1 male/female ratio has created a rather 'hearty' male atmosphere which has declined over last few years; still quite a few rugger-buggers but not as many as before. Situation has improved with the advent of a JCR Women's Officer, an SCR Women's Adviser and an active Target Schools Scheme, which is intent upon encouraging more women, state school, and disabled students to apply. Recently joined access scheme aimed at encouraging students from 'non-traditional' backgrounds to apply. SCR very committed to widening intake. General tolerant attitude; not many out-and-out rebels.

Reputation as a strong rowing college. Many other sports to a high standard; namely, Rugby, netball, football and cross-country. Facilities are close by and very comprehensive, including two football pitches, a rugby and a hockey pitch, squash, tennis and netball courts, and an excellent boathouse. Facilities feature a college-run bar, recently enlarged, redecorated and taken over by college – bar staff very popular and reputedly best student bar in Oxford. College recently constructed a purpose built computer room for junior members which houses 4 modern computers and is continuing to develop it. JCR has Sky TV and video, a pool table, Coke machine and various games machines. Runs societies as diverse as The Brasenose Players, Christian Union, Women's Group, Wine Society, Left Caucus as well as its own wittily malicious student Noserag.

Pauper notes

Accommodation: Live in college (usually) 1st and 3rd years. Accommodation in college character rooms, attractive and well-equipped. Frewin Annexe good facilities, modern and warm. Accommodation in Frewin for some 2nd years soon to be built: much cheaper than living out. Will be hardship fund for those forced to live out. Oxford very expensive; up to £50/week room shared house not uncommon. **Drink:** College bars; 4 central 'student' pubs – Turf, Kings Arms, White Horse (very small and cosy – crowded), the Bear (very Sloaney). **Eats:** College, 3 meals per day. Carfax chippy. Donna Kebab Van. **Ents:** Free college ents: bops, bands mainly. Usual smash hit cinemas, plus Penultimate Picture Palace and the Phoenix, both more arty. Lots student drama. **Sports:** Every college has its own sports ground and facilities – they vary in their facilities. **Hardship funds:** Strictly means tested. Have to be absolutely broke and preferably injured to get one. Access fund. Incoming legislation means have to have taken out a student loan to be eligible. **Travel:** A few travel grants; £5 return on bus to London (1½ hours). **Work:** Tight at the moment, and tight anyway because lots of students in town. Vacation grants available.

Informal name

BNC (in writing); Nose (sporting supporters).

Alumni (Editors' pick)

Colin Cowdrey (cricketer), Michael Palin (Monty Python), William Golding (novelist), Robert Runcie (ex-Archbishop of Canterbury), Walter Pater, Sir Arthur Evans, John Buchan, Lord Scarman.

CHRIST CHURCH

Christ Church, Oxford OX1 1DP (0865 276151)

Founded: 1525; women undergraduates first admitted 1980. Heat, light and laundry charges according to use. **Accommodation:** All undergraduates offered accommodation in college (sets or bedsits) for whole course. Standard charge £894 pa; accommodation with dinner is £6.67p per day. **Eating arrangements:** All meals in hall. Breakfast and lunch available on cash payment. **Gate/guest hours:** Undergraduates have own keys. Guests not admitted before 9 am, and must have left by 2 am. **Admission:** By entrance examination or interviews (see university undergraduate prospectus). Undergraduates not admitted to archaeology and anthropology; classics and English; electronic and structural materials engineering; geology/earth sciences; human sciences; metallurgy and science of materials; metallurgy, economics and management; modern history and English. **Scholarships:** The college will award scholarships and other prizes for meritorious

CAN'T FIND WHAT YOU'RE LOOKING FOR? USE THE INDEX!

work during residence. **Travel grants:** Limited assistance provided to encourage travel by undergraduates, irrespective of subject of study. **Book grants:** available for all undergraduates. **Library:** Over 100,000 volumes; collections of early printed books and manuscripts; large law library. **Other college facilities:** Picture gallery (Christ Church has a famous collection of Old Masters), music room, computer room, playing fields nearby, new sports pavilion, squash courts, tennis courts, boat house. Because Christ Church is both a college and cathedral it has a strong musical tradition. **Largest fields of study:** PPE, modern history, law, English, modern languages, classics, geography, physics, mathematics, chemistry, engineering.

European Community: 12½% first degree students take EC language as part of course and 12½% spend 6 months or more in another EC country. No formal exchange links.

College fees for 1992/93 (undergraduate) £2,983.

Undergraduates: *Men:* 278 *Women:* 133

Postgraduates: *Men:* 93 *Women:* 30

Teaching staff: *Men:* 33 fellows, 11 research fellows, 15 lecturers
Women: 2 fellows, 2 research fellows, 5 lecturers.

What it's like

One of the most architecturally outstanding and famous colleges in this university, which leads to much tourism and also a great deal of college pride. Easy access being in town-centre, although maintains relative peace and quiet. Large main college site means all college accommodation close together, rather than scattered around the town. Accommodation excellent – mostly large and beautiful rooms in good state of repair. Almost no cooking facilities for undergraduates but food served in hall is adequate. Mixed college residency but no mixed room sets. Large majority white, British students but some racial cross-section and a few overseas students, particularly graduates. Good relationship between college administrators and students – students have certain amount of say in college policies.

No overnight guests allowed officially but this rule seldom enforced. Probably less than 10% students have cars, mainly because of very restricted parking facilities. Active JCR – mainly socially rather than politically orientated; involved in charity work.

No counselling service within college, but college nurse offers a certain amount. University-wide counselling service good and confidential. Hardship grants available to those with financial difficulties.

Active drama society in college, but focus particularly on music and sport – music particularly including the cathedral choir; sport active in many areas, particularly rowing and rugby. Good sports facilities all within walking distance of college.

Large student population means good social cross-section and therefore a tendency to be quite insular but nevertheless easy to meet students from other colleges through societies etc.

College especially good for history and law – good law library open all night and excellent college library. Expected to cope with heavy workload but not enormous academic pressure. Most students go on to jobs, many well-paid in the city etc. Prestigious college – high graduate employment rate. Relatively low drop-out rate – a few students per year, perhaps 2 or 3. Students from independent schools predominate but much less so now than in the past. Male/female ratio 2:1 but evening out.

Pauper notes

Accommodation: Rooms in college excellent almost without exception. Single rooms to suite of 4 rooms per person and double rooms available in college. Married flats available; more graduate and undergraduate accommodation being built. **Drink:** JCR prices ⅔ of town pubs. Half price cocktails at discos and other social events. New bar 1991. Many popular pubs near, off licence outside college. **Eats:** Food cheap and of reasonable quality. As well as dining hall food, breakfast, lunch and tea are served daily in JCR. Good health-food shop directly by college. Many reasonable restaurants in town. **Ents:** Discos and other entertainments regularly held. Amusement machines, pool table and dart board in JCR. Also table football. Thriving drama group within college. 3 good independent cinemas in town. **Sports:** Excellent sports facilities 15 minutes by foot from college. Strong traditions of success in most sports, particularly rowing and rugby. Health centre/swimming pool at Temple Cowley does very cheap student package. College has own weights room, squash court and other free facilities. **Hardship funds:** Grants available from college and university by negotiation, if suitably broke. Also residence grant money for study abroad. **Travel:** Generous travel grants liberally distributed. Good student fares eg coach Oxford–London. **Work:** Officially permission needed for paid work 12 months of year, but never heard it enforced in vac!

Alumni (Editors' pick)

Lord Hailsham, Sir William Walton, OM, Sir Adrian Boult, CH, Norman St John Stevas, Sir Antony Acland, Sir Robert Armstrong, Judge James Pickles, Peter J F Green, Peter Jay, Mark Girouard, Lewis Carroll, Gladstone, Sir Alec Douglas Home, Antony Eden, Leon Brittan, Nigel Lawson, Hugh Cluarshie, Howard Goodall, Sir Robert Peel, W H Auden, ex-president Bhutto, Auberon Waugh, Anthony Howard.

CORPUS CHRISTI

Corpus Christi College, Oxford OX1 4JF (0865 276700)

Founded: 1517; women undergraduates first admitted 1979. **Accommodation:** All undergraduates and graduates are offered rooms in college or in annexes throughout their courses. Most undergraduates charged £760 pa (range £693–£789). Total charge likely to average at £1,420. **Eating arrangements:** All meals available in college except for Saturday dinner and Sunday breakfast. **Gate/guest hours:** Keys available to all members. Some restrictions on frequency and duration of entertainment of guests in college. **Admission:** No special provisions or requirements differing from those applying to Oxford generally. Undergraduates not admitted to archaeology and anthropology, botany, geography, geology (earth sciences, human sciences), music (except for organ scholars), oriental studies, zoology. Modern language students must offer Italian. **Travel grants:** Some available. **Library:** Old Library with unrestricted access but restricted borrowing hours. **Other college facilities:** Squash courts and playing fields; boathouse; music room, computer suite. **Largest fields of study:** Classics, history and PPE.

European Community: Approximately 4% of first degree students take an EC language and spend 6 months or more in another EC country, as part of their degree courses ie modern linguists and those combining languages with modern history, philosophy, classics or English. Members of the college can attend the courses run by the university's language laboratories – irrespective of their area of academic activity. Formal link with Siena under the Erasmus Scheme, open only to those studying languages; links in other subjects.

College fees for 1992/93 (undergraduate) £2,976.

Undergraduates: *Men:* 136 *Women:* 88

Graduates: *Men:* 57 *Women:* 25

Teaching staff: *Men:* 36 fellows, 2 research fellows, 13 lecturers.
Women: 2 fellows, 2 research fellows, 2 lecturers.

CAN'T FIND WHAT YOU'RE LOOKING FOR? USE THE INDEX!

What it's like

Its strength lies in its size: this is Oxford's smallest college. Atmosphere intimate and friendly and peculiar interests may be followed. Large beer cellar provides meeting place for all. JCR increasingly active and well supported. Fundamentally an academic college with propensity towards classics, but strong in PPE, English, history and medicine and gaining strength in sciences. (No tutors in zoological sciences.) Work load high in all subjects; library amongst best (open 24 hrs a day). Corpus average sporting college and facilities good – squash court, boathouse, tennis courts, playing fields and pavilion. All years now fully mixed and male:female ratio has increased to 1:1. Accommodation amongst Oxford's best, all undergraduates (and graduates) able to live in. Food compares favourably with other colleges. Discipline tactful; poor work not tolerated. No aristocratic pretensions. Public/state school ratio roughly equal. Tolerant college, if gossipy – slightly left wing bias though political discussion in JCR meetings is on the way out.

Pauper notes

Accommodation: Very good; one of few colleges where every undergrad able to live in. Overseas students and finalists given priority in staying in college accommodation during vac. Married quarters – college houses. **Drink:** Oxford pubs expensive: try Corpus beer cellar and those of other colleges. **Eats:** College food nutritional and cheap, veggie option. Kebab vans, chippy, fast food a whole array. Many good and cheapish Indian, Chinese, etc. **Ents:** Phoenix, PPP, Cannon cinemas, Oxford Playhouse. Attendance unpredictable at college events, plenty in other colleges and university. **Sports:** Men's rowing good, other sports variable. Nearest pool 2 miles away. **Hardship funds:** Special fund; book grants and vacation residence grants. **Travel:** Scholarships from college, university awards, good student travel centres. Good bus service to London and airports. **Work:** Can work on college maintenance staff; other temp work avail in Oxford.

More info?

Enquiries to Eric Dugdale 0865 276690 (or 276700 for messages).

Alumni (Editors' pick)

Sir Isaiah Berlin, Lord Beloff, William Waldegrave MP, J L Austin, Sir Robert Ensor, R Brinkley, G W Most (classics), Baron Hailey, Lord Clyde, E C Robertson-Glasgow, K H Bailey, Lord Cameron of Lochbroom, Brian Sedgemore MP, Michael Brock, Brough Scott.

EXETER

Exeter College, Oxford OX1 3DP (0865 279600)

Founded: 1314; women undergraduates first admitted 1979. **Accommodation:** All students accommodated in college for first year, and many offered a second year (usually for finals). College also has hostels, flats and houses available; generally able to house all who do not want privately rented accommodation. Most undergraduates charged £828 (range £739–£835). Lodging charge (including standard catering charge) up to £1,091 pa. **Eating arrangements:** Self-service breakfast and lunch and served dinner available in early 17th-century hall daily throughout term; cost is approx £3.85 per day if all meals are taken. Some self-catering facilities. **Gate/guest hours:** All members have late keys. No guests allowed between 2 and 8 am unless they have been booked in overnight. **Admission:** Undergraduates admitted for all subjects apart from biology, botany, human sciences, geography, oriental studies, zoology. **Scholarships:** and exhibitions awarded for meritorious work during undergraduate courses. **Travel grants:** Generous provision made from endowed funds for both academic and general purposes. **Library:** Well-stocked. **Hardship fund:** Well-endowed fund administered by the Rector and Tutors' Committee. **Other college facilities:** Bar, sports clubs, playing field, boathouse and multi-gym. College chapel has fine choir made up of students and boys from Cathedral school.

European Community: 12% first degree students take EC language as part of course and spend 6 months or more in another EC country. No formal exchange links. Many visiting EC students in residence.

College fees for 1992/93 (undergraduate) £3,017.

Undergraduates: *Men:* 221 *Women:* 90

Postgraduates: *Men:* 85 *Women:* 38

Teaching staff: *Men:* 31 fellows, 3 research fellows, 11 lecturers
Women: 4 fellows, 1 research fellow, 8 lecturers.

What it's like

Small and cosy; everyone knows everyone else. Central position gives good access to shops and facilities. Friendly, with thriving JCR and entertainments committee. Facilities are being slowly improved, eg a new staircase and lecture room built. Food is fairly good – dinner in 2 sittings; gowns worn for formal hall. Everyone has a late key. Cheap bar. Impressive fellows garden. Exeter has settled at around the top of the league tables, but non-academic pursuits are encouraged. JCR provides a wide range of facilities – newspapers, magazines, a drinks machine, table tennis table, pool table, televisions and video. Traditional links with West Country, but recently more people from Merseyside than from Devon. Healthy public/state school ratio.

Pauper notes

Accommodation: University married quarters. College owns flats, houses and hostels for students. **Drinks:** Cheap college bar. **Eats:** Town has many good places. College food improved, and fairly cheap. (Chefs have been on vegetarian courses.) **Ents:** Good local cinemas eg Phoenix. Excellent college entertainments committee. **Sports:** University sports centre. College has its own sports facilities including squash. **Hardship funds:** University hardship fund, plus many college funds. **Travel:** Easy to hitch to London. College has excellent travel grants. **Work:** Study grants. Work available behind college bar.

Alumni (Editors' pick)

J R Tolkien, Sir Michael Levy, Sir Roger Bannister, Robert Robinson, Tariq Ali, Richard Burton, Martin Amis, Alan Bennett, Nevil Coghill, Ned Sherrin, Russell Harty, William Morris, John Ford, Sir Charles Lyell, J A Froude, Edward Burne-Jones, Imogen Stubbs.

HERTFORD

Hertford College, Oxford OX1 3BW (0865 279400)

Founded: 1874; women undergraduates first admitted 1974. **Accommodation:** 200 places in college, 100 in college houses. Rent: 85% in accommodation where rent controlled by college. Standard charge £890.10 for 25 week year (including laundry and heating); fixed kitchen charge to a maximum £112 (for those living in college). **Eating arrangements:** Pay as you eat. **Gate/guest hours:** All students issued with gate keys. **Admission:** Generally places are offered unconditionally either on the basis of an interview in December or, if it is preferred, the Oxford Entrance Examination in November. In either case entry is competitive with the emphasis being on promise. **Academic features:** Engineering courses; Polish and

Linguistics courses. **Library:** Undergraduate and antiquarian libraries. **Hardship funds:** White, Boyd, Keasbey. **Other college facilities:** JCR complex, lecture theatre, sports ground, boathouse, orchestra, computer, bar, rowing, squash court.

European Community: 10% first degree students take EC language as part of course and 9% spend 6 months or more in another EC country. Formal exchange links with the British Institute in Paris for modern linguists.

College fees for 1992/93 (undergraduate) £3,147.

Undergraduates: *Men:* 212 *Women:* 136

Postgraduates: *Men:* 105 *Women:* 33

Teaching staff: *Men:* 26 fellows, 7 research fellows, 20 lecturers
Women: 3 fellows, 1 research fellow, 9 lecturers.

What it's like

Convivial; not the most impressive architecture or grounds in Oxford and facilities are adequate rather than extensive but it's very friendly. The pleasant atmosphere results from broad social mix of students from all regions and all backgrounds.

Accommodation is in shoe boxes in first year, in college houses or private accommodation in 2nd year, a relatively palatial room in 3rd year. Exceptionally well situated 2 minutes from town centre; 10 seconds from Kings Arms; 30 seconds from Bodleian Library.

Congenial atmosphere extends to discipline and to the attitude to overnight guests and drunkenness (barring excesses). Hertford people renowned for enjoying themselves. Numerous clubs, sports, political, social, benefit from not taking themselves too seriously and maintaining a sense of fun.

Work load averages 2 essays and tutorials a week. Pressure varies from subject to subject but is avoidable provided you keep your head above water, but pressure in finals. Generally academic work is not the dominant tenet of people's lives.

Generally people quickly develop a strong affinity to Hertford, find their niche and enjoy themselves. Very unsnobbish.

Pauper notes

Accommodation: Rooms in college for 1st/3rd year. About half second year accommodated. **Drink:** College bar cheap and very popular. Other college bars frequented. Pubs in city centre. **Eats:** College cheap; poor veg option. Town huge variety. **Ents:** Regular college bops and entertainments. Students ents go on all the time in different colleges. **Sports:** Hertford sports ground 1½ miles from college. Football, rugby, hockey, badminton traditionally strong. **Hardship funds:** Access funds on university scale. Keasbey grant for Hertford students and has just been doubled. **Travel:** A few college grants. **Work:** Some students get casual work in term, but not really enough time.

Alumni (Editors' pick)

Evelyn Waugh, John Donne, Gavin Maxwell, Thomas Hobbes, Jonathan Swift, Charles Ryder, Charles James Fox.

JESUS
Jesus College, Oxford OX1 3DW (0865 279700)

Founded: 1571; women undergraduates first admitted 1974. **Accommodation:** All undergraduates guaranteed college accommodation for all of their course. 154 rooms in college; flats for a further 233 undergraduates and graduates plus 12 flats for married graduates. Most undergraduates in college charged £685 pa including heat and light (range £627–£759). **Eating arrangements:** Continental breakfast, cafeteria lunch, cafeteria dinner and set dinner in hall. **Gate/guest hours:** 8 to 2 am. **Admission:** Undergraduates not admitted to fine art, oriental studies. **Scholarships:** Various scholarships and grants: Sankey scholarships to assist college members to meet expenses of being called to Bar. **Travel grants:** Charles Green Studentships for classical or other studies abroad; Dodd Benefaction for vacation travel abroad. **Other college facilities:** Library, bar, music room, 3 squash courts, sports field, computer rooms.

European Community: 5% first degree students take EC language as part of course and 5% spend a year in another EC country. Formal exchange links with Trier, Germany.

College fees for 1992/93 (undergraduate) £2,989.

Undergraduates: *Men:* 195 *Women:* 116

Postgraduates: *Men:* 91 *Women:* 38

Teaching staff: *Men:* 31 fellows, 15 research fellows, 12 lecturers
Women: 3 fellows, 3 research fellows, 5 lecturers.

What it's like

Founded by Queen Elizabeth in 1571. Compact, pretty college with 3 quads right in centre of Oxford. Handy for libraries, shops and entertainments but tends to attract tourists.

Good library, sociable common room, OK food served at convenient cafeteria, laundry facilities and a popular bar.

Accommodation is excellent and inexpensive. All first years live in as do some finalists. All third and second years live either in college or in modern self-catering college flats about 2 miles away.

Welsh connections now folklore, if anything Irish people more prominent. No admissions discrimination. Jesus people tend to come from wide range of backgrounds and schools. Politically centre/left and pretty sound.

Regular social events – easily the cheapest and most widely available in Oxford. Wide range of college societies and sporting clubs; drama and photographic societies recently formed and generously funded. Sporting record rapidly improving, especially in 'football' and Rugby; women's rowing and hockey. College squash and tennis courts and large sports ground.

Excellent academic standards; academic pressure being increased year by year. Nearly all subjects taught in college. Work loads and timetables vary. Student/don relationships good.

No visiting restrictions. Gates close at midnight, but college members have keys.

Worst point: tends to be socially isolated. Most people know your news (or think they do) before you know it yourself.

Best point: friendly, game for a laugh, unpretentious and cheap.

Pauper notes

Accommodation: Very high standard college accommodation. Cheapest and most available (100%) in university. **Drink:** Extremely popular bar. **Eats:** OK food. Very popular credit card system. All 'minority eaters' catered for but quality ropey. **Ents:** Free weekly ent in bar or JCR – discos, bands, talent nights and game shows. Weekly video in JCR. Lots on in Oxford. **Sports:** All free. A multigym and new ergometer recently acquired. Free pool table and bar games. **Hardship funds:** Student grants/loans etc. Guaranteed for academic 'stars'; Jesus is one of the richest colleges and as such is able to cushion its students (particularly the most academic ones among them) from financial hardship. **Travel:** Gratuitous grant x 1 max £300. All live nearby. Most cycle. **Work:** Academic pressure relatively intense. Students are sent down for persistent skiving.

CAN'T FIND WHAT YOU'RE LOOKING FOR? USE THE INDEX!

More info?

Enquiries to JCR President 0865 279700.

Alumni (Editors' pick)

T E Lawrence ('Lawrence of Arabia'), Lord Wilson of Rievaulx, James Burke, Magnus Magnusson, Paul Jones (Manfred Mann).

KEBLE

Keble College, Oxford OX1 3PG (0865 272727)

Founded: 1870; women undergraduates first admitted 1979. **Accommodation:** 2 years in college (normally first and second) during undergraduate course. Rent: 50% in college rooms where rent is controlled by college. Standard charge, £1,039.07 pa. **Eating arrangements:** Keble Hall (the longest in Oxford) can accommodate all who desire to eat there in one session. **Gate/guest hours:** Wicket gate keys available for all students. Visitors must leave by 1 am (guest rooms available for overnight stay). **Admission:** Pre A-level through entrance exam or conditional offer; post A-level on basis of grades achieved plus interview. Undergraduates not admitted for human sciences, music, oriental studies (except Japanese), geology. **Scholarships:** Awards given for meritorious work during undergraduate course. Organ and choral awards; periodic Third World scholarship. **Travel grants:** A number of study and travel grants are provided by Keble Association. **Library:** Butterfield's Victorian library was enhanced by a large extension opened 1981. **Other college facilities:** JCR, bar, music room, sports ground, boathouse, laundry, TV room, squash courts, weights room, darkroom, computer room. **Academic features:** Extension of provision for computer studies and Japanese. **Hardship funds:** There is a hardship fund for students in financial difficulty.

European Community: 9% first degree students take EC language as part of course and 9% spend 6 months or more in another EC country. No formal exchange links.

College fees for 1992/93 (undergraduate) £3,216.

Undergraduates: *Men:* 291 *Women:* 133

Postgraduates: *Men:* 97 *Women:* 27

Teaching staff: *Men:* 29 fellows, 2 research fellows, 18 lecturers
Women: 1 fellow, 1 research fellow, 9 lecturers.

What it's like

Keble is one of the largest Oxford colleges both in terms of student numbers and its physically imposing Victorian structure. All undergraduates are guaranteed two years in college accommodation and college is presently considering plans to increase its housing stock. Accommodation is good: two-thirds of the rooms are sets, all have central heating and a washbasin, and hot showers and baths are plentiful. One problem is the absence of cooking facilities, but three meals a day are provided seven days a week in hall, some choice but good value with vegetarian and vegan alternatives.

Junior Common Room (small student union) itself has good facilities and provides the focus for lively activity and debate. The JCR officers provide representation on internal and external bodies, and relations with the SCR are good. JCR offers useful information and welfare advice. The wide ranging social and geographical makeup of the students as well as the high state school intake makes Keble a friendly and open college. Post of JCR Womens' Officer created to ensure that the female perspective is considered in what has, for so long, been a predominantly male environment.

Academic performance has played an increasingly important factor in the college's self-assessment and work pressure can be high. Drop-out rate is approx 2%. Extra-curricular activity does not seem to have been unduly hindered – the college sporting achievements remain very high; music and drama also flourish.

Pauper notes

Accommodation: New accommodation on Keble grounds definitely going ahead. **Drink:** College bars still good price. Bar price freeze 1992 – (Tetley 85p). Good pubs: Lamb and Flag less than 2 mins walk from college. Good local beer: Morrells. **Eats:** Taylors (good pittas), Nosebag (more expensive). Nearby Pizza Hut (student nights) and Mr Roving as Roving Government Kebab Van, Heroes (sandwiches), St Giles Cafe (greasy, expensive and tasty!). **Ents:** Plenty about. Student nights vary. Numerous college drama productions within university, Oxford Venue (excellent gigs). Park End club (disco). **Sports:** Everything and anything available at all levels, usually free. **Hardship fund:** SCR sympathetic to specific cases. College supports loan for those in extraordinary need. **Travel:** Travel scholarships available from college. Hitching not too difficult. **Work:** Pub work, local shops, language and other teaching available. Term-time work discouraged.

More info?

Enquiries to Peter Boyd (0865 272727).

Alumni (Editors' pick)

Sir Peter Pears, Rev. Chad Varah (father of Samaritans), Michael Croft, Imran Khan, Andreas Whittam Smith (founder of the *Independent*).

LADY MARGARET HALL

Lady Margaret Hall, Oxford OX2 6QA (0865 274300)

Founded: 1878; men undergraduates first admitted 1977. **Accommodation:** All but about 50 undergraduates live in college; single study bedrooms (some third years have private bathrooms). Standard accommodation charge 1992/93: £1,014 pa plus meals as taken. **Eating arrangements:** All meals in hall on 'copytex' system. JCR kitchen/pantries on all floors. **Gate/guest hours:** Gate closed at midnight. All members of college issued with keys. Guest hours: weekdays 9 am to midnight; weekends 9 to 2 am. **Admission:** For pre A-level candidates a choice between sitting the entrance examination or interviews with a view to an offer conditional upon A-level results. For post A-level candidates interviews and, in some cases, short written tests. Undergraduates not admitted for geology, metallurgy, geography, and for oriental studies other than Hebrew. **Scholarships:** About 25 scholarships awarded to undergraduates in residence; organ scholarship; various college essay prizes. **Travel grants:** Armorel Holiday Gifts (total about £1,000 pa) to help needy undergraduates to have a good holiday. Maude Royden long vacation travelling exhibition (normally £200). Other grants in connection with academic work. **Hardship funds:** Limited grants available for unexpected hardship during course. **Library:** Open 24 hours; over 50,000 books on open shelves; law reading room; science reading room. **Other college facilities:** Bar, music practice rooms, 2 grand pianos and several upright pianos, tennis courts, croquet lawn, boathouse. Squash court, shared facilities for other sports.

European Community: Only students in modern languages and joint courses learn an EC language and spend a period in another EC country as part of their course. No formal exchange links.

College fees for 1992/93 (undergraduate) £3,140.

Undergraduates: *Men:* 178 *Women:* 186

Postgraduates: *Men:* 68 *Women:* 43

CAN'T FIND WHAT YOU'RE LOOKING FOR? USE THE INDEX!

Teaching staff: *Men:* 20 fellows, 4 research fellows, 9 lecturers, 5 professors and supernumerary fellows *Women:* 14 fellows, 2 research fellows, 1 lecturer, 2 professors and supernumerary fellows.

What it's like

Notably relaxed college with 50-50 male-female ratio and beautiful, expansive gardens rolling down to the river where the college has its own punt house. 80% of students live in for 3 years; rooms are varied in shape and size but good basic standard with plenty of kitchens (legacy from its days as a women's college) and en-suite bathrooms in many rooms. Liberal atmosphere with good state–private school balance, an anti-discrimination statute and amiable tutor–student relations.

Its distance (10 mins walk) from the town centre isn't a problem to socialising and working there; instead LMH benefits from a good college spirit, spacious feel and excellent on-site facilities. Results are better than average and its absence from the tourist trail in the summer is a virtue never overestimated . . .

Pauper notes

Accommodation: Very good, with some double rooms for couples, many rooms recently refurbished. **Drink:** Cheap – recently rebuilt bar on-site. **Eats:** Good food at LMH, reasonably priced – vegetarian options. **Ents:** Many JCR social events. JCR owns its own PA and drum kit – recently rebuilt social venue. **Sports:** Good but relaxed. Own squash and tennis courts and football pitch on-site. **Hardship funds:** Principal's fund recently increased + JCR living out fund. **Travel:** Holiday fund in memory of a former undergraduate for students who have been unable to afford a good holiday in recent years. **Work:** Some work in college over vac – helping with conferences and in library.

More info?

Enquiries to JCR President.

Alumni (Editors' pick)

Benazir Bhutto, Lady Antonia Fraser, Diana Quick, Gertrude Bell, Dame Veronica Wedgwood, Dame Josephine Barnes, Elizabeth Longford, Eglantine Jebb, Baroness Warnock, Matthew Taylor MP, Andrew Q Hands, Barbara Mills (new DPP), Caryl Churchill.

LINCOLN

Lincoln College, Oxford OX1 3DR (0865 279800)

Founded: 1427; women undergraduates first admitted 1980. **Accommodation:** All undergraduates accommodated for two years, most for three years. Excellent purpose built block available for graduates. Standard charge, £1,100 pa; £44.18 per week, inclusive of dinner (except Saturdays). **Eating arrangements:** Meals in hall; also snacks in bar, teas in JCR. **Gate/guest hours:** Gate closes at midnight during term. College members have keys. **Admission:** Undergraduates admitted under uniform Oxford colleges' system. No preference between mode E and mode N for pre-A level applicants. No undergraduates admitted for biology, botany, geography, geology/earth sciences, human sciences, metallurgy, science of materials, economics and management, oriental studies, zoology, theology. **Scholarships:** Various, for undergraduates once in residence; graduate entrance scholarships, details on request. **Travel grants:** Up to £184 for undergraduates, £300 research grant for graduates; £190 for clinical medicals. **Hardship funds:** Grants and interest-free loans for graduates and undergraduates in financial difficulties. Commemoration Fund, Keith Murray Fund. **Library:** Especially strong in law, history, English, politics, and physiological and chemical sciences. **Other college facilities:** Playing field, squash court, multi-gym; computing facilities; music practice rooms; bar.

European Community: 10% first degree students take EC language as part of course and 10% spend 6 months or more in another EC country.

College fees for 1992/93 (undergraduate) £2,933.

Undergraduates: *Men:* 163 *Women:* 94

Postgraduates: *Men:* 97 *Women:* 46

Teaching staff: *Men:* 27 fellows, 6 research fellows, 17 lecturers
Women: 4 fellows, nil research fellows, 8 lecturers.

What it's like

Not one of the famous names of Oxford but offers a lot. One of the oldest colleges, very pretty with a striking library in the converted All Saints' Church. Ideally situated for the centre of town, with shops, pubs and the Bodleian all on the doorstep.

All students live in college or college-owned houses. Rooms vary from small and modern to lovely old suites of rooms. No complaints about college food; it's arguably the best in the university, with trout and duck served on normal evenings; vegetarians well catered for.

The college is one of the best endowed, shown by the sports facilities. Main ground is a good bike ride from the centre, but the pitches are in super condition with a large, modern pavilion. Nearer the centre there is a squash court and new multi-gym both in constant college use. Teams aspire to the first division for most sports (impressive for such a small college) and there's much enthusiasm. Lively Boat Club.

The social centre of college is the bar, which is a good one open till 11.00 six nights a week. Several ents events a term and an annual ball held after eights. The college is very friendly, tending towards insularity, and judges no one on appearances. Very lively JCR (student body); well attended meetings with free booze.

Ivor Collet, JCR President

Pauper notes

Accommodation: One of only 3 Oxford colleges to provide 100% accommodation. Also one of the cheapest, and rooms range from excellent (incl self-catering houses) to fairly reasonable. **Drink:** College bar subsidised, with good selection including weekly 'guest beers'. **Eats:** College food is excellent and popular. Snacks available in college bar. City centre usual range of snack bars, fast-food, etc. **Ents:** Fairly lively for a small college. Bops, videos, cabarets, boat parties, etc. **Sports:** Excellent new multi-gym; good pavilion and playing fields. Fairly successful sporting college, but it's all free, including boat club. **Hardship funds:** Excellent provision with a new scheme agreed between college and JCR. Generous help given. **Travel:** Good – travel grants easily available for holidays of *some* intellectual value. **Work:** Some work (well paid) available in college in term and vacation.

Alumni (Editors' pick)

Sir Peter Parker, John Le Carré, Edward Thomas, John Wesley, Richthofen, referred to as The Red Baron.

MAGDALEN

Magdalen College, Oxford OX1 4AU (0865 276000)

Founded: 1458; women undergraduates first admitted 1979. **Accommodation:**

All undergraduates can live in for at least 2 years. Most undergraduates charged £774 pa (range £594–£930). **Eating arrangements:** Cafeteria system, with formal dinner available once or twice a week. **Gate/guest hours:** Gate keys issued. **Admission:** Entry by interview (Mode N) or by examination (Mode E). Undergraduates not admitted to geography, geology, metallurgy. **Scholarships** and prizes awarded each year. College has both organ and choral awards. **Travel grants:** Funds for a number of purposes. **Hardship funds:** Very limited fund available. **Library:** Particularly large history and PPE sections, Denning law library; Old Library with fine collection of Renaissance and 18th-century volumes. **Other college facilities:** JCR shop, wine cellar and bar; 11 tennis courts (8 grass, 3 hard), 4 squash courts, 10 college punts, sports ground in beautiful riverside setting, with probably best cricket square in Oxford. Free membership of JCR computing scheme (4 x 286 IBM compatible computers; 2 x 24 pin dot matrix printers; range of software on hard disks; VAX and E-mail links; facilities soon to be expanded). Strong musical tradition. **Largest fields of study:** Biology, biochemistry, chemistry, engineering, English, law, literae humaniores, mathematics, medicine, modern history, modern languages, music, PPE, physics, psychology.

European Community: 12% first degree students take EC language as part of course and 4% spend 6 months or more in another EC country. No formal exchange links.

College fees for 1992/93 (undergraduate) £3,016.

Undergraduates: *Men:* 209 *Women:* 131

Postgraduates: *Men:* 154 *Women:* 63

Teaching staff: *Men:* 36 fellows, 3 research fellows, 16 lecturers, 11 professors *Women:* 3 fellows, nil research fellows, 4 lecturers.

What it's like

Strikingly beautiful (Great Tower and Cloisters) with extensive grounds (Addison's Walk, Deer Park, Fellows Garden etc) which give a sense of space rare in Oxford. New common room and bar act as focus for college – probably most thriving bar in town but not cheap. Most people thrive in their freedom and independence. No image/routine is imposed upon you – you can be who you want in Magdalen.

Modernisation programme continuing inc plumbing, central heating. New building scheme with aim of accommodating all students in college – also theatre, recital rooms, etc. Most accommodation good – some rooms palatial though most 1st years housed in infamous Waynflete Building. Sports facilities, brilliant.

Student body: 33% women, many foreign postgraduates and increasing state school intake.

Academically quite hot with pressure increasing but never to neurosis level. Arts often regarded as better than sciences but new Magdalen science park, so things may change.

Music and drama societies are very active and the college choir has a worldwide reputation. Services in chapel daily and well attended.

Pauper notes

Accommodation: Married quarters not easily available at Magdalen: no **really** cheap accom. Room ballot system means that you can choose room according to pocket. **Drink:** £1.10 a pint in college bar. **Eats:** Cheap food in hall. More expensive but better in spectacular college bar. **Ents:** College discos and bands frequently. Good college and univ theatre and brilliant cinema arrangements. **Sports:** Very good facilities. **Hardship funds:** Offered by both college and the university. College hardship fund has been drastically expanded this year, to take into account worsening student financial situation. **Travel:** Travel grants given by college are quite generous (cheap travel shop for students on the High St). **Work:**

GET HOLD OF THE PROSPECTUSES

Paid work and free accommodation in college is often available to students wanting to stay in Oxford during the vacations.

More info?
Enquiries to JCR President (0865 276011).

Alumni (Editors' pick)
Sir Peter Medawar, Sir John Betjeman, Lord Denning, A J P Taylor, Dudley Moore, Oscar Wilde, Lord Joseph, Joseph Addison, Edward Gibbon, Sir Charles Sherrington, Sir Robert Robinson, Dr Charles Daubeny, Sir Christopher McMahon, J Z Young, C S Lewis, R G Collinwood, Gilbert Ryle, Sir Peter Strawson, Kenneth Baker, Lord Gibson.

MANCHESTER

Manchester College, Mansfield Road, Oxford OX1 3TD
(0865 271006)

Founded: 1786; women undergraduates first admitted 1907. **Accommodation:** 80 students accommodated in college houses in college precincts. Standard charge £2,250 (including 18 meals per week). **Admission:** Mature students (over 25) only. Undergraduates not admitted for most science courses – check prospectus. **Special features:** Became part of the University in 1990 as college for mature students. **Library:** 3 libraries: Tate (general); Carpenter (world religions); Old (books before 1800); 40,000 volumes, 30 periodicals, 40 study places. **Other college facilities:** Chaplain, JCR bar. **Largest fields of study:** English.

European Community: 2% first degree students take EC language as part of course. No formal exchange links.

College fees for 1992/93 (undergraduate) £3,042.

Undergraduates: *Men:* 41 *Women:* 36

Postgraduates: *Men:* 6 *Women:* 1

Teaching staff: *Men:* 3 fellows, 1 lecturer *Women:* 3 fellows, 2 lecturers.

What it's like
Make no mistake about it, Manchester College is on an accelerated ascendency in Oxford University life. An ideally situated college slap-bang in the middle of town, it has a small but vibrant student community which is eager to 'get stuck in'.

Student accommodation is arguably second to none with full residence on offer for the full 3 years if needed. Rooms are either 15th century or thereabouts, or absolutely brand new circa 1992. The recently completed new quad offers homes for Manchester students as well as some All Souls Fellows.

Food at Manchester is beyond doubt the best of any Oxford college: a proud boast but one regularly endorsed by our guests.

Don't expect images of Lourdes if you visit our college – mature students will inspire you with their vitality – they come in all shapes, sizes, ages and sexes!
Tom Tobin, JCR President

Pauper notes
Drink: JCR bar – Kings Arms – it's near enough and isn't The Turf. **Ents:** JCR functions throughout the year. **Sports:** Croquet, punt, soccer, women's Rugby. 8's boat newly acquired, sailing too.

Alumni (Editors' pick)
Josiah Wedgwood (1750), John Datton (1802), Sir Henry Tate (1850).

CAN'T FIND WHAT YOU'RE LOOKING FOR? USE THE INDEX!

MANSFIELD
Mansfield College, Oxford OX1 3TF (0865 270999)

Founded: 1886; women undergraduates first admitted 1955. **Accommodation:** All undergraduates may reside in college for two years; college-owned or managed houses are available for the third year, with substantial subsidies on rent. Standard undergraduate charge £961 pa plus heating and meals. **Eating arrangements:** All meals available in hall, Monday to Saturday. Residents pay £25 per term in advance towards meals. Cooking facilities in all college houses and on some staircases. **Gate/guest hours:** Unrestricted. **Admission:** Entrance examination (pre-A level candidates) or interview mode of entry (pre- or post-A level candidates). Both modes of entry acceptable in most subjects. Undergraduates not accepted for modern languages, biological sciences, chemistry, medicine. **Scholarships:** Scholarships and exhibitions awarded at any stage of an undergraduate's course in recognition of high academic standards. Also a number of college prizes. **Travel grants:** 2 travelling scholarships. **Hardship funds:** An endowment plus limited provision from general funds; small grants to meet exceptional circumstances. **Library:** Spacious in relation to numbers. Strong in theology; other subjects have smaller but up-to-date collections. **Other college facilities:** Mansfield shares Merton sports grounds; own boat club. Billiard table, croquet, table tennis, bar. Refrigerators on all staircases. **Largest fields of study:** Engineering, English, geography, history, law, maths, PPE, theology.

European Community: 4 first degree students take EC language as part of course but none spends 6 months or more in another EC country. No formal exchange links.

College fees for 1992/93 (undergraduate) £3,330.

Undergraduates: *Men:* 110 *Women:* 53

Postgraduates: *Men:* 27 *Women:* 13

Teaching staff: *Men:* 14 fellows, 1 research fellow, 7 lecturers
Women: 2 fellows, 1 research fellow, 3 lecturers.

What it's like
It's often said to offer all of Oxford's advantages without many of the pitfalls. A small college on a quiet and spacious site, yet close to city centre, libraries and science area. New accommodation block consisting of 36 rooms, two kitchens and a computer room now completed. College is maintaining its progressive stance by a wide-ranging 'School Links Programme' designed to improve the female:male, state:independent school ratios.

Those who have found the college too small or who have wanted to extend their non-academic activities, have gone on to be prominent in university societies, music, drama and the SU. JCR and GCR (undergraduate and graduate bodies) enjoy good relations and work closely with the college authorities.

Pauper notes
Accommodation: Rent equalisation scheme and small living-out grants have just been introduced. **Drink:** College bar – run by students, therefore prices are kept as low as possible. **Eats:** Food (with veg options) provided on site; kitchens and newly improved cooking facilities allow self-catering. **Ents:** Frequent college events – discos/groups/beer. Active involvement in drama etc. **Sports:** Good/ extensive sports facilities shared with Merton College. **Hardship Funds:** Small college fund. **Travel:** A few travel scholarships awarded each year by college. **Work:** Difficult to find.

Alumni (Editors' pick)
Rev Prof G B Caird (Dean Ireland's professor of the exegesis of holy scripture, Oxford University), Rev Dr Alex Boraine (vice-president of Progressive Federal

Party, South Africa), Paul Crossley (pianist), C H Dodd (theologian, chairman of New English Bible translators), Michael White (music critic), Chris Cragg (*Financial Times*), Donald MacDonald (president of university boat club during the 'mutiny' year).

MERTON

Merton College, Oxford OX1 4JD (0865 276310)

Founded: 1264; women undergraduates first admitted 1980. **Accommodation:** Accommodation in college or college annexe guaranteed for three years; some bed sitting rooms, some sets of rooms. Most undergraduates charged £1,450 pa (range £1,386–£1,500). **Eating arrangements:** All meals available in hall. **Gate/guest hours:** Gate closed at midnight during term. Guests must leave college by midnight. **Admission:** Either by examination and interview (mode E) or by interview and conditional offer (mode N). **Scholarships:** Postmasterships and Exhibitions awarded at end of first (and later) years for distinguished work. **Travel grants:** Various travel grants to 'subsidise well thought out plans for vacation travel'. **Library:** Fine Old Library (over 60,000 volumes); medieval manuscripts and chained early printed books). **Other college facilities:** Music room and organ; nearby playing fields, sports pavilion, boathouse. **Largest fields of study:** Chemistry, literae humaniores, mathematics, modern history and physics.

European Community: Number of students learning an EC language or spending time in another EC country, not known.

College fees for 1992/93 (undergraduate) £2,900.

Undergraduates: *Men:* 164 *Women:* 92

Postgraduates: *Men:* 78 *Women:* 50

Teaching staff: *Men:* 44 fellows, 9 research fellows, 14 lecturers
Women: 2 fellows, 1 research fellow, 8 lecturers.

What it's like

Merton is going places. Its members are increasingly active outside college, especially in the fields of journalism and drama. Participation in a variety of college sports is widespread. Recent successes on a university level include basketball, fencing, American football, chess and table football. All major sports are catered for; among these are two Rugby teams, two cricket teams and several rowing eights, including a victorious women's crew.

College social life is improving with an increasingly varied social calendar including bops, a bands night and bar quizzes. There is also a flourishing classical music society, a well-supported choir and an annual Christmas Ball, that is unique amongst Oxford colleges.

JCR meetings have become a lively forum for change. In particular, there is an active approach towards Target Schools, and the Women's Group. Students work hard, and a relatively high proportion of undergraduates go on to read for a second degree. Generally relaxed atmosphere, small and friendly. No pressure to be anyone that you don't want to be.

Andy Webb, JCR President

Pauper notes

Accommodation: Good quality, cheap accommodation for virtually all undergraduates. Important as private market expensive. **Drink:** Bar is college social centre, relatively cheap drinks. **Eats:** Excellent food, heavily subsidised. Increasing attention given to vegetarians. **Ents:** Increasing and varied. Often free. Well attended. **Sports:** Well endowed, including college sports pavilion and weights room. Widespread participation in range of sports. **Hardship funds:** College will help in extreme circumstances. **Travel:** Travel grants available. All college undergraduate accommodation within 10 mins walk of college.

More info?

Enquiries to Andy Webb, JCR President.

NEW COLLEGE

New College, Oxford OX1 3BN (0865 248541)

Founded: 1379; women undergraduates first admitted 1979. **Accommodation:** About 80% of undergraduates housed in college (all first and second year, and some third year students). Standard charge, £1,183 pa (bed, breakfast and dinner). **Eating arrangements:** All 3 meals provided in hall. **Gate/guest hours:** Late keys available. **Admission:** Undergraduates admitted through Oxford Colleges Admissions system for all subjects except geography. **Study grants:** About 30 a year. **Hardship funds:** Limited help available. **Library:** Over 70,000 volumes. **Other college facilities:** 10 acre sports ground 400 yards from college; college punts and boathouse.

European Community: 12% first degree students take EC language as part of course and 12% spend 6 months or more in another EC country. No formal exchange links.

College fees for 1992/93 (undergraduate) £3,008.

Undergraduates: *Men:* 234 *Women:* 182

Postgraduates: *Men:* 119 *Women:* 52

Teaching staff: *Men:* 31 fellows, 4 research fellows, 11 lecturers
Women: 7 fellows, 5 research fellows, 4 lecturers.

What it's like

Despite being one of the oldest and largest of Oxford's colleges, New College provides a surprisingly relaxed and normal atmosphere. The Junior Common Room (JCR) is the name given to the collective body of students; the Common Room itself, called the Nelson Mandela Room, provides a place for students to meet, talk, watch television and read the newspapers. JCR welfare office provides information and a range of subsidised stationery.

It's a large and relaxed place, with beautiful grounds and excellent facilities. With the library, dining hall, and JCR bar (probably the most popular student bar in Oxford) all close to each other, and with many college-based clubs and societies, it is possible to spend a great deal of time in college. The musical side is well-renowned, as are college sports, particularly rowing. Many students get involved in university-wide activities and with other colleges.

Student body changing fast: active Target Schools Scheme has helped to increase numbers from state schools; also member of Oxford Access Scheme, which works to increase applications from educationally disadvantaged backgrounds.

It's not an intimidating place from the academic point of view, although it has a respectable academic record (to the amazement of the less academically minded of its members!). Tutors tend to rely on individual interest rather than official sanctions, so the amount of work you do is largely up to you.

New College, like the rest of Oxford, has its 'traditions' (wearing gowns for dinner, and calling the terms 'Michaelmas', 'Hilary' and 'Trinity'). Some find such traditions quaint, others silly. Some students come to Oxford to go out rowing early each morning and frequent Summer Balls; others do neither. New College provides an environment which allows you to get what you want out of

Oxford and find your own niche to fit in – probably why most students there swear they wouldn't be anywhere else.

Pauper notes

Accommodation: Very expensive in Oxford; very limited married accommodation; New College one of cheaper in university. **Drink:** Good brews – Morlands, Wadworths, Hook Norton. You don't have to drink Pimms. **Eats:** Good Indian and Chinese on Cowley Road. **Ents:** High profile college entz, always successful. Lots of culture, some good small bands and jazz. **Sports:** College facilities closest of any Oxford college, and as good; swimming pool, athletics stadium and ice rink in town.

More info?

Enquiries to Shirish Kulkarni (0865 279578).

Alumni (Editors' pick)

Nigel Rees, Tony Benn MP, Lord Longford, Len Murray, John Fowles, Hugh Gaitskell.

ORIEL

Oriel College, Oxford OX1 4EW (0865 276555)

Founded: 1326; women undergraduates first admitted 1985. **Accommodation:** First, second year and most third year undergraduates accommodated in college. Most charged £957 pa (range £809–£1,000). Average charge of £8.30 per day for room, six luncheons and seven dinners a week. **Eating arrangements:** All meals available in college. **Gate/guest hours:** Free access 24 hours a day for college members. Liberal guest rules. **Admission:** By way of mode E (entrance examination) or mode N (conditional/unconditional offer on the basis of extended interview). Full range of subjects available except human sciences, computation and fine arts. College prospectus available. **Scholarships:** Scholarships or exhibitionerships available on the basis of work within the college. **Travel grants:** Small grants available. **Library:** 70,000 books; liberal hours. **Other college facilities:** Facilities for all major sports; drama; music. **Largest fields of study:** Modern history, PPE, modern languages, natural sciences.

European Community: 13% students learn an EC language as part of their course, 2% spend 6 months or more in another EC country. Informal links with several EC universities/colleges; link with Bonn for students of German.

College fees for 1992/93 (undergraduate) £3,140.

Undergraduates: *Men:* 177 *Women:* 95

Postgraduates: *Men:* 81 *Women:* 28

Teaching staff: *Men:* 29 fellows, 3 research fellows, 27 lecturers
Women: 1 fellow, 1 research fellow, 3 lecturers.

What it's like

One of the oldest and friendliest of the Oxford colleges, conveniently situated in town centre. First admitted women in 1985; male:female ratio not bad for Oxford as a whole.

Accommodation of a high standard is available for 1st and 2nd years, in single and shared rooms. Gates locked at 12, but overnight keys are provided (a blind eye turned to overnight guests). College hall for lunch and dinner of a reasonable standard and price; also catering for vegetarians. Good library (open 24 hours a day); overshadowed by the lively, popular and (cheap) beer cellar – the venue for various entertainments during term, and a good meeting point for all years. JCR shop sells cheap stationery, food etc, 2 launderettes (not so popular) and a daily tea-bar for various delicacies for hungry, overworked students. TV room with weekly video shows (seats must be booked for popular soaps such as Neighbours).

Very good sporting reputation, especially for rowing. Has been head of the river in Torpids and Eights.

Many college societies for all interests, including an excellent dramatic society which produces famous annual summer play on the steps of 1st Quad – a must for all.

Oriel is not just a place to live. There is lively interest in the JCR and its workings, ents, and possibly the strongest college identity in Oxford.

Oriel has something for everyone, and, like all Oxford colleges, has the added advantage of being situated in one of the most beautiful cities in the country.

Pauper notes

Accommodation: College accommodation reasonably priced (soon may be able to accommodate all who want to live in). Living out more expensive. Cheap launderettes. **Drink:** All college bars are very cheap – especially Oriel. Pubs in town comparatively expensive. **Eats:** Many cheap restaurants catering for all tastes. **Ents:** Good college ents. Lots of cinemas, mainstream and otherwise. Millions of plays, good and bad. **Sports:** University sports centre free for all students (booking difficult), and there are good facilities on a college level too. **Travel:** Lots of travel grants from college. **Work:** Work available for college services eg bar. Tutors not keen on other work in term time. Students sometimes employed in summer in library/porters' lodge. Oxford full of opportunities for temp work especially tourism – many restaurants etc.

Alumni (Editors' pick)

Sir Walter Ralegh, Cecil Rhodes, Beau Brummel, A J P Taylor, Norman Willis, Cardinal Newman, Matthew Arnold.

PEMBROKE

Pembroke College, Oxford OX1 1DW (0865 276444)

Founded: 1624; women undergraduates first admitted 1979. **Accommodation:** About 280 rooms – all undergraduates will be able to live in college for at least 2 years. Rent: 60% in accommodation where rent controlled by college. Daily inclusive rate for living in college is £7.77 (heated room) or £7.14 (unheated). This does not include lunch (about £1.50 per day if taken in hall) or dinner on Saturday. **Eating arrangements:** Hall – formal breakfast and dinner, informal 'snack lunch'. JCR pantry for morning coffee and teas. **Gate/guest hours:** Gate closes at midnight, guests out by 2 am. **Admission:** For post A-level candidates on basis of interview and school reports. For pre A-level candidates admission either by entrance examination or by interview and school reports (acceptance is conditional on A-level grades). **Scholarships:** Up to 24 awards given at the end of the first year of undergraduate course based on performance in course work and examination. Any successful candidate who is qualified for an award from one of college's trusts may have his/her scholarship or exhibition named after and financed by that fund. **Travel grants:** Limited funds available for small number of grants. **Library:** Working collection of about 30,000 books covering all subjects taught; closes at 2 am. **Other college facilities:** Sports ground (1 mile from college), boathouse, bar, photographic darkroom.

European Community: 10% first degree students take EC language as part of course and 10% spend 6 months or more in another EC country. No formal exchange links.

College fees for 1992/93 (undergraduates) £2,993

Undergraduates: *Men:* 207 *Women:* 114
Postgraduates: *Men:* 52 *Women:* 15

GET HOLD OF THE PROSPECTUSES

Teaching staff: *Men:* 34 fellows, 1 research fellow, 8 lecturers
Women: 2 fellows, 1 research fellow, 5 lecturers.

What it's like

After settling for mediocrity in the 1980s, Pembroke has exploded into the 1990s and enjoyed a great deal of success along the way. Student life is based around an active JCR which organizes excellent ents at every available opportunity, and runs a wide variety of music, religious and dining societies (including The Teasel Club, Oxford's oldest dining society). The JCR also provides excellent sporting facilities and has its own art collection, which includes a Francis Bacon masterpiece. Work at Pembroke is like the Loch Ness monster – few people believe in it, and even fewer have seen it. Sport, on the other hand, is very much in evidence with the college contributing very highly to the university teams, and running a wide variety of college teams to suit all interests and abilities. Sporting success has recently come from darts team, while hockey and rowing are extremely strong. Relations between JCR and SCR are friendly enough and the regulations are seldom enforced. Amenities aren't good in Old College, but this is compensated for by the excellent New Building, which was built overlooking the river a few years ago. With so much going on in college it is possible for Pembroke to be a little insular. However, this is compensated for by the great college spirit, the fact that there are no college stereotypes; and Pembroke's attitude to life which is down to earth and relaxed. In summer, Chapel Quad becomes a blissful haven of croquet players and tanned finalists. All in all, Pembroke is a great place to be.

Jason Britton, JCR President

Pauper notes

Accommodation: All first years live in college; accommodation varies enormously. Second years have to live in nearby rented accommodation. All finalists can live in the recently built Sir Geoffrey Arthur Building, which overlooks the river and houses the best student accommodation in Oxford. **Drinks:** College bar among the best in Oxford, although prices aren't as low as most bars. Most students tend to use local pubs, unless there is a special reason not to (i.e. ents.). Pubs include, The Old Tom with its excellent garden, The Folley Bridge Inn, and The Marlborough Arms. **Eats:** All meals can be taken in hall, where breakfast is by far the best value. Some complain about formal hall every evening, with gowns and Latin Grace, but most get used to it soon enough. All finalists self cater due to the excellent facilities in the New Building. Self catering facilities in the main college building are appalling. **Ents:** Own committee takes care of ents, however, more recently the college authorities have been very active in preventing ents taking place. When they do occur they are normally very well attended and a great source of gossip for weeks. The 'Event' which takes place every two years and is the Pembroke equivalent of a summer ball, is excellent value for money. **Sports:** Own extensive facilities, and is currently enjoying a revival. Hockey, rowing, Rugby and darts are extremely strong. Everyone who wants to play a sport, whether seriously or for fun, catered for. **Hardship funds:** Available to those in need, while vacation grants are more freely available. **Travel:** Pembroke's excellent location means it is within walking distance of most of Oxford. Although owning a bike is recommended, it is by no means essential. **Work:** Not allowed to work (financially!) during term time; harder and harder to find in vacation. College development officer seeks vacation placements in business and industry for Pembroke students.

QUEEN'S

The Queen's College, Oxford OX1 4AW (0865 279120)

Founded: 1341; women undergraduates first admitted 1979. **Accommodation:** All undergraduates are accommodated in a room in college buildings for all three

CAN'T FIND WHAT YOU'RE LOOKING FOR? USE THE INDEX!

(or four) years of their course. (Over 100 large rooms in main buildings; 50 rooms in modernised Queen's Lane quadrangle; 77 study bedrooms in modern and spectacular Florey Building; 52 rooms in the newly modernised Iffley Road building opposite university sports complex; 24 rooms in 6 self-catering houses and 12 self-catering rooms for post-graduates in a house in Banbury Road). Standard charge, £928 pa. **Eating arrangements:** Breakfast available in hall, Florey Building and Iffley Road building; lunch and dinner in hall. Meals charged at cost of materials only. **Gate/guest hours:** Undergraduates can have their own keys. **Library:** Over 140,000 volumes, including good coverage of all undergraduate subjects. **Other college facilities:** Chapel with superb modern pipe organ and concert piano; convenient sports field; boathouse with several good 'eights'; tennis courts; squash courts; beer cellar. **Travel grants:** Some vacation travel grants available. **Admission:** By the procedures common to all Oxford colleges. Information is available from the Tutor for Admissions or from the Oxford Colleges' Admissions Office. Undergraduates not admitted for English, geography, metallurgy, fine arts. **Scholarships:** Various scholarships and exhibitions offered, to students on any course, for distinguished work; College bursaries for excellence in non-academic activities (sports, etc); choral, organ or instrumental awards offered for distinguished performance (not restricted to students reading music).

European Community: 16% first degree students take EC language as part of course and 16% spend 6 months or more in another EC country. No formal exchange links.

College fees for 1992/93: (undergraduates) £2,951

Undergraduates: *Men:* 178 *Women:* 116

Postgraduates: *Men:* 65 *Women:* 29

Teaching staff: *Men:* 34 fellows, 5 research fellows, 19 lecturers
Women: 1 fellow, nil research fellows, 5 lecturers.

What it's like

Probably one of the most flourishing of Oxford colleges, Queen's stands imposingly on the High Street; its cupola and quad designed by Hawksmoor who supervised the building at Blenheim Palace. Accommodation is now available to all students for three years, either in college itself or the two modern annexes (one of which is brand new) which house the first years. Academic pressure is significantly less marked than at other colleges yet Queen's still tends to do extremely well especially in modern languages, maths and law. It has regular success in sporting competitions and college societies include a popular drama society and a publicly-acclaimed choir. There is also a dark-room for students' use. Facilities are good although those living in cannot self-cater. College food is more than adequate for most, being cheap, available every day and quite edible! The beer cellar is among the best in Oxford, and popular entertainments are organised ranging from discos and bands to day-trips to France. The JCR is active if mainly apolitical. Its former 'northern insularity' image has now disappeared and it can be considered cosmopolitan and highly active.

Gregor Fergusen

Pauper notes

Accommodation: College rents comparatively inexpensive. **Drink:** Beer cellar, wide variety at excellent prices and the main college focal point. Few feel the need to drink elsewhere but if you fancy a change there are several good pubs close by. **Eats:** Good selection of food at subsidised price. Breakfast & lunch are self-service, dinner set menu. **Ents:** Renowned in Oxford for the quality and variety of its JCR organised ents. Close to town centre with all the usual cinemas and theatres. **Sports:** Excellent football, Rugby and cricket pitches conveniently situated by the river across from the college boathouse. New tennis and squash courts. **Travel:** Generous funding for those with course-related excuses. **Work:** Most need to work in the long vac.

WANT TO HELP WITH THE NEXT EDITION – SEE PAGE 76

Alumni (Editors' pick)

Rowan Atkinson (comedian), Leopold Stokowski (conductor), Brian Walden (TV presenter), Gerald Kaufman (politician), Bishop of Durham.

REGENT'S PARK

Regent's Park College, Pusey Street, Oxford OX1 2LB (0865 59887)

Founded: 1810; women undergraduates first admitted 1922 (ministerial) and 1978 (non-ministerial). **Accommodation:** Available for all students; standard charge £1,246 pa. **Eating arrangements:** Meals in hall. **Gate/guest hours:** All students given keys. **Admission:** By the procedures common to all Oxford colleges. Undergraduates not admitted for sciences. **Library:** 33,000 approx, 40 current periodicals, 25 study places and Angus Library of historic Baptist materials. **Scholarships:** Some scholarships available. **Other college facilities:** Kitchens on each level. Games room. TV room, JCR etc. **Travel grants:** Available. **Hardship Funds:** Some. **Largest fields of study:** Theology, but arts subjects generally.

European Community: 5% first degree students take EC language as part of course and 5% spend 6 months or more in another EC country. Special links with Bonn.

College fees for 1992/93 (undergraduates) £3,147

Undergraduates: *Men:* 34 *Women:* 21

Postgraduates: *Men:* 7

Teaching staff: *Men:* 6 fellows, 1 research fellow, 9 lecturers *Women:* 3 lecturers.

What it's like

Close to the city centre, with a small but attractive quadrangle framed by neo-classical buildings of the 20th century on three sides, and by houses from the 18th century and earlier on the fourth. Undergraduates able to live in college throughout their whole course if they so choose. A small, friendly community offering strong pastoral support to its members. About one third of college members preparing for ordination in the Baptist ministry, with other undergraduates and graduates reading a range of arts degrees with other careers in mind. Thoroughly ecumenical, the college offers, but does not impose, opportunities for all its members to think about a Christian world-view and Christian service in society today. Plenty of social events throughout the term and sport and drama encouraged. Excellent food during the week, self-catering at weekends in kitchens provided for student use.

Pauper notes

Accommodation: Most live in at reasonable rates. **Drink:** Temporary bar for events, otherwise 'drinks cupboard' available. **Eats:** Food good with vegetarian meals available at both lunch and dinner. **Ents:** Usually one event a week organised by social committee, discos twice a term, end of year mini-ball. **Sports:** Usual team and indoor sports well catered for. **Hardship funds:** Some bursaries available. **Travel:** Special travel grants available. **Work:** (non academic). Not encouraged during term.

ST ANNE'S

St Anne's College, Oxford OX2 6HS (0865 274800)

Founded: 1878; men undergraduates first admitted 1979. **Accommodation:**

CAN'T FIND WHAT YOU'RE LOOKING FOR? USE THE INDEX!

Single study-bedrooms for majority of undergraduates; first and final year students guaranteed college rooms. Standard maintenance charge, £1,302 pa. **Eating arrangements:** All meals available in hall but not compulsory; limited self-catering facilities in college houses. **Gate/guest hours:** No gate hours. Guests may stay overnight if signed in. **Admission:** College has tutorial fellows in all the main subjects. **Scholarships:** Scholarships and Exhibitions awarded for good academic work and success in examinations. **Hardship funds:** Hardship fund available – grants made on *ad hoc* basis. **Travel grants:** Limited funds available to undergraduates during their course but they must submit their proposed programme and have their tutor's recommendation. **Library:** One of the largest college libraries in Oxford, with Chinese section, and law library. **Other college facilities:** Extensive computer systems. Sports facilities shared with St John's, squash courts with St Antony's; new boathouse on river for rowers. **Largest fields of study:** English, history, law, mathematics, modern languages, PPE.

European Community: 13 students learning an EC language and spending time in another EC country.

College fees for 1992/93 (undergraduates) £3,126

Undergraduates: *Men:* 243 *Women:* 199
Postgraduates: *Men:* 85 *Women:* 58

Teaching staff: *Men:* 26 fellows, 4 research fellows, 9 lecturers
Women: 13 fellows, 4 research fellows, 6 lecturers, 1 letrice.

What it's like

Good male/female ratio contributes to friendly atmosphere while wide cross section of students ensures very little prejudice. Excellent college ents (frequent discos, wine tasting, cocktail evenings etc), videos twice a week. Cheap, efficient and well-stocked bar open nightly provides focal centre of college social life. Various societies – drama, music, religious, political, photographic etc. Freshers encouraged to come up early – special social events arranged. Also system of student sponsors for freshers. Accommodation is generally good, most live in. All single rooms. No gate or guest restrictions. Reasonable cheap food. Alternative student-run JCR buttery open at meal times. Sports facilities shared with St John's. College raised money to build a boathouse. One of Oxford's best college libraries, friendly staff, open 8.30–2 am during week.

Pauper notes

Accommodation: Most live in. **Drink:** College bar student run and cheap. **Eats:** Vegetarian meals available every night in college. JCR buttery. **Ents:** One college social event/week on average. Subsidised, generally well organised and well attended. Videos shown twice weekly. Very active social committee. **Sports:** Multi-gym recently purchased. **Hardship funds:** Extant but not well publicised. **Travel:** Large availability of funds for travel abroad. **Work:** Student run bar and buttery employ student helpers. Pubs locally employ undergraduates. Library helpers employed throughout term.

Alumni (Editors' pick)

Maria Aitken, Frances Cairncross, Baroness Young, Iris Murdoch, Libby Purves, Tina Brown, Elizabeth Turner, Joanna Richardson, Naomi Mitchison, Dame Cicely Saunders, Edwina Currie.

ST CATHERINE'S

St Catherine's College, Oxford OX1 3UJ (0865 271700)

Founded: 1962; women undergraduates first admitted 1973. **Accommodation:** 288 rooms in college, 30 bedsits in nearby college houses. It is normal for a first year undergraduate to live in college. Rent: 66% in accommodation where rent controlled by college. Standard charge £950.49 pa, plus meals. **Eating arrangements:** Hall, buttery, individual staircase facilities. **Gate/guest hours:** Unrestricted. **Admission:** Undergraduates not admitted for classics, theology. **Scholarships:** Awarded for academic excellence at end of first year. **Travel grants:** Limited number for undergraduates for use in long vacation. **Other college facilities:** JCR has debating pit, bar, buttery, TV room and private dining room; Bernard Sunley Building with lecture and film theatre, outdoor and indoor theatres, music room (with harpsichord and grand piano), squash courts and 6 tennis courts, several college punts, nearby playing fields at Marston.

European Community: Modern language students (about 15 per year) study an EC language and spend 6 months or more in another EC country as part of their course. No formal exchange links.

College fees for 1992/93: (undergraduates) £3,041

Undergraduates: *Men:* 298 *Women:* 160

Postgraduates: *Men:* 111 *Women:* 27

Teaching staff: *Men:* 30 fellows, 11 research fellows, 25 lecturers
Women: 2 fellows, 1 research fellow, 9 lecturers.

What it's like

Catz was originally founded in the 19th century as a society to matriculate poor students into Oxford University who could not afford the then astronomical cost of living in a college. When the government started paying for higher education, it was felt that the society was no longer necessary in its old form, and thanks to some generous donations from various sources, St Catherine's College was founded.

It comprises a set of low buildings – angular yet graceful – and some beautiful gardens. It is about five minutes from the city centre, but surroundings are more typical of the beautiful Oxfordshire countryside than of an urban environment. The architect, Arne Jacobsen, designed everything, from bricks to SCR's cutlery.

The background of the college has led to it being one of the more liberal in Oxford – it was one of the first to go co-ed – and its open-plan layout allows more freedom than at some of the older establishments. Students can live in college for two years, and the rooms are comfortable, if a little small. Self-catering facilities are also provided. It is one of Oxford's largest colleges, but has a great sense of community, despite the diversity of students' backgrounds.

The social life is lively: there are ents every other week, and a special event each term, the most popular being Catz night in November, where the entire college gets kegged on cheap cocktails. There are a number of societies, including the film soc, which screens a film each week. The college has punts, a weights room and squash, tennis and netball courts on site, and the sports field a 15-minute walk away.

Catz is strongest in sciences, but it also has a large proportion of arts students (it's just that they don't tend to work as hard).

Richard Baldry

Pauper notes

Accommodation: College-owned property cheapest (£5.10 per night). Married quarters only in college houses. Quite expensive to live out. **Drink:** Catz bar is one of the cheapest college bars in Oxford. Beer 70p–£1.00 per pint including Courage & Ind Coope real ales. **Eats:** Hall – 3 course evening meal except Sundays £2.50 or less with tickets, lunch £1.35, breakfast £1.20. Vegetarians catered for in hall. Pete's Cafe – more flexible, usually cheaper. Self-catering facilities are the best in Oxford's colleges. **Ents:** Catz has a reputation for good ents with discos, bands, etc – entry is free but restricted to JCR members and guests. Oxford theatrical productions are cheap (about £2) and frequent. **Sports:** Catz has squash courts, tennis and netball courts, weights room, punts, shared boathouse, sports field

(1 mile away). **Hardship funds:** Administered by the Master. College offers unlimited assistance in proven cases of difficulty. **Travel:** Travel scholarships are available for a wide range of projects. **Work:** Behind bar and in library during term. Available serving conference guests and gardening on campus during vacation.

Informal name:
Catz.

Alumni (Editors' pick)
A A Milne, Sarah R Wheale, John Birt, Simon Winchester, Peter Mandellson.

ST EDMUND HALL

St Edmund Hall, Oxford OX1 4AR (0865 279000)

Founded: 1317; women undergraduates first admitted 1978. **Accommodation:** All undergraduates may spend at least 2 of their 3 years in college (in study bedrooms). Standard charge £870 pa for 25 weeks; £5 per night for any extra. £1,464 for 25 weeks including heating, breakfast and dinner – refunds available if meals not taken. **Eating arrangements:** Cafeteria style service, formal dinner every Sunday night; formal guest dinner three nights per term. **Gate/guest hours:** No restrictions. **Admission:** Pre A-level candidates may apply for conditional offers or may take the entrance examination. There is no quota on any mode of entrance and the majority of subjects have no preference between them. Post A-level candidates apply on basis of school record, A-level grades and interview. Undergraduates are not admitted for theology, classics, biology, zoology, human sciences, oriental studies. **Academic features:** Particular strengths in Eastern European studies and material and earth sciences. College welcomes applicants for Joint Schools. **Special features:** The Ruskin Master of Drawing is a fellow of the college. **Scholarships and Bursaries:** Awards after first year of study. Musical bursaries. Support for academic projects. Small grants for travel and for developing language abroad. **Library:** Library (restored Early English church) with some 50,000 volumes, microfilm/fiche reader, microscope; word processing facilities are available. **Other college facilities:** Boathouse, tennis courts and hockey pitches, football in university park.

European Community: 12% first degree students take EC language as part of course and 12% spend 6 months or more in another EC country. No formal exchange links, but participation in Erasmus scheme.

College fees for 1992/93: (undergraduates) £3,101

Undergraduates: *Men:* 260 *Women:* 140

Postgraduates: *Men:* 77 *Women:* 18

Teaching staff: *Men:* 40 fellows, 2 research fellows, 12 lecturers, 1 lektor *Women:* 4 fellows, 1 research fellow, 6 lecturers, 1 lectrice.

What it's like
Teddy Hall, the oldest undergraduate house in the English speaking world, is universally acclaimed as Oxford's friendliest college. The very intimate community and strong Hall spirit for which it is famed have not resulted in insularity, but instead have tended to give Aularians (the ancient name of Hall Members) the confidence to be very outgoing. There is a resultant high representation of Aularians in most of the university's societies and all of its teams. Everyone can find a niche in its relaxed and tolerant community, where individuality is valued.

The tradition of strong debate in the JCR has resulted in easily the best attended JCR meetings but without any party-political biases.

GET HOLD OF THE PROSPECTUSES

Known as *the* party college, Teddy Hall's frequent ents are legendary, and draw students from all the other colleges.

A strong resurgence in journalism has joined the college's longer established tradition of being at the forefront of sport and drama.

Physically, the college is well endowed. Centrally located, its picturesque mediaeval front quad complements the modern quad behind, and the main university libraries are mere steps away. The college library is a serene eleventh century Norman church.

HH Maharaj Akaash
The President of the Junior Common Room

Pauper notes

Accommodation: First and third years guaranteed accommodation in college and 2 annexes. Limited second year rooms allocated by ballot. Flats for married students. **Drink:** The bar is the college's social focus and is always rated the university's best. Comparatively inexpensive. **Eats:** Food variable. Vegetarian option at all sittings. Fortnightly Guest Nights are excellent with fierce competition for limited tickets. **Ents:** Possesses Wolfson Hall, the largest student venue in Oxford, which is used to its full potential; frequent discos and bands. Cocktail evenings. Videos screened weekly. Known as Oxford's Green Room for its preeminence in drama. **Sports:** Completely dominates Oxford sports, especially athletics, Rugby, and rowing. Excellent facilities. **Hardship funds:** Available upon consideration of individual circumstances. **Travel:** Limited grants available. **Work:** Limited grants available.

More info?

Enquiries to JCR President (0865 279027).

Informal name:

Teddy Hall.

Alumni (Editors' pick)

Sir Robin Day, Terry Jones (Monty Python), Hugo MacNeill, Stuart Barnes.

ST HILDA'S

St Hilda's College, Oxford OX4 1DY (0865 276884)

Founded: 1893; women only. **Accommodation:** All first year, some second, and all final year undergraduates can live in college accommodation in study/bedrooms. Standard charge, £1,223 pa. **Eating arrangements:** Maintenance fee includes meal tickets for a certain number of meals in hall; additional tickets can be bought as required (breakfast £1.05; main meal £1.63). **Gate/guest hours:** During week, open to all 9 am–11 pm and to accompanied visitors 11 pm–2 am; overnight visitors may be signed in. **Admission:** By entrance examination and interview or by conditional offer on the basis of interview and in some cases submission of school written work. **Academic features:** The college will consider applications for any of the undergraduate courses offered in the university. **Travel grants:** About £6,000 given this year. M C Wise grants for undergraduates' travel abroad and graduate research, open to all subjects; Christina Keith travel grants for classics students; K O Morgan travel grants and graduate research grants for historians. **Hardship funds:** Funds available (grants and interest-free loans). Laura Ashley bursaries for mature students. **Library:** Good range of books for most honour schools. **Other college facilities:** Small chapel, buttery, tennis court,

CAN'T FIND WHAT YOU'RE LOOKING FOR? USE THE INDEX!

croquet lawn, harpsichord, pianos, punts, computers and printers (with access to university computing facilities), JCR bar, washing machines and spin dryers, cooking facilities. **Largest fields of study:** English, modern languages, history, mathematics, biological science.

European Community: 15% first degree students take EC language as part of course and 15% spend 6 months or more in another EC country. No formal exchange links.

College fees for 1992/93: (undergraduates) £3,094

Undergraduates: *Women:* 375

Postgraduates: *Women:* 59

Teaching staff: *Men:* 15 college lecturers
Women: 32 fellows, 5 research fellows, 6 lecturers.

What it's like

St Hilda's continues to cultivate a reputation for being relaxed, friendly and welcoming and full of go-getting women who make a great contribution to university life. Just one success story is the new O.U.S.U. (Oxford University Student Union) President. Effectively the last all-female Oxford college, the undergraduates are proud of their status and appreciate the supportive, community atmosphere. The college is open plan, lying over six acres of gardens alongside the River Cherwell; river, lawns and our own punts conspire to make summer term extremely pleasant.

As at all Oxford colleges, work is pressurised, but help and encouragement are always on hand from tutors and friends. The emphasis seems to be on co-operation rather than competition and your academic life can be as stimulating as you want it to be.

We do our level best to relieve candidate and fresher stress, something to bear in mind when you come for interview. Once you get here, accommodation is in single furnished rooms; not the lap of luxury, but at least not ancient and draughty. You are guaranteed a college room for first and final years; rent includes 20 breakfasts and 20 meals per term. The food is excellent; good quality and value for money with snack and vegetarian options and a formal dinner once a week. A kitchen is always nearby if you prefer to cook for yourself and snacks-between-meals can be bought in the bar or buttery. Other amenities include a computer room, two laundries, two common rooms, two TVs and one video, tennis courts and the aforementioned punts. The Boat Club is thriving with pro and fun crews and lots of parties, but there are many other things to do if rowing isn't your scene – what about standing for a committee post, auditioning for Drama Cuppers or organising the Arts Festival?

The city centre is ten minutes away, but the situation of the college is such that it remains a peaceful retreat from smog and noise. Head away from town and you are immediately in an area full of interesting shops and a variety of restaurants/fast food outlets, an off-licence just across the road, a liberal smattering of pubs, a cinema, a main supermarket and a venue for bands and club nights. Come and go as you please; late or overnight guests welcome provided you sign them in, and yes, men are allowed!

Founded in 1893, we are about to celebrate our centenary in grand style. With plans going ahead including improvements to the already excellent library and the construction of the Jaqueline Du Pré music building, a high profile 1993 will benefit students for years to come.

So there you have it; we rest our case!

Lisa Anscomb, JCR President

Pauper notes

Accommodation: Not the cheapest, but reasonable. **Drink:** Our college bar, one of Oxford's cheapest; fine range of spirits! **Eats:** Excellent value and quality in college; good healthy range and veggie alternative which often proves more popular than carnivore option. **Ents:** Regular college ents – cheap! **Sports:** College tennis courts, punts, boat club. **Hardship funds:** At college's discretion; not vast; stringent assessment but applications encouraged. **Travel:** Travel grants quite easy to come by, £50 Europe, £100 worldwide. **Work:** Term: opportunity to invigilate in library, do bar shifts. Vac: College will employ students for conference coverage; kitchens, silver service etc. Wages not brilliant, convenient if you need to be around college during vac.

More info?

Enquiries to Kay Hatfield (Schools Liaison Officer 1992/93). Preferable to write.

Alumni (Editors' pick)

Marjory-Anne Bromhead (economist at World Bank), Nicola Le Fanu (composer), Kate Millett (feminist writer), Beryl Smalley (historian), A Bullard (vice-president, Amcon Corp, USA), Dame Helen Gardner (critic), Barbara Pym (novelist), D K Broster, Jacqueline Du Pré (cellist), Catherine Heath (writer), Hermione Lee (broadcaster).

ST HUGH'S

St Hugh's College, Oxford OX2 6LE (0865 274900)

Founded: 1886; men undergraduates first admitted 1987. **Accommodation:** All undergraduates offered accommodation (study bedroom) for at least 3 years. Rent: 75% in accommodation where rent controlled by college. Standard charge, £1,084 pa. **Eating arrangements:** Meal tickets are bought as required. **Gate/guest hours:** All undergraduates have keys. Visitors out by 2 am. Overnight guests at weekend by arrangement. **Admission:** College welcomes applications from all kinds of school. Undergraduates not admitted for human sciences or theology. **Scholarships:** Up to 26 scholarships and exhibitions awarded annually to matriculated undergraduates; various essay prizes; organ scholarship (£200 plus free vacation lodgings) and instrumental award. **Travel grants:** Limited amount of money available for students attending required courses. **Library:** Recently modernised; separate law and science reading rooms. **Other college facilities:** JCR bar, bar billiards, tennis, croquet, rowing, particularly large and pleasant garden, computer.

European Community: 10% first degree students (modern languages and joint courses) take EC language as part of course and 10% spend 6 months or more in another EC country. No formal exchange links.

College fees for 1992/93: (undergraduates) £3,128

Undergraduates: *Men:* 222 *Women:* 155

Postgraduates: *Men:* 74 *Women:* 61

Teaching staff: *Men:* 24 fellows, 2 research fellows, 12 lecturers
Women: 13 fellows, 3 research fellows, 9 lecturers, 4 British Academy fellows.

What it's like

St Hugh's is now establishing itself as one of Oxford's most energetic, egalitarian, and educationally exciting colleges. Set in 14 acres of landscaped grounds in north Oxford it provides a supportive environment in which to enjoy the university as a whole. Extensive modern facilities include computer rooms, music rooms, dark room.

The atmosphere is relaxed, with both students and staff considerate and tolerant of each other. Something essential in such a small community.

Fifteen minutes' walk from town, less if you're a cyclist. Can be a bit insular, but many students very outgoing and active outside college. Admissions are evenly

CAN'T FIND WHAT YOU'RE LOOKING FOR? USE THE INDEX!

split between the sexes as well as the state and private school sectors. Academic standards are rising under new Principal.

Pauper notes

Accommodation: Everyone housed. Cost c£400 per term. **Drink:** Newest and cheapest bar in Oxford, extensive facilities, friendly atmosphere. **Eats:** Average food for all needs/diets in college. Lots of places to eat out in Oxford. **Ents:** Excellent regular ents (music, live bands, jazz etc) in college, 2 weekly videos and lots of active societies. **Sports:** Active football and cricket clubs. Tennis, croquet and weights all on site. Swimming pool nearby as are shared hockey/football/cricket grounds. Very active boat club. **Hardship funds:** Available in extreme cases – see Bursar. **Travel:** Lots of small (£50–£200) grants available for summer trips. **Work:** Same as any other medium-sized city.

More info?

Enquiries to Nikki Watson (0865 274900).

Alumni (Editors' pick)

Barbara Castle, Jane Glover, Catherine Johnston, Emily Davison (early suffragette), Dame Peggy Ashcroft, Mary Renault.

ST JOHN'S

St John's College, Oxford OX1 3JP (0865 277300)

Founded: 1555; women undergraduates first admitted 1979. **Accommodation:** Accommodation in college offered to all undergraduates for all 3 years (Jacobean, Victorian and modern rooms). Most undergraduates charged £1,590 pa for room and 3 meals (range £1,578–£1,791). **Eating arrangements:** Breakfast, lunch and early dinner self-service in hall, semi-formal dinner. Snacks available from college bar. **Gate/guest hours:** Late keys issued. **Admissions:** Conditional, pre A-level offers; by entrance examination; and post A-level unconditional offers. Undergraduates not admitted for geology, metallurgy. **Scholarships:** Awards offered on University examination results annually; organ scholarships and choral scholarships annually. **Travel grants:** Awarded annually on tutors' recommendations. Book grants open to all undergraduates. Instrumental awards. **Hardship funds:** Funds and grants occasionally available. **Library:** 12,000 older books, and working library of 30,000 volumes, many rare books and manuscripts. **Other college facilities:** Sports ground a mile from the college, tennis court, pavilion; boathouse in Christ Church meadow.

European Community: 12% first degree students take EC language as part of course and 12% spend 6 months or more in another EC country. Formal exchange links in Munich, Geneva and Pisa – open to all undergraduates.

College fees for 1992/93: (undergraduates) £2,948

Undergraduates: *Men:* 237 *Women:* 111
Postgraduates: *Men:* 133 *Women:* 41

Teaching staff: *Men:* 48 fellows, 6 research fellows, 16 lecturers, 1 lektor
Women: 3 fellows, 6 research fellows, 5 lecturers, 1 lektorin.

What it's like

The rumours about the wealth of St John's are all true, and as a student the material advantages are obvious – accommodation for all undergraduates, good kitchen facilities, cheap food in hall, and facilities to rival any in Oxford (a well-stocked library, an excellent computer room, 2 squash courts on site and so on). As one of the larger colleges, the sporting facilities are good – a sports ground only a mile away with rugby, football and hockey pitches in addition to two tennis courts and a boathouse on the River Isis.

But what sets St John's apart from the rest of Oxford is not the legendary work ethic, which is shared by Univ. and Merton (and which comes from other students, rather than directly from tutors), but an apparently endless supply of ambition – almost everyone becomes involved in extra-curricular activities, and it seems that the desire to achieve highly in finals is matched by endeavour beyond the library. Such dynamism leads to enthusiastic JCR debates and committed sports teams, although for some people these are only valued for CV points. In many ways St John's is a college of the 1980s, where materialism and competitiveness are as prevalent as altruism and philosophical thought. The result is a vibrant and exciting place to earn a degree.

Pauper notes

Accommodation: College accommodation for all undergrads – cheap by Oxford standards (£3.80–£5.00 per day). Married flats ('Hart-Synot House') ¾ mile away. **Drink:** Sub-pub prices in college bar; the Lamb and Flag next door. **Eats:** Cheap food in hall (3 course dinner £1.80) + bar food. Veg. options. **Ents:** Within college great dinners, bops, karaoke, hypnotists, garden party. **Sports:** Croquet lawn and 2 squash courts within college, sportsground 1 mile away. **Hardship funds:** £50 book grant pa for everyone, undefined hardship fund. **Travel:** Travel grants available c £150 for summer trips.

Alumni (Editors' pick)

Robert Graves, Philip Larkin, John Wain, Kingsley Amis.

ST PETER'S

St Peter's College, Oxford OX1 2DL (0865 278900)

Founded: 1929; women undergraduates first admitted 1979. **Accommodation:** All first year plus some third year (on a ballot) and JCR Committee and Club Secretaries in college. 75–80 more places in college houses. **Rent:** 60% in accommodation where rent controlled by college. Most undergraduates charged £900 pa (range £900–£1,096): £1,597 including all meals. **Eating arrangements:** Breakfast normally residents only. Lunch buffet-type, pay as you go. Dinner, pay as you go; one formal sitting (7.15) and one earlier informal sitting (6.15). **Gate/guest hours:** No restrictions except as to noise and good order. The gate is locked at 11.00 pm, keys available. **Admission:** Pre A-level candidates may sit an entrance examination. Post A-level candidates must (pre A-level candidates, may) apply instead on the basis of A-level results (known or future), school record, and interview. College welcomes applications from older candidates, especially in PPE. Undergraduates not accepted for classics, PPP, experimental psychology, human sciences, oriental studies, Russian, metallurgy. **Scholarships:** Organ scholarship and two choral awards annually at entrance. Other awards (including instrumental award) for students in residence. **Travel grants:** Grants are made annually to members of the college from the Christian Deelman Fund and by St Peter's Society. **Library:** Ample reading space, mainly undergraduate texts, with a few older and more specialist works. Separate Law Library. **Other college facilities:** Music room, usual athletics and other facilities, JCR.

European Community: Modern linguists (some 8 per year) only take EC language as part of course and spend 9 months in another EC country. No formal exchange links.

College fees for 1992/93: (undergraduates) £3,195

Undergraduates: *Men:* 212 *Women:* 77

Postgraduates: *Men:* 67 *Women:* 42

CAN'T FIND WHAT YOU'RE LOOKING FOR? USE THE INDEX!

What it's like

It's in the centre of Oxford, just off the major pedestrianised shopping and eating areas, a small collection of buildings that includes the ancient 'New Inn Hall' and a new accommodation block. Oxford doesn't have to be intimidating or posh, St Peter's is a friendly, lively stress free place. The 'typical'?? description of a student here would be – apolitical, keen socialite and college member, definitely not a genius, coming from all backgrounds and going in all directions! Work atmosphere relaxed with tutors giving fair demands and deadlines; good communication between the Master governing body and the students.

Close by are cinemas, restaurants, libraries (including a comprehensive college library open 9am–7pm every day) and top night spots. These supplement hectic social calendar organised by the students as 'in college' entertainments – ranging from fancy do's and college ball to sweaty bops and singalongs in the bar. In the undergraduate common room (JCR) we have local bands, hold karaokes, blind date etc. The bar is widely renowned in Oxford as one of the best. Good quality, cheap beer and always something happening. JCR has TV, video, pool and football tables, photocopier, games machines and newspapers.

Drama and music excellent standard – 3 shows this year at the Edinburgh festival and a number of productions each term in college – well funded by college and student body. Sports options cater for all types and standards, all both male and female; standards in top teams high, but comedy teams always well attended!

College is encouraging women to apply. The ratio in the 1st year is M:F 2:1. Last year's Presidents of JCR and MCR both female. There is a college women's officer and student women's reps organise events, talks and classes in self defence. The college has helpful structure for counselling and advice set up at all levels, from 1st year welfare reps to the Master himself. Female nurse on site during the day.

R Bradshaw, JCR President

Pauper notes

Accommodation: 1st year guaranteed live in, and one other year, normally 3rd. Rooms generally good. New building excellent. **Eats:** New catering system this year – very good food at cheap prices – pay as you eat 'key' system. All types of eats places – sandwiches to 3 course within 100 yards of college. **Hardship funds:** Well publicised university access fund; (academic and choral) scholarships available. **Travel:** Travel grants and scholarships. **Work:** Jobs around town not easy but are there.

More info?

Enquiries to Robin Bradshaw (0865 278912).

Informal name:

SPC.

Buzz-words:

Yorkie – humiliating 10–0 defeat at table football, or seven ball defeat at pool – loser buys winner a Yorkie; Sharking – on the pull.

Alumni (Editors' pick)

Sir Rex Hunt, Rev W Awdry, Sir Paul Reeves, Peter Wright.

SOMERVILLE

Somerville College, Oxford OX2 6HD (0865 270600)

Founded: 1879; women only. **Accommodation:** Most undergraduates accommodated in older or modern study bedrooms (some live out for one year); small independent nursery for children of college members. Most undergraduates charged

£1,261 pa (minimum £1,203). £1,480 pa for rent and food. **Eating arrangements:** Cafeteria system in hall. Meals paid for on ticket system. **Gate/guest hours:** Every undergraduate is given a key. **Special features:** GEC lecturer in engineering. **Admission:** Candidates are considered for either mode E or mode N; Somerville has not expressed a preference for either mode. Undergraduates not admitted for anthropology, geography, theology (but philosophy with theology is accepted). **Scholarships:** Various scholarships and exhibitions, both open and closed, awarded at any time in an undergraduate's career for work of especial merit (usually worth £200 and £150 pa respectively) – also Bousfield Scholarships, open to candidates from GPDST schools, and the Dorothy McCalman Scholarship (£100) for candidates who have earned their living for 3 years. **Travel grants:** Various college travel grants and awards. **Hardship funds:** Limited funds available for *unexpected* financial difficulties. **Library:** Over 100,000 volumes, with strong science, history, literature, languages and philosophy collections; also an ICL computer room, electronic calculators and microfiche reader. **Other college facilities:** JCR bar, tennis and croquet, 1 new boat, organ and several pianos.

European Community: 6% of students learn an EC language as part of their course and spend 6 months or more in another EC country. EC students come as undergraduates, visiting students or on the Erasmus programme.

College fees for 1992/93: (undergraduates) £3,099

Undergraduates: *Women:* 348

Postgraduates: *Women:* 45

Teaching staff: *Women:* 24 fellows, 4 research fellows, 6 lecturers.

What it's like

The unique atmosphere is relaxed, friendly, co-operative, and supportive and undergraduates' descriptions range from 'a dynamic base in which individuals develop with a common sense of identity' to 'like a comfy pair of slippers'! It can be best experienced by visiting on one of the Open Days or by speaking to undergraduates (for both of which you simply need to contact the JCR).

It remains, as yet, one of the last remaining single-sex colleges within a mixed university. As such, many students feel that it provides the best of both worlds – encouraging individuals to become involved in the many different societies and organisations across the university (Somerville is renowned as being the most out-going college); whilst also providing an excellent 'home-base' in which to make friends and to study. Indeed, whilst some of the undergraduates are not convinced about what a single-sex college will entail when they are accepted, in a referendum last year 84% of current undergraduates voted that they wanted the college to remain single-sex.

It's slightly out of town, backing on to the Jericho area of Oxford. Having been founded in 1879 by Mary Somerville for the education of women, it has a great variety of buildings, ranging from Victorian to the more modern. Accommodation good and improving; the purchase and refurbishment of houses have meant that a declining proportion of those in the second year are forced to 'live out' (accommodation is guaranteed in the first and final years of your course). Also the college provides good, cheap food and the JCR provides comparatively excellent self-catering facilities and other amenities. There are two laundries, numerous televisions and a video recorder, a sewing machine, typewriter, photocopier, an ICL computer room with a laser printer, a music room and one of Oxford's few creches.

Academically the workload is heavy and students are pushed to achieve. The tutors and fellows are enthusiastic and generally good-humoured and sympathetic and relations between the SCR and JCR are mostly very good, but challenging. The library is one of the most beautiful and well-equipped in Oxford and is accessible 24-hours a day (excellent for essay crises).

WANT TO HELP WITH THE NEXT EDITION – SEE PAGE 76

Socially it's one of the most active colleges in Oxford with a thriving, and extremely cheap bar – very popular is the 'Happy Hour' held on Friday and Saturday nights where prices on pints and shorts are slashed. There is also a pool table and team. Entertainments are of high quality and attract students from all over Oxford. There are active sports clubs and rowing is the best for women in Oxford. There are lively drama, arts and music societies. The college has a very relaxed attitude to overnight guests.

Jenni Borg, JCR President

Pauper notes

Accommodation: All first and third years guaranteed accommodation. Increasing accommodation for second years who want to 'live in'. Possibility of a cross-subsidisation scheme for those who have to 'live out', this is fun but expensive. There are excellent kitchen facilities provided by the JCR and very good provision of bathrooms. **Drink:** Very cheap and often packed bar. Lots of nearby pubs – Eagle & Child, Lamb & Flag, Horse & Jockey and the Jericho Tavern situated behind the college often has live bands. **Eats:** College food generally high standard and cheap. Close to cheap 'greasy spoon', St Giles Cafe. **Ents:** Excellent range and frequency; joint events often held with other colleges. Close to the Phoenix cinema; and only a short walk from town. **Sports:** Somervillians active in many university teams, notably hockey. The best women's rowing in Oxford – Somerville has been Head of the River for the past five years. **Hardship funds:** College and university funds available: Access funds, hardship funds, vacation residence funds open to all students. Some scholarships also available. College is sympathetic. **Travel:** Generous travel grants available and also specific subject grants. **Work:** Officially no Oxford undergraduate should undertake work whilst they are students. Unofficially jobs are easy to find in the vacation, but almost impossible to keep up during term-time. Some form of debt usual.

Alumni (Editors' pick)

Indira Gandhi, Iris Murdoch, Vera Brittain, Ann Oakley, Joyce Gutteridge, Victoria Glendinning, Kate Mortimer, Dr Cicely Williams, Anne Scott James, Dame Kiri Te Kanawa, Winifred Holtby, Dorothy Sayers, Dorothy Hodgkin FRS, Shirley Williams, Esther Rantzen, Margaret Thatcher.

TRINITY

Trinity College, Oxford OX1 3BH (0865 279900)

Founded: 1555; women undergraduates first admitted 1979. **Accommodation:** All undergraduates accommodated in college or in new student block about a mile away if they wish. Most undergraduates charged £1,127 pa (range £1,120–£1,400); £46.61 pw for room and dinner. **Eating arrangements:** All meals can be taken in hall. **Gate/guest hours:** Gate keys issued to college members. **Admission:** Candidates admitted through any of the usual modes of entry. Undergraduates not admitted for geography, PPP, music, experimental psychology, human sciences, oriental studies. **Scholarships:** College scholarships and exhibitions based on academic achievement after end of first year. Designated college for Jardine Scholars from Hong Kong, Japan and Bermuda, and Inlaks Scholars from India. **Travel grants:** J H Britton Travelling Bursaries; Lingen Fund (for classical studies); college funds for academically approved projects. One annual Whitehead Travelling Scholarship of £1,700 for a finalist. **Hardship funds:** Keasbey Grants, Abbott's and university hardship funds. Some college funds. **Library:** Open 24 hours (keyholders at night). Combined arts, science and law library. **Other college facilities:** Computer rooms, beer cellar, darkroom, music society (organ, 2 pianos), squash court, boathouse, playing grounds and pavilion; unusually spacious lawns and gardens.

European Community: 10% first degree students take EC language as part of course and 10% spend 6 months or more in another EC country. No formal exchange links.

College fees for 1992/93: (undergraduates) £2,969

Undergraduates: *Men:* 182 *Women:* 83

Postgraduates: *Men:* 50 *Women:* 33

Teaching staff: *Men:* 25 fellows, 4 research fellows, 19 lecturers
Women: 3 fellows, 1 research fellow, 3 lecturers.

What it's like

Centrally located, architecturally attractive college in extensive gardens. Accommodation of a reasonable standard; almost all undergraduates housed for 3 years, though some second years live off-site in college houses. Complaints about lack of fridges and the fact that there is only one kitchen. Library's all-day opening; extension in bar opening hours very popular. Relatively high proportion from independent schools and a generally deserved reputation for being middle of the road – academically, politically and in sport. Small, relaxed and friendly though some complain of a certain apathy which leads them to venture outside college. On the whole traditional but most of its students find it an excellent place to spend their time at Oxford.

Alumni (Editors' pick)

Cardinal Newman, Jeremy Thorpe (former leader of Liberal Party), Sir Terence Rattigan (playwright), Lord Clark ('Civilisation'), Anthony Crosland, Miles Kington, William Pitt the Elder, A V Dicey, W Anson (both great constitutional lawyers), R Hillary (author), Sir Hans Krebs (biochemist), R Porter (immunology) – both Nobel Laureates, Lord North, Sir Arthur Quiller-Couch, Sir Angus Ogilvy, Ross and Norris McWhirter, Marmaduke Hussey, Robin Leigh-Pemberton.

UNIVERSITY COLLEGE

University College, Oxford OX1 4BH (0865 276602)

Founded: 1249; women undergraduates first admitted 1979. **Accommodation:** Every undergraduate lives in college for his or her first 2 years; accommodation for remainder at Staverton Road site (all undergraduates can be accommodated). Standard charge £3,003 pa. **Admission:** Undergraduates not admitted for geography, theology, human science, history and English; modern language combinations must include Russian. College has one of largest numbers of science undergraduates in university; it also specialises in Russian and psychology. **Hardship funds:** Small loans or grants available.

European Community: Only modern language students study EC language as part of course (5–10%) and take optional year in another EC country. Informal exchange arrangement with Tübingen in classics.

College fees for 1991/92: (undergraduates) £2,968

Undergraduates: *Men:* 271 *Women:* 120

Postgraduates: *Men:* 84 *Women:* 36

Teaching staff: *Men:* 40 fellows, 5 research fellows, 15 lecturers
Women: 6 fellows, 1 research fellow, 4 lecturers.

CAN'T FIND WHAT YOU'RE LOOKING FOR? USE THE INDEX!

What it's like

It's normally painted as a rather staid institution, cold architecture, dryly academic, well respected but no place for a good time. This reputation needs an overhaul! There are few better places in Oxford and if colleges do have characters gradually perpetuated over the years then a kinder representation would be that it's down-to-earth and friendly. There's a startling level of keen intelligence, not necessarily of the intellectual kind (most people couldn't give a fig about Godard, Sartre or even Marx) but also a penetrating common sense that pervades the place. And, to be fair, although quite a serious college in attitude, there's equally a rewarding sense of fun and tolerance. Beer cellar, the envy of other colleges, can be terrifically vibrant, unintimidating even for the quiet type. Food allows students to have a moan but complaints run along the line of the old joke – 'God the food's awful – and such small portions.' Ambitious drama club, outstanding music society, active and valuable women's group, hugely successful rowing and rugby teams. JCR meetings have moved away from irrational, unpleasant, Luddite shouting matches of old, to a more amiable atmosphere of coherent and amusing discussion. The hierarchy likes to subscribe to the motto of 'work hard, play hard', a cliché that surprisingly springs to life when acted out in the discerning, quick-witted and enlightened environment that is University College.

Owain Thomas, JCR President

Pauper notes

Accommodation: College (and the whole of Oxford) is costly but on a par with most other colleges. College accommodation for 3 years if wanted. **Drink:** Beer Cellar run by the JCR. Best beer cellar in Oxford by a long chalk – pubs quite popular eg Eastgate, Wheatsheaf next door. Bullingdon Arms Cowley Road, The Cricketers Iffley Road, Star Royal Rectory Road. Cheap and unpretentious. **Eats:** College food. **Ents:** College ents cheap and frequent. PPP Cinema – but very few bands in Oxford. Comedy at Apollo Theatre (eg Harry Enfield etc). **Sports:** Free college sports facilities, plus gym on Iffley Road and squash court on site. **Hardship funds:** Available in dire circumstances. Parker Fund, claims for grants adjudicated by a committee. Also a fund that primarily gives out loans. **Travel:** NUS card, college travel grants sometimes. Keasby Bursary fund for student travel. **Work:** Work for college bursary/works dept in vac. Also in college beer cellar.

Alumni (Editors' pick)

V S Naipaul, Richard Ingrams, Shelley (poet), Clement Attlee, Roger Utley, Bill Clinton, Andrew Morton, Peter Snow.

WADHAM

Wadham College, Oxford OX1 3PN (0865 277946)

Founded: 1613; women undergraduates first admitted 1974. **Accommodation:** All first and third year students and a few second year can be accommodated in college (shared sets, sets and bedsitters). £1,284 pa covers all accommodation charges and dinner (breakfast and lunch extra). **Eating arrangements:** Self-service breakfast, lunch and dinner in Hall or student refectory. **Gate/guest hours:** No restrictions. **Admission:** Follows the general pattern of Oxford entrance. Undergraduates not admitted for fine art, theology, geography or metallurgy. **Scholarships:** Scholarships awarded for meritorious performance in university examinations and consistently excellent performance in tutorials. **Travel grants:** Various travel grants. **Library:** Library with space for 135 readers. **Other college facilities:** Computer room, JCR cafeteria and bar, launderette, organ and grand piano, squash court, weight-training room; sports ground 1½ miles from college. **Hardship funds:** Some assistance with research expenses for graduates. Loans or grants available according to circumstances. Some travel grants. **Structural features:** Large modern library.

European Community: 40% first degree students take EC language as part of course and 40% spend 6 months or more in another EC country. No formal exchange links, except assistantships. Erasmus initiatives.

College fees for 1992/93: (undergraduates) £3,061

Undergraduates: *Men:* 261 *Women:* 162

Postgraduates: *Men:* 105 *Women:* 38

What it's like

Reasonably large and very diverse student community. Its enviable male:female ratio and enlightened admissions policy mean everyone is made to feel welcome. Wadham cliché/in-joke that it is 'an island of normality in a sea of intellectual and class snobbery' still holds true. SU dynamic and politically active: reputation for left-wing 'soundness' offset by best student bops in Oxford and almost terminal laid-backness of some members. SCR usually sympathetic and tutors generally likeable. College facilities are okay: SU subsidised launderette, TV, video, vending/games machines and own PA system! Sports ground 15 mins by bike, library open 24 hours. New SU shop stocks everything from condoms to washing powder to stationery.

Accommodation ranges from old, quaint and airy to newer, goldfishbowl-like and warm, to brand new, disinfected and well-equipped (ie kitchens). New building finished last year means all 1st years and finalists live in . . . although all 2nd years left to the mercy of Oxford's rapacious housing monopolies.

Graduates go on to do everything/anything/nothing: recent batch of Wadham student journos now making names for themselves in national papers. Wadhamites are extremely active in journalism, politics, arts, sports . . . they're everywhere, in every university society from tiddlywinks to Cherwell to Labour Club – and sometimes even in the library.

The gardens are breathtaking; the food less so.

Pauper notes

Accommodation: No cheap accommodation. All second years forced to live out and increase overdrafts. 80 more students living on campus this year. East Oxford is cheapest area but living in college cheaper than that. **Drink:** College surrounded by pubs. Wadham's new bar looks like railway carriage but cheap and friendly, other college bars a good bet for cheap pints. In some you have to pretend to go to that college. **Eats:** College lunch good value for pie/chips/beans! Veg food better than meat in college. Kings Arms good for food (next door). Also St Giles Cafe (greasy, trucker atmosphere) a big favourite of Wadhamites. Plenty of kebab/potato vans, burger bars, Indians, Chinese etc in town. **Ents:** Wadham's ents are excellent. Range from 'bops' to quizzes, Blind Date, cabaret, trips to seaside, live bands both from college's 'famous' – ball every 3 years. Good cheap Indie venues; far too much low-cost student drama; free SU discos renowned as best in university. Excellent alternative cinemas: Phoenix and PPP. **Sport:** Own sports ground ½ mile; most sports catered for; public pools £1 a go. Sport good – so many teams varying from taking yourself very seriously to laughing a lot. Women's football extremely good laugh and good results. **Hardship funds:** Domestic Bursar sometimes sympathetic to rent arrears sob-stories. Wadham has a hardship fund, but is inadequate. (Also apply to university). Wadham's hardship fund only accepts applications after student loan taken up. Debt is a serious problem – we provide a lot of counselling etc, but without a magic wand. What can you do? **Travel:** Travel grants available. Oxford on arterial routes to almost anywhere – hitching good. NUS cards get reductions on nearly all travel. Oxford well-connected by standard rail/coach/motorways. Car a nuisance as parking non-existent and fines

CAN'T FIND WHAT YOU'RE LOOKING FOR? USE THE INDEX!

exorbitant. Some travel grants awarded each year. **Work:** Oxford rule states that students must *not* work during termtime – sad reality is that some do. College manual labour in vac. Tour guides needed in summer and A-level tutoring; some pub work and waitressing.

More info?

Get students' Alternative Prospectus.
Enquiries to SU President (0865 277969).

Alumni (Editors' pick)

Christopher Wren, Michael Foot, Alan Coren, Melvyn Bragg, Sue Brown (first woman to cox Blues boat).

WORCESTER

Worcester College, Oxford OX1 2HB (0865 278300)

Founded: 1714; women undergraduates first admitted 1979. **Accommodation:** Two years out of three accommodated in single study bedrooms in college. 65% in accommodation where rent controlled by college. Most undergraduates charged £1,400 pa for room, breakfast and one main meal, 25 weeks (range £1,200– £1,500). **Eating arrangements:** Bar lunches available; choice of self-service or formal dinner. **Gate/guest hours:** Gates shut between 2.30 am and 6.00 am. **Admission:** College welcomes both pre- and post-A level candidates, and keen to have applications from schools with no previous connection. Undergraduates not admitted for biochemistry, engineering and materials, human sciences, metallurgy and science of materials, metallurgy, economics and management. **Scholarships:** Scholarships and exhibitions are awarded for exceptionally good work. Two instrumental awards are available each year to any undergraduate. Book bursaries of £50 available to all undergraduates. **Travel grants:** About £10,000 available annually for travel with some reasonable academic purpose. Additional travel grants for geologists. **Library:** Separate law library and a number of valuable antiquarian collections. Undergraduate library including individual reading cubicles. **Other college facilities:** Beer cellar, buttery, 26 acres of college grounds including gymnasium equipped with 9-station multigym, squash courts, 7 tennis courts, playing fields; boathouse. **Largest fields of study:** Biological sciences, chemistry, classics, engineering, English, geology, history, law, maths and maths and computation, modern languages, physics, PPE.

European Community: 10% first degree students take EC language as part of course and spend 6 months or more in another EC country. No formal exchange links.

College fees for 1992/93: (undergraduates) £3,052

Undergraduates: *Men:* 213 *Women:* 122

Postgraduates: *Men:* 79 *Women:* 23

Teaching staff: *Men:* 28 fellows, 5 research fellows, 13 lecturers, 8 professional fellows *Women:* 1 fellow, 4 research fellows, 5 lecturers, 2 professional fellows.

What it's like

West of city centre, with imposing Quad and renowned gardens. Lake and sports fields in situ. Accommodation either old, interesting and cold or new, warm and well-equipped. Washing facilities good and cheap. Cooking facilities non-existent except in newly built Sainsbury Building. Students live in for first two years. Relations with SCR good. Renovated library open all night. Separate law library. College shop operates erratic hours. Food reasonable. Very popular cheap cellar bar. JCR apolitical but organises social events and negotiates actively. Restrictions on overnight guests largely ignored. Contraceptive and pregnancy advice from college doctor (plus woman doctor). Active drama group and music society. High participation in sports. Squash courts. New weights room. Top subjects: law, modern languages (which includes a year abroad). Courses traditional. Subject changes possible. Work-load substantial, not oppressive. Drop out rate low. Mixed from 1979, women gradually increasing. First woman fellow elected 1984. Women's group recently started and fairly active. Thumbnail sketch of typical student (from Oxford University Alternative Prospectus): 'The archetypal Worcester student is happy, well-adjusted, effortlessly brilliant, modest to the point of self-effacement, Byronic in his wasted talents, a sparkling conversationalist and wit, and a respectable table-football player and.' . . . And probably from a public school.

Pauper notes

Accommodation: Some 3rd year live-out accommodation at cheap rates. Generally college accommodation affordable, live-out very expensive. **Drink:** Local pubs just below London prices, college bars generally good value. Worcester bar cheaper than most. Nearby Brewhouse, own brews. **Eats:** Worcester food quite cheap but edible. Caters OK for vegetarians and very well for people with weird allergies. Formal hall offers better food with service at the same price as informal hall in return for a jacket and gown. Very good local restaurants. **Ents:** Oxford does not have a major venue for big concerts, but minor pop and cult bands do play here. Worcester ideally placed for cinemas and theatres. Social committee active – arranging discos/bands in bar and various theme parties. **Sports:** Free sports facilities on site (football, rugby, hockey pitches, tennis, squash, basketball). Only Oxford college to have facilities on site. **Hardship funds:** Generally large grants given to those who are truly needy rather than lots of small grants to many, also vacation grants for those who *have* to stay up late/come up early. **Travel:** Cheap bus fares to London. Travel scholarships available for educationally-related trips. **Work:** Officially against University regulations to work in term time and generally too little time to do so (although some do). Still easier to find work in Oxford than in much of the country but becoming increasingly difficult. Commuting to London (by bus/train) is possible but very hard work.

Alumni (Editors' pick)

Sir Alistair Burnet, Thomas de Quincey, Richard Lovelace, John Sainsbury, Rupert Murdoch, Donald Carr, Richard Adams, Anna Markland, David Kirk (ex-Captain of New Zealand rugby team), now commentator with ITV, Lord Palumbo, most of the Sainsbury family.

PAISLEY COLLEGE

See Paisley University

PAISLEY UNIVERSITY

University of Paisley, High Street, Paisley PA1 2BE (041 848 3000)
Map A, C3

Student enquiries: Student Records and Admissions Office and Public Relations Office

Main study areas – as in What to Study section: *(First degree):* Accountancy, biochemistry, biology, business studies, chemical engineering, chemistry, civil engineering, computing, electrical & electronic engineering, information technology, mathematical studies, mechanical & production engineering, physics, social policy and social welfare. *Also:* Business economics, land economics, operational research, personnel administration.

European Community: EC languages (French, German and Spanish) are core part of BA business and management, options in business economics, marketing and accounting. French/German/Spanish available as supplementary courses. Individual business economics, computing and engineering students have spent 6 months or more in another EC country supported by Comett and TEMPUS. Formal exchange links between departments of computer science and economics and management with a number of French and German universities/colleges.

Application: PCAS for 1993 start, UCAS thereafter. **Special features:** Visiting professors: Professor I Macpherson (Chemistry), Professor J Woods (Land Economics), Professor M Faulds (Applied Social Studies), Professor K Carpenter (Chemistry and Chemical Engineering) and Professor T Anderson (Biology). Specialist centres for alcohol studies, environmental and waste management; technology and business; land value information; microelectronics educational development; development and enterprise; heavy structures. **Largest fields of study:** Technology, engineering, sciences and business. **Founded:** 1992 as a university; previously Paisley College, founded 1897. **Main awards:** BA, BSc, BEng. **Awarding body:** Paisley University. **Site:** Paisley town centre. **Access:** M8 motorway, rail and air. **Academic features:** Courses in electronic systems; quality management and technology; industrial chemistry. Credit accumulation transfer scheme (CATS). **Accommodation:** 296 places in hall (approx cost: £20.50 pw). 180 university-owned flats with total of 286 places (approx cost: £11–£35 per month). 350+ rooms/digs (cost varies). **Library:** 120,000 volumes, 1,000 periodicals, up to 420 study places; recommended books reference only and overnight loan. New group reading room available. **Welfare:** 2 student advisory officers; safety officer, occupational health nurse; welfare officer; nursery. **Hardship funds:** Loan funds available for students in temporary difficulties, Access funds. **Careers:** Personal careers counselling service; Careers Information Centre. **Amenities:** SU building with a variety of affiliated clubs and societies, sports facilities, extensive computing facilities, Educational development unit (incl. closed circuit TV). **Employment:** Industry, commerce, local government, HM government, multinationals.

Duration of first degree course(s) or equivalent: 3–4 years (full-time); 4–5 (sandwich); **others:** 4½ years (Honours: mechanical and manufacturing, electrical and electronic, civil engineering) **Total first degree students 1991/92:** 4,758 **Overseas students:** 96 **Mature students:** 1,250 **Male/female ratio:** 2:1 **Teaching staff: full-time:** 245 **part-time:** 38 **Total full-time students 1991/92:** 4,092 **Postgraduate students:** 183 **Tuition fees for 1992/93** (first degrees): Home: £696 (if no grant), £1,855 (classroom), £2,770 (lab/studio); Overseas: £5,000.

What it's like

The University of Paisley (it used to be called Paisley College) is expanding at a rate of knots. In 1993 it should merge with Craigie College in Ayr.

The University is in the centre of town and approximately five minutes walk from the train station. Travel to Glasgow and surrounding areas is easy.

Students' Association building (called 'The Buroo') provides main source of entertainment. Facilities include two brand new extended bars, snack bar, video games, pool tables, large video screen and satellite TV. Regular discos, quiz nights, pool competitions, comedy nights and less frequent special events. Wide variety of sporting, political, religious and social clubs and societies.

Accommodation ranges from cheap and very nasty university accommodation, to expensive private sector flats in most big towns.

University's student advisory service offers careers advice, a welfare service and information on access funds. SA provides an independent professional and confidential welfare service.

WANT TO HELP WITH THE NEXT EDITION – SEE PAGE 76

"Small active left-wing confronts inactive reactionary majority"

As with all other colleges and universities, student poverty is a crisis in Paisley. Widespread occupations of college properties showed the extent of student anger throughout Britain. The situation can only get worse. It is rumoured that the West of Scotland will be the testing ground for new government policy of grant cuts and if so, the effect on Paisley students will be devastating.

Kirstie Davy, President SA

Pauper notes
Accommodation: Some university accommodation houses couples/families. **Drink:** The union (the Buroo). **Eats:** The Union (the Buroo). **Ents:** Paisley Arts Centre, Glasgow Film Theatre. **Sports:** The Lagoon centre; University Thornly Park Development. **Hardship Funds:** Access funds/SA hardship fund. **Travel:** Trains to Glasgow approximately every ten minutes. **Work:** Stewarding in the union/very little else; Paisley very high unemployment.

More info?
Get students' Alternative Prospectus.
Enquiries to Kirstie Davy, President SA (041 889 9940).

Alumni (Editors' pick)
Gavin Hastings (Scottish/British Lions rugby football international); Douglas Druburgh (junior world curling champion).

PLYMOUTH UNIVERSITY

University of Plymouth
(1) **Drake Circus, Plymouth PL4 8AA (0752 600600)**
(2) **Faculty of Arts & Design, Earl Richards Road North, Exeter EX2 6AS (0392 412211)**
(3) **Rolle Faculty of Education, Exmouth, EX8 2AT (0395 265344)**
(4) **Seale-Hayne Faculty of Agriculture, Food & Land Use, Newton Abbot TQ12 6NQ (0626 52323)**
Map A, C9

Student enquiries: Admissions Registry at appropriate campus

Main study areas – as in What to Study section: *(First degree):* Accountancy, agriculture, architecture, art & design, biology, biotechnology, business studies,

CAN'T FIND WHAT YOU'RE LOOKING FOR? USE THE INDEX!

chemistry, civil engineering, computing, drama, economics, education, electrical & electronic engineering, English, environmental science, European studies, fine arts, food science and nutrition, geography, geology, history, hotel & catering management, law, maritime studies, mechanical and production engineering, mathematical studies, microbiology, nursing, physics, politics and government, professions allied to medicine (PAMs), psychology, social policy and social welfare, sociology. *Also:* Astronomy, media studies, ocean sciences, personnel management, surveying, oceanography, performance arts.

European Community: 8% first degree students take EC language as part of course and 1% spend 6 months or more in another EC country. Formal exchange links with 17 EC universities/colleges: Eire (1); France (5); Germany (4); Greece (2); Netherlands (2); Spain (3). Approved Erasmus programme 1992/93. Courses in international business and business studies with a language involve work and/or study in EC. French, German, Spanish and Italian are available within the combined degree. Agriculture students can study French.

Application: PCAS for 1993 start, UCAS thereafter; except fine art and design, ADAR. **Largest fields of study:** Technology, science, human sciences, business studies, agriculture, education, arts and design. **Special features:** Navigation simulator, computer aided engineering facilities, diving school. Extensive participation in European Space Agency satellite communication and broadcasting programme. **Academic features:** Extensive combined honours scheme covering science, social science, arts and marine studies. Participation in International Student Exchange Programme. Credit accumulation and transfer scheme; many international links. **Founded:** 1992, as a university; previously Polytechnic South West, formed from merger of Plymouth Poly, Rolle College, Exeter College of Art and Seale-Hayne College. **Main awards:** BA, BSc, BEd, BEng, MEng. **Awarding body:** Plymouth University. **Site:** Main campus in Plymouth city centre, three faculty campuses located in Exeter, Exmouth and outskirts of Newton Abbot, each with its own academic welfare support services and social amenities. **Access:** Road and rail links to all sites good. Cheap coach fares to London and other major cities. **Accommodation:** Approx 750 places in hall on Plymouth campus (self-catering); 325 places in hall on Exmouth campus; 150 catered and 48 self-catering places on Newton Abbot campus. Priority given to first years. Approx cost: £29–£36 pw (Plymouth campus); £29–£35 pw, plus catering contract £70 per term (Exmouth campus); £33–£51 pw (Newton Abbot campus); payable termly in advance. Assistance given in finding private accommodation for those not allocated places in halls. Rent: 16% in accommodation where rent controlled by university. **Library:** 350,000 volumes, 2,200 journals, 820 study places; short loan collection, inter-library loans, film and video hire. Computer-based on-line information services. **Other learning facilities:** Study skills course, comprehensive computing service, audio-visual workshop and TV studio. **Welfare:** Counselling, chaplaincy, medical and other welfare services on each campus. **Careers:** Careers education programme; careers fair; information rooms; computer-assisted guidance system. **Amenities:** SU main building and offices on Plymouth site with facilities on other campuses including bars, shops, welfare and support services. Weekly campus newspaper. **Sporting facilities:** Sports halls and facilities for outdoor sports at Plymouth (including squash courts) and Newton Abbot. 13-acre playing field at Exmouth for soccer, rugby, hockey, netball and tennis. **Employment:** Good record of graduate employment (many courses vocational).

Duration of first degree course(s) or equivalent: 3 years; **others:** 4 years (BEd/sandwich courses) **Total first degree students 1991/92:** 9,289 **BEd students:** 614 **Overseas students:** 317 **Mature students:** 3,066 **Male/female ratio:** 3:2 **Teaching staff: full-time:** 670 **Total full-time students 1991/92:** 10,509 **Postgraduate students:** 1,043 **Tuition fees for 1992/93** (first degrees): Home: £759 (if no grant), £1,855 (classroom), £2,770 (lab/studio); Overseas: £4,550 (classroom), £5,250 (lab/studio).

GET HOLD OF THE PROSPECTUSES

What it's like – Plymouth

It's situated on the very edge of the city centre on a fairly compact campus, 5 mins walk from BR, coach stations and main shopping areas. Two halls of residence are on campus, other halls exist but only a third of first years are allocated places in halls. Other accommodation available and good university accommodation office on campus. Good student services with counselling, careers and chaplaincy. Sports grounds good but situated out of town, free buses are provided on Weds and Sats. Good courses especially in maritime and business fields with international visiting opportunities. Fairly good student/staff relationships. Plymouth is an excellent city to live in, in an excellent location with Dartmoor, beaches and the sea all within easy reach. Students integrate very well with each other and locals.

SU small but active with two bars, two shops and a number of other services. Excellent academic and welfare advice centre. Very wide range of clubs and societies to join, very strong in watersports. Good social life, SU band nights weekly, student run nightclubs, good restaurants.

Pauper notes

Accommodation: SU noticeboards, Western Evening Herald (Thurs). Hard to find, but available. **Drink:** Excellent range of ciders, local Dartmoor ales. Union bar far cheaper than town. Some clubs have promo nights weekly. **Eats:** Curries, excellent food on Barbican, especially veggie at Café des Artistes. **Ents:** SU has band nights weekly, few big names venture as far as Plymouth. Good variety of nightclubs. Couple of cinemas and good theatres. **Sports:** Uni sports centre 4 miles from campus. Squash courts on campus. Excellent watersports facilities and centre. **Travel:** Good hitching from Marsh Mills roundabout. Frequent trains and buses to London. Free women's minibus twice nightly. **Work:** Some in SU, local pubs, a few seasonal tourism jobs.

More info?

Get UPSU Handbook. Enquiries to any UPSU Executive Member (0752 663337).

What it's like – Exmouth

Exmouth's a great place to live, as long as you realise that you often have to make your own fun. Beach long and sandy; cliff walks excellent; good relations with town. Site very small. Most students enjoy living in mixed/single sex halls; officially no visitors after midnight (ha! ha!). Good staff/student relations; they drink together. SU active in social, academic, welfare and rag areas; less interested in politics, more into local causes and partying (left of centre though). Welfare advice and counselling available.

Students mostly state school, from all over country; 7 women to 1 man. Typical BEd wants to be a teacher; BA a secretary. Increasingly open gay and lesbian community. Rolle College rugby teams tend to dominate bar. Exmouth full of 60s remnants. Town increasingly student, though run by Tory fuddy-duddies.

Most active societies are soccer, hockey, music/acting performance societies, debating, CU, film and video. Exeter good for theatre, clubs, etc. SU capable of backing good bands (Jools Holland, Polly Harvey, Alan Parker, Fat and Frantic).

BA courses adventurous and quite rite-on (ethically sound); workload easy in first year, BEds work much harder, steadily. BA lecturers popular, unpatronising. Both degrees highly regarded.

Pauper notes

Accommodation: Two-thirds first years in halls. Rest in town. Halls no longer subsidised, but an entertaining time is guaranteed. **Drink:** Excellent SU bar, good beer, frequent promotions; good local ales. Best pubs are in Exeter (not far). **Eats:** Refectory recently refurbished; food considered passable by most. Not very imaginative. Loads of take-aways and good pub food in Exmouth. Double-Locks – best pub food in UK. **Ents:** SU bar has very popular bard nights, Club Monday: great for any type of performer; debating society often heated. Most people drink

CAN'T FIND WHAT YOU'RE LOOKING FOR? USE THE INDEX!

in the bar; Sky TV; occasional cabaret. Exeter good for bands and clubs. **Sports:** Good pitches, gym and weights room on campus. Soccer, rugby and hockey very active. Access to many water-sports (mostly at Plymouth). **Hardship funds:** SU in desperate cases lends students £50. Welfare unit at SU can help with sound advice. **Travel:** Excellent for hitching to London and North and Midlands. Buses and trains to Exeter. **Work:** Work in bar, refectory, local pubs. Loads of summer work in pubs, clubs, holiday camps, teaching foreign students etc.

More info?

Enquiries to SU President (0395 264783).

Alumni (Editors' pick)

Anna Tait (art editor of Photographic Journal), Chris Cook, Steve Mattheson (artists), Dave Sawyer, Pam St Clements ('Pat' in EastEnders).

PORTSMOUTH POLY

See Portsmouth University

PORTSMOUTH UNIVERSITY

University of Portsmouth, University House, Winston Churchill Avenue, Portsmouth PO1 2UP (0705 876543) Map A, E8

Student enquiries: Assistant Registrar (Admissions)

Main study areas – as in What to Study section: (*First degree*): Accountancy, architecture, art & design, biology, business studies, chemistry, civil engineering, computing, economics, electrical & electronic engineering, English, environmental science, environmental studies, geography, geology, history, hotel & catering management, information technology, Latin-American studies, mathematical studies, mechanical and production engineering, modern languages, nursing studies, pharmacology, pharmacy, physics, politics and government, professions allied to medicine (PAMs), psychology, social policy and social welfare, sociology, town and country planning. *Also:* Biomedical sciences, film studies, media studies, quantity surveying, Russian studies.

European Community: 20% first degree students take EC language as part of course and 15% spend 6 months or more in another EC country. Formal exchange links with over 50 EC universities/colleges: Belgium (1); France (17); Germany (17); Greece (1); Netherlands (2); Spain (14); many open to non-language specialists. Approx 60% of students (engineering, science, business and social science) can study EC languages as an assessed part of the degree. Tuition in French, German, Spanish and Italian available to all students on a supplementary basis (Institute of Linguists qualifications are available). Approved Erasmus programme: mobility grants support 132 students in other EC institutions. Library is designated European Documentation Centre, automatically receiving all EC publications.

Application: PCAS for 1993 start, UCAS thereafter; except design (PCAS or ADAR). **Academic features:** A range of extended 4 year full-time courses, including foundation year, leading to honours degrees in business, science and engineering. **Largest fields of study:** Engineering, science, business. **Founded:** 1992, as a university; previously Portsmouth Poly, founded 1870 as Portsmouth and Gosport School of Science and Art. **Main awards:** BA, BSc, BEng, MEng. **Awarding body:** Portsmouth University. **Site:** Main campus near town centre, Milton site 2½ miles away (business studies, economics, information science, education, management). **Access:** Free minibus or public transport to Milton site. **Accommodation:** 1,162 places in halls; 800 rooms/digs; 68 hostel places; 5,000 flats/bedsitters. Approx cost: Halls £34 pw (self-catering), £54 pw (breakfast and evening meal). **Library:** Central university library, and branch library; total of 500,000 volumes, 3,500 periodicals, 900 study places; short loan library. **Welfare:** Head of student services; 3 student counsellors, 2 doctors and sick bay, psychiatrist, solicitor, 3 chaplains. **Hardship funds:** Paul Burrell Fund – short-term loan of £100 max. **Special categories:** Residential facilities for married students, 40-place nursery (£2.90 per half day, £29.00 per week full-time). **Careers:** Information, advice and placement service, 4 careers advisers. **Amenities:** SU shop, bank, bars, travel bureau; Royal Naval Unit, Army Officer Training Corps and University Air Squadron; Chichester festival theatre; naval museum, D-Day museum, HMS Victory, HMS Warrior and Mary Rose; beaches, seaside resort and countryside near by. **Sporting facilities:** Wide range of sports; excellent sailing on Solent.

Duration of first degree course(s) or equivalent: 3 years or 4 years **Total first degree students 1991/92:** 7,485 **Number of BEd students:** 120 **Overseas students:** 334 **Mature students:** 1,627 **Male/female ratio:** 3:2 **Teaching staff: full-time:** 574 **part-time:** 240 **Total full-time students 1991/92:** 8,653 **Postgraduate students:** 978 **Tuition fees for 1992/93** (first degrees): Home: £1,855 (classroom), £2,770 (lab/studio); Overseas: £4,096 (classroom), £5,012 (lab/studio).

What it's like

Situated on two main sites around Portsmouth varying from modern tower blocks to beautiful old listed buildings to ex-army barracks. There is currently a surplus of private rented accommodation. Student social life is hectic with ents every night – discos, bands, theatre, folk and films. Over 150 clubs and societies offer everything from underwater hockey to instant liberalism. Water sports especially popular. Commercial Road is good shopping centre and Kings Theatre offers new play every 2 weeks; also Theatre Royal, Hornpipe Theatre – community arts centre with student concessions. Surveying, engineering and science courses excellent, offering good sandwich courses. Cultural, literary and language studies homely with friendly atmosphere. A new faculty of health studies has been set up. Portsmouth a navy port and some pubs are services-orientated though most are full of friendly students, especially SU bars. SU provides some of best student services.

Pauper notes

Accommodation: No squats; halls of residence fairly cheap; 3 housing co-ops charge about half the price of private accommodation. Cheap emergency accommodation in one of the halls. **Drink:** SU cheapest. Most pubs have a cheap night. Local brews: Friary Meux. **Eats:** SU very cheap £1 special. Some pubs good value. **Ents:** SU ents hall for bands, discos. Gaiety showbar – cheap discos. Hornpipe – alternative plays, music, films. **Sports:** 46 different sports via SU. Transport to and from games arranged by SU. **Hardship funds:** Three hardship funds. **Travel:** SU travel shop offers discount for students. No travel funds known to be available. **Work:** Lots of summer work: ferries, fairground etc. Pub jobs during term time. Union also employs casual staff: restaurant, bars and security. On-site job-shop finding work for students.

PRINCE OF WALES'S INSTITUTE

**The Prince of Wales's Institute of Architecture,
14–15 Gloucester Gate, Regent's Park, London NW1 4HG
(071 961 7380) Map D, B1**

Student enquiries: The Secretary

Main study areas – as in What to Study section: *(First degree):* Architecture.

European Community: No students take an EC language as part of course

CAN'T FIND WHAT YOU'RE LOOKING FOR? USE THE INDEX!

or spend time in another EC country. Institute has a base in Italy and good contacts in France (also in Hungary and other central European countries). Contacts likely to be extended through exchanges and involvement in practical programmes.

Application: Direct (may change, so check). **Academic features:** Personal tuition; live projects; all staff practising artists/architects. Summer school and foundation course from 1992; postgraduate course from 1993; first degrees to be offered thereafter. **Structural features:** Relationships with schools of architecture and construction internationally. **Special features:** Artist in residence, Kate Montgomery. **Largest field of study:** Architecture and building arts. **Founded:** 1992. **Main awards:** Foundation certificate at present. **Awarding body:** Prince of Wales's Institute. **Site:** Single site on the edge of Regent's Park. **Access:** Camden Town underground station, buses. **Accommodation:** Student accommodation (King's College) at Hampstead. **Approx cost:** £50 pw; meals pay-as-you-eat. **Rent:** 66% are in accommodation where rent controlled by the Institute. **Library:** 3,500 books, all main architecture and building journals. **Other learning facilities:** Well equipped workshops. **Careers:** Information, advice and placement service. **Employment:** Roles in construction. **Welfare:** Some health facilities at King's College. Personal tutor system. Staff being trained for in-house counselling. **Hardship funds:** Limited bursaries. **Amenities:** All central London galleries etc. Local cinemas. RIBA nearby. **Sporting facilities:** None on-site. Local facilities in Regent's Park.

Duration of foundation course: 1 year. **Total foundation students 1991/92:** 30 **BEd students:** None. **Overseas students:** 4 **Mature students:** 17 **Male/female ratio:** 2:1 **Teaching staff: full-time:** 2 **part-time:** 2 plus up to 30 visiting lecturers **Total full-time students 1991/92:** 30 **Postgraduate students:** 0 at present **Tuition fees for 1992/93 (foundation course):** Home: £650; Overseas: £4,500.

QUEEN MARGARET COLLEGE

Queen Margaret College, Clerwood Terrace, Edinburgh EH12 8TS (031 317 3000) Map A, D3

Student enquiries: Admissions

Main study areas – as in What to Study section: *(First degree):* Communication studies, food science & nutrition, hotel & catering management, library & information studies, nursing studies, professions allied to medicine (PAMs), speech sciences. *Also:* Consumer studies.

European Community: Number of students learning an EC language or spending time in another EC country, not known. Erasmus links in occupational therapy and physiotherapy.

Application: PCAS for 1993 start, UCAS thereafter. **Founded:** 1875. **Main awards:** BA, BSc. **Awarding body:** Queen Margaret College. **Academic features:** Expanding research degree programme. **Largest fields of study:** Health care, business management and information. **Structural features:** Business development centre. **Site:** 24-acre landscaped site about 5 miles from Edinburgh city centre; located in former grounds of a stately home. **Accommodation:** 427 places in halls of residence. Approx cost: £28 pw (self-catering), £44 pw (half board). **Library:** 80,000 volumes, 800 current periodicals, 300 study places; books in heavy demand held in reserve only. **Welfare:** Doctor, student counsellor, accommodation officer. **Hardship funds:** Student welfare fund available. **Special categories:** Advisory interviews for students considering applying to any courses. College publishes guide for mature students. **Careers:** Information, advice and placement service, careers adviser. **Amenities:** Students' Association; licensed bar; theatre; bank; college shop, representative from Edinburgh bookshop one day a week. **Sporting facilities:** Swimming pool, tennis courts, squash court, gymnasium.

Duration of first degree course(s) or equivalent: 4 years; **others:** 3 years (ordinary degrees) **Total first degree students 1991/92:** 2,000 **Overseas students:** 100 **Mature students:** 175 **Male/female ratio:** 1:4 **Teaching staff: full-time:** approx 140 **Total full-time students 1991/92:** 2,000 **Postgraduate students:** 20 **Tuition fees for 1992/93** (first degrees): Home: £696 (if no grant), £1,855 (classroom), £2,770 (lab/studio); Overseas: £4,900.

What it's like

Modern attractive and expanding college, in its own grounds, 4 miles west of Edinburgh's centre. Campus borders a residential area yet the grounds have a feeling of open space. Woodland, gardens, tennis and squash courts, swimming pool and games field; campus is very self-contained. Facilities include library, expanding information technology centre, gym, theatre, kitchens and food and science labs, drama and media studios and photography facilities, also the Students' Association Union building. Student executives, 3 of which are sabbatical, one always available for advice and to maintain the smooth running of the Union.

More than a fifth of the 2,200 students live in high quality halls, amongst the cheapest in Scotland with a reputation for being the cleanest. Shopping facilities within walking distance of the campus and buses stop outside the college gates so the attractions of Edinburgh are never far away.

Pauper notes

Accommodation: Halls of various prices (half-board, self-catering, or self-contained flats). One shop on campus; small yet well-stocked, shuts at 4 pm. Laundry facilities and all halls have kitchens. Overnight guests allowed at weekends. **Drink:** SA Union bar. Lively and friendly atmosphere. **Eats:** 2 campus refectories and the Union all provide a variety of hot meals and snacks cheaply. Plenty of pubs and restaurants in Edinburgh from vegetarian to Mexican to Tunisian (wide price range). **Ents:** Union ents provide infrequent live bands (sound proofing problems), comedians and hypnotists from time to time. Other attractions include drink promotions, weekly film nights, regular twice-weekly discos. Freshers lasts for 2 weeks at the beginning of term and is very cheap. Access to the numerous cinemas, theatres, pubs and clubs of Edinburgh. **Sports:** Gym, squash courts, tennis courts and swimming pool at college (equipment at a small annual fee). Various clubs from skiing to scuba diving (some affiliated with other Edinburgh colleges). New clubs budgeted for if more than 12 people are interested. **Hardship funds:** College loan system for students with good reasons. Access fund. **Travel:** Edinburgh offers many student concessions on trains and buses. The numerous black cabs can work out cheaper than the bus if 4 or 5 share. **Work:** Many students have part-time work mainly in pubs and restaurants which frequently provide taxis back to campus late at night. A lot of courses involve placements in industries.

Informal name:

QMC

QUEEN MARY AND WESTFIELD

**Queen Mary and Westfield College, University of London,
Mile End Road, London E1 4NS (071 975 5555) Map D, C1**

Student enquiries: Academic Registrar

CAN'T FIND WHAT YOU'RE LOOKING FOR? USE THE INDEX!

Main study areas – as in What to Study section: *(First degree):* Aeronautical engineering, biochemistry, biology, biotechnology, business studies, chemistry, civil engineering, computing, dentistry, drama, economics, electrical & electronic engineering, English, environmental science, European studies, geography, history, law, mathematical studies, mechanical and production engineering, medicine, metallurgy and materials science, microbiology, modern languages, nursing studies, physics, physiology, politics and government, zoology. *Also:* Astronomy, informatics, Rumanian, Russian.

European Community: Number of students learning an EC language or spending time in another EC country not known but includes science and engineering students. Formal exchange links with 25 EC universities/colleges: Belgium (1); France (2); Germany (8); Greece (1); Italy (8); Netherlands (3); Spain (2). Approved Erasmus programme 1991/92. College library has European Documentation Centre. European chair from Jean Monnet Action Programme. Internal newsletter, Euronews. Involvement in wide range of European Commission research and development programmes and headquarters of European Centre for Pollution Research. Many courses include language tuition from scratch, others for more advanced including Italian as a subsidiary subject. Language lab, including self tuition material, available for all students.

Application: UCCA for 1993 start, UCAS thereafter. **Structural features:** Part of London University. **Academic features:** Georgian available under the course unit system. Wide-ranging European studies options; business studies may be combined with a variety of other subjects. Course–unit system allows students to make up 'tailor-made' degree programme. Unusual BSc course in basic medical sciences; students study alongside trainee doctors and dentists, to gain general scientific grounding. **Special features:** Large number of visiting professors. English department unusual in high proportion of women academics. Only campus college in central London. **Founded:** 1989, from merger of Westfield College (1882) and Queen Mary College (1887). **Main awards:** BA, MEng, BEng, BSc, BSc(Econ), BSc(Eng), LLB. **Awarding body:** London University. **Site:** Mile End Road. **Access:** Stepney Green or Mile End underground stations 5 minutes walk. Docklands Light Railway Bow Road station and bus or 10 minutes walk; buses. **Accommodation:** 700 places in halls of residence at South Woodford, similar number in flats and halls within 5 miles of campus, including rooms with en suite bathrooms in new canal-side campus residences. 460 in college self-catering accommodation (more building underway). Accommodation office also deals with private sector. Rent: 20% in accommodation where rent controlled by university. **Library:** 500,000 volumes, 2,500 periodicals, intensive use collection on 3-hour loan only. Libertas computerised system for both catalogue and lending. 5 departmental libraries. **Specialist collections:** European documentation centre. **Other learning resources:** Language laboratory; Livenet, computer facilities. **Welfare:** Health centre; chaplains, counsellors, creche. **Hardship funds:** Small short-term loans to tide students over – further assistance might be available in extreme cases. **Careers:** Information, advice and placement service. **Amenities:** Bookshop, travel centre and bank on site; SU building with snackbar, bars, gymnasium, squash courts, 'Nightline' (telephone information and confidential listening service), chaplaincy (and ecumenical chapel); London University central facilities (including swimming pool) accessible; sports ground in Essex, close to central London by tube on the Central Line.

Duration of first degree course(s) or equivalent: 3 years; **others:** 4 years **Total first degree students 1991/92:** 4,830 **Overseas students:** 1,234 **Mature students:** 21% **Male/female ratio:** 3:2 **Teaching staff: full-time:** c500 **Total full-time students 1991/92:** 5,703 **Postgraduate students:** 1,138 **Tuition fees for 1992/93 (first degrees):** Home: £1,855 (classroom), £2,770 (lab/studio); Overseas: £6,150 (classroom), £7,450 (lab/studio).

What it's like

Situated in East End, 1 mile from the city; its impressive architecture dating back to 1880s is hard to miss. Easy access to centre of London, plenty of local culture. Canary Wharf 5 minutes.

New self-catering halls opened overlooking Regents Canal on the Mile End site in 1989, part of a much larger on-site residence development. Self-catering/private rented accommodation plentiful. Main halls at South Woodford (20 minutes by tube plus half-hourly night buses). Large overseas community, well integrated.

Active SU recently refurbished catering/bar facilities; expansions planned. Nightly entertainments programme. Welfare and counselling services. East London Nightline run from QMWSU. Over 100 clubs and societies, squash court, multigym and sports hall on site. New sports ground at Theydon Bois (on tube).

Renowned for science, engineering and law but many top quality smaller scale arts and social science departments. New faculty of basic medicine sciences for pre-clinical students of St Bartholomew's and the London Hospital Medical School. New arts building to open 1992/93. Course unit system provides flexibility. Language courses require a year spent abroad, usually very profitable experience. Quality of teaching varies. Work assessed by annual exams with fixed level of passes required to proceed. Generally unpopular system of having to take a year out to retake – no September resits.

Students of fairly mixed background, but noticeable tendency towards London-based students. Large numbers of American associate students. No notorious racism or sexism.

Pauper notes

Accommodation: Private rented plentiful. Some empty houses ripe for squatting. **Drink:** SU bar has wide range of drinks. Good East End pubs. 'Firkin' pubs at Hackney, Plaistow, selling the famous Dogbolter and the Barbican. **Eats:** Excellent local Indian cuisine. Cheap vegetarian wholefood at 'The Cherry Orchard', Bethnal Green. Local eel pie & mash shops a must. **Ents:** Regular discos, weekly gigs of up and coming bands, plus cabaret slots. **Sports:** Multigym and squash courts on campus. Wide range of clubs and societies. Good local sports centres. **Hardship funds:** SU operates Hardship Fund administered by committee. **Travel:** Alice Mutta Travel Prize worth £180 for interesting project, plus expenditure fund. STA branch in SU. **Work:** Work behind union bar and in union shop.

Informal name:

QMW.

Alumni (Editors' pick)

Peter Hain, Geoffrey Drain, Sir Roy Strong, Judge Alan Lipfriend, Martin Cross, Rhys Williams, Dr Adam Neville, Lady Falkender, Ruth Prawer Jhabvala, Malcolm Bradbury, Andrea Newman, Simon Gray, Eva Figes, Christopher Holmes, Mel Gingell, Patrick Moore, Dr Paul Dean, Sir Norman Lindop, Elizabeth Andrews, Bruce Dickinson (formerly of Iron Maiden).

RADA

Royal Academy of Dramatic Art, 62–64 Gower Street, London WC1E 6ED (071 636 7076) Map E, C2

Student enquiries: Admissions Secretary

Main study areas – as in What to Study section: Drama.

European Community: No students learn an EC language or spend time in another EC country.

Application: Direct. **Founded:** 1904, by Sir Herbert Beerbohm Tree; Royal Charter in 1920. **Main awards:** Diploma, Honours Diploma. **Awarding body:**

RADA. **Site:** Gower Street, in heart of London University area. **Access:** Goodge Street, Euston Square, Russell Square, Tottenham Court Road or Warren Street underground stations. **Academic features:** Acting course (9 terms, autumn term intake); stage management course (6 terms, yearly intake). **Access:** Central site, close to bus routes and several tube stations. **Accommodation:** No responsibility taken by Academy. **Library:** 13,000 volumes, 10 periodicals. **Specialist collections:** G B Shaw collection. **Centres of excellence:** Vanbrugh Theatre Club. **Welfare:** Access to all essential services. **Hardship funds:** Bursary fund. **Careers:** Information, advice and placement service. **Amenities:** Three fully-equipped theatres, the Vanbrugh, the GBS and Studio 14; broadcasting studio, speech laboratory, video-tape, scenery and property workshops, design office and wardrobe, common rooms, canteen, bar. **Employment:** Theatre.

Duration of first degree course(s) or equivalent: 9 terms (acting); **others:** 6 terms (stage management) **Total first degree students 1991/92:** 130 **Overseas students:** 10 **Mature students:** 6 **Male/female ratio:** 1:1 **Teaching staff: full-time:** 18 **part-time:** 80 **Total full-time students 1991/92:** 130 **Tuition fees for 1992/93:** £5,460.

What it's like

You need talent, luck and determination. 2,000 apply for about 28 places: competition for female places even more intense (introduction to one of harsh realities of the theatre). Once in, pace is hectic with everybody working long hours to accommodate evening tutorials, singing lessons, rehearsals, performances, etc, etc. Timetable includes classes on voice and movement, fencing, tumbling, dialect – anything an actor is likely to need. Demanding, pressured, requires mental and physical fitness; especially for stage management students who work almost 7-day week on constant stream of productions. This course includes set design and construction, props, lighting, sound. Staff/student relations very good. Professional directors from outside work on productions in GBS or larger Vanbrugh theatres. At start of 3-year course, rehearsals are evenly matched with classes but in 3rd year, productions take over full-time. 2 full years of public performances – unmatched by any other drama school. Best tuition and best showcase for talents in UK – if you can get in. Because of size tight student community where lasting friendships develop. Students come from large variety of backgrounds and from all over the world (UK, Ireland, NZ, USA, Canada). Excellent well-stocked library. No accommodation provided.

Pauper notes

Drink: Bar on premises not subsidised; ULU (Malet St). **Eats:** Good canteen on site. Plenty of cafes, stalls etc in the area. **Ents:** Plays are free to students on course; also freebies to rep and west end shows. **Sports:** Use of ULU. **Hardship funds:** Limited.

Alumni (Editors' pick)

Alan Bates, Sir John Gielgud, Dame Flora Robson, Susannah York, Sir Richard Attenborough, Glenda Jackson, Joan Collins, Ben Cross, Robert Lindsay, Lisa Eichhorn, Jonathan Pryce, Juliet Stevenson, Kenneth Branagh, Anton Lesser, John Hurt, Richard Briers, Albert Finney, Anthony Hopkins, Sir Anthony Quayle.

RAPID RESULTS COLLEGE

The Rapid Results College, Tuition House, 27–37 St George's Road, London SW19 4DS (081 947 7272) Map D, B4

Student enquiries: Student Services Manager

Main study areas – as in What to Study section: *(First degree):* Law.

GET HOLD OF THE PROSPECTUSES

European Community: No students learn an EC language or spend time in another EC country.

Application: Direct. **Founded:** 1928. **Main awards:** LLB. **Awarding body:** London University (External). **Site:** Tuition House is at Wimbledon, South West London. **Access:** Wimbledon station (BR and underground). **Academic features:** Distance learning courses that are self-contained and do not require additional textbooks. Includes full tutorial service with written or telephone contact with specialist tutors. **Careers:** Information and advisory service.

Duration of first degree course(s) or equivalent: minimum of 3 years **First degree students:** No limit to entry numbers. **Tuition fees for 1992/93 (first degrees):** Home: £556 (intermediate), £596 (final parts 1 or 2); Overseas: £556 (intermediate), £596 (final parts 1 or 2).

RAVENSBOURNE COLLEGE

Ravensbourne College of Design and Communication, Walden Road, Elmstead Woods, Chislehurst, Kent BR7 5SN (081 468 7071)
Map D, D4

Student enquiries: Admissions Officer

Main study areas – as in What to Study section: *(First degree):* Art & design. **Also:** Television operations and engineering.

European Community: No students learn an EC language; some spend time in another EC country. 3 formal exchange links in France, Germany and Netherlands. Approved Erasmus programme.

Application: ADAR. **Founded:** 1962, ex Bromley College of Art and Beckenham School of Art. **Main awards:** BA. **Awarding body:** Royal College of Art. **Site:** 1 mile from Chislehurst; 18 acre main site. **Access:** British Rail from Charing Cross to Elmstead Woods. **Accommodation:** 105 places in hall (mixed); list of local addresses. Approx cost: £40.00 pw. 18% in accommodation where rent controlled by college. **Library:** 20,000 volumes in total, 140 periodicals; slide library. **Other learning resources:** Desktop publishing and computer image generation laboratories. New television studios equipped to broadcast standard. **Careers:** Information and advice service. **Amenities:** All workshops necessary for art and design courses (plus process and dye labs, printing rooms, etc); SU bar; television studios/facilities. **Sporting facilities:** Sports centre at Crystal Palace.

Duration of first degree course(s) or equivalent: 3 years **Total first degree students 1991/92:** 370 **Overseas students:** 29 **Male/female ratio:** 3:2 **Teaching staff:** full-time: 40 part-time: 60 **Total full-time students 1991/92:** 614 **Tuition fees for 1992/93 (first degrees):** Home: £2,770; Overseas: £5,703.

What it's like

Chislehurst. The town is quiet, a few local pubs, the word nightlife wasn't around when Chislehurst was built, so students make their own: party, party! The college has a good atmosphere. SU bar is packed on event nights which are Tuesdays and Thursdays. SU puts on bands from Indie to R'n'B, funk to house. All kinds of discos, barn dances, 'pub sing-along' nights. The main attraction is the cheap beer, happy hours, and a friendly atmosphere. Film Club.

Easy access to London via BR, only 15 minutes journey. Bromley is close, pubs not too bad, new leisure centre; very nice, not too expensive. College very relaxed until degree shows approach. Very good reputation in industry.

Basically, because there are only 630 students, there's a lot of inter-departmental co-operation, so everyone gets to know one another.

WANT TO HELP WITH THE NEXT EDITION – SEE PAGE 76

"Lots of graduates take menial work (eg milkman) so they can continue painting"

Counselling tutor on hand one day a week. SU small, striving to increase number of people involved, so more active politically as well as socially. At Ravensbourne you get out what you put in!

David Woolston

Pauper notes

Accommodation: Only two-thirds of 1st years in halls, so get to know one and crash out there. Halls – single rooms £40 a week – shared (2) £35. College accommodation list ever increasing for new students. **Drink:** SU bar excellent, cheapest around. Excellent atmosphere. Quite a few good local pubs, bit expensive compared to bar. **Eats:** New canteen, good, cheap food on site, eg £1 for a filling hot lunch. Vegetarians well catered for. Chislehurst – not much use for students. A few bars and cafés. Bromley best bet for fast food. **Ents:** SU bar packed on event nights (Tuesday–Thursday), cheap, sometimes free, entry. Film club; every 2 or 3 weeks there's a band. Discos, barn dances, fancy dress extravaganzas. Not a lot outside college – only cinemas and pubs. **Sports:** No on-site sports. Excellent sports centre in Bromley, 5 min walk from halls. **Hardship fund:** Access fund available once a year – only given to those who *really* need it. **Travel:** Whatever BR and LRT say, we have to pay. Good bus and trains – night buses from London. **Work:** Local shops.

Informal name:
RCDC

Alumni (Editors' pick)
Karen Franklin (Clothes Show); Maria Cornego (fashion designer).

READING UNIVERSITY

University of Reading, Whiteknights, Reading RG6 2AH
(0734 875123) Map A, E8

Student enquiries: Sub-Dean of the Faculty in which you wish to study

Main study areas – as in What to Study section: (*First degree*): Accountancy, agriculture & horticulture, American studies, archaeology, art & design, biochemistry, biology, biotechnology, botany, business studies, chemistry, classics, computing, drama, economics, education, electrical & electronic engineering, English, environmental science, fine arts, food science and nutrition, geography, history, information technology, law, linguistics, mathematical studies, mechanical engineering, microbiology, modern languages, music, philosophy, physics, physiology, politics and government, psychology, sociology, speech sciences, zoology. *Also:* Building surveying, crop science, estate management, medieval studies, meteorology, surveying – general practice, typography.

European Community: 10% first degree students take EC language as part of course and 9% spend 6 months or more in another EC country. Formal exchange links with over 42 EC universities/colleges in: Belgium, Denmark, Eire, France, Germany, Italy, Netherlands and Spain; most open to non-language specialists. Approved Erasmus programme 1993/94. Languages available as option in first year of all arts/social science degrees and all years of humanities degrees. Courses in eg law with French law, physics with French/German/Italian.

Application: UCCA for 1993 start, UCAS thereafter. **Founded:** 1892. Bulmershe College of HE added 1989. **Main awards:** BA, BSc, BEng, LLB, BA(Ed). **Awarding body:** Reading University. **Site:** Whiteknights: 300 acres on southern outskirts of Reading; also buildings at Bulmershe Court. **Access:** Easy access to M4; frequent bus service from campus to town. Good trains and buses to London and elsewhere. **Accommodation:** 4,700 students in halls of residence; most first years accommodated. Also self-catering flats. Accommodation office helps students to find flats and houses outside university. Facilities for disabled students. **Library:** Main library with 600,000 books and pamphlets, 4,000 periodicals; extra copies of course books most in demand kept in reserve collection; various faculty libraries including education. **Specialist collections:** Overstone Library (economics, literature and history); Stenton Library (history); Cole Library of early medicine and zoology; Finzi poetry collection. **Other learning facilities:** Computer centre; university museums (English rural life, Greek archaeology, and zoology), language laboratories. **Welfare:** Counselling service and health centre (with doctors, dentists and psychiatrist), learning resource centre, tutor system, nightline, legal advice (through students' union), chaplains. **Hardship funds:** Fund available. **Careers:** Advisory service. **Amenities:** Union building with bars, shops, travel and insurance services etc; many athletic and social clubs; boathouses on Thames; sailing and canoeing on Thames and nearby gravel pits; sports hall. Reading film theatre, bookshop, banks, playing fields on the campus, playgroup, nursery.

Duration of first degree course(s) or equivalent: 3 years; 4 years (languages, art, food technology, typography) **Total first degree students 1991/92:** 6,276 **Total BA(Ed) students:** 519 **Overseas students:** 1,517 **Mature students:** 19% **Male/female ratio:** 1:1 **Teaching staff: full-time:** 650 approx **part-time:** 30 approx **Total full-time students 1990/91:** 8,244 **Postgraduate students:** 3,362 **Tuition fees for 1992/93 (first degrees):** Home: £1,855 (classroom), £2,770 (lab/studio); Overseas: £5,320 (classroom), £7,055 (lab/studio).

What it's like

Situated on the edge of the town, mainly on the Whiteknights Park; an open, green campus. Reading is not particularly a student town; its main virtue is proximity to London and Oxford, but it has good shopping facilities and excellent rail, coach and motorway connections. Inter-site travel poor. Getting about during the rush hour is a problem.

University accommodation trying to catch up with increasing student numbers. More high-quality conference-standard accommodation being built; more expensive. Most first years able to live in; some final years do. No visiting restrictions. Overseas students get some priority over self-catering but not accommodation in general. Reading not cheap.

SU good facilities; not very political; good on welfare, excellent for sporting and non-sporting clubs. It provides entertainments and services with cheap bars, shops and a very thorough student welfare service. Hall – JCRs – very strong. Most activities found on campus. SU central on campus, runs mini markets in Student Union; 3 + 1 SU bars; safety bus for evening transport.

CAN'T FIND WHAT YOU'RE LOOKING FOR? USE THE INDEX!

Disability awareness. Good support network eg accommodation priority; special arrangements for exams. Flat campus, access to buildings variable.

Courses vary. Some very specialised eg land management, meteorology. Others, increasingly, modular. Flexibility in first year to change subjects. Workload realistic. Life at university and Reading is largely what you make it.

Pauper notes

Accommodation: 14 halls of residence, student houses (self-catering limited but increasing). Student flats. Married quarters. **Drink:** All halls have a bar (cheaper than pubs, more expensive than union). SU has 3 bars at main site; one at Bulmershe. Various local pubs but prices very expensive. **Eats:** Reasonable service offered by university. Union catering expanding – cheap snacks, hot and cold plus vegetarian. Town has usual takeaways with some restaurants. **Ents:** Comprehensive and varied ents programme – some live music weekly discos and free jazz nights in SU. Film theatre on campus (2 films/week). **Sports:** Sports centre on campus. Cheap sports sales in SU. Some swimming pools give NUS discount. Over 200 clubs/societies (100+ sports – football good).**Hardship fund:** Access fund. Good educational trusts hunt-help by SU welfare office. **Travel:** Easy to hitch to and from. Excellent travel office gives student fares. Good communications but very busy at peak times. **Work:** Work in SU bar. Some part-time jobs available, temping during the summer.

Buzz-words:

The Nob (The Queen's Head – local pub); The Ath Pav (The Athletic Pavilion where SU sports clubs have a drink after matches).

Alumni (Editors' pick)

Andy Mackay (composer and performer, Roxy Music), Baroness Pike (chairman, Broadcasting Complaints Commission), Christine Rolfe (first known woman slaughterhouse supervisor), Sir Richard Trehane (ex-Milk Marketing Board), Steve Vines (Observer labour editor), Jim Bacon (BBC weatherman), Sue Turner (controller of children's programmes Thames TV), Gillian Freeman (novelist and biographer), Phil Vesty (Olympic walker), Richard Livsey (Liberal MP for Brecon), Clive Ponting (former civil servant), Elspeth Huxley, Sir Noel Stockdale (chairman ASDA/MFI group), Vasso Papandreou (European Commissioner), Susanne Charlton (BBC weatherperson), David Wright (arts officer for Bucks county council), Graham Ritchie (general manager, Belgrade Theatre, Coventry), Beverley Goddard (Olympic sprinter), Jennie Orpwood (wheelchair disabled Olympic swimmer).

RIPON & YORK ST JOHN

University College of Ripon & York St John
(1) The College, Lord Mayor's Walk, York YO3 7EX (0904 656771)
(2) The College, College Road, Ripon HG4 2QX (0765 602691)
Map A, E5

Student enquiries: Registrar (York address)

Main study areas – as in What to Study section: *(First degree):* Art and design, American studies, biology, drama, education, English, environmental science, geography, history, linguistics, music, professions allied to medicine (PAMs), religious studies and theology. *Also:* Physical education, women's studies.

European Community: 8% first degree students take EC language as part of course and 8% spend 6 months or more in another EC country. Formal exchange links with 6 EC universities/colleges: France (2); Greece (1); Italy (1); Netherlands (2). Contemporary Europe studies, with semester at Grenoble University, France, or the Free University of Amsterdam available to selected students.

Application: UCCA for 1993 start, UCAS thereafter. **Special features:** Modular degrees on semester pattern. **Largest fields of study:** Education. **Founded:** 1975, amalgamation St John's College York and The College Ripon. **Main awards:** BA, BSc, BA (QTS), BSc (QTS). **Awarding bodies:** Leeds University. **Site:** Campuses close to centres Ripon and York (25 miles apart). **Access:** Good road and rail links: A1, M1, M62. Regular inter-site campus buses. **Accommodation:** 420 (York) and 280 (Ripon) places in hall; 280 (York) and 60 (Ripon) places in college houses, flats; lodgings at both sites. Approx cost: Halls of residence £50 pw (incl all meals). **Library:** Library on each site; 175,000 volumes, 600+ periodicals, 330 study places, course books for reference and loan, on-line searches. **Specialist collections:** 19th century children's books. Local studies collection. **Other learning facilities:** Religious education centre, AV materials, slide and record library; CCTV unit and video equipment, computing facilities on both campuses. **Welfare:** Doctor, dentists, 2 chaplains. Chapel on each campus. **Careers:** Information, advice and placement. **Amenities:** SU both sites – bars, coffee bars, shops, gymnasia, Olympic standard pool, squash courts, dry-slope skiing; extensive playing fields. Arts centres, galleries and museums in York. **Employment:** Education, retail management, leisure services, public service admin, social and community work, journalism, the media.

Duration of first degree course(s) or equivalent: 3 years **others:** 4 years BA/BSc (QTS) **Total first degree students 1991/92:** 1,644; **BEd and BA (QTS) students:** 601 **Male/female ratio:** 1:3 **Teaching staff: full-time:** 134 **part-time:** not known **Total full-time students 1991/92:** 2,105 **Postgraduate students:** 61 **Tuition fees for 1992/93** (first degrees): Home: £1,855 (classroom), £2,770 (lab/studio). Overseas: £4,790 (classroom), £7,040 (lab/studio). First year students also pay £350–£400 validation fee.

What it's like

Main campus in York, just outside city walls with clear view of Minster and 5 sites around the city – 3 residential. Ripon campus 25 miles away is much quieter, set in spacious grounds, good community relations. Minibus service links the two campuses 4 times daily.

All new students accommodated in halls (21-meal package included in residence fees), kitchen areas provided in all halls. College also rents other houses, but not enough. York rents rising.

Female/male 4:1 at York, less healthy at Ripon at 8:1. Mature students steadily increasing but no crèche yet, exchange programmes to both Europe and America every year: international flavour to campus atmosphere.

Well-developed SU provides wide variety of clubs and societies, entertainments, welfare services, two shops, two bars, part and full-time staff. Focal point for social life, some political activity, much apathy. Professional counselling network on both campuses, run by staff and students. College as a whole has a very friendly atmosphere.

York has much to offer: top tourist city; 365 pubs, clubs, restaurants, two theatres, a 10 screen cinema, market, art gallery, bowling alley, monuments, museums. London is 2 hrs by train. Ripon is very different: a quiet market town, different campus atmosphere reflects this. Has pubs, a market, restaurants, no train station, buses regularly to Harrogate.

Leeds University validates degrees. Most courses modular. High application rate – 12 for each place. Well regarded nationally, low drop-out rate. Attracts students from all over Britain, most from comprehensives or colleges of FE. Overall picture is one of healthy academic development with much social interaction.

Pauper notes

Accommodation: Internal option for all new students; external provided by college and housing agencies. Rents increasing. **Drink:** Yorkshire home of good beer. **Eats:** York – anything at any price; Ripon – Valentino's cheap Italian,

Indian, Dominic's nice but pricy. Special discount in over 50 places in Ripon and York arranged by SU. **Ents:** York – Theatre Royal, cinema, Spotted Cow, Fibbens – live music. **Sports:** York – on campus pool, tennis courts, squash courts, 2 gymnasia 5 mins walk. Ripon – on-site gym, pool in city. Harrogate for further facilities. **Hardship funds:** Access fund, Bursar, number of funds to help those in trouble. **Travel:** York main line InterCity, 2 hrs to London. Ripon – bus to Harrogate and Leeds. **Work:** Campus vacation work and much local in Ripon and York.

Alumni (Editors' pick)

Jeff Squires, Geoff Cooke.

ROBERT GORDON INSTITUTE

See Robert Gordon University

ROBERT GORDON UNIVERSITY

The Robert Gordon University, Schoolhill, Aberdeen AB9 1FR
(0224 633611) Map A, D2

Student enquiries: Assistant Registrar (Student Administration)

Main study areas – as in What to Study section: *(First degree):* Architecture, art & design, business studies, chemistry, computing, electrical and electronic engineering, food science & nutrition, hotel & catering management, information technology, library & information studies, mathematical studies, mechanical and production engineering, pharmacy, physics, professions allied to medicine (PAMs), public administration, social policy and social welfare. *Also:* Building studies, building surveying, European business studies, legal and administrative studies, offshore engineering, publishing studies, quantity surveying.

European Community: 10% first degree students learn an EC language as part of their course and 7% spend 6 months or more in another EC country. A number of formal exchange links (France and Germany), all open to non-specialists, and more developing elsewhere in Europe. French and German languages incorporated into a number of degrees, including European business administration.

Application: PCAS for 1993 start, UCAS thereafter. **Special features:** 1 year exchange programmes with Oregon State University; Illinois Institute of Technology. **Academic features:** Courses in technology and business; legal and administrative studies; publishing studies; business computing; consumer product management. **Largest fields of study:** Art, architecture, engineering, business studies, pharmacy. **Founded:** 1992, as a university; previously Robert Gordon Institute, designated in 1903 as one of the Scottish Central Institutions. **Main awards:** BA, BSc, BEng. **Awarding body:** Robert Gordon University. **Site:** 8 sites in or near Aberdeen city centre. **Accommodation:** 500 places for first years in halls of residence (segregated) and self-catering flats; 375 self-catering flats. Approx cost: £45 pw hall; £33 pw flats. 316 private flats. Approx cost: £30–£35 per week. Rent: 25% in accommodation where rent controlled by the university. **Library:** 160,000 volumes in total, 1,600 periodicals, 410 study places. **Welfare:** Accommodation officer, student counsellors, careers officer, chaplaincy, medical advisory service. **Hardship funds:** Access funds and short term loan scheme. **Careers:** Information and advice service. **Amenities:** SA with bar, games room, etc; most sports (facilities available at Kepplestone).

Duration of first degree course(s) or equivalent: 3 and 4 years for honours; **others:** Business studies 4 years 1 term, computer science 5 years for honours. **Total first degree students 1991/92:** 3,000 **Overseas students:** 150 **Mature students:** 158 **Male/female ratio:** 3:2 **Teaching staff: full-time:** 320 **Total full-time students 1991/92:** 4,800 **Postgraduate students:** 350 **Tuition fees for 1992/93 (first degrees):** Home: £696 (if no grant), £1,855 (classroom), £2,770 (lab/studio); Overseas: £4,600 (classroom), £5,120 (lab/studio).

What it's like

Scotland's second largest central institution spread over six sites throughout the city. Aberdeen has a large student population and RGU students mix easily with Aberdeen university, ACFE and Northern College students. Increasing in size and reputation despite cutbacks at other institutes. Courses range from fine art to mechanical and offshore engineering with a highly practical slant on most, particularly attractive to employers. Relatively easy to change from degrees to honours degrees and vice versa. Assessment varies from course to course, but exams play a large part, along with lab work, practical etc.

SA building has 1 bar/disco, and a lounge bar/art gallery, TV room, pool room, laundry, canteen, Cable TV and has over 30 clubs and societies, ranging from hockey to fencing to Chinese boxing to boardgames. SA campaign on many student issues as well as discussing them with the governors. Produces 'The Review', Aberdeen's leading monthly student newspaper. Students from all over UK, with quite large overseas contingent. Atmosphere hardworking, but lively, and employment prospects are good.

Pauper notes

Accommodation: Some short-life 'hard to let' flats available. **Drink:** RGIT union, Prince of Wales (real ale), Ma Cameron's, Caledon Bar (for architecture and art students). **Eats:** RGU, Radars, La Lombarda (Italian). **Ents:** Aberdeen Exhibition and Conference Centre for more famous bands and music hall for smaller but well known. SA ents, Odeon/Cannon cinemas, Capitol (cheap films and bands), HM Theatre (occasional student discounts), lively student clubs, Ritzy on a Monday night, the Pelican Club. **Sports:** SA clubs and societies, RGC swimming pool, Use of Aberdeen Leisure Centre, Wednesday afternoons. **Hardship funds:** Institute administers several funds – contact SA first. **Travel:** BR railcard. **Work:** Usual part time jobs in bars, tutoring, babysitting.

More info?

Get students' Alternative Prospectus.
Enquiries to President/Deputy President, SA (0224 644239).

ROEHAMPTON INSTITUTE

Roehampton Institute, Roehampton Lane, London SW15 5PU
(081 392 3000)
(1) Digby Stuart College, Roehampton Lane, London SW15 5PH
(2) Froebel Institute College, Roehampton Lane, London SW15 5PJ
(3) Southlands College, Wimbledon Parkside, London SW19 5NN
(4) Whitelands College, West Hill, London SW15 3SN
Map D, A3

Student enquiries: Admissions Officer (Senate House, Roehampton Institute)

Main study areas – as in What to Study section: *(First degree):* Art & design,

CAN'T FIND WHAT YOU'RE LOOKING FOR? USE THE INDEX!

biology, business studies, dance, drama, education, English, environmental studies, geography, history, mathematical studies, modern languages, music, psychology, religious studies & theology, social policy and social welfare, sociology. *Also:* Consumer science, sports studies, women's studies.

European Community: 18% first degree students take EC language as part of course and 16% spend 6 months or more in another EC country. Formal exchange links with some 14 EC universities/colleges in Belgium and France (for language students only). Approved Erasmus programme. French and Spanish tuition available for non-language students; German and Italian soon. New degree in marketing, French and Spanish.

Application: UCCA for 1993 start, UCAS thereafter. **Special features:** Most Degrees are combinations of 2 subjects with over 200 possible combinations. Several single subject degree programmes also offered. **Largest fields of study:** Education, English, business studies and psychology. **Founded:** 1975, ex Digby Stuart (1874), Froebel Institute (1892), Southlands (1872) and Whitelands Colleges (1841). Affiliated to Surrey University. **Main awards:** BA, BA(QTS), BSc. **Awarding body:** Surrey University. **Site:** 4 sites in Wimbledon/Roehampton area. **Access:** Bus, train and underground. **Accommodation:** 1,252 places in mixed and segregated halls (most first years normally accommodated). Rent: 45% of students housed in accommodation where rent controlled by Institute. **Library:** Library at each site; 400,000 volumes in total, 1,000 periodicals, 525 study places. **Specialist collections:** Early childhood archive. **Welfare:** Welfare officer, doctor, chaplains. **Careers:** Counsellor on site. **Amenities:** SU building at each site. **Sporting facilities:** Facilities in and near colleges for wide variety of sports.

Duration of first degree course(s) or equivalent: 3 years (BA/BSc); 4 years BA(QTS) and BA with modern languages **Total first degree students 1991/92:** 3,524 **BA(QTS) students:** 759 **Overseas students:** 28 **Mature students:** 21% **Male/female ratio:** 1:3 **Teaching staff:** 250 **Total full-time students 1991/92:** 3,636 **Postgraduate students:** 463 **Tuition fees for 1992/93 (first degrees):** Home: £1,855 (classroom), £2,770 (lab/studio); Overseas: £5,415 (classroom), £6,522 (lab/studio).

What it's like

Formed from four colleges, Digby Stuart, Southlands, Whitelands and Froebel. It offers the same academic and recreational facilities as larger institutions but with the advantage to students who might need more support and guidance of a smaller college. Teaching takes place in all four colleges (a free bus service is provided to transport students).

Digby Stuart – 15% of funding comes from the Society of the Sacred Heart, a Catholic college, although you don't need to be Catholic. The Catholic ethos is apparent and mass is available daily, but people are free to enjoy their own faith.

A good situation geographically, close enough to central London to enjoy the benefits of metropolitan life but far enough away not to be caught up in the rat race. Close to Richmond, Putney, Kingston and Wimbledon for shopping trips, nights out and work.

SU offers range of weekly activities, discos, bands, bar games, theatre productions and lots of clubs and societies as well as information on welfare topics and talks on specific topics.

A student counselling service and a fully equipped welfare room now open so all students should be happy and problem free.

Pauper notes

Accommodation: Offered to most first years and final years; all second years live out. Help available in finding places from the accommodations officer. **Drink:** Staff/student social club. Beer prices not too bad, pretty reasonable for London. **Eats:** Food not bad in residence; vegetarians catered for; lots of places to eat outside, including places that deliver free. **Ents:** Local cinemas, student restaurants. London life is entertainment itself! **Hardship fund:** Now available on application. **Sports:** Well-established field sports. Amateur sport encouraged. **Travel:** BR (Barnes Station). Good buses. Hitching not recommended. **Work:** Jobs in the bar; work available in Putney and Richmond.

Informal name:

Digby

Alumni (Editors' pick)

Ashley Ward (English athletics international), Vivien Leigh. Pope John Paul II visited here in 1982.

ROSE BRUFORD COLLEGE

Rose Bruford College of Speech and Drama, Lamorbey Park, Sidcup, Kent DA15 9DF (081 300 3024) Map D, D4

Student enquiries: Admissions Officer

Main study areas – as in What to Study section: *(First degree):* Drama and theatre arts. **Also:** Stage management/technical theatre.

European Community: No students learn an EC language or spend time in another EC country. Formal exchange arrangements being developed in Amsterdam. Plans to tour and invite visiting European groups.

Application: Direct. **Academic features:** Degrees in theatre (programmes for actors, writers and directors) and in technical theatre. Courses accredited by National Council for Drama Training. **Founded:** By Rose Bruford in 1950. **Main awards:** BA. **Awarding body:** Kent University. **Sites:** Lamorbey Park, Sidcup, Kent and Deptford. **Access:** British Rail (Charing Cross 30 min); easy access from A20 or M2. **Accommodation:** College is non-residential. Students live locally in flats or lodgings. Rent: no student accommodated where rent is under college control. **Library:** 24,000 books, 12,000 slides, 100 periodicals, 30 reading places; audiovisual and photocopying facilities; tuition in library use and research methods. Dynex computerised cataloguing and circulation system. **Welfare:** Accommodation officer on site; local doctors and dentists. **Careers:** Agents, theatre managers and related employers invited to college productions. Continuing placement facilities to past students. **Hardship funds:** Small funds administered by college and SU. **Amenities:** Barn theatre; cinemas and swimming pool locally; grass tennis courts and extensive grounds; nearby banks and shops; plus all London facilities. **Employment:** Theatre and allied fields.

Duration of first degree course(s) or equivalent: 3 years **Total first degree students 1992/93:** 240 **Overseas students:** 2 **Male/female ratio:** 1:2 **Teaching staff: full-time:** 16 **part-time:** large number of visiting tutors **Total full-time students 1992/93:** 262 **Tuition fees for 1992/93 (first degrees):** Home: £2,770; Overseas: £6,000.

What it's like

The new theatre degree course has now established itself and improved links are being created between the actors and the technical theatre arts students, to build more unity throughout the college.

The SU has an active committee to represent students in all areas of concern. As the college is reasonably small, c230, it has only a few facilities available to larger institutions.

The college has no accommodation itself and students live in rented houses across SE London. Everything is expensive and with a tremendous workload, once you graduate, you will be fully prepared for a career in theatre.

Here's to an exciting three years!

Jane Miller

CAN'T FIND WHAT YOU'RE LOOKING FOR? USE THE INDEX!

Pauper notes

Accommodation: College ensures suitable lodgings nearby. **Drink:** A popular place with students – Ye Olde Black Horse, Halfway Street, Sidcup. **Eats:** Canteen facility on Sidcup site; Greenwich cafes, Little Mo's Cafe, Deptford. **Ents:** Close to central London, always something to see at college. **Sports:** Good summer sports facilities on campus, swimming pools nearby. **Hardship funds:** College has trust funds. **Travel:** Expensive – student rail card a must. Hitching not advisable. College vans – must be over 21. **Work:** Working during term time is difficult with the workload. Holiday jobs almost essential.

Informal name:

RBC

Alumni (Editors' pick)

Freddie Jones, Tom Baker, Nerys Hughes, Angharad Rees, Barbara Kellerman, Gary Oldman, Emma Wray, Janet Dibley, Jon Iles, Diane Louise Jordan.

ROYAL ACADEMY OF MUSIC

Royal Academy of Music, Marylebone Road, London NW1 5HT (071 935 5461) Map E, B1

Student enquiries: Admissions Officer

Main study areas – as in What to Study section: *(First degree):* Music.

European Community: Language tuition available for all undergraduates; required for opera and singing students. Formal exchange links with conservatoires in France and Germany. Member of a consortium of 12 leading European conservatoires established to set up a permanent exchange programme.

Application: Direct (except BMus joint with Kings College, through UCCA for 1993 start, UCAS thereafter). **Special features:** Many distinguished visiting musicians; Alberni Quartet and Amadeus Quartet. Five international chairs – Witold Lutoslawski, Composition and Contemporary Music; Christopher Hogwood, Early Music; Sir Colin Davis, Conducting and Orchestral Studies; Andras Schiff, Piano Studies and Lynn Harrell, Cello Studies. International composer festivals. **Academic features:** Joint centre for advanced performance studies established by the Academy and King's College, London; new joint vocal faculty with Royal College of Music. **Founded:** 1822. **Main awards:** BMus(Perf), Certificate of Advanced Studies, MMus. **Awarding body:** Royal Academy of Music and London University. **Site:** Central London. **Access:** Baker Street or Regent's Park underground stations. **Accommodation:** 44 places in halls of residence (mixed), plus new purpose-built hostel. Rent: 9% in accommodation where rent controlled by academy. **Library:** approx 175,000 items in total, 40 periodicals and approx 10,000 books. **Specialist collections:** Sir Henry Wood, Sullivan Archive and Otto Klemperer collections of orchestral scores. **Welfare:** Student services; counsellor. **Careers:** Information and advice. **Amenities:** Local music shop within a few yards; refurbished concert hall, opera theatre; 5 organs; RAM Magazine; canteen, students' club (licensed); social/sports facilities. **Hardship funds:** Substantial awards and funds available, particularly for postgraduate students.

Duration of first degree course(s) or equivalent: 4 years **Total first degree students 1991/92:** 313 **Overseas students:** 26 **Mature students:** 34 **Male/female ratio:** 9:11 **Teaching staff: full-time:** 6 **part-time:** 107 **Total full-time students 1991/92:** 469 **Postgraduate students:** 156 **Tuition fees 1992/93 (first degrees):** Home: £2,770; Overseas: £7,660.

WANT TO HELP WITH THE NEXT EDITION – SEE PAGE 76

What it's like

Housed in a pink wedding cake off busy Marylebone Road, close to Madame Tussauds, but with a little more life! Atmosphere serious but social. Practice the order of the day (every day!) for students looking to make the grade as professional musicians. Excellent personal tuition from some of the finest members of the profession and resident academic staff. Staff/student relations good. Performing ability is most important but there are courses in written musical disciplines. Easy to change courses. Work load fair. Many students from independent schools; about 100 students have a car. Most musical tastes and abilities catered for: Baroque; Jazz; Big B; Rock music.

It has an exciting social and sporting life, and its location, in the heart of the West End of London, makes it ideal for the best shopping and nightlife.

Pauper notes:

Accommodation: None. **Drink:** Own bar – 'one of cheapest in London ' – and 7 pubs within 100 yards! **Eats:** As Drink. **Ents:** West End – ideal for ent. **Sports:** West End – ideal for sports. **Hardship fund:** Admin always willing to listen. **Travel:** Students encouraged to travel. **Work:** If there is a case, then something can always be worked out.

Informal name:

RAM.

ROYAL ACADEMY SCHOOLS

Royal Academy of Arts, Piccadilly, London W1V 0DS (071 439 7438)
Map E, B3

Student enquiries: Secretary

Main study areas – as in What to Study section: *(Not at first degree level):* Art & design.

European Community: Number of students learning an EC language or spending time in another EC country, not known.

Special feature: Postgraduate only.

Application: Direct. **Founded:** 1768. **Main awards:** Postgraduate diploma. **Awarding body:** Royal Academy Schools. **Site:** Piccadilly. **Access:** Piccadilly underground station; various buses. **Academic features:** All courses are of 3 years' duration, with annual examinations; the majority of teaching is done by visiting tutors. All courses are postgrad. **Accommodation:** Schools secretary will advise. **Library:** 15,000 volumes, various periodicals. **Specialist collections:** Old master drawings/prints. **Welfare:** Doctor, psychiatrist, chaplain. **Careers:** Advice service. **Amenities:** St James' Church (the artists' church) opposite; National Gallery and other galleries within easy reach. **Employment:** Teaching.

Total full-time students 1991/92: 60 (postgraduate) **Tuition fees 1992/93:** £4,560 (Home/Overseas)

What it's like

Situated in the West End behind the Academy Gallery and next to the Museum of Mankind. Entrance to the college is via Burlington Gardens.

The only 3 year, full-time, postgraduate course in the country and is an independent college, not state-run. Intake of approximately 15 painters and 3–4 sculptors a year. Although these are the only basic courses offered, there is a printmaking department which is basic but covers all areas of the medium and technicians are available for help and advice.

Keeper has liberal attitude towards the individual student. Students not obliged to take up the rather more academic side of the course, ie life drawing, unless they choose to. The spaces available are getting bigger due to degree course cuts and all students are guaranteed a reasonable working area. The schools have a regular turnover of Academicians who come in to tutor and outside artists also occasionally visit.

Being situated in the centre of London, access to all the large galleries is very good, and many other independent galleries such as those in Cork Street are all a few moments away; therefore the possibilities for seeing all kinds of art work are vast.

There are links with the Royal Academy Gallery itself with at least two annual student shows in the Diploma Gallery which attract a large public. Entrance to Academy exhibitions for students is free. A small bar in the canteen and parties can be arranged.

The Royal Academy Schools are basically a set of studio spaces with regular tutoring, but being a small institution it does not operate in the same way that other colleges do. As a result of this, students are not hampered by the machinations of a larger college or university and there is more room for student influence in the running of the school.

Visiting hours are between 1.00 and 2.00 or 4.00 and 4.30.

Pauper notes

Drink: Subsidised real ale at college bar. **Eats:** Canteen very cheap by London standards. Plenty of cheap alternatives in area. **Ents:** Free admission to all RA exhibitions. **Grants:** DES money available for RA Schools fees and maintenance. **Hardship funds:** Available to those without DES grants. **Travel:** Travel scholarships to selected students. Occasional visits to far-away lands.

ROYAL AGRICULTURAL COLLEGE

Royal Agricultural College, Cirencester GL7 6JS (0285 652531)
Map A, D7

Student enquiries: Admissions Secretary

Main study areas – as in What to Study section: *(First degree):* Agriculture and forestry, biology, business studies, economics, environmental studies, town & country planning. *Also:* crop technology and ecology, estate management, equine studies, international agribusiness management.

European Community: 44% first degree students take EC language as part of course (compulsory on international agribusiness management, international agriculture and equine business management courses; all degree students have access to evening language tuition in French/German/Spanish/Russian, taken by some 14%). 10% spend 6 months or more in another EC country, many others go worldwide. Formal exchange links with 7 EC universities/colleges in France, Germany, Netherlands and Spain (Institut Supérieur Agricole de Beauvais; Lycée Agricole de Libourne-Montagne; Ecole Supérieure d'Agriculture d'Angers; Fachhochschule Nurtingen; Wageningen University; Larenstein International Agricultural College; Universidad Politécnica de Valencia).

Application: Direct but UCCA for some courses (for 1993 start, UCAS thereafter). **Academic features:** Course in international agricultural and equine business management, combining agriculture, equine studies and business management. **Special features:** Combination of technical and business teaching. Some courses lead to membership of Royal Institution of Chartered Surveyors – Rural Practice Division. **Largest fields of study:** Rural economics and estate management, agriculture, business studies and equine management. **Founded:** 1845. **Main awards:** BSc, Diploma in rural estate management (DREM). **Awarding bodies:** Reading University, Bath University and Buckingham University (BSc),

Royal Agricultural College (DREM). **Site:** 1 mile from Cirencester. **Accommodation:** 309 beds in halls. Approx cost: £2,040–£2,940 pa full board. 33% students in accommodation where rent controlled by college. **Library:** 17,500 volumes, 600 periodicals, 160 study places. **Other learning resources:** Own farm, 770 hectares. **Welfare:** Doctor, student welfare officer, chaplain, personal tutors. **Hardship funds:** Various bursaries available. Grants generally available. **Careers:** Information, advice and placement. **Amenities:** Common rooms, bar, snack bar, student union. **Sporting facilities:** Sports pitches including floodlit all-weather hockey and tennis, facilities for squash, rowing, water sports and field sports, gym. **Employment:** Farm, plantation, nursery and estate management, private and government land agency, leisure management, conservation, rural investment, advisory and development agriculture, food industry, retailing, marketing.

Duration of first degree course(s) or equivalent: 3 years or 4 years (sandwich) **Total first degree students 1991/92:** 633 **Overseas students:** 16 **Mature students:** 38 **Male/female ratio:** 7:2 **Teaching staff: full-time:** 53 **part-time:** 8 **Total full-time students 1991/92:** 843 **Postgraduate students:** 95 **Tuition fees, first degrees, 1992/93:** Home: £3,600–£4,998; Overseas: £5,250–£7,050.

What it's like

The Cotswolds provide a great atmosphere for the college which is set in private grounds, one mile outside Cirencester. Accommodation for approximately 300 students, mainly first years. Remaining students live in cottages within about a 10-mile radius of the college.

The library is computerised and there are computers available for student use.

Range of sporting clubs and other activities can be arranged; floodlit all-weather pitch and a multi-gym.

Pauper notes

Accommodation: Single study bedrooms in college. Digs, cottages, flats in 'Ciren' area. **Drink:** Lots of good pubs and numerous local brews. College bar not subsidised but provides a meeting place for students. **Eats:** College food is reasonably priced and good. Lots of places in 'Ciren'. **Ents:** Not a lot on campus. Students go to Oxford, Stratford, Bristol, Bath, Cheltenham. **Sports:** Most sports catered for on campus, otherwise 'Ciren' and locality. **Hardship funds:** None as such College helps arrange employment part-time. **Travel:** Bursaries available; student fares through SU. **Work:** In term time, limited but available in Cirencester and locality. In vacation most have jobs as work experience – mostly on farm, relief milking, lambing and harvest jobs.

More info?

Enquiries to Jane Keay (0285 652531).

Informal names

RAC; Cirencester

ROYAL COLLEGE OF ART

Royal College of Art (RCA), Kensington Gore, London SW7 2EU (071 584 5020) Map E, A3

Student enquiries: The Registrar

Main study area – as in What to Study section: *(not at first degree level):* Art and design including arts administration, illustration, natural history illustration and ecological studies, information and technical illustration, computer related design, vehicle design, tapestry, visual Islamic and traditional arts, bronze casting and history of design.

CAN'T FIND WHAT YOU'RE LOOKING FOR? USE THE INDEX!

European Community: Number of students learning an EC language or spending time in another EC country, not known but college encourages student exchanges and all students have access to language tuition. Approved Erasmus programme 1992/93.

Special features: A postgraduate university institution with Royal Charter. **Main awards:** MA, MDes, MPhil, PhD, and DrRCA. **Academic features:** Project or thesis work, following individual student proposals, forms an increasing proportion of degree work. PhD work may be carried out in any discipline provided resources exist; minimum period of study is 2 full-time equivalent years.

Application: Direct. Entry for Masters courses by competitive examination; usually about 300 places a year. Candidates normally aged over 21 with a first degree send in portfolios of recent work. Applications for Masters and PhD by end of January.

Application for state bursaries in the case of English and Welsh candidates is made through RCA but award is not automatic. Scottish candidates should apply to Scottish Education Department and Northern Irish candidates apply to Ministry of Education, Northern Ireland. (For addresses see *How to go about it*.)

Home students only are eligible for UK state bursaries. All financial arrangements should have been made before the student arrives.

Accommodation: College provides none. Rent: college controls no student rents. Student Housing and Welfare Officer can help students find accommodation, and advise on student welfare.

Duration of Master's degree course(s): 2 years **Male/female ratio:** 5:4 **Teaching staff: full-time:** 198 **part-time:** 92 **Total postgraduate degree students 1991/92:** 700 **Tuition fees, 1992/93:** Home: £2,842; Overseas: £7,750.

What it's like

It is still the only exclusively postgraduate college in Britain teaching both art and design. It is a prestigious educational institution with a high profile and a growing international reputation for quality.

The reality of being a student here is far from glamorous; the majority of courses last for only two years so there is a lot of hard work, pressure and financial hardship. The most exciting element of college life for Royal College students is the opportunity to meet other postgraduates from a great variety of art and design areas.

As everywhere, students at the RCA are suffering acute financial hardship. Money, space and resources are getting tighter, but at present the college is well funded. The college has a student fund which helps students suffering hardship due to unforeseen circumstances, and an access fund which helps UK students with costs of accommodation and travel. However, your two years at the RCA could well prove to be two of the most expensive years of your life.

As a graduate student I know that the experience of studying here is well worth all the financial hardship and practical worries. It is an exciting place to study and some of the people you meet here are truly inspiring. The college has recently appointed a new Rector and positive changes are on the way.

Pearl John, Student Union President RCA

Pauper notes:

Accommodation: Difficult to find and expensive. The college has no halls of residence, but accommodation and welfare office very helpful in finding homes with dependable landlords, and rents which are just about affordable. **Drink:** The Art Bar, SU run, so prices reasonable. **Eats:** College canteen meals and snacks throughout the day, food not great and quite expensive. **Ents:** The Art Bar runs regular events, including jazz nights, karaoke, weekly discos, and big parties for Hallowe'en, Christmas, and so on. **Sports:** SU has very few facilities but we are affiliated to Imperial College, a massive institution, close by, with great facilities for sports and events which we can use at cut price.

GET HOLD OF THE PROSPECTUSES

Informal name:
RCA

Alumni (Editors' pick)
David Hockney, Peter Blake, Ian Dury, David Gentleman, The Emmanuels, Zandra Rhodes, Kenneth Grange, Nick Butler, Len Deighton, Henry Moore, Ridley Scott, Barbara Hepworth, Edward Burra, Briget Riley.

ROYAL COLLEGE OF MUSIC

Royal College of Music (RCM), Prince Consort Road, South Kensington, London SW7 2BS (071 589 3643; Fax: 071 589 7740)
Map E, A3

Student enquiries: Admissions Tutor

Main study areas – as in What to Study section: *(First degree):* Music.

European Community: 5% first degree students learn an EC language; singers study application of French, Italian, German, Russian, Spanish. None spend time in another EC country.

Application: Direct. **Academic features:** BMus performance degree. Prizes available – winners perform at public recitals in London concert halls. Postgraduate courses in performance, composition, electroacoustic performance. **Structural features:** New Britten Theatre opened 1986. College has formal relationships with many musical organisations. **Special features:** Many visiting musicians including John Williams, George Benjamin, Grigory Zhislin, Evelyn Glennie, Eileen Croxford, John Lill, Rostropovich, Dorothy DeLay (violin) and William Pleeth (cello), Geoffrey Parsons (accompaniment), visiting professors; various master classes. **Founded:** 1883, by Prince of Wales (later Edward VII). **Main awards:** BMus, GRSM, DipRCM(Perfs), ARCM (PG), MMus (RCM). **Awarding bodies:** London University, Royal Schools of Music, Royal College of Music. **Site:** South Kensington. **Access:** South Kensington and Gloucester Road underground stations; various buses. **Accommodation:** 1 hall of residence (mixed) Robert Mayer Hall; also Queen Alexandra's House (women only) has a number of places available for RCM students, accommodating chiefly first year students (preference given to those living outside London). Approx cost: £750–£900 per term. **Library:** Reference and loan collections; over 250,000 volumes, including rare early printed material and manuscripts. **Specialist collections:** Portraits of musicians; Instrument Museum. **Other learning resources:** Extensive reference library and research facilities. **Welfare:** Counsellor, doctor, dentist, FPA, psychiatrist, Alexander Technique, chaplain. **Careers:** Information and advice. **Amenities:** Nearby music shop gives 10% discount to RCM students; facilities of London University (including Imperial College swimming pool). **Employment:** Orchestral; teaching; freelance playing.

Duration of first degree course(s) or equivalent: 4 years **Total first degree students 1991/92:** 331 **Overseas students:** 95 **Male/female ratio:** 3:4 **Teaching staff: full-time:** 13 **part-time:** c160 **Total full-time students 1991/92:** 480 **Postgraduate students:** 149 **Tuition fees for 1992/93** (first degrees): Home: £2,770; Overseas: £5,310–£8,310.

What it's like

Life for students at the Royal College of Music has inevitably become far more interesting and varied over the years, as college has expanded and standard of musicianship improved. The opening of new Britten Opera Theatre for example, has attracted talented singers from all over the world. About 20% of students at college are from overseas, in fact there are around 35 countries represented. This is a great advantage as we can learn so much from our foreign counterparts, not only from a musical point of view but also about other cultures.

SA has also grown considerably over last few years. Every full-time student of college is automatically a member. SA is responsible for many things, managing students' bar, arranging parties, student conductors' concerts, football matches and other social events. RCM drama association is integral part of SA. Everything from costumes to choreography, lighting to directing is taken on by students.

The 'Gowrie Report' suggested Royal College should merge with Royal Academy of Music to create a 'new and better conservatoire'; Royal College students decided that this venture was more of a cost-cutting exercise than a true realisation of student needs and fought unanimously against it. The idea was eventually shelved. This created a solid and coherent attitude among students: we defended our rights to keep the Royal College the wonderful institution we know it to be.

I am positive that the Royal College of Music will continue to produce the high standard of musical education it always has, and I'm sure anyone would be hard pushed to find a student who was not extremely proud to be here.

Paul Keohone

Pauper notes

Accommodation: Robert Mayer Hostel, Queen Alexandra's House. **Drink:** Very good Merrydown Cider! **Eats:** RCM canteen very convenient, reasonable (not cheap) prices. Imperial College eating facilities very good value. **Ents:** RCM film club. Student entry to most London cinemas, theatres, etc. **Sports:** Imperial College facilities – very cheap and near RCM. **Hardship funds:** RCM Union offers interest free loans of up to £500. **Travel:** No student fares (except railcard). London Transport travel cards save money. **Work:** Various off campus; RCM Appointments Office offers lots of playing and teaching work.

Alumni (Editors' pick)

Holst, Britten, Tippett, R Vaughan Williams, Andrew Lloyd-Webber, Oliver Knussen, Rick Wakeman, Colin Davis, Peter Pears, Janet Baker, Barry Douglas, Julian Bream, James Galway, Gwyneth Jones, Joan Sutherland, John Lill, Elizabeth Maconchy, Neville Marriner, Sarah Walker, David Willcocks.

ROYAL FREE

Royal Free Hospital School of Medicine, University of London, Rowland Hill Street, London NW3 2PF (071 794 0500) Map D, B1

Student enquiries: Registrar

Main study areas – as in What to Study section: *(First degree):* Medicine.

European Community: No students learn an EC language or spend time in another EC country.

Application: UCCA for 1993 start, UCAS thereafter. **Structural features:** Part of London University. **Special features:** BSc course open to those who have successfully completed first 2 years of MBBS course; integration of clinical and pre-clinical teaching. **Founded:** 1874. **Main awards:** BSc, MBBS. **Awarding body:** London University. **Site:** Hampstead. **Access:** Belsize Park underground and Hampstead Heath BR stations. **Accommodation:** London University accommodation office will assist. Halls of residence plus College hall with 80 places. **Rent:** 20% in accommodation where rent controlled by university. **Library:** 27,000 volumes, 360 periodicals, 230 study places; reference copies of course books. **Centres of excellence:** Academic department of medicine (liver diseases and gastroenterology); department of neurological science; haematology, immunology. **Welfare:** Doctor, dentist, FPA, psychiatrist, chaplain, hospital chapel. **Amenities:** SU bar, squash courts. **Sporting facilities:** Athletics ground at Enfield. **Employment:** Some pre-registration house officer posts after graduating.

Duration of first degree course(s) or equivalent: 5 years **Other:** 6 years (including BSc) **Total first degree students 1991/92:** 535 **Overseas students:** 30 **Male/female ratio:** 1:1 **Teaching staff: full-time:** 92 **part-time:** 12 **Total full-time students 1991/92:** 580 **Postgraduate students:** 119 **Tuition fees for 1992/93 (first degrees):** Home: £1,000 (if no grant), £2,770 (pre-clinical), £4,985 (clinical); Overseas: £7,500 (pre-clinical), £13,500 (clinical).

What it's like

All subjects taught at Royal Free Hospital in Hampstead. Pre-clinical students live in London University halls in Bloomsbury, the student house in Islington and 100 new places in new halls in West Hampstead, mainly for first years and clinical students. Extremely difficult to find suitable accommodation in Hampstead. Libraries well-stocked and late study possible. SU not NUS affiliated but very active. Student facilities at hospital include 2 squash courts, 450 seat assembly hall, and bar. Also collective membership of hospital recreation centre. Social events (discos, live bands, annual beer-races) held at hospital; active sports clubs, Dramsoc, orchestra and rag week. Fully confidential counselling. Continuous assessment throughout course. If 2-year pre-clinical course is successfully completed you can study for one-year intercalated BSc. Drop-out rate moderate (approx 8–10 from first year). First-time success rate for finals about 95%. Good balance between work and relaxation. One of the friendliest medical schools with good tutor/student relationships.

Pauper notes

Accommodation: Halls of residence; SU accommodation officer. Some cheap properties on short term lease to School. **Drink:** Bar owned by medical school. Good local brew Highgate Mild. **Eats:** Curry Paradise just around corner from hospital. Local trendy Hampstead restaurants. **Ents:** Good cinemas locally, Dingwalls in Camden Town and Camden Palais. **Sports:** Squash courts and recreation centre (gym and pool) on site. Sports ground at Enfield. Rowing at ULU boathouse, Chiswick. Swiss Cottage Sports Centre – 2 swimming pools – cheap for students, well equipped. **Hardship funds:** Some special grants/bursaries for hard-up students; apply to registry. Access funds. **Work:** Auxiliary nursing, portering, lab work available in summer vacation.

Informal name:

The Free

Alumni (Editors' pick):

Dr Hillary Jones (TV-am).

ROYAL HOLLOWAY AND BEDFORD

Royal Holloway and Bedford New College, University of London, Egham Hill, Egham, Surrey TW20 0EX (0784 434455) Map A, F8

Student enquiries: Schools Liaison Officer

Main study areas – as in What to Study section: *(First degree):* Biochemistry, biology, botany, business studies, classics, computing, drama, economics,

CAN'T FIND WHAT YOU'RE LOOKING FOR? USE THE INDEX!

English, environmental science, European studies, geography, geology, history, mathematical studies, microbiology, modern languages, music, physics, politics & government, psychology, public administration, sociology, zoology. *Also:* Electronics, Japanese studies, media arts, operational research.

European Community: 18% first degree students take EC language as part of course and 20% spend 6 months or more in another EC country. Formal exchange links with 17 universities in EC: Belgium (2), Denmark (1), France (4), Germany (3), Italy (5), Netherlands (1); Portugal (1) – all open to non-language specialists. New student mobility programme in music. European studies degree. Most undergraduates have access to basic language training (French, German, Italian, Spanish). New course unit system means many students will be able to add a language as part of their degree.

Application: UCCA for 1993 start, UCAS thereafter. **Structural features:** Part of London University. **Largest fields of study:** Biology, English, geography, history, maths, French and social studies. **Founded:** 1985, from merger of Bedford College (1849) and Royal Holloway College (1886) – both founded as women's colleges, co-ed from 1960s. **Main awards:** BA, BMus, BSc. **Awarding body:** London University. **Site:** 100 acre parkland campus. Founder's building in style of Château of Chambord. Many newly completed buildings. **Access:** Egham station (Waterloo–Reading line); buses. Close to Heathrow airport, M3, M4 and M25. **Accommodation:** 2,000 places in halls including 200 places in self-catering houses and flats; all students in first year and most in third year offered places in residence. Rent: 50% in accommodation where rent controlled by university. **Library:** Main library; several departmental collections; 400,000 volumes in total, 1,500 periodicals, 400 study places; restricted loan collections. **Other learning resources:** 300 computer workstations for student use. **Welfare:** Wardens, counsellor to students, doctors, FPA, psychiatrist, chaplains, interdenominational chapel. **Hardship funds:** Limited loans and grants from the Principal's Hardship Fund. **Special categories:** Residential facilities for some married students. Extracurricular College certificate in computing and quantitative skills available by modular study. **Careers:** Information, advice and placement. **Amenities:** Purpose-built SU building; orchestra and choirs. **Sporting facilities:** Wide variety of sports (including rowing); playing fields on site.

Duration of first degree course(s) or equivalent: 3 years; **Total first degree students 1991/92:** 2,965 **Overseas students:** 201 **Mature students:** 576 **Male/female ratio:** 1:1 **Teaching staff: full-time:** 278 **part-time:** 26 **Total full-time students 1991/92:** 3,813 **Postgraduate students:** 415 **Tuition fees for 1992/93** (first degrees): Home: £725 (if no grant), £1,885 (classroom), £2,770 (lab/studio); Overseas: £5,900 (classroom), £7,100 (lab/studio).

What it's like

'London University's Country Campus', 30 minutes from central London. Housed on a campus near Windsor based on amazing Victorian 'founders' building. An established centre of academic excellence. Geology and physics departments are both pre-eminent in their research fields and the arts faculty is one of the best in the university. New buildings include sciences, life sciences, maths/arts and new SU building. Also new residences – one of the most popular of the new buildings is Reid Hall, where every study bedroom has a shower/toilet en suite.

SU active, mostly social rather than political. Over 100 clubs and societies ranging from political to social, religious to sporting. It also provides a varied and enjoyable ents programme of events most days in the week, as well as an alternative comedian practically every week. Operates four bars around campus, good prices.

Pauper notes

Accommodation: College accommodation increased: Self catering, en-suite bathrooms, very nice. Local area expensive. Married residence 50 yards from campus.

"Most ex-students have very fond memories, as shown by attendance at ex-students' association"

Drink: Best place for cheapies – union bars. Stumble Inn on campus has nice pub atmosphere and cheap prices. **Eats:** SU coffee bar – cheap and varied. 'Girovend' credit card food system on campus; vegetarian on menu. Local places – Windsor, Staines 'load of bull'. **Ents:** New cabaret venue open on campus. Drama dept does lots of plays. Very active ents. Lot of fringe theatre, 3 cinema groups, bands and alternative comedy every week. **Sports:** Campus playing field and small gymnasium. Egham Sports Centre good but expensive, Staines nearest swimming. **Hardship funds:** A few are available. SU has just set up a welfare fund. **Travel:** French and ski societies do good cheapies. **Work:** College employs students during vacs, plenty of bar work etc during term with SU and local area.

More info?

Get students' Alternative Prospectus.
Enquiries to General Secretary, SU (0784 435035).

Buzz word

RHUL (SU)

Alumni (Editors' pick)

Ivy Compton-Burnett, Richmal Crompton, Felicity Lott, Janet Fookes MP, David Bellamy, Kathleen Lonsdale, Jean Rook, Marie Patterson, George Eliot.

ROYAL NORTHERN COLLEGE OF MUSIC

Royal Northern College of Music, 124 Oxford Road, Manchester M13 9RD (061 273 6283) (Fax 061 273 7611) Map A, D6

Student enquiries: Secretary for Admissions

Main study areas – as in What to Study section: *(First degree):* Music. *Also:* Performance arts.

European Community: 20% first degree students take EC language as part of course (all singing students); some language classes may be open to other students. None spend time in another EC country as a formal course requirement. Formal exchange links with conservatoires in Paris, Lyon, Copenhagen and Frankfurt (in addition to Prague and Belgrade) open to all students. Annual orchestral tours, especially to France.

Application: Direct. **Special features:** All undergraduate courses are 4 years

CAN'T FIND WHAT YOU'RE LOOKING FOR? USE THE INDEX!

(2 years broad musical education, 2 years specialisation); college runs a joint course with Manchester University. **Founded:** 1973, ex Northern School of Music and Royal Manchester College of Music. **Main awards:** GMusRNCM(Hons), GRNCM, PPRNCM. **Awarding body:** Royal Northern College of Music. **Site:** Fine modern buildings 1 mile south of city centre. **Access:** Buses from city centre. **Accommodation:** 176 study bedrooms (residence recommended for first year students). Approx cost: £60 per week (with meals). Rent: 20% (ie most first-year undergraduates) in accommodation where rent controlled by college. **Library:** Extensive reference and lending sections of books and performing material. Vast record collection with playback facilities for records, tapes, CDs and videos. Microfilm and microfiche facilities. **Specialist collections:** Henry Watson Collection of Musical Instruments; Library of Jascha Horenstein; original manuscripts of Alan Rawsthorne, and a unique collection of Scandinavian music. **Other learning facilities:** Electronic studio, keyboard laboratory, professionally-staffed recording studio. **Welfare:** Chaplain, counsellors, instrument purchase loan scheme. **Hardship fund:** Bursaries may be awarded from college trust funds. **Careers:** Advisory service. **Amenities:** Opera theatre, concert hall, recital room; Junior Common Room; roof garden; refectory with bar. Full programme of public events takes place throughout the academic year. **Sporting facilities:** Tennis, football and cricket at hall of residence. **Employment:** Primarily music performance; private teaching; school teaching and music librarianship (after further study); music and arts in general.

Duration of first degree course(s) or equivalent: 4 years **Total first degree students 1991/92:** 410 **Overseas students:** 32 **Mature students:** 120 **Male/female ratio:** 1:1 **Teaching staff: full-time:** 38 **part-time:** 75 **Total full-time students 1991/92:** 565 **Postgraduate students:** 102 **Tuition fees for 1992/93** (first degrees): Home: £2,770; Overseas: £5,775.

What it's like

It's the youngest of the four British Royal Schools of Music and boasts some of the most up-to-date facilities and opportunities for music students in Britain. Facilities include a fully staffed opera theatre, with its own workshop, concert hall, recital room, lecture theatre, comprehensive practice room facilities and its own hall of residence.

Students actively encouraged to seek external work with local orchestras and music clubs. Through its close links with BBC Philharmonic, Hallé, Liverpool Philharmonic and Camerata Orchestras, RNCM students are ideally placed to take advantage of this forward looking policy. In what is a highly competitive field, RNCM is a surprisingly friendly place, perhaps due to its large refectory area where students congregate. SU organises many social events, including two annual Balls, parties and sports.

Pauper notes

Accommodation: Cheapest housing in Moss-Side, Hulme and Whalley range. Fair number of squats in Hulme. Most popular student areas are Chorlton and Withington. **Drink:** Many good locals; SU bar (cheap) and university and poly SUs. **Eats:** Approx 30 Indian restaurants in Rusholme (most cheap and very good). Good vegetarian. **Ents:** Lots of cinemas (student discount). Student reductions at most theatres. Royal Exchange Theatre very good. Lots of socials at SU. **Sports:** Use of university and poly facilities – Moss-Side Leisure Centre very cheap and convenient. **Hardship funds:** College and SU have limited resources for small loans and scholarships available. **Travel:** College fund for studying abroad. **Work:** Gigs and teaching relatively easy to find by the time you've been at college for a couple of years.

Alumni (Editors' pick)

Peter Donohoe, Jane Eaglen, Brodsky Quartet, Howard Jones.

GET HOLD OF THE PROSPECTUSES

ROYAL SCOTTISH ACADEMY

Royal Scottish Academy of Music & Drama, 100 Renfrew Street, Glasgow G2 3DB (041 332 4101) Map A, C3

Student enquiries: Secretary and Treasurer

Main study areas – as in What to Study section: *(First degree):* Drama, music. *Also:* Theatre design.

European Community: No students learn a language or spend time in another EC country.

Application: Direct. **Special features:** Many top professional concert artists and theatre directors in recitals, productions and master classes. **Academic features:** BA musical studies. **Founded:** 1847. **Main awards:** BA, BEd, DipRSAMD, Dip Dramatic Art, Dip Stage Management Studies. **Awarding body:** Glasgow University, Royal Scottish Academy of Music & Drama. **Site:** Central Glasgow. **Accommodation:** 30 places in mixed hall (20 places for first years). Approx cost: £44.30 pw; assistance in locating private accommodation. **Library:** 80,120 music volumes, 13,750 books, 7,570 sound recordings, 26 study places, 9 listening booths. **Welfare:** Doctor, student adviser. **Hardship funds:** RSAMD Trust. **Careers:** Information and advice. **Amenities:** Theatre (500 seats); closed circuit TV studio; recital room; concert hall; choir (Academy Chorus); regular recitals by distinguished artistes on premises; orchestras. **Employment:** Professional orchestral musicians; members of opera companies; theatre; teaching (music and drama); solo concert artists and actors.

Duration of first degree course(s) or equivalent: 3 years; **others:** 2 and 4 years
Total first degree students 1991/92: 267 **BEd students:** 54 **Overseas students:** 8
Mature students: 65 **Male/female ratio:** 2:3 **Teaching staff: full-time:** 43 **part-time:** 115 **Total full-time students 1991/92:** 397 **Postgraduate students:** 45
Tuition fees for 1992/93 (first degrees): Home: £2,770; Overseas: £6,600.

What it's like

Impressive orange brick building in a good vantage point on corner of Hope and Renfrew Streets. Full of modern facilities. Used by public for performances in the New Athenaeum or the Chandler Studio Theatres, or for concerts in the Stevenson Concert Hall. Extensive library on top, complete with hi-fi, CD players and video equipment. TV studio with cameras, lighting, sound and editing. Large technical dept. Practice rooms for music and drama students. Small canteen and smaller common room. Noticeable lack of SU bar in the building. Plenty of nightclubs and bars, good gay community. Lot of visiting companies and musicians in the Academy. Plenty going on locally in the arts. Large shopping centres. Academy in town centre; Glasgow Central and Queen Street rail stations nearby, also Cowcaddens Subway and Buchanan bus station; buses to most places in city (prices average). Easy access to parts of Scotland eg Loch Lomond only 30 minutes away. Few drop-out once they have started the course although people drop out for lack of funds or fear of future lack of funds a week *before* their first term. Lack of social cohesion in music school and minimal interaction between music and drama students. Can feel claustrophobic but few students are unhappy. RSAMD is widely respected and opportunities after graduating verge on the excellent.

Greg Haiste, Vice President SRC

Pauper notes

Accommodation: Some music student accommodation available, prospective students given list of places for rent by office but mainly up to students themselves. Glasgow can be expensive – southside and West End popular. **Drink:** Art School, The Waldorf, The Variety (pubs everywhere). Cheap beer can be found but Glasgow getting very trendy. **Eats:** Academy canteen not subsidised. Cheap

CAN'T FIND WHAT YOU'RE LOOKING FOR? USE THE INDEX!

local places easily found. **Ents:** Lots of cheap theatre and music. Arthouse cinema at Glasgow Film Theatre. Nightlife good. Generally lots to do – Glasgow now a major cultural centre. **Sports:** Kelvin Hall Sports Centre, easy to take tube. **Hardship funds:** Academy loan scheme. **Travel:** No travel scholarships as such. Hitching good on M8. Buses average. Discounts on train with railcard. Tube 50p anywhere. **Work:** Ushering in college, music teaching, plenty bars and restaurants. A job is often needed in these hard times.

More info?

Enquiries to Mark Stevenson, SRC President/Greg Haiste, SRC Vice President (041 332 5080).

Alumni (Editors' pick)

Hannah Gordon, Moira Anderson, Sheena Easton, Tom Conti, Sir Alex Gibson, Bill McCue, Fulton Mackay, James Loughran, Margaret Marshall, Isobel Buchanan, Ian Richardson, Victor & Barry, Bill Paterson, Christine Cairns, Kathleen Livingstone, Neil Mackie, Bryden Thomson, Judith Howarth, David Hayman, Mary Marquis, Phyllis Logan, Denis Lawson, John Cairney, John Grieve, Ruby Wax.

ROYAL VETERINARY COLLEGE

Royal Veterinary College, University of London, Royal College Street, London NW1 0TU (071 387 2898) Map D, B1

Student enquiries: Registrar

Main study areas – as in What to Study section: *(First degree):* Veterinary studies.

European Community: No students learn an EC language or spend time in another EC country as part of their course (components of compulsory vacation work may be taken overseas). Formal exchange links with Royal Veterinary & Agricultural University Copenhagen (food hygiene) and Veterinary Faculty, Munich University (veterinary clinics).

Application: UCCA for 1993 start, UCAS thereafter. **Structural features:** Part of London University. **Academic features:** Individual project in final year forms part of the final degree examination. **Founded:** 1791. **Main awards:** BVetMed, BSc. **Awarding body:** London University. **Site:** Pre-clinical studies at Camden Town, north London; clinical studies on 575 acre campus at Hawkshead, near Potters Bar, Herts. **Access:** Buses and tubes to Camden Town site (Camden Town, Mornington Crescent, Euston and King's Cross stations); BR stations for Hawkshead (Brookmans Park, Potters Bar) about 20 mins by train from King's Cross. **Accommodation:** London University intercollegiate halls for students at Camden campus: majority of pre-clinical students are accommodated within walking distance of the college; halls of residence at Hawkshead with 90 study bedrooms for clinical students; plus further 30 expected. **Library:** Library and reading rooms at both sites; reference copies of standard texts; public library in Camden High Street; London University library. **Other learning facilities:** Computer suites at Camden and Hawkshead with teaching packages including word-processing, statistics, simulation programmes. Animal hospitals at both sites. Large animal practice at Hawkshead. **Welfare:** Camden students may register with health services of University College or London University Central Institutes. Physician visits Hawkshead regularly during term. **Amenities:** ULU building in Malet Street, college refectory, and common rooms at Camden Town and Hawkshead. Playing fields and swimming pool at Hawkshead.

Duration of first degree course(s) or equivalent: 5 years **Total first degree students 1991/92:** 372 **Overseas students:** 24 **Mature students:** 40 **Male/female**

ratio: 2:3 **Teaching staff:** 70 **Total full-time students 1991/92:** 413 **Postgraduate students:** 80 (full and part-time) **Tuition fees for 1992/93 (first degrees):** Home: £2,770 (pre-clinical), £4,985 (clinical); Overseas: £7,410 (pre-clinical); £13,638 (clinical).

What it's like

The college is split site at Camden (Central Camden) and Potters Bar (northern suburb) as are the course and student population.

In the first two years 'real' student life can be embraced with London providing endless entertainment, and the numerous houses of residence plus centre of London University allowing a massive scope for socialising; both of which do ease the somewhat tedious 'pre-clinical' work load.

In the final three years 'clinical' studies are taught and with the majority of students living out (though these are in halls) a more domesticated 'country life' is appreciated with increased professionalism as you reach the final year.

For a college of our size (approx. 400 students) there is a good range of clubs and work-hard, play-even-harder mentality when the students socialise, with all the years and a number of nationalities/mature students mingling.

London being the city that it is, things are becoming increasingly expensive but with pre-clinical work experience being a reasonable money spinner, London life can be liked to a great extent. Being a five-year vocational course we do not get preferential treatment from some banks, and whilst most students leave college considerably overdrawn we are well placed in the profession.

So if you want to be a vet (and there are postgraduate places), enjoy your work, have no qualms about a split city/country life, and would like life in a small self-sufficient community college, come to the RVC.

Tony Beck

Pauper notes

Accommodation: Intercollegiate halls during 1st year, possibly 2nd. College hall in final 3 years, though living out is reasonably priced. **Drink:** ULU bars and other unions (especially UCL), the Rising Sun (Euston Road) can be happening. **Eats:** Campus/college food OK. UCL/ULU are good when in London. **Ents:** Good and lively college social events. **Sports:** Field station has playing field, squash court, swimming pool. Use of all ULU and Imperial/QMH facilities. **Hardship Funds:** Access fund. **Travel:** Variety of scholarships for projects abroad. **Work:** Hard but possible to do part-time, though first two years good vocational opportunities. In final three years a lot of minimally paid vocational study making this more difficult.

More info?

Enquiries to Tony Beck (0707 662255).

Informal name:

RVC

ST ANDREWS UNIVERSITY

University of St Andrews, College Gate, St Andrews, Fife KY16 9AJ (0334 76161) Map A, D2

Student enquiries: Schools Liaison Office

Main study areas – as in What to Study section: *(First degree):* Anthropology, biochemistry, biology, biotechnology, botany, chemistry, classics, computing, economics, English, fine arts, geography, geology, history, Latin American studies, mathematical studies, medicine, microbiology, modern languages, Near East and Islamic studies, pharmacology, philosophy, physics, physiology, politics and government, psychology, religious studies and theology, zoology. *Also:* Astronomy, electronics, Hispanic studies, physical education, Scottish studies.

European Community: 22% first degree students take EC language as part of course, and 10% spend 6 months or more in another EC country. Some 25 formal exchange programmes under Erasmus, many with multiple links, involving 10 other EC countries eg Belgium (Latin), Denmark (Latin, philosophy), France (history, art history, languages, biology, maths, physics), Germany (classical philology, Arabic, applied maths, biotechnology, geography), Greece (history, art history, biology), Italy (languages, classical philology, philosophy, biology, chemistry, biochemistry), Netherlands (classical philology, geography), Portugal (biochemistry, biotechnology), Spain (history, art history, biology, geography). Tuition in French/German/Spanish available to all students. Strong in joint honours courses, eg social sciences or history or philosophy with French/German/ Spanish, biology or maths/statistics with French/German, psychology with French, geography with French/Spanish.

Application: UCCA for 1993 start, UCAS thereafter. **Academic features:** Many new single and joint honours courses including MA in modern languages (1, 2 or 3 languages); 4 year honours system gives great flexibility – final choice of subject(s) can be delayed until end of second year. General entrance requirements are relaxed for mature students. **Largest fields of study:** Physical sciences, biology, modern languages, social sciences, history. **Founded:** 1411. **Main awards:** BD, MA, BSc, MTheol. **Awarding body:** St Andrews University. **Site:** St Andrews town centre, North Haugh site half mile west of the town. **Access:** Nearest station is Leuchars (5 miles away) on main London–Aberdeen line, then bus; good road links. **Accommodation:** 2,200 places in halls; 600 student flats; 80 lodgings (all first years offered and encouraged to live in hall). **Library:** 730,000 volumes, 10,000 periodicals, 680 study areas. **Other learning facilities:** Computing laboratory, Gatty marine laboratory, language centre. **Welfare:** Doctor, FPA, chaplain, student counsellor. **Hardship funds:** Application to Hebdomadar. **Special categories:** Limited residential facilities for married and disabled students. **Careers:** Information, advice and placement service. **Amenities:** SU with coffee and snack bars, newspaper, arts and crafts area etc; St Andrews Festival organised by town and gown. **Sporting facilities:** Modern physical education centre; excellent playing fields; 6 squash courts; 5 golf courses (including 'Old' course); local leisure complex complete with indoor swimming pool.

Duration of first degree course(s) or equivalent: 4 years Honours; 3 years Ordinary **Total first degree students 1991/92:** 3,850 **Overseas students:** 451 (plus 158 postgrad) **Mature students:** 353 **Male/female ratio:** 1:1 **Teaching staff: full-time:** 335 **part-time:** 40 **Total full-time students 1990/91:** 4,444 **Postgraduate students:** 594 **Tuition fees for 1992/93 (first degrees):** Home: £1,855 (classroom), £2,770 (lab); Overseas: £5,355 (classroom), £7,015 (lab).

What it's like

Small university of about 4,300, in historic town on east coast of Scotland (little industry or economic activity apart from golf, university and RAF Leuchars). Town small, with good mix of historic and new. Academic departments spread over town, sciences on 1960's campus-style North Haugh site.

Cosmopolitan university – 10% overseas, 40% English, 5% Northern Irish, 45% Scottish. All first years in halls; most others in private or university-owned flats.

Flexible course structure and entry by faculty requires no honours specialisation (within reason) until third year. Exemption system means few first year students (unless they do no work) sit exams at the end of the year. Psychology, mediaeval history, chemistry and maths have excellent reputations, amongst others.

A very close-knit community. Over 150 active student societies from silly (The Tunnocks Caramel Appreciation Society) to serious (Amnesty International). Strong debating tradition and acclaimed Dramatic Society – the Mermaids.

Traditions abound: Raisin Weekend, Red Gowns, Pier Walks and May Morning Dip in the North Sea.

Students' Association provides services, both social and support, for all students. Athletic Union provides excellent facilities for almost all sports.

Highlights of the social calendar are the balls: the Union Ball, the Debates Ball, residence balls and society balls, like Canmore. Easiest to crash is the Graduation Ball in July, when the college lawns are covered by marquees.

You might never leave St Andrews for good, but find yourself drawn back again and again.

Pauper notes

Accommodation: University accommodation good value, private flats vary, can be difficult to find. **Drink:** Students Association cheapest. **Eats:** Lots of atmosphere, coffeeshops, pizzas and wholefood places. Indians are quite expensive; Chinese food is more affordable. **Ents:** One film theatre, The Byre Playhouse very prestigious. Student productions full of imagination. Union Theatre has regular bands and smaller scale ents occur frequently in the Union bar. **Sports:** Athletic union free to students. Local swimming pools and golf courses offer concessions. **Hardship funds:** Through the university via The Hebdomadar. **Travel:** SA runs cheap travel service. Nearest BR station is Leuchars (5 miles away on East Coast line). **Work:** Mostly bars and waitress service, but jobs go fast.

Alumni (Editors' pick)

Sir Hugh Cortazzi, Colin Young, Fay Weldon, Alastair Reid, Eric Anderson, James Michener, Siobhan Redmond, Zoe Fairbairns, Michael Forsyth, Allan Stewart, Alex Salmond.

ST BARTHOLOMEW'S

The Medical College of St Bartholomew's Hospital, University of London, West Smithfield, London EC1A 7BE (071 982 6000)
Map E, D2

Student enquiries: Admissions Officer

Main study areas – as in What to Study section: *(First degree):* Medicine.

European Community: No languages, exchanges or links yet.

Application: UCCA for 1993 start, UCAS thereafter. **Structural features:** Part of London University. **Academic features:** Teaching during first 2 years at Queen Mary and Westfield College, with new innovative curriculum, including project work, integrated teaching, and self-directed learning. Clinical course (years 3–5) centred at St Bartholomew's Hospital. New intercalated BMedSci course open to students who have completed 4th year of MBBS. **Founded:** 1123. **Main awards:** MBBS. **Awarding body:** London University. **Site:** West Smithfield, Charterhouse Square and QMW. **Access:** Barbican and St Paul's underground stations. **Accommodation:** 206 single study bedrooms in Charterhouse Square; some college flats for clinical students. Approx cost: £40 pw. **Rent:** 60% in accommodation where rent controlled by college. Accommodation guaranteed for all first and final year students. **Library:** One on the Charterhouse Square site, clinical and media resources libraries on hospital site. **Other learning resources:** Self-teaching tape/slide programmes; computer self-teaching programmes; interactive video discs. **Amenities:** Recreational facilities in College Hall (TV lounge, bar, etc). Social club (bar, billiards room, etc) in the Robin Brook Centre for Medical Education on the hospital site. Extensive audio-visual learning and computing facilities. **Hardship funds:** Limited funds available. **Sporting facilities:** Squash courts and gymnasium in Charterhouse Square; swimming pool in nearby nurses' home; athletic grounds in Chislehurst, Kent.

CAN'T FIND WHAT YOU'RE LOOKING FOR? USE THE INDEX!

Duration of first degree course(s) or equivalent: 5 years; **others:** 6 years (with intercalated BSc or BMedSci) **Total first degree students 1991/92:** 369 (plus students in years 1 and 2, studying at QMW) **Overseas students:** 11 **Mature students:** 39 **Male/female ratio:** 1:1 **Teaching staff:** 200 **Total full-time students 1991/92:** 413 **Postgraduate students:** 44 (full-time); 75 (part-time) **Tuition fees for 1992/93 (first degrees):** Home: £755 (if no grant), £2,770 (pre-clinical), £4,985 (clinical); Overseas: £7,450 (pre-clinical), £13,620 (clinical).

What it's like

Beautiful, unique college, hidden in the heart of the city – allowing the best of both worlds. The hospital, 200 yards away, is in City and Hackney Health Authority; its patients are the richest and poorest giving great diversity. Pre-clinical studies at Queen Mary & Westfield.

1st years and final years guaranteed a place on campus and then you can stay in Brent House, Hackney – our self-contained flats (lively, friendly, cheap and very convenient) or move out into Hackney/Stoke Newington which has some of the most central and cheap student digs in London. Some overseas students and 10% postgraduates. Some car parking available – usually only for finalists.

Campus library is open 9 am–10 pm 5 days/wk. SU shop open every day and near by are all-purpose shops some open from 9 am–11 pm 7 days/wk. Nearby Smithfield allows students to take advantage of the multitude of all night cafés – great for the 4 am munchies!

Very active SU, involved in all aspects of college life, representing the students, to staff and entertainments. Welfare officer and student health officer take care of any personal/social problems confidentially – being a small college very conscious of students' welfare and not much opportunity to be lonely or isolated.

Most active societies drama and mountaineering clubs. Popular sports include rugby, football (men), hockey (men/women), netball, water sports and rowing, and many more. Barbican Centre on doorstep offers huge range of drama, cinema, music and art exhibitions. Easy access to north and central London. 2 balls a year and twice weekly entertainment on campus. ULU is near, offering additional facilities. Friendly bar with unusual opening hours forms a very special social crux.

Students encouraged to comment on any problems, and generally well listened to; student reps in most areas including representation at your interviews.

Personality is important and ability to communicate. Any old medical school can churn out doctors; Barts aims to produce doctors who understand the concepts of health care. Everyone guaranteed a job after they qualify; wide-ranging contacts in many UK hospitals – and internationally.

Pauper notes

Accommodation: Cheap, lively hall with no petty regulations (rooms guaranteed for first years and finalists). New college-owned flats for 100 students. Student-run accommodation service helps find cheap lodgings in N and E London. **Drink:** Real ale pubs abound. Unique bar in hall, 'Eugenes', very popular. **Eats:** Cheap eating at college hall and hospital. Huge greasies available at all-night cafés. Outstanding pub food at 'Fox and Anchor'. Wide variety of food types available locally. **Ents:** Regular discos, bands and review acts in hall bar. Regular quality productions by Drama Soc. Student reductions at next-door Barbican Centre. **Sports:** On site multigym, swimming pool, water polo. Boathouse at Chiswick. Rugby, soccer, hockey, cricket at Chislehurst. Sailing at Burnham. **Hardship funds:** Funds administered by SU and college for students in need. **Travel:** A number of college grants available for student electives. **Work:** Wide variety of jobs in hospital including some specifically reserved for particularly needy students eg graduates without grants. Jobs in city wine bars etc.

Informal name

Barts

GET HOLD OF THE PROSPECTUSES

Alumni (Editors' pick)

William Harvey, John Abernethy, James Paget, Richard Gordon, Graham Chapman, Percival Pott, Thomas Vicary, W G Grace, Graham Gardner, Penfolds (as in Australian wine).

ST GEORGE'S

St George's Hospital Medical School, University of London, Cranmer Terrace, London SW17 0RE (081 672 9944) Map D, B4

Student enquiries: Registry

Main study areas – as in What to Study section: *(First degree):* Medicine.

European Community: No students learn an EC language or spend time in another EC country.

Application: UCCA for 1993 start, UCAS thereafter. **Structural features:** Part of London University. **Founded:** 1751. **Main awards:** MB, BS, BSc. **Awarding body:** London University. **Site:** Tooting. **Access:** Tooting Broadway underground station; buses. **Accommodation:** 256 places in mixed hall of residence (all first years accommodated; 30% total). **Library:** 17,000 monographs, 30,000 journal volumes, 500 periodicals, 400 study places. **Welfare:** Student counsellor, student health service, chaplains. **Amenities:** Hospital chapel; bookshop managed by school club; bar and common rooms, banks. **Sporting facilities:** 6 squash courts and gymnasium; Olympic standard public swimming pool just off site; playing fields.

Duration of first degree course(s) or equivalent: 5 years; 6 years (with intercalated BSc) **Total first degree students 1991/92:** 753 **Overseas students:** 22 **Mature students:** 62 **Male/female ratio:** 4:3 **Teaching staff: full-time:** 147 **part-time:** 194 **Total full-time students 1991/92:** 794 **Postgraduate students:** 112 **Tuition fees for 1992/93 (first degrees):** Home: £775 (if no grant), £2,770 (pre-clinical), £4,985 (clinical); Overseas: £7,055 (pre-clinical), £12,990 (clinical).

What it's like

Large complex of buildings with all pre-clinical and approximately half clinical teaching on site. Mixed self-catering halls of residence are seven minutes' walk from the Medical School, with room for 256 students (first years are guaranteed places). Halls life is good (socially) and easy (financially and domestically). Central London is easily accessible by tube (about 20 minutes' ride).

Tooting is good for eating and drinking; theatre, film and cabaret require a short five minute bus journey.

SU has fortnightly discos held in the Medical School (featuring the longest student bar in London) with many events in between (plays, films, happy hours) and special events (Christmas revue, rag week, freshers fortnight). The bar serves the usual plus guest beers, and hot and cold food.

Most sports and leisure interests are catered for and new clubs are constantly becoming active, inactive and reactive (depending on demand). The sports ground is at Cobham (Surrey) and there is a sports hall on site with squash courts and multigym. Successful clubs include hockey, football, basketball and rowing; all clubs are remarkably active socially!

The work load in the first year is relatively light compared to the rest of the course. Failures are not by a set rate, although the chances of an appeal for a second retake are dwindling. Once through the first year, being thrown out is unlikely. Also a third of students are offered a chance of doing an intercalated BSc at the end of the pre-clinical course. A clinical BSc is also offered. Student–staff relations are relaxed and friendly.

CAN'T FIND WHAT YOU'RE LOOKING FOR? USE THE INDEX!

If you want to become a capable and caring physician, and still enjoy every moment of your five years, come to St George's.

Sarah Jarvis

Pauper notes

Drink: Tooting Tavern, Selkirk, King's Head, Corner Pin. **Eats:** Lots of Indian (many weekend buffets). **Ents:** SU events, Ritzy in Brixton for films. **Sports:** Tooting Leisure Centre next door. Centre on site. **Hardship funds:** Can sometimes be arranged by grovelling. Access Funds. **Work:** Work in hospital available (clerical and nursing).

Informal name:

George's

Alumni (Editors' pick)

Henry Gray, Edward Wilson, Edward Jenner, Thomas Young, John Hunter, Mike Stroud.

ST MARK & ST JOHN

College of St Mark & St John, Derriford Road, Plymouth PL6 8BH (0752 777188) Map A, C9

Student enquiries: Admissions Officer

Main study areas – as in What to Study section: *(First degree):* Art & design, education, English, geography, history, humanities, information technology, linguistics, mathematical studies, philosophy, religious studies and theology, sociology. *Also:* Film studies, public relations.

European Community: 2% first degree students learn an EC language as part of their course; some spend 6 months or more in another EC country. Formal exchange links with 1 EC college in Brest, France. French offered to all students; other languages likely to be introduced.

Application: UCCA for 1993 start, UCAS thereafter. **Academic features:** Modular framework for all BA courses, allowing full and part-time study. **Special features:** Urban Learning Foundation with teaching practice and community work opportunities in east London. Specialist centres for design and technology, health and physical recreation, international education, information technology in education, primary teaching, mathematics teaching, religious education. English as a Foreign Language offered. BA students may spend 1 term in USA. Policy of overseas visiting academics. **Founded:** St John's, Battersea, 1840; St Mark's, Chelsea 1841, amalgamation as the College of St Mark and St John in Chelsea, 1923. New location in Plymouth, 1973. **Main awards:** BA, BEd. **Awarding body:** Exeter University. **Site:** 5 miles Plymouth city centre. 53-acre site overlooking Dartmoor National Park, Plymouth Sound and City of Plymouth. **Access:** Good bus services. **Accommodation:** Priority to first and final year students for on-campus accommodation; others found approved lodgings by college accommodation officer. Rent: 70% in accommodation where rent controlled by college. **Library:** Over 100,000 volumes, 450 periodicals, plus extensive microfilm and audio-visual materials. 185 study places, plus 'out of hours' work area. **Welfare:** Careers office, chaplain, nursing officer (SRN), student welfare centre, welfare counsellors. **Special categories:** Crèche during half terms. Christian Fellowship and study groups. **Careers:** Specialist careers adviser and information room. **Amenities:** Joint common room with bar and snack bar, games and TV rooms, SU shop, launderette, minibus, printing service, specialist bookshop, part-time banking service, chapel, drama theatre, Plymouth (arts centre, theatre, orchestras). **Sporting facilities:** Floodlit all-weather sports area and pitches; sports centre including carpeted sports halls for badminton, basketball, 5-a-side soccer, netball, tennis, volleyball etc, plus gym, weight training room, 3 squash courts, climbing wall, indoor 25-metre pool; also Dartmoor, coasts and rivers of Devon and Cornwall for sailing, canoeing, climbing etc.

Duration of first degree course(s) or equivalent: 3 years; **Other:** 4 years (BEd); **Total first degree students 1991/92:** 1,100 **Number of BEd students:** 550 **Overseas students:** 150 **Mature students:** 375 **Male/female ratio:** 2:3 **Teaching staff:** full-time 84 part-time: 30 **Total full-time students 1991/92:** 1,155 **Postgraduate students:** 75 **Tuition fees for 1992/93 (first degrees):** Home: £759 (if no grant), £1,855 (classroom), £2,770 (lab/studio); Overseas: £5,320.

What it's like

New site opened in 1973 in rural, picturesque position 5 miles from city centre, within easy reach of moors, sea and Cornwall. Reasonable public transport. Modern comfortable accommodation, including recently built student village and four newly built residences. 24 hour visiting and few regulations. First and final years offered on-campus accommodation. Wide range of subjects, main ones, education, geography, English, history, recreation and community and a developing postgraduate sector. SU active politically, socially and academically; runs shop, minibus, launderette, various machines and services and magazine. Over 40 clubs and societies. New and expanding sports centre on campus with swimming pool, 2 sports halls, gymnasium, squash courts, multi-gym, plus extensive sports ground; new full-sized astro-turf pitch being built. Good shopping in city, lots of hypermarkets for good bargains; plus theatres, cinemas, pubs and Arts Centre. Good relationship with admin and teaching staff. High proportion of mature students on some courses; high proportion of overseas students. Library open Saturday. Confidential counselling and welfare service.

Pauper notes

Accommodation: Good campus accommodation – halls and student village – off campus approved lodging system; or go private. **Drink:** Joint common rooms (JCR), bar; Lion and Lamb slightly more expensive, The George (off campus) best nearest pub – some students drive into town or Dartmoor. **Eats:** Average square meals are fairly reasonable. Other things are notoriously expensive eg fruits, yoghourt; good vegetarian at art centre. **Ents:** Very good campus entertainment, bands, films, discos etc – off campus, 3 main theatres, 2 cinemas, 1 alternative film centre – lots and lots of nightclubs. **Sports:** On campus very well catered for; leisure centre attached – student reductions given. **Hardship funds:** Access fund (government). **Travel:** A lot hitch from college to town (harder to do if vice-versa). Cheap fare because of competing bus companies. **Work:** Very limited on campus; bar staff and union staff vacancies – best to go in town in local pubs and shops.

More info?

Enquiries to Stephan Hawksworthy (0752 761125).

Informal name:

Marjon

Alumni (Editors' pick)

Cat Stevens, Peter Duncan, Ron Pickering.

CAN'T FIND WHAT YOU'RE LOOKING FOR? USE THE INDEX!

S MARTIN'S COLLEGE

S Martin's College of Higher Education, Lancaster LA1 3JD
(0524 63446) Map A, D5

Student enquiries: Academic Registrar

Main study areas – as in What to Study section: *(First degree):* Education, English, geography, history, nursing studies, professions allied to medicine (PAMs). *Also:* Social ethics, religious studies.

European Community: 10% first degree students take EC language as part of course and 5% spend 6 months or more in another EC country. Formal exchange links with University of Extremadura (Spain), open to non-language specialists. French, German and Spanish (for practical communication) available to all undergraduates.

Application: UCCA for 1993 start, UCAS thereafter. **Structural features:** Associate College of Lancaster University. **Academic features:** Degree courses in Christian ministry and in nursing studies with a nurse training specialism (RGN, RMN, RNMH). BA/BSc with QTS includes first subjects in art & design, biology, English, geography, history, maths, music and religious studies; wide range of second subjects. **Other features:** Centres for educational computing and for moral and social education resource. **Founded:** 1963, as C of E college of education. **Main awards:** BA, BSc, BA/BSc with QTS. **Awarding body:** Lancaster University. **Site:** Pleasant, single open campus 5 minutes from city centre. **Access:** InterCity rail (London-Glasgow) or motorway (M6); frequent local bus service. **Accommodation:** Most first years accommodated. 500+ places in halls, plus 92 places in city centre hall. Rent: 30% in accommodation where rent controlled by college. **Library:** 160,000 volumes, 550 periodicals, 160 study places. Wide range of non-book materials. Students can use Lancaster University library. **Other learning resources:** Computer laboratories, AVA resource centre and centres for teaching resources, primary education, reading and language, science resource, religious & moral education resource, art and ceramic studios, music recital and rehearsal rooms; plus individual departmental resource facilities. **Welfare:** Student welfare officer, doctor, resident nurse, chaplain, SU solicitor; chapel, medical centre, counselling service. **Careers:** Information and advice service on site. **Amenities:** Bookshop on campus, SU bar and social club; shop; new drama studio; separate Student Union building; chapel; medical centre. Good art, ceramic, music and drama facilities. **Sporting facilities:** Various sports pitches (including floodlit all-weather pitch), tennis and squash courts, gymnasia, multi-gym with equipment for aerobic exercise. **Employment:** Teaching, youth and community work. Nursing – general, psychiatric, mentally handicapped. Radiography and occupational therapy – NHS or private.

Duration of first degree course(s) or equivalent: 3 years (BA, BSc and accelerated BA with QTS); **Others:** 4 years (most BA/BSc with QTS & BA Nursing Studies); 2 years (accelerated BSc with QTS) **Total first degree students 1991/92:** 2,100 **BA/BSc with QTS students:** 650 **Mature students:** 200 **Male/female ratio:** 2:3 **Teaching staff: full-time:** 140 **part-time:** 35 **Total full-time students 1991/92:** 2,400 **Postgraduate students:** 300 **Tuition fees for 1992/93 (first degrees):** Home: £1,855 (classroom), £2,770 (lab/studio); Overseas: £5,320 (classroom), £7,055 (lab/studio). In addition first year students pay £340 validation fee.

What it's like

It's a C of E college, ¼ mile from Lancaster, with a very pleasant campus. Close links with the community and much involvement with local projects. Lancaster has the usual high street stores, pubs for all tastes, restaurants for all palates, a good range of theatre, music and films. Well situated for coastal and countryside activities. 75% of first years can live in one of six 'warm' halls (mixed, except one all female). Meals and daily cleaning included in hall fees. Each hall has irons, kettles etc for communal use. New hall of residence opened this year. Fully caters for 250 students, with its own laundry facility. Self-catering residence in town centre for 90 students.

Other campus facilities include medical centre, laundry, TV lounges, games room with pool table etc, coffee bar, book shop and general shop. Two bars for alcoholic and non-alcoholic drinks are linked with disco and ents.

SU Ents responsible for the weekly discos, quiz and games nights and visiting bands, also for major events like the 'Easter Ball', 'Freshers Ball', 'Christmas Cracker' and 'Going Down Ball'.

Active SU (affiliated to NUS) strives to meet student needs in all areas, eg welfare, entertainments, clubs and societies, magazine, needs of women and minority groups. Range of sports clubs and subject related societies; others include Community Action Group, Labour Club, Video/Film. Strong links with SCAN (Student Cancer Appeal Nationwide); many students participate in a variety of events associated with this. Access to university facilities, including library, sports centre, theatre, clubs and societies.

A place of opportunities where people can be themselves and participate in or initiate those activities which interest them.

Pauper notes

Accommodation: Well above average on campus. Provided for most first years if required. **Drink:** Social and JCR bars relatively cheap. Vast range of pubs in town. 3 coffee bars on campus open 10–4 weekdays. **Eats:** Refectory – full meals. Coffee bars have range of snack meals. Keen catering officer, vegetarian provision. **Ents:** Discos, local bands, films, society organised evenings. **Sports:** Adequate sports facilities plus new multi-gym. Easy access to university facilities and town sports centre. **Travel:** Trust funds and travel scholarships through the chaplaincy. **Work:** Social club, JCR discos, JCR bar, plus minibus shuttle service home from evening events.

More info?

Enquiries to SU President, Richard Boxford or SU Welfare Officer, Michelle Timperley (0524 65827).

Alumni (Editors' pick)

David Coates, Elizabeth Dent, Nicholas Rigby.

ST MARY'S COLLEGE

St Mary's College, Strawberry Hill, Twickenham TW1 4SX
(081 892 0051) Map D, A4

Student enquiries: The Registrar

Main study areas – as in What to Study section: *(First degree):* Biology, chemistry, drama, education, English, environmental science, geography, history, mathematical studies, religious studies and theology, sociology. **Also:** Classical studies, Irish studies, sports sciences.

European Community: No students learn an EC language or spend time in another EC country as part of their course. French, German, Greek and Italian taught as supplementary course. BA QTS students can exchange through Erasmus scheme.

Application: UCCA for 1993 start, UCAS thereafter. **Special features:** College of Surrey University. Voluntary College, Christian (RC) foundation. **Largest fields of study:** English, history, sports science, education. **Founded:** 1850, moved 1925 to present site. **Main awards:** BA, BSc, BAQTS. **Awarding body:** Surrey

University. **Site:** 18th century 'Gothic' house built by Horace Walpole in Strawberry Hill just outside Twickenham town centre. **Access:** Bus and British Rail (Strawberry Hill Station). **Accommodation:** 450 places on campus (segregated), accommodation officer helps with rooms locally. Approx cost: £1,687–£1,805 pa inclusive of 9 meals per week (term time only). **Library:** 150,000 volumes, 700 periodicals, 234 study places, reference copies of course books. **Other learning facilities:** TV studio, CCTV, computer centre, theatre, learning resources centre. **Welfare:** Medical centre, 1 nurse, visiting doctors; personal tutors, chaplain, wardens. **Careers:** Information and advice. **Amenities:** Campus bookshop, SU shop, bar, coffee lounge, refectory open to resident and non-resident students. **Sporting facilities:** Good sports facilities (gymnasium, dance studio, exercise physiology laboratory, sports hall, floodlit all-weather playing area).

Duration of first degree course(s) or equivalent: 3 years; **others:** 4 years **Total first degree students 1991/92:** 708; **Total BA (QTS):** 212 **Overseas students:** 40 **Mature students:** approx 200 **Male/female ratio:** 2:3 **Teaching staff: full-time:** 97 **part-time:** 13 **Total full-time students 1991/92:** 1,576 **Postgraduate students:** 146 **Tuition fees for 1992/93 (first degrees):** Home: £1,855 (classroom), £2,770 (lab/studio); Overseas: £4,870 (classroom), £5,780 (lab/studio). In addition, first year students pay £360 validation fee.

What it's like

Steeped in history and tradition, part of the college still consisting of the beautiful 18th-century mansion, St Mary's provides a classic setting for study with added advantage of being within half an hour's journey from central London. Spacious college grounds are 'home for a year' for vast majority of first years who choose to live in; all college accommodation no more than five minutes' walk to heart of campus. Halls of residence single sex, but opportunities abound for fruitful interactions between individuals, nowhere more so than at the thrice-weekly disco. Other SU events include Christmas and Going-Down balls and hugely popular bonfire night. Sporting facilities excellent. Movement studies, English and RS the most significant disciplines at St Mary's. Recent developments include introduction of Irish studies and environmental science.

Any attempt to define typical St Mary's student is bound to end in disappointment. They could be of British/Irish/Malaysian origin, and of any religious background, the Catholic tradition of the college being far from oppressive; they may or may not intend becoming a teacher and could be studying virtually any combination of subjects.

SU role is to ensure a fair deal for all St Mary's students as well as encouraging friendly atmosphere within college. External issues of particular interest to St Mary's students include Amnesty International and Friends of Birzeit (a West-Bank university).

St Mary's caters for students preferring the cosy ambience of a smaller college to larger, more anonymous institutions.

Pauper notes

Accommodation: Many students live in single-sex accommodation on campus; others in local area, housing is good value – £45 per week. **Drink:** St Mary's is famous for its ale appreciation. Atmospheric bar with animated drinking and tapes galore. **Eats:** Lots of ethnic, vegetarian, pizza, kebab shops galore. Local curry house 'Modern Tandoori' is famous for after-pub snacks. **Ents:** SU has mental discos, good live music and lazer raves. Good theatre in college. Party scene in college amazing. London is just around the corner with kicking nightclubs. **Sports:** Excellent facilities on campus (including a new health fitness research gym). **Hardship funds:** College access fund. Local banks give good overdrafts. **Work:** Loads of part-time work – shops etc.

More info?

Enquiries to Stuart Allen, President (081 892 0051).

WANT TO HELP WITH THE NEXT EDITION – SEE PAGE 76

Alumni (Editors' pick)

Robert Ackerman, Patricia Mordecai, Tom O'Connor, David Bedford, Rowena Roberts, Mick Melia (Eddie the landlord in 'EastEnders'), Robert Beck (Brookside C4), John Callander (President of Commonwealth Institute), Julian 'Corkey' Kelly (Irish reggae star), Geoffrey (from Rainbow).

ST MARY'S HOSPITAL

St Mary's Hospital Medical School, University of London, Paddington, London W2 1PG (071 723 1252) Map E, A2

Student enquiries: The Admissions Secretary

Main study areas – as in What to Study section: *(First degree):* Medicine.

European Community: No students learn an EC language or spend time in another EC country.

Application: UCCA for 1993 start, UCAS thereafter. **Structural features:** Part of Imperial College of Science, Technology and Medicine, London University. **Academic features:** Offers both pre-clinical and clinical studies and courses for intercalated BSc. Small number of clinical students admitted after pre-clinical studies at Oxford or Cambridge. **Founded:** 1854, becoming part of London University in 1900; merged with Imperial College 1988. **Main awards:** BSc, MBBS. **Awarding body:** London University. **Site:** Near Paddington station. **Access:** Paddington and Edgware Road underground stations. **Accommodation:** 240 places available in mixed hall. Approx cost: £41.50 pw (self-catering). Rent: 50% in accommodation where rent controlled by university. **Library:** 30,000 volumes, 245 periodicals, 168 study places, departmental libraries. **Welfare:** Student health service, university chaplains. **Hardship funds:** Limited endowed funds are available to assist students in financial distress. **Amenities:** SU bookshop (second-hand), nearby local bookshop specialising in medical textbooks. **Sporting facilities:** Excellent cricket, rugby, soccer and hockey at the sports ground in Teddington; swimming pool; 2 squash courts; multi-purpose recreation hall. Mountain hut in Snowdonia. Access to Imperial College and University of London union facilities, eg rowing and sailing. **Employment:** Postgraduate office assists graduate students to find first 2 house officer posts and offers advice on subsequent career development.

Duration of first degree course(s) or equivalent: 5 years; **others:** 6 years (with intercalated BSc) **Total first degree students 1991/92:** 574 **Overseas students:** 41 **Mature students:** 28 **Male/female ratio:** 6:5 **Teaching staff: full-time:** 73 **part-time:** 150 **Total full-time students 1991/92:** 627 **Postgraduate students:** 138 (inc 85 p-t) **Tuition fees for 1992/93 (first degrees):** Home: £755 (if no grant), £2,770 (pre-clinical), £4,985 (clinical); Overseas: £7,750 (pre-clinical), £12,990 (clinical).

What it's like

Founded in 1854. Course leads to degrees of Bachelor of Medicine and Bachelor of Surgery (MB.BS), also clinical medicine courses for students from Oxbridge. Many students encouraged to take an additional intercalated or clinical BSc course. 5 minutes' walk from Paddington, close to Hyde Park and central London attractions. Renowned for friendliness, one immediately feels welcome.

Pre-clinical teaching, lasting 2 years, on basis of lectures, practicals and tutorials studying basic medical sciences including anatomy (fun dissection classes), physiology, biochemistry and pharmacology. Course is intensive, a lot of work is expected. On the whole teaching is very good and most cope, sometimes organisation would help! Clinical teaching, lasting 3 years, is ward-based, it's up to the individual to gain the maximum from what is offered on your firm of medical staff.

SU very active, Nursing and Physiotherapy Schools are affiliated. Many facili-

CAN'T FIND WHAT YOU'RE LOOKING FOR? USE THE INDEX!

ties, including swimming pool, weights room and a sports ground at Teddington. Formidable sporting record in United Hospitals' competitions – especially in rugby, rowing and hockey. Music and drama has an impressive reputation. About 50 clubs and societies, for a diversity of activities, ensures never a dull moment. Clubs vary from rugby, waterpolo, rifle shooting, rowing to music, photography, aerobics, wine tasting, mountaineering. Community at St Mary's is small, comprises students, doctors, nurses, physiotherapists and staff involved in research. Now the fourth constituent college of Imperial College of Science, Technology and Medicine, this community is unlikely to change and will keep its identity as always.

Pauper notes

Accommodation: Guaranteed for first year students. First class hall – Wilson House – reasonable cost, first years and clinicals. **Drink:** Mainly SU bar, 'The Heron', 'The Exchange', 'Monkey Puzzle', 'Crockers', 'The Flem'. **Eats:** Hospital canteen, Micky's, Just-a-Bite, Paddington Tandoori, Toula's, Wong Kei – Chinese, Paradise – Indian, McDonald's, Wimpy etc. **Ents:** Film Soc, fringe and pub theatres, West End etc, discos and Balls in Med School, Band nites featuring Mary's All Stars and small outside bands. Reduced rates into ents in London and SU run ents, eg Freshers Week, Balls, discos. Sky TV in Wilson House. **Sports:** Swimming pool, squash courts, sports hall and sports ground. **Hardship funds:** Scholarships only for matures. Hardship (access) fund. Local banks very helpful. **Travel:** Numerous SU elective scholarships. **Work:** Not advised as too much study and playing to do! Some work in SU bar, SU shop and in local area. Also clinical trials (a bit dodgy) and auxiliary nursing.

More info?

Get students' Alternative Prospectus.
Enquiries to SU President (Marc Swan) or SU Secretary (Cath Ashworth) (071 723 1251 ext 5196).

Informal name:

Mary's.

Buzz-words:

WHIPS (lager/beer).

Alumni (Editors' pick)

J P R Williams, Sir Roger Bannister, Sir Almroth Wright, Sir Alexander Fleming, Sir Rodney Porter.

SALFORD COLLEGE

University College Salford, Frederick Road, Salford M6 6PU
(061 736 6541) Map A, D6

Student enquiries: Central Admissions Unit

Main study areas – as in What to Study section: *(First degree):* Art and design, business studies, chemistry, communication studies, computing, drama and theatre arts, electrical and electronic engineering, hotel and catering management, mechanical and production engineering, music, professions allied to medicine (PAMs), social policy and social welfare. *Also:* Audio and video systems, band musicianship, popular music recording, prosthetics and orthotics.

European Community: 25% first degree students take EC language as part of course and 10% spend 6 months or more in another EC country. Formal exchange links with 3 EC universities/colleges in Clemont-Ferrand (France), Kiel (Germany) and Barcelona (Spain); all open to non-language specialists. Erasmus exchange programmes for business, engineering and performing arts students.

Application: PCAS for 1993 start, UCAS thereafter. **Academic features:** Broad range of teaching methods; all courses vocationally oriented with work placement projects. New degree courses in TV and radio, pop music and recording. **Structural features:** Federal partnership with Salford University, allowing students to share most facilities on both campuses. **Special features:** Visiting professor: David Plowright (ex Granada TV); professional patrons include George Martin (Beatles producer), Brian Redhead (BBC) and Jack Rosenthal (TV). **Largest field of study:** Health studies, performing arts and media studies. **Founded:** 1896; previously (1961–1991) Salford College of Technology. **Main awards:** BA, BSc, BEng. **Awarding body:** Salford University. **Site:** Main site at Frederick Road; other sites at Adelphi (performing arts and media) and Irwell campus (art and industrial design). **Access:** Good access from A6; Salford Crescent railway station 300m away; excellent bus service from Manchester city centre, 10 mins away. **Accommodation:** 800 places in halls of residence; private student houses sublet by college throughout Salford. **Approx cost:** £30–£35 pw, plus fuel and meals. **Library:** 54,000 books, 714 periodicals, 375 study places. Specialist collections; HMSO, British Standards, specialist music collections. **Other learning facilities:** Language labs, IT/computer suite, CD Rom facility, commercial student restaurant (recommended in Which Good Food Guide). **Careers:** Information and advice service; placement service on sandwich courses. **Employment:** Business and management, paramedical, design and media industries. **Welfare:** Chaplaincy, legal and welfare advisers, nurses, accommodation service, overseas student welfare officer. **Special facilities:** Nursery provision (children aged 2–4, weekdays in term time). **Hardship funds:** Access funds for full-time students in case of financial hardship. **Amenities:** Students encouraged to set up and run clubs and societies. **Sporting facilities:** Indoor sports/aerobics hall.

Duration of first degree course (or equivalent): 3 or 4 years. **Total first degree students 1991/92:** 807 **BEd students** 0 **Overseas students:** 29 **Mature students:** 40% **Male/female ratio:** 1:1 **Teaching staff: (full and part-time):** 66 **Total full-time students 1991/92:** 2,440 **Postgraduate students:** 20 **Tuition fees for 1992/93 (first degree):** Home: £1,855 (classroom), £2,770 (lab/studio); Overseas: £4,850.

Alumni (Editors' pick)

John Cooper Clarke (poet), Albert Finney, Bill Beaumont, Paul Fryer, Paula Dunne, Peter Williams, C S Lowry.

SALFORD UNIVERSITY

University of Salford, Salford, Greater Manchester M5 4WT
(061 9745 5000) Map A, D6

Student enquiries: Registrar

Main study areas – as in What to Study section: (*First degree):* Accountancy, aeronautical engineering, biochemistry, biology, business studies, chemistry, civil engineering, computing, economics, electrical & electronic engineering, English, environmental science, environmental studies, geography, history, information technology, mathematical studies, mechanical and production engineering, metallurgy and materials science, modern languages, physics, politics and government, sociology. *Also:* Arabic, biomedical electronics, construction engineering, interpretation and translation, quantity surveying.

European Community: All students have the chance to study an EC language outside their degree; most departments offer the opportunity to take a language within a degree and to spend six months to one year working/studying abroad. Opportunities exist in Belgium, Denmark, Eire, France, Germany, Greece, Italy, Netherlands, Portugal and Spain. Erasmus/Lingua exchange links with some thirty EC universities/colleges.

Application: UCCA for 1993 start, UCAS thereafter. **Academic features:** Applicants with arts or science backgrounds accepted on BEng in construction management, BSc in information technology. New 4-year degree programmes run jointly by university and local colleges of technology; students spend 2 years at college then, if suitable, complete degree at university in a further 2 years (1 year plus 3 years for technological physics course). Over 40% of students take integrated courses which include industrial or professional training. Most degree programmes include 'student capability schemes' designed to improve skills in teamwork, verbal and written communication and presentation. **Special features:** Integrated chairs where professors work part-time in university and part-time in senior positions in their company: aeronautical and mechanical engineering (British Aerospace and Danichi-Sykes); chemistry and applied chemistry (Unilever); physics (British Nuclear Fuels); transport management (British Rail); information technology (British Telecom). **Founded:** Granted Royal charter in 1967. **Main awards:** BA, BSc, BEng, MEng. **Awarding body:** Salford University. **Site:** 34-acre campus a mile from Salford town centre, 2 miles from Manchester city centre. **Access:** Motorway links, buses and trains from Manchester. Main line railway station on campus. Manchester International airport in easy reach. **Accommodation:** 540 places in halls; 2,400 self-catering flats; 100 lodgings; 800 flats/bedsitters houses (all single first year students who apply for accommodation by 8th September provided with accommodation and one further year guaranteed in university controlled accommodation). Approx cost: £43 pw halls, £23 pw student houses, £50 pw lodgings. 80% in accommodation where rent controlled by university. **Library:** 300,000 volumes in total, 2,000 periodicals, 750 study places, reference collection of recommended student texts. **Welfare:** Health centre, psychotherapist, 3 professional welfare officers, overseas students' adviser. **Hardship funds:** Hardship loan scheme operates. **Special categories:** Some residential facilities for married and disabled students. **Careers:** Information (excellent library of employers' material, videos and reference books), advice and placement through 'milk round'. **Amenities:** Restaurants, snackbars, bookshop, union shop and bank on campus; SU building with bar, insurance and travel bureaux; nursery provision; Salford City Art Gallery and Lowry Collection near campus. **Sporting facilities:** Sports hall with 6 squash courts, fitness room, badminton etc. Outdoor playing fields at student village. **Employment:** Industry, commerce and public service.

Duration of first degree course(s) or equivalent: 3 years; **others:** 4 years (integrated) **Total first degree students 1991/92:** 3,677 **Overseas students:** 395 **Male/female ratio:** 7:3 **Teaching staff: full-time:** 368 **part-time:** 65 **Total full-time students 1991/92:** 5,029 **Postgraduate students:** 1,352 **Tuition fees for 1992/93 (first degrees):** Home: £1,855 (classroom), £2,770 (lab); Overseas: £5,320 (classroom), £7,055 (lab).

What it's like

Green, single modern campus, closer to the centre of Manchester than Manchester University's campus, and within two miles of all the university accommodation. Accommodation guaranteed for first year, 65% of students in university accommodation. *No* first years in crash accommodation at the start of 1992/1993 session.

The University is thriving, independent with a colourful history and strong links with industry. Many courses have industrial sandwich years (home and abroad). Specialising in engineering, modern languages, technology and sociology, graduates have a fine employment record, among the best in the country, mainly into industry. Arts and social science is growing rapidly.

SU has a student advice centre with three members of staff and four student officers who can help with any problem at all: financial, legal, accommodation, visas, personal or academic; it also provides a legal adviser, overseas counsellor, student counsellor and various health campaigns, e.g. AIDS awareness, safe sex, womens' health etc. Union runs campus shop, launderette, hairdressers, opticians and provides print shop; also produces monthly magazine, SCALP and weekly newsletter Profile.

SU very active (but not political) with emphasis on clubs, societies, entertainments and other student services. More than 90 different clubs or societies. Massive participation in outdoor pursuits. Very active community services section – includes Christmas parties for senior citizens, children; English lessons for partners of overseas students; work with ex-offenders; work with the disabled. Sports policy is to provide for as many as possible, then to achieve excellence.

Over 20% of students from overseas – contribute greatly to university life. Students from all over the globe come to Salford to study. SU overseas secretary gives advice and organises a Welcome Week and various international events. Over 15 different overseas societies.

Salford is a small, but very friendly university. People enjoy themselves.

Pauper notes

Accommodation: Over 3,500 rooms in university accommodation; some married quarters. List of accommodation in private sector (which is cheap in this part of Manchester) and housing advice from SU. **Drink:** 3 main bars, 2 smaller lounges – 1 pub. Late bar till 2.00am three nights a week at The Pavilion, where 2,000 students live – cheaper than local pubs – Theakston's, McEwan's, Tennent's, Tetley – lots of promotion nights. Local pubs a bit rough. **Eats:** 'The Cage' at the Pavilion – run by the union – open every night – range of cheap meals. Lots of takeaways and restaurants in Manchester. **Ents:** SU Thurs/Sat superb video disco at Village – often have live bands, theme nights (beach party, toga party, 60s and 70s nights) plus specialised discos (Indie/House etc.) many top current and classic films. Free special evenings on Tuesdays with cabaret/competitions, music etc. In town: Manchester excellent for cheap student nightlife – lots of cheap cinemas, concerts, theatres and nightclubs and loads of students. (Over 50,000 in Greater Manchester). Union provides free coaches back to student residences after all late night events and all through Freshers' Fortnight. **Sports:** Union runs leisure centre – weights room, sports hall, fitness centre, snooker room, sunbed, sports shop, video library, squash courts, outdoor play area, all very cheap. Good facilities. **Hardship funds:** Some interest-free loans from university. **Travel:** Union travel bureau on campus, offers all possibilities especially cheap air travel/train and coach. Open 9–4.30 Mon.–Fri. **Work:** Union on ents. team – selling tickets etc. and work at concerts. Bar work and library work.

More info?

Get students' Alternative Prospectus.
Enquiries to Alex Buss (061 736 7811).

Alumni (Editors' pick)

John Howard, Ieuan Evans, Sarah Greene.

SANDHURST

Royal Military Academy Sandhurst, Camberley, Surrey GU15 4PQ (0276 63344) Map A, F8

Student enquiries: (Officers' Enquiries) Careers for Army Officers, Ministry of Defence (DAR1d), Empress State Building, Lillie Road, London SW6 1TR.

Main study areas – as in What to Study section: Strategic studies.

European Community: Most students spend time in another EC country.

CAN'T FIND WHAT YOU'RE LOOKING FOR? USE THE INDEX!

Special features: All British army officers, male and female, graduate and non-graduate, are trained at Sandhurst. All entrants join 44 week commissioning course. All officers under training hold officer cadet status, excepting those awarded a university cadetship who hold the rank of second lieutenant. After commissioning, officers usually attend specialist courses before starting a period of regimental duty. Students are organised into platoons and companies. **Academic features:** Courses are designed to teach basic military skills and develop qualities of leadership. Distinguished civilian academic staff in addition to serving officers. **Founded:** 1802 as Royal Military College, Sandhurst. Womens Royal Army Corps College incorporated in 1984. **Accommodation:** Provided for 100% students. **Library:** 100,000 books, 350 periodicals. **Specialist collection:** Military history. **Other learning resources:** Audio-visual equipment; closed circuit TV recording and playback studios. **Sporting facilities:** Squash, badminton and rackets courts; playing fields; indoor swimming pool; gymnasium; physical and recreational training; adventurous training pursuits; rowing and sailing (own canoes, dinghies and sailing boats); facilities for golf, boxing, field sports; many 'indoor' clubs, parachuting, caving and climbing, fencing, judo and horse-riding.

Total students 1991/92: 1,000 approx of which 500 are graduate entrants **Male/female ratio:** 9:1 **Staff:** 108 military; 35 civilian; **Total full-time students:** 700 **Number of postgraduate students:** 360.

What it's like

It is set in one of the most beautiful estates in the south of England. A young officer who recently 'survived' the course had this to say about his experience: 'Sandhurst dismantles you bit by bit, kicks you around for a couple of weeks, and then reassembles you in slightly more soldierlike fashion. It then goes on to teach you a great deal. In retrospect, of course, it was tremendous fun and very hard, in that you can experience frustrations as well as enjoyment and real satisfaction.'

Sandhurst is not for the faint-hearted.

You will almost certainly become fitter than at any previous time of your life through physical pursuits like military exercises and adventurous training exercises. The 'physical' is, however, counter-balanced by study. You will learn about military history, organisation and military tactics, and comment intelligently on world events. You will become proficient in handling weapons and cross country navigation – as well as learning how to behave as an officer. 'Behave like an officer' has been made fun of in countless films, cartoons and comedy sketches. In reality it means that you will be courteous and caring.

If you successfully negotiate Sandhurst and gain your commission you will then go on a 'Special to Arm' course with the Regiment or Corps of your choice. The length of this course will depend on which branch of the Army you have chosen to join. It is designed to give you a general appreciation of your Regiment or Corps, and the specialist knowledge you will need before taking your first command.

Alumni (Editors' pick)

Winston Churchill, General Haig, General Montgomery, King Hussein of Jordan, David Niven.

SCHOOL OF PHARMACY

The School of Pharmacy, University of London,
29/39 Brunswick Square, London WC1N 1AX (071 837 7651/8)
Map E, C1

Student enquiries: The Registrar

Main study areas – as in What to Study section: *(First degree):* Pharmacology, pharmacy. *Also:* Toxicology.

European Community: No students learn an EC language. European exchanges have taken place with German and Italian students. More planned.

Application: UCCA for 1993 start, UCAS thereafter. **Structural features:** Part of London University. **Special features:** 3-year BPharm degree course designed to teach to honours level while equipping student vocationally for pharmaceutical profession; 4-year BSc course in toxicology and pharmacology includes 1 year industrial experience. **Founded:** 1842, instituted in 1925. **Main awards:** BPharm, BSc. **Awarding body:** London University. **Site:** Central London (between Southampton Row and Grays Inn Road). **Access:** Russell Square underground station. **Accommodation:** School is near several intercollegiate halls. Advice on other accommodation from university accommodation office. Rent: 70% undergraduates (other than those living at home) in accommodation where rent controlled by university. **Library:** 26,000 volumes, 200 periodicals, 74 study places; recommended books in reserve collection. **Other learning facilities:** Computer centre. **Welfare:** London University health service. **Careers:** Information, advice and placement. **Amenities:** SU with shop and second-hand book service, ULU nearby; also British Museum etc. **Employment:** Pharmacists in general practice, hospitals and industrial organisations; toxicologists in industrial and government laboratories, or with environmental, regulatory and law enforcement authorities.

Duration of first degree course(s) or equivalent: 3 years (BPharm) and 4 years (BScTox) **Total first degree students 1991/92:** 356 **Overseas students:** 35 **Mature students:** 16 **Male/female ratio:** 9:11 **Teaching staff: full-time:** 47 **part-time:** 4 **Total full-time students 1991/92:** 455 **Postgraduate students:** (78 f-t 84 p-t) **Tuition fees for 1992/93 (first degrees):** Home: £2,700; Overseas: £7,055

What it's like

Its academic excellence is respected throughout the world. Just as importantly it is a very friendly college so virtually everyone knows everyone else by the end of first year. All staff internal and on hand if students experience any work problems.

Social functions very popular with both internal and external students, which enables one to meet people from other institutions. SU apolitical, very active socially, and in looking after its own members' interests. Main events: annual ball, garden party, bonfire party, Christmas panto and party and, of course, the best freshers and rag weeks in the country.

The Ball is always held at a prestigious location (eg. Hyde Park Hotel). The garden party and bonfire party are held at the school's sports ground which is shared with the Royal Free Hospital at Myddleton House and are always superb fun. The Christmas panto and party produce many a laugh both for students and lecturers alike.

Rag week highlight of the second term; usual charity is Great Ormond Street Children's Hospital. A few of the functions include a bed push down Oxford Street and a three-legged pub crawl.

Regular Friday night 'Bop-till-u-Drop' disco, renowned throughout London University for its atmosphere, held in student common room which has its own cheap bar, pool table, table-tennis table etc.

Many clubs and societies within the union: football, hockey, rugby, film, Islamic, Afro-Caribbean, netball, Indian, Chinese, Jewish, Christian Union and Welsh.

Successful sporty teams and the highlight of the year is when everyone travels to the BPSA sports weekend.

All societies hold their own functions in each term, such as meals, pub crawls and even trips to places such as Paris and Alton Towers! Besides having our own societies we are also affiliated to ULU which offers many other varied activities.

Students have a happy and enjoyable time whilst in London, making lifelong friends within their colleges and with students from other faculties as well. Being at 'The Square' is like being part of one big family where everyone helps out, so all can have three years of untroubled education and a varied and happy social life.

CAN'T FIND WHAT YOU'RE LOOKING FOR? USE THE INDEX!

Pauper notes

Accommodation: 6 intercollegiate halls within 5 mins walk; most 2nd and some 3rd years live out. **Drink:** Bar very cheap and cheerful. ULU bar near as well as numerous good pubs. **Eats:** Good quality cheap refectory in college – many restaurants within 5 mins walk (Chinese, Indian, Greek, Italian, hamburgers etc). **Ents:** Crowded, noisy, lively, discos every Friday night. Numerous other events including pantomime, rag week, midsessional ball etc. **Sports:** At college there are football, netball, rugby, hockey; ULU nearby with multitude of societies and sports facilities. **Hardship funds:** None available. **Travel:** No cheap fares. **Work:** Jobs in pharmacy during vacations, but not much time otherwise for work during term due to intensive nature of course.

Informal name:

SOP or The Square.

SCOTTISH AGRICULTURAL COLLEGE

Scottish Agricultural College, Auchincruive, Ayr, Scotland KA6 5HW (0292 520331) Map A, C3

Student enquiries: Academic Registrar

Main study areas – as in What to Study section: *(First degree):* Agriculture, horticulture and forestry, biotechnology, environmental studies. *Also:* Aquaculture.

European Community: Under 10% first degree students take EC language as part of course (while at Strathclyde University); majority of BTechnology students spend 6 months or more in another EC country, a few others. Many formal links with EC universities/colleges but not for exchanges.

Application: UCCA for 1993 start, UCAS thereafter or direct. **Academic features:** Emphasis on student-centred learning in small groups; communication, numeracy and business/computing literacy emphasised. Links with Glasgow, Strathclyde, Edinburgh, Napier and Aberdeen universities. **Largest field of study:** Food, land and the environment. **Founded:** 1990, ex North of Scotland, West of Scotland and East of Scotland Agricultural Colleges, founded circa 1900. **Main awards:** BSc, BTechnology. **Awarding bodies:** Aberdeen University, Glasgow University. **Site:** 3 campuses at Aberdeen, Edinburgh (both urban, on university campuses) and Auchincruive (rural, 3 miles from Ayr). **Access:** Rail, road and air links at each centre. **Accommodation:** 120 places on-site at Auchincruive and halls of residence. Approx cost: £49 half board. 20% students in accommodation where college controls rent. Flats, farm cottages etc nearby, variable cost. **Library:** 45,000 books, 500 periodicals, 200 study places. **Other learning facilities:** Laboratories, poultry farm, several farms, 2 countryside interpretation centres, food processing plant, glasshouse units, aboretum. **Careers:** Information and advice service. **Employment:** Land-based industries – management, education, research. **Welfare:** Student services manager, doctors, welfare officers at each site. **Hardship funds:** Access funds; local trusts, usually with residential qualifications. **Amenities:** Range of clubs and societies at each centre; use of all university facilities. **Sporting facilities:** Full range of sports facilities plus access to golf courses, water sports, hill-walking and climbing.

Duration of first degree course (or equivalent): Standard: 4 years; other: 3 years **Total first degree students 1991/92:** 183 **Overseas students:** 5% **Mature students:** 5% **Male/female ratio:** 4:1 **Teaching staff:** full-time: 90 **Total full-time students 1991/92:** 1,150 **Postgraduate students:** 105 **Tuition fees for 1992/93** (first degrees): Home: £2,770 (£755 if no grant). Overseas: £7,055.

What it's like

There's still an agriculture base to the college but it's fast disappearing into horticulture, leisure management, poultry and other obscurities. Numerous opportunities to learn almost any subject with a more profitable conclusion.

College area small so you can reach most of the departments on foot with ease. Roads are lit by night for those who get lost in the trees. There are good facilities for the keen students among us: between 16 and 30 computers and printers are available depending on the day of the week, and at weekends. The library has a good but somewhat limited selection of books etc. For leisure management students there is a dire lack of information partly due to the fact that the course is only in its second year.

Sense of humour vital for preservation of student/student and student/lecturer relations. Most of the lecturers meet this requirement.

Sport is one of the busiest pastimes. A ruthless rugby team, a formidable football team and an extremely dangerous hockey team consisting of ladies and a few brave gentlemen. The sports hall provides: football, basketball, volleyball, badminton and a modern multi-gym. In the metropolis of Ayr there is 10-pin bowling, several martial arts clubs, fencing, archery, Ayr rugby club not to mention heaps of watering holes and a host of night clubs.

College food has improved. Accommodation is available for the select few in Wilson Hall. Numerous B&Bs nearby if you don't get a place. Good washing facilities for people and clothes in halls. Four telephones in the halls, two in the bar and one in the main building.

SU active. Creche available. A number of overseas students from Europe, Africa, Canada, etc.

Student bar magnet for all so if you're hard up and looking for a dance with a pretty milk maid it's the place to be. Most take advantage of the cheap booze to the full and some find it hard to leave.

Pauper notes

Accommodation: Nothing cheap. **Drink:** Student bar. **Eats:** College food; refectory sells vegetarian lunch and tea. **Ents:** College disco and dances; cinema in Ayr. **Sports:** Swimming pool in Ayr; numerous sports on and off campus. **Hardship funds:** Access funds. **Travel:** Bus, ferry, train discounts. **Work:** Nothing substantial.

Alumni (Editors' pick)

'Doddy' Weir – Scottish rugby international.

SCOTTISH COLLEGE OF TEXTILES

The Scottish College of Textiles, Galashiels, Selkirkshire TD1 3HF (0896 3351) Map A, D3

Student enquiries: Admissions Office

Main study areas – as in What to Study section: *(First degree):* Art & design, business studies, chemistry, computing, information technology. *Also:* Clothing technology, textile technology.

European Community: No students learn an EC language at present; language options due to be introduced. 10% spend 6 months in another EC country as part of their course.

Application: UCCA for 1993 start, UCAS thereafter. **Structural features:** Faculty of Heriot-Watt University. **Academic features:** Degree courses include manufacturing computing (textiles), quality management, industrial design (textiles); colour chemistry; textiles with marketing clothing (technology, marketing, management and product design). **Largest fields of study:** Textile design, clothing

CAN'T FIND WHAT YOU'RE LOOKING FOR? USE THE INDEX!

studies. **Founded:** 1883; joined Heriot-Watt University 1990. **Main awards:** BA, BSc. **Awarding body:** Heriot-Watt University (and Clothing Institute, Textile Institute, Clothing and Footwear Institute). **Site:** Outskirts of Galashiels. **Access:** Bus from Edinburgh (34 miles). **Accommodation:** 130 places in mixed halls. Approx cost: £1,050 pa (self-catering) £1,510 pa (bed & breakfast and evening meal). Rent: 70% in accommodation where rent controlled by college. 72 places in flats on campus, 230 places in flats off-campus. Approx cost £950 pa self-catering. All first year students accommodated in halls. **Library:** 18,000 volumes, 420 periodicals, 90 study places. **Specialist collections:** Fabric samples and shawls. **Other learning facilities:** Outstanding handloom weaving workshop, extensive studios, textile and clothing workshops, IBM 4331 computer, micro-computing lab, computer-aided textile design centre. **Centres of excellence:** Textile design and technology, clothing studies. **Welfare:** Welfare centre with careers' officer and students' counsellor; college chaplaincy; other services with local practitioners. **Hardship funds:** Small trust fund. **Careers:** Information and advice. **Amenities:** College bookshop, student/staff social club. **Sporting facilities:** Wide range of sports. **Employment:** Textile and clothing design, retail management, technology and merchandising; management, marketing, information technology, computer programming.

Duration of first degree course(s) or equivalent: 4 years **Total first degree students 1991/92:** 418 **Overseas students:** 13 **Mature students:** 28 **Male/female ratio:** 1:4 **Teaching staff: full-time:** 52 **part-time:** 14 **Total full-time students 1991/92:** 767 **Postgraduate students:** 39 **Tuition fees for 1992/93** (first degrees): Home: £1,855 (quality management), £2,770 (other degrees); Overseas: £5,420 (quality management), £6,288 (other degrees).

What it's like

It's modern, purpose-built, on outskirts of Galashiels, a small country town, 33 miles (and 1½ hours by bus) south east of Edinburgh. Excellent facilities for study and recreation with specially designed laboratories and design studios. It is now the Faculty of Technology of Heriot-Watt University. Very well equipped textile technology and colour chemistry departments. Specialist rooms for behavioural science, personnel management, work study; language laboratories and computer suite in management department. Design and technology departments have vast hand weaving shed, complemented by extensive modern high-speed weaving and knitting looms allowing students first-hand experience of designing commercial fabrics. Pleasant library, lecture theatre, recreation hall, refectory, licensed club room. Halls of residence on hillside near college unsegregated with full board facilities. Students may have visitors of either sex on Friday and Saturday evenings. Plenty of student flats in Galashiels, but increased student numbers making them more difficult to get. High ratio of women to men. Aims of SRC: adequate facilities within college, and welfare, social and cultural facilities. Social and sporting links kept with Heriot-Watt; inter-site visits by bus and mini-bus. Usual sports and activities including football, rugby, hockey, camera, squash, badminton, tennis, pool. Student body international – includes Americans, Irish, Germans, Swiss, Indians and Pakistanis. Regular dances/discos and annual charities week. Employment prospects for SCOT graduates in textile industry excellent. Most courses now industrially orientated with industrial placement in 2 BSc and clothing courses.

Pauper notes

Accommodation: Halls. Many prefer flats but increasingly difficult. **Drink:** Student/staff club – cheap, good beer/food – Belhaven beers. **Eats:** Halls and refectory food cheap with a good choice. Hall dining room open to non-resident students at cost of £2.00 per meal. **Ents:** Regular discos/band in club, regular visits to Heriot-Watt University for social events. **Sports:** Badminton, aerobics, 5-aside football etc in college sports hall. Local swimming pool. Active football/ Rugby teams. **Hardship funds:** Difficult to get from college. **Travel:** Student fares on buses. Special bus to Edinburgh leaving college car park 4.00pm Fridays (no stops). **Work:** Local bars and clubs. Student/staff club also uses students.

More info?
Enquiries to Clive Gillanders (0896 51869).

Informal name:
SCOT.

Alumni (Editors' pick)
Sir Russell Fairgrieve MP, Lord R Sanderson of Bowden, Sir Alan Smith.

SHEFFIELD HALLAM UNIVERSITY

Sheffield Hallam University, Pond Street, Sheffield S1 1WB (0742 720911); Telex 54680 SHPOLY G; Fax 532096 Map A, E6

Student enquiries: Student administration

Main study areas – as in What to Study section: *(First degree):* Accountancy, agriculture, horticulture and forestry, art & design, business studies, chemistry, civil engineering, communication studies, computing, education, electrical & electronic engineering, English, environmental studies, European studies, fine arts, food science & nutrition, geography, geology, history, hotel & catering management, information technology, law, mathematical studies, mechanical and production engineering, metallurgy and materials science, modern languages, nursing, physics, politics & government, professions allied to medicine (PAMs), psychology, public administration, social policy and social welfare, town and country planning. *Also:* Biomedical technology, construction design, film and media studies, recreation management, surveying, tourism, women's studies.

European Community: 5% first degree students take EC language as part of course and 3% spend 6 months or more in another EC country. All students have the option of learning an EC language. Possible to spend time in another EC country on some courses; by 1995, all students will be able to do so. Approved Erasmus programme 1992/93. Formal exchange links with a number of EC universities/colleges.

Application: PCAS for 1993 start, UCAS thereafter; except art and design ADAR. **Academic features:** Emphasis on applied and vocational courses; high proportion of sandwich courses. Access and credit accumulation and transfer schemes in operation. **Largest fields of study:** Technology, business and management, education, health and welfare, environmental and cultural subjects. **Founded:** 1992, as a university; previously Sheffield Poly, founded 1969 ex colleges of technology, art and 3 colleges of education. **Main awards:** BA, BEd, BEng, MEng, BSc. **Awarding body:** Sheffield Hallam University. **Site:** 5 sites in or near Sheffield city centre. **Access:** City centre site, opposite central rail and bus stations. Good public transport and free internal inter-site transport available. **Accommodation:** 2,500 places; majority in self-catering rooms; priority given to first year students. Extensive register of student flats/bedsits/lodgings. Approx cost: Student residences: £25 pw (shared rooms, no meals) to £65 (single room, fully catered). Self-catered, private sector: £25–£40 per week per person. **Library:** 1 library on each site; 500,000 volumes in total, 2,200 periodicals; multi-site catalogue on microfiche. 1,370 study places. Extensive short loan and reference collection. **Specialist collections:** European documentation, antique books, audio-visual statistical data, government publications, British Standards, EEC papers. **Other learning facilities:** TV and media resources centres. Microcomputing and over 250 terminals to mainframe throughout university. **Welfare:** 3 doctors, FPA, solicitor, 3 chaplains, 2 counsellors. **Special categories:** Day nursery (1 to 5 year olds). **Careers:** Information, advice and placement. Also sandwich training placement support. **Amenities:** Purpose-built SU in town centre; union facilities on each site; theatre, film studios, national exhibitions. Close to open countryside and Peak District National Park. **Sporting facilities:** Excellent sporting resources: tennis courts, hockey pitches and running tracks, Alan Rouse Climbing Wall. Sheffield hosted World Student Games in 1991, so enormous sports complexes available. **Employment:** Due to comparatively high number of applied/vocational courses, good employment prospects.

Duration of first degree course(s) or equivalent: 3 full-time, 4 years sandwich, up to 5 years part-time **Total first degree students 1991/92:** 11,700 **BEd students:** 1,200 **Overseas students:** 300 **Mature students:** 4,700 **Male/female ratio:** 3:2 **Teaching staff: full-time:** 847 **part-time:** 104 **Total full-time students + sandwich 1991/92:** 12,400 **Postgraduate students:** 380 **Tuition fees for 1992/93** (first degrees): Home: £1,855 (classroom), £2,770 (lab/studio); Overseas: £4,800 (classroom), £5,700 (lab/studio).

What it's like

Sheffield to many people means knives and forks; still being made, but not so much now. New air of prosperity to the city. Millions of pounds of development in the city centre and the lower Don Valley. Industrial city; more than compensated by its greenness, the Peaks and the Dales are a short drive away. Sheffield has nightclubs and pubs galore – the famous Sheffield One that has to be sampled to be believed. Clubs, pubs and plenty of curries and kebab places, as well as the ubiquitous chippie. There are cultural delights too – the Crucible Theatre does not exist solely for the snooker tournament! Five cinemas as well as multiplex cinema, Crystal Peaks outside the city.

By the way, Sheffield is built on seven hills, like Rome.

Pauper notes

Accommodation: Lack of private accommodation as student numbers increase. **Drink:** Union bars cheapest bitter/lager; Yorkshire Grey – a must. **Eats:** Curry. **Ents:** Student nights in most discos, SU discos on sites every week, Saturday night poly 'Sheffield 1' disco. **Sports:** Most sports on sites, clubs etc well funded by union. **Hardship funds:** Access funds. **Travel:** Sheffield Union Travel Shop; near to M1, good for hitching. **Work:** Mainly in pubs in evening.

Alumni (Editors' pick)

Bruce Oldfield, David Mellor.

SHEFFIELD POLY

See Sheffield Hallam University

SHEFFIELD UNIVERSITY

University of Sheffield, Western Bank, Sheffield S10 2TN
(0742 768555) Map A, E6

Student enquiries: Undergraduate Admissions Office

Main study areas – as in What to Study section: *(First degree):* Accountancy, American studies, anatomy, archaeology, architecture, art & design, Asian studies, biochemistry, biology, biotechnology, botany, business studies, chemical engineering, chemistry, civil engineering, computing, dentistry, economics, electrical & electronic engineering, English, environmental science, environmental studies, geography, history, information technology, law, linguistics, mathematical studies, mechanical and production engineering, medicine, metallurgy and materials science, microbiology, modern languages, music, pharmacology, philosophy, physics, physiology, politics and government, professions allied to medicine (PAMs), psychology, social policy and social welfare, sociology, speech sciences, town & country planning, zoology. *Also:* Catalan, cancer studies, criminology, ecology, genetics, Japanese, Korean, landscape, medical biochemistry, medieval studies, Slavonic studies, software and systems engineering, urban studies.

European Community: 5% first degree students take EC language as part of course and 2% spend 6 months or more in another EC country. Formal exchange links with 19 EC universities/colleges: Denmark (2); France (7); Germany (4); Portugal (2); Spain (4); plus Erasmus links across the EC with a number of departments. Increase in language options in all disciplines. New courses in mechanical engineering and computer science both with an EC language. Developing joint qualifications with EC partners. Approved Erasmus programme 1992/93.

Application: UCCA for 1993 start, UCAS thereafter. **Academic features:** New courses in biomedical science; Catalan; chemistry with industrial studies and with European studies; criminology, Korean, molecular biology, neuroscience. **Founded:** University Charter in 1905; previously three constituent colleges (founded 1828, 1879 and 1884), then University College 1897–1905. **Main awards:** BA, BMus, BSc, MBChB, BDS, BMedSci, LLB, BEng, BScTech, MEng. **Accommodation:** 2,552 places in halls. Approx cost: £50 pw (includes 2 meals per day in hall and full board at weekends). Another 1,830 places in university flats. Approx cost: up to £35 pw. All single first year students from outside Sheffield accommodated if they wish. Rent: 4,400 students housed in accommodation where rent charged is under the control of the university. **Library:** Major branch network and most departments have their own (duplicate) libraries; 950,000 books and periodicals. **Other learning facilities:** Audiovisual and television centre, computing centre, centre for English cultural tradition and language, drama studio, English language teaching centre, language labs, computer-aided design lab. **Hardship funds:** Both SU and university run schemes to help students in financial hardship. **Sporting facilities:** Goodwin athletics centre with excellent sports complex (playing fields, 2 sports halls, 2 all-weather floodlit pitches, heated indoor swimming pool, 8 squash courts), additional 38 acres of playing fields 5 miles away; sailing at Ogston reservoir (20 miles from campus).

Duration of first degree course(s) or equivalent: 3 or 4 years; **others:** dentistry 4 or 5 years; medicine 5 or 6 years; architecture 6 years **Total first degree students 1991/92:** 8,684 **First degree overseas students:** 654 **Mature students:** 1,241 **Male/female/ratio:** 4:3 **Teaching staff:** full-time: 872 part-time: 103 **Total full-time students 1991/92:** 10,530 **Postgraduate students:** 1,846 **Tuition fees for 1992/93** (first degrees): Home: £756 (if no grant), £1,855 (classroom), £2,770 (lab/studio), £4,985 (clinical); Overseas: £5,320 (classroom), £7,055 (lab/studio), £12,990 (clinical).

What it's like

Sheffield is a lively and growing city, which boasts more park space within its boundaries than any other major European city. The much heralded Super Tram promises to make access to the city centre much better. Culturally it's very active; sports facilities second to none.

It's a non-campus university. Like Rome, it's built on seven hills; impressive Pennine peaks are a mere 30 minutes' bus ride away. Main academic buildings just 10 minutes' walk from city centre and within 15 minutes' walk of each other, including halls of residence, in pleasant leafy suburbs. University is still expanding. Good bus services link sites and accommodation. SU has excellent community liaison office with community action and conservation volunteers. Sheffielders are especially friendly and welcoming. SU now with one of the largest nurseries in the country 'one of only three examples of a good practice'. SU plays a big role; up to 20 events each week in range of venues, including multi-purpose Octagon Centre, also has new radio station, Forge FM. Regular programme of major bands. Relations between university and SU generally good.

Pauper notes

Accommodation: Six good halls; flats and university houses high standard, rents average to slightly expensive for north. **Drink:** SU has excellent bars (cheapest in city) and its own two pubs, the Fox and Duck in Broomhill, a main student area, and The Rising Sun in Fulwood, a quieter area. Local pubs tend to be friendly including several Jazz and Irish pubs. The 'Frog and Parrot' brews strongest beer in world, on site. Local brewery, Ward's, supplies many pubs, the beer is OK. **Eats:** Growing Asian and Latin American scene, excellent Italian and American Diners, many cheap takeaways. Some good veggie restaurants and very cheap Castle Market in town centre. **Ents:** SU gigs do over 120,000 tickets a year on campus. Lots of clubs, some jazz and Irish music. Cinema at Crystal Peaks; SU has its own purpose-built showing arts, house and mainstream films four nights a week. Crucible and Lyceum Theatres very active, as is University Drama Studio at the SU. **Sports:** 55 Clubs, well funded and expanding. University facilities free, good and expanding. Excellent pool. **Hardship funds:** University loans. Access funds administered second and third terms. **Travel:** Excellent travel shop, ferry, coach, rail and flights, very cheap. Well connected rail network and buses out to the Peaks. Good national rail links. **Work:** Relatively high youth unemployment, occasional vacation work. Careers service usually helpful in finding holiday work.

More info?

Enquiries to SU Reception (0742 724076).

Alumni (Editors' pick)

David Blunkett, Amy Johnson, Jane Irving, Tony Miles, Willy Hamilton MP, Tim Robinson, Sir Peter Middleton, Jack Rosenthal, Carol Barnes, Roger Humm.

SHRIVENHAM

Royal Military College of Science Shrivenham, Swindon SN6 8LA (0793 782551) Map A, E8

Student enquiries: Academic Registrar, RMCS

Main study areas – as in What to Study section: *(First degree):* Aeronautical engineering, civil engineering, electrical and electronic engineering, information technology, mechanical engineering. *Also:* Aeromechanical systems, command and control, communications and information systems; information systems engineering, information systems management; diagnostic radiography and therapeutic radiography.

European Community: No students learn an EC language or spend time in another EC country.

Application: UCCA for 1993 start, UCAS thereafter. **Structural features:** faculty of Cranfield. **Special features:** LEA places and Shrivenham scholarships for civilian students. **Founded:** 1946. Became a faculty of Cranfield Institute of Technology in 1984. **Main awards:** BEng, BSc. **Awarding body:** Cranfield. **Site:** Campus at Shrivenham. **Access:** A420. **Accommodation:** 370 single rooms in halls plus annexe. Rent: 100% in accommodation where rent controlled by college. **Library:** 100,000 books, 65,000 reports, 850 periodicals. **Welfare:** Resident nurse in medical centre; doctor in Shrivenham village. Resident student services co-ordinator. C of E and RC churches on site. Each student has own academic adviser. **Amenities:** Heated outdoor swimming pool, stables, small theatre, range of sports facilities including squash courts and golf course in excellent grounds; a wide range of recreational social clubs and societies.

Duration of first degree course(s) or equivalent: 3 years; others: 4 years **Total first degree students 1991/92:** 451 **Overseas students:** 23 **Male/female ratio:** 20:1 **Teaching staff:** 104 **Total full-time students 1991/92:** 696 **Postgraduate students:** 245 **Tuition fees for 1992/93** (first degrees): Home: £2,770; Overseas: £5,900 (BSc), £6,900 (engineering).

What it's like

Situated in the beautiful countryside of the Vale of the White Horse, this campus college runs undergraduate courses for military and civilian students in equal proportion.

RMCS has most of the facilities enjoyed by other colleges and universities – library (no need for any student to buy books), some free stationery, tutoring and counselling, and so on. On-site full board accommodation available for the majority of students; limited self-catering places. Some students live out.

Swindon (7 miles) and Oxford (23 miles) are the nearest towns for cinemas, nightclubs, fitness centres, main shops, etc.

Pauper notes

Accommodation: College accommodation relatively cheap, convenient for lectures. **Drink:** Subsidised bars on campus. Several local, friendly pubs within walking distance. **Eats:** Student bar serves cheap food, as do many of the pubs. **Ents:** Wednesday night parties, Balls every term. Multi-screen cinemas, ice rink, and other leisure facilities at West Swindon. Water chutes and large entertainment venue at the Oasis. **Hardship funds:** These are available. **Travel:** Close to M4 and M5. **Sports:** Cheap membership, includes gliding, golf, hiking, etc. **Work:** Limited.

SILSOE COLLEGE

Silsoe College, Silsoe, Bedford MK45 4DT (0525 860428) Map A, F7

Student enquiries: Student Recruitment Executive

Main study areas – as in What to Study section: *(First degree):* Agriculture, business studies, environmental studies, mechanical and production engineering. *Also:* Food, technology, water resources.

European Community: 100% first degree students take EC language as part of course (compulsory part of first year); 20% spend 6 months or more in another EC country. Formal exchange links with 3 universities/colleges (Beauvais, Deventer, Montpellier). Approved Erasmus programme 1991/92.

CAN'T FIND WHAT YOU'RE LOOKING FOR? USE THE INDEX!

Application: UCCA for 1993 start, UCAS thereafter. **Structural features:** faculty of Cranfield. **Founded:** Silsoe College in 1962 (formerly National College of Agricultural Engineering). Now forms Faculty of Agricultural Engineering, Food Production and Rural Land Use of Cranfield Institute of Technology. **Main awards:** BEng, BSc. **Awarding body:** Cranfield. **Site:** Silsoe, midway between Luton and Bedford (20 km south of Cranfield). **Access:** A6 and M1. **Accommodation:** 276 places in halls of residence (all first year students are offered place on campus). **Library:** 37,000 books and pamphlets, 300 periodicals, 49 study places. **Other learning resources:** Language unit, college farm, computer facilities, workshop areas, teaching laboratories. **Welfare:** Doctor, dentist, nurse, student services adviser. **Hardship fund:** Douglas Bomford Trust Education Awards, Merricks Trust, Whitworth Scholarship, Elizabeth Nuffield Educational Fund. **Careers:** Careers information and advice given by Head of Student Services. **Amenities:** Restaurant, SU with bar, vehicle repair shop, shop, etc; many societies including motor club, brewing and ploughing clubs, sailing, shooting, parachuting etc. **Sporting facilities:** Wide range on campus (eg soccer, cricket, rugby, tennis and squash). **Employment:** At home and overseas within rural sector, local authorities, food and agricultural industries; research and teaching institutes; engineering and agricultural consultants.

Duration of first degree course(s) or equivalent: 3 or 4 years **Total first degree students 1991/92:** 154 **Overseas students:** 15 **Mature students:** 20 **Male/female ratio:** 4:1 **Teaching staff: full-time:** 55 **part-time:** 4 **Total full-time students 1991/92:** 500 **Postgraduate students:** 346 **Tuition fees for 1992/93** (first degrees): Home: £2,770; Overseas: £5,900–£6,900.

What it's like

The campus is set amongst 30 acres of landscaped lawns and wooded areas in the pleasant mid-Bedfordshire village of Silsoe. Bedford and Luton both 10 miles away with easy bus access. Buildings modern low-level; college farm adjacent. Of 400 students, third are undergraduates reading for agricultural/environment engineering, rural resources management and marketing.

Courses made up of study units, seminars, visits and practical work. Study facilities good: computerised library, good computing facilities, labs; glasshouses, workshop facilities. Acres of trial and project land. Social life good and varied with discos, live bands and bar.

Sporting facilities basic, many clubs and societies, different religions and cultures provided for.

Undergraduates guaranteed accommodation (self-catering at weekends). College food good and varied. Many students have transport. Major bus and railway stations within easy access.

Pauper notes

Accommodation: Quite expensive, limited married quarters. No local squats; some cheap farm cottages. **Drink:** College bar, good cheap bar, Star and Garter in village, students always welcome. Need cars for most others: Crosskeys, Polloxhill, jazz on Sunday nights; Jolly Coopers, Flitton, good food. **Eats:** On campus good varied food, veggie and ethnic, but expensive. Nearest chip shop 4 miles. Chinese and Indian 5 miles – Flitwick. **Ents:** Films shown weekly in college. Cheap cinema in Bedford, Mondays. Ten screen point Milton Keynes, student reductions. **Sports:** Sports centre, 4.5 miles. On campus weights, badminton and squash courts, and outdoor pitches. **Hardship funds:** Hardship fund available. **Travel:** M1 close, good hitching. Good bus links, no student fares. Nearest train station Flitwick 5 miles, direct to London. **Work:** College bar work during term. Local stores, eg Tesco. Pub work in vicinity.

More info?

Enquiries to SU General Secretary (0525 60428/61601).

GET HOLD OF THE PROSPECTUSES

SLADE

Slade School of Fine Art, University College London, Gower Street, London WC1E 6BT (071 387 7050 ext 510) Map E, C1

Student enquiries: The Secretary

Main study areas – as in What to Study section: *(First degree):* Art & design, fine arts. *Also:* Film, media, theatre design.

European Community: 1% first degree students take EC language as part of course and 4% spend 6 months or more in another EC country. Formal exchange links with 2 German universities/colleges (Düsseldorf, Frankfurt).

Application: UCCA for 1993 start, UCAS thereafter. **Structural features:** Part of University College, London University. **Special features:** All staff are practising artists. **Academic features:** 4-year degree courses composed mainly of studio work plus history of art as a mandatory subject (at University College) and one other subject from a list of options. **Founded:** 1871. **Main awards:** BA. **Awarding body:** London University. **Site:** Gower Street, Bloomsbury. **Access:** Warren Street or Euston Square underground stations; buses. **Accommodation:** Apply to University College London accommodation office for hostel places. Rent: 60% undergraduates in accommodation where rent controlled by university. **Library:** Donaldson Library of University College; 4,500 periodicals and 60 study places; Slade/Duveen fine art reference library; slide collection of University College. **Welfare:** Professional welfare officer; all other facilities from student health association. **Careers:** Information and advice service. **Amenities:** Automatic membership of University College SU which has own premises with bar, television, music rooms etc; also central collegiate building with theatre, indoor sports facilities; Slade itself maintains a close relationship with all major galleries in London. **Employment:** Artists and related fields.

Duration of first degree course(s) or equivalent: 4 years **Total first degree students 1991/92:** 102 **Overseas students:** 5 **Mature students:** 13 **Male/female ratio:** 1:1 **Teaching staff: full-time:** 10 **part-time:** 25 **Total full-time students 1991/92:** 190 **Postgraduate students:** 100 **Tuition fees for 1992/93** (first degree): Home: £2,770, £795 if no grant; Overseas: £7,995.

What it's like

Small art college within a large university. Reputation on international level: all tutors/lecturers are practising artists, working alongside rather than teaching their students. Studios for first year work are separated from studios for years 2, 3, 4 – their studios being arranged into (1) Painting and life studio; (2) Sculpture; (3) Media.

Theoretical studies virtually non-existent, art history archaic. Postgraduate studios for painting, sculpture, printing, theatre design and media. Facilities for sound recording, computer graphics and general workshops. Access increasingly dependent on which department you are in.

In spite of traditional reputation there are few constraints. Tutors very willing to discuss problems. Shortage of space, but the setting within the quadrangle of University College and the West End more than make up for any of the college's disadvantages.

Pauper notes

Accommodation: Extremely difficult if you aren't in halls. Squats increasingly temporary. Halls epitome of studentdom. However this should not put you off. **Drink:** UCL union and ULU very cheap for London. **Eats:** Food is very bad in college. UCL union is best. Otherwise the whole of London is open to you – very cheap places. **Ents:** You'd have to be boring to be bored in London. **Sports:** Very good sporting societies, outside college probably a bit expensive, swimming pool at ULU. **Hardship funds:** Don't count on them, but there is money available if you really need it. **Travel:** Scholarship abroad available yearly. Opportunities for exchange half-yearly trips in third year. **Work:** Not known.

Alumni (Editors' pick)

Augustus John, Stanley Spencer, Gwen John, Derek Jarman, Stuart Brisley, Christopher le Brun, Rachel Whiteread.

SOAS

School of Oriental & African Studies, University of London, Thornhaugh Street, Russell Square, London WC1H 0XG (071 637 2388) Map E, C1

Student enquiries: Registrar

Main study areas – as in What to Study section: *(First degree):* African studies, anthropology, archaeology, Asian studies, economics, fine arts, geography, history, law, linguistics, music, Near East and Islamic studies, politics and government, religious studies and theology. *Also:* Unique range of African and Asian languages/studies, eg Bengali and Burmese to Sanskrit, Swahili and Urdu; African and Asian medical related studies, phonetics.

European Community: French (taught at University College London) may be combined with a number of Asian or African languages taught at SOAS. Undergraduates may study for a year at certain universities elsewhere in the EC under the Erasmus scheme.

Application: UCCA for 1993 start, UCAS thereafter. **Structural features:** Part of London University. **Largest fields of study:** Geography, law, history, Far Eastern languages, Arabic, anthropology, economics, politics. **Founded:** 1916. **Main awards:** BA, LLB. **Awarding body:** London University. **Site:** Central London university site. **Access:** Russell Square, Goodge Street underground stations; buses. **Accommodation:** Inter-collegiate halls; self-catering flats. 5% in accommodation where rent controlled by university; further 20% in university halls. **Library:** 750,000 items, 600 study places; reserve and short loan collections. **Specialist collections:** Regional libraries on Africa, Far East, South and South-East Asia, Near and Middle East; subject collections on art, law, geography, social sciences. **Welfare:** Doctors, dentists, FPA, psychiatrist, chaplains, counsellor, optician, behavioural psychologist; free legal advice centre. **Careers:** London University careers advisory service. **Amenities:** All facilities of ULU union building (including swimming pool); University church and prayer room; Percival David collection of Chinese art. **Sporting facilities:** Sports ground at Greenford; boat house at Chiswick and sailing club; squash courts, gymnasium.

Duration of first degree course(s) or equivalent: 3 years; 4 years for some languages **Total first degree students 1991/92:** 1,000 **Overseas students:** 90 **Mature students:** 175 **Male/female ratio:** 3:4 **Teaching staff:** 200 **Total full-time students 1991/92:** 1,350 **Postgraduate students:** 329 **Tuition fees for 1992/93** (first degrees): Home: £1,855; Overseas: £6,300.

What it's like

SOAS has an international reputation in its field – though little known in rest of country. Founded in 1916, in order to train administrators for the empire, it is unique in Western world in combining fields of Asian and African studies.

Unfortunately, college doesn't seem to have completely thrown off its past and there have been complaints that some courses and departments are Eurocentric in their approach.

GET HOLD OF THE PROSPECTUSES

Student population is a mixture. Students come from all over the world, many pursuing postgraduate courses, but there is a large proportion of mature students. In addition FCO and MOD staff take crash courses in languages and politics, and business types do college's new diploma in Japanese and Japanese economy. It would seem that such courses are seen as the future by the college's authorities – profit rules!

For a time in mid-80s, SOAS's existence seemed threatened by Thatcher's cuts, but having survived that, numbers are rising and it seems likely that college will expand.

SOAS is now housed in original building (mainly now used for administration), attached to a new (late 70s) building of lecture rooms and staff offices which surrounds the college's five-storey library (open six days a week). It's located in a surprisingly pleasant area of central London, off Russell Square, where students laze and the rugby team train. All handy for the British Museum and Library and a short walk from Oxford Street and Tottenham Court Road.

Work mainly assessed by end-of-year exams – though some courses are partially or wholly graded on essays and/or dissertations. Teaching is by a combination of lectures and seminars with regular tutorials. Staff are quite approachable for help!

SU small but active – and has a radical reputation. There is very little in way of faction-fighting and bureaucracy which can dog other unions. If you're willing to get involved there's a chance for individuals to shine. Largest societies are the Africa Society, Palestine Society, Women's Group and the Lesbian and Gay Society. Understandably, the union has a reputation for supporting liberation campaigns in Asia and Africa, though it's also active in national and local campaigns.

SOAS ents are improving and cover a wide range from Thrash Indie bands through to World Music. African and Asian bands and discos frequently take place. The Film Society shows many films from Africa and Asia not seen anywhere else. The Women's Group and the Lesbian and Gay Society frequently organize events aimed at a specific audience/theme and enjoy a lot of support, from within the college and from students from other colleges.

The union is comprised of left-orientated people (not necessarily Labour Party supporters) also Greens and fellow-travellers. All exec. members are friendly and approachable. It is easy for students to meet each other. The societies bring people with the same interests together and the larger ents events bring those with differing interests together. SOAS has a large proportion of overseas students and its degrees have both a national and international standing.

Pauper notes

Accommodation: Squatting increasingly popular with SOAS students and they help each other out. College accommodation in intercollegiate halls – gets booked up early so think ahead. **Drink:** SOAS bar very cheap, and lots of other SU bars near by. ULU has a beer festival in Autumn term. SOAS now has a real ale society. **Eats:** SOAS food cheap but not very good. Locally – Greenhouse vegetarian restaurant. First Out – lesbian and gay vegetarian café, cheap but not cheap. **Ents:** SOAS ents improving. SOAS societies especially Lesbian and Gay and Africa Society put on v. good events. Locally – Scala cinema £2.50 students before 4.30 pm. Asia nightclub in Islington – World Music Thursday nights, recommended. **Sports:** Small gym at SOAS. Squash courts. ULU facilities near by – pool, weights, badminton and squash courts. **Hardship funds:** Some – but very hard to get hold of – not specifically for people going bust either, so don't count on it. **Travel:** London Transport expensive. Bicycling is popular with students but roads are getting busier. Helmets a must. **Work:** SOAS has work on offer in bar, cloakroom, shop. Outside – bar and shop work is easy to come by but pay is pretty bad. Avoid agencies – they get you work but rip you off.

More info?

Enquiries to Debbie Mortimer, SU Co-President (071 580 0916).

CAN'T FIND WHAT YOU'RE LOOKING FOR? USE THE INDEX!

Informal name:
SOAS.

Alumni (Editors' pick)
Paul Robeson, Walter Rodney.

SOUTH BANK POLY
See South Bank University

SOUTH BANK UNIVERSITY

South Bank University, Borough Road, London SE1 0AA
(071 928 8989) Map E, D3

Student enquiries: Central Registry

Main study areas – as in What to Study section: *(First degree):* Accountancy, architecture, biology, biotechnology, business studies, chemical engineering, chemistry, civil engineering, computing, education, electrical & electronic engineering, English, environmental science, European studies, food science & nutrition, geography, hotel and catering management, information technology, law, mathematical studies, mechanical and production engineering, modern languages, nursing studies, politics and government, professions allied to medicine (PAMs), sociology, town and country planning. *Also:* Banking technology, construction management, energy studies, estate management, fire safety engineering, highways engineering, quantity surveying, water engineering.

European Community: Number of first degree students taking EC language as part of course not known. Students on language degrees (with international studies/business) spend 6 months or more in another EC country. Formal exchange links with EC universities/colleges: France (10 including 6 open to non-language students); Germany (4 including 2 open to non-language students); Greece (1, open to non-language students); Italy (2, 1 open to non-language students); Netherlands (1, open to non-language students); Spain (1). Approved Erasmus programme 1992/93. Students on many courses have the opportunity to take a language option (eg various engineering courses, business studies, hotel management). European studies available with various engineering specialisms.

Application: PCAS for 1993 start, UCAS thereafter. **Academic features:** Education route (leading to additional award of Cert Ed) available on some BEng courses. 4-year BA in home economics and resource management, available with industry route (sandwich) or teaching route (full-time). Courses in: engineering with European studies; fire safety engineering and risk management; radiography. Numerous foundation courses taught at local colleges for students without standard qualifications, leading into degree courses. **Founded:** 1992 as a university; previously South Bank Poly, founded 1970, ex 6 colleges of further education. **Main awards:** BA, BEd, BEng, BSc, LLB. **Awarding body:** South Bank University. **Site:** 2 main locations in central South London. **Access:** Elephant & Castle, Stockwell, London Bridge and Waterloo stations. **Accommodation:** Approx 720 places in halls (priority to first year students); 250 in head-leasing scheme; list of private lodgings. Approx cost: £45.£44–£46 pw in hall; £29–£49 pw in head-leasing properties; £45+ pw in private sector. Apply to accommodation officer early. **Rent:** 11% in accommodation where rent controlled by university.

WANT TO HELP WITH THE NEXT EDITION – SEE PAGE 76

Library: 2 main libraries, 280,000 volumes and other catalogued items; 29,500 bound volumes of periodicals and some 2,225 subscriptions to periodicals; 1,370 study places. Specialist collections in education, law, computing and the built environment. OYNIX software system on MIPS computer for cross referencing. **Other learning facilities:** Courses, individual tuition or supervised self-pacing language lab sessions (programmed tapes, video-cassettes, direct reception of foreign broadcasts and audio-interactive microcomputers). Computing facilities include DEC system 1091; VAX 8650 clustered with 2 VAX 11/785 computers; VAX 11/750 for general purpose computing; microcomputers in departmental computing labs. **Welfare:** Housing service, professional counsellors, 2 chaplains, visiting medical officers, nursery for children under 5, careers service. **Hardship funds:** Limited hardship funds available. **Careers:** Information and counselling. **Amenities:** Active students union; new union building. 2 sports halls and gymnasia on main sites, 21-acre sports ground at Dulwich, nearby South Bank arts complex.

Duration of first degree course(s) or equivalent: 3 or 4 years **Total first degree students 1991/92:** 6,310 **Number of BEd students:** 421 **Overseas students:** 400 **Male/female ratio:** 2:1 **Teaching staff: full-time:** 600 **part-time:** 500–700 **Total full-time students 1991/92:** 8,793 **Postgraduate students:** 2,276 **Tuition fees for 1991/92** (first degrees): Home: (£716 if no grant), £1,855 (classroom), £2,770 (lab/studio); Overseas: £5,600 (classroom), £5,800 (lab/studio).

What it's like

Mixmatch of split sites: three main ones are Borough Road (science, engineering, school of bakery), London Road (social studies, languages, law), and Wandsworth Road (built environment). Public transport provides easy access with the exception of Wandsworth Road, a bit more isolated. London Road business school is externally in the style of the Technopark but internally looks like an H-block. Borough Road has town hall cakey appearance, Wandsworth is more of an architectural oddity. Uni accommodation limited, so apply early. Otherwise it's digs or bedsits which vary in quality and can be pricey. SU facilities improved tenfold in new building. Increased space so far incorporates new 'club' venue. When new large upstairs is completed, this will be one of the largest student venues in London. Usual range of sports activities and numerous culturally based societies. Sports at both main sites, playing fields at Dulwich quite a trek away. Courses are practical, including industrial placements and studies abroad. Lots of access courses; many mature students. Library services adequate with completion of new library, but be prepared to queue. Ents programmes are in hand.

Pauper notes

Accommodation: Students sharing can find cheap houses. **Drink:** SU has cheapest booze, Goose and Firkin is popular (landlord brews own potent beer, and live ents most nights) but pricey. **Eats:** Uni food just adequate. SU outlets cheaper and becoming more popular due to wider variety. **Ents:** Society socials, bands, comedy, discos, live screenings at least six days a week. Films most Wednesday afternoons. Drama Society active at local fringe theatre. **Hardship fund:** Arranged by uni. **Travel:** No travel grants. **Work:** Part-time jobs going around town and also in SU in bars and ents.

SOUTH WEST POLY

See Plymouth University

CAN'T FIND WHAT YOU'RE LOOKING FOR? USE THE INDEX!

SOUTHAMPTON INSTITUTE

Southampton Institute of Higher Education, East Park Terrace, Southampton, Hampshire SO9 4WW (0703 229381) Map A, E8

Student enquiries: Head of Student Administration Services

Main study areas – as in What to Study section: *(First degree):* Business studies, computing, European studies, fine arts, information technology, public administration, sociology. *Also* Graphic design, leisure studies, maritime studies, transport studies.

European Community: 25% first degree students take EC language as part of course and 5% spend 6 months or more in another EC country. EC language tuition involved in business studies and European policy degrees; part time language courses available.

Application: PCAS for 1993 start, UCAS thereafter. **Special features:** Courses in yacht and small craft design and in European policy. **Founded:** 1968. **Main awards:** BA, BSc. **Awarding body:** Nottingham Trent University. **Site:** Two campuses at Southampton city centre and at Warsash (maritime). **Access:** Near BR station. **Accommodation:** 250 places at Warsash. **Approx cost:** £16–£42, without meals. Details of private accommodation on request, cost variable. **Library:** 3 libraries; 70,000+ books, 1,000+ periodicals, 600+ study places. **Specialist collections:** Godden Collection (antiques, ceramics), CD Roms. **Other learning facilities:** Test tank, computer suite, 1 manned model ships, metrology lab, language labs, advanced manufacturing technology centre. **Careers:** Information, advice and placement service. **Welfare:** Community services, including health centre and chaplain; Student union welfare officer. **Hardship funds:** Access funds. **Amenities:** Student union block with bank, book shop, bar, games rooms. **Sporting facilities:** Sports hall, fitness suite, sports field (12 acres) 3 miles from campus.

Duration of first degree course (or equivalent): Standard: 3 years; others: 4 or 5 years **Total first degree students 1991/92:** 1,395 **Overseas students:** 172 **Mature students:** 2,266 **Male/female ratio:** 2:1 **Teaching staff, full time and part time:** Not known **Total full-time students 1991/92:** 3,513 **Postgraduate students:** 159 **Tuition fees for 1992/93** (first degrees): Home: £1,885 (classroom); £2,770 (lab/studio); Overseas: £5,000.

What it's like

It's on 2 campuses – one in city centre, other 10 miles away at Warsash. Halls of residence only at Warsash, otherwise students live in private rented sector, average rent £27–35. Libraries open until 9.00 pm and Saturday morning. Good student scene. Lots of cheap restaurants, student nights at clubs. Lot of students from Hampshire area. Lots of new courses eg European policy.

Joanna Watson

Pauper notes

Accommodation: Halls of residence on Warsash campus only. **Drink:** SU. Mainly lagers and cheap spirits. **Eats:** Loads of foreign exotic eateries. On campus so/so. Bar food excellent. **Ents:** Very cheap cruises around Isle of Wight. Guildhall balls 5 a year. Discos, nightclubs etc. cheap for students. **Sports:** All usual sports spread in different locations all over city's large recreation areas. **Hardship funds:** Hardship fund, also access fund. **Travel:** Cheap travel on city buses. **Work:** Bar jobs, supermarkets & factory temp. work on & off campus.

Informal name:

SIHE.

Alumni (Editors' pick)

Humphries (yacht), R Parkes (HCC wicket keeper).

GET HOLD OF THE PROSPECTUSES

SOUTHAMPTON UNIVERSITY

University of Southampton, Southampton SO9 5NH
(0703 595000) Map A, E8

Student enquiries: Academic Registrar (0703 592379)

Main study areas – as in What to Study section: *(First degree):* Accountancy, aeronautical engineering, archaeology, biochemistry, biology, botany, business studies, chemistry, civil engineering, computing, economics, electrical & electronic engineering, English, environmental science, European studies, food science and nutrition, geography, geology, history, industrial relations, Latin American studies, law, linguistics, marine technology, mathematical studies, mechanical and production engineering, medicine, modern languages, music, nursing studies, pharmacology, philosophy, physics, physiology, politics and government, professions allied to medicine (PAMs), psychology, public administration, social policy and social welfare, sociology, zoology. *Also:* Actuarial studies, astronomy, Iberian studies, operational research, oceanography, population studies, space.

European Community: 8% first degree students take EC language as part of course and 7% spend 6 months or more in another EC country. Most faculties have links with institutions in other EC countries, notably France, Germany, Italy and Spain; many provide exchange opportunities under ERASMUS programme. New courses in contemporary Europe, European law, MEng with European studies. Languages may be taken in combination with many other subjects.

Application: UCCA for 1993 start, UCAS thereafter. **Special features:** Concert hall, theatre and art gallery on campus. **Founded:** 1952. **Main awards:** BA, BEng, BM, BN, BSc, BSc(Social Sciences), LLB, MEng. **Awarding body:** University of Southampton. **Site:** 2 miles from Southampton city centre. **Accommodation:** 1,200 places in halls; 1,600 places (self-catering). 90% first year students accommodated. Approx cost (30 weeks): £1,494 pa (half board), £1,059 pa (self-catering). Rent: 40% in accommodation where rent controlled by university. **Library:** Main library with 3 subsidiary subject libraries; 83,000 volumes in total, 1,600 study places; short-loan collection. **Specialist collections:** Agriculture to 1900, local history, parliamentary papers, history of relations between Jewish and non-Jewish peoples, Wellington papers, Mountbatten papers. **Other learning facilities:** IBM 3090/150; over 800 workstations for students' use; advanced network. **Welfare:** Doctor, education and welfare office, FPA, psychiatrist, chaplain, university counsellors, legal advice centre. **Special categories:** Residential facilities for married and disabled students, 44-place nursery. **Careers:** Information, advice and placement service. **Amenities:** SU shop, travel agency, launderette, banks, concert hall, theatre, art gallery etc. **Sporting facilities:** Excellent playing fields and sailing facilities, 6 squash courts and sports hall, multi-gym, table-tennis room. **Employment:** Comparatively high proportion of graduates enter industry and commerce.

Duration of first degree course(s) or equivalent: 3 years; **others:** 4 years (language courses, MEng, double honours courses, nursing, sociology and social policy); 5 years (medicine, MEng with tripartite diploma) **Total first degree students 1991/92:** 6,570 **Overseas students:** 980 **Mature students:** 590 **Male/female ratio:** 3:2 **Teaching staff: full-time:** 715 **part-time:** 60 **Total full-time students 1991/92:** 7,914 **Postgraduate students:** 1,344 **Tuition fees for 1992/93** (first degrees): Home: £755 (if no grant), £1,855 (classroom), £2,770 (lab/studio), £4,985 (clinical); Overseas: £5,320 (classroom), £7,055 (lab/studio), £12,990 (clinical).

What it's like

Campus is a mixture of modern and traditional buildings set in rolling pastures and trickling brook, three miles out of city centre. It is in the residential area, shops near by, centre is 10 mins bus ride away.

Most academic buildings on campus; medical sciences building (preclinical medics, biologists and biochemists) is 8 mins walk away. Other campus facilities include theatre, concert hall, art gallery and banks.

Halls all off campus, within walking distance. Nearly all first years offered a place in halls (choice of self-catering or fully catered) usually in single study/bedrooms. All halls have good facilities (bars, shops, launderette) and are cheap.

All courses/facilities are of high standard, in particular the pioneering medical course and the prestigious engineering department. Students represented on all faculty boards and most other university committees. Hartley Library has just been extensively altered giving more space and easier access to its resources.

SU provides for social, cultural and fun interests of its members through over 200 clubs and societies, discos, bands and talks. Welfare service is of exceptional standard with advice, help and campaigning on student issues (finance/housing) and more general issues (AIDS, anti-racism etc). Politics present but not overwhelming, lying somewhere between left and right.

Pauper notes

Accommodation: Halls for 1st years; private rented accommodation has good choice of price/standard/area. Number of married quarters, good accommodation for people with disabilities. **Drink:** SU and hall bars (members only) competitive compared with wide variety of local pubs. **Eats:** SU coffee bar. Many take-aways near campus and in centre. Cheap veggie/ethnic shops/restaurants in town. **Ents:** Excellent on campus. Ents department run by SU. SU discos, bands, cabarets, films. Discount for students at campus theatre. Rest of town variable. **Sports:** Union has use of good sports grounds 2 miles from campus. Squash, sports hall and multi-gym on site. No swimming pool yet. **Hardship funds:** SU/University hardship fund. University hardship fund, overseas students only, will organise loan if grant late. **Travel:** SU Travel Centre has all mod cons. **Work:** Seasonal work, eg boat show in summer, some bar work.

More info?

Get students' Alternative Prospectus.
Enquiries to SU's Education and Welfare Officer (0703 586122 ext 235).

Alumni (Editors' pick)

Jon Potter, T G Thomas, John Nettles, Baroness Hooper, Lord Tonypandy, Jenny Murray, Chris Packham, Kathy Tayler, John Sopel, John Denham MP, Alan Whitehead, Roger Black, Stuart Maister.

SPURGEON'S COLLEGE

Spurgeon's College, South Norwood Hill, London SE25 6DJ
(081 653 0850) Map D, C4

Student enquiries: Registrar

Main study areas – as in What to Study section: *(First degree):* Religious studies and theology.

European Community: No students learn an EC language (other than New Testament Greek) but some spend time during their course in another EC country, as an optional element.

Application: Direct. **Special features:** Theological college; a small denominational college, devoted primarily, though not exclusively, to the training of men and women to serve as ordained Baptist ministers. Strong vocational bias. Ministerial applicants are mature men and women supplied by the churches and are not accepted straight from school. Students seeking theological training for purposes other than the Baptist ministry are accepted straight from school. A part-time degree course in theology is also available to applicants who have already received some theological education. **Main awards:** BA. **Awarding body:** Wales University. **Accommodation:** Mainly for single students though some available for married couples and families. Rent: 33% in accommodation where rent controlled by college. **Library:** 40–45,000 volumes. **Other learning resources:** Extensive audio-visual equipment.

Duration of first degree course(s) or equivalent: 3 years; others: 4–5 years (part-time) **Total first degree students 1991/92:** 79 **Overseas students:** 6 **Mature students:** 79 **Male/female ratio:** 13:1 **Teaching staff: full-time:** 10 **part-time:** 4 **Total full-time students 1991/92:** 77 **Postgraduate students:** 15 (part-time) **Tuition fees for 1992/93** (first degrees): Home and Overseas: £4,976.

What it's like

A theological college for the training of Baptist ministers and other Christian workers. Situated in South London so all the facilities of central London are close. Crystal Palace National Sports Complex is five minutes away by car. 30 students in hall of residence; another 40 live locally. In addition many part-time training and correspondence courses are available. Unmarried students live in. Food and living expenses included in fees. All students are mature: school leavers not generally accepted. Some overseas students, but few female students. Social activities are organised for students and their spouses. There is a well-stocked computer-catalogued library and a bookshop on site; sports facilities include: tennis, snooker and table-tennis. Football, cricket and rugby matches are arranged against other colleges.

Pauper notes

Accommodation: College tries to assist in finding accommodation. Rooms automatically available on campus for single students. **Drink:** Not on campus!! **Eats:** Available on site, included in maintenance fee. The economically/gastronomically astute may be able to provide for themselves more cheaply. **Ents:** Student rates at Fairfield Halls/Warehouse Theatre in Croydon. **Sports:** Tennis court and croquet lawn on site. Crystal Palace sports stadium. **Hardship funds:** Students operate their own fellowship fund. **Travel:** Buy student railcard. **Work:** Some vacation work available on campus, otherwise local shop work.

SSEES

School of Slavonic & East European Studies, University of London, Senate House, Malet Street, London WC1E 7HU (071 637 4934)
Map E, C1

Student enquiries: Registrar

Main study areas – as in What to Study section: *(First degree):* European studies, history, modern languages. *Also:* Bulgarian, Czech/Slovak, Finnish studies, Hungarian, Jewish studies, Polish, Romanian, Russian, Serbo-Croat.

European Community: 14% first degree students take EC language as part of course and 7% spend 6 months or more in another EC country. Formal exchange links with Cologne University. Joint degrees in Russian with French/German/Polish, Romanian and Italian/French. Students can take course units in other EC languages as offered by other colleges of university by intercollegiate arrangement.

Application: UCCA for 1993 start, UCAS thereafter. **Structural features:** Part of London University. **Special features:** Visiting lecturers teach each language; Soviet television by satellite. **Academic features:** 4-year courses for students without an A- or A/S-level in particular language; first year is then intensive language year. Language and social sciences students spend a period of study abroad. All degrees by course units. **Largest fields of study:** Russian, East European studies, history. **Founded:** 1915, becoming a university institute in 1932. **Main awards:** BA. **Awarding body:** London University. **Site:** Heart of London University area. **Access:** Goodge Street, Tottenham Court Road, Russell Square underground stations; buses. **Accommodation:** London University accommodation office and intercollegiate halls of residence. School has none of its own. **Library:** 290,000 volumes, 1,400 periodicals, 70 study places; reference facilities for course books. **Specialist collections:** Romanian and Hungarian literature; pre-1800 Russian and Church Slavonic books. **Other learning resources:** Language laboratory. **Welfare:** London University health service. **Careers:** Information, advice and placement; careers computer. **Amenities:** Student common room, bar and canteen. All facilities of ULU in Malet Street.

Duration of first degree course(s) or equivalent: 4 years (languages); **others:** 3 years (History and contemporary East European studies) **Total first degree students 1991/92:** 380 **Overseas students:** 9 **Mature students:** 85 **Male/female ratio:** 1:1 **Teaching staff: full-time:** 47 **part-time:** 9 **Total full-time students 1991/92:** 430 **Postgraduate students:** 100 **Tuition fees for 1992/93** (first degrees): Home: £1,855 (£795 if no grant); Overseas: £5,600.

What it's like

Yes, SSEES is indeed one of the smallest colleges within the London University. It is also one of the very few that is classified as an 'institute' rather than a 'school', though you wouldn't think it looking at its name. This difference means nothing to the average SSEES student. However, our 'smallness' (c500 students) means a great deal. Our facilities, predictably, are not boundless but with ULU just a stagger away they are, surprisingly, sufficient. Also, it is very difficult not to get to know/be known by everybody here and SSEES camaraderie is infamous.

Lecture loads vary from just 3–4 hours a week for history finalists to well over 20 for Russian first year 'intensives'. Those of us studying even more esoteric languages (Bulgarian, Polish, Hungarian) often find ourselves with very little company apart from the tutor during lectures while some history courses (open to history students throughout the university) seem to need Wembley Stadium to seat everybody. Postgraduates don't tend to hide from undergraduates here, socially as well as academically, and our new(-ish) Social Science Department is evidence that the rumour that we're expanding is true.

Our bar has also expanded and been repainted and it remains the presumed centre of SSEES social life. It's certainly the focus of post-match revelry for sports teams. Most popular societies: mountaineering, drama, Polish (not necessarily in that order); rising high alongside our college magazine, 'Ceasefire', is our monthly monitor of East European affairs, 'Eurus', both produced entirely by students. Last year our Mount Society made an expedition to the Isle of Skye, our hockey team toured in Malta and no one escaped participation in our November Rag Week. Few other colleges have such reputations (and names) which stun enquirers into silence.

Pauper notes

Accommodation: No college accommodation, but good intercollegiate halls near by can be used for up to 2 years of a course. **Drink:** SSEES bar, run by students, has short hours, but good parties and promotions which should not be missed. Many college and hall bars near by; bars in ULU building. Some very pleasant pubs in the vicinity. **Eats:** SSEES canteen for tea, coffee, sandwiches and a limited selection of hot meals, including vegetarian dishes. Wider selection at ULU or other nearby college canteens. **Ents:** Near the West End; best selection of clubs, theatres, cinemas, concerts in the country, but tend to be expensive. Cheaper entertainments in outer London. SSEES throws good parties. **Sports:** Despite small size, fields teams competing with some success in football, hockey and rugby. **Social societies:** (current list): Drama, Russian, Jewish, Photographic,

TransCaucasian, Polish, Balkan, History and Mountaineering societies. **Work:** Bar work in SSEES enjoyable but not financially very rewarding. Some work in ULU, or in shops near by.

Alumni (Editors' pick)

Jonathan Ross.

STAFFORDSHIRE UNIVERSITY

Staffordshire University, College Road, Stoke-on-Trent ST4 2DE (0782 744531) Map A, D6

Student enquiries: Assistant Registrar (Admissions)

Main study areas – as in What to Study section: *(First degree):* American studies, art & design, biology, business studies, chemistry, computing, economics, electrical and electronic engineering, English, environmental science, European studies, fine arts, geography, geology, history, information technology, law, mathematical studies, mechanical and production engineering, modern languages, philosophy, physics, politics and government, psychology, social policy and social welfare, sociology. *Also:* Ceramic technology, environmental chemistry, estate management, humanities, sports studies, surveying, women's studies.

European Community: Number of students learning an EC language or spending time in another EC country, not known. Language options available for courses including: applied sciences, design, engineering, international relations, politics, computing, marketing and economics. Formal links in Belgium (engineering, sociology, law, economics); Eire (engineering, computing, women's studies); France (engineering, humanities, sociology, law, business studies, management); Germany (humanities, sociology); Greece (engineering, sociology); Italy (engineering); Portugal (engineering, law); Spain (engineering, humanities, sociology, law). Approved Erasmus programme 1992/93.

Application: PCAS for 1993 start, UCAS thereafter; ADAR for art and design. **Academic features:** Extended engineering degrees for students with A-levels in subjects other than maths and physics. Applied science modular programme. **Largest fields of study:** Business studies, computing, design, law. **Founded:** 1992 as a university; previously Staffordshire Poly, founded 1970, ex Stoke-on-Trent Colleges of Technology and Art and Stafford College of Technology. **Main awards:** BA, BSc, BEng, LLB. **Awarding body:** Staffordshire University. **Site:** Split on 2 sites. **Access:** Easy access to both sites by road (M6) and rail (Stoke-on-Trent and Stafford stations both on main line routes to London). **Accommodation:** Over 1,700 university places, majority single study bedrooms. Extensive stocks of approved private housing locally. Rents from £27 pw. **Library:** Large libraries on each site. **Other learning resources:** Extensive computing facilities, language, science and engineering laboratories, design and fine art studios. Study skills support. **Welfare:** Counsellors, nurses and chaplaincy service. Local GPs visit each site weekly. **Amenities:** SU with office on each site, snack bars, shops, minibus service, travel company; banking facilities on Stafford site; cinema and art gallery on Stoke campus and New Victoria Theatre close. **Sporting facilities:** New sports hall on Stoke site, together with playing fields. Stafford students have concessionary access to new local leisure centre complex.

Duration of first degree course(s) or equivalent: 3 years; **others:** 4 years (sandwich courses; extended engineering degrees); 5 years (sandwich extended engineering degrees) **Total first degree students 1991/92:** 6,695 **Overseas students:** 200 **Mature students:** 2,500 **Male/female ratio:** 3:2 **Teaching staff: full-time:** 460 **part-time:** 30 **Total full-time students 1991/92:** 7,320 **Postgraduate**

students: 875 Tuition fees for 1992/93 (first degrees): Home: £1,855 (classroom) £2,770 (lab/studio); Overseas: £4,750 (classroom), £5,120 (lab/studio).

What it's like

Stoke is the larger site both in student numbers and size of the premises; great pressure on inadequate SU facilities. An industrial town based around the Potteries and what's left of mining and steel industries. Easy to get out into countryside Peak District and to major cities, particularly if you can afford a car; railway station right next to uni.

Stafford is a market town 17 miles south of Stoke. Very pleasant; more up-market than surrounding areas. Move of humanities to Stoke means a male-dominated student body left in Stafford.

Much accommodation in Stoke is in long, terraced streets in urban renewal area. Stafford is better but costs more. Some halls in Stoke are a long way from uni, though uni provides limited bus service to them (best to make sure of a floor to kip on in Stoke on Monday nights, which is student night at the local night spots and no bus).

SU offers facilities from banking to launderettes and minibuses for student societies. Regular comedy, gigs and a disco – students come from all over the UK and overseas. Staffordshire can be a good place to see the world from – it's cheap. Uni is on the up.

Pauper notes

Accommodation: Halls. Some good, some hideous. Local accommodation is good in Stoke but hard to come by in Stafford. **Drink:** SU. Good, cheap bars and local pubs. Banks, Marstons Pedigree. **Eats:** Campus food not brilliant. Few local places offer discount; local vegetarian and vegan foods as well as good Italian, Indian etc. **Ents:** Regular live music at both SUs; thriving local music scene in Stoke. Plenty of theatres, cinemas and gig venues. **Sports:** Sports centre at Leek Road, swimming pool nearby – good value for money. Local authority offers students 'recreation key', allowing cheap/free use of local recreation facilities. **Hardship funds:** Government access funds only – uni has no known criteria. **Travel:** Good access: London 1 hr 40 mins, Manchester and Birmingham less than 1 hr, so possible for nights out. **Work:** Some student work in pubs, cinemas, nightclubs etc.

STAFFS POLY

See Staffordshire University

STIRLING UNIVERSITY

The University of Stirling, Stirling FK9 4LA
(0786 67043) Map A, C2

Student enquiries: Director, Schools and Colleges Liaison/Student Recruitment Officer

Main study areas – as in What to Study section: *(First degree):* Accountancy, biochemistry, biology, botany, business studies, communication studies, computing, economics, education, English, environmental science, environmental studies, European studies, history, industrial relations, mathematical studies, microbiology, modern languages, philosophy, politics & government, psychology, religious studies and theology, social policy and social welfare, sociology, zoology. *Also:* Aquaculture, EFL and ELT, film studies, Hispanic studies, human resources management, Japanese, personnel administration, Scottish literature, Scottish studies, technological economics.

European Community: 30% first degree students take EC language as part of course and 8% spend 6 months or more in another EC country. Formal exchange links with over 25 EC and EFTA universities/colleges: Austria (1 in film and media studies); Belgium (1 in business); Denmark (2 in English); France (8 in business, languages, marketing); Germany (4 in film and media, business, languages, marketing); Greece (2 in biology, English); Italy (1 in biology); Netherlands (3 in business and management); Spain (4 in biology, business, languages, film and media, marketing); Sweden (1 in human resources management). Approved Erasmus programme 1992/93. Number of exchanges increasing each year. All undergraduates have option to study French, German or Spanish as part of their degree (minor or subsidiary) and increasing number of European-orientated course options.

Application: UCCA for 1993 start, UCAS thereafter. **Special features:** Semester system (2 semesters, 15-weeks per academic year); concurrent education (teacher training) courses; continuous assessment policy. **Academic features:** Wide range of single and combined honours degrees. **Founded:** 1967. **Main awards:** BA, BSc, BAcc. **Awarding body:** Stirling University. **Site:** 300-acre site c.2 miles north-east of Stirling. **Access:** A9; buses from Stirling direct to campus. **Accommodation:** 1,500 places in halls of residence; 600 flats. First years accommodated. Rent: 80% in accommodation where rent controlled by university. **Library:** 400,000 volumes, 2,400 periodicals, 800 study places; reference collection. Computerised catalogue and issue system. **Specialist collections:** Rare books (19th century); government publications. **Welfare:** Doctor, chaplains, counsellors and academic advisers on site; other services available locally. **Hardship fund:** Some small funds available. **Special categories:** Limited residential facilities for married and disabled students. **Careers:** Information and advice. 2 careers advisers. **Amenities:** Bookshop on campus, chaplaincy centre, students' association with shop and travel service; bank, supermarket, chemist, post office; MacRobert Arts Centre; particularly good facilities for disabled students (wheelchair routes, paraplegic toilets). **Sporting facilities:** Gannochy sports centre with wide range of indoor and outdoor sports; swimming pool, golf course and tennis centre on campus.

Duration of first degree course(s) or equivalent: 4 years (honours); **others:** 3 years (general) **Total first degree students 1991/92:** 3,200 **Male/female ratio:** 1:1 **Teaching staff: full-time:** 297 **part-time:** 15 **Total full-time students 1991/92:** 4,000 **Postgraduate students:** 730 **Tuition fees for 1992/93** (first degrees): Home: £755 (if no grant), £1,855 (classroom), £2,770 (lab/studio); Overseas: £5,320 (classroom), £7,055 (lab/studio).

What it's like

Situated on the Airthrey Estate, Stirling is home to approximately 4,500 students. Backed by a massive hill, surrounded by woods, with a lake (sorry, loch) in the middle, it's easy to see why it's called one of Europe's most beautiful campuses.

It has an extremely active union with a wide variety of clubs and societies to cater for the 90 nationalities that form the University's population. Sports facilities were excellent even before the new Scottish National Tennis Centre was opened.

An academic institution nationally renowned for allowing students a flexibility in course choice hard to better elsewhere.

Students tend to buy necessities on campus and leave weekly shopping until they visit the town centre. Plenty of pubs and restaurants, and if you're bored with the town you can easily travel to Glasgow or Edinburgh for the day.

Pauper notes

Accommodation: Breezeblock/wooden chalets: Rents increasing yearly to market levels. **Drink:** Good selection lagers and beers. Plenty promos. **Eats:** Excellent value foods in SA eateries. Veggie food available. **Ents:** Very active ents scene, good enough to keep most students on campus. **Sports:** Excellent sports facilities on campus. Plenty sports clubs. **Hardship Funds:** Access fund available off-campus students. **Travel:** Exchange programme 3rd year, otherwise it's the travel shop. **Work:** Bar work on campus/town. Shops tend not to employ students unless they can guarantee availability for long period.

Buzz-words:
Heavy (pint of local beer).

Alumni (Editors' pick)
Tommy Sheridan, Dr John Reid MP, Stewart Hepburn, Mike Connarty MP.

STRATHCLYDE UNIVERSITY

The University of Strathclyde, Glasgow G1 1XQ (041 552 4400)
Map A, C3

Student enquiries: Registry

Main study areas – as in What to Study section: *(First degree):* Accountancy, architecture, biochemistry, biology, biotechnology, business studies, chemical engineering, chemistry, civil engineering, computing, economics, education, electrical & electronic engineering, English, environmental science, European studies, food science and nutrition, geography, history, hotel & catering management, industrial relations, information technology, law, marine technology, mathematical studies, mechanical and production engineering, metallurgy and materials science, microbiology, modern languages, pharmacology, pharmacy, physics, politics and government, psychology, public administration, social policy and social welfare, sociology, speech sciences, town and country planning. *Also:* Building technology, community arts, forensic chemistry, horticulture, international business, laser physics, offshore engineering, operational research, orthotics, prosthetics, Scottish studies, Soviet and East European studies, sports studies, tourism.

European Community: 20% first degree students learn an EC language as part of their course, 15% spend 6 months or more in another EC country. EC languages may be combined in the wide range of subjects; 7 languages may be studied by any student on self-serve basis in language laboratory. Erasmus exchange links with 30+ EC universities/colleges: Belgium (2); Denmark (2); Eire (1); France (7); Germany (6); Greece (2); Italy (8); Portugal (1); Spain (2) all open to non-language specialists. Approved Erasmus programme 1992/93.

Application: UCCA for 1993 start, UCAS thereafter. **Academic features:** Flexible credit-based system for all courses. Student's performance assessed by course work as well as final examination; practical training and experience are features of many degree courses. **Founded:** 1964. Applied scientific education on city centre campus since 1796. Jordanhill College of Education merged with university, 1993. **Main awards:** BA, BArch, BSc, BEng, BEd, LLB, MEng. **Awarding body:** Strathclyde University. **Site:** Glasgow city centre (John Anderson campus) and west end (Jordanhill campus). **Accommodation:** 25% students live in halls of residence (both mixed and segregated). Apply as soon as possible to residence and catering services (many students live at home). **Library:**

600,000 volumes, 1,230 study places, short loan collection. **Specialist collections:** Business information centre, rare books and manuscripts in Andersonian Library. **Welfare:** Health clinics on site; consultant psychiatrist; chaplaincy centre; student advisers. **Hardship funds:** A fund available. **Special categories:** Limited number of flats for married students; playgroup run by students' association. **Careers:** Information and advice service. **Amenities:** 10-storey Students' Association building with entertainment/sport/catering/support facilities. **Sporting facilities:** Sports centre with large twin-court games hall; gymnasium, swimming pool; 7 football pitches; artificial grass floodlit pitch for hockey, soccer and club training; athletics club has over 40 sections covering most indoor and outdoor sports.

Duration of first degree course(s) or equivalent: 4 years (honours); **others:** 5 years (MEng) 3 years (ordinary) **Total first degree students 1991/92:** 7,773 **Overseas students:** 934 **Mature students:** 600 **Male/female ratio:** 7:5 **Teaching staff: full-time:** 642 **part-time:** 60 **Total full-time students 1991/92:** 9,607 **Postgraduate students:** 1,834 full-time **Tuition fees for 1992/93** (first degrees): Home: £1,855 (classroom), £2,769 (lab/studio); Overseas: £5,400–£6,300 (classroom), £7,200 (lab/studio).

What it's like (John Anderson campus)

Attractively landscaped city centre campus lying between George Square and magnificent Glasgow cathedral. Modern, sought after residences on campus. Further residences and other university accommodation off campus including married quarters. University located on a series of hills though not all buildings accessible by wheelchair. Well served by all forms of public transport. SA has purpose-built union building with 10 levels. 5 distinct bars/lounges selling wide variety of snacks and meals; games room; major band venue on level 8 capable of holding 800 people; film society; debating chamber; suites available for hire; bank and shopping mall in building; launderette and child care facility organised by SA. Over 150 different sports and non-sports clubs boasting over 6,000 members.

Students from west of Scotland mix well with high proportion of overseas students. Very high numbers of mature students add character to student mix. Elective classes available; university is proud of its technological eminence though arts and other faculties also strong. New Graduate Business School.

Pauper notes

Accommodation: Halls competitively priced but otherwise limited amount of accommodation, price of which has increased dramatically in recent years in keeping with new yuppie image of city. **Drink:** SU bars, various trendy yuppy bars situated throughout the city. Cheapest drink is in the union. Most popular beer is Tennents or McEwan's. Most popular soft drink is Irn Bru. **Eats:** Union caters for all types of food including vegetarian. Drink outlet in one bar shut to allow Moslems to use it. **Ents:** Glasgow has a thriving music scene which is mirrored in the Union. Films – Glasgow Film Theatre (student discount), Plays – Citizens Theatre/Trongate. **Sports:** Massive sports union with full facilities. Sports centres in central Glasgow tend to be private. **Hardship funds:** Administered by the university as a separate department. **Travel:** Bus and train transcards are fairly economical. **Work:** Bars, shops and many new tourist-orientated businesses. Students are employed as staff in the union itself. Some city-centre work.

Alumni (Editors' pick)

John Logie Baird, Sir Monty Finniston, Bobby McGregor, Frank Clement. Also Manager of the Great Wall Hotel in Peking; Geologist with British Antarctic Survey; Computer Manager with Burroughs Ltd, Melbourne, Australia; Architect in Qatar; David Livingstone, John Reith, Sir Ian McGregor, Sir Adam Thompson; Malcolm Bruce, Douglas Henderson, Dick Douglas, Maria Fyfe, Clive Soley (MPs); James Kelman (writer).

CAN'T FIND WHAT YOU'RE LOOKING FOR? USE THE INDEX!

Buzz-words

'Poke' – paper bag; 'Ned' – trouble-maker; 'Butty'/'piece' – sandwich; 'Lumber' – boy/girlfriend; 'hen' – woman.

SUNDERLAND POLY

See Sunderland University

SUNDERLAND UNIVERSITY

University of Sunderland, Langham Tower, Ryhope Road, Sunderland SR2 7EE (091 515 2000) Map A, E4

Student enquiries: Admissions Officer

(International students contact International Office, Unit 4, Technology Park, Chester Road, Sunderland SR2 7PS; Tel (44) 91 515 2688; Fax (44) 91 510 0990)

Main study areas – as in What to Study section: *(First degree):* Accounting, American studies, art & design, biochemistry, biology, biotechnology, business studies, chemistry, civil engineering, communication studies, computing, economics, education, electrical and electronic engineering, English, environmental studies, fine arts, geography, geology, history, information technology, mathematical studies, mechanical and production engineering, microbiology, modern languages, pharmacology, pharmacy, philosophy, physics, physiology, politics and government, professions allied to medicine (PAMs), psychology, religious studies and theology, social policy and social welfare, sociology, strategic studies. *Also:* Medical laboratory science.

European Community: Number first degree students taking EC language or spending 6 months or more in another EC country, not known. Links with over 60 universities/colleges across the EC – including student exchanges. Approved Erasmus programme.

Application: PCAS for 1993 start, UCAS thereafter; ADAR for art and design. **Special features:** students from over 50 countries. UK students have chance to study abroad on a number of courses; exchange programmes with universities/colleges in America, Japan and Russia, as well as EC. Main library and life sciences building are accessible to mobility-impaired students. **Academic features:** Franchise scheme; modular credit scheme. **Largest fields of study:** Science (including pharmaceutical science), humanities, engineering. **Founded:** 1992, as a university; previously Sunderland Poly, founded 1969. **Main awards:** BA, BEd, BSc, BEng. **Awarding body:** Sunderland University. **Site:** 4 town centre sites within 10 min walk. **Accommodation:** 870 places in halls, 72 in campus flats and 1,000 in university houses; priority given to first and final years students. Approx cost: From £20 pw (self-catering); from £40 pw (part board depending on number sharing); university houses, £24–£32 pw. Rent: 33% in accommodation where rent controlled by university. **Library:** Main central library; 230,000 volumes, 1,800 periodicals, 650 study places. Art and design library, 14,000 books, 60 study places, 80,000 slides and photos. **Other learning resources:** Art gallery; language laboratories; media resources unit; computer network with operators, programmers and advice allowing access to mini-computers and to main computer. **Welfare:** Counselling service, professional welfare officer; solicitor through SU;

chaplain; nursing sister on call for first aid; day nursery. **Hardship funds:** Some funds available from SU. **Careers:** Information, advice and placement. **Amenities:** SU with numerous societies (including ski club) and shop; bookshop on site; Sunderland arts centre; Crowtree leisure centre; university swimming pool/sports/recreation facilities.

Duration of first degree course(s) or equivalent: 3 years; 4 years sandwich (4–5 years part-time); BEd, 2 years full-time, 3 years part-time **Other:** 4–5 years part-time **Total first degree students** 1991/92: 5,837 full-time, 966 part-time **BEd students:** 771 full-time, 150 part-time **Overseas students:** 371 **Male/female ratio:** 3:2 **Teaching staff: full-time:** 400 **part-time:** 20+ **Total full-time students** 1991/92: 7,133 **Postgraduate students:** 210 full-time, 457 part-time **Tuition fees for 1992/93** (first degrees): Home: £1,855 (classroom), £2,770 (lab/studio); Overseas: £3,000 (classroom), £4,000 (lab).

What it's like

It's a splinter-site campus with over 40 buildings scattered over Sunderland, all within walking distance. Most students live in private houses. About 1,000 live in halls.

Student numbers increasing yearly; proportions of men to women about 6:4; large number of overseas students (from over 50 different countries); also large number of local and mature students. All in all it's a very varied student population.

The standard of university buildings varies immensely in terms of age, size and facilities, but university is still expanding. Academically the poly is under-rated at a national level – it's strong in most areas, particularly in pharmacy, technology, engineering, fine arts, business studies. Courses range from OK to excellent. Computer resources reasonable; library very strained; lecture halls often packed.

SU very active. SU services include 2 bars (very cheap!), shop and travel office (both also cheap), entertainments, professional welfare services, nightline, and late night transport for women. SU has no union building yet; subsidises activities of over 90 clubs and societies (sporting, political, cultural). Uni student services overstretched. Crèche good, limited places.

The town is very much orientated towards students – with a few exceptions in the form of non-recommended pubs. Most nightclubs offer cheap student nights, and some shops and restaurants offer student discount. The cheap cost of living in the North East is a definite bonus, making the paltry student grant stretch a little further.

Though Sunderland suffers the unfortunate reputation of being 'the place students go when they fail their A-levels and nowhere else will have them', this image does not do it justice. Most develop a fierce loyalty to both the university and the town, and many choose to stay here on completion of their degree.

Pauper notes

Accommodation: Halls of residence (1,000 beds; possibly more 1994), private housing (rents c. £30; quality varies). University operates head tenancy scheme where the uni becomes landlord/lady and makes sure of basic standards. Some lodgings with families. **Drink:** Union has two bars, cheapest in town (98p a pint). Good town pubs. Local brew, Vaux; Samson and Double Maxim recommended. **Eats:** Lots of pizza/kebab/Chinese/Indian/chip shop take-aways. Some good restaurants, predominantly Italian. **Sports:** University sports facilities limited, but include pool, gyms, tennis courts and sports field. Local facilities include Crowtree Leisure Centre (most indoor sports), Puma Tennis Centre (indoor), Silksworth Sports Complex (ski and athletics). **Ents:** Good. Union runs weekly discos, comedy, bands, Rag events, plus Balls, quiz nights and the unusual. Local nightclubs run student nights. Local theatre and cinema is limited. **Hardship funds:** Access Fund, strict criteria. Hardship loans available for short term problems. **Travel:** University sites all in walking distance of each other. Some students live out of city centre and catch reasonably cheap, regular bus service in.

CAN'T FIND WHAT YOU'RE LOOKING FOR? USE THE INDEX!

Work: Poor choice of work during term time or vacation. Bar/serving jobs always available and limited shop/factory work.

More info?

Enquiries to SU Executive Committee (091 514 5512).

Alumni

Steve Cram.

SURREY UNIVERSITY

The University of Surrey, Guildford, Surrey GU2 5XH
(0483 300800) Map A, E8

Student enquiries: Undergraduate Admissions Office

Main study areas – as in What to Study section: *(First degree):* Biochemistry, biology, biotechnology, chemical engineering, chemistry, civil engineering, computing, dance, economics, electrical & electronic engineering, European studies, food science & nutrition, hotel & catering management, information technology, law, linguistics, marine technology, mathematical studies, mechanical and production engineering, metallurgy and materials science, microbiology, modern languages, music, nursing, physics, professions allied to medicine (PAMs), psychology, sociology. *Also:* bioprocess engineering, offshore engineering, retail management, sound recording, toxicology, Russian studies.

European Community: 11% first degree students currently take EC language as integral part of course; engineering and science degrees with integral language component from 1992. All such students spend 6 months or more in another EC country, and opportunities for other students to take professional training abroad. Formal exchange links with 8 EC universities/colleges: France (4); Germany (4). Actively participates on Erasmus, Comett programmes. European language teaching centre established with aim of providing language teaching to all students regardless of course. French, German, Italian and Spanish available for beginners.

Application: UCCA for 1993 start, UCAS thereafter (except for some industrial-sponsored applicants). **Academic features:** BSc/BEng incorporate foundation year for those without subject qualifications. BSc chemistry for Europe (France/German); physics with environmental protection. **Special features:** Most first degree courses offer periods of industrial/professional training in UK or abroad. Applications from mature students are welcomed. Queen's Award for Export granted for invisible exports (fees from overseas students and technology transfer contracts). **Founded:** 1966, from Battersea College of Technology. **Main awards:** BMus, BSc, BA, BEng, MEng. **Awarding body:** Surrey University. **Site:** 1 mile outside Guildford. **Access:** 10 mins' walk from station, bus from Guildford, A3. **Accommodation:** 2,488 segregated places in halls. Most first years accommodated. Approx cost: £31.50 pw (single). Rent: 60% in accommodation where rent controlled by university. **Library:** 386,000 volumes, 2,300 current periodicals, 550 study places. **Other learning resources:** Computing facilities include Alliant Supercomputer, Hewlett Packard UNIX-based general purpose, 4 IBM compatible PC clusters, 1 Apple-Mac cluster; these connected together and to over 1,000 terminals across campus (simple VDUs to sophisticated work stations and local area networks). Very high ratio of terminals/students. **Welfare:** 2 student counsellors, doctor, FPA, psychiatrist, welfare officer, chaplain. **Hardship funds:** Available only in exceptional circumstances, in final year of course. **Special

categories: Limited residential facilities for married and disabled students. **Careers:** Information, advice and placement. **Amenities:** SU house with print-room, games-room, restaurants, bars, canteen; bookshop, grocer, post office, launderette, bank, restaurants, hairdresser on campus.

Duration of first degree course(s) or equivalent: 3 years; **others:** 4 years (including professional training); 4½ years for MEng courses **Total first degree students 1991/92:** 3,403 **Overseas students:** 331 **Mature students:** 510 **Male/female ratio:** 5:4 **Teaching staff:** full-time: 321 part-time: 39 **Total full-time students 1991/92:** 5,287 **Postgraduate students:** 1,884 **Tuition fees for 1992/93** (first degrees): Home: £755 (if no grant), £1,885 (classroom), £2,770 (lab/studio); Overseas: £6,750 (classroom), £7,100 (lab/studio).

What it's like

It's a medium sized campus built on the grassy Cathedral hillside, overlooking Guildford. Fifteen minutes' walk to railway station (only 35 minutes' train journey to London), and 20 minutes' walk to the bus station. The university is built on a hill and so is not ideal for disabled students.

First, final and overseas students are at present housed in university accommodation. The standard is OK to very good; most rooms have a sink; some have en-suite facilities. Between 10–28 share a kitchen with single and mixed floors. A good community exists on campus. There is also a separate residence site 3 miles from university. On-site students are normally unable to have a car on campus.

Campus has an expensive launderette, small shop, plus bookshop, hairdresser, post office and a Nat West Bank. There is a large library, open until 10pm; so is the sports hall. The Union has excellent entertainments (some free), and nightly discos. It produces a weekly student magazine, and there is a campus radio station.

The university gives social advice and support, plus university health centre with family planning advice, confidential counselling service and a student run 'night help line'. The Union also houses a full time welfare officer.

Guildford is expensive, three nightclubs offering student discount. There is a good number of pubs, a theatre, cinema, concert hall and lovely countryside. The university is a social centre – an easy place to make friends.

Basically a technological university with music and dance the only balancing arts. Courses are generally 'up to date', most having a period of placement in industry, some abroad, offering valuable experience. Workload varies from OK to hard – generally combining yearly exams with assessed course work.

Pauper Notes

Accommodation: University accommodation is at the moment provided for all first/final/overseas students. There are a few married family flats. Practically no provision for single parents but nursery on site (long waiting list). Off campus accommodation expensive (£40–£50) and in short supply. **Drinks:** Four bars in the Union provide a range of drinking environments (quiet to disco) with a wide range of beers and spirits. Most pubs are expensive. Good local brews – Gales HSB. **Eats:** University – and Union – run various catering outlets; vegetarian catered for; town, good choice but expensive. **Ents:** Very good on site, with cabaret, free Sunday night band, lunchtime concerts, discos, balls and annual festivals. Town offers theatre, cinema and concert hall. **Sports:** Very good cheap facilities; friendly and competitive events. **Hardship funds:** University and access fund. SU has own hardship fund. **Travel:** Travel office in SU offering student fares. **Work:** Some available on site in the bars and catering outlets, with a little down town.

More info?

Enquiries to President SU (0483 509223).

Alumni (Editors' pick)

Alan Wells (sprinter).

CAN'T FIND WHAT YOU'RE LOOKING FOR? USE THE INDEX!

SUSSEX UNIVERSITY

University of Sussex, Falmer, Brighton, Sussex BN1 9RH
(0273 678416) Map A, F8

Student enquiries: Admissions Office, Sussex House

Main study areas – as in What to Study section: *(First degree):* African studies, American studies, anthropology, Asian studies, biochemistry, biology, biotechnology, business studies, chemistry, computing, economics, electrical & electronic engineering, English, environmental science, environmental studies, European studies, fine arts, geography, history, law, linguistics, mathematical studies, mechanical and production engineering, modern languages, music, philosophy, physics, politics and government, psychology, social policy and social welfare, sociology. *Also:* Astrophysics, conservation, intellectual history, Japanese, media studies, medicinal chemistry, neuroscience, Russian and East European studies.

European Community: 19% first degree students take an EC language as part of course and spend 6 months or more (normally a year) in another EC country (which may include parts of France in West Indies or Indian Ocean). Year abroad is normally 3rd year of 4 year course. Almost all subjects can be taken with a language and year abroad. Previous language qualification essential; language centre for language reinforcement and acquisition of minority language skills (eg Portuguese, Greek). Many subjects may be combined with European Studies. Formal exchange links (including ECTS) in Belgium (3); Denmark (2); Eire (2); France (26); Germany (19); Greece (1); Italy (8); Netherlands (5); Portugal (2); Spain (6); Sweden (1). 29 approved Erasmus programmes 1992/93. ECTS (history) links with all other EC countries.

Application: UCCA for 1993 start, UCAS thereafter. **Academic features:** Combinations possible of science and engineering with a language, management studies or North American studies. **Special features:** International students community; many from EC and US. **Largest fields of study:** English, engineering, computing, mathematics, physics, biology, chemistry, history, economics, law, psychology, French. **Founded:** 1961. **Main awards:** BA, BSc, BEng, LLB, MPhys, MEng. **Awarding body:** Sussex University. **Site:** 4 miles from Brighton town centre. **Access:** Bus, train. **Accommodation:** Housing office will assist all first year students to find accommodation, usually on campus. **Library:** 607,100 volumes, 3,500 periodicals, 1,000 study places, short loan collection, audio-visual section. **Welfare:** Health service, sick bay on campus, personal counselling unit. **Hardship funds:** Special funds for disabled. **Special categories:** Residential facilities for disabled students; crèche and nursery. **Careers:** Information and advice (also for vacation work). **Amenities:** SU with concert hall, bar, vegetarian restaurant, shop, television studio, campus student radio station; Gardner Arts Centre, banks, launderette. **Sporting facilities:** Sports centre for most indoor sports; playing fields, tennis courts, etc adjoining campus, sports injury clinic. **Employment:** Research, teaching, central and local government, welfare, financial, commercial, communications, manufacturing, media.

Duration of first degree course(s) or equivalent: 3 or 4 years **Total first degree students 1991/92:** approx 5,000, overseas students (outside EC): 371 **Male/female ratio:** 1:1 **Teaching staff: full-time:** approx 404 **part-time:** approx 14 **Total full-time students 1991/92:** approx 5,000 **Postgraduate students:** approx 2,000 **Tuition fees for 1992/93** (first degrees): Home: £700 (if no grant), £1,855 (classroom), £2,770 (lab/studio); Overseas: £5,600 (classroom), £7,150 (lab/studio).

What it's like

Award-winning red-brick architecture amidst trees and beautiful South Downs, 3 miles from Brighton centre. Many arts taught with pro-feminist, left emphasis, challenging established ideas. Interdiscipline system means varied (if sometimes superficial) education without excessive role learning. Emphasis on independent research. Euro and American Studies students have third year abroad. Science more formal, structured and conservative; excellent reputation for attracting research grants. Still one of Britain's more radical universities. Active SU with vibrant campaigns against student loans, etc. Campaigning societies (eg anti-apartheid, women's group and lesbian and gay) very active. Radical, anti-racist and anti-sexist atmosphere predominates. Union societies representing a wide range of political affiliations. Many mature students; many from overseas. Facilities for disabled students somewhat lacking but constantly under review. Link-Up (Student Community Action Group) connects students to outside world through community-based projects. Aids Campaign based at Sussex. Brighton: excellent student town, lively 'alternative' social scene. Has many antique and junk shops, plus all the delights of a posh seaside town. Major problems for average student: finding somewhere to live.

Pauper notes

Accommodation: Campus: mainly single self-catering, but some doubles and family flats. No petty regulations on visitors. Local: appalling housing crisis in Brighton area; rents expensive; big trouble. **Drink:** Six campus bars. Many and varied watering holes in Brighton. **Eats:** Plenty of choice in all price ranges. Veggie, canteen and snacks on campus. Brighton has many good cheap places. **Ents:** Good 'alternative' circuit in Brighton. Many alternative pubs and clubs. Campus has regular club nights, bands, films and own Gardner Arts Centre. **Sports:** Plenty of facilities, wide range of activities for all levels of participation. Competitive and non-competitive sports. **Hardship funds:** Government access funds hopelessly inadequate; union has little money. **Travel:** Buses very expensive; buses/trains to Brighton/Lewes. Hitching on and off campus OK in pairs. **Work:** Good in summer – but wages too low to sustain decent standard of living. Recession has hit Brighton too.

Alumni (Editors' pick)

Ian McEwan, Bernard Coard, Howard Brenton, Brendan Foster, Neil from 'The Young Ones', Virginia Wade, Kathy Foster, Howard Barker, Julia Somerville, Peter Jones, Brian Behan, Peter Hain.

SWANSEA

University of Wales – Swansea, Singleton Park, Swansea SA2 8PP (0792 205678) Map A, C8

Student enquiries: Schools Liaison Office

Main study areas – as in What to Study section: *(First degree):* American studies, anthropology, biochemistry, biology, biotechnology, botany, business studies, chemical engineering, chemistry, civil engineering, classics, computing, economics, electrical & electronic engineering, English, environmental studies, geography, history, law, mathematical studies, mechanical and production engineering, metallurgy and materials science, microbiology, modern languages, philosophy, physics, politics and government, psychology, social policy and social welfare, sociology, zoology. *Also:* Marine biology, mediaeval studies, operational research, Russian studies, Welsh studies.

European Community: 20% students learn an EC language and spend 6 months or more in another EC country. Formal exchange links with 81 EC universities/colleges: Belgium (3); Denmark (4); Eire (4); France (20); Germany (16); Greece (3); Italy (9); Netherlands (8); Portugal (3); Spain (10). Also Tempus links with Hungary (3), Bulgaria (2), Czechoslovakia (1), Poland (2) and (former) Yugoslavia

CAN'T FIND WHAT YOU'RE LOOKING FOR? USE THE INDEX!

(1). European Business Management School 20% first year students have access to EC language tuition which can be combined with a number of subjects. Biology, chemistry, computer science, engineering, geography, history, mathematics and politics offer a year in Europe.

Application: UCCA for 1993 start, UCAS thereafter. **Structural features:** Part of Wales University. **Academic features:** 4-year engineering degree for students with arts-based A-levels. **Special features:** School of Postgraduate Medical Studies. Mass Spectrometry Research Unit; Institute of Numerical Analysis; Hayter Centre for Russian and East European studies. **Largest fields of study:** Arts and pure science. **Founded:** 1920. **Main awards:** BA, BSc, BSc(Econ), BEng, MEng. **Awarding body:** Wales University. **Site:** 2 miles to west of Swansea, near Gower Peninsula (designated area of outstanding natural beauty). **Access:** Bus from Swansea city centre. **Accommodation:** 1,150 places in halls (both segregated and mixed); 1,675 places in self-catering flats and houses; 2,500 flats/bedsitters; majority of first year students accommodated. Approx cost: From £21 pw shared self-catering to £55 pw single room in halls. Rent: 46% in accommodation where rent controlled by university. **Library:** Main library plus departmental libraries; over 600,000 volumes in total, 4,000 periodicals, 1,100 study places in library complex + 150 in maths/physics/applied science buildings. **Welfare:** Doctor, dentist, chaplains; legal and financial advice through students' union. Student counsellor. **Hardship funds:** Cases of financial hardship treated on individual merit. **Special categories:** Resident welfare facilities for married and disabled students. Special study centre for blind and visually handicapped students (CCTV reader, braille embosser, ten four-track tape recorders). Ramps, lifts and toilets for students in wheelchairs. Staff tutor for disabled students. **Careers:** Information, advice and placement. **Amenities:** SU building with shop, launderette, dark room, radio station, etc; closed circuit television unit; large arts centre on campus; access to recently opened Swansea leisure centre. **Sporting facilities:** Modern indoor sports centre; gymnasia, swimming pool, rifle range; wide range of sports especially soccer and rugby; surfing and canoeing on Gower beaches. **Employment:** Industry, commerce, education and public service.

Duration of first degree course(s) or equivalent: 3 years; **others:** 4 years (eg MEng, philosophy, courses combining languages, European business and management studies. **Total first degree students 1991/92:** 5,654 **Overseas students:** 428 **Mature students:** 800 **Male/female ratio:** 6:5 **Teaching staff:** 500 **Total full-time students 1991/92:** 5,459 **Postgraduate students:** 1,067 **Tuition fees for 1992/93** (first degrees): Home: £750 (if no grant), £1,855 (classroom), £2,770 (lab/studio); Overseas: £5,320–£7,055.

What it's like

Located in Singleton Park, UCS Campus can be very picturesque. It encompasses all facilities except teacher training centre (20 minutes' walk). Six halls of residence: 3 on campus (breakfast only), 3 off (1 for overseas students only), 20 minutes' walk and meals provided. Hendrefoilan Student Village houses 1,750 (30 minutes' walk from campus, women's minibus provided by SU). It's a self-catering complex with facilities including a union-run shop, bar, launderette, tennis courts and car park. Rented accommodation reasonable. Rapid expansion of student numbers has placed great pressure on accommodation. Over 500 overseas students, plus mature students. Very mixed backgrounds reflected in relaxed atmosphere at college. SU very active, excellent Welfare service including cheap, full-time crèche, counselling service, first sabbatical women's officer in University of Wales and only sabbatical overseas officer in the country. Union services include: shop, two bars, launderette, coffee bar, travel office and printing. Over 100 societies, Labour Club, Green Action, RAG, Community Action, Women's Group, Macabre etc. Semi-student city, very friendly – plenty of pubs, clubs, cinemas and theatres. Gower Peninsula only 7 miles away for walks, surfing, rock climbing etc. Ents programme good with many big names and regular discos. Quite easy to change course in first year as often made up of three subjects. Language and American studies get a year abroad but not many sponsored or sandwich course students. Easy to get year out (University of Wales five-year rule). Work assessed differently from course to course (course work, single or split finals). Work rate reasonable. Quality of degree generally excellent.

Pauper notes

Accommodation: Big pressure on accommodation. Bedsit land in Uplands, Brymill, Mumbles. Generally OK – average rent £30 and rising. Student village best all-round value for money. **Drink:** Student Village again – cheapest beer in Swansea. Union bar in village and new Union bar in Mandela House. Cheapest Union bar in Wales. Local pubs varied, usually friendly and reasonably priced. Several 'Student' pubs. Löwenbräu, 1664, Brain's Beer, Felinloel and Directors in abundance. **Eats:** College refectory not good. Over 30 Indian/Chinese restaurants. Plenty of variety for all tastes, vegetarian, vegan, ethnic. **Ents:** Union ents good. Also range of cheap clubs – student nights in most of the big ones. 14 cinemas plus Film Society. Blues, jazz, folk, rock/pop scene in town, but requires investigation. Swansea Fringe Festival annually. Theatres provide excellent mix of well-known and new productions. Outdoor and indoor markets. **Sports:** Leisure centre good and cheap. Very cheap campus sports centre. All easy to get to. **Hardship funds:** Little joy from college. **Work:** Casual/seasonal work, but in these times very hard to get.

More info?

Enquiries to Ken Penton (0792 295466).

Informal name:

UCS.

Alumni (Editors' pick)

Donald Anderson MP, John Morgan, Lamin Mybe, Mark Wyatt, Paul Thorburn, Gwynne Howell, Mavis Nicholson, Alun Richards, Ian Bone (Head of Class War), Nigel Evans MP, Half of Manic Street Preachers, Hadyn Tanner.

SWANSEA INSTITUTE

Swansea Institute of HE, Townhill Road, Swansea SA2 0UT
(0792 203482) Map A, C8

Student enquiries: Registry

Main study areas – as in What to Study section: *(First degree):* Accountancy, art & design, business studies, computing, economics, education, electrical & electronic engineering, English, information technology, law, nursing studies. *Also:* Leisure management, media studies, visual arts, urban studies.

European Community: 2% first degree students take EC language as part of course and 2% spend 6 months or more in another EC country. Some formal exchange links with EC universities/colleges.

Application: PCAS for 1993 start, UCAS thereafter. **Founded:** 1976, ex Colleges of Art, Technology and Education. **Main awards:** BA, BSc, BEd, BEng, BNursing, LLB. **Awarding bodies:** Wales University; London University. **Site:** 3 main campuses, 1 in town centre; 2 outside. **Access:** Public transport. **Accommodation:** 260 places in mixed halls of residence. 60% of students are home based. **Library:** 3 libraries (Mount Pleasant and Townhill sites); 120,000 volumes in total; 820 periodicals, 400 study places. **Specialist collections:** Salmon collection of 17th, 18th and 19th century books. **Other learning facilities:** Visual aid centre, print room and resources centre. **Welfare:** Student counsellor, doctor, chaplains. **Hardship funds:** Access fund (almost £60,000 pa). Also college emergency fund gives frequent assistance to students. **Careers:** Careers counsellor. **Amenities:** SU bar and coffee bar, gymnasia, Swansea leisure centre. **Employment:** Teaching, business, nursing, accountancy, engineering, computing, law, vocational art, tourism and recreation.

Duration of first degree course(s) or equivalent: 3 years **Other:** 4 years **Total first degree students 1991/92:** 1,200 **Total BEd students:** 500 **Overseas students:** 20 **Mature students:** 250 **Male/female ratio:** 2:3 **Teaching staff: full-time:** 120 **part-time:** 20 **Total full-time students 1991/92:** 2,400 **Postgraduate students:** 50 **Tuition fees for 1992/93** (first degrees): Home: £1,855 (classroom), £2,770 (lab/studio); Overseas: £5,319.

What it's like

4 sites, Townhill and Mount Pleasant are main campuses; Alexandra Road and Penybryn are annexes. All close to each other. Wide range of courses, business studies, education, stained glass, ceramics and technology most popular. Extensive range of diploma courses. Recreational facilities poor. Townhill campus has a gymnasium but few other facilities; compensated by free use of Swansea Leisure Centre for students during the day and passport to leisure scheme all round Swansea with SU card. Halls only cater for c.240 students so apply really early. SU very active but developing – now has 2 sabbatical officers. Provides many facilities including two coffee bars, materials and stationery shops. Private accommodation difficult because of close proximity of university. Libraries at Townhill and Mount Pleasant open 9.00 am–9.00 pm, closed at weekends, limited vacation hours. All sites close to town centre and the famous Gower Peninsula is only a 15-minute bus ride away. SU has about 35 societies including many sports. Confidential counselling services. Good relationships between staff and students are a priority. Overseas students encouraged, students from all ethnic minorities. Students from all over UK, Europe, China, Nigeria, America, etc. Drop-out rate is relatively low. A close-knit atmosphere as students tend to live in the same area. Expanding college, hoping to get university status within five years.

Pauper notes

Accommodation: Halls relatively cheap but definitely not the Ritz. Bed-sits, flats etc, moderate but very scarce; grab places before the univ does. **Drink:** SU bar at Townhill. Juke box, pool tables. Quite cheap – plastic glasses. Loads of local pubs. Some welcome students. Majority are student dominated. **Eats:** College refectories not bad in general. SU coffee bars for snacks and drinks. Lots of Chinese, Indian, Cantonese and Greek food. Local chippies very good, cheap and everywhere. Some health food shops and restaurants; few veggies. **Ents:** Different ents each Wednesday. Cinema discount with SU card. Lots of good pubs and clubs; student night every night somewhere in Swansea. **Sports:** Free use of Swansea Leisure Centre with SU card and passport to leisure scheme. **Hardship funds:** Institute emergency fund and access funds but need extenuating circumstances to get anything. Grovel to understanding bank managers. Abundance of tight-fisted cashpoint machines. **Travel:** M4 express hitch route to the East. Good overall communication including coach and train services. Shared lifts always advertised. **Work:** Local department stores, bar/restaurant work. Summer jobs not bad but pay poor.

Alumni (Editors' pick)

Mervyn Davies.

TEESSIDE POLY

See Teesside University

TEESSIDE UNIVERSITY

University of Teesside, Middlesbrough, Cleveland TS1 3BA
(0642 218121) Map A, E4

Student enquiries: Admissions Officer

Main study areas – as in What to Study section: *(First degree):* Accountancy, art & design, biochemistry, biotechnology, business studies, chemical engineering, chemistry, civil engineering, communication studies, computing, electrical & electronic engineering, English, European studies, history, information technology, law, mathematical and production engineering, mechanical and production engineering, metallurgy & materials science, modern languages, nursing studies, philosophy, politics and government, professions allied to medicine (PAMs), psychology, public administration, social policy and social welfare, sociology. *Also:* Building & construction, criminology, sports studies.

European Community: 5% first degree students take EC language as part of course and 2% spend up to a year in another EC country. Formal exchange links with universities/colleges in Belgium, Denmark, France, Germany, Greece, Netherlands, Portugal and Spain – mostly open to all students. Approved Erasmus and Comett programmes. Internationally orientated courses eg international business, government and policy in Europe. Languages built into some degrees, and offered as an option in many others. All students have access to EC language tuition by system of late afternoon classes open to all staff and students.

Application: PCAS for 1993 start, UCAS thereafter; except art and design (ADAR). **Academic features:** New courses in business economics, health sciences, law and finance, journalism, sports sciences, radiography, manufacturing and business. **Largest fields of study:** Business studies, humanities, social studies, computer science, engineering. **Founded:** 1992 as a university; previously Teesside Poly, founded 1930. **Main awards:** BA, BSc, BEng, LLB. **Awarding body:** Teesside University. **Site:** Middlesbrough town centre and Flatts Lane, Normanby (4 miles away). **Access:** Nearby bus and railway stations; A19 road; Teesside international airport. **Accommodation:** 727 places in mixed and segregated official residence (70% reserved for first years) comprising 191 places in self-catering houses, approx cost: £29.14 pw; 221 places in halls offering b&b for 5 days, approx cost £35.74 pw; 145 places in highrise block, approx cost £19 pw (plus electricity); and 170 places in halls (mainly shared study bedrooms) offering limited self-catering facilities, approx cost £31.14 pw. **Private sector:** Head tenancy scheme run by the University, private sector self-catering furnished properties and lodgings. Total places 1,200. Rents negotiated annually. All private sector accommodation is inspected. **Library:** Main site and Flatts Lane centre; 200,000 volumes; plus 8,000 annually. 1,800 periodicals; 500 study places (main site), 65 (Flatts Lane). **Other learning facilities:** Computer centre with networks of PCs and the library with networks of Macintoshes, all to be connected to the University – wide network based on a fibre-optic backbone. **Welfare:** Occupational nurse, accommodation officer, student liaison officer, student financial adviser, student counsellor, chaplains. **Special categories:** Limited residential facilities for the disabled; 66-place nursery (enquire when applying). **Careers:** Information and guidance on vocations, jobs and further courses. **Amenities:** Recreation unit, amenities block with SU bars, coffee bar, shop, refectory, welfare unit.

Duration of first degree course(s) or equivalent: 3 years; 4 years sandwich **Total first degree students 1991/92:** 4,263 **Overseas students:** 200 **Male/female ratio:** 2:1 **Teaching staff: full-time:** 800 **part-time:** 300 **Total full-time students 1991/92:** 5,457 **Postgraduate students:** 600 **Tuition fees for 1992/93** (first degrees): Home: £800 (if no grant), £1,855 (classroom), £2,770 (lab/studio); Overseas: £4,250.

CAN'T FIND WHAT YOU'RE LOOKING FOR? USE THE INDEX!

What it's like

It's on two main sites, though the university is now basing some of its courses at some local and some not so local FE Colleges – so beware! The main site is in Middlesbrough Centre, and the other is at Flatts lane, five miles away at the foot of the Eston Hills. The university library is inadequate in terms of size and book provision, though does have a lot of journals.

There is a lack of purpose built accommodation for first years, although private sector housing, both through the university and landlords, usually suffices. Avoid problems if you can, by looking for accommodation as soon as you know you're coming.

Facilities for students with disabilities seem inadequate.

Teesside is not a cultural desert. It has a cinema and the town hall is a regular stopping place for some big productions. Near by are ten-screen cinemas, bowling alleys, an arts centre and bingo.

Locals are not always friendly, but the surrounding area is great. The North Yorkshire Moors are near by, as are Whitby, York, Newcastle and Redcar.

SU employs around 30 full time staff, and around 120 part time staff. It runs many services for its members, with 2 shops, 3 bars, a pizzeria, print shop, insurance agent, welfare officer and a women's minibus service. It has the largest nursery of any HE institution, but demand is high.

John Gibson, General Secretary

Pauper Notes

Accommodation: Usually problems at the beginning of the year, with the lack of bed-space. **Drink:** Cheapest drink in town, cheaper than local pubs and night-clubs. **Eats:** Great variety of fast foods and restaurants. **Ents:** SU ents are cheap and varied. Amateur theatre plays at Stockton, and town hall has varied events. **Sports:** Wide range of sports clubs run by the SU. Local facilities available to students. **Hardship funds:** University access funds; SU welfare loans and hard-ship payments scheme. **Travel:** Coach travel from London (5 hours) and BR becoming ever more expensive. Middlesbrough on some direct routes now, not just a branch line. **Work:** Could be a problem, as Teesside has one of the highest unemployment rates in Britain. SU offers many the opportunity of part time employment.

Alumni (Editors' pick)

David Bowe MEP, Stephen Hughes MEP.

THAMES POLY

See Greenwich University

THAMES VALLEY UNIVERSITY

Thames Valley University
(1) **Ealing Campus, St Mary's Road, Ealing, London W5 5RF**
   (081 579 5000) Map D, A2
(2) **Slough Campus, Wellington Street, Slough, Berkshire SL1 1YG**
   (0753 534585)

Student enquiries: Information Centres on either campus

Main study areas – as in What to Study section: *(First degree):* Accountancy, American studies, business studies, computing, economics, English, European studies, fine arts, geography, history, hotel and catering management, information technology, law, library & information studies, modern languages, music, nursing studies, psychology. *Also:* Arts management, criminology, leisure, publishing.

European Community: Approx 55% first degree students take EC language as part of course and 30% spend 6 months or more in another EC country. Formal exchange links with some 24 EC universities/colleges: France (5); Germany (7); Italy (1); Netherlands (3); Portugal (2); Spain (6), many open to non-language specialists. BA applied languages Europe, in collaboration with University of Aix-en-Provence and Fachhochschule Koln or Universidad Granada. Approved Erasmus programme. Increasing number of courses allow 1 semester study abroad in EC.

Application: PCAS for 1993 start, UCAS thereafter. **Academic features:** New degree courses in criminal justice, social sciences, European law, information systems. **Founded:** 1992, as a university; previously West London Poly, founded 1991 ex Ealing College, Queen Charlotte's College of Health Care Studies, London College of Music, Thames Valley College. **Main awards:** BA, BSc. **Awarding body:** Thames Valley University. **Site:** Ealing and Slough. **Access:** Easily reached by road and public transport. **Accommodation:** Accommodation officer arranges flats and lodgings locally. **Library:** 215,600 volumes, 1,500+ periodical titles, 570 study places. **Welfare:** Student services provides medical, counselling and welfare services. **Careers:** Information and advice service. **Amenities:** Well-equipped students union on both sites. University employment agency – First Employment Services Ltd.

Duration of first degree course(s) or equivalent: 3 or 4 years **Total first degree students 1991/92:** 3,421 **Overseas students:** 800 **Mature students:** 40% **Male/female ratio:** 3:4 **Teaching staff: full-time:** 442 **part-time:** 407 **Total full-time students 1991/92:** 6,500 **Postgraduate students:** 1,622 **Tuition fees for 1992/93 (first degrees):** Home: £1,855 (classroom), £2,770 (lab/studio); Overseas: £5,319.

What it's like

It's a two-site campus university, Ealing and Slough. Ealing campus is 30 minutes out of central London by tube; within easy walking distance of Ealing Broadway and South Ealing tubes. Slough campus is 17 miles away along M4. Good train and bus links. Slough caters for many non-degree as well as degree courses. Both sites have friendly atmosphere; impersonality of larger institutions avoided. Lively, effective SU has expanded rapidly with new offices, larger facilities and extra staff. SU runs a wide range of social events and activities and supports a large number of clubs: standard sporting (most activities catered for), cultural and political groups; also ethnic groups (Afro-Caribbean, Asian etc student association). SU deals with wide range of problems such as financial, accommodation and academic. No halls of residence. Rents are high locally, but SU and student services try to deal with all problems. Low drop-out rate. Comprehensive student support services. Courses are student driven/orientated and innovative; eg DAMM (Design and Media Management), the first of its type in the world, was set up here. Improving facilities for students with disabilities. Good relationship between SU and college. Free handbooks to all students on enrolment; freshers' pack available to all students. SU has non-sexist and non-racist policy. Confidential counselling service available in SU and student services.

Pauper notes

Drink: Excellent, friendly student bar; much cheaper (£1–£2 per pint) than local pubs. Firkin pubs popular – lively, drink-inducing atmosphere, eg Ferret & Firkin, Lots Road. **Eats:** Cheap food (including vegetarian) in student refectory, SU shop and bar. Some restaurants give student discounts, eg Bella Pasta in Ealing Broadway. **Ents:** Wide and increasing range of SU-based events – discos, cabaret, live bands. Waterman Centre, Broadway Boulevard – cheap student night Tuesdays, £1 plus cheap drink. Plenty of local cinemas; local arts centre

(Watermans); easy access to central London for theatre, films etc. **Sports:** Very good /cheap facilities for all major and minor sports. Student discounts if have TVU sports card at some centres, eg Gurnell swimming pool and Ealing squash courts. **Hardship fund:** Access funds – limited money therefore limited help. Money to specific students. **Travel:** Good foreign placements on various courses, eg USA, Russia, Mexico and Europe. A must for every student is a Young Persons Railcard. **Work:** Student bar; use students as security in bar and some students to help in SU, especially during freshers' week.

TRINITY & ALL SAINTS

Trinity & All Saints College, Brownberrie Lane, Horsforth, Leeds LS18 5HD (0532 584341) Map A, E5

Student enquiries: Admissions Officer

Main study areas – as in What to Study section: *(First degree):* Business studies, communication studies, economics, education, English, geography, history, mathematical studies, modern languages, psychology, public administration, religious studies and theology, sociology. *Also:* Physical education, public media, recreation studies.

European Community: 11% first degree students take EC language as part of course and 11% spend 6 months or more in another EC country. Erasmus exchange links with 5 EC universities/colleges: France (languages, business management and public media); Germany and Portugal (languages and public media). Other formal links with Germany (1); Netherlands (2); Spain (2). Approved Erasmus programme 1992/93.

Application: UCCA for 1993 start, UCAS thereafter. **Structural features:** A college of Leeds University. **Academic features:** Courses designed to lead to specific career outcomes – all students combine an academic and a professional subject. Two six-week attachments for non-initial teacher training students. All courses starting 1994 will be modular. **Largest fields of study:** Public media, business management and administration, education. **Founded:** 1966. **Main awards:** BA, BSc, BA (with QTS), BSc (with QTS) **Awarding body:** Leeds University. **Site:** Single campus in semi-rural surroundings. **Access:** Bus stop at door (direct services Leeds and Bradford); rail station 10 mins walk (Leeds to Harrogate line). **Accommodation:** 8 halls of residence; 330 study bedrooms. Plentiful private accommodation nearby. Approx cost: £49.80 pw (incl 3 meals/day). **Rent:** 25% (all first years) in accommodation where rent controlled by college. **Library:** 100,000 volumes, 800 periodicals, 170 study places. **Other learning facilities:** Computer labs, sound radio studio, video editing suite, TV studio, photography dark rooms, science labs, primary and secondary education bases. **Welfare:** College counsellor (half-time); sick bay, local GP visits. Special coordinator for mature/access students. **Special facilities:** Nursery – run for students as part of early years education course. **Hardship funds:** Dean of Students disburses about £15,000 to needy students each year. **Careers:** Information and advice available. **Amenities:** Self-contained SU building with performing centre, 2 bars and coffee bar. Recreational and cultural activities, including performing arts, golf, car maintenance, modern languages, keep fit etc. **Sporting facilities:** Double gym, 5 squash courts, all-weather pitch, rugby & soccer, cricket, fitness centre. **Employment:** Teaching, management, marketing, journalism, broadcasting, recreation, finance.

Duration of first degree course(s) or equivalent: 3 years **others:** 4 years (BA/BSc with QTS) **Total first degree students 1991/92:** 1,440 **Number of BA/BSc (education) students:** Approx 600 **Overseas students:** 9 **Mature students:** 280 **Male/female ratio:** 2:5 **Teaching staff: full-time:** 90 **part-time:** 30 **Total full-time**

students 1991/92: 1,600 **Postgraduate students:** 130. **Tuition fees for 1992/93** (first degrees): Home: £1,855 (classroom), £2,770 (lab/studio); Overseas: £4,575.

What it's like

It was built in the sixties and fairly modern in design. Accommodation good, as is the food. Each first year is offered a chance to live in hall but the numbers involved mean that some might have to share or live in locality. Halls of residence mixed; each room fitted with a wash basin, wardrobe, cupboard, a desk, easy chair and bed.

Atmosphere on campus that of a small community, where everyone knows everyone else; relationship between staff, both domestic and academic, and students is good. Social life good, with activities taking place on campus. It's within the bounds of Leeds and Bradford, both university cities, with a number of student orientated events.

Travel good; 5 bus services pass college gates. Horsforth BR station 15–20 mins walk away. Leeds/Bradford airport 2 miles away. (College good for plane spotters.)

Pauper notes

Drink: College bar; wide selection of beers, lagers and ciders at cheap prices. Local pubs good – geared to younger generation. **Eats:** Cheap eats: The Outside Inn, Horsforth, good food, big portions and very reasonably priced. **Ents:** Cinemas in and around Leeds give discounts, also Bradford Museum of Film & Photography. Most nightclubs have student nights. **Travel:** West Yorkshire metro system operates cheap off-peak fares on bus and rail: you can travel round all west Yorkshire for approx 75p. **Hardship funds:** Apply through Dean of Students. **Work:** Availability not known.

TRINITY COLLEGE CARMARTHEN

Trinity College, Carmarthen SA31 3EP
(0267 237971/2/3) Map A, C7

Student enquiries: Registrar

Main study areas – as in What to Study section: *(First degree):* Education. *Also:* Rural environment studies.

European Community: Number of students spending time in another EC country as part of their course not known. Formal exchange links with Eire (Limerick), Italy (Florence).

Application: PCAS for 1993 start, UCAS thereafter. **Special features:** Conference centre. 50 USA students follow special course as part of their degree programme. **Academic features:** BEd in bilingual education in Wales. **Founded:** 1848 Church Voluntary College. **Main awards:** BEd, BA, BSc. **Awarding body:** Wales University. **Site:** On outskirts of West Wales market town of Carmarthen. Within easy reach of the Pembrokeshire and Brecon Beacons national parks. **Accommodation:** Hostels on campus for most first, third and fourth-year students. Approx cost: £30–£42 pw. **Learning resources:** Microcomputers; film cameras and closed circuit TV; 130-acre farm. Modernised language lab; modern theatre. **Careers:** Guidance given. **Sporting facilities:** Heated swimming pool, gymnasia, weights room; multi-purpose floodlit all-weather playing surfaces; strong rugby tradition.

Duration of first degree course(s) or equivalent: 3 years; 4 years (BEd); **BEd students:** 704 **Overseas students:** 60 **Mature students:** 150 **Male/female ratio:** 1:2 **Teaching staff: full-time:** 83 **Total full-time students 1992/93:** 1,392 **Postgraduate students:** 100 **Tuition fees for 1991/92** (first degrees): £1,855 (Home); £4,842 (Overseas).

CAN'T FIND WHAT YOU'RE LOOKING FOR? USE THE INDEX!

What it's like

Bilingual (English/Welsh) college in West Wales close to climbing, hill walking, rivers, forests and sea. East Dyfed School of Nursing on campus. SU bar. Daily religious services (voluntary). Accommodation on the whole is poor and in need of repair. However college now redecorating and has built a new self-catering hostel for 3rd and 4th years. Excellent sporting facilities – 2 gymnasia, indoor heated swimming pool, rugby, soccer and hockey pitches, athletics track, tennis and netball courts, all-weather match cricket as well as grass wickets and five concrete practice wickets. Active drama societies, orchestra, choir, folk groups, brass and woodwind ensembles. Opportunities for learning Welsh.

Small college so everyone knows everyone else. Live music every weekend in SU. Disco, Twmpaths (Welsh folk dancing).

A must for anyone who knows how to have a good time.

Pauper notes

Accommodation: Campus hostels. Digs in town. **Drink:** Cheap in SU bar. 56 pubs in town. **Eats:** Good food on campus and veg food. **Ents:** Excellent groups videos, discos on campus. **Sports:** Good gyms, weights, pool. Outdoor pursuits. Huge local leisure centre. **Travel:** Railway station and buses. **Work:** Not that much.

More info?

Get students' Alternative Prospectus.
Enquiries to Trinity SU (0267 237794).

Alumni (Editors' pick)

Barry John, Carwen James.

TRINITY COLLEGE OF MUSIC

Trinity College of Music, Mandeville Place, London W1M 6AQ (071 935 5773) Map E, B2

Student enquiries: Registrar

Main study areas – as in What to Study section: *(First degree):* Music. *Also:* Performance arts.

European Community: Language classes in French, German and Italian for singing students, as well as French and Italian song and German Lieder.

Application: Direct. **Academic features:** Jazz and electronic, IT and early music departments. DipTCL for teachers and performers; MMus (performance and related studies); specialist short courses for overseas students. **Special features:** College was founded to provide training in church music, but is a conservatoire for training teachers and performers for a variety of careers in music. **Largest fields of study:** Piano, singing and orchestral instruments. **Founded:** 1872. **Main awards:** GTCL, DipTCL, FTCL, LTCL. **Awarding body:** Trinity College. **Site:** Just off Manchester Square, central London. **Access:** Bond Street underground station; buses. **Accommodation:** 40 places in mixed hall (priority to those outside London area); registrar's assistant will help first years. Approx cost: £550–£800 per term in hall. Rent: no student accommodated where college controls rent. **Library:** 4,000 volumes, 12 periodicals, 30 study places. **Other learning resources:** Recording studio. **Specialist collections:** Barbirolli Collection of scores. **Welfare:** Doctor, FPA, psychiatrist, physiotherapist, welfare officer. **Careers:** Information, advice and placement. **Employment:** Music teaching and performing.

Duration of first degree course(s) or equivalent: 3 years; **others:** 4 years **Total first degree students 1991/92:** 330 **Overseas students:** EC – 22; others – 13

Male/female ratio: 1:2 **Teaching staff: full-time:** 8 **part-time:** 104 **Total full-time students 1991/92:** 391 **Postgraduate students:** 51 **Tuition fees for 1992/93** (first degrees): Home: £2,770; Overseas: £6,300.

What it's like

Trinity is a small but perfectly formed friendly college with around 400 students who study all aspects of music. Although student population is on the whole made up of British nationals, there is a strong overseas contingent from countries as diverse as Iceland and Indonesia.

Trinity has long history of music education. It started life as a conservatoire for church music in 1872 and has expanded rapidly ever since. It has pioneered practical music exams, an early music department, and a junior department. The college itself consists of two buildings a couple of minutes walk from each other in heart of the West End.

Regular public concerts are given by the symphony orchestra and chamber groups at various venues in and around London. 'See press for details'!

Student facilities leave a lot to be desired, in fact they are all but non-existent. There is a common room with a coffee machine, pool table and a couple of video games and that's just about it. Plenty of sandwich shops nearby, and the union sells food two days a week.

Active SU has two representatives on the governing body. It supports several clubs and societies as well as dealing with welfare problems.

Pauper notes

Accommodation: Henry Wood House has places for 28 students, other accommodation found in a number of other Church-run hostels otherwise students find their own digs. **Drink:** College bar; most students go to Angel where they drink Samuel Smith's Ale. **Eats:** Buzz (Thayer Street), SU baked potatoes twice a week. Stockpot (Italian run). **Ents:** Social societies such as Rats, The Pork Pie Society, a curry appreciation club and a Video Club. Students often get in cheap to a number of Concert halls etc. **Sports:** Football, cricket teams; nearest sports complex ULU. **Hardship funds:** Access funds. **Travel:** Day trips and other continental trips arranged by SU. **Work:** Part-time shop work etc is readily available as well as part-time teaching. Students also supplement their grants by playing gigs.

Informal name:

Trinity or TCM.

Alumni (Editors' pick)

Heather Harper, Margaret Price, John Hancorn, Manoug Parikian, Gilbert Biberian – composer/guitarist, Steve Sidwell – 'Wham', Winston Rollins – 'Aswad', Mark Nightingale – 'Harry Connick Jnr', Joe Loss.

ULSTER UNIVERSITY

University of Ulster, Cromore Road, Coleraine, County Londonderry, Northern Ireland BT52 1SA (0265 44141) Map A, B4

Student enquiries: Admissions Officer

Main study areas – as in What to Study section: *(First degree):* Accountancy, American studies, art & design, Asian studies, biochemistry, biology, business studies, civil engineering, communication studies, computing, drama, economics, education, electrical & electronic engineering, English, environmental science, European studies, fine arts, food science & nutrition, geography, history, hotel & catering management, mathematical studies, mechanical and production engineering, modern languages, music, nursing studies, philosophy, politics & govern-

CAN'T FIND WHAT YOU'RE LOOKING FOR? USE THE INDEX!

ment, professions allied to medicine (PAMs), psychology, social policy and social welfare, sociology, speech sciences. *Also:* Advertising and public relations, building, interpretation and translation, Irish studies, media studies, medical laboratory science, sports studies, surveying, tourism.

European Community: 12% first degree students take EC language as part of course and 2% spend 6 months or more in another EC country. Formal exchange links with 22 EC universities/colleges in France (11); Germany (8); and Spain (3). Approved Erasmus programme 1992/93; participating in 20 Erasmus and Lingua exchange programmes, of which 15 are open to non-language specialists. Year in EC country available, with additional diploma, on courses in geography, environmental science, European regional development and modern and contemporary history. Language options (and possibly a year abroad) available on some other courses.

Application: UCCA for 1993 start, UCAS thereafter; direct for BSc Nursing for registered nurses (professional development in nursing) and BTech; ADAR for art and design. **Academic features:** New courses in government and law, visual communication, software engineering, business with computing. **Founded:** 1984 ex New University of Ulster and Ulster Polytechnic. **Main awards:** BA, BEd, BSc, BMus, BEng, MEng, BTech. **Awarding body:** Ulster University. **Site:** Main campuses at Jordanstown, 7 miles NE of Belfast, and Coleraine, 55 miles N of Belfast. Also campuses in Belfast and Londonderry; close to the heart of the city in both cases. **Access:** All campuses have road and rail connections. Air and sea routes from UK. **Accommodation:** 680 residential places at Jordanstown, majority allocated to first year students at Jordanstown: 280 places at Coleraine; also 103 residential places at Magee College. Other students live at home, in rented accommodation or accommodation provided by Student Housing Association. **Library:** Library on each site; main libraries at Coleraine and Jordanstown; 556,000 volumes in total; 5,100 periodicals. **Other learning resources:** Education technology unit; computer services; social skills training centre. **Welfare:** Counsellors; doctors, chaplains. **Special categories:** Residential facilities for married and disabled students (Jordanstown); creche and day nursery (Coleraine, Jordanstown and Magee College). **Careers:** Information, advice and placement. **Amenities:** SU with extensive leisure facilities; Belfast museums and galleries; Ulster Orchestra concerts; Riverside Theatre at Coleraine. **Sporting facilities:** Sports centres on Coleraine and Jordanstown sites with full facilities including swimming and diving pools at Jordanstown.

Duration of first degree course(s) or equivalent: 3 years; **others:** 4 years (eg sandwich; courses including period abroad); 5 years (MEng) **Total first degree students 1991/92:** 9,285 **BEd students:** (Part-time only) 150 **Overseas students:** 169 **Mature students:** 25% of full-time degree students **Male/female ratio:** 6:7 **Teaching staff:** 776 **Total full-time students 1991/92:** 9,986 **Postgraduate students:** 718 (f-t), 2,454 (p-t) **Tuition fees for 1992/93** (first degrees): Home: £1,855 (classroom), £2,770 (lab/studio); Overseas: £4,130 (classroom), £5,500 (lab/studio).

What it's like

4 campuses. Belfast campus has all the advantages of the city's wide ranging services. Students work in bright, airy buildings of ex-art college. Atmosphere relaxed, facilities adequate; art and design subjects dominant in the academic programme. Almost 20% of students on foundation (pre-entry programmes). Jordanstown, 7 miles north of Belfast, is the largest campus (4,326 ft/2,829 pt). High reputation for industry. Very high proportion of part-time students. Facilities good. Student village with 760 places attractive but, for N Ireland, pricey. Business management and science and technology most important courses. Campus well integrated with European, American/Canadian and Far East students.

Coleraine is university headquarters. Campus of the 60s situated close to 2 of N Ireland's main holiday resorts, Portstewart and Portrush, much favoured by students for accommodation outside the summer months. Student facilities have markedly improved. All major faculties present at Coleraine, which has a high reputation in sports and excellent facilities. Academic courses strongly favour continuous assessment. Magee campus transferred over 5 years. New buildings now surround the 19th century college, which has proved a major success in attracting mature students to foundation, degree and postgraduate courses.

Pauper notes

Accommodation: 1,000 students in halls of residence. South side of city holds large student population with good services but rents high for only fair accommodation. **Drink:** Univ bar £1.15 a pint; outside £1.35. **Ents:** Good social life on campus. Wide range univ ents. Good bars in the city. **Eats:** Awful all round. **Sports:** Good except Magee & ADC. **Hardship funds:** Available. **Travel:** Deals with Ulsterbus/NIR. Cheap taxis from city to Jordanstown site, morning and afternoon. **Work:** Good. Union employs 70–80 students part-time, mainly from hardship list.

Informal name:

UU.

Alumni (Editors' pick)

Mark Robson (commentator), Pat Jennings (footballer), Will Cooper (rock star).

UMDS

United Medical & Dental Schools of Guy's & St Thomas's Hospitals, Lambeth Palace Road, London SE1 7EH (071 922 8013)
Map E, D3, C4

Student enquiries: Undergraduate Admissions Officer

Main study areas – as in What to Study section: *(First degree):* Dentistry, medicine.

European Community: Formal exchange links with University of Lille. As an alternative to the intercalated BSc course, students can opt in the third year to learn a language and develop knowledge of health care delivery in another European country.

Application: UCCA for 1993 start, UCAS thereafter. **Structural features:** School of London University. **Special features:** Students admitted for both pre-clinical and clinical studies (some places for students who have completed pre-clinical studies at other UK medical schools). Dental students taught mainly at Guy's and medical students on both sites. **Main awards:** MBBS, BDS. **Awarding body:** London University. **Founded:** 1982 from medical schools of Guy's (1726) and St Thomas's (12th century). **Site:** St Thomas's Hospital (south of Westminster Bridge) and Guy's Hospital (south of London Bridge). **Accommodation:** School accommodation for 435 students; university halls of residence also available. All first-years are guaranteed a room. Rent: 25% in accommodation where rent controlled by university. **Library:** Substantial libraries on both sites together with computer-assisted and audio-visual learning facilities. **Welfare:** Doctor, dentist, counsellors, chaplain, student advisers and tutors. **Careers:** Various pre-registration posts reserved for UMDS students at hospitals in or near London. **Sporting facilities:** Swimming pools, gymnasium, squash courts and 2 sports grounds. Playing fields 10 minutes and 40 minutes by train from London Bridge/Waterloo.

Duration of first degree course(s) or equivalent: 5 years **Total first degree**

WANT TO HELP WITH THE NEXT EDITION – SEE PAGE 76

students 1991/92: 1,570 **Overseas students:** 55 **Mature students:** 120 **Male/female ratio:** 3:2 **Teaching staff:** full-time 200 part-time: 400 **Total full-time students 1991/92:** 1,650 **Postgraduate students:** 300 **Tuition fees for 1992/93** (first degrees): Home: £775 (if no grant), £2,770 (pre-clinical), £4,985 (clinical); Overseas: £7,450 (pre-clinical), £13,840 (clinical).

" True Dickensian atmosphere at a snip..... "

What it's like

UMDS was formed from two of London's most prestigious medical schools: Guy's and St Thomas's. Now in our fourth year of complete amalgamation we are reaping the benefits of union and most of the hatchets and rivalry have been buried.

St Thomas's is very attractively situated opposite Westminster and only 10 minutes away from the West End. Guy's is a short bus journey away at London Bridge and has peaceful gardens and courtyards.

Teaching is evenly split between the campuses, both being well equipped with lecture theatres and boasting between them brand new anatomy and physiology departments. UMDS has four libraries, two student bars, shops, laundries, canteens and two playing fields and the historic Gordon Pathology Museum (one of the largest in the country).

The course is traditional in structure; however, clinical experience (including GP and nursing attachments) is becoming an increasing part of preclinical years. Dental school is situated on the Guy's campus and contains most of its own teaching facilities. Pastoral guidance is provided throughout the course by a tutor/guidance scheme. Clinical teaching is provided by two of London's largest and well-respected hospitals.

Sport is inevitably strong following amalgamation and successes at university level are matched by the variety on offer (from polo to korfball).

The schools have a very active drama society with regular shows and an appearance at Edinburgh Festival. Music is also strong and college bands and concert groups are provided with rehearsal rooms and a PA system.

UMDS hosts one of the largest summer balls in London and the annual Hallowe'en ball is always eagerly anticipated. There are social events on at least

GET HOLD OF THE PROSPECTUSES

one campus every week and if that doesn't keep you happy, then London also has plenty to offer in entertainment.

London has never been a great place for student accommodation but UMDS has campus halls for students and nearly everyone finds somewhere they're happy with.

London is the most exciting and dynamic city in the country and a training at UMDS not only gives you the opportunity to enjoy the capital but also to receive a high-quality medical education in modern surroundings.

Richard Simcock, Anne Ward

Pauper notes

Accommodation: Student halls at both campuses. Most are pleasant, modern and cheap. **Drink:** Guy's new bar one of cheapest in London. Wealth of local friendly pubs. **Eats:** Two subsidised restaurants, also cheap hospital canteens (if you dare!). Every aspect of world cuisine within easy reach. **Ents:** Very active SU. Hops every week, 2 annual balls, film club on both campuses and college bands. West End in easy reach, regular shows. **Sports:** Two gyms, swimming pool, squash courts, two playing fields, mountaineering hut, boat club on Thames. **Hardship funds:** Some scholarships available. **Travel:** Biking between campuses quick, easy and cheap. Anywhere in London in easy reach by bus. **Work:** Some do nursing work in hospital but plenty of part-time work available in London. **European Community:** 2 delegates for European Medical Students' Association (EMSA) in Brussels, 1991; night classes in French (and maybe German). 2 NAMS delegates.

Informal name:

UMDS; Guy's and Thommies.

Alumni (Editors' pick)

David Owen, Somerset Maugham, John Keats, Jeffrey Tate (conductor), Lord Butterfield, Addison (as in disease), Florence Nightingale, Sir William Gull (possibly Jack the Ripper).

UMIST

**The University of Manchester Institute of Science & Technology
PO Box 88, Sackville Street, Manchester M60 1QD
(061 236 3311) Map A, D6**

Student enquiries: Registrar

Main study areas – as in What to Study section: *(First degree):* Aeronautical engineering, biochemistry, biotechnology, business studies, chemical engineering, chemistry, civil engineering, computing, electrical & electronic engineering, environmental studies, information technology, linguistics, mathematical studies, mechanical and production engineering, metallurgy and materials science, modern languages, physics. *Also:* American business studies, building, computational linguistics, ophthalmic optics, operational research, paper science, quantity surveying, textiles.

European Community: 8% first degree students take EC language as part of course and 8% spend 6 months or more in another EC country. Formal exchange links with 30 EC universities/colleges: Belgium (1); Denmark (2); France (10);

Germany (9); Greece (1); Italy (2); Portugal (3); Spain (2). Approved Erasmus programmes 1992/93. Languages may be combined with eg paper science, biochemistry, computational physics, chemical engineering, chemistry, maths, physics, management, textiles, electronics, environmental science.

Application: UCCA for 1993 start, UCAS thereafter. **Academic features:** BEng (3-year) and MEng (4-year) courses in major engineering disciplines. Large and prestigious school of management. Many joint courses including languages, environmental studies and management. Only degree course in paper science, with management and language options. **Largest fields of study:** Science and technology, engineering management sciences. **Founded:** 1824, faculty of Manchester University since 1905, charter awarded 1956. **Main awards:** BSc, BEng, BScMEng, MEng. **Awarding body:** Manchester University. **Site:** Centre of Manchester. **Access:** Bus, train and metrolink; 25 mins from Manchester Airport. **Accommodation:** Over 6,800 places in halls and university self-catering residences (shared with Manchester University). Approx cost: £1,600 pa (halls), £1,100 pa (self-catering). Rent: 36% in accommodation where rent controlled by university. **Library:** Over 226,000 volumes; also resources of main university library and public libraries. **Centres of excellence:** John Rylands University Library at Manchester, Nuffield Radio Astronomy labs at Jodrell Bank. **Welfare:** Services include doctors, dentists, psychiatric adviser, clinical psychologist, counsellors and nurses. Purpose-built chapel for all denominations. **Hardship funds:** UMIST student hardship loan fund, access funds. **Sponsorship:** Sponsorship Information Service. **Careers:** Information, advice and placement. **Amenities:** SU building with bar, shop, travel bureau, halls, lounges, and welfare office including overseas student adviser; wide range of clubs and societies; sports centre; students may also join Manchester University SU.

Duration of first degree course(s) or equivalent: 3 years; **others:** 4 years **Total first degree students 1991/92:** 3,929 **Overseas students:** 595 **Mature undergraduate students:** 12% **Male/female ratio:** 7:3 **Teaching staff: full-time:** 405 **part-time:** 5 **Total full-time students 1991/92:** 5,226 **Postgraduate students:** 1,297 **Tuition fees for 1992/93** (first degrees): Home: £1,855 (classroom), £2,770 (lab); Overseas: £5,320 (classroom), £7,055 (lab).

What it's like

Campus university, in the heart of Manchester. 2 mins walk from all the record stores, fast food shops and department stores you'll ever need. Pubs (The Old Garratt, Lass O'Gowrie) and SU bars all no more than 60 seconds away from campus.

SU facilities range from dark room, bar etc to the copyshop with computer typesetting facilities and full photocopying. SU Travel Bureau among the most popular in Manchester, offering special student discounts. Popular Coffee Shop packed every lunchtime. SU fortnightly newspaper, *Grip*, written, produced, composed and arranged by students who also develop the photographs and typeset the text. SU disco (Sharansky's) has eclectic selection of music night to night, Acid House to Heavy Metal catered for. Regular bar promotions ensure that UMIST SU has cheapest bars in Manchester. All entertainment organised by students who DJ, set up lighting rigs, act as roadies for bands, mix and publicise. UMIST Union has about 60 societies and very active community action and rag group.

About 21% overseas students, 30% women and 24% post-graduates. Worldwide reputation for science research. A separate university with its own campus and union; students can also take full advantage of the facilities of Manchester University, concerts, societies, sports facilities and halls.

Pauper notes

Accommodation: University halls offer to UMIST and univ students, Hulme flats. **Drink:** Lass O'Gowrie (Charles St), Robin Hood (Moss Side), The Clarence (Irish pub on Wilmslow Rd), King's Arms (Chorlton-on-Medlock, brews Dobbins beer in cellar). **Eats:** Chicago Diner (East Didsbury), Chinese restaurants in

Chinatown (loads of them), massive Asian quarter in Rusholme has all manner of dishes at wildly varying prices. **Ents:** Free concert and movie tickets if reviewing for SU newspaper, 7 theatres, 7 cinemas, 5 art galleries, Cornerhouse is trendy but not expensive, free SU disco on Thursday. **Sports:** McDougall Sports Centre, Armitage centre, Sugden centre featuring squash, pool etc. **Hardship funds:** Institute fund and SU welfare loans. **Travel:** SU travel office open to enquiries.

Alumni (Editors' pick)

Sir John Cockroft, Sir Alan Veale, Gary Bailey, Sir William Barlow, David Clark MP, Keith Oates.

UNIVERSITY COLLEGE LONDON

University College London, Gower Street, London WC1E 6BT
(071 387 7050) Map E, C1

Student enquiries: Registrar

You can look up Institute of Archaeology, National Hospitals College and Slade separately.

Main study areas – as in What to Study section: *(First degree):* Anatomy, anthropology, archaeology, architecture, biochemistry, biology, biotechnology, botany, business studies, chemical engineering, chemistry, civil engineering, classics, computing, economics, electrical and electronic engineering, English, environmental studies, European studies, fine arts, geography, geology, history, Latin-American studies, law, linguistics, marine technology, mathematical studies, mechanical and production engineering, medicine, microbiology, modern languages, Near East and Islamic studies, pharmacology, philosophy, physics, physiology, professions allied to medicine (PAMs), psychology, speech sciences, town and country planning, zoology. *Also:* Biosocial science, Egyptology, human genetics, neuroscience, Romanian, Scandinavian studies.

European Community: Number of students learning an EC language or spending time in another EC country as part of their course, not known. Formal exchange links with numerous EC universities/colleges including Denmark (Copenhagen); Italy (Venice, Pisa); plus universities of Aix-Marseille III (law with French law), Cologne (law with German law) and Florence (law with Italian law). Approved Erasmus programme. BA modern European studies; courses in maths, physics and chemistry with a European language. Sophisticated new language centre.

Application: UCCA for 1993 start, UCAS thereafter. **Structural features:** Part of London University. **Academic features:** 3- or 4-year LLB course available. MEng (4 yrs) in chemical engineering, biochemical engineering, electronic and electrical engineering. **Special features:** School of medicine offers clinical studies to students who have completed pre-clinical studies at Oxbridge. **Founded:** 1828; merged with Middlesex Hospital Medical School and Institute of Archaeology. **Main awards:** BA, BSc, BSc(Econ), BSc(Eng), MBBS, LLB, BEng, MEng. **Awarding body:** London University. **Site:** Heart of London University area in Bloomsbury. **Access:** Warren Street, Euston Square, Goodge Street underground stations, buses. **Accommodation:** 713 places in halls, more than 1,700 in other accommodation; London University Accommodation Office deals with rooms, digs, flats, bedsits, lodgings. All first year undergraduates guaranteed either college or university accommodation. **Library:** Main library in ten departments – 900,000 volumes, 7,000 periodicals, 1,162 study places; special reference facilities for some course books; extensive specialist collections. **Centres of excellence:** Both University College and its school of medicine (formerly University College Hospital School of Medicine) have national and international reputations. **Welfare:** Doctor, dentist, psychiatrist, solicitor, chaplain, student counselling service. **Hardship funds:** Funds available but not for first year students. **Careers:** Information, advice and placement service. **Amenities:** Central London. **Sporting facilities:** 60-acre athletic ground at Shenley.

Duration of first degree course(s) or equivalent: 3 years; **others:** 4 years **Total first degree students 1991/92:** 6,628 **Overseas students:** 1,276 **Male/female ratio:** 5:4 **Teaching staff:** 750 **Total full-time students 1991/92:** 9,026 **Postgraduate students:** 2,529 **Tuition fees for 1992/93** (first degrees): Home: £795 (if no grant), £1,855 (classroom), £2,770 (lab/studio), £4,985 (clinical); Overseas: £6,250 (classroom), £7,995 (lab/studio), £8,970 (anatomy and pre-clinical), £14,215 (clinical).

What it's like

The portico is the centrepiece of the college and can be viewed from the Gower Street entrance. The main campus is situated on Gower Street; much of it is unsuitable for students with disabilities. UCL's academic reputation ranks second only to Oxbridge, many of our departments being on a par with their Oxbridge counterparts. UCL has over 60 departments and 9,000 students.

UCL has both purpose-built and converted halls of residence and student houses. It tries to accommodate all first years and as many third years as possible. Although UCL rents are increasing, still lowest of any London college.

UCL is a cosmopolitan environment in the heart of a cosmopolitan environment – London. Standards are generally very high in all aspects of college life, but particularly in terms of research. Over 50% of students attain first or upper second class degrees. Around a quarter of students are postgraduates. The heart of Bloomsbury is one of the best places to study. Students come from all backgrounds, although those from private school sector may be in a slight majority. Easy to integrate into UCL life.

Pauper notes

Accommodation: Housing rights and advice pack produced by union. Good student halls, cheaper (only just!) than the rest of London University. New block of flats for married students, and two bungalows for students with families. **Drink:** Mainly SU bars ('Gordons' ground floor), second floor bar (recently renovated), Steve Biko Bar, Windeyer Café-bar, Huntley St Medic's Union Bar. **Eats:** SU veggie food quite good. Veggie Indians on Drummond Street nearby excellent. Lots of variety in food available in SU and cheap. **Ents:** Recently renovated disco area (named 'The G-spot') and many bands eg Resque, Bleach, The Dylans, etc. Film Soc get many of latest films which are still in West End. Top fringe theatre, Bloomsbury Theatre, on campus; students get 10 weeks of use. Also studio theatre called 'Theatre Workshop' used by students for a different production each week all year round. **Sports:** University of London pool in Bloomsbury precinct, massive sports ground at Shenley, Herts and at Chiselhurst in Kent. Recently expanded fitness centre with very cheap rates for students. Plans for new sport/leisure centre on campus. **Hardship funds:** Access funds inadequate, but allocated second and third terms. Financial workshops and counselling. **Travel:** Many departments award travel scholarships for long vacation. Travel agent on campus. Most students use the tube. **Work:** Some work in SU. Application forms at reception. Some work available outside SU and in college, if persistent in looking.

Informal name:

UCL.

GET HOLD OF THE PROSPECTUSES

Alumni (Editors' pick)

David Lodge, David Storey, Clare Francis, Jonathan Miller, Lloyd Cole (Commobins) lasted 1 term, Jonathan Dimbleby, David Gower, Carol Thatcher, Geoffrey Dear (former Chief Constable of West Midlands Police), David Johnson (Features editor, Daily Telegraph), Margaret Hodge (Leader, Islington Council).

WALES COLLEGE OF MEDICINE

University of Wales College of Medicine, Heath Park, Cardiff CF4 4XN (0222 747747; Fax 0222 742914) Map A, D8

Student enquiries: Registrar and Secretary

Main study areas – as in What to Study section: *(First degree):* Dentistry, medicine, nursing studies.

European Community: No students learn an EC language or spend time in another EC country as part of their course. Formal exchange links with Hanover and Munster.

Application: UCCA for 1993 start, UCAS thereafter. **Structural features:** Part of Wales University. **Special features:** Offers 6-year medical and dental courses (students usually admitted direct to second year); pre-clinical studies at Cardiff. 3 and 4 year courses in nursing. **Founded:** 1931. **Main awards:** MBBCh, BDS, BN. **Awarding body:** University of Wales. **Site:** Part of complex shared with University Hospital of Wales, 2 miles from city centre. **Access:** By road. **Accommodation:** 213 places in hall, 23 study bedrooms in hostels, 18 flatlets 2 miles from campus. Accommodation available from Warden for all clinical students. Approx cost: £22.50 pw halls, £36.50–£38.50 pw flatlets. **Library:** Main and dental libraries; 100,000 volumes, 1,100 current periodicals, 190 study places, audiovisual facilities. **Centres of excellence:** Tenovus Cancer Research Centre; Institute of Nephrology; Department of Medical Genetics. **Welfare:** Doctor, dentist, psychiatrist, chaplain, 2 student counsellors, international development officer. **Special categories:** Some residential facilities for married students; crèche at University of Wales College of Cardiff. **Careers:** Information and advice (pre-registration house officer posts in Welsh hospitals virtually automatic). **Amenities:** Medical bookshop on campus, music and drama societies. Staff and students' social club. **Sporting facilities:** Athletics facilities of Cardiff University.

Duration of first degree course(s) or equivalent: 5–6 years MB, BCh; 3–4 years BN, 5–6 years BDS **Total first degree students 1991/92:** 791 **Overseas students:** 51 **Mature students:** 10 **Male/female ratio:** 6:7 **Teaching staff: full-time:** 267 **part-time:** 31 **Total full-time students 1991/92:** 920 **Postgraduate students:** 399 **Tuition fees for 1992/93** (first degrees): Home: £2,770 (pre-clinical and BN), £4,985 (clinical); fee may be lower if no grant; Overseas: £7,055 (pre-clinical and BN), £12,990 (clinical).

What it's like

Situated on a 53-acre purpose-built (1970) campus some two and a half miles north of the city centre, UWCM provides teaching facilities for students in medicine, dentistry, bachelor of nursing courses and Project 2000. The campus is easily accessible and is on most main bus routes.

The medical and dental pre-clinical courses are at nearby University of Wales College Cardiff (UWCC) and therefore most 1st year pre-clinical, and some 2nd year pre-clinical students are accommodated by UWCC halls of residence, which include self-catering or full-board facilities.

Accommodation is provided for approximately one-third of clinical students on campus offering single study bedrooms with shared catering and laundry facilities. There is a small number of places for married students. Other students usually choose to find lodgings, which are plentiful in the neighbourhood.

SU and bar (Med Club) are located on ground floor of the 'on-site' hall of residence. SU is essentially apolitical but very active socially, and fields teams in most major sports (not just rugby!). It enjoys exceptionally good relations with college authorities and unlike many other medical student associations it is an autonomous body within the NUS. Students are also able to make full use of the fine facilities offered at UWCC.

UWCM is highly regarded nationally and internationally with an excellent teaching record and a high pass rate. It has over 200 academic staff, and teaching takes the form of lectures, seminars and tutorials, with an emphasis on clinical skills.

Free transport for students is provided to hospitals around the Cardiff area. Most students have opportunity to study in hospitals throughout Wales, as well as undertaking an elective period either abroad or in UK. Examinations take the form of traditional and multiple choice papers as well as vivas. Students are assessed by course work before presentation for degree exams. Resits are possible, but there is no fixed failure rate. Medically trained members of staff act as student counsellors, who treat all information confidentially.

The city has a large student population, and has much to offer. Cardiff is the cultural and sporting centre of Wales, boasting the National Museum of Wales, and the headquarters of Welsh National Opera. It has a fine castle, a superb civic buildings as well as seven cinemas and four theatres including the 2,000-seat St. David's Hall. Cardiff is an excellent shopping centre and has numerous pubs, clubs and restaurants.

Students come here from a wide variety of backgrounds: 40% Welsh students, 50% from other UK countries and 10% overseas students (1989) with a male: female ratio of nearly 1:1. There is no discrimination of any description.

The Students Club has been recently refurbished and redecorated to cope with the amalgamation with the South East Wales Institute of Nursing giving UWCM approximately 1,700 students. The club prides itself on its apolitical, areligious, adiscriminatory, a great place for a party policy.

Pauper Notes

Accommodation: Campus hall £22 week, others pay £25–25 per week in rented houses. Small number of houses/flats for married students. **Drink:** Med Club cheapest prices in Cardiff. Brains is local brew, but many other excellent local beers. **Eats:** Excellent variety of restaurants in town, now with many vegetarian and ethnic eateries. Many offer 10% student discount. **Ents:** new 9-screen cinema due to open. Wed afternoons half-price for students at all cinemas. Student stand-by tickets at reduced cost for most theatres. **Sports:** All SU sports club free; National Sports Centre very reasonable. Sports and social club on campus has membership fee, but also reasonable. **Travel:** Free transport to hospitals in Cardiff area. Scholarships available to help fund electives. **Work:** Preclinical students have similar holidays to other students; clinical students have little/no time to supplement grants with outside work due to long academic terms.

Ian Daniels, President UWCMSC

More info?

Get students' Alternative Prospectus.
Enquiries to Ian Daniels, President UWCMSC (0222 742125).

Informal name

UWCM

GET HOLD OF THE PROSPECTUSES

Alumni (Editors' pick)

Dr. Gareth Crompton, J.N. Parry, John Peters, Doreen Vermeulencranch, Professor B. Knight.

WALES POLY

See Glamorgan University

WALES UNIVERSITY

This is a federal university consisting of 6 colleges: Aberystwyth, Bangor, Cardiff, Lampeter, Swansea and Wales College of Medicine. All select and teach their first degree students themselves. You can look them all up separately. Some other institutions also offer Wales University degrees.

WARWICK UNIVERSITY

The University of Warwick, Coventry CV4 7AL (0203 523523)
Map A, E7

Student enquiries: Academic Registrar

Main study areas – as in What to Study section: *(First degree):* Accountancy, American studies, archaeology, biochemistry, biology, business studies, chemistry, civil engineering, classics, computing, drama and theatre studies, economics, education, electrical & electronic engineering, English, environmental science, European studies, film studies, fine arts, geography, history, Latin-American studies, law, mathematical studies, mechanical and production engineering, microbiology, modern languages, music, philosophy, physics, politics and government, psychology, religious studies and theology, social policy and social welfare, sociology. *Also:* Caribbean studies, comparative literature, film studies, medicinal chemistry, operational research, physical education, virology.

European Community: 9% first degree students take EC language as part of course although 80% students have a language option (all arts courses, maths, physics, accounting, economics). 5% spend 6 months or more in another EC country. Formal exchange links with some 29 EC universities/colleges: Belgium (3); Denmark (1); Eire (1); France (10); Germany (5); Greece (1); Italy (4); Netherlands (3); Spain (1). All are open to non-language specialists. Approved Erasmus programme 1992/93.

Application: UCCA for 1993 start, UCAS thereafter. **Academic features:** BA courses in ancient history, classical archaeology; English & Spanish-American literature; French with film studies; philosophy with classical civilisation; chemistry with medicinal chemistry. Chemistry with European studies (French), European engineering degrees. **Special features:** High percentage of mature students. University provides adult and continuing education courses locally and validates an open access scheme; range of part-time degrees by day and/or evening study. Resident German writer, and writer in translation; many visiting professors; quartet in residence. Successful science park; close links with industry and local community. **Founded:** 1964. **Main awards:** BA, BA with qualified teacher status, BSc, LLB, BEng, MEng. **Awarding body:** University of Warwick. **Site:** 2½ miles southwest of Coventry city centre. **Access:** Buses from Coventry and Leamington Spa to campus. **Accommodation:** 2,173 places in mixed halls; 1,331 places in campus flats; 20 in student house; 1,500 places in 300 university-managed off-campus houses available through university's property leasing scheme. Majority of first year students accommodated. Approx cost: £29–£38 pw halls; £25.95 pw for periods of 30 weeks and 39 weeks. Rent: 65% in accommodation where rent controlled by university. **Library:** 3 libraries; nearly 700,000 volumes in total, 4,000 periodicals, 1,200 study places in central library; short-term loan period for books in heaviest demand. **Specialist collections:** Business information service; modern records centre. **Other learning resources:** Computing centre; language centre. **Welfare:** Doctors, dentists, opticians, psychiatrist, chaplains, law centre (in school of law), 3 student counsellors and personal tutor system. **Special categories:** Crèche with 20 places. **Careers:** Careers library, individual counselling, employers' recruitment visits. **Amenities:** Modern SU building, newspaper, travel and insurance offices; refectory; university arts centre is largest arts complex outside London (theatres, concert hall, music centre, cinema, art gallery, sculpture court, bookshop, restaurant and bars); shops and services on campus; facilities of Coventry (Belgrade Theatre, international 50-m swimming pool); museums and art galleries. **Hardship fund:** Small fund administered by Vice-Chancellor. **Sporting facilities:** Extensive playing fields, tennis courts, dri-pla floodlit area, running track, trim track, sports centre (two 25-m pools, squash courts, etc). **Employment:** Significant proportion of graduates enter financial areas.

Duration of first degree course(s) or equivalent: 3 years **others:** 4 years (BEng/MEng; BA (QTS); languages) **Total first degree students 1991/92:** 6,192; **Total BA(QTS) students:** 930 **Overseas students:** 1,468 **Mature students:** 733 **Male/female ratio:** 1:1 **Teaching staff:** 630 **Total full-time students:** 7,909 **Postgraduate students:** 5,093 **Tuition fees for 1992/93** (first degrees): Home: £1,855 (classroom), £2,770 (lab/studio); Overseas: £5,320 (classroom), £7,055 (lab/studio).

What it's like

With one of the largest student unions in the country Warwick can boast not only an excellent academic record but also excellent facilities. There's little 'hall affinity' and SU is the focal point of most student activity. SU provides excellent and professional welfare service (rapidly expanding), a 7 day a week student run ents programme, 230 clubs and societies (70 of which are sporting), a shop, Endsleigh Insurance, student run travel shop, building society, opticians, launderette, 6 bars, 3 catering outlets, take-away pizza, an academic affairs unit and, most recently, an employment centre (which found jobs for over 200 students in summer vacation).

Union tends to be moderate labour; Warwick has prominent and powerful voice in NUS and student politics, generally taking a consistent and sensible line. Most active societies: Labour Club, Music Societies, Rag and Film Society. We also have the award-winning radio station (W963) and newspaper (the *Warwick Boar*). Future work includes a further £40,000 to combat student hardship and a lift for those with disabilities to allow access to the whole of the building, along with a mass campaign to stop voluntary membership.

Ents: Discos 2–3 nights a week (usually free), comedy, cabaret, quizzes and drama. Saturday nights see Warwick's unique whipround system of two up-and-coming live bands in return for a donation (depending on what you think of the band). Recent bands include Debbie Harry, Snap, Alison Moyet, De La Soul and the Shamen.

The campus itself is pleasant with a balance between buildings and environment . . . lakes, fields and woods complement the campus environment. Accommodation on campus (about 3,500 places which is soon to go up to about 4,000) is all of good quality with sheets being laundered and all are self-catering (which most prefer). About one-fifth of the rooms have en suite bathrooms and practically all have their own washbasin. About 50% of third years get onto campus, with all first years (except clearing) guaranteed a place on campus. Most off-campus students live in Leamington or Coventry.

GET HOLD OF THE PROSPECTUSES

It's 3 miles from Coventry and 8 miles from Leamington Spa; travel links are good with frequent and cheap public transport from campus to Coventry and Leamington Spa. This is complemented by an efficient hitching system for students living in Leamington Spa. Car parking on campus is increasingly difficult, however, with charges on some car parks as the university presses the 'environmental friendliness' of public transport and funds the bus system to keep fares low. Few on-campus students are allowed cars.

Top courses include maths, history, politics, law and business studies, all internationally renowned. Workload depends on the course but most are reasonable with assessment based on long essays and examination. Changing courses and doing a varied degree is reasonably easy. Students come from all over the country and from varying social backgrounds; neither the university nor SU now allow discrimination on the grounds of gender, sexual preference, race or disability. Warwick offers excellent opportunities to all its students. I would thoroughly recommend you take them up.

Ian R. Corfield, President

Pauper notes

Accommodation: £25 to £38/week off campus, plus bills and transport. **Drink:** Courage, S&N. Local: M+B, Ansells. **Eats:** SU hot meals, sandwich bars, pizza restaurant and take-away, baked potato outlet, caters to all budgets. **Ents:** Cheap ents programme, large arts centre and cinema. **Sports:** Union runs whole sports programme; 2 university-run sports centres including pools and tracks. **Hardship funds:** Very little: university arranged. Access funds available. **Travel:** 50p hitch to Leamington. Bus: 50p to Coventry, 90p to Leamington (50p on bus pass). **Work:** Union priority on student employment in all outlets. Vacation conference work and some off-campus work.

More info?

Enquiries to Jacky Wooding (0203 417220 ext 130).

Alumni (Editors' pick)

Sting (for 1 term), Steve Heighway, Dave Nellist (Militant MP), David Davis MP, Jeff Rooker MP, Timmy Mallett (TV personality), Stephen Pile (journalist), Simon Mayo (DJ).

WELSH AGRICULTURAL COLLEGE

Welsh Agricultural College, Llanbadarn Fawr, Aberystwyth, Dyfed SY23 3AL (0970 624471) Map A, C7

Student enquiries: Admissions Office

Main study areas – as in What to Study section: *(First degree):* Agriculture, horticulture and forestry, environmental studies. *Also:* Countryside management, equine studies, wildlife management.

European Community: EC languages not yet available to first degree students, though planned for the future. Formal exchange links with Friesland College of Agriculture in Netherlands.

Application: PCAS for 1993 start, UCAS thereafter. **Academic features:** All courses are modular, with strong emphasis on student-centred learning. **Special features:** Close links with University College of Wales, Aberystwyth (shared SU, joint courses etc). **Largest field of study:** Agriculture, countryside management, equine studies. **Founded:** 1971. **Main awards:** BSc. **Awarding body:** Wales

University. **Site:** Single campus, shared with 2 other institutions, overlooking Cardigan Bay. Outskirts of Aberystwyth town and ½ mile from university college campus. **Access:** A44, A487; BR link to Shrewsbury; Holyhead and Fishguard ferries to Northern Ireland and Eire. **Accommodation:** 150 single study bedrooms on site, 50 places off-site. Approx cost: £55 (with breakfast and evening meal). Some 300 places in private accommodation. Approx cost: £35 (no meals). Some 50% students in accommodation where rent controlled by the college. **Library:** 40,000 books, 800 periodicals, 35 study places. Specialist collections in agriculture, countryside management and equine studies. **Other learning facilities:** Specialist science labs, riding school, 3 farms, glasshouse complex, computer lab, mechanisation workshop. **Careers:** Information, advice and placement service. **Employment:** Agriculture, countryside management, equine industry. **Welfare:** Local GPs; tutorial service for students; welfare officer on campus. **Special facilities:** Creche. **Hardship funds:** Student support fund and industrial sponsorship available. **Amenities:** Wide range provided by Aberystwyth Guild of Students (linked with university college), including arts centre, student bars, restaurant, bank etc; over 50 societies and clubs. **Sporting facilities:** 50 acres playing fields close by; Snowdonia within easy reach; sports hall provide for all major sports.

Duration of first degree course (or equivalent): 4 years. **Total first degree students 1991/92:** 80 **Overseas students:** 4 **Mature students:** 10 **Male/female ratio:** 2:1 **Teaching staff: full-time:** 26 **Total full-time students 1991/92:** 450 **Postgraduate students:** None **Tuition fees for 1992/93** (first degrees): Home £2,770; Overseas £5,547.

What it's like

Located at Llanbadarn Fawr village on the outskirts of Aberystwyth, the Welsh Agricultural College is well positioned for access to the open countryside and coastline of Wales and is within easy reach of the Snowdonia National Park.

A small closely knit campus with a good mix of students. Originally catering for education in agriculture, it's now in the forefront of developing new courses such as countryside management and equine studies.

The college itself provides an excellent environment for learning and the young teaching staff are very enthusiastic and have a very 'open door' attitude.

The college bar is an excellent meeting point with a good juke box and TV. Beer promotions are often on offer and also bands and discos are arranged. The town of Aberystwyth is a small friendly place with shops catering for all tastes and plenty of pubs. No night clubs as such exist in Aber but some of the pubs have late licences (till 1.00 a.m. some nights).

All sports catered for: traditionally rugby is the WAC game but good football, hockey, cricket and shooting teams. Many students are involved in outdoor activities and we have a very active mountaineering club.

Accommodation on campus is generally good and the college refectory food is just about palatable. There is a good shop on site and holds good stock of essentials like bread, pies, paper, pens. If you prefer to live out then there is plenty of student accommodation in town (approximately 30% of the population of Aberystwyth are students) but can be expensive. Just come and have a look, you might get to like the pace of life at WAC.

Ken Latham, Student President

Pauper notes

Accommodation: Plenty of student houses in Aberystwyth; good campus accommodation. **Drink:** Cheap beer at College Bar; plenty of local pubs in town. **Eats:** Cheap food in town, own food on campus, refectory good but basic. **Ents:** Cheap, good bands at the university arts centre, bands and disco on campus. **Sports:** Very good sports facilities, pool in village, good sports grounds. **Hardship funds:** All usual funds are available, regular meetings. **Work:** Local bar work, farm work available.

GET HOLD OF THE PROSPECTUSES

Informal name

WAC.

Buzz-words:

None, but good opportunity to study Welsh.

WELSH COLLEGE OF MUSIC AND DRAMA

Welsh College of Music and Drama, Castle Grounds, Cathays Park, Cardiff CF1 3ER (0222 342854/6; Fax 0222 237639) Map A, D8

Student enquiries: Chief Administrative Officer

Main study areas – as in What to Study section: *(First degree):* Drama, music. *Also:* Stage management, stage design.

European Community: Languages taught to singing students (11%). No students spend time in another EC country.

Application: Direct. **Special features:** Visiting Professors: Christopher Adey, Mary Hammond, Anthony Hopkins, Janet Price, Elizabeth Vaughan, John Mitchison. **Academic features:** 2-year BEd in music, 4-year BEd in music and drama in conjunction with Cardiff Institute; considerable emphasis is laid on practical studies. BA performing arts (music). BA and performers courses for drama. **Founded:** 1949, as Cardiff College of Music, gaining its present title in 1971. **Main awards:** BA, BEd, Performers Diploma Music and Drama. **Awarding body:** Wales University. **Site:** Cardiff city centre. **Access:** Site close to main bus and railway station. **Accommodation:** Apply to Student Accommodation Service (University College, 58 Park Place, Cardiff CF1 3AT, tel: 0222 874000). Rent: no students in accommodation where rent controlled by the college. **Library:** 10,000 volumes, 35 periodicals, 34 study places. **Welfare:** Doctor, chaplain. **Careers:** Information, advice and placement service. **Amenities:** Theatre on site; studios and workshops, Studio Theatre, refectory; recreational facilities of Cardiff (eg national sports centre). Concert and opera ticket concessions; strong practical association with BBC, WNO; twinned with Sherman Theatre. **Employment:** Teaching and professional work.

Duration of first degree course(s) or equivalent: 3 years; **others:** 4 years BEd **Total first degree students 1991/92:** 98 **Total BEd students:** 51 **Male/female ratio:** 1:3 **Teaching staff: full-time:** 16 **part-time:** 11 **Total full-time students 1991/92:** 329 **Postgraduate students:** 48 **Tuition fees for 1992/93** (first degrees): Home: £2,770; Overseas: £5,319.

What it's like

Situated in Cathays Park next door to Cardiff Castle, only a five-minute walk to the city centre. All courses have a large emphasis on practical work and performance – students performing regularly in the college's Bute Theatre, St David's Hall, Sherman Theatre, Llandaff Cathedral and many other venues. BEd, BA, Graduate Diploma, performance and ACC courses are on offer in music, drama, stage management, design and directing. Changing courses within the same department is easily done – all course tutors are approachable and are always ready to listen to students' suggestions. Staff/student relationships are good, especially as most lessons are one to one, and lectures tend to be conducted in small groups. The BEd courses and all the stage management and design courses have had a 100% employment rate for graduates over the past four years. Other courses also have a good employment rate for grads.

College nurse comes in every lunch-time and there is a counsellor on hand if need be.

College bar open five nights a week – it's the cheapest beer in Cardiff. Regular

WANT TO HELP WITH THE NEXT EDITION – SEE PAGE 76

entertainment in the bar, often provided by students, local bands, discos and karaoke. SU societies include the footy society (1991 winners of the inter-college tournament), the women's rugby team, the shove-ha'penny society and many more. If you can't find a club or society to suit you then start your own. Being a student city, the social life outside college is excellent. The university SU is just across the road from the college and they provide a wide range of entertainment in their nightclub and bars, as well as providing a venue (the Great Hall) for big name bands. Students from college are welcome over there.

Sharon Guy, Student President

Pauper notes

Accommodation: Average rent £30 pw; no halls. Rented accommodation getting hard to find as most colleges in the area are taking in more students each year. It's best to come down a good 4 weeks before term starts to get digs sorted. **Drink:** College bar very cheap. Lots of studenty pubs around – The Woody and The Rummer are particular favourites with students in this college. Brains and Bass tend to be the most popular brewers. **Eats:** College canteen not bad for the prices. Outside college there's an abundance of good (and a few bad!) curry houses, Chinese, pizza parlours, chippy's etc . . . A good selection of vegetarian places around. **Ents:** Good and cheap in all the SU bars around Cardiff. Town is a bit more expensive but a wide variety of ents around to cater for all. **Sports:** Apart from the sports societies in college, there's the National Sports Centre of Wales nearby and the university sports facilities (Uni students have priority). **Hardship funds:** College tries to help people in financial trouble through access funds and loans; SU emergency loan scheme. **Travel:** Most places are within walking distance. Cathays station across the road; main BR and bus stations within walking distance. No student travel cards on local buses. **Work:** During term time easy to find work in the numerous pubs. The theatres nearby employ a lot of students from this college. Full-time holiday jobs not so easy to come by unless you apply early.

Informal name

WCMD.

Buzz-Words

Butty – not a sandwich but a mate

Alumni (Editors' pick)

Anthony Hopkins, Sir Geraint Evans, Hugo E Blick, Victor Spinetti, Peter Gill, Hywell Gwyfryn, Geraint Morris, Jane Freeman, Maldwyn Davies, Caryl Thomas, Sioned Williams, David Gwesyn Smith, Kenneth Smith, Iris Williams.

WEST HERTS COLLEGE

Watford Campus, Hempstead Road, Watford, Herts WD1 3EZ (0923 57500) Map A, F8

Student enquiries: Faculty of Visual Communication (0923 57661)

Main study areas: *(First degree):* Management, packaging technology, printing, publishing.

European Community: Languages are optional for first degree students; number taking up options not known. 10% spend 6 months or more in another EC country. No formal exchange links with EC universities/colleges, although many international links.

Application: PCAS for 1993 start, UCAS thereafter. **Special features:** Postgrad publishing diploma. **Largest fields of study:** Printing and packaging technology.

GET HOLD OF THE PROSPECTUSES

Founded: 1874. **Main awards:** BSc. **Awarding body:** Hertfordshire University. **Site:** Watford town centre and 3 other sites. **Access:** Watford Junction station (British Rail). **Accommodation:** Welfare officer will assist in finding lodgings in and around Watford; none provided by college. **Library:** Main library, plus 2 site libraries; 45,000 volumes in total, 350 periodicals, 100 study places. **Specialist collections:** Publishing, Printing technology and management library. **Other learning facilities:** Computer unit; reprographic unit. **Welfare:** Medical advisory service, counselling service. **Careers:** Information, advice and informal placement service. **Amenities:** Social centre and bar, bookshop on site. Concert hall, live theatre, cinemas, Division 1 football in Watford. London facilities 20 minutes train ride away. **Employment:** Publishing, printing and packaging industries, their suppliers and customers.

Duration of first degree course(s) or equivalent: 4 years sandwich **Total first degree students 1991/92:** 120 **Overseas students:** 12 **Mature students:** 8 **Male/female ratio:** 6:1 **Teaching staff (degree): full-time:** 20 **part-time:** 4 (college as a whole: 200 full-time, 200 part-time) **Total full-time students 1991/92:** 3,500 **Postgraduate students:** 150 **Tuition fees for 1992/93** (first degrees): Home: £1,855; Overseas: £5,475.

What it's like (Watford)

It's made up of six sites, all near town centre. There is no college accommodation but there is a welfare/housing officer to help you out. There is also a YMCA and YWCA. Town's entertainment is pretty standard: one nightclub – Kudos – a general release cinema and loads of pubs. Rag week is best week in the year. Print department is one of best in world and attracts many overseas students. Relations between different nationalities very friendly. Employment easy to come by, especially after print courses.

Pauper notes

Accommodation: None. All private housing expensive (£40–£45 per week). **Drink:** College bar cheapest in town with good real ales though it shuts early. The Horns and Blakes are good student places. Benskins and Greene King good local brews. **Eats:** Cheap food at student snack bar in college; lots of kebabs, Greek, Chinese, curry and burgers in town. **Ents:** Live bands at college, Pump House Theatre. Not much else in Watford. **Sports:** Lots of swimming-pools and golf centres (pitch + putt course) locally. **Hardship Funds:** See welfare officer. **Travel:** Good hitching to most parts of the UK on the M1, A1 and M4. **Work:** Part-time jobs often available – details from Association Office.

WEST LONDON INSTITUTE

West London Institute (College of Brunel University), 300 St Margarets Road, Twickenham, Middlesex TW1 1PT (081 891 0121) Map D, A3

Student enquiries: Academic Registry

Main study areas – as in What to Study section: *(First degree):* American studies, business studies, drama, education, English, environmental studies, geography, geology, history, music, nursing studies, professions allied to medicine (PAMs), religious studies and theology. *Also:* Leisure management, sports studies.

European Community: No students learn an EC language or spend time in another EC country as part of their course.

Application: PCAS for 1993 start, UCAS thereafter. **Structural features:** College of Brunel University. **Academic features:** Modular scheme with art, film/TV studies, computer studies, IT in education as minor subjects. Degrees in physiotherapy and occupational therapy; community health (including eg district nursing, health visiting, occupational health nursing). **Special features:** Associate student scheme for mature students returning to education; access links with further and adult education institutes. **Founded:** 1976, ex Borough Road College (1798), Chiswick Polytechnic (1850), Maria Grey College (1878) and West Middlesex School of Physiotherapy (1987). **Main awards:** BA, BEd, BSc. **Awarding body:** Brunel University. **Site:** 2 campuses: Lancaster House in Isleworth; Gordon House in Twickenham. **Access:** BR and underground; close to Heathrow, M25, M4 and M3; free inter-campus transport. **Accommodation:** 300+ places in halls; college list of approved lodgings. Accommodation for first year students a priority (10–15% first degree students home-based). Approx cost: £49.90 pw halls (part-board) £40–45 pw (self-catering lodgings). **Library:** 2 libraries; 160,000 volumes, 1,000 periodicals; short loan facilities. **Other learning facilities:** Integrated learning area/multi-media rooms with eg CD Roms, PCs, videos, sound systems. Media resources centre with CCTV, VTR; computer service; micro computer laboratories; learning resource areas. **Welfare:** 2 doctors, 2 nurses, 3 chaplains, 4 counsellors (part-time). **Hardship funds:** SU and other funds available; staged payments possible for fees. **Careers:** Careers officer and library. **Amenities:** Media store, SU shops, club bars; bookshops, orchestras, studio opera, choir, student societies, recreation officer. Easy access to West End, Richmond Park, Twickenham RFC, good swimming pools etc. **Sporting facilities:** New sports hall, incorporating 2 international size basketball courts, 8 badminton courts etc; 3 rugby pitches, 2 football pitches, 2 hockey pitches and additional floodlit training facilities; cricket pitch, lacrosse pitch, tennis courts, athletics track (tartan) and associated facilities. School of PE piloting Sports Council scheme, as one of 3 national centres, with its national coaching centre and biomechanics and sports psychology labs.

Duration of first degree course(s) or equivalent: 3 years; 4 years (BEd and BA/BSc with QTS) **Total first degree students 1991/92:** 1,360 **Total BEd students:** 360 **Overseas students:** 30 **Mature students:** 130 **Male/female ratio:** 2:3 **Teaching staff: full-time:** 180 **part-time:** 180 **Total full-time students 1991/92:** 2,430 **Postgraduate students:** 240 **Tuition fees for 1992/93** (first degrees): Home: £1,855 (classroom), £2,770 (lab/studio); Overseas: £5,319 (classroom).

What it's like

Split-site campus – approx 1 mile apart. River Thames flows past the Gordon House campus; Borough Road campus on Great West Road (easy access Heathrow and London) but noise caused by jet aircraft can be problem, especially during summer term.

5 halls of residence house approx 300 students – mainly first years. Rented accommodation outside halls quite expensive and scarce, especially Richmond and Twickenham areas. Hounslow cheaper but distinctly less pleasant. Libraries on both sites scarcely adequate.

Despite excellent reputation for sports studies and high-class sports teams, lack of actual pitches for football, rugby and hockey quite startling.

Usual social life – discos and bands – organised regularly by SU. SU sees itself as being there for the welfare and well-being of its student membership.

With London/West End being so close (via Hounslow and Richmond stations) there are plenty of distractions from academic side of student life. Loadsa pubs, wine bars, restaurants, theatres, cinemas and horse and dog tracks provide scope for frittering away grant cheques. Staff–student relationships generally very amicable but, of course, there have been exceptions over the years. It's not a bad place to get a degree.

Pauper notes

Accommodation: Very difficult to find cheap accommodation in Richmond and Twickenham environs; some less expensive digs in Hounslow area. **Drink:** Fullers

Brewery is just up the road in Chiswick. ESB (Extra Special Bitter) is not the weakest tipple known to man! **Eats:** College catering facilities expensive but range of food good; Maria Grey campus superior. Richmond has wide range of tastes and price. Minars Tandoori Restaurant, Hounslow, reasonable price, excellent food, including vegetarian. **Ents:** Bear Cat Cabaret Club, Turks Head Pub, St Margarets Road (off campus). London ensures plenty of cheap entertainment, ie pub bands/cabaret etc. **Sports:** Two swimming pools close to campus/sports hall on Borough Road campus. Large leisure centre at Brentford, on a smaller scale plus leisure centre in Old Isleworth near the MG campus. **Hardship funds:** Access welfare fund. Small short-term loans. **Travel:** Rail and coach cards available with NUS cards. **Work:** Increasingly difficult to find vacation work although some on campus, ie portering and cleaning staff.

Informal name:
WLIHE.

Buzz-words:
MG – Maria Grey campus; Boro' Rd – Lancaster House campus.

Alumni (Editors' pick)
M Naylor, Kathy Cook, B C Rose, P Stimpson, Brian Hooper, Alan Pascoe, Dave Otley, Martin Cross, Phil Bainbridge.

WEST LONDON POLY
See Thames Valley University

WEST SURREY COLLEGE

West Surrey College of Art & Design, Falkner Road, Farnham, Surrey GU9 7DS (0252 722441) Map A, E8

Student enquiries: Admissions Officer.

Main study areas – as in What to Study section: *(First degree):* Art & design, fine arts. *Also:* Animation, film studies.

European Community: Number students learning an EC language not known; small number spend time in another EC country. Exchange links with EC universities/colleges in France, Germany and Italy. Comett exchanges for animation students with computer animation industry in Europe.

Application: ADAR; also PCAS for 1993 start, UCAS thereafter. **Academic features:** Unique BA Animation. **Largest fields of study:** Fine art, communication and media studies, 2 and 3 dimensional design. **Founded:** 1969, ex Farnham and Guildford schools of art. **Main awards:** BA. **Awarding body:** West Surrey College. **Site:** Within Farnham town centre. **Special features:** Most academic staff are practising artists, designers, film makers, media and crafts people. Many students major award winners (eg Fine Young Sculptors Arena), participate in festivals, trade fairs and receive external commissions. **Accommodation:** 332 hostel places (101 on campus); assistance in finding lodgings. **Rent:** 13% in accommodation where rent controlled by college. **Library:** 50,000 volumes, 200,000 slides, 4,000 videos, 300 periodicals. **Welfare:** Doctor, professional welfare officer. **Careers:** Information, advice and informal placement. **Amenities:** Redgrave Theatre at Farnham and Yvonne Arnaud Theatre at Guildford; many galleries and arts centres in area. **Sporting facilities:** Games hall on site; sports centres at Farnham, Guildford and Alton.

CAN'T FIND WHAT YOU'RE LOOKING FOR? USE THE INDEX!

Duration of first degree course(s) or equivalent: 3 years; **others:** 5 years (part-time BA fine art) **Total first degree students 1991/92:** 1,016 **Overseas students:** 35 **Mature students:** 612 **Male/female ratio:** 2:3 **Teaching staff: full-time:** 48 **part-time:** 29 **Total full-time students 1991/92:** 1,321 **Postgraduate students:** 0 **Tuition fees for 1992/93** (first degrees): Home: £2,770; Overseas: £5,450.

What it's like

It's near the town centre of Farnham; 50 mins by BR from London. Very good reputation, especially in audio visual dept (animation has won many awards, including a BAFTA award). Three dimensional design dept has a very good reputation and offers one of the few glass degree courses in the country. Most courses offer limitless expression within your work and a chance to experiment with media other than that on your chosen course. Due to the size there's a good community feeling but apathy is sometimes a problem. Farnham's a small, middle-class town in pleasant surroundings but limited entertainments for young people. SU provides bands, discos, parties, films, cabarets, sports clubs etc, with limited financial support. Accommodation can be a problem (hard to find and quite pricey). Three college hostels, the Main Hostel (behind the college), West Street Hostel (about 2 mins away), Shortheath Hotel (1½ miles away). International exchange programmes yearly, the number of foreign and mature students is increasing. Good complementary studies dept; very low failure and drop-out rate. Well stocked and expanding library. Students tend to be politically aware and sensitive to a huge variety of issues. Local transport is terrible, hence the need for bikes; Farnham well served by trains, coaches and major roads.

Pauper notes

Accommodation: Hostels/shared rooms for 1st years. Some single rooms in 3rd year. Student houses, bedsits and landlady type lodgings. **Drink:** SU bar (Grapes Club) – cheap. Large selection of spirits, beers, real ales and lagers. In student pubs change every year. **Eats:** Lots of restaurants around town – Indian, Chinese, Italian, Nepalese. College canteen expensive. **Ents:** SU bops, discos, bands, cabarets, films etc. **Sports:** Farnham has well equipped sports centre. No student reductions. Sports clubs at college. **Hardship funds:** SU welfare fund lends money to tide over. **Travel:** Regular exchange programme with European colleges. STA at Surrey University. **Work:** Vacation work in restaurants, supermarkets and cleaning.

Informal name:

WSCAD.

Alumni (Editors' pick)

Adrian Knowles (picture editor, Amateur Photographer), Terence Hudson (animator), Lindsey Hullen, Poni Amin (lecturer, Malaysia), Annabelle Jankel (cucumber animation – Max Headroom), Dave Banks (editorial photographer – Face, etc), Jankel and Morton (Max Headroom), Mark Bauer (Grand Prix, Annely).

WEST SUSSEX INSTITUTE

West Sussex Institute of Higher Education, The Dome, Upper Bognor Road, Bognor Regis, West Sussex PO21 1HR (0243 865581) Map A, F8

Student enquiries: Marketing Officer; Admissions Office

Main study areas – as in What to Study section: *(First degree):* Art & design, dance, education, English, geography, history, music, religious studies and theology, social policy and social welfare. *Also:* Choreography, related arts, performance arts, sports studies.

European Community: No first degree students take EC language as part of course; a few spend a term in another EC country. Formal exchange links with 11 EC universities/colleges: Belgium (1); France (1 for sports studies); Germany (1 for English with art minor); Portugal (3 including fine art and design); Spain (5). Approved Erasmus programme.

Application: UCCA for 1993 start, UCAS thereafter. **Structural features:** Accredited College of Southampton University. **Founded:** 1977, ex Bishop Otter College Chichester and Bognor Regis College. **Main awards:** BA, BEd, BSc. **Awarding body:** Southampton University. **Site:** 2 sites (Chichester and Bognor Regis). **Access:** Both sites within walking distance of respective town centres. **Accommodation:** Many first years and some final year students have opportunity of living in halls. Approx cost: £49 pw, including 2 meals/day. Rent: 25% full-time students in accommodation where rent controlled by institute. **Library:** Library on each site. 170,000 volumes in total, 800 periodicals, 120 study places; restricted loan collections. **Specialist collections:** Gerard Young local history collection, art slides, official education documents, 19th-century British parliamentary papers, Historical Association pamphlets, music scores, Open University course material. **Other learning resources:** 2 Nimbus networks, 50 work stations; video-edit suite, mobile video production unit; 2 dark rooms. **Welfare:** Accommodation officers, health centre, doctors, counsellors, chaplain, welfare officer for international students. **Special provision:** Limited nursery facilities and half-term play scheme. **Hardship funds:** Co-ordinator of Student Services can advise on short-term loans for students in temporary need. **Careers:** Information and advice, both individually and as part of course. **Amenities:** SU with many societies, travel and insurance bureaux. Chapel, art collection. **Sporting facilities:** Sports hall and pitches.

Duration of first degree course(s) or equivalent: 3 years; 4 years BEd **Total first degree students 1991/92:** 1,700; **BEd students:** 860 **Overseas students:** 60 **Mature students:** 37% (57% on BEd) **Male/female ratio:** 1:3 **Teaching staff: full-time:** 104 **part-time:** 3 **Total full-time students 1991/92:** 1,880 **Postgraduate students:** 340 **Tuition fees for 1992/93** (first degrees): Home: £700 (if no grant), £1,855 (classroom), £2,770 (lab/studio); Overseas: £5,500.

What it's like

It's made up of two colleges, The Bognor Regis College and the Bishop Otter College in Chichester, both are reasonably accessible. Attempts are made to house the majority of first year and a small number of final year students in halls of residence. All other students live in accommodation found in either town. Intersite transport is provided. Both colleges have a very friendly atmosphere for study and a good social life. Selection of BA and BEd degrees; some international students.

Ideally placed for the south coast countryside, but parking is a problem; normally no student cars on campus. Many clubs and societies provided by the SU for a wide range of sporting and cultural activities. A small, friendly college which offers a good alternative to the larger establishments around the country.

Pauper notes

Accommodation: Hall accommodation for most first years (often in shared rooms) and some final years. **Drink:** SU bar on each site for cheap drinks; nice pubs in both Chichester and Bognor but expensive. Ballards Brewery and Gales HSB excellent local beers. **Eats:** Food at college is not the highest quality. Several good eating places in town – especially Chichester. **Ents:** Ents at colleges with bands performing regularly and various other events throughout the year. Chichester town lacks alternative entertainments and Bognor has a couple of night clubs.

CAN'T FIND WHAT YOU'RE LOOKING FOR? USE THE INDEX!

Sports: Sports at college very good; both towns have leisure centre. Chichester has access to swimming pool. **Hardship funds:** Little provision although due to the increasing financial difficulties faced by students, support systems are improving. **Travel:** Little. Hitching difficult. Cycling easiest and cheapest means of travel. **Work:** Bar work easily available on either campus.

WESTMINSTER COLLEGE

Westminster College, Oxford OX2 9AT (0865 247644) Map: A, E7

Student enquiries: The Registrar

Main study areas – as in What to Study section: *(First degree):* Education, religious study and theology.

European Community: 10% first degree students take EC language as part of course (BEd students with French as work subject; students exchanging with Belgium and Denmark also have intensive language tuition). 10% spend 4 months in another EC country. Formal exchange links with France (4); also for non-specialists with Belgium and Denmark. Short exchanges, including projects in schools, in France, Denmark and Netherlands, all open to non-specialists. Approved Erasmus programme 1992/93.

Application: UCCA for 1993 start, UCAS thereafter. **Academic features:** Courses validated by Oxford University. **Special features:** Visiting professors from USA. **Largest fields of study:** Education (primary school teachers). **Founded:** 1851. **Main award:** BEd, BTheol. **Awarding body:** Oxford University. **Site:** Single site with 100 acres overlooking Oxford. **Access:** Just off Oxford ring road; Oxford rail station. **Accommodation:** 520 places on site: approx cost £65 per week (room + 15 meals). Plenty of private accommodation in neighbourhood (accommodation officer helps). **Library:** 60,000 volumes, 450 periodicals, 100 study places. **Specialist collections:** Archives of Methodist education. **Other learning facilities:** TV studio, drama area, primary classrooms, information technology facilities. **Careers:** Information, advice and placement service. **Employment:** Mainly teaching, social services, pastoral work. **Welfare:** Nurse and sick bay. **Special facilities:** Playgroup one afternoon/week. **Hardship funds:** Samaritan fund available.

Duration of first degree course(s) or equivalent: 3 years (standard), 4 years (other). **Total first degree students 1991/92:** 710 **Total number of BEd students:** 590 **Mature students:** 40 **Male/female ratio:** 7:3 **Teaching staff:** full-time: 65; **part-time:** 20 **Total full-time students 1991/92:** 895 **Postgraduate students:** 150 **Tuition fees for 1992/93 (first degrees):** Home: £1,855 (classroom), £2,770 (lab); Overseas: approx £5,000.

What it's like

It's sited on the top of Harcourt Hill (cardiac hill?!), a good half-hour walk from the centre of Oxford – 38 purpose-built houses in extensive gardens, backed by over 40 acres of playing fields.

Majority of first year students offered residential accommodation, a shared double room. After living out in the second year, they can return to a single college room for their final year(s). However, as student numbers increase this may change. Houses have 12/13 students each; single sex, there are 2 toilets, 2/3 showers and a bath. Meals in dining hall on cafeteria system; one formal meal (where everyone sits down together) every week. Each house is fitted with a small kitchen (ie. a fridge and a cooker) for self-catering at the weekends only. There is one new laundry room with 6 washing machines and 4 tumble driers, but with 450 resident students (and same number of non-residents) you have to choose your time!

About 25% of total number of students are 'mature', although this counts as anything from 22+.

SU is not political, but fairly active on a practical welfare and social level. Excellent sporting facilities on campus: a nine-hole golf course, tennis courts, swimming pool, squash courts, hockey, football, rugby and cricket pitches; there are also two gyms. You are also eligible to join the Oxford Union (famed debating society & cheap bar, but costs £80 for life-membership), and can participate in any student activities offered by Oxford university, to say nothing of the lectures, available through our 'academic association'.

First 2 years of BEd course not too demanding, study is in the subject area chosen, with minimal school contact. Years 3 and 4 are more rigorous, with Block School Experience for 5/6 weeks at a time. Theology degree has recently undergone further changes, and there is a wide variety of combinations available, with a lot of independent study, particularly in the 2nd and 3rd years. About 40 foreign exchange students in any academic year, with the BEd French off to France, an exchange with colleges in the States; Erasmus scheme links led to a theological exchange with Leuven in Belgium.

Students mostly from the Midlands and the South, although we have a good Welsh contingent, and some from as far as Sunderland and Scotland. There are quite good links with Oxford Brookes University, although it is on the other side of Oxford – bring a bicycle with you! Individuals in Oxford University can be very friendly, but the institution as a whole can seem a little off-ish. The female:male ratio is about 8:1 within college, so if you're here to look for a man, think again! This should make sex discrimination unheard of, but these things seem to take a while to eradicate totally. Generally staff/student relations are good.

Because of its size, and perhaps because of its Methodist foundations there is a really good community atmosphere here. Everyone is really friendly and the older year groups do their best to settle in the freshers. The college has increased its numbers quite dramatically over the last few years, and is having some teething troubles in accommodating all the new students, particularly in the area of car parking, dining arrangements, and day student facilities.

Pauper notes

Accommodation: Cheap end of town out towards poly, majority of students live in Botley. **Drink:** Bar from Xmas '92 but not heavily subsidised. Morrells (rugby team sponsors), Morland, Brakspears. **Eats:** Melting-pot of cultures – loads of varied scoff. Good variety of price/type: The Randolph to Bretts Burgers! **Ents:** Good student rates for theatres but not cinemas. **Sports:** Excellent facilities on campus. **Hardship funds:** Good at treating each student on own merits. **Travel:** Women-only night bus and taxi service. **Work:** Summer jobs in various departments of college more scarce than a couple of years ago. Dining hall/library/office on site. Casual work in Oxford.

More info?

Enquiries to Paul Robson, President SU (0865 200067).

Informal name

Westie. WSIHE.

WESTMINSTER UNIVERSITY

University of Westminster, 309 Regent Street, London W1R 8AL (071 911 5000) Map E, B2

Student enquiries: Central Student Administration

Main study areas – as in What to Study section: *(First degree):* Architecture, art & design, biology, biotechnology, building studies, business studies, civil engineering, computing, economics, English, environmental science, geography, history, industrial relations, information technology, law, linguistics, mathematical studies, mechanical and production engineering, modern languages, physiology, politics and government, professions allied to medicine (PAMs), psychology, social policy and social welfare, sociology, town and country planning. *Also:* Artificial intelligence, Chinese, electronic engineering, film studies, medical laboratory science, photography, quantity surveying.

European Community: 20% first degree students take EC language as part of course and 10% spend 6 months or more in another EC country. Some links with EC universities/colleges plus specific schools. Approved Erasmus programme 1992. All students can use Polylang (extensive teach-yourself labs); modularisation of courses allows languages to be included in all degree courses.

Application: PCAS for 1993 start, UCAS thereafter. **Academic features:** Modern engineering foundation (1 year); BSc computer systems technology; BA housing studies; BSc in photographic and electronic imaging sciences; BA in film, video and photographic arts. **Largest fields of study:** Engineering science, built environment, business studies, languages, communication, design and media, social sciences. **Founded:** 1992 as a university; previously Central London Poly, founded 1838. **Main awards:** BA, BSc. **Awarding body:** Westminster University. **Site:** 13 main sites in central London (W1/NW1) and Harrow. **Access:** All major sites within 15 minutes walk of each other, apart from Harrow site (15 minutes by tube). All are on major bus and tube lines. **Accommodation:** 301 places in hall, some places in flats. Rent: 6% in accommodation where rent controlled by university. **Library:** 8 libraries, 262,000 volumes, 2,500 periodicals, 1,060 study places. Sophisticated Libertas on-line catalogue system. **Welfare:** Doctor, FPA, psychiatrist, international students officer, student adviser, student counsellor, chaplain, accommodation adviser. 20 place nursery. **Hardship funds:** Central fund administered by Hardship Committee. Loans, nursery bursaries and grants may be awarded to students facing unexpected financial hardship. **Careers:** Careers centre in Bolsover Street. **Amenities:** SU in Bolsover Street with staff/ student bar, gymnasia, squash courts, rifle range, billiards room, table tennis room; sports ground at Chiswick.

Duration of first degree course(s) or equivalent: 3 years; 4 years (language and sandwich courses) **Total first degree students 1991/92:** 7,000 **Mature students:** 750 **Male/female ratio:** 5:4 **Teaching staff:** full-time: 600 part-time: 400 **Total full-time students 1991/92:** 6,000 **Postgraduate students:** 600 **Tuition fees for 1992/93 (first degrees):** Home: £1,855 (classroom), £2,770 (lab/studio); Overseas: £4,950 (classroom), £5,300 (lab/studio).

What it's like

Sites are spread throughout central London and at large faculty in Harrow. Law, languages, computing and most sciences have good reputations, as do photography and media courses run by faculty of communication.

Main advantage of studying in London is accessibility of wide range of arts and entertainment venues and cosmopolitan nature of the capital although all are expensive. Main disadvantage is acute housing shortage making finding a decent, affordable place to live a full-time job, especially with no housing benefit and static grants.

SU supports a wide range of political and cultural clubs and societies as well as over thirty different sports clubs. It produces a weekly magazine (McGarel), distributed free to students, that gives information on what's on and matters of interest to students. There are two union bars, one at central London site (Bolsover Street) and another at Harrow.

The Union's main campaigns are concerned with protecting and enhancing facilities, especially the nursery, and this year obviously the student hardship campaign will be our priority.

GET HOLD OF THE PROSPECTUSES

Pauper notes

Accommodation: Near bottom of league for student accommodation, housing only 3% of the students. High rents account for more than whole grant. Squatting becoming popular by necessity but obviously more difficult. Union will help. **Drink:** Union bar has wide selection and is cheap! Camel Club, Bolsover Street. **Eats:** Food generally nasty at Westminster, vegetarians and ethnic minorities not generally catered for. Windezer Cafe (Middlesex Hospital). **Ents:** Union organises club nights, cabarets, bands and discos for every night of the week. **Sports:** Union organises about 30 sports clubs. ULU has pool which students can use. **Hardship Funds:** Administered through student services, and very difficult to get. **Work:** SU bar a possibility.

More info?

Enquiries to Alison Woodmason (071 636 6271).

Alumni (Editors' pick)

Quentin Crisp, Pink Floyd, Red Box, Pamela Armstrong, Bernard Wiltshire, Fred and Judy Vermorel, Peter Brunivels, Margaret Harker, Alexander Fleming, Vic Reeves, Paul Gascoigne.

WIMBLEDON SCHOOL OF ART

Wimbledon School of Art, Merton Hall Road, London SW19 3QA Tel (081 540 0231) Fax (081 543 1750) Map D, B4

Student enquiries: Registrar

Main study areas – as in What to Study section: *(First degree):* Art & design. *Also* Theatre design.

European Community: No students learn an EC language or spend time in another EC country. Some exchange programmes with colleges in other EC countries.

Application: ADAR. **Academic features:** 3 year BA courses in fine art (painting and sculpture) and theatre (theatre design, technical arts or costume). All include mandatory courses in history of art and contextual studies. Normally students must have completed foundation course. **Special features:** Programme of visiting lectures by professional artists and designers. **Largest fields of study:** Theatre. **Founded:** 1890. **Main awards:** BA. **Awarding body:** Surrey University. **Site:** Main site plus annexe for foundation course. **Access:** Wimbledon station or bus for main site; South Wimbledon or Merton Park stations + 77a bus for annexe. **Accommodation:** College provides no accommodation nor controls rent in any accommodation. Approx cost locally: £50–£55 pw. **Library:** 26,000 books, 100 periodicals, 57 study places; slide collection, video tapes. **Welfare:** Trained student counsellor and assistant, information held on all other services. **Careers:** Departmental advice service. **Amenities:** SU with common rooms, shop, canteen, etc; workshop theatre.

Duration of first degree course(s) or equivalent: 3 years **Total first degree students 1991/92:** 341 **Overseas students:** 81 **Mature students:** 50 **Male/female ratio:** 2:3 **Teaching staff: full-time:** 27 **part-time:** 26 **Total full-time students 1991/92:** 539 **Postgraduate students:** 62 **Tuition fees for 1992/93 (first degrees):** Home: £2,770; Overseas: £5,724. Registration and conferment fee added to all fees.

CAN'T FIND WHAT YOU'RE LOOKING FOR? USE THE INDEX!

What it's like

It's situated in quiet, leafy suburbia, 5 minutes walk from Wimbledon Chase station and 15/20 minutes from Wimbledon or South Wimbledon. Far enough out of London for a small town feeling yet close enough for galleries or going out at night (10 minutes by rail to Waterloo).

Foundation course in the annexe in Palmerston Road, Wimbledon; some facilities are shared. The staff on all courses are very experienced and helpful, some are well known and respected in the art world. One of the largest regular part-time staffs in the country and occasional visiting artists and lecturers with fresh views and a great deal of energy. Facilities generally excellent; sculpture dept is well equipped to do large-scale works in stone, steel, wood or plaster and a life room of its own. The painting dept has large studio spaces, a well equipped film and video room, a photography dept with full-time technical staff and part-time specialist tutors. Facilities open to other depts. Preparation and woodwork rooms for making stretchers, stretching canvas, grinding paint etc, a painting seminar room bookable in advance for large-scale works, exhibitions, discussions and a permanent life room with usually three models. Print dept has two large areas which together can cater for all major fine art printing methods – and these facilities can be used freely by BA painting students. Theatre dept also very well equipped; own theatre, bang up to date facilities for lighting and sound. Individual studio spaces for students, a model making workshop, large props workshop and in-theatre wardrobe, in addition to usual facilities, there are a number of industrial sewing machines and separate areas for pattern cutting, fitting etc. Palmerston Road site is a large building equipped to give students a grounding in almost all aspects of painting, sculpture and design.

Well stocked library with friendly and efficient staff, comprehensive slide library, video collection with viewing facilities available to any student on request, 2 complementary studies seminar rooms, lecture theatre/projection room, space in the foyer for exhibitions and a well stocked school shop with good discounts. Materials are not free but many of them are covered by a levy which is paid once a year.

Canteen not bad; a bit plain and uncomfortable. Student common room small and a bit grubby. However, the college is undertaking a large building project with SU which involves getting an architect to redesign these 2 areas to make them more inviting. Common room contains a pool table, darts board and a video game but no tea or food machines and no bar. SU social evenings popular. Social life very much up to the students. Pub down the road packed with students. 2 or 3 parties a term, organised by SU in the theatre, often with bands; touring theatre and ballet companies perform there at the start of tours; because of work done for them by the design and wardrobe depts, these evenings tend to be free. Only other entertainment is film and video club which tries to put on a film every week. Essentially a place for working. However, atmosphere is very friendly; large number of private parties which all students are usually invited to.

Almost no student housing provided, but housing officer is useful for finding houses and generally people have no problem getting somewhere reasonable. But look as soon as you get the housing list and if you're using a housing agency find out just what you'll get for your money.

Pauper notes

Accommodation: Ask housing officer. **Drink:** Leather Bottle and Prince of Wales. **Eats:** Vegetarian cafe; Greek, Italian, Chinese, Indian and McDonalds. **Ents:** Theatre, cinema and central London 10 min; SU film soc, and parties. **Sports:** YMCA. **Shops:** School shop for materials. **Work:** Restaurants and summer bar work in Wimbledon if you can get it.

Alumni (Editors' pick)

Louise Belson (freelance designer with RSC), Rolf Langenfass (designer, Vienna Opera), Iona McLeish (freelance designer, Pal Joey), John Pascoe, James Acheson (Oscar winner 1988), Raymond Briggs, Raymond Brooks.

GET HOLD OF THE PROSPECTUSES

WINCHESTER SCHOOL OF ART

Winchester School of Art, Park Avenue, Winchester SO23 8DL
(0962 842500) Map A, E8

Student enquiries: Academic Registrar

Main study areas – as in What to Study section: *(First degree):* Art & design, fine arts.

European Community: All full-time first degree students take EC language and go on exchanges as part of course; all exchanges are of 3 months' duration and almost all are to EC. Formal exchange links with EC universities/colleges in: France (8); Germany (2); Netherlands (1); Spain (3). Approved Erasmus programme and Comett placements. Own studios in Barcelona, currently housing MA courses.

Application: ADAR for full-time BA studio courses. Direct for other degree courses. **Special features:** Teaching staff are practising painters, sculptors, designers. **Academic features:** Normally entrants must have completed foundation course or appropriate BTEC course for entry to full-time BA studio courses. Applications from mature and overseas candidates without standard UK qualifications are welcomed. **Founded:** 1870 to provide training for local Winchester craftsmen. **Main awards:** BA. **Awarding body:** Southampton University. **Site:** Winchester town centre. **Accommodation:** 56 hostel places. Approx cost: from £35 pw. Rent: 10% in accommodation where rent controlled by college. **Library:** 22,000 volumes, 150 periodicals, 80 study places; slide and video collections; automated link with Hartley Library, Southampton University. **Careers:** Information service by careers adviser/academic staff. **Amenities:** Second-hand bookshops nearby; excellent learning facilities including CAD/CAM equipment; SU; recreation centre and park adjacent to college. 1 hour by train from London galleries and exhibitions.

Duration of first degree course(s) or equivalent: 3 years **Total first degree students 1990/91:** 430 **Overseas students:** 15 **Mature students:** 130 approx **Male/female ratio:** 1:2 **Teaching staff: full-time:** 26 **part-time:** 100 **Total full-time students 1990/91:** 470 **Postgraduate students:** 50 **Tuition fees for 1992/93** (first degrees): Home: £2,770; Overseas: £6,250.

What it's like

Small but rapidly expanding college with a forward-looking management. Set in beautiful surroundings on the banks of the River Itchen, very close to the town centre. A 60s style building with 80s additions (further extensions planned for next year). Car parking is a problem, usually limited to students who live outside Winchester. Accommodation is very expensive. A few student houses still remaining. Roughly equal numbers of students in flats, houses, halls and lodging houses; most places are self-catering. SU provides washing facilities.

The main buildings house BA, postgraduate and MA courses; with the new MA fine art course using the main fine art studios for 3 months during the summer and working for the remaining 9 months in the college's Barcelona studio in Spain. Many part-time tutors have good links with London studios and are working artists. Good work placements for textile students, and lots of opportunities to study in European colleges on an exchange basis. All BA students travel to foreign lands ie Paris, Barcelona, Florence, Milan, Russia – fine art also have access to a cottage in Cornwall for drawing excursions during the summer term.

SU provides regular parties, bands, entertainments, cheap beer and pool room. Lots of pubs in Winchester of various quality. Live music regularly at the Railway Inn and the Mash Tun. Easy access to Southampton clubs and theatres etc. SU has one sabbatical officer and a committee of students who are always open to suggestions and voluntary help.

CAN'T FIND WHAT YOU'RE LOOKING FOR? USE THE INDEX!

Remember – Winchester School of Art is relatively small and everyone knows everything on the grapevine.

Pauper notes

Accommodation: Becoming increasingly difficult to find; few student houses, only 2 hostels, mostly rented accommodation, very expensive. **Drink:** City full of pubs, many of distinctive individual character and good food, especially in out of town country pubs. Local brew, Marstons. SU brew Allied Breweries. Good places – The Willow Tree, The Bush, The Mash Tun, Prince of Wales, Railway Inn, Vine, Greens Wine Bar (live jazz bands). **Eats:** Refectory, pub grub, 4 pizza places, Muswells, various Chinese and Indian restaurants and take-aways, 3 chip shops, Blue Dolphin, Olivers and Chinese chip shop; cheap health food from 'The Grainstore' (Parchment Street – close to college). **Ents:** SU only alternative night-out in Winchester; 3 theatres plus Tower Arts Centre; Theatre Royal shows films regularly, no main cinema; one nightclub – tries to cater for students and an early closing club/pub called Minsters. Many sports clubs and societies. SU tries to cater for these, especially bands. Southampton bigger and better. **Sports:** Very good recreation centre situated close to college with excellent new leisure pool complex. Competitive/fun football team. Group and individual sport available; cheapest on day-user ticket or with SU. **Hardship funds:** Access fund. **Travel:** Courses comprise many compulsory European study visits; exchanges with New York, Barcelona, Paris, Moscow, Holland, Germany, Italy. **Work:** Jobs available but becoming more difficult to obtain – mainly barwork, cleaning, shopwork and waiter/waitressing.

Informal name:
WSASU.

Alumni (Editors' pick)
Brian Eno.

WOLVERHAMPTON POLY
See Wolverhampton University

WOLVERHAMPTON UNIVERSITY

The University of Wolverhampton, Wulfruna Street, Wolverhampton WV1 1SB (0902 321000) Map A, D6

Student enquiries: Admissions Unit

Main study areas – as in What to Study section: *(First degree):* Accountancy, American studies, art & design, biochemistry, biology, biotechnology, business studies, chemistry, civil engineering, communication studies, computing, drama, economics, education, English, environmental science, European studies, fine arts, geography, history, hotel and catering management, information technology, law, mathematical studies, mechanical and production engineering, microbiology, modern languages, music, nursing studies, philosophy, physics, physiology, politics and government, professions allied to medicine (PAMs), psychology, religious studies and theology, social policy and social welfare, sociology, strategic studies. *Also:* Building, leisure studies, licenced retail management, photography, physical education, sports studies, surveying, women's studies.

European Community: 6% first degree students take EC language as part of course and 1% spend 6 months or more in another EC country. Formal exchange links with over 50 EC universities/colleges including Paris, Madrid, Barcelona, Berlin, Athens, Amsterdam. Exchanges open to students on most courses. Approved Erasmus programme 1992/93. Two courses with simultaneous awards and equal time spent in UK and EC: BA European business administration (with Netherlands diploma), and BSc European computing (with French diploma) ECTS scheme in management studies. Member of Text Consortium (for student exchange and transfer in Europe); student mobility encouraged. EC language tuition available to 100% undergraduates.

Application: PCAS for 1993 start, UCAS thereafter, except art and design (ADAR). **Academic features:** Credit accumulation and transfer scheme, and BA/BSc modular degree scheme enable students to select individually-tailored programmes of study; virtually all courses are modular (leading to CertHE, DipHE and BA/BSc). Work placements encouraged. Strong emphasis on continuing education and the development of international links. **Largest fields of study:** Business and social science. **Founded:** 1992 as a university; previously Wolverhampton Poly, founded 1969, ex former Colleges of Technology and Art, and 4 teacher training institutions. **Main awards:** BA, BEd, BSc, BEng, LLB. **Awarding body:** Wolverhampton University. **Site:** Main Wolverhampton site plus 4 other sites. **Access:** Free shuttle service; public transport. **Accommodation:** 1,350 hostel places, priority to first years. Approx cost: £45 pw (part board), £30 pw (self-catering). Rent: 8% in accommodation where rent controlled by polytechnic. **Library:** Libraries on each site; over 372,000 books and 5,000 journals in total; over 1,200 study places, computerised databases. **Specialist collections:** Regional history of West Midlands, company and legal reports, European Documentation Centre Collection. **Other learning resources:** Computer centre; resource based learning provision. **Welfare:** Advice on all sites, networked with other agencies and health consultancy service; access to dentist, FPA, psychiatrist, professional welfare officer, overseas student counsellor, chaplains, industrial relations officer; financial adviser, academic counselling based on Higher Education Shop which also advises applicants. **Careers:** Information and advice service. **Amenities:** SU premises on each site (coffee bar, TV rooms, sports facilities (including swimming pool at Walsall), bank, stationery and travel, shops, bars); Wolverhampton sports stadium (Olympic standard); art gallery, museums, cinema at Dudley and Wolverhampton, theatre and concert hall in Wolverhampton, arboretum at Walsall.

Duration of first degree course(s) or equivalent: 3 years; **others:** 4 years **Total first degree students 1991/92:** 10,516 (inclusive of p-t) **BEd students:** 1,389 **Overseas students:** 650 **Male/female ratio:** 1:1 **Teaching staff: full-time:** 450 **part-time:** 10 **Total full-time students 1991/92:** 8,140 **Postgraduate students:** 1,062 **Tuition fees for 1992/93 (first degrees):** Home: £1,855 (classroom), £2,770 (lab/studio); Overseas: £4,950. Registration fee of £50 payable in first year.

What it's like

It's on 5 sites but the main one is in the centre of Wolverhampton. Others are at Compton Park (1½ miles), Dudley (7 miles), Walsall (9 miles), and Telford, the newest and smallest (15 miles). Travel between sites should be provided by the university – not always reliable.

Accommodation provided for a limited number of freshers, Wolverhampton site only one that's self-catering. Halls' service basic and expensive. Rented accommodation varied yet plentiful.

Courses widespread. Highly innovative combined studies allows combination of almost every course in poly; modular scheme works well, allowing students to pick and choose. Workloads realistic and can be quite low if year's work carefully planned. Continuous assessment and examinations.

Students come from all over England and Wales. Minimal numbers from independent schools. Large number of European and overseas students, particularly on law course. Low drop-out rate speaks volumes for the quality of the courses and the social life provided, relative to the reputation that preceded them.

CAN'T FIND WHAT YOU'RE LOOKING FOR? USE THE INDEX!

SU very active socially: top bands; seven bars, some of the busiest in town. Politically it's fairly quiet apart from the occasional outburst from the active hunt saboteurs.

Pauper notes

Accommodation: Expensive halls, not great standard. Plenty private but varied quality. **Drink:** Fairly cheap (£1 pint). V. good Union. Bass & Courage. Local pubs – Banks. **Eats:** Campus food poor. Union supply meals from all bars. **Ents:** Excellent, varied comedy, major venue. Cheap, plentiful. **Sports:** V. poor. Sports centre facilities at all sites. **Hardship funds:** V. good welfare service both uni and SU. **Travel:** Travel shop run by SU. **Work:** Well paid bar work at union bars. Some available in town.

Informal name

Wally poly.

WORCESTER COLLEGE

Worcester College of HE, Henwick Grove, Worcester WR2 6AJ (0905 748080) (Fax: 0905 748162) Map A, D7

Student enquiries: Academic Registrar

Main study areas – as in What to Study section: *(First degree):* Art and design, biology, computing, drama and theatre arts, economics, education, English, environmental science, geography, history, mathematical studies, music, psychology, sociology. *Also:* Home economics, physical education, urban studies.

European Community: No students learn an EC language or spend 6 months or more in another EC country, but some exchange visits.

Application: PCAS for 1993 start, UCAS thereafter. **Special features:** Primary Teaching Centre. Opportunity for 2nd year students to spend term in USA. Sponsorship/bursary scheme for BA/BSc students. **Academic features:** BA English studies, geographical studies, historical studies, social sciences; BSc biological sciences, environmental sciences. **Founded:** 1946. **Main awards:** BA, BSc, BEd. **Awarding body:** Coventry University. **Site:** 55-acre campus 2 miles from Worcester town centre. **Access:** Bus service from Worcester. **Accommodation:** 580 places in mixed and single sex halls of residence. Approx cost: £45 pw. New self-catering hall for 200 students. **Library:** 100,000 volumes, 500 periodicals, 280 study places. **Other learning resources:** Media services primary centre. **Welfare:** Medical and health centre (doctor, FPA), chaplain, counselling service, advisory tutor system. **Careers:** Information and advice service. **Amenities:** SU bar, shops, newspaper, dance studios, drama studio, computer centres. **Sporting facilities:** Playing fields, tennis courts, gymnasia, floodlit hard playing area on site. **Employment:** Teaching, commerce, industry, public service, administration, buying/marketing, management services, information and library work, personnel and welfare.

Duration of first degree course(s) or equivalent: 3 years; 4 years (BEd) **Total first degree students 1991/92:** 1,400; **BEd students:** 600 **Mature students:** 200 **Male/female ratio:** 2:3 **Teaching staff: full-time:** 100 **part-time:** 30 **Total full-time students 1991/92:** 1,250 **Postgraduate students:** 250 **Tuition fees for 1992/93 (first degrees):** Home: £1,855 (classroom), £2,770 (lab/studio); Overseas: £5,019. Additional £50 registration fee in first year.

What it's like

It's a single site college in mature grounds of shrubs and playing fields. Short walk from banks of the river Severn and city centre. Most first years and many finalists live on campus in halls – some modern flats, generally relaxed attitude to friends staying overnight. On-site facilities include shops – cheap laundry, computer rooms and medical centre. Typical but picturesque smallish provincial city; many shops, nightclubs, theatre, cinema, restaurants and a multitude of pubs to suit all tastes.

BEd courses recognised as some of the best in the country, female dominated. Academic study travel opportunities exist mainly to Europe but as far afield as the Shetlands and Tunisia. Exchange programmes to Hungary, Finland and the USA.

Good staff-student relationships – students seen as individuals not just one of the crowd. Tutors only too willing to help if you need it. Trained counsellors can help with any problems you may have – sympathetically and confidentially – active and approachable SU will also help in any way they can.

SU bar – 'The Dive' – is the 'Mecca' of our universe. SU organises many ents – great Freshers and Rag Week. Wide range of clubs and societies. Students come from all over the country – all types of background – slight Northern bias – no typical student here.

On the whole a very relaxed and friendly place. Most students are happy socially and academically. Who knows, you may even get a good degree out of it – a great many do.

As for breaking the ice . . . What ice?

Pauper notes

Accommodation: 10-meal licence in rooms in halls of residence. Some shared rooms. Self-catering flats only available to final year students. **Drink:** SU bar cheapest place in a city full of pubs. World's strongest beer brewed at 'The Brewery Tap'. 'Little Pub Company' pubs surround us. **Eats:** Canteen and snack bar on campus. Lots of various restaurants with veggie options. 'Desperate Dan Cow-Pies' sold at 'The Little Sauce Factory'. **Ents:** Theatre, cinema, nightclubs, live bands in pubs; but the best ents are always right here at college. Have 5 balls per year, frequent live bands, and a film every Sunday. **Sports:** County cricket ground, racecourse (horses), rowing and canoe clubs on river, banger racing circuit, rugby and football clubs, leisure centres. **Hardship funds:** SU helps with financial difficulties. **Travel:** Good train and bus services all over the country. **Work:** Work available on campus eg SU bar/shop etc. Fair amount of local jobs available, particularly in pubs and food outlets.

More info?

Get students' Alternative Prospectus.
Enquiries to President SU (0905 748522 or 748523).

Informal name

WCHE.

Buzz-words

Hines (Hines Building); The Dive (SU Bar).

WRITTLE

Writtle College, Chelmsford, Essex CM1 3RR (0245 420705)
Map: A, G7

Student enquiries: Student Registration Officer

Main study areas – as in What to Study section: *(First degree):* Agriculture and horticulture. *Also*: Equine studies, landscape studies, leisure studies, recreation studies, rural environment studies, soil science, tourism, urban estate management, water resources.

European Community: 10% students take EC languages as part of course, 5% spend 6 months or more in another EC country. Formal exchange links with 6 EC colleges. Some work experience in EC for BSc (horticulture) students.

Application: PCAS for 1993 start, UCAS thereafter. **Academic features:** Modular courses; flexible learning methods. **Structural features:** Partners with Hertfordshire University (BSc Hort), Anglia Poly University (BSc Hons Rural Res Dev) and Essex University (BSc Ag). **Founded:** 1893. **Main award:** BSc. **Awarding bodies:** Anglia Poly University, Essex University, Hertfordshire University. **Site:** Single campus. **Access:** Just off A414 at Writtle. Chelmsford railway station 2 miles. **Accommodation:** On-site for 200; approx cost £65/week single room, all meals. 500 places in cottage/flat lodgings; approx cost £40/week, no meals. Rent: 45% in accommodation where rent controlled by college. **Library:** 40,000 volumes, 300 periodicals, 50 study places. **Specialist collections:** Agriculture, horticulture and rural resources. **Other learning facilities:** 500-acre estate including 3 farms; separate fruit farm, commercial glass, equestrian centre, amenity centre, farm shop, engineering workshops, labs. **Careers:** Information, advice and placement service. **Employment:** Management in horticulture, leisure, agriculture etc. **Welfare:** Health centre, counselling. **Amenities:** Recreation centre. New bar/disco/social centre. **Sports:** Sports hall, squash, tennis, fitness centre on site.

Duration of first degree course(s) or equivalent: 4 years (BSc Hort), 3 years (BSc Rural Res), 1 year (BSc – top-up courses) **Total first degree students 1991/92:** 228 **Overseas students:** 150 **Mature students:** 100 **Male/female ratio:** 3:1 **Teaching staff: full-time:** 90 **Part-time:** 10 **Total full-time students 1991/92:** 650 **Postgraduate students:** 10 **Tuition fees for 1992/93 (first degrees):** Home: £2,770; Overseas: £5,319.

WYE COLLEGE

Wye College, University of London, Ashford, Kent TN25 5AH (0233 812401) Map A, G8

Student enquiries: The Registrar

Main study areas – as in What to Study section: *(First degree):* Agriculture, horticulture, biochemistry, biology, biotechnology, business studies, botany, economics, environmental science, environmental studies, zoology. *Also:* Agricultural/horticultural business management, agricultural economics, countryside management.

European Community: No students learn an EC language although French available to all undergraduates (non-examined). Optional course available to some degree streams an 'introduction to agriculture, food and environment in France' taught in French. No students spend 6 months or more in another EC country as part of their course but business studies students may, in sandwich year. Formal exchange links with Denmark (Copenhagen), France (Montpellier, Toulouse) and Spain (Barcelona) as well as ad hoc links with a number of others. Approved Erasmus programme.

Application: UCCA for 1993 start, UCAS thereafter. **Structural features:** Part of London University. **Academic features:** Courses in agriculture and the environment, rural environment, countryside management, business studies, plant and animal science, biochemistry. **Special features:** Research into the impact of human activity in the environment eg recycling organic waste, Channel Tunnel, sustainable agriculture; and into aspects of food production in developed and developing countries. **Largest fields of study:** Agriculture, environmental science, countryside management and business management. **Founded:** 1894. 1900 admitted to London University as a constitutional 'School'. **Main awards:** BSc. **Awarding body:** London University. **Site:** Combination of medieval and modern buildings in Wye town centre. **Access:** Wye station; M20 from London, A28 from Ashford. **Accommodation:** 404 places in mixed halls of residence (all new undergraduates can live in hall for their first year). Approx cost: £1,710 pa (breakfast and evening meal 5 days pw). Rent: 60% in accommodation where rent subsidised by college. **Library:** 39,000 books, 600 periodical titles, 120 study places. **Specialist collections:** European Documentation Centre, historical collection of agricultural and horticultural books. **Other learning resources:** Labs, glasshouses, field laboratories; 325 hectares of arable and grassland including sites for amenity and conservation, 5 hectares horticultural crops and orchards. **Welfare:** College medical officer, resident nursing sister, counselling service, college chaplain, Directors of Study, Wardens (halls of residence and hostels). **Hardship funds:** Principal's Fund is available should hardship arise once the course has started. **Special categories:** Limited accommodation for married students; 3 undergraduate rooms with wheelchair access. **Careers:** Information and advice service through both London University Careers Advisory Service and Wye College. **Amenities:** SU building with bar, music room, photographic facilities and many active clubs and societies; cultural facilities of Canterbury 11 miles away; situated in an area of outstanding natural beauty. **Sporting facilities:** Tennis courts, playing fields, swimming pool, squash courts. **Employment:** Agricultural and horticultural industries; civil service; local government; scientific research establishments; conservation and resource management.

Duration of first degree course(s) or equivalent: 3 years **Total first degree students 1991/92:** 440 **Overseas students:** 24 **Mature students:** 56 **Male/female ratio:** 1:1 **Teaching staff: full-time:** 64 **part-time:** 6 **research:** 48. **Total full-time students 1991/92:** 681 **Postgraduate students:** 241 **Tuition fees for 1992/93 (first degrees): Home:** £1,855 (classroom), £2,770 (lab); **Overseas:** £6,357 (classroom), £7,839 (lab).

What it's like

It's a London University college, unique in its situation and style of life. Wye provides students with London University qualifications while remaining in a very beautiful part of the Kent countryside. Students come from a wide geographical area and varied social backgrounds but generally all are in some way involved with the countryside. The result is a very harmonious community comprising 600 undergraduates (50:50 mix of male to female) and approximately 200 postgraduates.

The college represents the agricultural and horticultural part of London University, but the undergraduate courses extend into business management and environmental-type courses providing a wider outlook over all land/business careers. Courses are run on a unit system, with some assessment on course work during the year, and exams in the summer. Failure rates low.

There's a wide variety of people studying at the college. SU very active, but not politically aligned, mainly due to the rather easy-going nature of the students. Any group of students who wish to form a society can be sponsored by the union (over 50 at the time of writing). The SU's biggest success has been in fund raising for charity in Rag Week, usually by fairly unconventional means.

Wye has its own farm estate to give students real practical knowledge, plus many well equipped lecture rooms. The staff usually have worked in their field of study in the private sector. All students have a director of studies to help them if they run into trouble.

1st years accommodated in 3 halls of residence all within easy walking distance from lectures, SU, village shops, and local BR station. It's not necessary for 1st year students to own a car, but it is useful in the 2nd and 3rd years when Wye students tend to live further away from the college in the large number of rented houses available. Highlights of 1st year are Freshers Week and Rag Week (in the Christmas term) and Cricket Week (after exams in the summer). There are approximately 5 black tie Balls in the year (It is a very good idea to lay your hands on the appropriate clothing!), and there is nearly always a live band or a disco in the union every week of the term. 1st year students quickly feel at home in Wye's relaxed and easy-going atmosphere. It remains at the top of its class in teaching, facilities and in the superb participation the union achieves amongst students, and the enjoyment students get out of Wye.

Ralph Rayner, Student Press Officer

Pauper notes

Accommodation: 3 halls of residence for undergrads. Single rooms (unless otherwise stated by the applicant). Includes cleaners, kitchens, bathrooms, and breakfast on week days. Price – reasonable and includes weekday evening meals at the canteen. **Drink:** Union bar – good standard bitters and lagers (well run by students) controlled and maintained well with an unprecedented percentage of students using the union compared to other universities. Local pubs – plenty of them, friendly atmospheres and more specialised, varied types of beer etc. **Eats:** At the canteen (OK but not spectacular!). Local pubs – excellent and reasonably priced. Local restaurants in Wye, Canterbury (12 miles) and Ashford (4 miles). **Ents:** Very active SU – discos, live bands, theme nights and official balls (It's a wonder anyone does any work at all). Also cinema and theatre in Canterbury. **Sports:** Rugby, hockey, cricket, football, squash courts, tennis courts, swimming pool, gymnasium, riding, clay shooting, beagling all available on campus. There are also annual ski trips, paintball games – in fact anything is possible! **Hardship funds:** For exceptional financial problems. **Travel:** 60 miles from London. Road – M25, M11, M20. Rail – Ashford BR and Wye BR Network SE.

Alumni (Editors' pick)

Sir Peter Mills, MP; Professor Chris Baines; Professor Bill Hill FRS.

YORK UNIVERSITY

University of York, Heslington, York YO1 5DD
(0904 430000; Fax 0904 433433) Map A, E5

Student enquiries: Undergraduate Admissions Office
(0904 433535; Fax 0904 433538)

Main study areas – as in What to Study section: *(First degree):* Archaeology, biochemistry, biology, chemistry, computing, economics, education, electrical and electronic engineering, English, environmental science, environmental studies, history, information technology, linguistics, mathematical studies, modern languages, music, pharmacology, philosophy, physics, physiology, politics and government, psychology, social policy and social welfare, sociology. *Also:* Avionics, Chinese, Hindi, Swahili.

European Community: All first degree students can take EC language as part of first year course through the university's 'Languages for All' programme; 8% spend 6 months or more in another EC country. Formal exchange links with 10 EC universities/colleges: in France (history, language and linguistics), Germany (biology, maths, language and linguistics) and Italy (English and music). Formal combined courses include history with French, information technology with business management and language, maths and biology can both be taken with a year in Germany, chemistry with a year in Europe. Approved Erasmus programme 1992/93.

Application: UCCA for 1993 start, UCAS thereafter. **Academic features:** BEng (sandwich) in electronic engineering; 3-4 year BEng physical electronics; BA linguistics and Chinese/Hindi/Swahili/Swedish; 4 year BSc biology with 1 year in Germany; 4 year BSc (sandwich) in biology and biochemistry; 3 year BA in English/history of art. Combined degree in environmental economics and environmental management and in music technology; information technology courses for students without science or maths at A-level. **Special features:** College system. Institute for Applied Biology, Centre for Women's Studies. Resident quartet – the Sorrell Quartet. **Main awards:** BA, BEng, BSc, MEng, MSci. **Awarding body:** York University. **Site:** 86-hectare site about 2 miles from city centre. **Access:** Bus from York station (London King's Cross 1¾ hours); signposted turnings off A64. **Accommodation:** Approx 3,000 places on or near campus. Seventh college recently opened. Approx cost: £770 pa (all meals extra). 70% in accommodation where rent controlled by university. **Library:** 455,000 volumes, 2,200 periodicals; 725 reading places (university library) + 390 (college libraries); multiple copies of course books; reserve collection. **Open learning facilities:** Audiovisual centre, computing service, language teaching centre. **Amenities:** Over 100 student societies; social functions, discos, community action projects; student newspaper, television and radio; 3 studios for pottery, printmaking and painting for use of all students; drama studio, open-air chess board and 'Boules' terrain; children's nursery; all colleges have rooms adapted for disabled students. **Sporting facilities:** 40 acres of playing fields on site; 400-metre 7-lane athletics track; boathouse on the River Ouse for rowing; York's 3-swimming pool complex half a mile away. **Hardship funds:** Reduced fees for self-financing students. Access funds available.

Duration of first degree course(s) or equivalent: 3 years; **others:** 4 years **Total first degree students 1991/92:** 3,658 **Overseas students:** 300 **Mature students:** 13% **Male/female ratio:** 11:9 **Teaching staff: full-time:** 334 **part-time:** 16 **Total full-time students 1991/92:** 4,626 **Postgraduate students:** 986 (f-t) 333 (p-t) **Tuition fees for 1992/93 (first degrees):** Home: £906 (if no grant), £2,006 (classroom), £2,921 (lab/studio); Overseas: £5,320 (classroom), £7,055 (lab/studio).

What it's like

York, the city, is beautiful, historic, and overflowing with beer (365 pubs!). As a small city, though, it is fairly quiet. The campus reflects that, with no SU building, relatively poor sporting facilities, and few big gigs. It's a fairly small campus divided into seven colleges, each with own bar and social centre; so it's easy to make friends, if a little claustrophobic at times.

York's great advantage is accommodation; the university guarantees to house 70% of all students, including all first years, and so far they're managing. Campus itself has most of the facilities you'd need (laundries, shop, hairdressers!), and is relatively good for disabled access (though that's not saying a lot). There is a nursery, but fees are a bit high. The main hassle is that the campus library doesn't open on Sundays.

Also, York has a very good academic reputation. The courses can be a little inflexible (no modular system as yet), but they are (mostly) good quality, and the staff-student ratio is still relatively high. Assessment and work load varies wildly (science students have a harder time). The university is fairly flexible about course transfers and time off, and runs a number of foreign exchange schemes. It encourages people to take higher degrees.

The stereotypical York student is a white, middle class ex-public-school southerner, and there is some truth in that. Certainly, most senior staff are white, middle class ex-Oxbridge southerners, and few are women either. But there are plenty of students who don't fit the model, and there's little (overt) discrimination.

The welfare system supposedly relies on supervisors, which can be a problem; but in reality, the university and the SU provide a wide range of other help and support, including counselling.

There are dozens of active societies, including independent media and a very successful Film Soc, as well as college Junior Common Rooms which organise many social events. New Barbican Centre in town accommodates symphony orchestras, Russ Abbott and The Chippendales.

On the whole, provided you're not a big city animal, York is a good place to take a degree and an excellent place to live!

Pauper notes

Accommodation: Campus cheap, town now £38/week on average. **Drink:** Best place to drink anywhere – top pubs. **Eats:** Campus – expensive, not too good. Town – varies, lots of good stuff (good curry houses!) **Ents:** Not a lot. Plenty of cinemas, but few G/G venues. **Sports:** Mediocre sports hall on campus, good one 15 minutes away. **Hardship funds:** Both union and university quite helpful. **Travel:** A few scholarships. STA shop on campus. Hitching not bad. **Work:** Lots of pub work, not a lot else.

More info?

Get students' Alternative Prospectus.
Enquiries to SU (0904 433723/4).

Alumni (Editors' pick)

Tony Banks, Michael Brown and Harriet Harman (MPs), Harry Enfield and Victor Lewis-Smith (comedians), Moray Welsh (cellist), Paul Roberts (pianist), Genista McIntosh (Director of the National Theatre), Trevor Jones and Dominic Muldowney (composers), Tom Gutteridge and Sebastian Cody (TV producers).

Aberdeen University *Map A, D2*
Aberystwyth *Map A, C7*
ALRA *Map D, B3*
Anglia Poly University *Map A, F7*
Architectural Association *Map E, C2*
Aston University *Map A, E7*

Bangor *Map A, C6*
Bangor Normal College *Map A, C6*
Bath College *Map A, D8*
Bath University *Map A, D8*
Bedford College *Map A, F7*
Belfast University *Map A, B4*
Birkbeck College *Map E, C1*
Birmingham Conservatoire *Map A, E7*
Birmingham University *Map A, E7*
Bolton Institute *Map A, D5*
Bournemouth University *Map A, E9*
Bradford & Ilkley *Map A, E5*
Bradford University *Map A, E5*
Bretton Hall *Map A, E5*
Brighton University *Map A, F8*
Bristol Old Vic *Map A, D8*
Bristol University *Map A, D8*
Bristol UWE *Map A, D8*
British Institute in Paris
British School of Osteopathy *Map E, C3*
Brunel University *Map A, F8*
Buckingham University *Map A, E7*
Buckinghamshire College *Map A, E8*
Buckland *Map A, E7*

Camberwell College of Arts *Map D, C2*
Camborne School of Mines *Map A, B9*
Cambridge University *Map A, F7*
  Christ's
  Churchill
  Clare
  Corpus Christi
  Downing
  Emmanuel
  Fitzwilliam
  Girton
  Gonville & Caius
  Jesus
  King's
  Lucy Cavendish

  Magdalene
  New Hall
  Newnham
  Pembroke
  Peterhouse
  Queens'
  Robinson
  St Catharine's
  St Edmund's
  St John's
  Selwyn
  Sidney Sussex
  Trinity
  Trinity Hall
  Wolfson
Canterbury Christ Church College *Map A, G8*
Cardiff *Map A, D8*
Cardiff Institute *Map A, D8*
Central England University *Map A, E7*
Central Lancashire University *Map A, D5*
Central Saint Martins *Map E, C2*
Central School of Speech and Drama *Map D, B1*
Charing Cross and Westminster *Map D, A2*
Charlotte Mason *Map A, D5*
Chelsea *Map E, B4*
Cheltenham & Gloucester College *Map A, D7*
Chester College *Map A, D6*
City University *Map E, D1*
Colchester Institute *Map A, F7*
Courtauld Institute *Map E, C2*
Coventry University *Map A, E7*
Cranfield *Map A, F7*
Cranwell *Map A, F6*
Crewe & Alsager *Map A, D6*

Dartington *Map A, C9*
Dartmouth *Map A, C9*
De Montfort University *Map A, E6*
Derby University *Map A, E6*
Duncan of Jordanstone *Map A, D2*
Dundee Institute *Map A, D2*
Dundee University *Map A, D2*
Durham University *Map A, E4*

East Anglia University *Map A, G6*
East London University *Map D, D1*
Edge Hill *Map A, D5*

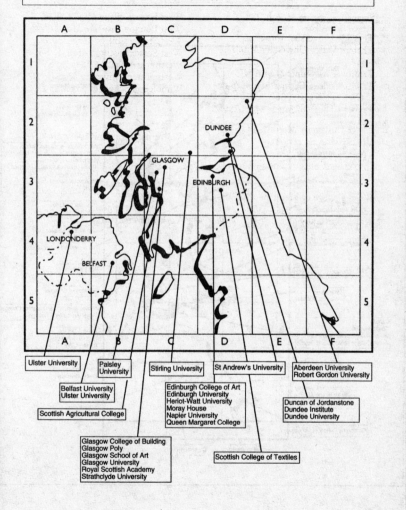

NORTHERN IRELAND AND SCOTLAND
Map A (i)

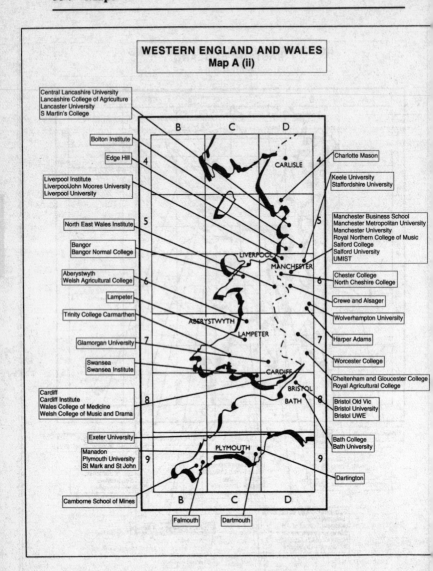

WESTERN ENGLAND AND WALES
Map A (ii)

Central Lancashire University
Lancashire College of Agriculture
Lancaster University
S Martin's College

Bolton Institute

Edge Hill

Liverpool Institute
LiverpoolJohn Moores University
Liverpool University

North East Wales Institute

Bangor
Bangor Normal College

Aberystwyth
Welsh Agricultural College

Lampeter

Trinity College Carmarthen

Glamorgan University

Swansea
Swansea Institute

Cardiff
Cardiff Institute
Wales College of Medicine
Welsh College of Music and Drama

Exeter University

Manadon
Plymouth University
St Mark and St John

Camborne School of Mines

Charlotte Mason

Keele University
Staffordshire University

Manchester Business School
Manchester Metropolitan University
Manchester University
Royal Northern College of Music
Salford College
Salford University
UMIST

Chester College
North Cheshire College

Crewe and Alsager

Wolverhampton University

Harper Adams

Worcester College

Cheltenham and Gloucester College
Royal Agricultural College

Bristol Old Vic
Bristol University
Bristol UWE

Bath College
Bath University

Dartington

Falmouth

Dartmouth

CARLISLE

LIVERPOOL
MANCHESTER

ABERYSTWYTH
LAMPETER

CARDIFF
BRISTOL
BATH

PLYMOUTH

B C D

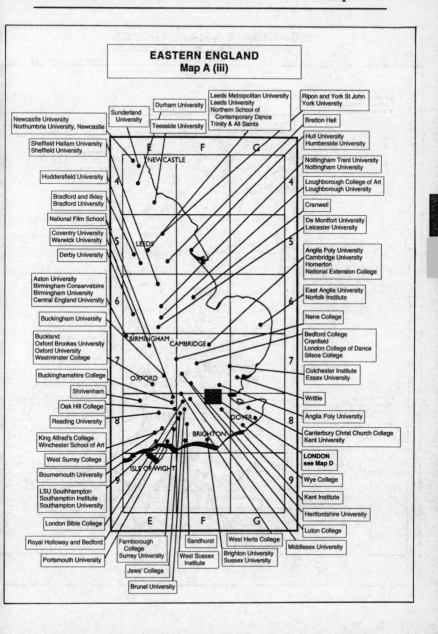

EASTERN ENGLAND
Map A (iii)

Newcastle University
Northumbria University, Newcastle

Sunderland University

Durham University

Teesside University

Leeds Metropolitan University
Leeds University
Northern School of
Contemporary Dance
Trinity & All Saints

Ripon and York St John
York University

Bretton Hall

Sheffield Hallam University
Sheffield University

Huddersfield University

Bradford and Ilkley
Bradford University

National Film School

Coventry University
Warwick University

Derby University

Aston University
Birmingham Conservatoire
Birmingham University
Central England University

Buckingham University

Buckland
Oxford Brookes University
Oxford University
Westminster College

Buckinghamshire College

Shrivenham

Oak Hill College

Reading University

King Alfred's College
Winchester School of Art

West Surrey College

Bournemouth University

LSU Southhampton
Southampton Institute
Southampton University

London Bible College

Royal Holloway and Bedford

Portsmouth University

Farnborough
College
Surrey University

Jews' College

Brunel University

Sandhurst

West Sussex
Institute

West Herts College

Brighton University
Sussex University

Hull University
Humberside University

Nottingham Trent University
Nottingham University

Loughborough College of Art
Loughborough University

Cranwell

De Montfort University
Leicester University

Anglia Poly University
Cambridge University
Homerton
National Extension College

East Anglia University
Norfolk Institute

Nene College

Bedford College
Cranfield
London College of Dance
Silsoe College

Colchester Institute
Essex University

Writtle

Anglia Poly University

Canterbury Christ Church College
Kent University

LONDON
see Map D

Wye College

Kent Institute

Hertfordshire University

Luton College

Middlesex University

NEWCASTLE

LEEDS

BIRMINGHAM   CAMBRIDGE

OXFORD

DOVER

BRIGHTON

ISLE OF WIGHT

E   F   G

4   4

5   5

6   6

7   7

8   8

9   9

MOTORWAYS & MAJOR ROADS
Map B

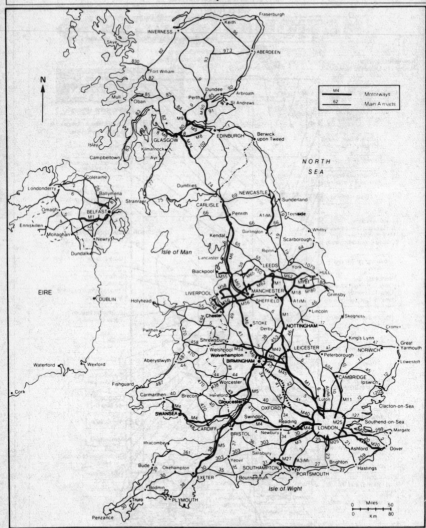

COACH SERVICES Map C (i)

NATIONAL EXPRESS »

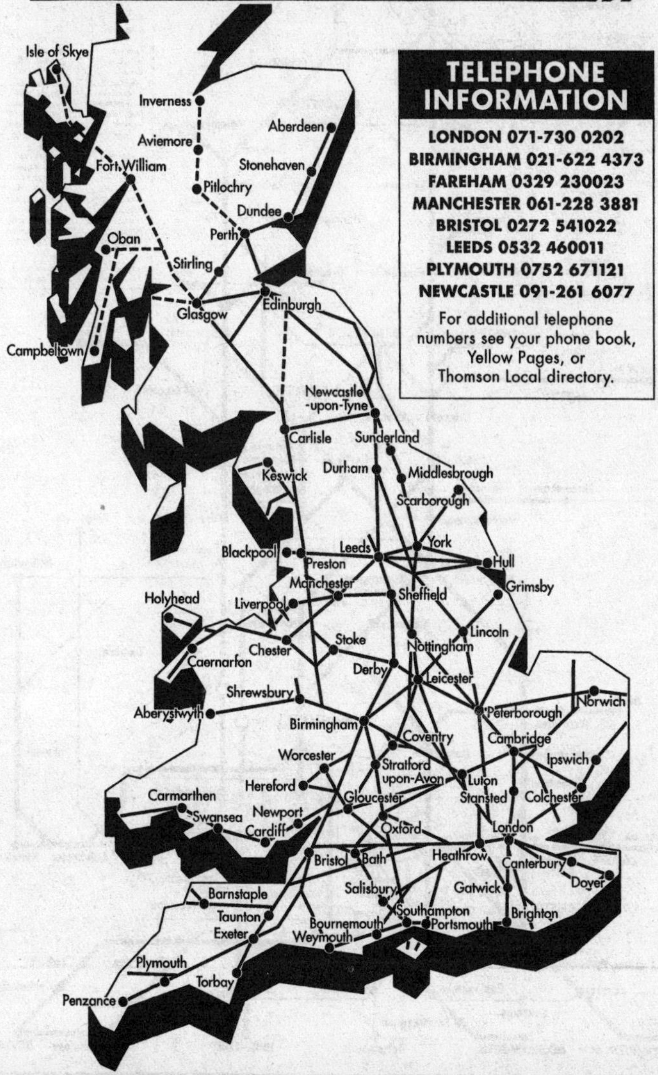

TELEPHONE INFORMATION

LONDON 071-730 0202
BIRMINGHAM 021-622 4373
FAREHAM 0329 230023
MANCHESTER 061-228 3881
BRISTOL 0272 541022
LEEDS 0532 460011
PLYMOUTH 0752 671121
NEWCASTLE 091-261 6077

For additional telephone
numbers see your phone book,
Yellow Pages, or
Thomson Local directory.

RAIL SERVICES
Map C (ii)

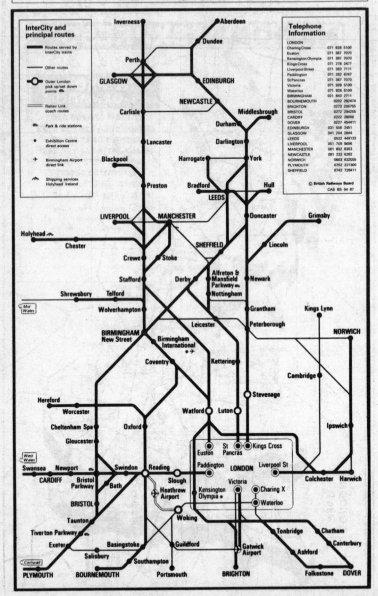

InterCity and principal routes

Routes served by InterCity trains

Other routes

Outer London pick up/set down points

Railair Link coach routes

Park & ride stations

Exhibition Centre direct access

Birmingham Airport direct link

Shipping services Holyhead Ireland

Telephone Information

LONDON
Charing Cross   071 928 5100
Euston   071 387 7070
Kensington Olympia   071 387 7070
Kings Cross   071 278 2477
Liverpool Street   071 283 7171
Paddington   071 262 6767
St Pancras   071 387 7070
Victoria   071 928 5100
Waterloo   071 928 5100
BIRMINGHAM   021 643 2711
BOURNEMOUTH   0202 292474
BRIGHTON   0273 206755
BRISTOL   0272 294256
CARDIFF   0222 28000
DOVER   0227 454411
EDINBURGH   031 556 2451
GLASGOW   041 204 2844
LEEDS   0532 448133
LIVERPOOL   051 709 9696
MANCHESTER   061 832 8353
NEWCASTLE   091 232 6262
NORWICH   0603 632055
PLYMOUTH   0752 221300
SHEFFIELD   0742 726411

© British Railways Board
CAS 85 54 87

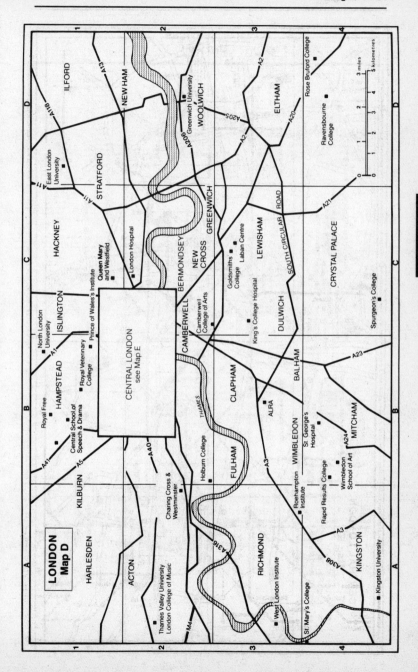

LONDON Map D

ILFORD

NEW HAM

A13

A118

D

East London University

A11

STRATFORD

A11

HACKNEY

ISLINGTON

HAMPSTEAD

North London University

A1

Royal Free

A41

A5

KILBURN

Central School of Speech & Drama

Royal Veterinary College

Prince of Wales's Institute

London Hospital

Queen Mary and Westfield

CENTRAL LONDON see Map E

HARLESDEN

ACTON

Thames Valley University London College of Music

A40

M4

A316

Charing Cross & Westminster

Holburn College

THAMES

FULHAM

CAMBERWELL

BERMONDSEY

NEW CROSS

GREENWICH

Greenwich University

A206

WOOLWICH

A205

A2

A2

ELTHAM

A20

Rose Bruford College

Ravensbourne College

SOUTH CIRCULAR ROAD

A21

CRYSTAL PALACE

Spurgeon's College

Goldsmiths College

Laban Centre

LEWISHAM

King's College Hospital

DULWICH

Camberwell College of Arts

CLAPHAM

BALHAM

ALRA

WIMBLEDON

St George's Hospital

A3

A23

A24

MITCHAM

Roehampton Institute

Rapid Results College

Wimbledon School of Art

RICHMOND

West London Institute

St. Mary's College

A308

A3

KINGSTON

Kingston University

3 miles

5 kilometres

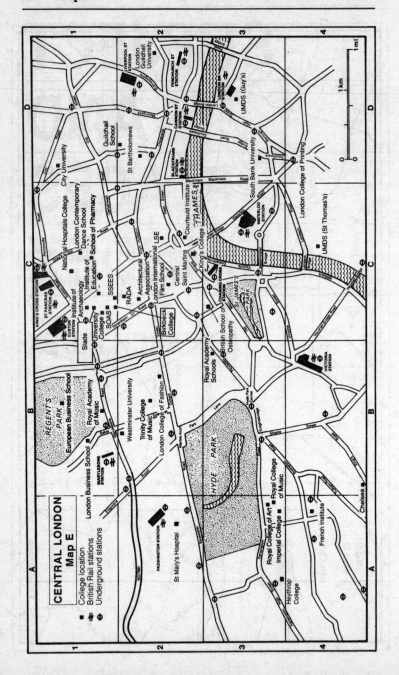

SUBJECT
AND
PLACES
INDEX

A SEARCH INDEX

HOW TO USE THE SUBJECT AND PLACES INDEX

This is a search index designed to help you find out where subjects are taught and what they are.

Where's your subject taught?
We spotlight the prospectuses of institutions teaching a subject as all (or a major part) of a first degree course.

If you know what you want to study, all you need to do is look up the places in *Where To Study*, make a shortlist and write for the prospectuses.

Beware. After the prospectuses have crashed through your letter box you still may be unable to find the subject you want. This is usually because they use another name for it – they can use whatever fancy name they please. Persevere and you should eventually find it.

What subjects interest you?
This could help you if you are not sure what to study. For instance if you look up French you will see that its study area is Modern Languages. You can then look up the article on Modern Languages in *What to study*. Use the index to help you browse.

GET HOLD OF THE PROSPECTUSES

A

ACCOUNTANCY
Possible prospectuses: Aberdeen Univ, Aberystwyth, Anglia Poly Univ, Aston Univ, Bangor, Belfast Univ, Birmingham Univ, Bournemouth Univ, Bradford Univ, Brighton Univ, Bristol Univ, Bristol UWE, Buckingham Univ, Cardiff, Central England Univ, Central Lancashire Univ, City Univ, Coventry Univ, De Montfort Univ, Derby Univ, Dundee Inst, Dundee Univ, East Anglia Univ, East London Univ, Edinburgh Univ, Essex Univ, European Bus Sch, Exeter Univ, Glamorgan Univ, Glasgow Poly, Glasgow Univ, Greenwich Univ, Heriot-Watt Univ, Hertfordshire Univ, Holborn Coll, Huddersfield Univ, Hull Univ, Humberside Univ, Kent Univ, Kingston Univ, Lancaster Univ, Leeds Metropolitan Univ, Leeds Univ, Liverpool John Moores Univ, Liverpool Univ, London Guildhall Univ, Loughborough Univ, LSE, Luton Coll, Manchester Metropolitan Univ, Manchester Univ, Middlesex Univ, Napier Univ, Nene Coll, Newcastle Univ, North London Univ, Northumbria Univ, Nottingham Trent Univ, Nottingham Univ, Oxford Brookes Univ, Paisley Univ, Plymouth Univ, Portsmouth Univ, Reading Univ, Robert Gordon Univ, Royal Agricultural Coll, Salford Univ, Sheffield Hallam Univ, Sheffield Univ, South Bank Univ, Southampton Inst, Southampton Univ, Stirling Univ, Strathclyde Univ, Sunderland Univ, Swansea Inst, Teesside Univ, Thames Valley Univ, Ulster Univ, Warwick Univ, Wolverhampton Univ.
See also: Business studies.
Study area: Accountancy.

ACOUSTIC ENGINEERING
Possible prospectuses: Cambridge Univ, Salford Univ, Southampton Univ.
See also: Electrical engineering.
Study area: Electrical and electronic engineering; mechanical and production engineering.

ACOUSTICS
See: Acoustic engineering; electronic engineering; music; physics; speech sciences.

ACTING
Possible prospectuses: ALRA, Bretton Hall, Bristol Old Vic, Central Sch Speech/Drama, Manchester Metropolitan Univ, RADA, Welsh Coll Music/Drama.
See also: Drama.
Study area: Drama and theatre arts.

ACTUARIAL STUDIES
Possible prospectuses: City Univ, Glasgow Poly, Heriot-Watt Univ, Kent Univ, LSE, Southampton Univ.
See also: Mathematics; social sciences; statistics.
Study areas: Mathematical studies.

ADMINISTRATION
See: Business administration; estate management; housing administration; personnel administration; public administration.

ADVERTISING
Possible prospectuses: Bournemouth Univ, Buckinghamshire Coll, Humberside Univ, Luton Coll, Napier Univ, Ulster Univ.

ADVERTISING DESIGN
See: Graphic design.

AERODYNAMICS
Possible prospectuses: Cambridge Univ, Cranfield (p/g only), Cranwell, Dartmouth, Kingston Univ, Manchester Univ.
Study area: Aeronautical engineering.

AERONAUTICAL ENGINEERING
Possible prospectuses: Bath Univ, Belfast Univ, Bristol Univ, Bristol UWE, Brunel Univ, Cambridge Univ, City Univ, Coventry Univ, Cranfield (p/g only), Cranwell, Dartmouth, Farnborough Coll, Glasgow Univ, Hertfordshire Univ, Humberside Univ, Imperial Coll, Kingston Univ, Loughborough Univ, Manadon, Manchester Univ, North East Wales Inst, Queen Mary & Westfield, Royal Coll Art (p/g only), Salford Univ, Shrivenham, Southampton Univ, UMIST.
Study area: Aeronautical engineering.

AESTHETICS
See: Fine arts; philosophy.

AFRICAN STUDIES
Possible prospectuses: Birmingham Univ, Kent Univ, Liverpool Univ, SOAS, Sussex Univ.
See also: Archaeology; Asian studies; Near East studies.
Study area: African studies.

AFRO-ASIAN STUDIES
See: African studies; Asian studies.

AGRICULTURAL BOTANY
Possible prospectuses: Aberystwyth, Belfast Univ, Glasgow Univ, Hertfordshire Univ, Imperial Coll, Leeds Univ, Newcastle Univ, Reading Univ, Royal Agricultural Coll, Scottish Agricultural Coll, Wye Coll.
See also: Agriculture; botany.
Study area: Agriculture, horticulture and forestry.

AGRICULTURAL CHEMISTRY
See: Chemistry; agriculture.

AGRICULTURAL ECONOMICS
Possible prospectuses: Aberdeen Univ, Aberystwyth, Bangor, Belfast Univ,
Edinburgh Univ, Exeter Univ, Glasgow Univ, Harper Adams, Manchester
Univ, Newcastle Univ, Nottingham Univ, Reading Univ, Royal Agricultural
Coll, Scottish Agricultural Coll, Silsoe Coll, Wye Coll.
See also: Economics; agriculture.
Study areas: Agriculture, horticulture and forestry; economics.

AGRICULTURAL ENGINEERING
Possible prospectuses: Anglia Poly Univ, De Montfort Univ, Harper Adams,
Newcastle Univ, Silsoe Coll, Writtle.

AGRICULTURE
Possible prospectuses: Aberdeen Univ, Aberystwyth, Anglia Poly Univ, Bangor,
Belfast Univ, Edinburgh Univ, Glasgow Univ, Harper Adams, Newcastle Univ,
Nottingham Univ, Plymouth Univ, Reading Univ, Royal Agricultural Coll,
Scottish Agricultural Coll, Sheffield Hallam Univ, Silsoe Coll, Welsh
Agricultural Coll, Writtle, Wye Coll.
Study area: Agriculture, horticulture and forestry.

AGRONOMY
See: Agriculture.

AIRCRAFT ENGINEERING
See: Aeronautical engineering; air transport engineering.

AIR FORCE
Possible prospectuses: Cranwell.

AIR TRANSPORT ENGINEERING
Possible prospectuses: City Univ, Cranfield (p/g only), Cranwell, Loughborough
Univ, Queen Mary & Westfield.

AKKADIAN
Possible prospectuses: Cambridge Univ, Liverpool Univ, Manchester Univ,
SOAS, University Coll London.
See also: Near East studies.
Study area: Near East and Islamic studies.

AMERICAN STUDIES
Possible prospectuses: Aberystwyth, Belfast Univ, Birmingham Univ,
Canterbury Christ Church Coll, Central Lancashire Univ, Crewe & Alsager,
Derby Univ, Dundee Univ, East Anglia Univ, Essex Univ, Exeter Univ, Hull
Univ, Keele Univ, Kent Univ, King Alfred's Coll, Lancaster Univ, Leeds Univ,
Leicester Univ, Liverpool Inst, Liverpool Univ, Manchester Univ, Middlesex
Univ, Nene Coll, Nottingham Univ, Reading Univ, Ripon & York St John,
Sheffield Univ, Staffordshire Univ, Sunderland Univ, Sussex Univ, Swansea,
Thames Valley Univ, Ulster Univ, Warwick Univ, West London Inst,
Wolverhampton Univ.
Study area: American studies.

AMHARIC
See: Asian studies.

ANALOGUES
See: Computing; electrical engineering; electronic engineering.

ANALYTICAL
See: individual subjects, eg chemistry.

ANATOLIA
See: Archaeology.

ANATOMY
Possible prospectuses: Aberdeen Univ, Belfast Univ, Birmingham Univ, Bristol
Univ, Cambridge Univ, Cardiff, Dundee Univ, Edinburgh Univ, Glasgow Univ,
King's Coll London, Leeds Univ, Manchester Univ, Newcastle Univ, Queen
Mary & Westfield, Sheffield Univ, University Coll London.
See also: Medicine; human biology.
Study area: Anatomy.

ANCIENT HISTORY
Possible prospectuses: Belfast Univ, Birkbeck, Birmingham Univ, Bristol Univ,
Cambridge Univ, Cardiff, Edinburgh Univ, Exeter Univ, Keele Univ, Kent
Univ, King's Coll London, Lampeter, Leicester Univ, Liverpool Univ,
Manchester Univ, Newcastle Univ, Nottingham Univ, Oxford Univ, Reading
Univ, Royal Holloway & Bedford, St Andrews Univ, Swansea, University Coll
London, Warwick Univ.
See also: Classics; history.
Study areas: History; classics.

ANGLO SAXON
Possible prospectuses: Cambridge Univ.

ANIMALS
See: Agriculture; animal science; veterinary studies; zoology.

ANIMAL SCIENCE
Possible prospectuses: Aberdeen Univ, Aberystwyth, Bangor, East Anglia Univ, East London Univ, Edinburgh Univ, Glasgow Univ, Harper Adams, Imperial Coll, Leeds Univ, Leicester Univ, Newcastle Univ, Nottingham Univ, Reading Univ, Royal Agricultural Coll, Royal Vet Coll, Scottish Agricultural Coll, Welsh Agricultural Coll, Wolverhampton Univ, Writtle, Wye Coll.
Study area: Zoology.

ANIMATION
Possible prospectuses: Edinburgh Coll Art, Humberside Univ, National Film Sch (p/g only), Royal Coll Art (p/g only), West Surrey Coll.
See also: Film studies.

ANTHROPOLOGY
Possible prospectuses: Brunel Univ, Cambridge Univ, Durham Univ, East Anglia Univ, Edinburgh Univ, Goldsmiths' Coll, Hull Univ, Keele Univ, Kent Univ, LSE, Manchester Univ, Oxford Brookes Univ, Oxford Univ, St Andrews Univ, SOAS, Sussex Univ, Swansea, University Coll London.
See also: Social anthropology.
Study area: Anthropology.

APPLIED
See: individual subjects, eg biology.

AQUACULTURE
Possible prospectuses: Aberdeen Univ, Glasgow Univ, Scottish Agricultural Coll, Stirling Univ.

ARABIC
Possible prospectuses: Aberdeen Univ, Cambridge Univ, Durham Univ, Edinburgh Univ, Exeter Univ, Glasgow Univ, Leeds Univ, Manchester Univ, Oxford Univ, St Andrews Univ, Salford Univ, SOAS, Westminster Univ.
Study area: Near East and Islamic studies.

ARAMAIC
See: Near East studies.

ARCHAEOLOGY
Possible prospectuses: Bangor, Belfast Univ, Birmingham Univ, Bournemouth Univ, Bradford Univ, Bristol Univ, Cambridge Univ, Cardiff, Durham Univ, East London Univ, Edinburgh Univ, Exeter Univ, Glasgow Univ, Inst Archaeology, King Alfred's Coll, King's Coll London, Lampeter, Leicester Univ, Liverpool Univ, Manchester Univ, Newcastle Univ, Nottingham Univ, Oxford Univ, Reading Univ, Sheffield Univ, SOAS, Southampton Univ, University Coll London, Warwick Univ, York Univ.
See also: Anthropology.
Study area: Archaeology.

ARCHITECTURE
Possible prospectuses: Architectural Association, Bath Univ, Belfast Univ, Brighton Univ, Cambridge Univ, Cardiff, Central England Univ, De Montfort Univ, Duncan of Jordanstone, Dundee Univ, East London Univ, Edinburgh Coll Art, Edinburgh Univ, Glasgow Sch Art, Glasgow Univ, Greenwich Univ, Heriot-Watt Univ, Huddersfield Univ, Humberside Univ, Kent Inst, Kingston Univ, Leeds Metropolitan Univ, Leeds Univ, Liverpool John Moores Univ, Liverpool Univ, Manchester Metropolitan Univ, Manchester Univ, Newcastle Univ, North London Univ, Nottingham Univ, Oxford Brookes Univ, Plymouth Univ, Portsmouth Univ, Prince of Wales's Inst, Robert Gordon Univ, Royal Coll Art (p/g only), Sheffield Univ, South Bank Univ, Strathclyde Univ, Teesside Univ, University Coll London, Westminster Univ.
Study area: Architecture.

ARMY
Possible prospectuses: Sandhurst.

ART
Possible prospectuses: Aberystwyth, Anglia Poly Univ, Bangor Normal Coll, Bretton Hall, Bristol UWE, Camberwell Coll, Canterbury Christ Church Coll, Cardiff Inst, Central Lancashire Univ, Central Saint, Cheltenham & Gloucester Coll, Chester Coll, Colchester Inst, Coventry Univ, Derby Univ, Duncan of Jordanstone, East London Univ, Edinburgh Coll Art, Falmouth, Glamorgan Univ, Goldsmiths' Coll, Heriot-Watt Univ, Homerton, Humberside Univ, Kent Inst, Leeds Metropolitan Univ, Liverpool Inst, London Guildhall Univ, Manchester Metropolitan Univ, Middlesex Univ, Nene Coll, North East Wales Inst, Nottingham Trent Univ, Plymouth Univ, Portsmouth Univ, Reading Univ, Ripon & York St John, Robert Gordon Univ, Roehampton Inst, Royal Academy Sch (p/g only), St Mark & St John, S Martin's Coll, Salford Coll, Sheffield Hallam Univ, Slade, Staffordshire Univ, Sunderland Univ, Swansea Inst, Ulster Univ, West London Inst, West Sussex Inst, Wimbledon Sch Art, Winchester Sch Art, Wolverhampton Univ, Worcester Coll.
See also: Graphic design; photography; silversmithing; textiles; three-dimensional design.
Study area: Art and design.

ART HISTORY
See: Fine arts.

ARTIFICIAL INTELLIGENCE
Possible prospectuses: Aberdeen Univ, Cranfield (p/g only), Edinburgh Univ, Essex Univ, Hertfordshire Univ, Middlesex Univ, Sussex Univ.
Study area: Computing.

ASIAN STUDIES
Possible prospectuses: Cambridge Univ, De Montfort Univ, Edinburgh Univ, Hull Univ, Manchester Univ, Newcastle Univ, North London Univ, Oxford Univ, SOAS, Sussex Univ, Ulster Univ.
See also: Near East studies; South East Asian studies.
Study area: Asian studies.

ASSYRIOLOGY
See: Archaeology; Near East studies.

ASTRONAUTICS
See: Aerodynamics; space.

ASTRONOMY
Possible prospectuses: Cambridge Univ, Cardiff, Central Lancashire Univ, Glasgow Univ, Hertfordshire Univ, Keele Univ, Leicester Univ, Manchester Univ, Newcastle Univ, Plymouth Univ, Queen Mary & Westfield, St Andrews Univ, Sheffield Univ, Southampton Univ, University Coll London.
Study area: Physics.

ASTROPHYSICS
Possible prospectuses: Aberystwyth, Belfast Univ, Birmingham Univ, Bristol Univ, Cambridge Univ, Cardiff, Central Lancashire Univ, Cranfield (p/g only), Edinburgh Univ, Glasgow Univ, Hertfordshire Univ, Imperial Coll, Kent Univ, King's Coll London, Leeds Univ, Leicester Univ, Liverpool John Moores Univ, Manchester Univ, Newcastle Univ, Queen Mary & Westfield, Royal Holloway & Bedford, St Andrews Univ, Southampton Univ, Sussex Univ, UMIST, University Coll London.
Study area: Physics.

AUDIO-VISUAL COMMUNICATION
See: Communication studies; electronic engineering; art.

AUTOMOTIVE ENGINEERING
Possible prospectuses: Birmingham Univ, Brunel Univ, Coventry Univ, Cranfield (p/g only), Hertfordshire Univ, King's Coll Hospital, Loughborough Univ, Royal Coll Art (p/g only), Sheffield Hallam Univ, Sunderland Univ.
Study area: Mechanical and production engineering.

AVIONICS
Possible prospectuses: Cranfield (p/g only), Cranwell, Glasgow Univ, Hertfordshire Univ, Humberside Univ, Queen Mary & Westfield, Salford Univ, York Univ.
See also: Aeronautical engineering.

B

BACTERIOLOGY
Possible prospectuses: Birmingham Univ, Brunel Univ, Edinburgh Univ, Glasgow Poly, Glasgow Univ, Manchester Univ, Reading Univ.
Study area: Microbiology.

BANKING
Possible prospectuses: Bangor, Birmingham Univ, Buckingham Univ, Cardiff, Central England Univ, City Univ, Humberside Univ, Liverpool John Moores Univ, London Guildhall Univ, Loughborough Univ, Middlesex Univ, Napier Univ, Stirling Univ, Teesside Univ, Trinity & All Saints, Ulster Univ.
See also: Business studies; economics.
Study area: Business studies.

BANTU LANGUAGE
Possible prospectuses: SOAS.
Study area: African studies.

BEHAVIOURAL SCIENCE
Possible prospectuses: Brunel Univ, Glamorgan Univ, Huddersfield Univ, Manchester Metropolitan Univ, Manchester Univ, Nottingham Univ, Portsmouth Univ, Reading Univ, Teesside Univ, Ulster Univ, Westminster Univ.
See also: Psychology; zoology.
Study area: Psychology; zoology.

BENGALI
Possible prospectuses: SOAS.
See also: Asian studies.
Study area: Asian studies.

BERBER
See: African studies.

BIBLICAL STUDIES
Possible prospectuses: Aberdeen Univ, Bangor, Belfast Univ, Birmingham Univ, Cambridge Univ, Edinburgh Univ, Glasgow Univ, Heythrop Coll, Jews' Coll, King's Coll London, London Bible, Manchester Univ, National Extension Coll, Oak Hill Coll, St Andrews Univ, Sheffield Univ, Spurgeon's Coll, Stirling Univ.
See also: Religious studies; theology.
Study area: Religious studies and theology.

BIOCHEMICAL ENGINEERING
Possible prospectuses: Birmingham Univ, Bradford Univ, Cranfield (p/g only), Heriot-Watt Univ, Imperial Coll, Luton Coll, Surrey Univ, Swansea, Teesside Univ, UMIST, University Coll London.
See also: Biochemistry; biotechnology; chemical engineering.
Study area: Biochemistry; biotechnology; chemical engineering.

BIOCHEMISTRY

Possible prospectuses: Aberdeen Univ, Aberystwyth, Anglia Poly Univ, Bangor, Bath Univ, Belfast Univ, Birmingham Univ, Bradford Univ, Bristol Univ, Bristol UWE, Brunel Univ, Buckingham Univ, Cambridge Univ, Cardiff, Central Lancashire Univ, Coventry Univ, Dundee Univ, Durham Univ, East Anglia Univ, East London Univ, Edinburgh Univ, Essex Univ, Glamorgan Univ, Glasgow Poly, Glasgow Univ, Greenwich Univ, Heriot-Watt Univ, Hertfordshire Univ, Huddersfield Univ, Imperial Coll, Keele Univ, Kent Univ, King's Coll Hospital, King's Coll London, Lancaster Univ, Leeds Univ, Leicester Univ, Liverpool John Moores Univ, Liverpool Univ, Luton Coll, Manchester Metropolitan Univ, Manchester Univ, Newcastle Univ, North London Univ, Nottingham Trent Univ, Nottingham Univ, Open Univ, Oxford Univ, Paisley Univ, Portsmouth Univ, Queen Mary & Westfield, Reading Univ, Royal Holloway & Bedford, St Andrews Univ, Salford Univ, Sheffield Univ, Southampton Univ, Stirling Univ, Strathclyde Univ, Sunderland Univ, Surrey Univ, Sussex Univ, Swansea, Teesside Univ, Ulster Univ, UMIST, University Coll London, Warwick Univ, Wolverhampton Univ, Wye Coll, York Univ.
Study area: Biochemistry.

BIOLOGICAL CHEMISTRY

Possible prospectuses: Aberystwyth, Anglia Poly Univ, Central Lancashire Univ, Dundee Univ, Essex Univ, Glasgow Poly, Heriot-Watt Univ, Hertfordshire Univ, Hull Univ, Imperial Coll, Kent Univ, King's Coll London, Leicester Univ, Manchester Univ, North London Univ, Nottingham Univ, Queen Mary & Westfield, Salford Univ, Stirling Univ, Warwick Univ.
See also: Biotechnology.
Study area: Biochemistry.

BIOLOGY

Possible prospectuses: Aberdeen Univ, Aberystwyth, Anglia Poly Univ, Aston Univ, Bangor, Bath Univ, Belfast Univ, Birkbeck, Birmingham Univ, Bolton Inst, Brighton Univ, Bristol Univ, Bristol UWE, Brunel Univ, Buckingham Univ, Cambridge Univ, Canterbury Christ Church Coll, Cardiff, Cardiff Inst, Central Lancashire Univ, Chester Coll, Coventry Univ, Crewe & Alsager, De Montfort Univ, Derby Univ, Dundee Inst, Dundee Univ, Durham Univ, East Anglia Univ, East London Univ, Edge Hill, Edinburgh Univ, Essex Univ, Exeter Univ, Glamorgan Univ, Glasgow Poly, Glasgow Univ, Greenwich Univ, Heriot-Watt Univ, Hertfordshire Univ, Homerton, Hull Univ, Imperial Coll, Keele Univ, Kent Univ, King's Coll Hospital, King's Coll London, Lancaster Univ, Leeds Univ, Leicester Univ, Liverpool John Moores Univ, Liverpool Univ, LSU Southampton, Luton Coll, Manchester Metropolitan Univ, Manchester Univ, Napier Univ, Nene Coll, Newcastle Univ, North London Univ, Nottingham Trent Univ, Nottingham Univ, Open Univ, Oxford Brookes Univ, Oxford Univ, Paisley Univ, Plymouth Univ, Portsmouth Univ, Queen Mary & Westfield, Reading Univ, Ripon & York St John, Roehampton Inst, Royal Agricultural Coll, Royal Holloway & Bedford, St Andrews Univ, S Martin's Coll, St Mary's Coll, Salford Univ, Sheffield Univ, South Bank Univ, Southampton Univ, Staffordshire Univ, Stirling Univ, Strathclyde Univ, Sunderland Univ, Sussex Univ, Swansea, Ulster Univ, University Coll London, Warwick Univ, Wolverhampton Univ, Worcester Coll, Wye Coll, York Univ.
See also: eg Botany; zoology.
Study area: Biology.

BIOMEDICAL ELECTRONICS
Possible prospectuses: Brunel Univ, Central Lancashire Univ, Hertfordshire Univ, Kent Univ, Salford Coll, Salford Univ.
Study area: Electrical and electronic engineering.

BIOMEDICAL SCIENCE
Possible prospectuses: Aberdeen Univ, Anglia Poly Univ, Belfast Univ, Bradford Univ, Bristol UWE, Brunel Univ, Cardiff Inst, De Montfort Univ, Hull Univ, King's Coll Hospital, King's Coll London, Leicester Univ, Liverpool John Moores Univ, Portsmouth Univ, Salford Univ, Sheffield Hallam Univ, Sheffield Univ, Sunderland Univ, Swansea, UMIST, Westminster Univ, Wolverhampton Univ.

BIOPHYSICS
Possible prospectuses: Aberdeen Univ, Cambridge Univ, East Anglia Univ, East London Univ, Imperial Coll, King's Coll London, Leeds Univ, Liverpool John Moores Univ, Luton Coll, Portsmouth Univ.
Study area: Biology.

BIOSOCIAL SCIENCE
Possible prospectuses: Sussex Univ, University Coll London.
See also: Human sciences.
Study areas: Biology; sociology.

BIOTECHNOLOGY
Possible prospectuses: Aberdeen Univ, Anglia Poly Univ, Birmingham Univ, Bristol Univ, Bristol UWE, Cardiff, Central Lancashire Univ, Cranfield (p/g only), De Montfort Univ, Dundee Inst, Dundee Univ, East London Univ, Glamorgan Poly, Glasgow Poly, Heriot-Watt Univ, Hertfordshire Univ, Huddersfield Univ, Hull Univ, Imperial Coll, Kent Univ, King's Coll London, Leeds Univ, Leicester Univ, Liverpool John Moores Univ, Liverpool Univ, Luton Coll, Nottingham Univ, Plymouth Univ, Queen Mary & Westfield, Reading Univ, St Andrews Univ, Scottish Agricultural Coll, Sheffield Hallam Univ, Sheffield Univ, South Bank Univ, Strathclyde Univ, Sunderland Univ, Surrey Univ, Sussex Univ, Swansea, Teesside Univ, UMIST, University Coll London, Westminster Univ, Wolverhampton Univ, Wye Coll.
See also: Biochemical engineering; biochemistry.
Study area: Biotechnology.

BOTANY
Possible prospectuses: Aberdeen Univ, Aberystwyth, Bangor, Belfast Univ, Birkbeck, Birmingham Univ, Bristol Univ, Cambridge Univ, Cardiff, Dundee Univ, Durham Univ, East Anglia Univ, East London Univ, Edinburgh Univ, Exeter Univ, Glasgow Univ, Imperial Coll, King's Coll London, Leeds Univ,

Leicester Univ, Liverpool Univ, Manchester Univ, Newcastle Univ,
Nottingham Univ, Oxford Univ, Reading Univ, Royal Holloway & Bedford, St
Andrews Univ, Sheffield Univ, Southampton Univ, Stirling Univ, Swansea,
University Coll London, Wye Coll.
*See also: **Agriculture; biology; horticulture.***
Study area: Botany.

BREWING
Possible prospectuses: Heriot-Watt Univ.
*See also: **Microbiology.***
Study area: Microbiology.

BUILDING AND CONSTRUCTION
Possible prospectuses: Bath Univ, Bolton Inst, Brighton Univ, Bristol UWE,
Central Lancashire Univ, Coventry Univ, Cranfield (p/g only), Dundee Inst,
Glamorgan Univ, Glasgow Coll Building, Glasgow Poly, Heriot-Watt Univ,
Leeds Metropolitan Univ, Liverpool John Moores Univ, Loughborough Univ,
Luton Coll, Middlesex Univ, Napier Univ, Nene Coll, Northumbria Univ,
Nottingham Trent Univ, Oxford Brookes Univ, Paisley Univ, Reading Univ,
Robert Gordon Univ, Salford Univ, Sheffield Hallam Univ, South Bank Univ,
Southampton Inst, Teesside Univ, Ulster Univ, UMIST, Westminster Univ,
Wolverhampton Univ.
*See also: **Architecture; building surveying; building technology; civil
engineering.***

BUILDING STUDIES
Possible prospectuses: Anglia Poly Univ, Bolton Inst, Brunel Univ,
Buckinghamshire Coll, Central Lancashire Univ, Coventry Univ, Dundee Univ,
Glamorgan Univ, Glasgow Coll Building, Glasgow Poly, Greenwich Univ,
Heriot-Watt Univ, Liverpool John Moores Univ, Luton Coll, Napier Univ,
Northumbria Univ, Nottingham Trent Univ, Reading Univ, Robert Gordon
Univ, Royal Agricultural Coll, Sheffield Hallam Univ, South Bank Univ,
Southampton Inst, Teesside Univ, Ulster Univ, UMIST, University Coll
London, Westminster Univ, Wolverhampton Univ.
*See also: **Architecture; building surveying; building technology; civil
engineering.***

BUILDING SURVEYING
Possible prospectuses: Brighton Univ, Bristol UWE, Central England Univ,
Central Lancashire Univ, De Montfort Univ, Glamorgan Univ, Glasgow Coll
Building, Glasgow Poly, Greenwich Univ, Heriot-Watt Univ, Leeds
Metropolitan Univ, Liverpool John Moores Univ, Loughborough Univ, Luton

Coll, Napier Univ, Northumbria Univ, Nottingham Trent Univ, Reading Univ, Robert Gordon Univ, Royal Agricultural Coll, Salford Univ, Sheffield Hallam Univ, South Bank Univ, Westminster Univ, Wolverhampton Univ.
See also: Quantity surveying.

BUILDING TECHNOLOGY
Possible prospectuses: Bristol UWE, Central Lancashire Univ, Coventry Univ, Cranfield (p/g only), Glamorgan Univ, Glasgow Coll Building, Glasgow Poly, Heriot-Watt Univ, Liverpool Univ, Loughborough Univ, Luton Coll, Napier Univ, Nottingham Trent Univ, Reading Univ, Robert Gordon Univ, South Bank Univ, Strathclyde Univ, Ulster Univ, UMIST, Wolverhampton Univ.

BULGARIAN
Possible prospectuses: SSEES.
Study area: Modern languages.

BURMESE STUDIES
Possible prospectuses: SOAS.
See also: Asian studies.
Study area: Asian studies.

BUSINESS
See: Accountancy; business administration; business studies; economics; law; mathematics.

BUSINESS ADMINISTRATION
Possible prospectuses: Aberystwyth, Anglia Poly Univ, Aston Univ, Bath Univ, Belfast Univ, Birmingham Univ, Bolton Inst, Bradford & Ilkley, Bradford Univ, Brighton Univ, Bristol UWE, Brunel Univ, Buckinghamshire Coll, Cardiff, Cardiff Inst, Central Lancashire Univ, Coventry Univ, De Montfort Univ, Derby Univ, Dundee Inst, East London Univ, European Bus Sch, Farnborough Coll, Glamorgan Univ, Glasgow Poly, Greenwich Univ, Harper Adams, Heriot-Watt Univ, Hertfordshire Univ, Huddersfield Univ, Humberside Univ, Keele Univ, Kingston Univ, Leeds Metropolitan Univ, Liverpool John Moores Univ, London Business Sch (p/g only), Loughborough Univ, Luton Coll, Manchester Business Sch (p/g only), Manchester Metropolitan Univ, Middlesex Univ, Napier Univ, Nene Coll, Newcastle Univ, North Cheshire Coll, North East Wales Inst, Northumbria Univ, Nottingham Trent Univ, Oxford Brookes Univ, Portsmouth Univ, Reading Univ, Robert Gordon Univ, Royal Agricultural Coll, Salford Coll, Salford Univ, Scottish Coll Textiles, Sheffield Hallam Univ, Southampton Inst, Staffordshire Univ, Stirling Univ, Strathclyde Univ, Sunderland Univ, Swansea Inst, Teesside Univ, Thames Valley Univ, Trinity & All Saints, Wolverhampton Univ.
Study area: Business studies.

BUSINESS ECONOMICS
Possible prospectuses: Aberystwyth, Anglia Poly Univ, Birmingham Univ, Bradford Univ, Brunel Univ, Buckingham Univ, Cardiff, Central Lancashire Univ, Coventry Univ, Dundee Inst, Durham Univ, East London Univ, European Bus Sch, Exeter Univ, Glasgow Poly, Heriot-Watt Univ, Hertfordshire Univ, Hull Univ, Leicester Univ, Liverpool Univ, London Guildhall Univ, Luton Coll, Manchester Univ, Middlesex Univ, North London Univ, Nottingham Trent Univ, Paisley Univ, Queen Mary & Westfield, Reading Univ, Robert Gordon Univ, Salford Univ, Scottish Coll Textiles,

Southampton Univ, Staffordshire Univ, Stirling Univ, Sunderland Univ, Surrey Univ, Swansea Inst, Teesside Univ, Thames Valley Univ, Westminster Univ, Wolverhampton Univ.
Study areas: Business studies; economics.

BUSINESS STUDIES
Possible prospectuses: Aberystwyth, Anglia Poly Univ, Aston Univ, Bedford Coll, Birmingham Univ, Bolton Inst, Bournemouth Univ, Bradford & Ilkley, Bradford Univ, Brighton Univ, Bristol UWE, Brunel Univ, Buckingham Univ, Buckinghamshire Coll, Canterbury Christ Church Coll, Cardiff, Cardiff Inst, Central England Univ, Central Lancashire Univ, Cheltenham & Gloucester Coll, City Univ, Coventry Univ, De Montfort Univ, Derby Univ, Dundee Inst, East Anglia Univ, East London Univ, Edinburgh Univ, European Bus Sch, Exeter Univ, French Inst, Glamorgan Univ, Glasgow Poly, Greenwich Univ, Heriot-Watt Univ, Hertfordshire Univ, Holborn Coll, Huddersfield Univ, Hull Univ, Humberside Univ, Kent Univ, King's Coll London, Kingston Univ, Leeds Metropolitan Univ, Leeds Univ, Liverpool John Moores Univ, London Coll Printing, London Guildhall Univ, Loughborough Univ, Luton Coll, Manchester Business Sch (p/g only), Manchester Metropolitan Univ, Middlesex Univ, Napier Univ, Nene Coll, North East Wales Inst, North London Univ, Northumbria Univ, Nottingham Trent Univ, Oxford Brookes Univ, Plymouth Univ, Portsmouth Univ, Queen Mary & Westfield, Reading Univ, Robert Gordon Univ, Roehampton Inst, Royal Agricultural Coll, Salford Coll, Salford Univ, Scottish Coll Textiles, Sheffield Hallam Univ, Sheffield Univ, South Bank Univ, Southampton Inst, Staffordshire Univ, Stirling Univ, Strathclyde Univ, Sunderland Univ, Sussex Univ, Swansea, Swansea Inst, Teesside Univ, Thames Valley Univ, Trinity & All Saints, Ulster Univ, UMIST, University Coll London, Warwick Univ, West London Inst, Westminster Univ, Wolverhampton Univ, Wye Coll.
Study area: Business studies.

BYZANTINE STUDIES
See: Classics; history.

C

CANADIAN STUDIES
See: American studies.

CARBON DATING
See: Archaeology.

CARIBBEAN STUDIES
Possible prospectuses: Kent Univ, North London Univ, Warwick Univ.

CARING
See: Education; medicine; nursing; social administration.

CARPET DESIGN
Possible prospectuses: Heriot-Watt Univ, Wolverhampton Univ.
See also: Textiles.
Study area: Art and design.

CATALAN
Possible prospectuses: Cambridge Univ, Cardiff, Liverpool Univ, Queen Mary & Westfield, Sheffield Univ.
See also: Spanish.
Study area: Modern languages.

CATERING
Possible prospectuses: Bournemouth Univ, Central England Univ, Central Lancashire Univ, Cheltenham & Gloucester Coll, Colchester Inst, Glasgow Poly, Huddersfield Univ, Manchester Metropolitan Univ, Middlesex Univ, Napier Univ, North London Univ, Oxford Brookes Univ, Queen Margaret Coll, Robert Gordon Univ, Salford Coll, Sheffield Hallam Univ, South Bank Univ, Surrey Univ, Thames Valley Univ, Ulster Univ, Wolverhampton Univ.
See also: Dietetics; hotel and catering management.
Study area: Hotel and catering management.

CELL BIOLOGY
Possible prospectuses: Aberdeen Univ, Aberystwyth, Anglia Poly Univ, Birmingham Univ, Bradford Univ, Brunel Univ, Cambridge Univ, East Anglia Univ, Essex Univ, Glasgow Poly, Glasgow Univ, Hertfordshire Univ, Imperial Coll, Keele Univ, Kent Univ, King's Coll London, Kingston Univ, Leicester Univ, Liverpool Univ, Manchester Univ, Oxford Brookes Univ, Plymouth Univ, St Andrews Univ, Sheffield Univ, Stirling Univ, Surrey Univ, University Coll London, Wolverhampton Univ, York Univ.
See also: Microbiology.
Study areas: Biology; microbiology.

CELLULAR PATHOLOGY
Possible prospectuses: Bradford Univ, Bristol Univ, Bristol UWE, Glasgow Poly, Reading Univ, St Andrews Univ.
See also: Pathology.
Study areas: Microbiology; dentistry; medicine.

CELTIC STUDIES
Possible prospectuses: Aberdeen Univ, Aberystwyth, Belfast Univ, Cambridge Univ, Edinburgh Univ, Glasgow Univ, Manchester Univ.
See also: Irish studies; Scottish studies; Welsh studies.

CENTRAL EUROPEAN STUDIES
See: European studies.

CERAMIC SCIENCE
See: Chemistry.

CERAMICS
Possible prospectuses: Bath Coll, Bretton Hall, Brighton Univ, Bristol UWE, Buckinghamshire Coll, Camberwell Coll, Canterbury Christ Church Coll, Cardiff Inst, Central England Univ, Central Saint Martins, Cheltenham & Gloucester Coll, Crewe & Alsager, De Montfort Univ, Duncan of Jordanstone, Dundee Univ, Edinburgh Coll Art, Falmouth, Glasgow Sch Art, Heriot-Watt Univ, Leeds Univ, Liverpool Inst, Loughborough Coll, Manchester Metropolitan Univ, Middlesex Univ, Portsmouth Univ, Robert Gordon Univ, Royal Coll Art (p/g only), Sheffield Univ, Staffordshire Univ, Sunderland Univ, Ulster Univ, West Surrey Coll, Westminster Univ, Wolverhampton Univ.
See also: Three-dimensional design.
Study area: Art and design.

CHEMICAL ENGINEERING
Possible prospectuses: Aston Univ, Bath Univ, Belfast Univ, Birmingham Univ, Bradford Univ, Cambridge Univ, Edinburgh Univ, Exeter Univ, Glamorgan Univ, Heriot-Watt Univ, Hertfordshire Univ, Huddersfield Univ, Imperial Coll, Leeds Univ, Loughborough Univ, Newcastle Univ, Nottingham Univ, Oxford Univ, Paisley Univ, Sheffield Univ, South Bank Univ, Strathclyde Univ, Surrey Univ, Swansea, Teesside Univ, UMIST, University Coll London.
Study area: Chemical engineering.

CHEMICAL PHYSICS
Possible prospectuses: Bristol Univ, East Anglia Univ, Edinburgh Univ, Glasgow Univ, Imperial Coll, Kent Univ, Liverpool Univ, Manchester Univ, Open Univ, Sheffield Univ, Southampton Univ, Sussex Univ, UMIST, University Coll London.
Study areas: Physics; chemistry.

CHEMISTRY

Possible prospectuses: Aberdeen Univ, Anglia Poly Univ, Aston Univ, Bangor, Bath Univ, Belfast Univ, Birkbeck, Birmingham Univ, Bradford Univ, Brighton Univ, Bristol Univ, Bristol UWE, Brunel Univ, Cambridge Univ, Cardiff, Central Lancashire Univ, Coventry Univ, Crewe & Alsager, De Montfort Univ, Derby Univ, Dundee Inst, Dundee Univ, Durham Univ, East Anglia Univ, Edinburgh Univ, Essex Univ, Exeter Univ, Glamorgan Univ, Glasgow Poly, Glasgow Univ, Greenwich Univ, Heriot-Watt Univ, Hertfordshire Univ, Huddersfield Univ, Hull Univ, Imperial Coll, Keele Univ, Kent Univ, King's Coll London, Kingston Univ, Lancaster Univ, Leeds Metropolitan Univ, Leeds Univ, Leicester Univ, Liverpool John Moores Univ, Liverpool Univ, Loughborough Univ, Manchester Metropolitan Univ, Manchester Univ, Napier Univ, Newcastle Univ, North East Wales Inst, North London Univ, Northumbria Univ, Nottingham Trent Univ, Nottingham Univ, Open Univ, Oxford Brookes Univ, Oxford Univ, Paisley Univ, Plymouth Univ, Portsmouth Univ, Queen Mary & Westfield, Reading Univ, Robert Gordon Univ, St Andrews Univ, St Mary's Coll, Salford Coll, Salford Univ, Scottish Coll Textiles, Sheffield Hallam Univ, Sheffield Univ, South Bank Univ, Southampton Univ, Staffordshire Univ, Stirling Univ, Strathclyde Univ, Sunderland Univ, Surrey Univ, Sussex Univ, Swansea, Teesside Univ, UMIST, University Coll London, Warwick Univ, Wolverhampton Univ, York Univ. *Study area:* Chemistry.

CHINESE

Possible prospectuses: Cambridge Univ, Durham Univ, Edinburgh Univ, Leeds Univ, Newcastle Univ, Oxford Univ, SOAS, Westminster Univ, York Univ. *See also: Asian studies.*

CHIROPODY

Possible prospectuses: Belfast Univ, Brighton Univ, Cardiff Inst, Central England Univ, Derby Univ, Glasgow Poly, Huddersfield Univ, LSU Southampton, Nene Coll, Plymouth Univ, Queen Margaret Coll, Salford Coll, University Coll London, Westminster Univ. *Study area:* Professions allied to medicine (PAMs).

CHOREOGRAPHY

Possible prospectuses: West Sussex Inst. *Study area:* Dance.

CHURCH HISTORY

Possible prospectuses: Aberdeen Univ, Cambridge Univ, Edinburgh Univ, Glasgow Univ, Lampeter, London Bible, Manchester Univ, Oak Hill Coll, St Andrews Univ, Spurgeon's Coll. *Study area:* History.

CIVIL ENGINEERING

Possible prospectuses: Aberdeen Univ, Aston Univ, Belfast Univ, Birmingham Univ, Bolton Inst, Bradford Univ, Brighton Univ, Bristol Univ, Bristol UWE, Cambridge Univ, Cardiff, City Univ, Coventry Univ, Cranfield (p/g only), Dundee Inst, Dundee Univ, Durham Univ, East London Univ, Edinburgh Univ, Exeter Univ, Glamorgan Univ, Glasgow Poly, Glasgow Univ, Greenwich Univ, Heriot-Watt Univ, Hertfordshire Univ, Imperial Coll, Kingston Univ, Leeds Univ, Liverpool John Moores Univ, Liverpool Univ, Loughborough Univ, Manchester Univ, Middlesex Univ, Napier Univ, Nene Coll, Newcastle

Univ, North East Wales Inst, Nottingham Trent Univ, Nottingham Univ,
Oxford Brookes Univ, Oxford Univ, Paisley Univ, Plymouth Univ, Portsmouth
Univ, Queen Mary & Westfield, Salford Univ, Sheffield Hallam Univ, Sheffield
Univ, Shrivenham, South Bank Univ, Southampton Univ, Strathclyde Univ,
Sunderland Univ, Surrey Univ, Swansea, Teesside Univ, Ulster Univ, UMIST,
University Coll London, Warwick Univ, Westminster Univ, Wolverhampton
Univ.
See also: Engineering.
Study area: Civil engineering.

CLASSICAL STUDIES
Possible prospectuses: Aberystwyth, Birkbeck, Birmingham Univ, Bristol Univ,
Durham Univ, Edinburgh Univ, Exeter Univ, Glasgow Univ, Keele Univ, Kent
Univ, King's Coll London, Lampeter, Liverpool Univ, Manchester Univ,
Newcastle Univ, North London Univ, Nottingham Univ, Open Univ, Reading
Univ, Royal Holloway & Bedford, St Andrews Univ, St Mary's Coll, Swansea,
Warwick Univ.
See also: individual subjects, eg **Arabic.**

CLASSICS
Possible prospectuses: Belfast Univ, Birkbeck, Birmingham Univ, Bristol Univ,
Cambridge Univ, Durham Univ, Edinburgh Univ, Exeter Univ, Glasgow Univ,
Kent Univ, King's Coll London, Lampeter, Leeds Univ, Liverpool Univ,
Manchester Univ, Newcastle Univ, North London Univ, Nottingham Univ,
Oxford Univ, Reading Univ, Royal Holloway & Bedford, St Andrews Univ,
Swansea, University Coll London, Warwick Univ.
Study area: Classics.

CLIMATE
See: Geography; meteorology.

CLOTHING
See: Fashions; textiles.

COASTAL ENGINEERING
See: Civil engineering.

COGNITIVE SCIENCE
Possible prospectuses: Bangor, Dundee Univ, Exeter Univ, Hertfordshire Univ,
Oxford Brookes Univ, Portsmouth Univ, Sheffield Univ, Sussex Univ,
Westminster Univ.
See also: Psychology.
Study area: Psychology.

COMMERCE
Possible prospectuses: Birmingham Univ, Dundee Inst, Edinburgh Univ,
Glasgow Poly, Heriot-Watt Univ, Manchester Metropolitan Univ, Napier Univ,
Robert Gordon Univ, Scottish Coll Textiles, Thames Valley Univ.
See also: Business studies.
Study area: Business studies.

COMMUNICATION ENGINEERING
Possible prospectuses: Bath Univ, Birmingham Univ, Bradford Univ, Cardiff
Inst, Coventry Univ, Cranwell, Essex Univ, Glamorgan Univ, Greenwich Univ,
Heriot-Watt Univ, Huddersfield Univ, Hull Univ, Humberside Univ, Imperial
Coll, Kent Univ, Leeds Metropolitan Univ, Liverpool John Moores Univ,

Manchester Univ, Napier Univ, Nene Coll, North London Univ, Northumbria Univ, Plymouth Univ, Portsmouth Univ, Ravensbourne Coll, Robert Gordon Univ, Salford Univ, Sheffield Univ, Shrivenham, Southampton Univ, Staffordshire Univ, Strathclyde Univ, Sunderland Univ, UMIST.
Study area: Electrical and electronic engineering.

COMMUNICATION STUDIES
Possible prospectuses: Anglia Poly Univ, Bangor Normal Coll, Bournemouth Univ, Bradford Univ, Bristol UWE, Brunel Univ, Cardiff, Cardiff Inst, Central Sch Speech/Drama, Coventry Univ, Edge Hill, Glamorgan Univ, Glasgow Poly, Glasgow Sch Art, Goldsmiths' Coll, Huddersfield Univ, Humberside Univ, Kent Inst, Kent Univ, Lancaster Univ, Leeds Univ, Leicester Univ, Liverpool Univ, London Guildhall Univ, Loughborough Univ, Luton Coll, Middlesex Univ, Napier Univ, North Cheshire Coll, North London Univ, Nottingham Trent Univ, Queen Margaret Coll, Sheffield Hallam Univ, Stirling Univ, Sunderland Univ, Teesside Univ, Thames Valley Univ, Trinity & All Saints, Ulster Univ, Wolverhampton Univ.
See also: Media studies.
Study areas: Communication studies; art and design.

COMMUNITY ARTS
Possible prospectuses: Bretton Hall, Dartington, Heriot-Watt Univ, Strathclyde Univ.
Study area: Art and design.

COMMUNITY STUDIES
See: Public administration; social work; sociology; town planning; urban studies; youth and community work.

COMPARATIVE LITERATURE
Possible prospectuses: Anglia Poly Univ, Bradford Univ, Buckingham Univ, East Anglia Univ, Essex Univ, Kent Univ, Manchester Univ, Middlesex Univ, Warwick Univ.

COMPUTER ENGINEERING
Possible prospectuses: Aston Univ, Bangor, Birmingham Univ, Bolton Inst, Bournemouth Univ, Bradford Univ, Bristol Univ, Brunel Univ, Buckinghamshire Coll, City Univ, Coventry Univ, Cranfield (p/g only), Cranwell, Dartmouth, Derby Univ, Dundee Inst, Glasgow Poly, Greenwich Univ, Heriot-Watt Univ, Huddersfield Univ, Hull Univ, Kent Univ, Leicester Univ, Liverpool John Moores Univ, Loughborough Univ, Luton Coll, Napier Univ, Nottingham Trent Univ, Portsmouth Univ, Queen Mary & Westfield,

Robert Gordon Univ, Sheffield Hallam Univ, Sheffield Univ, South Bank Univ, Staffordshire Univ, Strathclyde Univ, Sunderland Univ, Sussex Univ, Swansea Inst, Teesside Univ, Westminster Univ, York Univ.
See also: Computer technology.
Study areas: Computing; electrical and electronic engineering.

COMPUTER SCIENCE
Possible prospectuses: Aberdeen Univ, Aberystwyth, Anglia Poly Univ, Aston Univ, Belfast Univ, Birmingham Univ, Bradford Univ, Brighton Univ, Bristol Univ, Bristol UWE, Brunel Univ, Buckingham Univ, Cambridge Univ, Cardiff, Central Lancashire Univ, City Univ, Coventry Univ, Cranfield (p/g only), Cranwell, Dartmouth, De Montfort Univ, Derby Univ, Dundee Inst, Dundee Univ, Durham Univ, East Anglia Univ, East London Univ, Edinburgh Univ, Essex Univ, Exeter Univ, Glamorgan Univ, Glasgow Poly, Glasgow Univ, Goldsmiths' Coll, Greenwich Univ, Heriot-Watt Univ, Hertfordshire Univ, Hull Univ, Imperial Coll, Keele Univ, Kent Univ, King's Coll London, Kingston Univ, Lancaster Univ, Leeds Univ, Leicester Univ, Liverpool John Moores Univ, Liverpool Univ, Loughborough Univ, LSE, Luton Coll, Manchester Metropolitan Univ, Manchester Univ, Napier Univ, Nene Coll, Newcastle Univ, North East Wales Inst, North London Univ, Nottingham Trent Univ, Nottingham Univ, Open Univ, Oxford Brookes Univ, Paisley Univ, Portsmouth Univ, Queen Mary & Westfield, Reading Univ, Robert Gordon Univ, Royal Holloway & Bedford, St Andrews Univ, Salford Coll, Salford Univ, Scottish Coll Textiles, Sheffield Hallam Univ, Sheffield Univ, Shrivenham, South Bank Univ, Southampton Inst, Southampton Univ, Staffordshire Univ, Stirling Univ, Strathclyde Univ, Sunderland Univ, Surrey Univ, Sussex Univ, Swansea, Swansea Inst, Teesside Univ, Ulster Univ, UMIST, University Coll London, Warwick Univ, Westminster Univ, Wolverhampton Univ, York Univ.
See also: Computing.
Study area: Computing.

COMPUTER TECHNOLOGY
Possible prospectuses: Aberystwyth, Anglia Poly Univ, Bath Univ, Birmingham Univ, Bradford Univ, Brighton Univ, Bristol Univ, Brunel Univ, Coventry Univ, Cranfield (p/g only), Cranwell, Dartmouth, De Montfort Univ, Derby Univ, Dundee Inst, Essex Univ, Glasgow Poly, Heriot-Watt Univ, Imperial Coll, Kent Univ, Liverpool Univ, Loughborough Univ, Luton Coll, Manchester Metropolitan Univ, Manchester Univ, Napier Univ, Nottingham Trent Univ, Open Univ, Paisley Univ, Portsmouth Univ, Robert Gordon Univ, Salford Univ, Scottish Coll Textiles, Sheffield Hallam Univ, Sheffield Univ, Southampton Inst, Staffordshire Univ, Sunderland Univ, Surrey Univ, Teesside Univ, Thames Valley Univ, Warwick Univ, Westminster Univ, Wolverhampton Univ.
See also: Computer science.
Study area: Computing.

COMPUTING
Possible prospectuses: Aberdeen Univ, Aberystwyth, Anglia Poly Univ, Aston Univ, Bangor, Bath Univ, Birkbeck, Bolton Inst, Bournemouth Univ, Bradford Univ, Brighton Univ, Bristol UWE, Brunel Univ, Buckinghamshire Coll, Cambridge Univ, Cardiff, Cardiff Inst, Central England Univ, Central Lancashire Univ, Cheltenham & Gloucester Coll, Chester Coll, Coventry Univ, Cranwell, Dartmouth, De Montfort Univ, Derby Univ, Dundee Inst, Dundee Univ, East Anglia Univ, East London Univ, Essex Univ, Exeter Univ,

Glamorgan Univ, Glasgow Poly, Greenwich Univ, Heriot-Watt Univ, Hertfordshire Univ, Huddersfield Univ, Humberside Univ, Imperial Coll, Kent Univ, Leeds Metropolitan Univ, Leeds Univ, Leicester Univ, Liverpool John Moores Univ, Liverpool Univ, London Guildhall Univ, Loughborough Univ, Luton Coll, Manchester Metropolitan Univ, Manchester Univ, Middlesex Univ, Napier Univ, Nene Coll, Newcastle Univ, North East Wales Inst, North London Univ, Northumbria Univ, Nottingham Trent Univ, Open Univ, Oxford Brookes Univ, Oxford Univ, Paisley Univ, Plymouth Univ, Queen Mary & Westfield, Reading Univ, Robert Gordon Univ, Royal Coll Art (p/g only), St Andrews Univ, Salford Univ, Scottish Coll Textiles, Sheffield Hallam Univ, South Bank Univ, Southampton Inst, Staffordshire Univ, Stirling Univ, Sunderland Univ, Surrey Univ, Sussex Univ, Teesside Univ, Thames Valley Univ, UMIST, University Coll London, Warwick Univ, West London Inst, Westminster Univ, Wolverhampton Univ, Worcester Coll.
See also: Computer science.
Study area: Computing.

CONFLICT
See: War studies.

CONSERVATION
Possible prospectuses: Birkbeck, Bournemouth Univ, Camberwell Coll, Cardiff, Cheltenham & Gloucester Coll, Edinburgh Coll Art, Hertfordshire Univ, Napier Univ, Royal Agricultural Coll, Royal Coll Art (p/g only), Silsoe Coll, South Bank Univ, Stirling Univ, Sussex Univ, Swansea Inst, Welsh Agricultural Coll, Writtle Coll, Wye Coll.
See also: Archaeology; biology; ecology; environmental studies.

CONSTRUCTION
See: Building and construction.

CONSUMER STUDIES
Possible prospectuses: Glasgow Poly, Leeds Metropolitan Univ, Liverpool John Moores Univ, Manchester Metropolitan Univ, North London Univ, Northumbria Univ, Robert Gordon Univ, Roehampton Inst, Ulster Univ.

CONTROL ENGINEERING
Possible prospectuses: Aberdeen Univ, Birmingham Univ, Bolton Inst, Brunel Univ, City Univ, Coventry Univ, Cranfield (p/g only), Dartmouth, Glasgow Poly, Huddersfield Univ, Hull Univ, Humberside Univ, Imperial Coll, Leicester Univ, Loughborough Univ, Napier Univ, North East Wales Inst, Open Univ, Reading Univ, Robert Gordon Univ, Salford Univ, Sheffield Hallam Univ, Sheffield Univ, South Bank Univ, Staffordshire Univ, Strathclyde Univ, Sunderland Univ, Sussex Univ, Teesside Univ, UMIST, Westminster Univ.
Study areas: Computing; electrical and electronic engineering.

CORROSION
See: Materials science.

COSMETIC TECHNOLOGY
See: Chemistry.

COUNSELLING
See: Social work.

COUNTY PLANNING
See: Town and country planning.

CRIMINOLOGY
Possible prospectuses: Hull Univ, Liverpool John Moores Univ, Middlesex Univ, Sheffield Univ, Teesside Univ.
Study area: Law; sociology.

CROP TECHNOLOGY
Possible prospectuses: Aberystwyth, Bangor, Bath Univ, Edinburgh Univ, Harper Adams, Newcastle Univ, Nottingham Univ, Reading Univ, Royal Agricultural Coll, Scottish Agricultural Coll, Wolverhampton Univ, Writtle, Wye Coll.
Study areas: Agriculture, horticulture and forestry.

CULTURAL STUDIES
Possible prospectuses: Aberdeen Univ, Birmingham Univ, Cheltenham & Gloucester Coll, East London Univ, Falmouth, Greenwich Univ, Lancaster Univ, Liverpool John Moores Univ, Middlesex Univ, Norfolk Inst, North London Univ, Portsmouth Univ, Sheffield Hallam Univ, Staffordshire Univ, Sussex Univ, Trinity & All Saints, Warwick Univ, West Surrey Coll, Wolverhampton Univ.

CUNEIFORM STUDIES
See: Near East studies.

CYBERNETICS
Possible prospectuses: Loughborough Univ, Reading Univ.
See also: Computing; control engineering.

CZECH/SLOVAK
Possible prospectuses: Cambridge Univ, Glasgow Univ, Oxford Univ, SSEES.
Study area: Modern languages.

D

DANCE
Possible prospectuses: ALRA, Bedford Coll, Birmingham Univ, Bretton Hall, Brighton Univ, Coventry Univ, Crewe & Alsager, De Montfort Univ, Laban Centre, London Coll Dance, London Contemp Dance Sch, Loughborough Univ, Middlesex Univ, Northern Sch Cont Dance, Roehampton Inst, Surrey Univ, West Sussex Inst.
See also: Drama; movement studies; performance arts.
Study area: Dance.

DANISH
Possible prospectuses: East Anglia Univ, Edinburgh Univ, Hull Univ, University Coll London.
See also: Scandinavian studies.
Study area: Modern languages.

DATA PROCESSING
Possible prospectuses: Anglia Poly Univ, Bolton Inst, Bradford Univ, Bristol UWE, Cranfield (p/g only), Dartmouth, Glasgow Poly, Humberside Univ, Leeds Univ, Manchester Univ, Napier Univ, Nene Coll, Open Univ, Oxford Brookes Univ, Scottish Coll Textiles, Sheffield Univ, Staffordshire Univ, Teesside Univ, Thames Valley Univ, Ulster Univ, UMIST.
See also: Computing.
Study area: Computing.

DECISION THEORY
Possible prospectuses: Brunel Univ, Hertfordshire Univ, Manchester Univ.
See also: Business studies; economics; politics.

DEMOGRAPHY
See: Geography; sociology.

DENTISTRY
Possible prospectuses: Belfast Univ, Birmingham Univ, Bristol Univ, Dundee Univ, Glasgow Univ, King's Coll Hospital, King's Coll London, Leeds Univ, Liverpool Univ, London Hospital, Manchester Univ, Newcastle Univ, Queen Mary & Westfield, Sheffield Univ, UMDS, Wales Coll Medicine.
Study area: Dentistry.

DESIGN
See: individual subjects, eg **interior design, industrial design.**

DEVELOPMENTAL
See: individual subjects, eg **biology.**

DEVIANCE
See: Psychology; sociology; statistics.

DIETETICS
Possible prospectuses: Cardiff Inst, Glasgow Poly, King's Coll London, Leeds Metropolitan Univ, North London Univ, Queen Margaret Coll, Robert Gordon Univ, Surrey Univ.
See also: Nutrition.
Study areas: Food science and nutrition; professions allied to medicine (PAMs).

DIGITAL MICROELECTRONICS
Possible prospectuses: Anglia Poly Univ, Birmingham Univ, Bradford Univ, Dundee Inst, Dundee Univ, Edinburgh Univ, Glasgow Poly, Heriot-Watt Univ, Imperial Coll, Kent Univ, Liverpool John Moores Univ, Open Univ, Queen Mary & Westfield, UMIST.
See also: Computing; electronic engineering.

DIVINITY
See: Theology; religious studies.

DRAMA
Possible prospectuses: Aberystwyth, ALRA, Bangor Normal Coll, Bedford Coll, Birmingham Univ, Bolton Inst, Bretton Hall, Brighton Univ, Bristol Univ, Central Sch Speech/Drama, Chester Coll, Crewe & Alsager, De Montfort Univ, Derby Univ, East Anglia Univ, Edge Hill, Exeter Univ, Glamorgan Univ, Glasgow Univ, Goldsmiths' Coll, Guildhall, Homerton, Huddersfield Univ, Hull Univ, Kent Univ, King Alfred's Coll, Lancaster Univ, Leeds Univ, Liverpool Inst, Liverpool John Moores Univ, Loughborough Univ, Manchester Metropolitan Univ, Manchester Univ, Middlesex Univ, Nene Coll, North Cheshire Coll, Northumbria Univ, Nottingham Trent Univ, Plymouth Univ, Queen Mary & Westfield, RADA, Reading Univ, Ripon & York St John, Roehampton Inst, Rose Bruford Coll, Royal Holloway & Bedford, Royal Scottish Academy, S Martin's Coll, St Mary's Coll, Salford Coll, Sussex Univ, Ulster Univ, Warwick Univ, Welsh Coll Music/Drama, West London Inst, Wolverhampton Univ, Worcester Coll.
See also: Dance; performance arts.
Study area: Drama and theatre arts.

DUTCH
Possible prospectuses: Cambridge Univ, Hull Univ, Liverpool Univ, University Coll London.
Study area: Modern languages.

E

EARTH SCIENCES
Possible prospectuses: Aberdeen Univ, Aberystwyth, Anglia Poly Univ, Birmingham Univ, Cambridge Univ, Cheltenham & Gloucester Coll, Derby Univ, East Anglia Univ, Glasgow Univ, Greenwich Univ, Hertfordshire Univ, Hull Univ, Imperial Coll, Kingston Univ, Leeds Univ, Liverpool John Moores Univ, Liverpool Univ, Manchester Univ, Nene Coll, Open Univ, Oxford Brookes Univ, Oxford Univ, Plymouth Univ, Portsmouth Univ, Royal Holloway & Bedford, St Andrews Univ, Sheffield Univ, Southampton Univ, Staffordshire Univ, Stirling Univ, University Coll London, West London Inst, Wolverhampton Univ.
See also: Geology.
Study areas: Geology; environmental science.

ECOLOGY
Possible prospectuses: Aberdeen Univ, Anglia Poly Univ, Bedford Coll, Cardiff, Derby Univ, Dundee Univ, Durham Univ, East Anglia Univ, East London Univ, Edinburgh Univ, Harper Adams, Hertfordshire Univ, Huddersfield Univ, Hull Univ, Humberside Univ, Imperial Coll, King's Coll London, Lancaster Univ, Leeds Univ, Leicester Univ, Liverpool John Moores Univ, Loughborough Univ, Luton Coll, Manchester Univ, North London Univ, Open Univ, Queen Mary & Westfield, Royal Agricultural Coll, Royal Holloway & Bedford, St Andrews Univ, Sheffield Univ, Stirling Univ, Sunderland Univ, Sussex Univ, Ulster Univ, University Coll London, Westminster Univ, Wolverhampton Univ, Worcester Coll, Writtle, York Univ.
See also: Biology; botany; zoology.
Study areas: Biology; environmental science.

ECONOMETRICS
Possible prospectuses: Aberdeen Univ, Birmingham Univ, Brunel Univ, Essex Univ, Heriot-Watt Univ, Kent Univ, Leeds Univ, Liverpool Univ, Loughborough Univ, LSE, Manchester Metropolitan Univ, Manchester Univ, Nottingham Univ, Reading Univ, Sheffield Univ, Southampton Univ, Staffordshire Univ, Surrey Univ, Warwick Univ, York Univ.
See also: Economics; mathematics.
Study area: Economics.

ECONOMIC HISTORY
Possible prospectuses: Aberdeen Univ, Aberystwyth, Belfast Univ, Birmingham Univ, Bristol Univ, Cambridge Univ, East Anglia Univ, Edinburgh Univ, Essex Univ, Exeter Univ, Glasgow Poly, Glasgow Univ, Hull Univ, Kent Univ, Leeds Univ, Leicester Univ, Liverpool Univ, LSE, Manchester Metropolitan Univ, Manchester Univ, Newcastle Univ, Nottingham Univ, Open Univ, Portsmouth Univ, Queen Mary & Westfield, Reading Univ, Royal Holloway & Bedford, St Andrews Univ, Salford Univ, Sheffield Univ, SOAS, Southampton Univ, Staffordshire Univ, Strathclyde Univ, Sussex Univ, Swansea, University Coll London, Warwick Univ, Westminster Univ, York Univ.
See also: History.
Study area: History.

ECONOMICS
Possible prospectuses: Aberdeen Univ, Aberystwyth, Anglia Poly Univ, Bangor, Bath Univ, Belfast Univ, Birkbeck, Birmingham Univ, Bradford Univ, Brighton Univ, Bristol Univ, Bristol UWE, Brunel Univ, Buckingham Univ, Cambridge Univ, Cardiff, Central England Univ, Central Lancashire Univ, City Univ, Coventry Univ, De Montfort Univ, Derby Univ, Dundee Inst, Dundee Univ, Durham Univ, East Anglia Univ, East London Univ, Edinburgh Univ, Essex Univ, European Bus Sch, Exeter Univ, Glasgow Poly, Glasgow Univ, Goldsmiths' Coll, Greenwich Univ, Heriot-Watt Univ, Hertfordshire Univ, Holborn Coll, Hull Univ, Humberside Univ, Keele Univ, Kent Univ, Kingston Univ, Lancaster Univ, Leeds Metropolitan Univ, Leeds Univ, Leicester Univ, Liverpool John Moores Univ, Liverpool Univ, London Guildhall Univ, Loughborough Univ, LSE, Manchester Metropolitan Univ, Manchester Univ, Middlesex Univ, Nene Coll, Newcastle Univ, North London Univ, Northumbria Univ, Nottingham Trent Univ, Nottingham Univ, Open Univ, Oxford Brookes Univ, Oxford Univ, Paisley Univ, Plymouth Univ, Portsmouth Univ, Queen Mary & Westfield, Reading Univ, Robert Gordon Univ, Royal Agricultural Coll, Royal Holloway & Bedford, St Andrews Univ, Salford Univ,

Sheffield Univ, SOAS, Southampton Univ, Staffordshire Univ, Stirling Univ, Strathclyde Univ, Sunderland Univ, Surrey Univ, Sussex Univ, Swansea, Swansea Inst, Thames Valley Univ, Trinity & All Saints, Ulster Univ, University Coll London, Warwick Univ, Westminster Univ, Wolverhampton Univ, Worcester Coll, Wye Coll, York Univ.
Study area: Economics.

EDUCATION
Possible prospectuses: Aberystwyth, Anglia Poly Univ, Bangor, Bangor Normal Coll, Bath Coll, Bath Univ, Bedford Coll, Belfast Univ, Birmingham Univ, Bolton Inst, Bradford & Ilkley, Bretton Hall, Brighton Univ, Bristol Univ, Bristol UWE, Brunel Univ, Cambridge Univ, Canterbury Christ Church Coll, Cardiff, Cardiff Inst, Central England Univ, Central Lancashire Univ, Central Sch Speech/Drama, Charlotte Mason, Cheltenham & Gloucester Coll, Chester Coll, Crewe & Alsager, Derby Univ, Durham Univ, East Anglia Univ, East London Univ, Edge Hill, Exeter Univ, Glasgow Univ, Goldsmiths' Coll, Greenwich Univ, Heriot-Watt Univ, Hertfordshire Univ, Homerton, Huddersfield Univ, Hull Univ, Inst Education (p/g only), Jews' Coll, Keele Univ, King Alfred's Coll, King's Coll London, Kingston Univ, Lancaster Univ, Leeds Metropolitan Univ, Liverpool Inst, Liverpool John Moores Univ, Liverpool Univ, Loughborough Univ, LSU Southampton, Manchester Metropolitan Univ, Manchester Univ, Middlesex Univ, Moray House, Nene Coll, North East Wales Inst, North London Univ, Northumbria Univ, Nottingham Trent Univ, Open Univ, Oxford Brookes Univ, Plymouth Univ, Reading Univ, Ripon & York St John, Roehampton Inst, St Mark & St John, S Martin's Coll, St Mary's Coll, Sheffield Hallam Univ, South Bank Univ, Stirling Univ, Strathclyde Univ, Sunderland Univ, Swansea, Swansea Inst, Trinity & All Saints, Trinity Coll Carmarthen, Ulster Univ, Warwick Univ, West London Inst, West Sussex Inst, Westminster Coll, Wolverhampton Univ, Worcester Coll, York Univ.
Study area: Education.

EGYPTOLOGY
Possible prospectuses: Oxford Univ, University Coll London.
*See also: **Archaeology; history; Near East Studies.***

ELECTRICAL ENGINEERING
Possible prospectuses: Aberdeen Univ, Aston Univ, Bangor, Bath Univ, Belfast Univ, Birmingham Univ, Bolton Inst, Bradford Univ, Brighton Univ, Bristol Univ, Bristol UWE, Brunel Univ, Cambridge Univ, Cardiff, Cardiff Inst, Central Lancashire Univ, City Univ, Coventry Univ, Cranwell, Dartmouth, Derby Univ, Dundee Inst, Dundee Univ, Durham Univ, East Anglia Univ, East London Univ, Edinburgh Univ, Essex Univ, Exeter Univ, Glamorgan Univ, Glasgow Poly, Glasgow Univ, Greenwich Univ, Heriot-Watt Univ, Hertfordshire Univ, Huddersfield Univ, Humberside Univ, Imperial Coll, Kingston Univ, Leeds Univ, Leicester Univ, Liverpool John Moores Univ, Liverpool Univ, Loughborough Univ, Luton Coll, Manadon, Manchester Metropolitan Univ, Manchester Univ, Middlesex Univ, Napier Univ, Nene Coll, Newcastle Univ, North East Wales Inst, Northumbria Univ, Nottingham Trent Univ, Nottingham Univ, Oxford Brookes Univ, Oxford Univ, Paisley Univ, Plymouth Univ, Portsmouth Univ, Queen Mary & Westfield, Robert Gordon Univ, Salford Univ, Sheffield Hallam Univ, Sheffield Univ, South Bank Univ, Southampton Univ, Staffordshire Univ, Strathclyde Univ, Sunderland

Univ, Surrey Univ, Sussex Univ, Swansea, Teesside Univ, Ulster Univ,
UMIST, University Coll London, Warwick Univ.
See also: Electronic engineering; engineering.
Study area: Electrical and electronic engineering.

ELECTROMECHANICAL ENGINEERING
Possible prospectuses: Aston Univ, Cranwell, Dartmouth, Dundee Inst,
Glasgow Poly, Heriot-Watt Univ, Imperial Coll, Lancaster Univ, Leeds Univ,
Loughborough Univ, Manchester Metropolitan Univ, Manchester Univ, Robert
Gordon Univ, Southampton Univ, Strathclyde Univ, Sussex Univ, UMIST.
See also: Engineering.
Study area: Mechanical and production engineering.

ELECTRONIC ENGINEERING
Possible prospectuses: Aberdeen Univ, Aberystwyth, Aston Univ, Bangor, Bath
Univ, Belfast Univ, Birmingham Univ, Bolton Inst, Bournemouth Univ,
Bradford Univ, Brighton Univ, Bristol Univ, Bristol UWE, Brunel Univ,
Cambridge Univ, Cardiff, Cardiff Inst, Central England Univ, Central
Lancashire Univ, City Univ, Coventry Univ, Cranwell, De Montfort Univ,
Derby Univ, Dundee Inst, Dundee Univ, Durham Univ, East Anglia Univ,
East London Univ, Edinburgh Univ, Essex Univ, Exeter Univ, Glamorgan
Univ, Glasgow Poly, Glasgow Univ, Greenwich Univ, Heriot-Watt Univ,
Hertfordshire Univ, Huddersfield Univ, Hull Univ, Humberside Univ, Imperial
Coll, Kent Univ, King's Coll London, Kingston Univ, Lancaster Univ, Leeds
Metropolitan Univ, Leeds Univ, Leicester Univ, Liverpool John Moores Univ,
Liverpool Univ, Loughborough Univ, Luton Coll, Manadon, Manchester
Metropolitan Univ, Manchester Univ, Middlesex Univ, Napier Univ, Newcastle
Univ, North East Wales Inst, North London Univ, Northumbria Univ,
Nottingham Trent Univ, Nottingham Univ, Oxford Brookes Univ, Oxford
Univ, Paisley Univ, Plymouth Univ, Portsmouth Univ, Queen Mary &
Westfield, Ravensbourne Coll, Reading Univ, Robert Gordon Univ, Salford
Univ, Sheffield Hallam Univ, Sheffield Univ, Shrivenham, South Bank Univ,
Southampton Univ, Staffordshire Univ, Strathclyde Univ, Sunderland Univ,
Surrey Univ, Sussex Univ, Swansea, Swansea Inst, Teesside Univ, Ulster Univ,
UMIST, University Coll London, Warwick Univ, Westminster Univ, York
Univ.
See also: Electrical engineering; engineering.
Study area: Electrical and electronic engineering.

ELECTRONIC MECHANICS
Possible prospectuses: Brunel Univ, East London Univ, Glasgow Poly, Heriot-
Watt Univ, Imperial Coll.
See also: Electronic engineering.
Study area: Electrical and electronic engineering.

ELECTRONICS

Possible prospectuses: Aberystwyth, Anglia Poly Univ, Aston Univ, Bangor, Birmingham Univ, Bolton Inst, Bradford Univ, Brighton Univ, Bristol UWE, Brunel Univ, Cardiff, Cardiff Inst, Central Lancashire Univ, Coventry Univ, Cranwell, Dartmouth, De Montfort Univ, Dundee Inst, Dundee Univ, Durham Univ, Edinburgh Univ, Essex Univ, Glamorgan Univ, Glasgow Poly, Glasgow Univ, Greenwich Univ, Heriot-Watt Univ, Hertfordshire Univ, Huddersfield Univ, Imperial Coll, Keele Univ, Kent Univ, Kingston Univ, Lancaster Univ, Leeds Metropolitan Univ, Leeds Univ, Liverpool John Moores Univ, Liverpool Univ, Loughborough Univ, Manchester Metropolitan Univ, Manchester Univ, Middlesex Univ, Napier Univ, North East Wales Inst, Northumbria Univ, Nottingham Trent Univ, Nottingham Univ, Open Univ, Oxford Brookes Univ, Paisley Univ, Queen Mary & Westfield, Reading Univ, Robert Gordon Univ, Royal Holloway & Bedford, St Andrews Univ, Salford Univ, Sheffield Univ, Southampton Univ, Staffordshire Univ, Sussex Univ, Swansea Inst, Teesside Univ, Ulster Univ, UMIST, Warwick Univ, Wolverhampton Univ, York Univ.
Study area: Physics.

EMBROIDERY

Possible prospectuses: Central England Univ, Glasgow Sch Art, Loughborough Coll, Manchester Metropolitan Univ, Royal Coll Art (p/g only), Ulster Univ.
See also: Textiles.
Study area: Art and design.

EMBRYOLOGY

See: Biology; medicine.

ENERGY ENGINEERING

Possible prospectuses: Cranfield (p/g only), Glamorgan Univ, Heriot-Watt Univ, Imperial Coll, Leeds Univ, Napier Univ, South Bank Univ, Sunderland Univ.

ENERGY STUDIES
Possible prospectuses: Brighton Univ, Brunel Univ, Coventry Univ, Cranfield (p/g only), Glamorgan Univ, Glasgow Poly, Heriot-Watt Univ, Leeds Univ, Manchester Univ, Nene Coll, Newcastle Univ, South Bank Univ, Sunderland Univ.
Study area: Chemical engineering.

ENGINEERING (GENERAL)
Possible prospectuses: Aberdeen Univ, Anglia Poly Univ, Aston Univ, Bolton Inst, Bournemouth Univ, Brighton Univ, Bristol UWE, Brunel Univ, Camborne Sch Mines, Cambridge Univ, Cardiff, Central England Univ, Central Lancashire Univ, City Univ, Coventry Univ, Cranfield (p/g only), Dartmouth, De Montfort Univ, Dundee Inst, Durham Univ, East London Univ, Edinburgh Univ, Exeter Univ, Glamorgan Univ, Glasgow Poly, Greenwich Univ, Heriot-Watt Univ, Hull Univ, Humberside Univ, Imperial Coll, Kingston Univ, Lancaster Univ, Leicester Univ, Liverpool John Moores Univ, Liverpool Univ, Loughborough Univ, Luton Coll, Manadon, Manchester Metropolitan Univ, Manchester Univ, Middlesex Univ, Napier Univ, Nene Coll, Newcastle Univ, North East Wales Inst, Northumbria Univ, Nottingham Trent Univ, Oxford Brookes Univ, Oxford Univ, Paisley Univ, Portsmouth Univ, Queen Mary & Westfield, Reading Univ, Robert Gordon Univ, Sheffield Hallam Univ, Shrivenham, Silsoe Coll, South Bank Univ, Southampton Inst, Staffordshire Univ, Sunderland Univ, Surrey Univ, Sussex Univ, Ulster Univ, UMIST, Warwick Univ, Westminster Univ, Wolverhampton Univ.
See also: Electrical engineering; mechanical engineering.

ENGINEERING MATHEMATICS
Possible prospectuses: Aberdeen Univ, Bristol Univ, Brunel Univ, Cranfield (p/g only), Dartmouth, Glasgow Poly, Heriot-Watt Univ, Loughborough Univ, Napier Univ, Nottingham Univ, Open Univ, Queen Mary & Westfield, Swansea.
See also: Mathematics.

ENGLISH
Possible prospectuses: Aberdeen Univ, Aberystwyth, Anglia Poly Univ, Bangor, Bangor Normal Coll, Bedford Coll, Belfast Univ, Birkbeck, Birmingham Univ, Bolton Inst, Bretton Hall, Brighton Univ, Bristol Univ, Bristol UWE, Buckingham Univ, Cambridge Univ, Canterbury Christ Church Coll, Cardiff, Central England Univ, Central Lancashire Univ, Cheltenham & Gloucester Coll, Chester Coll, Crewe & Alsager, De Montfort Univ, Derby Univ, Dundee Univ, Durham Univ, East Anglia Univ, Edge Hill, Edinburgh Univ, Essex Univ, Exeter Univ, Glamorgan Univ, Glasgow Univ, Goldsmiths' Coll, Hertfordshire Univ, Homerton, Huddersfield Univ, Hull Univ, Humberside Univ, Keele Univ, Kent Univ, King Alfred's Coll, King's Coll London, Kingston Univ,

Lampeter, Lancaster Univ, Leeds Univ, Leicester Univ, Liverpool Inst, Liverpool John Moores Univ, Liverpool Univ, Loughborough Univ, LSU Southampton, Luton Coll, Manchester Metropolitan Univ, Manchester Univ, Middlesex Univ, Nene Coll, Newcastle Univ, North East Wales Inst, North London Univ, Northumbria Univ, Nottingham Trent Univ, Nottingham Univ, Open Univ, Oxford Brookes Univ, Oxford Univ, Plymouth Univ, Portsmouth Univ, Queen Mary & Westfield, Reading Univ, Ripon & York St John, Roehampton Inst, Royal Holloway & Bedford, St Andrews Univ, St Mark & St John, S Martin's Coll, St Mary's Coll, Salford Univ, Sheffield Hallam Univ, Sheffield Univ, South Bank Univ, Southampton Univ, Staffordshire Univ, Stirling Univ, Strathclyde Univ, Sunderland Univ, Sussex Univ, Swansea, Swansea Inst, Teesside Univ, Thames Valley Univ, Trinity & All Saints, Ulster Univ, University Coll London, Warwick Univ, West London Inst, West Sussex Inst, Westminster Univ, Wolverhampton Univ, Worcester Coll, York Univ.
Study area: English.

ENTOMOLOGY
See: Biology; zoology.

ENVIRONMENTAL ARCHAEOLOGY
Possible prospectuses: Bradford Univ, Edinburgh Univ, Inst Archaeology, Lampeter, Luton Coll, Sheffield Univ.
Study area: Archaeology.

ENVIRONMENTAL CHEMISTRY
Possible prospectuses: Aberystwyth, Bristol Univ, Brunel Univ, Edinburgh Univ, Glasgow Poly, Hertfordshire Univ, Portsmouth Univ, Staffordshire Univ, Swansea.

ENVIRONMENTAL ENGINEERING
Possible prospectuses: Bath Univ, Brighton Univ, Brunel Univ, Cardiff, Cardiff Inst, Dundee Inst, Edinburgh Univ, Glamorgan Univ, Harper Adams, Imperial Coll, Leeds Univ, Liverpool Univ, Loughborough Univ, Luton Coll, Middlesex Univ, Newcastle Univ, Nottingham Univ, Portsmouth Univ, Sheffield Hallam Univ, Silsoe Coll, South Bank Univ, Southampton Univ, Staffordshire Univ, Strathclyde Univ, Sunderland Univ, Surrey Univ, Univ Coll London.
Study area: Environmental science.

ENVIRONMENTAL HEALTH
Possible prospectuses: Bristol UWE, Cardiff Inst, Greenwich Univ, King's Coll London, Leeds Metropolitan Univ, Luton Coll, Manchester Metropolitan Univ, Middlesex Univ, Nottingham Trent Univ, Open Univ, Salford Univ, South Bank Univ, Strathclyde Univ, Ulster Univ.

ENVIRONMENTAL SCIENCE
Possible prospectuses: Aberdeen Univ, Aberystwyth, Anglia Poly Univ, Birkbeck, Birmingham Univ, Bradford Univ, Brighton Univ, Bristol UWE, Brunel Univ, Buckingham Univ, Central Lancashire Univ, Colchester Inst, Coventry Univ, Crewe & Alsager, Dundee Inst, Dundee Univ, East Anglia Univ, East London Univ, Edinburgh Univ, Essex Univ, Glamorgan Univ, Glasgow Univ, Greenwich Univ, Heriot-Watt Univ, Hertfordshire Univ, Huddersfield Univ, Hull Univ, Kent Univ, King's Coll London, Kingston Univ, Lancaster Univ, Leeds Univ, Liverpool John Moores Univ, London

Guildhall Univ, Loughborough Univ, Luton Coll, Manchester Metropolitan
Univ, Manchester Univ, Middlesex Univ, Nene Coll, Newcastle Univ, North
East Wales Inst, North London Univ, Nottingham Univ, Open Univ, Oxford
Brookes Univ, Paisley Univ, Plymouth Univ, Portsmouth Univ, Queen Mary &
Westfield, Reading Univ, Ripon & York St John, Royal Holloway & Bedford,
St Mary's Coll, Salford Univ, Sheffield Univ, South Bank Univ, Southampton
Univ, Staffordshire Univ, Stirling Univ, Sunderland Univ, Sussex Univ, Ulster
Univ, UMIST, Warwick Univ, Welsh Agricultural Coll, West Sussex Inst,
Westminster Univ, Wolverhampton Univ, Worcester Coll, Wye Coll, York
Univ.
Study area: Environmental science.

ENVIRONMENTAL STUDIES

Possible prospectuses: Aberdeen Univ, Aberystwyth, Anglia Poly Univ, Bangor
Normal Coll, Bedford Coll, Belfast Univ, Bolton Inst, Bradford Univ, Bretton
Hall, Bristol UWE, Cardiff, Central Lancashire Univ, Charlotte Mason,
Cheltenham & Gloucester Coll, Crewe & Alsager, De Montfort Univ, Derby
Univ, Duncan of Jordanstone, East Anglia Univ, Edinburgh Coll Art,
Greenwich Univ, Harper Adams, Hertfordshire Univ, Humberside Univ, Keele
Univ, Leeds Univ, Liverpool Inst, London Guildhall Univ, Luton Coll,
Manchester Metropolitan Univ, North East Wales Inst, North London Univ,
Northumbria Univ, Open Univ, Oxford Brookes Univ, Portsmouth Univ,
Queen Mary & Westfield, Reading Univ, Roehampton Inst, Royal Agricultural
Coll, Salford Univ, Scottish Agricultural Coll, Sheffield Univ, Silsoe Coll, South
Bank Univ, Stirling Univ, Sunderland Univ, Sussex Univ, Swansea, UMIST,
Univ Coll London, Welsh Agricultural Coll, West London Inst,
Wolverhampton Univ, Wye Coll, York Univ.
See also: Environmental archaeology.
Study area: Environmental studies.

EQUINE STUDIES

Possible prospectuses: Coventry Univ, De Montfort Univ, Humberside Univ,
Nene Coll, Royal Agricultural Coll, Welsh Agricultural Coll, Writtle.

ERGONOMICS

Possible prospectuses: Aston Univ, Glasgow Poly, Loughborough Univ, Univ
Coll London.

ESTATE MANAGEMENT

Possible prospectuses: Aberdeen Univ, Bristol UWE, Cambridge Univ, Central
England Univ, City Univ, De Montfort Univ, East London Univ, Edinburgh
Coll Art, Greenwich Univ, Harper Adams, Heriot-Watt Univ, Kingston Univ,
Liverpool John Moores Univ, Luton Coll, Newcastle Univ, North East Wales
Inst, Northumbria Univ, Nottingham Trent Univ, Oxford Brookes Univ,
Plymouth Univ, Portsmouth Univ, Reading Univ, Royal Agricultural Coll,
Sheffield Hallam Univ, Silsoe Coll, South Bank Univ, Staffordshire Univ, Ulster
Univ, Westminster Univ, Writtle, Wye Coll.
See also: Urban estate management.

ETHICS

See: Philosophy, theology.

EUROPEAN BUSINESS STUDIES
Possible prospectuses: Anglia Poly Univ, Aston Univ, Birmingham Univ, Bournemouth Univ, Brighton Univ, Bristol UWE, Buckingham Univ, Buckinghamshire Coll, Cardiff Inst, Central Lancashire Univ, Coventry Univ, De Montfort Univ, Derby Univ, East London Univ, European Business Sch, Glamorgan Univ, Glasgow Poly, Greenwich Univ, Heriot-Watt Univ, Hertfordshire Univ, Hull Univ, Humberside Univ, Kent Univ, Kingston Univ, Lancaster Univ, Leeds Metropolitan Univ, Liverpool John Moores Univ, London Guildhall Univ, Loughborough Univ, Luton Coll, Manchester Metropolitan Univ, Middlesex Univ, Nene Coll, North London Univ, Northumbria Univ, Nottingham Trent Univ, Oxford Brookes Univ, Plymouth Univ, Portsmouth Univ, Reading Univ, Robert Gordon Univ, Royal Agricultural Coll, Sheffield Hallam Univ, South Bank Univ, Staffordshire Univ, Strathclyde Univ, Sunderland Univ, Swansea, Teesside Univ, Thames Valley Univ, Ulster Univ, Westminster Univ, Wolverhampton Univ, Writtle.
Study areas: Business studies; European studies.

EUROPEAN STUDIES
Possible prospectuses: Aberdeen Univ, Aberystwyth, Anglia Poly Univ, Aston Univ, Bath Univ, Bedford Coll, Belfast Univ, Bolton Inst, Bradford Univ, Bristol Univ, Bristol UWE, Brunel Univ, Buckingham Univ, Cardiff, Central Lancashire Univ, Coventry Univ, Derby Univ, Dundee Univ, East Anglia Univ, Edge Hill, Edinburgh Univ, Essex Univ, Greenwich Univ, Hertfordshire Univ, Hull Univ, Keele Univ, Kent Univ, King's Coll London, Leicester Univ, Liverpool Inst, Liverpool John Moores Univ, Loughborough Univ, LSE, LSU Southampton, Manchester Metropolitan Univ, Manchester Univ, North East Wales Inst, North London Univ, Northumbria Univ, Nottingham Trent Univ, Nottingham Univ, Open Univ, Plymouth Univ, Queen Mary & Westfield, Royal Holloway & Bedford, St Andrews Univ, Sheffield Hallam Univ, South Bank Univ, Southampton Inst, Southampton Univ, SSEES, Staffordshire Univ, Stirling Univ, Strathclyde Univ, Surrey Univ, Sussex Univ, Teesside Univ, Thames Valley Univ, Ulster Univ, Univ Coll London, Westminster Univ, Wolverhampton Univ.
*See also: **Scandinavian studies.***
Study area: European studies.

EXPLORATION
Possible prospectuses: Camborne Sch Mines, Cardiff, Univ Coll London.
*See also: **Mining; geology.***
Study area: Geology.

F

FASHION

Possible prospectuses: Bradford & Ilkley, Bretton Hall, Brighton Univ, Bristol UWE, Central England Univ, Central Lancashire Univ, Central Saint Martins, Cheltenham & Gloucester Coll, De Montfort Univ, Derby Univ, East London Univ, Edinburgh Coll Art, Heriot-Watt Univ, Kent Inst, Kingston Univ, Liverpool John Moores Univ, London Coll Fashion, Manchester Metropolitan Univ, Middlesex Univ, Northumbria Univ, Nottingham Trent Univ, Ravensbourne Coll, Royal Coll Art (p/g only), Southampton Inst, Ulster Univ, West Surrey Coll, Westminster Univ, Winchester Sch Art.
See also: Textiles.
Study area: Art and design.

FERMENTATION
See: Biochemistry; brewing; microbiology.

FILM MAKING TECHNIQUES
See: Film studies.

FILM MUSIC
Possible prospectuses: London Int Film Sch, National Film Sch (p/g only).

FILM STUDIES
Possible prospectuses: Canterbury Christ Church Coll, Cardiff, Central Saint Martins, Coventry Univ, Derby Univ, East Anglia Univ, Edinburgh Coll Art, Glasgow Univ, Humberside Univ, Kent Inst, Kent Univ, London Coll Printing, London Int Film Sch, Manchester Metropolitan Univ, Middlesex Univ, Napier Univ, National Film Sch (p/g only), North Cheshire Coll, North London Univ, Northumbria Univ, Portsmouth Univ, Reading Univ, Royal Coll Art (p/g only), Sheffield Hallam Univ, Staffordshire Univ, Stirling Univ, Swansea Inst, Warwick Univ, West Surrey Coll, Westminster Univ.
Study area: Art and design.

FINANCE
Possible prospectuses: Aberystwyth, Aston Univ, Bangor, Belfast Univ, Bournemouth Univ, Bradford Univ, Brighton Univ, Bristol UWE, Brunel Univ, Buckingham Univ, Cardiff, Central England Univ, Central Lancashire Univ, Cheltenham & Gloucester Coll, City Univ, Coventry Univ, Dundee Inst,

Dundee Univ, East London Univ, European Business Sch, Glamorgan Univ, Greenwich Univ, Heriot-Watt Univ, Huddersfield Univ, Humberside Univ, Lancaster Univ, Leeds Metropolitan Univ, Liverpool John Moores Univ, London Guildhall Univ, Loughborough Univ, LSE, Luton Coll, Manchester Metropolitan Univ, Manchester Univ, North London Univ, Nottingham Trent Univ, Paisley Univ, Plymouth Univ, Portsmouth Univ, Robert Gordon Univ, Royal Agricultural Coll, Salford Univ, Sheffield Hallam Univ, South Bank Univ, Staffordshire Univ, Stirling Univ, Strathclyde Univ, Swansea Inst, Teesside Univ, Thames Valley Univ, Ulster Univ, Westminster Univ, Wolverhampton Univ, York Univ.
See also: Accountancy; business studies; economics.
Study area: Business studies.

FINE ART
See: Art; painting; photography; printmaking; sculpture.

FINE ARTS
Possible prospectuses: Aberdeen Univ, Aberystwyth, Anglia Poly Univ, Birkbeck, Birmingham Univ, Bolton Inst, Brighton Univ, Bristol Univ, British Institute in Paris, Buckingham Univ, Camberwell Coll, Cambridge Univ, Cardiff Inst, Central England Univ, Central Lancashire Univ, Central Saint Martins, Cheltenham & Gloucester Coll, Chester Coll, Courtauld Inst, Coventry Univ, De Montfort Univ, Derby Univ, Dundee Univ, East Anglia Univ, East London Univ, Edinburgh Coll Art, Edinburgh Univ, Essex Univ, Exeter Univ, Falmouth, Glasgow Univ, Goldsmiths' Coll, Hull Univ, Humberside Univ, Kent Inst, Kent Univ, Kingston Univ, Lancaster Univ, Leeds Metropolitan Univ, Leeds Univ, Leicester Univ, Liverpool John Moores Univ, Manchester Metropolitan Univ, Manchester Univ, Middlesex Univ, Newcastle Univ, Northumbria Univ, Nottingham Trent Univ, Nottingham Univ, Open Univ, Oxford Brookes Univ, Oxford Univ, Plymouth Univ, Portsmouth Univ, Reading Univ, Robert Gordon Univ, St Andrews Univ, Sheffield Hallam Univ, Slade, SOAS, Southampton Inst, Staffordshire Univ, Sunderland Univ, Sussex Univ, Swansea Inst, Thames Valley Univ, Ulster Univ, Univ Coll London, Warwick Univ, West Surrey Coll, Winchester Sch Art, Wolverhampton Univ.
Study area: Art and design.

FINNISH STUDIES
Possible prospectuses: Hull Univ, SSEES.
See also: Scandinavian studies.
Study area: European studies.

FIRE SAFETY
Possible prospectuses: Edinburgh Univ, South Bank Univ.

FISHERIES MANAGEMENT
See: Wild life management.

FISHERY SCIENCE
Possible prospectuses: Aberdeen Univ, Edinburgh Univ, Humberside Univ, Plymouth Univ, Scottish Agricultural Coll.

FLYING
Possible prospectuses: Cranwell.
See also: Aeronautical engineering.

FOOD SCIENCE
Possible prospectuses: Belfast Univ, Bournemouth Univ, Bradford Univ, Cardiff, Cardiff Inst, Duncan of Jordanstone, Dundee Univ, Glasgow Poly, Harper Adams, Huddersfield Univ, Humberside Univ, Leeds Univ, Loughborough Univ, Manchester Metropolitan Univ, North London Univ, Nottingham Univ, Oxford Brookes Univ, Plymouth Univ, Queen Margaret Coll, Reading Univ, Robert Gordon Univ, Sheffield Hallam Univ, Silsoe Coll, South Bank Univ, Strathclyde Univ, Surrey Univ, Ulster Univ.
See also: Nutrition.
Study area: Food science and nutrition.

FOOTWEAR
Possible prospectuses: De Montfort Univ.
See also: Textiles.
Study area: Art and design.

FORENSIC SCIENCE
See: Chemistry.

FORESTRY
Possible prospectuses: Aberdeen Univ, Bangor, Edinburgh Univ, Royal Agricultural Coll.
Study area: Agriculture, horticulture and forestry.

FRENCH
Possible prospectuses: Aberdeen Univ, Aberystwyth, Anglia Poly Univ, Aston Univ, Bangor, Bath Univ, Bedford Coll, Belfast Univ, Birkbeck, Birmingham Univ, Bradford Univ, Bristol Univ, Bristol UWE, British Institute in Paris, Brunel Univ, Buckingham Univ, Cambridge Univ, Cardiff, Central Lancashire Univ, Central Sch Speech/Drama, Cheltenham & Gloucester Coll, Coventry Univ, Crewe & Alsager, De Montfort Univ, Derby Univ, Durham Univ, East Anglia Univ, East London Univ, Edge Hill, Edinburgh Univ, Essex Univ, European Business Sch, Exeter Univ, French Inst, Glasgow Poly, Glasgow Univ, Goldsmiths' Coll, Heriot-Watt Univ, Huddersfield Univ, Hull Univ, Humberside Univ, Keele Univ, Kent Univ, King's Coll London, Kingston Univ, Lampeter, Lancaster Univ, Leeds Metropolitan Univ, Leeds Univ, Leicester Univ, Liverpool Inst, Liverpool John Moores Univ, Liverpool Univ, London Guildhall Univ, Loughborough Univ, LSU Southampton, Luton Coll, Manchester Metropolitan Univ, Manchester Univ, Middlesex Univ, National Extension Coll, Nene Coll, Newcastle Univ, North London Univ, Northumbria Univ, Nottingham Trent Univ, Nottingham Univ, Oxford Brookes Univ, Oxford Univ, Plymouth Univ, Portsmouth Univ, Queen Mary & Westfield, Reading Univ, Ripon & York St John, Roehampton Inst, Royal Holloway & Bedford, St Andrews Univ, Salford Univ, Sheffield Hallam Univ, Sheffield Univ, South Bank Univ, Southampton Univ, SSEES, Staffordshire Univ, Stirling Univ, Strathclyde Univ, Sunderland Univ, Surrey Univ, Sussex Univ, Swansea, Teesside Univ, Thames Valley Univ, Trinity & All Saints, Ulster Univ, UMIST, Univ Coll London, Warwick Univ, Westminster Univ, Wolverhampton Univ, York Univ.
Study area: Modern languages.

FRESHWATER BIOLOGY
See: Marine biology.

FUEL SCIENCE
See: Chemistry; energy studies.

FURNITURE DESIGN
Possible prospectuses: Buckinghamshire Coll, Central England Univ, De Montfort Univ, Edinburgh Coll Art, Heriot-Watt Univ, Kingston Univ, Leeds Metropolitan Univ, London Guildhall Univ, Loughborough Coll, Middlesex Univ, Nottingham Trent Univ, Ravensbourne Coll, Royal Coll Art (p/g only), Ulster Univ.
Study area: Art and design.

FURNITURE PRODUCTION
Possible prospectuses: London Guildhall Univ.

G

GENDER STUDIES
Possible prospectuses: Anglia Poly Univ, Bolton Inst, Coventry Univ, Edinburgh Univ, North London Univ.

GENETICS
Possible prospectuses: Aberdeen Univ, Aberystwyth, Belfast Univ, Birmingham Univ, Cambridge Univ, Cardiff, East Anglia Univ, Edinburgh Univ, Glasgow Univ, Hertfordshire Univ, Leeds Univ, Leicester Univ, Liverpool Univ, Manchester Univ, Newcastle Univ, Nottingham Univ, Queen Mary & Westfield, St Andrews Univ, Sheffield Univ, Sussex Univ, Swansea, Univ Coll London, York Univ.
See also: Biology.
Study area: Biology.

GEOCHEMISTRY
Possible prospectuses: Aberystwyth, Anglia Poly Univ, Cambridge Univ, Greenwich Univ, Imperial Coll, Leicester Univ, Manchester Univ, Reading Univ, Royal Holloway & Bedford, St Andrews Univ.
See also: Geology; chemistry.
Study area: Geology.

GEOGRAPHY
Possible prospectuses: Aberdeen Univ, Aberystwyth, Anglia Poly Univ, Bedford Coll, Belfast Univ, Birkbeck, Birmingham Univ, Bradford Univ, Brighton Univ, Bristol Univ, Bristol UWE, Cambridge Univ, Canterbury Christ Church Coll, Central Lancashire Univ, Cheltenham & Gloucester Coll, Chester Coll,

Coventry Univ, Crewe & Alsager, Derby Univ, Dundee Univ, Durham Univ, East Anglia Univ, Edge Hill, Edinburgh Univ, Exeter Univ, Glamorgan Univ, Glasgow Poly, Glasgow Univ, Greenwich Univ, Homerton, Huddersfield Univ, Hull Univ, Humberside Univ, Keele Univ, Kent Univ, King's Coll London, Kingston Univ, Lampeter, Lancaster Univ, Leeds Univ, Leicester Univ, Liverpool Inst, Liverpool John Moores Univ, Liverpool Univ, London Guildhall Univ, Loughborough Univ, LSE, LSU Southampton, Luton Coll, Manchester Metropolitan Univ, Manchester Univ, Middlesex Univ, National Extension Coll, Nene Coll, Newcastle Univ, North London Univ, Northumbria Univ, Nottingham Trent Univ, Nottingham Univ, Open Univ, Oxford Brookes Univ, Oxford Univ, Plymouth Univ, Portsmouth Univ, Queen Mary & Westfield, Reading Univ, Ripon & York St John, Roehampton Inst, Royal Holloway & Bedford, St Andrews Univ, St Mark & St John, S Martin's Coll, St Mary's Coll, Salford Univ, Sheffield Hallam Univ, Sheffield Univ, SOAS, South Bank Univ, Southampton Univ, Staffordshire Univ, Strathclyde Univ, Sunderland Univ, Sussex Univ, Swansea, Thames Valley Univ, Trinity & All Saints, Ulster Univ, Univ Coll London, West London Inst, West Sussex Inst, Westminster Univ, Wolverhampton Univ, Worcester Coll.
Study area: Geography.

GEOLOGY
Possible prospectuses: Aberdeen Univ, Aberystwyth, Anglia Poly Univ, Belfast Univ, Birkbeck, Birmingham Univ, Bristol Univ, Camborne Sch Mines, Cambridge Univ, Cardiff, Cheltenham & Gloucester Coll, Derby Univ, Durham Univ, East Anglia Univ, Edinburgh Univ, Glamorgan Univ, Glasgow Univ, Greenwich Univ, Hertfordshire Univ, Imperial Coll, Keele Univ, Kingston Univ, Leeds Univ, Leicester Univ, Liverpool John Moores Univ, Liverpool Univ, Luton Coll, Manchester Univ, Middlesex Univ, North London Univ, Open Univ, Oxford Brookes Univ, Oxford Univ, Plymouth Univ, Portsmouth Univ, Queen Mary & Westfield, Royal Holloway & Bedford, St Andrews Univ, Sheffield Hallam Univ, Southampton Univ, Staffordshire Univ, Sunderland Univ, Teesside Univ, Univ Coll London, West London Inst.
Study area: Geology.

GEOPHYSICS
Possible prospectuses: Aberystwyth, Bath Univ, Belfast Univ, Camborne Sch Mines, Cambridge Univ, Durham Univ, East Anglia Univ, Edinburgh Univ, Imperial Coll, Lancaster Univ, Leeds Univ, Leicester Univ, Liverpool Univ, Manchester Univ, Newcastle Univ, Open Univ, Southampton Univ, Univ Coll London.
See also: Geology; physics.
Study area: Geology.

GERMAN
Possible prospectuses: Aberdeen Univ, Aberystwyth, Anglia Poly Univ, Aston Univ, Bangor, Bath Univ, Bedford Coll, Belfast Univ, Birkbeck, Birmingham Univ, Bradford Univ, Bristol Univ, Bristol UWE, Brunel Univ, Buckingham Univ, Cambridge Univ, Cardiff, Central Lancashire Univ, Central Sch Speech/Drama, Coventry Univ, De Montfort Univ, Derby Univ, Durham Univ, East Anglia Univ, East London Univ, Edinburgh Univ, Essex Univ, European Business Sch, Exeter Univ, Glasgow Poly, Glasgow Univ, Goldsmiths' Coll, Heriot-Watt Univ, Huddersfield Univ, Hull Univ, Humberside Univ, Keele

Univ, Kent Univ, King's Coll London, Kingston Univ, Lampeter, Lancaster
Univ, Leeds Metropolitan Univ, Leeds Univ, Leicester Univ, Liverpool John
Moores Univ, Liverpool Univ, London Guildhall Univ, Loughborough Univ,
LSU Southampton, Luton Coll, Manchester Metropolitan Univ, Manchester
Univ, Middlesex Univ, National Extension Coll, Nene Coll, Newcastle Univ,
North London Univ, Northumbria Univ, Nottingham Trent Univ, Nottingham
Univ, Oxford Brookes Univ, Oxford Univ, Plymouth Univ, Portsmouth Univ,
Queen Mary & Westfield, Reading Univ, Royal Holloway & Bedford, St
Andrews Univ, Salford Univ, Sheffield Hallam Univ, Sheffield Univ, South
Bank Univ, Southampton Univ, SSEES, Staffordshire Univ, Stirling Univ,
Strathclyde Univ, Sunderland Univ, Surrey Univ, Sussex Univ, Swansea,
Teesside Univ, Thames Valley Univ, Ulster Univ, UMIST, Univ Coll London,
Warwick Univ, Westminster Univ, Wolverhampton Univ, York Univ.
Study area: Modern languages.

GLASS
Possible prospectuses: Buckinghamshire Coll, Central England Univ, Edinburgh
Coll Art, Heriot-Watt Univ, Manchester Metropolitan Univ, Royal Coll Art (p/g
only), Sheffield Univ, Staffordshire Univ, Sunderland Univ, West Surrey Coll,
Wolverhampton Univ.
See also: Three-dimensional design.
Study area: Art and design.

GOLDSMITHING
See: Silversmithing.

GOVERNMENT
See: Politics.

GRAPHIC DESIGN
Possible prospectuses: Aberystwyth, Anglia Poly Univ, Bath Coll, Bournemouth
Univ, Bradford & Ilkley, Brighton Univ, Bristol UWE, Camberwell Coll,
Cardiff Inst, Central England Univ, Central Lancashire Univ, Central Saint
Martins, Cheltenham & Gloucester Coll, Colchester Inst, Coventry Univ, De
Montfort Univ, Derby Univ, Duncan of Jordanstone, Dundee Univ, Edinburgh
Coll Art, Falmouth, Glasgow Sch Art, Goldsmiths' Coll, Heriot-Watt Univ,
Humberside Univ, Kent Inst, Kingston Univ, Leeds Metropolitan Univ,
Liverpool John Moores Univ, London Coll Printing, Luton Coll, Manchester

Metropolitan Univ, Middlesex Univ, Norfolk Inst, Northumbria Univ,
Nottingham Trent Univ, Plymouth Univ, Portsmouth Univ, Ravensbourne
Coll, Reading Univ, Robert Gordon Univ, Royal Coll Art (p/g only), Salford
Coll, Southampton Inst, Staffordshire Univ, Teesside Univ, Thames Valley
Univ, Ulster Univ, West Surrey Coll, Westminster Univ, Wolverhampton Univ.
Study area: Art and design.

GREEK, ANCIENT/CLASSICAL

Possible prospectuses: Aberystwyth, Belfast Univ, Birkbeck, Birmingham Univ,
Bristol Univ, Cambridge Univ, Durham Univ, Edinburgh Univ, Exeter Univ,
Glasgow Univ, Kent Univ, King's Coll London, Lampeter, Leeds Univ,
London Bible, Manchester Univ, Newcastle Univ, Nottingham Univ, Oxford
Univ, Reading Univ, Royal Holloway & Bedford, St Andrews Univ, Swansea,
Univ Coll London.
See also: Classics.
Study area: Classics.

GREEK MODERN

Possible prospectuses: Birmingham Univ, Cambridge Univ, Edinburgh Univ,
King's Coll London, Oxford Univ.
Study area: Modern languages.

GUJARATI

Possible prospectuses: SOAS.
See also: Asian studies.
Study area: Asian studies.

H

HARBOURS

See: Civil engineering.

HAUSA

Possible prospectuses: SOAS.
See also: African studies.
Study area: African studies.

HEALTH

Possible prospectuses: Aberdeen Univ, Anglia Poly Univ, Bangor, Bournemouth
Univ, Bristol UWE, Central Lancashire Univ, Chester Coll, City Univ,
Coventry Univ, Crewe & Alsager, Derby Univ, Dundee Univ, East London
Univ, Glasgow Poly, Hull Univ, Humberside Univ, Leeds Metropolitan Univ,
Liverpool John Moores Univ, Liverpool Univ, Luton Coll, Manchester
Metropolitan Univ, North East Wales Inst, North London Univ, Open Univ,
Oxford Brookes Univ, Plymouth Univ, Queen Margaret Coll, Robert Gordon
Univ, Roehampton Inst, S Martin's Coll, Sheffield Hallam Univ, South Bank
Univ, Sunderland Univ, Teesside Univ, West London Inst, West Sussex Inst,
Wolverhampton Univ.

HEBREW
Possible prospectuses: Aberdeen Univ, Belfast Univ, Cambridge Univ, Cardiff, Edinburgh Univ, Glasgow Univ, Jews' Coll, Liverpool Univ, London Bible, Manchester Univ, Oxford Univ, St Andrews Univ, SOAS, Univ Coll London.
See also: Near East studies; religious studies.
Study area: Near East and Islamic studies.

HELLENISTIC STUDIES
See: Classics; Greek, Ancient.

HIGHWAY/TRAFFIC
See: Civil engineering; town planning; transport studies.

HINDI
Possible prospectuses: Cambridge Univ, SOAS, York Univ.

HINDUSTANI
See: Asian studies.

HISPANIC STUDIES
Possible prospectuses: Aberdeen Univ, Belfast Univ, Birkbeck, Birmingham Univ, Bristol Univ, Cardiff, Edinburgh Univ, Glasgow Univ, Hull Univ, King's Coll London, Leeds Univ, Liverpool Univ, Manchester Univ, North London Univ, Nottingham Univ, Portsmouth Univ, Queen Mary & Westfield, St Andrews Univ, Salford Univ, Sheffield Univ, Southampton Univ, Stirling Univ, Swansea, Thames Valley Univ, Wolverhampton Univ.
See also: Iberian studies; Portuguese; Latin American studies; Spanish.
Study areas: European studies; Latin American studies.

HISTORY
Possible prospectuses: Aberdeen Univ, Aberystwyth, Anglia Poly Univ, Bangor, Bangor Normal Coll, Bedford Coll, Belfast Univ, Birkbeck, Birmingham Univ, Bolton Inst, Bradford Univ, Brighton Univ, Bristol Univ, Bristol UWE, Buckingham Univ, Cambridge Univ, Canterbury Christ Church Coll, Cardiff, Central Lancashire Univ, Cheltenham & Gloucester Coll, Chester Coll, Coventry Univ, Crewe & Alsager, De Montfort Univ, Derby Univ, Dundee Univ, Durham Univ, East Anglia Univ, Edge Hill, Edinburgh Univ, Essex Univ,

Exeter Univ, Glamorgan Univ, Glasgow Univ, Goldsmiths' Coll, Hertfordshire
Univ, Homerton, Huddersfield Univ, Hull Univ, Humberside Univ, Keele
Univ, Kent Univ, King Alfred's Coll, King's Coll London, Kingston Univ,
Lampeter, Lancaster Univ, Leeds Univ, Leicester Univ, Liverpool Inst,
Liverpool John Moores Univ, Liverpool Univ, LSE, LSU Southampton, Luton
Coll, Manchester Metropolitan Univ, Manchester Univ, Middlesex Univ, Nene
Coll, Newcastle Univ, North East Wales Inst, North London Univ,
Northumbria Univ, Nottingham Trent Univ, Nottingham Univ, Open Univ,
Oxford Brookes Univ, Oxford Univ, Plymouth Univ, Portsmouth Univ, Queen
Mary & Westfield, Reading Univ, Ripon & York St John, Roehampton Inst,
Royal Holloway & Bedford, St Andrews Univ, St Mark & St John, S Martin's
Coll, St Mary's Coll, Salford Univ, Sheffield Hallam Univ, Sheffield Univ,
SOAS, Southampton Univ, SSEES, Staffordshire Univ, Stirling Univ,
Strathclyde Univ, Sunderland Univ, Sussex Univ, Swansea, Teesside Univ,
Thames Valley Univ, Trinity & All Saints, Ulster Univ, Univ Coll London,
Warwick Univ, West London Inst, West Sussex Inst, Westminster Univ,
Wolverhampton Univ, Worcester Coll, York Univ.
See also: Economic history; social history.
Study area: History.

HISTORY OF ART
See: Fine arts.

HISTORY/PHILOSOPHY OF SCIENCE
Possible prospectuses: Belfast Univ, Cambridge Univ, Keele Univ, Kent Univ,
King's Coll London, Lancaster Univ, Leeds Univ, Leicester Univ, Open Univ,
St Andrews Univ.
Study area: History.

HOME ECONOMICS
Possible prospectuses: Bath Coll, Cardiff, Duncan of Jordanstone, Leeds
Metropolitan Univ, Liverpool John Moores Univ, Manchester Metropolitan
Univ, Middlesex Univ, North London Univ, Queen Margaret Coll, Robert
Gordon Univ, Sheffield Hallam Univ, South Bank Univ, Trinity & All Saints,
Ulster Univ, Worcester Coll.

HORTICULTURE

Possible prospectuses: Central Lancashire Univ, De Montfort Univ, Greenwich Univ, Harper Adams, Hertfordshire Univ, Lancs Coll Agric, Nottingham Univ, Reading Univ, Scottish Agricultural Coll, Strathclyde Univ, Writtle, Wye Coll. *Study areas:* Agriculture, horticulture and forestry.

HOTEL AND CATERING MANAGEMENT

Possible prospectuses: Bournemouth Univ, Brighton Univ, Buckingham Univ, Cardiff, Cardiff Inst, Central England Univ, Central Lancashire Univ, Cheltenham & Gloucester Coll, Colchester Inst, Duncan of Jordanstone, Dundee Univ, Glasgow Poly, Huddersfield Univ, Leeds Metropolitan Univ, Manchester Metropolitan Univ, Middlesex Univ, Napier Univ, North London Univ, Nottingham Trent Univ, Oxford Brookes Univ, Plymouth Univ, Portsmouth Univ, Queen Margaret Coll, Robert Gordon Univ, Salford Coll, Sheffield Hallam Univ, South Bank Univ, Strathclyde Univ, Surrey Univ, Thames Valley Univ, Ulster Univ, Wolverhampton Univ. *Study area:* Hotel and catering management.

HOUSING ADMINISTRATION

Possible prospectuses: Bristol UWE, Edinburgh Coll Art, Edinburgh Univ, Heriot-Watt Univ, Humberside Univ, Salford Univ, Sheffield Hallam Univ, South Bank Univ, Stirling Univ, Ulster Univ, Westminster Univ. *See also: Estate management.*

HUMAN BIOLOGY

Possible prospectuses: Aberdeen Univ, Aston Univ, Cambridge Univ, East London Univ, Hertfordshire Univ, King's Coll London, Leeds Metropolitan Univ, Liverpool Inst, Liverpool Univ, Loughborough Univ, Manchester Univ, Nene Coll, Nottingham Trent Univ, Oxford Brookes Univ, Plymouth Univ, S Martin's Coll, Wolverhampton Univ. *See also: Anatomy; physiology.* *Study areas:* Anatomy; biology; physiology.

HUMAN COMMUNICATION
Possible prospectuses: Coventry Univ, De Montfort Univ, Kent Univ, Lancaster Univ, Leicester Univ, Manchester Metropolitan Univ, Queen Margaret Coll, Sheffield Univ, Ulster Univ.
*See also: **Communication studies; psychology.***
Study areas: Communication studies; psychology.

HUMAN MOVEMENT
See: Movement studies.

HUMAN SCIENCES
Possible prospectuses: Bradford Univ, Brunel Univ, City Univ, East London Univ, Kingston Univ, Loughborough Univ, Nottingham Trent Univ, Open Univ, Oxford Univ, Plymouth Univ, Surrey Univ, Sussex Univ, Teesside Univ, Univ Coll London.
See also: Biosocial science.

HUMANITIES
Possible prospectuses: Bangor Normal Coll, Birkbeck, Bolton Inst, Bradford Univ, Bretton Hall, Brighton Univ, Bristol UWE, Cambridge Univ, Cheltenham & Gloucester Coll, Crewe & Alsager, De Montfort Univ, Derby Univ, East London Univ, Edge Hill, Glamorgan Univ, Glasgow Univ, Greenwich Univ, Hertfordshire Univ, Hull Univ, Humberside Univ, Kent Univ, Kingston Univ, Liverpool John Moores Univ, Luton Coll, Manchester Metropolitan Univ, North London Univ, Northumbria Univ, Nottingham Trent Univ, Open Univ, Oxford Brookes Univ, Plymouth Univ, Roehampton

Inst, Royal Academy Music, Royal Coll Art (p/g only), St Andrews Univ, Southampton Univ, Staffordshire Univ, Stirling Univ, Sussex Univ, Swansea Inst, Teesside Univ, Thames Valley Univ, Trinity Coll Carmarthen, Ulster Univ, Wolverhampton Univ.

HUNGARIAN
Possible prospectuses: Cambridge Univ, SSEES.
Study area: Modern languages.

HYDRAULIC ENGINEERING
See: Civil engineering.

I

IBERIAN STUDIES
Possible prospectuses: Manchester Univ, Southampton Univ, Univ Coll London.
See also: Hispanic studies; Portuguese; Spanish.
Study area: European studies.

ICELANDIC
Possible prospectuses: Univ Coll London.
See also: Scandinavian studies.
Study area: Modern languages.

ILLUSTRATION
See: Graphic design.

IMMUNOLOGY
Possible prospectuses: Aberdeen Univ, Brunel Univ, Edinburgh Univ, Glasgow Univ, King's Coll London, Manchester Univ, Plymouth Univ, Strathclyde Univ, Univ Coll London.
See also: Bacteriology; microbiology.
Study area: Microbiology.

INDIAN STUDIES
See: Asian studies.

INDONESIAN STUDIES
Possible prospectuses: SOAS.
Study area: Asian studies.

INDUSTRIAL DESIGN
Possible prospectuses: Bournemouth Univ, Brunel Univ, Cardiff Inst, Central England Univ, Central Saint Martins, Colchester Inst, Coventry Univ, Cranfield (p/g only), De Montfort Univ, East London Univ, Glasgow Sch Art, Heriot-Watt Univ, Imperial Coll, Loughborough Univ, Manchester Metropolitan Univ, Napier Univ, Northumbria Univ, Open Univ, Ravensbourne Coll, Royal Coll Art (p/g only), Salford Coll, Scottish Coll Textiles, Sheffield Hallam Univ, South Bank Univ, Staffordshire Univ, Teesside Univ, Westminster Univ, Wolverhampton Univ.
See also: Three dimensional design.
Study area: Art and design.

INDUSTRIAL ENGINEERING
Possible prospectuses: Cranfield (p/g only), East London Univ, Heriot-Watt Univ, Hertfordshire Univ, Imperial Coll, Manchester Univ, Napier Univ, Nottingham Trent Univ, Royal Coll Art (p/g only), Surrey Univ, Teesside Univ, Wolverhampton Univ.
Study area: Mechanical and production engineering.

INDUSTRIAL RELATIONS
Possible prospectuses: Bradford Univ, Brunel Univ, Cambridge Univ, Cardiff, Coventry Univ, Glasgow Univ, Humberside Univ, Kent Univ, Lancaster Univ, Leeds Univ, LSE, Scottish Coll Textiles, Southampton Univ, Stirling Univ, Strathclyde Univ, Westminster Univ.
See also: Business studies; economics; law; sociology.
Study area: Industrial relations.

INDUSTRIAL STUDIES
Possible prospectuses: Aberdeen Univ, Bradford Univ, Central England Univ, Loughborough Univ, Napier Univ, Nene Coll, Nottingham Trent Univ, Nottingham Univ, Sheffield Hallam Univ.

INFORMATICS
Possible prospectuses: Brighton Univ, City Univ, Heriot-Watt Univ, Kent Univ, Lampeter, Leeds Metropolitan Univ, Plymouth Univ, Queen Mary & Westfield, Sheffield Hallam Univ, Westminster Univ.

INFORMATION DESIGN
See: Graphic design.

INFORMATION SCIENCE
Possible prospectuses: Aberystwyth, Cambridge Univ, Coventry Univ, Cranfield (p/g only), Hull Univ, Imperial Coll, Luton Coll, North London Univ, Open Univ, Portsmouth Univ, Robert Gordon Univ, South Bank Univ, Staffordshire Univ, Strathclyde Univ, Thames Valley Univ, Westminster Univ.

INFORMATION STUDIES
Possible prospectuses: Aberystwyth, Belfast Univ, Brighton Univ, Brunel Univ, Central England Univ, East London Univ, Falmouth, Hertfordshire Univ, Leeds Metropolitan Univ, Liverpool John Moores Univ, Liverpool Univ, Loughborough Univ, Luton Coll, Manchester Metropolitan Univ, Nene Coll, North London Univ, Northumbria Univ, Queen Margaret Coll, Robert Gordon Univ, Scottish Coll Textiles, Sheffield Univ, Shrivenham, Southampton Inst, Thames Valley Univ.
See also: Library studies.
Study area: Library and information studies.

INFORMATION TECHNOLOGY
Possible prospectuses: Aberystwyth, Aston Univ, Belfast Univ, Bradford Univ, Brighton Univ, Bristol UWE, Brunel Univ, Buckinghamshire Coll, Canterbury Christ Church Coll, Cardiff Inst, Central England Univ, Central Lancashire Univ, Cheltenham & Gloucester Coll, Chester Coll, Coventry Univ, Cranfield (p/g only), Dartmouth, De Montfort Univ, Derby Univ, Edge Hill, Essex Univ,

European Business Sch, Exeter Univ, Glamorgan Univ, Glasgow Poly, Greenwich Univ, Heriot-Watt Univ, Huddersfield Univ, Humberside Univ, Imperial Coll, Kingston Univ, Lancaster Univ, Liverpool Inst, London Guildhall Univ, Loughborough Univ, Luton Coll, Manchester Metropolitan Univ, Manchester Univ, Middlesex Univ, Napier Univ, North Cheshire Coll, North East Wales Inst, North London Univ, Northumbria Univ, Nottingham Trent Univ, Open Univ, Paisley Univ, Portsmouth Univ, Reading Univ, Robert Gordon Univ, St Mark & St John, Salford Coll, Salford Univ, Scottish Coll Textiles, Sheffield Hallam Univ, Sheffield Univ, Shrivenham, South Bank Univ, Southampton Inst, Staffordshire Univ, Strathclyde Univ, Sunderland Univ, Surrey Univ, Swansea Inst, Teesside Univ, Thames Valley Univ, UMIST, West London Inst, Westminster Univ, Wolverhampton Univ, York Univ.
Study area: Information technology.

INSTRUMENTATION
Possible prospectuses: Brunel Univ, Cranfield (p/g only), Glasgow Poly, Heriot-Watt Univ, Luton Coll, Manchester Metropolitan Univ, Open Univ, Robert Gordon Univ, Sheffield Hallam Univ, Teesside Univ.

INSURANCE
See: Actuarial studies; business studies.

INTERIOR DESIGN
Possible prospectuses: Brighton Univ, Buckinghamshire Coll, Cardiff Inst, Central England Univ, Chelsea, De Montfort Univ, Duncan of Jordanstone, Dundee Univ, Edinburgh Coll Art, Glasgow Sch Art, Heriot-Watt Univ, Kent Inst, Kingston Univ, Leeds Metropolitan Univ, London Guildhall Univ, Manchester Metropolitan Univ, Middlesex Univ, Napier Univ, North London Univ, Nottingham Trent Univ, Ravensbourne Coll, Royal Coll Art (p/g only), Salford Coll, Teesside Univ, West Surrey Coll.
Study area: Art and design.

INTERNATIONAL BUSINESS
Possible prospectuses: Aston Univ, Bournemouth Univ, Bristol UWE, Buckinghamshire Coll, Central Lancashire Univ, Coventry Univ, Greenwich Univ, Heriot-Watt Univ, Liverpool John Moores Univ, Luton Coll, Manchester Metropolitan Univ, Newcastle Univ, Northumbria Univ, Paisley Univ, Plymouth Univ, Sheffield Hallam Univ, South Bank Univ, Staffordshire Univ, Strathclyde Univ, Surrey Univ, Teesside Univ, UMIST, Westminster Univ, Wolverhampton Univ.
See also: Business studies.

INTERNATIONAL RELATIONS
Possible prospectuses: Aberdeen Univ, Aberystwyth, Birmingham Univ, Bradford Univ, City Univ, Coventry Univ, Hull Univ, Keele Univ, Kent Univ, Lancaster Univ, LSE, Manchester Metropolitan Univ, Nottingham Trent Univ, Open Univ, Reading Univ, St Andrews Univ, Scottish Coll Textiles, South Bank Univ, Southampton Univ, Staffordshire Univ, Surrey Univ, Sussex Univ, Thames Valley Univ, Ulster Univ, Warwick Univ.
See also: Politics; war studies.
Study area: Politics and government.

INTERPRETATION AND TRANSLATION
Possible prospectuses: British Institute in Paris, Heriot-Watt Univ, Luton Coll,
Salford Univ, Thames Valley Univ, Ulster Univ.
Study area: Modern languages.

INVESTMENT
See: Business studies.

IRANIAN STUDIES
See: Near East studies.

IRISH STUDIES
Possible prospectuses: Aberystwyth, Belfast Univ, Liverpool Univ, Manchester
Univ, North London Univ, St Mary's Coll, Ulster Univ.
See also: Celtic studies.
Study area: European studies.

ISLAMIC STUDIES
Possible prospectuses: Durham Univ, Edinburgh Univ, Exeter Univ, Lampeter,
Manchester Univ, Newcastle Univ, Oxford Univ, St Andrews Univ, SOAS.
Study area: Near East and Islamic studies.

ITALIAN
Possible prospectuses: Aberystwyth, Anglia Poly Univ, Belfast Univ,
Birmingham Univ, Bristol Univ, Cambridge Univ, Cardiff, Central Lancashire
Univ, Durham Univ, Edinburgh Univ, European Business Sch, Exeter Univ,
Glasgow Univ, Hull Univ, Kent Univ, Lancaster Univ, Leeds Univ, Leicester
Univ, Luton Coll, Manchester Univ, National Extension Coll, Nene Coll,
Oxford Univ, Plymouth Univ, Reading Univ, Royal Holloway & Bedford,
Salford Univ, Sheffield Hallam Univ, SSEES, Strathclyde Univ, Sussex Univ,
Swansea, Univ Coll London, Warwick Univ, Westminster Univ.
Study area: Modern languages.

J

JAPANESE
Possible prospectuses: Cambridge Univ, Cardiff, Durham Univ, Edinburgh
Univ, Glasgow Poly, Lancaster Univ, Leeds Univ, Liverpool John Moores
Univ, Luton Coll, Oxford Univ, Royal Holloway & Bedford, Sheffield Hallam
Univ, Sheffield Univ, SOAS, Stirling Univ, Sussex Univ, Ulster Univ.
See also: Asian studies.
Study area: Asian studies.

JEWELLERY
Possible prospectuses: Buckinghamshire Coll, Central England Univ, Central
Saint Martins, Crewe & Alsager, Duncan of Jordanstone, Dundee Univ,
Edinburgh Coll Art, Glasgow Sch Art, Heriot-Watt Univ, London Guildhall
Univ, Loughborough Coll, Middlesex Univ, Robert Gordon Univ, Royal Coll
Art (p/g only), Sheffield Hallam Univ, Ulster Univ.
See also: Silversmithing; three-dimensional design.
Study area: Art and design.

JEWISH STUDIES
Possible prospectuses: Jews' Coll, Manchester Univ, SOAS, SSEES, Univ Coll London.
*See also: **Hebrew.***
Study area: Religious studies and theology.

JOURNALISM
Possible prospectuses: Cardiff, Central Lancashire Univ, City Univ, Falmouth, London Coll Printing, Luton Coll, Napier Univ, Nottingham Trent Univ.
*See also: **Communication studies.***

JURISPRUDENCE
*See: **Law.***

L

LABOUR
*See: **Business studies; economics; industrial relations; law; politics; sociology.***

LAND ADMINISTRATION
*See: **Estate management.***

LAND ECONOMY
Possible prospectuses: Aberdeen Univ, Cambridge Univ, Harper Adams, Hull Univ, Luton Coll, Paisley Univ, Royal Agricultural Coll, Scottish Agricultural Coll, Sheffield Hallam Univ, Wye Coll.

LAND SURVEYING
*See: **Quantity surveying.***

LANDSCAPE ARCHITECTURE
Possible prospectuses: Central England Univ, Cheltenham & Gloucester Coll, Edinburgh Coll Art, Greenwich Univ, Heriot-Watt Univ, Leeds Metropolitan Univ, Manchester Univ, Sheffield Univ.

LANDSCAPE STUDIES
Possible prospectuses: Edinburgh Coll Art, Heriot-Watt Univ, Hertfordshire Univ, Kingston Univ, Manchester Metropolitan Univ, Manchester Univ, Reading Univ, Sheffield Univ, Writtle.
See also: Architecture; geography; horticulture.

LANGUAGES
See: individual languages (eg *French*) or regional studies (eg *African studies*).

LASER
See: Physics.

LATIN
Possible prospectuses: Aberystwyth, Belfast Univ, Birkbeck, Birmingham Univ, Bristol Univ, Cambridge Univ, Durham Univ, Edinburgh Univ, Exeter Univ, Glasgow Univ, Hull Univ, Kent Univ, King's Coll London, Lampeter, Leeds Univ, Manchester Univ, Newcastle Univ, Nottingham Univ, Oxford Univ, Reading Univ, Royal Holloway & Bedford, St Andrews Univ, Swansea, Univ Coll London, Warwick Univ.
See also: Classics.
Study area: Classics.

LATIN AMERICAN STUDIES
Possible prospectuses: Aberdeen Univ, Bristol Univ, Cambridge Univ, Essex Univ, Glasgow Univ, Goldsmiths' Coll, King's Coll London, Leeds Univ, Liverpool Univ, Manchester Univ, Newcastle Univ, North London Univ, Portsmouth Univ, St Andrews Univ, Southampton Univ, Univ Coll London, Warwick Univ.
See also: Hispanic studies; Iberian studies; Portuguese; Spanish.
Study area: Latin American studies.

LAW
Possible prospectuses: Aberdeen Univ, Aberystwyth, Anglia Poly Univ, Belfast Univ, Birkbeck, Birmingham Univ, Bournemouth Univ, Bristol Univ, Bristol UWE, Brunel Univ, Buckingham Univ, Buckland, Cambridge Univ, Cardiff, Central England Univ, Central Lancashire Univ, City Univ, Coventry Univ, De Montfort Univ, Derby Univ, Dundee Univ, Durham Univ, East Anglia Univ, East London Univ, Edinburgh Univ, Essex Univ, Exeter Univ, Glamorgan Univ, Glasgow Poly, Glasgow Univ, Greenwich Univ, Hertfordshire Univ,

Holborn Coll, Huddersfield Univ, Hull Univ, Keele Univ, Kent Univ, King's
Coll London, Kingston Univ, Lancaster Univ, Leeds Metropolitan Univ, Leeds
Univ, Leicester Univ, Liverpool John Moores Univ, Liverpool Univ, London
Guildhall Univ, LSE, Luton Coll, Manchester Metropolitan Univ, Manchester
Univ, Middlesex Univ, Napier Univ, National Extension Coll, Nene Coll,
Newcastle Univ, North London Univ, Northumbria Univ, Nottingham Trent
Univ, Nottingham Univ, Oxford Brookes Univ, Oxford Univ, Plymouth Univ,
Queen Mary & Westfield, Rapid Results Coll, Reading Univ, Robert Gordon
Univ, Sheffield Hallam Univ, Sheffield Univ, SOAS, South Bank Univ,
Southampton Inst, Southampton Univ, Staffordshire Univ, Strathclyde Univ,
Surrey Univ, Sussex Univ, Swansea, Swansea Inst, Teesside Univ, Thames
Valley Univ, Univ Coll London, Warwick Univ, Westminster Univ,
Wolverhampton Univ.
Study area: Law.

LEATHER TECHNOLOGY
Possible prospectuses: Nene Coll.

LEISURE STUDIES
Possible prospectuses: Anglia Poly Univ, Bolton Inst, Bournemouth Univ,
Bradford & Ilkley, Buckinghamshire Coll, Canterbury Christ Church Coll,
Cardiff Inst, Cheltenham & Gloucester Coll, Coventry Univ, Farnborough Coll,
Heriot-Watt Univ, Humberside Univ, Leeds Metropolitan Univ, Luton Coll,
Moray House, North Cheshire Coll, North London Univ, Southampton Inst,
Thames Valley Univ, Ulster Univ, West London Inst, Wolverhampton Univ,
Writtle.

LEVANT
See: Archaeology.

LIBRARY STUDIES
Possible prospectuses: Aberystwyth, Brighton Univ, Central England Univ,
Leeds Metropolitan Univ, Liverpool John Moores Univ, Loughborough Univ,
Manchester Metropolitan Univ, North London Univ, Northumbria Univ,
Robert Gordon Univ, Thames Valley Univ.
See also: Information studies.
Study area: Library and information studies.

LIFE SCIENCE
See: Biology.

LINGUISTICS
Possible prospectuses: Bangor, Birkbeck, Brighton Univ, Cambridge Univ,
Central Lancashire Univ, Durham Univ, East Anglia Univ, Edinburgh Univ,
Essex Univ, Exeter Univ, Hertfordshire Univ, Kent Univ, Lancaster Univ,
Leeds Univ, Manchester Univ, Newcastle Univ, Reading Univ, Ripon & York
St John, St Mark & St John, Sheffield Univ, SOAS, Southampton Univ, Surrey
Univ, Sussex Univ, UMIST, Univ Coll London, Westminster Univ,
Wolverhampton Univ, York Univ.
See also: individual languages, eg *French.*
Study area: Linguistics.

LITERATURE
See: individual languages, eg *Chinese.*

LOGIC
See: Mathematics; philosophy.

M

MALAY
Possible prospectuses: SOAS.
Study area: Asian studies.

MANAGEMENT
Possible prospectuses: Aberdeen Univ, Aston Univ, Birkbeck, Birmingham Univ, Bradford Univ, Bristol UWE, Brunel Univ, Cambridge Univ, Cardiff, Central Lancashire Univ, City Univ, Coventry Univ, Cranfield (p/g only), Cranwell, Dundee Inst, Dundee Univ, East London Univ, Edge Hill, European Business Sch, Glamorgan Univ, Glasgow Poly, Glasgow Univ, Heriot-Watt Univ, Hertfordshire Univ, Holborn Coll, Hull Univ, Humberside Univ, Keele Univ, Kent Univ, King's Coll London, Kingston Univ, Lancaster Univ, Leeds Metropolitan Univ, Leeds Univ, Liverpool Univ, London Business Sch (p/g only), Loughborough Univ, LSE, Luton Coll, Manadon, Manchester Business Sch (p/g only), Manchester Univ, Napier Univ, Newcastle Univ, North London Univ, Nottingham Trent Univ, Nottingham Univ, Oxford Brookes Univ, Oxford Univ, Paisley Univ, Reading Univ, Robert Gordon Univ, Royal Agricultural Coll, Royal Holloway & Bedford, St Andrews Univ, Salford Univ, Scottish Coll Textiles, Sheffield Hallam Univ, Sheffield Univ, Silsoe Coll, South Bank Univ, Stirling Univ, Strathclyde Univ, Sunderland Univ, Sussex Univ, Swansea, Teesside Univ, Thames Valley Univ, Trinity & All Saints, Ulster Univ, UMIST, Warwick Univ, Westminster Univ, Wolverhampton Univ, Writtle, Wye Coll.
See also: Business studies; economics; estate management; hotel and catering management; public administration.
Study area: Business studies.

MANUFACTURING ENGINEERING
Possible prospectuses: Aberdeen Univ, Anglia Poly Univ, Aston Univ, Bath Univ, Belfast Univ, Birmingham Univ, Bolton Inst, Bradford Univ, Bristol Univ, Bristol UWE, Brunel Univ, Cambridge Univ, Cardiff, Cardiff Inst, Central England Univ, Coventry Univ, Cranfield (p/g only), Derby Univ, Dundee Univ, Durham Univ, East London Univ, Exeter Univ, Glamorgan Univ, Glasgow Poly, Heriot-Watt Univ, Hertfordshire Univ, Huddersfield Univ, Hull Univ, Humberside Univ, Imperial Coll, Kingston Univ, Leeds Metropolitan Univ, Leeds Univ, Liverpool John Moores Univ, Liverpool Univ, Loughborough Univ, Luton Coll, Manchester Metropolitan Univ, Manchester Univ, Middlesex Univ, North East Wales Inst, Northumbria Univ, Nottingham Trent Univ, Nottingham Univ, Paisley Univ, Plymouth Univ, Portsmouth Univ, Salford Coll, Salford Univ, Sheffield Hallam Univ, Staffordshire Univ, Strathclyde Univ, Sunderland Univ, Teesside Univ, Ulster Univ, UMIST, Warwick Univ, Westminster Univ, Wolverhampton Univ.
See also: Production engineering.
Study area: Mechanical and production engineering.

MARINE ARCHITECTURE
Possible prospectuses: Newcastle Univ, Strathclyde Univ, Univ Coll London.
See also: Naval architecture; naval engineering.
Study area: Marine technology.

MARINE BIOLOGY
Possible prospectuses: Aberdeen Univ, Bangor, Heriot-Watt Univ, Hull Univ,
Liverpool Univ, Newcastle Univ, Portsmouth Univ, Queen Mary & Westfield,
St Andrews Univ, Southampton Univ, Stirling Univ, Swansea.
See also: Maritime studies.
Study area: Biology.

MARINE ENGINEERING
Possible prospectuses: Cranfield (p/g only), Dartmouth, Heriot-Watt Univ,
Liverpool John Moores Univ, Liverpool Univ, Manadon, Newcastle Univ,
Surrey Univ.
Study area: Marine technology.

MARITIME STUDIES
Possible prospectuses: Bangor, Cardiff, Dartmouth, Liverpool John Moores
Univ, Manadon, Plymouth Univ, Southampton Inst.
Study area: Maritime studies.

MARKETING
Possible prospectuses: Aberystwyth, Aston Univ, Bournemouth Univ, Bradford
Univ, Central Lancashire Univ, Coventry Univ, De Montfort Univ, Derby
Univ, European Business Sch, Glamorgan Univ, Glasgow Poly, Greenwich
Univ, Harper Adams, Hertfordshire Univ, Huddersfield Univ, Humberside
Univ, Kingston Univ, Lancaster Univ, London Guildhall Univ, Loughborough
Univ, Luton Coll, Manchester Metropolitan Univ, Newcastle Univ, North
London Univ, Oxford Brookes Univ, Paisley Univ, Plymouth Univ, Robert
Gordon Univ, Roehampton Inst, Royal Agricultural Coll, Salford Univ, Scottish
Coll Textiles, Silsoe Coll, Staffordshire Univ, Stirling Univ, Strathclyde Univ,
Sunderland Univ, Teesside Univ, Ulster Univ, UMIST, Westminster Univ,
Wolverhampton Univ, Writtle.
See also: Business studies.
Study area: Business studies.

MATERIALS SCIENCE
Possible prospectuses: Aston Univ, Bath Univ, Birmingham Univ, Brunel Univ,
Cambridge Univ, Coventry Univ, Cranfield (p/g only), Cranwell, Dundee Univ,
Durham Univ, Greenwich Univ, Heriot-Watt Univ, Imperial Coll, Leeds Univ,
Liverpool Univ, Loughborough Univ, Manchester Metropolitan Univ,
Manchester Univ, North East Wales Inst, Nottingham Univ, Open Univ,

Oxford Univ, Queen Mary & Westfield, Robert Gordon Univ, Sheffield Hallam Univ, Sheffield Univ, Shrivenham, Strathclyde Univ, Sunderland Univ, Surrey Univ, Swansea, UMIST, Wolverhampton Univ.
See also: Chemistry; engineering; metallurgy.
Study area: Metallurgy and materials science.

MATERIALS TECHNOLOGY
Possible prospectuses: Birmingham Univ, Bradford Univ, Brunel Univ, Coventry Univ, Cranfield (p/g only), Cranwell, Heriot-Watt Univ, Imperial Coll, Leeds Univ, Loughborough Univ, Manchester Univ, Northumbria Univ, Nottingham Univ, Open Univ, Plymouth Univ, Robert Gordon Univ, Sheffield Hallam Univ, Sheffield Univ, Surrey Univ, Swansea, UMIST.
Study area: Metallurgy and materials science.

MATHEMATICS
Possible prospectuses: Aberdeen Univ, Aberystwyth, Anglia Poly Univ, Aston Univ, Bangor, Bangor Normal Coll, Bath Univ, Belfast Univ, Birkbeck, Birmingham Univ, Bolton Inst, Bradford Univ, Brighton Univ, Bristol Univ, Brunel Univ, Buckingham Univ, Cambridge Univ, Canterbury Christ Church Coll, Cardiff, Central Lancashire Univ, Cheltenham & Gloucester Coll, Chester Coll, City Univ, Coventry Univ, Crewe & Alsager, De Montfort Univ, Derby Univ, Dundee Inst, Dundee Univ, Durham Univ, East Anglia Univ, East London Univ, Edge Hill, Edinburgh Univ, Essex Univ, Exeter Univ, Glamorgan Univ, Glasgow Poly, Glasgow Univ, Goldsmiths' Coll, Greenwich Univ, Heriot-Watt Univ, Hertfordshire Univ, Homerton, Hull Univ, Imperial Coll, Keele Univ, Kent Univ, King's Coll London, Kingston Univ, Lancaster Univ, Leeds Univ, Leicester Univ, Liverpool Inst, Liverpool John Moores Univ, Liverpool Univ, London Guildhall Univ, Loughborough Univ, LSE, LSU Southampton, Luton Coll, Manchester Metropolitan Univ, Manchester Univ, Middlesex Univ, Napier Univ, Nene Coll, Newcastle Univ, North London Univ, Northumbria Univ, Nottingham Trent Univ, Nottingham Univ, Open Univ, Oxford Brookes Univ, Oxford Univ, Paisley Univ, Plymouth Univ, Portsmouth Univ, Queen Mary & Westfield, Reading Univ, Robert Gordon Univ, Roehampton Inst, Royal Holloway & Bedford, St Andrews Univ, St Mark & St John, S Martin's Coll, St Mary's Coll, Salford Univ, Sheffield Hallam Univ, Sheffield Univ, Shrivenham, South Bank Univ, Southampton Univ, Staffordshire Univ, Stirling Univ, Strathclyde Univ, Sunderland Univ, Surrey Univ, Sussex Univ, Swansea, Teesside Univ, Trinity & All Saints, Ulster Univ, UMIST, Univ Coll London, Warwick Univ, West Sussex Inst, Westminster Univ, Wolverhampton Univ, Worcester Coll, York Univ.
Study area: Mathematical studies.

MECHANICAL ENGINEERING
Possible prospectuses: Aberdeen Univ, Aston Univ, Bath Univ, Belfast Univ, Birmingham Univ, Bradford Univ, Brighton Univ, Bristol Univ, Bristol UWE, Brunel Univ, Cambridge Univ, Cardiff, Cardiff Inst, Central England Univ, Central Lancashire Univ, City Univ, Coventry Univ, Cranfield (p/g only), Cranwell, Dartmouth, De Montfort Univ, Derby Univ, Dundee Inst, Dundee Univ, Durham Univ, Edinburgh Univ, Exeter Univ, Glamorgan Univ, Glasgow Poly, Glasgow Univ, Greenwich Univ, Heriot-Watt Univ, Hertfordshire Univ, Huddersfield Univ, Hull Univ, Humberside Univ, Imperial Coll, Kingston Univ, Lancaster Univ, Leeds Univ, Leicester Univ, Liverpool John Moores Univ, Liverpool Univ, Loughborough Univ, Luton Coll, Manadon, Manchester

Metropolitan Univ, Manchester Univ, Middlesex Univ, Newcastle Univ, Northumbria Univ, Nottingham Trent Univ, Nottingham Univ, Oxford Brookes Univ, Oxford Univ, Paisley Univ, Plymouth Univ, Portsmouth Univ, Queen Mary & Westfield, Reading Univ, Robert Gordon Univ, Salford Univ, Sheffield Hallam Univ, Sheffield Univ, Shrivenham, Silsoe Coll, South Bank Univ, Southampton Univ, Staffordshire Univ, Strathclyde Univ, Sunderland Univ, Surrey Univ, Sussex Univ, Swansea, Teesside Univ, Ulster Univ, UMIST, Univ Coll London, Warwick Univ, Westminster Univ.
See also: Engineering.
Study area: Mechanical and production engineering.

MEDIA AND PRODUCTION
See: Graphic design.

MEDIA STUDIES
Possible prospectuses: Birmingham Univ, Bournemouth Univ, Bristol UWE, Brunel Univ, Canterbury Christ Church Coll, Central England Univ, City Univ, Coventry Univ, De Montfort Univ, Durham Univ, Edge Hill, Exeter Univ, Falmouth, Glamorgan Univ, Glasgow Poly, Huddersfield Univ, Humberside Univ, Kent Inst, King Alfred's Coll, Liverpool John Moores Univ, London Coll Printing, Loughborough Univ, Luton Coll, Manchester Metropolitan Univ, Napier Univ, Nene Coll, North Cheshire Coll, Northumbria Univ, Plymouth Univ, Portsmouth Univ, Royal Holloway & Bedford, St Mark & St John, Salford Coll, Sheffield Hallam Univ, Slade, Staffordshire Univ, Stirling Univ, Sunderland Univ, Sussex Univ, Swansea Inst, Thames Valley Univ, Trinity & All Saints, Ulster Univ, West Surrey Coll, West Sussex Inst, Westminster Univ, Wolverhampton Univ.
See also: Communication studies.
Study area: Communication studies.

MEDICAL LABORATORY SCIENCE
Possible prospectuses: Bradford Univ, Bristol UWE, Cardiff Inst, De Montfort
Univ, Leeds Metropolitan Univ, Manchester Metropolitan Univ, Portsmouth
Univ, Sunderland Univ, Ulster Univ, Westminster Univ.

MEDICINAL CHEMISTRY
Possible prospectuses: Brunel Univ, Dundee Univ, Essex Univ, Exeter Univ,
Glasgow Univ, Hertfordshire Univ, Huddersfield Univ, Leicester Univ,
Loughborough Univ, Newcastle Univ, Sussex Univ, UMIST, Univ Coll
London, Warwick Univ.

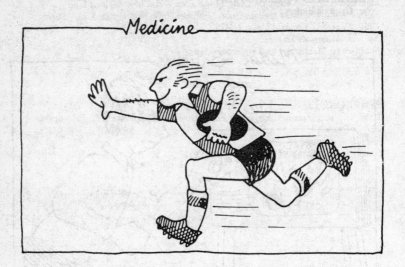

Medicine

MEDICINE
Possible prospectuses: Aberdeen Univ, Belfast Univ, Birmingham Univ, Bristol
Univ, Cambridge Univ, Charing Cross & Westminster, Dundee Univ,
Edinburgh Univ, Glasgow Univ, Imperial Coll, King's Coll Hospital, King's
Coll London, Leeds Univ, Leicester Univ, Liverpool Univ, London Hospital,
Manchester Univ, Newcastle Univ, Nottingham Univ, Oxford Univ, Queen
Mary & Westfield, Royal Free, St Andrews Univ, St Bartholomew's, St
George's, St Mary's Hospital, Sheffield Univ, Southampton Univ, UMDS, Univ
Coll London, Wales Coll Medicine.
Study area: Medicine.

MEDIEVAL STUDIES
Possible prospectuses: Birmingham Univ, Cambridge Univ, Cardiff, Edinburgh
Univ, Lancaster Univ, Liverpool Univ, Manchester Univ, Oxford Univ,
Reading Univ, St Andrews Univ, Sheffield Univ, Southampton Univ, Swansea.
See also: History.
Study area: History.

MEDITERRANEAN STUDIES
Possible prospectuses: Birmingham Univ, Bristol Univ.
See also: Archaeology.
Study area: Archaeology.

MESOPOTAMIA
See: Archaeology.

METALLURGY
Possible prospectuses: Birmingham Univ, Brunel Univ, Camborne Sch Mines,
Cambridge Univ, Cranfield (p/g only), Greenwich Univ, Imperial Coll, Leeds
Univ, Liverpool Univ, Loughborough Univ, Manchester Metropolitan Univ,
Manchester Univ, Newcastle Univ, North East Wales Inst, Oxford Univ,
Salford Univ, Sheffield Hallam Univ, Sheffield Univ, Strathclyde Univ, Surrey
Univ, Swansea, Teesside Univ, UMIST.
See also: Materials science.
Study areas: Metallurgy and materials science.

METAPHYSICS
See: Philosophy.

METEOROLOGY
Possible prospectuses: Dartmouth, Edinburgh Univ, Imperial Coll, Plymouth
Univ, Reading Univ.
See also: Geography.
Study area: Geography.

MICROBIOLOGY
Possible prospectuses: Aberdeen Univ, Aberystwyth, Belfast Univ, Birmingham
Univ, Bradford Univ, Bristol Univ, Bristol UWE, Brunel Univ, Cambridge
Univ, Cardiff, Central Lancashire Univ, Dundee Univ, Durham Univ, East
Anglia Univ, East London Univ, Edinburgh Univ, Glasgow Poly, Glasgow
Univ, Heriot-Watt Univ, Hertfordshire Univ, Imperial Coll, Kent Univ, King's
Coll London, Leeds Univ, Leicester Univ, Liverpool John Moores Univ,
Liverpool Univ, Manchester Metropolitan Univ, Manchester Univ, Napier
Univ, Newcastle Univ, North London Univ, Nottingham Univ, Plymouth
Univ, Queen Mary & Westfield, Reading Univ, Royal Holloway & Bedford, St
Andrews Univ, Sheffield Univ, Strathclyde Univ, Sunderland Univ, Surrey
Univ, Swansea, UMIST, Univ Coll London, Warwick Univ, Wolverhampton
Univ.
See also: Bacteriology; biochemistry; biology; genetics; virology.
Study area: Microbiology.

MICROELECTRONICS
Possible prospectuses: Aberdeen Univ, Anglia Poly Univ, Bradford Univ, Brunel Univ, Derby Univ, Dundee Univ, Edinburgh Univ, Glasgow Poly, Middlesex Univ, Northumbria Univ, Nottingham Trent Univ, Open Univ, Oxford Brookes Univ, Paisley Univ, Robert Gordon Univ, UMIST.
See also: Electronics; computer science.
Study area: Computing.

MIDDLE EAST STUDIES
See: Near East studies; Asian studies.

MIDWIFERY
Possible prospectuses: Bradford Univ, Central Lancashire Univ, Derby Univ, Greenwich Univ, King Alfred's Coll, King's Coll London, Liverpool John Moores Univ, Newcastle Univ, Northumbria Univ, Oxford Brookes Univ, South Bank Univ.
Study area: Nursing.

MINERAL PROCESSING TECHNOLOGY
Possible prospectuses: Birmingham Univ, Camborne Sch Mines, Imperial Coll, Leeds Univ, Leicester Univ, Nottingham Univ.
See also: Geology; mining.

MINERALOGY
See: Geology.

MINING
Possible prospectuses: Camborne Sch Mines, Exeter Univ, Imperial Coll, Leeds Univ, Leicester Univ, Nottingham Univ.

MODERN LANGUAGES
See: individual languages (eg *French*) or regional studies (eg *Scandinavian studies*).

MOLECULAR BIOLOGY
Possible prospectuses: Aberdeen Univ, Bath Univ, Birkbeck, Bradford Univ, Bristol Univ, Bristol UWE, Dundee Univ, Edinburgh Univ, Glasgow Univ, Hertfordshire Univ, Hull Univ, Kent Univ, King's Coll London, Liverpool Univ, Manchester Univ, Royal Holloway & Bedford, Sheffield Univ, Stirling Univ, UMIST.
Study area: Biology; microbiology.

MORAL PHILOSOPHY
See: Philosophy.

MOVEMENT STUDIES
Possible prospectuses: Brighton Univ, Bristol Old Vic, Cardiff Inst, Dartington, Greenwich Univ, Heriot-Watt Univ, Laban Centre, Leeds Metropolitan Univ, Liverpool Univ, Moray House, Nene Coll, Ripon & York St John, Trinity Coll Music.
See also: Dance; drama; physical education.

MUSIC
Possible prospectuses: Aberdeen Univ, Anglia Poly Univ, Bangor, Bangor Normal Coll, Bath Coll, Belfast Univ, Birmingham Conservatoire, Birmingham Univ, Bretton Hall, Brighton Univ, Bristol Univ, Cambridge Univ, Canterbury Christ Church Coll, Cardiff, Central England Univ, City Univ, Colchester Inst, Crewe & Alsager, Dartington, De Montfort Univ, Derby Univ, Durham Univ, East Anglia Univ, Edinburgh Univ, Essex Univ, Exeter Univ, Glasgow Univ, Goldsmiths' Coll, Guildhall, Homerton, Huddersfield Univ, Hull Univ, Keele Univ, King Alfred's Coll, King's Coll London, Kingston Univ, Lancaster Univ, Leeds Univ, Liverpool Inst, Liverpool Univ, London Coll Music, Manchester Univ, Middlesex Univ, Nene Coll, Newcastle Univ, Northumbria Univ, Nottingham Trent Univ, Nottingham Univ, Open Univ, Oxford Brookes Univ, Oxford Univ, Reading Univ, Ripon & York St John, Roehampton Inst, Royal Academy Music, Royal Coll Music, Royal Holloway & Bedford, Royal Northern Coll Music, Royal Scottish Academy, S Martin's Coll, Salford Coll, Sheffield Univ, SOAS, Southampton Univ, Sunderland Univ, Surrey Univ, Sussex Univ, Thames Valley Univ, Trinity Coll Music, Ulster Univ, Warwick Univ, Welsh Coll Music, West London Inst, West Sussex Inst, Wolverhampton Univ, Worcester Coll, York Univ.
Study area: Music.

MUSIC TECHNOLOGY
Possible prospectuses: Bretton Hall, Edinburgh Univ, Leeds Metropolitan Univ, London Guildhall Univ, Salford Coll, Surrey Univ.
Study area: Music.

MYCOLOGY
See: Botany.

MYTHOLOGY
See: Anthropology; classics; psychology.

N

NAUTICAL STUDIES
See: Maritime studies.

NAVAL ARCHITECTURE
Possible prospectuses: Glasgow Univ, Newcastle Univ, Southampton Univ, Strathclyde Univ, Univ Coll London.
See also: Marine architecture; naval engineering.
Study area: Marine technology.

NAVAL ENGINEERING
Possible prospectuses: Dartmouth, Manadon, Univ Coll London.
See also: *Marine engineering.*
Study area: Marine technology.

NAVY
Possible prospectuses: Dartmouth, Manadon.

NEAR EAST STUDIES
Possible prospectuses: Cambridge Univ, Durham Univ, Manchester Univ, Oxford Univ, St Andrews Univ, SOAS.
See also: *Asian studies.*
Study area: Near Eastern and Islamic studies.

NEUROBIOLOGY
See: *Biology; physiology; psychology.*

NEUROSCIENCE
Possible prospectuses: Aberdeen Univ, Cardiff, Central Lancashire Univ, Edinburgh Univ, Glasgow Univ, Manchester Univ, Nottingham Univ, St Andrews Univ, Sheffield Univ, Sussex Univ, Univ Coll London.

NORSE
See: *Anglo Saxon.*

NORWEGIAN
Possible prospectuses: East Anglia Univ, Edinburgh Univ, Hull Univ, University Coll London.
See also: *Scandinavian studies.*
Study area: Modern languages.

NUCLEAR SCIENCE
Possible prospectuses: Manchester Univ, Westminster Univ.
Study area: Physics.

NUCLEAR TECHNOLOGY
Possible prospectuses: Dartmouth, Imperial Coll, Manchester Univ.
Study area: Physics.

NURSING
Possible prospectuses: Anglia Poly Univ, Birmingham Univ, Bournemouth Univ, Bradford Univ, Brighton Univ, Bristol UWE, Buckinghamshire Coll, Canterbury Christ Church Coll, Central England Univ, City Univ, Coventry Univ, De Montfort Univ, Derby Univ, Dundee Inst, East London Univ, Edinburgh Univ, Glasgow Poly, Glasgow Univ, Greenwich Univ, Hertfordshire Univ, Hull Univ, King Alfred's Coll, King's Coll London, Leeds Metropolitan Univ, Liverpool John Moores Univ, Liverpool Univ, Luton Coll, Manchester Metropolitan Univ, Manchester Univ, Middlesex Univ, Nene Coll, North East Wales Inst, Northumbria Univ, Nottingham Univ, Oxford Brookes Univ, Plymouth Univ, Portsmouth Univ, Queen Margaret Coll, Queen Mary & Westfield, Robert Gordon Univ, S Martin's Coll, Sheffield Hallam Univ, South Bank Univ, Southampton Univ, Surrey Univ, Swansea Inst, Teesside Univ, Thames Valley Univ, Ulster Univ, Wales Coll Medicine, Wolverhampton Univ.
Study area: Nursing studies.

NUTRITION
Possible prospectuses: Bradford Univ, Cardiff Inst, Central Lancashire Univ, Glasgow Poly, Huddersfield Univ, Humberside Univ, King's Coll London, Leeds Metropolitan Univ, Newcastle Univ, North London Univ, Nottingham Univ, Oxford Brookes Univ, Queen Margaret Coll, Robert Gordon Univ, South Bank Univ, Southampton Univ, Surrey Univ, Ulster Univ.
Study area: Food science and nutrition.

O

OCCUPATIONAL PSYCHOLOGY
See: Psychology.

OCCUPATIONAL THERAPY
Possible prospectuses: Canterbury Christ Church Coll, Coventry Univ, Derby Univ, East Anglia Univ, Exeter Univ, Glasgow Poly, Liverpool Univ, Luton Coll, Nene Coll, Northumbria Univ, Oxford Brookes Univ, Portsmouth Univ, Queen Margaret Coll, Ripon & York St John, Robert Gordon Univ, S Martin's Coll, Salford Coll, Sheffield Hallam Univ, South Bank Univ, Southampton Univ, Ulster Univ, West London Inst.
Study area: Professions allied to medicine (PAMs).

OCEANOGRAPHY
Possible prospectuses: Aberdeen Univ, Bangor, Dartmouth, East Anglia Univ, Liverpool Univ, Plymouth Univ, Southampton Univ.
Study areas: Geography; maritime studies.

OFFICE ORGANISATION
Possible prospectuses: Buckinghamshire Coll, Central Lancashire Univ, Glasgow Poly, Humberside Univ, Luton Coll, Northumbria Univ, Scottish Coll Textiles, Thames Valley Univ.
See also: Business studies.
Study area: Business studies.

OFFSHORE ENGINEERING
Possible prospectuses: Cranfield (p/g only), Heriot-Watt Univ, Imperial Coll, Newcastle Univ, Robert Gordon Univ, Strathclyde Univ, Surrey Univ.
Study area: Marine technology.

OPERATIONAL RESEARCH
Possible prospectuses: Belfast Univ, Coventry Univ, Essex Univ, Exeter Univ, Hertfordshire Univ, Hull Univ, Kent Univ, Lancaster Univ, Leeds Univ, Loughborough Univ, Manchester Univ, Nottingham Trent Univ, Paisley Univ, Royal Holloway & Bedford, Salford Univ, Southampton Univ, Staffordshire Univ, Strathclyde Univ, Swansea, UMIST, Warwick Univ, Westminster Univ.

OPHTHALMIC OPTICS
Possible prospectuses: Aston Univ, Bradford Univ, Cardiff, City Univ, Glasgow Poly, UMIST.

ORGANISATIONAL BEHAVIOUR
Possible prospectuses: Bradford Univ, European Business Sch, Humberside Univ, Luton Coll, Queen Margaret Coll, Thames Valley Univ.
Study areas: Business studies; psychology.

ORGANISATIONAL STUDIES
Possible prospectuses: Aston Univ, Bradford & Ilkley, Central Lancashire Univ, Heriot-Watt Univ, Lancaster Univ, Luton Coll, Queen Margaret Coll, Reading Univ, Thames Valley Univ.

ORIENTAL STUDIES
See: Asian studies.

ORNITHOLOGY
See: Zoology.

ORTHOPTICS
Possible prospectuses: Coventry Univ, Glasgow Poly, Liverpool Univ, Sheffield Univ.
Study areas: Professions allied to medicine (PAMs).

OSTEOPATHY
Possible prospectuses: Brighton Univ, British Sch Osteopathy, Kingston Univ.

P

PACKAGING TECHNOLOGY
Possible prospectuses: Hertfordshire Univ, Sheffield Hallam Univ, West Herts Coll, West Surrey Coll.

PAINTING
Possible prospectuses: Aberystwyth, Anglia Poly Univ, Bath Coll, Bretton Hall, Brighton Univ, Bristol UWE, Camberwell Coll, Canterbury Christ Church Coll, Cardiff Inst, Central England Univ, Central Lancashire Univ, Central Saint Martins, Chelsea, Cheltenham & Gloucester Coll, Coventry Univ, De Montfort Univ, Duncan of Jordanstone, Dundee Univ, East London Univ, Edinburgh Coll Art, Falmouth, Glasgow Sch Art, Goldsmiths' Coll, Heriot-Watt Univ, Humberside Univ, Kent Inst, Kingston Univ, Lancaster Univ, Liverpool Inst, Liverpool John Moores Univ, Loughborough Coll, Manchester Metropolitan Univ, Middlesex Univ, Newcastle Univ, Norfolk Inst, Northumbria Univ, Portsmouth Univ, Reading Univ, Robert Gordon Univ, Royal Academy Sch

(p/g only), Royal Coll Art (p/g only), Sheffield Hallam Univ, Slade,
Staffordshire Univ, Ulster Univ, West Surrey Coll, West Sussex Inst,
Wimbledon Sch Art, Winchester Sch Art, Wolverhampton Univ.
Study area: Art and design.

PAMs
See: individual subjects eg *podiatry*.

PAPER SCIENCE
Possible prospectuses: UMIST.

PARASITOLOGY
Possible prospectuses: Aberdeen Univ, Glasgow Univ, Imperial Coll, King's
Coll London.
Study area: Biology.

PATHOLOGY
Possible prospectuses: Aberdeen Univ, Belfast Univ, Bradford Univ, Bristol
Univ, Cambridge Univ, Dundee Univ, Edinburgh Univ, Glasgow Univ, Leeds
Univ, Manchester Univ, Reading Univ, St Andrews Univ.

PEACE STUDIES
See: War studies.

PERFORMANCE ARTS
Possible prospectuses: Birmingham Univ, Bretton Hall, Brighton Univ, Bristol
Old Vic, Cheltenham & Gloucester Coll, Coventry Univ, Dartington, De
Montfort Univ, Glasgow Univ, Kent Univ, Laban Centre, Liverpool John
Moores Univ, Loughborough Univ, Middlesex Univ, North Cheshire Coll,

Performance Arts

Nottingham Trent Univ, Plymouth Univ, RADA, Royal Northern Coll Music,
S Martin's Coll, Salford Coll, Trinity Coll Music, Ulster Univ, Welsh Coll
Music/Drama, West Sussex Inst.
See also: Dance; drama and theatre arts.

PERSIAN
Possible prospectuses: Cambridge Univ, Edinburgh Univ, Manchester Univ,
Oxford Univ, SOAS.
See also: Near East studies.
Study area: Near East and Islamic studies.

PERSONNEL ADMINISTRATION
Possible prospectuses: Anglia Poly Univ, Aston Univ, Bradford Univ, East
London Univ, Glamorgan Univ, Humberside Univ, Keele Univ, Luton Coll,
Napier Univ, Paisley Univ, Plymouth Univ, Robert Gordon Univ, Scottish Coll
Textiles, Stirling Univ, Strathclyde Univ, Teesside Univ.

PETROLEUM ENGINEERING
Possible prospectuses: Aberdeen Univ, Imperial Coll, Luton Coll, Robert
Gordon Univ, Strathclyde Univ.
See also: Energy studies.
Study area: Chemical engineering.

PETROLOGY
See: Geology.

PHARMACOLOGY
Possible prospectuses: Aberdeen Univ, Bath Univ, Bradford Univ, Bristol Univ,
Cambridge Univ, Cardiff, Central Lancashire Univ, Dundee Univ, East London
Univ, Edinburgh Univ, Glasgow Univ, Hertfordshire Univ, King's Coll
London, Leeds Univ, Liverpool Univ, Manchester Univ, Nottingham Univ,
Portsmouth Univ, St Andrews Univ, School Pharmacy, Sheffield Univ,
Southampton Univ, Strathclyde Univ, Sunderland Univ, University Coll
London, York Univ.
See also: Pharmacy.
Study area: Pharmacology.

PHARMACY
Possible prospectuses: Aston Univ, Bath Univ, Belfast Univ, Bradford Univ,
Brighton Univ, Cardiff, De Montfort Univ, King's Coll London, Liverpool
John Moores Univ, Manchester Univ, Nottingham Univ, Portsmouth Univ,
Robert Gordon Univ, School Pharmacy, Strathclyde Univ, Sunderland Univ.
See also: Pharmacology.
Study area: Pharmacy.

PHILOSOPHY
Possible prospectuses: Aberdeen Univ, Anglia Poly Univ, Belfast Univ, Birkbeck, Birmingham Univ, Bolton Inst, Bradford Univ, Bristol Univ, Cambridge Univ, Cardiff, Cheltenham & Gloucester Coll, City Univ, Crewe & Alsager, Dundee Univ, Durham Univ, East Anglia Univ, Edinburgh Univ, Essex Univ, Glamorgan Univ, Glasgow Univ, Hertfordshire Univ, Heythrop Coll, Hull Univ, Jews' Coll, Keele Univ, Kent Univ, King's Coll London, Lampeter, Lancaster Univ, Leeds Univ, Liverpool Univ, London Bible, LSE, Manchester Metropolitan Univ, Manchester Univ, Middlesex Univ, National Extension Coll, Nene Coll, North London Univ, Nottingham Univ, Open Univ, Oxford Univ, Reading Univ, St Andrews Univ, St Mark & St John, S Martin's Coll, Sheffield Univ, Southampton Univ, Staffordshire Univ, Stirling Univ, Sunderland Univ, Sussex Univ, Swansea, Teesside Univ, Ulster Univ, University Coll London, Warwick Univ, Wolverhampton Univ, York Univ.
Study area: Philosophy.

PHILOSOPHY OF SCIENCE
See: History of science.

PHONETICS
See: Linguistics.

PHOTOGRAPHY
Possible prospectuses: Bradford & Ilkley, Derby Univ, Edinburgh Coll Art, Falmouth, Glasgow Sch Art, Heriot-Watt Univ, Humberside Univ, Kent Inst, London Coll Printing, Manchester Metropolitan Univ, Middlesex Univ, Napier Univ, Nottingham Trent Univ, Royal Coll Art (p/g only), Sheffield Hallam Univ, Slade, Staffordshire Univ, West Surrey Coll, Westminster Univ, Wolverhampton Univ.
Study area: Art and design.

PHYSICAL EDUCATION
Possible prospectuses: Bangor, Bangor Normal Coll, Bedford Coll, Birmingham Univ, Brighton Univ, Canterbury Christ Church Coll, Cardiff Inst, Cheltenham & Gloucester Coll, Chester Coll, Crewe & Alsager, Edge Hill, Exeter Univ, Greenwich Univ, Heriot-Watt Univ, Leeds Metropolitan Univ, Leeds Univ, Liverpool Inst, Liverpool John Moores Univ, Liverpool Univ, Loughborough Univ, Moray House, Nottingham Trent Univ, Reading Univ, Ripon & York St John, St Mark & St John, St Mary's Coll, Sheffield Hallam Univ, Trinity & All Saints, Warwick Univ, West London Inst, West Sussex Inst, Wolverhampton Univ, Worcester Coll.
See also: Sports studies.

PHYSICAL SCIENCE
See: individual sciences (eg *Chemistry*).

PHYSICS
Possible prospectuses: Aberdeen Univ, Aberystwyth, Aston Univ, Bath Univ, Belfast Univ, Birkbeck, Birmingham Univ, Brighton Univ, Bristol Univ, Bristol UWE, Brunel Univ, Cambridge Univ, Cardiff, Central Lancashire Univ, Coventry Univ, Crewe & Alsager, De Montfort Univ, Derby Univ, Dundee Inst, Dundee Univ, Durham Univ, East Anglia Univ, Edinburgh Univ, Essex Univ, Exeter Univ, Glasgow Poly, Glasgow Univ, Greenwich Univ, Heriot-Watt Univ, Hertfordshire Univ, Hull Univ, Imperial Coll, Keele Univ, Kent Univ, King's Coll London, Kingston Univ, Lancaster Univ, Leeds Univ, Leicester

Univ, Liverpool John Moores Univ, Liverpool Univ, Loughborough Univ, Manchester Metropolitan Univ, Manchester Univ, Napier Univ, Newcastle Univ, North East Wales Inst, North London Univ, Northumbria Univ, Nottingham Trent Univ, Nottingham Univ, Open Univ, Oxford Brookes Univ, Oxford Univ, Paisley Univ, Plymouth Univ, Portsmouth Univ, Queen Mary & Westfield, Reading Univ, Robert Gordon Univ, Royal Holloway & Bedford, St Andrews Univ, S Martin's Coll, Salford Univ, Sheffield Hallam Univ, Sheffield Univ, Shrivenham, Southampton Univ, Staffordshire Univ, Strathclyde Univ, Sunderland Univ, Surrey Univ, Sussex Univ, Swansea, UMIST, University Coll London, Warwick Univ, Westminster Univ, Wolverhampton Univ, York Univ.
Study area: Physics.

PHYSIOLOGY
Possible prospectuses: Aberdeen Univ, Belfast Univ, Birmingham Univ, Bristol Univ, Cambridge Univ, Cardiff, Central Lancashire Univ, Crewe & Alsager, Dundee Univ, East Anglia Univ, East London Univ, Edinburgh Univ, Glasgow Univ, Hertfordshire Univ, King's Coll London, Leeds Univ, Leicester Univ, Liverpool Univ, Loughborough Univ, Manchester Metropolitan Univ, Manchester Univ, Newcastle Univ, Oxford Univ, Queen Mary & Westfield, Reading Univ, Royal Holloway & Bedford, St Andrews Univ, Sheffield Univ, Southampton Univ, Sunderland Univ, University Coll London, Westminster Univ, York Univ.
Study area: Physiology.

PHYSIOTHERAPY
Possible prospectuses: Bath Univ, Birmingham Univ, Bradford Univ, Brighton Univ, Bristol UWE, Coventry Univ, East Anglia Univ, East London Univ, Glasgow Poly, Hertfordshire Univ, Keele Univ, King's Coll London, Leeds Metropolitan Univ, Liverpool Univ, Luton Coll, Manchester Univ, Northumbria Univ, Nottingham Univ, Queen Margaret Coll, Robert Gordon Univ, Salford Coll, Sheffield Hallam Univ, Southampton Univ, Teesside Univ, Ulster Univ, University Coll London, West London Inst, Westminster Univ, Wolverhampton Univ.
Study area: Professions allied to medicine (PAMs).

PLANETARY PHYSICS
See: Astrophysics.

PLANT SCIENCE
See: Botany.

PLASTICS
See: Polymers.

PODIATRY
Possible prospectuses: Belfast Univ, Brighton Univ, Cardiff Inst, Central England Univ, Derby Univ, Glasgow Poly, LSU Southampton, Nene Coll, Queen Margaret Coll, Salford Coll, Sunderland Univ, University Coll London, Westminster Univ.
Study area: Professions allied to medicine (PAMs).

POLISH
Possible prospectuses: Cambridge Univ, Glasgow Univ, SSEES.
Study area: Modern languages.

POLITICAL ECONOMY
See: Economics.

Politics

BEING IN POLITICS MEANS NEVER HAVING TO SAY YOU'RE SORRY

POLITICS
Possible prospectuses: Aberdeen Univ, Aberystwyth, Aston Univ, Bath Univ, Belfast Univ, Birkbeck, Birmingham Univ, Bradford Univ, Bristol Univ, Bristol UWE, Brunel Univ, Buckingham Univ, Cambridge Univ, Cardiff, Central England Univ, Central Lancashire Univ, Coventry Univ, De Montfort Univ, Dundee Univ, Durham Univ, East Anglia Univ, Edinburgh Univ, Essex Univ, Exeter Univ, Glasgow Poly, Glasgow Univ, Goldsmiths' Coll, Greenwich Univ, Huddersfield Univ, Hull Univ, Keele Univ, Kent Univ, Kingston Univ, Lancaster Univ, Leeds Univ, Leicester Univ, Liverpool John Moores Univ, Liverpool Univ, London Guildhall Univ, Loughborough Univ, LSE, LSU Southampton, Manadon, Manchester Metropolitan Univ, Manchester Univ, Middlesex Univ, Newcastle Univ, North London Univ, Northumbria Univ, Nottingham Univ, Open Univ, Oxford Brookes Univ, Oxford Univ, Plymouth Univ, Portsmouth Univ, Queen Mary & Westfield, Reading Univ, Royal Holloway & Bedford, St Andrews Univ, Salford Univ, Sheffield Hallam Univ, Sheffield Univ, SOAS, South Bank Univ, Southampton Univ, Staffordshire Univ, Stirling Univ, Strathclyde Univ, Sunderland Univ, Sussex Univ, Swansea, Teeside Univ, Thames Valley Univ, Ulster Univ, Warwick Univ, Westminster Univ, Wolverhampton Univ, York Univ.
Study area: Politics and government.

POLLUTION
Possible prospectuses: Bradford Univ, Cranfield (p/g only), Glamorgan Univ, Hertfordshire Univ, Luton Coll, South Bank Univ, Teeside Univ.
See also: Ecology; environmental science; environmental studies.

POLYMERS
Possible prospectuses: Aberdeen Univ, Birmingham Univ, Brunel Univ, Cranfield (p/g only), Heriot-Watt Univ, Lancaster Univ, Loughborough Univ, Manchester Metropolitan Univ, Manchester Univ, Napier Univ, North East Wales Inst, North London Univ, Queen Mary & Westfield, Scottish Coll Textiles, Sheffield Univ, Sussex Univ, UMIST.
See also: Chemistry; materials science.
Study areas: Chemistry; chemical engineering; metallurgy and materials science.

PORTUGUESE
Possible prospectuses: Aberystwyth, Belfast Univ, Birmingham Univ, Cambridge Univ, Cardiff, Edinburgh Univ, Glasgow Univ, King's Coll London, Leeds Univ, Liverpool Univ, Manchester Univ, Oxford Univ, Portsmouth Univ, Salford Univ, Sheffield Hallam Univ, Southampton Univ.
See also: Hispanic studies; Iberian studies; Latin American studies.
Study area: Modern languages.

PRINTING AND TYPOGRAPHY
Possible prospectuses: Hertfordshire Univ, Kent Inst, Liverpool Inst, London Coll Printing, Manchester Metropolitan Univ, Napier Univ, Reading Univ, West Herts Coll.
Study area: Art and design.

PRINTMAKING
Possible prospectuses: Anglia Poly Univ, Bretton Hall, Brighton Univ, Bristol UWE, Camberwell Coll, Central England Univ, Central Lancashire Univ, Central Saint Martins, Chelsea, Cheltenham & Gloucester Coll, Derby Univ, Duncan of Jordanstone, Dundee Univ, Edinburgh Coll Art, Falmouth, Glasgow Sch Art, Heriot-Watt Univ, Humberside Univ, Kent Inst, Kingston Univ, London Coll Printing, Loughborough Coll, Manchester Metropolitan Univ, Middlesex Univ, Norfolk Inst, Northumbria Univ, Portsmouth Univ, Reading Univ, Robert Gordon Univ, Royal Coll Art (p/g only), Sheffield Hallam Univ, Slade, Staffordshire Univ, West Herts Coll, West Surrey Coll, Winchester Sch Art, Wolverhampton Univ.
Study area: Art and design.

PROBATION
See: Social work.

PRODUCT DESIGN
Possible prospectuses: Bournemouth Univ, Brunel Univ, Buckinghamshire Coll, Cardiff Inst, Central Lancashire Univ, Central Saint Martins, Coventry Univ, East London Univ, Glasgow Sch Art, Glasgow Univ, Heriot-Watt Univ, Hertfordshire Univ, Huddersfield Univ, Leeds Metropolitan Univ, Loughborough Univ, Northumbria Univ, Nottingham Trent Univ, Ravensbourne Coll, Robert Gordon Univ, Salford Coll, Sheffield Hallam Univ, Staffordshire Univ, Strathclyde Univ, Teesside Univ, Westminster Univ, Wolverhampton Univ.

PRODUCTION ENGINEERING
Possible prospectuses: Aston Univ, Birmingham Univ, Bradford Univ, Brighton Univ, Bristol UWE, Brunel Univ, Cambridge Univ, Cardiff Inst, Central England Univ, Coventry Univ, Cranfield (p/g only), De Montfort Univ, East London Univ, Glamorgan Univ, Glasgow Poly, Heriot-Watt Univ, Imperial Coll, Kingston Univ, Liverpool John Moores Univ, Loughborough Univ, Luton Coll, Manchester Metropolitan Univ, Manchester Univ, Newcastle Univ, North East Wales Inst, Nottingham Trent Univ, Nottingham Univ, Paisley Univ, Portsmouth Univ, Robert Gordon Univ, South Bank Univ, Staffordshire Univ, Strathclyde Univ, Sunderland Univ, Teesside Univ, UMIST, Warwick Univ, Westminster Univ, Wolverhampton Univ.
Study area: Mechanical and production engineering.

PROFESSIONS ALLIED TO MEDICINE (PAMs)
See: individual subjects eg *podiatry.*

PROGRAMMING
See: Computing; computer science.

PSYCHOLOGY
Possible prospectuses: Aberdeen Univ, Aston Univ, Bangor, Belfast Univ, Birkbeck, Birmingham Univ, Bolton Inst, Bradford Univ, Bristol Univ, Bristol UWE, Brunel Univ, Buckingham Univ, Cambridge Univ, Cardiff, Cardiff Inst, Central Lancashire Univ, Cheltenham & Gloucester Coll, Chester Coll, City

Univ, Cranfield (p/g only), Crewe & Alsager, Dundee Univ, Durham Univ, East London Univ, Edinburgh Univ, Essex Univ, Exeter Univ, Glamorgan Univ, Glasgow Poly, Glasgow Univ, Goldsmiths' Coll, Hertfordshire Univ, Huddersfield Univ, Hull Univ, Humberside Univ, Keele Univ, Kent Univ, Lancaster Univ, Leeds Univ, Leicester Univ, Liverpool Inst, Liverpool John Moores Univ, Liverpool Univ, London Guildhall Univ, Loughborough Univ, LSE, Luton Coll, Manchester Metropolitan Univ, Manchester Univ, Middlesex Univ, Nene Coll, Newcastle Univ, North London Univ, Northumbria Univ, Nottingham Trent Univ, Nottingham Univ, Open Univ, Oxford Brookes Univ, Oxford Univ, Plymouth Univ, Portsmouth Univ, Reading Univ, Roehampton Inst, Royal Holloway & Bedford, St Andrews Univ, Sheffield Hallam Univ, Sheffield Univ, Southampton Univ, Staffordshire Univ, Stirling Univ, Strathclyde Univ, Sunderland Univ, Surrey Univ, Sussex Univ, Swansea, Teesside Univ, Thames Valley Univ, Trinity & All Saints, Ulster Univ, University Coll London, Warwick Univ, Westminster Univ, Wolverhampton Univ, Worcester Coll, York Univ.
Study area: Psychology.

PUBLIC ADMINISTRATION
Possible prospectuses: Anglia Poly Univ, Aston Univ, Bangor Normal Coll, Birmingham Univ, Brunel Univ, De Montfort Univ, Durham Univ, Essex Univ, Glamorgan Univ, Glasgow Poly, Hull Univ, Kent Univ, Leeds Univ, Liverpool Univ, LSE, Luton Coll, Manchester Metropolitan Univ, Manchester Univ, Nottingham Trent Univ, Open Univ, Robert Gordon Univ, Royal Holloway & Bedford, Sheffield Hallam Univ, Southampton Inst, Southampton Univ, Staffordshire Univ, Strathclyde Univ, Teesside Univ, Trinity & All Saints.
See also: Social administration.
Study area: Public administration.

PUBLIC HEALTH
Possible prospectuses: Cardiff Inst, Glasgow Poly, Luton Coll, Open Univ, South Bank Univ, Sunderland Univ.
See also: Environmental health.

PUBLIC RELATIONS
Possible prospectuses: Bournemouth Univ, Leeds Metropolitan Univ, Luton Coll, St Mark & St John, Ulster Univ, Westminster Univ.

PUBLISHING
Possible prospectuses: London Coll Printing, Napier Univ, Oxford Brookes Univ, Robert Gordon Univ, Thames Valley Univ, West Herts Coll.

Q

QUALITY CONTROL
See: Production engineering.

QUANTITY SURVEYING
Possible prospectuses: Anglia Poly Univ, Bath Univ, Bristol UWE, Central England Univ, Central Lancashire Univ, Dundee Inst, Glamorgan Univ, Glasgow Coll Building, Glasgow Poly, Greenwich Univ, Heriot-Watt Univ, Kingston Univ, Leeds Metropolitan Univ, Liverpool John Moores Univ,

Loughborough Univ, Luton Coll, Napier Univ, Nene Coll, North East Wales Inst, Northumbria Univ, Nottingham Trent Univ, Portsmouth Univ, Reading Univ, Robert Gordon Univ, Salford Univ, Sheffield Hallam Univ, South Bank Univ, Staffordshire Univ, Ulster Univ, UMIST, Westminster Univ, Wolverhampton Univ.

R

RADAR
See: Electronic engineering.

RADIO
See: Electronic engineering.

RADIOGRAPHY
Possible prospectuses: Anglia Poly Univ, Bradford Univ, Bristol UWE, Canterbury Christ Church Coll, Central England Univ, Derby Univ, Glasgow Poly, Hertfordshire Univ, Keele Univ, King's Coll London, Kingston Univ, Liverpool Univ, Portsmouth Univ, Queen Margaret Coll, Robert Gordon Univ, S Martin's Coll, Salford Coll, Sheffield Hallam Univ, South Bank Univ, Southampton Univ, Teesside Univ, Ulster Univ.
Study areas: Professions allied to medicine (PAMs).

RECREATION STUDIES
Possible prospectuses: Birmingham Univ, Bournemouth Univ, Cardiff Inst, Cheltenham & Gloucester Coll, Coventry Univ, Heriot-Watt Univ, Loughborough Univ, Luton Coll, Moray House, North Cheshire Coll, St Mark & St John, Sheffield Hallam Univ, Staffordshire Univ, Thames Valley Univ, Trinity & All Saints, West Herts Coll, Writtle.
See also: Sports studies; tourism; town planning.

RELIGIOUS STUDIES
Possible prospectuses: Aberdeen Univ, Aberystwyth, Bangor, Bangor Normal Coll, Birmingham Univ, Bristol Univ, Cambridge Univ, Canterbury Christ Church Coll, Cardiff, Cheltenham & Gloucester Coll, Chester Coll, Crewe & Alsager, Derby Univ, Edge Hill, Edinburgh Univ, Exeter Univ, Glamorgan Univ, Greenwich Univ, Homerton, Hull Univ, Kent Univ, King's Coll London, Lampeter, Lancaster Univ, Leeds Univ, Liverpool Inst, Liverpool Univ, London Bible, Manchester Univ, Middlesex Univ, National Extension Coll, Newcastle Univ, Oak Hill Coll, Oxford Univ, Ripon & York St John, Roehampton Inst, St Andrews Univ, St Mark & St John, S Martin's Coll, St Mary's Coll, SOAS, Spurgeon's Coll, Stirling Univ, Sunderland Univ, Trinity & All Saints, Warwick Univ, West London Inst, West Sussex Inst, Wolverhampton Univ.
See also: Biblical studies; theology.
Study areas: Religious studies and theology.

RENAISSANCE STUDIES
See: History.

RETAIL MANAGEMENT
Possible prospectuses: Bournemouth Univ, Dundee Inst, Loughborough Univ, Manchester Metropolitan Univ, Oxford Brookes Univ, Queen Margaret Coll, Robert Gordon Univ, Surrey Univ, Ulster Univ.

RISK
See: Actuarial studies.

RUMANIAN
Possible prospectuses: Birmingham Univ, SSEES, University Coll London.
Study area: Modern languages.

RURAL ENVIRONMENT STUDIES
Possible prospectuses: Aberdeen Univ, Anglia Poly Univ, Cheltenham & Gloucester Coll, Edinburgh Univ, Harper Adams, Hertfordshire Univ, Napier Univ, North East Wales Inst, Plymouth Univ, Reading Univ, Royal Agricultural Coll, Silsoe Coll, Trinity Coll Carmarthen, Writtle, Wye Coll.
Study area: Environmental studies.

RUSSIAN
Possible prospectuses: Bangor, Belfast Univ, Birmingham Univ, Bradford Univ, Bristol Univ, Cambridge Univ, Durham Univ, Edinburgh Univ, Essex Univ, Exeter Univ, Glasgow Univ, Heriot-Watt Univ, Keele Univ, Leeds Univ, Liverpool John Moores Univ, Manchester Univ, Northumbria Univ, Nottingham Univ, Oxford Univ, Portsmouth Univ, Queen Mary & Westfield, St Andrews Univ, Sheffield Univ, SSEES, Strathclyde Univ, Surrey Univ, Sussex Univ, Swansea, Thames Valley Univ, Westminster Univ, Wolverhampton Univ.
See also: Russian studies; Slavonic studies.
Study area: Modern languages.

RUSSIAN STUDIES
Possible prospectuses: Belfast Univ, Birmingham Univ, Cambridge Univ, East Anglia Univ, Essex Univ, Glasgow Univ, Leeds Univ, Liverpool Univ, Manchester Univ, Portsmouth Univ, St Andrews Univ, Sheffield Univ, SSEES, Sunderland Univ, Surrey Univ, Sussex Univ, Swansea, Wolverhampton Univ.
See also: Russian; Slavonic studies.
Study areas: Modern languages; European studies.

S

SAFETY
See: Environmental health.

SANSKRIT
Possible prospectuses: Cambridge Univ, Edinburgh Univ, Oxford Univ, SOAS.
See also: Near East studies.
Study area: Near East and Islamic studies.

SCANDINAVIAN STUDIES
Possible prospectuses: East Anglia Univ, Edinburgh Univ, Hull Univ, University Coll London.
See also: individual languages (eg *Danish*).

SCIENTIFIC/TECHNICAL GRAPHICS
Possible prospectuses: Falmouth.
See also: Graphic design.

SCOTTISH STUDIES
Possible prospectuses: Aberdeen Univ, Edinburgh Univ, Glasgow Univ, St Andrews Univ, Stirling Univ, Strathclyde Univ.
See also: Celtic studies.

SCULPTURE
Possible prospectuses: Anglia Poly Univ, Bath Coll, Bretton Hall, Brighton Univ, Bristol UWE, Camberwell Coll, Central Lancashire Univ, Central Saint Martins, Chelsea, Cheltenham & Gloucester Coll, Coventry Univ, De Montfort Univ, Duncan of Jordanstone, Dundee Univ, East London Univ, Edinburgh Coll Art, Falmouth, Glasgow Sch Art, Goldsmiths' Coll, Heriot-Watt Univ, Humberside Univ, Kent Inst, Kingston Univ, Liverpool Inst, Liverpool John Moores Univ, Loughborough Coll, Manchester Metropolitan Univ, Middlesex Univ, Newcastle Univ, Norfolk Inst, Northumbria Univ, Portsmouth Univ, Reading Univ, Robert Gordon Univ, Royal Academy Sch (p/g only), Royal Coll Art (p/g only), Sheffield Hallam Univ, Slade, Staffordshire Univ, Ulster Univ, West Surrey Coll, West Sussex Inst, Wimbledon Sch Art, Winchester Sch Art, Wolverhampton Univ.
Study area: Art and design.

SECRETARIAL STUDIES
See: Office organisation.

SEISMOLOGY
See: Geology.

SEMICONDUCTORS
See: Electronic engineering.

SEMITIC LANGUAGES
Possible prospectuses: Aberdeen Univ, Manchester Univ, SOAS.
See also: individual languages (eg *Arabic*).
Study area: Near East and Islamic studies.

SERBO-CROAT
Possible prospectuses: Cambridge Univ, Glasgow Univ, Nottingham Univ, SSEES.
See also: Yugoslav studies.
Study area: Modern languages.

SHIPBUILDING
See: Naval architecture; marine architecture.

SILVERSMITHING
Possible prospectuses: Buckinghamshire Coll, Camberwell Coll, Central
England Univ, Crewe & Alsager, De Montfort Univ, Duncan of Jordanstone,
Dundee Univ, Edinburgh Coll Art, Glasgow Sch Art, Heriot-Watt Univ,
Liverpool Inst, London Guildhall Univ, Loughborough Coll, Robert Gordon
Univ, Royal Coll Art (p/g only), Staffordshire Univ, Ulster Univ, West Surrey
Coll.
See also: Jewellery; three dimensional design.
Study area: Art and design.

SINHALESE
Possible prospectuses: SOAS.
See also: Asian studies.

SLOVAK
See: Czech/Slovak.

SLAVONIC STUDIES
Possible prospectuses: Cambridge Univ, Glasgow Univ, Hull Univ, Leeds Univ,
Manchester Univ, Nottingham Univ, Sheffield Univ, SSEES.
Study area: European studies.

SOCIAL ADMINISTRATION
Possible prospectuses: Anglia Poly Univ, Bangor, Birmingham Univ, Brighton
Univ, Bristol Univ, Cardiff, Central Lancashire Univ, Dundee Univ, Durham
Univ, East London Univ, Edinburgh Univ, Essex Univ, Glasgow Poly, Glasgow
Univ, Goldsmiths' Coll, Hertfordshire Univ, Hull Univ, Kent Univ, Lancaster
Univ, Leeds Metropolitan Univ, Leeds Univ, Loughborough Univ, LSE, Luton
Coll, Manchester Metropolitan Univ, Manchester Univ, Middlesex Univ,
Newcastle Univ, Nottingham Trent Univ, Nottingham Univ, Open Univ,
Paisley Univ, Plymouth Univ, Portsmouth Univ, Robert Gordon Univ,
Roehampton Inst, Sheffield Hallam Univ, Sheffield Univ, Southampton Univ,
Stirling Univ, Strathclyde Univ, Teesside Univ, Ulster Univ, Warwick Univ,
Westminster Univ, Wolverhampton Univ, York Univ.
Study areas: Social policy and social welfare.

SOCIAL ANTHROPOLOGY
Possible prospectuses: Belfast Univ, Brunel Univ, Cambridge Univ, East Anglia
Univ, Edinburgh Univ, Goldsmiths' Coll, Hull Univ, Keele Univ, Kent Univ,
LSE, Manchester Univ, St Andrews Univ, SOAS, Sussex Univ, Swansea, Ulster
Univ, University Coll London.
See also: Anthropology.
Study area: Anthropology.

SOCIAL BIOLOGY
Possible prospectuses: Roehampton Inst.
See also: Biosocial science; human sciences.

SOCIAL HISTORY
Possible prospectuses: Aberdeen Univ, Aberystwyth, Belfast Univ, Birmingham
Univ, Central Lancashire Univ, East Anglia Univ, Edinburgh Univ, Exeter
Univ, Glasgow Poly, Hull Univ, Kent Univ, Lancaster Univ, Leicester Univ,
Liverpool Univ, Luton Coll, Manchester Metropolitan Univ, Manchester Univ,
Newcastle Univ, Nottingham Univ, Open Univ, Reading Univ, St Andrews

Univ, Sheffield Univ, Staffordshire Univ, Strathclyde Univ, Sussex Univ, Swansea, York Univ.
See also: Economic history; history.
Study area: History.

SOCIAL POLICY
See: Social administration; social work.

SOCIAL PSYCHOLOGY
See: Psychology.

SOCIAL SCIENCE
Possible prospectuses: Aberdeen Univ, Belfast Univ, Bradford & Ilkley, Bradford Univ, Bristol UWE, Brunel Univ, Cambridge Univ, City Univ, Coventry Univ, Derby Univ, Dundee Inst, East Anglia Univ, East London Univ, Edge Hill, Edinburgh Univ, Essex Univ, Glamorgan Univ, Glasgow Poly, Glasgow Univ, Goldsmiths' Coll, Hertfordshire Univ, Hull Univ, Humberside Univ, Keele Univ, Kent Univ, Kingston Univ, Leeds Metropolitan Univ, Liverpool John Moores Univ, Liverpool Univ, Loughborough Univ, Luton Coll, Manchester Metropolitan Univ, Manchester Univ, Middlesex Univ, Newcastle Univ, North London Univ, Nottingham Trent Univ, Open Univ, Oxford Brookes Univ, Paisley Univ, Plymouth Univ, Queen Margaret Coll, Reading Univ, Ripon & York St John, Robert Gordon Univ, Royal Holloway & Bedford, Salford Univ, Sheffield Hallam Univ, South Bank Univ, Southampton Inst, Southampton Univ, Staffordshire Univ, Stirling Univ, Sunderland Univ, Surrey Univ, Sussex Univ, Swansea, Thames Valley Univ, Ulster Univ, Westminster Univ, Wolverhampton Univ, York Univ.
See also: individual subjects (eg *economics, politics, sociology*).

SOCIAL STATISTICS
See: Statistics; sociology.

SOCIAL STUDIES
Possible prospectuses: Birmingham Univ, Bradford Univ, Bretton Hall, Central Lancashire Univ, Coventry Univ, Durham Univ, East London Univ, Hertfordshire Univ, King Alfred's Coll, Lancaster Univ, Liverpool John Moores Univ, Liverpool Univ, Luton Coll, Manchester Metropolitan Univ, Manchester Univ, Newcastle Univ, Nottingham Trent Univ, Nottingham Univ, Open Univ, Paisley Univ, Robert Gordon Univ, Sheffield Hallam Univ, South Bank Univ, Southampton Inst, Staffordshire Univ, Stirling Univ, Strathclyde Univ, Sussex Univ, Swansea, Swansea Inst, Teesside Univ, York Univ.
See also: Social science.

SOCIAL WORK
Possible prospectuses: Anglia Poly Univ, Bath Univ, Birmingham Univ, Bradford Univ, Buckinghamshire Coll, Cardiff, Cardiff Inst, Central England Univ, Central Lancashire Univ, Cheltenham & Gloucester Coll, Coventry Univ, Derby Univ, East Anglia Univ, East London Univ, Exeter Univ, Glasgow Poly, Glasgow Univ, Heriot-Watt Univ, Hertfordshire Univ, Hull Univ, Humberside Univ, Kingston Univ, Lancaster Univ, Leeds Metropolitan Univ, Liverpool John Moores Univ, Liverpool Univ, Luton Coll, Manchester Metropolitan Univ, Manchester Univ, Middlesex Univ, Moray House, Nene Coll, Newcastle Univ, North East Wales Inst, North London Univ, Northumbria Univ, Nottingham Trent Univ, Paisley Univ, Plymouth Univ, Portsmouth Univ,

Reading Univ, Robert Gordon Univ, S Martin's Coll, Salford Coll, Sheffield Hallam Univ, South Bank Univ, Southampton Univ, Staffordshire Univ, Stirling Univ, Strathclyde Univ, Sussex Univ, Teesside Univ, Ulster Univ, West London Inst, West Sussex Inst, York Univ.
Study area: Social policy and social welfare.

SOCIOLOGY
Possible prospectuses: Aberdeen Univ, Anglia Poly Univ, Aston Univ, Bangor, Bath Univ, Bedford Coll, Belfast Univ, Birmingham Univ, Bradford Univ, Bristol Univ, Bristol UWE, Brunel Univ, Buckinghamshire Coll, Cambridge Univ, Cardiff, Central England Univ, Central Lancashire Univ, Cheltenham & Gloucester Coll, City Univ, Crewe & Alsager, Durham Univ, East Anglia Univ, East London Univ, Edinburgh Univ, Essex Univ, Exeter Univ, Glamorgan Univ, Glasgow Poly, Glasgow Univ, Goldsmiths' Coll, Greenwich Univ, Huddersfield Univ, Hull Univ, Humberside Univ, Keele Univ, Kent Univ, Kingston Univ, Lancaster Univ, Leeds Metropolitan Univ, Leeds Univ, Leicester Univ, Liverpool Inst, Liverpool John Moores Univ, Liverpool Univ, London Guildhall Univ, Loughborough Univ, LSE, LSU Southampton, Luton Coll, Manchester Metropolitan Univ, Manchester Univ, Middlesex Univ, Nene Coll, Newcastle Univ, North London Univ, Northumbria Univ, Nottingham Univ, Open Univ, Oxford Brookes Univ, Plymouth Univ, Portsmouth Univ, Reading Univ, Robert Gordon Univ, Roehampton Inst, Royal Holloway & Bedford, St Mark & St John, St Mary's Coll, Salford Univ, Sheffield Univ, Southampton Univ, Staffordshire Univ, Stirling Univ, Strathclyde Univ, Sunderland Univ, Surrey Univ, Sussex Univ, Swansea, Teesside Univ, Thames Valley Univ, Trinity & All Saints, Ulster Univ, Warwick Univ, Westminster Univ, Wolverhampton Univ, Worcester Coll, York Univ.
Study area: Sociology.

SOFTWARE ENGINEERING
Possible prospectuses: Aberdeen Univ, Aberystwyth, Anglia Poly Univ, Central England Univ, Central Lancashire Univ, City Univ, Coventry Univ, Cranfield (p/g only), De Montfort Univ, Derby Univ, Glamorgan Univ, Glasgow Univ, Greenwich Univ, Heriot-Watt Univ, Hertfordshire Univ, Huddersfield Univ, Hull Univ, Kent Univ, Leicester Univ, Liverpool John Moores Univ, Nene Coll, Newcastle Univ, North London Univ, Paisley Univ, Robert Gordon Univ, Salford Coll, Sheffield Hallam Univ, Sheffield Univ, South Bank Univ, Staffordshire Univ, Stirling Univ, Teesside Univ, Ulster Univ, UMIST, Westminster Univ, Wolverhampton Univ, York Univ.
See also: Computing study area; computing.

SOIL SCIENCE
Possible prospectuses: Aberdeen Univ, Aberystwyth, Bangor, Edinburgh Univ, Hull Univ, Luton Coll, Manchester Univ, Newcastle Univ, Reading Univ, Royal Agricultural Coll, South Bank Univ, Writtle.

SOLID STATE ELECTRONICS
See: Electronics.

SOLID STATE PHYSICS
See: Physics.

SOUTH AMERICA
See: Latin American studies.

SOUTH EAST ASIAN STUDIES
Possible prospectuses: Edinburgh Univ, Hull Univ, Newcastle Univ, North London Univ, SOAS.
See also: Asian studies.
Study area: Asian studies.

SOVIET STUDIES
See: Russian studies.

SPACE
Possible prospectuses: Aberystwyth, Kent Univ, Leicester Univ, Southampton Univ.
See also: Astronomy.
Study area: Physics.

SPANISH
Possible prospectuses: Aberdeen Univ, Aberystwyth, Anglia Poly Univ, Belfast Univ, Birmingham Univ, Bradford Univ, Bristol Univ, Bristol UWE, Buckingham Univ, Cambridge Univ, Cardiff, Central Sch Speech/Drama, Coventry Univ, De Montfort Univ, Derby Univ, Durham Univ, Edinburgh Univ, Essex Univ, European Business Sch, Exeter Univ, Glasgow Poly, Glasgow Univ, Goldsmiths' Coll, Heriot-Watt Univ, Hull Univ, Humberside Univ, King's Coll London, Kingston Univ, Leeds Univ, Liverpool John Moores Univ, Liverpool Univ, London Guildhall Univ, Luton Coll, Manchester Metropolitan Univ, Manchester Univ, Middlesex Univ, National Extension Coll, Nene Coll, Newcastle Univ, North London Univ, Northumbria Univ, Nottingham Univ, Oxford Univ, Plymouth Univ, Portsmouth Univ, Queen Mary & Westfield, Royal Holloway & Bedford, St Andrews Univ, S Martin's Coll, Salford Univ, Sheffield Hallam Univ, Sheffield Univ, South Bank Univ, Southampton Univ, Staffordshire Univ, Stirling Univ, Strathclyde Univ, Sussex Univ, Swansea, Thames Valley Univ, Trinity & All Saints, Ulster Univ, University Coll London, Westminster Univ, Wolverhampton Univ.
See also: Hispanic studies; Iberian studies; Latin American studies.
Study area: Modern languages.

SPANISH STUDIES
See: Hispanic studies; Iberian studies; Latin American studies; Spanish.

SPEECH SCIENCES
Possible prospectuses: Central Sch Speech/Drama, City Univ, De Montfort Univ, Manchester Metropolitan Univ, Manchester Univ, National Hospitals Coll, Newcastle Univ, Reading Univ, Sheffield Univ, University Coll London.
Study area: Speech sciences.

SPEECH THERAPY
Possible prospectuses: Cardiff Inst, Central England Univ, Central Sch Speech/Drama, Leeds Metropolitan Univ, Manchester Metropolitan Univ, Manchester Univ, National Hospitals Coll, Queen Margaret Coll, Reading Univ, Sheffield Univ, Strathclyde Univ, Ulster Univ.
See also: Speech sciences.
Study area: Speech sciences.

SPORTS STUDIES
Possible prospectuses: Bangor, Bedford Coll, Birmingham Univ, Brighton Univ, Canterbury Christ Church Coll, Cardiff Inst, Cheltenham & Gloucester Coll, Chester Coll, Crewe & Alsager, Glasgow Univ, Heriot-Watt Univ, King Alfred's Coll, Leeds Metropolitan Univ, Liverpool John Moores Univ, Loughborough

Univ, Moray House, North Cheshire Coll, North London Univ, Northumbria Univ, Nottingham Trent Univ, Roehampton Inst, St Mary's Coll, Staffordshire Univ, Strathclyde Univ, Teesside Univ, Ulster Univ, Warwick Univ, West London Inst, West Sussex Inst, Wolverhampton Univ.
See also: Physical education.

STAGE MANAGEMENT
Possible prospectuses: ALRA, Bretton Hall, Guildhall, RADA, Rose Bruford Coll, Welsh Coll Music/Drama.
Study area: Drama and theatre arts.

STATISTICS
Possible prospectuses: Aberdeen Univ, Aberystwyth, Anglia Poly Univ, Bath Univ, Belfast Univ, Birkbeck, Birmingham Univ, Bradford Univ, Brighton Univ, Bristol Univ, Bristol UWE, Brunel Univ, Cardiff, Central Lancashire Univ, City Univ, Coventry Univ, Derby Univ, Dundee Inst, Dundee Univ, Durham Univ, East London Univ, Edinburgh Univ, Essex Univ, Exeter Univ, Glasgow Poly, Glasgow Univ, Goldsmiths' Coll, Greenwich Univ, Heriot-Watt Univ, Hertfordshire Univ, Hull Univ, Imperial Coll, Keele Univ, Kent Univ, Lancaster Univ, Leeds Univ, Leicester Univ, Liverpool John Moores Univ, Liverpool Univ, London Guildhall Univ, Loughborough Univ, LSE, Luton Coll, Manchester Univ, Middlesex Univ, Newcastle Univ, North London Univ, Northumbria Univ, Nottingham Univ, Open Univ, Oxford Brookes Univ, Paisley Univ, Plymouth Univ, Portsmouth Univ, Queen Mary & Westfield, Reading Univ, Robert Gordon Univ, Royal Holloway & Bedford, St Andrews Univ, Salford Univ, Sheffield Hallam Univ, Sheffield Univ, South Bank Univ, Southampton Univ, Staffordshire Univ, Strathclyde Univ, Surrey Univ, Sussex Univ, Swansea, Teesside Univ, Thames Valley Univ, Ulster Univ, UMIST, University Coll London, Warwick Univ, Westminster Univ, Wolverhampton Univ, York Univ.
See also: Mathematics.
Study area: Mathematical studies.

STRUCTURAL ENGINEERING
Possible prospectuses: Bradford Univ, Cranfield (p/g only), Edinburgh Univ, Glasgow Poly, Heriot-Watt Univ, Hertfordshire Univ, Manchester Univ, North East Wales Inst, South Bank Univ, UMIST, University Coll London.
Study area: Civil engineering.

SURVEYING
Possible prospectuses: Aberdeen Univ, Bristol UWE, Camborne Sch Mines, Central Lancashire Univ, East London Univ, Glamorgan Univ, Glasgow Poly, Greenwich Univ, Harper Adams, Heriot-Watt Univ, Hertfordshire Univ, Kingston Univ, Liverpool John Moores Univ, Loughborough Univ, Luton Coll, Napier Univ, Newcastle Univ, North East Wales Inst, Nottingham Trent Univ, Paisley Univ, Plymouth Univ, Reading Univ, Robert Gordon Univ, Royal Agricultural Coll, Salford Univ, Sheffield Hallam Univ, South Bank Univ, Staffordshire Univ, Teesside Univ, University Coll London, Westminster Univ, Wolverhampton Univ.
See also: Quantity surveying.

SWAHILI
Possible prospectuses: SOAS, York Univ.
See also: African studies.
Study area: African studies.

SWEDISH
Possible prospectuses: East Anglia Univ, Edinburgh Univ, Hull Univ, Lampeter, Surrey Univ, University Coll London, York Univ.
See also: Scandinavian studies.
Study area: Modern languages.

SYSTEMS ANALYSIS
Possible prospectuses: Bristol UWE, Cardiff, Cranfield (p/g only), East London Univ, Imperial Coll, Kent Univ, Luton Coll, Manchester Univ, North London Univ, Sheffield Hallam Univ, South Bank Univ, Staffordshire Univ, UMIST, Westminster Univ.
See also: Computer science; computing.
Study area: Computing.

T

TALMUD
See: Jewish studies.

TAMIL
Possible prospectuses: SOAS.
See also: Asian studies.
Study area: Asian studies.

TEACHING
See: Education.

TECHNICAL GRAPHICS
See: Scientific and technical graphics.

TELECOMMUNICATIONS ENGINEERING
Possible prospectuses: Anglia Poly Univ, Birmingham Univ, Bradford Univ, Coventry Univ, Essex Univ, Heriot-Watt Univ, Imperial Coll, Luton Coll, Napier Univ, Open Univ, Queen Mary & Westfield.
Study area: Electrical and electronic engineering.

TELEVISION
See: Communication studies; film studies; media studies.

TEXTILE TECHNOLOGY
Possible prospectuses: Bolton Inst, De Montfort Univ, Heriot-Watt Univ, Huddersfield Univ, Leeds Univ, Nottingham Trent Univ, Scottish Coll Textiles, UMIST, Wolverhampton Univ.
Study area: Chemical engineering.

TEXTILES
Possible prospectuses: Bolton Inst, Bretton Hall, Brighton Univ, Bristol UWE, Cardiff, Central England Univ, Central Saint Martins, Chelsea, Cheltenham & Gloucester Coll, Crewe & Alsager, De Montfort Univ, Derby Univ, Duncan of Jordanstone, Dundee Univ, East London Univ, Edinburgh Coll Art, Glasgow Sch Art, Goldsmiths' Coll, Heriot-Watt Univ, Huddersfield Univ, Leeds Univ, Liverpool Inst, Liverpool John Moores Univ, London Coll Fashion,

Loughborough Coll, Manchester Metropolitan Univ, Middlesex Univ, Nottingham Trent Univ, Plymouth Univ, Robert Gordon Univ, Royal Coll Art (p/g only), Scottish Coll Textiles, Staffordshire Univ, Ulster Univ, UMIST, West Surrey Coll, Winchester Sch Art, Wolverhampton Univ, Worcester Coll.
Study area: Art and design.

THAI STUDIES
Possible prospectuses: SOAS.
Study area: Asian studies.

THEATRE DESIGN
Possible prospectuses: Bretton Hall, Bristol Old Vic, Central England Univ, Central Saint Martins, Central Sch Speech/Drama, Crewe & Alsager, Dartington, Glamorgan Univ, Glasgow Sch Art, Heriot-Watt Univ, Nottingham Trent Univ, RADA, Royal Scottish Academy, Slade, Welsh Coll Music/Drama, Wimbledon Sch Art.
Study areas: Art and design; drama and theatre arts.

THEOLOGY
Possible prospectuses: Aberdeen Univ, Aberystwyth, Bangor, Belfast Univ, Bristol Univ, Cambridge Univ, Cardiff, Cheltenham & Gloucester Coll, Chester Coll, Derby Univ, Durham Univ, Edinburgh Univ, Exeter Univ, Glasgow Univ, Greenwich Univ, Heythrop Coll, Hull Univ, Kent Univ, King's Coll London, Lampeter, Lancaster Univ, Leeds Univ, Liverpool Inst, Liverpool Univ, London Bible, LSU Southampton, Manchester Univ, Newcastle Univ, Nottingham Univ, Oak Hill Coll, Oxford Univ, Ripon & York St John, St Andrews Univ, St Mark & St John, S Martin's Coll, St Mary's Coll, Spurgeon's Coll, Trinity & All Saints, West Sussex Inst, Westminster Coll.
See also: Religious studies.
Study areas: Religious studies and theology.

THIRD WORLD STUDIES
Possible prospectuses: Derby Univ, Middlesex Univ, St Mark & St John, Staffordshire Univ.

THREE-DIMENSIONAL DESIGN
Possible prospectuses: Brighton Univ, Bristol UWE, Buckinghamshire Coll, Cardiff Inst, Central England Univ, Central Lancashire Univ, Coventry Univ, Crewe & Alsager, De Montfort Univ, Edinburgh Coll Art, Glasgow Sch Art, Heriot-Watt Univ, Humberside Univ, Kent Inst, Kingston Univ, Leeds Metropolitan Univ, Liverpool Inst, Loughborough Coll, Loughborough Univ, Manchester Metropolitan Univ, Middlesex Univ, Northumbria Univ, Open Univ, Plymouth Univ, Portsmouth Univ, Ravensbourne Coll, Reading Univ, Ripon & York St John, St Mark & St John, Salford Coll, Sheffield Hallam Univ, Staffordshire Univ, Sunderland Univ, Teesside Univ, West Surrey Coll, Westminster Univ, Wolverhampton Univ.
Study area: Art and design.

TOPOGRAPHICAL SCIENCE
Possible prospectuses: Glasgow Univ, Luton Coll, Swansea.

TOURISM
Possible prospectuses: Birmingham Univ, Bolton Inst, Bournemouth Univ, Brighton Univ, Canterbury Christ Church Coll, Cardiff Inst, Cheltenham & Gloucester Coll, Derby Univ, Hertfordshire Univ, Humberside Univ, Leeds Metropolitan Univ, Luton Coll, Manchester Metropolitan Univ, Napier Univ,

North Cheshire Coll, North London Univ, Northumbria Univ, Oxford Brookes Univ, Sheffield Hallam Univ, Staffordshire Univ, Strathclyde Univ, Thames Valley Univ, Ulster Univ, West Herts Coll, Westminster Univ, Wolverhampton Univ, Writtle.

TOWN AND COUNTRY PLANNING
Possible prospectuses: Aston Univ, Birmingham Univ, Bristol UWE, Cardiff, Central England Univ, Cheltenham & Gloucester Coll, Coventry Univ, Duncan of Jordanstone, Dundee Univ, Edinburgh Coll Art, Heriot-Watt Univ, Hertfordshire Univ, Luton Coll, Manchester Univ, Newcastle Univ, Nottingham Univ, Oxford Brookes Univ, Portsmouth Univ, Reading Univ, Royal Agricultural Coll, Sheffield Hallam Univ, South Bank Univ, Strathclyde Univ, University Coll London, Westminster Univ.
See also: Environmental studies.
Study area: Town and country planning.

TOXICOLOGY
Possible prospectuses: Aberdeen Univ, Anglia Poly Univ, Bradford Univ, Hull Univ, Luton Coll, School Pharmacy, Surrey Univ.
Study area: Pharmacology.

TRANSLATION
See: Interpretation and translation.

TRANSPORT STUDIES
Possible prospectuses: Aston Univ, Cardiff, Cranfield (p/g only), Hertfordshire Univ, Huddersfield Univ, Loughborough Univ, Napier Univ, Plymouth Univ, Southampton Inst, Ulster Univ.

TURKISH
Possible prospectuses: Cambridge Univ, Manchester Univ, Oxford Univ, SOAS.
See also: Near East studies.
Study area: Near East and Islamic studies.

TYPOGRAPHY
See: Printing and typography.

U

UNITED STATES
See: American studies.

URBAN ESTATE MANAGEMENT
Possible prospectuses: Bristol UWE, De Montfort Univ, Glamorgan Univ, Heriot-Watt Univ, Liverpool John Moores Univ, Luton Coll, North East Wales Inst, Nottingham Trent Univ, Oxford Brookes Univ, Portsmouth Univ, Reading Univ, Sheffield Hallam Univ, South Bank Univ, Westminster Univ, Writtle.
See also: Estate management.

URBAN STUDIES
Possible prospectuses: Aberdeen Univ, Aston Univ, Bristol UWE, Coventry Univ, Edge Hill, Edinburgh Coll Art, Kent Univ, Leeds Metropolitan Univ, Liverpool John Moores Univ, Liverpool Univ, Loughborough Univ, Manchester Univ, Middlesex Univ, North London Univ, Open Univ, Oxford Brookes Univ, Portsmouth Univ, Reading Univ, Sheffield Hallam Univ, Sheffield Univ, Sunderland Univ, Swansea Inst, Worcester Coll.

URDU
Possible prospectuses: Luton Coll, SOAS.
See also: Asian studies.
Study area: Asian studies.

V

VALUATION
See: Estate management; quantity surveying; surveying.

VETERINARY STUDIES
Possible prospectuses: Bristol Univ, Cambridge Univ, Edinburgh Univ, Glasgow Univ, Liverpool Univ, Royal Vet Coll.
Study area: Veterinary studies.

VICTORIAN STUDIES
Possible prospectuses: Lampeter, Open Univ, Sunderland Univ.
Study area: History.

VIETNAMESE STUDIES
Possible prospectuses: SOAS.
See also: Asian studies.
Study area: Asian studies.

VIROLOGY
Possible prospectuses: Glasgow Univ, Manchester Univ, Reading Univ, Surrey Univ, Warwick Univ.
Study area: Microbiology.

VISUAL COMMUNICATION
See: Graphic design.

W

WAR STUDIES
Possible prospectuses: Aberystwyth, Bolton Inst, Bradford Univ, Cranwell, Dartmouth, King's Coll London, Manadon, Manchester Univ, Sandhurst, Sunderland Univ, Wolverhampton Univ.
See also: History; internatinal relations; politics.
Study area: Strategic studies.

WATER RESOURCES
Possible prospectuses: Hertfordshire Univ, Luton Coll, Napier Univ, Silsoe Coll, South Bank Univ, Writtle.

WELFARE STUDIES
See: Social administration; social work.

WELSH STUDIES
Possible prospectuses: Aberystwyth, Bangor, Bangor Normal Coll, Cardiff, Glamorgan Univ, Lampeter, Manchester Univ, North East Wales Inst, Swansea.
See also: Celtic studies.

WILDLIFE MANAGEMENT
Possible prospectuses: Edinburgh Univ, Hertfordshire Univ, Welsh Agricultural Coll.

WOMEN'S STUDIES
Possible prospectuses: Anglia Poly Univ, Central Lancashire Univ, Cheltenham & Gloucester Coll, Coventry Univ, East London Univ, Edge Hill, Edinburgh Univ, Glamorgan Univ, Lancaster Univ, Liverpool John Moores Univ, Liverpool Univ, Middlesex Univ, North London Univ, Ripon & York St John, Roehampton Inst, Sheffield Hallam Univ, Staffordshire Univ, Wolverhampton Univ.

WOOD TECHNOLOGY
Possible prospectuses: Buckinghamshire Coll, Luton Coll.

Y

YOUTH AND COMMUNITY WORK
Possible prospectuses: Bradford & Ilkley, Canterbury Christ Church Coll, Crewe & Alsager, Derby Univ, Greenwich Univ, Heriot-Watt Univ, Humberside Univ, Leeds Metropolitan Univ, Luton Coll, Moray House, North East Wales Inst, Plymouth Univ, Reading Univ, St Mark & St John, S Martin's Coll, Ulster Univ.
Study area: Social policy and social welfare.

YUGOSLAV STUDIES
Possible prospectuses: SSEES.
See also: Serbo-Croat; Slavonic studies.
Study area: European studies.

Z

ZOOLOGY
Possible prospectuses: Aberdeen Univ, Aberystwyth, Bangor, Belfast Univ, Birmingham Univ, Bristol Univ, Cambridge Univ, Cardiff, Dundee Univ, Durham Univ, East Anglia Univ, East London Univ, Edinburgh Univ, Glasgow Univ, Imperial Coll, King's Coll London, Leeds Univ, Leicester Univ, Liverpool Univ, Manchester Univ, Newcastle Univ, Nottingham Univ, Oxford Univ, Portsmouth Univ, Queen Mary & Westfield, Reading Univ, Royal Holloway & Bedford, St Andrews Univ, Sheffield Univ, Southampton Univ, Stirling Univ, Swansea, University Coll London, Westminster Univ, Wye Coll.
See also: Animal science.
Study area: Zoology.

ZULU
See: African studies.

WHAT TO STUDY

Here over 70 university teachers define their own study areas and outline how they are taught at first degree level. Try browsing, then list the study areas that interest you. You can then check whether the university and colleges you might want to go to teach what interests you by looking them up in the *Where to Study* section. Remember that each university labels its degree courses as it chooses, so before you apply, get hold of the prospectus to check directly that what you want to study is in fact taught there.

WHAT TO STUDY

About Study Areas, Subjects and Subject Mixes, Professor Sir Graham Hills, Strathclyde University
Accountancy, Professor M Bromwich, LSE
Aeronautical Engineering, Professor Donald McLean, Southampton University
African Studies, Richard Rathbone, SOAS
Agriculture, Horticulture and Forestry, Professor W Holmes, Wye College
American Studies, Dr Michael Dunne, Sussex University
Anatomy, Professor Anthony Firth, St Mary's Hospital Medical School, London
Anthropology, Professor Adam Kuper, Brunel University
Archaeology, Dr S W Hillson, University College London
Architecture, Sandra Morris, Architectural Association School of Architecture
Art and Design, Bernard Gay
  • Fine Art • Graphic Design • Photography
  • Textiles/Fashion • Three-Dimensional Design
Asian Studies, Dr Ian Brown, SOAS
Biochemistry, Professor Robert Freedman, Kent University
Biology, Dr N Maclean, Southampton University
Biotechnology, Dr J H Parish, Leeds University
Botany, Professor D M Moore, Reading University
Business Studies, Alan Munro, London Guildhall University
Chemical Engineering, Dr J R Backhurst, Newcastle University
Chemistry, Dr L D Pettit, Leeds University
Civil Engineering, Emeritus Professor Sir Alan Harris, Imperial College
Classics, Dr Oswyn Murray, Balliol College, Oxford University
Communication Studies, Robert Ferguson, Institute of Education
Computing, Professor D Conway, De Montfort University
Dance, Dr Richard Ralph, London Contemporary Dance School
Dentistry, Jane R Goodman, Eastman Dental Hospital
Drama and Theatre Arts, Malcolm Griffiths, Nottingham Trent University
  • Acting, Malcolm Griffiths • Drama, John Marshall, Bristol University
  • Theatre design, Malcolm Griffiths
Economics, Professor David W Pearce, University College London
Education, Professor David Bridges, East Anglia University
Electrical and Electronic Engineering, Dr J C Earls
English, Professor Patrick Parrinder, Reading University
Environmental Sciences, Dr Ian F Spellerberg, Southampton University
Environmental Studies, Emeritus Professor A D G Smart, University College London
European Studies, Dr Juliet Lodge, Hull University
Fine Arts, Dr Alex Potts, East Anglia University
Food Science and Nutrition, Professor R A Lawrie, Nottingham University
Geography, Professor M D I Chisholm, Cambridge University
Geology, Professor T R Owen, Swansea, University of Wales
History, Dr Maurice Keen, Balliol College, Oxford University
Hotel and Catering Management, Professor J O'Connor, Oxford Brookes University
Industrial Relations, Professor K F Sisson, Warwick University
Information Technology, Professor R S Burgess, Northumbria University, Newcastle
Latin American Studies, Professor Simon Collier, Vanderbilt University, USA
Law, Professor Geoffrey Wilson, Warwick University

Library and Information Studies, Dr Margaret Evans, Loughborough University
Linguistics, Dr Michael Garman, Reading University
Marine Technology, Emeritus Professor J B Caldwell, Newcastle University
Maritime Studies, Dr Alston Kennerley, Plymouth University
Mathematical Studies, R Daniel Hirsch, London Guildhall University
Mechanical and Production Engineering, Emeritus Professor M W Thring, Queen Mary & Westfield College London
Medicine, Dr David Sturgeon, University College and Middlesex School of Medicine
Metallurgy and Materials Science, Vernon John, City University
Microbiology, Professor John Postgate, Sussex University
Modern Languages, Professor Dennis Ager, Aston University
Music, Professor Brian Trowell, Oxford University
Near Eastern and Islamic Studies, Professor H T Norris, SOAS
Nursing Studies, Professor Penny Prophit, formerly of Edinburgh University
Pharmacology, Dr Robin Hoult, King's College London
Pharmacy, Dr Robin Hoult, King's College London
Philosophy, Professor Antony Flew, Reading University
Physics, Dr P E Hodgson, Oxford University
Physiology, Dr D J Begley, King's College London
Politics and Government, Peter Dawson, LSE
Professions Allied to Medicine (PAMs), Dr Jackie Campbell, Nene College
Psychology, Professor Keith Oatley, Glasgow University
Public Administration, Barry J O'Toole, Loughborough University
Religious Studies and Theology, Professor John R Hinnells, SOAS
Social Policy and Social Welfare, Professor Olive Stevenson, Nottingham University
Sociology, Dr Jason Ditton, Glasgow University
Speech Sciences, Dr Karen Bryan, Dr Jane Maxim & Dr Sheila Wirz, National Hospitals College of Speech Sciences
Strategic Studies, Dr Gerald Segal, International Institute for Strategic Studies
Town and Country Planning, Professor Margaret Roberts
Veterinary Studies, Professor Lord Soulsby, Cambridge University
Zoology, Professor R McNeill Alexander, Leeds University

About Study Areas, Subjects and Subject Mixes:

Professor Sir Graham Hills, Strathclyde University

To enter university or college is to step on to a new stage, a higher platform of opportunity and attainment. It is a world of greater challenges which, when overcome, lead to greater achievements. It is a world in which the undergraduate takes a giant step towards the confident, likeable, knowledgeable, skilful person that he or she must become to live a fruitful life. The ensuing journey is essentially the same whatever subjects are studied and whatever courses are followed. At the end of your course you will be on your own. You will swim without being supported. Real life will have begun.

So whilst the academic context in which all this happens is nevertheless important, it is not vitally so. Some classicists eventually become computer linguists. A surprising number of engineers become accountants. Occasionally even a medical doctor becomes something else, for example, an author. It is a fact that most graduates quickly find employment in subject areas far from those they studied so diligently. It is in that sense, therefore, that it is less important what you study than how you do it and how it enables you to blossom into that gifted person you, your parents and your friends wish you to become.

Some undergraduates will nevertheless enter higher education with firm intentions to undertake specialised study, say of chemistry, politics or accounting. They may well have gained entry to higher education on the basis of success already obtained in areas of scientific or other specialisations. Those intending to become medical doctors, veterinary or dental surgeons, electronic engineers and so on will not have much choice in the matter. Their courses will be laid out in front of them, although, even here, there may be some scope for variations in the later years.

It is in relation to this issue that the intending undergraduate will need to study in detail what is on offer in the wide range of courses offered by universities and colleges. Some of the courses will reflect some seemingly haphazard combination of disparate courses and subjects. Others will reflect a deeply held view that most young people should not specialise before they have to. Keeping one's options open seems sensible and it is common practice in many other countries. It enables the student to shed some of the experiences and prejudices of school. It enables the student to explore new subjects not encountered before. It also enables the student to consider what jobs are likely to be available and to target his or her courses accordingly.

One famous example of this is the Oxford course, which combines philosophy, politics and economics (PPE), a combination of subjects which has attracted large numbers of students who have subsequently gone on to specialise in government, law, administration or business. In earlier times it was usual to take a first, general degree which, as its name implies, required prowess in more than one subject, often three subjects, after which the student then proceeded to an honours or postgraduate degree. That degree is still commonly found in Scotland. It is generally unclassified (no honours) but even it could be taken with honours, thereby preserving the subject breadth to the very end. This tendency towards breadth in Scottish higher education is encouraged by an equivalent breadth in the secondary schools. The argument between breadth and depth ie between Scotland and England, will continue for some time. It is my belief that breadth will win.

In higher education, the extent of breadth varies from one subject grouping to another or, in administrative terms, from faculty to faculty. A faculty is a collection of similar (cognate) subjects which enjoy similar outlooks and similar methods (for example the use of laboratories). Thus the family of sciences will normally contain mathematics, physics, chemistry, bioscience, geology, perhaps computing science, pharmacy and pharmacology. These subjects mix well but they also tend to specialise further in themselves, for example, into theoretical chemistry, particle physics, or immunology. The tendency to ever greater specialisation and fragmentation can be a problem for scientists. It may need to be compensated by an insistence on general, foundation courses at the level of first or second year where the essentials of the neighbouring sciences can be brought into the course. This is the case at MIT or Stanford in the United States. At both these institutions early specialisation is frowned upon.

In the arts and humanities the same attitudes prevail. English, history, modern languages are often the basis of single separate degrees. But many institutions will now expect, indeed insist, that a range of subjects are studied in the early years. The same is true for the social sciences and business studies.

For engineers, doctors, vets and the like the arrangements are different again. Their students would also benefit from a breadth of outlook but the professional bodies which control and validate the degrees and grant the graduates chartered status often insist on specified courses which cramp the students' ability to range widely and to choose freely. Even here, things are changing and it should be possible for intending students to enjoy more choice in their professional subjects. In the even more vocational subjects, such as music, nursing or architecture, great emphasis is placed on specialised performance. Whether this is ultimately good or bad is not yet clear and will continue to be debated.

There is a view that all students should read a general degree before going on to specialise in anything. That would mean that most specialised professional courses would be the basis of a second degree. It would then be impossible to be an undergraduate student in say law or medicine. That is the case in other countries now but not yet so in Britain.

One of the questions to be answered by all intending undergraduates in Britain is therefore 'Do I want to keep my options open or would I like to specialise?' If you want to do research you will have to specialise but not necessarily at the beginning. It is worth remembering that premature specialisation may cut you off from other careers yet to be encountered.

On the other hand, if you are keen to be an astrophysicist then no-one should stop you from being one. Somewhere you will find an undergraduate course in it.

These remarks therefore have to do with the shape of your undergraduate course. Is it to be broadly based? Is it to be a flat pyramid? Or is it to be a tall spike of achievement? Most experienced educators would wish it to be all of these things and it usually can be. Even the broadest courses will end up with a project the extent and depth of which will be up to you.

To mention options is to consider choice and there are administrative penalties to pay for wide variations. Nowadays most institutions of higher education offer their courses in modular form on a common timetable so that in principle at least, any combination of courses can be taken. Academic guidance is invariably offered to those who need it or want it but ultimately the choice is yours. This arrangement of course options is progressive by nature. As each module is assessed the examination successes are accumulated as credits. Credit accumulation then leads to your degree and, in Britain, to the class of your degree.

This matter of classes of degree is largely a British phenomenon. All honours degrees in Britain are classified into first, upper second, lower second and third class honours and there may be a pass degree also. Much is made of the need to get a first or at least an upper second. A double first, in say, politics and economics is the sort of success that a good career could be launched on. This arrangement reflects an elitist view of education in which academic excellence is everything. One must not belittle achievement but there are those who note that this kind of attitude reflects only academic prowess and leaves other qualities primarily unrecognised and unrewarded. Whilst, therefore, it is immensely worthwhile to obtain a first, it is not a disaster to get a third.

What do employers think? They will inevitably be guided by the performance indicators of the examinations at universities and colleges. But, in time, the results of these examinations dim. It is said that you get your first job entirely on the basis of your initial qualifications but that you get your last job entirely on the basis of your personality. It is a fact of life that most men and women are highly intelligent but with a variable capacity to succeed in academic examinations. To use their intelligence is a life-long characteristic dependent on many other qualities. These qualities are therefore encouraged during undergraduate study, especially by many of the extra-curricular, non-academic activities available at most universities and colleges.

When considering your higher education you will therefore be confronted with a seemingly limitless range of choices of subjects and subject mixes. You may be bewildered by that choice but you will have some idea of what you like and what you are good at. What you do not study now can perhaps be studied later. It is a poor person who once educated does not stay a student all of his or her life.

You will be pleasantly surprised at what you discover you can do.

Remember to build on success – nothing is so successful at motivating you to do more. In the end you will emerge as a clever, gifted and, I would hope, confident and charming personality.

I want to stress the word confident. To be under-confident is almost as dangerous as being over-confident. Confidence is bred from achievement and from the strengthening by that achievement of your regard for yourself. To like yourself is not to be a latter-day Narcissus but to be someone who knows their potential as well as their shortcomings. The three or four years as an undergraduate will have an important part to play in this business of building you up (or building you down).

In the worst case, a diffident undergraduate can be confronted by a seemingly unscalable wall of knowledge. The professors seem to find it easy but you find it impossibly difficult. This kind of encounter is inevitable but should not be too frequent. The respect (one could say awe) in which knowledge is held does not help. There are knowledge-mongers who perpetuate the idea that the more difficult the knowledge or the concept appears to be the more valuable or important it is. Many text books are written more to impress the author's peers than to help the ordinary reader. So one must be wary of the people and circumstances that belittle or discourage the beginner.

In short, knowledge is not everything. It too has its defects. It wears out or degrades with time. Nowadays it can be as conveniently stored in a computer's database as stuffed into the human head. A lot of mathematics and science takes abstract, and at first obscure, forms because that was once the only way of expressing the complexities of the real world. These forms should be differentiated from the simpler concepts they are intended to describe. It is the concepts that matter. They stimulate the imagination and allow the human mind to enter the scene of science. Unless that happens, these subjects will wither away. Again most experienced educators are aware of the dangers of over-emphasising the knowledge base or the content as it is called. In selecting your courses and institutions you will have regard for the way in which these fundamental issues are dealt with. Too many demands on the knowledge base is the way of demotivation and a denting of that confidence.

Using the knowledge is the way to differentiate between what is useful and what is not, what is valuable and what is not. A sense of values is an essential part of good judgement which is another plank on which confidence is built. Using knowledge is applying it to useful purposes. It is usually an enjoyable experience in which mistakes are made from which you will learn. The process of learning belongs to the human side of education. It is a skill to be acquired and when acquired is likely to last a lifetime. The acquisition of this skill and others like it is part of the permanent development of the individual. It is therefore the most valuable part of the experience of higher education.

Subjects, courses and institutions vary in the way they approach these matters. If you find learning an easy process then perhaps it doesn't matter where you go or what you do. But for many students this will not be so. They should be careful in their choice of options. In my opinion, it is at least as important for all students to become skilled as to become knowledgeable. Skills add to competence and that is yet another basis for the confidence which I believe all young people should strive to develop.

So bear these things in mind when you approach your higher education.

Do you want to be a specialist or a generalist? Do you want to develop your personality as well as your knowledge base? Think carefully about those needs and ask yourself quite selfishly, 'What is best for me?'.

Accountancy
Professor M Bromwich, LSE

For well over two decades the accountancy profession has been growing very rapidly especially in the area of advice and consultancy. Recently the profession has suffered from the problems experienced by the economy, though the difficulties have been less than those experienced by many other industries.

However, because of the economic environment many newly qualified accountants have found more difficulty in moving on to other areas of accounting to enhance their careers as was the usual practice. This has meant that the market for trainee accountants has become somewhat more difficult. Recently the major growth has been in management accounting, which seeks to help management make decisions and control these decisions, in consultancy, where the skills offered by the accounting firms extend far beyond accountancy and tax.

Much of accounting is concerned with providing financial information to those who make decisions and who wish to monitor their existing plans. Thus, accounting is useful to almost everyone from those planning household expenditure, investors, the trade unions for wage negotiation to senior managers evaluating a vast capital project like a new factory or a new car model. This does not mean that the better known aspects of accounting are no longer of importance. One of accounting's major contributions to society is its ability to handle and summarise large amounts of data. The mechanics of this – book-keeping – used to be tedious but this work is now done by computer, thereby freeing accountants to concentrate on analysing the meaning of the accounting figures so produced. That book-keeping is the foundation of accountancy means that those who wish to take up the subject as a career need to be fairly comfortable with figures. More important necessary abilities are to be able to discern what accounting figures mean, to perceive the trends implicit in them and to be able to communicate persuasively with others. Thus, in the present environment the ability to ensure adequate cash is flowing into the business is at a premium.

These abilities are needed in full strength in the auditing sphere of what is known as financial accounting. The objective of auditing is to ensure that organisations have kept their accounts properly, that these contain the information they are required to produce, that they have not been subject to fraud, are likely to be able to continue in operation in the future and to advise management on the status of its financial management systems. Efficiency audits which go further than this and attempt to consider organisational effectiveness are likely to be an important task of auditors in the future.

There are some very difficult problems to be solved with regard to the other major areas of financial accounting, the production of accounting reports for the general public. First, as these reports are used by many different people for many different purposes, should there be special reports for special purposes or should the accountancy profession attempt to provide a general purpose set of accounts for use by all? A second problem is how should the effects of price changes be reflected in accounts? Among the large number of other problems which remain to be solved is that of attempting to say what published financial reports should contain for this is still a matter of substantial choice by their preparers.

The other major area of activity of accountants is that of management accounting which is concerned with providing information to help organisations make decisions and to monitor those already made. Many of the problems of financial accounting (such as allowing for the effects of inflation) plague its internal variant, but there are many problems which are of especial urgency to management accountants. How, for example, does one modify management accounting to reflect the major trend towards automating and computerising both manufacture and planning for manufacture?

That many of these problems have, as yet, no entirely satisfactory solutions is one reason why many accounting degrees concentrate on the basic disciplines underlying accounting such as economics, elementary statistics, behavioural studies, law and the more theoretical aspects of accounting. The objective of this is to give students the theoretical foundations which will help them to understand these problems and aid them in finding and understanding their solutions. Another reason why accounting degrees concentrate on the more theoretical aspects of the subject is that after graduating from accounting courses those who wish to make their career in the subject have to study in some depth the existing techniques of accounting and to take professional examinations (after approximately 3 years for graduates and 4 years for foundation course students). It would be a misallocation of resources for degree studies to cover the same ground. The professional examinations cover a wide range of subjects with the contemporary emphasis being especially on management subjects. There is also a strong trend away from part-time study for these examinations toward block release from work for such studies. Reflecting the wide range of disciplines covered in accounting degrees, there is usually no restriction on the A-levels required of potential accounting students.

This ability to understand future developments in the subject provided by accounting degrees and the opportunities to study other related disciplines such as law in some depth is what attracts many to accounting degrees. The unsolved problems of accounting provide plenty of intellectual excitement and ensure the development of reasoning and independent judgement. Most courses have a similar core of economics, elementary statistics, law and accounting. Operations research, which is the use of quantitative techniques to help in decision making, usually forms part of this core. Given the wide range of disciplines which impact on decisions, different accountancy degrees specialise in exploring the interaction of accounting with various disciplines. Many degrees stress the relation between accounting and economics. Indeed some would say that accounting is mainly microeconomics writ large. Some courses attempt to integrate accounting and business studies. Others concentrate on the sociological and psychological aspects of accounting, others combine computing and accounting and yet others explore the interaction between law and accounting. It is of importance for potential students to bear this in mind when selecting an accounting course. Most of these courses provide a good general introduction to financial management and therefore graduates are often recruited as management trainees and in many other careers not directly related to accountancy.

There still seems to be a high demand for accountants of all varieties. It is possible to specialise in financial accountancy either within an organisation or within the auditing profession. Management accounting makes a good alternative career whether in industry or the public sector. Most areas of the accounting profession offer opportunities for foreign travel and the ability to specialise in one area of accounting, such as tax advice. Often accountants, after success in their chosen branch of accounting, move on to become managing directors or chairmen of large companies reflecting the necessary wide experience of all aspects of the business acquired by senior accounting personnel.

Aeronautical Engineering

Professor Donald McLean, Southampton University

Telling anyone about aeronautical engineering is about as easy as defining an elephant: you can recognise it when you see it, but you can't describe it. The reason why it is so difficult is that aeronautical engineering is a very big subject. A large number of specialised technical disciplines go to make up the subject, but each of those disciplines can become a lifetime study for some of us. Yet to be any good at aeronautical engineering means that you must have an understanding of all of them. You must learn about the physical principles involved when anything flies, or when it moves through space where there is no real atmosphere. You have to learn the techniques needed to analyse and design aerospace vehicles. But it is that very variety and the great complexity of these vehicles which gives aeronautical engineering its special grand dimension: as an engineering subject it calls forth the greatest imagination and enthusiasm from everyone who works in it. The kind of vehicles you may be lucky enough to deal with can range from those which operate in the earth's atmosphere, to those which go beyond it. Such atmospheric vehicles are called aircraft and they range in type from the helicopter, which is slow in the air (sometimes even stationary), to Concorde, which is fast (but never hovers). Some spacecraft travel at super high speeds and operate outside earth's atmosphere, but often in the atmosphere of some other planet. In between the helicopter and Concorde there are the single-engined and twin-engined general aviation aircraft which don't fly very fast, very far, or very high, but which are the most common aircraft type in the world: in total, they fly ten times the number of hours flown by all the commercial passenger and large transport aircraft operating in the world, and by the fighters, the bombers, and the strike aircraft of all the military air forces. These commercial jet transports fly millions of people daily in safety and comfort over millions of miles at affordable cost. And then there are all the different types of military aircraft whose performance is evidently a function of their intended missions. Although each of these aircraft types has its special problems, because each operates in a different speed regime, and although research is carried out continuously on them in industrial design offices, university laboratories, and military research establishments, each type is linked by a common core of technical specialisations and disciplines which are used as the basic subjects of any British aeronautical degree. Typically, degrees have a first year devoted to subjects like mathematics, mechanics, computing, elasticity, thermodynamics, fluid mechanics, properties of materials and basic electricity which are common to all engineering subjects. In the second year all the aeronautical subjects, like aerodynamics, aircraft structures, propulsion system dynamics and stability and control, which every aeronautical engineer should know something of, are dealt with. And the final year is usually devoted to optional subjects and a project which are chosen by the student to help him specialise in his or her chosen branch of aeronautical engineering.

If you study a supersonic passenger aircraft, such as Concorde, you will find that such very high speed flight can only be achieved if it has been arranged for the air to flow over the wing, the fuselage, and the vertical fin, in a fashion which causes the efficient creation of forces and moments. But at such very high speeds, the air reacts chemically with the metal surface of the aircraft which then begins to heat up. Arranging for that heat to be dissipated before the aircraft's structure is affected, and before the passengers and crew are caused discomfort, is a major technical problem. In Concorde it was solved by using the engines' fuel as a coolant for the aircraft's surface. When we study how and why the shape of an aircraft can be arranged so that these forces and moments are produced satisfactorily by the air flow we are concerned with **aerodynamics**. From aerodynamics, for example, we learn why high speed aircraft must have swept wings. To study aerodynamics effectively means that you have to be able to get access to a wind tunnel in which a model aircraft or an airfoil can be used to obtain good measurements which apply to a real aircraft. For a good understanding of aeronautical engineering, a knowledge of aerodynamics is indispensable, and familiarity with wind tunnel techniques is most helpful in learning about aero-dynamics. So, try to study where there are plenty of wind tunnels but be warned; such facilities are expensive, so they are heavily used for laboratory classes, projects and even for staff research. In the future it may be possible to obtain the same data from computer simulation using computational fluid dynamics.

You may wonder why it is so important to know such forces and moments in such detail: the answer is that the aircraft's motion and, therefore, its flight path will be governed by them. Whenever we study aircraft motion, and the corresponding aircraft trajectory which occurs as a consequence of such forces and moments, we are then dealing with flight dynamics. Here we are concerned with the aircraft's performance, how fast it will fly, how high it will climb, how long it can fly, and how far it can fly. But in the atmosphere the air is never still, so the motion of the aircraft is always being disturbed by the very air through which it flies. Thus, the aircraft has to be controlled at every moment of its flight if it is to maintain its desired path. That continuous control can be provided by a human pilot or by an automatic flight control system. (Never call it an autopilot: that was the trade name – like Hoover – of the automatic flight control system used in the Zeppelin airships.) Whenever such human or automatic control is being studied it is necessary to know the degree of stability of the aircraft. This property is often indicated by means of the measured flying qualities of the aircraft, but with many modern aircraft, the aircraft simply cannot be designed with flying qualities which will allow a pilot to fly it safely and, as a result, automatic flight control systems have to be fitted so that the aircraft can be flown. This important topic, **stability** and **control**, is an essential part of all aeronautical engineering degree courses, although the design of the automatic control systems may be dealt with separately under Avionics. Very few aeronautical departments have a test aircraft, but even if they had it would be prudent to use **simulation**, nearly always carried out on a digital computer. You must expect to use digital computers as routinely as using a pencil. All UK courses provide a one-week test flight course.

Of course, when an aerospace vehicle is moving around it has to be structurally sound: its frame and surface must be strong enough to withstand the stresses which result from the very great forces to which a vehicle is subject whenever it is manoeuvred, or whenever it meets atmospheric turbulence. Even spacecraft orbiting outside the earth's atmosphere can be subjected to torque disturbances caused by gravity gradients and solar pressure. Thus, the study of the behaviour of materials, the stresses and strains within that material, the study of vibration, and the deflection and twisting of the structural elements, are referred to as **structural analysis**. It is an important subject for every aeronautical engineer and it is taught in every aeronautical engineering course. Equally important is the study of how a vehicle is accelerated: **propulsion**. Every engine is governed by the laws of thermodynamics and every course will give a brief introduction to propulsion, including reciprocating petrol engines and their associated propellers, the turbojet, the ramjet and, perhaps, the rocket motor. Some courses have specialised option subjects in propulsion which are particularly useful if you want to work with aircraft or spacecraft engines.

Aircraft and spacecraft carry a considerable amount of systems equipment for auxiliary power, heat exchanging, life support, fire extinguishing, communication, navigation, and flight control not to mention the wide variety of weapons systems fitted to military aircraft. Some of these systems are described by the neologism, **avionics** (a compound word from *aviation electronics*). How such systems work, and how aerospace vehicles depend upon them, are usually covered in degree courses but there are also specialist courses in avionics systems or aerospace systems engineering. The core subjects of an aerospace systems course are likely to include mathematics, computation, communication theory, electromagnetism, system dynamics, signal analysis, power and actuator systems, as well as aerodynamics, propulsion, and structural design.

Avionics systems courses involve the five principal areas of modern aeronautical engineering, namely: aerodynamics and structures, propulsion, communication and guidance, flight control systems, and information systems. If you understand that a little more than half the cost of a modern military aircraft (and sometimes as much as a third of the cost of a commercial passenger aircraft) is spent on such systems you will be able to appreciate how important such new courses are going to be in helping provide British industry with the well-educated aeronautical engineers it needs to successfully respond to the great challenges of aerospace in the future.

HELPFUL READING: O G Sutton, *Mastery of the Air* (Hodder and Stoughton, 1965); this is an up-dated version of an earlier book published by Penguin books in 1948. It was then called 'The Science of Flight'. J D Anderson, *An Introduction to Flight* (McGraw-Hill, 1978); R Shevell, *Fundamentals of Flight* (Prentice-Hall, 1983); both these books are elementary text-books, but each provides a good introduction to aeronautical engineering. C H Gibbs-Smith, *Aviation* (HMSO, Science Museum, 1985); an excellent historical account of the development of aeronautical engineering; B Sweetman, *Aircraft 2000* (Hamlyn Publishing, 1984); a good look at what present research in aeronautical engineering will accomplish. P P Wegener *What Makes Airplanes Fly* (Springer-Verlag, 1991) gives an excellent account of basic aeronautical knowledge.

African Studies

Richard Rathbone, SOAS

You have to be *exceptionally* boring to find Africa dull. African art, music and literature, all more and more available in the West, convey some of the excitement of this huge continent. Africa isn't like anywhere else. Understanding even a little of the lives of Africans demands imaginative minds that don't think that Britain is the centre of the universe. First of all you will have to cope with a *continent* not a country. Africa is massive and the historical experiences of its peoples have been immensely different. Africa boasts a virtually uncountable number of cultures, languages and styles of life. Second, you will be presented with a set of populations whose lives have changed more dramatically in the last two hundred years than any other large collection of people. Travelogue films on TV always harp on the vanishing world of the Bushmen or the herders of the encroaching Sahara. Romantic stuff; but romance always ignores the fact that such rural people are ruled from cities with motorways, fax machines and stock exchanges. When rural people look at the sky they see not only firecrowned bishop birds, but 747s coming in to land at the nearest international airport. Not many people carry spears when there are no tourists about. People your age are more likely to wear personal stereos and 501s than loincloths.

That doesn't mean that Africa is becoming a sort of tropical Croydon. The challenge of African studies is understanding how 500 million people have retained their cultural, spiritual and personal individuality in the midst of rapid change. Just about everything is relevant to that understanding. Geography helps us to grasp the immensity of the task the ancestors of modern Africans undertook when they progressively colonised often unpromising ecosystems like rain-forests or desert fringes. It also helps us to imagine the developmental possibilities of this potentially rich continent. The history of Africa, the birthplace of all our *Homo sapiens* ancestors, forces us to think about how states emerged, and perhaps even more challengingly, why some African peoples set their faces against such political organisation. It also forces us to think about why African historical development has been so unlike that of Europe. Even before the intervention of Islam and then Europe into Africa, it's clear that African political, social and economic organisations had their own striking individuality. Looking at Africa before the slave trade and colonialism allows us to tease out which elements of the dramatic changes were imposed upon Africa and which are the results of Africa's own robust initiatives.

Some of the answers to those questions will emerge from a concentration on social anthropology. This discipline helps us to get to grips with extremely varied but always original forms of African social organisation, the centrality of family relationships in their widest sense and, no less importantly, with how Africans have understood both the visible and invisible world. Understanding the root of African thought is crucial. A keen student of Africa wants more than descriptions, however good. What would you think about an African student studying Britain without learning English? Trying to learn, however basically, one of Africa's major languages equips you with the tools to begin to understand some of the words and concepts which shape African thought. The languages are not as difficult as you might think.

Many of you are interested in modern Africa because its sad problems are all that British press sensationalism is interested in. If you look at Africa through the discipline of political science you will again find a huge kaleidoscope of contrast. African states have emerged through exciting and sometimes bloody opposition to colonialism. Some are grim,

repressive states like South Africa or Zaire, others are relatively democratic and open like Senegal or Tanzania. Why do we hear so little about
the success stories? Again the economists will surprise you with a continent in which Sudanese famine plays much less of a role than hard-won
development and the improvement in people's standards of living of the
sort that has been evident in Botswana and Zimbabwe. It's certainly true
that studying modern Africa will help you understand some of the great
problems of today like the north–south divide, the population and
resource crises, military intervention and South Africa, but it's not all
gloomy. It's an environment, after all, from which an African novelist
has recently won the Nobel prize for literature, in which the Bhundu
Boys and all the musical innovators from Mali we've been enjoying in
Britain recently and some of the greatest athletes in the world have
developed their skills.

African Studies is usually approached through a combined studies
format. You'll get advice about good combinations from the teachers at
individual colleges and universities. Be warned we are all fanatics. We've
all worked in Africa and can't put it down. Studying Africa makes for a
kind of commitment which is unusual in higher education. Students get
infected too and there is no known cure. Why is it so infectious? Firstly
there are few better opportunities to embark on comparative, multidisciplinary studies which use some of the skills you've acquired at school
but demand you use them in a totally different environment. Secondly
Africa comes to matter a lot to those who study it. It's not a place, but
an excitingly varied collection of populations. And these people are
exciting, warm and original. The more you learn about the things
they think are important, the more you wonder about your own society's
values and styles. Above all, as with all study, there is a lot to learn
and a lot of it is hard, but the slog is always accompanied by the
availability of Africa's art, its music, its literature. If any of this begins to
sound interesting, read some of the novels I have suggested. If it stops
being interesting then you are, as I suggested in the beginning, exceptionally boring.

HELPFUL READING: Fiction: Chinua Achebe, *Things Fall Apart*
(Heinemann, 1958); Chinua Achebe, *Anthills of the Savanna* (Heine-
mann, 1987); M Dikobe, *The Marabi Dance* (Heinemann, 1973);
Bessie Head, *A Collector of Treasures* (Heinemann, 1977). **Non-fiction:**
S E Akpabot, *Football in Nigeria* (Macmillan, 1985); D Coplan, *In
Township Tonight! South Africa's black city music and theatre* (Long-
man, 1985); John Dunn (ed), *West African States* (CUP, 1978); Paulin J
Hountondji, *African Philosophy, Myth and Reality* (Hutchinson,
1983); John Mack, *Madagascar. Island of the Ancestors* (British
Museum, 1986); Ali A Mazrui, *The Africans. A triple heritage* (BBC
Publications, 1986); P Richards, *Indigenous Agricultural Revolution:
ecology and food production in West Africa* (Hutchinson, 1985);
Landeg White, *Magomero* (CUP, 1987); John Iliffe, *The African Poor:
a History* (CUP, 1987).

Agriculture, Horticulture and Forestry

Professor W Holmes, Wye College

The study of natural resources, and their management to provide food, fibre and other materials is of major importance throughout the world. The current emphasis on the environment makes it even more important that the physical, biological and economic principles underlying the production of crops, trees, and animals, and their interactions with the environment, are well understood.

Agriculture, horticulture and forestry and related subjects studied at degree level deal with these subjects in a very effective way. General courses give a broad training and open the way to many careers. There are also specialist courses in sciences (agricultural botany, agricultural biochemistry, agricultural zoology, animal science, horticultural science, wood science); courses emphasising economics (such as agricultural economics, agricultural business management, agricultural and food marketing); environmental courses (agriculture and environmental science, forestry and natural resources, terrestrial ecology) and in agricultural engineering.

Before you start, you must of course have a genuine interest in the subject. You might have grown up on a farm but this is certainly not essential. The subject may appeal because you like the growing of plants or you like working with animals. Or, you may wish to apply your skills and interests in biology, or chemistry, or economics, or geology, or mathematics, or physics to the real life situation. Or you may just like the countryside and country pursuits. Whatever your motivation, evidence of a keen interest and that you have read something about the subject will help to impress the selectors; a vague sentimental interest in nature and the open air is not enough.

For most courses, it is preferred that you spend at least one year after school, gaining practical experience on a farm, a horticultural holding or an agricultural research station before you start. Even farmers' sons and daughters are encouraged to gain experience away from home. The majority of students find it enjoyable and rewarding to learn some of farming's manual skills and to live through the annual cycle of events. Moreover many employers consider such experience to be essential. As an alternative, a few courses provide for the student to take a sandwich year to gain his or her practical experience in the middle rather than before the course begins.

Courses in the UK normally last 3 or 4 years, in addition to the practical year, with a progression from basic studies in the first year to more applied studies in the later years. For example, a course in agriculture will probably include the study of biology, biochemistry and economics together with introductory aspects of agriculture and statistics in the first year. Soil science, crop production, animal production, farm mechanisation and farm management would be second-year courses. Advanced aspects of crop and animal production, and of farm management together with selections from more specialist topics (eg animal breeding, marketing, plant pathology or intensive horticultural crop-ping) might occupy the final years. In addition most final year courses include a project, in which the student pursues a particular interest in some detail and submits a report or dissertation as part of the final examination.

Courses in horticulture, plant science and agricultural botany concentrate on plants. The horticultural courses include production and amenity horticulture, economics, management and marketing as well as the sciences of plant nutrition, plant physiology and plant pathology. Courses in plant science and agricultural botany are more science oriented: they omit management and devote the additional time to experimental techniques and frequently to the conduct of small scale investigations.

Similarly, courses in animal science and agricultural zoology provide for more detailed study of the anatomy, physiology and biochemistry of farm animals and of the parasites and insects of agricultural importance but omit some of the more practical aspects of animal husbandry and management. Since some of the work is conducted with smaller organisms, practical laboratory projects may be included.

Courses in agricultural economics are intended primarily for planners or consultants rather than for farm or estate managers whose needs are usually met by courses in agriculture, agricultural business management or horticulture. These courses therefore start from a base of economics, mathematics and statistics and progress to advanced economics, agrarian development, agricultural policy, economic statistics, management and marketing with relatively brief reference to agricultural technology. Courses in agricultural business management and land economy depend more heavily on economics, management techniques and legal aspects and they give less emphasis to scientific subjects.

Of course it is not all work. The faculties of agriculture are usually small communities of from 400–800 students, sometimes in a rural setting. They usually have a strong community spirit with good sports facilities, a wide range of other student activities and excellent staff/student relationships.

A good degree gained in this wide field of study opens a remarkable variety of career opportunities. Some graduates are soon running their own business in farming or horticulture, many are managing businesses for larger organisations or estates. A further large proportion is involved in advisory work either with state or EC organisations or with commercial companies. Education, research and government posts at home or overseas also provide many opportunities.

These subjects lead to a wide range of interesting and useful careers in Britain, Europe and in the tropics. Indeed if you wish to apply science to the benefit of mankind, what better opportunity, apart from medicine, than in the oldest technology, agriculture.

HELPFUL READING: Books which give a general description of British agriculture include *Freams Agriculture* (John Murray, 1983); Michael Haines, *An Introduction to Farming Systems* (Longman, 1982), and *Farming UK* (HMSO, 1987). There are weekly journals like

The Farmers Weekly and *The Grower*, while serious newspapers have many articles on agricultural topics such as the Common Agricultural Policy and agricultural development overseas.

American Studies

Dr Michael Dunne, Sussex University

The term, American studies, is somewhat misleading; for though the adjective American can be applied to the whole of the Western Hemisphere, in this country American studies denotes primarily the investigation of the past and present society of the USA. Canada, the USA's larger though sparsely populated northern neighbour, has not normally been included in American studies syllabuses and has more usually appeared as part of British Imperial and Commonwealth history and relations. In recent years, however, courses on Canadian history, society and culture have grown and are increasingly to be found in combination with traditional American studies. As for the huge and populous areas of South and Central America and the Caribbean, these are most often grouped into Latin American studies. In this latter case a number of separate departments or institutions of Latin American studies exist; alternatively, the study of Latin America is pursued in departments of Hispanic or Romance language and literature as part of the dispersion of the Spanish and Portuguese-speaking peoples. If, therefore, you are seeking hemispheric or Pan American perspectives on today's United States you would be well advised to investigate the offerings of universities which give instruction in Spanish, Portuguese and French (the latter for Canada and the Caribbean). Furthermore, if your concern is to study the indigenous, non-European (pre-Colombian) peoples and languages of the Americas, then you should survey the opportunities provided by departments of anthropology and ethnology.

One consequence of this academic map-drawing is that most American (ie USA) studies departments have emphasized the British or, more generally, northern European roots of contemporary United States society. Recently, however, and as another reflection of both changing attitudes and demographic facts, the Latin, African and (increasingly) Asian contributions to American life have been steadily recognized in the growing number of university courses on Hispanic Americans, the African diaspora and the nature and legacies of slavery, and the salience of newer ethnic groups from the western Pacific rim: Japan, Korea, China, Vietnam, and the Philippines.

These changes and qualifications show that geographic considerations merge into chronological ones; and American studies is no exception. In this study area the concentration is upon events and issues since the Era of the Revolution, the War of Independence and the establishment of the federal government under the US Constitution (1763–1789). So while many American studies departments provide general and specialist options in British North American colonial culture and society, if your main interests lie in the pre-Independence period or in imperial relations, then you may be better served in the more traditional straight history departments.

These geographical and chronological axes help to explain one of the most striking characteristics of American studies, namely its concern (preoccupation might be a better word) with definitions of national identity. 'What is an American?' was a question posed by an observer of the new-born United States, the Frenchman Crèvecoeur; and the early decades of American studies after World War II echoed with the rephrasing and inconclusive answering of that conundrum. Nor has its resonance faded: women's studies, ethnic studies, black (African American) studies are, in the United States especially, conscious and vigorous movements to redirect academic as well as popular concern away from the presumptions and values which originally informed analyses of American history and literature. That such fields of intellectual study and social activity have not been institutionalised to the same extent in this country as they have in the United States is one measure of the difference between those putative cousins, the British and the Americans. At the same time the elasticity of American studies in British universities does offer room for exploring such important subjects by combining long-established disciplines such as history, literary analysis, sociology, anthropology, and geography with newer insights drawn from psychology, semiology and linguistics.

These comments should not be taken to mean that American studies departments provide instruction in every branch of social enquiry! Rather they are intended to point to the possibilities of combining area and interdisciplinary studies. For the simple truth is that American studies still retains its links with long-established modes of academic investigation – what are called the disciplines. In most American studies departments academic interests are likely to cluster around one of three nuclei: literature, history and (increasingly) a number of the social sciences, especially politics, sociology, economics and geography. The existence of these specialisms means that students are trained to become experts in particular disciplines by applying those disciplines to American materials. But the underlying theory is by no means exclusively American: literature specialists, historians and social scientists will be incorporating the latest thinking from outside the USA, notably from continental Europe.

From these perspectives it may be easily seen that American studies is no more outlandish than studying European history, English literature or international relations. Conversely and more positively, American studies does distinguish itself by the strength and success of its efforts to relate the study of history, literature, politics, sociology and so forth to one another. Thus you will find courses on gender in American society, on the south and the west, on black culture and black consciousness, on class and social mobility – in all of which the diachronic and synchronic methods of structuralism are employed in redrawing conceptual and disciplinary boundaries. Thus the west is understood not merely as California and the Pacific coast, nor even Hawaii of today; it is also the west in the imagination of the eighteenth century enlightenment; gender is not merely the definition of contemporary women and men but a critical concept in the study of the ideologies of equality and freedom at the time of the Revolution. So too with race and class: similarities and dissimilarities are explored across time and place by examining people's lives, their social relations and their artefacts.

Much of the material (or data, evidence) of American studies reflects its concern with questions of social formation and reproduction. How does the mass media operate? What is the social function of the leisure industry? What is the influence of television upon politics, especially presidential elections? What are the preconceptions and dangers in basing academic enquiry upon printed (and predominantly book-form) sources? These sorts of theoretical questions explain why American studies embraces film and broadcasting; the press and journalism; oral history and folklore; music and the visual and plastic arts.

Not all departments of American studies treat every one of these subjects in equal depth. Nor indeed is American studies taught at degree-level only in American studies departments. The organization of American studies varies from one university to another. In some universities American studies constitute a separate department; in others different departments (usually history and literature) offer or pool courses, which can then be taken by students specializing in American studies. In both these models it is usually necessary to take courses either from a range of disciplines (eg from a list of both history and literature topics) or from specially-designed interdisciplinary courses embracing work in a number of different study-areas (eg popular images of the Frontier). With the growth of modular degrees, such mix-and-match options are likely to grow, with American studies courses taken as major or minor components in joint degrees. Generally speaking, it is advisable to seek out separately-organized American studies departments, for these are more likely to offer integrated patterns of study, have a larger number of Americanists (specialists in the study of the USA) and enjoy better resources and library facilities. Such American studies departments, with their own designed degree-programmes, are also more likely to provide for a period of study in the United States. When consulting school and college advisers, reading through prospectuses and syllabuses, questioning interviewers and admissions officers you should look out for teaching and resource strengths in particular areas. Try to find out the possibilities for research in depth *and* for bridging traditional gaps (say between high and popular culture, between painting and photography, between economic or legislative history and sociological theory, between the geography of physical space and the location of social inequality). In this way you will be making your own contribution to the shape and development of American studies.

HELPFUL READING: Hugh Brogan, *Penguin History of the United States of America* (1990); Marcus Cunliffe, *The Literature of the United States* (1991 – also published by Penguin); Angela Y. Davis, *Women, Race and Class* (1982).

Anatomy

Professor Anthony Firth, St Mary's Hospital Medical School, London

Anatomy does not form a body of knowledge clearly distinct from other biomedical sciences such as physiology or biochemistry, for all of these concern themselves with the problem of how living things work. However, anatomy takes a distinctive approach to investigation of this problem. The word 'anatomy' means 'cutting apart'; the anatomical approach is to explore the structure of living organisms as a way of getting at how they work. Anatomists tend to think in terms of shapes and relationships in space as the most striking and exciting aspects of living things – their imagination tends to be visual and spatial rather than abstract.

The earliest anatomists relied on dissection of dead organisms ('dissection' is another word meaning 'cutting apart') as their main method of study, and dissection of the dead bodies of people or of domestic animals still forms the core of many anatomy courses in medical, dental or veterinary science. Research in anatomy has more or less exhausted all but the small print of this 'gross anatomy' and has largely moved on to other things, although each generation of medical students still discovers anew the fascination of exploring the elegant intricacy of the human body.

Whether or not students of biology outside the health sciences come across anatomy as a formal subject in their courses, they use the methods of structural study which typify the anatomical approach to biology. These now range from naked-eye observations during dissection to high-resolution microscopic examination of cells and their components. The first effective use of the electron microscope on biological materials in the 1950s both emphasised the power of the visual approach and also underlined its limitations. With these instruments it is possible to reveal the organisation not only of cell interiors but also of the large molecules such as DNA and proteins which characterise living tissue, but until quite recently this ability to see fine structural detail has been offset by the maddening difficulty of finding out anything precise about the chemical nature of the structures so revealed. For example, despite the hundreds of articles which have been published about the structure of the seamlike junctions between cells of the surface-covering sheets called epithelia, none of the chemical compounds of these junctions has yet been identified.

This kind of problem is rather akin to that which once confronted astronomers who could see stars very clearly through telescopes but could say nothing about their chemical composition. The astronomers made headway against this problem by recognising that particular elements leave tell-tale absorption lines at characteristic frequencies in the spectrum. Over the last generation, and particularly in the last ten years, biologists have learned to characterise the molecular composition of microscopic structures by a range of methods which allow the presence of specific molecules to be revealed by light or electron microscopy. This hybrid science of histochemistry is an extraordinarily powerful tool, for it has allowed specific chemical information to be obtained with all the precision about structure and spatial relationships which characterises microscopic science. At first this could only be exploited for a fairly limited number of biologically interesting chemicals which were sufficiently distinctive for them to be stainable by chemical reactions which failed to stain other substances: starch and neutral fats are good examples. The most interesting molecules of living systems, the nucleic acids and proteins, could be identified as classes but it seemed impossible to label selectively a single species of protein or a single gene in a chromosome. Something could be done with those proteins which happened to be catalysts, the enzymes, as they could often be manipulated to yield a visible and insoluble reaction product which could be recognised by light or electron microscopy. Enzyme histochemistry has been with us for about thirty years and grows in subtlety and usefulness every year; it can show us not only where enzymes are within a cell, but also which reactions they can catalyse and even how fast they can do it.

However, the real explosion of biological microscopy owes its existence to a group of methods collectively and repulsively described as 'specific ligand binding histochemistry'. These exploit the ability of certain classes of molecules to recognise and bind very selectively to other molecules of biological interest. For example, the group of proteins called antibodies, made by cells of the immune system, are characterised by the ability of a particular antibody type to bind very selectively to a particular site on a specific protein or some other molecule of moderate complexity. A wide range of methods can be used to label this antibody so that it can be used as a visible probe. In light microscopy a spectacular result is obtained by using labels such as fluorescein which glow brilliantly when exposed to ultraviolet light of the correct wavelength; cells or other structures which have bound the fluorescein-labelled antibody literally 'light up'. Similar stratagems using labels such as colloidal particles of gold allow the extension of these immunohistochemical methods to electron microscopy. Our ability to culture clones of antibody-making cells derived from a single original cell now allows us to make single-specificity antibodies against single components of complex and unpurifiable mixtures of molecules, ability to make these monoclonal antibodies being only limited by practical considerations of time and expense. Similarly, another family of specific probes can be directed against the genes themselves; genetic engineering methods allow single genes or groups of genes to be grown in bacterial cells, and these mass-produced 'cloned DNA' molecules can be labelled and used to light up matching gene sequences within cells. Short sequences of synthetic DNA can be used in a similar way.

This fusion of microscopy with the 'new biology' of cloned DNA and monoclonal antibodies has revolutionised biomedical research in just a few years. If anatomy is defined as 'what anatomists do', then most biologists are becoming anatomists as labelled probes and microscopes become ubiquitous tools of experimental biology. Good anatomy has always been concerned with the relationship between form and function rather than with the sterile description of form for its own sake, and these new histochemical methods enable us to paint our maps of the body in functionally defined and vivid colours.

For students entering biology these are exciting times. Those training for medicine and allied professions meet both the traditional and the new anatomy. They study the human body by dissecting the dead, by examining pictures generated by an ever-growing range of non-invasive imaging methods such as x-radiographs, computerised tomography, ultrasound and magnetic resonance imaging. They explore living anatomy by examining their own bodies and those of other students. They study the mature and the developing body by microscopic means which increasingly depend on the chemically specific and functionally informative methods of histochemistry. For all biologists form and function are becoming unified by new methods in microscopy. Whether we work on the unfolding of the genetic program of development, the functional organisation of the brain, the subtly disordered biology of cancer cells, or the means by which Amoeba achieves the extraordinarily complex task of crawling across a piece of glass, our approach leans heavily on the central insight of anatomy: that form is the visible aspect of invisible functions and so can serve as a road to understanding them.

HELPFUL READING: Edited B Alberts et al, *Molecular Biology of the Cell* (New York, Garland, 1989 (2nd edition)).

Anthropology

Professor Adam Kuper, Brunel University

Anthropologists have a romantic image. They are pictured camping in an Amazonian rain forest, or sailing on a frail barque between two little Pacific islands, accompanying a picturesquely attired party intent on some exotic ritual exchange. In Germany, students are flocking to study anthropology, apparently because they believe it is the Green Party of the social sciences. But it is true that not everyone finds the romance irresistible. My mother believed that anthropologists were driven crazy by isolation in the bush. When I began working in the Kalahari Desert she suffered gloomy forebodings – and who shall say she was wrong? But few people have much idea what anthropologists are really up to, and they are surprised to discover that we may also do field studies rather closer to home, in Greek islands, Irish villages, or even Midlands factories.

Anthropology is about the evolution, unity and diversity of the human species. One branch of anthropology, physical anthropology, is concerned largely with the biological evolution of human beings. However, the main differences between human communities over the past 100,000 years at least have been cultural rather than biological, and the other main branches of anthropology concern themselves with the study of cultural development and variation. Archaeologists drive deep shafts back in time, reconstructing cultural processes in the distant past. Social or cultural anthropologists study contemporary human communities, charting their customs and practices and attempting to explain them.

The central experience of anthropologists is always fieldwork. Ideally they spend one or two years alone in an exotic community, participating as far as possible in the life of the people, speaking their language and forging bonds of friendship and trust. This sometimes trying, often inspiring, always important experience of immersion in a totally strange way of life is then laboriously relived at home, and translated into a formal analysis either of the community or, more usually today, of an aspect of its life. (But a number of anthropologists do slip the academic restrictions and produce lively impressionistic and personal accounts of their experience, such as Nigel Barley's humorous reminiscences of fieldwork in West Africa and Indonesia.)

Fieldwork – ethnography – is only one aspect of the anthropologist's work. The challenge to field-workers is not only to make sense of their observations, but to relate what they have seen to studies made of similar institutions elsewhere. The ultimate goal is to further our understanding of social and cultural processes at large.

Social anthropology is a comparative social science, living on particularly intimate terms with history and sociology, though there are also fecund links with other disciplines. It can often be studied in association with another subject, sometimes in the traditional company of physical anthropology and archaeology, but otherwise together with ancient history, linguistics, African or Asian languages, psychology or sociology.

First-year students are sometimes shocked by their sudden, unjudging exposure to the variety of ways in which people think it proper and sensible to order their lives but this is itself a profoundly educational experience and the discipline provides rich insights into other cultures. Students are also given a training in social science approaches and techniques, which often provides a basis for further independent academic development or opens the way to a career in the media, market research, social work, teaching or, in some cases, to the adventure of anthropological research.

Applied anthropology is a growing field. Government departments or development agencies are the usual employers but in the USA today more than half of professional anthropologists are employed by the private sector. Anthropologists advise on problems of development abroad and are often to be found on teams of planners associated with development projects. Others have come to specialise in community relations at home, particularly in multi-cultural environments and they may contribute to policy-making in fields as diverse as medical or educational services and town planning.

For some anthropologists, the ultimate justification of our studies is a moral one. Lévi-Strauss has suggested that the study of anthropology offers two advantages:

First, they encourage us to take a level-headed and unbiased view of customs and ways of life remote from our own – without, however, attributing to them absolute merits such as no society can claim to possess. Second, they dissuade us from taking for granted the 'rightness' or 'naturalness' of our own customs, as can easily be the case if we know of no others, or know of them only partly and with bias.

HELPFUL READING: Claude Lévi-Strauss, *Triste Tropiques* (Harmondsworth: Penguin, 1976); Adam Kuper, *Anthropology and Anthropologists: the Modern British School* (London: Routledge and Kegan Paul, 1983). The Royal Anthropological Institute publishes a lively bi-monthly magazine, *Anthropology Today.* Subscription is £8 (£15 for libraries), payable to the Royal Anthropological Institute, 50 Fizroy Street, London W1P 5HS.

Archaeology
Dr S W Hillson, University College London

Lost cities, great ancient works of art in gold and precious stones, the sumptuous tombs of forgotten kings. If you study archaeology, you can certainly learn about such exciting and exotic things, but most archaeologists spend most of their time dealing with much more mundane objects such as broken pottery and bones – the accumulated waste of ordinary households, farms and towns. What keeps us fascinated is the light that archaeology can shed on everyday life in ancient communities, rather than the lives and works of the great and powerful. This is one of the major differences between archaeology and history. Written history is mostly about rulers and the nobility, military and religious life. Archaeology is based on physical remains rather than records and the great bulk of the material which survives from the past represents the common people. Most ancient objects, even those which may seem to us to be ugly, poorly made or badly damaged, have a story locked up in them. There is a real thrill in taking a small, broken fragment out of the ground, and bringing this story out with careful detective work. If you want to find out how people live, a good way is to look in their household refuse, and much of archaeology is tied up with the recovery and sophisticated analysis of ancient domestic rubbish.

Archaeology is an unusually broad subject, bridging the arts and the sciences. It ranges throughout the world, wherever people have lived, and extends from the earliest artifacts made by our extinct relatives some two and a half million years ago, through the period of historical records, including the industrial revolution and up to the present day. The basic approach is scientific, because objects must be excavated and studied in as methodical and objective a manner as possible, but there is also room for the artistic appreciation of beautiful artifacts and for interpretations which involve history, philosophy and sociology. An expanding field is 'science-based archaeology'; applying techniques which originated in the more traditional sciences. Physics is used to date objects and to locate buried sites. Chemistry helps to discover ancient methods of manufacture and trade routes. Biology is applied in the study of health, hygiene and diet in ancient communities. With all these different strands to archaeology, it can be difficult to define the core of the subject.

If you apply to study archaeology, you will find a bewildering range of degree courses and options. Some courses are highly specialised, such as classical archaeology, medieval archaeology, Egyptology, Near Eastern archaeology and archaeological conservation (the restoration and preservation of artifacts). These are really for people who already know the area of archaeology in which they would like to concentrate. The majority of people are less sure and apply for general archaeology courses, but the coverage of these also varies considerably. The subject is so wide that very few institutions have the staff to cover the full range, or even a substantial part of it. Look very carefully at what options are available before you apply. The majority of courses deal with the archaeology of Europe, Mediterranean and Middle Eastern countries. It is much harder to find course options on the archaeology of Africa, eastern Asia and Australasia, and the Americas. Some departments specialise in prehistory, whilst others concentrate on the classical or medieval periods. Relatively few institutions have specialist options in the various science-based archaeology subjects but some departments concentrate on them and several BSc degrees in archaeology are offered. Because of all these variations, it is a good idea to visit archaeology departments in good time before you apply. Most departments will be very pleased to arrange this. I certainly see many people each year in this way.

Despite the rather exotic nature of the material, much of an archaeology course follows the traditional pattern of classes but one of the distinctive features of the subject is practical work. You are likely to do a lot of fieldwork because it is the basis of all archaeology. Fieldwork is one of the main attractions for most professional archaeologists and students, ranging from a regional field survey to full excavation of a particular site. Depending on the course, you may travel widely with your fieldwork. There may also be a lot of practical work in the drawing office and laboratory. You could be identifying and piecing together sherds of pottery, learning to interpret aerial photographs, practising drawing site plans, learning to sort and identify animal bone fragments, or using a microscope to identify pollen grains. Archaeological conservation involves a specialised training with a great deal of laboratory work, learning various treatments and restoration techniques. Most students enjoy handling ancient objects very much. The fieldwork and practical content of courses varies, and it is well worth finding out what facilities are available in a particular department and how much hands-on experience of artifacts and other remains there is.

What kinds of people do archaeology? Archaeology is at present rarely taught at A and AS level, so school or college leavers come with all sorts of different combinations of subjects including both arts and sciences. There is no 'best' combination and most subjects are relevant to some aspect of archaeology. Some students have had little or no previous experience of archaeology, whilst others have been helping on excavations for years. Thousands of people are actively involved as amateurs on archaeological projects, either in their own local societies or as volunteers on professionally run excavations. If you are thinking of studying archaeology you would be well advised to try a little excavation beforehand. The archaeology bug can bite at any age and, although some students started digging in their early teens, an increasing number of people are well established in another career before they decide that their real interests lie in archaeology. You will certainly meet people from a wide variety of backgrounds, age groups and nationalities.

HELPFUL READING: Kevin Greene *Archaeology: an introduction* (Batsford, 1983); Keith Branigan (Ed.) *The Atlas of Archaeology* (Macdonald & Co, 1982); Andrew Sherratt (Ed.) *The Cambridge Encyclopedia of Archaeology* (Cambridge University Press, 1980).

Architecture

Sandra Morris, Architectural Association School of Architecture

Architecture is the world around us. It is the room in which we live, the house across the road, the city in which we walk each day. It is equally the Dogong village carved into the rock, the Bedouin tent, the Eskimo igloo, another world of architecture in which architects have had no hand. The urge to build a shelter, to create a personal space, we are dependent on the architect and his team to provide us with an environment in which we can feel comfortable, happy and relaxed.

The development of any city is a history of complex issues. Buildings do not simply emerge fully fledged from the mind of an architect, but reflect the social, economic and aesthetic issues of their day. To walk round a Georgian square is to experience a certain lifestyle. An understanding of the predominant issues that have determined form, structure and materials is essential to any criticism of architecture.

An architect is not just a skilled technician but a highly creative person whose skills enable him or her to communicate intentions and aspirations through drawings, and to organise the various components of a building into an integrated whole. At best the architect is still an artist, in the same way that Brunelleschi or Alberti were artists of the Renaissance.

There are many ways of approaching architecture and as many ways of teaching it. No-one expects a student beginning a course to be able to 'draw a building'. What every school looks for are the students with an eye and a lively imagination, who know how to select from among the myriad images with which we are bombarded every day of our lives what is important for them. Drawing skills can be acquired, but ideas are more difficult to come by. It is the quality of the ideas that will finally distinguish the architect from the draughtsman.

Most architectural schools – and there are over thirty to choose from in the UK – operate a selection system based on a personal interview. Once a student has fulfilled the academic requirements, a place will be offered on the basis of suitability for the course. A portfolio of drawings, paintings, photographs is the surest way of convincing a panel that you have the motivation and commitment to undertake a five-year full-time course and another two years of practical training in an architect's office.

Architecture is not a subject that can be spoon-fed or learned from books – although books on architecture and by architects should certainly be an important feature of any architect's life. From day one a student can expect to be looking at things in a new and spatial way, to be making associations with art, cinema and literature, to be solving simple three dimensional problems. But architecture is not an abstract art. Although, like the artist, the architect uses form, mass and colour, his art is functional. He is also responsible for choosing structures and materials which other people will assemble in order to create the building he has designed. So the student must discover how different materials behave in particular circumstances and respond to stress and tension. He will work on the technical aspects of his design and perhaps build a detail of it in steel, concrete, glass, whatever is appropriate. The workshop can become an important place for acquiring technical knowledge and a feel for materials. An understanding of what a specific material will do in certain conditions, of how sunlight will hit a wall or lie across a floor at a certain time of day, can be the key to experiencing a building.

Looking at End of Year Exhibitions in architectural schools can be both inspiring and overwhelming. It is a very important way of helping a student to select the right school, but it is sometimes hard for a beginner to believe that he or she will one day be capable of making drawings as beautiful as those on the walls. It is always important to remember that the drawing is only a tool, the real significance of which lies in its ability to communicate with clarity.

The architect must always understand the needs of those who will inhabit his spaces, and ensure that his building is sympathetic to its context, whether urban or rural. In the Dogong village, the villagers themselves build according to their needs. The architect still has a great deal to learn from the techniques of other cultures, which is why it is so important for every student to have access through lectures and exhibitions to work that is being done by other architects all over the world. But he can never assume that what has been right for one set of people will be appropriate for another. It is up to you, the architects of tomorrow, to ensure that architecture in Britain is in the forefront of all our concerns. It is a responsible and challenging role to undertake.

HELPFUL READING: Kenneth Frampton: *Concise History of Modern Architecture*; Stein Eiler Rasmussen: *Experiencing Architecture*; Rayner Banham: *Theory & Design in the First Machine Age*; Robert Harbison: *Eccentric Spaces*.

Art and Design

Bernard Gay

Academically able and talented young people who can dedicate themselves to a future concerned with influencing and improving the quality of life through design or who can contribute to the cultural ethos of society through the visual arts will find rewarding and interesting careers in the world of art and design.

Many academically able applicants who have a desire to be makers and doers as well as thinkers embark on careers of study in art and design despite the education system in Britain rather than because of it. No gifted young person at school should allow themselves to be dissuaded from the idea of such a career if they feel their abilities, interests and inclinations lie in that direction. It is often the case that the most gifted sixth formers will be discouraged from considering courses in art and design and persuaded to consider what are regarded as more academically respectable subject areas. In fact art and design requires high intellectual ability combined with visual awareness and the capacity to translate ideas into material form.

The term art and design embraces five separate areas of study and practice: they are fine art, graphic design, textiles/fashion, three dimensional design, photography. These umbrella titles give no idea of the diversity of courses of study which they embrace. The majority of

ART & DESIGN DEGREE COURSE STUDY AREAS AND SPECIALISATIONS

Study area	Area of specialisation
Fine art	*includes* painting; printmaking; sculpture; some photography, film and in some courses other media studies
Graphic design	*includes* visual communication; graphic design; typography; illustration; advertising design; media and production; information design; scientific and technical graphics
Photography	*includes* photographic arts; applied photography; film and television; visual communication; photographic sciences (this last does not require a foundation course)
Textiles/fashion	*includes* woven and printed textiles; fashion; contour fashion; design of carpets and related textiles; embroidery; footwear design; fashion administration and marketing; knitwear
Three-dimensional design	*includes* ceramics; furniture; glass; industrial design (engineering); industrial design (transportation); interior design; jewellery; silver and metal; silversmithing; theatre design; and wood, metal, ceramics and plastics

courses are pursued in schools and colleges of art and in the new universities. The duration of the degree courses is either of three years full time study or four years on sandwich courses when a substantial period is spent in industry or in a related professional practice. There are a number of routes of entry to degree courses; for many, the preferred route is the foundation course.

As an alternative to the degree, applicants may embark on vocational courses, nationally validated by the Business and Technician Education Council (BTEC). BTEC awards a diploma and a higher diploma, the higher diploma course attracts a mandatory grant.

Fine Art

Fine art is an infinitely more variable study than used to be the case. Painting, sculpture and printmaking remain as hitherto the principal areas of practice, but fine art can now embrace film, photography, video, animation, elements of sound and movement, performance, and a large range of other media and practice. The nature of a particular course will be determined by the teaching staff many of whom are likely to be visiting part-time teachers who are successful practising artists. The content and structure of a course of study will reflect their interests and professional practice.

There are such important differences in content and approach in fine art courses that students will be well advised to investigate carefully the nature and philosophy of any course before committing themselves to it.

The majority of courses have in common a firmly structured beginning but will allow and encourage increasing freedom as study progresses, offering students the opportunity through practice to discover their personal language and direction and the media through which their ideas can be best expressed.

The initial stages of a course are likely to be exploratory; students will be confronted with a wide range of approaches and methods of working though they will not be required to acquire predetermined specific skills to any high degree. In fact the development of a particular skill or technique as an end in itself is likely to be discouraged. While in recent years there has been less concern with training in established disciplines and techniques, there has recently been a re-emergence of more traditional attitudes. The majority of courses, however, remain open-ended and will encourage students to discover those areas of visual art most appropriate to their particular talent and inclinations.

After the initial stages of the course have been completed, where work is likely to have been based on projects and assignments, it is usual for students to opt for a particular area or studio and for the teaching to be carried forward by means of tutorials and by means of a personal critical dialogue between the student and usually several individual members of staff. All courses contain an academic element of study broadly related to the history of art and design and it is usual for each student to complete a thesis on an agreed subject of their own choice. These studies are separately assessed and contribute to the grade of the final degree. Final assessment is usually conducted through a display of the work carried out during the course of study.

Graphic Design

No one can be unaware of the sustained impact of the mass media in our society. We are daily bombarded with visual and verbal messages. This is the world of the graphic designer who through the whole range of communication media will engage in art form to persuade, manipulate, transform, and educate the public.

A large number of degree and vocational courses is available for the student who wants to work in the graphic/communication design field. Courses are different in emphasis from each other. Some concentrate on illustration, the drawn image, print making and fine printing, others will specialise in film, photography, video, and animation. The majority will be concerned with the graphic image and typography in advertising; some will concentrate more on the visual image, others more on typography and the printed image. All will be concerned with the development of original and personal solutions to communication design problems.

Some graphic designers, those who specialise in the illustration of books, for example, will be engaged in private practice, freelancing, working with an author or a publisher as commissioned. The majority are likely to work in an organisation or agency designing and operating within constraints set by a client. For such a designer creative identity is concerned with problem solving within the parameters set by the particular project. The designer will be required to practise to a high level of ability over a wide range of techniques, methods and media.

Graphic design, the title which has traditionally covered the work of designers in mass media, is now often referred to as communication design which better explains the technology including computer-based printing and image making and television which, with other photo-based imagery, now dominates the graphic design world. Students who engage in this form of study need a good visual sense, a command of the spoken and written word, creative flair, and the ability to visualise ideas and images.

A good course will familiarise the aspiring designer with the technologies, techniques and methods employed by other designers while nourishing and promoting the natural aptitudes and abilities of the individual student.

Photography

Recently photography has grown in scale and importance. It has always been recognised as a science, a technical skill and a craft. It is now increasingly regarded as a significant art form in its own right. Courses at degree and vocational level are available to accommodate those students who see their futures in one of the numerous specialist areas of professional photographic practice.

As in other areas of art and design education, the content and orientation of courses will depend to some extent upon the special interests of the staff and the nature and level of specialist resources available. Photographic technology, photographic sciences, medical and technical photography, photographic journalism, fashion photography, film and photographic arts, applied photography, visual communication photography, film and television, and holography are some of the many major study areas covered by existing courses. They are also likely to cover the history of photography, the history of art, communication studies and other appropriate contextual studies such as the literary arts, the history of ideas, and social studies. Courses will certainly contain studies in the technical theory of photography. The balance between theoretical and practical work will vary between one course and another.

Employment opportunities for graduates are wide, ranging from employment in the photographic industry, in large photographic and film units in industry, or in medical illustration departments in hospitals. Careers can also be made as a professional photographer, film maker, sponsored photographic artist, teacher, film critic, archivist, researcher, or film librarian.

Students with an interest in the photographic arts who are not certain that they want to pursue a course dedicated only to photography will, if they read the notes on other art and design degree and vocational courses (or study individual college prospectuses), recognise that some fine art and graphic design courses offer a major option in some combination of photography, film and television.

Textiles/Fashion

For those considering a career in textiles or fashion design there is plenty of choice in the number and nature of courses at degree and vocational level. Courses vary in the emphasis they place on different aspects of the subject. Aspiring textile designers can specialise in printed, woven or knitted textiles. Some courses combine the study of textiles with fashion while others specialise in fashion. Most courses will ensure that students gain experience in more than one particular area before they commit themselves to a single specialisation. It will be found that these courses provide a broad and varied experience leading to interesting careers.

Fashion courses will provide opportunities to design for men and children as well as for women. Some teach fashion illustration or accessory design and there are courses which provide an emphasis on business studies and management. Students will learn to cut and make garments as a means to realise ideas. Many courses help develop considerable drawing skills. Some experience in the fashion industry is often part of the course and there is sometimes the opportunity to travel to fashion centres in other countries such as Paris, Florence, Frankfurt and New York.

Textile courses are equally as varied in character; the approach of some is near to fine art while others are closely linked to industry. A good colour sense, drawing ability and some interest in machinery, especially if weaving or knitting is seen as a specialism, are all necessary to the successful textile designer. Professional textile designers frequently free-lance, often working from home, so personal motivation, integrity, tenacity and a good business sense are all important. Textile and fashion designers need lively and creative minds balanced by common sense, and they need the ability to work as part of a team.

Three-Dimensional Design

This umbrella title covers a wide range of design practice embracing jewellery, ceramics, glass, furniture, interior design, product and indus-trial design; everything from Concorde to a paperclip. Every man-made thing is designed by someone and there are a substantial number of courses in art colleges and universities to train designers in all the varied disciplines.

Product and industrial design is concerned with the functional, ergo-nomic, and aesthetic qualities of manufactured products. Designers in this field are required to have an understanding of technological develop-ments, manufacturing processes, professional practice and management in industry. They must also have a good visual understanding and awareness and an open mind uncluttered by conventional solutions to design problems. Drawing ability and the capacity to explain ideas visually and verbally are necessary for success. Additionally such designers should be endowed with an acute social and environmental awareness and must be able to work as part of a highly trained team of industrial specialists all of whom will have a contribution to make to a design solution.

Interior designers have a similar social and environmental base to their professional practice. In this field the designer must be able and willing to temper creative ideas with the mundane but necessary understanding of structures and building regulations. As well as having a good visual sense and drawing ability, the interior designer must be able to project ideas by means of working and presentation drawings.

Furniture designers often work in an industrial situation and much that applies to product and interior designers applies to them though the furniture designer might also be a designer craftsman and so bridge the area between industrial and craft practice, which is the area relating to the jeweller, silversmith, and the practitioner in glass and ceramics.

In these specialist fields study will help students towards a critical awareness and sensitive response to the materials of their art. They will need to develop a creative appreciation of form and function and to master the manipulative skills and techniques to fashion the artefacts which they design.

Graduates may find themselves in industry but more usually will find themselves in individual workshop practices determining for themselves the nature of the work they produce and selling it through exhibitions or retail outlets, though on occasions they may work to commissions (silversmiths especially). These art- and design-based craft practices at their highest level demand dedication, highly developed sensibilities, imagination and a limitless appreciation of colour, line, scale, three dimensional form, two dimensional surface design, as well as technical knowledge, highly developed craft abilities and a personal understanding of the value and significance of the objects produced.

Other Opportunities in Art and Design

The above is an outline of the major areas of study in art and design but does not exhaust all possibilities. In three-dimensional design no mention has been made of a study such as wrought iron work, but there are courses concerned with the design and fabrication of wrought iron at both degree and vocational levels. No mention has been made either of picture restoration or the restoration of prints and drawings though courses in these studies are available. Finally, there is the history of art and design, the separate study area – **Fine Arts**. There are now combined degrees which have a major option in some aspect of the visual arts, eg a major option in history, criticism and appreciation through the study and practice of fine art.

Asian Studies
Dr Ian Brown, SOAS

To read for a degree in Asian Studies in practice means following a particular discipline or combination of disciplines – for example anthropology, economics, geography, history, languages, philosophy, politics or religious studies – with reference to one or more of the four major regions of Asia, that is the Far East (China, Japan, Taiwan and the Koreas); South East Asia (Vietnam, Thailand, Burma, Malaysia, Indonesia, the Philippines); South Asia (India, Pakistan, Bangladesh, Sri Lanka); and the Middle East (see *Near East and Islamic Studies*). The number and variety of courses subsumed under Asian Studies is therefore very great indeed. They include the study of subjects as diverse as the economic problems of contemporary India; ritual and religion in Indonesia; environmental problems in the rapidly expanding urban centres of Asia; the rise of anti-colonial movements in India, Vietnam or Indonesia in the first half of the twentieth century; Japanese language and literature; Buddhist thought; or contemporary political problems in the Middle East.

But why study Asia at all? To many people such courses may seem rather exotic or even esoteric fields of study that will provide the graduate with little or no introduction to a particular career. Whilst a few graduates from Asian Studies do in fact find employment in areas where their knowledge of Asia can be put to practical use – as diplomats, in certain branches of journalism, in overseas commerce or banking, with international organisations – it is true that the numbers involved are comparatively small. A degree in some aspect of Asian Studies is not primarily a vocational degree. But this is true of virtually all arts and social science degrees. Therefore the question posed at the beginning of this paragraph should perhaps be rephrased: why study, for example, the modern history of India rather than the modern history of Britain; why pursue a course in economics that in its orientation concerns itself with the contemporary problems of Asia rather than those of the western world; why study Japanese rather than French? Two answers may be offered to this question. First, I would suggest that the most important reason for undertaking an arts or social science degree is to train yourself to think critically and imaginatively, while developing a greater understanding of yourself and of the world in which we live. This can be achieved through close study of, for example, a particularly complex historical problem, or an area of literary criticism, or a field of political thought. The study of Asia provides a particularly rich and varied opportunity to train your mind in this way, partly because of the great cultural and historical diversity of the region, but more importantly because it involves achieving an understanding of societies and civilisations which are clearly and profoundly different from those of Europe. Brief examples may make the argument clear. To achieve an understanding of the thinking of an Indian peasant under British colonial rule or of a Chinese Emperor of the Ming dynasty; to appreciate the intricacies of contemporary Japanese politics; to comprehend fully the social, economic and political barriers to economic development in present-day India, in each case requires a student to work in cultures, societies and historical traditions outside his or her own experience. This provides a fascinating and exhilarating challenge. Once this challenge is met – and it is by no means an impossible one to surmount despite Rudyard Kipling's dictum concerning the east and west – a student will then be acquiring not only the trained and disciplined mind referred to above but also greater insight into his or her own culture, society and history. Intellectual horizons will be widened; invaluable and unique understandings acquired. The second important reason for studying Asia can be dealt with much more briefly. Asia is a region of great and increasing significance in world affairs. It need only be noted that almost 60% of the world's population live in Asia. Over 20% of the people on this planet live in China. In an increasingly volatile and interdependent world we all need to acquire a much greater understanding of Asia.

There are two final points. The first concerns languages. In some degrees in Asian Studies there is a strong emphasis on mastering the language and literature of a particular region as the entrance to understanding its culture. However, where the approach to Asia is through a discipline or combination of disciplines such as economics, history or politics, rarely is language training required at the undergraduate level, though it is possible to combine those disciplines with a language, as for example in a joint degree in Japanese and Far East history. For those who wish to undertake a single subject Asian language degree no previous knowledge of the language is required, although evidence of linguistic interest and competence is sought, and for this reason A-level language or languages are often necessary for admission. The second point is that only a small proportion of the applicants for degrees in some branch of Asian Studies have had substantial previous experience of Asia. For the large majority of applicants, previous knowledge of the region is usually slight and indirect, arising, for example, from school-level geography, from those parts of the British and European A-level history syllabus which touch on European involvement in Asia, from a reading of Asian literature in translation, or most usually from an interest in contemporary world affairs, particularly the problems of poverty and underdevelopment. If in any of these ways you have had an initial contact with Asian Studies, and that contact has stimulated your interest, then the reading suggested below should enable you to explore further. And, of course, those offering courses in Asian Studies will be pleased to provide additional detailed guidance.

HELPFUL READING: Edgar Snow, *Red Star over China* (Harmondsworth: Penguin, 1972); Milton Osborne, *Southeast Asia: an introductory history* (Sydney: George Allen and Unwin, 1979); Dilip Hiro, *Inside India Today* (London: Routledge and Kegan Paul, 1976); Bernard Lewis, *The Arabs in History* (London: Hutchinson, 1968).

Biochemistry

Professor Robert Freedman, Kent University

If you decide to study biochemistry, you will be getting to grips with what many historians of science believe to be one of the major intellectual achievements of the century – the interpretation of living organisms and the phenomena of life in terms of the properties, activities and interactions of the molecules of which they are made. Biochemistry (the word and the science both date from this century) is essentially a search for an understanding of life in chemical terms. This makes it both an exciting and a demanding subject for study. Exciting, because biochemistry is now the central biological science, as ideas and techniques from biochemistry are now the basis of research in medicine, agriculture, biotechnology and the pure biological sciences. Demanding, because biochemistry involves the use of a wide range of techniques (many of them physical techniques) to understand biological phenomena in terms of chemical and molecular principles. So a student of biochemistry needs a good knowledge of chemistry, some aptitude for quantitative physical thinking, and an interest in a broad range of biological phenomena from cell structure and physiology, to genetics and evolution.

Biochemistry graduates play an important part in the pharmaceutical, agrochemical, food, cosmetics and fine chemical industries and in the laboratories of hospitals, police forces, public health authorities etc. Biochemists in all these professions read textbooks and journals, and buy equipment and specialised chemicals, and so there is a further set of varied careers which directly support active science. Work in scientific publishing and scientific instruments combines closeness to the cutting edge of the science with a flavour of the commercial world.

Biochemistry deals with four kinds of questions, of increasing depth and complexity. The first question is simply, 'Of what kinds of molecules are living things made? What are the detailed structures of these molecules?' A century ago this led to the recognition of proteins, carbohydrates, fats and later nucleic acid as the major ubiquitous components of all living things. But questions of this kind are still being asked as biochemists probe the detailed three-dimensional structures of molecules containing hundreds of thousands of atoms, or when they try to establish the identities of newly discovered powerful hormones and other transmitters which the body manufactures in only tiny amounts.

In the last few years it has become possible to isolate and purify proteins which, in trace amounts, act as key messengers in the immune system, produced by one set of cells to switch on others. From very limited structural information on these 'cytokines' it is now possible to track down the genes coding for them, to isolate these genes and transfer them to other cells where they can be 'overexpressed' so that a research scientist can rapidly generate more of the pure protein in a test-tube than could ever be produced from the natural source. Most of what we now know about the structure of interferon and its anti-viral and anti-cancer properties is derived from studies on material produced in this way.

The second question follows on from the first. If you know the nature of the molecules making up living things, it is natural to ask what the chemical reactions are which lead to the construction of these molecules. How exactly do green plants convert CO_2 and water into carbohydrates? How do cows convert grass into beef and milk? How do some bacilli sour milk by converting milk sugars into acids, while other micro-organisms perform the welcome task of turning sugars into CO_2 and ethanol? These questions deal with the area known as 'metabolism' and much of biochemistry concerns the establishment of 'metabolic pathways' – route maps explaining all the chemical interconversions which take place in an organism. The whole network is immensely complex, but after a while you will be able to pick out the main highways; the catabolic pathways by which foodstuffs are broken down into a small number of simple units, the downtown interchanges such as the Krebs tricarboxylic acid cycle which links many of the central metabolites, and the anabolic or biosynthetic pathways which lead to the formation of new complex materials from the simpler building blocks.

Much of metabolism was worked out in the period from 1910 to 1960 but there is still exciting exploration going on in this area even if there are no 'dark continents' left. We introduce hundreds of tons of new chemical pesticides and industrial wastes into the environment each year; how are these new molecules metabolised by the plants and micro-organisms in rivers, sea and land? We develop new drugs, cosmetics and food additives; what changes do these undergo in the body? Are they converted into harmless waste products or into toxic metabolites? All these problems provide new and pressing questions for metabolic research.

Biochemistry's third question arises from the second. If we know the myriad chemical processes going on in a living organism, can we understand how these reactions are catalysed, how the energy-requiring processes are harnessed to the energy-yielding processes, how all the reactions in a single cell are regulated and controlled and how all the cells in a complex organism are integrated with each other? This question opens up the whole field of enzymes and their regulation, of hormones, like insulin and the steroids, of the molecular changes involved in physical work and exercise, and the molecular basis of nerve and brain function. As you will recognise, in this area biochemical knowledge is brought to bear on all the central questions of physiology.

Biochemical questions of the fourth kind are essentially old biological questions asked in a new way. If we know all about the composition of a living thing, and the reactions going on within it, and the way in which these are regulated and integrated, how is the information for all this stored and passed on to that organism's progeny? Thirty years ago this question could hardly be answered at all – now our knowledge is so extensive that the Sunday papers regularly record successes not just in understanding the molecular basis of heredity, but in altering it through 'genetic engineering'. Recently the defect in cystic fibrosis, the most common 'genetic' disorder in Britain, has been traced to a change in a specific gene, and the properties of the protein product of this gene can now be studied. This breakthrough will certainly generate new possibilities for therapy.

A more difficult question to answer is how it is that all the cells in an individual organism, which share the same genetic blueprint nevertheless turn out as very different specialised cells; this question of development and differentiation is occupying biochemists increasingly. And in similar ways, biochemical modes of thinking and experimenting are being applied in every area of biology, to answer questions in evolution and taxonomy for example, or to extend ecological knowledge by studying how organisms survive and flourish in extreme environments of high temperature, high acidity or high salt concentrations.

As a biochemistry student you will look at questions of all these kinds. Wherever you go you will study the central aspects of the structures of biological molecules, metabolism, enzymology and molecular biology. But beyond that the emphasis of your study will vary with the nature and context of the institution. In a university with major industrial connections, the advanced aspects of the course may have a strong applied flavour. Where a biochemistry department is part of a medical school, it will also be teaching medical students and the course may reflect their interests. In other institutions biochemistry comes under a larger biological sciences umbrella; in others again there is a strong link to physiology or to microbiology. So the precise emphasis of the course will depend on the context in which it runs, and this variation will be most marked in the final year.

It is possible to combine biochemistry with other subjects, or to extend a degree with a year of quite different experience. Some courses offer biochemistry with a related science (eg microbiology, physiology, pharmacology); others offer biochemistry with industrial training as 'sandwich' degrees. Some offer a bigger contrast eg biochemistry with management science, or biochemistry with a language and a year in Europe.

The teaching of biochemistry inevitably involves a lot of practical work. This is partly professional training in specific skills, but its main purpose is to give you some sense of the way in which biochemical knowledge is acquired, questioned and revised, by careful and critical experimentation. So you will spend part of your timetabled time working in the laboratory in addition to attending lectures and classes in small groups. Frequently the practical work develops from rather standardised exercises into more open-ended work, and at most places you will be encouraged to do an individual research project in your final year. For many students, the individual project is the highlight of their course, bringing together what they have learned from all sources and giving them a real chance to discover something new. You will not be studying biochemistry only, of course. Early on you will do a good deal of chemistry, some more general biology and probably some maths too.

Most students say they are attracted to biochemistry because they like both biology and chemistry (which makes sense), but it is clear that a broad science background is invaluable, and the best preparation is probably three sciences at A-level, such as chemistry and biology with either maths or physics.

A course in biochemistry should 'train your mind' so that you can tackle problems, recall, organise and express knowledge. But the same can probably be argued for any degree course. The best reason for choosing to study biochemistry is because you really enjoy finding out about an exciting, fundamental and wide-ranging subject.

Biology

Dr N Maclean, Southampton University

Biology, the study of life and living things, occupies a unique position in the spectrum of human interest and knowledge. Although undoubtedly a science, it has much in common with the arts, partly because nature appeals to our aesthetic as well as our rational senses, also because we ourselves are part of nature. For this reason many people who would not otherwise choose to study science finally settle on biology. On the other hand, with the rapid growth of molecular biology over the last decade, some who would previously have chosen to study physical sciences are now considering biology as a possible and challenging alternative. It should also be emphasised that many departments offer a choice of degree options in biology, botany, zoology, cell biology and applied biology, the choice of degree title depending on courses chosen for study.

Thus if you find yourself subscribing to any of the following categories then it may mean that biology should be your prime choice of subject. (1) Your interests straddle the two cultures of science and arts, (2) you are very keen on natural history, birds, plants, insects or whatever, (3) your greatest passion is conservation of the planet and its natural resources, (4) you are not at all keen about natural history or conservation, but you are intrigued by problems of living systems and how they work, (5) you are interested in medicine but don't want to become a 'doctor'.

Biology is often taken to represent 'soft' science rather than 'hard' science, that is a science where the number of variables in any one situation may be so great that the construction of an equation or formula is impossible. Although with the recent growth of molecular biology and biotechnology this is much less true than it once was, it is still sufficiently true to mean that biology may appeal to those with limited expertise in the physical sciences. But do not be beguiled into thinking that the softer science indicates a softer option. Ability to analyse and understand complex situations such as arise, for example, in evolutionary genetics, requires a sharp mind as well as considerable breadth of knowledge.

But the complex nature of many biological situations does have a significance for the career prospects of those who study this discipline. It is accepted by many experienced industrialists and management consultants that a training in biology is a good, perhaps even an ideal, preparation for a career in management. This follows from the realisation that most situations involving people are, by their nature, complex, and relatively difficult to define with precision. Someone who has been trained in the physical sciences may find their new skills of rather limited usefulness in tackling complex industrial decision making. On the other hand an entirely arts-based course of study may not provide the necessary training in analysis and directional strategy. So biology is not solely beneficial to those who proceed to a science-orientated career.

Let me now try and impart to you the flavour of modern biology in terms of what topics you might expect to study in depth. The central core in most departments would consist of cell biology, genetics, ecology, and the form and function of living organisms; students will often be encouraged or compelled to study computation and statistics on the one hand and biochemistry and physiology on the other. From this basic groundwork will stem a range of optional specialisations, for example, parasitology, taxonomy, evolution, cell and molecular biology, developmental biology, immunology, applied ecology, and advanced courses in genetics or comparative physiology. You will notice that the emphasis in biology has substantially shifted in the last decade or so from a direct focus on the organism to a focus on the nature of life and living systems. So instead of courses emphasising entomology, reptile biology or flowering plant families, there is much more importance attached to understanding cell structure and function on the one hand and ecological interactions on the other. Of course many departments have their own special areas of research expertise, but these are reflected more in higher degree course structures than in undergraduate ones. When you visit a department as a prospective student, you can do worse than enquire as to the areas in which the research strength of a department lies. It may not coincide at all with the area in which you would want to specialise.

A second way of imparting flavour is to describe to you two activities which all first year students experience in the department in Southampton. In the Easter vacation of their first year, all our undergraduates participate in a field course, either in Southern France or Southern Spain. In springtime in Spain the fields are ablaze with flowers and the sky often filled with migrating storks and eagles. Even students who have previously found taxonomy boring (probably the majority) find new excitement in identifying beetles, birds, or plants both in the field and in the laboratory. There is no better way to appreciate the strategies of evolution, the elaborate networks of ecology, or the problems of biological classification than to see and work with organisms in the field.

The second location is a genetics laboratory in which my students study the regulation of genes in bacterial cells. In the course of an afternoon we are able to carry through an experiment, involving the induction of beta galactosidase enzyme in mutant strains of *E. coli*, for which two eminent French scientists, Jacob and Monod, shared the Nobel Prize in 1965. One's belief in the molecular organisation of an operon is greatly strengthened by finding that one can manipulate it oneself in the laboratory.

Many of the key questions facing mankind now and in the future are essentially biological. How can we control our own population, avoid war, cure disease, conserve nature? To my mind one of the most exciting things about being a student of biology is that one learns so much more about oneself. You learn to understand your own anatomy, physiology, behaviour and evolution, but you also come to see yourself in the context of nature, as one amongst many other species, as a member of an evolved and evolving population of organisms, interacting at all times and levels with the other diverse organisms with which we share the planet. Whether you are managing staff in Marks and Spencer's or running field trials of agricultural crops, there is much to be gained from the bracing sense of perspective, both evolutionary and ecological, available to those who have learned to think deeply about biology.

HELPFUL READING: Ralph Buchsbaum, *Animals without back-bones* (Chicago University Press, 1987 (3rd edition)); *The Molecules of Life* – Readings from *Scientific American* (W H Freeman, 1986); Christian de Duve, *A Guided Tour of the Living Cell* (W H Freeman, 1985); R Dawkins, *The Selfish Gene* (Oxford University Press, revised edition 1989); J D Watson, *The Double Helix* (Penguin, 1981 (revised edition)).

Biotechnology

Dr J H Parish, Leeds University

Biotechnology is concerned with the application of the biological sciences to manufacturing processes. Some of the processes themselves (especially those concerned with the food and drink industries) are thousands of years old but the analysis of the processes by the application of scientific method and the use of scientific enquiry to expand the variety of biological products is relatively recent – largely because biological science, as opposed to natural history, is a relatively recent academic discipline. In order to try and specify modern biotechnology, a person who makes home-brew beer is not a biotechnologist but biotechnologists are employed by commercial breweries in order to optimise the performance of these companies by applying such subjects as fermentation technology and the molecular genetics of yeast to the brewing process.

There are four major academic foundations of biotechnology.

(1) Biochemistry: the subject emphasises a certain unity among living organisms. All organisms have energy-yielding metabolism whereby substrates are converted to products and energy is trapped by the synthesis of ATP, a chemical that represents the energy currency of a cell. Energy-yielding metabolism invariably involves oxidation/reduction (in our species reduced substrates such as cream cakes and fish and chips are oxidised to carbon dioxide and water) but the variety in different forms of life is considerable. All organisms convert substrates to the chemicals required for growth by processes that involve expenditure of ATP. All these chemical conversions are catalysed by enzymes. Finally the role of DNA in inheritance is common to all forms of life. (2) Genetic engineering: classical genetics is limited by the 'breeding barrier' (you can cross barley and rye, horses and donkeys, but not diverse species – such as carrots and elephants). However there are techniques for introducing a gene or a few genes (ie a piece of DNA) from one organism into cells of a totally unrelated host. The hosts are commonly microbes but can be animal or plant cells. There is a sense in which such genetic engineering is now classical: for some purposes genes are obtained by amplifying DNA sequences in the test tube by using the 'Polymerase Chain Reaction' (PCR). (3) Cell culture: traditionally, bacteria, yeasts and moulds have been the organisms used in industrial fermentations. To these can now be added cells of animals and plants and specialised examples of these are used for production of vaccines, antibodies and natural products. Additionally photosynthetic microbes (including algae) suggest an alternative (yet to be realised commercially) for the large scale fixation of CO_2. (4) Fermentation engineering and reactor design: these are specialised engineering subjects and biotechnology presents engineers with problems concerned with sterilisation, stirring, heat exchange and downstream processing of large volumes of aqueous materials.

The applications of biotechnology are varied so the following examples are necessarily incomplete. Genetic engineering allows the construction of micro-organisms and animal and plant cells in culture that contain cloned genes from a variety of sources. Further manipulation allows the expression of these genes. We can thus construct a bacterial or fungal strain that will produce proteins of animal origin and which is of established value. Examples are chymosin (an enzyme used in cheese manufacture obtained otherwise from calves) and several human proteins (such as insulin, tissue plasminogen activator and blood clotting factor VIII) of medical importance. The benefits of using fermentation technology (rather than material from the slaughterhouse, human post mortem remains or a blood bank) vary between the economic, humanitarian and medically desirable: in the case of a source for factor VIII, there is no danger of a microbe being infected by the AIDS virus. The implications of the ability to introduce and express foreign genes into plant and animal cells are rather different. If these cells are used to generate whole plants or if their genetic information is introduced into embryonic animals we obtain 'transgenic' higher organisms. A transgenic plant might have (for example) properties of resistance to pests, diseases or herbicides to improve agricultural productivity. Transgenic animals might be used to generate recombinant proteins in their milk. However the applications of genetic engineering mentioned so far do not define the limits of biotechnological potential. The ability to manipulate DNA in the laboratory either by altering the structure of cloned DNA or by synthesising the sequence chemically provides a method for altering or improving the performance of a protein for specific purposes. Such activities are referred to as 'protein engineering'. The starting points for a protein engineer are the cloned gene(s) involved and a knowledge of the structure and function of the protein(s) in question. One example of protein engineering is the modification of the enzyme present in biological washing powders to allow it to perform better at the relatively high temperatures used in washing machines. Examples that might have rather more importance for the human race involve the modification of proteins for medical use. One example is the development of hybrid interferons; another is the production by recombinant bacteria of antibody molecules with either improved specificity or smaller size that are likely to lead to dramatic improvements in the treatment of viral infections and possibly in the treatment of cancer. The generalisation that follows from all these examples from the sharp end of biotechnological research is that although the science of molecular biology has followed a progressive development over the past several years, it has generated a technological revolution. Just as the subject of synthetic organic chemistry generated novel chemicals, such as dyestuffs and plastics, that came to dominate parts of the chemical industry, molecular biology has entered a synthetic or creative phase that is leading to a domination of parts of the fermentation, pharmaceutical and agricultural industries.

Developments in biotechnology are driven by research in its underlying academic subjects. Although it is hazardous to sketch in a possible future scenario for scientific advances it is uncontentious to state that the excitement at the moment is at the molecular biological interface of the subject. There is one very high profile international project at the moment – the Human Genome Mapping Project (HUGO). Although the applications of the results from this vast enterprise are some way off, HUGO itself makes new demands on instrumentation, data acquisition and computation that have more direct impacts on biotechnological research. On a more modest scale, the field of the rational design of drugs is extremely active and the development of transgenic plants is leading to the development of strains that are disease resistant as well as producing (for example) fruit that have improved storage qualities through a lack of autolytic enzymes (ie the enzymes that make tomatoes go squashy).

How do you become a biotechnologist? For a school leaver there are two alternative routes. One is to apply for a BSc degree in biotechnology or applied molecular biology. You will find from the university prospectuses that different institutions give emphasis to different aspects of the subject. These reflect the fields of research expertise in the relevant department(s). For general guidance, it is more important to end up with a good degree than to worry about the fine tuning of the curriculum but any worthwhile course should certainly contain individually supervised practical research projects because the ability to plan and execute such a project is an essential skill for a biotechnologist. Biotechnology students must become familiar with the use of computers which are used routinely in analysis of genes, the interrogation of databases of protein and DNA sequence and structure as well as in automated instrumentation and control. The alternative route into biotechnology is to do a BSc degree in one of the foundation subjects or a combination of these. In some universities the biotechnology course will share a substantial amount of teaching with 'pure' molecular biology teaching. The graduate biochemist/geneticist/microbiologist has opportunities to obtain further training and experience in biotechnology either through a specialised MSc degree or by experience gained during industrial training or a PhD in an applied biological subject.

HELPFUL READING: *A Revolution in Biotechnology* edited by J L Marx (1989, Cambridge University Press) is comprehensive and comprehensible to an A-level scientist. *New Scientist* and *Trends in Biotechnology* both carry regular articles on current developments in biotechnology. Flipping through *New Scientist* in your local library represents the easiest route to savouring the current flavour of the subject.

Botany

Professor D M Moore, Reading University

This study area deals with plants. It has beginnings in the distant past, when primitive man learned to distinguish edible from inedible plants and in the middle ages, when *Materia Medica* summarised knowledge on the healing properties of plants – reflected until relatively recently in the requirement that medical students attend courses in botany. The need to identify useful plants gave rise to the field of taxonomy, which is concerned with describing the great diversity of plants in the world, assessing their relationships and evolution, and ordering them in some utilisable system of classification. External morphological features are still important in taxonomy but it is now very broadly based, using information on the chromosomes, chemistry, internal structure, physiology etc, as can be appreciated by reading V H Heywood, *Plant Taxonomy* (London: Arnold, 1976).

Of course the mosses, algae and fungi, ferns, conifers and flowering plants that inhabit the world today (see H C Bold, C J Alexopoulis, and T Delevorayas *Morphology of Plants and Fungi* (New York: Harper and Row, 1987)) are the only survivors of the myriad forms that have arisen and become extinct during the 630 million years since plant life first appeared. The remains of some of these plants have been preserved in the rocks as fossils, the study of which – palaeobotany – provides our only direct observations on the changes which have taken place in plants through the long course of evolution.

It is part of our common experience that different species of plants live together in communities, that is in various kinds of forest, grassland, heathland etc. The plant communities, which are each characterised by a particular structure and species-composition, are determined by the ability of the available species both to live together and to cope with the prevailing conditions of light, temperature, rainfall, soil etc. This study of the interactions of plants with each other, with the physical environment and with animals is the concern of ecology (see B D Collier, G H Cox, A W Johnson and P C Miller, *Dynamic Ecology* (London: Prentice-Hall International, 1974)). As your knowledge of this field improves, you will increasingly appreciate its fundamental relevance to matters of current public concern such as conservation and environmental planning. Information on the present habitats of plants permits identification of the plant remains (particularly pollen) preserved in peat deposits and lake muds and this is a powerful tool for finding out about changes in climates and vegetation during at least the last 15–20,000 years (see R G West, *Studying the Past by Pollen Analysis* (Oxford University Press, 1971)).

Apart from the study of plant populations, ecology is also concerned with evolutionary genetics, that is with the numbers of individuals having various inherited characteristics within a population, the extent to which they are adapted to the local environments and the degree to which the numbers are maintained, decreased or increased from one generation to the next. These factors, which are considered important in the evolution of the species, are affected by, for example, competition and plants' breeding systems; the latter frequently depend upon the relationship between plants and their pollinators (insects, bats, birds etc), providing a link with zoology.

Anatomy deals with both the diverse and the constant features of the internal structure of plants. As noted earlier, these characteristics are important in determining the taxonomic relationships between plant groups. The advent of the light microscope permitted the careful description of cells and tissues of plants, and the relatively recent use of scanning and transmission electron microscopes has not only provided more information but has also permitted study of the fine structure of cells, including the membranes and organelles which are involved in operating and controlling living functions. Your anatomical studies, therefore, can range from the minute structural features of plant tissues, as utilised in taxonomy and, for example, in forensic science and archaeology (see D F Cutler, *Applied Plant Anatomy* (London: Longman, 1978), to features of cells which are fundamental to plant functions and to all living organisms.

The structures and mechanisms involved in such basic processes as metabolism and reproduction will show you the strong link between plants and other living things. At this point you will need a knowledge of chemistry. There is a common biochemical basis in plants and animals, bacteria and viruses relating to such universal life activities as respiration (dependent upon the proper functioning of series of enzymes) and inheritance (largely dependent upon the nucleic acids DNA and RNA). Helpful books about this are E E Coon and P K Stumf, *Outlines of Biochemistry* (New York, London: Wiley, 1967) and W S Klug and M R Cummings, *Concepts of Genetics* (Columbus: Merrill, 1986).

An understanding of these fundamental properties of living organisms will enable you to tackle the study of plant physiology, which is largely concerned with metabolic processes that can only be carried out by plants. Paramount among these is photosynthesis, by which the sun's energy is harnessed by green plants to synthesise the food. It is utilised by most living organisms and without it life on this planet as we know it would be impossible (see D O Hall and K K Rao, *Photosynthesis* ed.4, (London: Arnold, 1988)). The uptake of water and mineral salts by plants – vital to their nutrition and their effect on the soil – and the movement of solutions and chemicals within the plant are other important concerns of plant physiology (F B Salisbury and C M Ross, *Plant Physiology* ed.4 (Belmont: Wadsworth, 1990). Through its interest in the production and distribution of auxins (plant hormones), physiology links with morphogenesis. This deals with the mechanisms controlling the orderly growth and development of the plant from a single cell to a fully-fledged flowering individual (see, for example, F A L Clowes, *Morphogenesis of the Shoot Apex* (Oxford University Press, 1972).

During your botany course you will be introduced to many facts and concepts. They will range from understanding the fundamental part played by plants in producing the world's food, whether cabbages or steak, to the diversity of plants and vegetation and the means by which they arose. Each of the fields within botany impinges upon and assists in understanding and interpreting the others. There are also strong links with other study areas. Furthermore, from the level of the cell through that of the individual to that of the community, plants interrelate with all other sorts of living organisms. At the end of your degree course you should appreciate this more clearly. To start your course, the most suitable A-levels are botany or biology, and preferably chemistry.

Business Studies

Alan Munro, London Guildhall University

What is Business Studies? Is it **about** business or **for** business? Is it academically respectable and intellectually demanding? These were popular questions in the late 1960s when undergraduate education in business studies started to take off. Even today for some considering the wide choice available in higher education the questions still remain. For most, however, courses in business studies are perceived to afford an educationally attractive and vocationally relevant experience as preparation for a successful business career. Potential applicants should not underestimate either the competition for places or the challenges they will face when embarking on courses.

Business studies, as a field of enquiry, is concerned with understanding business and its changing environment. In advancing our knowledge about business it is necessary to address problems and issues relevant to the manager of today and the future. These problems if not fully understood and resolved can, for the small firm, lead to insolvency or for the larger firm, a hostile 'takeover'. The factors that have been identified as significant for **successful** British companies are discussed by Walter Goldsmith and David Clutterbuck in *The Winning Streak* (Penguin 1984). Some of these factors relate for example to the personal characteristics of leadership and an ability to understand people, other factors relate to technical skills in finance, marketing, production control and communication. For these firms considerable emphasis is placed on improving the quality and availability of their products/services. The business must therefore be prepared for change and successful firms adapt and evolve over time. Today business is experiencing technological progress of a radical kind, with the most fundamental developments occurring in information technology and transportation. The implications for future managers are not obvious although it is generally accepted that the rapidly changing environment presents great opportunities.

Clearly then the scope, variety of business problems is immense; more importantly managers have to make decisions (to make no decision is a decision in itself!) ranging from future plans to current operating details. It is this scope which allows for both specialist and generalist studies of business and which creates problems for some of subject definition but real intellectual challenges to those who enter the field. As might be expected an understanding of business and its problems can be achieved by careful analysis of activities undertaken within business, and acquisition of relevant techniques. These activities normally include marketing, finance, distribution and production, also general management. In most courses an opportunity to specialise in at least one of these areas is normally available. Many business studies graduates continue this specialisation by taking relevant professional qualifications, eg in accounting, marketing etc.

To undertake the analysis special knowledge and familiarity with a number of disciplines is required. These disciplines provide what are essentially building blocks. They normally include economics, at both the micro and macro levels, since not only business efficiency and competitive market situations are involved but also the general economic environment and government policy in relation to it. The study of the behavioural sciences of psychology and sociology is essential. In business, individual and group decision-making is involved. The formation of attitudes including attitudes to risk as well as questions of motivation clearly affect the successful implementation of such decisions. More widely it is necessary to understand the nature and direction of social change externally and its influence within the firm on organisational structures. The complex nature of business, its evolution and interaction with its environment frequently requires expression in mathematical form. Statistics, mathematics and logical analysis are also building blocks which are relevant for forecasting market changes for a more sophisticated analysis of risk, and many other business operations. Many decisions within business take place within a framework of law, which sets constraints on action and decisions. All large businesses are multinational in scale and therefore the studying of language and different cultures frequently forms a contribution to business studies courses. These building blocks are then further developed to provide insights into the main activities within business, discussed earlier. For the student this often involves the selection of appropriate disciplines and a reconciliation of their different perspectives in relation to real problems faced by business. In this sense business studies is considered to be one of the best examples of an interdisciplinary field of enquiry.

Thus the ability to perform well in business requires an awareness of social, economic and industrial conditions, and the pressures associated with them in addition to special skills and knowledge. This awareness is not one which can be gained simply by studying, to ensure facility with techniques, or by even paying close attention to the results of detailed research. Direct involvement with industry and commerce is necessary. This involvement is an essential element in all undergraduate business studies courses and normally extends over the period of one year. It aims to provide you with a critical edge on your studies as well as an understanding of business, and the opportunity to assess your own personal abilities within a business context to aid you to plan for career development.

The opportunity to combine academic and vocational elements and the closeness of the world of work has meant that for many, business studies courses are the first stage in the development of a successful career. However the variety of courses offered means that you must examine carefully the content and structure of your selected course to see if it matches your own interests and career expectations. Remember it is **your** investment.

Chemical Engineering

Dr J R Backhurst, Newcastle University

> 'Well, I'm not bad at maths and physics and quite interested in chemistry so chemical engineering seemed a good idea.'

These words first appeared in an early edition of *The Student Book* and the quotation is heard just as often now, 15 years later. The reply is so familiar to those who interview prospective students that any response showing a more informed opinion is likely to come as a great surprise. The reason for the apparent ignorance of the subject is easy to understand since very few professional engineers find their way into school-teaching and the media persist with their image of oily rags and spanners. What then is chemical engineering and why should anybody consider it for a future career?

The Institution of Chemical Engineers produced a definition: 'Chemical engineering is the science of processes in which materials undergo a change, changes which can be chemical and/or physical.' This sort of statement can hardly be expected to fire enthusiasm into the hearts of those deciding upon their chosen paths, however factually correct it may be. The name 'chemical engineering' itself is rather misleading as it implies that it is only concerned with chemicals. Many university departments have incorporated the word 'process' into their names and this gives a much better impression of the subject. It is the engineering of processes with which the chemical engineer is concerned and the bold definition above gives no idea of the challenges which will be encountered and the excitement of a life being involved with the production of anything ranging from North Sea oil through chemicals and synthetic fibres to cosmetics and frozen foods. The scope of processes is very wide and a chemical engineer can, for example, be instrumental in both creating, developing and running a process to meet the demand of a world market.

Chemical engineering is an international discipline. The raw materials for industry have to be extracted from where they occur naturally. As resources are used at an ever-increasing rate, the search for new supplies is spread further, often to remote and ecologically hostile parts of the world. Oil, gas and uranium for energy supplies are familiar examples.

The UK chemical industry has an economic record of which it can be justly proud. Its products are not produced solely for the demands of a consumer society. Two of the major problems facing the world at present – problems which will assume even greater importance in the future – are the supply of food and energy. By means of modern fertilisers, herbicides and pesticides, large areas of previously barren land are now able to support food production. The expertise of our own industry is being offered to developing countries in the form of complete plants, which bring the additional benefits of employment and technology. The challenge of energy in the face of dwindling supplies of oil is attracting the attention of chemical engineers. Whilst atomic power must provide the bulk of the immediate solution, the possibilities of harnessing solar energy, wind power and energy from the waves of the sea are both technically difficult and exciting. Chemical engineers through the training they receive, are uniquely equipped to offer new processes and better techniques to the problems encountered in the important field of conservation of energy and raw materials.

Chemical plants are not noted for their great beauty but new plant complexes costing many millions of pounds are certainly impressive and great efforts are taken to ensure that they have a negligible effect in terms of pollution. Indeed, many new plants return their effluent in a cleaner condition than the river water to which it is discharged. Concern for the environment is fashionable at present but chemical engineers are uniquely placed to actually do something real to help to improve the quality of our life and surroundings. Capital investment in chemical plant is high and safety requirements rigorous. The lessons learned from disasters like the tragic explosion at Flixborough or the leakage at Bhopal some years ago are incorporated into both design methods and safety legislation. The safety record of the chemical industry is excellent, though the very small number of accidents do receive abnormally high publicity. This in turn tends to further improve the safety measures possibly, however, to the detriment of a good public image.

How do you become a chemical engineer? Training is usually, and preferably, undertaken in the form of a full-time degree course at university, although it is possible to become professionally qualified whilst working in industry and studying on a part-time basis. The problem in deciding which course is helped by the choice between three- or four-year courses, honours or ordinary degrees, sandwich courses or not – all information available in the prospectuses.

Normally the first two years of a chemical engineering course include an introduction to chemical process operations, heat and mass transfer, fluid flow, material and energy balances, fuel science, control, computing and further mathematics and chemistry. Most of these subjects will be new to you, though your A-level studies are an essential background. Laboratory work will probably be on a larger scale from anything you have encountered previously – though not on the industrial scale. Your first contact with the industrial world, apart from works visits, is likely to be during the long summer vacation when most departments arrange a period of industrial experience for students. Whilst this period is short, it does provide a valuable insight into the outside world and most students enjoy this part of the course.

The final year is likely to contain a design and research project as well as lecture courses on all aspects of chemical engineering. The projects are usually carried out by small teams of students supervised by a member of staff. Working as part of a team is a facet of industrial life and it is as well to realise the inherent difficulties at an early stage. The design project will introduce you to the flavour of the industrial design situation and will encourage you to apply the theoretical knowledge acquired earlier in the course. The research project enables you to demonstrate your initiative and originality in a practical way. Both of these projects are a challenge which students enjoy and find useful to their professional career.

Life as a chemical engineer is never mundane and a position can always be found which can offer everything demanded of a satisfying career. Do not imagine that all plants are designed and controlled by computers; important they may be, but it is people that make them work and it is dealing with people that makes life interesting. Research, development, design, production, sales, marketing, finance and even teaching are some of the possibilities. There is responsibility, opportunity for travel, and financial security. The demand for chemical engineers has been maintained and recent surveys show that starting salaries are amongst the highest of all the engineering disciplines. The economic health of the country tends to move in cycles and as you read this, you will be at least three years away from graduation by which time the employment situation should be better than it is now.

Traditionally, A-level subjects suitable for a chemical engineering course are mathematics, physics and chemistry, though other combinations are possible. Mathematics and chemistry are essential though entrance requirements and the courses available are flexible. Biology is sometimes offered instead of physics at A-level and it can provide a useful foundation for a course which includes biochemical engineering – a fast expanding area of industry. If you chose to take different A-levels at the start of your sixth-form career and now wish to become a chemical engineer, several universities offer a foundation year course designed to not only make good deficiencies in your knowledge, but to provide you with a genuine engineering course while you are doing it. You do not need to be a genius at all your A-level subjects to be a successful engineer. Sound common-sense is often more important than brilliance in the examination room, though if you do succeed in eventually attaining a first-class degree the world will be at your feet. Engineering is a challenge. The problems are real and often urgent, but remember that however desirable a project may be it must always make economic sense. If you feel that you can rise to the challenge, consider chemical engineering and enjoy the experience.

HELPFUL READING: available from the Institution of Chemical Engineers, 165–171 Railway Terrace, Rugby CV21 3HQ.

Chemistry

Dr L D Pettit, Leeds University

Chemistry is an area of study which touches human life at innumerable points. It is the science which forms a bridge between physics and biology as well as between earth sciences and life and medical sciences. It is therefore a **central science** which holds the key to an appreciation and understanding of life-cycles on the one hand through to man-made processes on the other.

The development of chemistry as a science has taken place at an increasingly rapid rate over the last two centuries, and has depended upon **quantitative** reasoning. Chemists of the nineteenth century could not have anticipated the contribution which their research would make to the applications of chemistry today – applications which range from microcircuits and developments in solid state devices to the use of hormones as a new generation of pesticides, and which even give a glimmering of understanding of the chemical basis of life itself. In many cases this rapid progress in the application of chemistry has itself created new crises for man (eg some forms of pollution; the effect of some pesticides on the environment, or the side effects of some pharmaceuticals), but chemists have immediately led the search for an answer to the resulting problems so that the advances could be controlled or harnessed to the benefit of man.

Superficially it is fairly easy to visualise the earth in terms of basic chemical concepts – it is an apparent equilibrium between solid, liquid and vapour phases surrounded by space and supplied with energy from the sun. However, the apparent position of the equilibrium is continually moving and small changes have profound effects on the processes of life.

For our survival in anything approaching an 'advanced state of civilisation' we must exploit the energy content of as much of our environment as possible, while minimising the effect on the equilibrium of that environment. In all aspects of this interaction chemistry plays a key role. In agriculture, for example, in our attempt to use the sun's energy in the way most beneficial – and palatable – to our present populations, we use fertilizers and pesticides and these lead on to problems of nitrogen fixation, the possibility of genetic engineering, and the applications of hormones and similar chemicals to control specific species. On another front, that of our demands for energy, our use of fossil and of nuclear fuels is fundamentally linked to their chemistry. Pollution that results from their use can itself be controlled only by a detailed knowledge of their chemistry and the application of chemical principles. We have inherited problems resulting from past attempts to harness energy resources, and we in our turn must be ever aware of the inheritance that we are leaving succeeding generations.

How are we to understand the 'energy crisis'? If the energy of the universe is conserved (the well known first law of thermodynamics), why are we in danger of running out of energy? The answer lies in the less well understood second law which relates to useful work which can be obtained from available energy. An understanding of these basic concepts of thermodynamics is essential to an understanding of the problems of our material needs and their possible solution. Hence, a sound grounding in mathematics and, to a lesser extent, physics is necessary if we are to grasp the fundamental quantitative concepts of chemistry, and to apply them in the service of mankind.

Because of our numbers and aspirations we consume vast quantities of chemicals, usually intentionally but often unintentionally. We thus have to live with the waste of our endeavours and adapt our lifestyles to the resulting shortages when scarce resources are depleted. Our environment and, on a more personal level, our metabolism is vulnerable to the corrupting results of so many of our endeavours, and the answer can only lie in the careful and responsible application of our knowledge of chemistry. What is more, we are continually needing new materials to replace those no longer available in sufficient quantities, or to take advantage of the advance of the frontiers of knowledge. We have seen an explosion in the use of plastics and synthetic organic polymers. The petrochemical industry is a particularly important industrial application of chemistry since petroleum products are too valuable as sources of organic molecules to be simply burnt for heat and advances in this field are far from exhausted. Inorganic polymers are also likely to become more important and the development of solid state technology is, in all probability, barely out of its infancy. Biological polymers, in particular proteins and nucleic acids, will continue to be an expanding topic. Already studies in this field have contributed enormously to our understanding of the chemical basis of life, of genetic diseases and of heredity. Through a study of biological systems we are beginning to understand the molecular mechanism for the production and transfer of energy within the living cell, and so to open the door to new methods of exploiting solar energy. This will lead to new sources of food supply at a time when existing sources are becoming over-strained.

For all these daunting tasks and exciting prospects chemistry is a key subject. However, the importance and fascination of chemistry goes beyond purely material applications of the science. In chemistry we make and study beautiful crystalline compounds and we are introduced to theoretical concepts and ideas which are both elegant and interesting from a philosophical point of view. A chemist is one who studies both the practical synthesis and reactions of substances and also the underlying theories which unite and classify such a wide variety of compounds.

Chemistry is therefore a fund of knowledge which can open up the whole field of related technologies. The preferred A-level subjects are chemistry with one or both of mathematics and physics. In general three science-based A-levels are required, although many institutions will consider students with two science and one arts-based A-level, or with only two good A-levels.

Amidst the rapid advances of today, science students are wise to choose a course that will **open** rather than **close** doors to them. They need to choose a starting point which is equally suited to continued specialisation or continued diversification, depending on the developing interest of the individual. Chemistry provides a basis upon which either more chemistry, or another science or technology can be built. It is also increasingly recognised as a sound training for an eventual career in management, administration or some other field completely outside science. As a quantitative science a study of chemistry can therefore prove to be a means of enriching the life of the recipient and also the basis for a rewarding and satisfying career.

Civil Engineering

Emeritus Professor Sir Alan Harris, Imperial College

The job of the civil engineer is the world – making it habitable, enabling it to support human life.

First the provision of clean water and the disposal of human and industrial waste – this more than anything else has permitted the increase of the world's population this last century. For food, civil engineers act indirectly except where irrigation is economic, but their role in satisfying the world's need for energy is central and ever expanding – engineering off-shore is a new field. They build the infrastructure needed for transport by land, sea and air, without which there would be little food and little energy. They are the servants of every sort of manufacture and finally they provide the structure of the shelter within which people may carry on their lives.

Their activity is the application of the practical intelligence to constructing things which serve these ends. This makes civil engineering an art and by art is to be understood the right making of what needs making. As an art it has certain peculiarities.

It has an insatiable appetite for exact knowledge, but only for such knowledge as clarifies or facilitates the task and that at a given time and place – information delivered in London on Thursday might be of value; in Edinburgh on Friday week, none. Its concern with knowledge is thus utilitarian, serving a practical need, as opposed to that of science which seeks knowledge for its own sake. It is nevertheless not helpful to see engineering as 'applied science'; there are as many branches of science founded by the quest of engineers for knowledge as the reverse – the steam engine preceded thermodynamics, aircraft flew before there was a science of aerodynamics. In both, the practice of the art profited hugely from the science which it instigated.

This need for exact knowledge requires that the typical civil engineer must master sophisticated intellectual techniques which he will use either in determining what is to be constructed, in checking its adequacy, in pursuing minimum cost, or in managing its construction. These techniques develop continuously; new ones are always being invented. You may not suppose that with a degree you are equipped for life.

None of the works of man incorporates more material than do those of civil engineering. A moon rocket may cost more in human labour, but for bulk of material an earth-fill dam has few rivals since the pyramids. The sheer magnitude of civil engineering works in terms of the material, labour and plant needed in their execution profoundly affects the nature of the art – it makes it anonymous, communal, a twentieth century folk-art. It is not without charm that there are several hundred people who can pass by even quite a small job and say to their family 'Do you see that job? That's my job; I did that.'

Civil engineers are in servitude to the purpose of the work and to the practicalities of construction; theirs cannot be an expressive art and it is fatuous for designers to see their work as self-expression – if they do, they are playing the fool with their clients' money and mocking the efforts of those on site. To ask an engineer who has just finished a bridge, 'What were you trying to say?' will not prompt a coherent reply.

Among the arts, then, civil engineering is perhaps the most useful, the most learned, the most substantial, the most servile, the most impersonal and the least expressive. Let us not forget that it sometimes achieves beauty, even a certain majesty, though the incidence of such is not less capricious than in any other category of the works of human hands. (This beauty has inspired contemporary architecture with, it has to be admitted, results which are often good and sometimes less good.)

The field is broad; there are firms, both designers and constructors, who deal with it all, but not many. But in any part, however narrow, of the field there is a wide range of functions needing different talents – research, design, analysis, detailing, costing, construction – and none of these can succeed without management. Whilst no one can hope to be expert in all, the well-rounded engineer will know something about each. The education of civil engineers will thus be broad, as will be their early practical experience but, according to their talents and character they can choose from this diversity a function in which to specialise, within which they may still deal with a wide range of types of work.

A hierarchy exists in the profession, as organised by the Institution, between three levels known, in the jargon of the day, as the chartered engineer, the technician engineer and the technician. The chartered engineer is a professional, capable of original thought and judgement and of accepting major responsibilities; the title will be conferred at about 27–28 years of age by the Institution. The technician engineer is an executive, fully understanding what he is asked to do and capable of carrying it out with little supervision. Engineers in both these categories will normally have a degree; there are paths between them. The technician is a practical man with the knowledge, skill and understanding needed to carry out the intentions of the chartered and technician engineers.

The classic group of A-level subjects seen as a proper preliminary to a civil engineering degree is mathematics, physics and chemistry. Mathematics is desirable and physics and chemistry are useful but many civil engineers see attractions in such subjects as economics, English or a foreign language as part of the mix.

The number of women in the profession is still small but is increasing. Experience shows that there is no need to distinguish between the sexes in the practice of civil engineering, where women have distinguished themselves right across the field, including running a site. Are there matters of ecology where the sensitivity of women engineers is irreplaceable?

One of the attractions of civil engineering as a career is that positions at the very top are open to members. Firms of civil engineering consultants are, of course, run by civil engineers; contractors have civil engineer directors and government ministries, municipalities, nationalised corporations, have large civil engineering departments under the direction of civil engineers. Another attraction is that the civil engineer may be concerned with works anywhere in the world.

There is a small but significant tendency to see a civil engineering degree as a liberal education in itself – the intellectual discipline, numeracy and sense of physical reality which it instils are beginning to be seen as a desirable basis for management and administration.

HELPFUL READING: *Civil Engineering – A Career Guide*, Institute of Civil Engineers, Great George Street, London SW1.

Classics

Dr Oswyn Murray, Balliol College, Oxford University

Classics, the study of the cultures of Greece and Rome, is the oldest non-vocational university subject; it was the original course in 'humanities' (the study of man rather than God) and is still a central arts discipline at most major UK universities. This long tradition raises two questions: firstly, what is the justification of the classics in the modern world, and secondly, what are its strengths and weaknesses, both now and for the future?

The justification of classics lies in the nature of the Western cultural tradition. The essential characteristic of our culture, what the sociologist Max Weber called its 'formal rationality', is a creation of the Greeks. It was transmitted to the whole of Europe through that first institution of European unity, the Roman Empire, and diffused through the rest of the world by the colonial expansion of Europe after the Renaissance, to become the basis of the first world civilisation. The Greeks were the first to separate clearly the three great functions of social civilisation – politics, religion and culture – as defined by the nineteenth century historian Jacob Burckhardt in his *Reflections on History*. In all essential aspects they set out the major branches of human investigation: biology, physics (atomic and field), medicine and mathematics in science; metaphysics, ethics, politics and logic (formal and informal) in philosophy; sociology, psychology and anthropology in the social sciences; sculpture, pottery, architecture and the concept of representation in the arts; tragedy, comedy, epic, personal lyric, pastoral, history, biography and the divide between truth and fiction in literature – to mention only the obvious areas. Where the Greeks were lacking, Rome often filled the gap, as in law and constructional engineering. Of course many of these activities (though not all) have transcended their beginnings, but the study of their classical origins reveals the interconnection between such different subjects and so the fundamental nature of Western man.

For obvious reasons, therefore, the Western world has always looked back to the Greco-Roman past as an ideal and often sought to restore it in the present. One recurrent phenomenon in our culture is the creative importance of the renaissance or rebirth. The renewal of classical influences has marked every major new departure in culture from the fourth century AD to at least the nineteenth century. We cannot of course know the future. We may wonder if the chain has been broken, but even so its existence in the past is a fact, so that in the arts no major area of Western thought or literature can be understood without some knowledge of the classics.

This explains the existence of classics courses in the majority of universities, both new and old, for some access to the classics is presupposed for any serious arts studies: hence, too, the great popularity of foundation courses and of options covering classical history and literature in translation. Recently, at a level involving linguistic knowledge, joint courses such as the school of classics and modern languages at Oxford and the joint English/Latin degree at Warwick have been successful, particularly in opening up opportunities for graduate research.

Language requirements vary between courses and universities. For literary studies prior knowledge of Latin or Greek is an obvious advantage, but all universities make provision for beginners in one or both languages. What is necessary is a keenness to learn. All universities teach in varying degrees in translation, often exclusively in translation for history and philosophy while in literature a combination of survey in translation with in-depth study in the original is typical. Many universities also now offer courses in Classical Studies, in which the thought, literature, art, history and archaeology of the classical world play a dominant role. But there are two warnings. Firstly, willingness to learn the language of any foreign culture is an essential part of understanding it. Secondly, even with subjects studied in translation, the standards of attainment and understanding are ultimately set in relation to those who know the languages (your teachers and the past scholars in your subject); if you become really interested in your course you will want to learn the languages in order to continue the dialogue with the past. It follows that the best A-level preparation for classics at university lies in Latin and, if possible, Greek; the various ancient history and classical civilisation A-level courses are also useful. If there is no provision for language work at your school, get in touch with the Joint Association of Classical Teachers (31–34 Gordon Square, WC1) for information on the many residential and non-residential courses for beginners in both languages: do it early, because they are very popular and great fun.

The strengths and weaknesses of classics lie in its self-confidence and the existence of a set of professional standards – which must be mastered in order to be manipulated, or they will become a prison-house of irrelevant conservatism. Classics is a European discipline; many of the books and articles you read will have been translated into English from French, German or Italian, or written by scholars who were not English-speaking by birth, and classics teaching in the UK is still dominated by the work of the refugees who came over from Germany and Italy in the 1930s. Increasingly you will meet students from other EC countries studying classics in England and you will undoubtedly travel to Greece and Italy during your time at university. In the past classics pioneered major techniques in the arts – for example textual criticism in literature, the critical study of history, and many of the early theories in anthropology and sociology. Today the situation is reversed and classicists need to be aware of advances in disciplines outside their own. Only classical archaeology still maintains something of its past supremacy as one of the most advanced areas of archaeology, with its enviable precision in stratigraphic techniques, dating by style, aerial photography, area surveys and underwater archaeology.

One last point: traditionally classics divides both into the two cultures of Greece and Rome and also into four major areas – literature, history, philosophy and archaeology. It is important to decide how you want to mix these various subjects and to choose your university accordingly.

HELPFUL READING: *The Oxford History of the Classical World* (Oxford University Press, 1986); E R Dodds, *The Greeks and the Irrational* (Cambridge University Press, 1951); Gordon Williams, *The Nature of Roman Poetry* (Oxford University Press, 1970); M I Finley, *Aspects of Antiquity*, 2nd edn (Pelican, 1977); E Panofsky, *Renaissance and Renascences in Western Art* (London: Paladin, 1970); John Boardman, *The Greeks Overseas* (London: Thames and Hudson, 1980).

Communication Studies

Robert Ferguson, Institute of Education

Communication is a fundamental factor in all our lives. At the very least, we have to communicate to live. Whether we are going to the shops or getting on a bus or sitting in a school or college classroom, we are engaged in the process of communication as a regular and continuing part of our existence. Much of this communication takes place through the spoken word and a lesser part of it takes place through reading and writing. But we also communicate through what we wear, the way we stand or sit and our attitude towards those with whom we communicate. All this is to do with us as individual senders of messages. But, of course, we are all also part of groups of various kinds. There is the family for some. For others there is the football team or the local club. Even the street corner where we meet our friends can be a place where groups communicate. And all this involves different kinds of language – different forms of communication.

Just as we all spend a great deal of our lives communicating with others, or sending messages, so we all spend a great deal of time receiving messages. Many of these messages come from outside our immediate circle of friends or family. They may come from institutions such as the school or the employment office, but by far the largest number of messages that we receive come to us from the mass media. These media include hoardings, the radio, the cinema, magazines, comics, pop records, videos, newspapers and overwhelmingly from the television set.

Communication studies is about the ways in which all these messages are sent and received. It is also about all the different theories which have been put forward to explain how the communication process works. Once we set about studying the communication process, we find out that what seemed a simple and clear issue becomes difficult and clouded. Communication on an interpersonal basis and communication via a mass medium such as television often involves misunderstandings and raises issues about whether those doing the communicating are trying to tell us something clearly or 'pull the wool over our eyes'. Communication studies is, in part, about trying to unravel some of these mysteries, especially in relation to the mass media.

There have been theorists of communication dating back as far as Aristotle and before, but the birth of communication studies as we now understand it is usually linked with the names of Shannon and Weaver and their model of communication. This dates from 1949, and it represents an approach to communication which is one-way and rather basic. They suggested that in every communication process there was a sender, a receiver and a message. The sender would transmit the message and the receiver would receive it, provided no 'noise' got into the system. By 'noise' they meant anything which stopped the receiver from getting that message in its pure form. But it did not take long before this model of communication and others like it were seen to be very inadequate. One of the main reasons for this was that messages were also about meaning, and this was an altogether more slippery concept to handle. It led to theories of communication which looked at the ways in which meanings could be produced by one group of people who had some influence over another group of people. Communication was perceived by some theorists as a political act.

So communication studies is about the ways in which communication processes, from writing to speech, from dress to music, help to sustain or break with patterns of authority and control. It is about the ways in which messages are designed to communicate or to reassure, to sustain relationships of power or to question them. Thus we may look at the ways in which communication takes place between international powers as they negotiate for peace, or the way in which communication takes place between an interviewer and a contestant in the *Miss World* Competition. Or we may analyse the kinds of messages which are given to us in an advertisement which have less to do with the product itself than a dream which we are being offered if we buy the product.

Communication studies is also about the way in which communication is organised and structured through major media organisations. It is concerned with patterns of control and responsibility in broadcasting and in the press. It is concerned with the ways in which information does or does not pass from one part of the world to another. In the coming years it will be increasingly concerned with satellite broadcasting and the laws which will or will not regulate the messages which are sent and received around the world.

Above all, communication studies is a critical activity. It is a means whereby the various theories about communication can be scrutinised. It involves the detailed study of various forms of communication, from the personal to the international. This in turn requires the development of skills in the various fields associated with other disciplines such as sociology, linguistics, anthropology, social theory and literary studies. It is essentially a synthetic field which cannot be tied down to any one discipline. This is both an attraction and a potential pitfall for those who wish to be involved in its study. For it requires a will to take on board a whole range of skills and disciplines. But it also means that it is difficult to keep a clear and structured perspective on a vast field whilst immersed in one or other of its many facets.

It should also be noted that many communication studies courses are about *making* messages as well as studying them. Practical work in video, film, sound and graphic communication are amongst the many activities which are offered. Students for such courses come from a whole range of subject fields. These would normally include English and may require a modern foreign language at A-level. But it would be unwise to generalise, and would-be students of communication should check the specific entry requirements of the place where they hope to study. A-level communication studies, for instance, is *not* a requirement in many institutions offering communication studies degrees!

HELPFUL READING: A good overview of the field which is relatively easy to understand is *Introduction to Communication Studies* by

John Fiske (Methuen, 1982). This is a paperback and it contains constructive suggestions for further reading and work at the end of each chapter.

Computing

Professor D Conway, De Montfort University

The computer and the microprocessor have become an integral part of all aspects of modern life. Society's information needs continue to grow at an alarming rate and our desire to harness IT in business and industry far outstrips the availability of skilled workers. Computing is still a relatively new area of study. The subject is developing rapidly and as a discipline available for study at degree level it has come of age – the first courses started over 21 years ago. Innovations in the subject continue to emerge with breathtaking rapidity, thus ensuring the discipline has the vigour and enthusiasm expected in a youthful subject. The present era has been referred to by many as the new 'industrial revolution'. Modern computers increasingly provide users with more and more power to process information with, surprisingly, associated reductions in cost. This provides mankind with the ability to extend the use of the mind, just as the industrial revolution provided the power to extend the use of the muscle.

What do computing professionals do?

Although the range of specific activities is great it is possible to describe the tasks as satisfying society's information needs. These are almost exclusively problem-solving activities which frequently involve a high level of interaction with other people. Many problems still involve the creation of new solutions and workers gain great satisfaction from the implementation of their own ideas. The tasks vary from generalised solutions with a wide range of applications to highly specific solutions. For example the generation of a word processing system on a PC has to provide an interface suitable for general users in both the home and office environment. This can then be specially tailored to make the facility available to blind workers, hence requiring a totally new approach to designing the interface with the user. Alternatively, you may be building a system to enable fashion knitwear designers to create garments for immediate distribution to sales outlets.

Who can do it?

There are few restrictions and with the wide range of application areas, computing can enable you to encompass many other special interests. Because of its creative content it places a high premium on intellectual capabilities. The emphasis on 'information' makes precision and logic an important feature of the work. Usually, because of the 'human' aspects, it is important to be good at communicating. It is not an area with inbuilt prejudices though, at present, women (who generally possess all the appropriate characteristics) tend not to take advantage of the opportunities, hence denying the UK a valuable source of skilled workers. With the high level of demand for professionals, work in this area normally involves a high level of commitment and most people find they work very hard.

There are now a wide range of courses available at degree level and, generally, computing professionals are expected to be of graduate calibre. (Although as supply is still well short of demand, about a third of these have taken non-computer orientated degrees.) Most relevant courses bear the title 'computer science', but there are others, eg information technology, systems analysis, software engineering, computing and business, information systems. Sometimes you can combine computing with law, accounting, physics etc. Even courses with similar titles can be quite different and you should examine the curriculum carefully and make sure the courses you apply for reflect the sort of emphasis you want, eg software, business orientated, industrially orientated, theoretical, computer technology. Some courses require prescribed studies at A-level, others just want intelligent applicants with good A-level grades. Almost all assume you know little about computers and start from scratch but assume all the students are literate, numerate and hard working.

The discipline has attracted much support from successive governments because the skilled manpower produced can make a significant contribution to the economic wealth of the nation. The courses provided are still leaders worldwide and graduates are able to compete in the multinational arena with those from the US and Japan. In spite of the highly vocational emphasis placed on the courses, there are, as well, clear avenues for personal development of other kinds. The use of computing in the medical field has enabled great achievements to be made in, for example, learning systems for the deaf, expert systems for diagnosis, automated artificial limbs. The present interest in 'artificial intelligence' poses problems relating to mankind's thought processes and the challenging goal of amplifying our brain power.

Finally, one must stress the responsibilities involved. Just as bulldozers enable us to make bigger holes more quickly, computers enable us to make more mistakes (in information) faster than ever before – for example, a large firm paid everyone twice one month! Power brings with it responsibility.

What will you study?

You will, of course, have to acquire skills and knowledge. It is important to know how the computer functions and to develop skills in programming, but the real interest lies in situations where you have to design your own 'information processing system'. This is a creative activity where the solutions are reflections of your style and precision. When the system is put to work you can participate in its testing and see it in action at first hand. It will be your responsibility to put it right and eventually you will experience great satisfaction when you feel you have a flawless system. The context of this design will vary considerably. There are three main areas. At the very applied end of the spectrum you could be designing a system for the users of a railway timetable which answers enquiries posed by travellers. Alternatively, you might be devising a system that allows programmers to manipulate objects on a graphical display, eg create the graphic image seen at the beginning of television programmes. In contrast the problem might be to devise an algorithm that enables you to specify the most likely diagnosis of an illness for a patient whose symptoms have been established by a doctor. In such a system subsequent events should be used to modify the algorithms so that the system 'learns' about the patients. The real excitement is in that the computers you use should give you the power to crack problems you previously felt were beyond your capabilities.

HELPFUL READING: *The Information Technology Revolution* Ed. Tom Forester (Blackwell); *Computer Studies through Applications* Kennewell (Oxford).

Dance

Dr Richard Ralph, London Contemporary Dance School

One of my own favourite questions to students coming to audition for my School goes as follows: 'Is there anything else you could possibly be happy doing as a career?' If the answer is 'yes' I tell the student to do that, as without any doubt it would be easier than a training and subsequent career in dance. For dancing – like a religious vocation, with which it has many parallels – chooses you rather than you choosing it. Young people suddenly discover that they need to move their bodies, to reach deep into their reserves of stamina, strength and courage – and to dance. It can come upon you at the advanced age of sixteen or seventeen or it might be something you wanted to do since infancy. But these days you are likely to have had the chance to study part-time, if only for a short period.

The basis of most professional dance courses is the learning of dance technique (this is usually either ballet or contemporary dance technique; other forms include jazz). This takes at least three hours of every day always following the same pattern and gives you a basic movement alphabet – the building bricks with which a choreographer will be able to express his or her art through you, or with which you will be able to communicate with others through movement.

Technique is a bit like doing scales, if you are a musician, or press-ups, if you are an athlete. It is a daily routine which stays with you as a dancer and which keeps the body fit, supple and responsive to the instructions your brain gives it. Of itself it is not necessarily artistic, but it makes art possible: for the choreographer will paint and compose with the dancers' bodies. It is important to emphasise the place of technique in a dance school because it consumes many of the dance student's waking hours.

As the body is trained painstakingly and methodically to master the full range of dance technique, it changes shape as the muscle is developed appropriately and as all spare tissue is reduced. (This is the process known as 'changing the body'.) The way that the movement is timed and phrased gracefully and beautifully in relation to music will also be learned and the inner ideas or 'feeling tones' and muscular habits connected with certain sequences will become second nature. But learning to dance is no automatic business of idle repetition and following the lead of the teacher; rather, it is a mental and physical activity requiring ferocious concentration and considerable endurance. It tests commitment severely and many fall by the wayside. In any professional dance course the main credit will be given on the basis of progress made in technique classes.

Physical aptitude is important to any dance student; your body has got to be strong, but people with less-than-ideal or 'difficult' bodies can work wonders, especially if they undertake an appropriately supervised course of corrective strengthening exercises with a physiotherapist, qualified osteopath or body conditioning expert. But there are certain weaknesses which carry the risk of injury and which rule out rigorous training. So a proportion of students are not accepted at audition for physical reasons. In ballet the stereotyped look is more necessary than in contemporary dance, which tends to be more individual with less emphasis on the *corps de ballet*.

As I hinted before, the most important qualification and the secret of eventual success in dance is an 'appetite' for movement: the burning need to express yourself physically. Even in an untrained body this can show itself unmistakably in the height of the leap, the length or depth of an extension, the follow through of a movement or exercise, or in a general sense of joy or even ecstasy. However, facial and physical beauty are of themselves not enough. The body as a whole must need to speak out in movement.

What I have described is a study in itself: a full-time job. But a course of theoretical studies as provided by most dance schools (especially those with degree courses) can actually speed your development as a dancer. Such subjects as music, anatomy and costume are obviously relevant, dealing as they do with the essential elements of the professional dancer's craft, but increasingly the dancer is being required to operate part-time as a community worker and teacher. Few companies do not include such work in their annual programme and some preparation for teaching is necessary at dance school. It also helps future dancers to know a little of the problems to be found in modern urban social life.

Equally important to most high-level professional dance courses is an emphasis upon personal and cultural development. All the best dance schools have good libraries, record and video collections. It is vital that young dance students know something of the history of dance – how it came to be as it is – and about other art forms. Students need to go to museums, theatres, concerts and films, preferably with some guidance from the School. All of these art forms provide vital resources for any dancer. Without some emphasis on developing the whole person the student could end up with a marvellous technique and nothing to say; developing interpretative artists must feed their mind and spirit.

A powerful sense of identity and considerable self-confidence are necessary to dance generally and contemporary dance in particular. The dancer is saying, 'Here I am; this is what I am doing; look at me.' And the 'I' is vitally important. There has to be somebody interesting to look at. All too often the hothouse intensity of the dance school produces a cold obsessiveness and a narrowing of horizons which ends up by actually threatening artistic values. So resolve to keep your mind active and your interest in the world around you alive.

Any good dance school will give prominence to the creative and interpretative aspects of dance. Choreography, or dance composition, is usually taught from an early stage. Of course it is mainly a matter of individual ability, but there is a basic craft which can be taught to all, and which will help dancers to understand the choreographers who will work with them in their professional careers, even if they are not destined to become established choreographers themselves. Even modest compositions can help dance students to develop as interpretative performers and to move creatively. For this reason it is encouraged. It is an excellent preparation for professional life for students to work with other dancers on group pieces and to find ways of working through the inevitable artistic and personal tensions that arise.

Repertory is a very popular subject, consisting in the learning of a dance which has already been performed. Once students have mastered the steps they learn how to perform it in front of other students and sometimes a public paying audience. It is important that students should always remember that they are studying a theatrical art form which is designed to be performed; although too much performance too early in the course is usually seen as inappropriate. The technical groundwork must be laid before it can be absorbed into interpretation.

In summary, the dancer's training is very tough and requires much dedication and there are already many good and fully trained dancers pursuing too few professional jobs. But such warnings are useless to those who have decided they must dance. And should you not achieve your ambition of dancing professionally, there is now a range of interesting dance-related careers open to the well-trained dancer. But here, too, commitment and love of dance are essential; and careful course selection when you are applying for your dance course can keep a range of career options open.

Dentistry

Jane R Goodman, Eastman Dental Hospital

Conversation at social gatherings often turns to how you earn a living. 'I'm a dentist' brings a response ranging from curiosity to horror, followed by compliments or complaints about their own practitioner, and details of recent dental experiences.

Dentistry for many patients is still an ordeal, which they undergo with some trepidation, and during which they may feel anxious and vulnerable. The dental surgeon has to reassure the patient while carrying out intricate work on what is probably the most sensitive area of the body.

A desire to work with people and an ability to communicate with them are therefore essential qualifications for dentistry. Manual dexterity, which may prove difficult to assess initially becomes highly developed during training. In the majority of cases a scientific training to A-level is necessary, although exceptions can be made to this. Family connections within the profession are strong, and maintaining this tradition, and that of the hospital where trained, is still considered by some to be important.

Dentistry as a university degree bears little resemblance to any others save perhaps medicine. Because of the nature of the subject, the course of five years is very structured. At the end of this time, however, one is able to start practising without any further period of study or apprenticeship, unlike other professions such as medicine, law or accountancy.

The degree of Bachelor of Dental Surgery (BDS) is divided into three parts – 1st, 2nd and 3rd BDS. A-levels in physics, chemistry and biology give exemption from 1st BDS. However, a few medical schools will offer this course to arts students and mature students who, having pursued other careers, wish to retrain. These students would at interview have to show that, despite lack of scientific training, they had the interest and ability to study dentistry.

The first year of basic medical sciences – anatomy, physiology and biochemistry, with the addition of dental histology – is tightly packed with lectures and practicals, culminating in the 2nd BDS examination, usually held in June. The anatomy concentrates on the head, neck and thorax regions and the histology deals with the structure of teeth and related tissues. Wherever possible the application of these subjects to the clinical work encountered in the following years is stressed, making the subjects more relevant and integrated. Having survived the first year – and at this stage there are some who drop out – one starts clinical training and treatment of patients under close supervision. One learns all the different aspects of operative dentistry: prosthetics (false teeth), conservation (fillings, crowns and bridges), periodontology (gums), orthodontics (correct positioning of teeth with braces), children's dental problems, and oral surgery (extraction etc). The practice of preventive dentistry for the community and individual is also encouraged. The theory of pharmacology and pathology, as well as a basic grounding in medicine and surgery, are taught during this period. Most schools will encourage students to have an elective period during which they can visit other units in this country or abroad.

In the final months of training the questions of how and where to practise raise themselves. The choice is varied. Although the majority of newly qualified dentists go straight into practice, there are openings in hospital and community services. Vocational training courses in general practice and community dentistry have been started in many centres throughout the country. Here trainees, on a day release basis from a chosen practice or clinic, attend lectures or seminars to improve their awareness of the possibilities within the service in which they have chosen to work. A few graduates, particularly those with an interest in science or basic medical subjects and with less of an interest in clinical work, may turn immediately to research.

In dental practice, whether as an associate member, with fewer management responsibilities, or a full partner of a group, one can pursue and develop particular interests and ideas. Although there is still a general lack of concern by the public in dental health, and routine treatment is necessary, more people are expressing an interest in and demanding advice on preventive dentistry. There is the satisfaction of having responsibility for patients attending one's practice and getting to know and interest them. At the same time one is running a business unit and administering the day-to-day workings of a group of personnel. There are, of course, good financial rewards in return for hard work, although these may decrease with middle age if one is unable to maintain the pace of work. Probably the main advantage of practice over the other branches of dentistry is personal independence, which is partly true of the National Health Service and even more so in the growing private sector.

To specialise in one of the branches of dentistry will involve climbing the career ladder in university or to a consultant post in a hospital. Oral surgery ranges from extractions under local anaesthesia to cosmetic surgery and treatment of head and neck cancer. Orthodontics, restorative dentistry and paediatric dentistry are other specialities for which the diploma of Fellowship of Dental Surgery (FDS) is necessary, but for oral surgery and oral medicine a medical degree is also required. One of the rewards of hospital work is the challenge of particularly difficult procedures, which with time, technical assistance and expertise one is able to perform. In paediatric dentistry one may be consulted about a patient with, for example, an unusual hereditary condition. This requires long-term treatment planning which takes into consideration the growth and development of the child, and alterations in the dentition. Restorative dentistry involves conservation of teeth, treatment of gum conditions and advanced crown and bridge work combined with removable prostheses, which includes precision dental engineering. The orthodontist, by means of removable or fixed appliances, moves teeth to provide better function and improved aesthetics. The community dentist will consider the provision of care on a wider population, taking into account the epidemiology of disease and changing health patterns. Recently training programmes for specialists have been established in this field. Specialisation enables one to develop new approaches to problems, to inform colleagues of innovations, and to influence people concerned with health services, both consumers and administrators. This ensures that the care available is of a high standard, and continues to improve.

Both in hospital and practice, as well as community dentistry, where the service is directed towards the special groups, the handicapped and the elderly, dentistry is basically a practical career. Preparing cavities and filling them, repositioning teeth, cutting soft tissue and bone all require manual dexterity accompanied by good communication skills. Major technological changes in the past two decades have led to more efficient equipment and the development of new materials. These wide ranging changes have greatly increased the scope of the work, and have made treatment easier for the patient and more interesting for the dentist.

Drama and Theatre Arts

Malcolm Griffiths, Nottingham Trent University

Theatre is an uniquely challenging art form and an equally challenging study. It combines personal exploration with social purpose, individual experimentation with collective responsibility, research with performance, images with words. The past decade has seen a marked increase in the number of applications for drama and theatre arts courses. This is partly the result of the successful development of theatre studies at A-level, partly the result of the growth of youth theatre activities throughout the country but chiefly because live performance now plays an important role in people's cultural and social lives. The interest in theatre in all its forms is increasing with the result that the demand for places has rocketed. Rock bands and West End musicals have harnessed technological wizardry to provide audiences with visual spectacles matching the impact of their sound systems. Theatre-in-Education companies and community theatre groups have brought exciting and relevant theatre to less traditional theatre spaces. High standard opera productions tour the country and attract audiences of all ages. Contemporary playwrights explore important aspects of today's world in innovative ways. Add to these the crucial contributions theatre makes to television, film and video and you will begin to capture the vitality and potency of theatre and the wide range of opportunities it offers. Whilst you may be aware of the controversies surrounding funding for the arts and the anger being increasingly felt at the way in which they are being devalued in political circles, it is important to recognise that the art of theatre in Britain is thriving.

Having decided to study drama or theatre arts, you will have begun your search for the most appropriate and attractive course and will have discovered that the situation is at best confused, if not downright daft. A galaxy of institutions in both the public and private sectors of higher education promote a bewildering range of degree and diploma courses. Some are widely recognised and acclaimed. Some are simply shady. With so many young people wanting to enter this area of study there are many opportunities for unscrupulous operators to take advantage of people's aspirations. The Business and Technician Education Council, the Conference of Drama Schools and the Standing Council of University Drama Departments represents the best available in their different areas. You should ensure that an institution you are thinking of applying to is recognised by one of these organisations.

If you have sought advice on how best to make a career in theatre you will have encountered two conflicting points of view. On the one hand people argue that a degree course provides an all-round education, that you should not specialise too soon, that many of our foremost theatre-workers never took any formal training but progressed through student drama societies and that, as theatre work is so precarious, you should ensure that you do not narrow down your career choices too far. Others argue that theatre has now emerged from the dark ages when people drifted into it with a kind of inspired amateurism, that vocationally-orientated courses can best help you acquire the skills and insights necessary to survive and build a successful career and that a professionally-rigorous course provides you with creative, intellectual and interpersonal challenges which are in themselves an all-round education. All, however, will agree that theatre is an exacting art form and that any drama or theatre arts course worth the candle will stretch your capabilities to the full – artistically, intellectually, technically and socially. This may make for a tough education but, provided you are determined, also makes for a rewarding one.

Whatever aspect you choose to study the following points should be considered before making your application:

- There is no uniformity of courses. Each has its strengths and weaknesses, principles and eccentricities. It is important to find out about these before committing yourself. Comparing prospectuses is useful but they are, of course, a form of advertising. Try to visit courses and form a first-hand idea of how they work. This takes time and money, but you owe it to your own future to make the right decision. Most courses have nothing to hide and welcome arranged visits. But don't turn up unannounced and expect the red carpet treatment. Above all, talk with current students. They are at the cutting edge and know what the course is really like.
- Contact your local regional theatre, arts association, youth drama groups and drama advisers to see whether they can help you with information.
- Check carefully with your local education authority about grants. Some courses carry only discretionary awards and these are becoming more and more difficult to obtain.
- Check the entry requirements carefully and what is expected in the way of interviews, auditions, portfolios of work etc. Some places charge a non-returnable audition fee.
- Try to discover the employment record of graduates. This information is generally available so think twice if you are being fobbed off with evasive replies.

Acting

The image of the successful actor or actress projected by the media and magazines is one of often far-fetched glamour. Real success can mean being able to afford to choose between work in theatre, films or television or to remain with a company over a number of years developing a particular form of theatre. The majority of performers, however, face a harsher reality where stretches of unemployment are broken by the occasional television engagement, promotional video or short repertory season. A career in acting requires a special toughness and determination in addition to real talent. If you succeed, it will be very rewarding. Should you fail, nobody else will shed a tear.

Drama schools are a comparatively recent phenomenon and have largely replaced the actor's traditional apprenticeship on the job with opportunities for developing skills, learning techniques, making mistakes and acquiring self-confidence before trying to survive in a highly competitive market. Although there will always be room for people with irrepressible natural talent, the importance of drama schools in nurturing ability and improving standards is now recognised. Schools are acutely aware that a professional actor needs to be adaptable to all kinds of theatre – compelling a pub audience in cabaret, projecting the nuances of a character's psyche in a large auditorium, devising a show with disabled children etc. Each school will try to prepare students to meet the exceptional range of responses and skills required, but each will have evolved its particular philosophy and style. It is here that care needs to be taken in selecting a course. All drama schools provide tuition in voice, movement and acting but how these three fundamentals are taught will differ widely. Movement teaching, for example, can vary from exercises drawn from gymnastics or acrobatics to precise schooling in dance. One school may place great emphasis on a highly individualistic approach focusing on students' technical and expressive proficiency and on the production of playtexts in order to give the student the experience to develop as a flexible and disciplined instrument of interpretation. Another will stress the essential collaborative aspect of theatre and develop work from a basis of group improvisation in order to increase students' creative responsiveness and social awareness. No drama school would claim to be able to turn you into a great actor but it can help you further your ambition by providing a thorough grounding, expertise and time.

Before deciding which course to apply to, you should consider what facilities the school has and how much work is done in radio, television and film as these will become a crucial source of your future livelihood. Also find out whether the school employs visiting professionals for projects or productions and whether it covers both past and contemporary theatre forms. *Going on the Stage* – a report to the Calouste Gulbenkian Foundation – is still a useful background book to consult and should be available through your local library.

In addition to drama schools there are a number of performing and creative arts courses which offer opportunities for more experimental approaches to performance in conjunction with, for example, dance, music and visual arts studies. These courses do not claim to provide the kind of training found at drama schools but to encourage students to create their own performance events and to learn through both practice and the wider debate on the arts.

Drama
John Marshall, Bristol University

Of all the arts, drama is perhaps the most public and popular. In the various forms of live theatre, film and television, more drama is seen now than ever before. Although this popularity may, in part, be attributed to the greater accessibility afforded by television it cannot disguise the very real significance of performed drama to society. Why should this be so? What made London audiences flock to the public playhouses in Elizabethan England? Why do millions of people watch *Eastenders*? How did Shakespeare ensure that the audience not only watched and listened to his plays but also returned to see his next one? How do soap operas work in terms of character, story line, dialogue, subject matter, setting, camera angles, editing and so forth? The serious asking of these questions and the rigorous thinking, exploring and analysis required to answer them is, in very simple terms, what constitutes the study of drama. To be able to comprehend fully the role of drama in society and to engage critically with text and performance it is necessary to gain knowledge and experience in a number of theoretical and practical areas which contribute to the informed study of drama. In the pursuit of textual analysis and practical criticism students may find themselves drawing on aspects of such diverse disciplines as art, architecture, history, religion, politics, physics, philosophy, psychology, sociology etc. This wide range of contributing knowledge is one of the exciting qualities of drama study at undergraduate level which places it deservedly within the area of liberal arts education and distinguishes it from the more specialised and specific actor training with which it is sometimes confused. For the most part drama degrees are not vocational, they are not designed to train students for particular professional posts in the theatre or television and should not be regarded as a fail-safe alternative to drama school. The candidate at interview who professes a yearning to act but wants a degree to 'fall back on' is unlikely to impress. It is rewardingly true that many drama graduates do proceed professionally but in most cases this follows an additional period of appropriate training.

The number of degree courses available in the subject has grown considerably since the first, forty years ago; and although many may have 'drama' in the title the courses may be very different in content and approach. It is, therefore, extremely important that candidates read course outlines very carefully in order to select the type of course which best suits their interest. For example, many departments acknowledge the significant contribution of television and film to the drama of the twentieth century and may incorporate not only the theoretical study necessary for the critical analysis of text and screening but also a complementary element of practical film or video making. Other courses may concentrate entirely on the process and products of the theatre and yet both degrees may be listed in handbooks as BA(Hons) Drama. Similarly, the variety of courses reflects the variety of approaches available to the study of drama and while most will combine a number of these the emphasis on the historical, critical, sociological and generic approach may be different in each case.

What courses will have in common, however, and what distinguishes drama from other apparently similar disciplines such as English, is the essential emphasis attached to performance. Although the printed text may represent the most tangible object for study it is only the written record of what the author intended the actors to say and, in a very limited way, to do. As such it qualifies as a piece of dramatic literature but it cannot record the effect in performance of the interpretative contributions of the actors, the director and the designer. Nor can it indicate such things as the influence of the audience or the venue or the means of finance and administration on the experience of performance. The analysis of these elements which make up the dramatic performance requires the acquisition and application of a vocabulary and methodology which is part of the undergraduate study of drama.

One of the methods which particularly characterises the study of drama is the practical exploration of aspects of performance and production. On most courses this is designed to enhance students' experience and understanding of the ways in which the practical, technical and interpretative skills of the theatre, film and television contribute to the production of drama. As such these activities, be they workshops or full productions, are as much part of the study methods necessary to the discipline of drama as those that may be regarded as traditionally academic. It is for this reason that most departments consider the division of drama study into 'practical' and 'academic' areas as artificial and misleading, for it seems to imply that some methods are more proper to degree study than others. The relationship between these study methods should perhaps be seen as equivalent to that of theory and experiment in the laboratory sciences where one informs upon the other.

It would be wrong, however, not to acknowledge that it is the opportunity to approach a subject through practice as well as theory that attracts very many students. Often the earliest interest in drama develops from the enjoyable participation in the school play or local youth theatre. In some schools this interest can be encouraged further by directing it towards GCSE-level drama and A-level theatre studies. Success in and enjoyment of these courses can be a good indication of whether a degree in drama would be a valid option. Not all students, of course, have the opportunity to take these subjects and it is important to realise that this in no way penalises candidates in their chances of acceptance. What admission tutors will be looking for, in addition to academic ability and suitability, will be a committed interest in the subject which is commensurate with local opportunity. In other words, a demonstrable and critical interest in theatre-going, cinema and television viewing as well as an active involvement in some area of theatre performance (not necessarily acting) or film/video making will be as important as A-level choice.

Drama study, in common with its professional relations, theatre, television and film, is apparently glamorous but in reality extremely hard work, not only intellectually but physically and emotionally as well. It is demanding in terms of time as well as effort but it is also sociable and pleasurable and to the outsider enjoyment can sometimes be confused with easiness. Don't be confused; be prepared to work long hours at reading as well as rehearsing and to give a great deal of yourself, not merely for your own benefit but for the collective advantage and development of others.

HELPFUL READING: A useful introduction to the subject is Martin Esslin's *An Anatomy of Drama* (London, Temple Smith, 1976).

Theatre Design
Malcolm Griffiths, Nottingham Trent University

Once the cinema had supplanted the theatre's meagre capacity for spectacle with visual splendour, fantasy and glamour and television had created a detailed authenticity which exposed the theatre's efforts as clumsy and unconvincing, it became necessary to rethink the purpose and aesthetics of design in the theatre. It has taken the sustained efforts of two generations of designers to achieve this new understanding and to demonstrate that theatre design is neither a poor derivative of fine art nor a slap-happy version of industrial design but a complex creative discipline in its own right.

Changes in theatre over recent decades – the building of new and different theatres throughout the country, the extensive growth of touring companies, the creation of the Theatre-in-Education movement, the new technology available, the new languages of performance explored by dance and experimental companies etc – have heightened the importance design plays in theatre production and in the audience's enjoyment. British theatre design is internationally renowned and the development of theatre design courses closely related to professional practice has meant that an undervalued area of theatre arts has now emerged as a major consideration in performance events. **British Theatre Design – the Modern Age** (published in 1989) will give you some idea of the artistic challenges faced by a theatre designer.

There are many qualities needed to make a good theatre designer – a feeling for space, mass, colour and texture; the ability to analyse playtexts, operas etc and imagine the performance they embody; an interest in research and social background; an understanding of lighting design; a knowledge of costume construction and of the development of fashion and morality in dress; an awareness of the qualities and possibilities of different materials; and an ability to collaborate, delegate, organise and manage a budget without losing sight of one's own creative purpose. Above all it requires a good eye, a good mind and a good pair of hands.

Although some drama schools and departments offer options in design, the major courses are situated in schools of art and design and normally expect applicants to have successfully completed an art and design foundation course.

Economics
Professor David W Pearce, University College London

You may not have thought of economics as the sort of subject that is relevant to organised crime or whether it is worth taking a postgraduate degree, or even to explaining just why one in four American men and women have extra-marital affairs. That is the beauty of economics. It creeps in everywhere and for a very simple reason. Basically, there is nothing (well, nearly nothing) you can do that does not imply an economic decision. Consider the petty thief and whether we should allocate

the much overstrained resources of the police force to catching him. Say
he has stolen £1,000. He is better off by £1,000 and his victim is worse off
by £1,000. Society as a whole is no worse off – we have merely redistrib-
uted money from one person to another. Now, if we set the police on
him, we have all the costs of catching the thief. And if he is caught, it gets
worse. Then we have the costs of criminal proceedings and, worse still, if
he is imprisoned, we have the (substantial) costs of looking after him and
hopefully rehabilitating him for re-entry into society. We can be fairly
sure it will all cost more than £1,000. So is it worth catching the marginal
criminal? It may look like a moral problem and it is, but the example
shows you that it is also an economic problem. There aren't enough
police to go round and we can't afford to give them all the resources they
would need to capture all the villains. So some crimes must go unsolved
for want of resources.

Of course, you wouldn't want economics alone to decide issues like
this (though some would). But you'll begin to see that dry statements like
'economics is about the allocation of resources' imply a rather dull and
turgid subject, whereas some of its aspects are a little more exciting. Take
the issue of taking a postgraduate degree or a professional qualification.
Is it worth it to you? Count the cost of being without work while you
secure the qualification, then work out the difference between what you
would have earned with the qualification and what you would have
earned without it. (You can find the statistics to do this, so long as you
know you are going to be a brain surgeon or a car park attendant.) On the
basis that you won't care too much now about what you will earn when
you are sixty-five, apply a factor which 'discounts' future earnings in each
case.

Compare the sum of these discounted earnings with what you forgo by
taking the course. If you are thinking about an undergraduate degree, the
answer will come out in favour of taking the qualification in most cases. If
your intended PhD is in Transylvanic gravestone inscriptions of the
fourteenth century, you may well find a negative rate of return (there
isn't very much demand for that sort of person, even in Transylvania).
There is even a good chance you are investing badly if you take an
economics doctorate, but check carefully.

So now you've done your very own personal 'cost-benefit analysis'.
You have even learnt a piece of economic jargon fairly painlessly. Of
course, you might want to justify your staying on at school to society.
What you now do is to point out that your extra earnings are some sort of
measure of your extra worth to society (debatable that one, but begin that
way) and then point to the enormous benefits other people will gain from
having you around (you'll be able to answer the four year old's questions
on the relative size of dinosaurs and man, or exactly what a balanced
budget multiplier is, and so on). If you win this argument (you might
not) you have demonstrated that you are an 'external benefit' to society
(they benefit at your cost) and you've gained a bit more jargon.

We'll leave the one on extra-marital affairs since you might prefer to
worry about the pre-marital ones first. But it is true that economists have
sought to explain why they take place (something one had always thought

psychology was concerned with). Not that the glamour should be exaggerated. Before you decide whether to criticise the health board for buying an expensive body scanner instead of buying more dialysis machines for kidney patients, you'll have to find out about marginal costs, programme budgets and quality-adjusted life years.

Moreover, you might find yourself dealing with a textbook that denies economics has anything to do with any of this. That would be a shame, but some economists are purists and think we can only answer questions about fact and prediction. They are the 'positivists' (and are very dull people). That is they say we can only talk about what would happen if something else happened. Well, we can disagree and we often do (though not as much as those silly jokes about economists suggest), but there is a richer field of prescriptive economics to be mined and, at the end of the day, you cannot divorce economics from what is desirable. Indeed, just think about it. If economics is about how best to allocate resources, what does 'best' mean? It could mean give it all to me. Or it could mean that we should make as much output as we can from the resources we've got. Or it could mean we should maximise output, but allow for the 'quality of life'. The 'best' allocation can only be defined by reference to some moral principle.

Economists are into everything. The only catch if you want to join us is that you have to take a short course in how to think in economic terms. That probably means a textbook in which the exciting bits are left out, though I've never seen why. Hopefully you'll stay with the textbook for a year or two but you may be able to insist to your lecturer that there are some everyday issues – crime, environment, health care, education – to which even the most rudimentary economics can be applied. And if the jargon gets you down a bit, just think: if *everyone* understood economics the supply of economists could be very large. The price of economists (their salaries) would fall as a result. And we wouldn't want that, would we? (By the way, you've just learned about supply and demand!).

HELPFUL READING: Guy Routh, *The Origin of Economic Ideas* (London: Macmillan, 1975); David Pearce, Anil Markandya and Ed Barbier, *Blueprint for a Green Economy* (London: Earthscan, 1989).

Education

Professor David Bridges, East Anglia University

With a few exceptions the study of education in undergraduate courses is associated with a preparation for a career in teaching, and typically it is in the context of a four year BEd programme (though some universities are re-designating these courses as BA or BA Ed). You don't have to teach at the end of a BEd course – some 15% to 20% of BEd graduates use the qualification as a stepping stone into advertising, accountancy, the professional theatre, banking and everything else that graduates of non-vocational courses enter by way of employment. A head hunter for management trainees from Marks and Spencer once told some of my students that they liked BEd graduates because the experience they had working with other adults and taking responsibility for children gave them an extra maturity. However, degrees in education involve a lot of practical work in schools, and if you are really unexcited by teaching or if you turn pale at the sight of a writhing mass of young humanity, then perhaps this is not the subject for you.

There are usually four main components to undergraduate courses in education. Let me say a little about each.

Main subject study   Degrees in education are effectively combined subject degrees in which the equivalent of two years of undergraduate study has to be devoted to a main academic subject, such as maths, English, music, science, to be found in the school curriculum. You will not be able for this purpose to take eg sociology, business studies or law. Your main subject will be studied in much the same way as it would be studied in any other purely academic degree course. Indeed in most cases you will be studying it alongside other undergraduates in the same subject area.

Teaching methodology   If you are preparing to teach in a secondary school this part of the course will concentrate on the teaching of your main subject with perhaps some attention to a subsidiary area of teaching. You will look at the requirements of the national curriculum and the newly developing system of assessment. You will become familiar with teaching resources – books, packages, videos, information technology, etc – and with a wide repertoire of teaching and learning styles including eg games and simulations, collaborative group work and field visits as well as 'chalk and talk'.

If you are preparing to teach in a primary school, the demands of this part of the degree are of course much wider, and you will have to gain some familiarity at your own level with a reasonable range of the subjects you will be expected to teach. Maths, science and English will be required components of the training of all primary teachers, but it will not end there. You will also have to take a selection of courses from eg expressive arts, history, geography, technology, religious studies and physical education. So be prepared to tackle some pretty diverse experiences!

Education theory or Education studies   These elements of a degree in education look two ways. In one direction they seek to root the study and practice of education in the academic discourse appropriate to a degree programme. In this regard the study of education looks in particular to the research and scholarship to be found in writing in the disciplines of psychology, sociology, philosophy and history. Indeed the study of education can provide an interesting inroad into the study of the social sciences in their own right. You will typically explore elements of child development, learning theory, motivation, the sociology of education (including eg school and community studies and investigations of ethnicity and education), ethics, theory of knowledge and the history of education. You will be expected to bring the same kind of demands for evidence, the same questioning and critical stance and the same discipline to this study as you would expect to bring to your main academic study – though, frankly, in the time available in the undergraduate course you will only be able to lay the foundations of study which you may be able to extend in an MA or MEd after you have had a few years in teaching.

At the same time, however, the study of education has to look to the real world of schools and classrooms and the practical concerns – your practical concerns – which it is reasonably expected to inform. The study of education in this context is an applied study which should help you to do your job better – not 'better' in the most crudely practical sense that you can for example write more clearly on the blackboard, but better in the sense that you have a wider understanding of what you are about, that you have thought out a defensible rationale for what you are doing, that you are capable of articulating and reflecting on your practice, discussing it with others and modifying it in the light of experience and changing circumstances. For many of us, these demands which arise from practice, far from undermining the purely intellectual appeal of the study of education add a special excitement and piquancy to its engagement.

School experience/teaching practice   This is the really practical end of the course where you will be working directly with children. To begin with you will probably work with individual children or pairs alongside other students and under the supervision of a teacher or one of your tutors. Gradually you will take responsibility for larger groups and have more of a role in planning the work you will do with them. Some of your teaching methods course will be school-based. You will probably have two substantial teaching practices, for example, a five week practice in the second year of your course and ten weeks in the fourth year. By the end of the course you should have experience of taking a whole class (primary) or whole classes (secondary) for a reasonably sustained period by yourself.

It is this last ingredient – the practice of teaching – which makes the degree in education a somewhat different experience from other purely academic degrees. Undoubtedly it confronts you with extra challenges. I don't think anyone faces their first class alone without some doubts as to whether they are going to be able to cope.

But it also has its satisfactions. It does take you out of what you can sometimes feel is a rather precious and inward looking undergraduate environment into the local community and into a position of real responsibility in which teaching colleagues, children – and often their parents too – need you and are depending upon your skill, imagination and resourcefulness. For some students, the exercise of that responsibility provides an important balance to other elements of their undergraduate experience.

School-based training

The government has recently introduced new requirements (so far applicable to secondary teacher training courses only) which will strengthen the participation of practising teachers in the teaching and oversight of teacher training courses and ensure that a high proportion of the course is actually based in schools. Many institutions are in the process of revising their courses to meet these requirements, so you will need to ensure that you have as up-to-date information as possible about any changes.

Electrical and Electronic Engineering

Dr J C Earls

To reflect upon the profession of electronic and electrical engineers after thirty years of involvement is curiously difficult. One can stress the very considerable contribution of the profession to society through developments in energy supply, communications, medical electronics, computers, automatic control systems etc, etc. I suppose it is true that many present-day electronic and electrical engineers had in mind the relevance of our profession to the well-being of humanity when they decided on such a career. But was that the primary force which influenced their decision? It is difficult to speak for others, but I would judge that many of us decided upon our career path for many other reasons – we had some involvement with electronics or electrical engineering as schoolchildren and found electronic or electrical devices interesting; or we assumed that 'being good' at physics and mathematics was a helpful indicator that we would make good engineers. Certainly there is an elegance about the study of electronic and electrical engineering which readily appeals to those who find mathematics and the natural sciences interesting subjects. Another force in our choice might well have been the obvious rapid technological change taking place within our profession (and this continues at an even greater pace now) which gave it an excitement and a challenge.

The origins of our profession go back centuries to the early observations on the phenomena of electricity and magnetism. It was not however until the 19th century that these phenomena were well understood and a collection of laws and theories could be systematically deployed in the creation of apparatus and machinery that we would now recognise. Early pioneers could be cited – Ohm, Faraday, Wheatstone, Kirchhoff etc, etc; they, with many others, laid the foundations of engineering principles upon which many modern developments are based – radio, radar, energy generation and transmission etc. In the early 20th century the profession was concerned with communication (telegraphy and radio) and with electrical energy generation and its use (lighting and transport). Up until the second world war (1939) there were very few undergraduate courses in electronic and electrical engineering; these subjects were usually part of general courses in engineering which embraced mechanical engineering and, in some cases, civil engineering. The 1939–45 war promoted a heightened interest in electronics and developments took place rapidly – the refinement of radar systems, and the creation of a whole new range of electronic circuits – based of course on the vacuum valve. The latter part of the war and the immediate years following saw the early precursors of the modern computer – though the principles had been first enunciated in the 17th century by Pascal and by Babbage in the early 19th century.

The transistor, the integrated electronic circuit, and the microprocessor in turn have revolutionised electronic and electrical engineering (and our lives) in the past thirty years. All the time new phenomena are being applied and the revolution continues – for example superconductivity is set to lead to new types of computer, and magnetic levitation is the basis of new forms of transport. Robots are in the factory and will soon be in our homes. It is an exciting time for engineers and for those they serve.

What sort of people are electronic and electrical engineers? Well you cannot tell by looking at them and it will not necessarily be easy to judge by talking to them. The evidence is best taken from the things they do and create. Some are in research and development – looking at fundamental electronic processes, investigating new materials and circuits, assessing new applications of systems already proved; others will be associated with the design of systems to meet particular commercial or industrial needs. All will have some form of management role, and the ability to be creative and resourceful will be important to their success. Because of the rapid rate of change in technology, all will require to be resilient and be prepared to learn and develop throughout their professional careers.

Clearly the form and style of courses for electronic and electrical engineers have necessarily reflected the changes and pressures within the profession. In 1979 the Committee of Enquiry into the Engineering Profession published its very thorough report 'Engineering our Future'. This resulted in the creation of the Engineering Council which maintains an overview of standards in the engineering profession. The report also had a significant influence upon all courses in engineering. Particular among these were the increased emphasis upon students gaining insight into real engineering problems during their study and a generally heightened stress upon undergraduates establishing individually, and collectively, links with industry. How is this manifest? Well there is much more attention paid to design, to project work and to case studies. Problems set are much more likely to be open-ended, solutions requiring the exercise of creativity and of judgement. Knowledge and the skills of analysis remain important but are now accompanied by the skills of communication and of group activity. The old-fashioned mould (if incorrect) of the introspective backroom-boy has been well and truly broken; the electronic and electrical engineers of today must not only be academically able but must be innovative, resourceful and be effective as a part of a team and as managers of people.

Because of rapid changes in the past and the continued rate of change there are a very wide range of courses in electronic and electrical engineering. In outline structure they are similar – three years duration for full-time courses, and four years for sandwich courses, most leading to the award of BEng or BSc (there are some new extended courses leading to an MEng, though comparatively speaking these are few). The variety exists in their content and level of specialisation – some remain fairly general and embrace a wide range of subjects, others are quite specialised, concentrating on such aspects as communications or computer technology. Most courses will be accredited by the Institution of Electrical Engineers and/or by the Institution of Electronic and Radio Engineers. Accreditation means that upon completion of the course the graduate will be exempt from the academic part of the requirements to be met for a Chartered Engineer.

Earlier I used the expression 'backroom-boy'; I was not intending to be sexist but it is true that few women have chosen engineering as a career. Happily the situation is changing and the number of women on engineering courses is rising quickly. Electronic and electrical engineering offers particularly attractive prospects for women because of the nature of the work (see Helpful Reading).

Since I graduated in 1953 I have witnessed, and happily I have been part of, many changes in the profession. Most of these changes have been technical – the dramatic development of the power of computers, the many new forms of communication, the transistor, then the integrated circuit, lasers, automation, the widespread use of electronics in medicine, vast increases in the power capacity of single generators, nuclear power and the harnessing of new power sources (wind and wave) etc, etc. Many of the changes have led to higher standards of living and have led to products that enrich our lives. They are the products of a society which seeks change, which is concerned for people and which recognises the value of technical expertise and innovation. Electronic and electrical engineers have made their contribution and will continue to do so. I have certainly found it to be fun and to be rewarding.

HELPFUL READING: *What is Different About Being a Woman in Electrical Engineering?* and *Have You Got What it Takes?* (Both these can be obtained free from the Schools Liaison Service, Institution of Electrical Engineers, Michael Faraday House, 6 Hills Way, Stevenage, Herts SG1 2AY; telephone 0438 313311.)

English

Professor Patrick Parrinder, Reading University

The study and teaching of imaginative literature is as old as recorded history. In British education this function was for long fulfilled by Greek and Latin literature, so that English as a university course did not come into its own until the twentieth century. As it did so, literature increasingly took over from historical language study as the core of the new discipline. Anglo-Saxon and Middle English are now – sadly, some would say – marginal to the curriculum in nearly all institutions. The enthusiasm of teachers and taught for the many varieties of contemporary literature has also led to the widespread abandonment of the chronological survey approach ('From *Beowulf* to Virginia Woolf') in favour of thematic and contextually-based options. There is now a marked difference between the single-subject degree courses offered in the more innovative and the more traditional English departments, so it pays to study the prospectus closely.

For the student, the initial attraction of an English course is likely to be the opportunity to immerse oneself in some of the most exciting, and most complex, works of poetry, fiction and drama in the language. Some of our motives for studying literature are quite properly introspective – a desire to know ourselves and to explore our cultural and psychic identity. But literary study is outward – as well as inward-looking. Literary criticism, as developed in the writings of such intellectual precursors as S T Coleridge, Matthew Arnold, T S Eliot and F R Leavis, combines formal analysis with the belief that the literary work offers a key to the nature of human experience. Theorists since Aristotle have argued that literature is not mere entertainment and that the impulses to make poetry, to tell stories and to act out our feelings in words play a central part in our lives.

The separation of literature from entertainment is central to the traditional justification of literary studies – but it is also notoriously productive of anxiety. The need to demonstrate that literary students are not wasting their time on trivia has led to a heavy (and at times stultifying) emphasis on the intellectual and moral benefits of 'high culture'. More recently it has been acknowledged that all social life involves feelings and attitudes which are reflected in, and reinforced by, the culture's systems of symbolic expression. 'High' and 'low' culture serve much the same functions in this respect. The notion of symbolic systems has permitted the extension of English studies beyond the so-called 'canon' of recognised major literary works to other texts including advertisements, popular romantic fiction and TV soap operas. Some teachers now argue for a broader redefinition of the subject as 'cultural studies' (throwing the criteria of aesthetic and literary merit out of the window), while others argue for a renewed connection between literary and language studies. At the same time, the subtlety and complexity of the verbal creations of the greatest writers, from Chaucer to the Nobel Prize winning Caribbean poet Derek Walcott, is the *raison d'être* of most English courses.

The reason why some kinds of writing are considered more literary than others is, at bottom, a question of language and form. Yet most varieties of current criticism give pride of place to the multiple meanings of literary texts, including below-the-surface meanings, the different meanings attached to them in different historical periods, and the meanings they may have for different readers. Since virtually every literary text contains or implies moral, psychological, religious, political and philosophical layers of significance as well as evoking an aesthetic response, the number of valid critical approaches is very considerable. You are likely to be introduced to several approaches (though some English departments are much more self-consciously pluralistic than others) and you will have the opportunity to find out others for yourself. The pressure to produce and reproduce convincing or at least plausible interpretations of texts, whether in essays, seminar discussions or in an extended dissertation, is fundamental to the training that English courses set out to provide.

In Joyce's *Dubliners* we learn – among other things – that there are two ways of opening a corked bottle of stout. You can use a corkscrew, or you can warm the bottle on the hob until the glass expands, the pressure inside builds up and the cork flies out. The object is to get at the liquid inside. At an earlier stage in the history of English studies the idea was that the fires of the critic's appreciative prose would gently warm up the bottle. Modern techniques of literary analysis often seem like patent corkscrews useful for opening large numbers of bottles in a hurry. Some literary theorists would deny that poems or novels are given objects like the stout in this imaginary bottle; the readers' task is not so much to empty the bottle as to fill it up with their own interpretations. Yet reading and re-reading can be a lifelong process, and no single reading or act of interpretation is final. An English degree must always be to some extent a crash course which risks leaving the liquid overheated or peppered with pieces of cork.

Which authors and texts will you be expected to study? Shakespeare is no longer invariably compulsory, though most single honours graduates will end up with a fairly wide knowledge of his complete works, together with a selection from the other canonical writers such as Chaucer, Donne, Milton, Pope, Swift, the Romantic poets, the Victorian novelists and the early twentieth-century Modernists. Such works as the *Canterbury Tales*, Spenser's *Faerie Queene*, *Paradise Lost*, Wordsworth's *Prelude* or the major novels of Dickens, George Eliot or Virginia Woolf may be studied in depth. The analysis of short unseen passages (formerly known as 'practical criticism') may be used to teach the skills of attentive reading and to develop versatility of response. In the final year you are likely to be given the opportunity of writing a dissertation or series of extended essays on subjects of your own choice. Occasionally the study of some literature in another language is required, and in fields such as medieval studies and the twentieth century the 'comparative' element, drawing on other European literatures, is sometimes strong.

Apart from the core of compulsory courses, the range of specialist options offered in many departments makes 'From *Beowulf* to Virginia Woolf' sound narrow. Anglo-Saxon, *Piers Plowman* and the Elizabethan sonnet sequences and verse romances continue to attract some of the best students, but the majority opt for the more modern subjects, which are likely to include American and post-colonial literatures, women's literature, 'minority' literatures, contemporary popular fiction, aspects of film and television studies, and some of the strands of literary theory. Broad intellectual movements such as feminism, structuralism and semiotics (ie theories of sign and symbol), hermeneutics (ie theories of interpretation) and post-modernism have had a marked impact on the teaching of many specialist options, though less on the core components of most degree courses. Current linguistic theories are probably less influential, though there is a small but growing number of courses in contemporary English language which fill the gap between the study of the language at GCSE and in the sixth form, and linguistic science as taught at university level.

For the more adventurous, many departments now allow students to take part of their English degree abroad, at a European exchange university. Another very new possibility is a placement with a local firm – for example, a newspaper or publishing house – where you can study the use of written language in commercial and media contexts. Creative writing and literary composition as such are very rarely part of the syllabus, though a number of departments run voluntary writing workshops. The creative atmosphere which a good English department can succeed in nurturing is a precious asset, but an English degree is only one (and not always the best) course of study open to a future novelist or poet. English in the UK is for the most part regarded as an intellectual discipline, less abstract than philosophy, less factual than history, yet closer to these subjects than to the creative and performing arts. Like many of the foregoing generalisations, however, this one is open to challenge, since English remains a vigorous, argumentative and open-ended discipline, with a tradition of engagement in wider cultural issues and a style of sharp, lively and sometimes volatile debate.

English graduates are able to follow the full range of careers open to those with an arts degree with a bias towards journalism, teaching, publishing, marketing and the media.

HELPFUL READING: P D Roberts, *How Poetry Works* (Harmondsworth: Penguin, 1986); F R Leavis, *The Common Pursuit* (London: Hogarth Press, 1984); A Jefferson and D Robey, eds, *Modern Literary Theory: A Comparative Introduction* (London: Batsford, 1986).

Environmental Sciences

Dr Ian F Spellerberg, Southampton University

An exciting, recent development in higher education has been the establishment of courses which cut across the boundaries of the well known and more traditional single disciplines. Environmental sciences is an example of a comparatively new and refreshing interdisciplinary science which is based on various aspects of the traditional science subjects such as biology, geography, chemistry, geology and oceanography. Environmental sciences and environmental studies are concerned with both the natural and built environments but whereas environmental sciences has a sound science component, environmental studies incorporates aspects of social sciences and the arts.

If you study for an environmental sciences degree, you will find that the course is interdisciplinary and not multidisciplinary. In other words, environmental sciences, like environmental studies, is not made up of randomly chosen bits of different subjects which have been 'Sellotaped' together. In all the traditional science subjects there are topics which are of practical relevance to our understanding of the environment and the processes which take place in the environment. Such topics can be brought together in an integrated fashion and so provide the all-important interdisciplinary basis for informed and integrated management. For instance, academically valid studies of water pollution in rivers and estuaries require an interdisciplinary approach, incorporating relevant aspects of environmental biology, physical geography, environmental chemistry and biological aspects of oceanography. Similarly, assessments of the environmental implications of alternative land use strategies require a sound knowledge of carefully selected aspects of geography, geology, environmental biology and elements of some subjects outside the boundaries of the traditional science disciplines such as environmental engineering and environmental law.

Environmental sciences deals with current issues about the natural and the built environment and is thus an attractive option for a wide range of students. But clearly any such interdisciplinary studies and training are not a soft option or an easy way to get a degree. Although the component parts of environmental sciences are generally the same as those taken by students specialising in single subject degree courses, environmental sciences students have to think about the integral links between subjects and have to draw upon resources provided by more than one subject when tackling interdisciplinary assignments. Environmental sciences therefore appeals to the highly motivated and enthusiastic students who are able to face the challenge of integrating aspects of more than one science discipline.

One of the many attractions of environmental sciences is that you may have the opportunity either to specialise in any one of the many areas, while retaining the interdisciplinary background or to retain a more general approach. You might, for example, specialise in waste resource management, economic geology, coastal management, nature conservation, hydrology, public health engineering, urban planning, ecological chemistry, land management, biological and chemical aspects of pollution or the economic aspects of sustainable development. Alternatively, many students choose environmental sciences because they simply want a good grounding in a broad variety of environmental topics. The value of such a grounding is obvious at a time when environmental education is becoming recognised as important and relevant to all walks of life.

Although environmental sciences is comparatively new, it is now a scientific discipline well recognised by industry, by the European Community and by international organisations such as UNESCO. It's not unusual these days to see advertisements by industry, local authorities and conservation agencies seeking an 'environmental scientist'. Further evidence for this recognition can be found in the growing amount of literature; there are now many books and scientific journals with titles incorporating the words 'environment' and 'environmental sciences'.

An interdisciplinary approach to the study of the natural and the built environments has increasing practical relevance because of the growing concern for human activities upon environmental resources and environmental processes. Thus concern about many environmental issues (such as global climate warming, deforestation, spread of desert conditions, disposal of toxic wastes, and losses of biodiversity) has prompted the need for more research and better ways of managing our resources. The increasing awareness of environmental problems is resulting in a greater participation in environmental organisations and in the creation of more environmental legislation, which must be based on sound knowledge of environmental processes. For example, environmental impact assessments (assessing the likely impact of proposed major developments) are comparatively new but have already stimulated the need for more people to be trained to manage interdisciplinary problems. Those engaged in assessing environmental impacts of motorways, electricity generating stations, marinas, or petroleum installations will be required to communicate effectively with biologists, geologists, geographers, or oceanographers and others who can contribute to the understanding of environmental impacts of urban, industrial and other developments.

Environmental sciences as a degree subject has a common core but, depending on where you study, there are different and unique components to the way that it is taught because the bias or structure will, in part, reflect the research interests of the teaching staff. This provides an added bonus of choice but it makes it essential that you find out all you can about the different courses. All course admission tutors offer a friendly information service about teaching, research projects, fieldcourses, entry requirements and the careers of their graduates. Ask them for a reading list and in addition note the books mentioned below.

There is no doubt that there is something special about environmental sciences students. Perhaps it is their enthusiasm, interest and concern in the many and varied environmental issues which always creates such a friendly and co-operative atmosphere when they are brought together as a group. Environmental sciences provides an agreeable and stimulating atmosphere for exercising the mind, enjoying debates and above all learning about a better approach to the management of our natural and built environments. The environmental scientists of the future will be playing an ever important role in bringing about a sustainable way of life and a wiser use of the world's resources.

HELPFUL READING: The World Commission on Environment and Development, *Our Common Future* (Oxford University Press, 1987); I G Simmons, *The Ecology of Natural Resources* (London: Edward Arnold, 1974, 1981); P R Ehrlich, A H Ehrlich and J P Holdren, *Ecoscience: population, resources, environment* (San Francisco: W H Freeman, 1970, 1977, 1983); W P Cunningham and B W Saigo, *Environmental Science* (Wm C Brown Publishers, 1990).

Environmental Studies

Emeritus Professor A D G Smart, University College London

Environmental studies, environmental science, environmentalism. Environment is not a precise term. What do we mean by it? Probably its most frequent use is to describe the habitat of a living species, but even here the context ranges widely – an anthill or a city, a microclimate or a weather system.

Thus the study of environment is potentially a huge subject, involving science, social science and the arts. You'll find aspects of it in many long-standing disciplines, for example in biology. But there are two developing areas – environmental studies and environmental science – in which the relationship between species (including man) and environment is treated more comprehensively, although the very complexity of the systems and the links between them inevitably leads to some specialisation. One division, broad as it is, focuses on the 'man-made environment' (sometimes equated with the built environment or, more appropriately, the urban and rural environment). This tends to be called environmental studies, whereas environmental science is more often concerned with the natural environment.

Why study the man-made environment? It is of the utmost social and political importance, an area of frequent controversy, where decisions have tended in the past to be made without adequate analysis and where mistakes can be costly in human and financial terms. Everybody has views about it and wants to be involved, but the buck has to stop somewhere. Policy-making and design for the man-made environment is a heavy responsibility, a true vocation.

Imagine a city of about one million people. Its population is growing slowly and the activities within it are quickly being dispersed as employment, housing and, to some extent, shopping move out to peripheral sites. The city's nineteenth century core is being depopulated, and there are decreasing numbers of suitable jobs for those whose circumstances force them to remain. Even though the local council long ago gave up building tall blocks of flats and is encouraging modernisation of housing instead, progress is disappointingly slow. The general surroundings in which people live in this core are deteriorating all the time, contrasting sharply with the more wealthy and leafy outer suburbs.

In the city's hinterland, farming is subject to more and more disturbance from people, especially at weekends, and from changes in ownership as landowners put their land up for sale in hopes of more profitable uses. The landscape is becoming shabby and derelict. Small towns and villages within commuting distance are growing quickly, their local communities swamped and their individual character at risk of being lost in a featureless suburbia.

Despite all this dispersal, the city centre thrives during the day-time, drawing in workers to the new office blocks there. But the approach roads are choked twice a day, there is a serious noise problem, pedestrians are at risk, and public transport is sometimes giving up the unequal struggle.

All in all, it is a well known situation. But there are some bright spots. The local authority is providing, against great odds, well designed community schools, playspaces, traffic-free areas and extra greenery, and voluntary groups are helping out with many kinds of community activities. There is new inner city housing, a new district centre and some workshops for small firms, inspired by far-sighted politicians, entrepreneurs and professionals. A polluted canal and the valley through which it runs is being reclaimed as a country park, a village green has been preserved, and a face-lift to an old market place is attracting shoppers back.

Anyone who is involved in helping to shape the future of our cities and countryside needs to understand the forces at work – social, economic and physical – and the issues to which they give rise: whether, for example, to devote scarce money to rebuilding old housing areas to modern standards (with long-term benefits) or to renovating them (with less disturbance to communities, but only short-term economies); whether to improve public transport and deter car commuters, with the risk that the city centre will become less attractive to car users, thus aiding and abetting more dispersal; whether to reduce pollution, possibly making it more costly for industry to operate in the inner core where jobs are so badly needed; whether to spend a lot on preserving historic buildings for which new uses are hard to find; and whether to save agricultural land despite this making housing sites more costly.

The people who help to make these key decisions may be planners, architects or other professionals whose education has been concerned with the planning, design and management of the man-made environment. Their degree courses will have included environmental studies and project work attuned to their special interests – humanities (history, geography, economics, sociology, social administration) and technology (design and construction processes, at the scale of the city or of its individual components). They will have found it an exacting education and if they had entered upon it under the impression that it was about the birds and the bees, they soon had to come to a point of decision.

Thus be sure that you understand the purpose of environmental studies courses. These aim to analyse the factors (social, economic and aesthetic) which make for quality in the man-made environment, and to promote good environmental planning, design and management. Preliminary reading will help you in this. And so will the sections of this book which deal more fully with some of the basic disciplines involved, such as architecture and landscape, town and country planning, geography, other social sciences, land management and building studies. As for course entrance requirements, most places tend to go for good A-level results rather than particular subjects.

HELPFUL READING: J B Cullingworth, *Town & Country Planning in Britain* (Allen & Unwin, 1985); N Fairbrother, *New Lives, New Landscapes* (Architectural Press, 1970); Peter Hall, *Urban and Regional Planning* (Allen & Unwin, 1985); HMSO series on careers in planning, architecture, building, etc; N Pevsner, *Pioneers of Modern Design from William Morris to Walter Gropius* (Harmondsworth: Penguin, 3rd revised ed 1977); *The Construction Team* (Building (Publishers) Ltd, 1983); *Building, a Professional Career* (Careers Consultants Ltd); R A Burgess & G White, *Building Production and Project Design* (Construction Press, 1979); also: S E Rasmussen, *Experiencing Architecture* (1962).

European Studies

Dr Juliet Lodge, Hull University

On the surface, the term 'European studies' seems self-explanatory. In reality, it covers a vast range of options. European studies exposes you to the many facets of life that have gone into producing the Europe of today and involves a broad examination of Europe's history, geography, culture, economics, philosophies, literature, politics and society.

European studies normally involves gaining fluency in at least one and usually two European languages besides your mother tongue. French, German and Spanish are the most popular but it is also possible to study Italian, Dutch, Russian etc. Language courses that form part of European studies degrees are increasingly practical in their orientation. Modern languages rather than linguistics or the literature of the 17th century are stressed, although you would also gain an appreciation of the literature of the country(ies) whose language(s) you were acquiring.

European society in all its ramifications tends to be studied both at a general level and in greater detail with reference to key European states. Western Europe, broadly conceived, and often Russia tends to be studied in greater detail than Eastern Europe.

Comparative politics and political economy or economic history rather than econometrics often form components of European studies degrees. The states most often studied include: Germany, France, Russia, the UK and possibly Italy, Spain and Sweden. You would normally learn about American and international politics as well.

You could not do a European studies degree without learning about the history, politics and economic origins of the European Community, and the origins, development and changing nature of East-West relations.

European studies degrees also normally involve a study of political philosophy from Plato, Machiavelli and Hobbes to Locke, Marx and Marcuse, for example. Major contemporary political trends – liberalism, socialism, communism, totalitarianism, fascism, feminism, etc – may also be studied from a variety of perspectives: literary, philosophical, historical, economic or political, for example.

It is now possible to take degree courses in subjects like chemistry or maths, for instance, that have a European studies component in them. You can also combine European studies with languages, or with law, history, art history, environmental studies, business studies, management, sociology, economics or politics.

Most European studies degrees offer you the chance to study relevant European elements from a number of different disciplines. You are likely to get a basic grounding in the history, politics and economic history of Europe whatever European studies course you follow.

Normally, you also spend a period of time in Europe either at a European university or working. Some courses sandwich two periods abroad into a four-year programme. During this time, you would be expected to write a dissertation of around 8,000 words (in English or one of your other European languages) on a topic relevant to your studies. Reasonable language proficiency is needed if you are to make the most of this. All European studies courses help you with your language before you go. On your return, you should be fluent in the language in which you have worked or studied.

Some of the most exciting courses in European studies are now offered by departments in the field of social science. These very often have a vocational component to them and they let you get right to the heart of European affairs.

If you are keen on politics, lobbying, trade, international affairs and business, for example, you can now take courses which build in a 'stage' at the European Parliament, for example. (A stage is the European term commonly used to refer to a period of unpaid internship.) This means that while continuing your studies in Brussels, you may also have working links with Members of the European Parliament. You get to see how Europe ticks. Periods working in Europe or as 'stages' or in partner European universities and polytechnics are highly illuminating, socially and personally rewarding. In addition, they are fun. As you become an active part of the trans-European student community, your circle of friends will grow, your intellectual horizons will alter and your experiences will challenge your preconceptions daily!

Among some of the best European studies courses are those which enable you to spend up to one year studying and gaining additional qualifications from partner universities in different parts of Europe. These courses normally last for four years. It is possible to graduate not only with a British but also with a European qualification.

If you want such a course, make sure that you look beyond language departments. The social sciences and law, and increasingly English and science departments, provide rich hunting grounds. If your main interest is language you would do well to choose a course that has a high European studies component and one which does not restrict you to the study of European literature. Many departments now offer the chance to study commercial language alongside literature, culture and politics.

In short, European studies courses offer you numerous options and they often benefit from excellent schemes such as Erasmus, Tempus and Lingua initiated by the Commission of the European Community. Erasmus is designed to promote student mobility. Many European studies courses from a wide variety of disciplines are linked to European universities through Erasmus networks. This is a sort of twinning arrangement which makes it possible for students to do parts of their degrees in a number of European states. Tempus, modelled on Erasmus, is being introduced to expand mobility and exchanges to Eastern Europe.

If you choose to do a course in European studies, you will be immersed in a dynamic and rapidly changing field. Your outlook is almost bound to change. You are likely to come into contact with students from all across Europe. You will have the chance of studying alongside them both at home and on the European continent. Your intellectual, social and employment horizons will expand considerably as a result.

In short, European studies is predominantly about understanding the

1990s. How and why Europe is shaped as it is. What its role and place in the world is. Where it is going. What problems it confronts. How it resolves them whether they are economic, political, environmental, social, cultural, scientific, commercial or technical. Europe encroaches on all aspects of our lives and all aspects of education.

Studying Europe and the dynamic changes within the European Community which may lead to a federal United States of Europe is enlightening, exhilarating and invigorating. The 1990s are set to be a new European Age. How better to understand and shape it than to study it first?

HELPFUL READING: J Lodge (ed), *The European Community and the Challenge of the Future*, (Pinter, London, 1991); Brian Morris, Klaus Boehm, Maurice Geller, *The European Community* 3rd edition, (Macmillan Press, London, 1991).

Fine Arts

Dr Alex Potts, East Anglia University

This area of study is often called art history, and with some justification. The visual arts – painting, sculpture and architecture – are usually studied from an historical point of view although critical analysis still plays a very important role. Even to be placed in an historical context, a work of art must be interpreted and this requires visual sensitivity – much as the reading of poetry requires a feeling for language. Of course no history can dispense with interpretation, no history is merely an objective recording of facts. Studying the history of art makes one all the more aware of this precisely because visual images can be so ambiguous, so difficult to interpret.

The history of art can be approached in a number of different ways and often one's approach varies with different periods and different art forms. Central to most discussions of the visual arts, however, are the notions of style and stylistic development (see Meyer Shapiro, 'Style' in A L Kroeber, ed, *Anthropology Today* – Chicago University Press, 1965; and in M Philipson, ed, *Aesthetics Today* – New York: World Publishing, 1961). We are all struck by the way visual forms change with time, one instance being changing fashions in clothes. The coherence of such changes is what enables the art historian to date a work of art on the basis of visual evidence, by classifying it with known objects in a similar style. Much more is involved, however, than placing works of art in chronological order. One wants to know, for example, why styles take on the particular aspect they do, how and why they change. This may be explored by focusing mainly on visual forms and defining their character and evolution, as in Heinrich Wolfflin's *Principles of Art History* (New York: Dover, 1950). Such preoccupation with style is a characteristic feature of art history.

No work of art, however, can be properly understood without reference to the ideas it expresses. These in turn must be illuminated by the social and cultural values of the society that produced the work of art. Some historians would go so far as to say that the visual arts should be conceived as the reflection of more general, social and cultural factors. But even though art history and social and cultural history are of necessity connected, links between the two that go beyond vague references to the spirit of the age can be hard to define. Jakob Burckhardt's celebrated *The Civilization of the Renaissance in Italy* (S G C Middlemore, trans, London: Phaidon, 1960), for example, though a basic text for anyone interested in Renaissance art and written by an authority on the subject, never actually specifies how the visual arts relate to the cultural values which he elicits from the writings and social and political history of the time. Recent attempts to link art and culture have often focused on subject matter, giving rise to a branch of art history variously called iconography and iconology (see Erwin Panofsky's *Studies in Iconology* – New York: Harper & Row, 1962). The religious beliefs embodied in an altar piece, for example, can be studied by looking at the subject depicted and the particular religious symbols used.

The interpretation of symbols and allegories, or iconographical analysis, is often as fruitful an approach to understanding a work of art as stylistic analysis. Content, however, can never be separated from style, for an idea is always modified by the way it is represented in a particular medium. Only by joint consideration of both styles and subject matter can one avoid a simplistic view of art as either pure form or mere illustration of cultural and social history (see Timothy J Clark's *Image of the People* – London: Thames & Hudson, 1973). Take a portrait, for example. Our understanding of it is undoubtedly aided if we know something about the particular person whom it represents. Some aspects, however, could be misunderstood if one interprets the portrait as a straightforward likeness. A certain rigidity, say, may owe more to the artistic conventions of the period than to the person's actual appearance.

Studying art and its history, you can see, will entail far more than learning how to identify and date works of art. This specialisation, connoisseurship as it is often known, can in any case perhaps best be learned by inspecting and classifying actual objects in museums or galleries. Studies in fine arts will involve you in trying to understand the varying character and significance of visual images from different historical periods. In most colleges you will be obliged to focus on a few select periods of Western European art, such as the Renaissance and the nineteenth century. A small number of institutions, however, do offer facilities enabling you to choose courses anywhere within the period from Greek times to the present day. One or two places also offer courses in non-Western art. As your studies proceed, you will find your awareness of different styles and their meanings becoming more precise, but this process will never be cut and dried. No amount of historical fact, for example, will teach you to distinguish between good and bad art. The attraction of the subject lies on the contrary in trying to come to terms with images whose significance has never been satisfactorily explained and which always demand new interpretations.

As entrance requirements, most courses ask for at least one foreign language to GCSE standard or equivalent, but few places specify particular A-level subjects. An A-level in history, English or a modern language can be as good a preparation for a fine arts course as one in art or art history.

HELPFUL READING: E H Gombrich, *Art and Illusion* (London: Phaidon, 1960).

Food Science and Nutrition

Professor R A Lawrie, Nottingham University

Prominent among the few unchanging aspects of the Earth is our need for food. It is essential for life. What is new is the relatively recent vast increase in the number of people who depend on sustenance for which the time and phase of consumption are substantially different. In our industrialized world there are few people nowadays who personally produce the food which they themselves require. Most depend on farmers and food factories. This circumstance, in turn, has created a much increased need to preserve the quality and safety of food from the time it is produced until the time it is eaten. It has thus become necessary to develop scientific understanding of food commodities so that control of their production and distribution can be effected with minimum wastage instead of being subject to the uncertainties which are unavoidable with traditional procedures based on empirical observation.

In the United Kingdom the systematized study of food has grown into a discipline in its own right since the end of the Second World War. A course in food science was established in the Royal Technical College, Glasgow, in 1949; and, as the University of Strathclyde, that body offered the first degree course in 1959. Since then about a dozen other degree courses in food science and technology have been established, a fact which clearly reflects the increasing opportunities for men and women trained in the subject.

It should be mentioned that the term 'food science' is sometimes used to refer to the extension of knowledge in the field and the term 'food technology' to the application of that knowledge; but, in practice, both terms are largely interchangeable.

Because the eating quality and nutritive value of food commodities are determined by a long sequence of events from conception in the animal or germination in the seed, through the phases of growth and maturity, harvesting, preservation and preparation to consumption and human nutrition, the field covered by food science and nutrition is exceedingly wide. A great variety of careers is available. These are satisfying in that they cater for most aptitudes and interests and in that they are evidently most important for the well-being and survival of mankind.

Careers in food science and nutrition can be successfully pursued in many contexts. Apart from the more obvious openings in the food industry itself, there are many opportunities in related spheres, such as the manufacture of food ingredients, food packaging and food plant. The aptitudes and interests of some men and women may be more appropriately displayed in the control of food products by legislation, analysis and public health. Posts are available in research institutes supported by government or trade associations, in educational establishments (technical colleges, polytechnics and universities), and in industry. Others, especially after their experience and expertise have developed, find fulfilling and remunerative roles as consultants. For those with a flair for writing and communication there are openings in presenting the science of nutrition and food to the public in journalism, publishing and advertising. Many young people wish to travel in the early years after qualification. For these, there are numerous opportunities in industrial firms overseas, and in research and teaching in developing countries.

Within all these broad areas the type of work available is also varied, eg product and process development, research, food control, management work study, scientific catering, teaching.

Not infrequently such posts require a knowledge of nutrition; but for those interested in dietetics as such (hospital almonry, nutritional catering, diet control), a diploma in dietetics is necessary; and courses for this are available.

A useful list of courses, at various levels up to degree, is published by the Institute of Food Science and Technology, 5 Cambridge Court, 210 Shepherds Bush Road, London W6 7NJ. The Institute is the incorporated professional body representing food science and technology in the United Kingdom. Membership is available in various grades, according to qualifications, experience and expertise. It confers recognition of status within the profession without academic qualifications.

HELPFUL READING: G C Birch, M Spencer and A G Cameron, *Food Science*.

Geography

Professor M D I Chisholm, Cambridge University

There was a time when geography was regarded as an easy option, skimming the surface of many interesting topics but never getting to grips with anything. Much has changed in the last twenty five years. Public debate about education often emphasises the disadvantages of specialisation, and in many universities interdisciplinary and multidisciplinary courses of study have been established in an attempt to meet this situation. The breadth of geographical study, bringing together topics concerning the physical environment (eg geology, soils, hydrology and climate) and socio-economic matters (eg patterns of economic development, urbanisation and industrial location), is now regarded as a strength rather than a weakness. This is particularly true given the growing importance of problems concerned with ecological management and the planning of cities and regions. Although maintaining a wide range of interests, geography also has developed some hard skills which have widespread application. Most departments teach basic statistics and introduce students to the use of computers; for these studies all that is required is a logical mind and an ability to think in numerical terms, something which many students with an arts background do readily enough. There is also growing emphasis on field observation and the use of basic laboratory techniques to analyse aspects of the natural environment (eg soil conditions and surface run-off).

Although there is a good deal of variation in detail, most university courses require the student to study across the whole field of the subject in his first year. Thereafter a choice of courses may be made, and attention can be increasingly focused on selected topics in either human geography or physical geography, or both. This offers a route to specialised studies in the third year for those who wish it. These specialised studies vary in character from one department to another, ranging from the study of particular regions/nations, through advanced statistical methods, microclimatology, hydrology, the processes of change in urban areas, and regional planning/development in selected countries. By careful selection of topics, students can also maintain a broad spread of interests, something that may be specially important for those who are undecided as to what they wish to do on completing their studies. Most departments emphasise global environmental concerns, and provide a good grounding in statistical methods, computing, and the rapidly developing field of GIS (geographical information systems) and remote sensing.

Over a three-year programme, students have the opportunity to study developed and developing regions, and to examine the phenomena of the physical environment in several climatic regions. Such studies in both human and physical geography are undertaken with staff who are personally familiar with the areas in question. In addition to study of the actual world and of the nature of geographical variation, another essential for the student is learning to conceptualise the world in abstract terms. The importance of distance as a basic organising principle for all economic and social interaction (eg freight traffic, telephone calls) and for the choice of optimum locations (eg for hospitals and factories) quickly becomes apparent; these are all fields where geography is applied to the solution of real problems. Other live and intriguing areas of study are how people perceive the environment and respond to their perception, modelling hillslope development, the water budget of river basins, climatology (though meteorology – concerned with weather and weather forecasting – is sometimes taught as a separate subject outside geography) and the analysis of soils, which provides an important background both to topographical evolution and agricultural development.

The overwhelming majority of students have an A-level in geography. In some universities there are faculty requirements limiting the possible range, but otherwise almost any combination of supporting A-levels is acceptable. The common ones on the science side are geology, physics, chemistry, biology and mathematics; on the arts side history, economics, English and languages figure prominently. After graduating, a remarkably wide range of jobs is open to geographers. While many still enter the teaching profession, having taken a one-year Certificate in Education, many others become planners (for which further training is also necessary), join the civil service or such organisations as the Soil Survey and River Boards, enter industry or commerce in a wide range of capacities. The job prospects for geographers are good over a wide and increasing range of employments.

HELPFUL READING: R Abler, J S Adams and P Gould, *Spatial Organisation* (Englewood Cliffs, New Jersey: Prentice-Hall, 1971); R J Chorley, ed, *Water, Earth and Man* (London: Methuen, 1979); P Haggett, *Geography: a modern synthesis* (New York, Evanston, San Francisco and London: Harper & Row, 1979).

Geology

Professor T R Owen, Swansea, University of Wales

Geology is the study of the Earth. It has to do with rocks, minerals and fossils, and with the interior of the Earth as well as its surface layers. It unravels the fascinating history of our planet, which goes back over 4,500 million years, and one can study rocks in West Greenland and Canada that are almost that old. The story is one of changing climates, changing patterns of land and sea, evolving life.

Any subject that goes into depth about all the above must be fascinating, but today geology is a lot more than that. It is adjusting after a major revolution following the revelation in 1967 of the concept of plate tectonics. This revolution can be compared with the impact of Darwin's theory of evolution in biology and with Einstein's theory of relativity in physics. I consider myself lucky to have lived at this time. In the words of Professor S Toulmin: 'In the world of science . . . the second half of the twentieth century is proving to be a period of perpetual revolution and scientists are learning to live with the fact.'

I came to college in the 1930s intending to study geography but had to take geology as my main subject because at that time there was no honours school in geography in my college. I say this because I want to assure anyone that you can take a degree in geology starting from scratch. It's a marvellous subject because it pulls together lots of other subjects – biology, geography, physics, chemistry, mathematics, etc. It helps a lot if you have studied some of these subjects at A-level, particularly if you want to become a professional geologist. But even without these background subjects you can really enjoy geology at college because geology is a cultural subject, a marvellous thinking exercise. It is both a 'doing' and a 'thinking' subject. A student of geology is a Sherlock Holmes. There are fascinating clues to be observed and problems to be solved.

Geology is also an outdoor subject. One studies rocks not only in the laboratory and the lecture room but also in the field. My student geological excursions are some of my most pleasant memories – the great thrill of finding my first fossils, of reaching the top of Snowdon, of making my first geological map in Spain or France, making marvellous friendships.

What about this geological revolution? It really all started at the beginning of the century when Alfred Wegener put forward his theory of continental drift. There followed a great debate but in general the theory was abandoned, mainly because there seemed to be no adequate mechanism for shifting continents. Then came a revival of interest with rapid exploration of ocean floors, the marvellous discovery of fossil magnetism in rocks and the theory of sea-floor spreading. The names of Blackett, Runcorn, Dietz, Hess, Matthews and Vine figure prominently in this exciting story. The revolution was proclaimed when the whole story was unfolded at the Goddard Symposium in 1967. We know now that the Earth's outer shell – the lithosphere – is broken into some seven major slabs or 'plates' (plus many more micro-plates) which are continually moving relative to one another. New oceanic crust is made when plates move away from one another. The Atlantic is widening whereas the Pacific is closing. When plates move towards one another, the denser plate – particularly when formed of oceanic crust – descends beneath the lighter plate, a process known as subduction. The descending plate melts and molten magma ascends to form lines of volcanoes. Deep-seated earthquakes are also a feature of subduction zones. The western zone of South America is a classic example. There are also areas of the world where plates are slipping sideways against one another. The San Andreas fault zone of California is an example as the recent tragic earthquake has shown.

We now have a coherent picture of geological processes. What were previously isolated geological items – volcanoes, earthquakes, mountain chains, sedimentary troughs, great fractures – can now be welded into a compact whole. Moreover, we can now truly follow the important geological principle, 'The present is the key to the past'. What is happening today helps us to unravel past geological history. The application of plate tectonics helps us to understand the British scene 500 million years ago. We now know that an ocean (long since closed completely) once separated Scotland from England and Wales. (Scottish devolution could have happened as early as 800 million years ago.)

The great advances in sea-floor studies around the British Isles are part of the new excitement in geology. Application of an exciting branch of geology called geophysics has given us a kind of X-ray picture of the deep structures beneath the North, Irish and Celtic Seas. New finds of oil and gas have resulted, finds of great importance to the UK economy. Moreover, all this new geological information has now to be incorporated into our revised reconstructions of British (and European) geological history. It may well be that the Atlantic Ocean once tried its best to begin where is now the North Sea.

I have not said anything about geology courses. There are various kinds in colleges, polytechnics and universities, and all sorts of combinations of subjects are permitted. One can combine geology with oceanography, geography, biological sciences, physics, chemistry, civil engineering, energy studies, etc. Or one can take geology in combination with arts subjects, if one chooses. Look at the prospectuses to find out what is possible. Field courses are a marvellous part of all geology courses. You'll enjoy them immensely.

Yes, geology has a new excitement – for everybody. Take geology as a first degree, either to be a geologist or, if you wish, just to get to know something about a truly fascinating Earth and the way it works. Mankind will one day derive tremendous benefits from these early days of the revolution. Why not join it now?

HELPFUL READING: Peter J Wyllie, *The Way the Earth Works* (New York: Wiley & Sons, 1976).

History

Dr Maurice Keen, Balliol College, Oxford University

St Thomas Aquinas defined man as 'a social and political animal' and history is the study of man's record as just that – and a little bit more too. A question that is often asked in history general papers is 'What is the difference between prehistory and history?' One answer is that pre-historians and archaeologists study tangible things that people of the remote past have left behind in the way of artefacts and the remains of buildings; in doing so they study man as a social animal, and very often, from their evidence, they also uncover something of the political structure of a past society. However, a new dimension of study – history – opens at the moment when the person studying the past can establish contact with statements that come direct from an articulate individual who lived in a past period and who can tell us of his or her internal reactions to the contemporary external environment. History is not just about man's experience as a species, but also about the experience of individuals with inner feelings and opinions and ambitions which are still communicable, even across major barriers of time.

Your first duty as a historian, therefore, will be to learn to listen. Moreover, you must learn to listen critically since you will hear a great many people talking, and people in the past were just as divided as they are now by differences of status, situation and attitude. Like people today, they were often the victims of their own prejudices, and they were equally prone to handling the truth carelessly. This is, of course, as true of historians themselves as it is of the people who made history, which is why in the study of history there is no substitute for the original sources.

Naturally it is important to read what other historians have said about their special fields, but history books are not to be mistaken for infallible guides to the final truth. They are valuable rather as interpreters, to put you in touch with the past and so into a position where you can form your own judgment about it. The final test of a history book is whether what the author says rings true when his words are set alongside those of the people about whom he is writing.

Because of the need to listen carefully, languages will be important to you as a historian. This is obviously true in the superficial sense: anyone who wants to specialise in French or Spanish history, for example, must be able to catch the special nuances of people's words. But a historian must also learn to speak the 'language of the past'. The different environments of past ages and the differences in the range of possibilities in social, economic and technological terms caused people to value different priorities and to talk and think about their situation in ways that are different from those natural to us. The historian must be able to grasp these differences imaginatively in order to understand what the people that he studies are saying.

This, I believe, is what above all makes history an educational subject in the best sense of the term. Many problems in any age – perhaps most of them – arise from men's inability to appreciate and to make allowance for differences of opinion and attitude that stem from differences in upbringing, in physical and economic environment, in cultural background and in individual reactions. The study of history cannot, of course, solve the problems that arise thus but it can and should teach us to approach them in an intelligent way. For the same reason the study of ancient history can be as relevant and educational as the study of the recent past: seeking to understand the ways of those remote in time is a useful introduction to understanding modern people who are divided from us by barriers of distance and culture. The process is, of course, a two-way one: what anthropologists can tell us about primitive societies of our own time may illuminate, for example, the thought-world of the early Anglo-Saxons.

Listening and looking imaginatively with a critical ear and eye, therefore, are the keys to understanding **how** things happened in the past. Just how different that is from understanding **why** things happened remains an endlessly debatable topic. In the end you will have to form your own judgment about it. Does history have an inner logic of its own? To what extent do such impersonal factors as physical environment, technological development and economic relations allow individual endeavour and action to have a decisive impact? In this century, a powerful school of historians, influenced by Marx, has believed and taught that we can perceive a coherence in history, based in the dynamic working out of impersonal factors, and that in the understanding of this lies the key to the improvement of the human condition. Other historians, as I myself, do not believe that history shows as efficient a measure of coherence as this, and claim simply that its study is a humanising exercise which helps us to understand more about both others and ourselves. These are only two lines of approach, around which a lot of debate focuses at present: there is of course an infinity of alternative approaches. History is a very broad and important subject (nothing that is human is irrelevant to it) and it is bound to raise controversy. It is also an exciting subject because it brings continual contact with people of the past.

History is a subject that requires a lot of patient work, and there are a number of ancillary skills which are very helpful. In terms of A-levels, you will obviously be wise to offer history and, if at all possible, a modern language (or Latin). For some degree courses you may need GCSE in a language as a course requirement for history. Mathematics or economics can be very useful: historians nowadays are much more statistically minded than they once used to be. Geography is another subject that can directly cross-fertilise with history. An A-level in classical studies or classical civilisation (offered by some GCSE boards) can be helpful, especially if the degree course covers ancient history.

The syllabuses of history courses vary a great deal, and so do regulations about the subjects that may be studied in combination with history. Some (eg York University) encourage students to spend a part of their time working on a long essay or mini-thesis, which can count towards the degree; some (eg Oxford University) lay emphasis on the study of British history as an essential part of the course; some (eg Durham University) offer a course in economic history as a degree course in its own right. Individual prospectuses will give you the relevant information and it is worth looking at them carefully.

HELPFUL READING: I Berlin, *The Hedgehog and the Fox* Ch.1 (London: Weidenfeld & Nicolson, 1953); E H Carr, *What is History?* (London: Macmillan, 1961); R G Collingwood, *The Idea of History* (Oxford University Press, 1946); J Le Goff and P Nora (eds.) *Constructing the Past* (Cambridge University Press, 1985).

Hotel and Catering Management

Professor J O'Connor, Oxford Brookes University

The provision of hospitality to the traveller has always been an important service and the origins of inn-keeping and tavern-keeping may be traced at least as far back as Ancient Rome. The profession of hotel and catering management as practised today is, however, vastly more diverse and complex than that pursued by the inn-keepers of Rome or the entrepreneurs who built the Savoy and the Ritz in London a century ago. Hospitality management, a term used to include hotel, catering and institutional management, is now truly international: our customers come from all over the world, many British companies have international interests and many young managers find it valuable to work abroad in the development of their careers. Whether pursued for profit or to provide a service, as in institutional management, hospitality is a business concerned with meeting the needs of consumers, with employing people with diverse skills and with investment, often heavy, in buildings, plant and other resources. The task of the modern hospitality manager is to make the best use of the investment of his employer and of his staff's skills in satisfying the needs of his consumers. This is more difficult today than it was at the turn of the last century and it will be more difficult still at the turn of this century when consumers will anticipate better value than ever before while being more discriminating and having a wider choice of services.

Education and training for hospitality management are constantly evolving. In the last twenty years some 40 courses have emerged in the UK. The structure and content of these courses varies significantly amongst the institutions. Most, but not all, are four-year sandwich courses; those which are not require students to gain industrial experience in their long vacations. A minority of courses specialise in preparation for one sector of the industry, eg institutional management or catering, but most are broadly based and aim at giving students the opportunity to become familiar with the industry in general before deciding upon a particular career pathway. The common core of all these courses is the study of the provision of food, drink and accommodation outside the home. These studies are technical and often scientific, involving laboratory work in training restaurants as well as the use of computers and scientific equipment. A second prime component will be business studies covering economics, accountancy and law. The third, and perhaps most important, cluster of studies will be those concerned with human behaviour, covering psychology, consumer studies and the management of people. Some institutions offer options in European languages. The range of subjects to be covered is therefore much wider than in the conventional honours degree and there is the additional demand upon students that they must integrate these studies into the vocational framework. To embark upon a course of this type and to complete it successfully requires motivation and flexibility in the student, but, since such attributes are essential for the hospitality manager, for those who possess them, the course and the subsequent career can be extremely rewarding. Most applicants to courses will prefer to test their suitability for the industry by seeking some work experience in the school holidays or at weekends. It is certainly not wise to enrol on a course of this nature unless you are quite clear that hospitality management is the career for you, with all that this implies in terms of unsocial and often long hours of work. It is a career which requires almost constant contact with people, whether customers or employees; you should, therefore, feel confident that you will enjoy working with and leading groups of people before embarking on this particular career pathway.

Entrance requirements for courses in this field do not usually demand specific A-level subjects, but applicants should enquire directly for details. Most courses are heavily over-subscribed so it is best to apply early, preferably by mid-December of the year preceding entry. Most admissions tutors like to interview candidates.

What will it be like after graduation? One thing is certain: your training will not be finished, thus you will probably decide to join a company with a graduate training scheme, usually of one or two years' duration, to widen your experience and develop managerial skills. Even if you are a born entrepreneur it is unwise to buy your own restaurant or hotel immediately. But I know many graduates who run their own businesses.

You may decide to work for an international hotel company, join the forces as a catering officer, enter hospital catering or go into the catering division of a large industrial company where you might be involved in anything from head office restaurants to supplying an oil rig. Pubs, clubs and students' residences all require trained management, as do hamburger chains or luxury hotels. Whatever you decide upon, don't expect every weekend off – you are likely to be most busy when everyone else seems to be on holiday!

HELPFUL READING: R Hayter, *Careers and Training in Hotels, Catering and Tourism* (Oxford, Butterworth-Heinemann and HCTC, 1992). *The Caterer and Hotelkeeper* publishes a career supplement each year, which is obtainable from booksellers or the publishers. The Hotel and Catering Training Company publishes *The College List* (HCTC, 1992). Videos, giving a general introduction to careers in the industry may be borrowed from your local Careers Office or from the HCTC. The Hotel, Catering and Institutional Management Association provides guidance on courses and publishes a reference book annually, obtainable from: HCIMA, 191 Trinity Road, London SW17.

Industrial Relations

Professor K F Sisson, Warwick University

Industrial relations is a relatively new subject. Only one or two offer degrees or joint degrees in the subject at undergraduate level, although the number of postgraduate courses is greater. More commonly industrial relations is offered as an option in its own right or key elements will be included in courses bearing such labels as industrial sociology, labour economics, organisational behaviour, and personnel management. The rapid growth in the number of such options and courses reflects the fact that industrial relations has become a subject of major economic, political and social importance.

So what is industrial relations? Essentially, it has to do with work or employment relationships, the organisations and groups which take part in the management or control of these relationships, and the processes which are involved. The typical syllabus is likely to include the study of the management strategies and policies; the structure and control of work organisations; trade unions (their membership, structure and organisation – both inside and outside the workplace); the structure and processes of bargaining and consultation; and the role of government. The latter, in particular, has been assumed as growing in importance in recent years. The government is not only the employer (or, at least, paymaster) of some 6.5 million people in the public services and nationalised industries, it also sets the legal framework and the economic context of industrial relations. For a more detailed list of the subjects covered, consult G S Bain, *Industrial Relations in Britain: Past Trends and Future Developments* (Oxford: Blackwell, 1983) or K Sisson, *Personnel Management in Britain* (Oxford: Blackwell, 1989) which are likely to be the standard texts for many courses.

The subject is anything but uncontroversial. Industrial relations touches on some of the most sensitive issues of the day – ways in which people are managed, the functions and power of trade unions, the role of the law, the contribution of collective bargaining in inflation, the prospects for industrial democracy, to name but a few. Clearly the outcome of such issues will have a significant effect on the balance of power between groups in society. Moreover, although many, but not all, who teach industrial relations might agree in broad terms with my definition of the subject, their method of approach to it is likely to be very different because they will inevitably hold different values about the issues involved.

Differences of approach are also likely according to the type of department which is offering the course or option in industrial relations. The increase in the number of universities offering the subject has, in many cases, been associated with the rapid growth in the number of first degree courses in business studies and management sciences. When industrial relations forms part of these courses there is a danger of teaching moving too quickly from description to prescription. That is to say, the institutions are described, industrial relations 'problems' identified – largely from a management perspective – and a range of possible solutions discussed. But the student is given insufficient time to study the processes at work and so develop an adequate framework within which to explain and interpret developments.

On the other hand, the teaching of industrial relations is also provided by more established academic departments like economics and sociology. Here there is likely to be greater emphasis on analysis and explanation but essentially from the point of view of the parent discipline. In this case the danger is that issues will be interpreted **only** in the light of the theories and explanatory frameworks of that discipline. For example, the economist might be tempted to treat trade unions as a special case of monopoly, while the sociologist might see them as essentially class organisations. Clearly both these approaches have something to offer, but exclusive preoccupation with one or the other is likely to give rise to limited understanding of the significance of trade unions. To concentrate on their economic aspects is to ignore the rights which trade unions have won to represent their members on a wide range of issues. Collective bargaining is not just concerned with pay or with hours of work; it often concerns such matters as discipline, dismissal, promotion, training and the organisation of work. Thus it is as much a political as an economic process. By the same token, if we see trade unions as essentially class organisations we are likely to overlook a large number of important organisations representing white collar and professional workers.

To sum up, industrial relations is not a discipline in the sense that many other subjects claim to be. Rather it is an area of study – and a very important area. It is by its very nature interdisciplinary and multidisciplinary, bringing insights from many of the social sciences together in an integrated fashion. It also requires a historical perspective. For these reasons it helps, but is not essential, to have done an A-level in one of the social studies. Those who teach industrial relations cannot and should not pretend that its study will provide easy answers. It does, however, provide an opportunity to gain much greater understanding of significant issues of today. For students who are prepared to think for themselves it can be immensely rewarding.

Information Technology

Professor R S Burgess, Northumbria University, Newcastle

Information Technology (IT) is a term introduced in the early 1980s to describe the coming together of other previously separate technologies and disciplines, namely computing, telecommunications and systems. Few people in the industrialised world have not had some contact with IT. IT is affecting us all, in the home, at work and in our social activities. Commerce, industry and government are becoming increasingly dependent on its application to function more effectively and efficiently. In the home we can access information via our television sets using teletext and programme some of our home appliances to be semi-automatic. Many of us are lucky enough to have a personal microcomputer to help us in our work or play. Our letter boxes regularly deliver us unwelcome bills produced by IT. Those privileged to have money in a bank can obtain cash at any time of the day through dispensers which are a part of the bank's IT system. IT helps us travel: road, air and rail traffic are controlled by computers as are airline reservation systems. Space travel would of course be impossible without computers and sophisticated telecommunications. IT provides us with some of our leisure activities through games machines. Many of our newspapers are produced using IT. Scientists were of course the first major users of computers back in the late 1940s and they would be unable to do much of their present day research without large computers. IT is having a major impact within the office in the form of word processing and electronic mail. Large businesses and government organisations have been using computers for nearly a quarter of a century for processing their financial and other data and this type of use has spread quickly to the smaller businesses. Perhaps the biggest impact of IT in the short-term future will be on manufacturing industry where the use of computer-aided design, real-time systems, computer-controlled machine tools and robots is expected to mushroom.

It is the fastest growing industry worldwide and this growth has occurred over the last 50 years. Indeed the growth has been exponential and there are no signs of it slowing down. Perhaps the two most significant advances responsible for this growth were the invention of the microchip (which dramatically reduced the cost of computing power), and the developments in telecommunications – in particular laser technology, which enables people to communicate with computers, and computers to communicate with each other over long distances. It is these two developments in particular that have brought IT into the home and onto the High Street and made IT all-pervasive. It is difficult to predict where IT is going and what will be the ultimate consequences for society. In the short term, three of the most significant and exciting developments will be in intelligent systems and voice and image recognition systems where machines and robots will be programmed to act and communicate more like humans.

However IT is not just about the technology of computers and telecommunications. To exploit this technology to the benefit of a particular application requires quantum leaps of human creative thought and effort so that the wood of an application can be seen for the trees of the technology. So not only is there a need for skilled manpower to create the technology but there is also a more significant requirement for skilled IT application specialists so IT may be successfully exploited. There is an acute shortage of well educated and skilled IT manpower in the UK and worldwide and all recent reputable reports suggest that the situation is getting worse rather than better. Therefore there will be good career prospects and rewards for IT graduates, both women and men, for the foreseeable future.

The majority of universities offer courses in IT at undergraduate level. Many of these courses will be offered by the computing departments but some may be offered by engineering or business studies departments. Such courses are offered under a variety of titles including computer engineering, computer science, computer studies, computing, business computing, industrial computing, information systems, information technology, software engineering and systems analysis. In some cases the title of the course will reflect the nature and emphasis of the course, but not always. All the courses will involve a study of the fundamental IT topics of telecommunications, computer systems hardware and software, programming and systems analysis and design. However some may have a greater emphasis on hardware and electronics (eg computer engineering and information technology courses), some on software and programming (eg software engineering, computer science and computing courses), some on systems analysis and design and business applications (eg business computing, information systems and systems analysis) and some on software and industrial applications (eg industrial computing). Courses may contain other supporting topics, such as mathematics, statistics, electronics, business applications, industrial applications or human behaviour and communications. There are also business studies courses with a major component of IT, aimed at producing graduates with the IT skills needed in modern business (often called business information technology). Before applying for a course, look closely at the course description to ensure the nature and emphasis of the course matches your likes and aspirations.

IT is a vocational subject and hence very practically-based. Many courses, particularly those in the new universities, are 4-year sandwich courses, the third year being spent in industry practising and enhancing the skills already learnt. A large proportion of your time will be spent in practical assignments such as: programming a microprocessor in assembler language; programming a robot; building an electronic circuit; interfacing a device to a microcomputer; programming a computer using a third or fourth generation programming language; interviewing staff who are role-playing users in order to determine the requirements of a proposed computer-based application system; specifying and designing a new computer-based application system using software aids. The practical nature of the course will usually culminate with a major individual project in the final year of the course.

Students who have successfully studied computing are at an advantage both in terms of obtaining a place and in their first year studies although it is not normally a prerequisite for entry. Many courses do not specify named subjects in their A-level requirements for entry, although a few specify mathematics. At present both the IT industry and undergraduate courses are very male dominated. There are many reasons why this is so but none of them are to do with IT being only suitable for men. None of the IT skills require male-only qualities. So come on you girls, IT can be for you as well as us men!

HELPFUL READING: Jacquetta Megarry, *Inside Information* (BBC, 1985); *About Information Technology* (Hobsons, 1986); Chris Evans, *The Mighty Micro* (Coronet, 1979) – a bit old, but a classic! Peter Zorkoczy, *Information Technology* (Pitman, 1990). Trevor Arden, *Information Technology Applications* (Pitman, 1991).

Latin American Studies

Professor Simon Collier, Vanderbilt University, USA

This study area is unlike most (though not quite all) the others discussed for your benefit in this guide. The big difference is that it isn't a **subject** in its own right so much as a number of subjects focused on a specific **region** of the world. Why study this particular region at all? You may well ask. Latin America (by which we usually mean the twenty republics of Central and South America) is not an area which is as well known as it might be in this country. If you follow the serious newspapers regularly, you see remarkably little reporting on events in Latin America. Only lurid and dramatic happenings get anywhere near the British headlines – the guerrilla campaign in Peru, the drug barons' activities in Columbia, or the short, sharp war between Britain and Argentina over the Falkland Islands in 1982 (**that** did get into the headlines, of course, and the background reports on that occasion may have taught people quite a lot about modern Argentina). In some ways, this normal absence of news from the region is rather surprising. The relationship between the UK and Latin America used to be very much stronger than it is today. If anything, it seems at present to be getting weaker. British trade with the region continues to decline, although the last thirty years have seen a definite growth in Latin American studies as an academic activity.

The chances are, therefore, that you have a fairly good reason for considering this study area at all. It may be that your family has had some sort of connection with one of the Latin American countries, or even that you yourself spent part of your childhood there and would like to return some day. It is possible that a particular Latin American theme has somehow taken your fancy – the ancient civilisations of the Aztecs and Incas, perhaps, or the work of the great Mexican mural-painters, or the glamorous and tragic story of Evita Peron, or the background to the Falklands conflict. It may just be that you are in an adventurous mood and are tempted to try something 'different' in the way of a first degree. It is a good temptation, but be careful. Sad though it is to have to say this, the number of possible careers directly connected with Latin America is strictly limited. So perhaps the best piece of advice that can be offered is, simply, that you should think long and hard before considering Latin American studies as a first degree.

But let us suppose that you have thought about it a bit, and want to take matters further. What kinds of things are involved in the study of Latin America? Certain subjects are unavoidable, and the first which must always be mentioned is language. Eighteen of the twenty Latin American republics speak Spanish, while Brazil, the largest country of the region, speaks Portuguese. (The tiny republic of Haiti, in the Caribbean, is French-speaking.) Mastery of Spanish or Portuguese (and if possible both) is quite essential for this study area. You should not be unduly deterred. They are not, for English-speakers, the most difficult languages in the world by a long chalk.

For most people, language is not an end in itself. It simply provides an instrument for communication and for further learning. The basic aim of Latin American studies is (indeed, must be) to enable you to build up a well-rounded and comprehensive picture of the region. There are several key subjects which can be called into play. Geography, for instance, can explain a great deal about the physical environment in which Latin Americans live and the ways in which this has helped or hindered their economic growth. Sociology, too, can probe some of the pressing dilemmas of the present day: the population explosion, over-rapid urbanisation, acute social stratification, and the extreme poverty which is still such a depressing feature of most of the Latin American countries. Politics and government, likewise, can shed light on some of the recurrent modes of political behaviour in the area, not least the tenacious phenomenon of militarism – the tendency to military dictatorship, sometimes very harsh, which was such a prominent feature in the 1970s, though the tide turned back towards democracy in the 1980s. The study of Latin American culture must also be included in the broad picture. The international impact of certain writers from the region has been outstanding in recent decades. The great Chilean poet Pablo Neruda, and that strangely compelling Argentine genius, Jorge Luis Borges, have perhaps been the best-known figures of recent decades, but a very impressive generation of novelists – Julio Cortazar (Argentina), Carlos Fuentes (Mexico), Mario Vargas Llosa (Peru), Isabel Allende (Chile), and Gabriel Garcia Marquez (Colombia), to name only five – has also staked a decisive claim to world attention.

Behind all these subjects there looms history, without which none of the others really falls into perspective. For those who study it, history is fascinating in itself, but from the angle of this study area it has the merit of helping to explain how things got to be the way they are. Latin America is often described, perhaps rather misleadingly, as part of the so-called Third World. If it is, it is easily the most developed part. But by the standards of Western Europe or the USA, Latin America remains a region of enormous problems, a region where 'development' remains the supreme imperative of modern times. Mass poverty of a kind no longer visible in Europe is still an all too normal feature of Latin American life.

What keys does the past provide for understanding Latin American underdevelopment? The nature of Spanish and Portuguese colonisation in the sixteenth century? The extremely lop-sided distribution of land in colonial times? The inability of the landowning elites, after independence, to 'modernise' the republics they now ruled? The influence of foreign economic interests – first British and later on American? All these question marks represent highly important historical debates, which are closely tied in, of course, with the kinds of issues examined by sociologists, economists and political scientists for the contemporary period.

Some of Latin America's dilemmas seem peculiarly her own; others look familiar enough from the viewpoint of Africa and Asia, too. The value of Latin American studies lies not in providing final or definite answers to the modern problems of the region, but in helping you to become very much better informed and more sensitive about the nature of the problems themselves. The opportunity to deepen your acquaintance with a richly colourful part of the world – exotic and puzzling, stimulating and depressing – is one which is well worth taking, providing that you really **want** to take it. Otherwise not. But if you are really keen, you probably will never regret it.

HELPFUL READING: Simon Collier, Harold Blakemore and Thomas E Skidmore, eds, *The Cambridge Encyclopedia of Latin America and the Caribbean* Second Edition (Cambridge University Press, 1992); J Franco, *The Modern Culture of Latin America* (London: Pall Mall Press, 1967).

Law

Professor Geoffrey Wilson, Warwick University

One of the problems with law as a subject of university study is that for most people still at school it is one of the great unknowns. Though there are A-level courses in law they give little idea of what a University course ought to be like and, in any event, there are more important subjects to do at school than law.

One of the most common reasons students applying for places give for reading law is that students are thinking of becoming solicitors or barristers. For those who eventually decide to practise as lawyers a law degree does have the practical advantage of providing them with the opportunity of getting exemption from the First Part of the professional examinations as well as giving them a better idea of what might be involved in practice, and laying a foundation of legal knowledge that should stand them in good stead as lawyers in the years to come. One does not have to study law to be a lawyer but three or four years on a law degree does provide the chance of a more thoughtful and grounded introduction to the way the law works than can readily be acquired by practising it. One of the motives of the legal profession in supporting legal education in degree courses is that it means they are getting recruits educated for them at someone else's expense; the notion that law studied in an academic environment provides a broader training also no doubt plays a part.

The study of law in a degree course has never been recommended entirely on the basis that it provides a good training for future lawyers. Most law schools would agree that the study of law has advantages for students who do not intend to practise, or who thought they might want to and then change their minds, or for those who simply do not know. They would point to the intellectual training involved in the close reading of texts, statutes and the judgments in decided cases, in the isolation of the relevant from the irrelevant and the identification and disposal of the main issues in complex problems and situations, and in the practice of rational argument according to the ground rules of English legal reasoning. They would emphasise too the special characteristics of legal reasoning that it is not simply abstract and academic, not simply logical, but reasoning with a view to reaching a decision; that even though it is conducted in an academic environment and at one remove from the real world, it is dealing with real world problems, real legislation, real cases, real facts, real judgments. It is, in short, reasoning of a practical kind. In this respect law as a degree subject can provide a convenient halfway house between school and the real world, not as academic as A-levels, not as practical as real-world decisions, but somewhere in between. The only hesitation one might have in endorsing this justification for the study of law is that, in the hands of some law teachers, in some law schools, real life situations have given way to hypothetical factual situations used as a means of testing students' understanding of basic legal principles which are so bizarre that an ability to deal with them has a closer analogy to the ability to master the detailed rules of a complicated board game than anything resembling a real life situation. Even this and the jokey names that go with them like Oddball who sets out to sell shoddy goods to Clueless which are eaten by his shaggy dog Wagtail and so on, like crosswords have their avid fans and supporters, but of course the more the emphasis is placed on the bizarre and the cardboard cut-out figures who take part in these turnabouts, the less one can really argue that the study of law is closely related to the study of real life. In this respect, as in others, a glance at a law school's examination papers may sometimes give a clue to the prevailing ethos in it.

To the arguments that law is a suitable subject of study for future lawyers and when done well provides a good general training in rational analysis, discussion and decision, most law schools would probably add the importance of law and the legal profession in the community at large. Here it stands shoulder to shoulder with other subjects which study important aspects of society, such as economics or politics, looking at society from one important perspective, that of the part law plays in it. And along with law, go the legal profession and the machinery of justice, criminal and civil. It does not need much effort to see that individuals, companies and groups cannot avoid the impact of law and lawyers which extends into family life, labour relations, the organisation of companies, commercial and business relationships, taxation, social security, the environment, consumer questions, the business of buying, selling and renting houses, and all the millions of contacts between them and public authorities of one kind or another. In other words the study of law is as important as the law itself.

For the most part English law schools concentrate on English law and the English legal system. But over the years there has been a growing interest in what goes on outside the United Kingdom as well. Courses in international law have long been common. To these have been added an increasing number of courses on foreign legal systems, in particular the European, such as France and Germany, and the European Community generally. One law school has even experimented with a course in Japanese law. The growing interest in foreign legal systems has been accompanied by the creation of formal links between UK law schools and law departments in foreign universities and the introduction of special degree courses which include a year abroad. These developments not only provide new opportunities for students, they may also break down some of the more parochial concerns that have been the hallmark of legal education since it was established in England in the nineteenth century.

Of course law schools vary in their strengths and weaknesses. Different schools emphasise different aspects of legal study and, as with other subjects, one needs to follow up a general interest in the prospect of studying law with a closer look at what each has to offer. Equally important to what is offered is the spirit of the place and here one is pretty well bound to be dependent on rumour and reputation, but even a day's visit may help and this goes for the question of studying law itself. Although there is a lot of law around for those still at school, it is largely invisible, but although it is invisible it is not inaccessible. All courts are open to the public. Many solicitors' firms welcome inquiries and some even offer opportunities for part time work. Visits of this kind can help to give some idea at least of the atmosphere in which the professional lawyer works.

As to the kind of person who is likely both to enjoy and do well at law that is more difficult. Law is a discipline: the reasoning is logical, rational and disciplined. It often has quite restricted views as to what is relevant in a particular situation which might not correspond to every man's scope, for imagination it is limited. It can appear pedantic, painstaking and inhibiting, but for those attracted by the prospect of pragmatic, concise and concrete argument about, not the whole world and its problems, but at least a part of it (or the whole of it but seen from a relatively limited perspective) it deserves very serious consideration, especially for those who look upon a degree course as the opportunity for a new start.

HELPFUL READING: *Report of the Ormrod Committee on Legal Education* (Cmnd 4995 London HMSO 1971); Sir Leslie Scarman, *New Dimensions of English Law* (London: Stevens, 1975); Glanville & Williams, *Learning the Law* (London: Stevens, 1978).

Library and Information Studies

Dr Margaret Evans, Loughborough University

What do courses in library and information studies offer students today? First, they provide a sound professional education that enables students to take up posts in the wide range of information careers now available. Information professionals are eagerly sought by all kinds of organisations, including libraries and information services, in both the public and private sectors, as well as all those organisations developing the management of their information resources, in such wide-ranging fields as marketing, charity and welfare, education or commerce. The market for information professionals is expanding rapidly, as the significance of information increases in our society, and the young information worker can anticipate a challenging and varied career. Inevitably therefore, as courses are vocationally oriented to a greater or lesser extent, you will learn a variety of skills as a preparation for an information-related career.

Some of these skills might surprise you. In the past, there was a great deal of emphasis on 'cataloguing and classification' in courses, as a means of organising knowledge for the library user. Professional librarians spent a great deal of their time in preparing material for use. Today there is rather less of this traditional 'cat and class' in degree programmes, as a result of the impact of computerisation on the organisation of information, which has freed librarians and information professionals for more creative professional work. You are as likely now to study the design of expert systems that help the information manager in accessing information as you are to learn about classifying books using a variety of classification schemes. The emphasis in most courses today is on the exciting developments in information management, made possible by the increasing sophistication of technology. This means that 'computer literacy' is essential for students: keyboard skills are developed in students from the very beginning of courses. However, most students coming into departments of library and information studies have either little or no previous computer experience and this is recognised in the teaching methods. Computer programming as such does not usually figure much, although for those who wish to specialise in this there is often the opportunity to do so.

Knowing how to organise information is one of the key skills expected by employers, but equally important is knowing how to manage that information in the context of a library or information service. The kinds of management skills developed in students are therefore very similar to those you would find on a business studies course. All libraries today are in the business of information provision, and even public libraries have to ensure they provide the kind of service expected by a demanding client group – the ratepayers. Many libraries or information services are also engaged in selling their services: university libraries, for example, are being encouraged to market their business information services to local industries. Information professionals therefore need to know what users want, be able to design services to meet those needs, and to monitor the quality of services and promote them to their potential users. Courses include a considerable element on the basic management skills needed to achieve this: resource management, managing people and marketing. Teaching methods often include the use of case study materials to emphasise the practical application of theories to the work situation in a variety of settings.

Inevitably, information professionals will spend a great deal of their time in communicating – to users, to other information services through the extensive national and international information networks, and also to information providers such as publishers or database producers. It is therefore essential to communicate effectively, whether verbally or in writing. There will usually be an element in courses that develops these skills and helps students to feel confident in their interactions with users and other information professionals. Report writing and abstracting, and presenting skills, feature considerably, often as an adjunct to other areas of study; as do foreign languages and, for those looking to the single European market for their career development, it makes considerable sense to take advantage of this aspect of a degree programme.

So far I have concentrated on the development of the various necessary skills, which can of course be transferable across a range of information-related careers (one of the many advantages of a degree course in library and information studies). There are as well huge areas of knowledge that you will gain. The history of knowledge and of information transfer is intrinsically fascinating and you will be introduced to the honourable contribution made to our culture by authors, publishers, libraries and other learned institutions. In addition to the 'core' areas of study, such as organising information, and managing libraries and information services, there is also a range of optional elements for specialist study that caters for students' particular subject and career interests. This includes subjects as varied as health and welfare information management, publishing, archives administration and records management, children's and school librarianship.

Added to the areas of knowledge that make up the library and information studies curriculum most courses offer either another 'minor' subject or will comprise one half of a joint honours degree programme; so you can add subjects such as English, geography, a modern European language, social science or computing to your repertoire. However, even in a single honours course, the range of study areas is both so broad and deep that most students find themselves intellectually fully stretched by their course!

Contacts between the real world of information provision and departments of library and information studies add considerably to the content of courses: these contacts can take many forms. Students are encouraged to take up work placements during the long vacations; to take a sandwich year out either in the UK or in institutions overseas; and to undertake project work in libraries and information services as part of their course assessment. Visiting information professionals also give lectures and take seminars.

Courses in library and information studies are stimulating and rewarding, both intellectually and vocationally. Graduates in this subject can feel confident that their broadly based liberal education has prepared them for an interesting and varied career.

HELPFUL READING: R C Benge, *Libraries and Cultural Change* (Bingley, 1979); A Toffler, *The Third Wave* (Collins, 1980); D J Urquhart, *Principles of Librarianship* (1981).

Linguistics

Dr Michael Garman, Reading University

First degree courses in linguistics started in this country only in 1964 but there are already many to be found, in a variety of forms. They range from single subject courses, through combined subject courses (often with a modern language), to packages where linguistics sits with a number of components (as in communication studies courses). This rapid growth (in what is still essentially a non-school subject) has led to a situation in which it will pay you well to select your course with some care (more of this later). But first we must look at the general area that any course would be expected to cover.

One obvious goal for students of language is acquiring fluent control of particular languages (often for practical reasons); another, perhaps less immediately obvious, is to understand language as such. Linguistics is more directly concerned with the second of these goals although it is impossible and undesirable to separate them entirely. As such, it is really a continuation of work that was begun by grammarians in the ancient world, as a branch of the study of man. But the methods and scope of the modern subject set it apart from the earlier traditions of language study. So when, and in what ways, did modern linguistics begin?

In one sense, towards the end of the eighteenth century: in 1786, Sir William Jones observed that Sanskrit, the ancient classical language of the Indian subcontinent, was 'possessed of a stronger affinity' with the European classical languages, Greek and Latin, 'both in the roots of the verbs and in the forms of grammar, than could possibly have been produced by accident'. For language scholars in Europe and elsewhere there was a unified research enterprise here, in uncovering the historical facts of this non-accident; the task, which filled the following century, was to place historical linguistic relationships on a scientific basis so that languages could be placed within 'families', and, where necessary, long-extinct linguistic forms could be reconstructed in a convincing way. This formative period, of comparative philology, saw the development of techniques of linguistic analysis which transformed the study of language and laid the basis of modern linguistics.

But in another sense it is the work of Ferdinand de Saussure, a Swiss-French comparative philologist, which marks the beginning of the modern subject, around the turn of this century. He recognised the limitations of a purely **historical** approach, based largely on **written** forms of languages, and dealing mainly with development of **individual**

words or sounds. In the 'structuralist' tradition that de Saussure inspired, the **whole language system** was the object of description, the system as it exists **at a particular point of time** (like the analysis of the pattern on the chess-board halfway through the game), and earlier emphasis on just the written forms of language was counteracted. This tradition saw the systematic description of thousands of previously unknown, or inadequately known, languages, most of them having no script, many imperilled by the advance of civilisation, scattered over North and South America, Africa below the Sahara, SE Asia and elsewhere. It was during this period, above all, that the main components of language structure and their associated fields of study became established in a recognisably modern form: **phonetics**, the study of speech, its acoustic properties and the neurophysiological basis of its production and perception; **phonology**, the study of the sound systems of particular languages; **morphology** and **syntax**, dealing with the grammatical elements (stems, affixes) of a language and the ways in which they combine to form words, phrases and sentences; and **semantics**, the study of meaning in language.

For most of us, though, there is another part to the answer. Our concern now, starting mainly with the work of Noam Chomsky in the late 1950s, is to go beyond the limits of a particular corpus of data, and to try to describe, not so much the data as the human reality which underlies it. We are as concerned with the next, unuttered, sentence, as with the one just recorded. And we have learned to build models of the language ability which we are trying to understand: while they are, as yet, only partially successful, these models have already taught us a good deal about what it means to **explain** (rather than **describe**) the nature of language. Furthermore, a particular feature of modern linguistics in this sense is the development of specialist research areas, many of which allow for the practical application of theoretical models. To mention some of the more important: **sociolinguistics** examines the nature of social and regional variation in language; **psycholinguistics** looks at the ways in which language abilities are developed and maintained in the individual, and the study of language development in young children has seen particularly vigorous activity in recent years; **second language learning** is another field in which psychological and linguistic factors have to be handled together, and where a great deal of research is currently going on; **language pathology**, the study of language disorders, is currently attracting the attention of an increasing number of linguists (and specialist degree courses have recently been established in this field. **Computational linguistics** is now making significant advances in the modelling of natural language performance, and the development of expert systems for automatic and flexible production and perception of speech by machine.

So, if you do decide on linguistics, you will be entering a world where great advances have been made, many of them quite recently, where practical applications are opening up, and where rapid developments are still taking place. The intellectual excitements are many, and career prospects are generally good, but there are reasons for you to be careful in your course selection: first, check whether the subject will be presented as complete and entire in itself (in a sense, it is, but the danger is that you may end up doing entirely theoretical linguistics with not much chance of deepening your knowledge of some language); secondly, try to find out if the course you are considering is dominated by one particular school of thought (in which case things may be presented in a very coherent fashion, but you will not easily discover the advantages of other approaches in a subject where it is far too easy to recognise just one golden path); above all, beware of the course which makes linguistics easy by leaving out the hard bits and putting in their place an assorted collection of attractive, but unfounded, speculations. After two millennia of language study we are getting close to some fascinating and difficult issues concerning an incredibly complex human ability: this is not the time to have your head filled with trivia!

HELPFUL READING: D Crystal, *What is Linguistics?* 3rd edn (London: Arnold, 1974); F Palmer, *Grammar* (Harmondsworth: Penguin, 1983); P Trudgill, *Sociolinguistics* (Harmondsworth: Penguin, 1983); J D O'Connor, *Phonetics* (Harmondsworth: Penguin, 1974); J Lyons, *Language and Linguistics* (Cambridge: CUP, 1981); D Crystal, *The Cambridge Encyclopaedia of Language* (Cambridge University Press, 1987); V Fromkin & R Rodman, *An Introduction to Language* (Holt, Rinehart & Winston, 1983).

Marine Technology

Emeritus Professor J B Caldwell, Newcastle University

This study area is about the sea, and mainly about designing and building things that go to sea. Ships, of course, but other things too; from boats and barges to the large structures and systems which will be needed as mankind looks increasingly to the sea for a multitude of purposes. The oceans have been described as our last resource, and the exploring and harvesting and preserving of this resource will pose some fascinating challenges to the marine technologist of the future.

Their work is a reflection of, and a response to, our need to use the sea. Throughout history the principal uses have been firstly to move people and goods and weapons around the globe, and secondly to harvest some of the many varieties of food which exist in the sea. The centre-piece of these activities is the ship in its multifarious forms, sizes and functions. Through many centuries the art of creating ships evolved by trial and error and experience, but with the industrial revolution came the need to design and build ships in new materials with new forms of propulsion, without the benefit of prior experience. And so there emerged the profession of naval architecture, signalled formally by the founding of the Institution of Naval Architects more than 130 years ago. Since then the main task of the naval architect has been the designing and building of all kinds of ships and craft for both civil and military uses, from ferries to frigates, tankers and trawlers, icebreakers and hydrofoils, containerships to cruisers. What is particularly fascinating is that, despite the antiquity of shipping, new concepts continue to appear. Wave-piercing catamarans and SWATH ships (small waterplane area twin hull) are very recent examples.

Nor should we overlook the part played by naval architects in the growing business of leisure activities at sea, whether on luxury cruise ships, or just messing about in boats. The design of both types of vessel depends on the same basic principles of naval architecture. And indeed it is through pleasure sailing in their young days that many boys (and some girls, too) have their interest aroused in ships and the sea, and take their first steps towards a career in naval architecture.

The naval architect is a special kind of engineer. Sea-going craft and structures are mobile communities with a job to do. They must be safe, habitable, efficient, economical both to build and to operate. They must as far as possible combine this 'fitness for purpose' with attractive appearance – there is still scope, thank goodness, for the naval architect to exercise his art as well as his science. His particular art is synthesis, the blending together of the often conflicting requirements of shipowner, shipbuilder, safety and legislative authorities, and seafarer. Within his field of work a variety of specialist skills has grown up (eg in structures, hydrodynamics, propeller design, computer applications) and most naval architects develop one or more of these specialisms alongside their general overview of design. But because the use of the sea is influenced by so many things – political, economic, social, legal, as well as by continuous development in science and technology – the naval architect, as the creator of the vehicles and systems, must have a wide-ranging and forward-looking view of life. In an age of increasing specialisation he must remain a determined and highly professional generalist.

Alongside the naval architect there has grown a very closely related profession, that of marine engineering. The marine engineer – and this is where the definitions can get a little confusing – can have two fairly distinct roles. One is as an operator of the machinery and systems on board ship; the other, which is the real counterpart of the naval architect, is as the designer and builder of this equipment. Again, variety is a feature of his work; ships can be propelled by steam turbines, gas turbines, slow- or medium-speed diesel engines and electric motors, and many combinations of these are possible. The basic source of energy to push a ship along has changed through the centuries from wind, muscle-power, coal, oil and other special chemical fuels to nuclear fission. It is one of the fascinations typical of marine technology that the days of wind propulsion, or of coal used in new forms, may come again if technological developments and relative fuel costs make them feasible and economic. More futuristic ideas currently being researched include 'magnetohydro-dynamic' propulsion, and even harnessing the energy in waves to push ships along! So just as the naval architect needs to take a broad informed view of the way in which progress in science and technology can contrib-ute, so also must the marine engineer seek to harness his skills and knowledge of mechanical, electrical and control engineering, dynamics, noise, vibrations and the like, to the special needs of the marine environment. It is one thing to design and install a land-based power system, quite another to ensure that a 20,000 kW marine diesel engine, with its many associated auxiliaries, will continue to work reliably for perhaps twenty years despite violent motions of the ship, extremes of temperature, a highly corrosive environment, with crews who increasingly are sensitive to noise or vibration and whose numbers steadily reduce.

Marine engineers and naval architects work closely together, and the professional education and training which they receive reflects their common interest in engineering for the sea. Mathematics and science – especially physics – provide the basis for degree-level education, not as ends in themselves, but for their usefulness when applied to solving the problems confronting the marine technologist. In most degree courses the general plan of study is similar. A foundation year of engineering science, mathematics, computing and some introductory work in marine technology is followed by an increasing emphasis through the second and third years on 'professional' studies. In the final year there may be a wide choice of specialised marine topics, and the student can begin to look forward to various career possibilities in choosing subjects for advanced study. Employment opportunities are many and varied, because all phases of the creative process – research, development, design, approval, production, commissioning, operation, trouble-shooting, education, training – require skilled professionals. And, as argued above, the scope of the work of the naval architect and marine engineer seems certain to increase.

This widening tapestry of marine activity now includes offshore, or ocean, engineering. This embraces a whole complex of engineering activities ranging from sea-bed technology (placing foundations for ocean structures, or pipes or cables) through underwater engineering (problems of submersible design, communication, visibility, life-support, safety etc), up to engineering on the surface (mothering craft, production platforms, artificial islands, protective structures, wave-energy devices etc). Of course many of the problems encountered in offshore engineering centre on the age-old difficulties of coping with the sea. So it is not surprising that naval architects and marine engineers – often working together with civil, mechanical, electrical, medical, electronic or other engineers – are finding new scope for their particular talents and interests.

What's in a name? If we use the term marine technology to embrace these three activities – naval architecture, marine engineering and ocean engineering – it serves to underline the essential community of interests between these disciplines. Technology itself, like money, is neutral; it is the use we make of it which is good or bad, and which can sometimes excite the proper opposition of the environmentalist. But civilised use of the sea is essential to the future of mankind. It is to this end that the marine technologist must direct his professional skills and his social responsibilities.

HELPFUL READING: *Careers in Naval Architecture* (London: Royal Institution of Naval Architects, 1992); *Careers in the Marine Engineering Profession* (London: Institute of Marine Engineers, 1986);

Oceans of Opportunity (London: Society for Underwater Technology, 1990); Tony Loftus, *The Last Resource: Man's Exploitation of the Oceans* (London: Penguin Harmondsworth, 1972); *Ships and Shipping of Tomorrow* (MacGregor Publications, 1983).

Maritime Studies

Dr Alston Kennerley, Plymouth University

With the waters of the world occupying some 70% of its surface area and the gradual decline in resources found on land, it was only to be expected that attention would increasingly be directed towards the exploitation of the sea's resources. The growth of marine-related activity over recent decades provides evidence enough for this, and it seems certain that the scale of man's involvement with the seas will continue to grow.

Maritime studies (or marine studies or nautical studies) is thus concerned with man's activity on and under the surface of the sea, and, of necessity, with the interface between the land and the sea, the coastline and ports. The nature of this activity may be expressed in general terms according to the uses man makes of the sea: for transportation, for exploitation of its living resources (sea food), for its non-living resources (energy and minerals), for recreation and for military purposes. None of these are new uses, but what is new is the extent to which these uses have been developed, and the global scale of activity and interest.

Each of these uses has scientific, technological, commercial, legal and social aspects, and it will be appreciated that in fact most traditional areas of study have a maritime dimension. Courses in maritime studies are designed to provide a marine emphasis and to embrace and integrate traditional areas of study.

Most established undergraduate courses in maritime studies have been built around the transportation use, with the ship as a focus. This alone provides quite a diversity of subjects which are important to all uses and provide a basis for career opportunities in most areas of marine activity.

Recently developed courses embrace an even fuller range of marine subjects, and by adopting a modular structure, permit prospective students to devise their own programme of studies, and move the emphasis of study from the transportation use to one of the other uses suggested above.

The sea is a much more demanding environment than the land and maritime studies courses provide an opportunity for the study of the natural environment in which ships and marine structures must operate, and in which living organisms must survive. The collective term ocean science is used to embrace several related subjects. Meteorology is concerned with the study of weather patterns, in this case in the marine context, with a view to predicting changes. Oceanography takes in many aspects of the oceans of the world but is particularly concerned with the nature of the waters, including the chemical composition, and the currents and tides. The deposits on the sea bed are studied in sedimentology. All these bear on marine pollution studies, the health of the seas now being recognised as of great importance.

Hydrography deals with the science of marine surveying, the process by which information about the sea bed is created. It includes marine cartography, the mapping of this information for use by mariners and others. Hydrographic charts are an essential tool for marine navigation, the subject concerned with the safe movement of ships across the seas. This is a broad subject which includes much more than the proper use of hydrographic information. Positioning, using the wide range of radio aids to navigation, is of course an important element, but it is now essential to include navigation management and communication, while also taking account of the natural environment, the ship and its cargo, and the density of shipping particularly in areas such as the Straits of Dover.

Marine technology is now used to indicate the scope of technological studies related to the sea. The traditional name given to the design of ships, naval architecture, demonstrates its links with the design of engineering structures, including for example those for offshore oil and gas extraction, with which it shares many principles. It is also concerned with the behaviour of marine vehicles in the sea, especially stability, and is closely related to shipbuilding. The study of the propulsion of ships, marine engineering, includes auxiliary machinery for ships' domestic services and deck machinery such as winches.

The handling and stowage of cargoes has both technological and scientific aspects, and is also a key element in the commercial success of shipping. Maritime business or sea transport is concerned with the commercial side of shipping including economics, finance, management and operation and has related studies in marine insurance, maritime law and port operations. There are connections here with the study of other forms of transport.

Some courses may cover other aspects of man's use of the sea and its resources. Fisheries studies will include: fisheries biology, especially the behaviour of fish; fishing technology, concerned with the design and use of fishing gear; marine acoustics, in the context of modern fish hunting; fish farming, fish processing, and fisheries economics, including marketing, management and the legal regime. Marine biology studies the organisms living in the sea, drawing on environmental aspects of oceanography and marine resources. Marine resources is concerned with both living and non-living resources, in terms of reserves, the scale of exploitation, reserve management and the legal framework.

Many of these maritime studies subject areas bear on the diverse and rapidly growing field of maritime recreation, which is increasingly important for the careers it offers. Such courses are likely to include boat design, management of facilities, boat safety and navigation, and, interpreting marine recreation widely, may cover a variety of marine sports. There may also be connections with tourism.

Britain has a significant maritime history, represented in the growing number of maritime museums and preserved ships. Courses in maritime history, which complement modern studies, range from regional to international studies. Included here are the histories of maritime trade, commerce and law, the history of maritime science (oceanography and navigation) and maritime technology, the social history of seafaring and the study of the military aspect in naval history.

From the foregoing it will be clear that courses in maritime or marine studies are very much applied studies and closely related to the modern uses that man makes of the seas. Such a range of subjects has the advantage of providing combinations suited to those who have backgrounds in the sciences or in social studies.

HELPFUL READING: To explore the content of maritime studies a little further start with one of the few books providing something of an overview; these should be available in most larger reference libraries. Perhaps the best is *The Times Atlas of the Oceans*, edited by A D Couper (Times Books, 1983), which has short articles on most of the subject areas indicated and provides suggestions for further reading. Also useful is *The Oxford Companion to Ships and the Sea*, edited by Peter Kemp (OUP, 1976). *The Commanding Sea*, edited by Clare Francis and Warren Tute (BBC and Pelham Books, 1981), has a more relaxed style and is well illustrated. For a more literary approach try one of the maritime anthologies such as *The Oxford Book of the Sea*, edited by Jonathan Raban (OUP, 1992), or *Men at Sea*, edited by Brandt Aymar (Barrie and Jenkins, 1989).

Mathematical Studies

R Daniel Hirsch, London Guildhall University

We all notice and are curious about the world and we all have the intelligence to understand and satisfy an increasing part of that curiosity. Indeed we see patterns and study them. For example, we see that three boys and four boys together form a group of seven boys, and that *therefore* three girls and four girls together form a group of seven girls. This we do at an early age, and we develop this ability quite naturally. We seek out patterns. And then we go further and ask if there are new properties that we may use to our advantage.

Mathematical study simply formalises this natural progress. It can lead to very practical and useful results such as applications of the calculus – marginal revenue for the accountant, velocity for the physicist – or matrix techniques, frequently employed in advanced statistics. It can also lead to further theoretical results, that is to say statements that are not immediately obvious and perhaps not immediately applicable – the work of logicians and algebraists of the last hundred years, culminating in the building of the computer, is an excellent example.

The investment of our time, energy and intellect in this advanced study yields great pleasure and proof of human achievement. It is available to all and most communities seek out and reward us for such progress.

Undergraduate work in mathematics, whether for application or theory, can be divided roughly into two categories, the analytic and the algebraic. The analytic approach consists of being given a particular system, for example the real numbers, and then cutting up or analysing its properties. Thus we may be led to fine (unexpected) details about the number system we use, so commonly; to differential equations that describe the physical, economic or social changes in the world; to study of optimising techniques etc. The algebraic approach consists of being given a particular structure and then examining what common properties are shared by all systems with that same structure – for example, your right hand gives a faithful copy of your left hand and the number 5 is associated with any other faithful copy. This structural approach leads to algebra, logic, computer science etc.

It is usual and clearly sensible to start off with a programme of study that includes all these elements in the first year. Thereafter we go our various ways and (usually) devote more of our time to that area of work that is most fun and where we feel we are going to make most progress. This can vary from finding out why you cannot trisect an angle, examining the foundations of geometry, to 'building' wind tunnels, constructing a transportation matrix, developing techniques of numerical analysis and generally to almost any mathematics that has stood up to the test of experience. It is not always easy but equally it is not always difficult. It is always fascinating whether you are 'good at maths' or not, for much of this depends on your natural ability and perception. You can start with sorting out a football coupon, go on to counting the number of people shaking hands at a party, and finish with a model of some hydrocarbon molecules. All you need is what you already have – human curiosity and intellect to satisfy it.

Enjoy it!

Mechanical and Production Engineering

Emeritus Professor M W Thring, Queen Mary and Westfield College London

Mechanical and production engineering are the very foundation of our industrial civilisation, providing the machines and the power to drive them that enable one man's work to achieve more than ten men could do unaided. The industrial revolution, in which Britain led the way for the first hundred years, was entirely dependent on the work of inventive engineers. It could have taken place with a different economic, religious or political system, but the development of steam engines and machine tools were essential. It is also true that steam and hot air engines were developed by engineers decades before scientists formulated the first and second laws of thermodynamics.

So far the industrial revolution has enabled the people who were replaced by machines in one industry to be employed in a new one which is a part of the rising standard of living. However, like all exponential growth, this growth of standard of living, and the use of fossil fuels and mineral ores on which it is based, must level off. Other factors limiting the rise in wealth of the developed peoples are space limitations, consumer resistance to new gadgets, and the fact that the undeveloped countries desperately need some share of the limited resources of the earth. The use of energy per capita in the poor areas is less than one-tenth of that in the rich areas.

The world's economic system is creaking badly, with rising unemployment in both rich and poor countries, loans on which even the interest is unpaid, and millions of humans starving while vast sums of money are spent every year on weapons, nuclear power, giant dams that make electricity no one can afford to buy and upset the environment irreversibly, supersonic flight and the space race. Failures, disastrous to humans, occur every year because man has used engineering for short-sighted purposes instead of looking to the future.

Thus mechanical and production engineers have a vital role to play in solving the problem of giving mankind a stable world in the 21st century. They can be in the forefront of developing the machines that will solve the following problems: to enable all adults in the world to have the opportunity of earning a fully adequate standard of living for themselves and their families using primarily local resources on a permanent basis; to use the limited mineral resources of the world in such a way that as they become exhausted the system can be maintained by recycling of metals and the use of renewable energy sources; to eliminate completely all potentially disastrous large systems and reduce to a very low level all small scale accidents; to reduce chemical pollution of air, land and water to undetectable levels, and not to burden the earth with any unnatural radioactive elements.

The mechanical engineer can play a central role in reducing the consumption of fossil fuels which cause the rise in CO_2 in the atmosphere which in turn is one of the main causes of the 'greenhouse effect'. This consumption can certainly be halved without any real sacrifices. Examples are given below. Similarly the mechanical engineer can develop refrigeration cycles which do not require the use of CFCs which are having such a disastrous effect on the ozone layer.

Of course the inventive engineer cannot solve these problems alone, but he or she must be at the spearhead of the solution because they are the only professionals who can foresee the machines that can be developed to solve them. Other professions constantly make wrong judgments because of their lack of engineering understanding. One example of this is that Britain has not developed the use of CHP (Combined Heat and Power, where boiling water from power stations is used for heating purposes instead of being thrown away) because those who drew up the terms of nationalisation of electricity did not understand the practical implications of the second law of thermodynamics. Another example is the export of tractors and high technology agriculture to the 'Third World'. Only the engineer can envisage the machines necessary to give really appropriate help to their agriculture: a possible machine is a 'mechanical bullock', a cultivator with legs that could be powered by steam from a boiler fired by agricultural refuse.

One of the most important problems of the developed countries is that our high standard of living is based on a steadily rising consumption of energy from fossil fuels (coal, oil and natural gas). The average use in the rich countries is about 6 tons of coal equivalent per head per year (TCE/c.a). Thirty years ago we all believed that nuclear fission energy would enable us to continue this extravagant use of energy even when fossil fuels were exhausted. Now we know that, because of the high capital cost of power stations and the thermodynamic limitations of generating electricity from heat, we can never hope to have electricity cheap enough to replace fossil fuels for low grade heating or use it for any rail-less transport. Moreover we have a much greater experience of the hazards of radioactive materials that are a necessary consequence of nuclear fission power generation.

The mechanical engineer has therefore to develop machines to achieve the following:

(1) enable us to use far less fossil fuel without losing any of the really valuable results of the industrial revolution. I have calculated that this could be done using only 1 TCE/c.a. in the developed countries with cold winters, while in the undeveloped countries about $\frac{1}{2}$ TCE/c.a. could bring them the most important benefits if the engineers really put their minds to it. The machines for these purposes have already been invented but need appropriate development. Examples are a diesel/electric parallel/hybrid car engine that could give over 100 mpg; aeroplanes using half as much fuel per passenger mile as present-day jets; a coal-fired steam loco giving smokeless combustion and as good efficiency and performance as a diesel loco. There is very much more coal in the world than oil and gas.

(2) enable people to avoid all hazardous situations in their work. We can develop 'Telechirs' (hands at a distance) so that all work down mines, undersea, in radioactive or explosive situations or in fires can be done with full manual skill and visual and tactile feedback by people sitting in comfortable control cabins in a safe place. This would have the further advantage of increasing many-fold the amounts of coal and oil available to us.

(3) enable us to relieve intelligent humans of totally boring and repetitive jobs. First generation robots are already being used for paint spraying, spot welding, feeding all kinds of machines on repetitive operations such as stamping, die casting, plastic moulding and lathes, and for grinding and inspection. Some simple assembly is being done, but we are a long way short of the human skill on this even when we use second generation robots with sensory adaptiveness. Second generation robots will certainly enable humans to avoid the more repetitive tasks, but the need to make long lasting consumer goods to save raw materials and fuel will reduce the number of identical objects being made and there must be a return to individual craftsmanship and personal responsibility to provide worthwhile jobs for all.

Every attempt to look into the future shows that we cannot have a peaceful, stable world in which one-third of the world's population uses over 80% of the energy and other limited resources while the remaining two-thirds has an ever falling standard of living as forests are cut down, deserts grow, soil blows away and even wood fuel for cooking vanishes. The mechanical engineer can provide the spearhead of the advance to solve these problems. Energy for electric lighting, water pumping, wood sawing and agriculture can be provided by windmills, solar concentrators, burning agricultural refuse and small hydropowered generators. In the case of solar or refuse heated boilers the steam can be condensed at 100°C and the boiling water used for cooking, thus saving the direct use of wood or charcoal. Leaf fractionation presses can act as 'mechanical cows' and produce 'grass milk' from any locally grown green leaves.

The use of high quality engineering design and invention to solve these problems, vital to the survival of humanity, can be just as exciting as the design of high technology gadgets or weapons and infinitely more satisfying to the conscience.

I hope that this survey of the problems that can be solved by mechanical and production engineers of the next generation shows that these subjects, far from being 'old hat', are the ones that would make the key contribution in the transition to a stable world in which man lives in peaceful equilibrium with his surroundings. 'Where there's a will there's a way.'

HELPFUL READING: M W Thring (1) *The Engineer's Conscience* (Northgate: MEP 1980); (2) *Robots and Telechirs* (Ellis Horwood 1983).

Medicine

Dr David Sturgeon, University College and Middlesex School of Medicine

The most important aspect of studying medicine is the enormous range of possible careers to which it can lead – from transplant surgeon to medical journalist, from general practitioner to research scientist.

You should realise that being a medical student is just the first step on a long road of learning, which continues after qualification, whether it be a three year general practice vocational training course, or the ladder of hospital specialist training. For a good overview of both the course structure, and career prospects, see the recommended reading.

The first two years, the pre-clinical course, are like an extension of A-levels, and certainly no more intellectually demanding. This does not mean that the subject matter is not different – it is. You will follow courses in biochemistry, physiology, anatomy, histology, cell biology as well as medical sociology and psychology. But the intellectual difficulty to passing exams in these subjects is no greater than at A-level.

You should not worry about exactly which subjects you have studied at A-level. The pre-clinical biological science subjects build only very indirectly on A-level knowledge. Very many students have not studied A-level biology, and indeed the minimum requirement at London

University is that a student should have A-level chemistry, mathematics and physics at GCSE level. Arts A-levels are, and should be, no bar to medical school entry, but check these requirements with the medical school of your choice.

There is one other important aspect of pre-clinical studies. There is a definite tension between the declared aim of providing a basis of scientific knowledge on which the clinical teaching can stand, and the interests of the pre-clinical teachers, in teaching their subjects as 'pure science' entities in themselves. As well as medical students, they will be teaching those studying for a three year degree in the same subject, often in the same lectures. Thus biochemistry is often taught for the sake of biochemistry 'per se', rather than with a specific clinical medical relevance.

In some courses (eg London) the bias is towards 'pure science', in others (eg Nottingham) greater efforts are made to integrate the pre-clinical and clinical courses, making pre-clinical studies more practically relevant.

The pre-clinical course can be a daunting time for many students, with intensive lectures and examinations, while at the same time there is little or no contact with patients. Some students, nonetheless, glimpse the fascination of the biology of human existence through the morass of facts. However, in many medical schools, this period also brings the opportunity to spend an optional third year (automatic at Oxbridge), studying one subject in greater depth, be it biochemistry or the history of medicine.

The three year clinical course is an introduction to the hospital specialities and brings you into contact with patients. Suddenly students must wear shirts and ties. A white coat and a stethoscope give the appearance of already being a doctor, a distinction many patients are determined to accord you despite the large badge saying 'medical student'. There are still many facts to be learnt, but now in the context of patients' illnesses. Practical skills must also be acquired – the art of taking a history, examining patients, the taking of blood. As a teacher, my contact with students is in psychiatry. However, I see the psychological medicine which I try to teach as being integral to the whole of medical practice. Relating to patients is the most challenging, but also the most rewarding part of the clinical course. This challenge is most acute in talking to patients who are having to cope with death and disability, two subjects which are largely taboo in 'everyday' life. It is not at all easy for both doctors and medical students to remain within the confines of these taboos when confronted with 'difficult' situations.

As a medical student, you will be under many pressures – not least to assimilate huge amounts of information – but you will also have to face these 'difficult' situations in all areas of medicine, from surgery to psychiatry. It is important to be aware of patients' feelings in these situations as well as using scientific knowledge to diagnose treatable illnesses and to be aware of the interaction between these feelings and illness. In my own field, I have been involved in studying the effects the emotional atmosphere in the family has on the relapse of patients with schizophrenic illnesses.

My job: To give you some idea of what you might end up doing if you choose psychiatry as a speciality, this is what I do.

> I have a number of patients in my care on a ward. I also see patients referred to me as out-patients and also patients on medical, surgical and other wards who have psychiatric or emotional difficulties. It is in these settings that I do most teaching of medical students. One afternoon a week I work in a health centre seeing GP referrals, and another afternoon I see patients with their families. I also find some time to do research and write books – and articles.

HELPFUL READING: Peter Richards, *Learning Medicine* (BMA, 1990); Peter Richards, *Living Medicine* (BMA, 1990).

Metallurgy and Materials Science

Vernon John, City University

Every single thing which is made, be it a humble paper clip or a highly complex construction composed of many thousands of components such as an aircraft, is produced from one or more materials. It is of the utmost importance that a good understanding of the science and technology of all materials exists in order that the selected materials are used wisely, effectively and economically. So the role played in industrial society by metallurgists, materials scientists and technologists is crucial and the possession of a degree in one of these study areas can lead to a wide range of career possibilities including research, development, manufacturing, management and marketing in spheres as diverse as microelectronics, aerospace, off-shore engineering and general manufacturing industry.

In the nineteenth century metals emerged as the major materials for engineering construction and metallurgy became an academic discipline (the first professorial chair in metallurgy in Britain was established a little under 100 years ago). Nowadays the spectrum of engineering materials comprises a wide range of metals and alloys, a continually increasing number of polymeric materials, ceramics (including new industrial ceramics) and glasses, stone, concrete, bituminous materials, timbers, and very many composite materials. This led to the creation of degree courses in materials science and technology. The pace of development in both materials and processing techniques is rapid and exciting. Some examples of developments of the last decade include materials for the electronics industry with impurity levels measured in parts per billion; single crystal turbine blades for aero gas turbines; ceramics which may be formed to shape by processes similar to those used for polymer materials; polymers for high temperature service; and high performance composites for aerospace applications.

The subject matter of degree courses in metallurgy and materials science develops from the basic A-level knowledge of physics, chemistry and mathematics but then, in my opinion, these two applied sciences are much more interesting than studies in the natural sciences. When I was an undergraduate I transferred from natural sciences to a degree course in metallurgy for this reason and have never regretted the change.

Now to the question, what is metallurgy and materials science? I will deal first with metallurgy – the study of all aspects of metals, from their extraction from ores through to the efficient utilisation of metals and alloys in engineering hardware. As you can imagine, this is an enormous spectrum of activity and it is convenient to divide it into a number of areas.

Extraction metallurgy is concerned with the production and refining of prime metals from their ores. The metallurgist in this sector is also involved with mineral dressing and the preparation of ore concentrates in a form suitable for successful extraction operations. This part of the subject is orientated towards chemistry, but there is also overlap with geology and mining.

Physical metallurgy, a major branch of the subject, deals with the structure, constitution and properties of metals and alloys. It is firmly based on theoretical physics and includes atomic structure and the crystalline nature of metals. The study expanded enormously after the 1940s and knowledge of the physical factors which affect the properties of materials has been increased beyond measure through the use of all the tools of modern research.

Mechanical metallurgy is a term which describes the study of metal-forming, that is the ways in which a metal or alloy can be converted into a useful shape by means of processes such as casting, rolling, forging and machining. There are many aspects to be considered in this field, including the analysis of the forces involved in the processing machinery and equipment, the analysis of the plastic deformation of the materials being processed, the structural and property changes which occur in the metal being shaped, and the advantages and limitations of the various shaping techniques. There is overlap here with mathematics, computing and branches of engineering – notably mechanical and production engineering.

In addition to the areas mentioned above, courses in metallurgy also contain other important topics including failure mechanisms and failure prevention, corrosion, welding technology, test and evaluation methods and selection criteria.

Materials science and/or technology is a broader study area than metallurgy, dealing with the range of materials available to the engineer, metallic and non-metallic. Like the courses in metallurgy, these deal with the structures of materials and the development of properties, the production and fabrication of materials, and behaviour in various engineering service conditions.

To me the most interesting and useful section of the subject area is materials/engineering. In this area basic materials knowledge is integrated with engineering design and manufacturing engineering. As engineering designs and the materials available become more sophisticated, it becomes increasingly important to use materials both effectively and efficiently. The selection of a material to fit a particular engineering requirement and the choice of a manufacturing process are complex problems, and solving them offers a perpetual challenge to the materials engineer and designer.

There are wide differences between many of these courses, some being highly theoretical and mainly containing applied physics, while others are more orientated towards materials engineering. I am of the opinion that many teachers of metallurgy and materials have taken the wrong path in recent years by deleting basic engineering studies in order to make room for larger doses of the more esoteric aspects of metal physics. I can do no better here than to quote from a speech made in 1978 by the then president of the Institution of Metallurgists:

> . . . much of the sophisticated fundamental academic metallurgy included in courses today, though intellectually challenging, is of little use in the practical world of industry and has displaced subject matter which was taught in earlier years and which is practical and of value.

Before selecting a course you need to decide whether to practise as an engineer or to remain fairly firmly within the world of science. Under Engineering Council regulations, only those courses with a substantial engineering content and a balance between theory and applications will be fully accredited as leading to Chartered Engineer status; these accredited courses lead to BEng and MEng. Courses with a greater bias towards science are expected to continue at some universities; they lead to BSc but will not have Engineering Council accreditation.

Any young person with an aptitude for science subjects could find this study area interesting and stimulating. After completing a course with a technological bias, the young graduate should be able to progress into a career in engineering with wide and varied possibilities and, in common with all other members of the engineering family, will be dealing with people as much as with things.

HELPFUL READING: J E Gordon, *The New Science of Strong Materials, or Why You Don't Fall Through the Floor* (Harmondsworth: Penguin, 1968).

Microbiology

Professor John Postgate, Sussex University

If you study microbiology, you will encounter a fascinating world of invisible, or barely visible, creatures who together encompass all the processes of which terrestrial life is capable.

What does that mean, you ask? Well, although fish and people, for example, live in very different environments, their life processes are really very similar: they breathe oxygen, they eat organic food, they reproduce sexually, they consist of enormous numbers of rather similar cells, they live out their lives and then die. Even plants are really much the same fundamentally, except that they mostly do not eat organic food; instead they use solar energy to make their organic matter from carbon dioxide. What makes microbes so different, then? Be patient – first I must tell you a little about what microbes are.

They are creatures, almost always single cells, which can only be seen satisfactorily through a microscope. A few, such as amoebae and certain sulphur bacteria, are just discernible with the naked eye; most microbes are visible only under a microscope; the viruses are so small that even the most powerful optical microscope is inadequate and scientists have to use the electron microscope to see them. Some microbes are very simple plants – yeast, moulds and certain algae are examples. Others, like the amoeba, are tiny primitive animals. But the majority, the bacteria, are neither plants nor animals; they constitute a different 'Domain' of living things, called the Prokaryotes. (Actually, they comprise two such Domains, and no one is quite sure where viruses fit in, but these are details you would learn later.)

Microbes are everywhere: in the air, in soil, in water, on our skin and hair, in our mouths and intestines, on and in the food we eat. They change, often improve, our food; they make us vitamins inside ourselves; they can protect us from undesirable microbes. Yet most people are scarcely aware that they exist and, as 'germs', they have a bad press. Their unpopularity arises for a very simple reason: a few kinds of microbe can actually cause disease, a few can actually spoil food, can actually destroy valuable materials. And these are about the only times most people notice them at all.

In a microbiology course you will naturally learn about microbes in disease, about the bacteria which cause 'old fashioned' illnesses such as tuberculosis, scarlet fever, typhoid and so on, illnesses that have become rare today because of the effectiveness of modern drugs and antibiotics. You will learn how our natural immunity to disease works and how, when it breaks down, we become ill. You will be taught precisely how drugs and antibiotics work to help us recover. You will discover that, though a few awkward bacterial diseases persist, the viruses are today's major problem: infinitesimal fragments of barely living material which can cause illnesses ranging in severity from the common cold to AIDS. And you will learn how the war against such nasties is slowly being won. Smallpox has been eradicated using a combination of hygiene and inoculations; polio is in retreat; modern genetic engineering is providing new ways to attack other virus diseases. And sooner or later you will turn your mind from people and learn of microbes in animals and plant diseases. You will be told of, and see, the ways in which microbes can attack non-living material, corroding concrete and iron pipes, spoiling leather, wood, paper and even glass or plastics; you will learn of the troubles they can cause in oil technology, mining, machining and even film processing, not to mention the part they play in food spoilage and water pollution.

But you will also learn of the good, useful side of microbes. You might at first find mundane and boring their crucially important part in sewage treatment and waste disposal, but persevere; in a pullulating morass of sewage sludge flourishes a fantastic newly-recognised Domain of living things called the Archeabacteria – but I do not have space for further enlightenment here. You will be told how microbes, including archeabacteria, clean up our fouled lakes, rivers and beaches, even deal with exotic industrial effluents; how they decompose plant material, corpses and excreta to renew soil fertility. How they make the soil fertile: they add essential nitrogen to soil, help plants to get at phosphate, keep up the supply of sulphur compounds which plants and animals need. How, by recycling the detritus of plants and animals they constantly renew the supplies of oxygen, carbon dioxide, nitrates and even water on which all life on this planet depends. So vital are microbes to the lives of higher organisms that our own nutrition depends on them and some animals – sheep, cows and termites, for example – carry microcosms of specialised microbes around in their guts, to digest materials which the animals alone could not tackle. Plants, too, often have 'helper' microbes in their roots or leaves; you will learn that symbiosis with microbes is the 'name of the game' in biology – a simple fact which non-microbiologists too often forget. Then you will learn about biotechnology, how we exploit these beneficial aspects of microbes, sometimes in new and fascinating ways: scientists can splice alien genes, even genes from animals or plants, into the DNA of microbes, which can then be made to produce valuable materials such as human insulin; bacteria which attack plants can actually be recruited to add new and useful genes to plants, creating new varieties.

The impact of microbes on our well-being, on our society, on our economy and industry, are all exciting topics, and they ensure that microbiologists have a better chance than many of finding good jobs. But for me, a lifelong professional microbiologist, there has always been a deeper fascination in the way microbes do these things. This brings me back to my opening remarks. You and I need air to breathe, organic matter to eat, and we must keep ourselves wet and reasonably warm (inside at least) to survive. Then we live out our lives and die. Yet most bacteria are potentially immortal: they only die if some stress kills them (you can get into quite a philosophical tangle here if you have a taste for that sort of thing). More practically, many bacteria need no air; some breathe sulphates or nitrates, others split, not burn, organic food. Yet others transform iron compounds or sulphur. Some live in boiling water, others in sub-zero brines. Spores of certain bacteria survive drying for at least 300 years; other bacteria are so fragile they die seemingly as soon as you look at them.

The microbiologist soon learns how constrained is the biology of mankind and gains new insights into the potential of terrestrial life, hints of what life was like in the early days of this planet's history and, most exciting, intimations of how life might have developed elsewhere in the universe.

HELPFUL READING: John Postgate, *Microbes and Man* (CUP, 1992).

Modern Languages

Professor Dennis Ager, Aston University

Despite the title, no degree courses are limited to the study of a foreign language. They involve the student in learning one or more languages, **and** in covering a programme of literary studies or studies of linguistics, history, politics, social and economic structure of the relevant country. The reason for this is not that learning a language is thought to be too easy – far from it! – or not intellectually demanding; rather that learning a language at an advanced level is a matter also of learning to see the world the way foreigners see it, from within their own cultural and historical traditions. There is no point in being a graduate in Arabic if you don't understand Islam; and a graduate in German who has never heard of Goethe or Hitler is literally not able to understand what Germans are talking about. Ideally, of course, a graduate in languages would be an expert in the history of the relevant country, in its present-day political, social and economic problems and in its relations with other countries, in its cultural, literary, intellectual and artistic achievements; and be able to assess and compare these with a similar awareness of his own country. In practice, within a three- or four-year degree course some selection has to be made and a lot of ground left to the initiative of the individual student; individual degree courses will therefore look very different from each other.

It is possible to start a language course from scratch at most universities and colleges, with the exception of French or German (although in some cases you can now start from GCSE or *ab initio* even in these languages). Success in language learning comes easily to some; they seem to have an ear for the sound patterns of foreign tongues and are able to reproduce particular sounds accurately and to perceive and use the quirks of a foreign grammar very quickly. For those of us who are less fortunate some effort is involved, but since the French and the Japanese are also human beings this effort is almost certain to be crowned, eventually, with success. There are very few people who are unable to achieve something approaching perfection in the linguistic skills in a foreign language; the recipe is a mixture of high motivation, persistence, intelligence and practice. Modern learning aids – language laboratories, video tape recorders, computer and calculator dictionaries – can speed up the process, as can carefully designed teaching sequences; but there is no substitute for understanding that a language is a means of communication between human beings, and that the spoken language is, in this function, vastly more important than the written. In a degree course, however, one is often dealing with more written material than spoken; and the necessity for precision and often finicky accuracy which is a characteristic of some languages in their written form imposes a discipline which is not necessarily characteristic of the spoken language. It is possible, for example, to make oneself understood in general outline in speaking German without too much attention to the difference between 'n' and 'm' at the end of adjectives;

in the written form, however, confusion of this sort is rightly seen as an indication of ignorance.

At degree level mastery of the skills of speaking, writing, reading and listening to the foreign language itself is often accompanied by practice in such skills as translating and interpreting; on some courses also by summarising or abstracting, essay writing and paraphrasing and final examinations are often now constructed to test a range of skills. Departments vary in the degree of importance they accord to the language skills; some delegate all the language learning work to a language centre and even conduct all their own lecturing in English; others carry out all the work in the foreign language, using native speakers in addition to their own staff. Colloquial assistants – young native speakers appointed to strengthen the learning of the spoken language – used to be a normal feature of all language departments; sadly in the present round of economies some are not being replaced. Many courses now last for four years, with an integrated year abroad – an absolutely essential experience for the linguist – and perhaps also with vacation courses.

Until about 30 years ago the language was always studied in order to understand its literature; and many degree courses today still concentrate heavily on literary criticism. It is usual to provide general survey courses, showing the nature of the literary production of the relevant country over, say, the last 400 years, and in addition to ask students to examine an author, or sometimes even one noteworthy book, in considerable depth. Departments with literary interests may concentrate on one aspect or period, may offer courses in practical criticism, and may organise lectures by topic, period, genre or author. Few such departments would claim their courses are vocationally useful; some indeed pride themselves that literary courses are essentially and necessarily useless, and that their graduates received an education which will enable them to derive personal pleasure from reading, to understand and assess intellectually what they read, and to be aware of the artistic achievements, in literature, of the foreign society. Nonetheless, career opportunities for all linguists, from whatever type of course, are varied; usually better than most other arts subjects, and, of course, they open up the prospect of work abroad. Some departments now offer courses in the other arts – film and drama, occasionally fine arts and music – in addition to literature; and yet others provide background lectures in history or institutions to enable students to 'place' the texts they study.

Linguistics is often studied as another accompaniment to language; usually the linguistics of the relevant language often limited to a survey of the historical development of the present-day language, medieval forms of the language and phonetics. Other departments offer a detailed analysis of the contemporary language, while others may be covering dialects or sociolinguistics, analysing the different ways the language is used by different social groups.

Logically, as language is a means of communication between human beings, a linguist should be interested in the nature of the interactions between human beings in the **foreign society**. These interactions take place within the social framework and against the background of the political and economic structure of society, as well as depending on personal relationships, family traditions and the working environment. Some popular courses in modern languages, regrettably only a few, enable students to study these matters, not as background to literature, but as main subjects. Studies of political history can be carried out, as can studies of literature, in a void – divorced from language; for linguists it is important that there be a close integration of these studies with the language, so that, although the techniques of the political scientist or the sociologist are used to analyse and comprehend the facts of the situation in a different society, the aims and purposes of the analysis remain those of the linguist; that is, the study of interaction and the improvement of one's understanding of the foreign society and people. Some caution needs to be exercised in looking at publicity material describing such 'non-literary' courses however: many really contain only the smallest component, usually called 'Institutions' or 'Intellectual History', not devoted to literature. Serious study of political history, social structure and policy, or economic trends, is as intellectually demanding as any other area of study, and needs adequate study time and adequate staff.

With the new Europe in mind, courses in eg international business, international management are more widely offered. Some of these offer dual qualifications, some split the undergraduate year between two or more centres in more than one country. Most are intended to train the Euro-managers of tomorrow and are often offered by a network of collaborating language departments and business schools here and abroad.

In essence the study of modern languages is a study of people, whether as individuals or in the mass, in the very aspect of existence which marks out the human being as unique and special. So studies of the framework of society should include the historical dimension and should examine the political, social and economic structure against which contemporary problems arise. Again, students will follow courses of a general survey kind and will balance this with detailed study of a particular topic or problem. Degree programmes with this type of syllabus tend to be regarded by employers and others as more vocationally relevant, enabling graduates to use their linguistic knowledge effectively and providing a wider understanding of the foreign country than can be obtained from courses limited to literary topics alone.

Potential students should read prospectuses of individual departments with care. Universities differ in orientation and course content; there are also differences of course structure to be aware of. You can study one language or two. It is often possible to study one language plus another subject, not a language – French plus civil engineering, German plus architecture – with no necessary link between the two subjects. A particularly popular combination is a language plus business studies or economics. Sometimes a link is made (eg in a Russian and sociology degree, the sociology is taught in Russian, and the Russian is the Russian of sociology); the titles vary considerably, as do the proportions of language-related work. Finally, languages often find a place within degrees in other subjects: historians find a knowledge of one or more invaluable, but their requirement is for reading ability; engineers, too, need languages but their prime need is for just enough French or Russian to get the gist of specialist reports plus enough spoken foreign language to understand the main point of a conversation or technical presentation. European studies degrees usually fall within this type, requiring only sufficient knowledge of French or German as will enable students to cope with original texts – the main interest is usually in politics or sociology or history.

Music

Professor Brian Trowell, Oxford University

We all know what an art is: a means of original creation and self-expression in some particular medium. In the case of a performing art such as music, we must add that it is a means of imaginative re-creation, of practical interpretation. The long training of the executant reminds us of an earlier meaning of 'art' in the sense that has given us the word 'artisan': a body of specialised practical training in the 'mystery' of a craft which was taught and regulated by a medieval trade union, a guild such as the shoemakers or goldsmiths. From the same period comes the usage preserved by our universities, in which an art was a body of higher learning and theoretical speculation, not in the modern sense of a liberal art or humane letters, but in the more general sense of a science, an organised complex of knowledge. Music, with its complexities of measurement and proportion, was then regarded (as in some respects it still may be) as an art allied to mathematics: geometry was mathematics made visible, music was mathematics made audible, and astronomy was mathematics in movement; all four were known as the 'quadrivium'. Today – though music has kept its mathematical associations and even increased them in the study of acoustics, temperament, electronic and computer applications, and complex notation – we have come to view music as a liberal or humane arts subject in the university curriculum. That is because music is an expressive art in the modern sense: its history and theory need to be studied as manifestations of what it was like to live, think and feel in cultures and periods different from our own, just as with any other art. We also need to re-interpret the old music that still forms the basis of our current repertory, from Purcell to Webern, to attempt the revival of forgotten or unexplored music and edit it for modern performance; and, besides restoring to the public its musical patrimony, we also have the duty of helping to elucidate and smooth away the difficulties that many modern composers face in getting their music performed and understood in a period of bewildering change. That involves us in the development of the theory of music and in musical analysis, though this branch of enquiry also enjoys a long history which must be studied in relation to the music of the past. As if that were not enough, we must also try to relate our studies of Western European music to our knowledge of non-Western music. Apart from the study of folk-music, which reminds us, amongst other things, that our horn or flute belongs to a family that is worldwide, we need to realise that there are other classical traditions of theory, aesthetics and notation in other lands, some of them older than our own.

Not all departments of music do all these things, but I have said enough to show some of the ramifications of the study of music in a university. Universities are primarily concerned with knowledge, with the interpretation of existing knowledge and the creation of new. One needs all kinds of knowledge to pursue the study of music in this way, from languages and 'straight' history to electronics and anatomy, and that is why the 'universitas' was invented, as a repository of universal learning. A professor or lecturer in music is pledged to advance musical learning, and a department of music will also contain a few – sometimes many – postgraduates, who are working to advance the boundaries of knowledge by research. In the close collegiate life of a university campus, and particularly in the intimacy of a music department with its collaborative music-making, this attitude of excitement over the acquisition of new knowledge inevitably spreads to the undergraduate members as well.

But music is a performing art as well as an arts subject. Its study at once is a science, an art in the modern sense, and a craft. That is not generally the case with arts subjects. Very few university English departments in this country teach 'creative writing': their approach is critical, historical, analytical. Historians do not go out of their universities and make history. (Perhaps they should, you may say: they seem to in France.) Yet music departments contain composers, and all music students have to be able to perform to a certain level, and some are good enough to specialise in performance, as in composition. That means that some parts of a university music curriculum overlap with the kind of studies taught at a high professional level by the music colleges, who in some cases, these days, number among their teachers historians and theoreticians of real distinction. The aspiring student, who may know very little about either type of musical education and may not be able to seek advice from recent graduates of both kinds of institution, can find it very hard to make the right decision.

The main emphases in the attitudes of music college and university department are clear enough. Common sense will tell the would-be professional performer (particularly the string-player) that he or she will form a more realistic view of future possibilities by constant comparison with fellow-students of high excellence. By the age of eighteen, though, an outstanding youngster may already have formed such a view, and indeed studied at a music college. Someone entering university with a very secure technique will not lose it (except through his or her own fault, playing in every concert in sight without practising). In a university in or near a large city with a college of music, a student may study with the same teachers that he or she would have met with by applying to the conservatory in the first place. For singers, it can be a positive advantage not to concentrate on vocal technique seriously at too early an age; many have profited by improving their musical skills first at a university and then going on to a college of music. Young conductors may gain invaluable experience by working with university groups. Performers in general get many more chances to perform in public on a university campus than they will at a music college – particularly pianists. At many universities there are choral, instrumental and organ scholarships which can help a little in these days of reduced grants. Those interested in the performance of early music, or of very new music (with expensive electronic facilities) may be much better served in a university; composers will find themselves working in a collegiate society which reflects the variety of interests and human types of the outside world much more widely than a monotechnical music college.

Against all this must be set the fact that a university course in England or Wales is normally of only three years, and that will contain a good deal of non-practical academic study which will not always allow adequate time for practice. In addition, there are wide variations from department to department in the provision for practical study (which you may have to pay for) and indeed for all aspects of the curriculum. Your guarantee in all this is the entrance interview, at which you should ask searching questions after careful prior study of any brochures or syllabus-descriptions that are sent to you. At this time of flux and reductions in university funding, you should also ask about the institution's plans for its music department over the next five years. You should also enquire about the nature of individual tutorial provision; do you have a personal tutor for everything, or can you count on expert tutorial advice for each separate subject?

If you wish to go first to a university and later to a music college, you should consider the matter of grants unusually carefully. If you wish to proceed to postgraduate study at a university, remember that to receive a British Academy studentship you will need a degree, not a diploma, though the two are regarded as equal in other professional respects. If you intend to enter the honourable, vitally important and potentially very rewarding career of school music-teaching, you would (if you took the university route) receive a mandatory year's grant for a Postgraduate Certificate of Education to cover the fourth year after a BMus. This route would normally allow you rather more study of the subject that you are going to teach, as opposed to ancillary matter connected with educational theory, than you would get in a department of education (good though some are); in school music, it is the ability to perform and direct that inspires enthusiasm and emulation . . .

Above all, if you are attracted by the university path, you should ask yourself whether, in addition to practical competence, you have a real intellectual interest in knowledge about music, and indeed about any of the many other subjects that you may take alongside music in a combined studies degree or as a subsidiary. These are not normally available in a music college. Try to learn another language on your way through the course, even if informally. Not only does so much great vocal music come with foreign words attached, but you will be able to read what foreign composers and scholars have written about music in their own authentic tone of voice.

Near Eastern and Islamic Studies

Professor H T Norris, SOAS

It is reported that T E Lawrence once remarked that a year spent in the Near East was worth at least ten years spent anywhere else. His adventures took place in Arabia which, viewed retrospectively, was a land of romance and nostalgia. Prior to the First World War, and even to the end of the 1960s in some parts of Southern Arabia, the Middle East and the Muslim World in Africa and in Southern and Eastern Asia were very much the habitat of Colonial Service adventurers, of desert explorers, both men and women, and pith-helmeted archaeologists and anthropologists. Many spectacled Orientalists studied and taught in closeted colleges, compiling lexicons and attempting poetic translations of Arabic, Persian and Turkish masterpieces. Arabic and Islamic Studies, in fact, have been respected academic disciplines in this country for many generations, the former since the seventeenth century.

Today our horizons are very different. Ours is the age of hostage taking, the Palestinian struggle, Salman Rushdie's *Satanic Verses*, the revival of fundamentalist Islam in Iran and in many parts of the Orient and Africa in protest against the West and its materialist values. Tourism has opened the whole Arab World to sightseers. The Alhambra is a visited building, Petra and Wadi Rumm in Jordan so commonplace a scenic backcloth, and the artistry of the Arab lute (*al-ud*) or the Algerian protest music group 'Rai' so familiar a sound on disc, that one is liable to forget how very recent was the rediscovery of the historical sites of the Arab world or their archaeological exploration.

All this is true, but whatever a student's reason for selecting Arabic, whether it be for a career in banking or in law or a fascination in the history and art of the Middle East, he or she will need to know something of the languages of Islam, especially Arabic. The latter is taught as a spoken language in many language schools and in courses on tapes. Nonetheless, in order to master the written language, whether medieval classical or modern literary Arabic, most students will need to devote three to four years of study to it at a university. The complexities of Arabic grammar, officially classical Arabic, are considerable and it takes time to explore the riches of Islamic literature, the ancient poets, the Koran, the mystical flights of the *Sufis*, not to speak of recent literature; Egyptian novels, Palestinian plays from the occupied territories, short stories from Tunisia, the exiled poets in Latin America and contemporary Arabic journalism. Ideally, a student needs to spend up to a year abroad to become fluent in a dialect, often very different from literary Arabic, whether in Tunisia, in Egypt, in Jordan or in the Gulf.

A student is able to study all, or most, of the subjects mentioned above at one or other of the universities where Arabic and Islamic Studies are taught in this country. He or she is advised to peruse the handbooks and, if the need arises, to ask for a detailed syllabus of the course. Enquiries should be made as to how the course is taught and when it is examined; whether by a single subject degree, by tripos or by course units, and whether Arabic and Islamic Studies might be combined with other Oriental languages or with other disciplines. At London University (SOAS), for example, Arabic is a four-year degree course with a choice of up to fourteen course units. It is common to combine it with politics, economics, law or another Oriental or African language. After a first year intensive study of modern literary Arabic, which, incidentally, can also be examined after one year to qualify, in part, for a Certificate in Arabic, a student can to some extent choose his or her subjects. At most British universities, now, where Arabic is taught, the majority of students who combine the language with a discipline (combined languages sometimes precludes it) will want to spend their second year in Egypt (for example the University of Alexandria) where there are now well organised courses and the cost of study there is paid by the local education authority if the student qualifies for a grant. It is an essential part of the degree course.

During the third and fourth years of study the subjects which a student may select range from the Arabic novel and contemporary poetry, to Islamic law, an Arabic dialect, Hispano-Arabic Literature, popular Arabic literature, Arab musicology, and the history and culture of the Islamic Middle East.

Apart from social sciences or arts subjects, Arabic can be combined at SOAS with Hebrew, Turkish, Berber and Hausa, and other combinations are possible. Most universities where Arabic is taught, have excellent libraries of lexicons, encyclopedias and language tapes, and there are normally facilities for an intensive study of the spoken language, particularly Egyptian and Gulf dialects.

An Arabic degree is a useful qualification. However, a student should be warned that the language is difficult and in order to understand it and use it correctly it is essential to combine it with a study of Islam. It is a mistake to think that Islam can be grasped without some knowledge of Arabic. The Koran needs to be read in Arabic. A translation is only a reflection of its poetry and its message. An Arabic student will need to be strongly motivated, though Arabic literature and Islamic culture have rich rewards to offer in compensation for much hard study. Students find it an adventure and it appeals to a variety of temperaments. Therefore expect every type of student, British or non-British, to be your boon companion when the wine cup of the Islamic East is passed to you in order to taste its nectar!

HELPFUL READING: *Islamic Surveys* (Edinburgh University Paperbacks); *The Cambridge History of Islam* (CUP); *The Arab Background Series* (Longman and Librairie du Liban); A J Arberry, *British Orientalists* (London, 1943) and *The Koran Interpreted* (Oxford, 1964); M Brett and W Forman, *The Moors* (Orbis, 1980); Peter B Clarke, *West Africa and Islam* (E Arnold, 1982); Michael Cook, *Muhammad* (Oxford, 1983); Leila Ahmad, *Edward W Lane* (Longman, 1978); B Lewis, *The Arabs in History* (Hutchinson University Library, 1950); L H Melikian, *Jassim, a Study of the Psychosocial Development of a Young Man in Qatar* (Longman, 1979); Dorothee Metlitzki, *The Matter of Araby in Medieval England* (Yale, 1977); Sari J Nasir, *The Arabs and the English* (Longman, 1979); R Nicholson,

A Literary History of the Arabs (Cambridge University Press, 1930); W Thesiger, *Arabian Sands* (Longman, 1959); J O Voll, *Islam, Continuity and Chance in the Modern World* (Westview and Longman, 1982); E L Ranelagh, *The Past We Share* (Quartet Books, 1979).

Nursing Studies

Professor Penny Prophit, formerly of Edinburgh University

At some time in life, every human being requires intelligent, kind, compassionate and competent care. It may come as a surprise to some that universities and colleges provide professional education in nursing, but on reflection it is obvious. This is especially true if you consider yourself a potential recipient of care, for nurses should gain their knowledge from a broad and liberal education, and from the level of competence in the discipline which such an education develops. Nurses are with patients in their most vulnerable moments, and the challenges of nursing are human challenges, demanding much of the nurse but also giving much. A degree course helps to prepare whole people to care for whole people, not just physically but also emotionally. In fact, nursing involves head, heart and hands. Nurses are best placed to be advocates for the patient, to interpret messages from other disciplines, and to assist the patient to cope with and find meanings in suffering and illness. Nursing is truly more than offering a pair of hands and feet: nursing is concerned with the human response to illness and with helping people to help themselves. As Florence Nightingale put it, 'Nurse the patient, not the disease'!

Nursing is an exciting and demanding profession: it is not a career choice for the fainthearted. Nurses are to be found not only in hospitals, but also in the community and in situations which focus on the promotion of better health. As the health care system increases in complexity and scope, and as knowledge and technology advance, the responsibilities of the nurse who professes a service to others will continue to expand and diversify. Degree programmes in nursing vary in emphasis and provide a vast array of opportunities, from working with sick children suffering from an illness such as cancer, to the fast-moving pace of accidents and emergency settings. There is the joy of helping at the birth of a baby, as well as the experience of sorrow associated with pain, suffering and death. In a very real sense, nursing is a preparation for living and provides wonderful opportunities for learning about life and oneself.

In their work nurses make use of knowledge from many areas. In some spheres, biological insights play a major role and in others, social and psychological perspectives are very important and more appropriate. Nurses work in a multidisciplinary team. They need all the skills involved in listening, communicating and comforting those who are often deeply troubled. They also need a thorough understanding of the problems faced by the handicapped and chronically ill, and of the stress endured by families trying to cope with sufferers in the community. How the sick, the disabled and people at risk cope with adversity depends to a large extent on the society in which they live. Ethnic and social differences between patients, and between patients and nurses, must be acknowledged and understood. The social sciences foster such understanding and a knowledge of theology and philosophy helps with the ethical and moral challenges often encountered in health care situations.

Though the UK was rather later than the USA and many of the developing countries in realising the need for degree level study, it is well ahead of its European partners. There are now numerous degree courses available. They came into being gradually and each new course is partially patterned on having an emphasis on the biological and natural sciences or on the social sciences. It is important to explore the focus of the various programmes offered. In some, nursing is situated in faculties of medicine or of social sciences. In others, nursing may be the major component in a social science degree. Yet others have sandwich courses with BSc or BA joint honours degrees, for example nursing with economics or sociology. There is no general agreement on the school subjects for entry; for some courses science subjects are important while others favour a much broader educational background, believing that there are advantages in having students whose interests and enthusiasms differ widely and whose supporting studies span a wide range of disciplines. Any talent, gift or strength a nurse possesses will be of benefit to patients.

It is said that we have the sick with us always. There are many career opportunities in nursing. They are particularly open to graduates, as evidence shows that nurses qualifying from degree programmes are highly proficient and competent clinical practitioners who have much to offer and obtain greater satisfaction in nursing. Both men and women enjoy the varied career opportunities nursing has to offer, not only in direct practice, but also in management and research opportunities.

International opportunities abound in nursing, whether in highly advanced technological settings, or by mission work in developing countries. An increasing number of nursing graduates obtain research degrees and take new masters degree courses.

The time is right, the opportunities are there; the challenges are for the person who wants to grow, to give, to care. How about you?

Pharmacology
Dr Robin Hoult, King's College London

Pharmacology concerns the uses of drugs and the ways in which they and other biologically active chemicals affect the body. Particular emphasis is on the molecular mechanisms by which these chemicals alter biological processes at the cell and tissue level. Pharmacology is highly relevant to everyday life, not only because of the important therapeutic uses of drugs but also because of issues such as drug misuse and addiction and is closely related to toxicology. Pharmacology is also exciting because research is proceeding at an ever-increasing pace, bringing with it the development of powerful new drugs as well as new insights into the molecular mechanism of the body's physiological functions.

Pharmacology is generally only offered as a degree subject in universities which have schools of medicine or pharmacy. Entry requirements are similar as for pharmacy (see below), although two good grades including chemistry may be sufficient for certain courses.

For the study of pharmacology it is necessary to have a good understanding of the functions and integration of living systems, particularly in mammals (physiology), and of the molecular basis of these systems (biochemistry and cell biology) because only with this fundamental knowledge can we begin to understand how drugs work and their applications in therapeutics. Thus, in the first year of most pharmacology degree courses it is usual to study biochemistry and physiology as well as some or all of the following: cell and molecular biology, organic chemistry, physical chemistry, statistics and design of experiments.

Chemistry is relevant to pharmacology for two main reasons. The first is that the principles of physical chemistry apply to the chemical systems of the body and to the molecular functions of cells, and the second is that the pharmacologist considers the actions of chemicals and drugs on body functions in terms of chemical interactions with specific receptor sites on tissues. Also, of course, it is the organic chemist who synthesises new substances (the potential new drug or medicine) which are later investigated by the pharmacologist.

Like all natural and medical sciences, pharmacology is above all an experimental subject – that is, most of our knowledge about drug action is based on careful measurement of effects of chemicals upon animals or man.

Much of this work, however, involves testing drugs on isolated tissues, organs or cell systems prepared from animals, rather than upon the whole animal itself. This means that a long time is spent in the laboratory learning experimental methods. A common problem is that even the simplest experiments often show variable results, usually due to the expected biological variation between animals, although sometimes it happens because of inexperience or error. As a result experiments may have to be performed many times to be sure of the real result and a good knowledge of statistics and experimental design is important for their interpretation.

The second and third years are generally spent on courses in specialised aspects of pharmacology and advanced courses in related subjects or disciplines. Many are concerned with specific categories of drugs in terms of their site of action in the body (eg chemotherapy of infectious and parasitic diseases; cardiovascular, renal or endocrine or central nervous system pharmacology; drugs affecting the blood, nervous, muscular or reproductive systems). Others cover the ways in which drugs work (eg drug receptors and membrane structure – these topics illustrate the close links between pharmacology and biochemistry; drug addiction; administration and metabolism of drugs; experimental techniques for analysis of drug action; interaction of drugs with nerves, hormones, etc). Thus there are two different approaches to the study of pharmacology – the systematic one, which concerns the application of drugs to organ systems and disease treatment, and the analytical one, which is concerned with the way in which drugs work at the molecular level.

In some courses eg King's College, London, students have the opportunity of an extra-mural year, working in an industrial or research laboratory, as part of a specialised research team. This option is offered between the second and third years, and is an exciting and useful preparation for the final year's study.

Many pharmacology graduates enter the pharmaceutical industry straight away as a BSc honours degree is a good starting point for several positions such as marketing, medical information and product registration (none of which involve laboratory work), as well as for pharmaceutical research. Other graduates continue their studies and obtain higher degrees, either by taking specialised MSc courses which offer specific career opportunities or by carrying out supervised research for a PhD degree (sometimes this can be done whilst employed in the pharmaceutical industry). PhD graduates usually continue to do research as a career, either in universities, hospitals, industry or in the scientific civil service (these options are also open to BSc graduates). Because of the multi-disciplinary nature of the subject, pharmacologists often carry out research in conjunction with scientists from other disciplines, such as biochemists, toxicologists, immunologists and molecular biologists.

HELPFUL READING: *Careers in Pharmacology* (London: British Pharmacological Society, 1989, available from the Society's secretariat, BPS Office, The Medical College, Charterhouse Square, London EC1M 6BQ).

Pharmacy

Dr Robin Hoult, King's College London

A definition of pharmacy which gives a good general idea of what undergraduate pharmacy courses are about is 'the application of physics, chemistry and biology to the study of medicinal products'. In other words pharmacy is concerned with every aspect of substances used to prevent or treat disease in humans and animals. Thus the pharmacist must be an expert in the production and quality-control of a wide range of both natural and synthetic substances and also in their application and dispensing for therapeutic purposes. This explains why a pharmacy degree involves the study of many subjects – and why stringent requirements have to be satisfied before anyone is allowed to practise as a pharmacist. In fact one year's practical training in a registered pharmacy is necessary before a pharmacist can register and practise on his own. This is taken either after graduation from a three-year course or is sandwiched into the degree course making a four-year course.

Pharmacy courses are offered by several universities, often ones with medical schools attached since some of the subjects which make up pharmacy are also common to medicine. Traditionally there is a quartet of sciences which form the basis of pharmacy and which are studied in the first two years of a pharmacy degree course. They are pharmaceutical chemistry, pharmacology, pharmaceutics and pharmacognosy. Pharmaceutical chemistry is concerned with the synthesis, properties and analysis of substances used in medicine, and its study may include compulsory foundation courses in chemistry and possibly physical sciences.

Pharmacology is the study of the effects and mode of action of chemicals which modify the functions of the living organism, particularly those which are used in the treatment of disease. A working knowledge of physiology, biochemistry and cell biology is necessary for its study and introductory courses in these subjects are generally offered in the first two years. The subject can also be studied independently (see above).

Pharmaceutics occupies a principal place in pharmacy courses and involves detailed study of the properties, formulation, preparation and presentation of medicinal drugs. Microbiology usually figures as a component of pharmaceutics, firstly because of the need to avoid inadvertent contamination of medicines with bacteria and fungi, and secondly because of the importance of disinfectants, vaccines, immunisations and antibiotics in medicinal practice.

Pharmacognosy, the final member of the quartet of sciences, is the study of natural products used in medicine or as sources of drugs. This is still a highly relevant subject even though most drugs are now synthesised rather than obtained from plant or animal sources. Other subjects on the pharmacy degree syllabus include medicinal chemistry, pharmaceutical engineering science, the law and practice of pharmacy, experimental pharmacology, biopharmacy (the principles affecting the absorption and fate of drugs in the body), computer science, forensic pharmacy, together with management and dispensing practice.

By the third year, courses usually become specialised and the student may undertake extended research or practical projects under supervision. Naturally, each institution has its own specialities and its own teaching style and atmosphere. One emerging speciality is clinical pharmacy, involving direct contact with hospital practice. However, lectures and practicals usually form the most important component of the formal instruction, generally supplemented by tutorials, directed reading and studies, and sometimes by self-instructional teaching materials.

For entry, three good A-levels are required from biology, chemistry, mathematics and physics. Students without biology at A-level must have a GCSE pass. Chemistry is very important both because of its relevance and because it is thought a good indicator of a student's likely performance; a good grade at A-level is usually obligatory.

Most of us think of a pharmacist as the person who is responsible for the dispensing of medicines in a chemist's shop (and who can give specialist advice about the choice of products for the treatment of minor illnesses), and indeed many students study pharmacy with this career specifically in mind. However, there are plenty of other career options either in hospital pharmacies or in industry (eg in the research and development of new drugs and in their production and marketing) or else in the academic field in either research or teaching.

HELPFUL READING: *Pharmacy: Effective Caring* (London: Royal Pharmaceutical Society, 1992, available from the Royal Pharmaceutical Society of Great Britain, 1 Lambeth High Street, London SE1 5JN).

Philosophy

Professor Antony Flew, Reading University

Philosophy is not a mainstream A-level subject. So if you decide to do degree work in it you and all the rest of your class will be, as near as makes precious little matter, starting level. But, just because there isn't anyone either teaching or learning the subject in your school, you may well not know what philosophy would involve. Or else, much worse, you may think you do know and be wrong.

No doubt you will have seen series or articles or TV interviews in which people in the eyes of the media were invited to sound off about their philosophies of life. The word 'philosophy' there was being used in a perfectly respectable sense. But it was a sense only rather distantly and rather indirectly related to that in which the word is construed when we speak of philosophy as a discipline pursued in universities and polytechnics.

It is difficult to explain to people who have never done any what, in this present sense, philosophy is. (Would you care to try to explain what mathematics would involve to someone who had been to a school in which no one had learnt any at all?) This difficulty is one of several good reasons why anyone considering this as a degree subject is well advised to try for one of the institutions – Keele, for instance, or Reading – giving students opportunities of sampling one or two new things before they have finally to commit themselves on what subject or subjects they will read for honours.

The same difficulty led one most distinguished and well-loved Cambridge professor, G E Moore, always to begin his replies to the question, 'What is philosophy?' by pointing towards his bookshelves: 'It is what all those are about.' So let me too start by saying that philosophy is the main subject of most of the writings of Plato; of Aristotle's *Metaphysics* and *Nicomachean Ethics*; of large parts of the works of St Thomas Aquinas, Duns Scotus and William of Ockham; of the *Discourse* and *Meditations* of Descartes; of Berkeley's *Three Dialogues* and *Principles of Human Knowledge*; of Hume's *Inquiry concerning Human Understanding*; of Kant's *Critique of Pure Reason*; and finally, in our own century, of Moore's own books, of Bertrand Russell's *Our Knowledge of the External World* and *Mysticism and Logic*, and of Wittgenstein's *Tractatus Logico-Philosophicus*.

If you do decide to do philosophy you will certainly be introduced to many of these classics. However, unless and until you have been thus properly introduced, you had perhaps best stick to books written fairly recently, and books written as introductions. Try, for instance, Bertrand Russell *The Problems of Philosophy* (first published 1912 but since 1967 available as an OUP paperback); and/or either Anthony O'Hear *What Philosophy Is* or Brenda Almond *The Philosophical Quest* (first published, respectively, 1985 and 1988, and both available from Penguin Books). And, whatever you do, don't set out for an interview without readying yourself to say something lively about some philosophy book which you have recently worked through. They probably want to sign you up. But you do need to give them some help!

You will not find many facts in any philosophy book, and those which you do find will be mainly facts about what particular philosophers have said. What you should find is arguments, and the more the better. So one good test for telling whether you are a person who could become fascinated by philosophy is to ask yourself whether you care about the validity or invalidity of arguments, and the sufficiency or insufficiency of evidence offered, as well as about the truth or falsity of conclusions reached, and the acceptability or otherwise of cases presented. If you do not, then certainly philosophy is not for you.

Consider, for example, the much disputed issues of 'freewill or predestination' and 'freewill or determinism'. The strictly philosophical questions here are not the questions of theological or scientific fact. They are not, that is, the questions: whether on the first day of creation God wrote what the last day of reckoning shall read; nor whether everything that happens, including everything which people do, could on the basis of a full knowledge of the laws of nature and the past condition of the whole universe, in principle be predicted. They are, rather, the questions: whether the idea of a creator God – not only all foreseeing, but also the sustaining cause of our every action and our very existence – is logically compatible with the ideas of human responsibility and human choice; and whether the sciences, and in particular the human sciences, logically presuppose or imply some form of determinism. If so, is this a sort of determinism logically compatible with our everyday talk and our everyday assumptions about human choice and action?

The philosophical questions about freewill and determinism and predestination, therefore, like other philosophical questions, though they may arise out of suggestions or discoveries about what is as a matter of fact the case, are themselves not questions of this factual sort, but questions about what does or does not follow from what, and what is or is not logically incompatible with what else. It is this fact which makes philosophy the outstandingly excellent pure mental training. Certainly it is not career-linked in the way in which law, say, and medicine both are. Certainly too it is not, unlike the usual school subjects, something which graduates can hope to earn their livings by teaching. But when you are competing for any of the other jobs done by arts graduates there is no call whatever to be shy about admitting that you read philosophy. Philosophy is, and is by many known to be, an incomparable exercise in intellectual gymnastics – just the right preparation for those intending to get to the top in either one of the new information industries or in some more ancient kind of administration.

If you are still worried either about making yourself unemployable or about broaching a quite unfamiliar subject, then you could compromise. What about a joint honours degree in which you combine your new way-out, other-worldly interest in philosophy with the study of some safe, familiar, bread-and-butter subject?

Physics

Dr P E Hodgson, Oxford University

I've always been interested by the idea that all the things of everyday life, including our own bodies, are made up of billions of tiny particles. I resolved to find out all I could about them and now, many years later, I'm more interested than ever.

Naturally physics was my favourite subject at school, though mathematics was a close second. It was so immensely satisfying to have clear-cut problems that could be solved precisely and definitely by applying general principles and theorems of great power. However one worked out the problem, the answer was always the same – so different from other areas of study where vague discussions went round and round and any rules were notable mainly for their exceptions.

Physics is written in the language of mathematics, so an easy familiarity with algebraic equations, vectors, trigonometry and the calculus is a basic requirement. Once this language is mastered, we see that it is an elegant and powerful way of saying difficult things about the world in a very simple way. One equation can sum up the behaviour of a vast range of phenomena, and from it we can easily calculate what will happen in many different circumstances. Mathematical studies thus form an essential basis and companion to the physics course. If you study physics at university you will probably spend about half your first year studying mathematics, and later on you will be using it continually.

A university physics course is not a soft option for the flabby-minded. It is tough, rigorous and demanding, and can easily provide a worthwhile challenge to the most flexible and energetic minds. Parts of it, mainly at the beginning, involve some rather routine learning, but it becomes more and more interesting as time goes on.

Most of the second year is spent on classical physics, and you have the chance of exploring Newton's classical mechanics in some detail. You will see how to calculate the paths of the planets and the orbits of satellites and projectiles. The kinetic theory of gases shows how the same laws apply to the realm of the very small, and by considering the collisions of a swarm of atoms we can understand the ways gases behave. Then we see how electricity and magnetism are unified by Maxwell's equations, and how a study of the frequencies of spectral lines gives us a glimpse into the structure of the atom itself. Perhaps at this stage we begin some elementary quantum mechanics and begin to wrestle with the unfamiliar ideas of wave packets and transition probabilities, and also start to study Einstein's relativity.

The third year is more interesting still. Modern physics, based on the pioneering work of Einstein and Planck, is explored in depth. We see how the ideas hammered out in the 1920s by Sommerfeld and Bohr, Dirac and Pauli provide a sound basis of understanding of the structure of atoms. A course in solid-state physics shows how, at least in principle, we can calculate the properties of all materials from what we know about their constituent atoms and the way they are bound together. Delving deeper, we learn how Rutherford discovered the nucleus of the atom and began to probe its structure. In the 1930s the unstable mesons were discovered and since then a whole host of elementary particles. We enter the subnuclear world in all its fascinating complexity. In the last decade our understanding has grown apace, and now we see that the particles we called elementary are themselves built up of even more elusive particles called quarks. Many puzzles remain, and the search goes on.

All too soon the course is over, and then what? I was lucky and was able to stay on and start research into the particles of the cosmic radiation. I climbed mountains in Switzerland and studied the way the nuclei broke up when they were hit by cosmic ray particles. Later on I made theoretical studies of nuclear reactions and nuclear structure, and I am still doing this now. I also give lectures and tutorials to the physics students at Oxford and try to pass on to them some of the interest and excitement of physics. The more I learn the more I marvel at the complexity and yet underlying simplicity of the world.

Of course, not everyone is able to stay on after the degree. Most physicists leave the university and they enter a wide variety of occupations where they can use their knowledge of physics. Some teach physics in schools. Others go into industry and help to make manufacturing processes as efficient as possible, and also initiate new processes and even whole industries such as the atomic energy and computer industries. Others range further afield. One of my students is now a psychologist, another a lawyer, another a priest, and certainly the habits of exact thinking learnt in physics are of enduring value to them. There are also branches of physics that may not receive much mention in the university course that yet can provide satisfying careers both in the university and outside, such as geophysics (concerned with the structure of the earth), astrophysics (the structure of the stars and galaxies) and atmospheric physics (the composition of the atmosphere and the weather).

Increasingly after graduation, with experience of life, one sees how profoundly physics has moulded our whole society. What would our lives be like without electricity, or television, or computers, to take a few examples? With this realisation comes a feeling of responsibility for seeing that as far as possible science is used for our good. We are aware of the damage that can be done by misapplied science, and this can only be prevented if people understand the potentialities of science. This in turn depends on scientists taking time off from their scientific work and explaining it in simple language.

At a deeper level we see that science raises, often in an acute form, all those problems about freedom and authority, power and responsibility, the individual and the state that we often discussed so inconclusively in our schooldays. As physicists we isolate one aspect of reality, mainly the quantitatively measurable, and find that it can be put in order. The much greater problems of life do not admit of such easy solutions. We also come to learn how science developed as an integral part of our Christian culture and realise that, from its first beginnings to the dominant position it occupies today, science is an organic part of the historical development of mankind.

So do not think that science, and particularly physics, is a dry, remote activity, fit only for desiccated robots who care nothing about other people. It is on the contrary a vital strand of our very humanity and if you have the essential ability and interest you can contribute more to your fellow man through the study of physics than in any other way.

HELPFUL READING: R P Feynmann, *Lectures on Physics* (Reading, Massachusetts and London: Addison-Wesley, 1963); S L Jaki, *The Relevance of Physics* (University of Chicago Press, 1970).

Physiology

Dr D J Begley, King's College London

> *General physiology is the basic biological science toward which all others converge. Its problem is to determine the elementary conditions of vital phenomena.*
>
> (Claude Bernard, *An Introduction to the Study of Experimental Medicine*, 1865)

Physiology is undoubtedly the most open-ended of the biological sciences and for this reason is also probably the most challenging. A physiologist is constantly attempting to explain how organisms work by a careful and critical analysis of well planned research and experiment. He can work at any number of levels within the organisation of a species. At the cellular level he can study how cells function or move, or how the nervous impulse is transmitted and how messages are received and interpreted by the cell. Alternatively he may focus on individual organs or tissues of the body (eg the brain or the liver) or on complete systems (eg the nervous or endocrine), studying how they control and regulate function. Or his interest can be in how several organs and systems interact (eg to maintain the constancy of the composition of the blood) or in the important area of developmental physiology (ie how the fertilised egg interprets and unfolds its genetic potential and develops into the mature adult). Or he may study the organism as a whole and its responses to external stimuli and environmental change.

In recent years, interest has certainly been concentrated on cellular physiology as powerful new research tools have increasingly miniaturised the scales at which living systems can be experimentally manipulated. Of course, there is still much to be discovered in other areas but studies into these must be built on firm foundations at cellular levels. Recent advances in cellular physiology have revolutionised the ways in which we examine and interpret higher function (eg in the working of the brain).

Because physiology forms the meeting point for a number of biological sciences, the physiologist utilises experimental methods and tools derived from related disciplines – for example the electron microscope from anatomy, radioactively labelled molecules from biochemistry, x-ray analysis from biophysics and from pharmacology new substances which mimic or modify the action of natural molecules in the body. It also means that the physiologist's armoury of experimental techniques is constantly expanding.

As a result of its interdisciplinary nature, physiology draws freely from and contributes widely to the other biological sciences. It is not uncommon, for instance, for the staff of a modern physiology department to be composed of academics whose initial training was perhaps in medicine, biology or physical science as well as in physiology.

A physiology undergraduate studies subsidiary subjects for at least the initial years of his course and the central nature of physiology allows him to take full advantage of courses offered in other biological sciences. Similarly physiology forms an essential but subsidiary part of subjects such as biology, zoology, botany and pharmacology, and a large number of physiology departments are actively involved in teaching medical as well as science students. This often enhances the already stimulating background for the undergraduate.

There is a large number of physiology departments in universities but it is not a subject offered by every institution and the emphasis placed on the subject can vary from department to department. Some may direct most of their research and teaching towards animal and comparative physiology, examining how similar functional problems are solved in different species; others may lay more emphasis on human physiology and the application of the science to medicine. The intending student would therefore be well advised to examine closely the various prospectuses available and to visit departments before making his final choices for application. The A-levels required by physiology departments may vary slightly but generally passes in biology and chemistry together with either physics or mathematics are acceptable.

HELPFUL READING: *Physiology – Education and Career* (London: Physiological Society, available from the Society whose address can be obtained from any university physiology department).

Politics and Government

Peter Dawson, LSE

Politics, political science, political theory and institutions, government – these are some of the names by which university departments teaching in this field are known and, although the specific subjects which they teach may differ, their broad concern is the same. The simplest way of describing this concern is to say that it is with the exercise of governmental power within and between nation states. Beyond that it is a concern with the processes by which power is acquired and used, and the restraints both material and ethical which may be placed upon it.

The oldest and most persistent strand of political studies is political philosophy with an ancestry which goes back at least as far as Aristotle and Plato. Political philosophy involves a concern – or 'engagement' – with the basic concepts of the discipline (eg politics, government, power, authority) and with the rights and obligations of both rulers and ruled, and much else. It cannot be assigned however to a separate and remote compartment. Philosophical considerations underlie all aspects of the study of politics and most enquiries tend to lead back to such concerns.

Some people distinguish political thought as a separate field from political philosophy. It entails an examination of the ideas of certain prominent thinkers and of their significance in their own and in subsequent times. Plato, Aquinas, Machiavelli, Rousseau and Marx would be just a few of the names which fall within this category.

Next there is a large area of empirical studies and theorising about them which may, for convenience, be divided into three parts. The first is the study of individuals and their motivation and behaviour in different political roles (eg voters or leaders). The second is the study of groups from the organised and articulate (eg political parties or pressure groups) to those with a possibly more diffuse voice who are less organised (eg racial or religious groups). Third is the study of governmental institutions – parliamentary assemblies, courts, cabinets, civil services – and constitutionally defined offices of leadership or direction (eg those of presidents, prime ministers and ministers). Public administration as an academic study is principally concerned with this third part.

These three types of study may be conducted in relation to the politics and government of our own or of any foreign country. Western European countries and North America have long been a subject of scrutiny, but with the growth since 1945 of Soviet, East European and Chinese studies and over the past twenty years of Third World studies there is now no country in the world whose political arrangements are not directly or indirectly the subject of research and publication.

Comparative politics – the methodical and simultaneous study of several political systems – has been one of the major developments of political science in recent years. The study has been aided by an accompanying elaboration of the concept of political systems. A primary concern in comparative politics is to show by examination of a number of countries how apparently similar institutions and structures may perform different functions or, conversely, how the same function may be performed by different structures. It becomes possible for example to analyse in some detail how political parties or the mass media perform widely varying roles in different countries, or how the functions attributed in the UK to Members of Parliament may elsewhere be performed by civil servants or influential, non-elected intermediaries.

Another aspect of comparative politics is the attempt to classify political societies and order them in generic groups. It tends to lead to an examination of such terms as totalitarianism, pluralism and participation.

Closely related to this approach is the examination of political ideas or bodies of widely held beliefs like nationalism, socialism or conservatism. But by now the circle is almost closed since this sort of concern brings one into close proximity again with political philosophy.

A final area of concern is international politics or international relations, which in some universities is taught within a separate department but elsewhere is covered under politics or government. Essentially it is the study of politics between states and of such institutions as the United Nations and the European Community which constitute forms of international government. The various approaches outlined above are equally appropriate in this field.

It must now be clear that the study of politics cannot be undertaken in isolation from other disciplines. It enjoys common and overlapping boundaries with numerous other subjects, sharing many of their concerns and using some of their methods of study. History, above all, has a prominent place. At a basic level a large part of what we are able to study is historical in that it is accomplished fact, but also at a more elaborate level we can only provide intelligible accounts of political arrangements by trying to understand how and why they have evolved, by recognising the phenomenon of change and seeking to discover its causes. Sociology, economics and law are close relatives of politics, while geography, anthropology and psychology are more distantly placed; and mathematics, including statistics and computer applications, is being admitted ever more frequently to the family circle.

What are the principal methods of studying politics as an undergraduate? It remains above all a 'book' subject, pursued by reading the works of other scholars, but there also exist opportunities, which vary from topic to topic, to use primary sources such as official publications and newspapers both contemporary and historical. Novels, plays, poetry and other artistic works may have their relevance and there is an increasing use of survey data (eg public opinion samples), which in some instances is prepared by students themselves. In recent years there has been some use of simulation techniques either involving role playing and/or using computers as a method of both research and of teaching.

Few universities specify particular A-level subjects for students wishing to specialise in political studies. British constitution and other directly related subjects have tended in the past not to be regarded as a specially favoured qualification. On the other hand A-level studies in history, a modern language or mathematics would provide a useful grounding for a potential student in this field.

A more detailed and very readable account of the study of politics is Jean Blondel, *The Discipline of Politics* (Butterworth, 1981). Alternatively, *Introducing Political Science* edited by Lynton Robins (published jointly by Longman and the Politics Association).

Professions Allied to Medicine (PAMs)

Dr Jackie Campbell, Nene College

When considering a vocational or professional course you not only have to choose the right course for your three years or so of study but you also have to make a decision as to your chosen career. In many ways this makes life difficult – you have to specialise very early in your student life – but it can also provide a focus and a motivation for your study.

What do you want from your career? – and what can you offer it? If you like working with people, are interested in the fields of health and medicine and enjoy the challenge of being responsible for your own decisions then one of the professions allied to medicine may be just what the health professional ordered.

'Professions allied to medicine', or PAMs, is a catch-all phrase used to describe a range of caring professions within a medical framework. These include physiotherapy, occupational therapy, chiropody (podiatry), speech therapy, radiography, dietetics and orthoptics amongst others. This wide range of careers can offer opportunities for all sorts of interests and expertise, from a scientific orientation through to emphasis on art and music. This range of opportunity is extended when you realise that even within a single profession there is enormous diversity – from the generalist to a large number of different specialists – working in hospitals, the community, industry or private practice.

The health professions in general have matched their enhancement of status within the medical services with their academic qualifications. Some professions, for example speech therapy and dietetics, are entirely graduate professions, other eg chiropody, radiography and occupational therapy are moving rapidly in that direction and you will find most of the new courses for these professions are at degree level although there are still diploma level courses available. Whatever course you choose though, make sure that it will make you eligible for state registration when you have qualified. Within the professions allied to medicine you don't *have* to be state registered to work outside the health service – anyone can theoretically set themselves up in the High Street as a 'physiotherapist' for example but you would have no opportunity for employment within the main stream of the profession and no support (including professional insurance) from the professional bodies.

What course you choose will obviously depend on which of the professions best suits your career aspirations but there will be certain features common to most. All courses at reputable colleges will provide professional training – teaching you the skills you need to do the job. These skills may include manual skills, such as using a scalpel or how to manipulate a joint, technical skills such as using X-ray equipment or administering local anaesthetic, evaluative skills that are necessary for initial patient assessment and communication skills so that you can not only talk to your patient but also communicate with other health professionals from a variety of disciplines that may be involved in the care of your patient. Some of your course will be college/university-based but you will also go out on placements where you will practise your skills in a work setting. Your final qualification to practise will depend on you being able to satisfy the statutory body responsible for your profession that you are 'competent to practise' and will include both practical and theoretical elements.

If you follow a degree course, you will learn all the sort of skills mentioned above but you will study for an academic qualification alongside your professional qualification. The academic elements will be closely linked to your professional needs and are designed to make you a reflective practitioner – one who thinks what they are doing, and why! This might include an element of health psychology, social policy, management and will usually entail a research project in the final year. At the end of your degree course you should be able to play a fuller role as an independent practitioner, making your own decisions and able to critically appraise your own work. In more general terms it also signals that you have achieved the academic level needed to attain any degree and could therefore equip you for employment outside your professional sphere.

All this is not easily won. It is sometimes a little galling to find that you have to attend a clinic session when your friends are off to the squash courts – again! Or that you have a heavier lecture timetable than anyone else in the entire world. But then your rewards are potentially great. You will be able to come home from work every day (exhausted – so it's good practice for that too!) and feel that you have made a difference to people's lives. You know that you will become a member of a respected profession which will give you professional independence yet provide you with opportunities to work as part of a wider team.

If this is the sort of career that appeals to you, then you need to explore in much more detail the range of professions on offer and what precisely is entailed in the ones that interest you most. You can do this via your local careers service or by contacting the professional bodies direct – a few of the addresses are given below. When you have found the one you think is for you, contact the appropriate department in your local health authority and ask if you can visit – most will be happy to arrange this. Most universities and colleges that offer PAMs courses will arrange open days or taster days for prospective students. Make sure you take advantage of these occasions to find out what it will really be like as a student there before you choose where to apply. Courses vary in content and educational philosophy so for example you may find that one course is assessed mainly by coursework, another may emphasise examinations or clinical practice may be more closely integrated with theoretical aspects in some courses than in others. In addition, some institutions suit some more than others so shop around and pick the one that's right for you.

FURTHER READING: *Health Care in the Public Sector* AGCAS Central Services Unit, Crawford House, Precinct Centre, Manchester M13 9EP; Stephen Moss (Ed), *Careers in Nursing and Allied Professions* Kogan Page, 1991; *Health Service Careers Directory*, HMSO.

USEFUL ADDRESSES (for further information): Society of Chiropodists, 53 Welbeck Street, London W1M 7HE. British Dietetic Association, Daimler House, Paradise Circus, Queensway, Birmingham B1 2BJ. College of Occupational Therapists, 6–8 Marshalsea Road, London SE1 1HL. General Optical Council, 41 Harley Street, London W1N 2DJ. British College of Optometrists, 10 Knaresborough Place, London SW5 0TG. British Orthoptists Society, Tavistock House North, Tavistock Square, London WC1H 9HX. Royal Pharmaceutical Society of Great Britain, 1 Lambeth High Street, London SE1 7JN. Chartered Society of Physiotherapists, 14 Bedford Row, London WC1R 4ED. College of Radiographers, 14 Upper Wimpole Street, London W1M 8BN. College of Speech and Language Therapists, Bath Place, Rivington Street, London EC2.

Psychology

Professor Keith Oatley, Glasgow University

'Know thyself' said the inscription on the temple at Delphi; and I suppose it is something like this idea that leads most of us into psychology. But how should we acquire that knowledge?

For most of this century the answer that has been widely accepted in psychology departments of universities is that we can best find out about ourselves using the methods of natural science. So psychology tends to be modelled on sciences like biology, and a common definition is 'Psychology is the study of behaviour and mental processes'. Just as biologists' and physiologists' interest is in how bodies of living things work, so psychologists concern themselves with how people behave and how their minds work.

A good deal of knowledge has indeed been produced in this way. Careful observation, results of experiments, and theories interpreting these kinds of evidence form the core of most psychology courses. A book specially written for people wondering whether to study psychology is A M Colman's *What is Psychology, The Inside Story* (Hutchinson). It emphasises this natural scientific viewpoint and gives a sample of what is to be expected in university and college psychology courses. Also with this viewpoint, but with more detail, is a book that is widely used at universities and colleges, *Introduction to Psychology* by R L Atkinson, R C Atkinson, E E Smith & E R Hilgard (Harcourt Brace Jovanovich). It, or an equivalent, is available in most public libraries.

Psychological research has made exciting advances in recent years. The observational and experimental study of childhood is an example which has important implications for education. Try M Donaldson's book *Children's Minds* (Fontana). Another approach which has become important at universities is cognitive psychology: the study of how knowledge is represented mentally, and used in such activities as seeing, conversing, understanding and thinking. A good book introducing cognitive psychology is *The Computer and the Mind: An Introduction to*

Cognitive Science (Fontana) by P Johnson-Laird. Despite the title this book is not too hard to approach. It explains how the computer has become important in helping us understand mental processes like thinking, memory, perception, language and so on. A series of books that describes in straightforward terms some of the recent advances in psychology, including its applications to practical problems, is *Psychology Survey* (British Psychological Society). Volume 5 was edited by J Nicholson and H Beloff; and the most recent, volume 6, is edited by H Beloff and A Colman.

So, one might think, this is how one could get to know about child development, thinking and suchlike, but still something remains elusive: these approaches have not necessarily given us knowledge of our own selves.

In using the methods of natural science investigators can stand more or less outside the system they are studying. We might be made of molecules, but we can still study molecular reactions in a test tube without interfering too much. We might ourselves be products of evolution, but we can study some evolutionary processes by looking at fossils or doing genetic experiments on fruit-flies. But with ourselves and our own minds, it's not clear that we can always stand outside in this way – or at least not without missing something important.

So for some psychologists, the methods of studying the natural world are not appropriate to investigating the human world, which after all is a world of culture as much as of nature. In the distinctively human world psychologists are not so much finding out about mental mechanisms as about what we as people are up to, by ourselves, with each other and in society. Rather than asking 'What makes a person tick?' we can ask about what things mean to people, or about how people construct their personal and interpersonal realities. Most characteristically this is the area of social psychology, and its closely related disciplines of sociology and anthropology. Try reading one of E Goffman's books, for example *The Presentation of Self in Everyday Life* (Pelican). The idea of looking for human meaning is also the impulse behind much clinical psychology, where understandings are applied to healing emotional crises to which we are subject at various times in our lives. A good introduction to these issues is J Kovel's *Complete Guide to Therapy: From Psychoanalysis to Behaviour Modification* (Pelican), or K Oatley's *Selves in Relation: An Introduction to Psychotherapy and Groups* (Methuen). Certainly, nearly all the time, there is lively discussion about how we should proceed – for a good taste of this, concerning one of psychology's best known inventions try L Kamin's *The Science and Politics of IQ* (Penguin).

Psychology is applied to an enormous range of practical problems (and there is even an important branch called applied psychology). With a BA or BSc in psychology you will be able to work in industry, communications or research, and psychologists are employed in fields as diverse as the media and the civil service. To work as a clinical, educational or applied psychologist, you will need to follow your first degree with a further one- to two-year course (MA or MSc) which will give you specific training and qualifications.

Doing an undergraduate course with at least half your time spent on psychology would be a typical requirement for going on to such a vocational course. Most British degree courses in which students spend the larger part of their time doing psychology are officially recognised by the British Psychological Society. Graduating from such a course qualifies you for membership of this Society, a professional body that looks after the interests of psychology in Britain. If you think you might want a career in psychology it is a good idea to check that courses for which you apply are recognised in this way. You can find out more about careers and qualifications by sending £1.25 to the British Psychological Society, St Andrews House, 48 Princess Road East, Leicester LE1 7DR requesting their booklet *How About Psychology? A Guide to Courses and Careers*.

As to what you need to be accepted for a psychology course at university or college, the requirements are usually quite flexible; typically maths at GCSE or equivalent, and usually three A-levels, or in Scotland four Highers, in arts or science subjects. Biology, sociology or indeed psychology itself at A-level are useful. But do not worry if you are not taking these particular subjects. The real qualifications are knowing a bit about psychology before you apply, eg from friends already at college or university, or from books like the ones I have mentioned, an interest in people, an enthusiasm for ideas, and a preparedness to think for yourself.

Public Administration

Barry J O'Toole, Loughborough University

Public administration is about the very essence of politics: it is about power. Power is the ability to get people to do something that they would otherwise not have done. Its sources can be physical strength or simply the ability to persuade. In public administration power is derived from authority. In other words, public officials, whether elected politicians or permanent functionaries, can get things done because they have the legitimate right, derived from election or law, to get those things done.

The study of public administration is concerned with the who, the why, and the how of this legitimate exercise of power. In Britain the study is all the more exciting because the public official, be that person politician, civil servant or local government officer, generally exercises power in secret. The world of the public official is a dark and hidden world – a world which is formally 'public', but which in reality is 'private'. It is a world governed by conventions, traditions and precedents – but it is a world in which conventions, traditions and precedents can be broken if it suits those people who operate within it.

Who are these people and what exactly do they do? First of all what are the institutions of public administration in Britain? Starting at the very top, in central government, there is the cabinet. The cabinet, which derives its legitimacy from parliament, and ultimately from the electorate, is the supreme policy-making body. In the cabinet sit the senior ministers of the government. These people are usually supported by huge departments of state which carry out their policies. In the departments are the civil servants. Civil servants are appointed by publicly known and non-party-political criteria; they serve the government of the day. At the very top of the civil service hierarchy they are responsible for advising ministers about policy and for putting those policies into effect. Civil servants derive their legitimacy from their official positions and from their expertise, in particular their expertise in how government works. They are not the 'faceless, pliable, sexless creatures' of myth; they are rather 'cloistered politicians' or 'statesmen in disguise'. In other words, they exercise a real and constant influence on public affairs.

Central government, in essence the cabinet and the civil service, is responsible for creating the policy framework within which the other organs of the state operate. These other organs of the state include the local authorities, the nationalised industries and the quasi-autonomous bodies (QUANGOs) such as the Sports Council or the National Health Service (certainly the most important of the semi-independent authorities).

Local government has the primary responsibility for implementing the practical aspects of public policy. The various local authorities are providers of education, public housing and social services; they build roads and footpaths; they cater for the arts, libraries and leisure; they take away our refuse and clean our streets; they police our neighbourhoods. In essence the local authorities provide much of the physical and social framework without which civilised society could not exist.

The people who carry the burden of responsibility for the provision of these services are the local councillors, deriving their legitimacy as elected politicians; and the local government officers, deriving their legitimacy from their official position and from their specific expertise in aspects of local service provision. These people work in bureaucratic structures, often in large departments, with long hierarchical chains and governed by volume upon volume of rules, regulations and procedures. However, any organisation is only as good as the people who work within it; and clearly there are other factors which play a part in how local government operates. Students of public administration are not simply concerned with structures and functions of local authority departments and the local council; they will also seek to raise questions about what sort of people local councillors and officials are; what motivates them; and what are the economic, political and social boundaries within which they work. In other words, public administration, at all levels, is about people, politics and power.

Much has been written about the role of power/authority/legitimacy in the study of politics. Public administration is about the practical aspects and applications of those concepts. Students of public administration will therefore be expected during their studies to deal with the theoretical elements of the study of politics as well as with the empirical evidence of political activity in public organisations. They will also be asked to tackle such problems as communications in organisations, motivation, decision theory, policy making and leadership. Who are the leaders in public organisations: temporary politicians or permanent officials? Who are the decision makers and policy determinators? Who is responsible for motivating public officials? How are they motivated: by pay or by power? All these questions, and many others, will be raised while studying public administration. Why are they important? They are important because the answers to them affect every aspect of our lives. What public people do has a direct bearing on the business of private individuals. Furthermore, these questions are important in another sense. As citizens in a democracy surely it is our duty to find out as much as we can about how those who have charge over our political destiny go about discharging their responsibilities. The more we know the less they are likely to be irresponsible. Therein lies the challenge of studying public administration: on the whole there is so little that is known.

Public administration may be taught in universities as part of a wider degree in politics or government or as an entirely separate degree. Whatever the model used the methodology for the study of public administration will draw upon the related disciplines of economics, history, management, philosophy and sociology amongst others. It is a varied, stimulating and rewarding subject and will stretch the critical and intellectual faculties to their fullest.

HELPFUL READING: Richard A Chapman, *Ethics in the British Civil Service* (Routledge 1988); Richard A Chapman, *The Art of Darkness* (University of Durham, 1988); John Greenwood and David Wilson, *Public Administration in Britain Today* (George Allen & Unwin, 1989).

Religious Studies and Theology

Professor John R Hinnells, SOAS

Religion is a potent driving force both in contemporary society and in past history. It has inspired some of the most noble, creative and generous actions. Equally it has been associated with the most savage cruelty, oppression and degradation. A balanced understanding of many major events commonly involves an appreciation of the religious factors at work. Whether it is in Northern Ireland, the Middle East, liberation movements in Latin America, independence movements in post-colonial Africa, the Church and 'Solidarity' in Poland or conflicts in the Punjab – religion and politics are commonly interwoven. Religion may inspire people, or it may be used by people, but it is commonly a significant dimension for the study of human life.

Many people describe contemporary British society as secular and say that religion is declining. I think that is wrong. Formal membership of the established churches may be dropping, but that is not an adequate measure of the state of religion in the country. Such an opinion ignores the growth of new religious movements, the ecstatic movements, what people (in biased tones) describe as the 'cults', and the central importance of religion in Asian and Afro-Caribbean communities here. Recent research has demonstrated that people who have migrated, or feel victims of prejudice, commonly reassert their identity in and through religious traditions. Much of contemporary British law, custom, values etc are (for better or worse) the product of a particular religious tradition. It is, in my opinion, impossible to understand our own society without an understanding of the plethora of religious influences which make it what it is.

Religion is crucial not only in the understanding of politics and society but also of the arts. Until recent times the Church was the main patron of the arts – painting, music, architecture, drama. The influence of a patron is often crucial. The Church not only commissioned works of art, it also dictated the form, content and style of much of that art. The Church often repressed the artist – not only through the mass destruction following the Reformation, but also in more recent times when its stance on, say, the depiction of the nude, the condemnation of some aspects of drama or literature, has been, frankly, narrow minded. Looking to other cultures, it is hardly possible to understand many of the art forms without the religion of which they are an essential part – whether it is the great civilizations of China and India, or of the small scale societies in Africa or the North American Indians. One of the fundamental failings of so many art histories, in my opinion, is that they study the arts as though they were produced for the 'antiseptic' atmosphere of most art galleries and museums, whereas in countless societies, including the pre-modern West, artefacts are produced to be used eg in rituals, to inspire devotion or to teach the illiterate.

Does a student have to be religious to study religion? Obviously many are, and in Britain that usually, but not always, means Christian. Some people study religion in order to find a faith for themselves; some study Christianity because they believe it will confirm or develop their faith. A few study religion because they want to enter the religious ministry. What must be emphasised is that a university or polytechnic is a secular institution and not a priestly seminary. Within a department of religious studies there will be people of various faiths, and many of none. In theory a student's own religious position should make no difference to their studies. That is, of course, an ideal situation – and neither students nor staff are ever ideal! Most people like to think they have no prejudices. In my experience that is self-delusion. We all have our prejudices. The danger time is when we are not aware of them. At least one major benefit of the study of religion is that it compels people to recognise their prejudices and to analyse them.

How should one study religion? There are as many answers to this question as there are departments which study it. In some departments religious studies means basically studying the Christian bible. One argument for this is that it, more than any other single document, has affected the course of western civilization. The scholarly methods used to study that text (or collection of texts) are intellectually demanding and diverse (eg languages, archaeology, literary studies, Roman history etc). But if you are interested in studying Asians in Britain then, frankly, it is not relevant. If you want both, make sure both are available.

For myself, I believe strongly that religion has to be studied from many points of view. The study must necessarily bring together a range of disciplines – anthropology, sociology, languages, history, art, archaeology, philosophy. It is only when there are students from these and other departments, people from different religions, as well as specialists in religion, that I find discussions come alive. Personally I accept the old dictum 'he who knows one knows none', ie that the study of any one religion is not the study of religion and such a focus precludes a balanced view of even that one phenomenon. It is only by a study of several that you see what is distinctive of each. But I am biased – comparative religion is my subject!

There are countless other branches to the study of religion not even hinted at yet. Religious studies more than any other subject wrestles with some of the ultimate issues: the concept of God; life after death; the nature of good and evil and ethical issues – what are the arguments for and against euthanasia, surrogate motherhood, nuclear power? If anyone thinks any of these are simple clear cut issues they have evidently not thought them through! Thinking things through is perhaps the most important part of studying religion.

What do people do after studying religion? The answer is 'almost anything'. In one year all my graduates, and postgraduates, went into business management. That was an unusual percentage, but it illustrates the point that not all students enter the religious ministry. Careers followed by my students in the last few years include teaching, social work, civil service, the media, publishing, the Foreign Office, the armed forces, airport management, personnel management. Quite a number go overseas. Doubtless colleagues could add considerably to the list. Generally employers respect the subject because it is widely seen as a serious, stringent academic discipline, involving a range of types of study thereby demanding an intellectual flexibility.

My strongest advice (apart from 'narrow minded people need not apply'!) is – think through what your motivations are, then visit the departments you think offer contrasting stimulations and judge for yourself at first hand which one suits you. Do not be misled by a prospectus, or by a beautiful location amid shady trees (or big city night life), or where your teacher went (places change). Because of the importance of religion, and the wide range of subjects it involves, there is no more stimulating, challenging, exciting and relevant subject in the curriculum. Try it!

HELPFUL READING: J Dunn, *Unity and Diversity in the New Testament* (SCM, 1981); J R Hinnells, *Handbook of Living Religions* (Penguin, 1985); Leroy Long Jr, *Survey of Christian Ethics* (Oxford, 1982); D Pailin, *Groundwork of Philosophy and Religion* (Epworth, 1986); N Smart, *Religious Experience of Mankind* (Fontana, 1971).

Social Policy and Social Welfare

Professor Olive Stevenson, Nottingham University

It is a pity that the world 'welfare', like 'charity', has been debased. It is a word of great importance and delicacy and expresses an aspiration that our citizens will 'fare well'. The much maligned phrase 'welfare state' carries an implication that through the organisation of service we will take responsibility for each other in times of need. It means that we do not want to leave it to chance or to informal acts of kindness, important though these things are. Industrialised societies generate social problems too large and too serious to be coped with by friends or voluntary activity alone. Every western country has welfare services organised by the state, even those which resist the intervention of the state as far as possible. So the phrase 'welfare state' is one to be proud of, not to sneer at. It is not about scroungers or creating dependency. These are minor matters in comparison with the central aim of creating a society in which the sick, elderly people, disabled people, and others who are socially vulnerable, are cared for generously and sensitively.

Since 1980 we have seen a shift to the right, unparalleled since the war in political ideology. There has been vigorous resistance to any increase in state involvement in welfare and a challenge to some of the assumptions which governments of both colours had accepted since 1945. This change of emphasis reflects a real shift in the prevailing political philosophy; it has been given force by an economic policy which stresses the need to reduce public expenditure in all areas, including welfare services. A recent manifestation of these changes is to be seen in the White Paper and subsequent legislation on community care. In this, whilst local authorities are to play a lead role in planning services, they are encouraged (perhaps compelled, by financial controls) to make much greater use of the private and voluntary sectors for the provision of services. We may expect, therefore, to see an expansion in these sectors, for example in residential care for vulnerable groups and in the provision of community services such as 'meals on wheels' and domiciliary support. It is likely that social policy graduates and social workers will increasingly find employment within these sectors, in addition to their traditional 'home' in the statutory sectors.

All this is central to social policy and social welfare studies. So whether you want to pursue a course in social policy (a more recent name for what is sometimes called social administration), or to qualify as a social worker, you will inevitably be drawn into a political debate to a greater extent than in the 1970s when the issues were less contentious.

Social policy and welfare studies draws upon a number of disciplines in the social sciences. You can expect a mixture, varying in balance, of philosophy, politics, economics and sociology, which are used selectively to focus upon the central issues and problems of the subject. For example: how do you define and measure poverty and social need? What factors create unemployment and what effect does it have on society, families and individuals? How do citizens obtain redress for their grievances? If you are undertaking an undergraduate or postgraduate social work professional qualifying course, to this will be added other subjects, mainly psychology and law, relevant to your chosen career. You will also undertake substantial periods of fieldwork, underpinned by teaching of social work theory and practice.

Despite some public scepticism in recent years, social science degrees are increasingly popular with students. Social scientists with an applied element in their studies continue to be needed across a wide range of public services. And public services will not – cannot – disappear, whatever the political rhetoric! They are integral to the fabric of a developed society. For example, if one thinks about the consequences – social, emotional and physical – of unemployment on the individuals concerned and on their families; or of the feelings and attitudes of young blacks in the inner cities who believe that our society has failed them; or of the growing numbers of frail elderly people in our society – these and many other social problems require intervention, both administrative and professional.

Realistically, students will be asking about job prospects. Many students are attracted to social policy degrees because they have a social work career in mind; it is an excellent preparation for professional training. But social policy also provides a good basis for a wide range of posts in the public sector like housing management, hospital administration, or the civil service. Many students look towards graduate entry into commerce and industry. Employers in the private sector value the skills in research methods and policy analysis, and the understanding of the structure and problems of contemporary society developed by a social policy degree.

If, at the end of your degree programme, you want to qualify as a social worker, your job prospects are good at present. Most students think of social work for local authorities as 'fieldwork in the community'. Much of this work focuses upon child protection. But there is another important area in which trained staff are urgently needed. This is in residential and day care where it is generally accepted that social workers have an important contribution to make to the care of the very vulnerable, dependent people – the very old, the young, disabled people, for example. The quality of this provision is vitally important; strenuous efforts are being made to increase the proportion of social work qualified staff in this sector. Qualifying as a social worker would also enable you to work in the probation service, which is expanding to meet government policy of keeping an increasing proportion of offenders out of prison. Many voluntary agencies, too, employ qualified social workers, whether they are large national bodies like the NSPCC or a small local organisation helping people to run self-help groups.

The position on A-level grades varies considerably across the range of educational institutions: you should check specific courses by consulting the prospectus or one of the student guides. It does not matter in what subjects you have your A-levels. If you are a mature student, different entry requirements will apply: again you should check with each university or college.

HELPFUL READING: V Coulshed, *Social Work: an Introduction to Practice* (London: Macmillan/British Association of Social Workers, 1991); N Johnson, *Reconstructing the Welfare State* (Hemel Hempstead, Herts: Harvester Wheatsheaf, 1990).

Sociology

Dr Jason Ditton, Glasgow University

Sociology is the scientific study of society, OK? You could make it sound more pretentious, but it wouldn't help much. In fact its very subject matter makes it difficult to define more exactly. You can see this if you compare social sciences with, for example, natural sciences. The units of physics, atoms, do not read physics books and then get together to confound the physicists' theoretical predictions, do they? But that is exactly what the units of sociology, people, do to social theorists' predictions. Look what happened to Marxism in Western Europe after the 1848 revolution: many of the policies which the dominant classes initiated after the revolution seem to have been formulated precisely to confound Marx's predictions of victory for the working-classes.

Sociology is a science, but it is obviously qualitatively different from the conventional natural sciences. Sociology has its 'units' for analysis and to be very precise these are not so much people as the interactions that take place between people. It is from these basic units – which are studied with normal scientific rigour, although out in the world rather than in the laboratory – that sociologists are able to build up low-level conceptual pictures of ideas like social status, social role, and social class, and from them middle-range theories of more general societal features like organisation, change and conflict. In turn these concepts help to build grand models capable of explaining the operation of, and differences between, various societies.

Well, that's what sociologists **do**. But, and this is the case with all disciplines which are by their very nature responsive to changes in their subject matter, you can get more of an idea of what sociology **is** by first erasing some common misconceptions. Firstly, sociology isn't new. So those who think it might be an easy course because sociologists haven't had time to write many books about it are in for a weighty surprise. (Don't worry, most of us started with the same cosy delusion.) The idea probably took root because most UK sociology courses are fairly new, which means that it doesn't matter much which A-levels you do although arts or social science subjects might help you through the first few weeks of a degree course. However, sociology isn't new. Most basic social theory, particularly the work of sociology's big Three – Karl Marx, Max Weber and Emile Durkheim – has a pedigree dating from the nineteenth century. If you want a taste of timeless social theory, read Karl Marx's *Communist Manifesto* (Harmondsworth: Penguin, 1967).

Of course, sociology is about people, but it is not – to dispel a common view of the discipline as half social work, half public relations – about 'dealing' with them. You won't get much of a chance to research real live people actively and personally on a typical three-year course, although you will get a chance to study systematically sociological analyses and descriptions of what life is like for other people. A brilliant example of what your and other people's life is like as seen through the eyes of a sociologist is Erving Goffman's *The Presentation of Self in Everyday Life* (Harmondsworth: Penguin, 1959).

Another common misconception is that sociology is obvious, that it is just common sense or, worse, merely trivial. Admittedly some sociological findings do seem obvious and pure common sense once sociologists have revealed them for everybody else, but that isn't the whole story. Everybody always knew, of course, that the newspapers and television coverage of news was biased against the working-class. But who could have backed his opinion with hard facts until the Glasgow University Sociology Media Group published their exhaustive and yet very readable study of the UK media? (For a short, lively and up-to-date account of the Group's work, see their *Really Bad News* – London: Writers and Readers, 1982.)

A final common but erroneous idea is that sociology analyses those bits of society which are left after economics, psychology and anthropology have carved off their bits. In fact the reverse is true. Sociology can be distinguished from all other disciplines through its ability not only to analyse society without the use of other disciplines (which is its chief function) but also to analyse competently the operations of all other disciplines. Natural science itself has become a target for some sociologists. They enquire: how do scientists make discoveries? Is it some sort of magical process? How is it that, occasionally, several scientists simultaneously but individually discover the same thing? Coincidence? If you want to know how it actually happens, take a look at Thomas Kuhn's *The Structure of Scientific Revolutions* (University of Chicago Press, 1970).

Finally, to judge sociology, don't just read those books with titles which begin with such phrases as 'An Introduction to . . .', or 'Teach Yourself . . .', or end with the words '. . . for Beginners' (except for *Marx for Beginners*, a good spoof by Rius, London: Beginners Books, 1976). No, read a bit of real sociology. For example why not take a look at those human warehouses which dominate current societal handling of certain groups – hospitals (the sick), prisons (the criminal), public schools and army camps (those in training), monasteries (those in retreat) and mental institutions (the insane)? One thing that they all have in common is that they have been studied, sociologically analysed and enchantingly described in Erving Goffman's *Asylums* (Harmondsworth: Penguin, 1968). Try reading it, and see this for yourself.

FURTHER INFORMATION: Get a free copy of a very useful 16-page leaflet, *Sociology: Information and Opportunities* from Nicola Boyne, the Executive Secretary, British Sociological Association, Unit 3G, Mountjoy Research Centre, Stockton Road, Durham DH1 3UR. And ask your Head of Sociology or Careers to get hold of a copy of the entertaining introductory sociology video, *So What's Sociology Anyway?* It can be obtained from Paul Littlewood, Sociology Department, Glasgow University, Glasgow G12 8RT (£29.99, or £10.00 to hire).

Speech Sciences

Dr Karen Bryan, Dr Jane Maxim & Dr Sheila Wirz,
National Hospitals College of Speech Sciences

When people talk to each other, a complex series of messages are sent out, received, understood and then responded to. The processes involved in human communication require the interaction of several brain functions, neuromuscular mechanisms, sight and hearing. Listening for most people involves paying attention to what is being said, to facial expression and body posture. Such complex processes may break down or not develop along normal patterns. Speech sciences is the study of these processes in both normal and abnormal human communication.

There are several degree courses in this area which usually appeal to students interested in speech therapy, audiology or the education of children with special needs. Not surprisingly, this science requires students to look at a range of widely differing subjects in order to acquire the integrated knowledge necessary to understand human communication. Speech sciences cross the boundaries between science and the arts, including anatomy, physiology, psychology, phonetics, linguistics, sociology, education, medical sciences and speech pathology and therapeutics.

In order to fulfil the demands of a course rooted in both the science and arts fields students need good analytical skills: in other words they need to enjoy problem solving. They also need an ability for creative and lateral thinking in order to put their scientific knowledge to realistic clinical use. However good an analysis of a communication problem is, there is still the need to present treatment in a form which is acceptable and enjoyable to the client. For example, a young child with delayed language development may need treatment through play to change their language pattern.

It may seem incredible that we still know so little about human communication but it is certainly the most complex of human functions and, perhaps, because of this complexity we are still only at the start of solving this particular jigsaw puzzle. As an example, let us consider how we understand just one word. We know that when it is heard, the acoustic and phonetic or speech sound properties have to be decoded. The brain then has to decide whether it has heard that particular word before. If it has then the word is processed to the semantic system where its meaning is retrieved. But even within this simple process, we still know very little about where words are stored in the brain and how they are stored in the semantic system.

For the student who is academically adventurous and sees research as a possible future goal this field still holds many possibilities. For that same reason this is not a field for those seeking ready made solutions. Clients with communication disorders may have the same diagnoses but the severity of the problem and the way in which it affects that particular client mean that an individual programme of therapy has to be worked out for each client. Many students wishing to enter the field feel that they want to help such individuals but such a desire to help must be coupled with a real curiosity about human behaviour and what can motivate the individual to change that behaviour. Clients with exactly the same diagnosis have very different degrees of severity and very specific individual needs. The child with cerebral palsy or the adult with multiple sclerosis both have problems with neuromuscular co-ordination but the treatment needed may vary from a programme to help mildly unintelligible speech to the provision of a complex computer system through which the client may communicate.

In common with other science degrees, speech sciences require practical work. This component has two different strands: work in the laboratory concerned with speech and audiological sciences and clinical work which takes place in a variety of settings. The practical work therefore has a dual purpose: to enable the student to understand normal and abnormal speech processes and to help the student apply that knowledge in a clinical setting. Knowledge used in a clinical environment also needs to be applied in a way which is appropriate for the client–therapist relationship; in other words the student learns how to apply personal and communication skills in a professional and effective way. The application of these skills also has to be implemented with a compassionate understanding for that particular individual. In some client groups the cause of the disorder may be a psychological disturbance, manifesting as, for example, a voice disorder. In such a case the student learns how to differentiate a voice disorder resulting from vocal abuse and poor vocal production from a voice disorder which requires counselling or referral to the psychiatric or psychology service.

Most courses in speech sciences begin with study of foundation subjects which usually include human anatomy and physiology, psychology, phonetics, linguistics and research design and statistics. In any science degree the last subject is usually a basic component without which the student is unable to understand research methodology and critically evaluate research.

Students are introduced to clinical work first by structured observation of normal communication – observing the development of children as babies, in nursery schools and at primary schools; maybe also observing elderly people so as to gain perspective of development across the whole life span. Students then go on to acquire their clinical skills in a variety of settings, most commonly community clinics, main stream and special schools, hospitals and rehabilitation centres. Some may have clinical placements in homes for the elderly, centres for adults with severe learning difficulties and psychiatric units. The timing and length of these clinical placements tends to vary between courses. Most courses mix weekly clinical placements with longer periods in a particular setting while others use a sandwich course model.

For anyone who likes problem solving and has an ability to listen and communicate, this area offers the possibility of a satisfying and varied professional life with continuing scope for widening knowledge. Research possibilities and postgraduate courses are available.

Degree courses in speech sciences, varying in length between 3 and 4 years. Different titles usually reflect something of the flavour of the course. These include: linguistics and language pathology, speech and language pathology, clinical communication studies, remedial linguistics, speech and psychology, medical sciences (speech) and speech sciences. Graduates with satisfactory clinical profiles can be recommended to the College of Speech and Language Therapists for a licence to practice as a speech and language therapist.

HELPFUL READING: These are not about speech sciences and speech therapy directly. Some are explorations of the issues of language development or of communication breakdown. But if you find them interesting and thought provoking then this may be the study area for you. Jean Aitchison, *The Articulate Mammal*, 3rd edition (Hutchinson, 1989); David Crystal, *Listen To Your Child* (Penguin, 1986); Diana Syder, *An Introduction to Communication Disorders* (Chapman and Hall, 1992).

Strategic Studies

Dr Gerald Segal, International Institute for Strategic Studies

War is the continuation of politics by other means and therefore the study of war is a continuation of the study of politics. The subject of strategic studies was once more generally known as war studies and was primarily the preserve of military historians dissecting ancient battles or arguing over the effectiveness of modern hardware. But especially in the past decade, the subject has had spectacular growth under its more modern headings of defence studies or security studies. Some have even gone as far as calling it peace studies. Whatever the name, most teachers, students and writers are concerned with the interaction between military power and politics.

As a result of this modernisation of the subject, people have been attracted to the subject for a number of reasons. Many are deeply concerned about the threat of war, especially nuclear war, and want to understand how to prevent or control it. Others have come to realise that it is impossible to understand politics or economics without understanding the impact that war has on both. The recent conflict in the Gulf with Iraq that threatened to shut oil supplies and affect Western economies is a case in point. The subject is also taught to military professionals to broaden their minds and produce 'thinking soldiers'. Many people are simply interested in a better understanding of issues that so dominate today's media, for example the wars in the Balkans, or negotiations intended to halt the proliferation of nuclear weapons.

Most people are attracted to the sweeping scope of the subject. In order to cover the issues, one needs a bit of history, economics, technology and politics. While each course will stress different dimensions, any good course will at least try to keep them all in perspective. While no specialised knowledge is required, what is most useful is a broad mind and a willingness to consider a range of problems and policies.

History is a usual starting point, if only because past wars have shaped the modern map and political realities and many wars, especially today, are fuelled by historical animosities. Without understanding the way in which the Second World War or colonial wars were fought, it is impossible to understand why the world is divided as it is. Why are there two

Koreas and why do the Arabs and Israelis fight over tiny bits of land? How do the Armenians remember their history and how does that affect conflict in the Caucasus in the 1990s. To what extent should we learn lessons from past wars, for example in preventing the type of appeasement that led to the outbreak of the Second World War? Others would suggest the main lessons for the modern day come from the First World War and the risks of conflict resulting from bungling and entangling alliances.

Economics is a fundamental aspect of strategic studies because states need certain levels of economic strength before they can fight certain types of war. Poor peasant economies, as in China or Vietnam, have used strategies of 'people's war' and defeated even the most developed and technologically advanced adversary. There are also smaller guerrilla movements which fight from the bush and avoid direct engagements. Rich states with their modern communications will also always be vulnerable to terrorism. But these rich states can afford modern weapons and develop nuclear arsenals, and even though this provides little defence against terrorism, the faster they grow economically, the less burdensome is the cost of war.

An obsession with technology is often the reason why some are attracted to strategic studies before they realise that it is only part of the subject. But without appreciating the impact of technology, the course of war and politics is hard to grasp. The invention of gunpowder helped destroy the feudal age of chivalry and castles. The invention of aircraft helped spread the impact of war and made cities more vulnerable to attack. The invention of new technologies of communication meant spying could be carried out from a distance and armed forces could be directed from the safety of a headquarters on a different continent. The invention of nuclear weapons revolutionised the strategy of war, making certain types of war unthinkable, and producing the no-peace-no-war called a cold war.

The link between strategic studies and politics is perhaps the strongest. On the level of domestic politics, there is the question of how important the armed forces are in running the state. Do military dictatorships have distinctive types of policies and do they make war more often? As modern, developed states have more complex relations between industry, the armed forces and government, then how important is the military-industrial complex in making policies? Some states are so politically divided that they degenerate into civil war and strategic studies seeks to understand why these wars are fought and who makes policy. Is there a 'national security state' that undermines democratic control or rule by an ideologically motivated movement?

The politics of international affairs is obviously a central dimension of the subject. States are often paranoid about their security while others may be genuinely covetous of their neighbours' land, people or resources. Strategic studies explains why wars break out, how they are managed and how they are ended. In the age of superpower crises, the concern was with such events as the 1962 Cuban missile crisis, the Soviet invasion of Afghanistan in 1979 or the American attacks on Libya in the 1980s. As the cold war ended, concern has shifted to controlling the transfer of conventional weapons, limiting the risks of nuclear proliferation, making more effective use of the UN Security Council for peacekeeping, and controlling the risks of ethnic conflict. States pursue these policies as continuations of their strategies of security, but they sometimes learn to develop common security rather than merely national security. In the end, strategic studies is about two sides of the same coin: war and peace.

HELPFUL READING: J Baylis et al, *Contemporary Strategy* (London: Croom Helm, 1987); B Buzan, *An Introduction to Strategic Studies* (London: Macmillan, 1987); E M Earle, ed, *The Makers of Modern Strategy*, 2nd edn (Princeton: Princeton University Press, 1986); L Freedman, *The Evolution of Nuclear Strategy*, 2nd edn (London: Macmillan, 1989). The annual editions of the International Institute for Strategic Studies' *Strategic Survey*.

Town and Country Planning

Professor Margaret Roberts

The overall aim of the planner is to see that our cities, towns and countryside are best arranged to meet people's needs – that there are enough and appropriate houses, schools, hospitals, factories, offices, shops, open spaces, roads, railways and so on. It is not, of course, the planners themselves who provide all these, but they meet their aim in two complementary ways. First, they have to deal with requests for planning permission to build. Secondly, planners can encourage the provision of what they know to be lacking in an area by using their knowledge to influence possible providers, especially through the plans which are regularly produced.

Sometimes such changes happen in a 'grand design' – like the massive development of London's docklands, or in the post-war programme of 'new town' building. But, mostly, land use change occurs through a continuous series of individual proposals for buildings or plots of land – to alter what is there already, or build for the first time. The planner has to reach a conclusion about each such proposed change – is it acceptable in planning terms? How does the planner decide?

The planner will in each case consider the proposed scheme, along with what the law requires and allows; the overall planning aims of the local authority; the planner's knowledge about the broader area in which the proposed development is to be located; and the problems and needs of the local community. To be able to do all this, the planning authority has to hold a very substantial and up-to-date bank of information about its area and community, and keep good links with local groups and organisations so that it knows their views.

People often want to become planners because they feel a commitment to making places better for people to live in. This commitment may well come from their own personal experience – say of life in a run-down inner city area, where every day they have seen people living in poor housing, children attending schools without enough play space, streets choked with cars alongside out-of-date public transport. Or perhaps they have grown up in the country and watched the landscape alter as farming methods changed, rural communities losing population as fewer people were needed to work the land, and the habitats of wild plants and animals being destroyed. But, to be effective, an intending planner has to acquire knowledge and skills, as well as a sense of purpose. The common core of planning courses is laid down by the planners' professional body – the Royal Town Planning Institute.

This core includes study of sociology. Britain today is a complex urban society containing a great variety of cultures, levels of wealth, and types of living arrangement. The planner needs to understand how people's life patterns and opportunities are affected by social structures. In recent years there have been important efforts made to attract people from a greater diversity of backgrounds into planning, so that the profession becomes representative of the whole community for which it is planning, and thus has a more solidly-founded understanding of everyone's requirements.

Also essential to a planner is some understanding of economics – of the production and distribution of wealth, of what determines variations in income levels, both of people and of whole areas. Planners have become increasingly involved in economic planning, especially at the local level, and in trying to encourage job creation which requires them to have some knowledge of the operations and motivations of firms.

Another group of subjects includes law, government and politics. Planning is founded on legal powers which are constantly being updated by the central government; and it is essential that all planners understand how their functions and responsibilities fit into the broader legal and political framework of Britain.

At some stage the student planner will look at what is called the development process – in other words the operations of organisations involved in the financing, building, letting and managing of development. This will include study of their objectives, how they are influenced by financial, legal and other factors, and how planners interact with them so the best possible outcome from development is secured for the community, as well as the individual developer.

Through the course, more will be learned about the physical aspects of planning, about natural resources and conservation, buildings and architecture, landscape and townscape, and the value of how things look as well as how they function. A deeper study will be made too of particular land uses – housing, transport, commercial, industrial and recreational – and of different types of policy – especially social and economic.

As well as the 'core' material, each course will have its own particular flavour or specialism. Some courses are specialised as a whole, for example urban planning. Others will offer students a choice of option subjects relating, say, to different kinds of planning work such as countryside planning, transport, recreation, conservation or housing. In most cases the specialism of a course will relate to the area in which it is located, and the planning needs of that city or region.

To bring all this to life for students there will be project work looking, in the way that a planner does, at a number of contrasting places – to see how they have been shaped in the past, what are the pressures for change, and how these may best be met. Studying all aspects of the way a settlement functions includes getting information from a variety of different sources in order to build up a picture of the place and its people. Information sources used will include statistics and reports, interviews, looking at buildings and their use, observing traffic flows, checking how satisfied people are with different facilities such as shops, playgrounds and so on. With the information thus brought together, students will try to apply the ideas and theories that have been discussed in their studies.

Skills needed by a planner are varied. A study of planning will equip you with the necessary skill and confidence you will need in writing and speaking, in maths, statistics and computing, in graphics, drawing and design. Project work will take you through all the methods a planner uses to analyse the needs and problems of different areas and groups of people, and to prepare planning proposals, schemes and plans. You will also get practice in dealing with applications for planning permission. There will be role playing, for example a public inquiry (which may be held when agreement cannot be reached on a planning matter).

You will certainly find that a planning course is stimulating. There is interest to be found in the wide range of subjects covered, and the intellectual challenge offered. There is satisfaction to be gained from its clear relevance to contemporary life. There is personal confidence to be won from the valuable knowledge and skills which you will acquire, many of which are not only useful to planning but are very versatile and applicable widely in life.

HELPFUL READING: David Kirby and Richard Carrick, *Planning in Britain, An Introductory Framework* (University Tutorial Press, 1985), which is very clear and helpful and is organised largely in terms of different land uses; *Town and Country Planning*, a report to the Nuffield Foundation (Nuffield Foundation, 1986), which discusses what planning is trying to do, how well it is working and what the main issues are for the future.

Veterinary Studies

Professor Lord Soulsby, Cambridge University

Veterinary medicine is concerned with the health and welfare of all animal species with the exception of one – man! This is a very wide field of endeavour, requiring extensive and intensive study, but the opportunities at the end of the course are remarkably diverse and can fit almost any aspiration.

The majority of applications for veterinary studies are motivated by a love of animals and the desire to enter veterinary practice having had some contact with a veterinary surgeon in practice, or having been influenced by books, television programmes or movies about veterinarians. However, there is an increasing number of young people who see veterinary medicine as one of the professions that addresses the complex issues of the inter-relationships between man and animals at national and international levels; particularly how animals fit into the scheme of things, be it as part of intensive food production, as essential sources of draught power in Third World countries or as companion animals.

The course is long, five years (six at Cambridge) so tenacity of purpose is also important. All veterinary courses start with detailed study of basic sciences such as anatomy, biochemistry, physiology and the like. These are necessary preparation for the clinical parts of the course which follows further study of disease-producing agents, how diseases occur and how animals resist infections. In many instances ill health in intensively managed livestock involves complex interactions between genetic factors, feeding and housing and is dealt with on the basis of maintaining health with maximum productivity and in which animal welfare is of increasing importance. In contrast ill health in companion animals is an individual rather than a herd problem and medical and surgical treatments are determined by factors other than economics.

Each veterinary school in the UK has a teaching hospital where students learn at first hand how to examine animals, diagnose their problems, advise owners and apply treatment under the supervision of clinical teachers. This must be the most exciting part of the course and the thrill of healing a sick animal is a unique and lasting experience.

Eventually the day of graduation as a veterinary surgeon comes when new members of the profession are admitted to the Royal College of Veterinary Surgeons, the body responsible for overseeing veterinary education in the UK. Each new graduate declares that he or she will be 'committed to the welfare of the animals under my care'. This is an important commitment as well as a solemn obligation and it has stood the test of time since the veterinary surgeon is regarded as an unbiased arbiter and is expected to act as such in his professional life.

The veterinary profession is numerically small; there are approximately 12,000 in the United Kingdom of which about 9,000 are actively working. The majority are in private veterinary practice and the rest are employed in government service, in university veterinary schools, in research institutes or by animal welfare societies. Those in research may become specialists in, for example, fish diseases, zoo animal medicine, farm animal, companion animal or wildlife studies or disciplines of the basic sciences. Quite a number of British veterinary graduates serve overseas, especially in developing countries where animals are especially important to agriculture, either as producers of meat and milk or the provision of motive power for transport or cultivation. Even in this world of mechanisation, on a global basis 85% of the energy required in agriculture is derived from animals; in the least developed countries 90% or more of energy is derived from animals.

Whatever the motivation and aspirations of the veterinarian-to-be, entry requirements are stringent and the number of applicants far exceeds the number of places available, about 450 nationally at this time. Generally at least two As and a B at A-level are required and all of the six veterinary schools in the UK conduct interviews, so some experience with a veterinary surgeon and strong motivation are important.

HELPFUL READING: *A Career as a Veterinary Surgeon* (The Royal College of Veterinary Surgeons, 32 Belgrave Square, London SW1X 8QP). Also available is a video (22 mins) *Do you want to be a Vet?*). *The British Veterinary Profession 1791–1948* by I Pattison (London: J A Allen, 1983); *Animals in Society: A Veterinary Viewpoint*, The Hume Memorial Lecture, November 1985 (University Federation for Animal Welfare, 1985); *Companion Animals in Society* (Oxford University Press, 1988). The novels by James Herriot provide an excellent humorous introduction to the life of a country veterinary surgeon in the late 1930s and 1940s.

Zoology

Professor R McNeill Alexander, Leeds University

Zoology is about animals, including the whole range from protozoans (although these are no longer formally included in the animal kingdom) to humans. It is about corals, beetles, dinosaurs, lions and all the rest.

Zoology is about all aspects of the structure and lives of animals. It includes the biochemistry of animals – not so much the universal processes of the tricarboxylic acid cycle and suchlike, which are studied mainly in biochemistry courses, but more special processes such as the metabolic tricks that enable tapeworms to live in the anaerobic environment of our guts. It includes the structure of animals, of their cells, their organs and their whole bodies, the amazing diversity of form in the animal kingdom and the ways in which structure is adapted to different ways of life. It is about how animal bodies work, dealing with all aspects of physiology but taking special notice of differences between animal groups. If you study physiology at university you will learn how 'typical' muscles (in practice that means frog muscles) work, but if you study zoology you will learn also about many other kinds of muscle: the muscles of insect wings with their built-in resonance, the special muscles that lock clams shut, and so on. Zoology includes the behaviour of animals, how their nervous systems control their behaviour and why particular behaviour patterns have evolved.

It includes animal ecology, the study of the interactions of animal populations with each other, with plants and with the physical environment. Behavioural ecology asks what are the best ways to behave, that will be favoured by natural selection: should a redshank eat every worm it finds or just the big juicy ones, should a stag fight a rival and risk injury, and so on. Finally zoology includes evolutionary theory, both the basic theory of how evolution works, and the evolutionary history of animals.

Biology courses include all forms of life, plants and micro-organisms as well as animals. This generally means that they have to concentrate on general principles and either rush through the animal kingdom or deal in detail with only a few selected animal groups. By choosing zoology instead of biology you will get a fuller treatment of animals and you will probably be able, if you wish, to get some knowledge of plants and micro-organisms by taking appropriate subsidiary courses.

Zoology is not all like the natural history programmes on television. It is about gorillas and whales and strange animals in exotic places, but there is a lot more to it than that. It involves painstaking work in laboratories with advanced, complex equipment. It involves difficult concepts, some of them mathematical. It involves muddy fieldwork (it usually rains) and messy, sometimes smelly dissections.

You should be prepared for dissection (that means cutting up **dead** animals). Some schools now do little or no dissection, and zoologists on degree courses do much less than in the past, but a limited amount of dissection is generally regarded as an essential (and very rewarding) part of a degree course in zoology. You cannot really appreciate how an animal is built until you yourself have taken it apart, and zoologists need dissecting skills for many kinds of research. Nearly all the zoologists I know have a profound respect for life and are careful not to cause pain to animals, but feel that it is justifiable to kill a few members of common species both for research and for teaching, and also of course to use animals that have died naturally. If you feel otherwise you probably ought to avoid zoology (and most other biological subjects).

Nearly all zoology lecturers believe that animals evolve and regard the theory of evolution by natural selection as the central theory that gives meaning to the whole subject. It is nevertheless possible (and not very uncommon) for students who do not believe in evolution to study the subject. They will not be penalised, provided that they remember that only scientific arguments have a place in science.

Zoology is not an easy option for students who have trouble with physics and mathematics. Zoologists use physics to explain how nerves, muscles and cilia work; to sort out the osmotic problems of life in fresh water; to understand the heat balance of desert animals; and for many other purposes. The mathematics we use is not just statistics (though that is important). We use mechanics to explain how people and other animals run, how fish swim and how birds fly; we use computer models to develop ecological theories; and we use calculus to work out optimum strategies for behaviour and reproduction. We also use chemistry as is well known. Most zoology lecturers assume that their students have a good basic knowledge of biology but may know less about some of the other sciences and teach accordingly.

Many people study zoology simply because they are interested in animals (an excellent reason). Others have more practical motives. Zoology is the essential basis for conservation work, and for understanding the effects of pollution. It deals with agricultural pests, with parasites that cause disease in humans and farm animals and with vectors (such as mosquitoes) that transmit diseases. It is important for commercial fisheries and for aquaculture. Finally, much of our understanding of humans comes from research done by zoologists on other species.

HELPFUL READING: Knut Schmidt-Nielsen, *How Animals Work* (Cambridge University Press), a brilliant little book on comparative physiology; Richard Dawkins, *The Blind Watchmaker* (Longman), a thought-provoking account of evolutionary theory; S L Gould and C G Gould, *Life at the Edge* (Freeman), about life in difficult environments.

INDEX